SHONEN JUMP MANGA EDITION

NARUTO

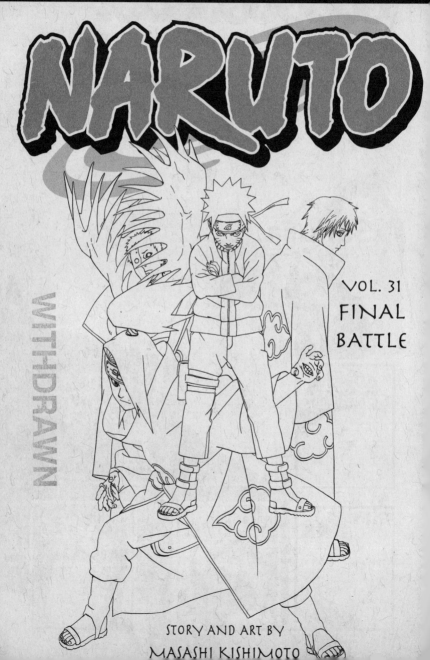

WITHDRAWN

VOL. 31
FINAL
BATTLE

STORY AND ART BY

MASASHI KISHIMOTO

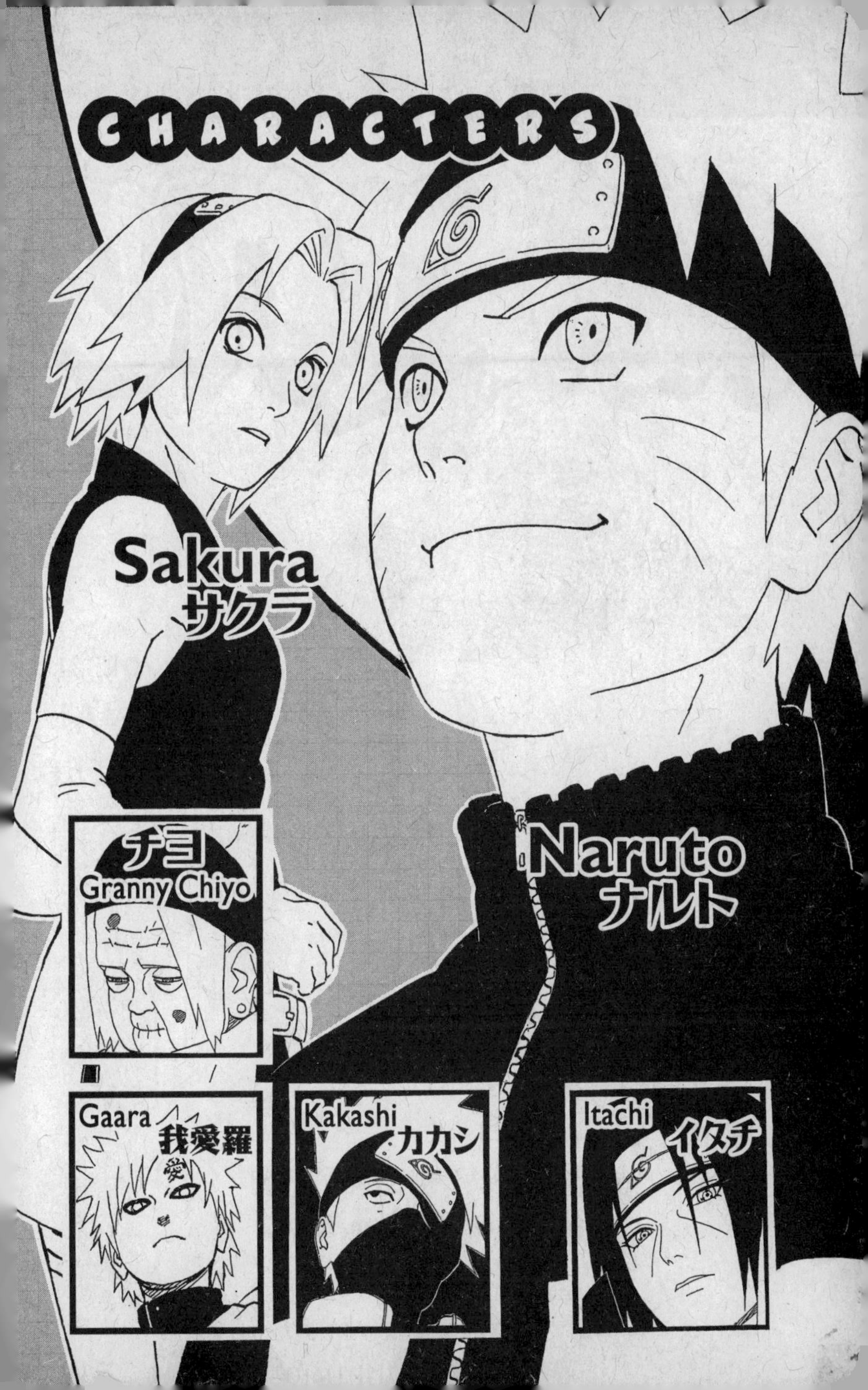
CHARACTERS
Sakura
サクラ
Naruto
ナルト
チヨ
Granny Chiyo
Gaara
我愛羅
Kakashi
カカシ
Itachi
イタチ

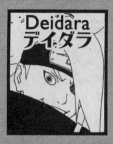

Might Guy
マイト・ガイ

Rock Lee
ロック・リー

Deidara
デイダラ

Tenten
テンテン

Neji
日向ネジ

Sasori
サソリ

The Story So Far...

Naruto, the biggest troublemaker at the Ninja Academy in the village of Konohagakure, finally becomes a ninja along with his classmates, Sasuke and Sakura. During the Chûnin Selection Exams, Orochimaru and his henchmen launch *Operation Destroy Konoha*. Naruto's mentor, the Third Hokage, sacrifices his own life to stop the attack, and Tsunade becomes the Fifth Hokage. Lured by Orochimaru, Sasuke leaves Konohagakure. Naruto fights valiantly against Sasuke, but cannot stop his friend from following the path of darkness...

Two years pass, and Naruto and his comrades grow up and undergo separate training programs, until Gaara falls into the hands of the Akatsuki. Naruto charges into the enemy's lair to rescue Gaara, but Deidara stops him. Sakura and Granny Chiyo remain in the cave locked in battle with Sasori!!

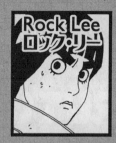

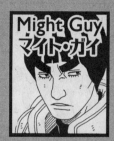

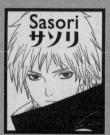

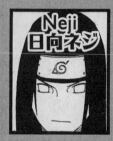

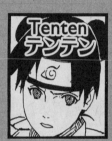

NARUTO

VOL. 31
FINAL BATTLE

CONTENTS

Number 272: Granny Chiyo vs. Sasori...!!

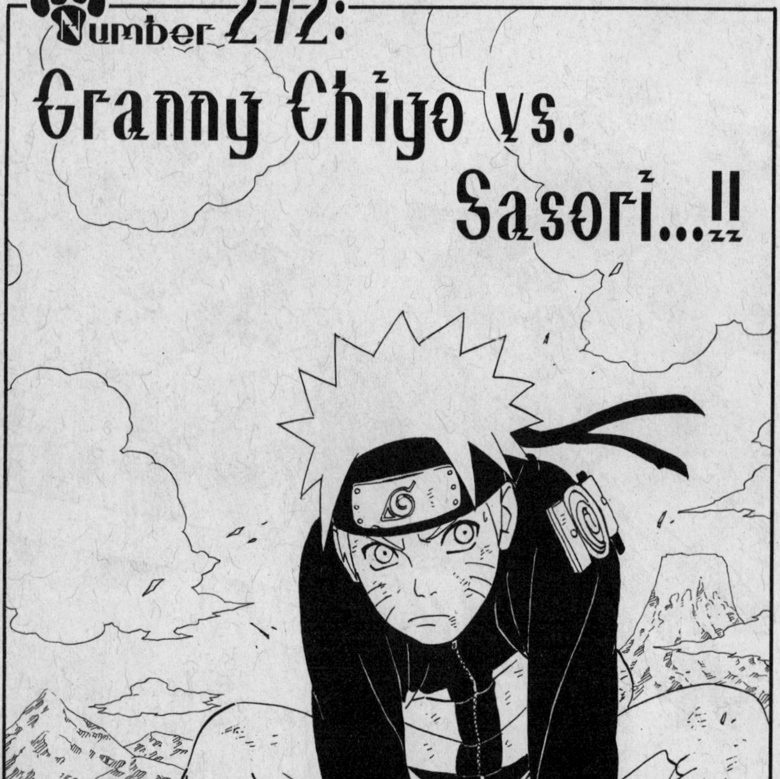

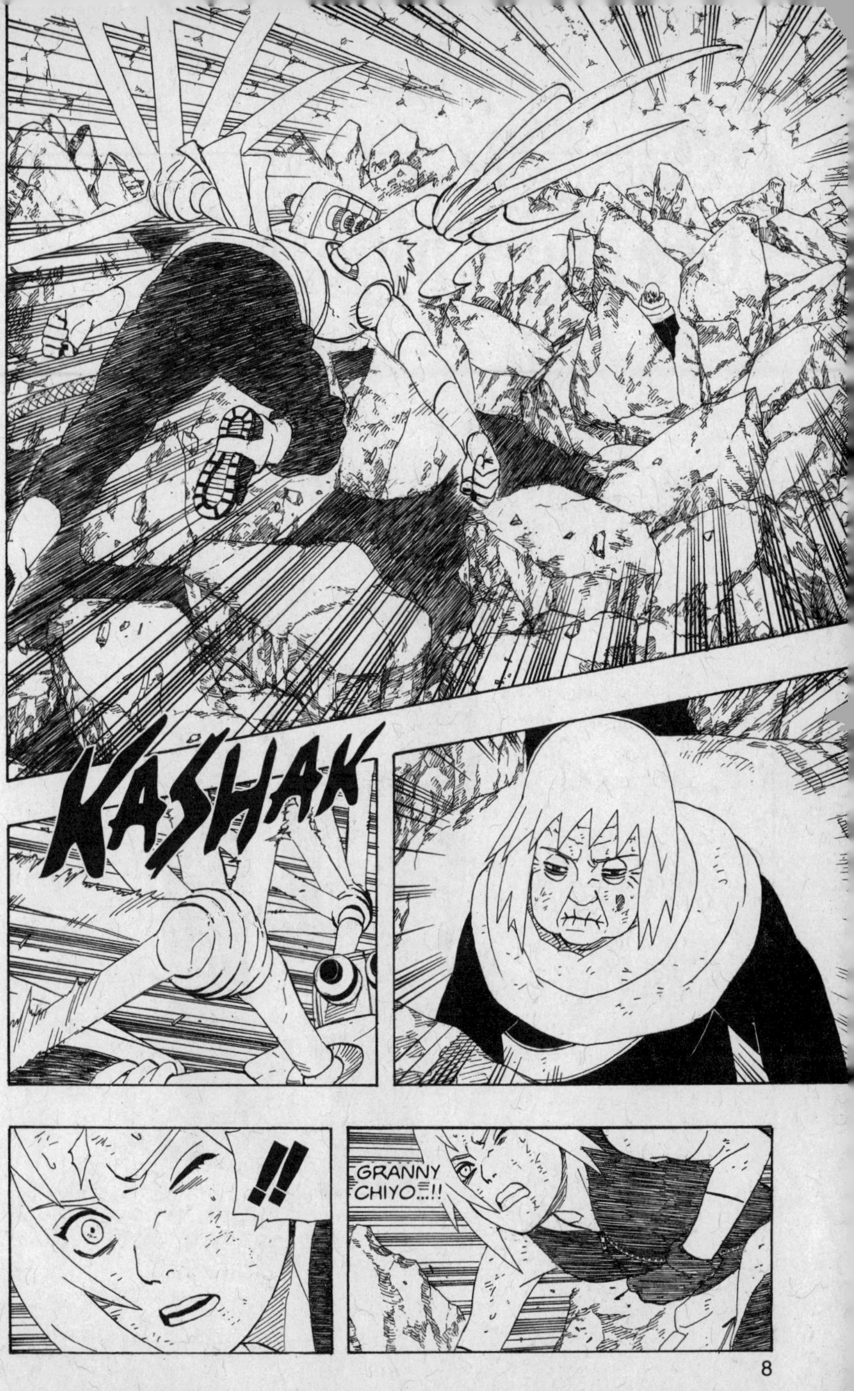
KASHAK
GRANNY CHIYO...!!
!!

READ THIS WAY

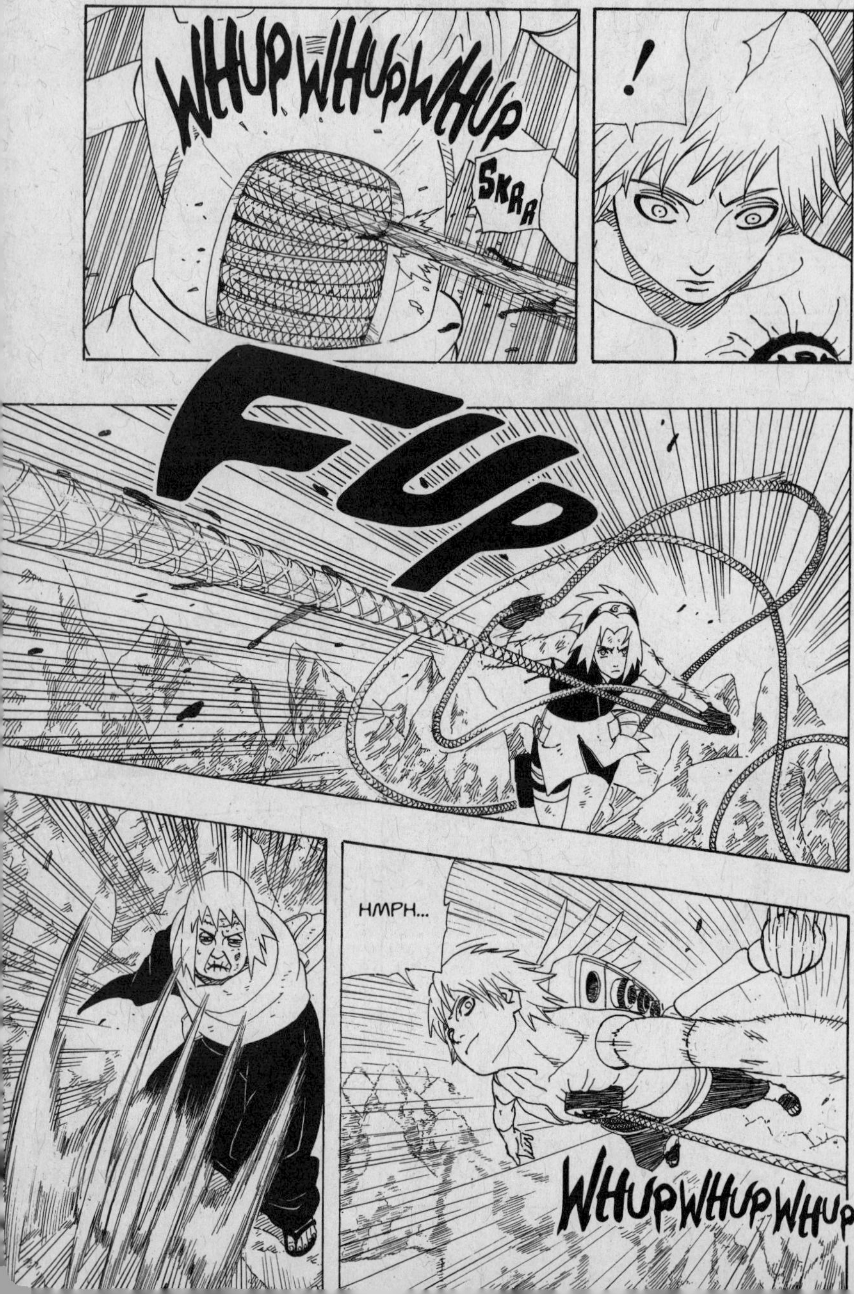
!
WHUP WHUP WHUP
SKRA
FUP
HMPH...
WHUP WHUP WHUP

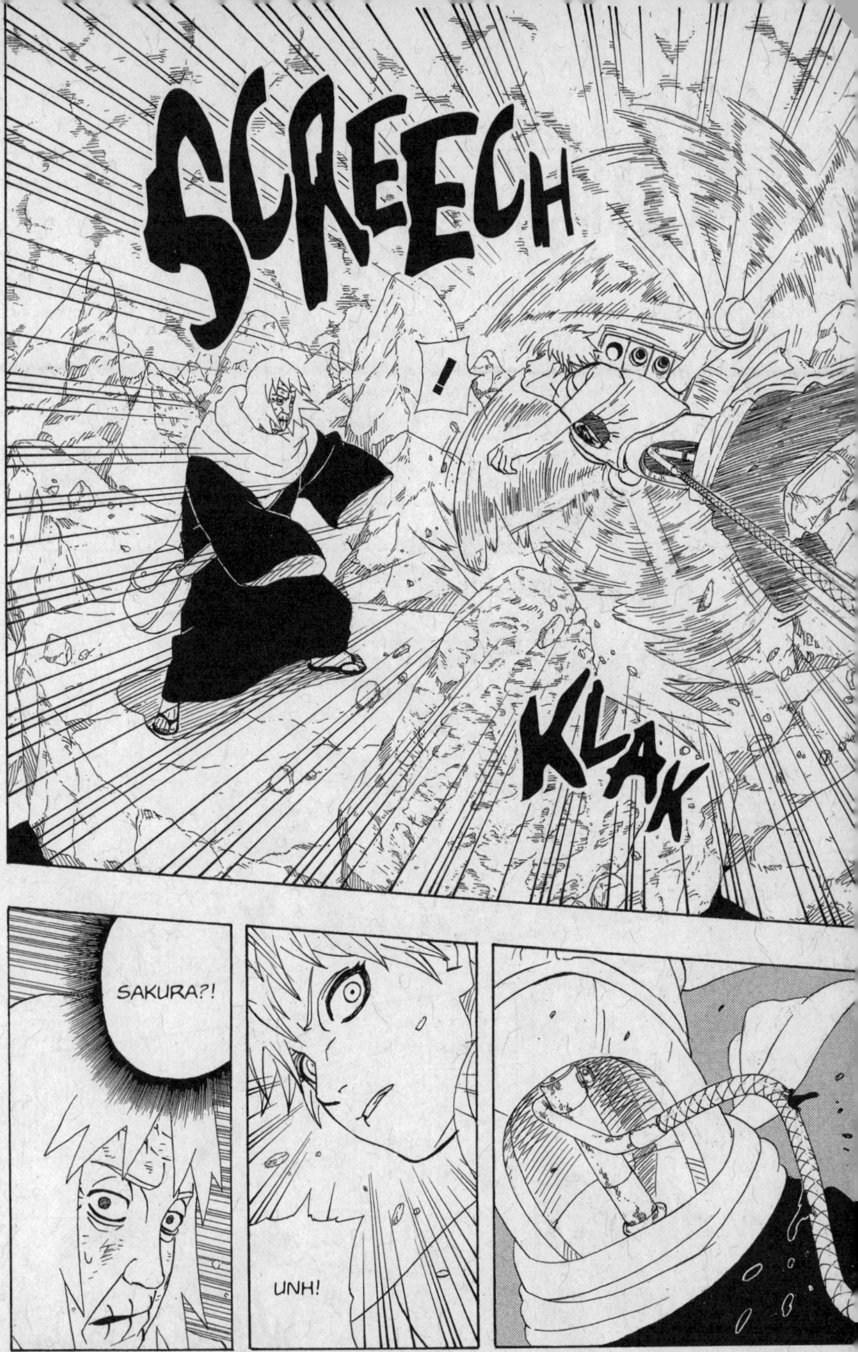
SCREECH
!
KLAK
UNH!
SAKURA?!

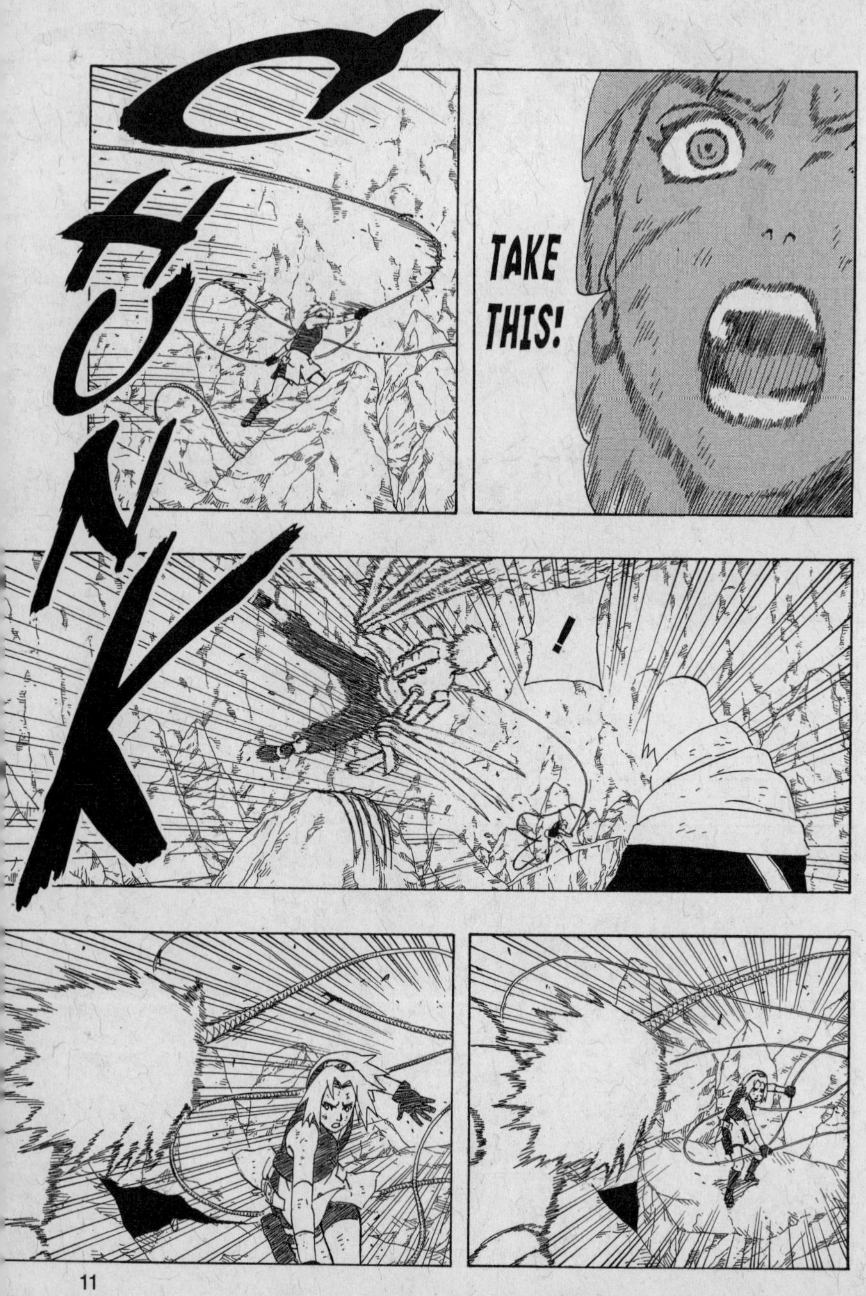
TAKE THIS!
CHUNK
!

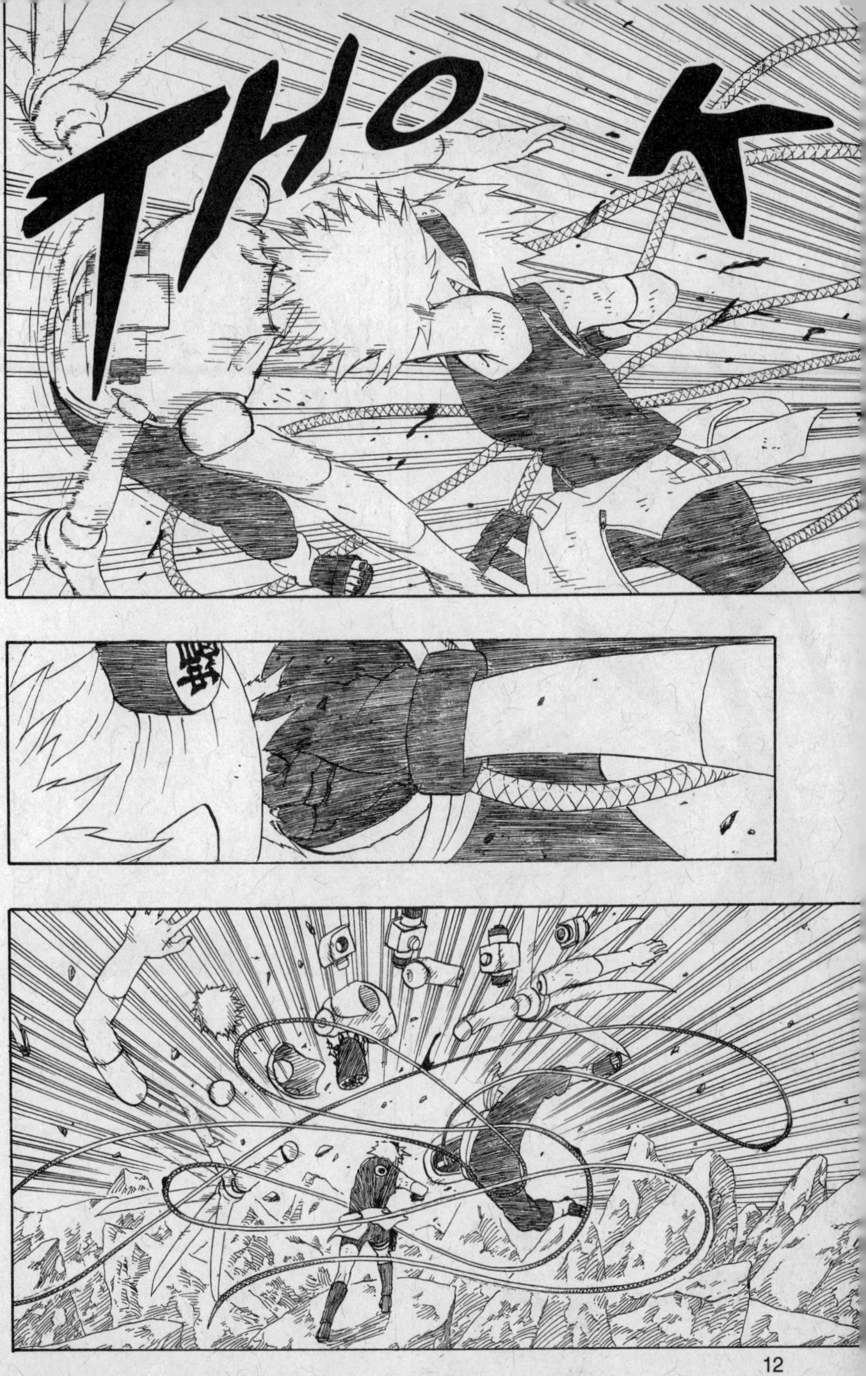
THOK

READ THIS WAY

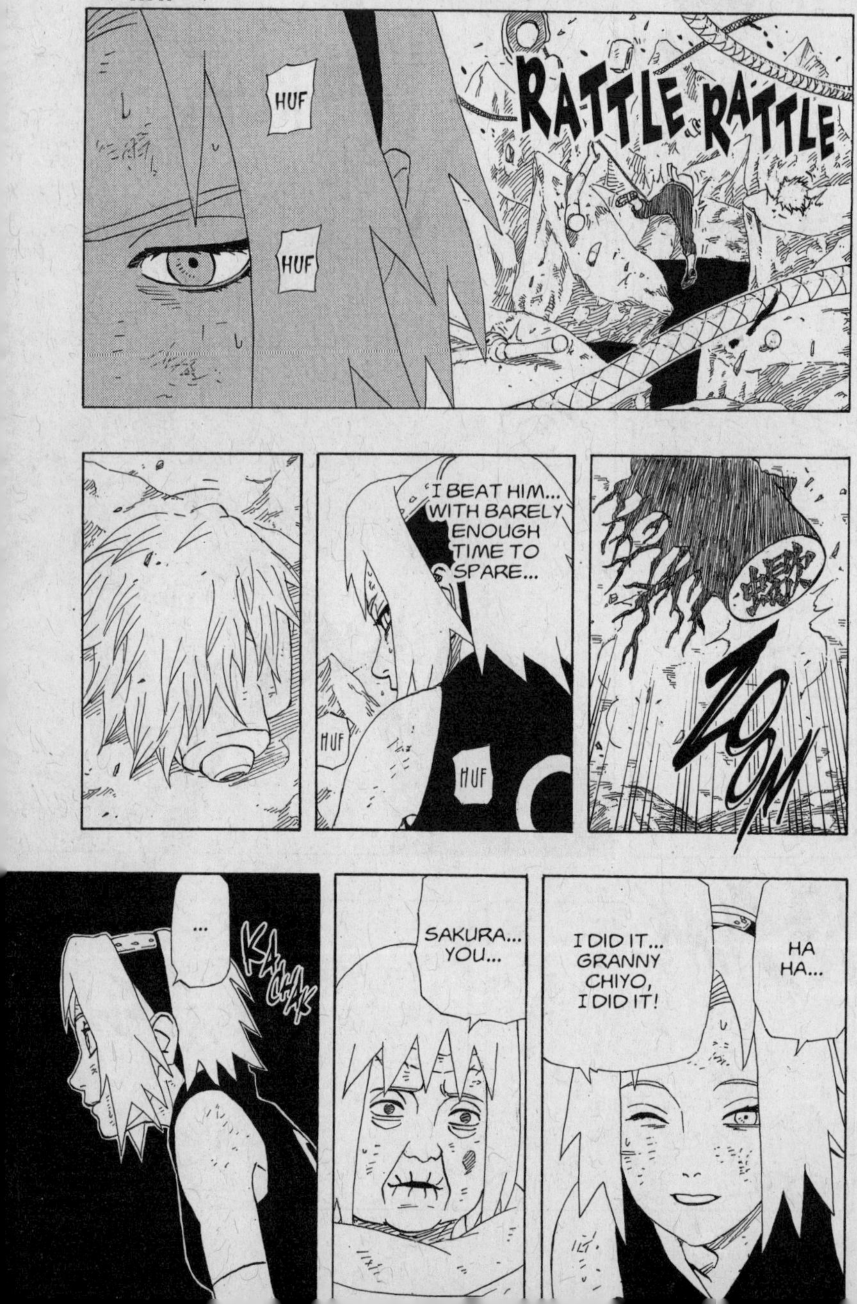
RATTLE RATTLE
HUF
HUF
ZOOM
I BEAT HIM... WITH BARELY ENOUGH TIME TO SPARE...
HUF
HUF
HA HA...
I DID IT... GRANNY CHIYO, I DID IT!
SAKURA... YOU...
...
KACHAK

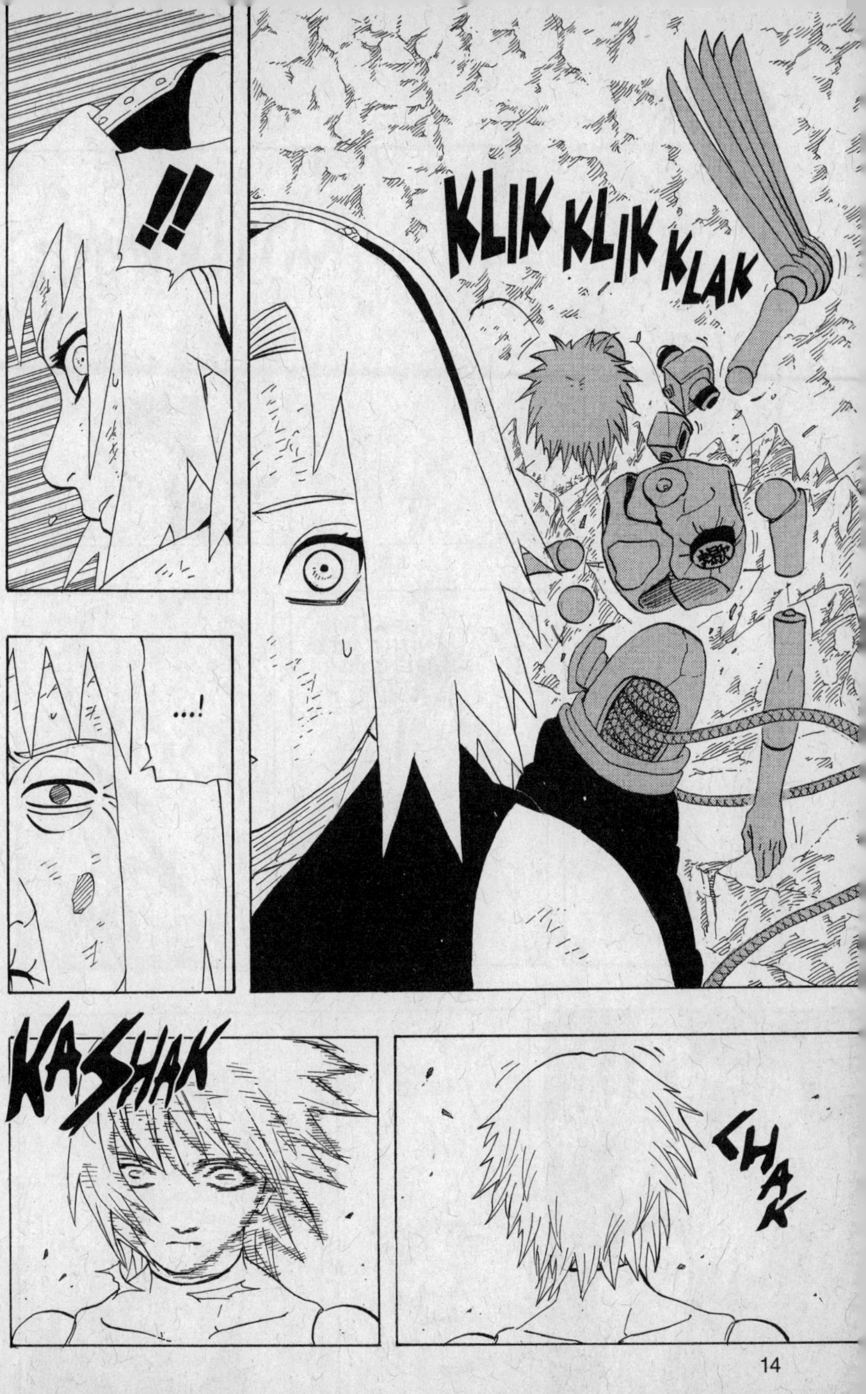
KLIK KLIK KLAK
!!
...!
CHAK
KASHAK

READ THIS WAY

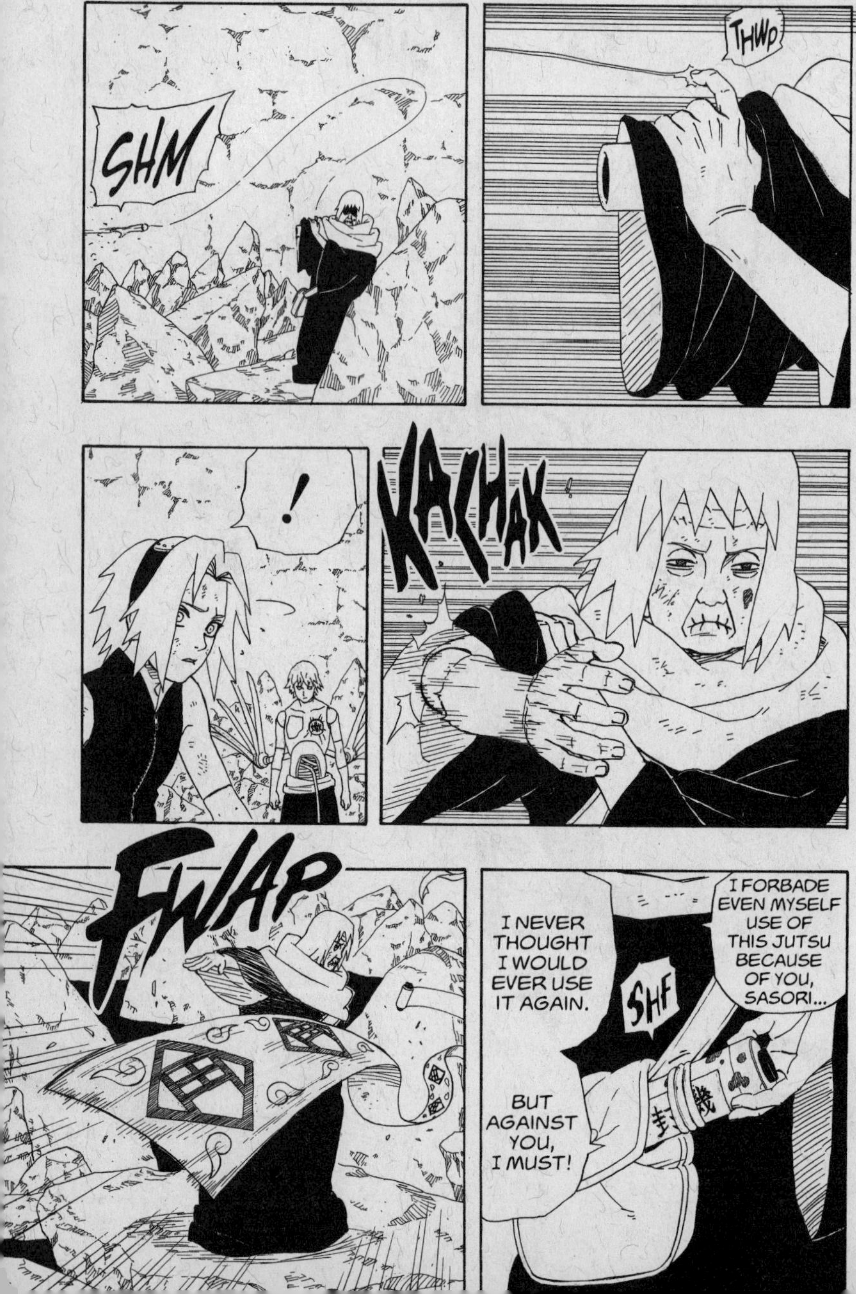
THWP
SHM
KACHAK
!
I FORBADE EVEN MYSELF USE OF THIS JUTSU BECAUSE OF YOU, SASORI...
I NEVER THOUGHT I WOULD EVER USE IT AGAIN.
SHF
BUT AGAINST YOU, I MUST!
FWAP

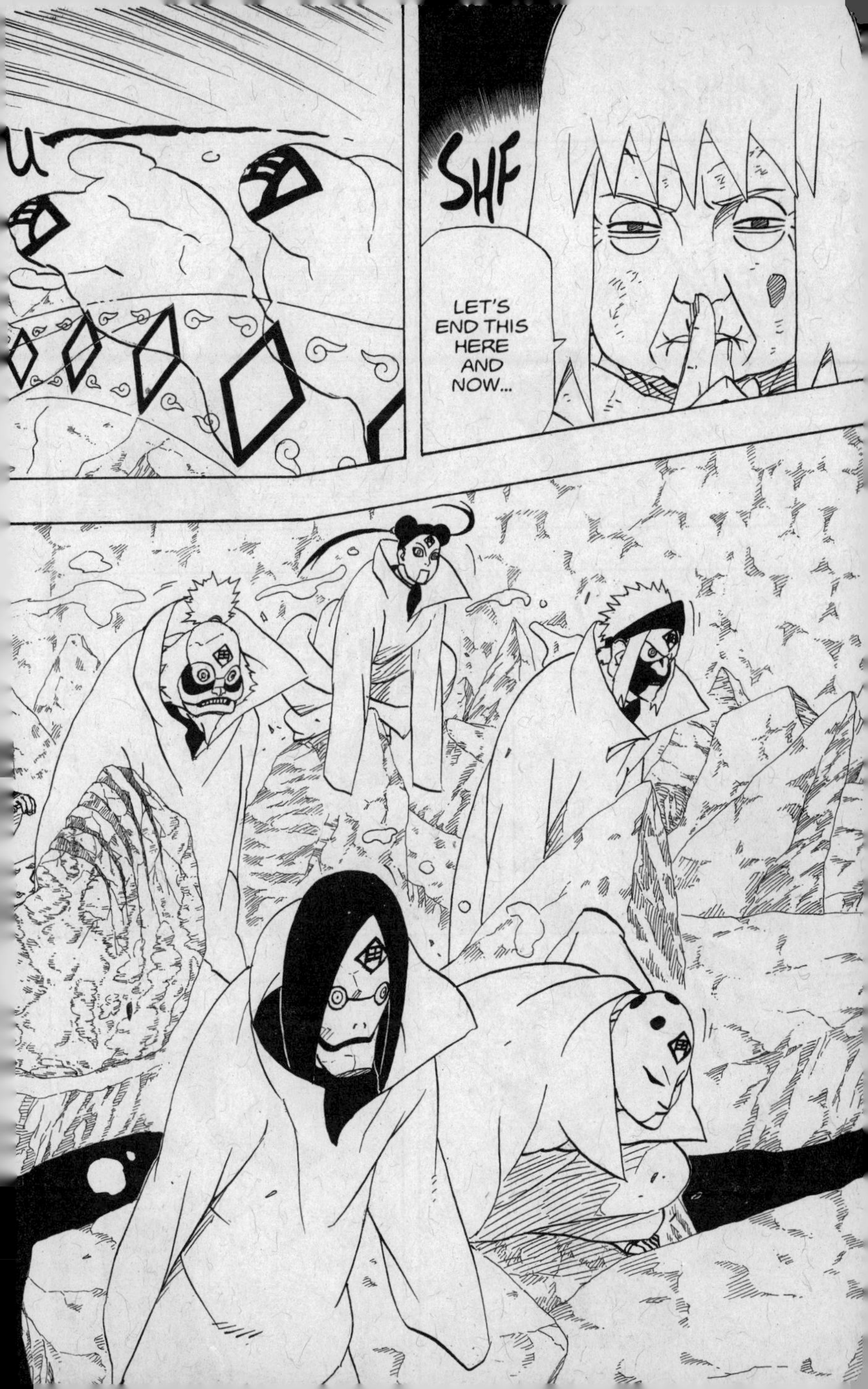
SHF
LET'S END THIS HERE AND NOW...
U

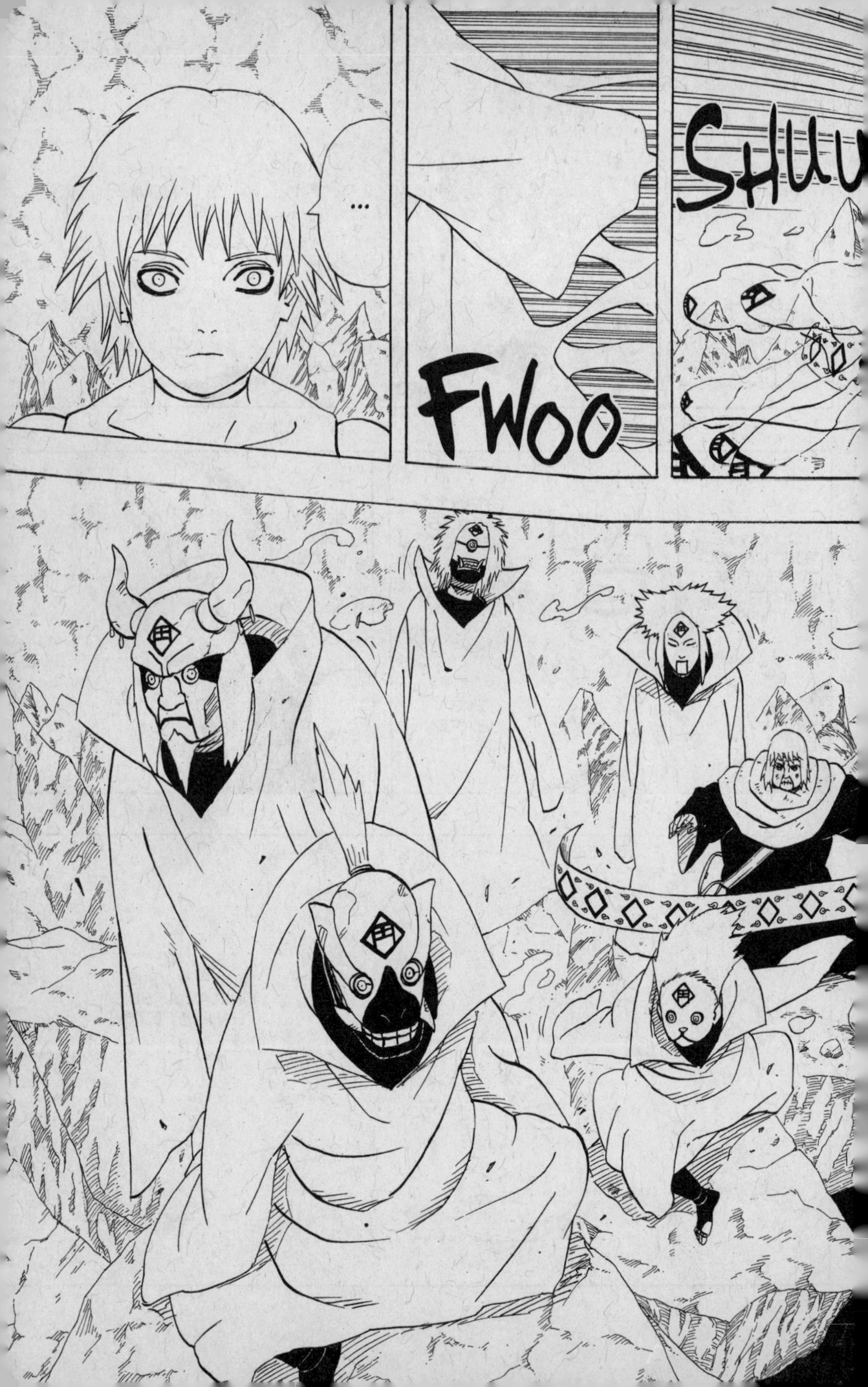
SHUU
FWOO
...

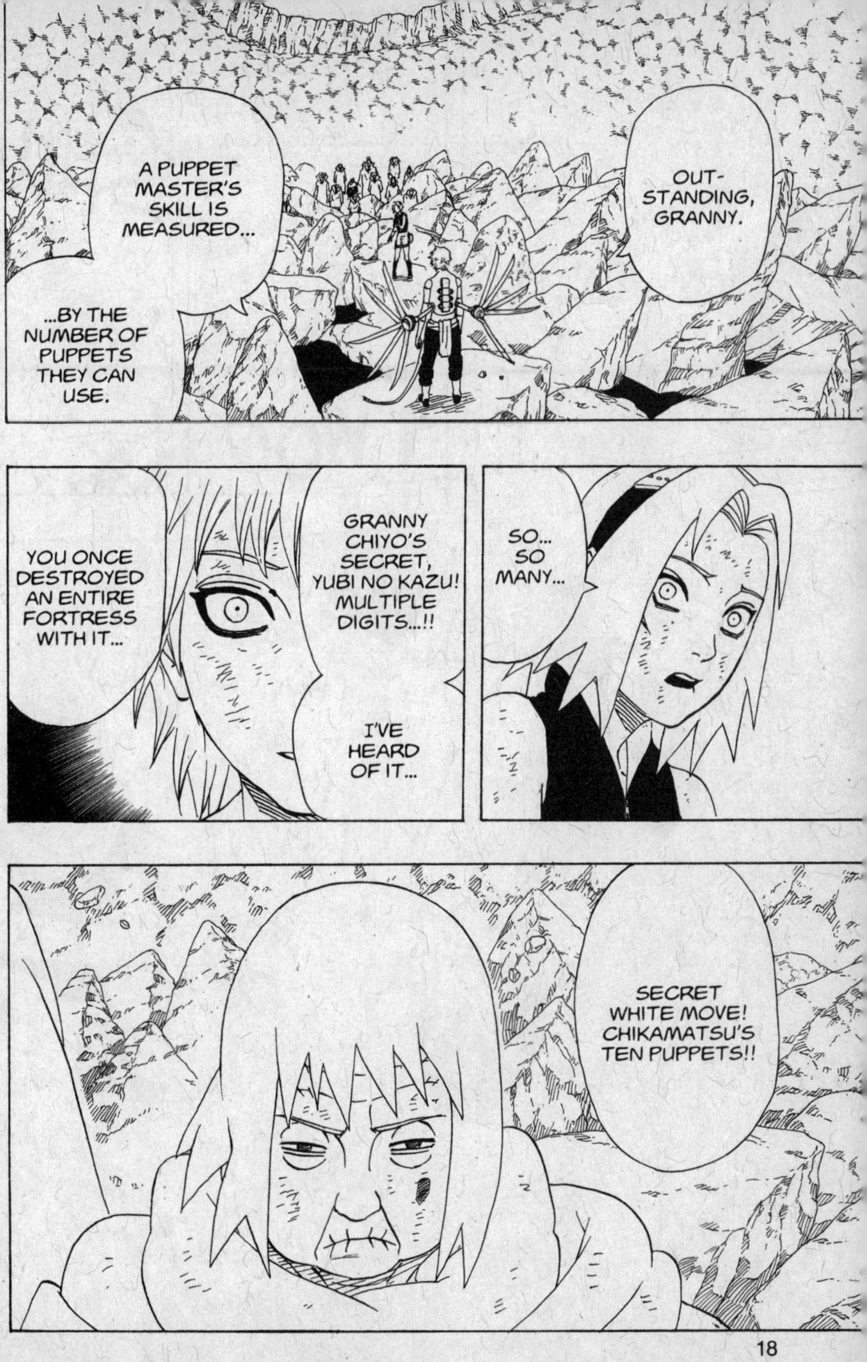
OUT-STANDING, GRANNY.
A PUPPET MASTER'S SKILL IS MEASURED...
...BY THE NUMBER OF PUPPETS THEY CAN USE.
SO... SO MANY...
GRANNY CHIYO'S SECRET, YUBI NO KAZU! MULTIPLE DIGITS...!!
I'VE HEARD OF IT...
YOU ONCE DESTROYED AN ENTIRE FORTRESS WITH IT...
SECRET WHITE MOVE! CHIKAMATSU'S TEN PUPPETS!!

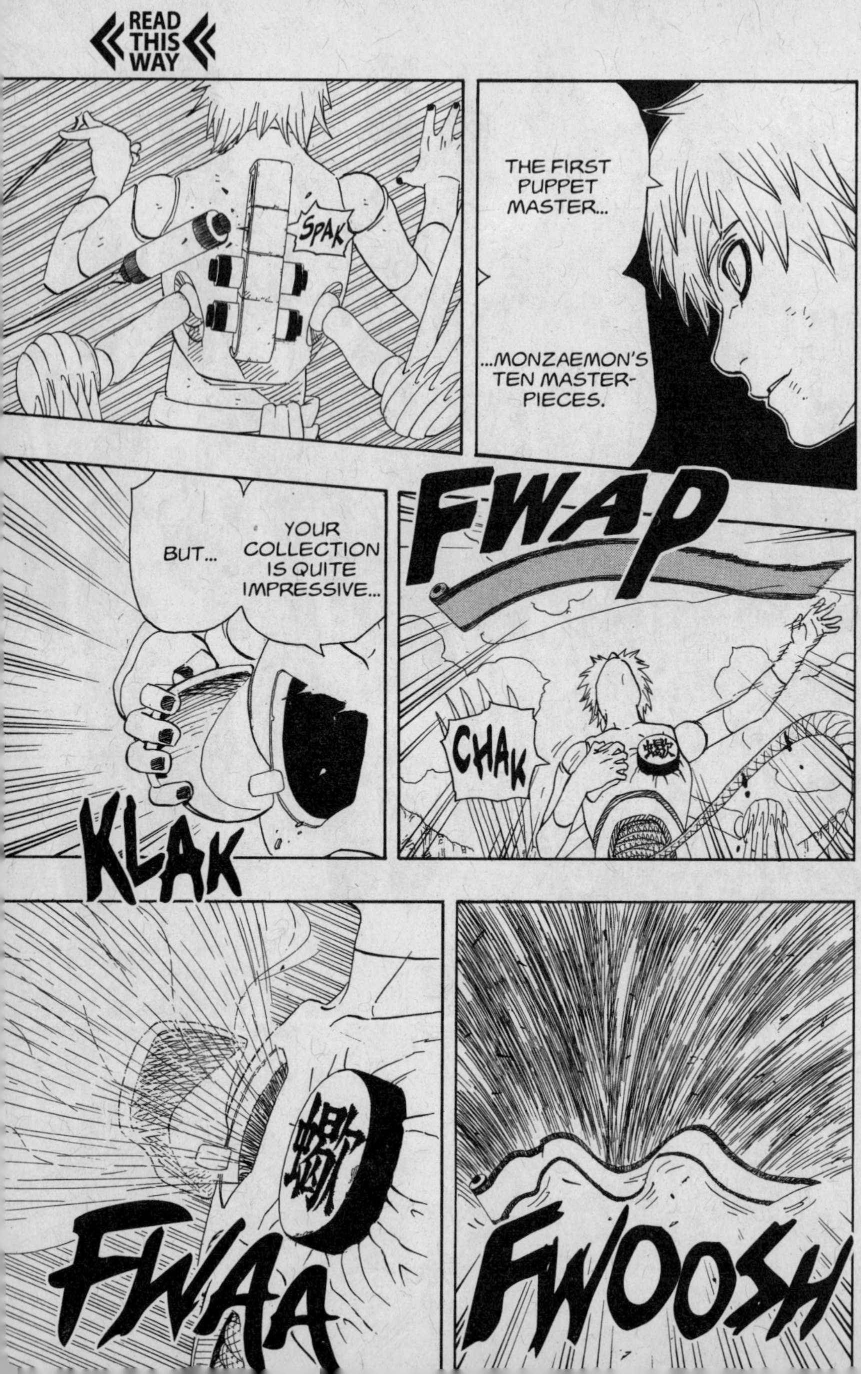
READ THIS WAY
THE FIRST PUPPET MASTER...
...MONZAEMON'S TEN MASTER-PIECES.
SPAK
FWAP
CHAK
BUT...
YOUR COLLECTION IS QUITE IMPRESSIVE...
KLAK
FWOOSH
FWAA

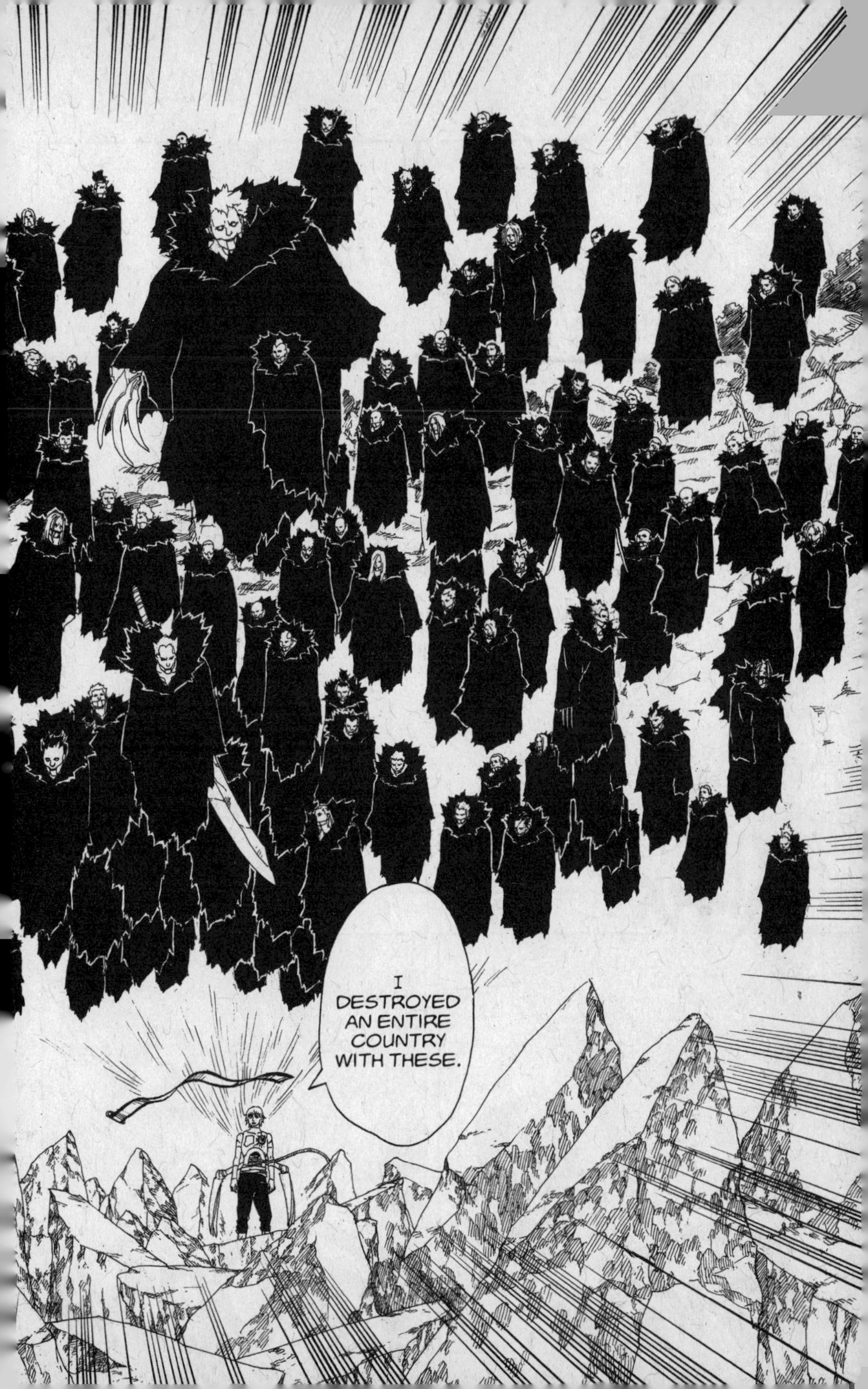
I DESTROYED AN ENTIRE COUNTRY WITH THESE.

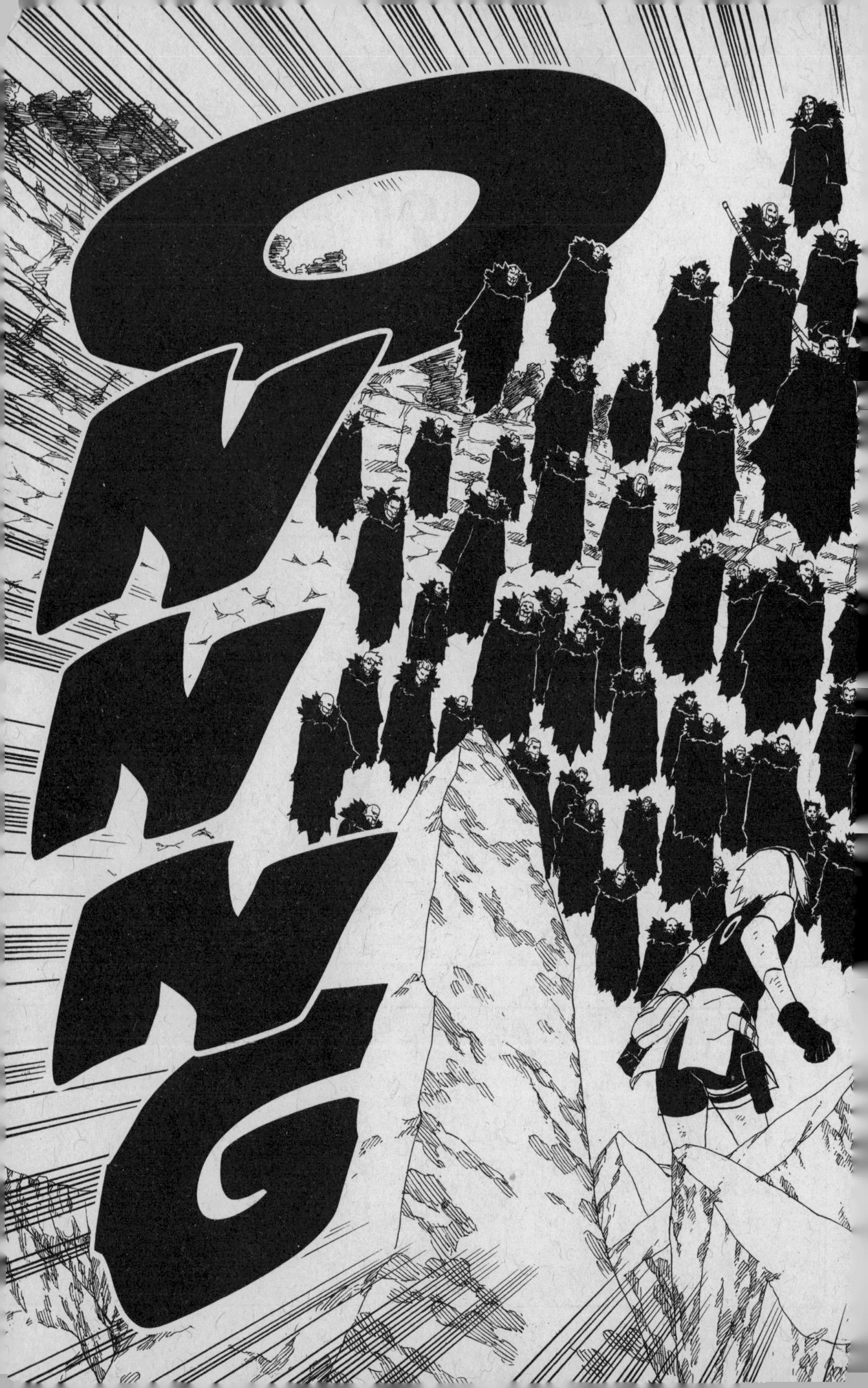

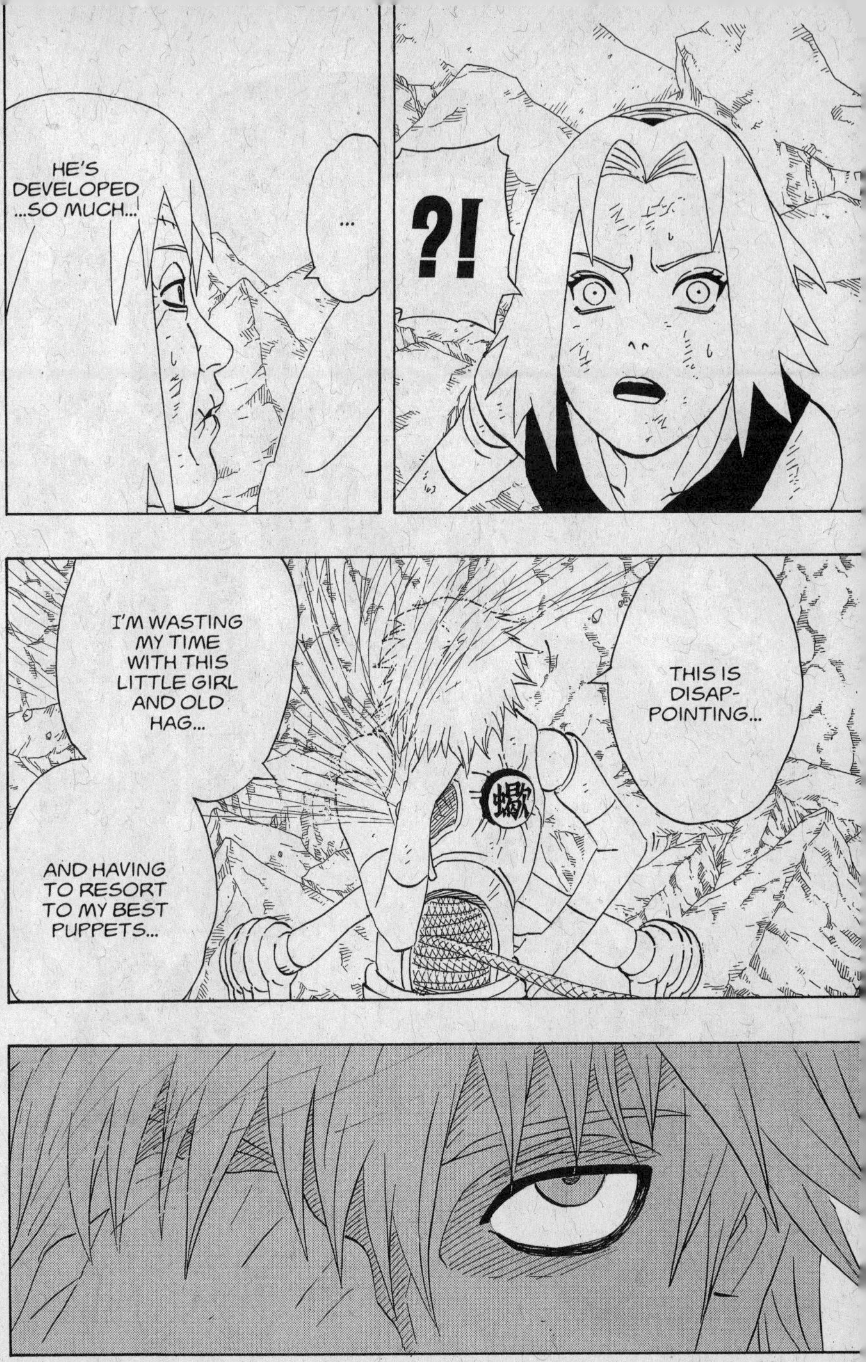
?!
...
HE'S DEVELOPED ...SO MUCH...
THIS IS DISAP-POINTING...
I'M WASTING MY TIME WITH THIS LITTLE GIRL AND OLD HAG...
AND HAVING TO RESORT TO MY BEST PUPPETS...

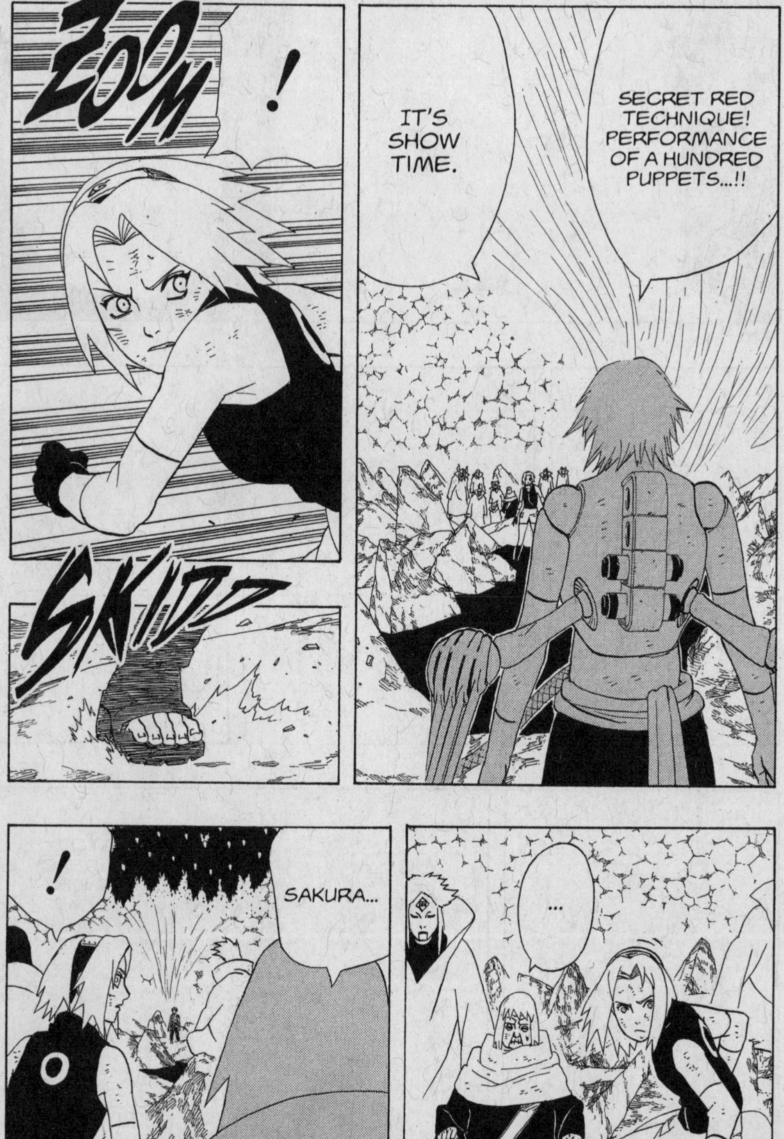
SECRET RED TECHNIQUE! PERFORMANCE OF A HUNDRED PUPPETS...!!
IT'S SHOW TIME.
ZOOM
!
SKIDD
...
SAKURA...
!

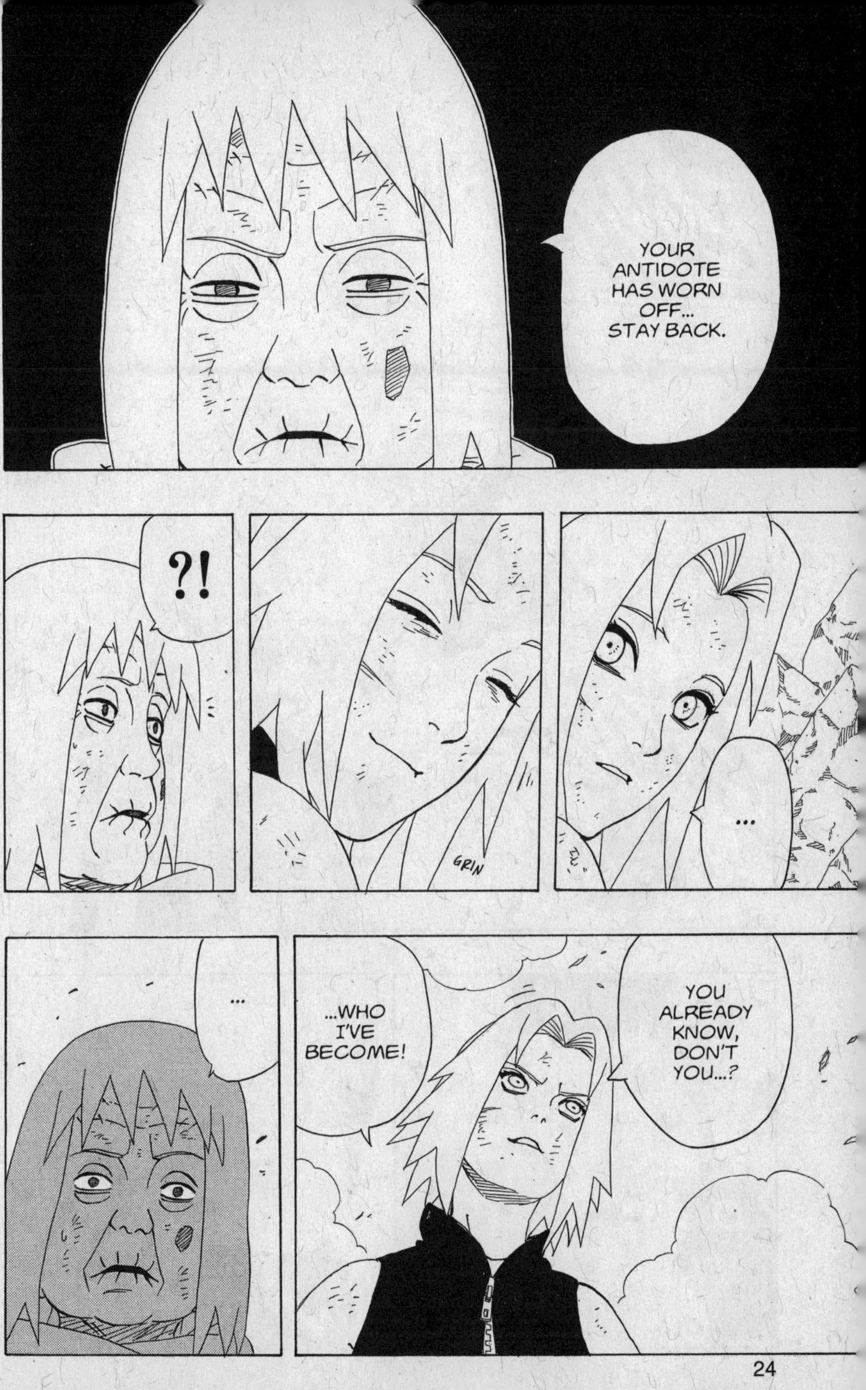
YOUR ANTIDOTE HAS WORN OFF... STAY BACK.
...
GRIN
?!
YOU ALREADY KNOW, DON'T YOU...?
...WHO I'VE BECOME!
...

READ THIS WAY

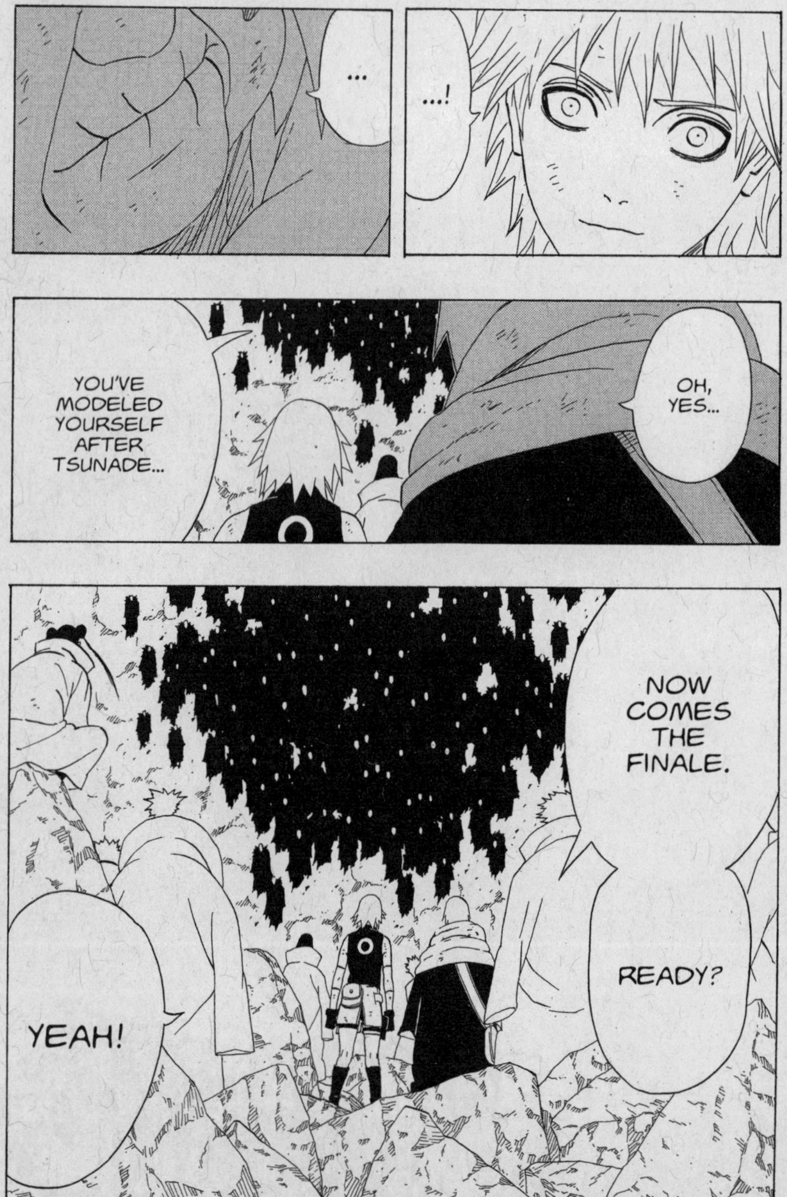

...!
...
OH, YES...
YOU'VE MODELED YOURSELF AFTER TSUNADE...
NOW COMES THE FINALE.
READY?
YEAH!

NARUTO

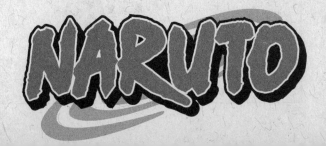

Number 273:

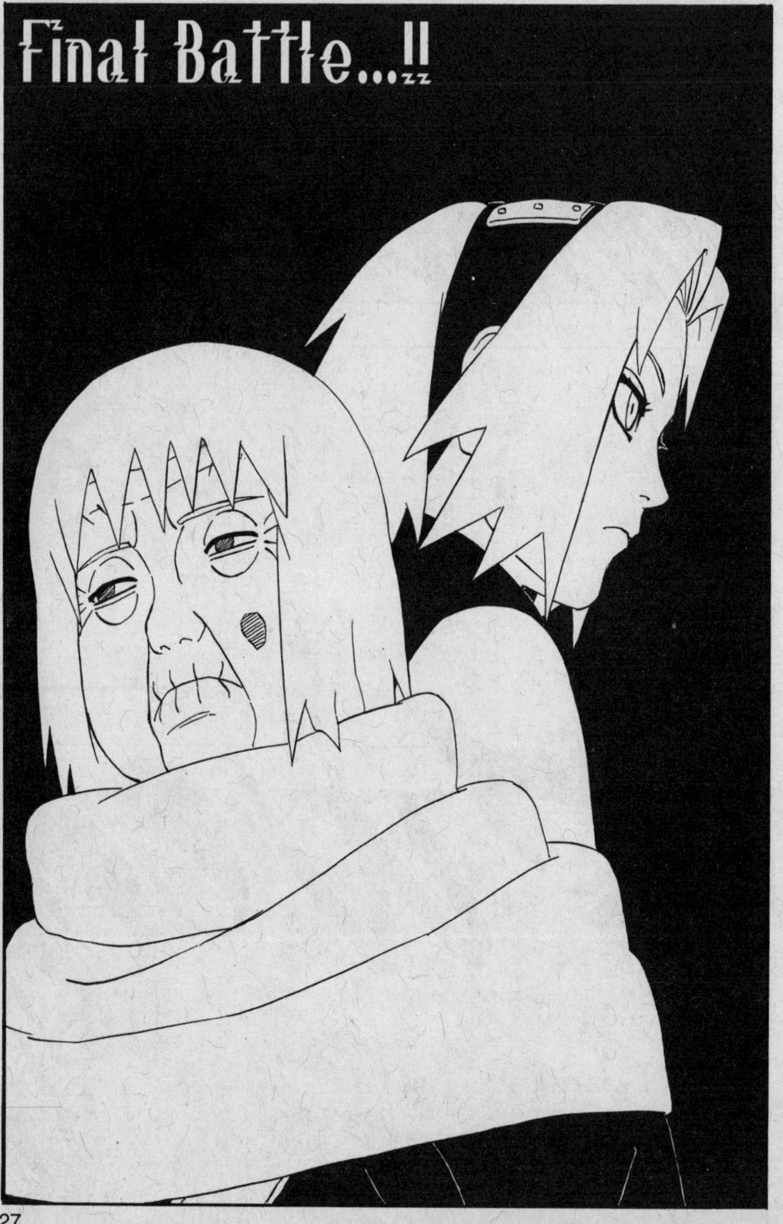
Final Battle...!!

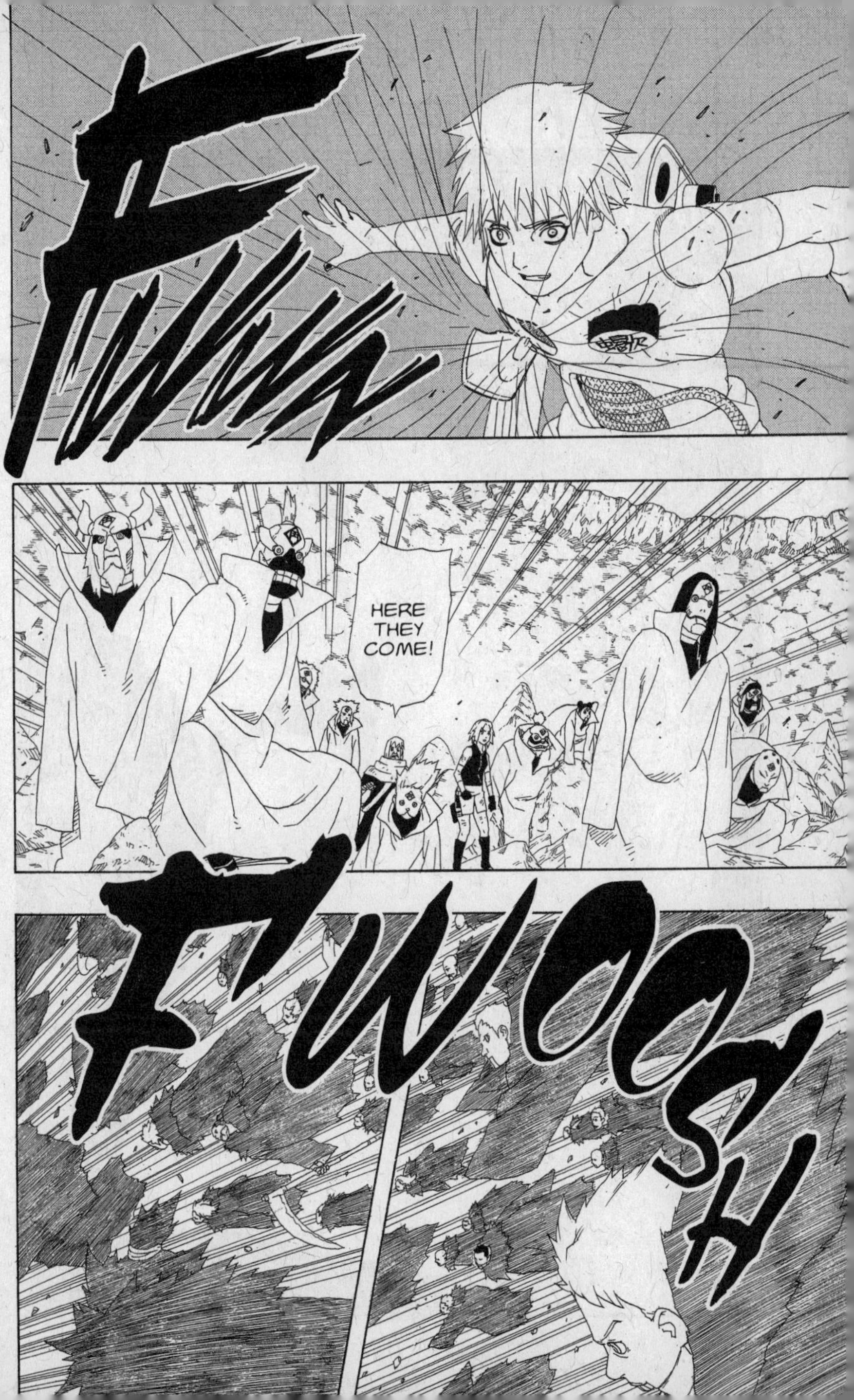
FWWA
HERE THEY COME!
FWOOSH

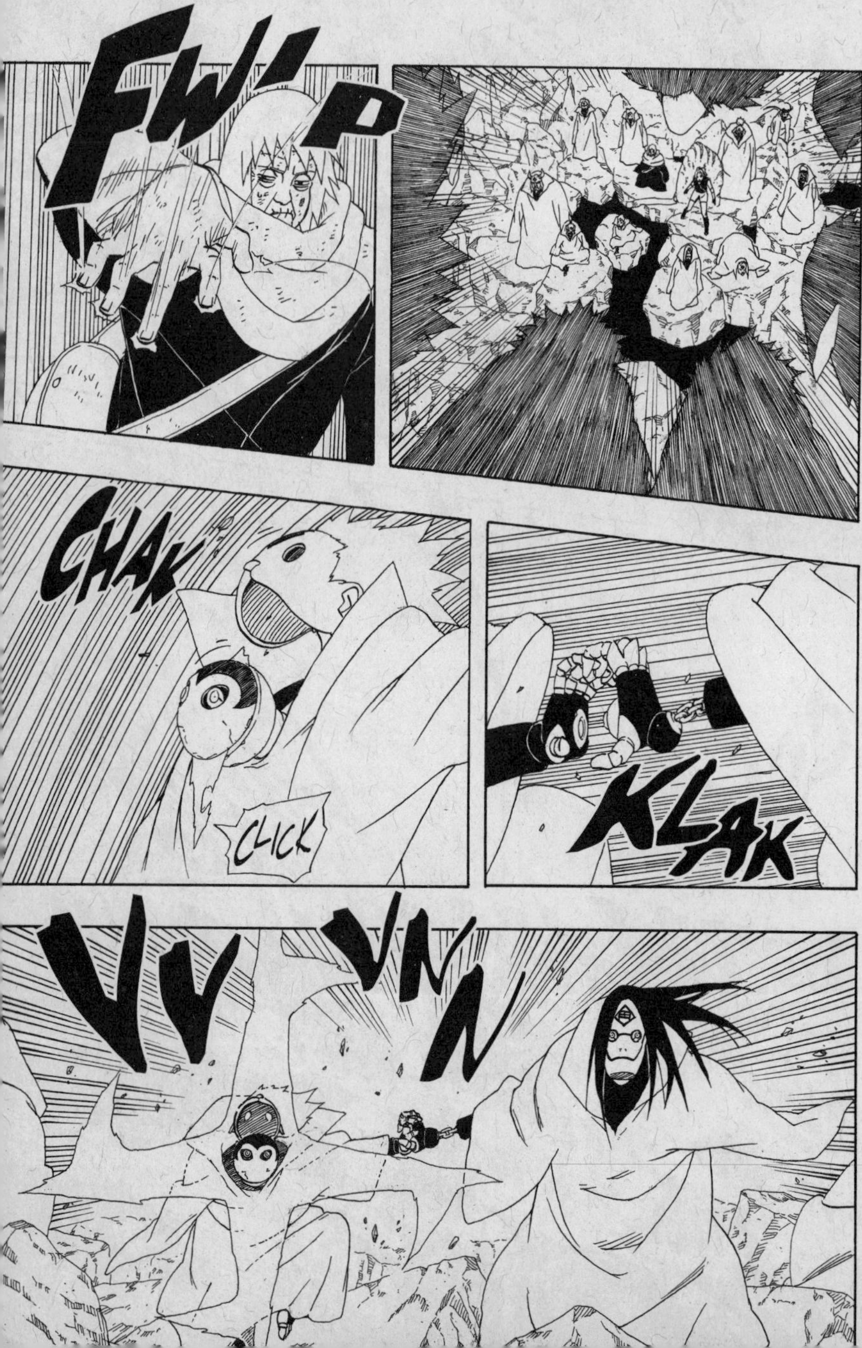
FW'P
KLAK
CHAK
CLICK
VVVNN

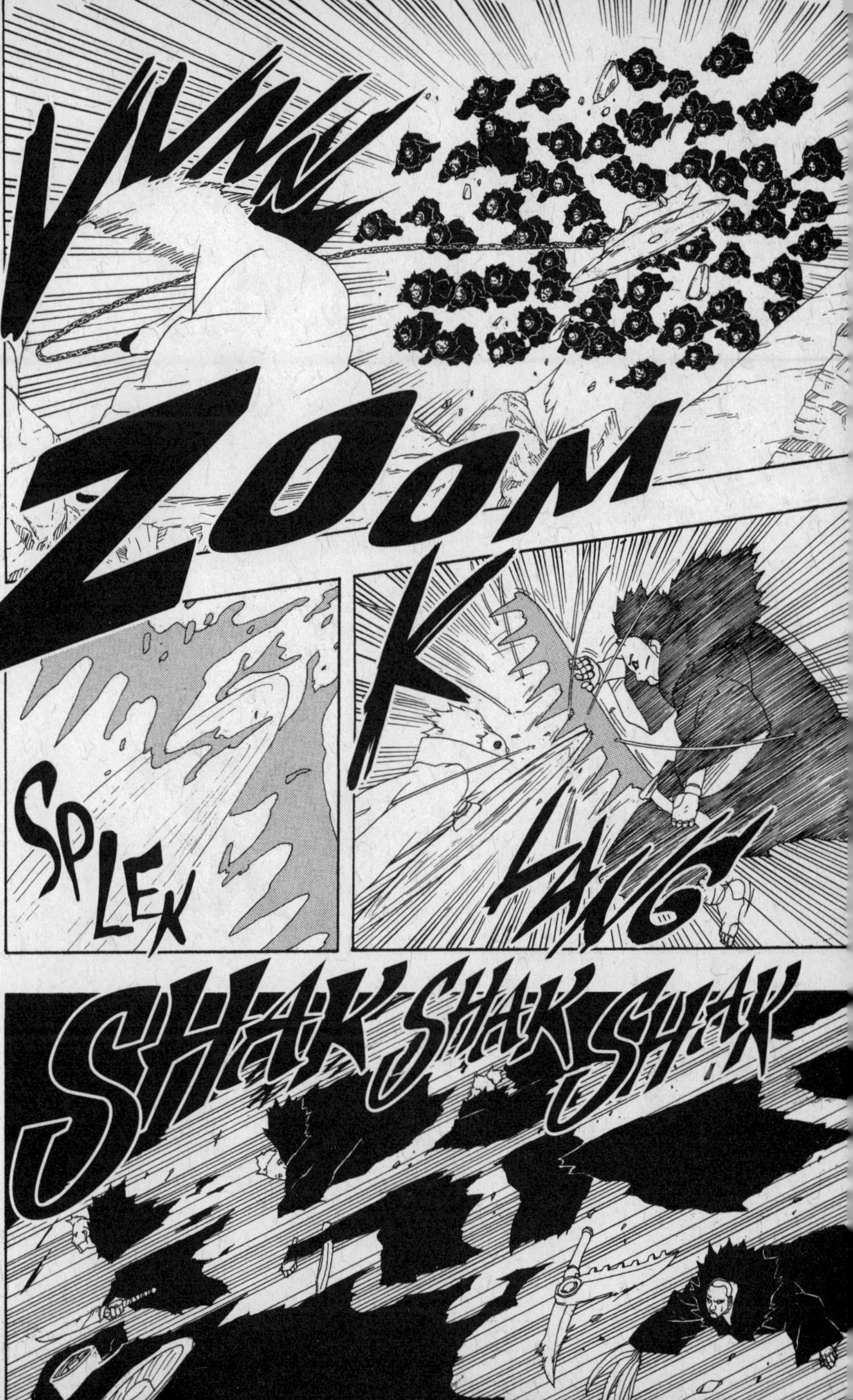
VWNN
ZOOM
SPLEK
SHAK SHAK SHAK

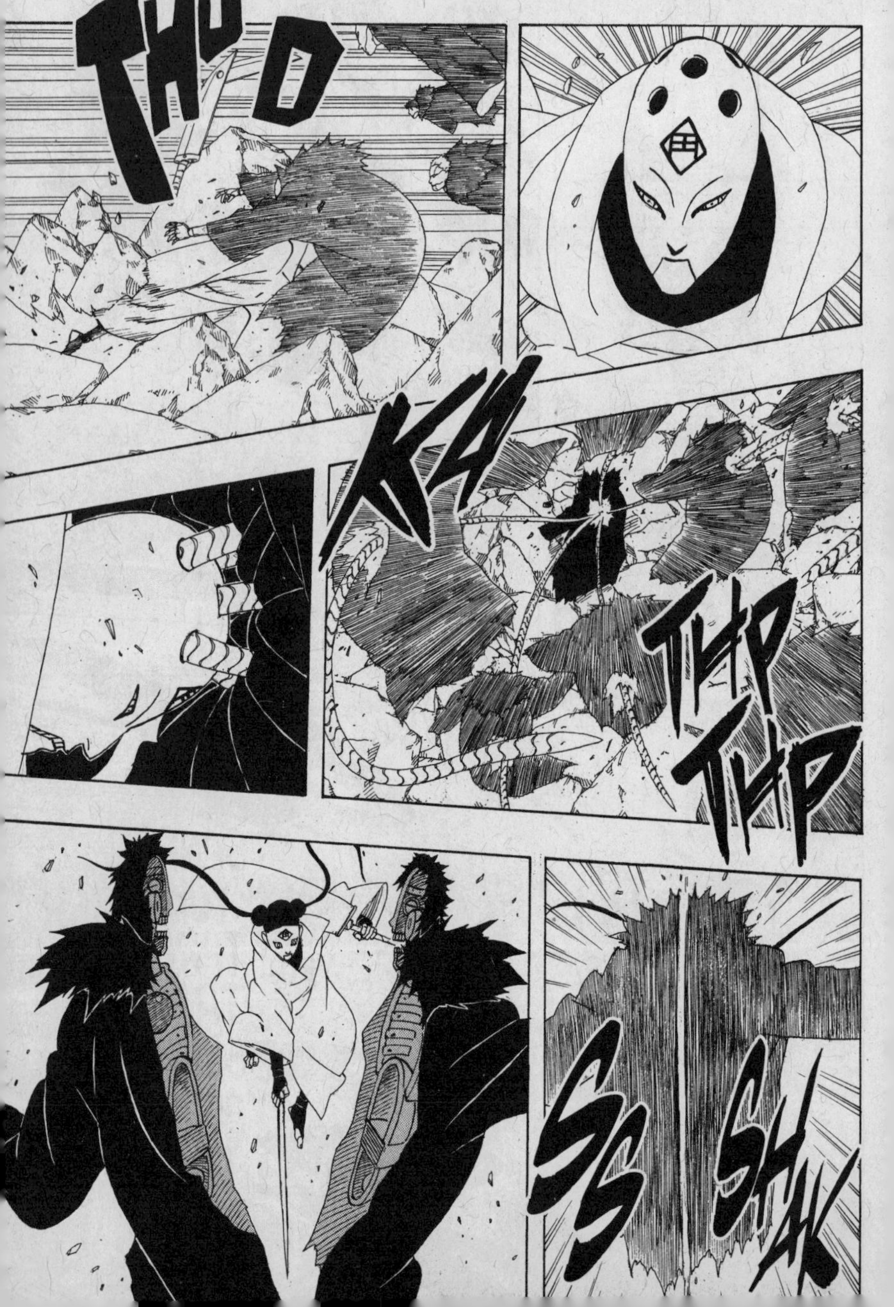
THUD
KA
THP THP
SHAK
SS

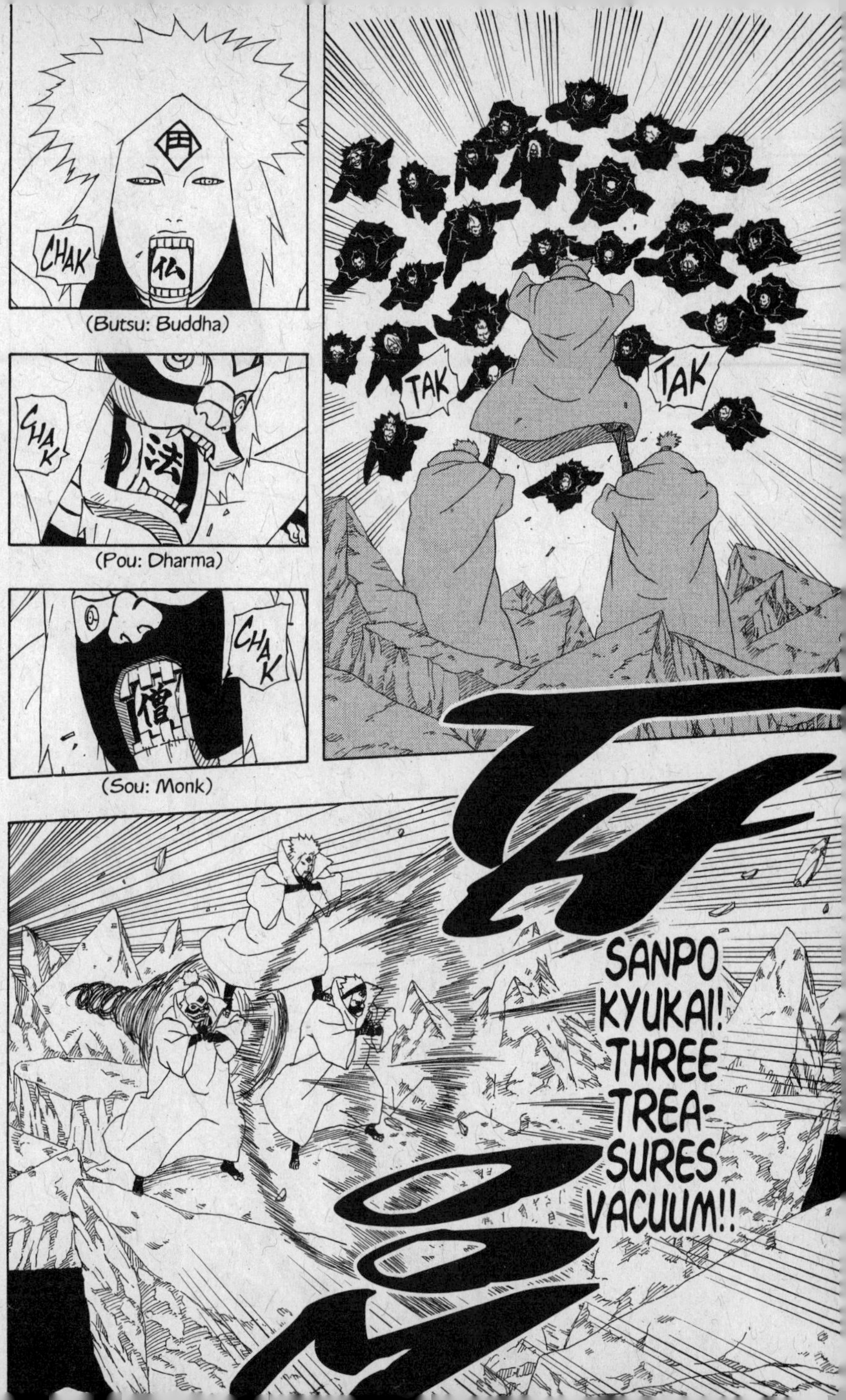

TAK
TAK
CHAK
仏
(Butsu: Buddha)
CHAK
法
(Pou: Dharma)
CHAK
僧
(Sou: Monk)
SANPO KYUKAI! THREE TREA-SURES VACUUM!!

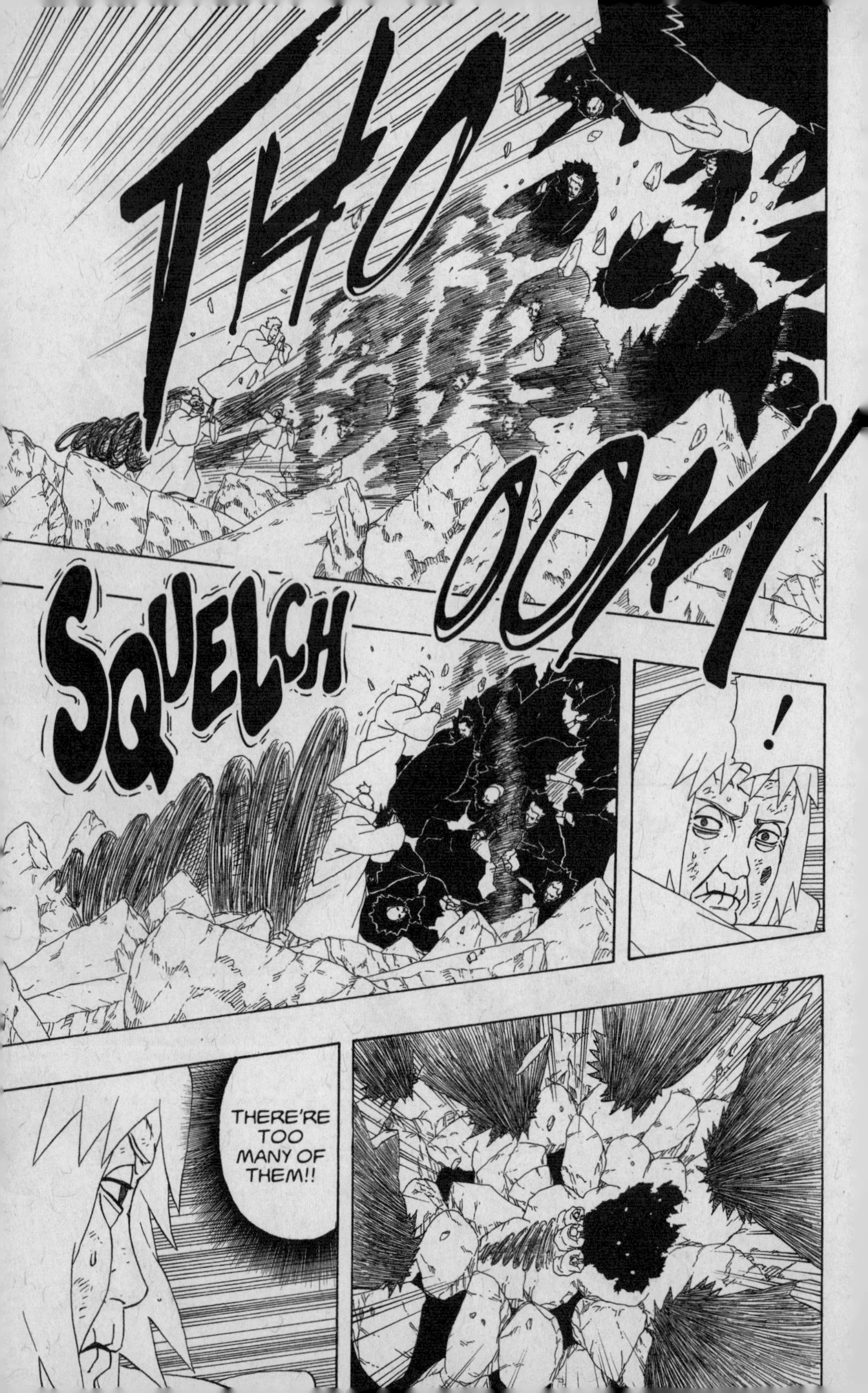
THOOOM
!
SQUELCH
THERE'RE TOO MANY OF THEM!!

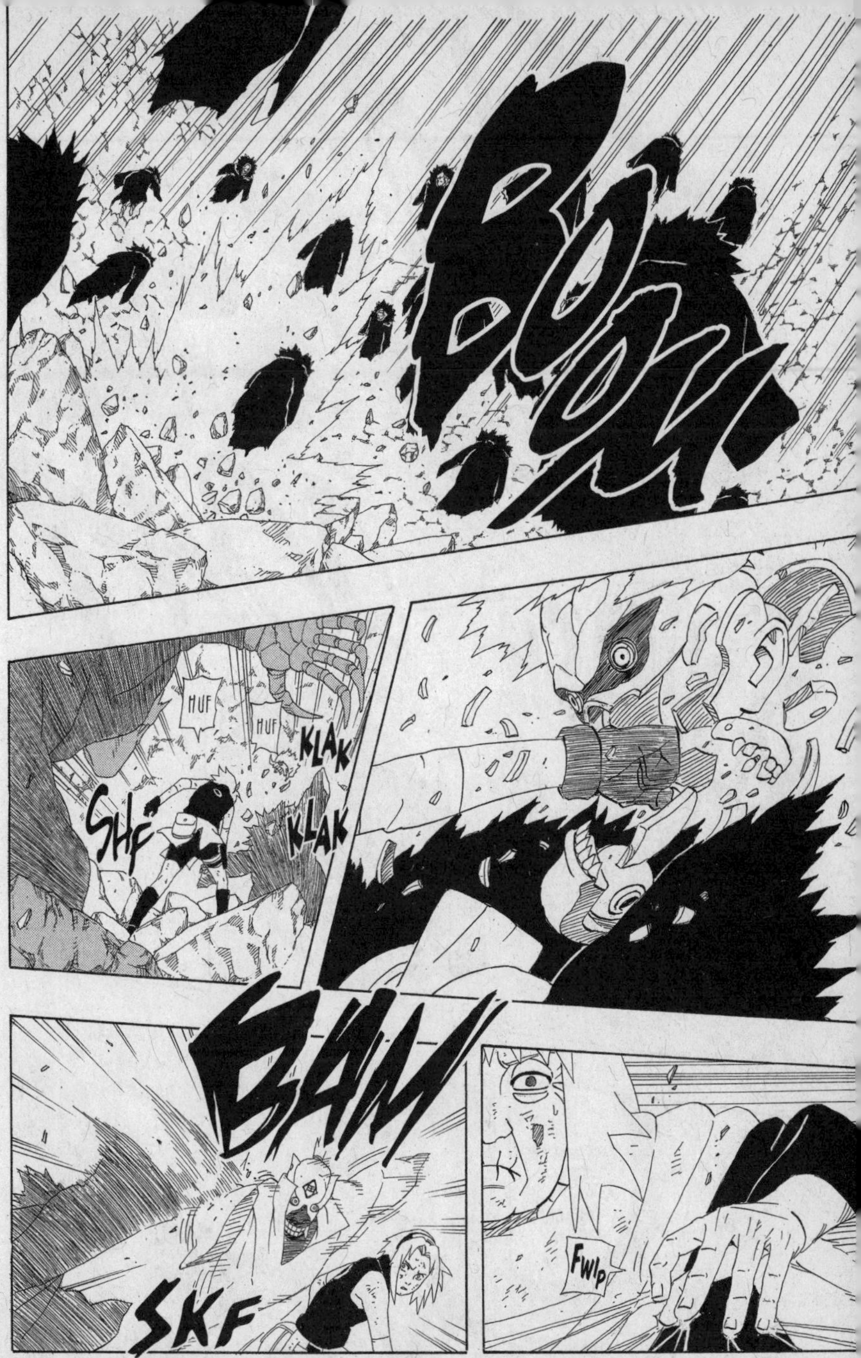
BOOM
BAM
HUF
HUF
KLAK
KLAK
SHF
FWIP
SKF

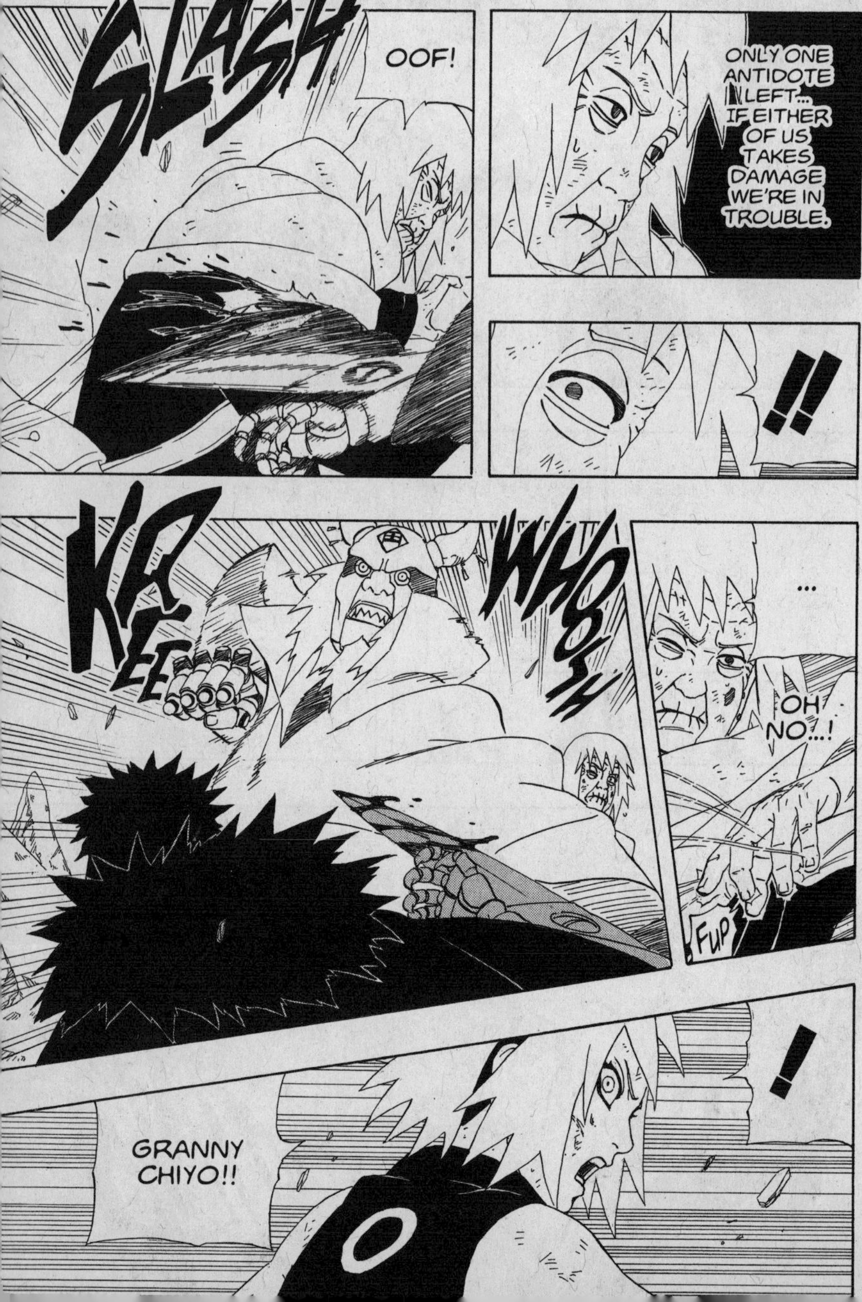
ONLY ONE ANTIDOTE LEFT... IF EITHER OF US TAKES DAMAGE WE'RE IN TROUBLE.
!!
SLASH
OOF!
...
OH NO...!
FUP
KREE
WHOOSH
!
GRANNY CHIYO!!

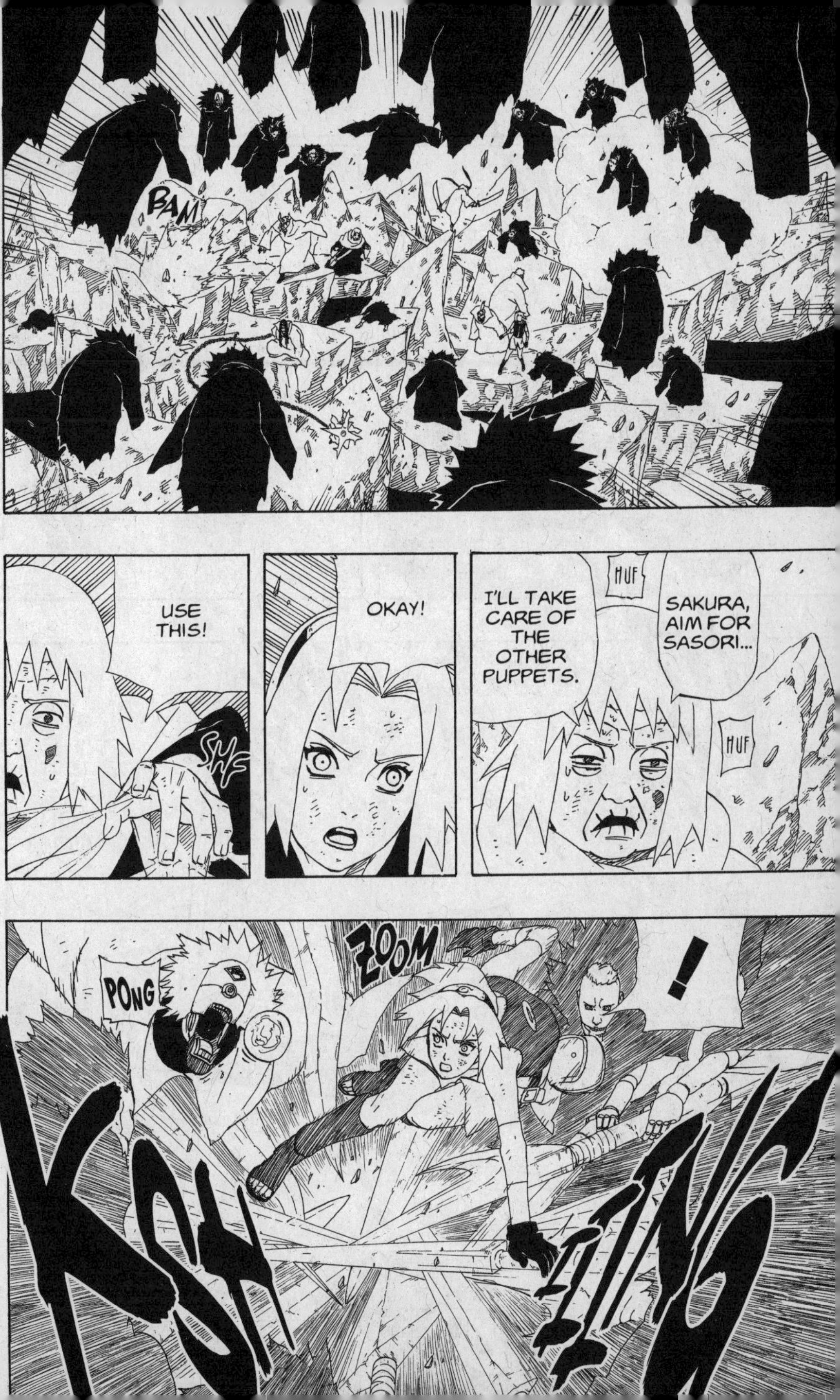
BAM
SAKURA, AIM FOR SASORI...
HUF
I'LL TAKE CARE OF THE OTHER PUPPETS.
HUF
OKAY!
USE THIS!
SHF
!
ZOOM
PONG

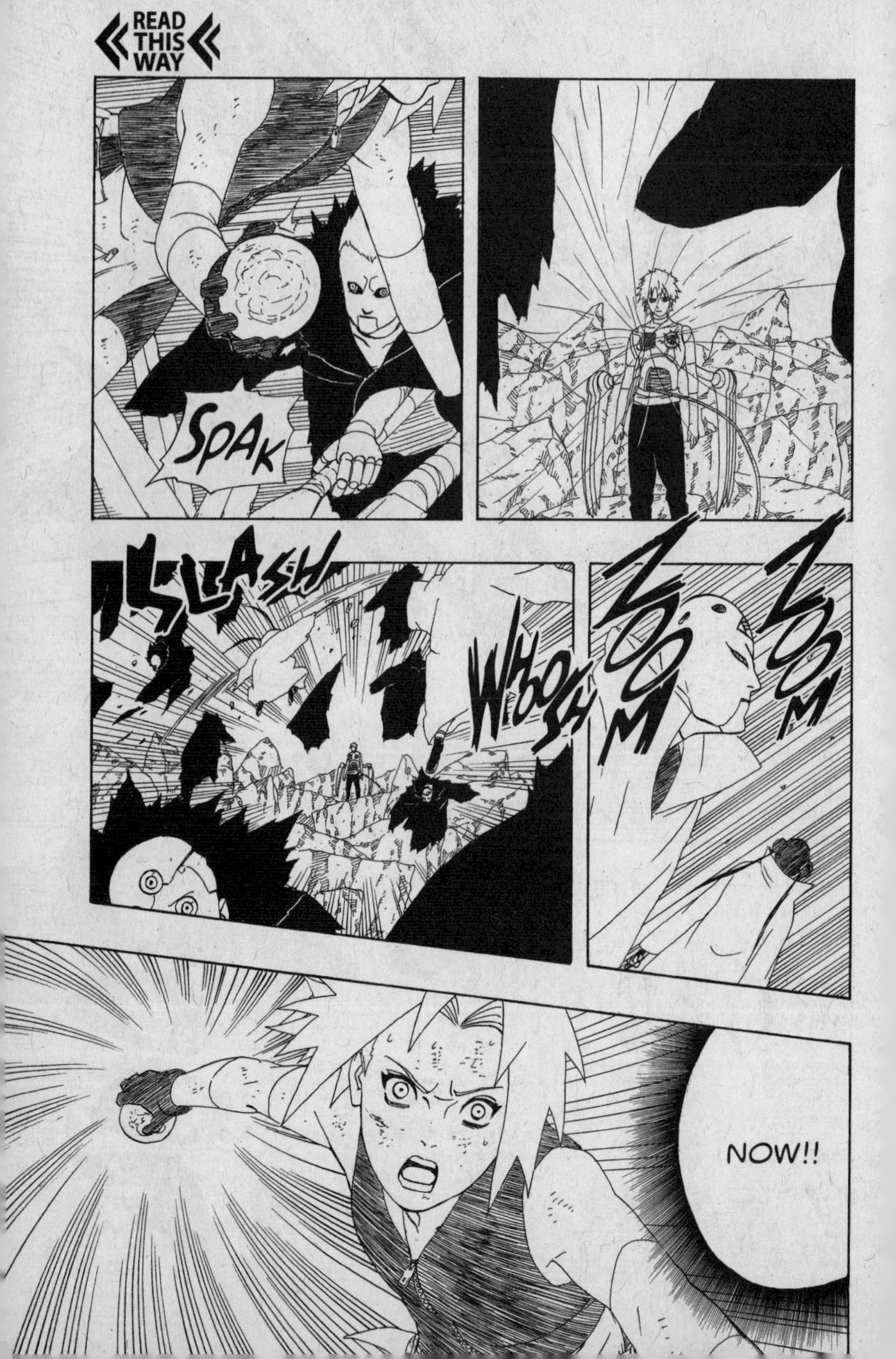
READ THIS WAY
SPAK
SLASH
WHOOSH
ZOOM
ZOOM
NOW!!

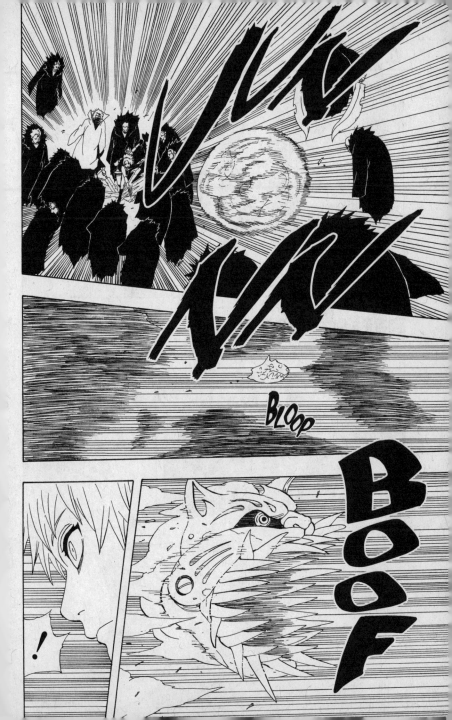

BLOOP

BOOF

READ THIS WAY

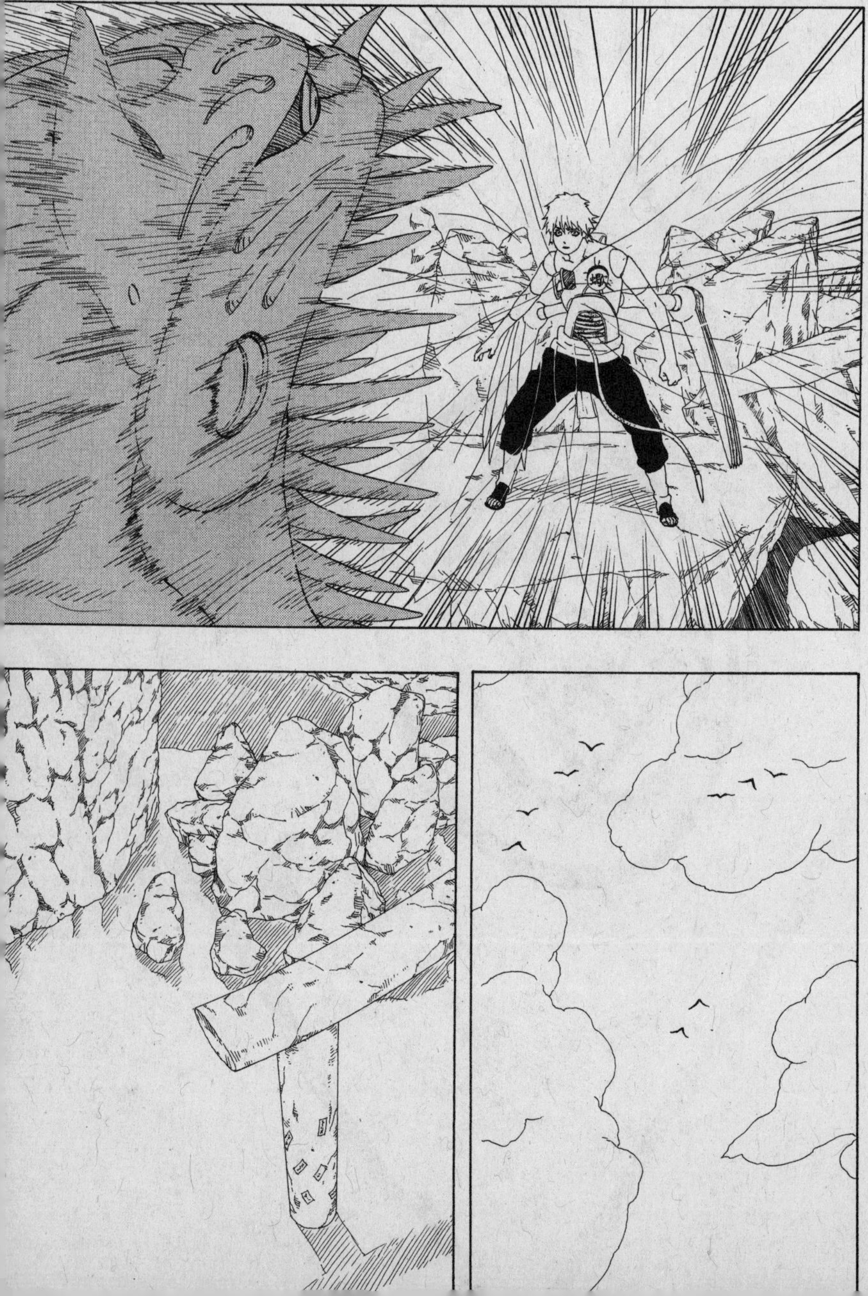

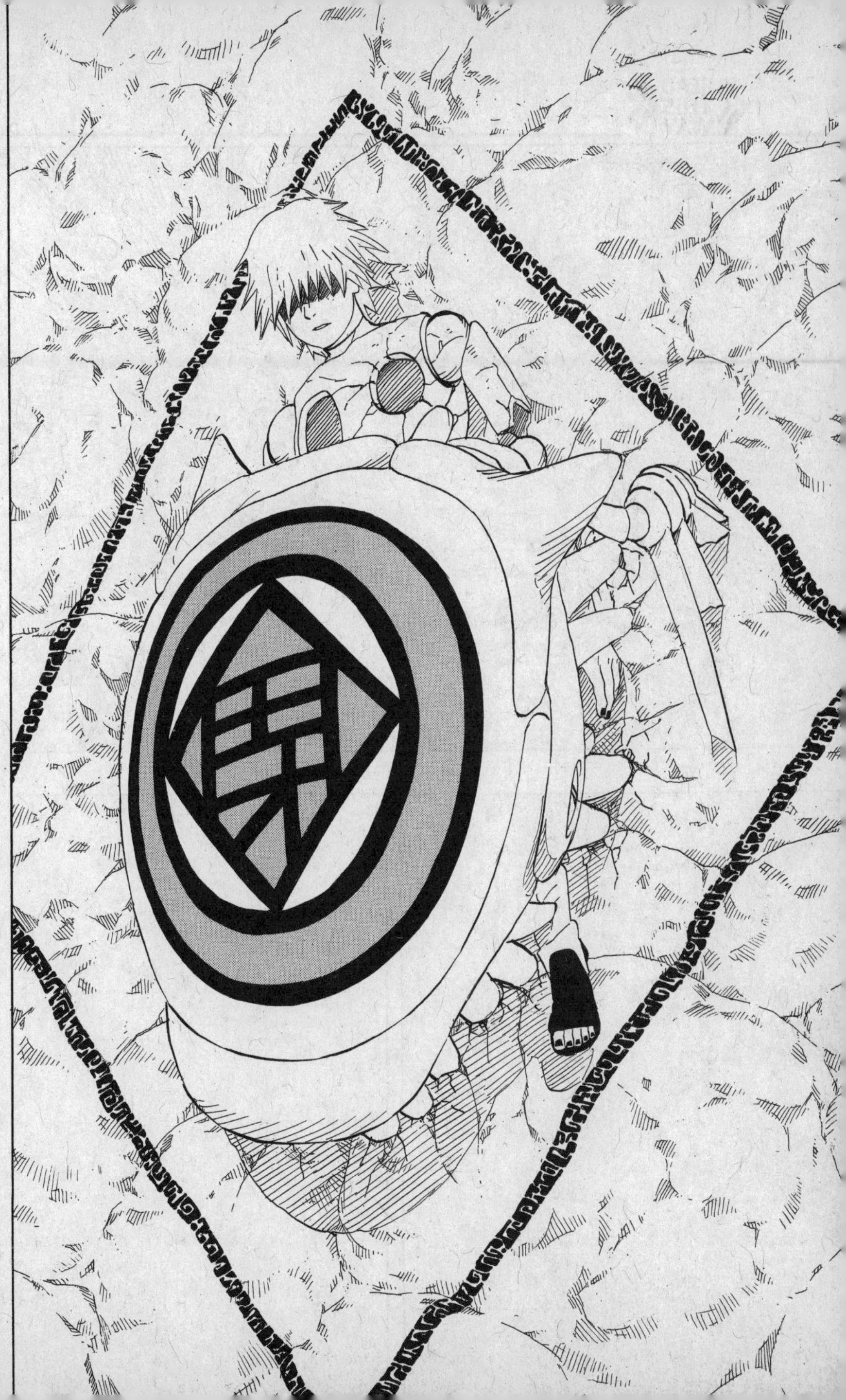

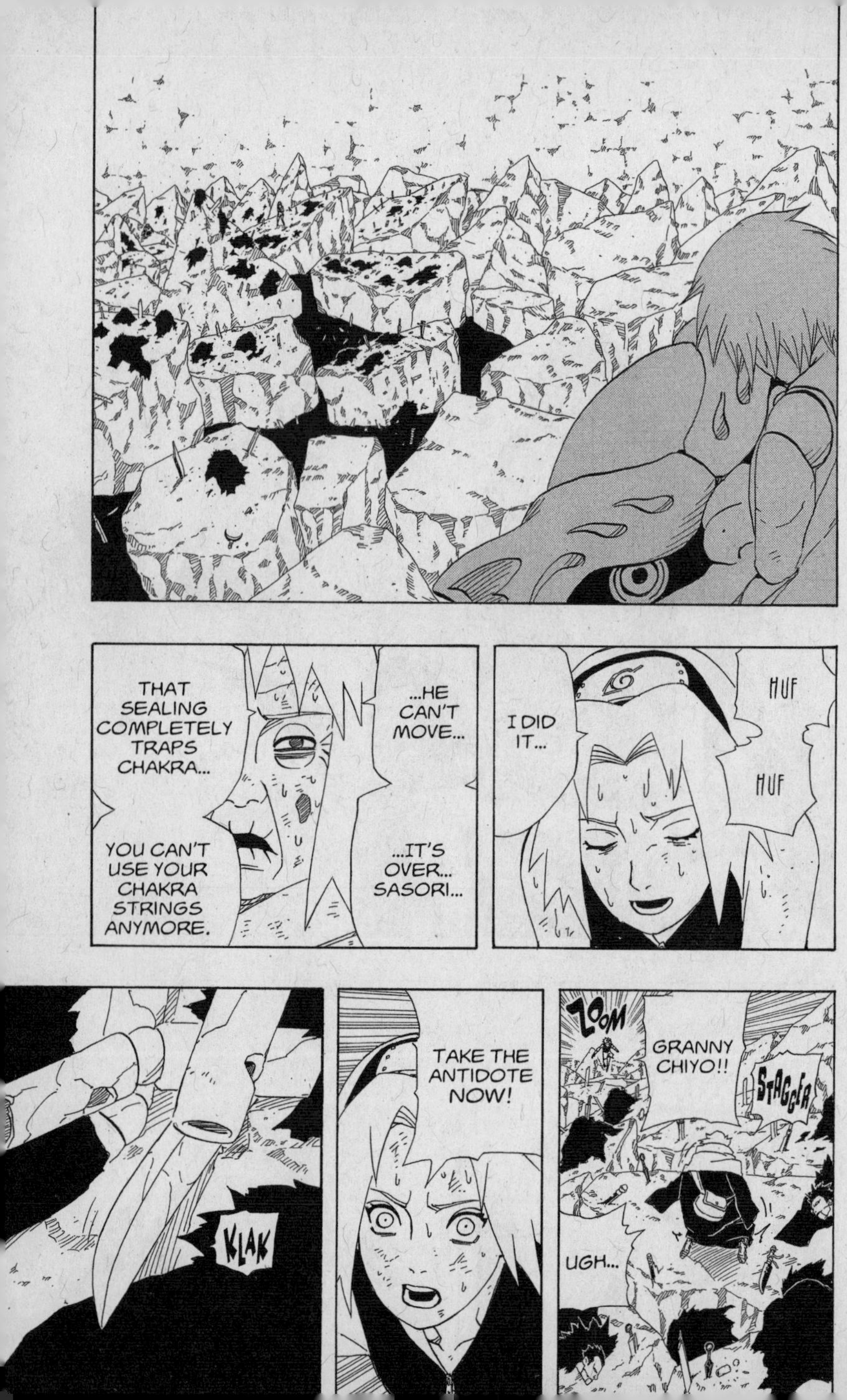

HUF
I DID IT...
HUF
...HE CAN'T MOVE...
...IT'S OVER... SASORI...
THAT SEALING COMPLETELY TRAPS CHAKRA...
YOU CAN'T USE YOUR CHAKRA STRINGS ANYMORE.
ZOOM
GRANNY CHIYO!!
STAGGER
UGH...
TAKE THE ANTIDOTE NOW!
KLAK

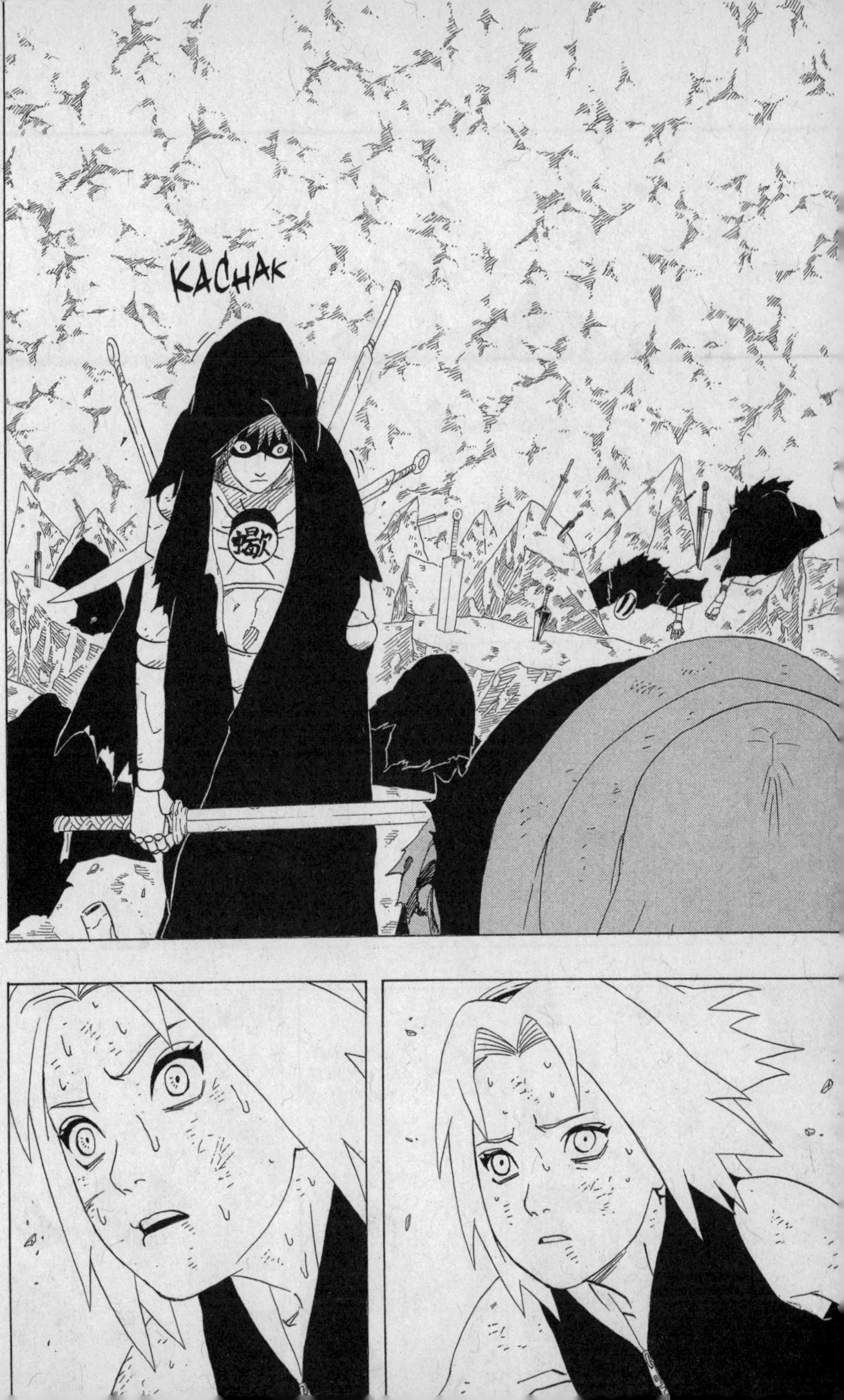
KACHAK

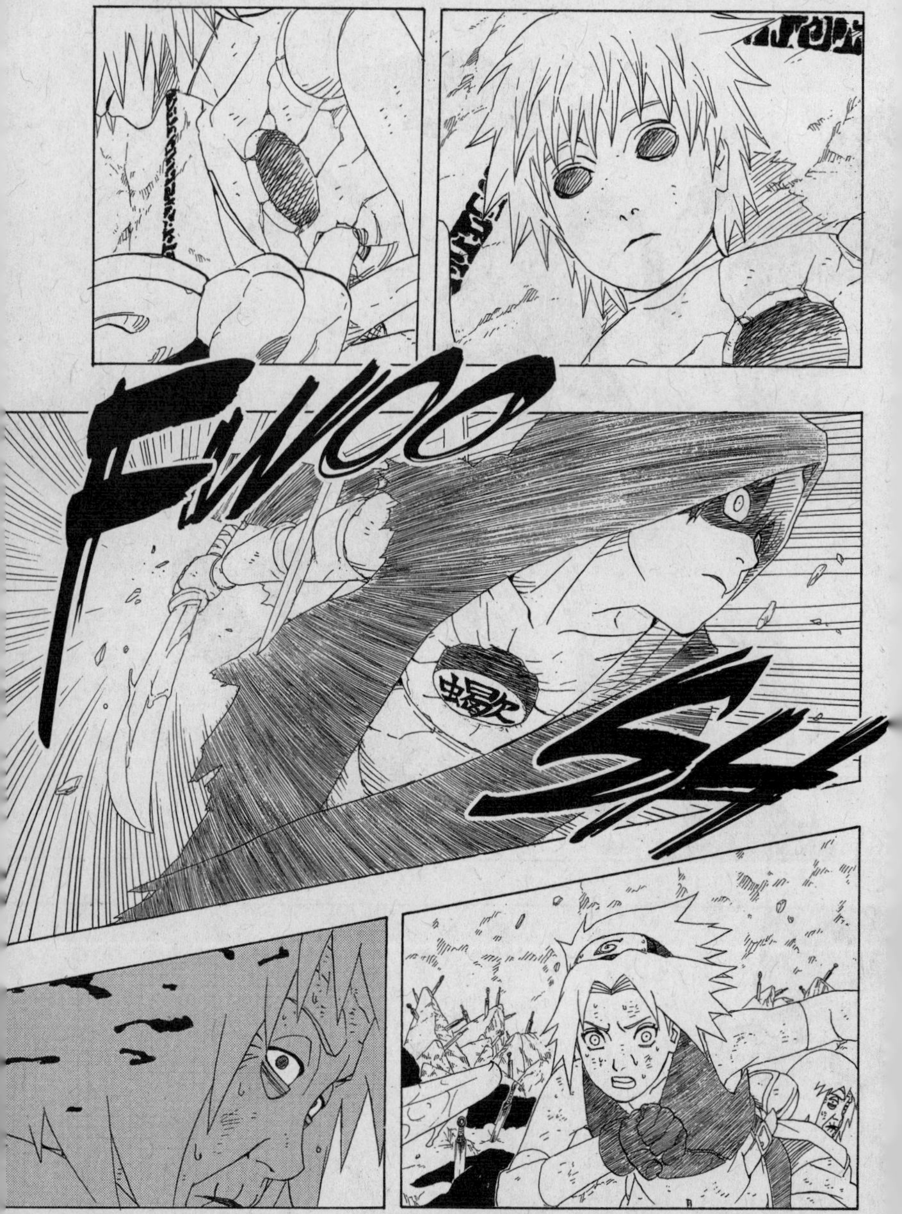
FWOOSH

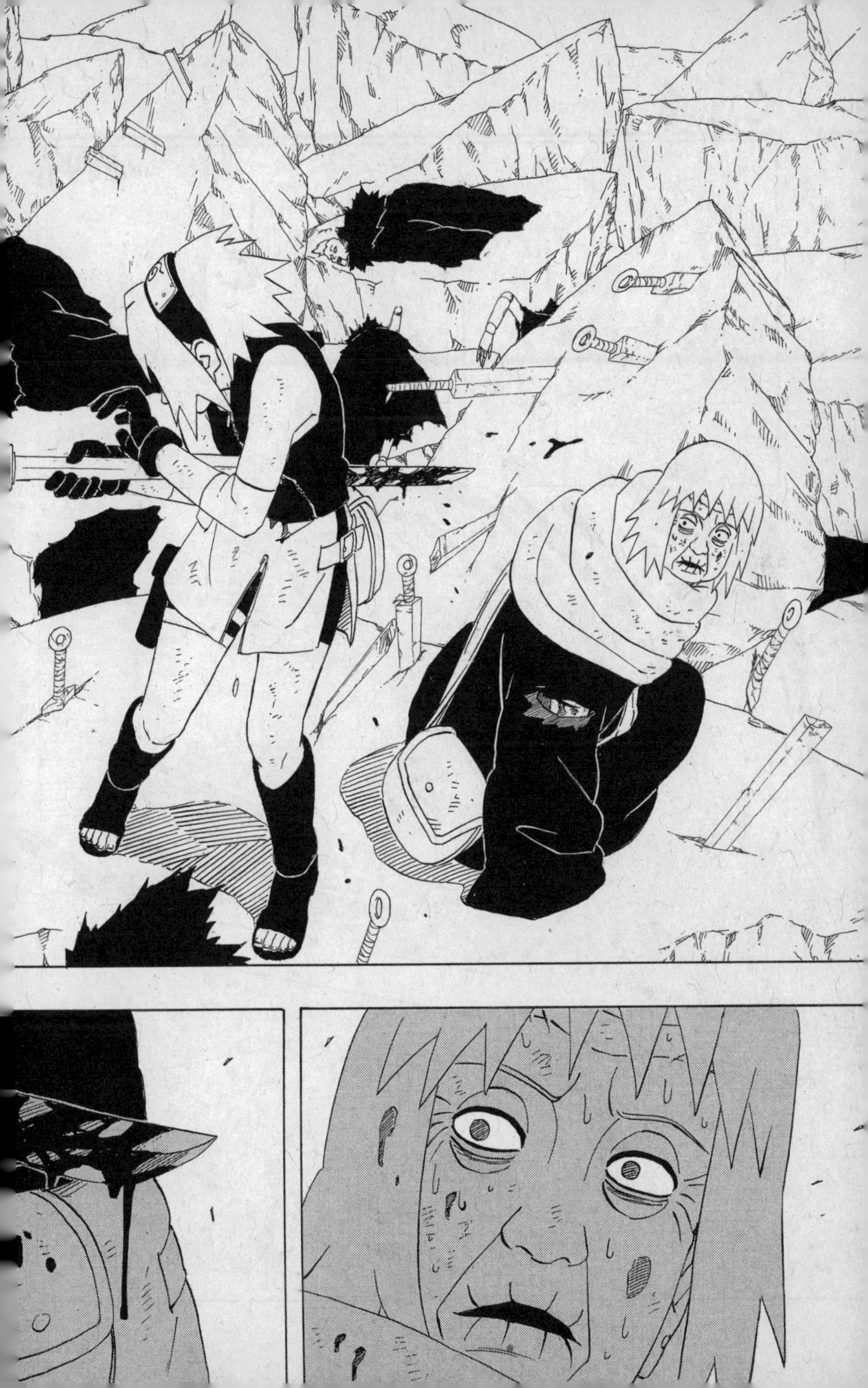

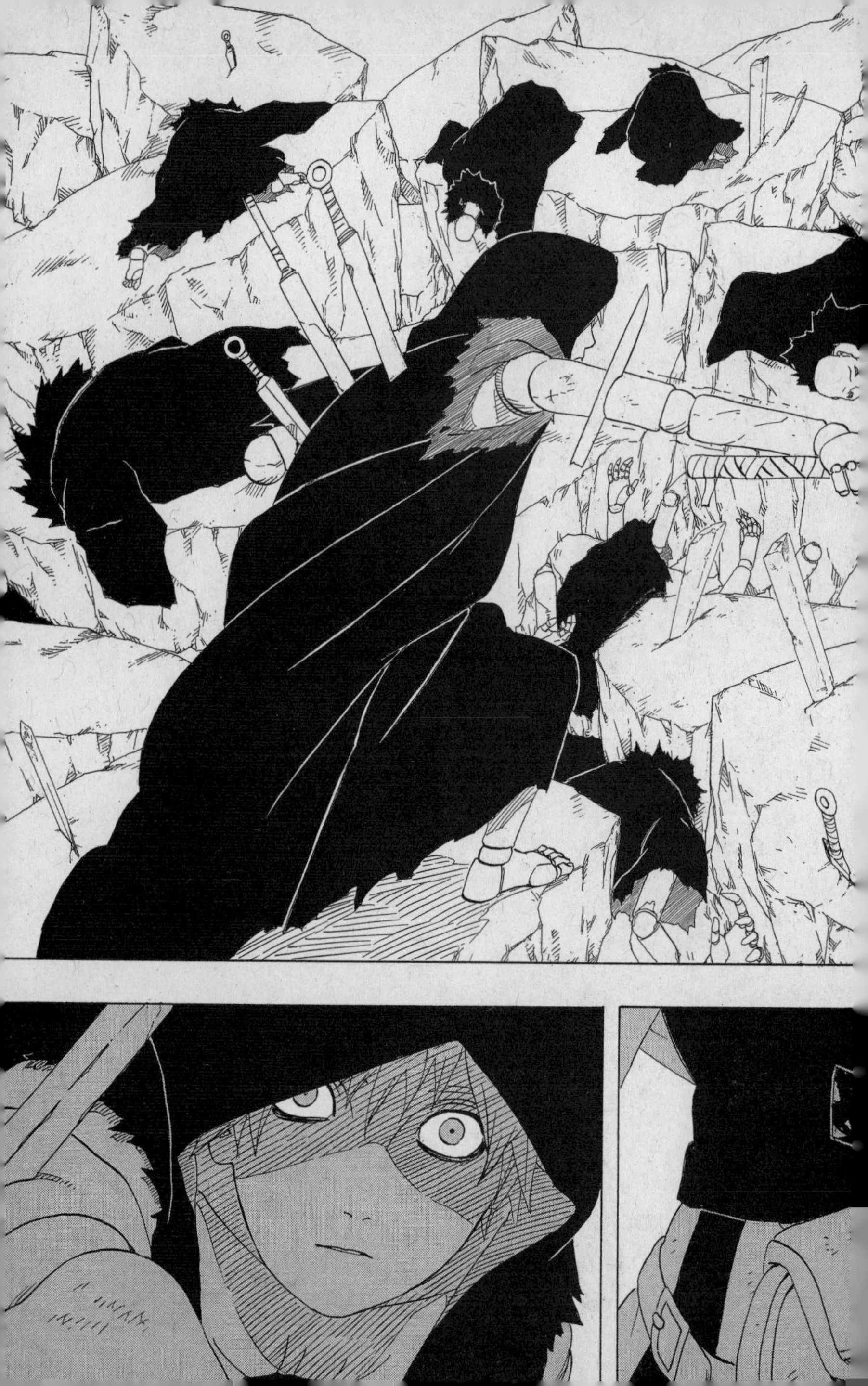

NARUTO

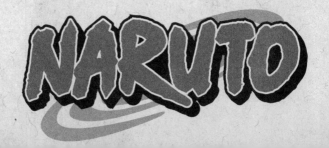

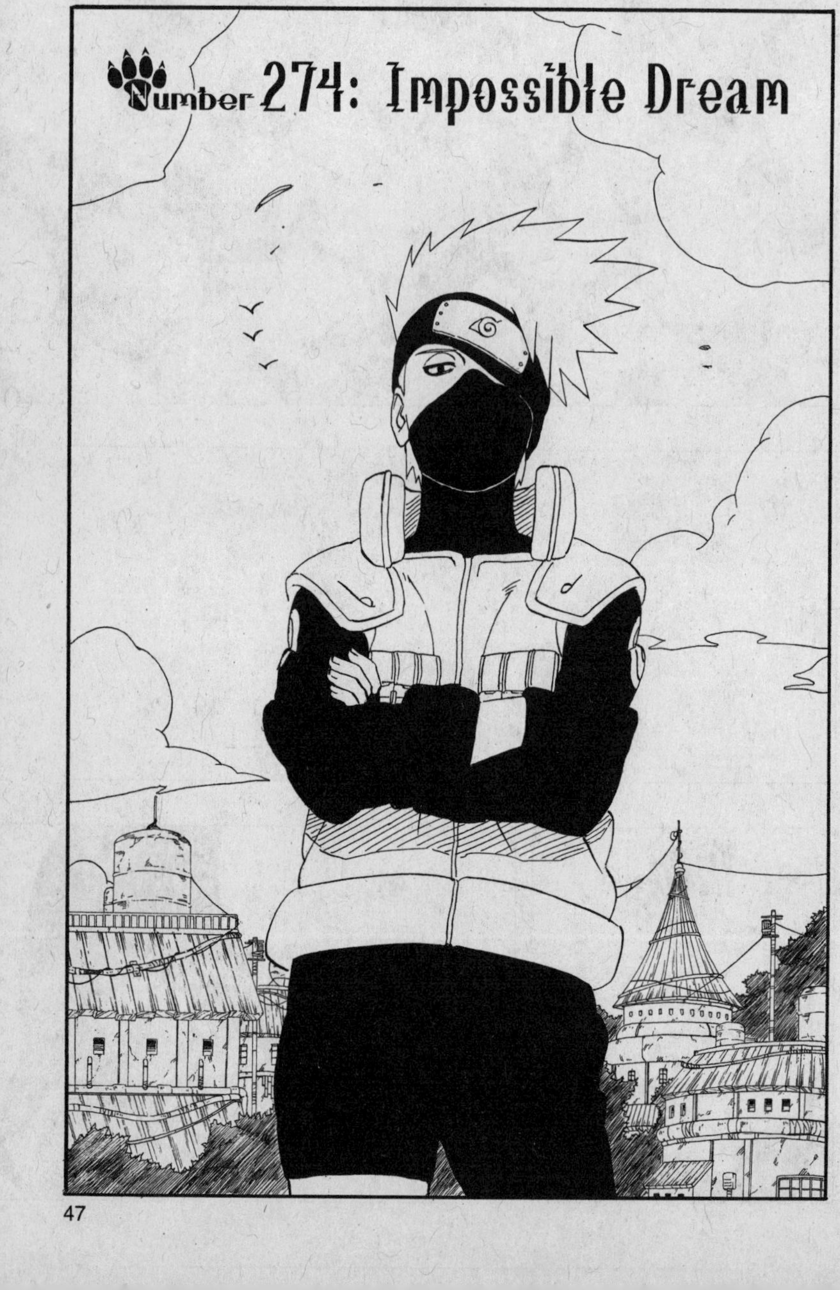
Number 274: Impossible Dream

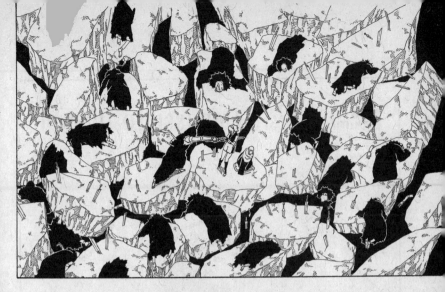

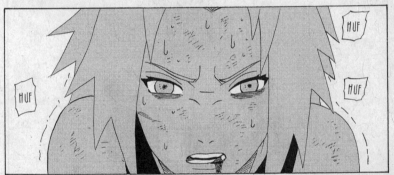

HUF

HUF

HUF

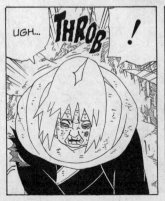

UGH... **THROB** !

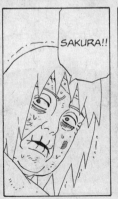

SAKURA!!

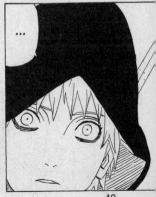

...

READ THIS WAY

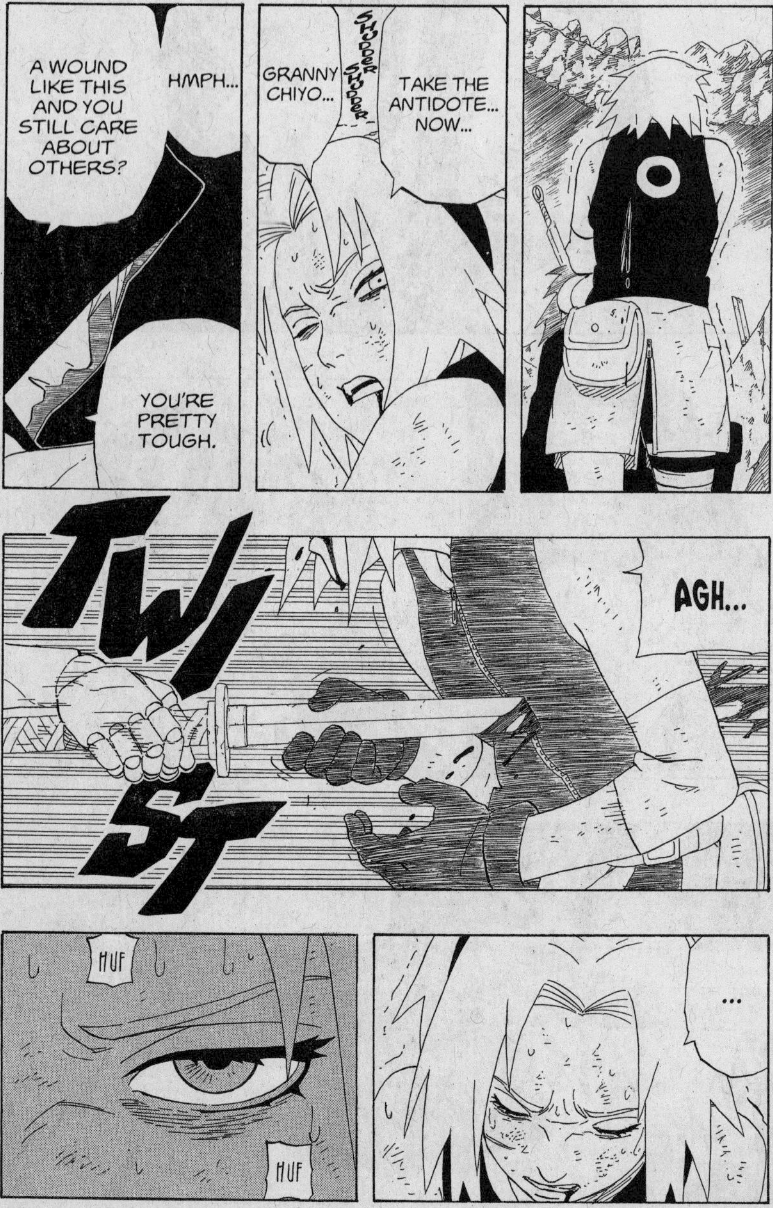
TAKE THE ANTIDOTE... NOW...
SHUDDER SHUDDER
GRANNY CHIYO...
HMPH...
A WOUND LIKE THIS AND YOU STILL CARE ABOUT OTHERS?
YOU'RE PRETTY TOUGH.
AGH...
TWIST
...
HUF
HUF

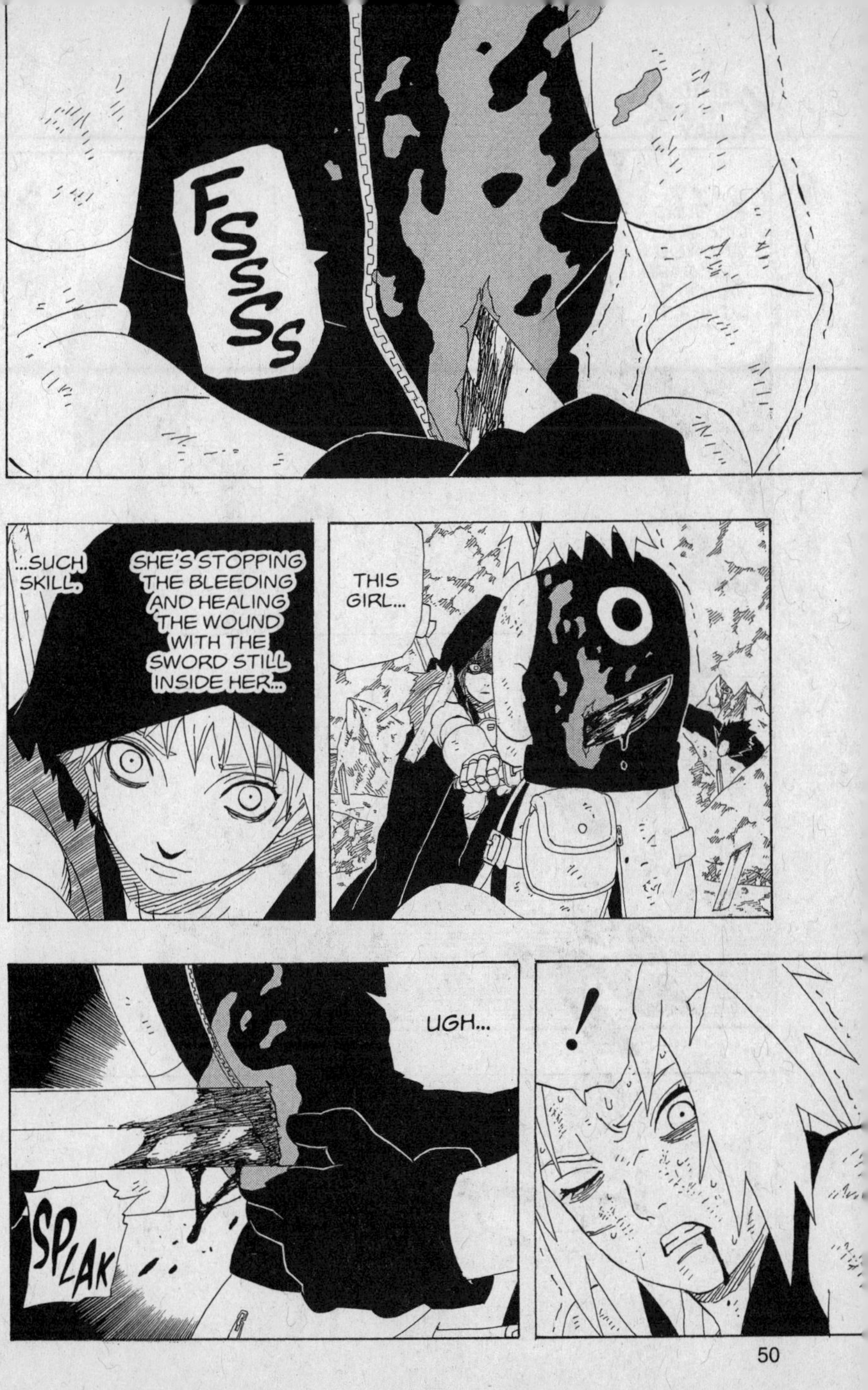
FSSSSS
THIS GIRL...
SHE'S STOPPING THE BLEEDING AND HEALING THE WOUND WITH THE SWORD STILL INSIDE HER...
...SUCH SKILL.
!
UGH...
SPLAK

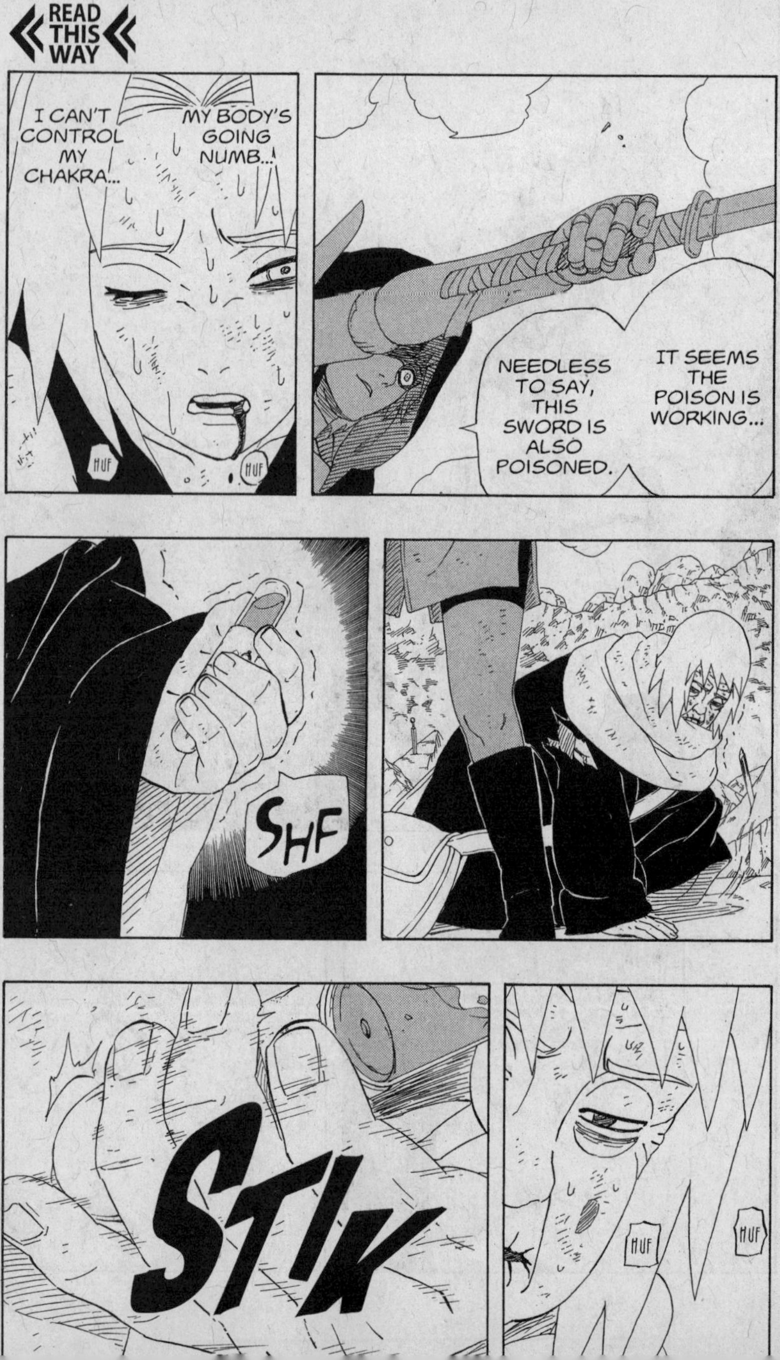
READ THIS WAY
NEEDLESS TO SAY, THIS SWORD IS ALSO POISONED.
IT SEEMS THE POISON IS WORKING...
MY BODY'S GOING NUMB...
I CAN'T CONTROL MY CHAKRA...
HUF
HUF
SHF
HUF
HUF
STIK

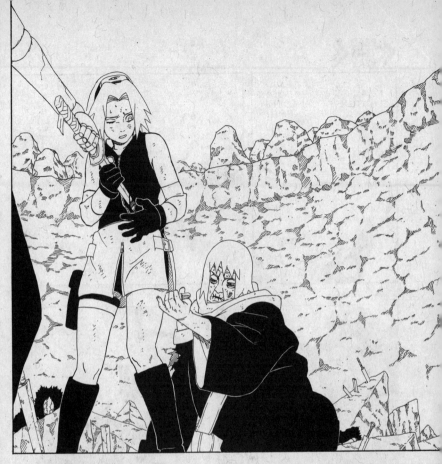

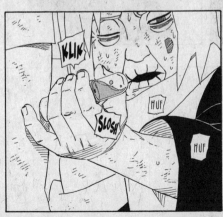

KLIK

HUF

SLOSH

HUF

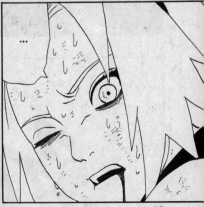

...

READ THIS WAY

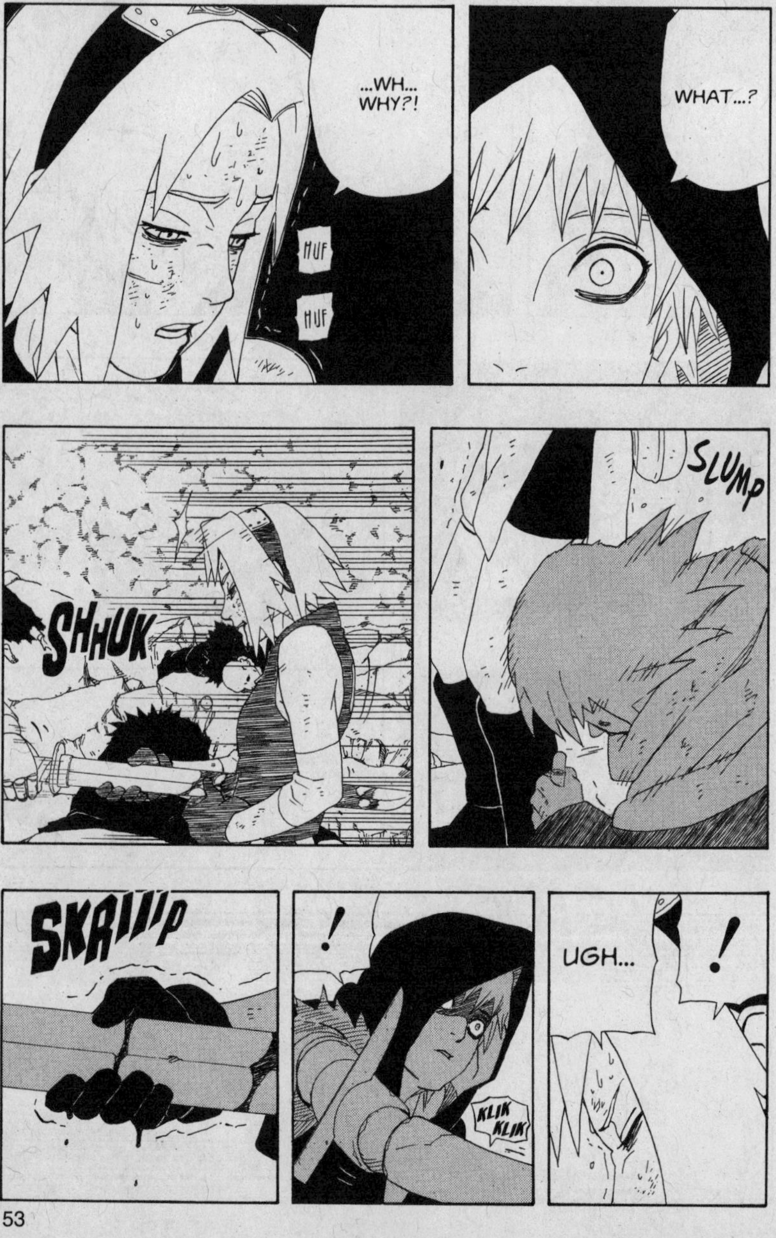
WHAT...?
...WH... WHY?!
HUF
HUF
SLUMP
SHHUK
UGH...
!
!
KLIK KLIK
SKRIIIP

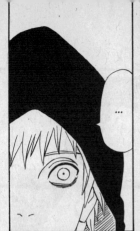

...

I WON'T LET GO.

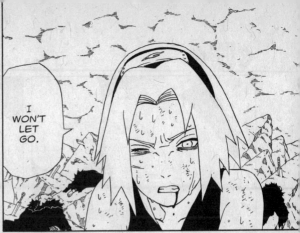

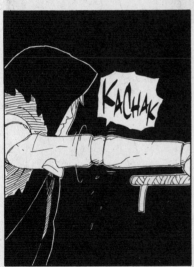

KACHAK

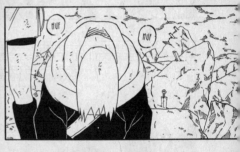

HUF

HUF

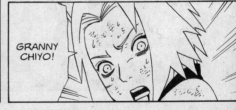

GRANNY CHIYO!

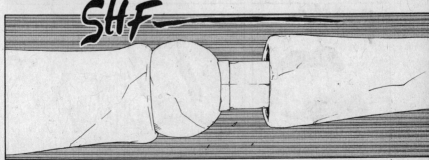

SHF

READ THIS WAY

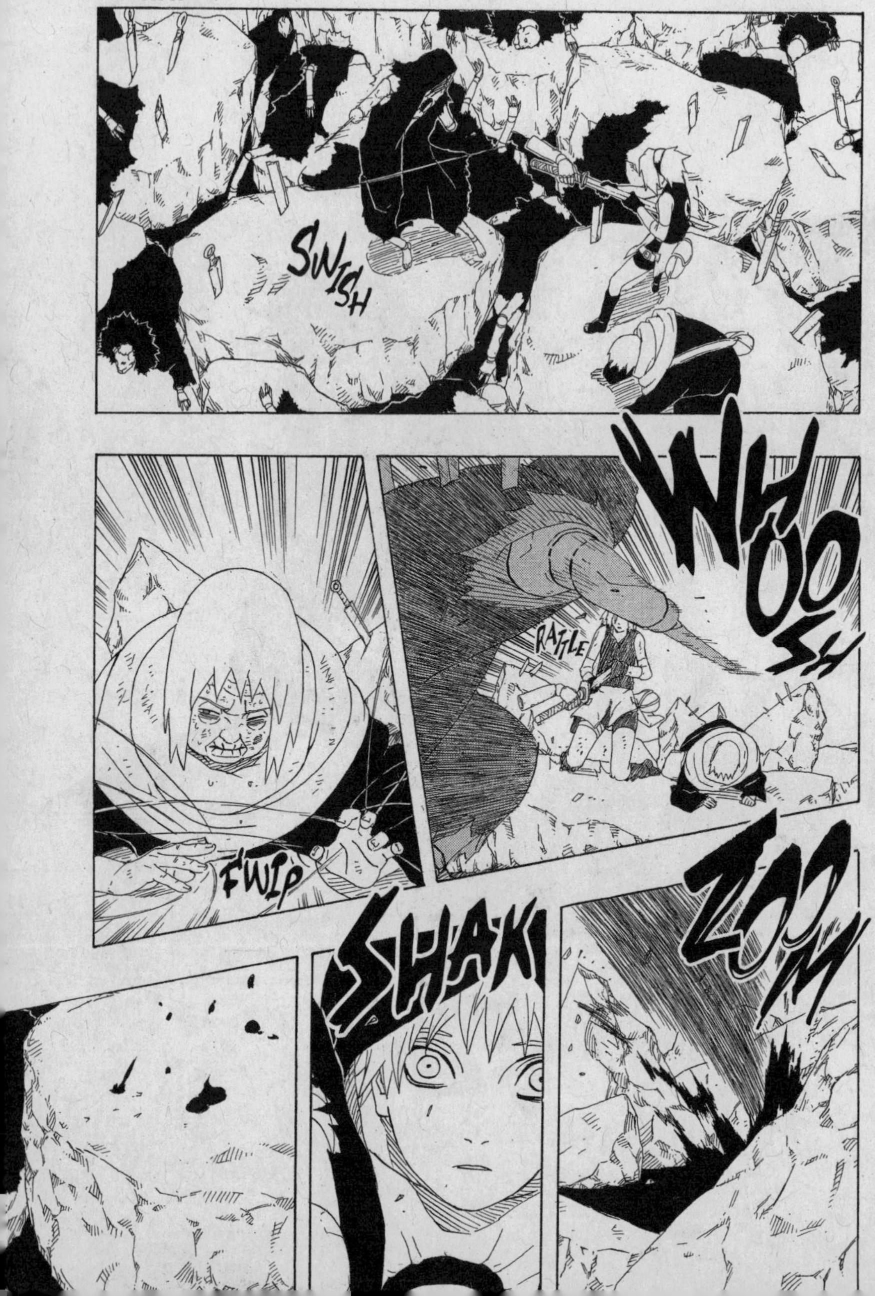
SWISH
WHOOSH
RATTLE
FWIP
ZOOM
SHAK

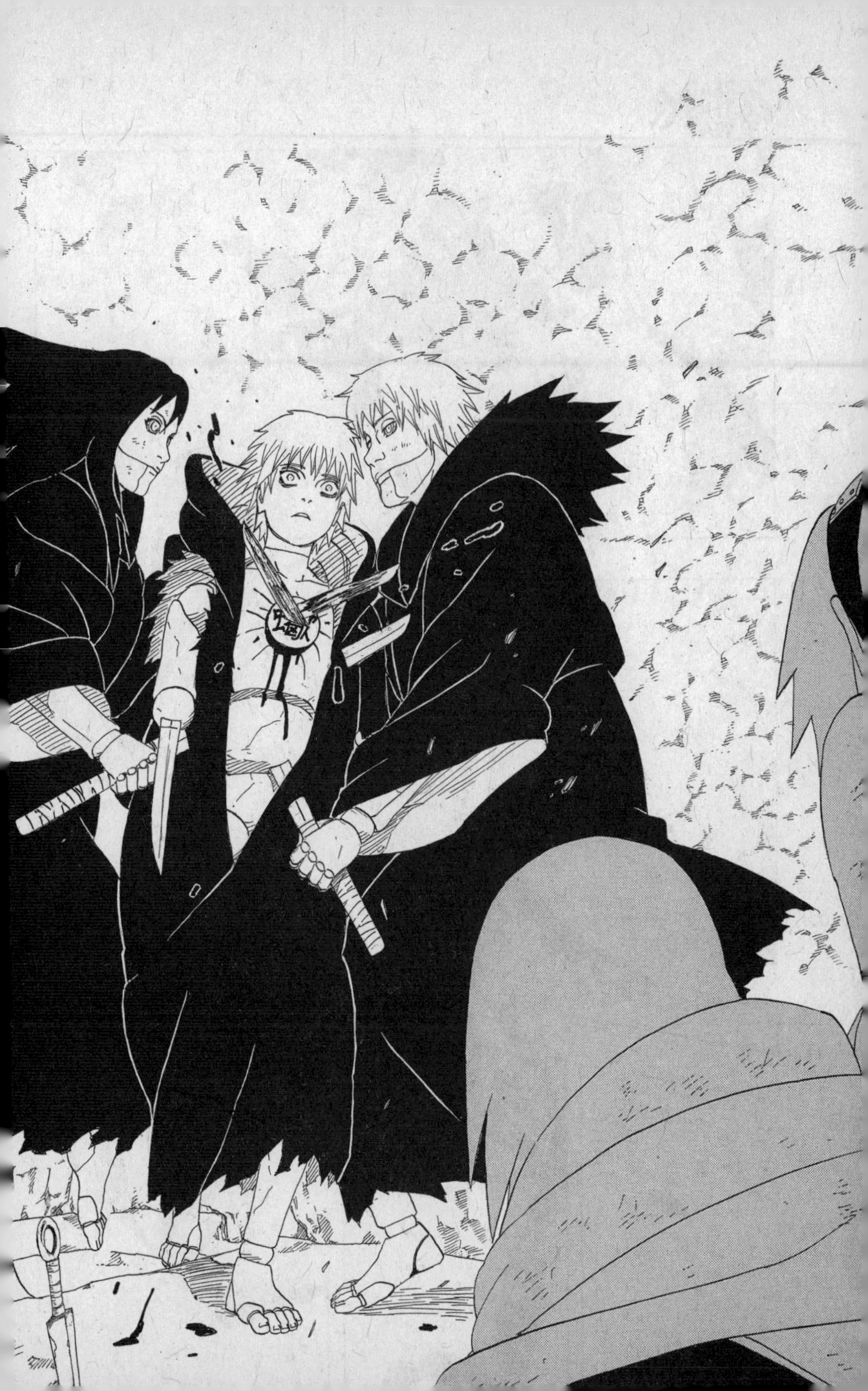

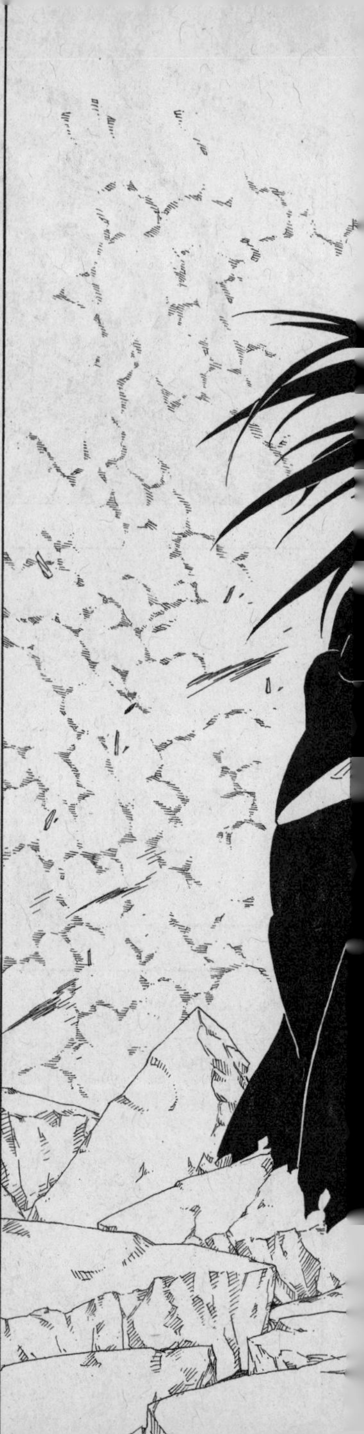

READ THIS WAY

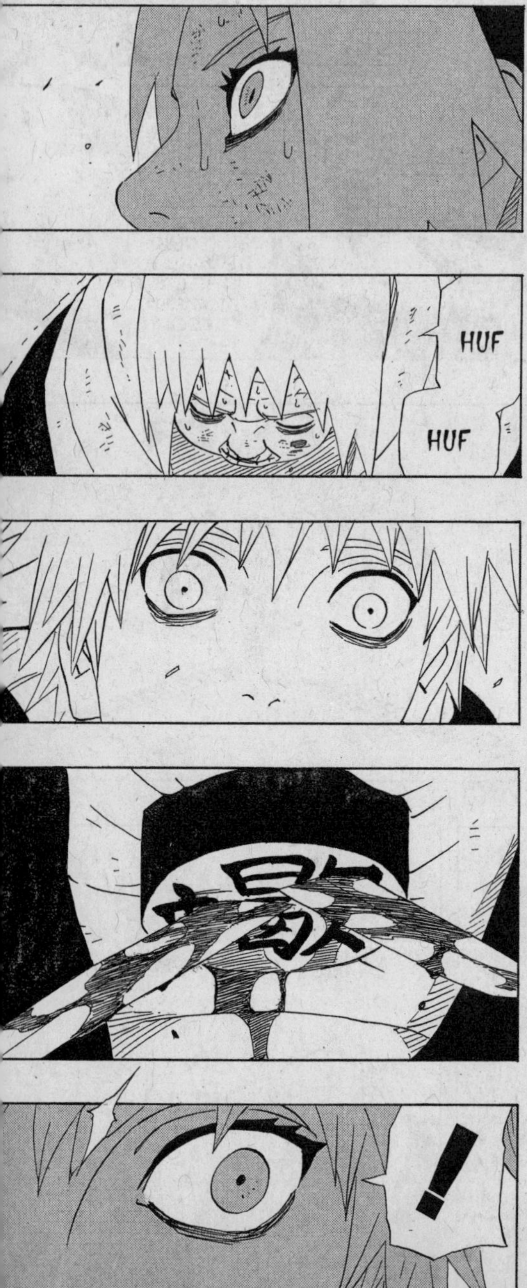
HUF
HUF
!

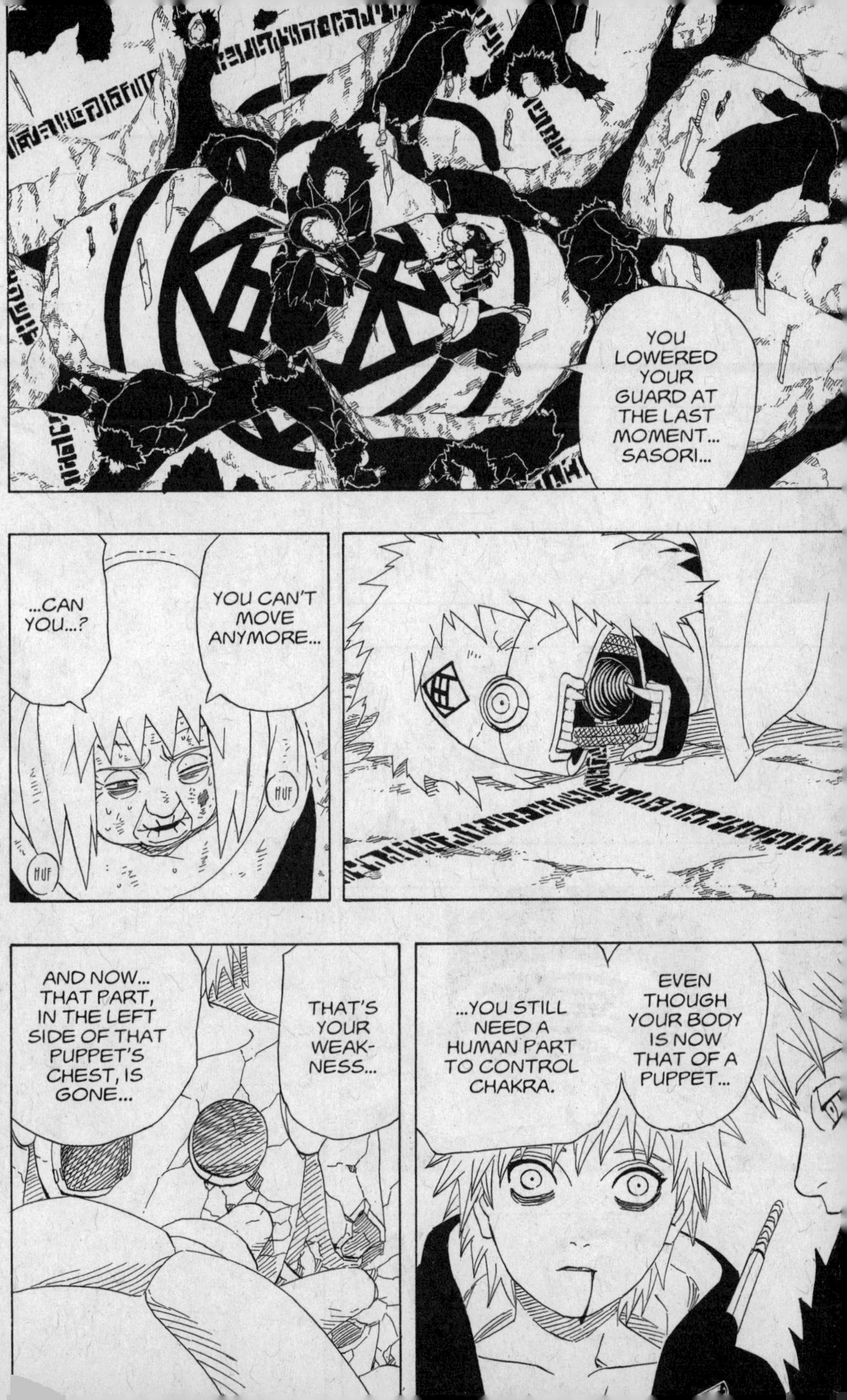
YOU LOWERED YOUR GUARD AT THE LAST MOMENT... SASORI...
YOU CAN'T MOVE ANYMORE...
...CAN YOU...?
HUF
HUF
EVEN THOUGH YOUR BODY IS NOW THAT OF A PUPPET...
...YOU STILL NEED A HUMAN PART TO CONTROL CHAKRA.
THAT'S YOUR WEAK-NESS...
AND NOW... THAT PART, IN THE LEFT SIDE OF THAT PUPPET'S CHEST, IS GONE...

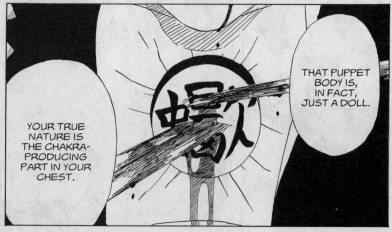

THAT PUPPET BODY IS, IN FACT, JUST A DOLL.

YOUR TRUE NATURE IS THE CHAKRA-PRODUCING PART IN YOUR CHEST.

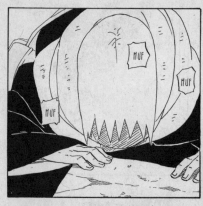

HUF

HUF

HUF

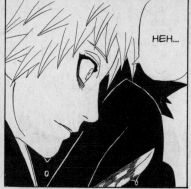

HEH...

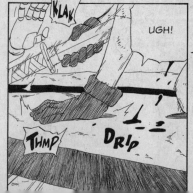

KLAK

UGH!

THMP

DRIP

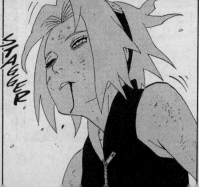

STAGGER

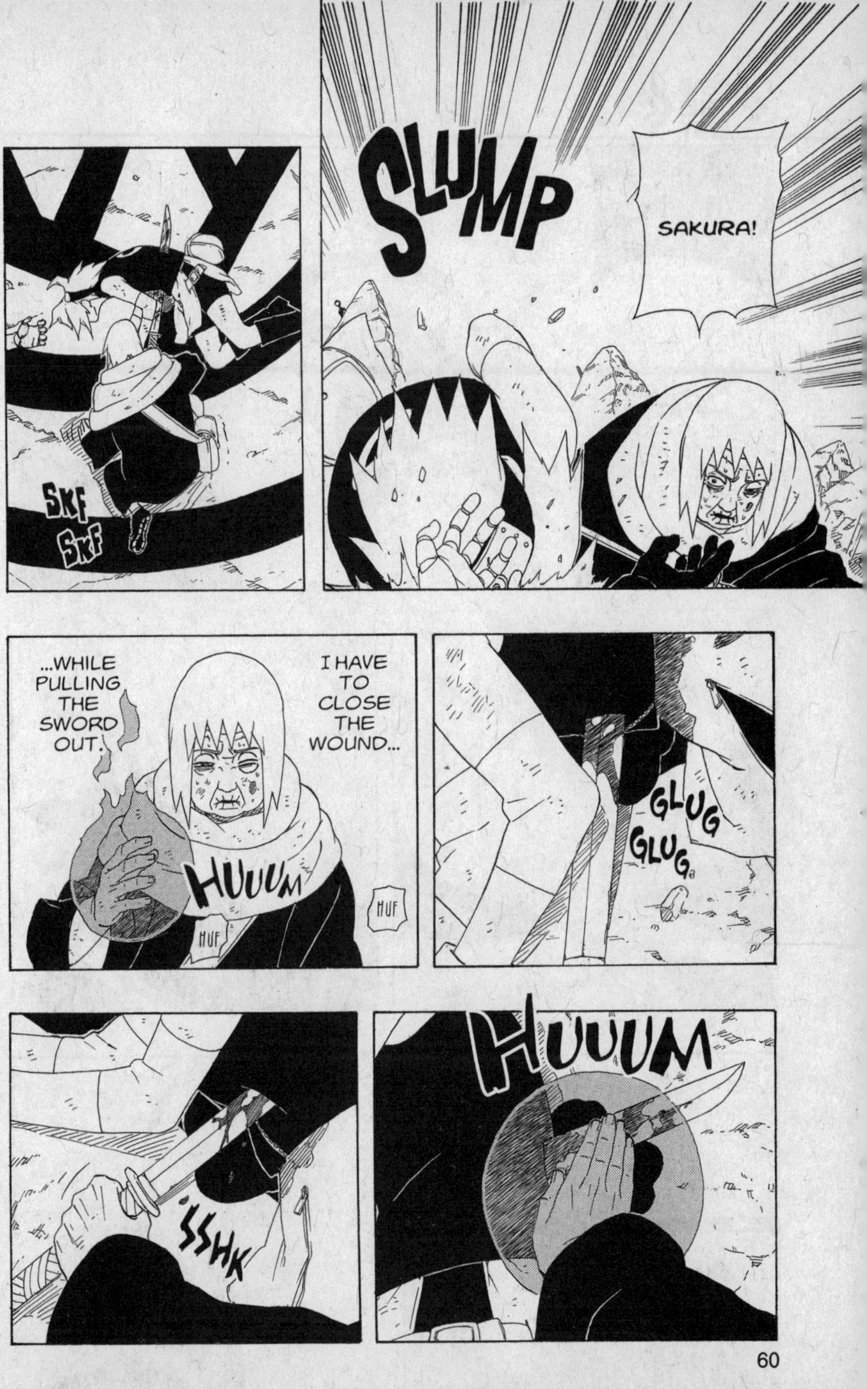
SLUMP
SAKURA!
SKF
SKF
GLUG
GLUG
I HAVE TO CLOSE THE WOUND...
...WHILE PULLING THE SWORD OUT.
HUUUM
HUF
HUF
HUUUM
SSHK

READ THIS WAY

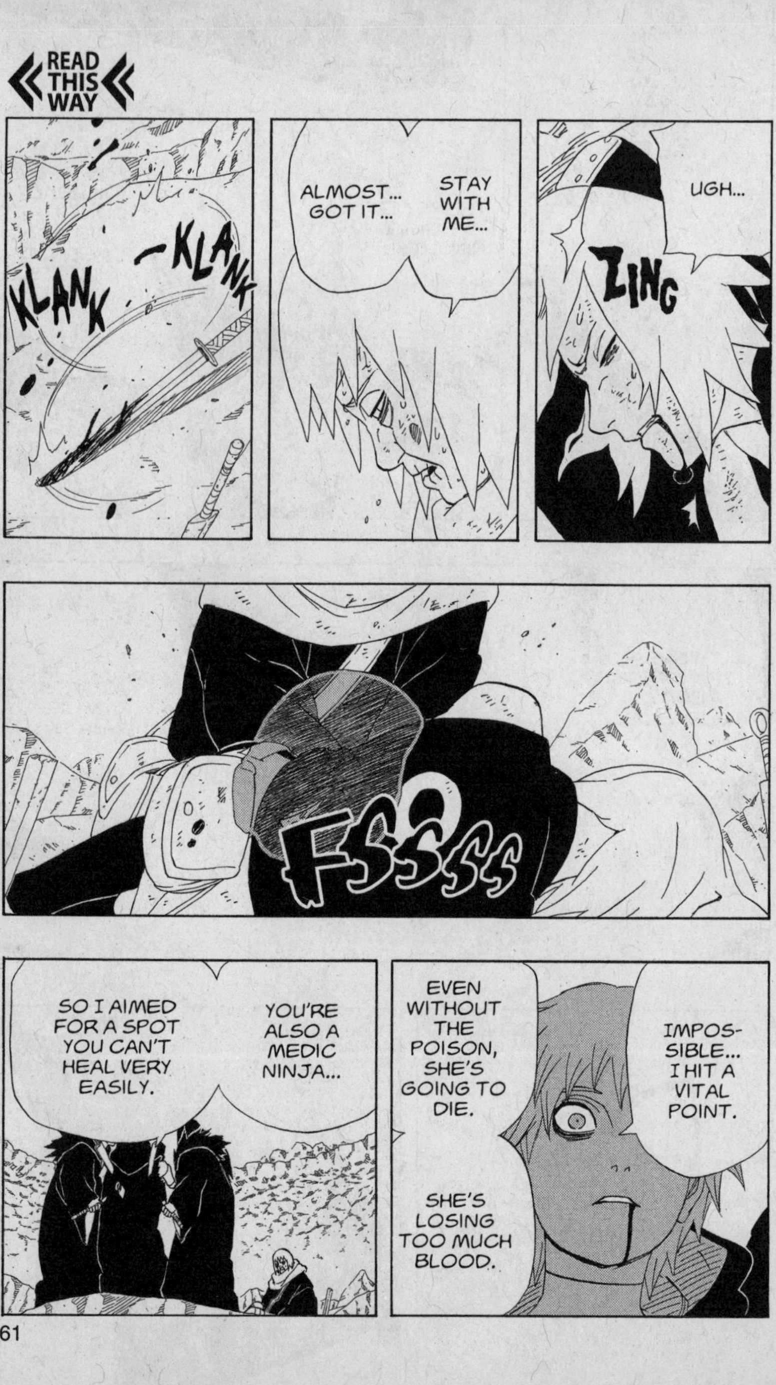
UGH...
ZING
STAY WITH ME...
ALMOST... GOT IT...
-KLANK
KLANK
FSSSS
IMPOSSIBLE... I HIT A VITAL POINT.
EVEN WITHOUT THE POISON, SHE'S GOING TO DIE.
SHE'S LOSING TOO MUCH BLOOD.
YOU'RE ALSO A MEDIC NINJA...
SO I AIMED FOR A SPOT YOU CAN'T HEAL VERY EASILY.

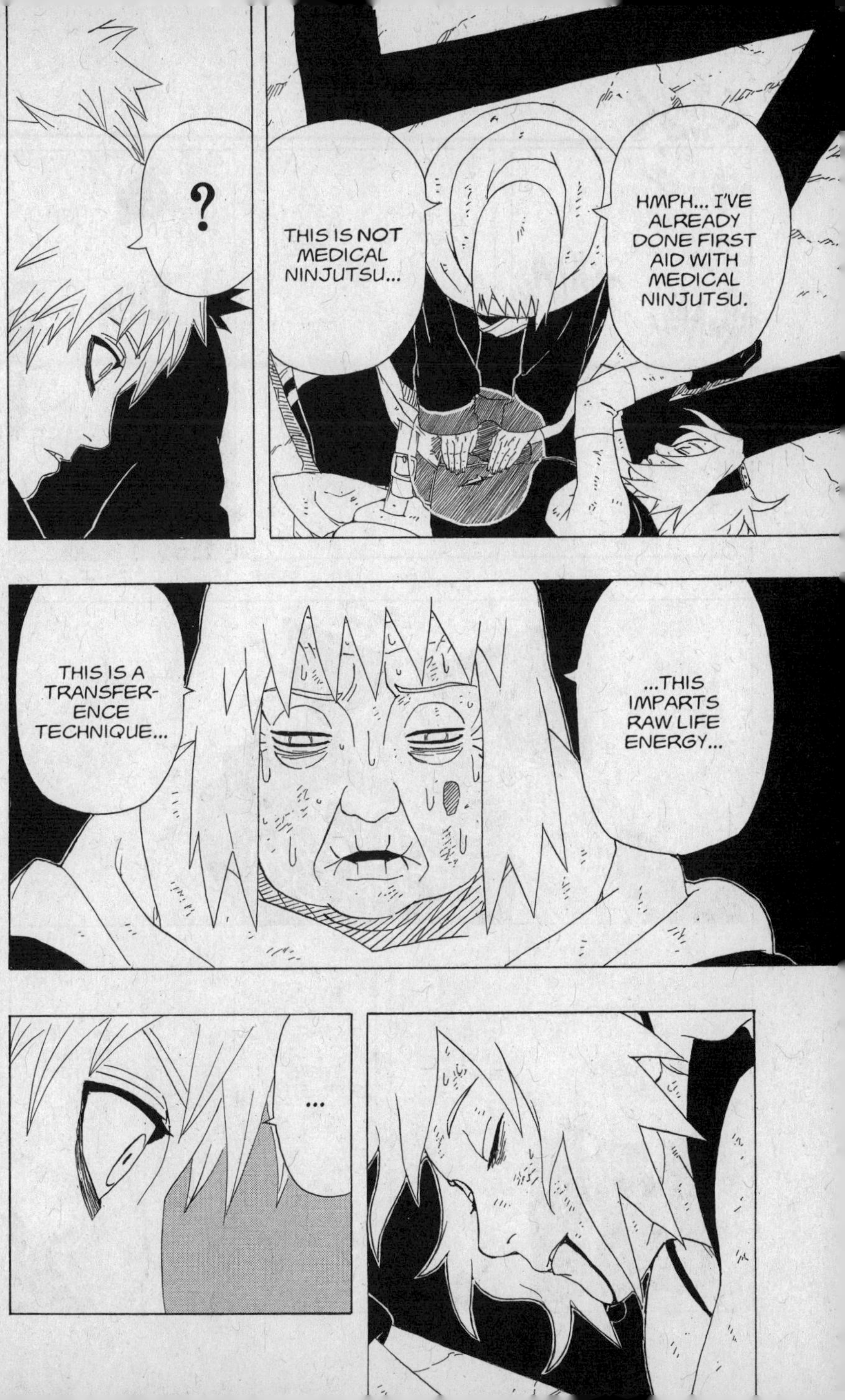
HMPH... I'VE ALREADY DONE FIRST AID WITH MEDICAL NINJUTSU.
THIS IS NOT MEDICAL NINJUTSU...
?
...THIS IMPARTS RAW LIFE ENERGY...
THIS IS A TRANSFERENCE TECHNIQUE...
...

READ THIS WAY

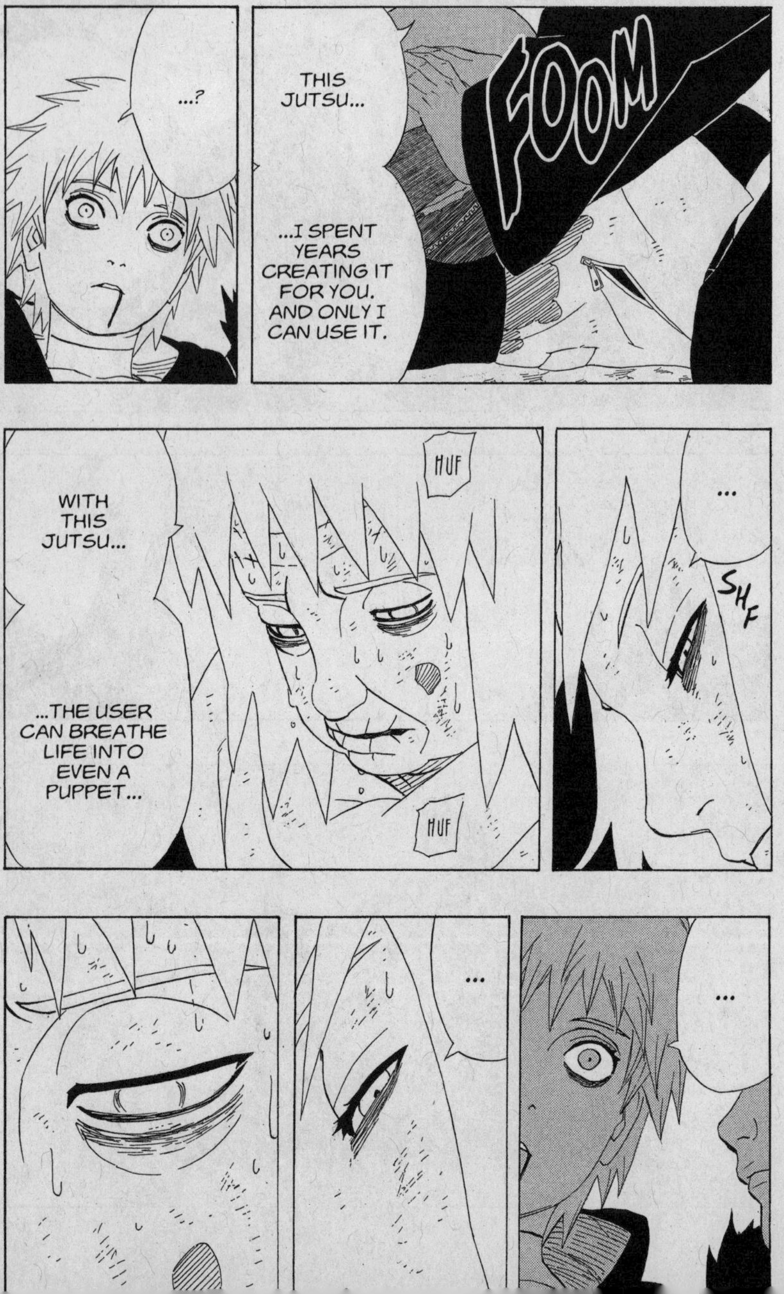
FOOM
THIS JUTSU...
...I SPENT YEARS CREATING IT FOR YOU. AND ONLY I CAN USE IT.
...?
...
SHF
HUF
WITH THIS JUTSU...
...THE USER CAN BREATHE LIFE INTO EVEN A PUPPET...
HUF
...
...

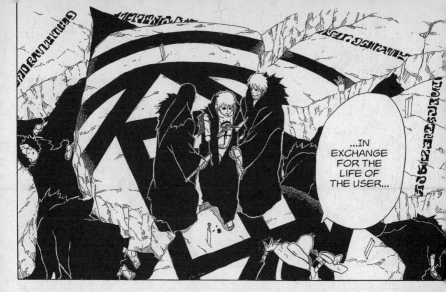

...IN EXCHANGE FOR THE LIFE OF THE USER...

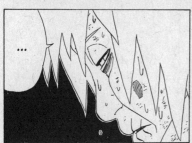

...

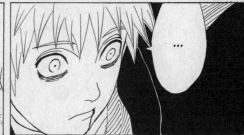

...

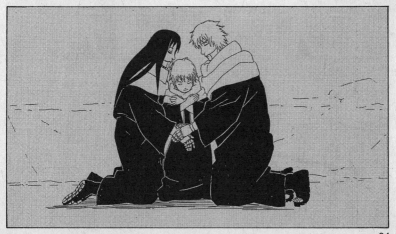

READ THIS WAY

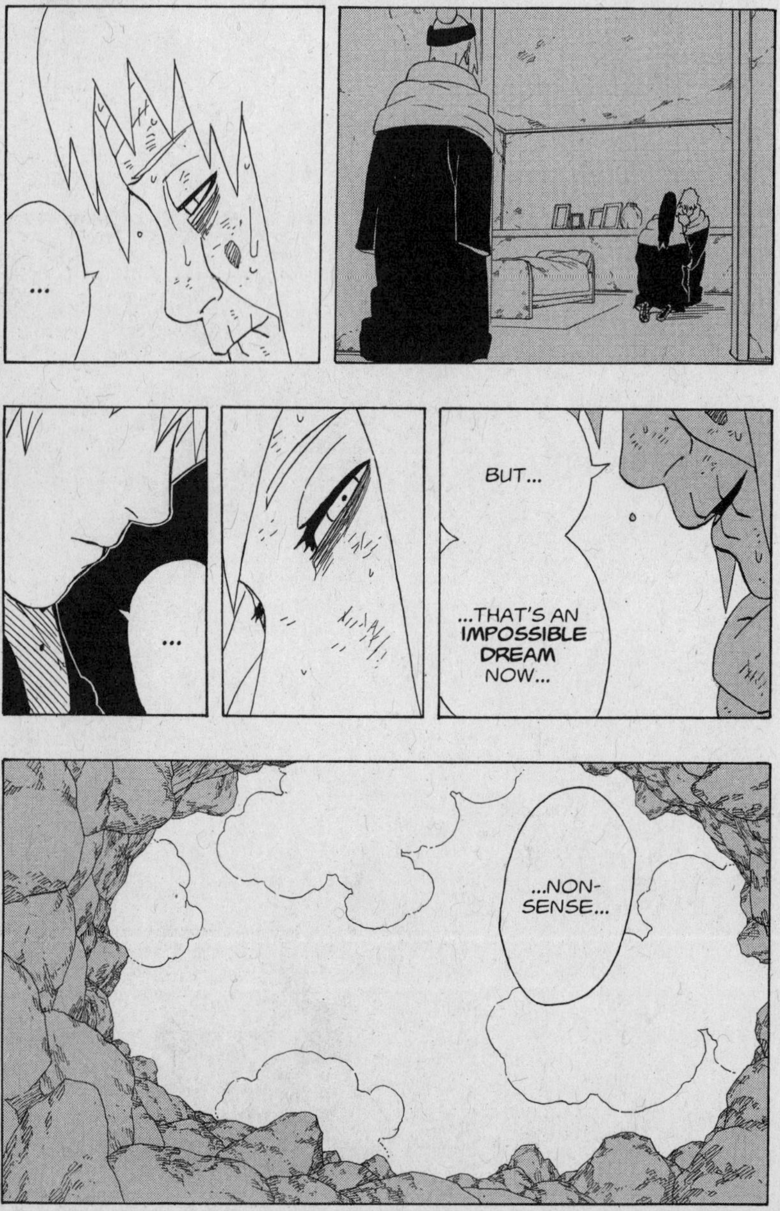
...
BUT...
...THAT'S AN IMPOSSIBLE DREAM NOW...
...
...NON-SENSE...

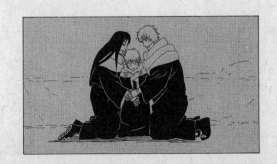

Number 275: Reward...!!

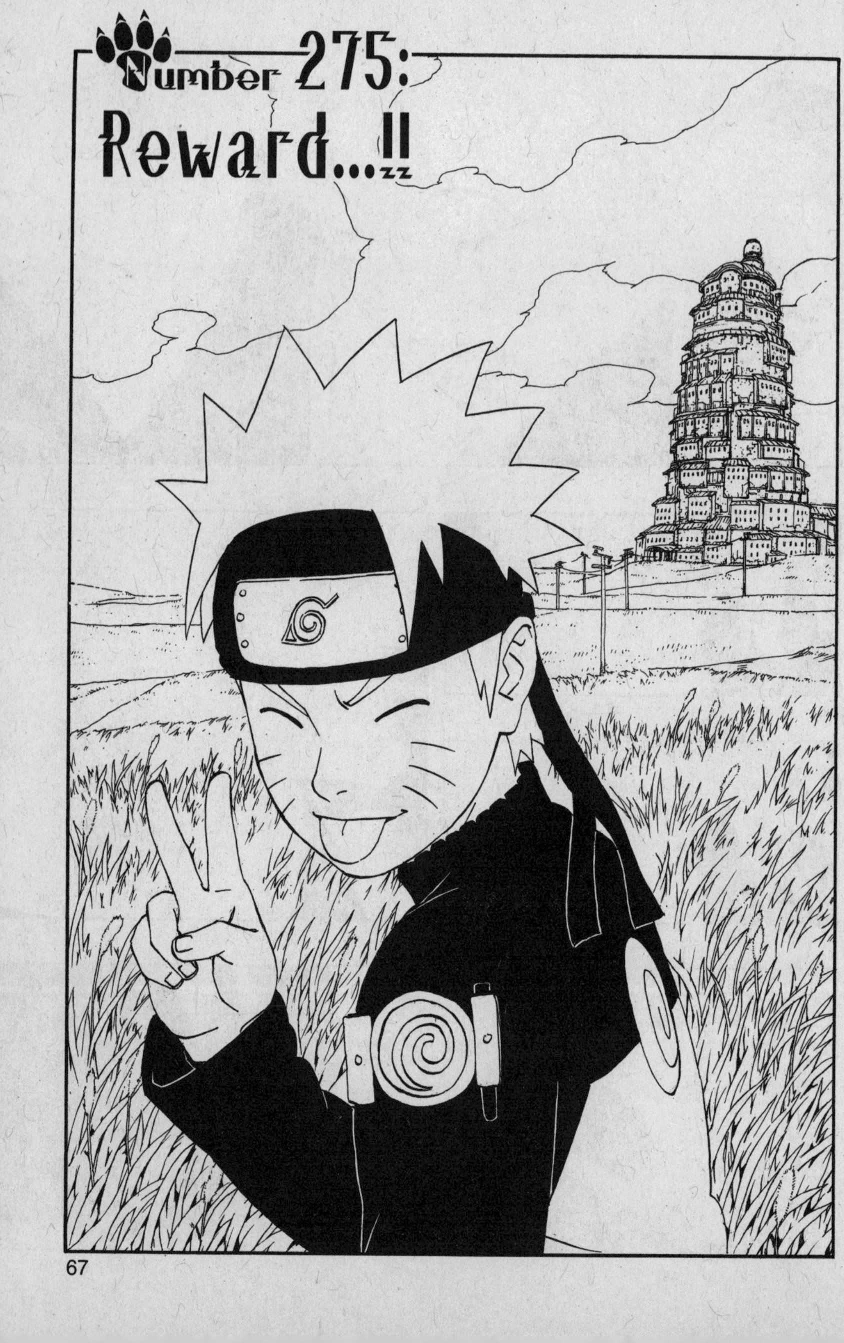

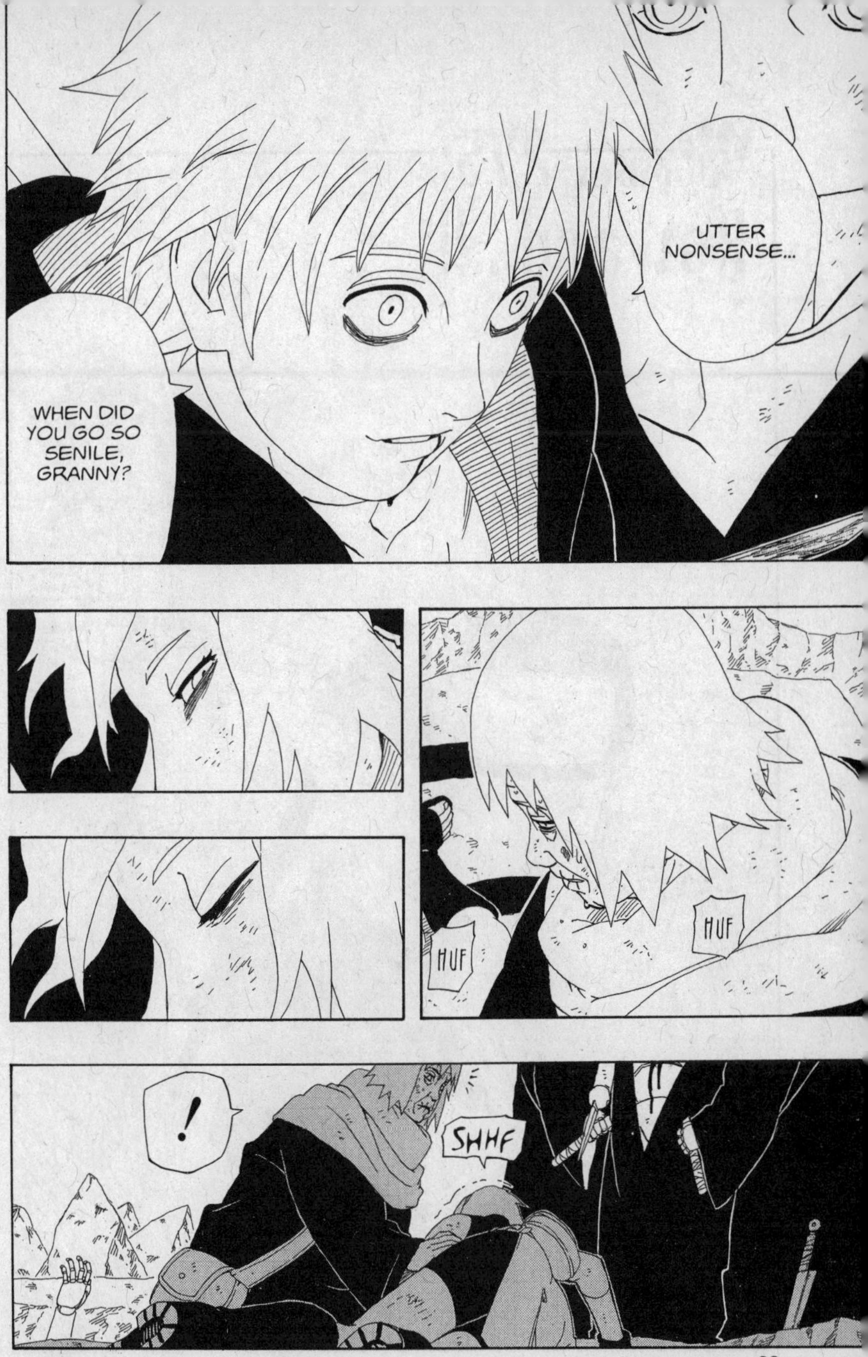
UTTER NONSENSE...
WHEN DID YOU GO SO SENILE, GRANNY?
HUF
HUF
SHHF
!

READ THIS WAY

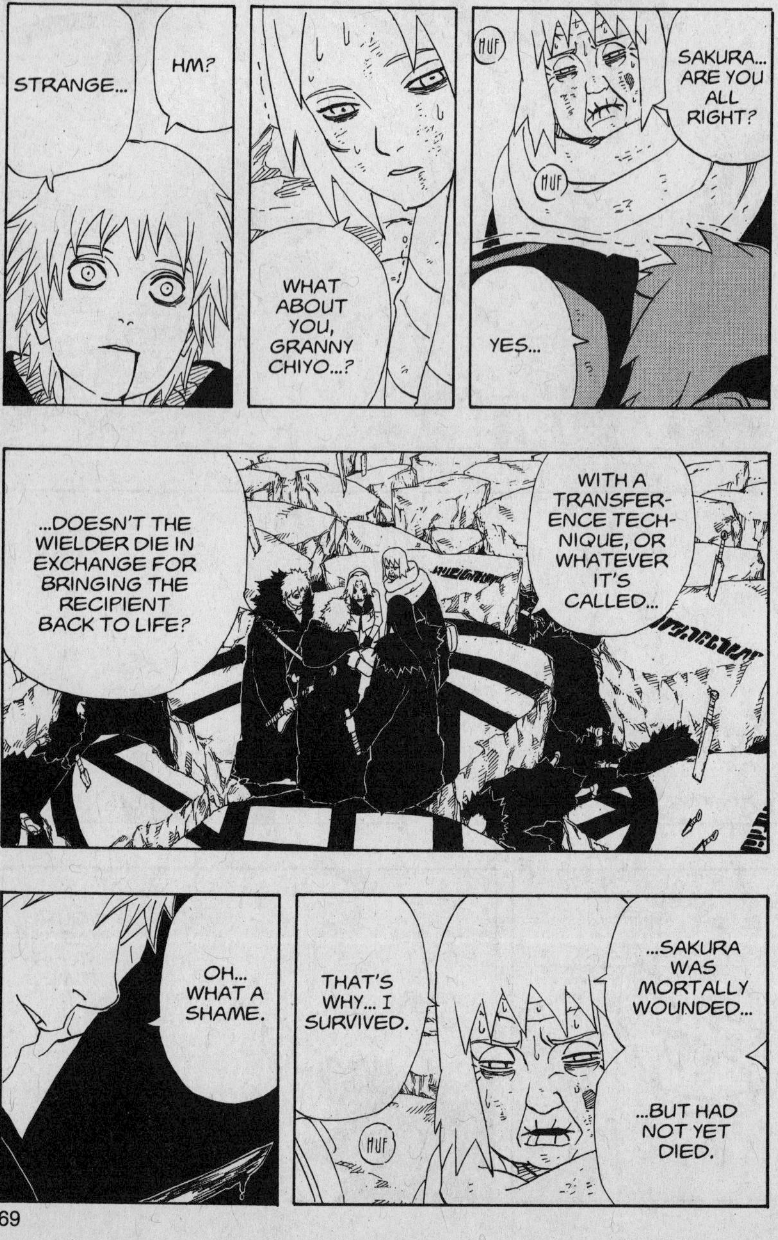
HUF
SAKURA... ARE YOU ALL RIGHT?
HUF
YES...
WHAT ABOUT YOU, GRANNY CHIYO...?
HM?
STRANGE...
WITH A TRANSFERENCE TECHNIQUE, OR WHATEVER IT'S CALLED...
...DOESN'T THE WIELDER DIE IN EXCHANGE FOR BRINGING THE RECIPIENT BACK TO LIFE?
...SAKURA WAS MORTALLY WOUNDED...
...BUT HAD NOT YET DIED.
THAT'S WHY... I SURVIVED.
HUF
OH... WHAT A SHAME.

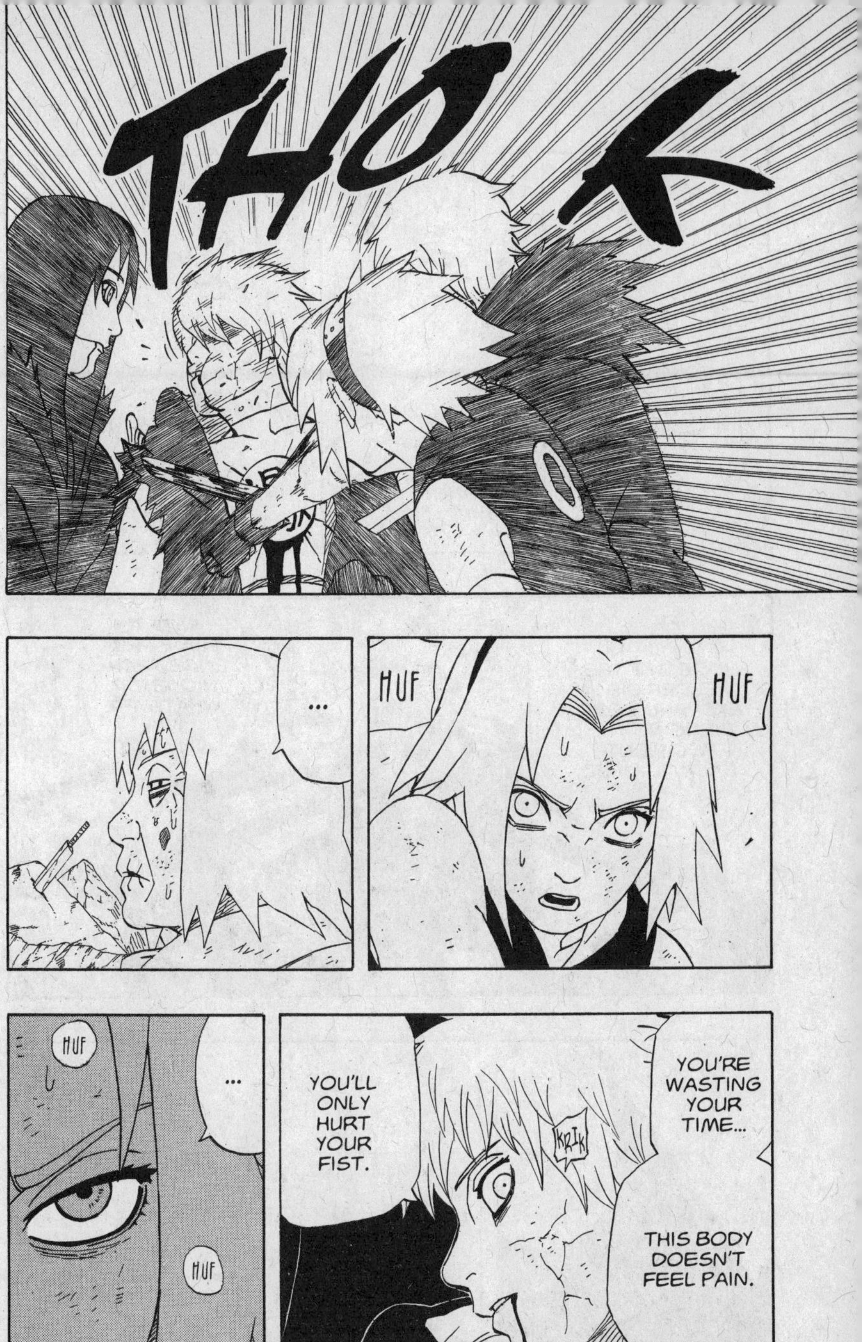
HUF
HUF
...
YOU'RE WASTING YOUR TIME...
YOU'LL ONLY HURT YOUR FIST.
KRIK
THIS BODY DOESN'T FEEL PAIN.
HUF
...
HUF

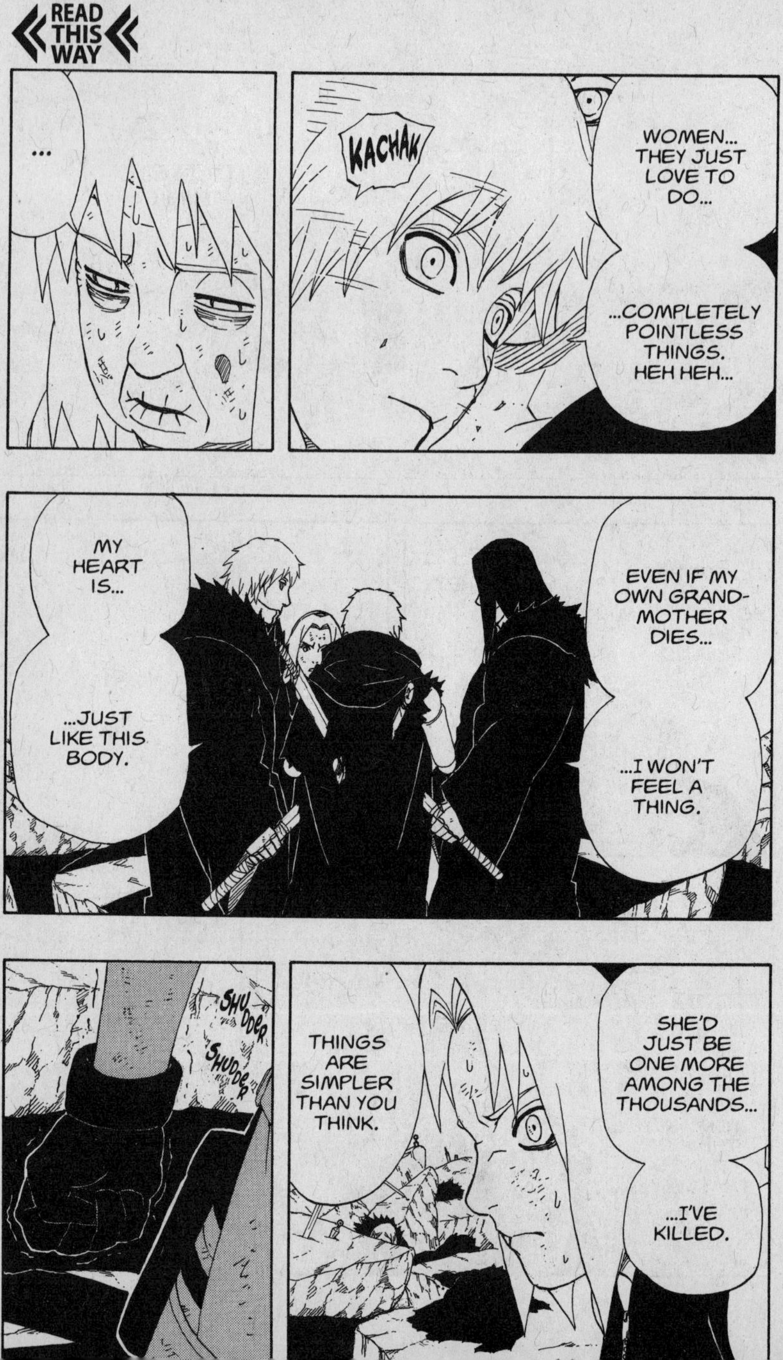
READ THIS WAY
KACHAK
WOMEN... THEY JUST LOVE TO DO...
...COMPLETELY POINTLESS THINGS. HEH HEH...
...
EVEN IF MY OWN GRAND-MOTHER DIES...
...I WON'T FEEL A THING.
MY HEART IS...
...JUST LIKE THIS BODY.
SHE'D JUST BE ONE MORE AMONG THE THOUSANDS...
...I'VE KILLED.
THINGS ARE SIMPLER THAN YOU THINK.
SHUDDER SHUDDER

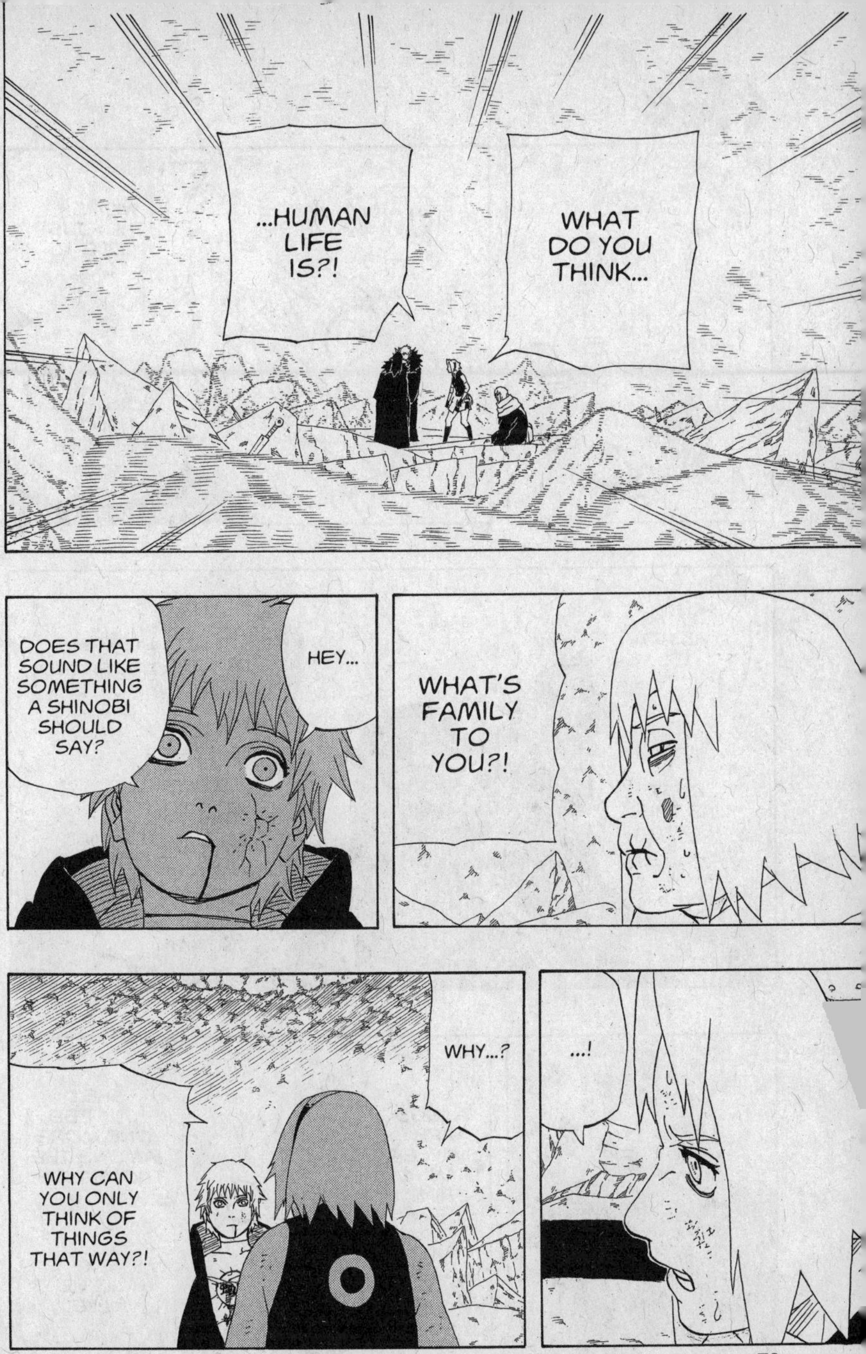

WHAT DO YOU THINK...
...HUMAN LIFE IS?!
WHAT'S FAMILY TO YOU?!
HEY...
DOES THAT SOUND LIKE SOMETHING A SHINOBI SHOULD SAY?
...!
WHY...?
WHY CAN YOU ONLY THINK OF THINGS THAT WAY?!

READ THIS WAY

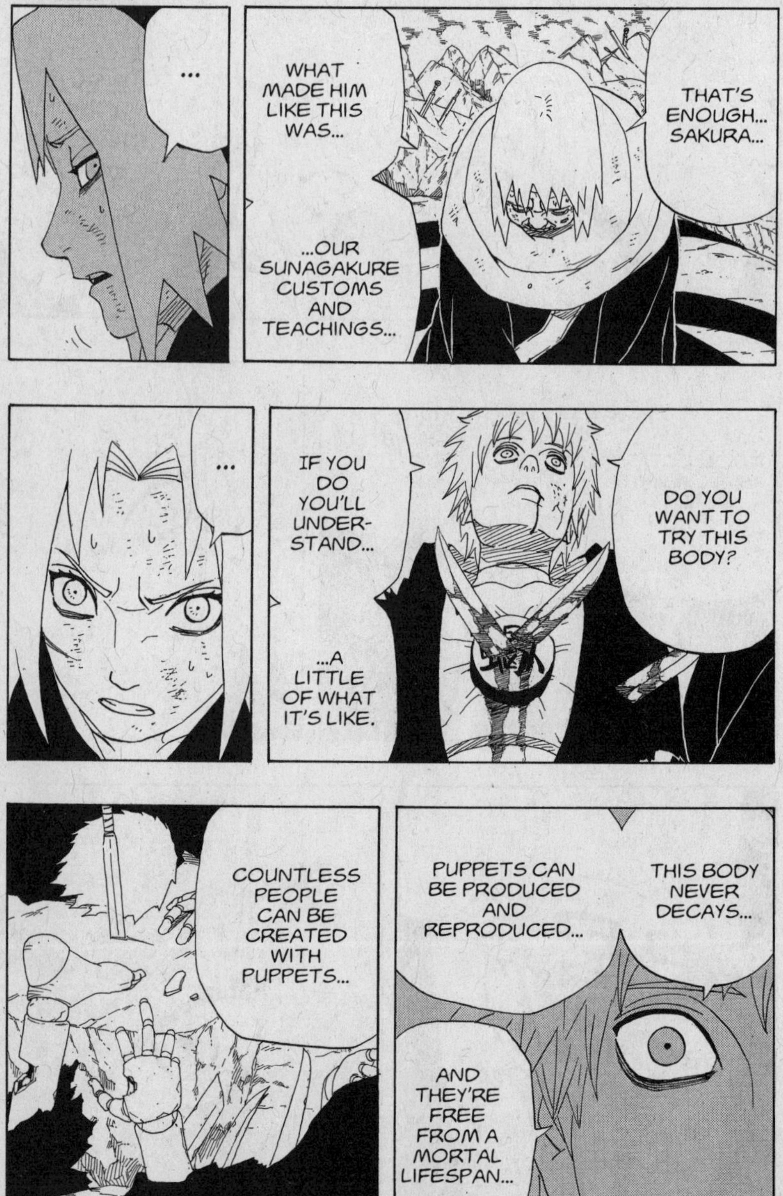
THAT'S ENOUGH... SAKURA...
WHAT MADE HIM LIKE THIS WAS...
...OUR SUNAGAKURE CUSTOMS AND TEACHINGS...
...
DO YOU WANT TO TRY THIS BODY?
IF YOU DO YOU'LL UNDERSTAND...
...A LITTLE OF WHAT IT'S LIKE.
...
THIS BODY NEVER DECAYS...
PUPPETS CAN BE PRODUCED AND REPRODUCED...
AND THEY'RE FREE FROM A MORTAL LIFESPAN...
COUNTLESS PEOPLE CAN BE CREATED WITH PUPPETS...

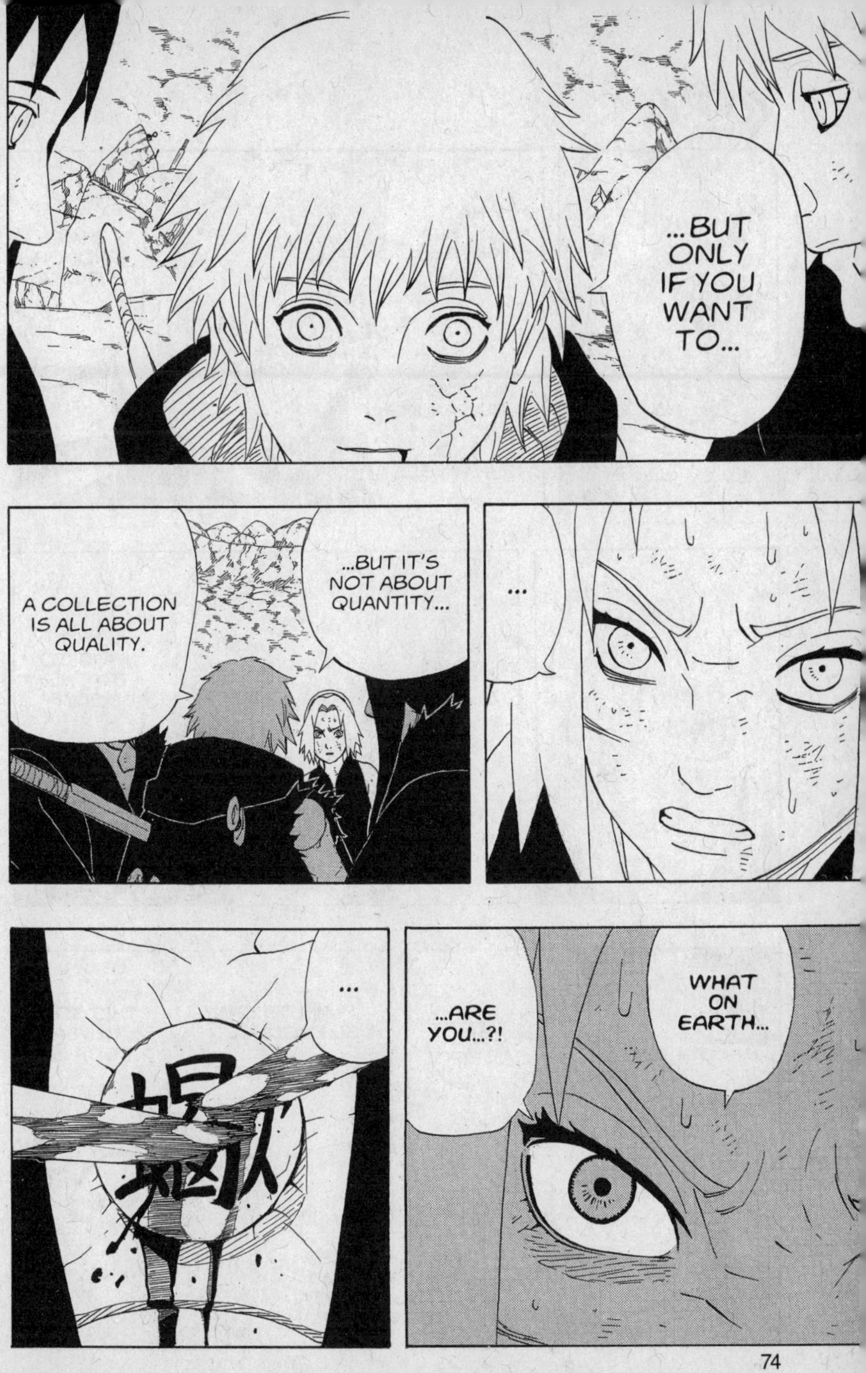
...BUT ONLY IF YOU WANT TO...
...
...BUT IT'S NOT ABOUT QUANTITY...
A COLLECTION IS ALL ABOUT QUALITY.
WHAT ON EARTH...
...ARE YOU...?!
...

READ THIS WAY

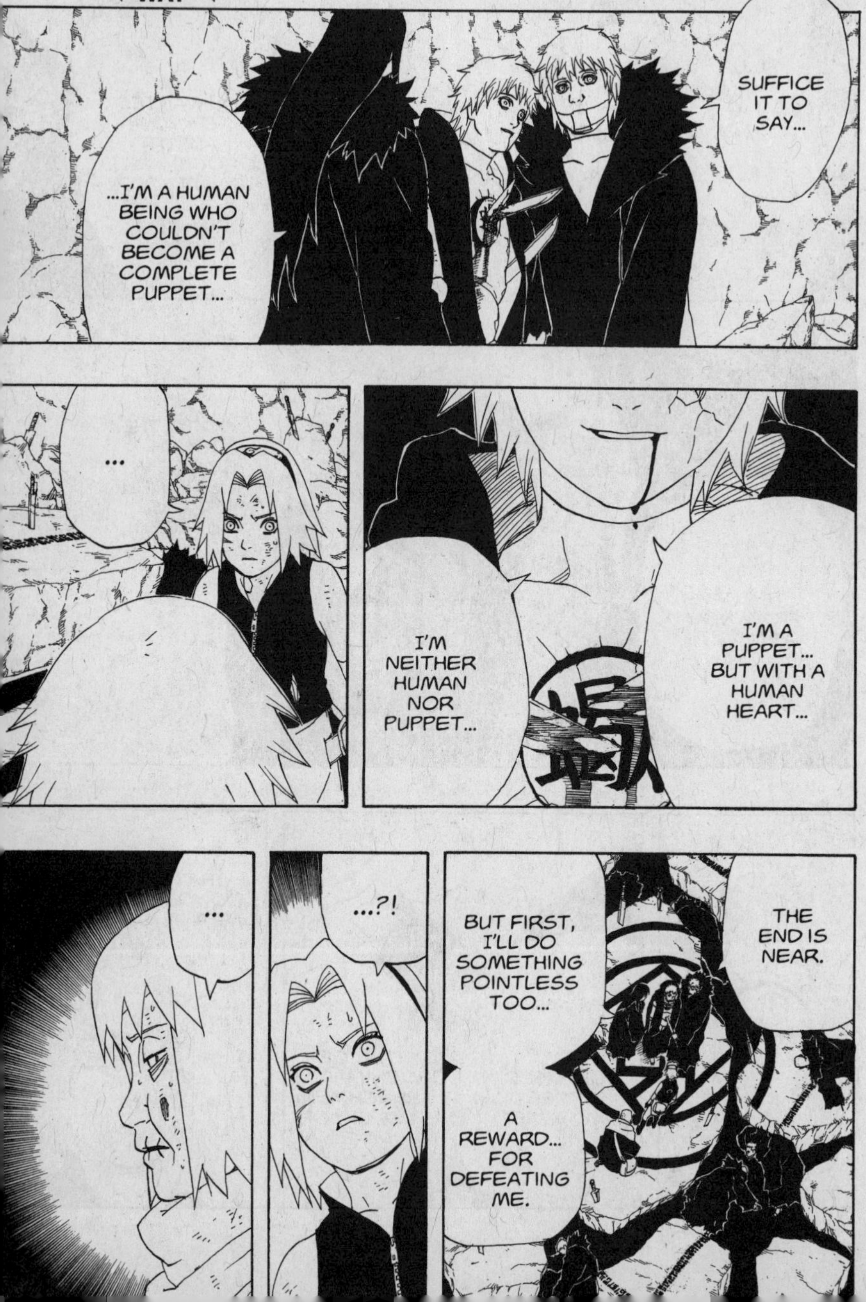
SUFFICE IT TO SAY...
...I'M A HUMAN BEING WHO COULDN'T BECOME A COMPLETE PUPPET...
I'M A PUPPET... BUT WITH A HUMAN HEART...
I'M NEITHER HUMAN NOR PUPPET...
...
THE END IS NEAR.
BUT FIRST, I'LL DO SOMETHING POINTLESS TOO...
A REWARD... FOR DEFEATING ME.
...?!
...

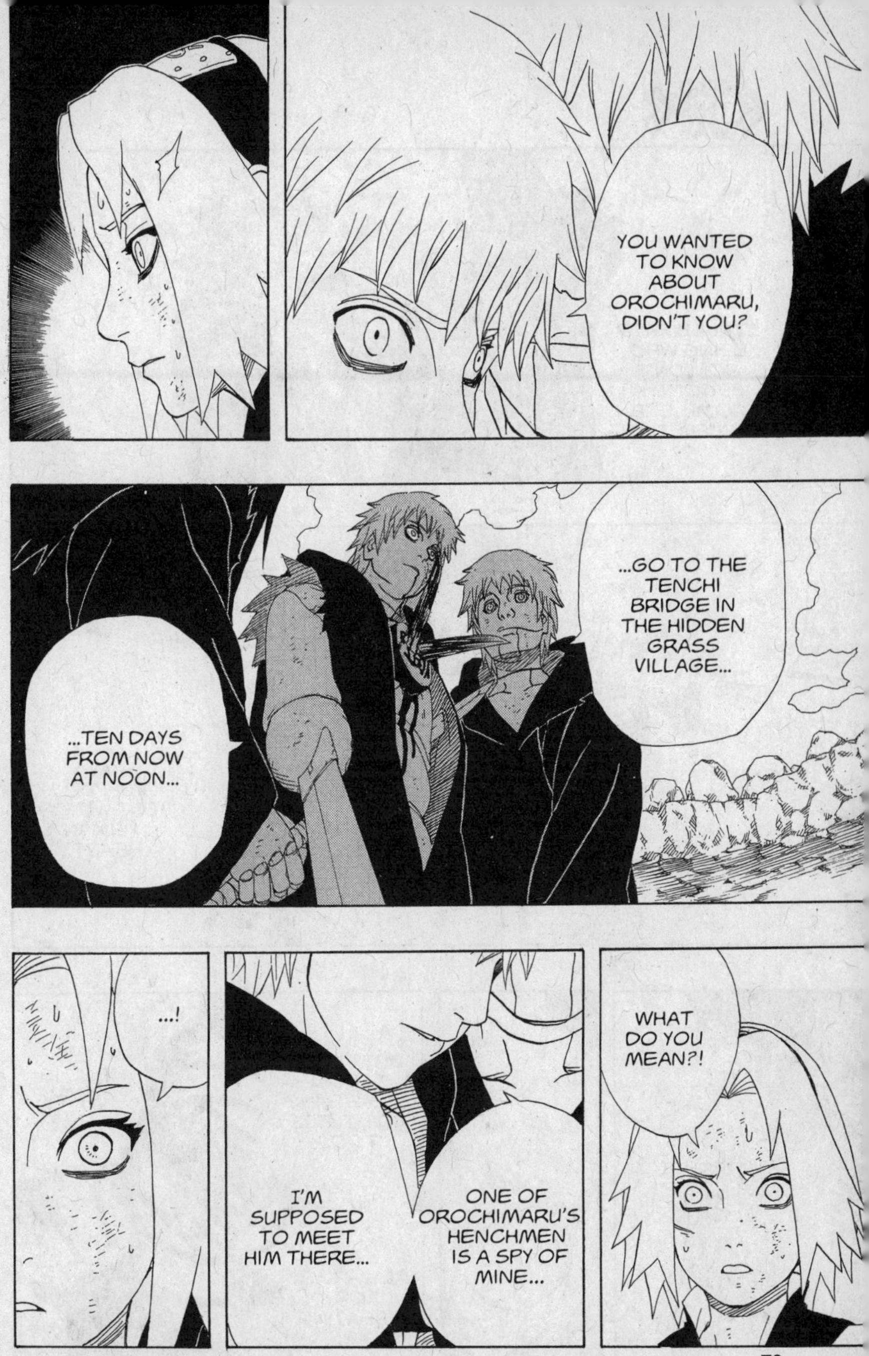
YOU WANTED TO KNOW ABOUT OROCHIMARU, DIDN'T YOU?
...GO TO THE TENCHI BRIDGE IN THE HIDDEN GRASS VILLAGE...
...TEN DAYS FROM NOW AT NOON...
WHAT DO YOU MEAN?!
ONE OF OROCHIMARU'S HENCHMEN IS A SPY OF MINE...
I'M SUPPOSED TO MEET HIM THERE...
...!

READ THIS WAY

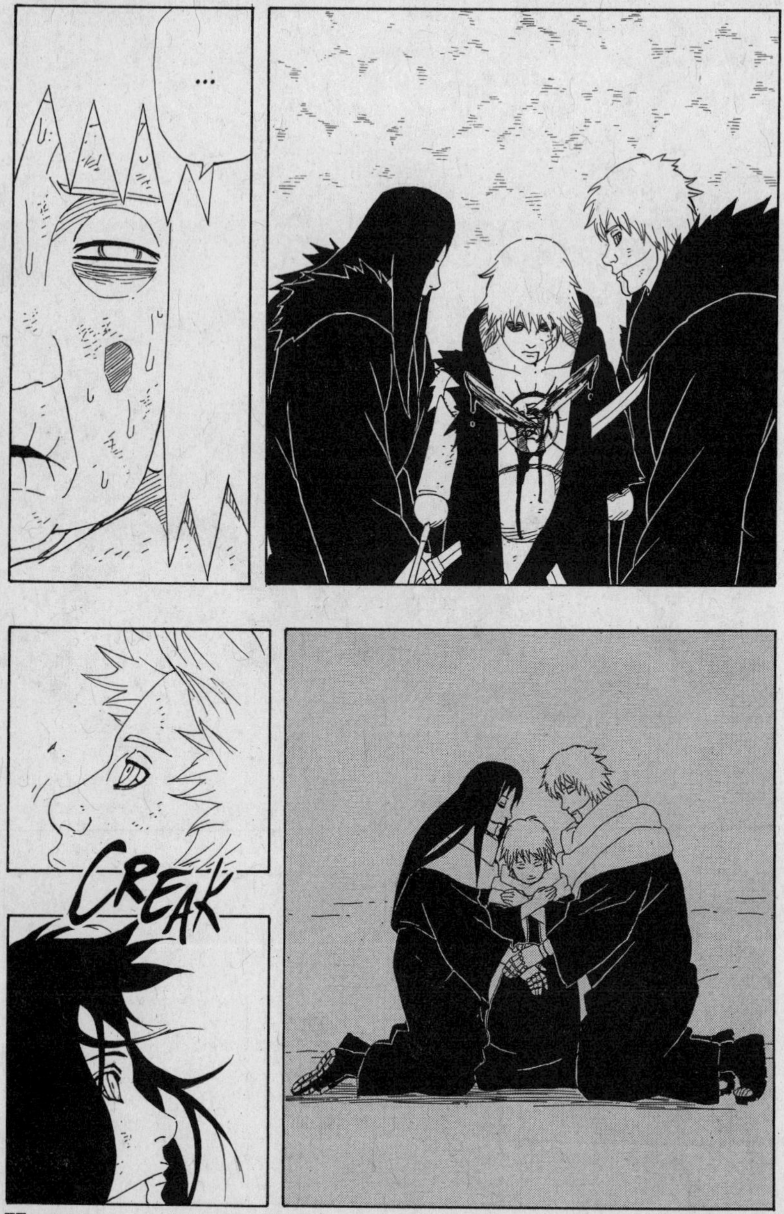
...
CREAK

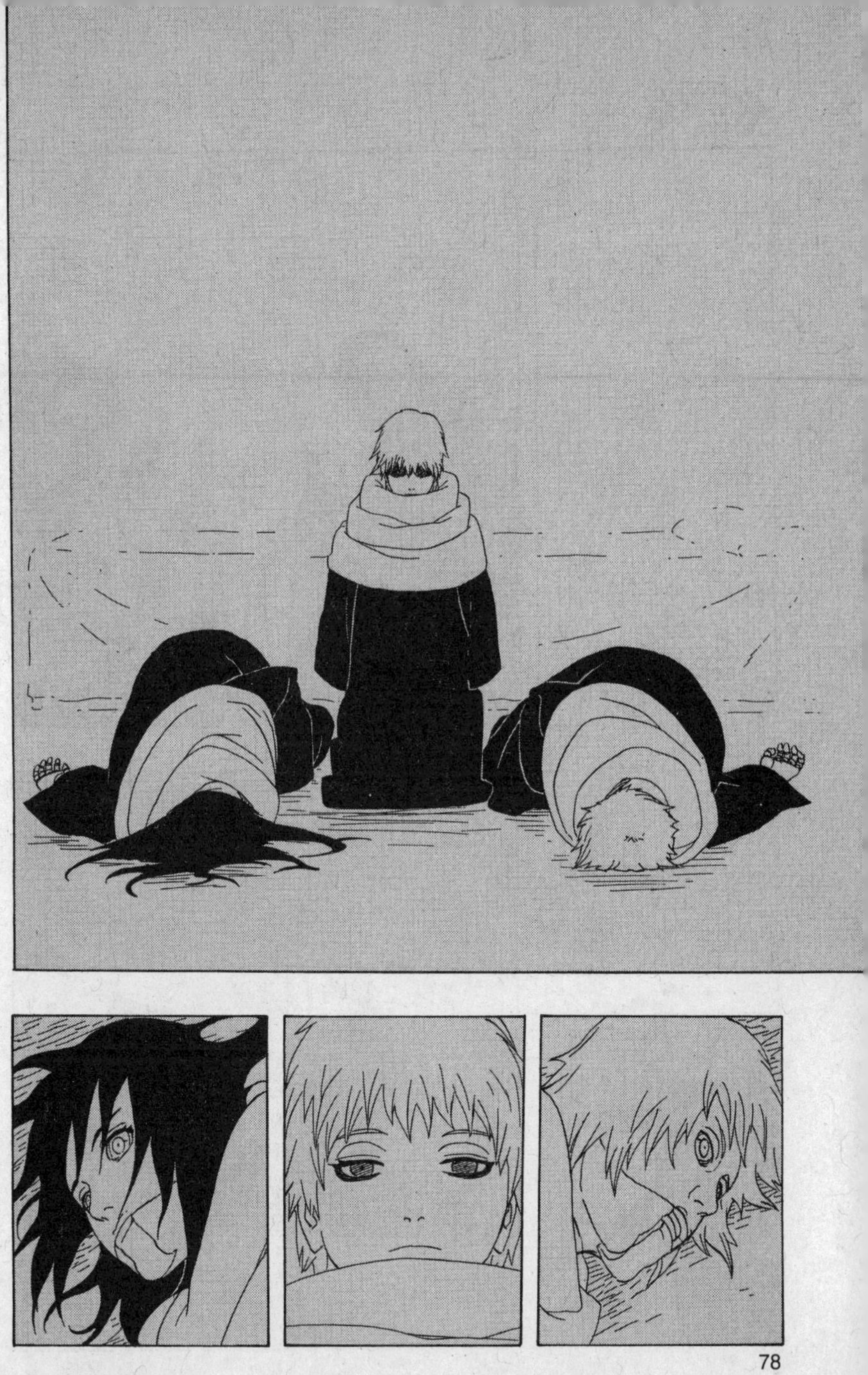

READ THIS WAY

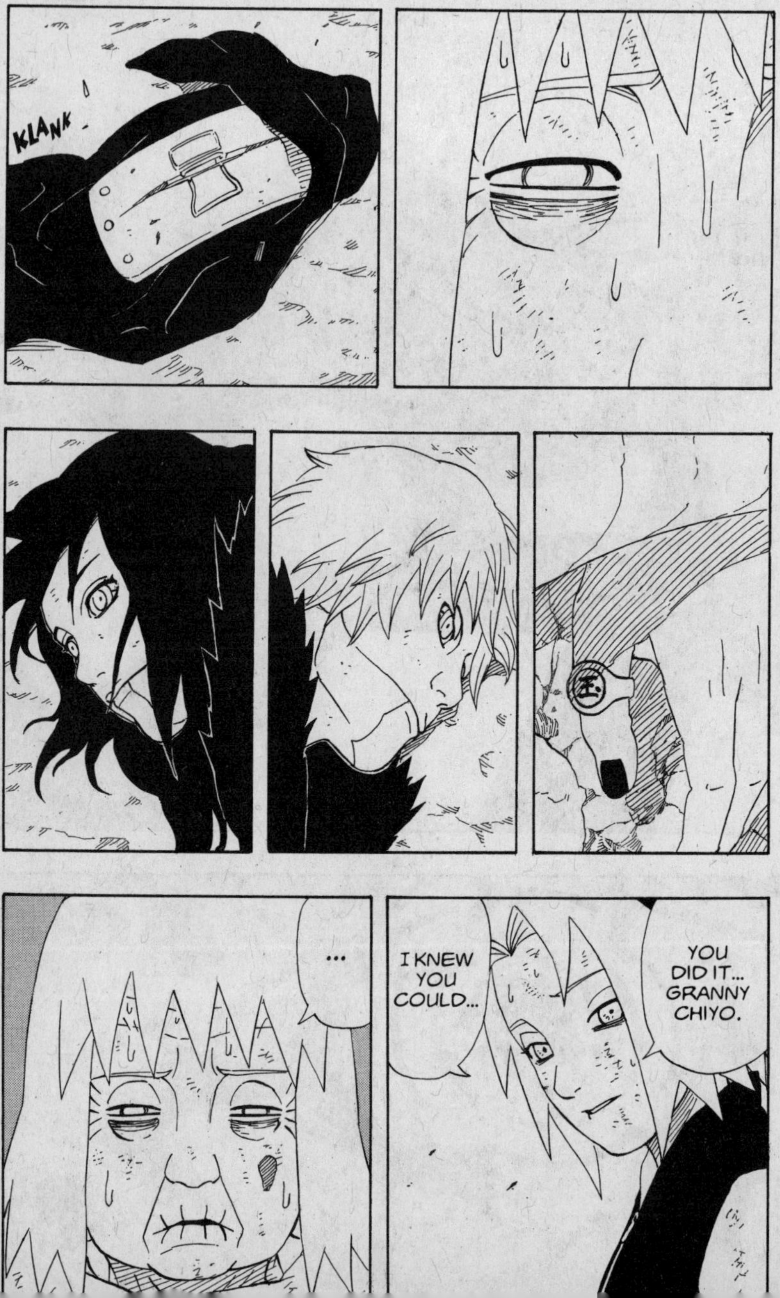
KLANK
YOU DID IT... GRANNY CHIYO.
I KNEW YOU COULD...
...

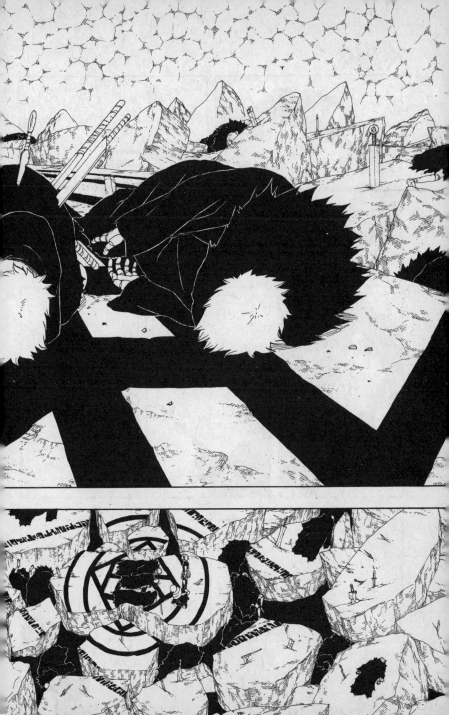

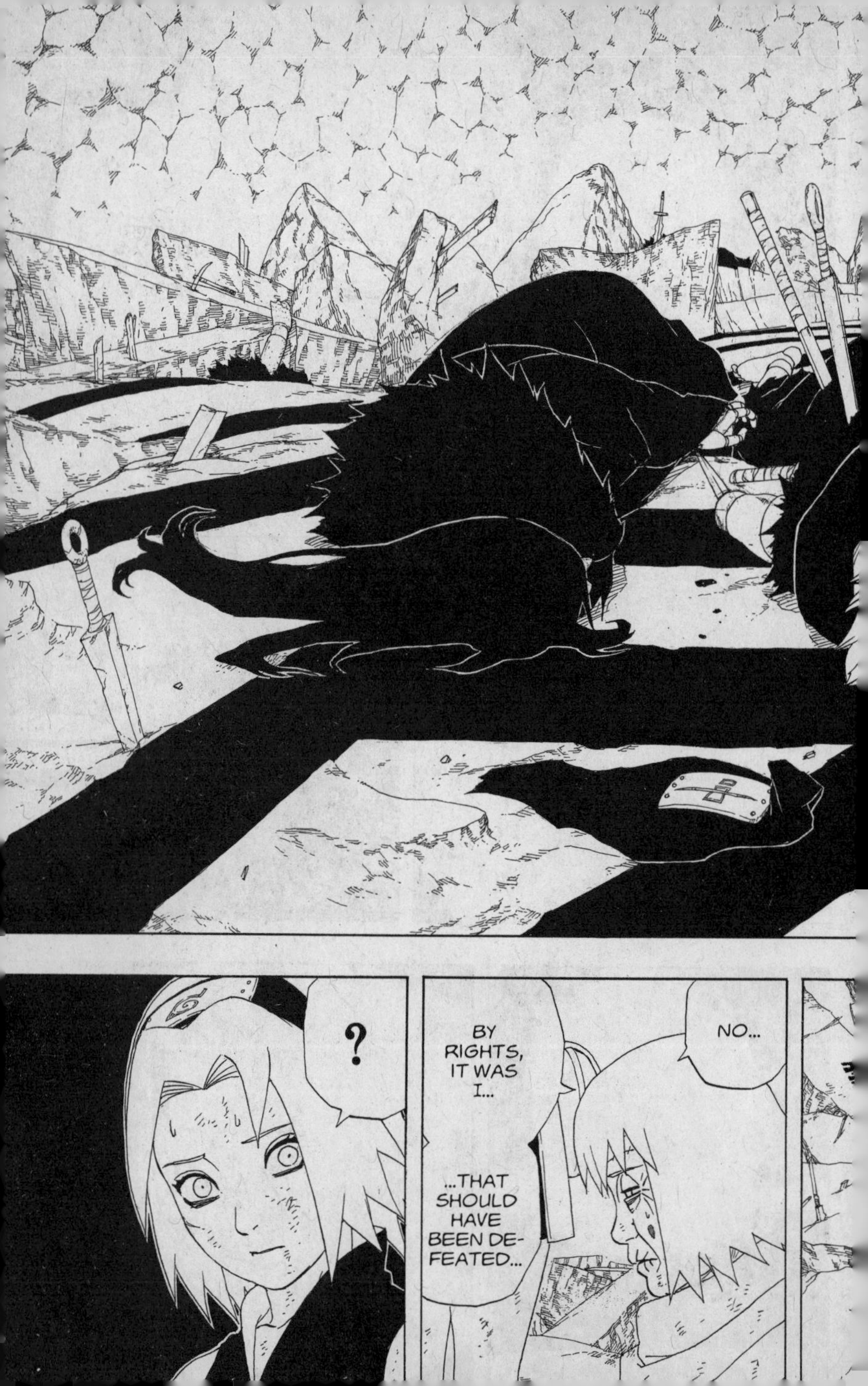
NO...
BY RIGHTS, IT WAS I...
...THAT SHOULD HAVE BEEN DE-FEATED...
?

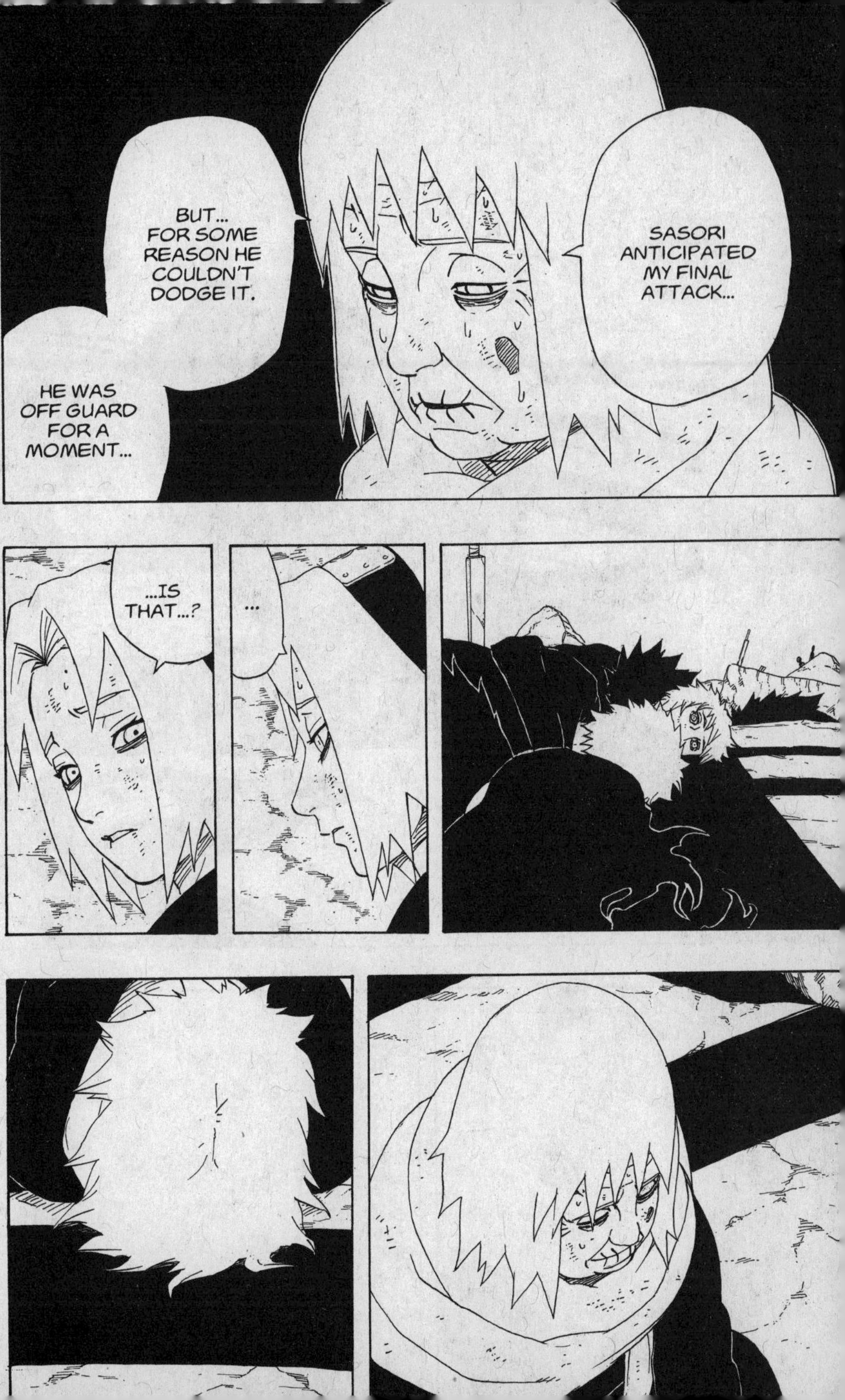
SASORI ANTICIPATED MY FINAL ATTACK...
BUT... FOR SOME REASON HE COULDN'T DODGE IT.
HE WAS OFF GUARD FOR A MOMENT...
...
...IS THAT...?

READ THIS WAY

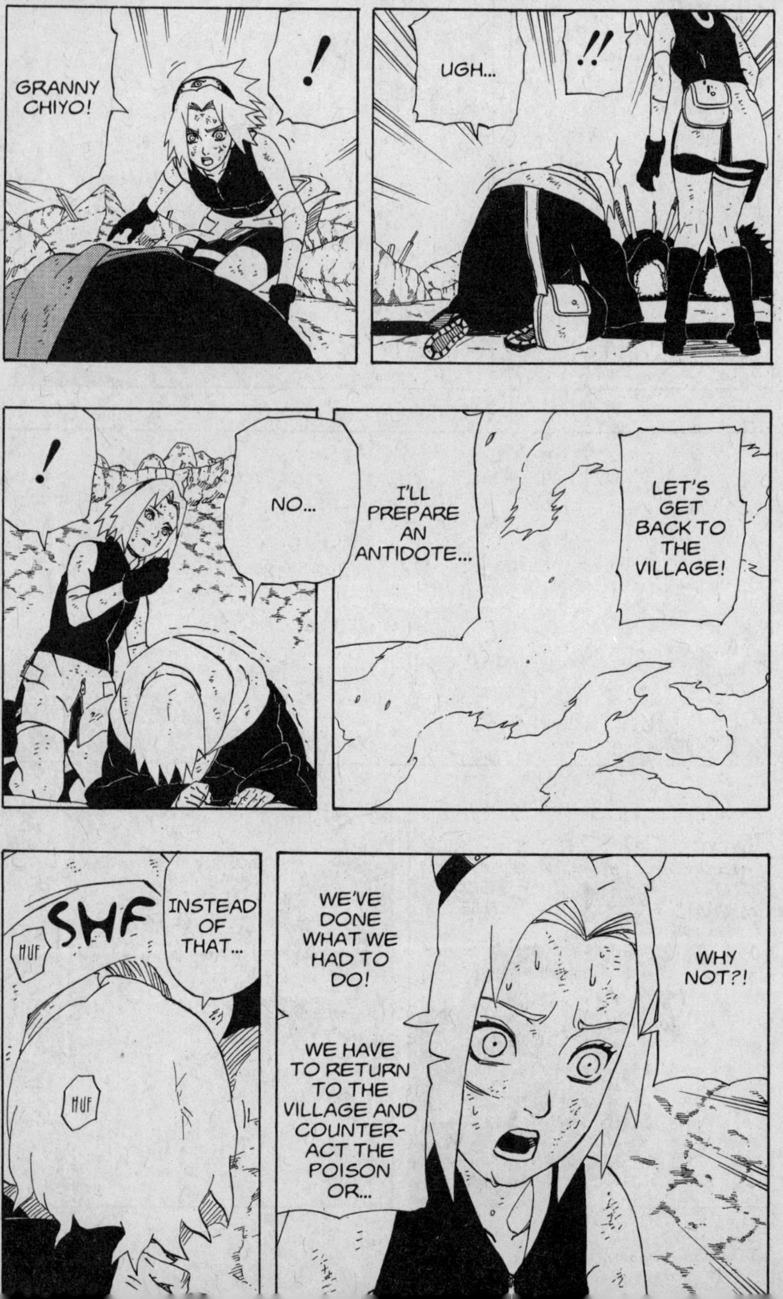
!!
UGH...
!
GRANNY CHIYO!
LET'S GET BACK TO THE VILLAGE!
I'LL PREPARE AN ANTIDOTE...
NO...
!
WHY NOT?!
WE'VE DONE WHAT WE HAD TO DO!
WE HAVE TO RETURN TO THE VILLAGE AND COUNTER-ACT THE POISON OR...
INSTEAD OF THAT...
SHF
HUF
HUF

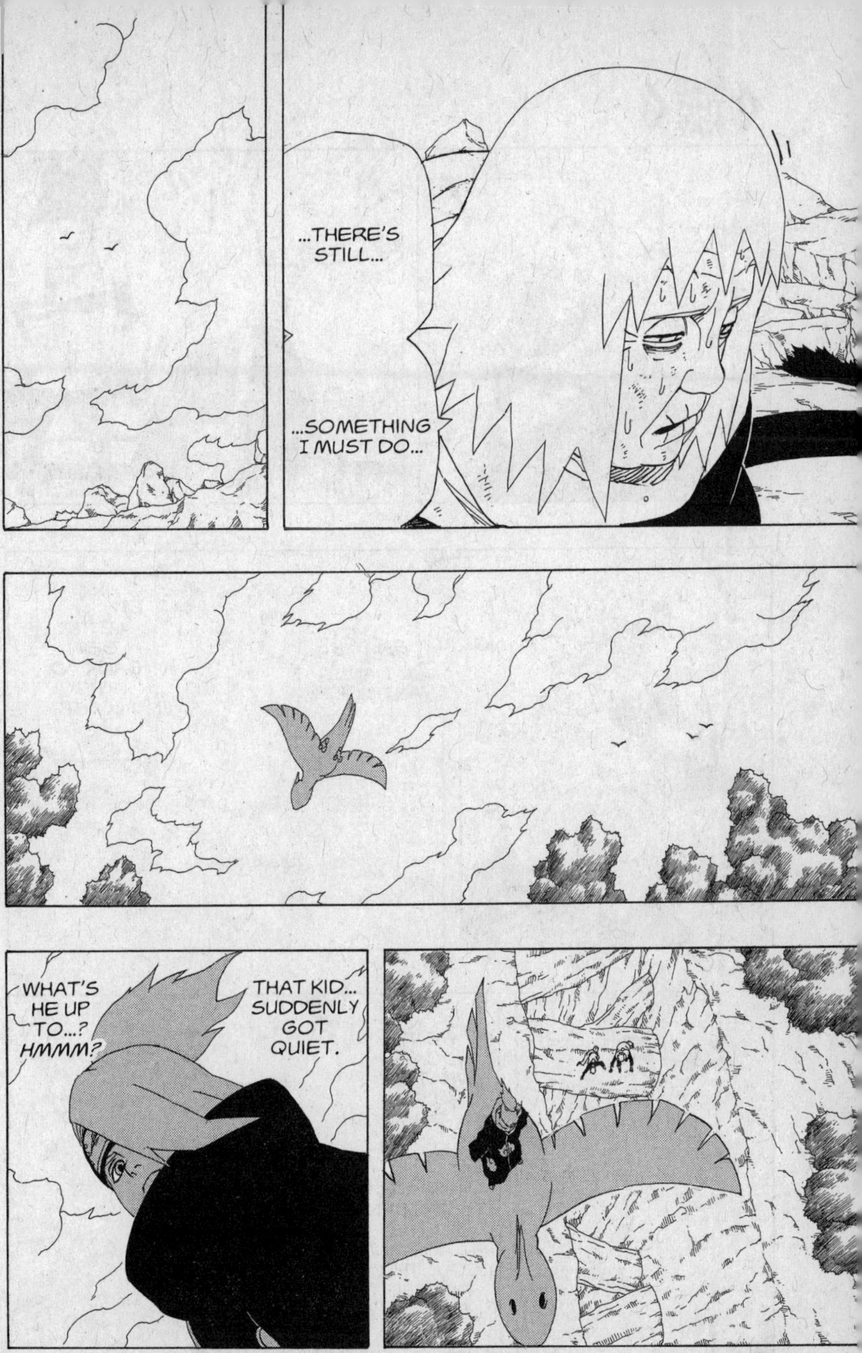
...THERE'S STILL...
...SOMETHING I MUST DO...
THAT KID... SUDDENLY GOT QUIET.
WHAT'S HE UP TO...? *HMMM?*

READ THIS WAY

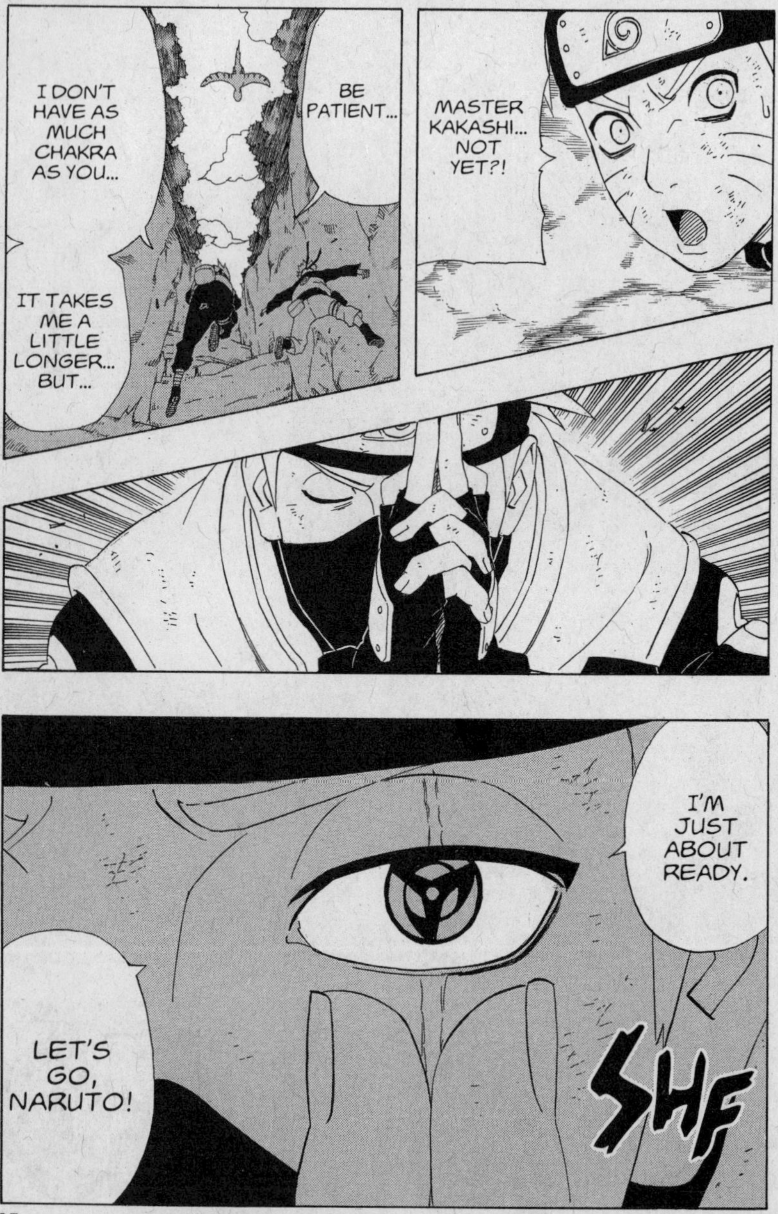

MASTER KAKASHI... NOT YET?!
BE PATIENT...
I DON'T HAVE AS MUCH CHAKRA AS YOU...
IT TAKES ME A LITTLE LONGER... BUT...
I'M JUST ABOUT READY.
SHF
LET'S GO, NARUTO!

NARUTO

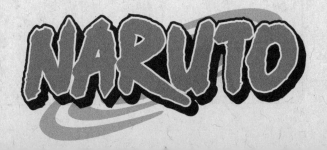

Number 276: New Sharingan!!

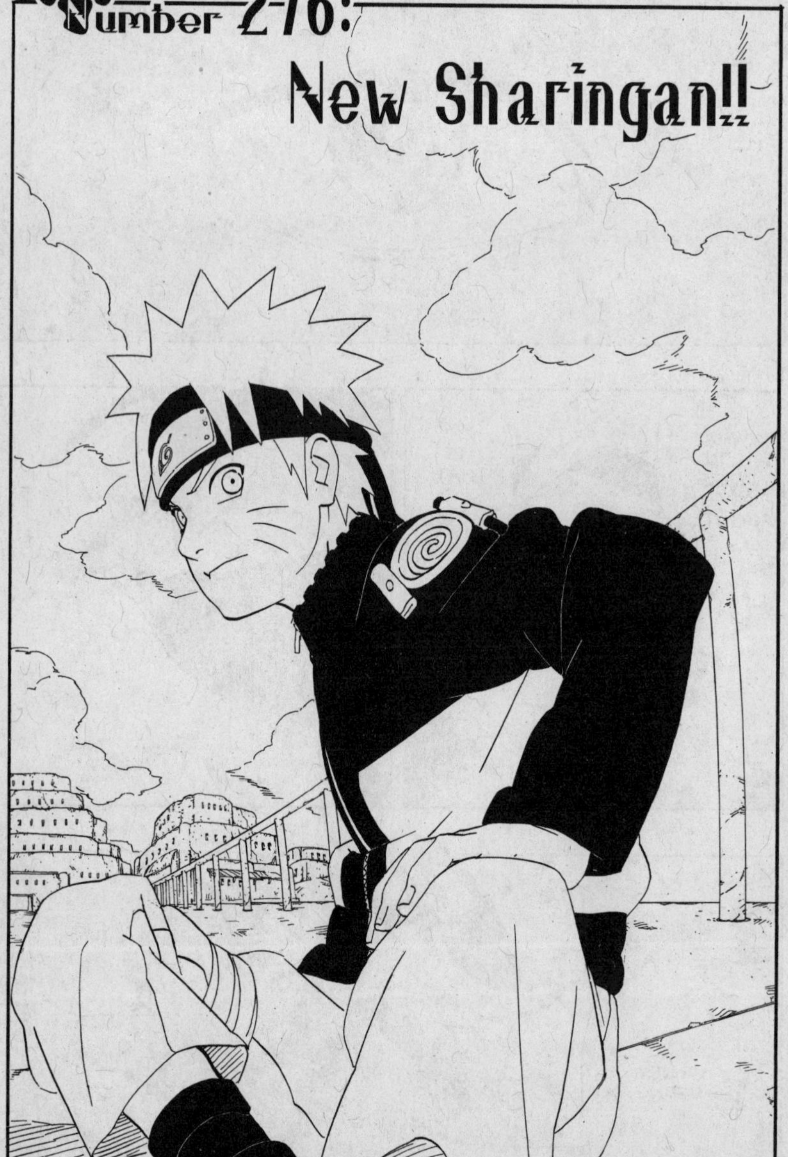

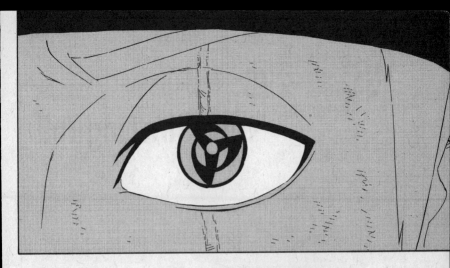

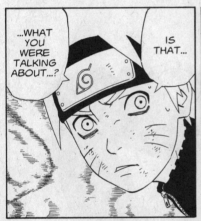

...WHAT YOU WERE TALKING ABOUT...?

IS THAT...

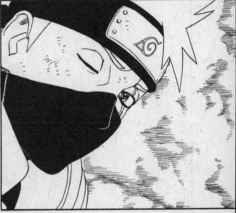

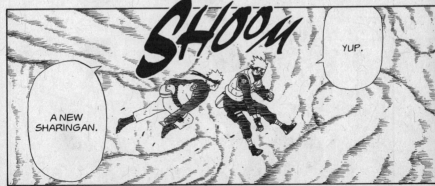

SHOOM

YUP.

A NEW SHARINGAN.

READ THIS WAY

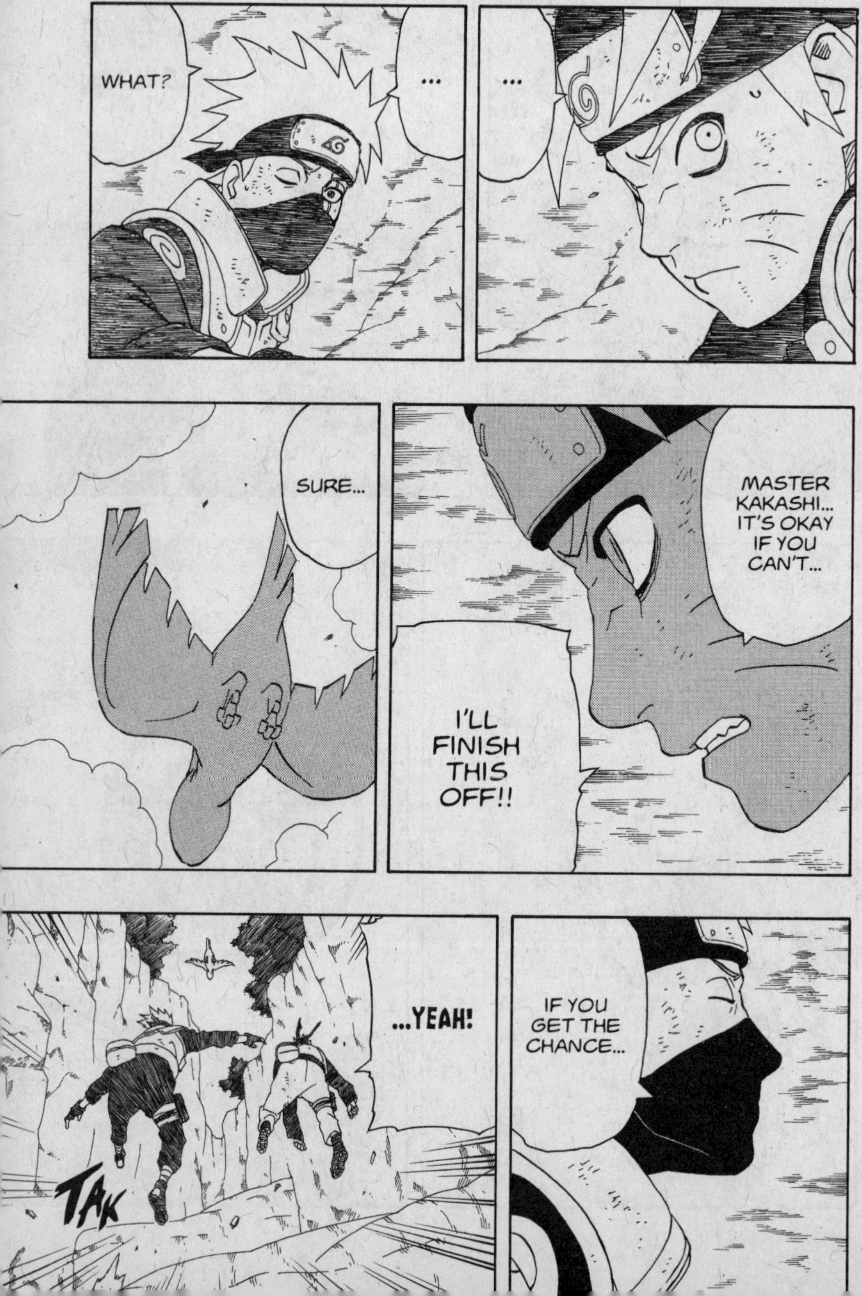
...
...
WHAT?
MASTER KAKASHI... IT'S OKAY IF YOU CAN'T...
I'LL FINISH THIS OFF!!
SURE...
IF YOU GET THE CHANCE...
...YEAH!
TAK

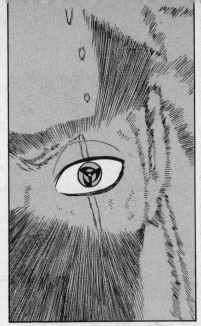

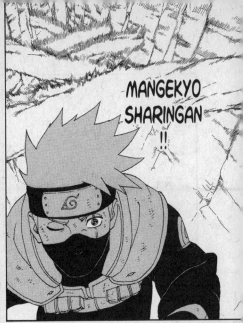

MANGEKYO
SHARINGAN
!!

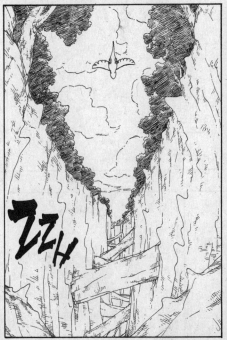

ZZH

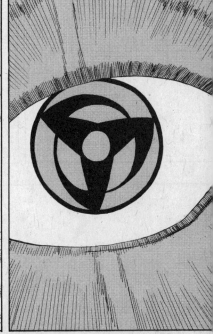

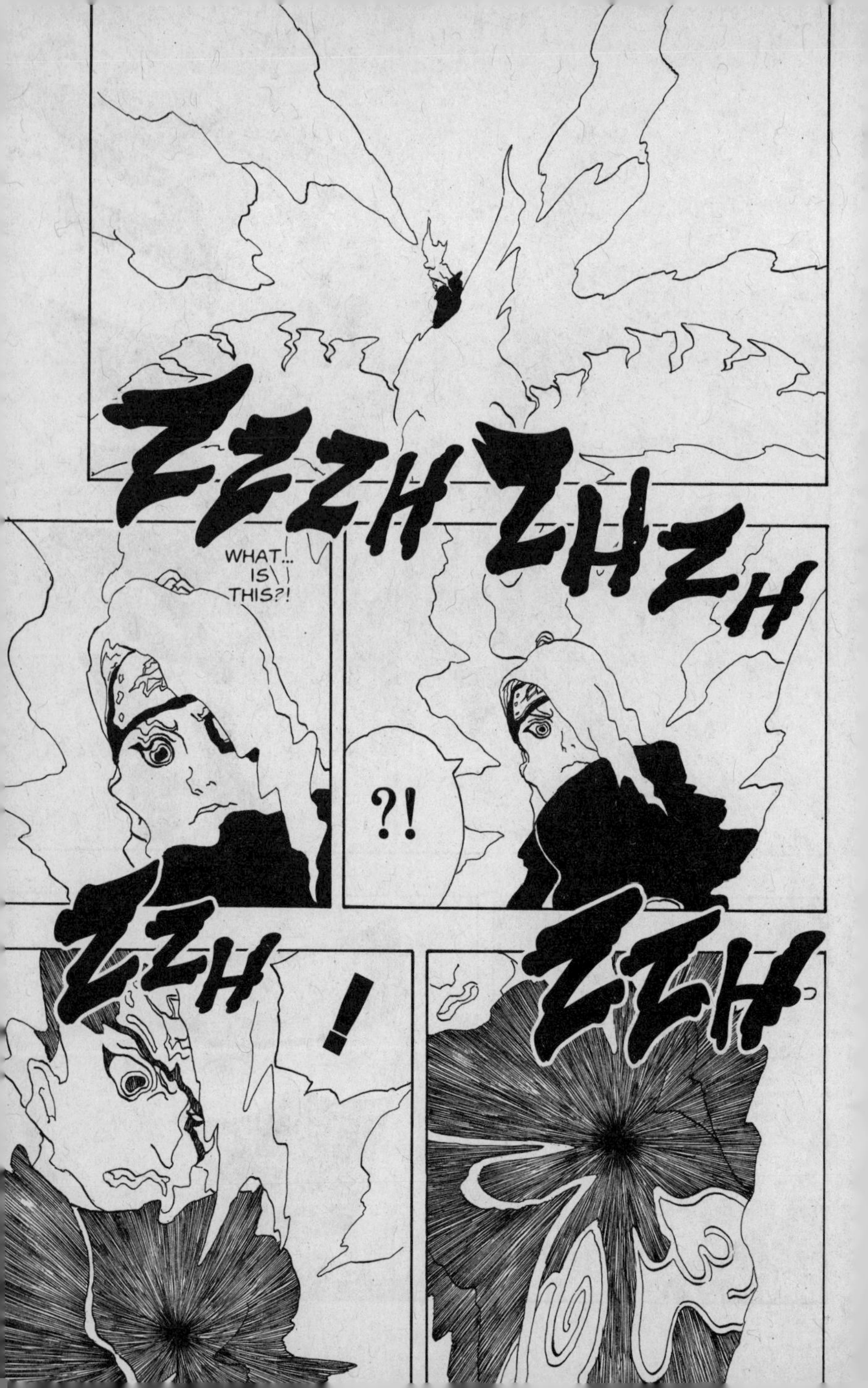
ZZZH ZHZHZH
?!
WHAT... IS THIS?!
ZZH
ZZH !

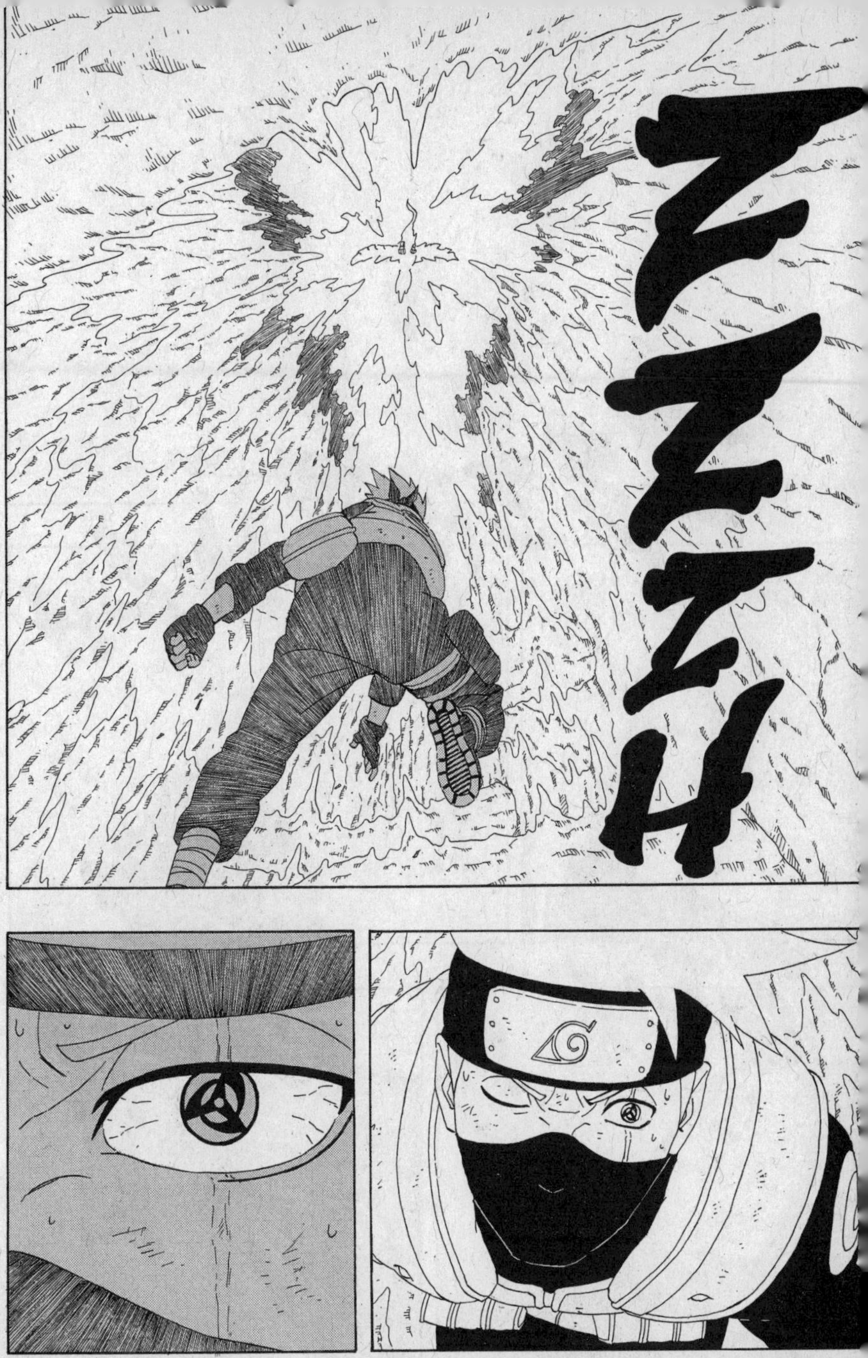
ZZZZZH

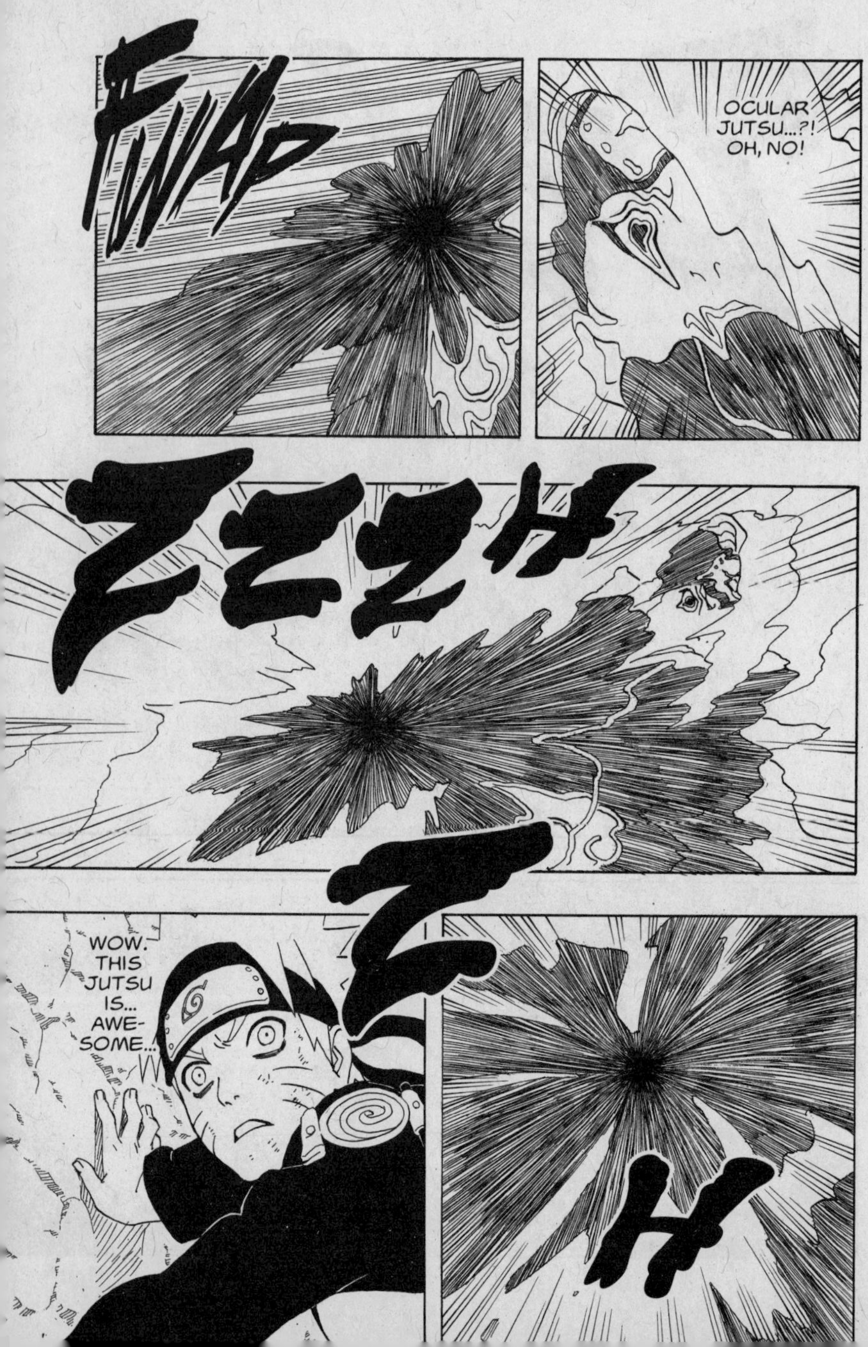
OCULAR JUTSU...?! OH, NO!
FWAP
ZZZZ
WOW. THIS JUTSU IS... AWE-SOME...
ZZH

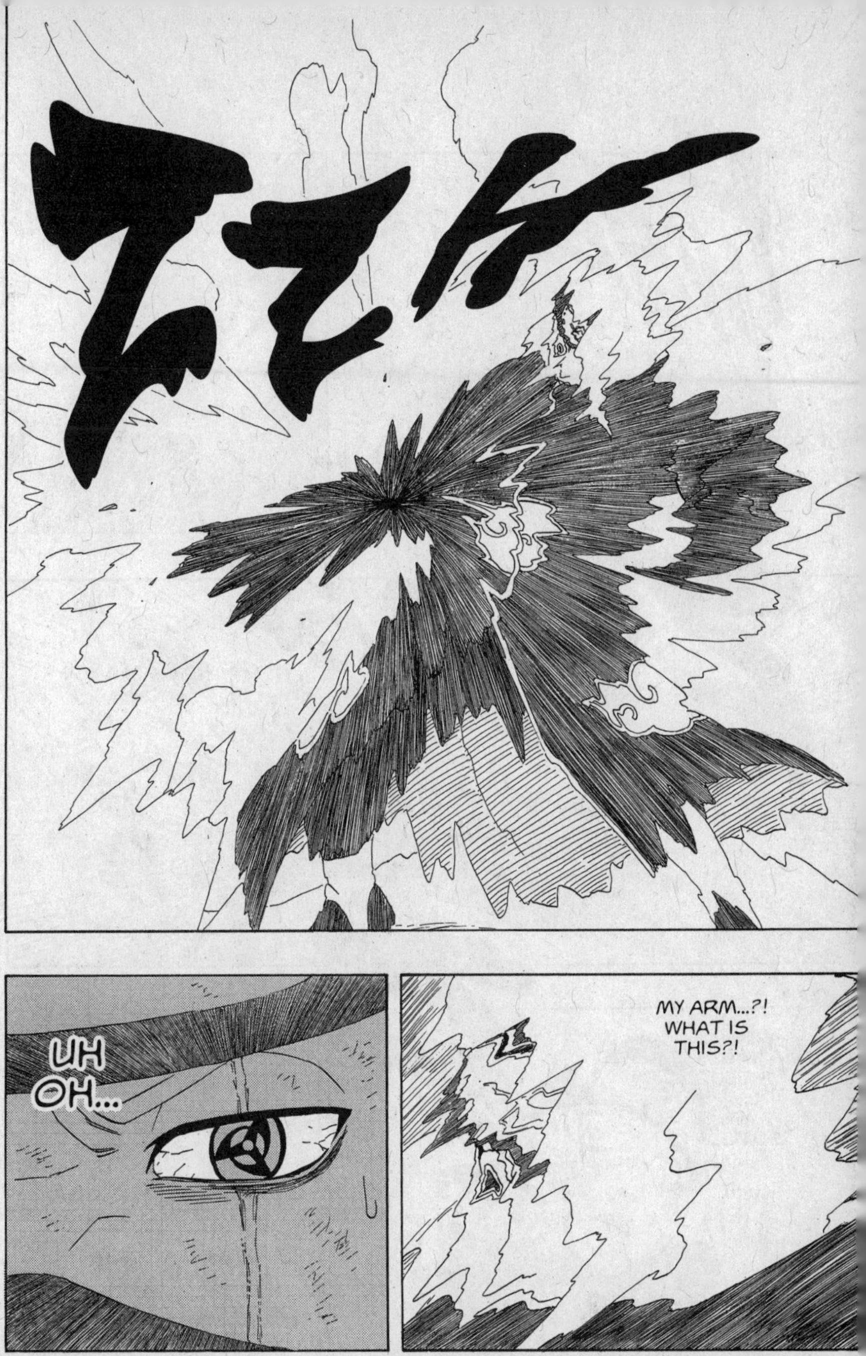
MY ARM...?! WHAT IS THIS?!
UH OH...

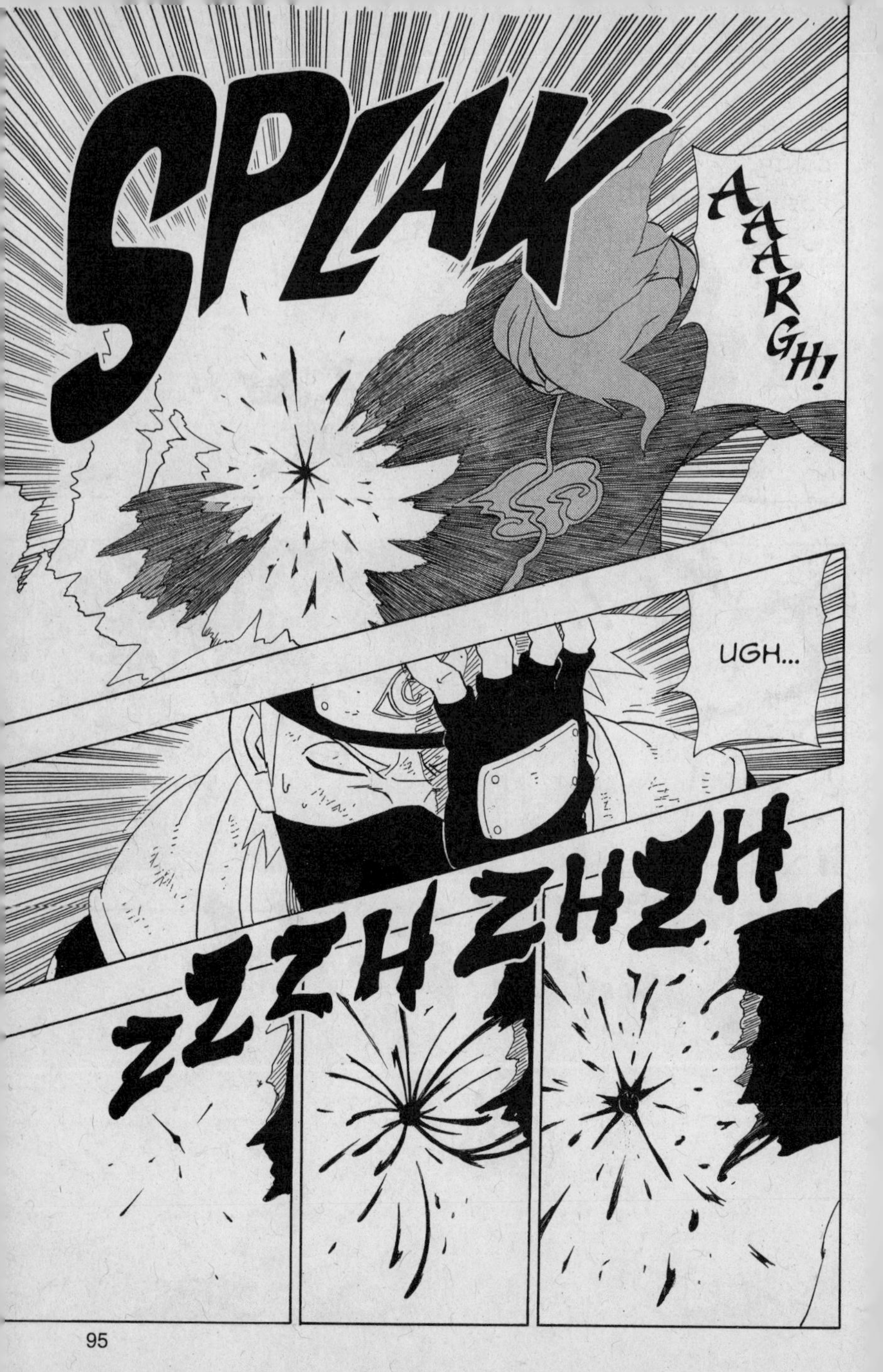
AAARGH!
SPLAK
UGH...
ZZZZH ZHZH

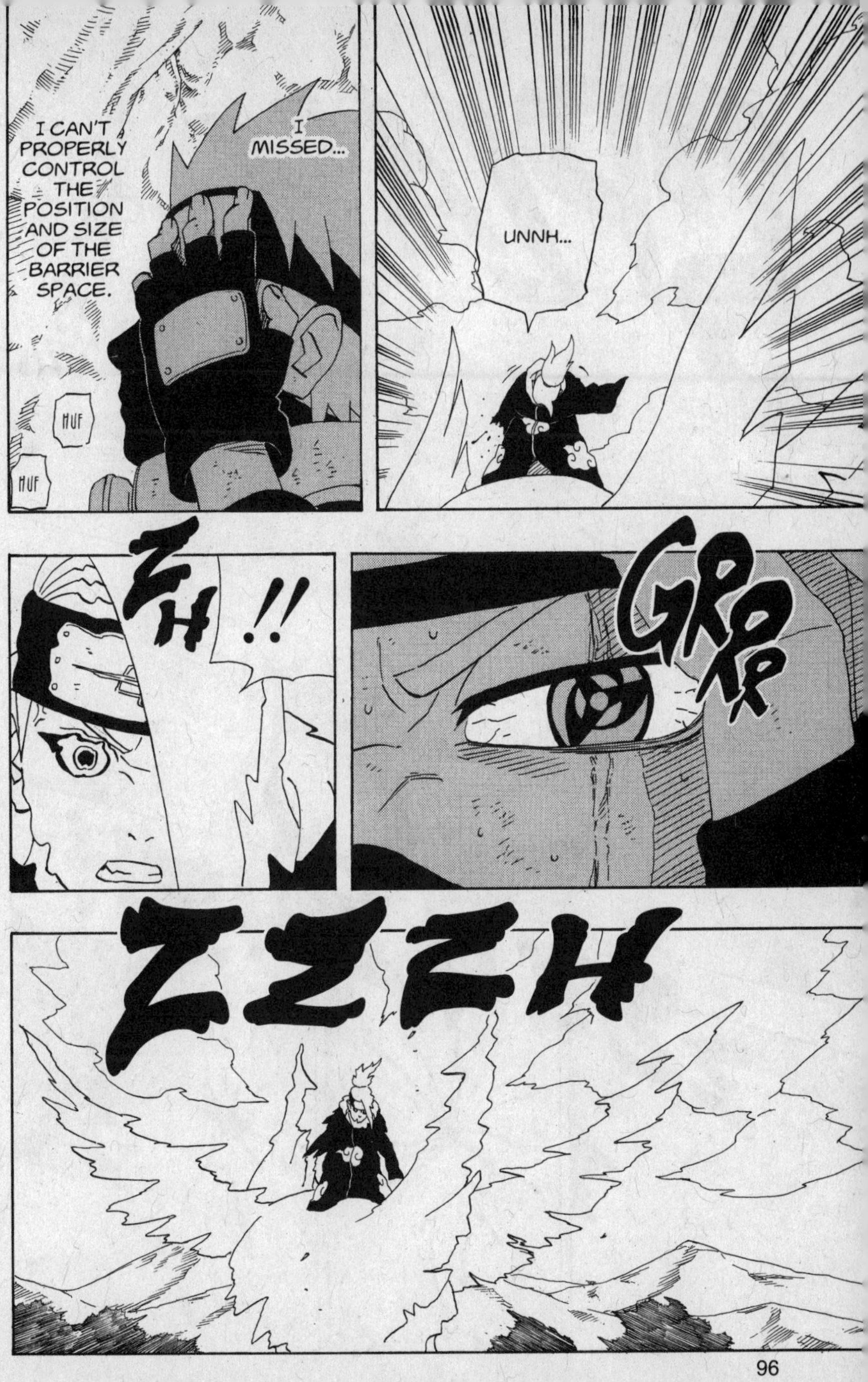
UNNH...
I MISSED...
I CAN'T PROPERLY CONTROL THE POSITION AND SIZE OF THE BARRIER SPACE.
HUF
HUF
GRRR
ZH !!
ZZZH

READ THIS WAY

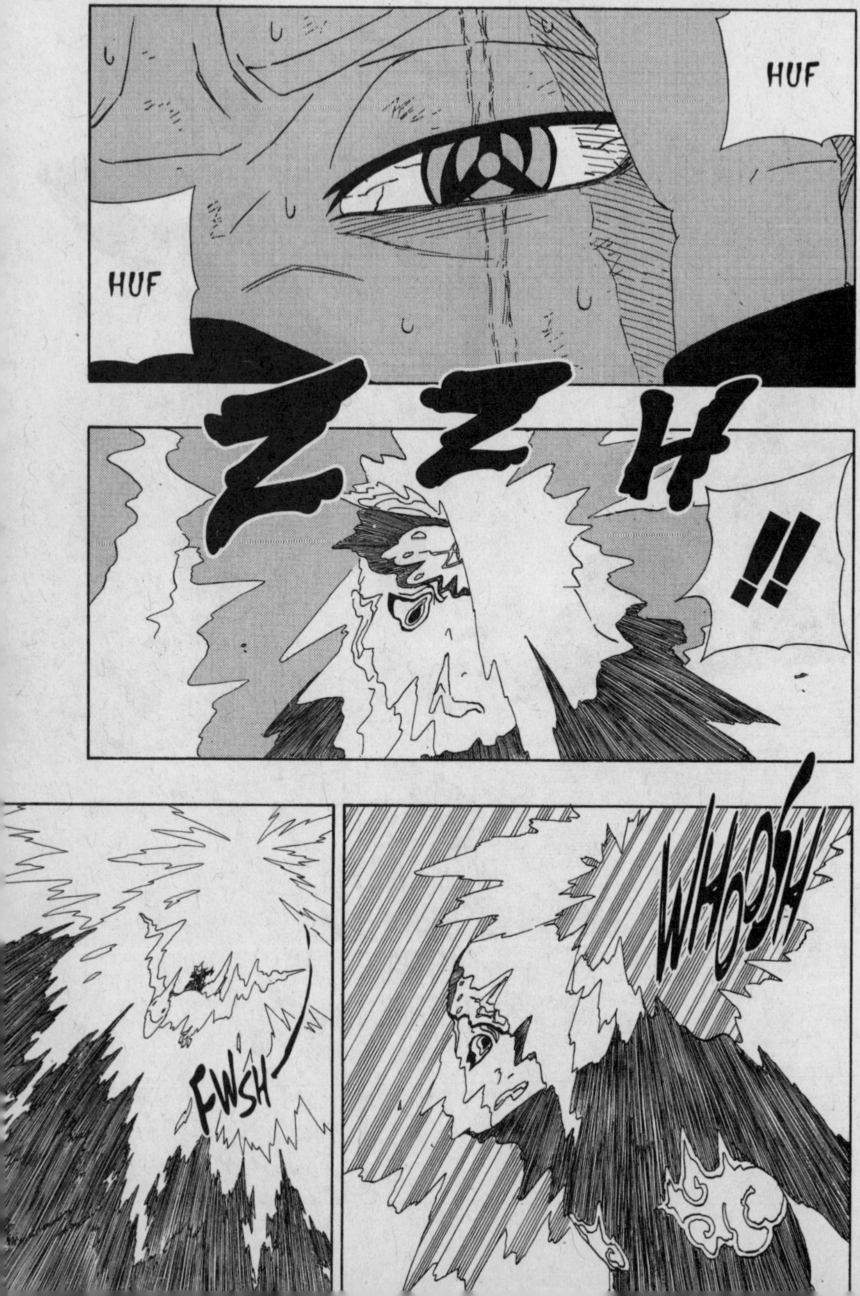
HUF
HUF
ZZH
!!
WHOOSH
FWSH

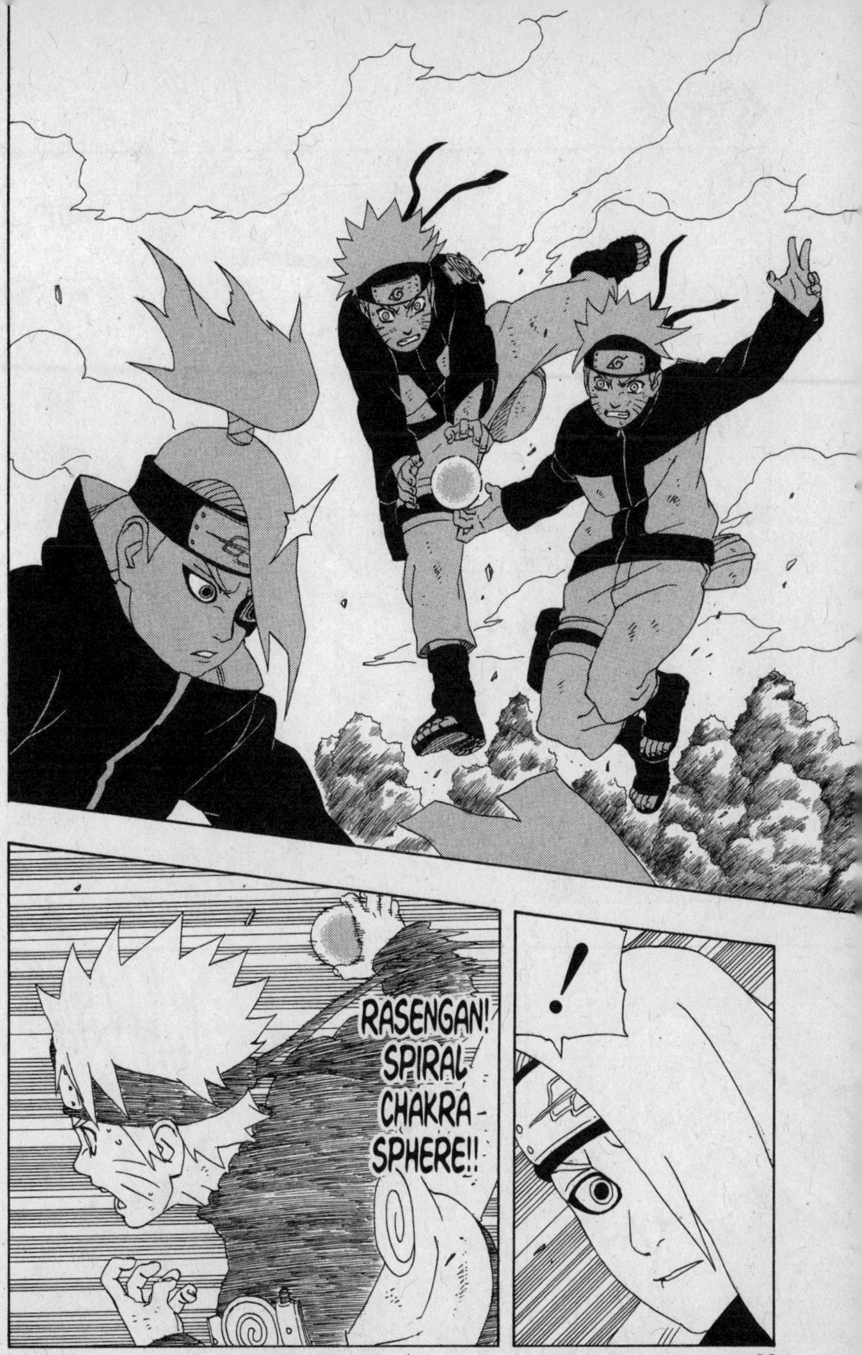
!
RASENGAN! SPIRAL CHAKRA SPHERE!!

READ THIS WAY

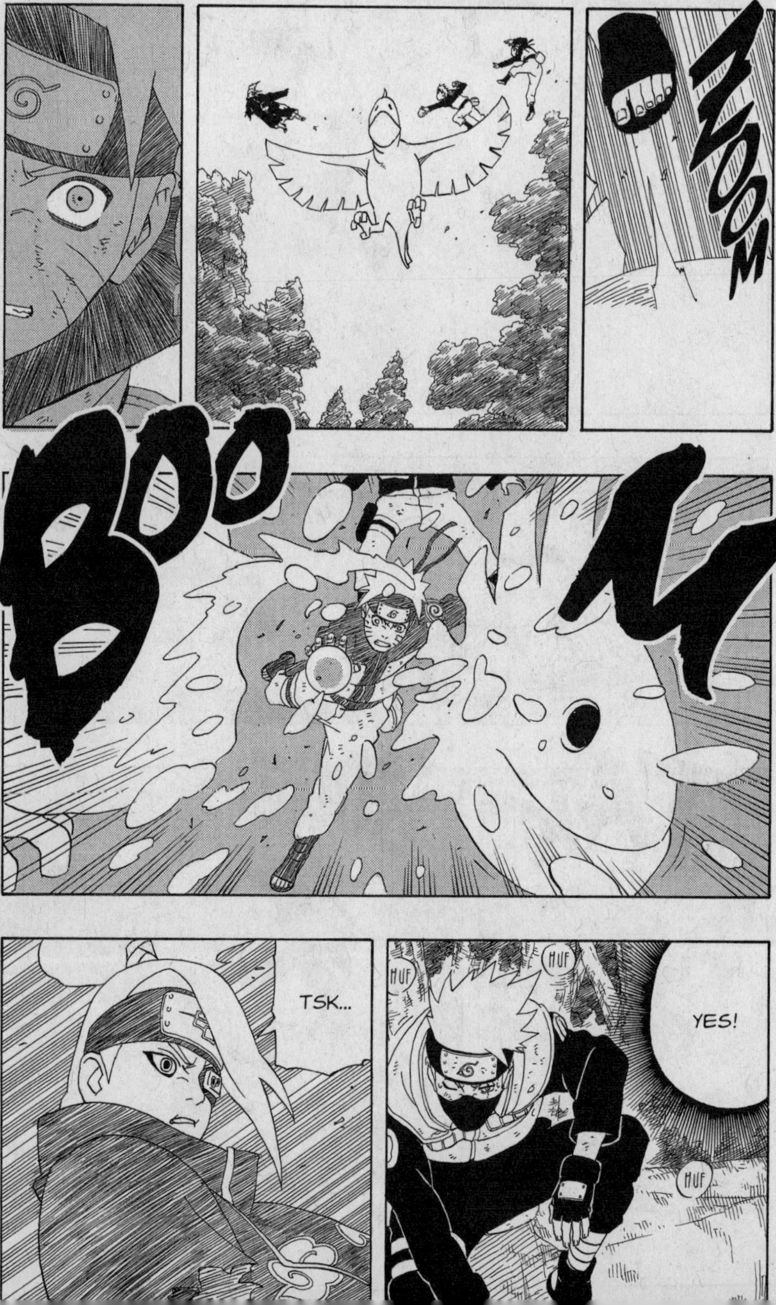
ZOOM
BOOOM
HUF
HUF
YES!
HUF
TSK...

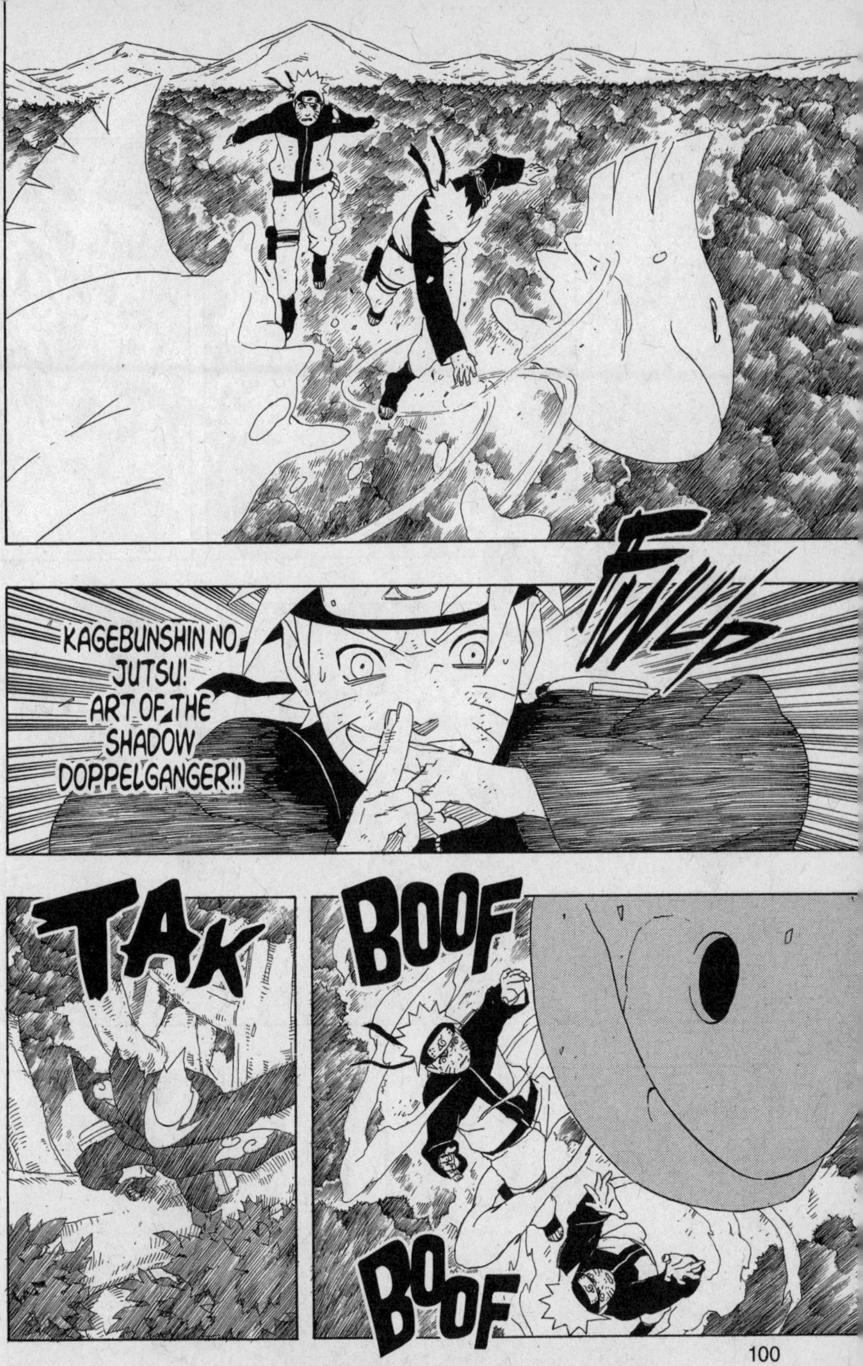
FWUP
KAGEBUNSHIN NO JUTSU! ART OF THE SHADOW DOPPELGANGER!!
BOOF
BOOF
TAK

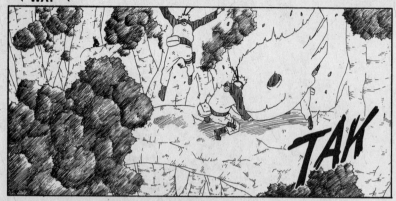

TAK

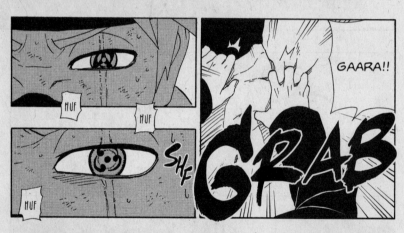

HUF

HUF

HUF

SHF

GAARA!!

GRAB

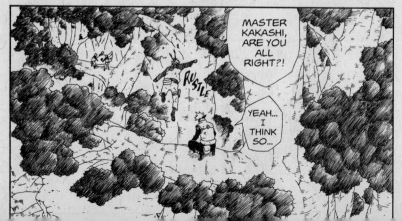

RUSTLE

MASTER KAKASHI, ARE YOU ALL RIGHT?!

YEAH... I THINK SO...

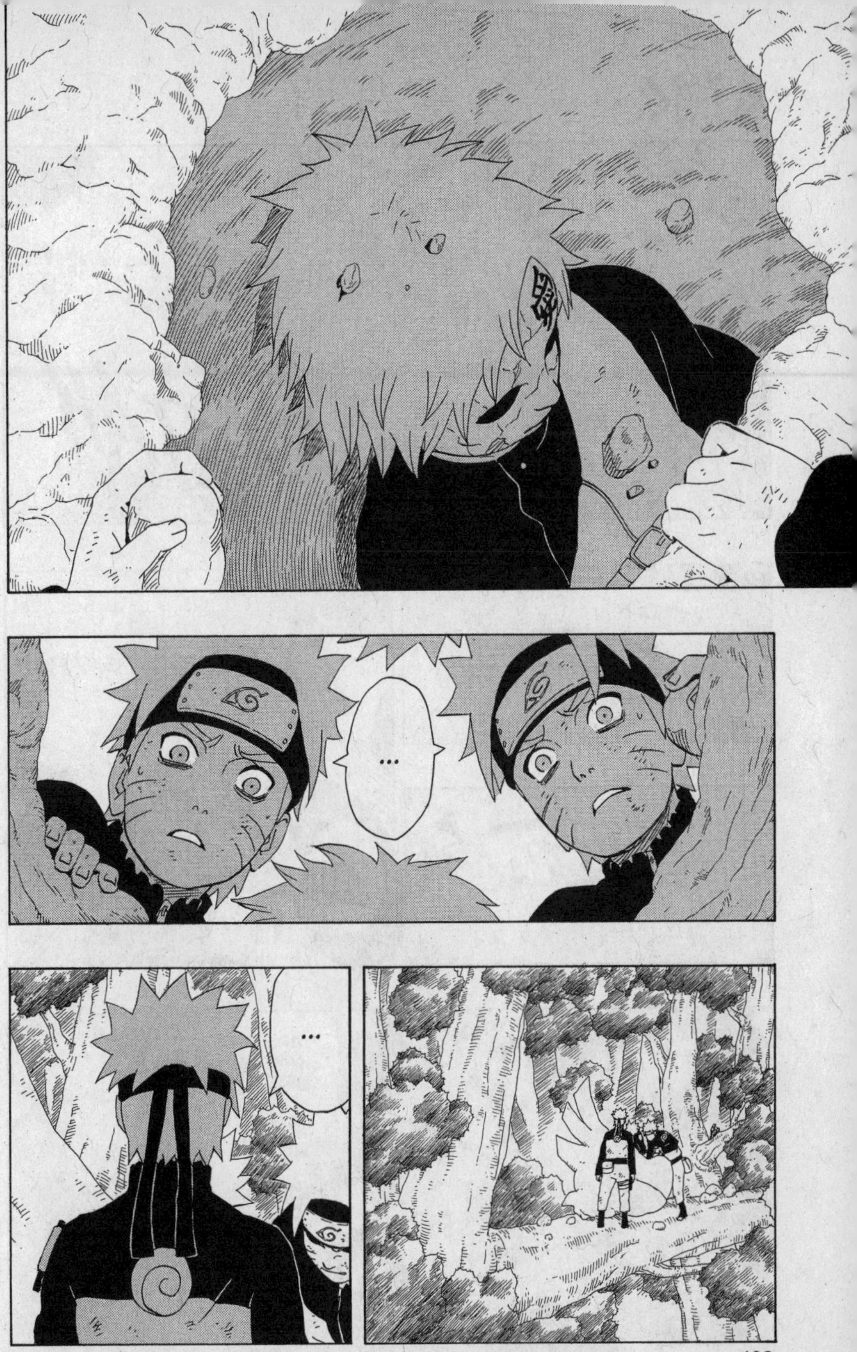
...
...

READ THIS WAY

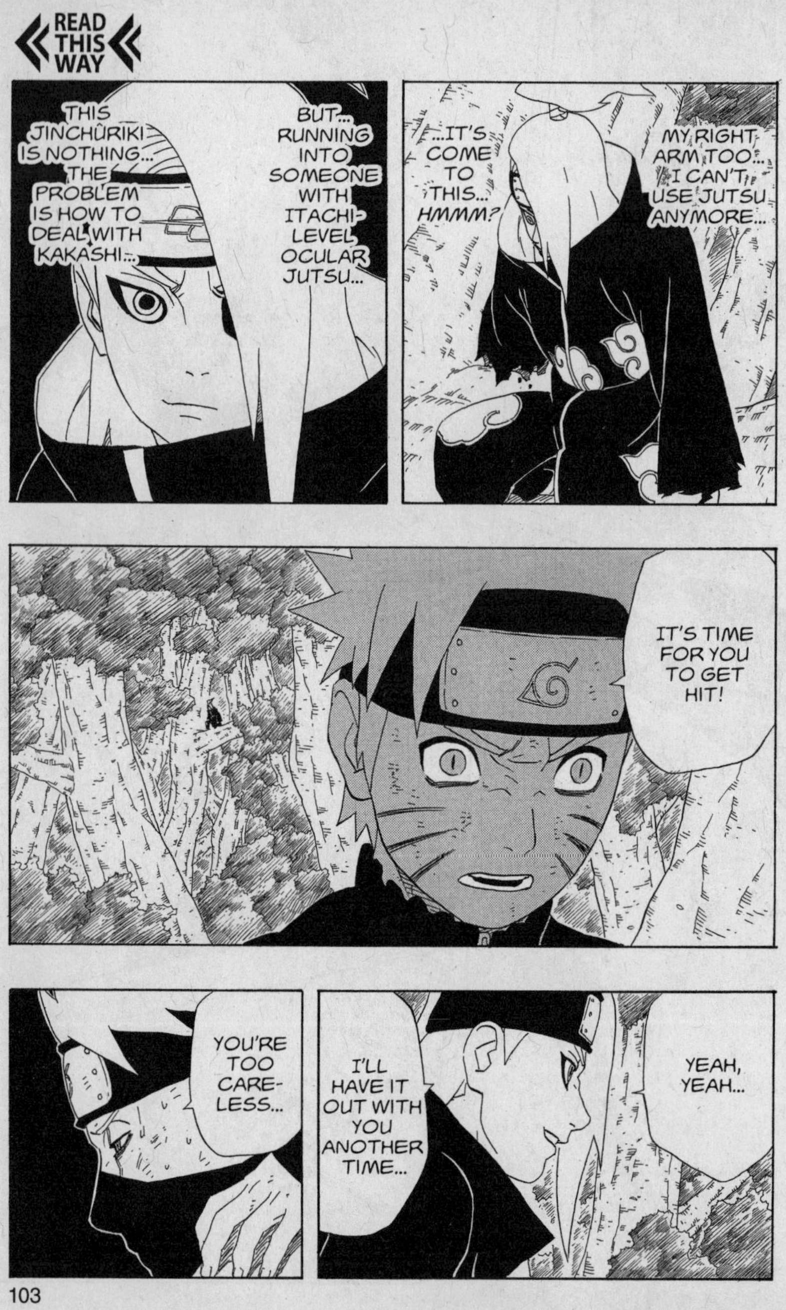
MY RIGHT ARM TOO... I CAN'T USE JUTSU ANYMORE...
...IT'S COME TO THIS... HMMM?
THIS JINCHÛRIKI IS NOTHING... THE PROBLEM IS HOW TO DEAL WITH KAKASHI...
BUT... RUNNING INTO SOMEONE WITH ITACHI-LEVEL OCULAR JUTSU...
IT'S TIME FOR YOU TO GET HIT!
YEAH, YEAH...
I'LL HAVE IT OUT WITH YOU ANOTHER TIME...
YOU'RE TOO CARE-LESS...

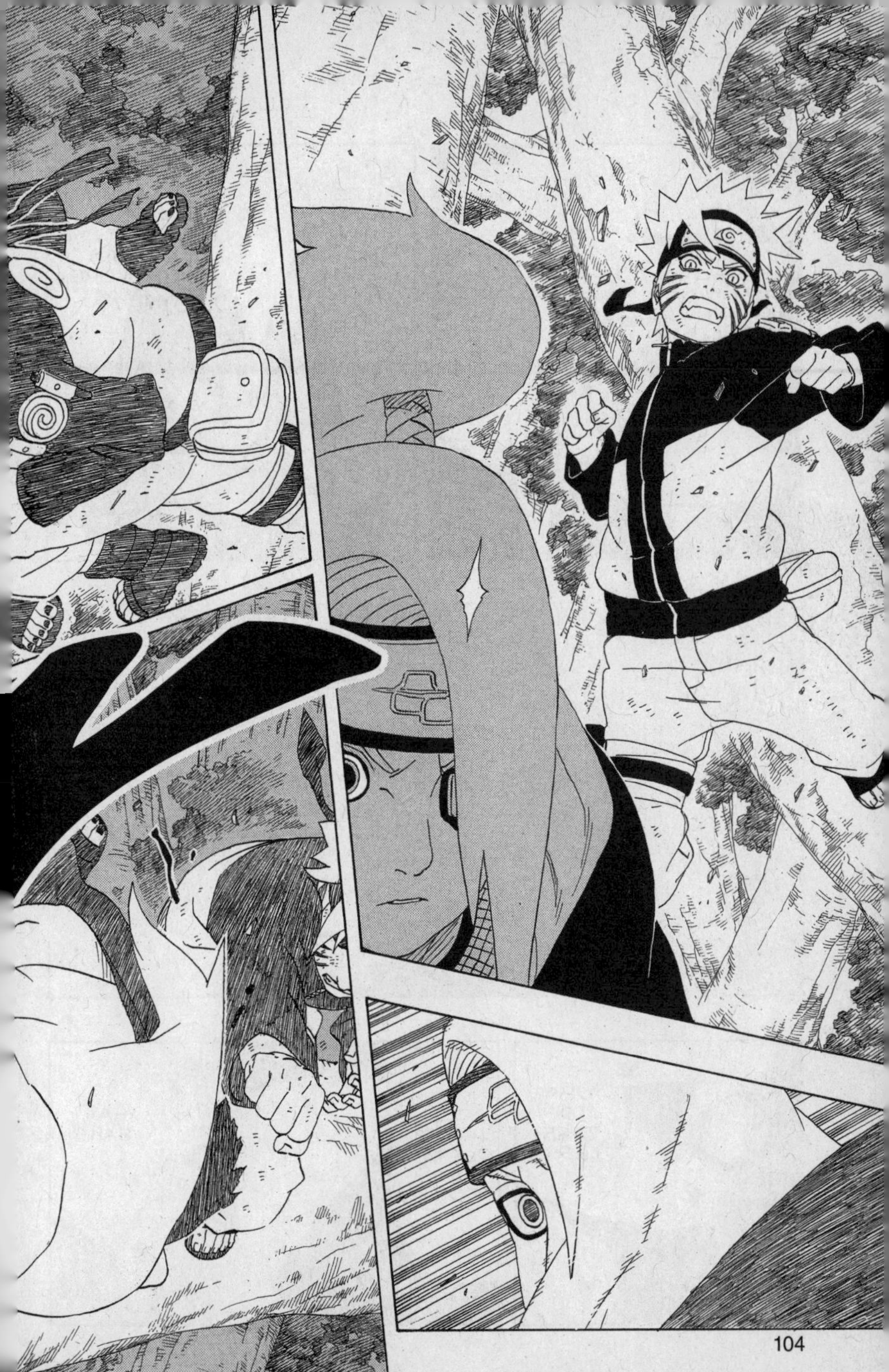

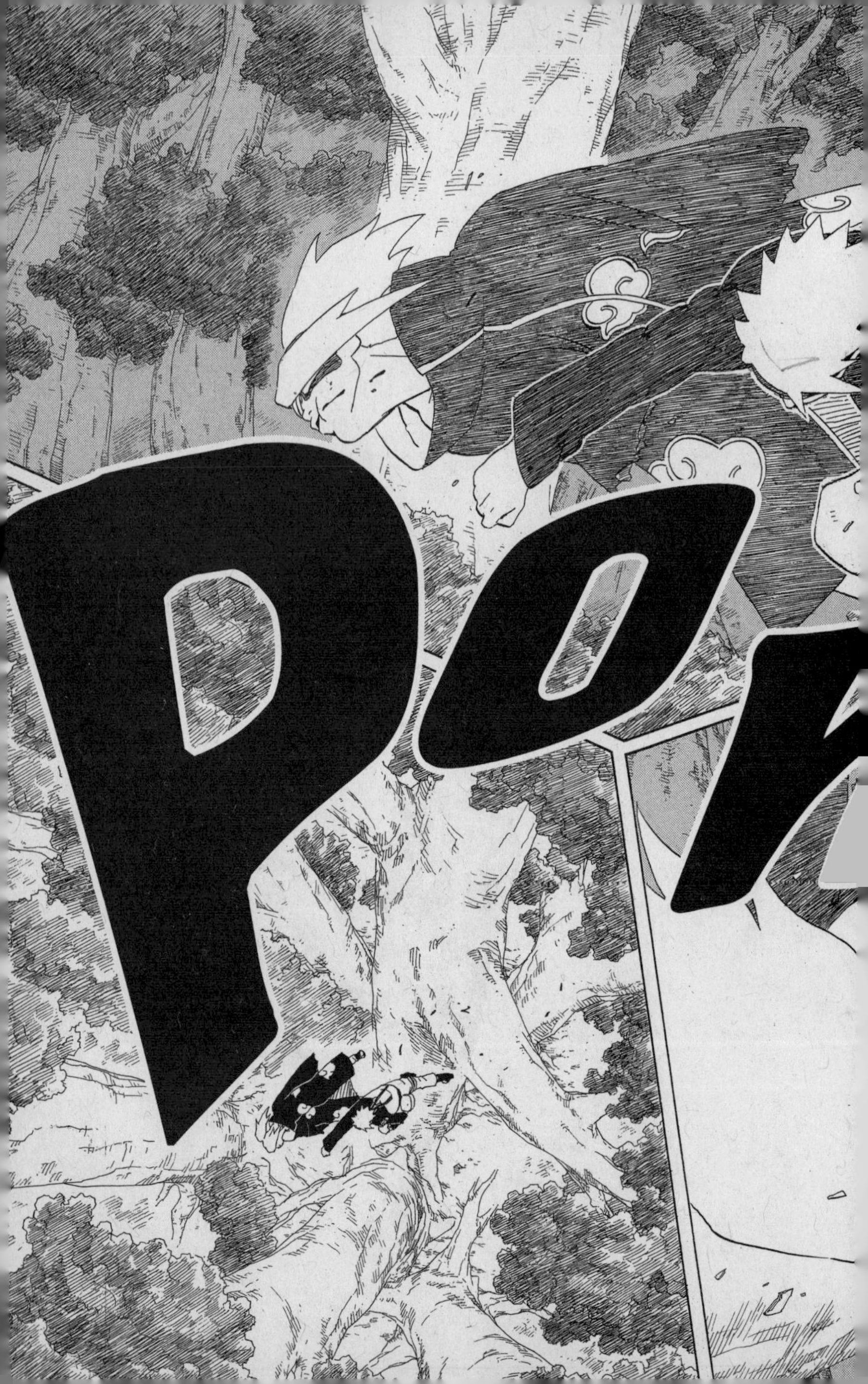
PO

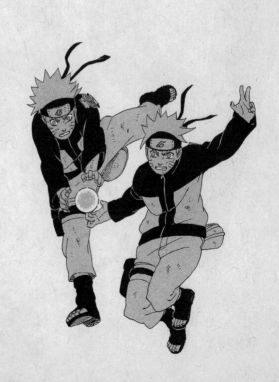

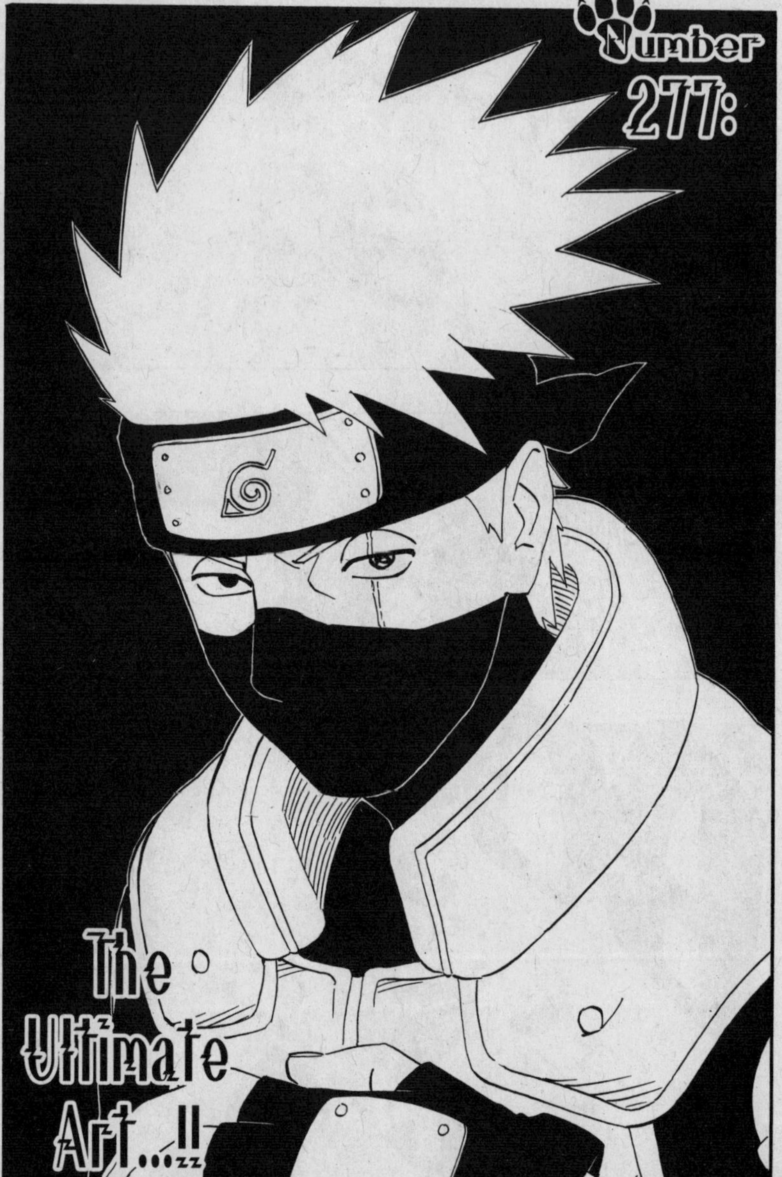
Number 277:
The Ultimate Art...!!

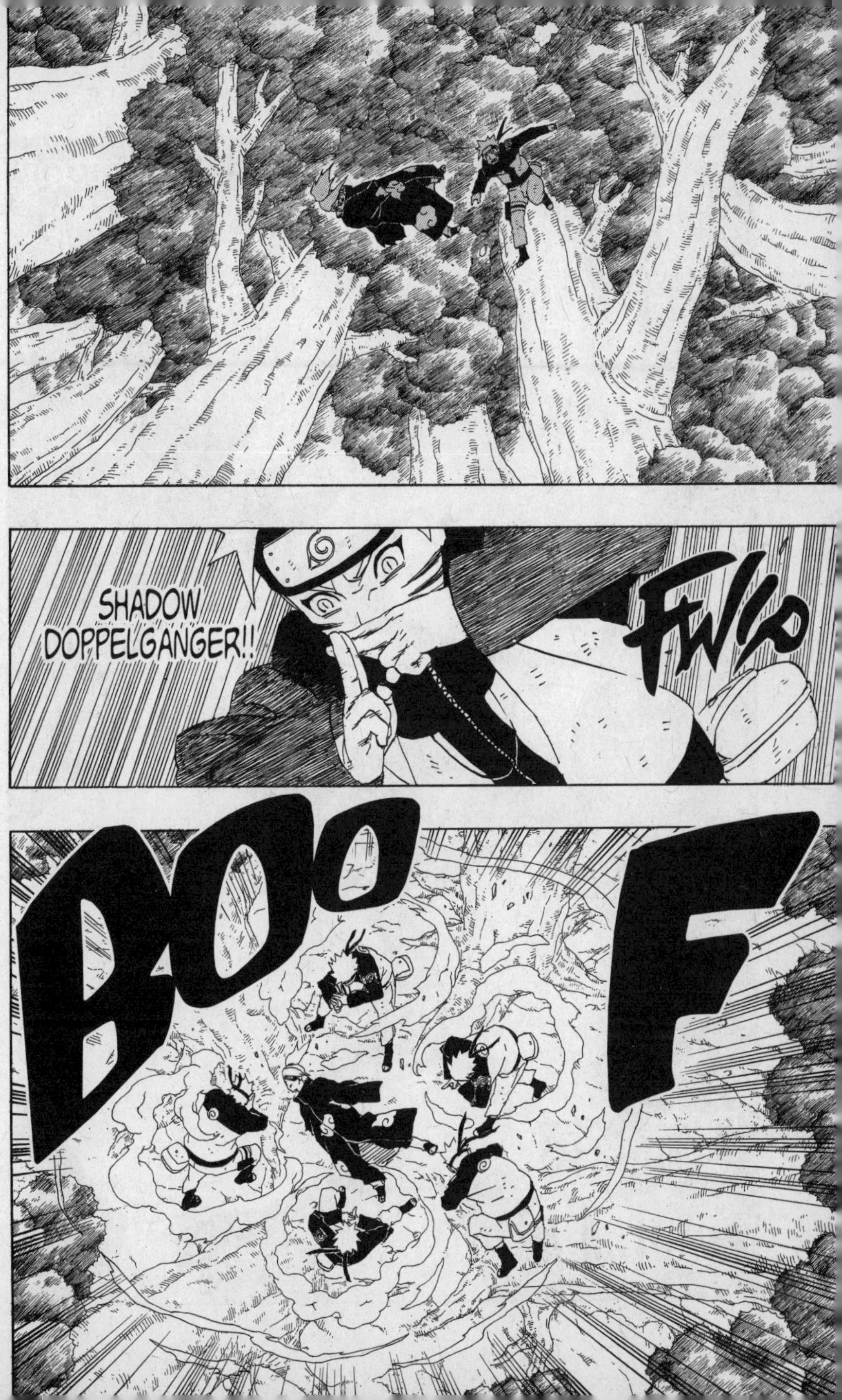
SHADOW DOPPELGANGER!!
FWIP
BOOF

READ THIS WAY

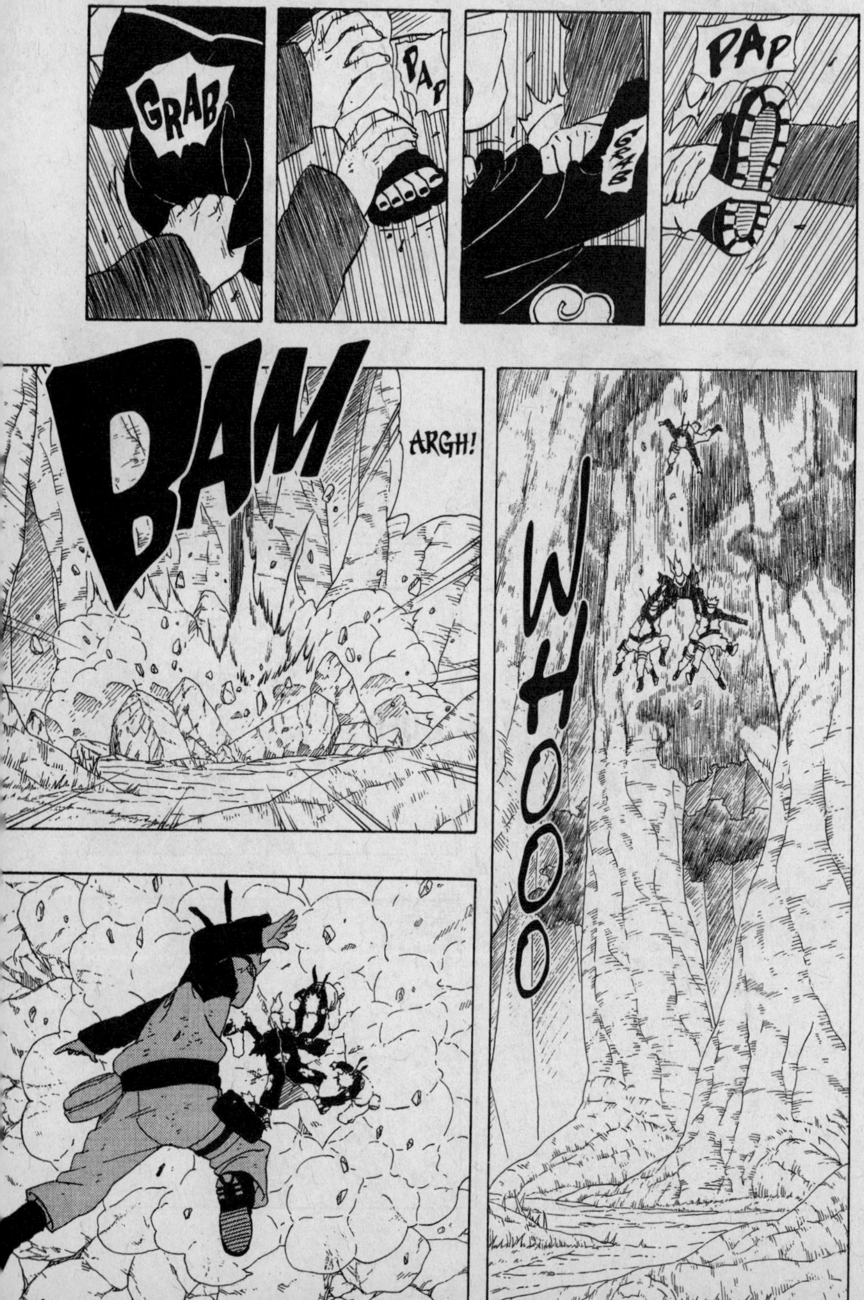
PAP
GRAB
PAP
GRAB
WHOOO
BAM
ARGH!

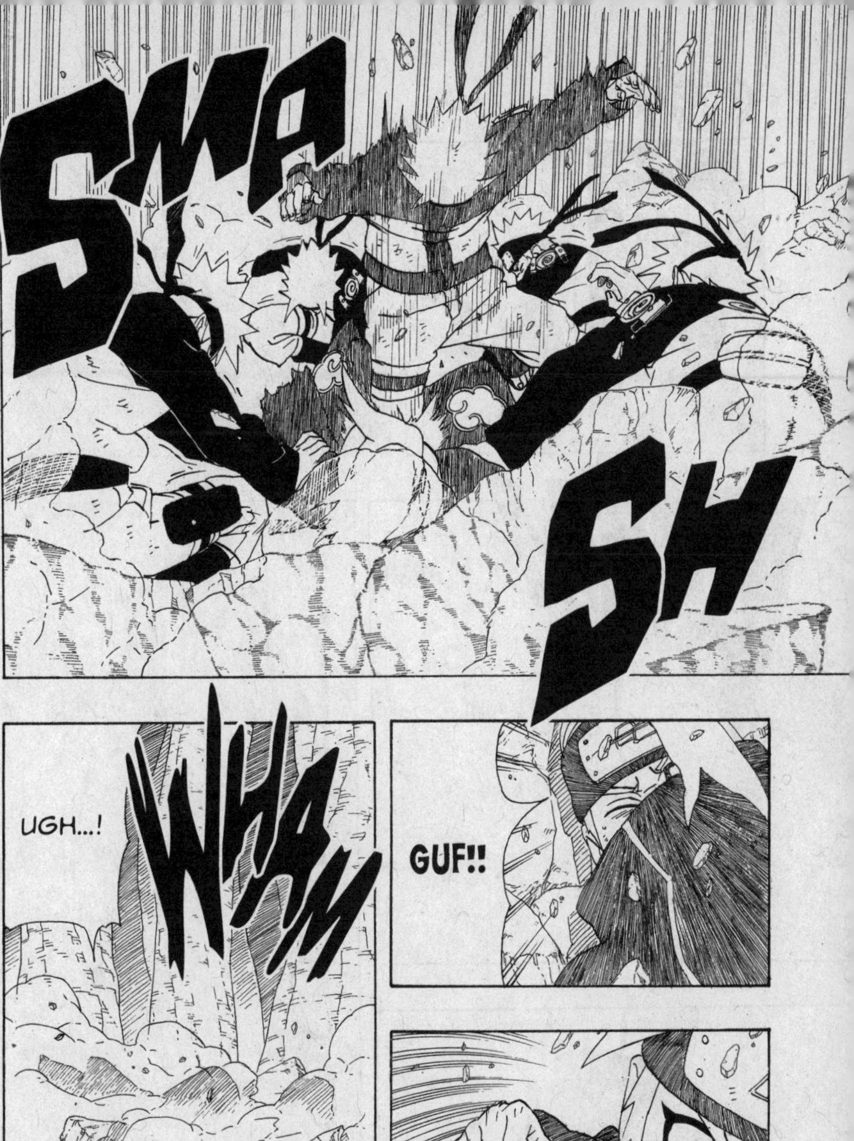
SMA
SH
GUF!!
UGH...!
WHAM

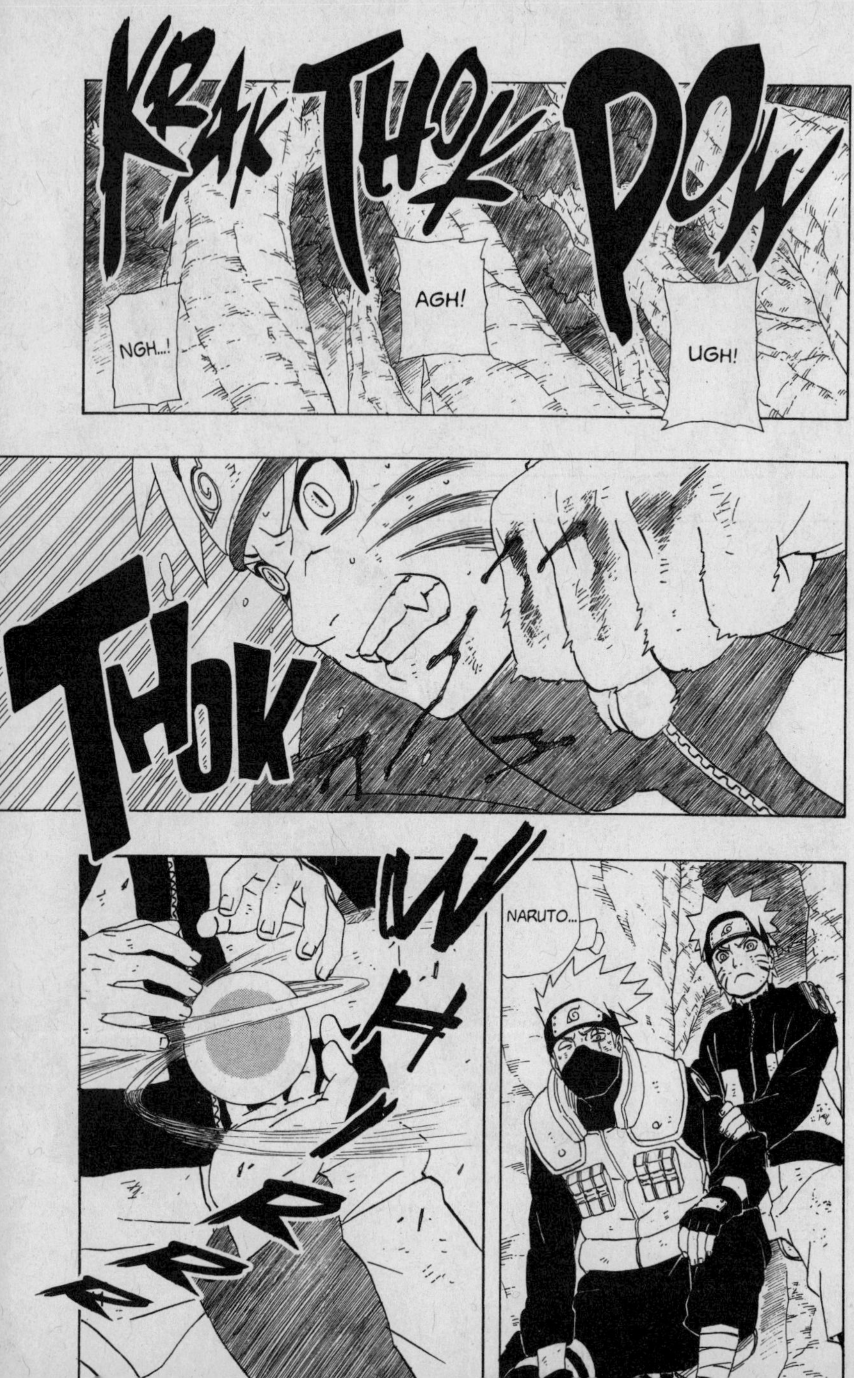

KRAK THOK DOW
UGH!
AGH!
NGH...!
THOK
NARUTO...
WHIRR

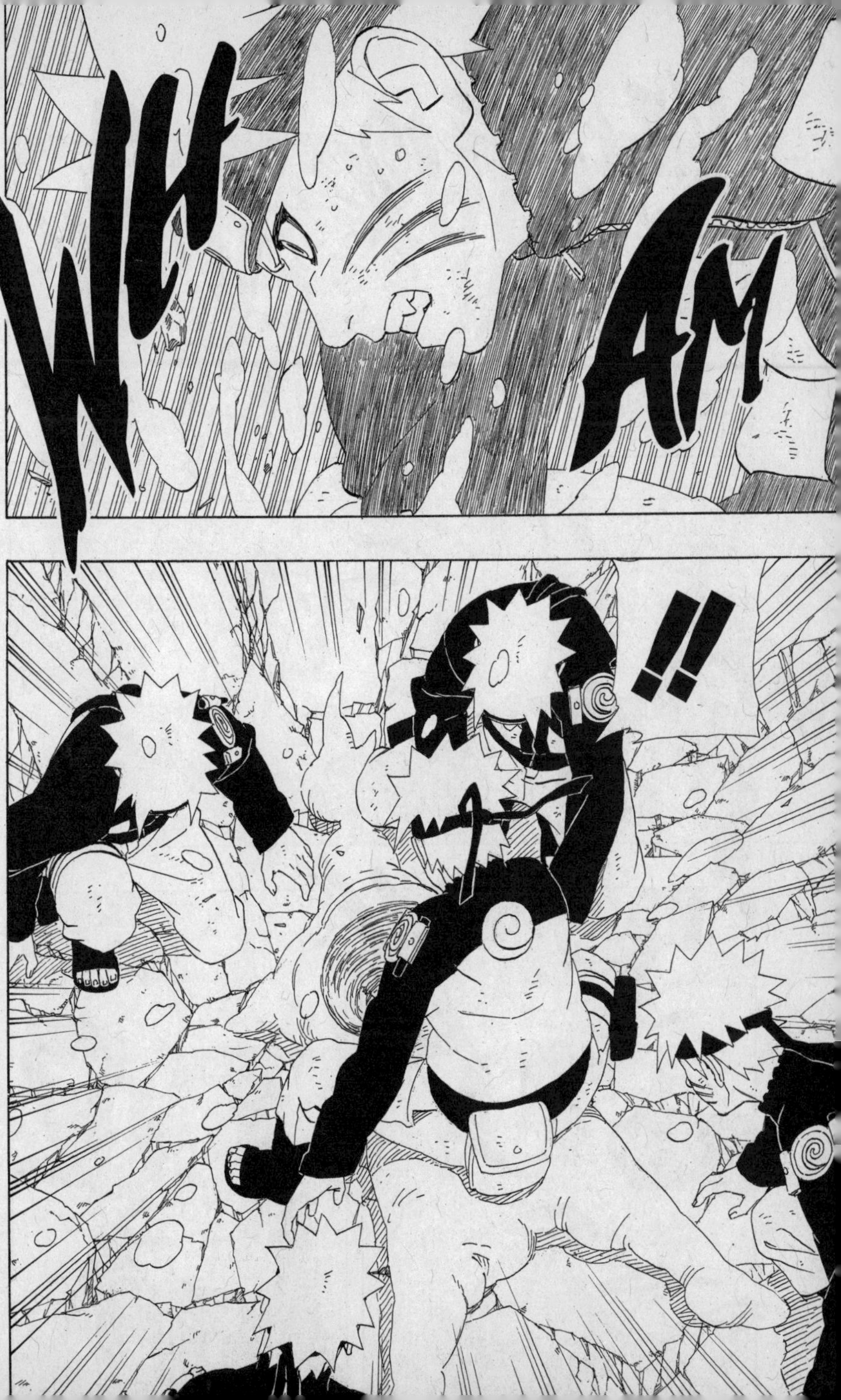
WHAM!!

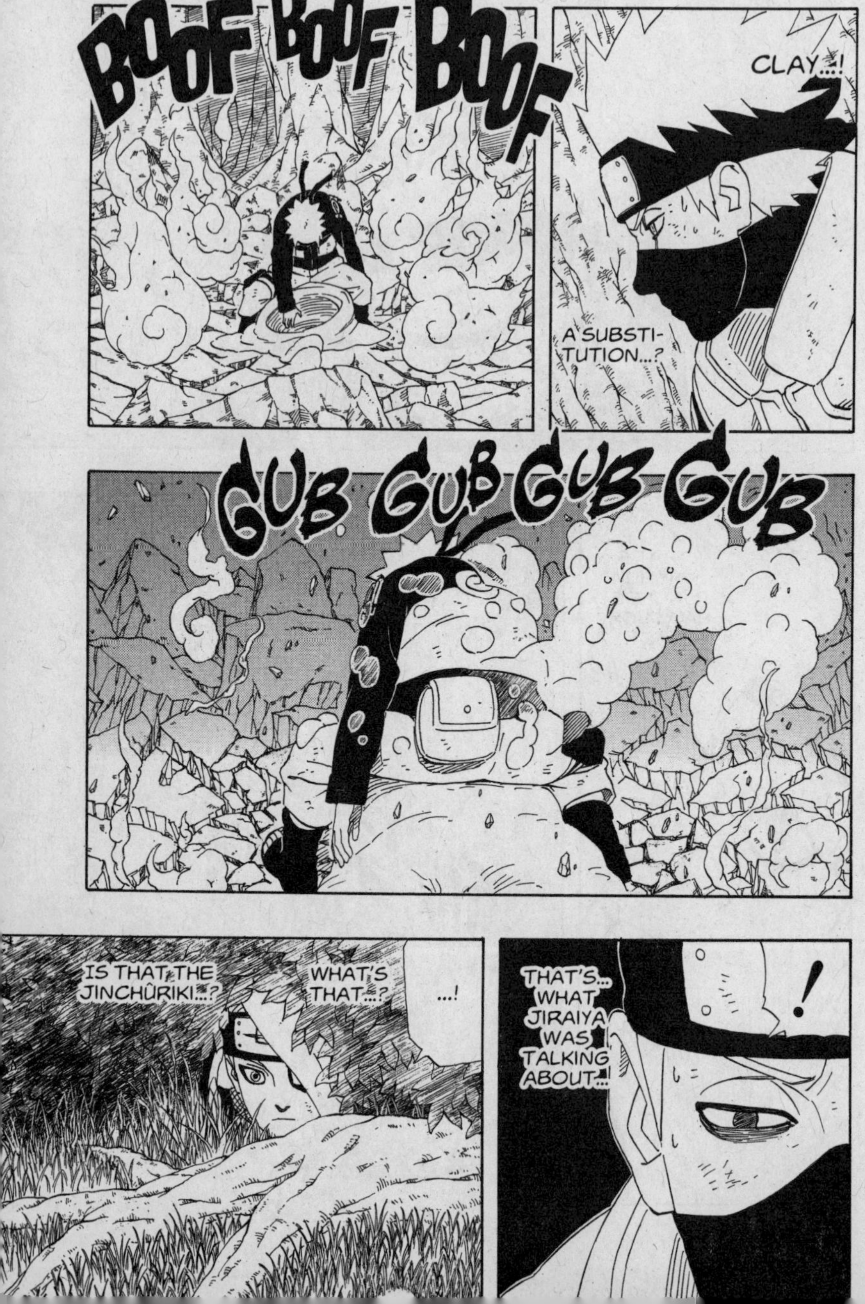
CLAY...!
A SUBSTI-TUTION...?
BOOF BOOF BOOF
GUB GUB GUB GUB
!
THAT'S... WHAT JIRAIYA WAS TALKING ABOUT...!
...!
WHAT'S THAT...?
IS THAT THE JINCHÛRIKI...?

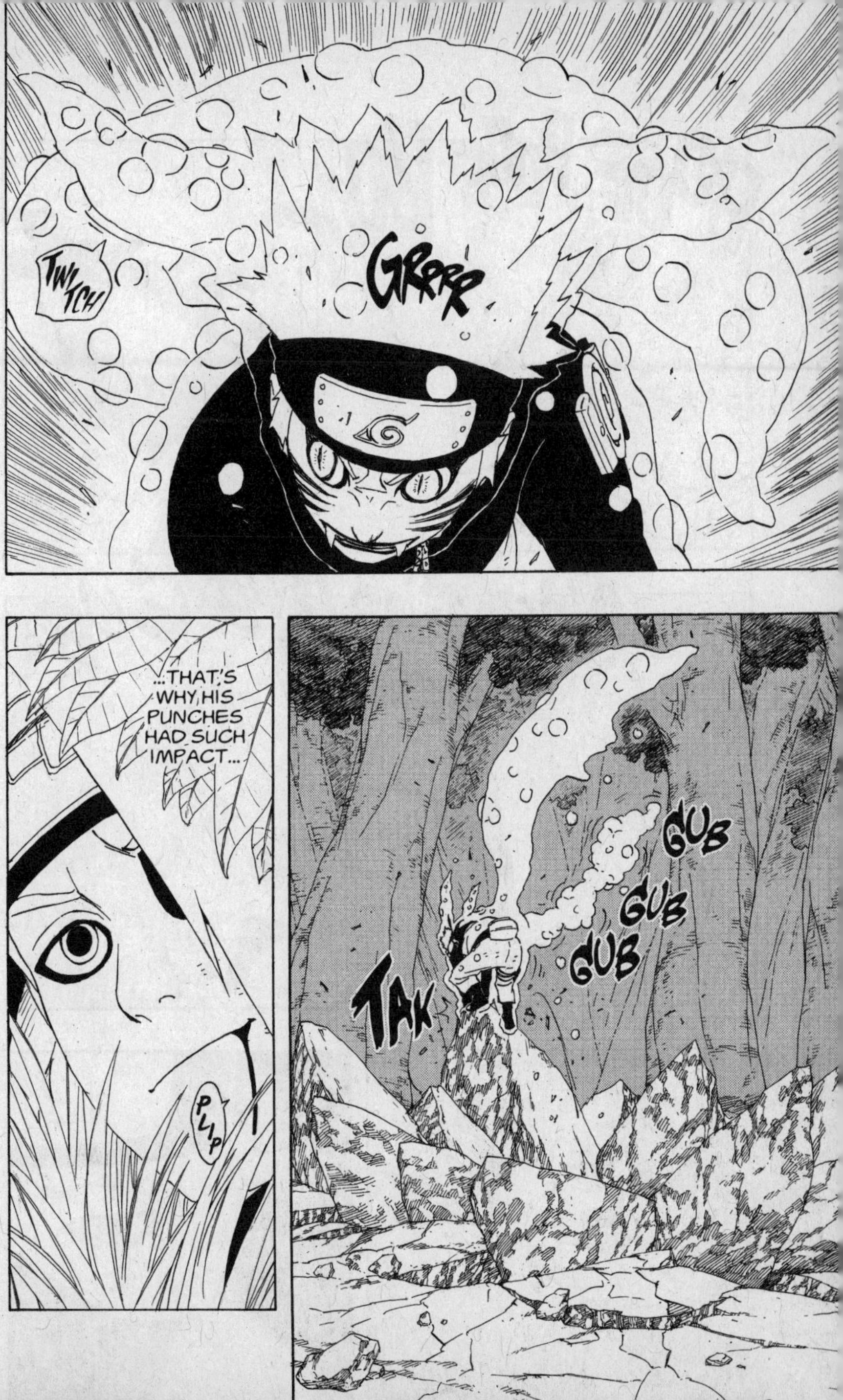
GRRRR
TWITCH
GUB
GUB
GUB
TAK
...THAT'S WHY HIS PUNCHES HAD SUCH IMPACT...
PLIP

READ THIS WAY

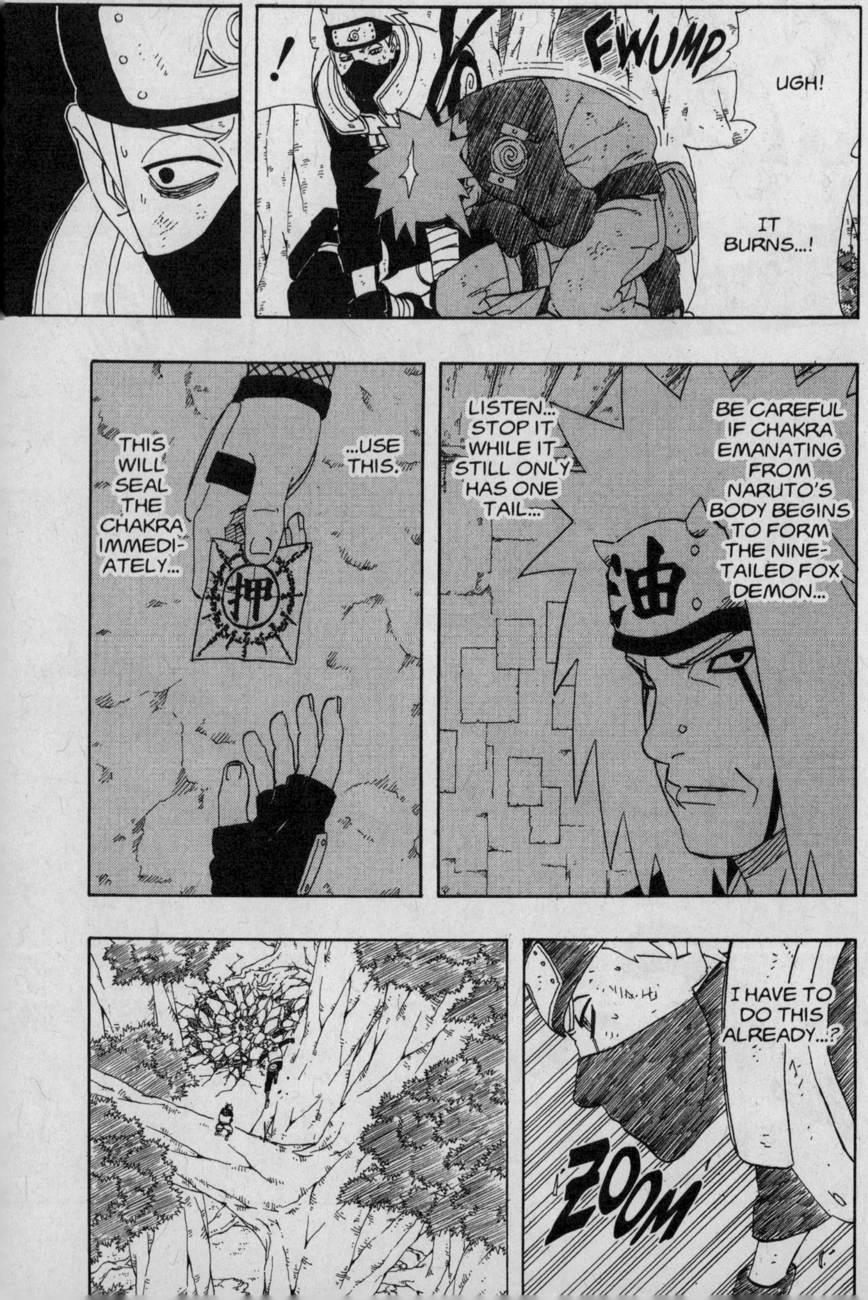
!
FWUMP
UGH!
IT BURNS...!
BE CAREFUL IF CHAKRA EMANATING FROM NARUTO'S BODY BEGINS TO FORM THE NINE-TAILED FOX DEMON...
LISTEN... STOP IT WHILE IT STILL ONLY HAS ONE TAIL...
...USE THIS.
THIS WILL SEAL THE CHAKRA IMMEDI-ATELY...
押
I HAVE TO DO THIS ALREADY...?
ZOOM

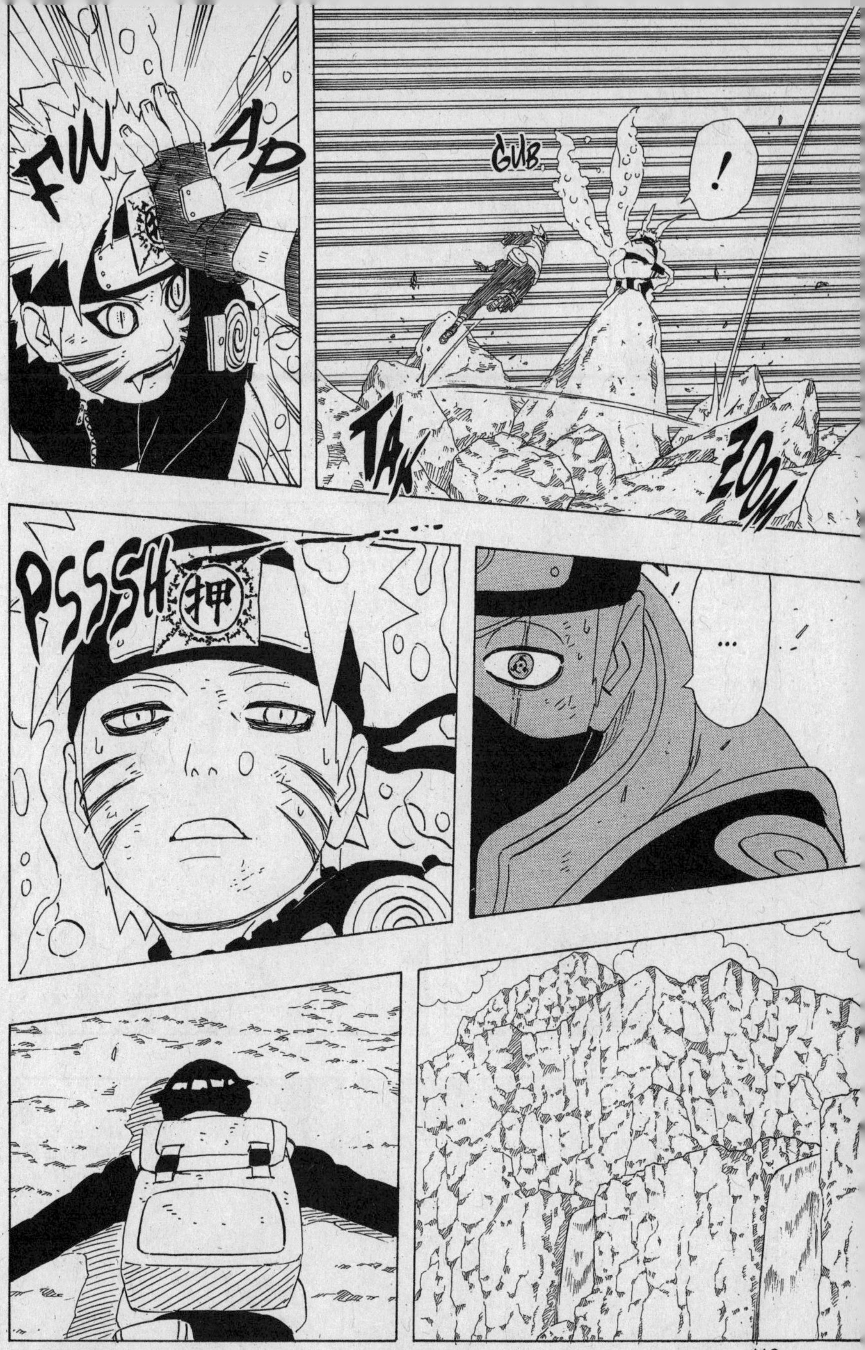
!
GUB
ZOOM
TAK
FWAP
...
PSSSH
押

READ THIS WAY

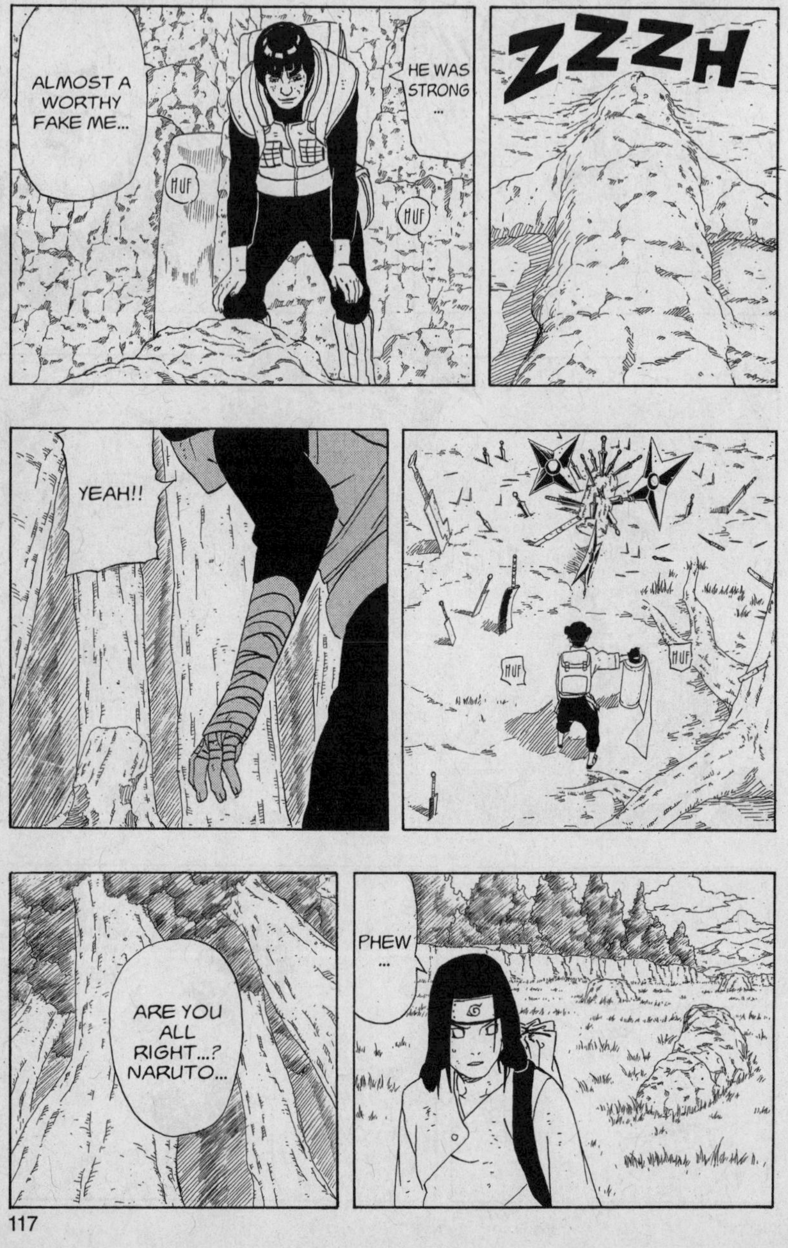
ZZZH
HE WAS STRONG ...
ALMOST A WORTHY FAKE ME...
HUF
HUF
HUF
HUF
YEAH!!
PHEW ...
ARE YOU ALL RIGHT...? NARUTO...

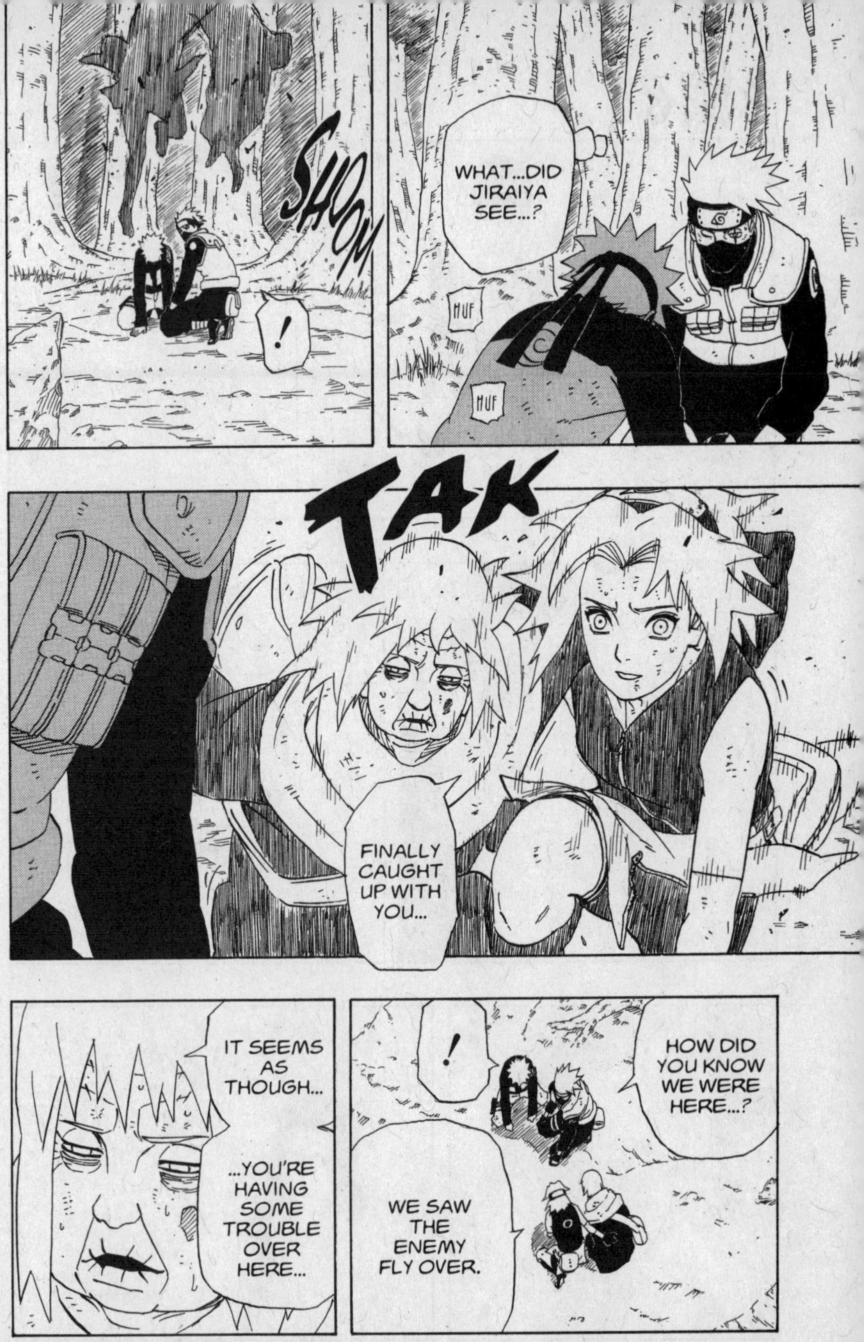
WHAT...DID JIRAIYA SEE...?
HUF
HUF
SHOOM
!
TAK
FINALLY CAUGHT UP WITH YOU...
!
HOW DID YOU KNOW WE WERE HERE...?
WE SAW THE ENEMY FLY OVER.
IT SEEMS AS THOUGH...
...YOU'RE HAVING SOME TROUBLE OVER HERE...

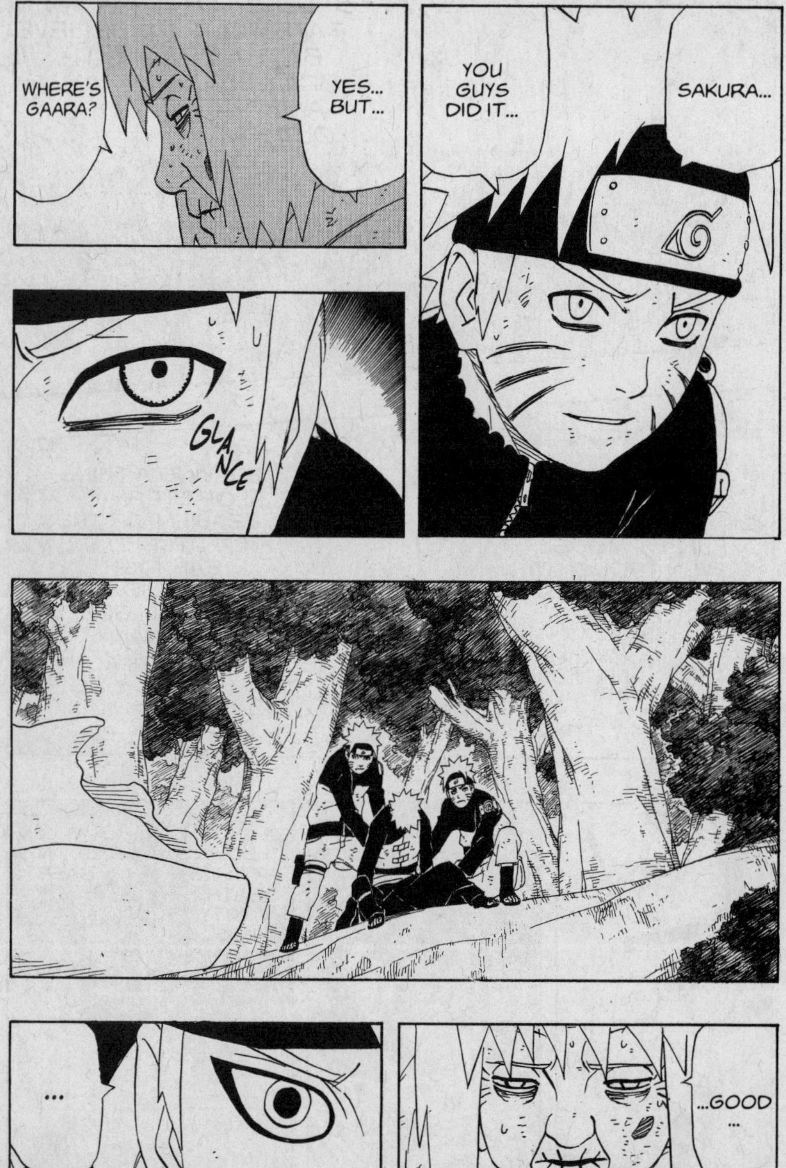
SAKURA...
YOU GUYS DID IT...
YES... BUT...
WHERE'S GAARA?
GLANCE
...GOOD ...
...

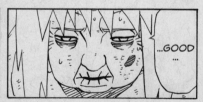

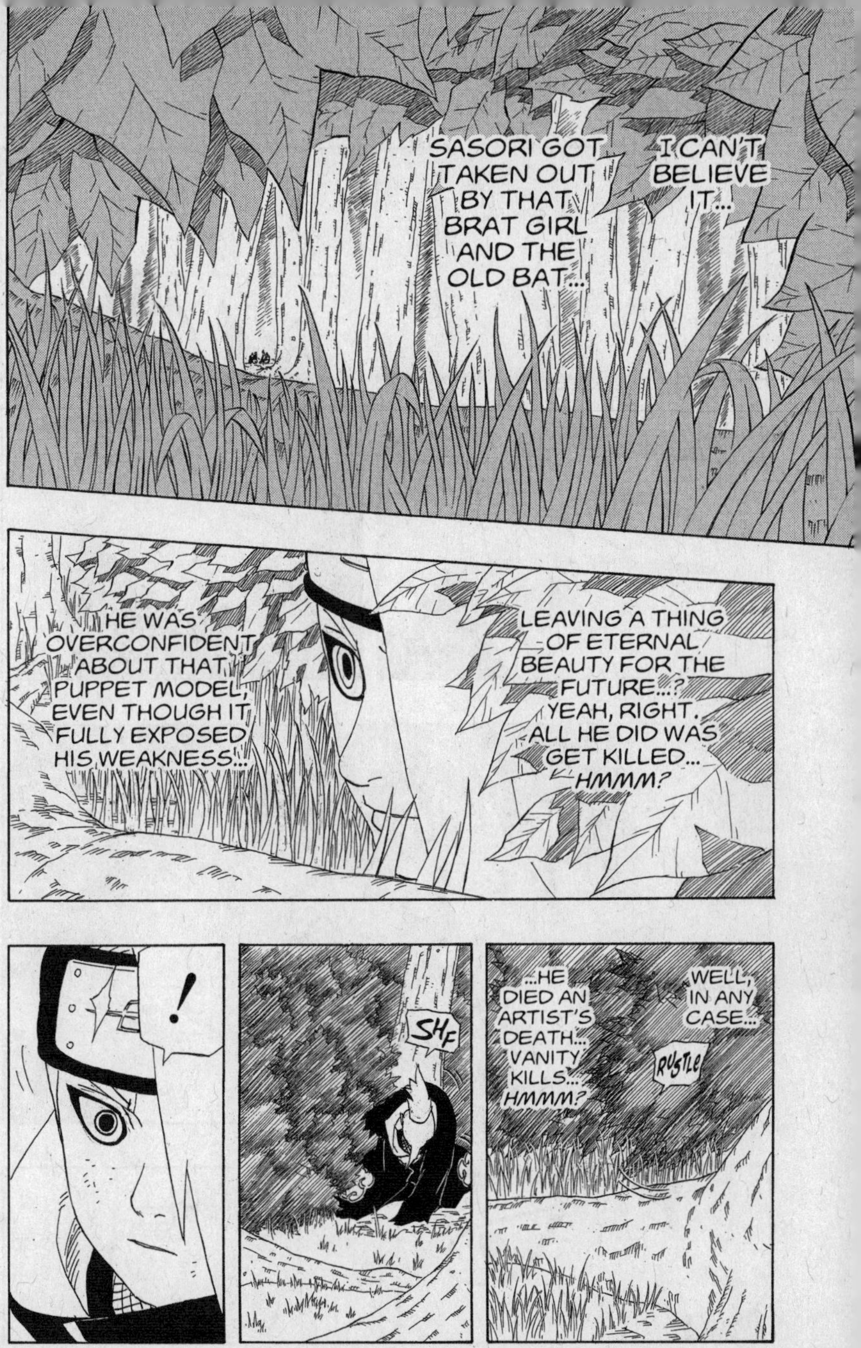
I CAN'T BELIEVE IT...
SASORI GOT TAKEN OUT BY THAT BRAT GIRL AND THE OLD BAT...
LEAVING A THING OF ETERNAL BEAUTY FOR THE FUTURE...? YEAH, RIGHT. ALL HE DID WAS GET KILLED... *HMMM?*
HE WAS OVERCONFIDENT ABOUT THAT PUPPET MODEL, EVEN THOUGH IT FULLY EXPOSED HIS WEAKNESS...
WELL, IN ANY CASE...
...HE DIED AN ARTIST'S DEATH... VANITY KILLS... *HMMM?*
RUSTLE
SHF
!

READ THIS WAY

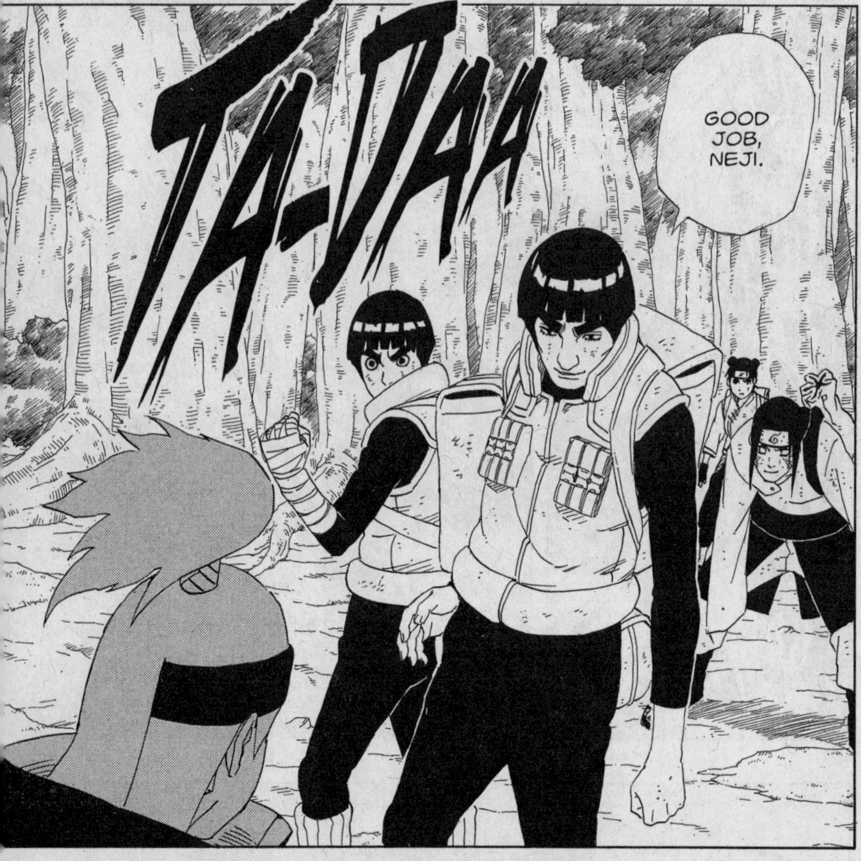
GOOD JOB, NEJI.
TA-DAA

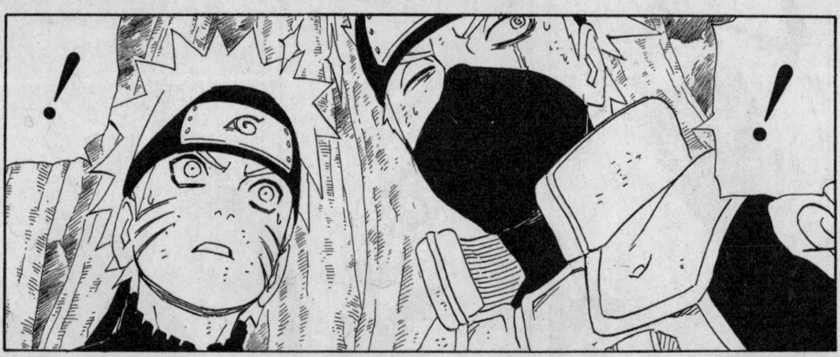
!
!

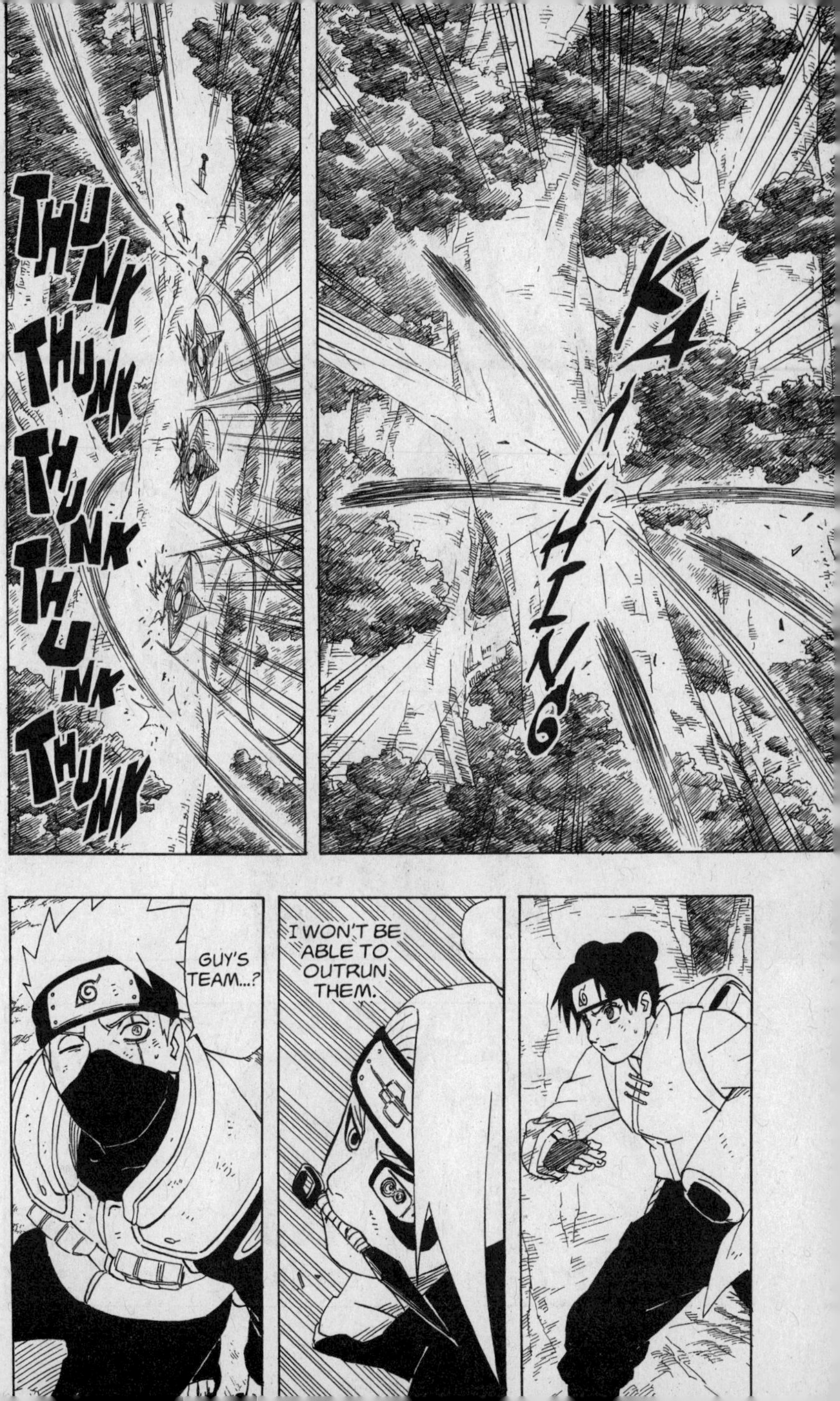
KA-CHING
THUNK
THUNK
THUNK
THUNK
THUNK
I WON'T BE ABLE TO OUTRUN THEM.
GUY'S TEAM...?

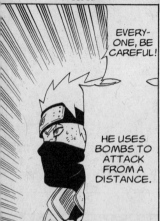

EVERY-ONE, BE CAREFUL!

HE USES BOMBS TO ATTACK FROM A DISTANCE.

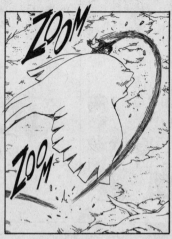

ZOOM

ZOOM

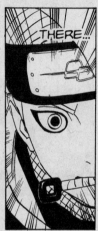

...THERE...

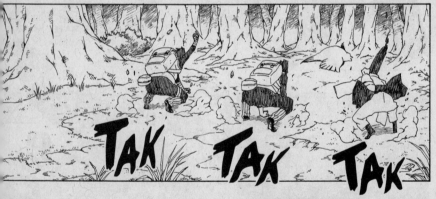

TAK TAK TAK

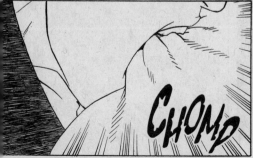

CHOMP

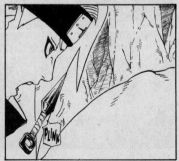

PLINK

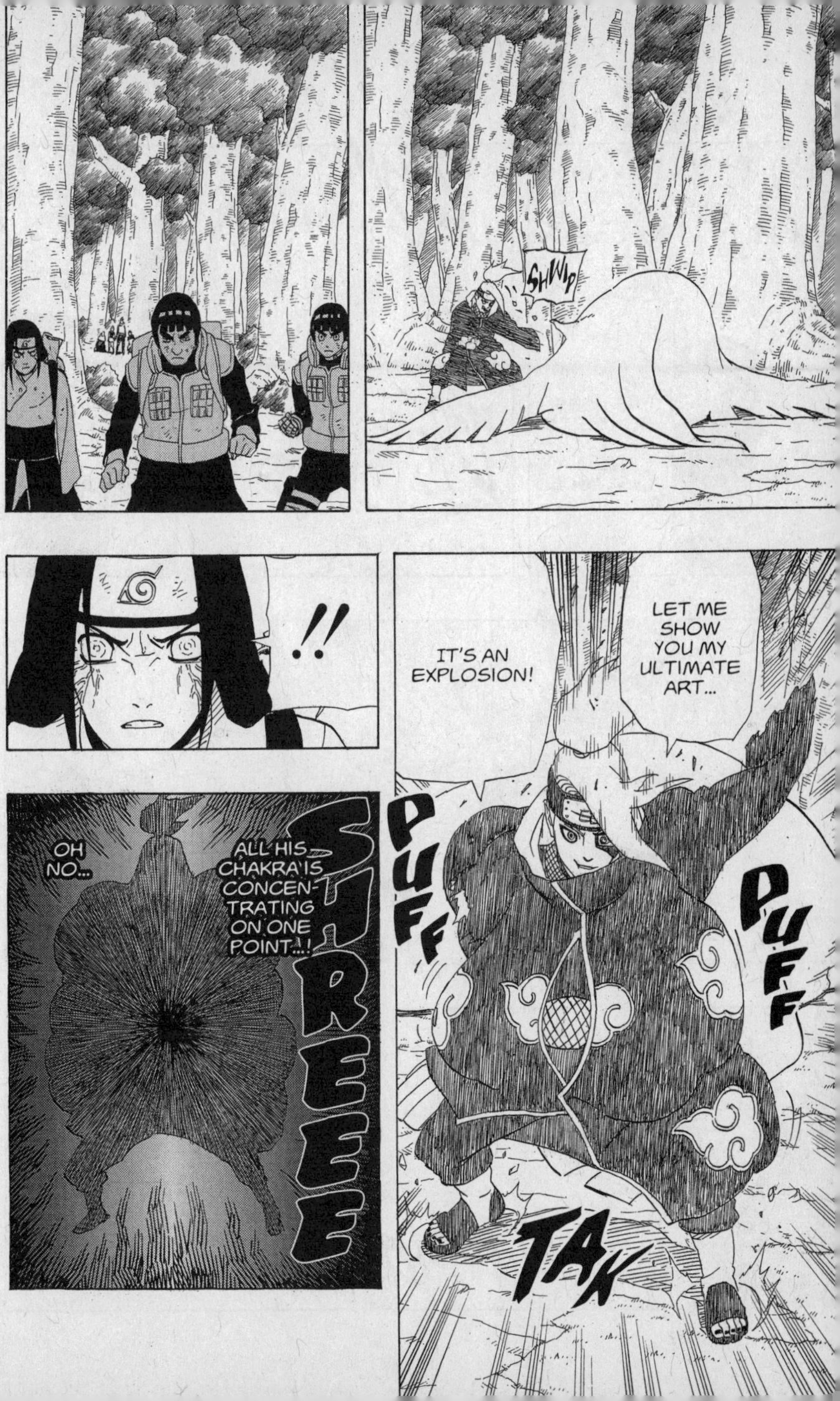
SHWIP
LET ME SHOW YOU MY ULTIMATE ART...
IT'S AN EXPLOSION!
PUFF
PUFF
TAK
!!
ALL HIS CHAKRA IS CONCEN-TRATING ON ONE POINT...!
OH NO...
SHREEE

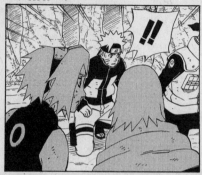

!!

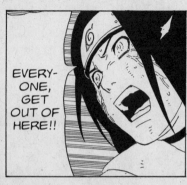

EVERY-
ONE,
GET
OUT OF
HERE!!

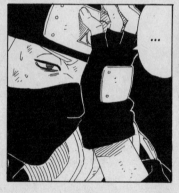

...

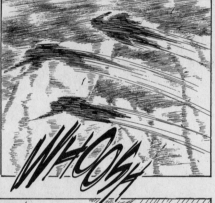

WHOOSH

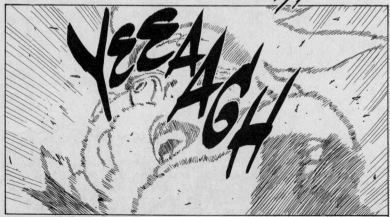

YEEA AGH

NARUTO

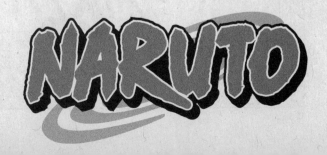

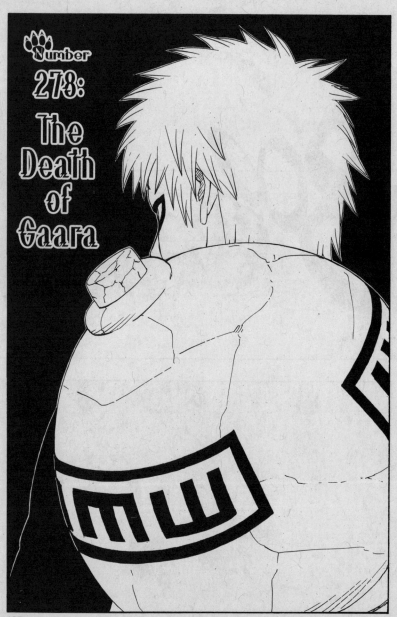

Number
278:
The
Death
of
Gaara

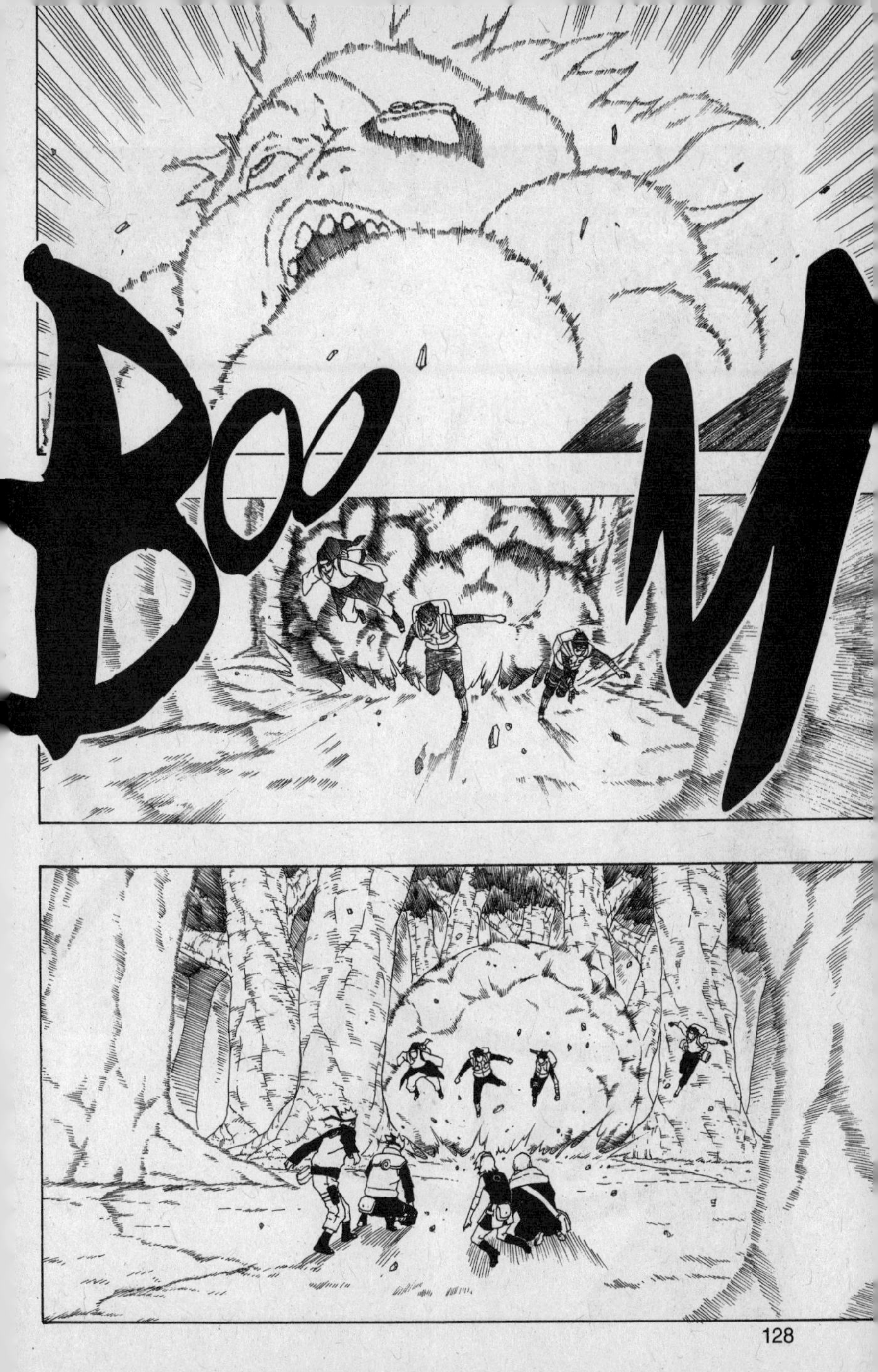
BOOM

READ THIS WAY

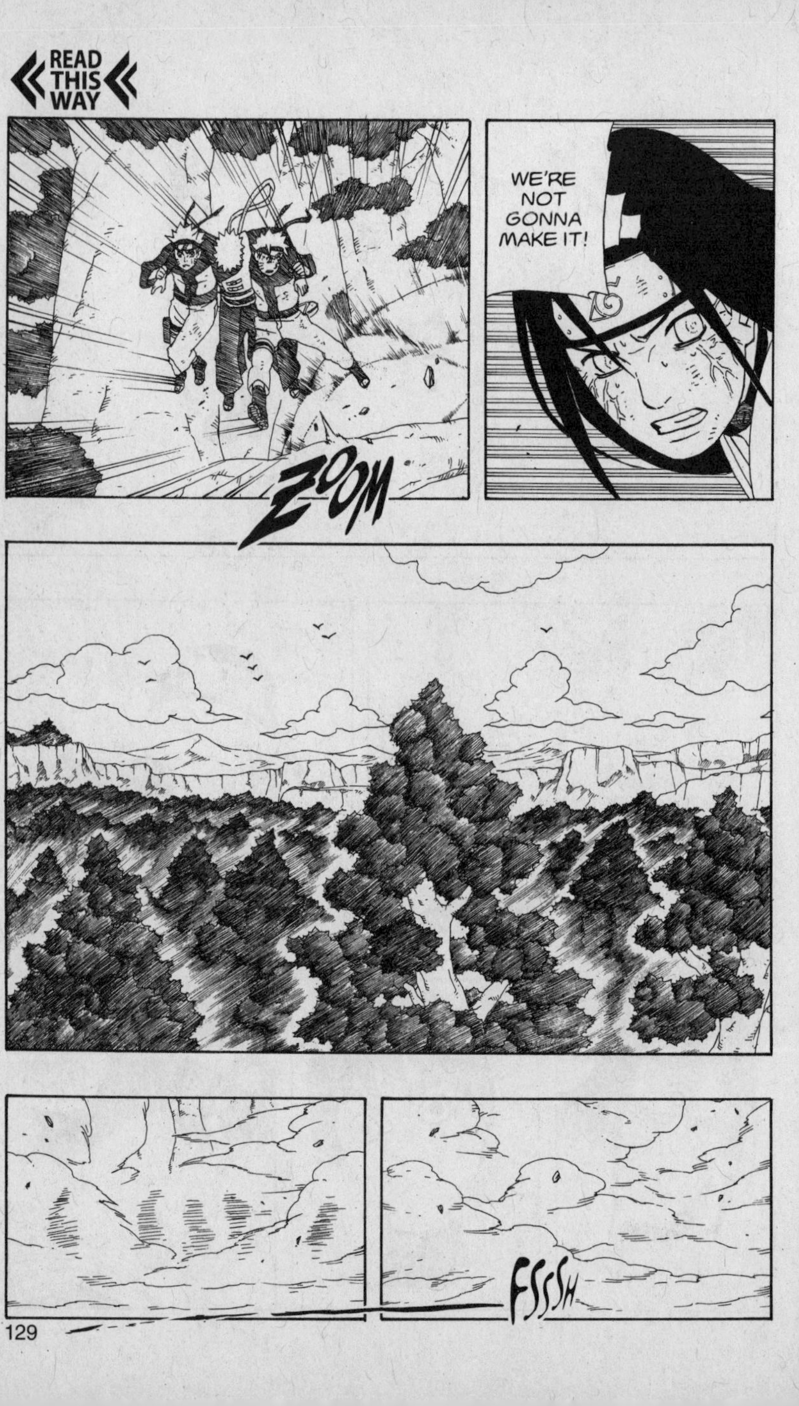
WE'RE NOT GONNA MAKE IT!
ZOOM
FSSSH

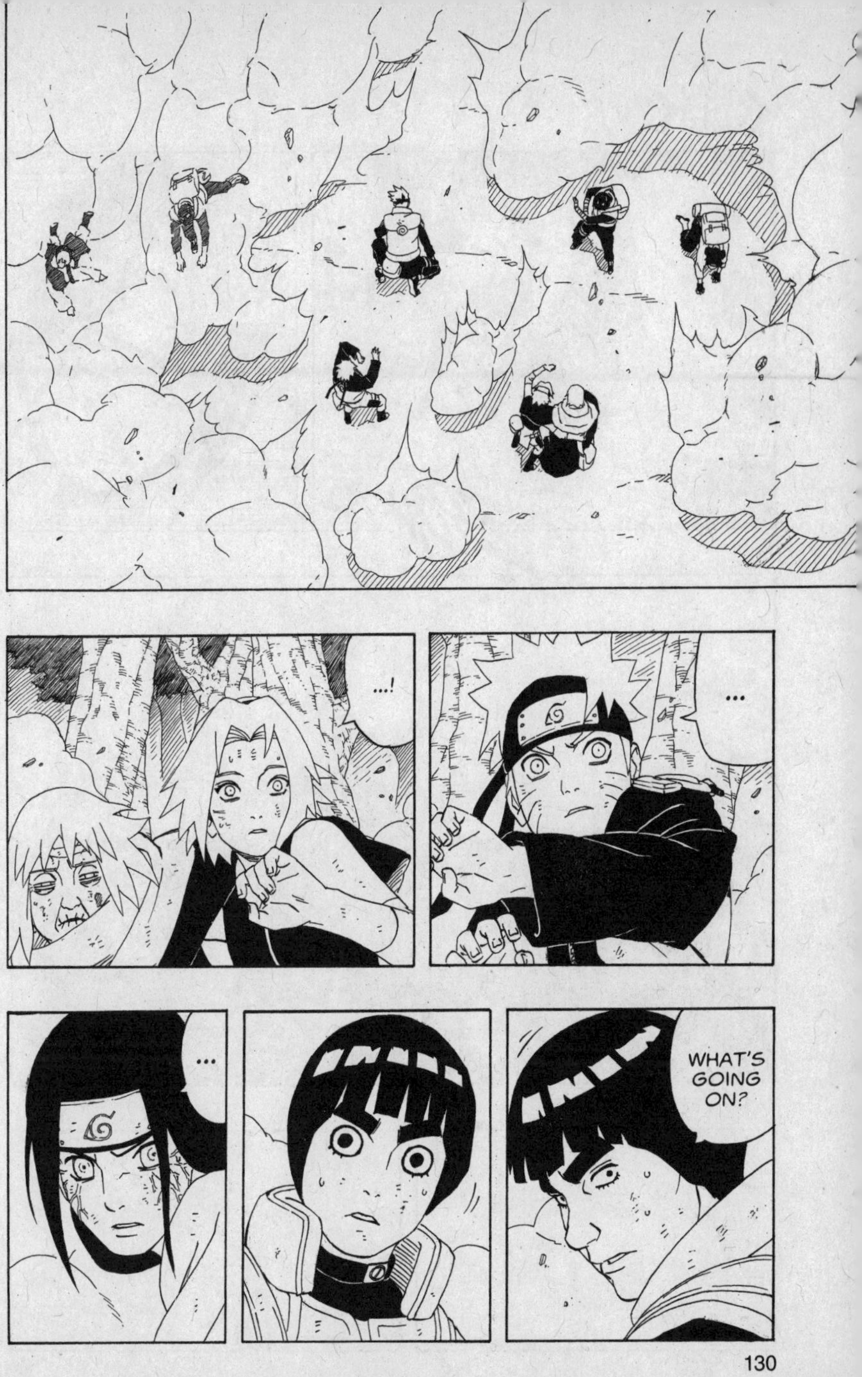
...
...!
WHAT'S GOING ON?
...

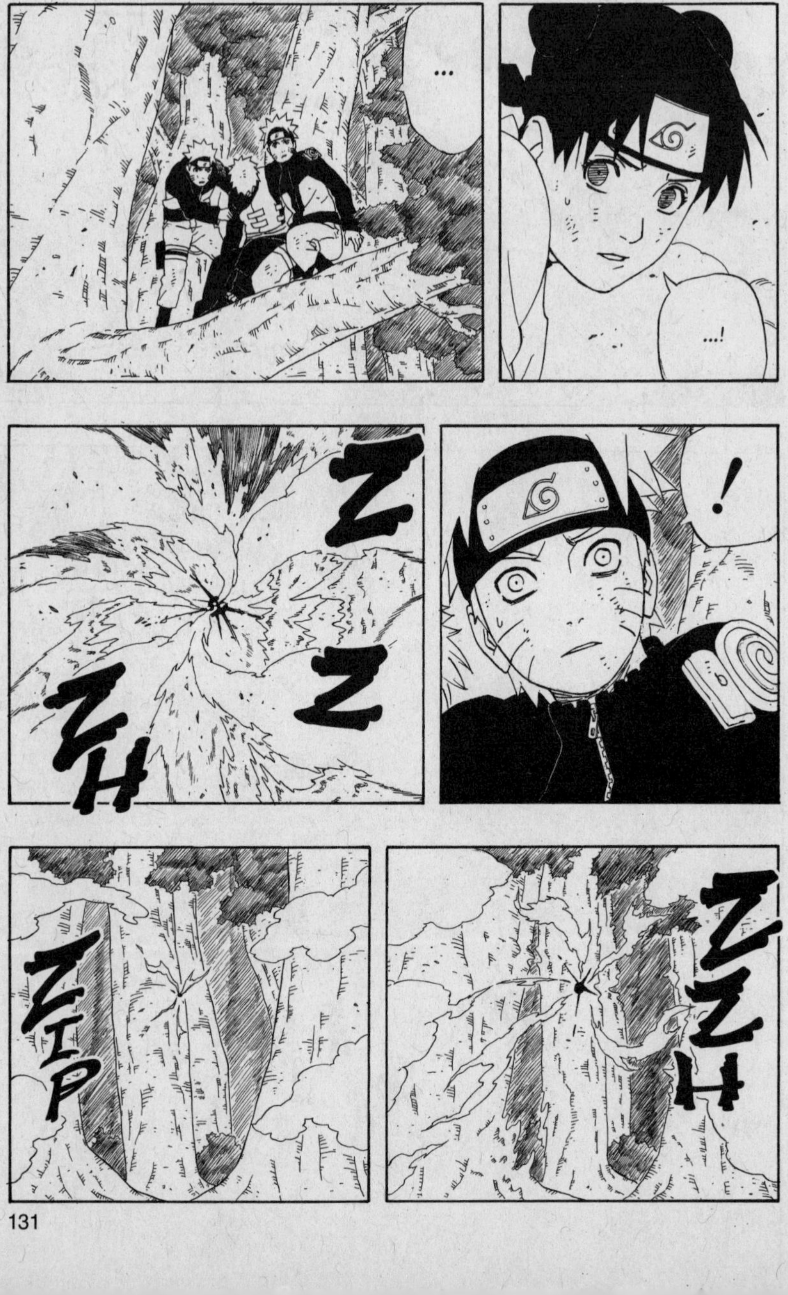

...!
...
!
ZZ
ZH
ZZZH
ZIP

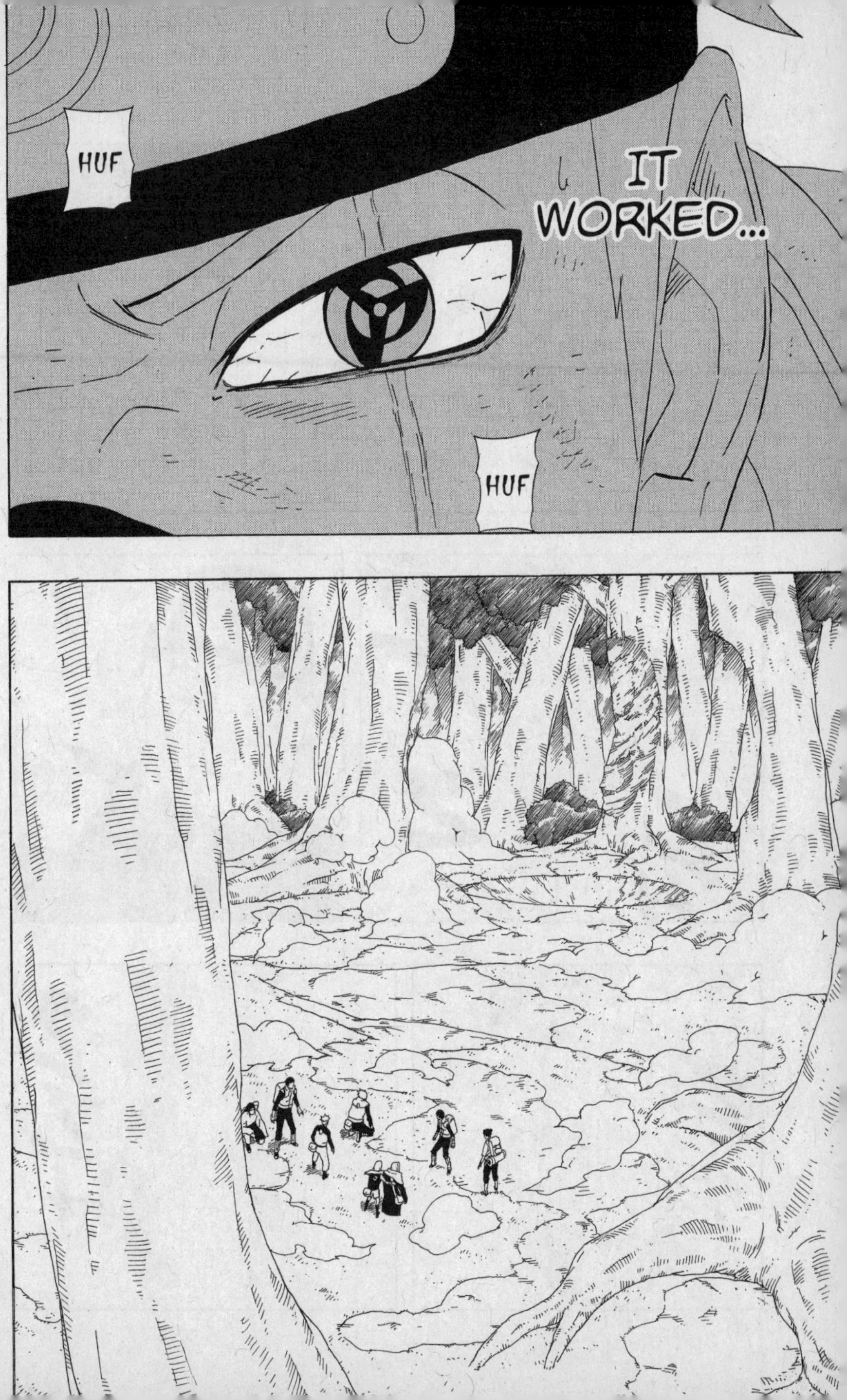
IT WORKED...
HUF
HUF

READ THIS WAY

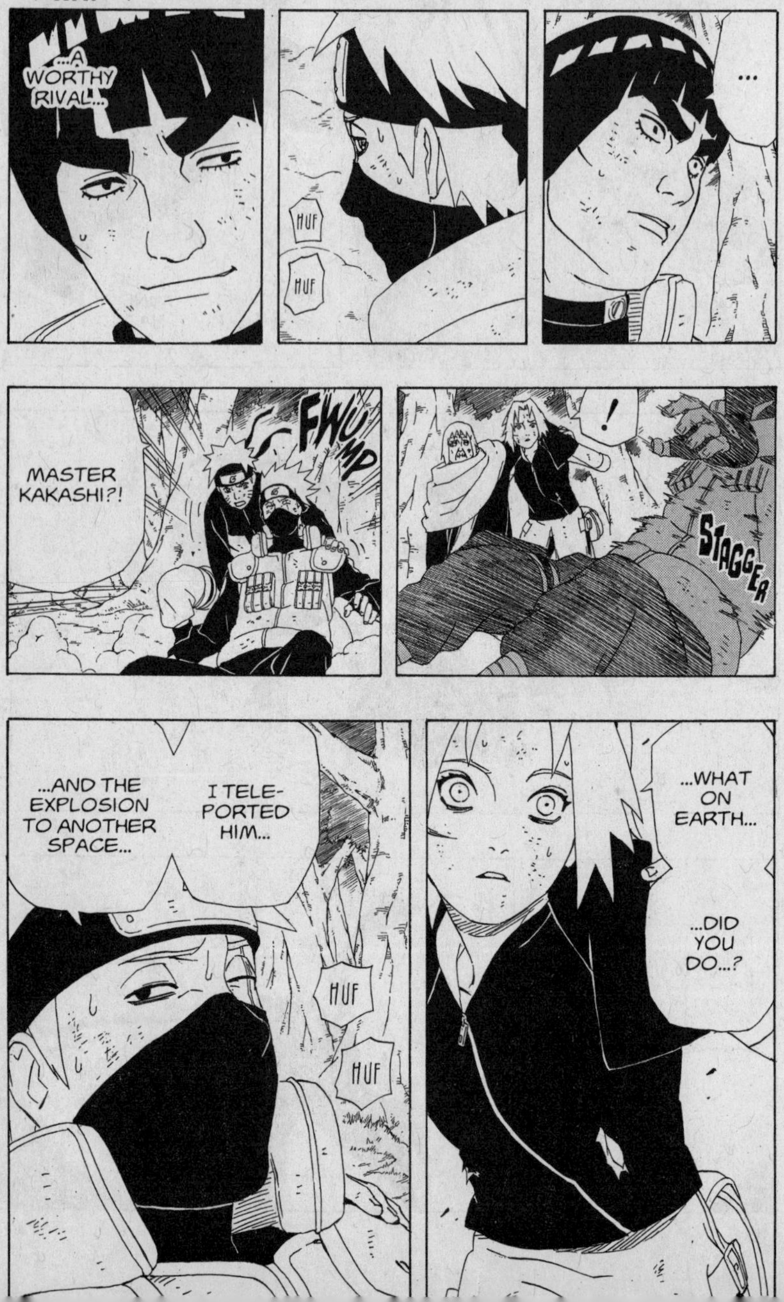
...
HUF
HUF
...A WORTHY RIVAL...
!
STAGGER
FWUMP
MASTER KAKASHI?!
...WHAT ON EARTH...
...DID YOU DO...?
I TELE-PORTED HIM...
...AND THE EXPLOSION TO ANOTHER SPACE...
HUF
HUF

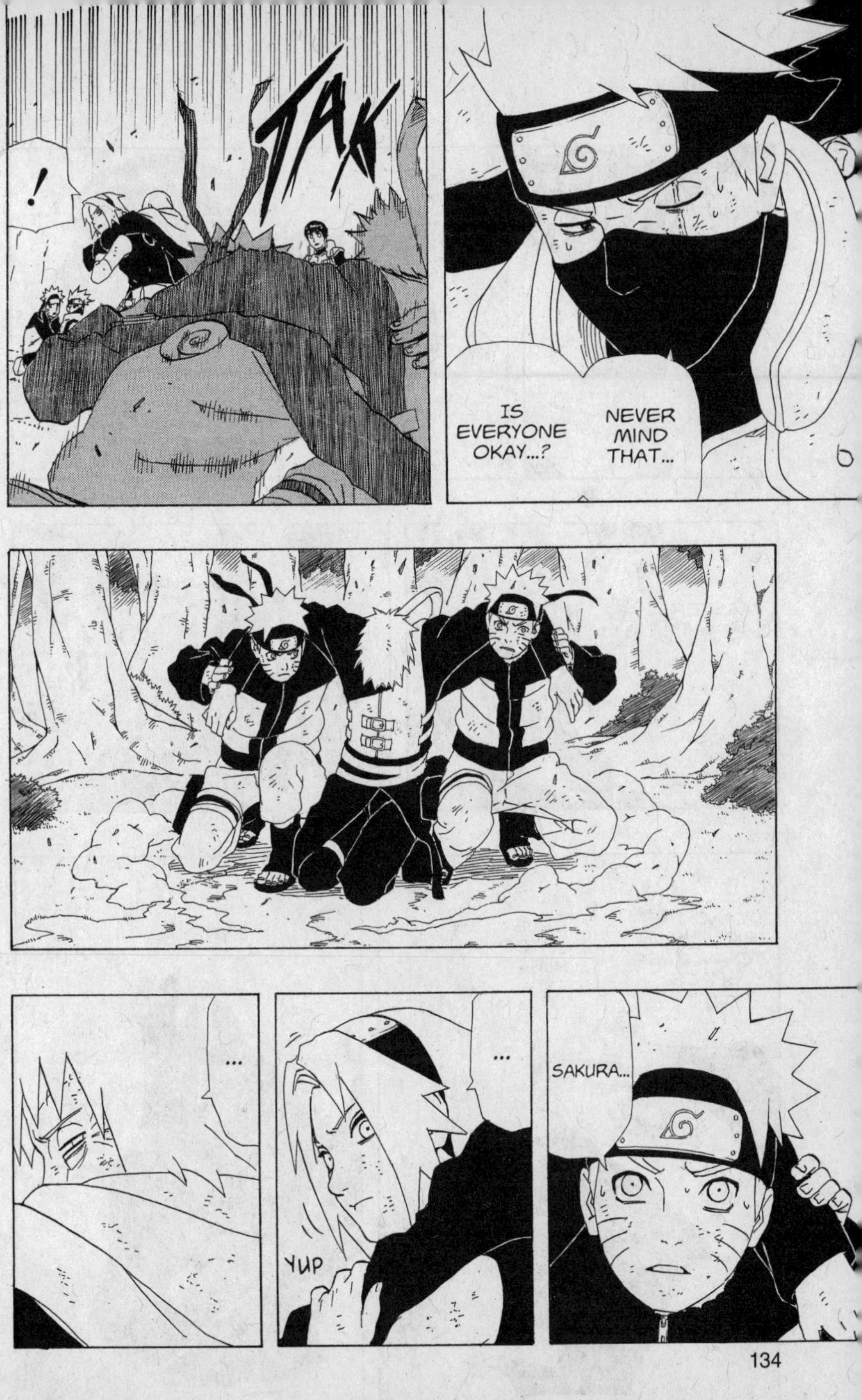
NEVER MIND THAT...
IS EVERYONE OKAY...?
TAK
!
SAKURA...
...
YUP
...

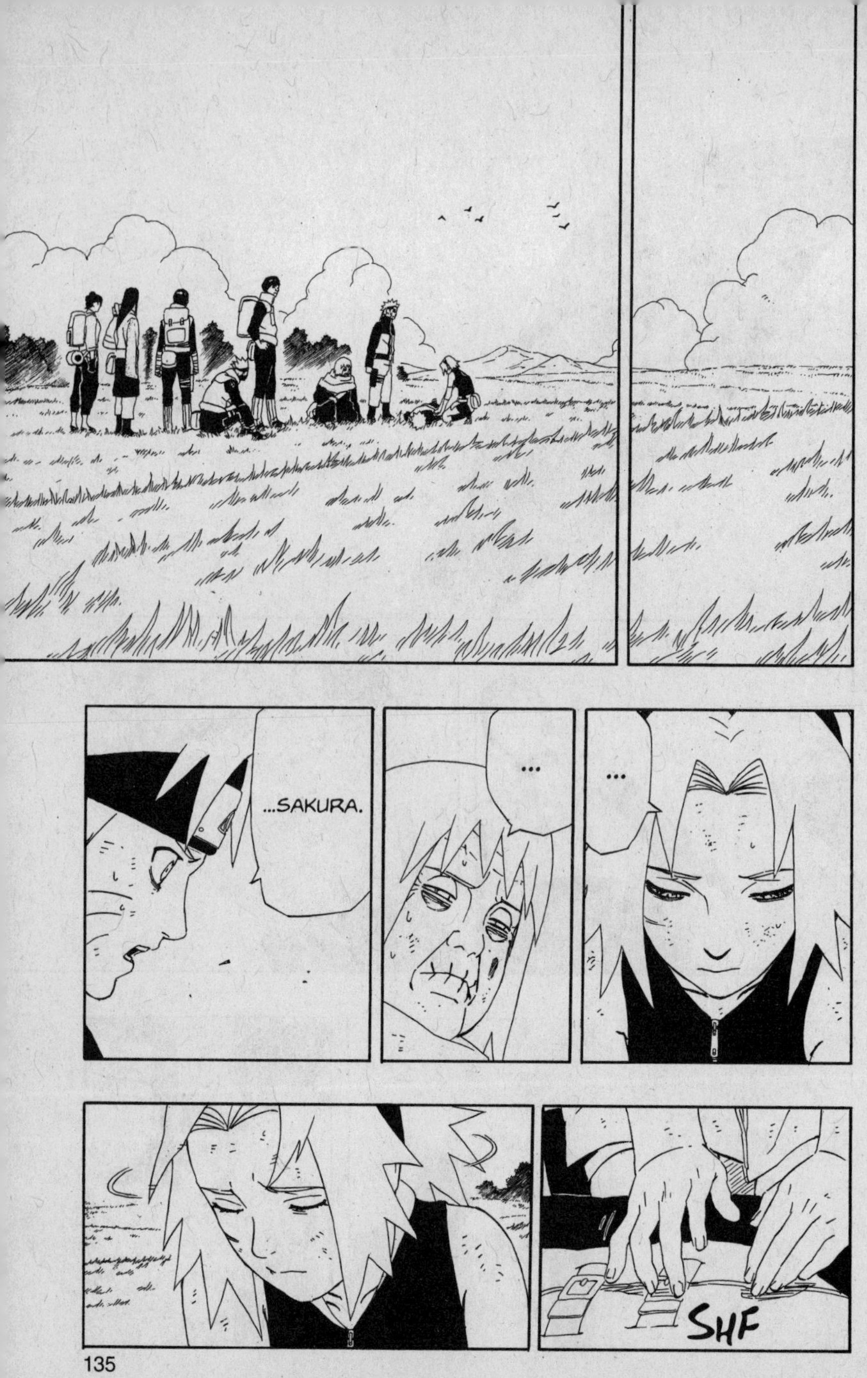
...
...
...SAKURA.
SHF

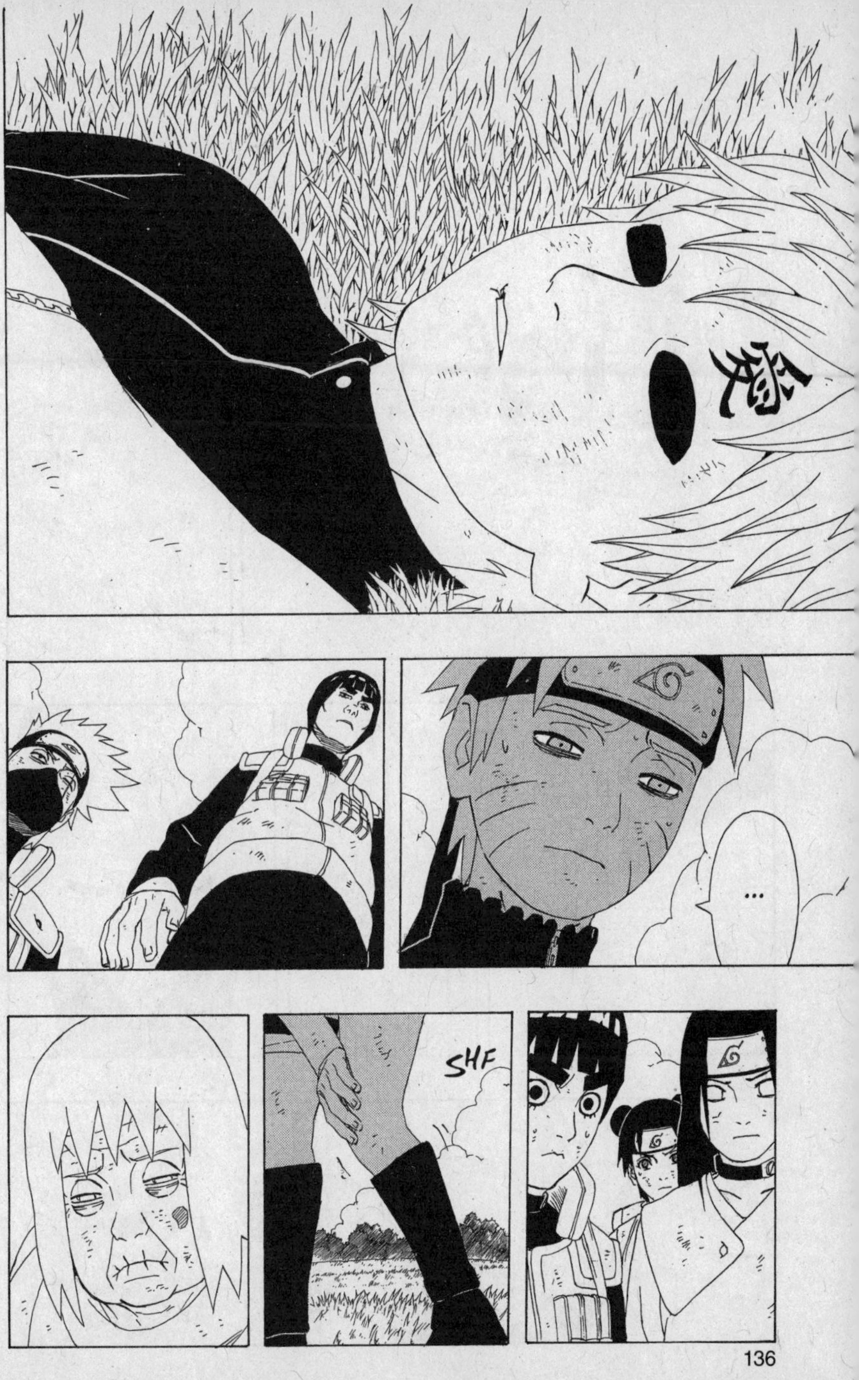
...
SHF

READ THIS WAY

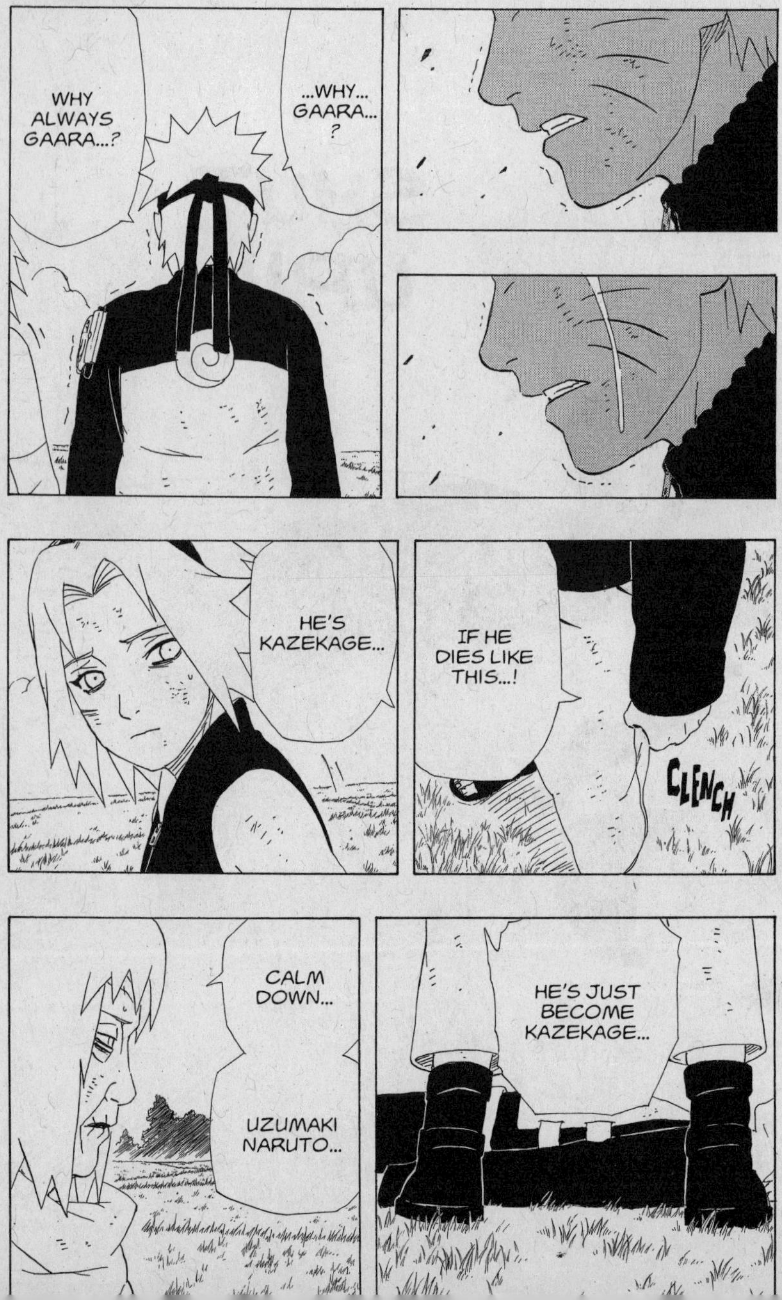
...WHY... GAARA...?
WHY ALWAYS GAARA...?
IF HE DIES LIKE THIS...!
CLENCH
HE'S KAZEKAGE...
HE'S JUST BECOME KAZEKAGE...
CALM DOWN...
UZUMAKI NARUTO...

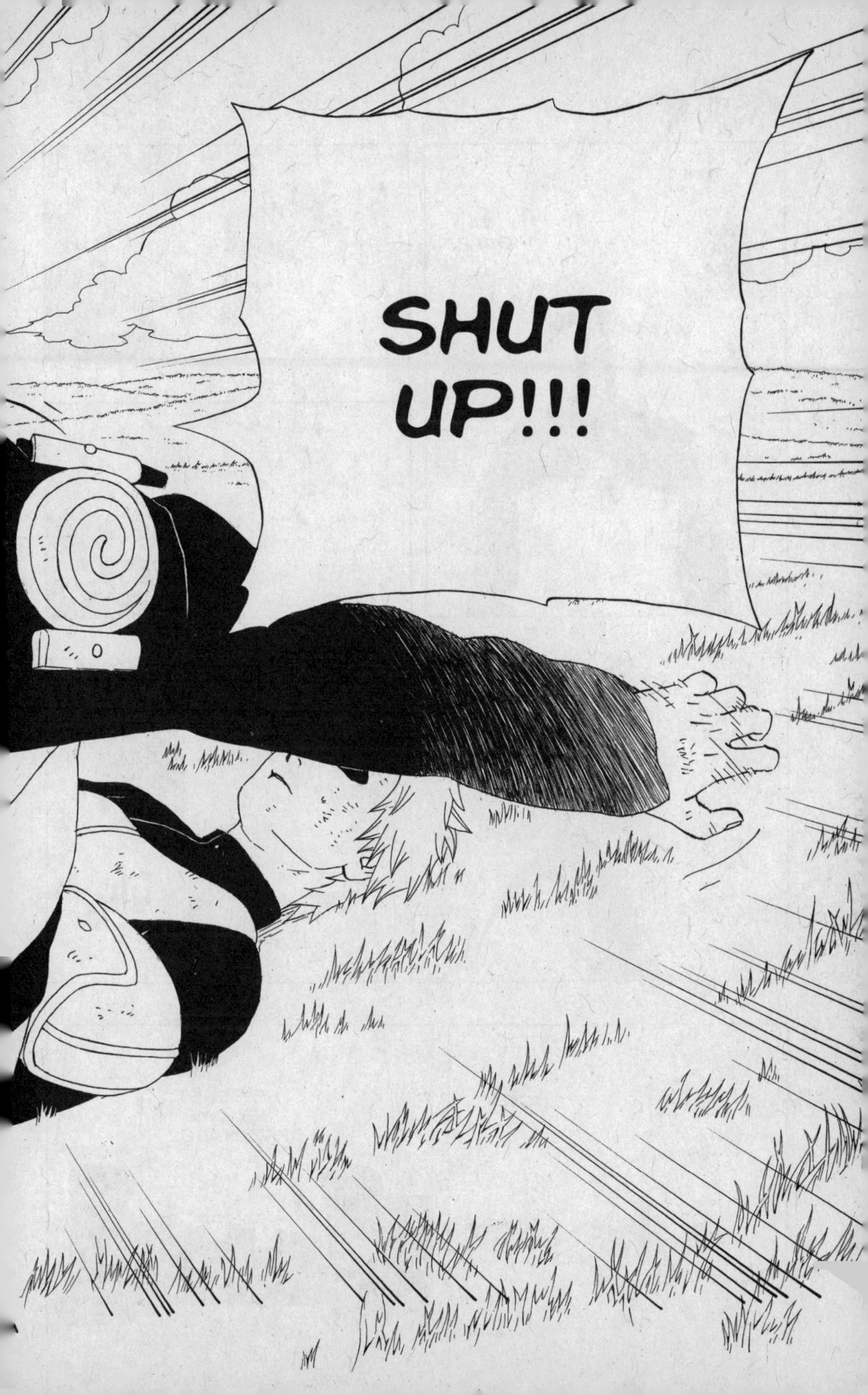
SHUT UP!!!

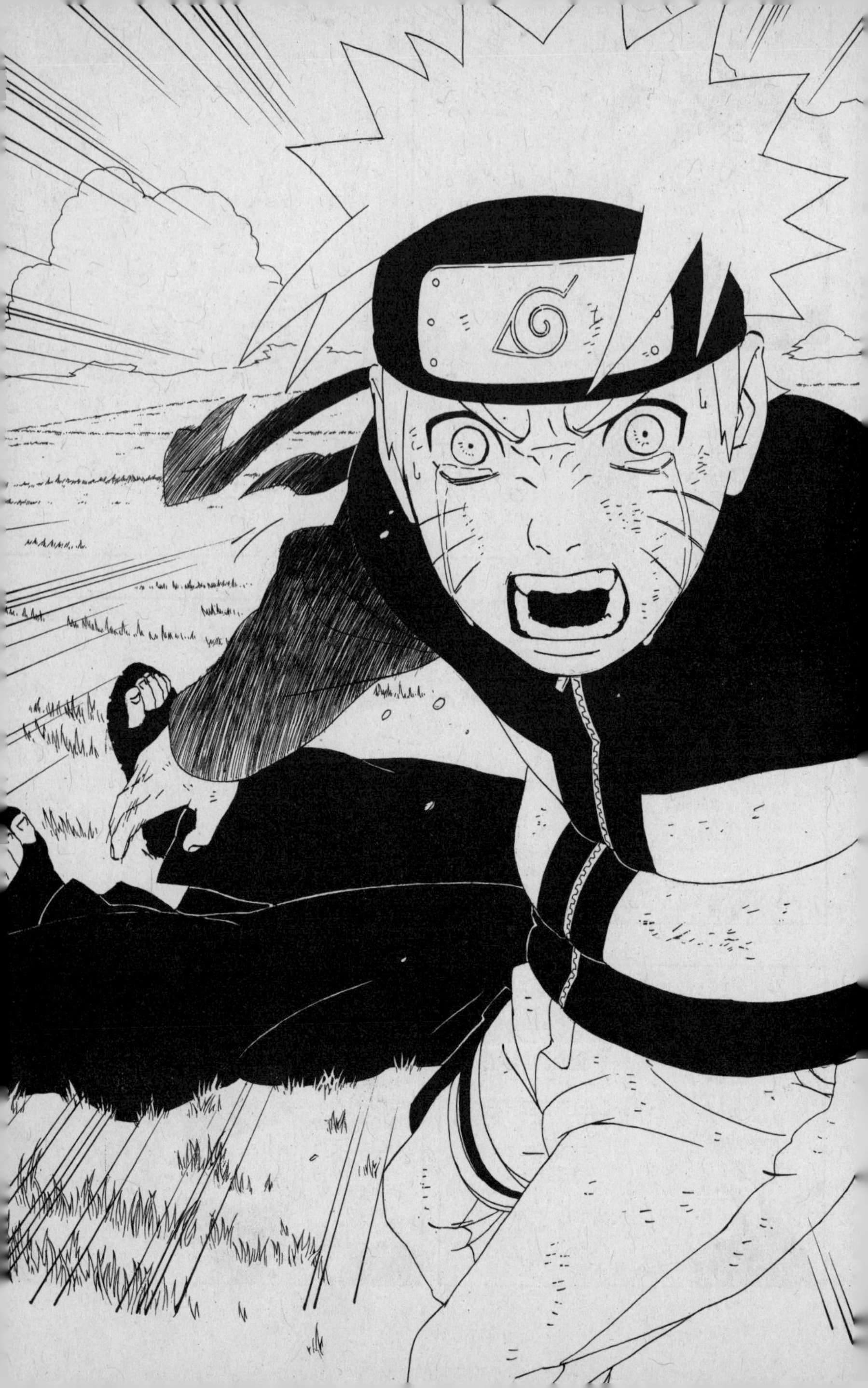

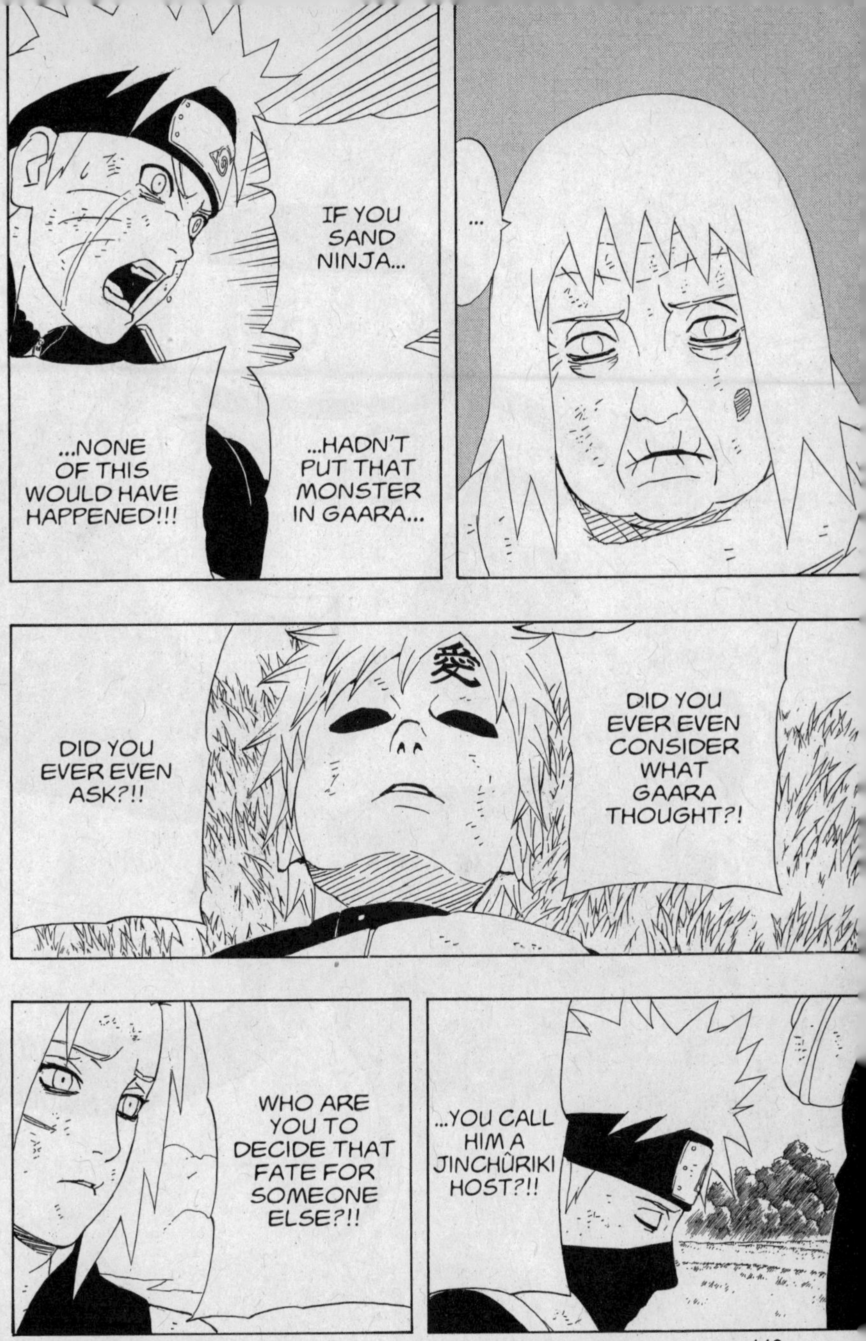
...
IF YOU SAND NINJA...
...HADN'T PUT THAT MONSTER IN GAARA...
...NONE OF THIS WOULD HAVE HAPPENED!!!
DID YOU EVER EVEN CONSIDER WHAT GAARA THOUGHT?!
DID YOU EVER EVEN ASK?!!
...YOU CALL HIM A JINCHÛRIKI HOST?!!
WHO ARE YOU TO DECIDE THAT FATE FOR SOMEONE ELSE?!!

READ THIS WAY

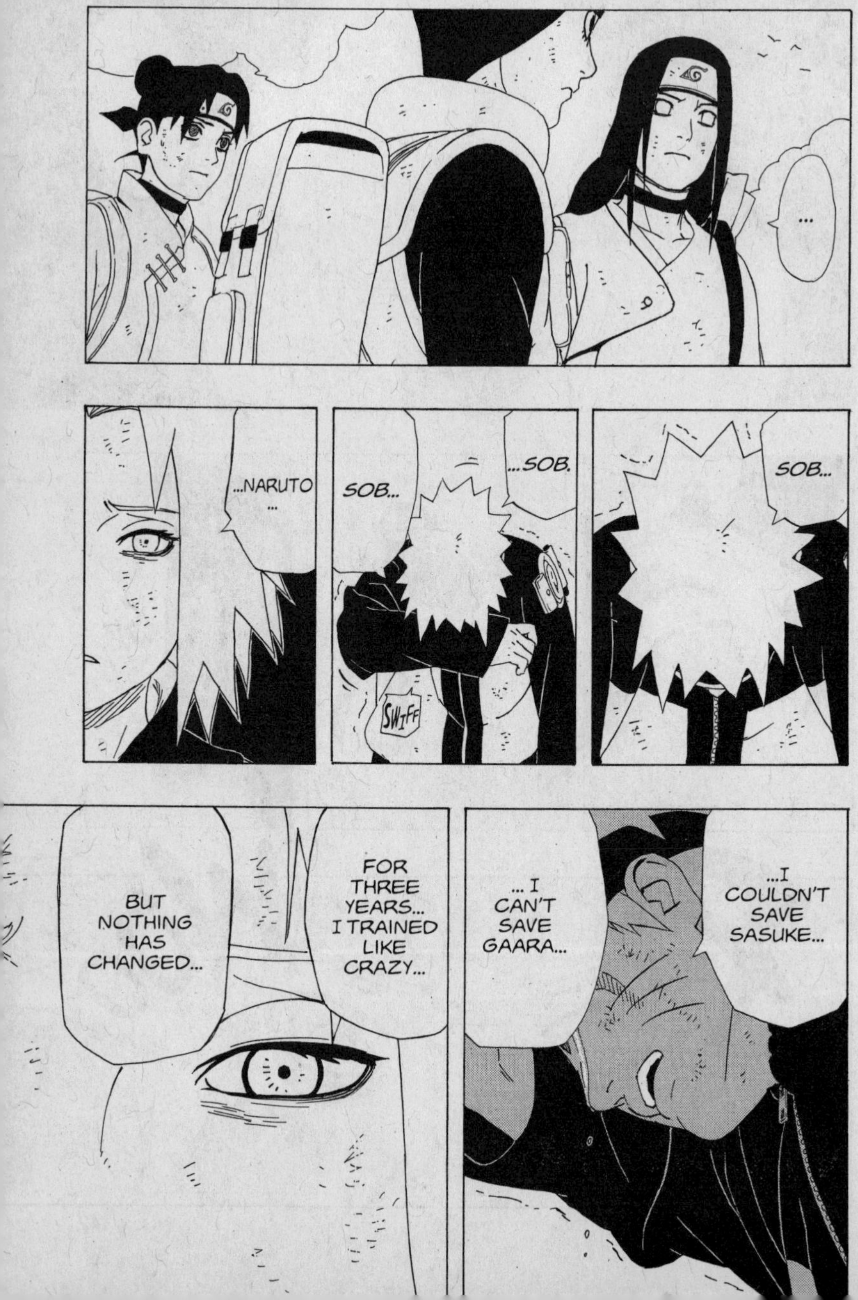
...
SOB...
...SOB.
SOB...
SWIFF
...NARUTO ...
...I COULDN'T SAVE SASUKE...
... I CAN'T SAVE GAARA...
FOR THREE YEARS... I TRAINED LIKE CRAZY...
BUT NOTHING HAS CHANGED...

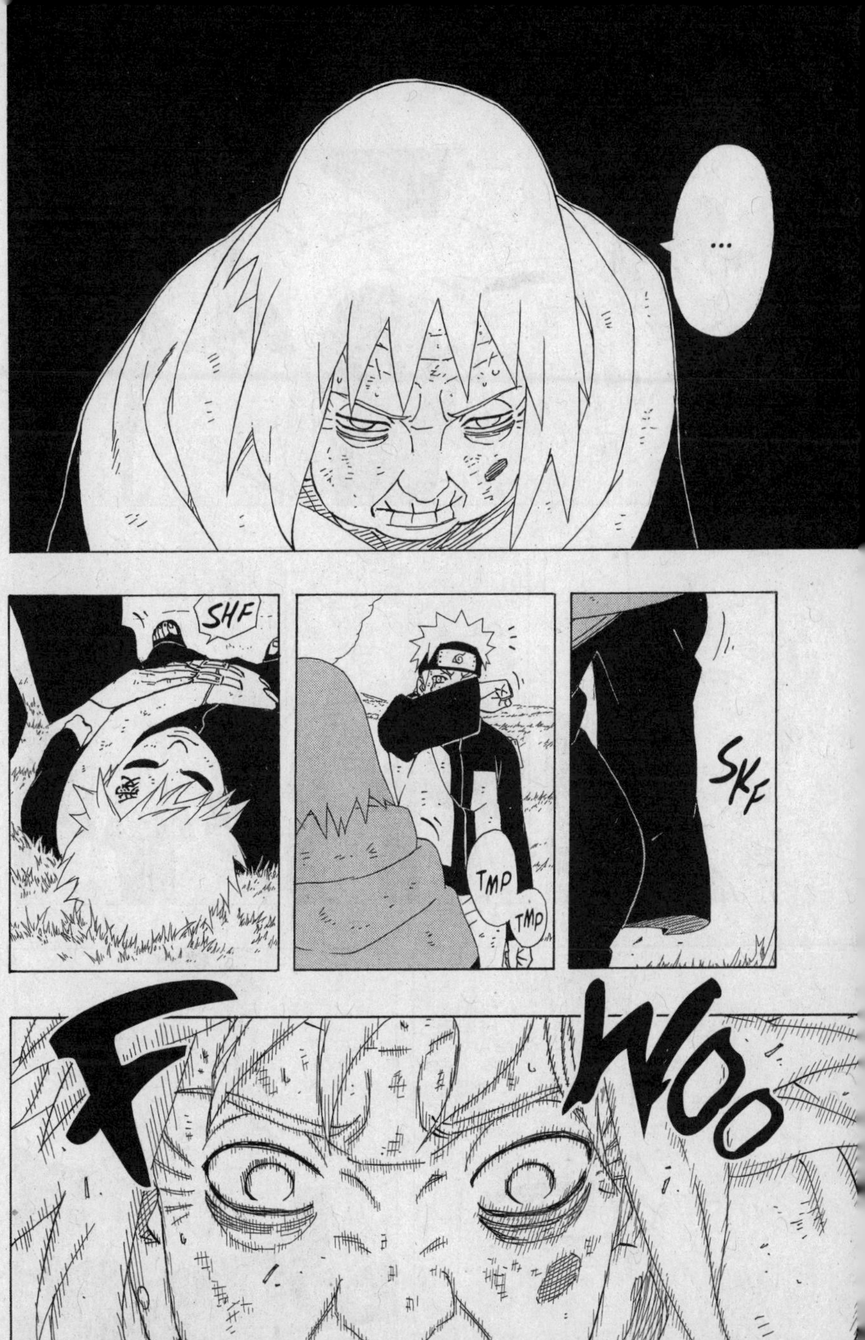
...
SKF
TMP
TMP
SHF
FWOO

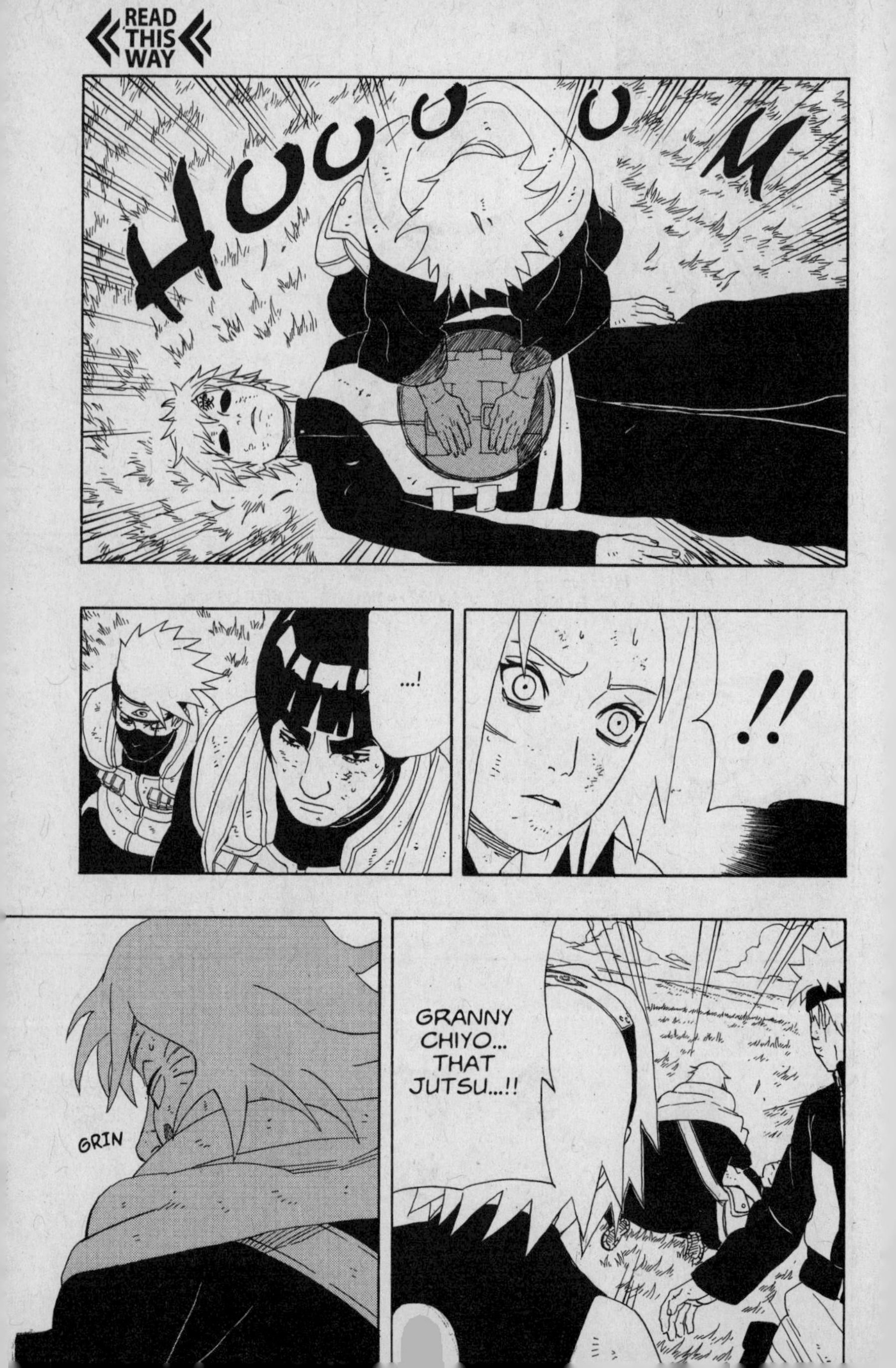
READ THIS WAY
HOOOOOM
!!
...!
GRANNY CHIYO... THAT JUTSU...!!
GRIN

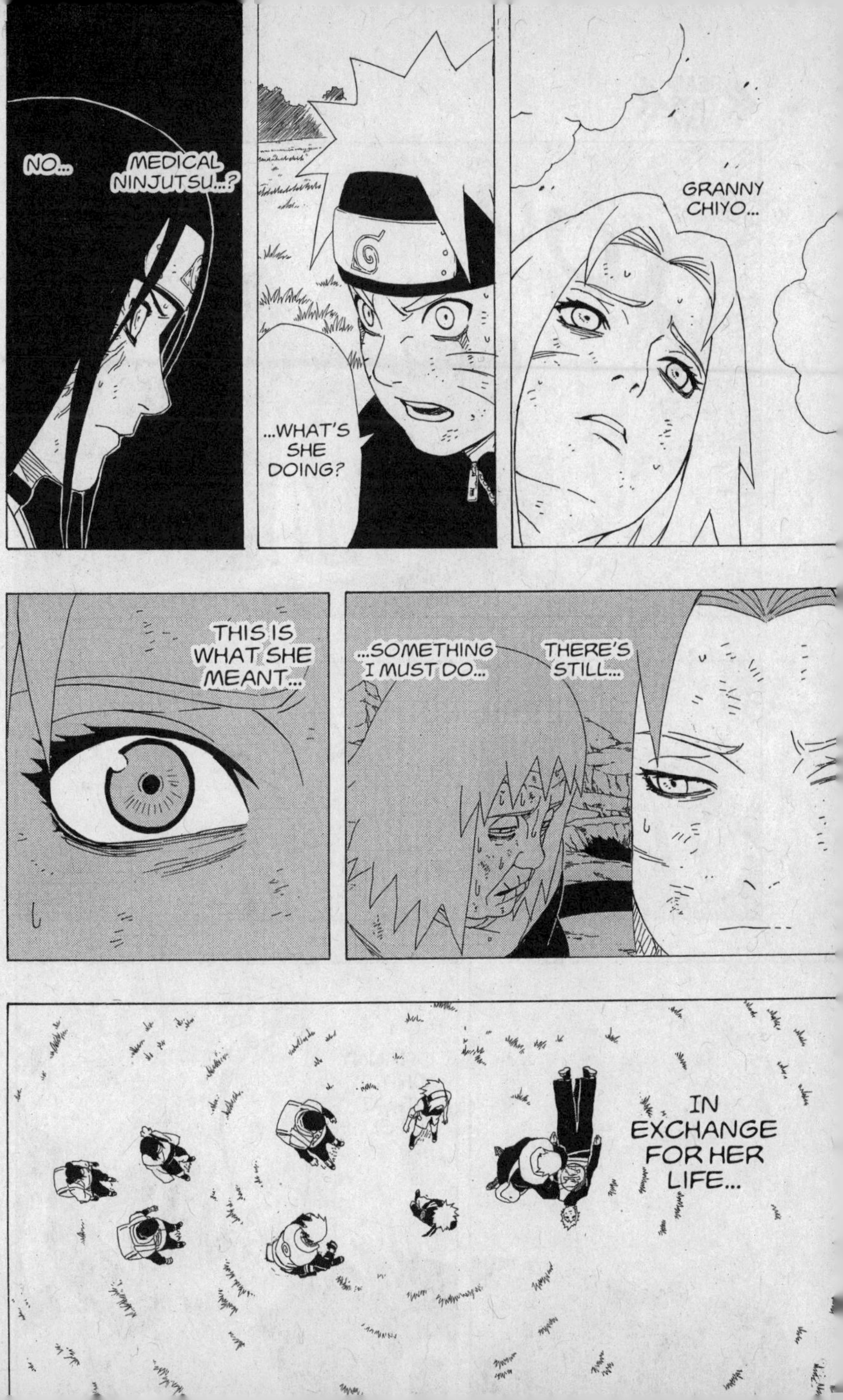
GRANNY CHIYO...
...WHAT'S SHE DOING?
MEDICAL NINJUTSU...?
NO...
THERE'S STILL...
...SOMETHING I MUST DO...
THIS IS WHAT SHE MEANT...
IN EXCHANGE FOR HER LIFE...

« READ THIS WAY «

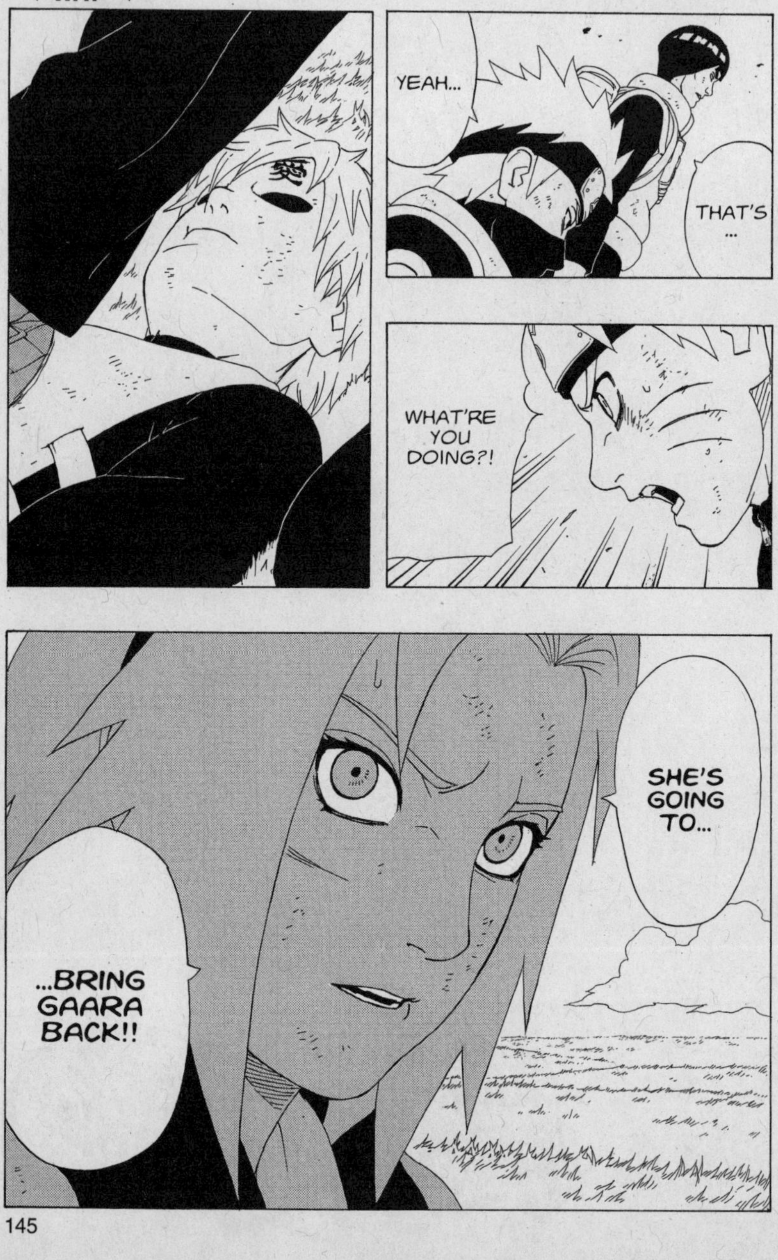
THAT'S ...
YEAH...
WHAT'RE YOU DOING?!
SHE'S GOING TO...
...BRING GAARA BACK!!

NARUTO

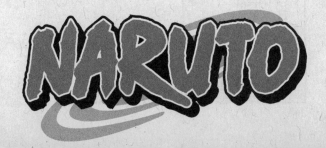

Number 279: Power & Miracles...!!

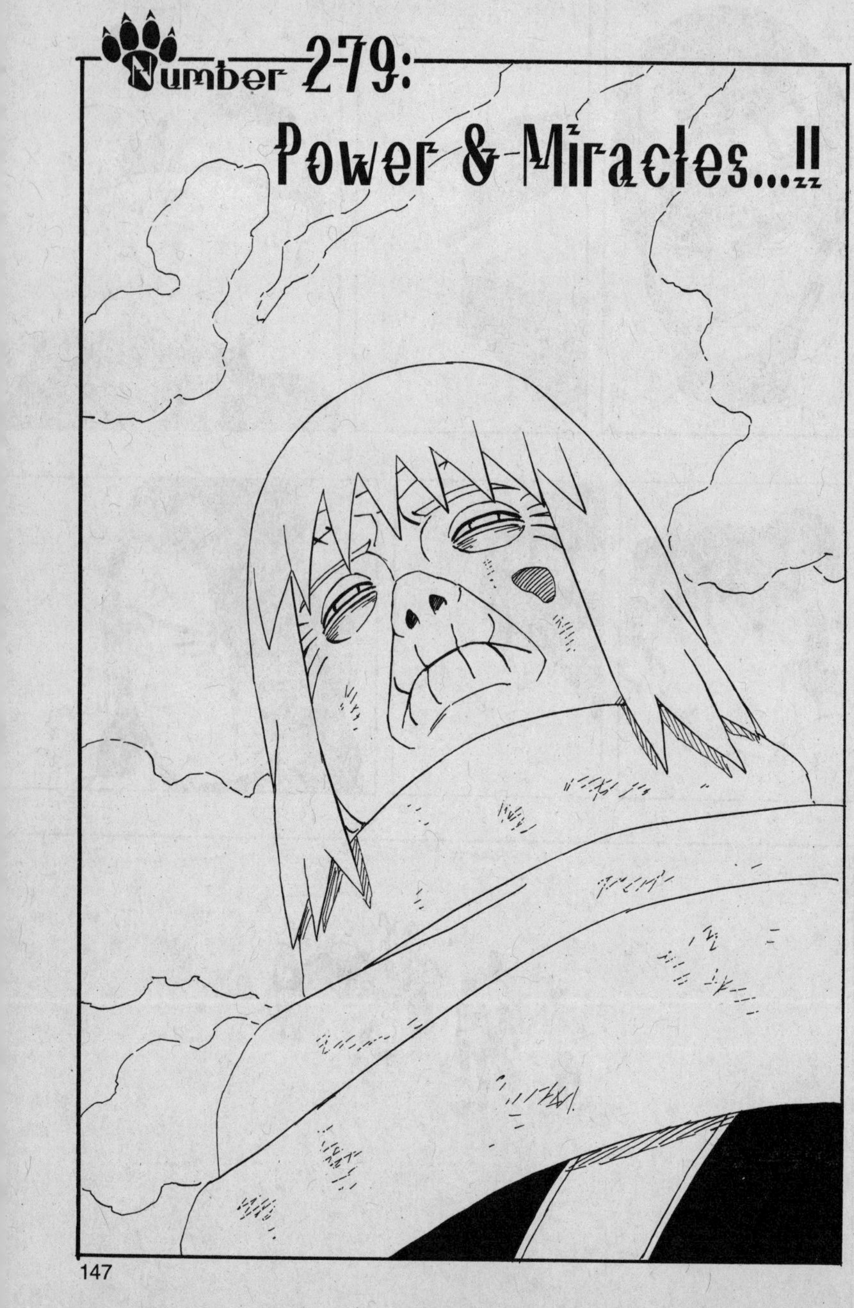

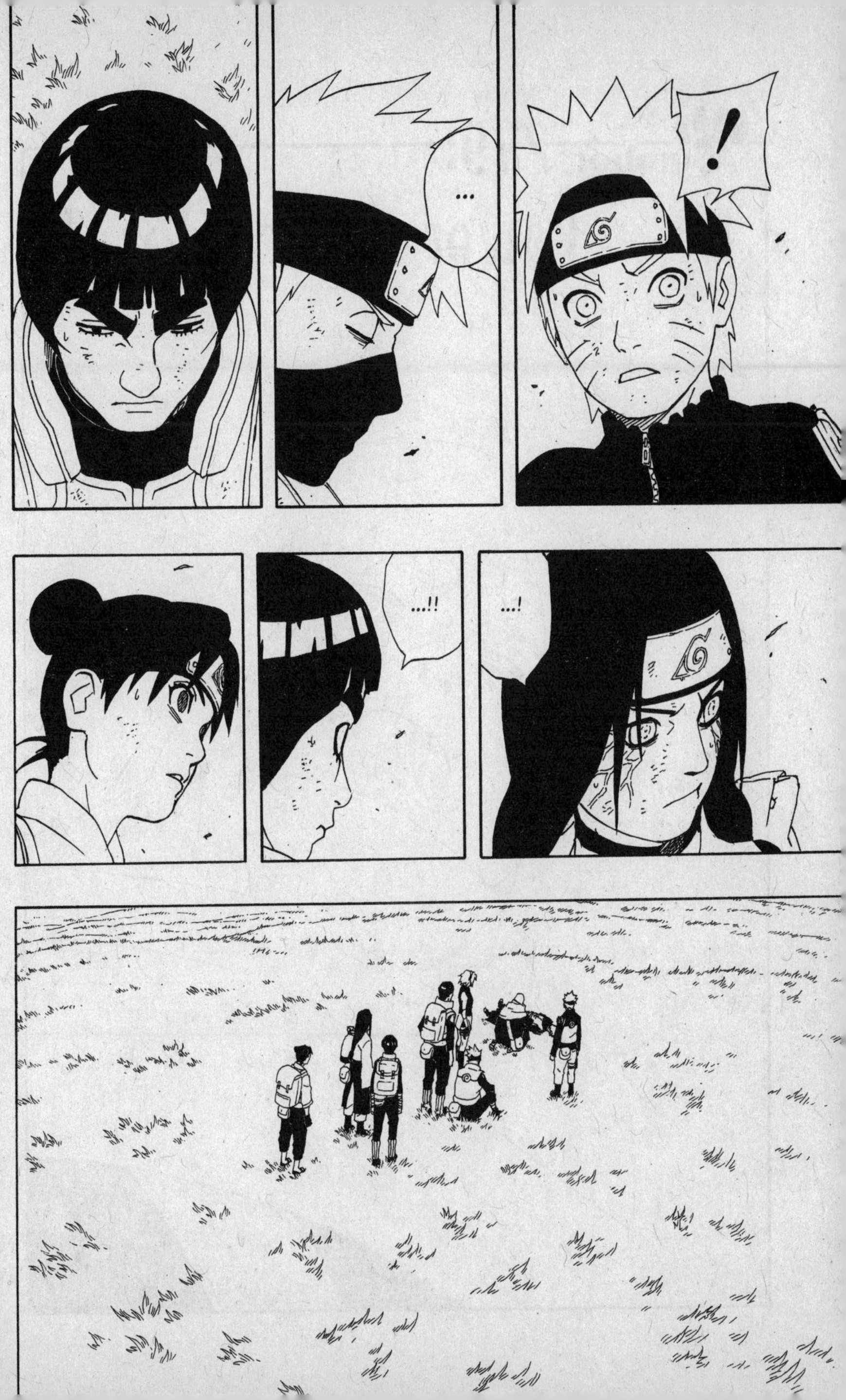
!
...
...!
...!!

READ THIS WAY

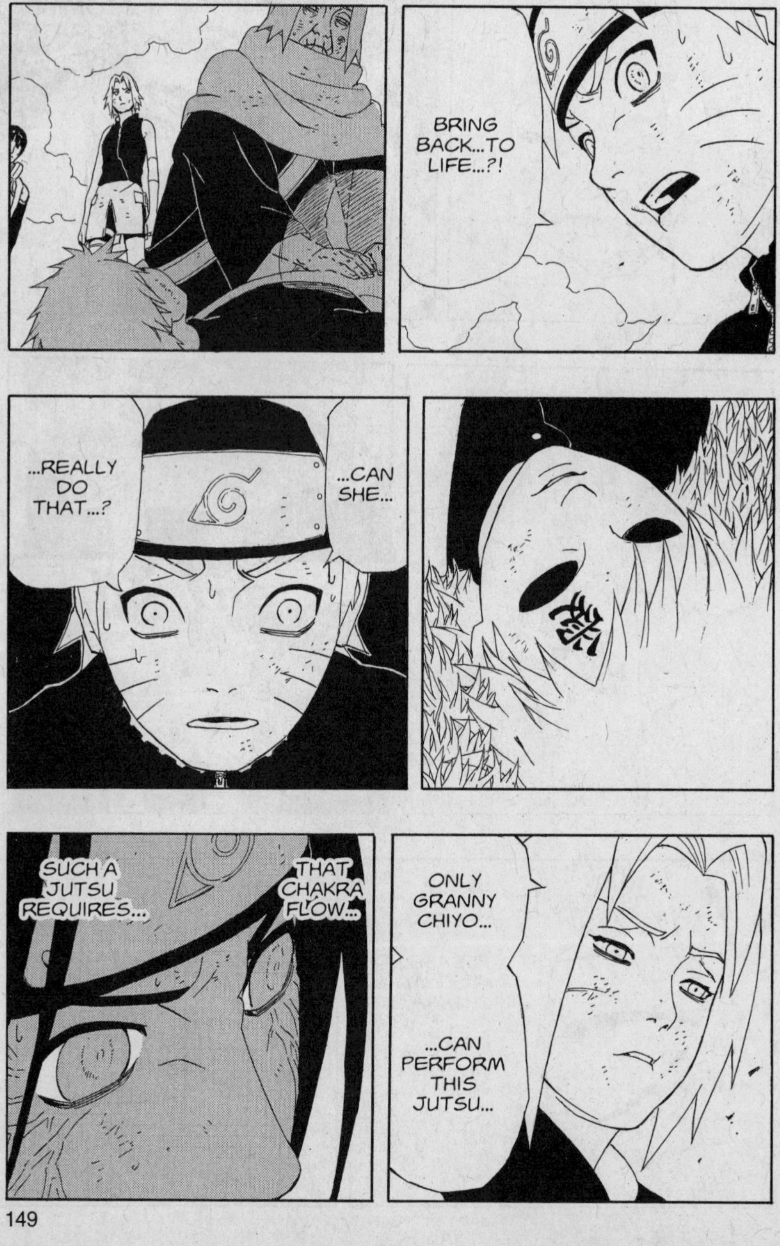

BRING BACK...TO LIFE...?!
...CAN SHE...
...REALLY DO THAT...?
ONLY GRANNY CHIYO...
...CAN PERFORM THIS JUTSU...
THAT CHAKRA FLOW...
SUCH A JUTSU REQUIRES...

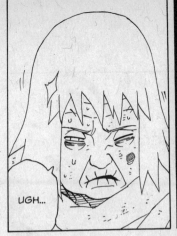

UGH...

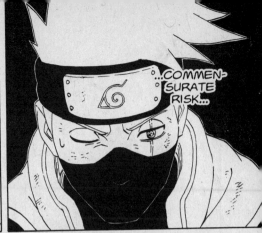

...COMMEN-SURATE RISK...

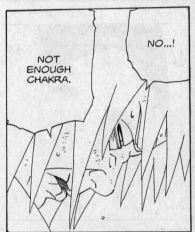

NO...!

NOT ENOUGH CHAKRA.

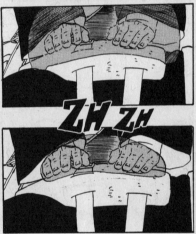

ZH ZH

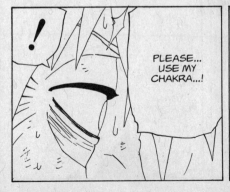

!

PLEASE... USE MY CHAKRA...!

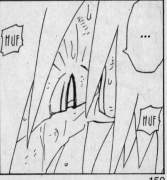

HUF

...

HUF

READ THIS WAY

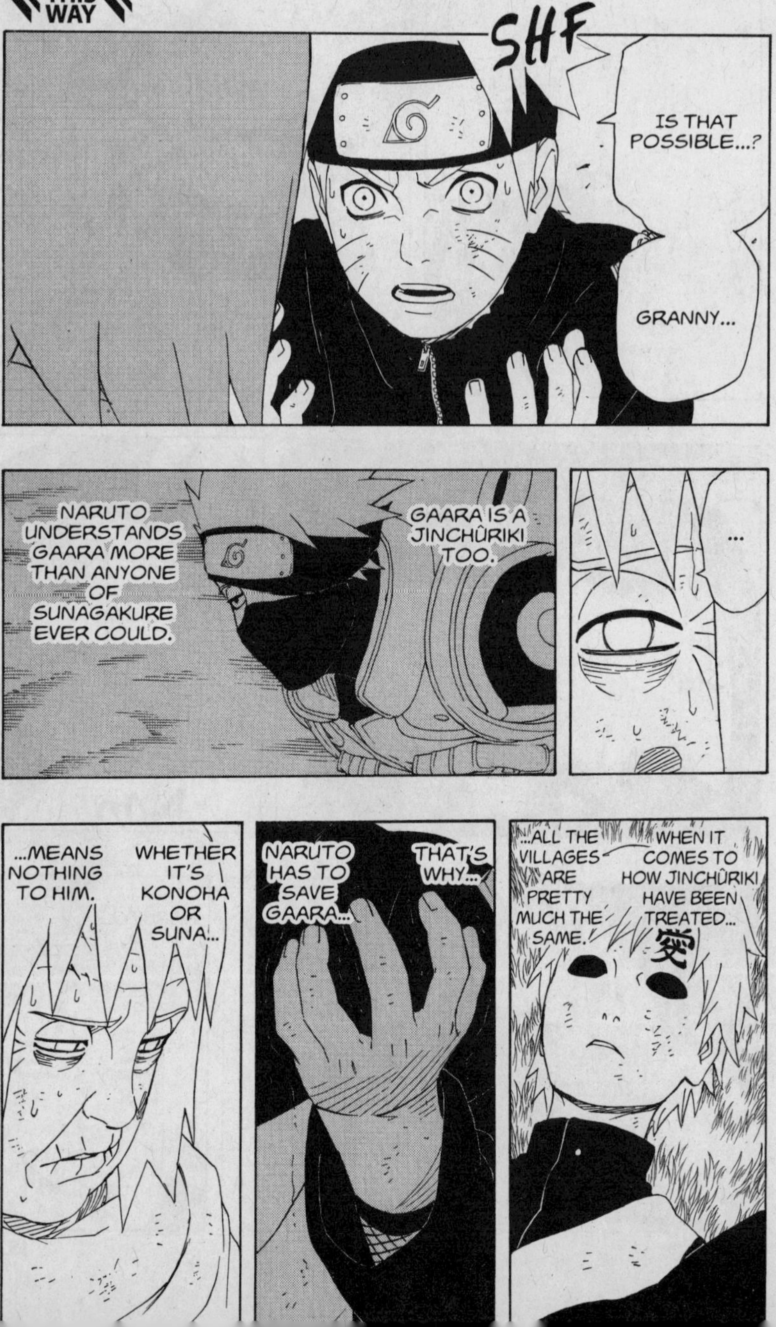
SHF
IS THAT POSSIBLE...?
GRANNY...
...
GAARA IS A JINCHÛRIKI TOO.
NARUTO UNDERSTANDS GAARA MORE THAN ANYONE OF SUNAGAKURE EVER COULD.
WHEN IT COMES TO HOW JINCHÛRIKI HAVE BEEN TREATED...
...ALL THE VILLAGES ARE PRETTY MUCH THE SAME.
THAT'S WHY...
NARUTO HAS TO SAVE GAARA...
WHETHER IT'S KONOHA OR SUNA...
...MEANS NOTHING TO HIM.

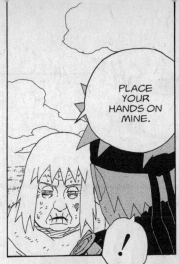

PLACE YOUR HANDS ON MINE.

!

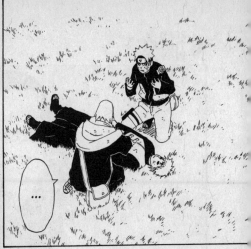

...

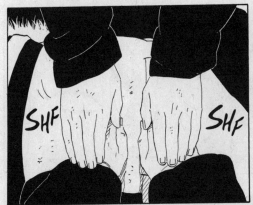

SHF SHF

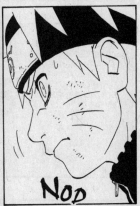

NOD

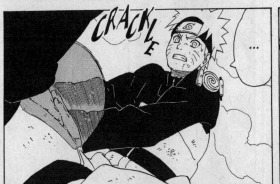

CRACKLE

...

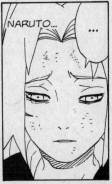

NARUTO...

...

READ THIS WAY

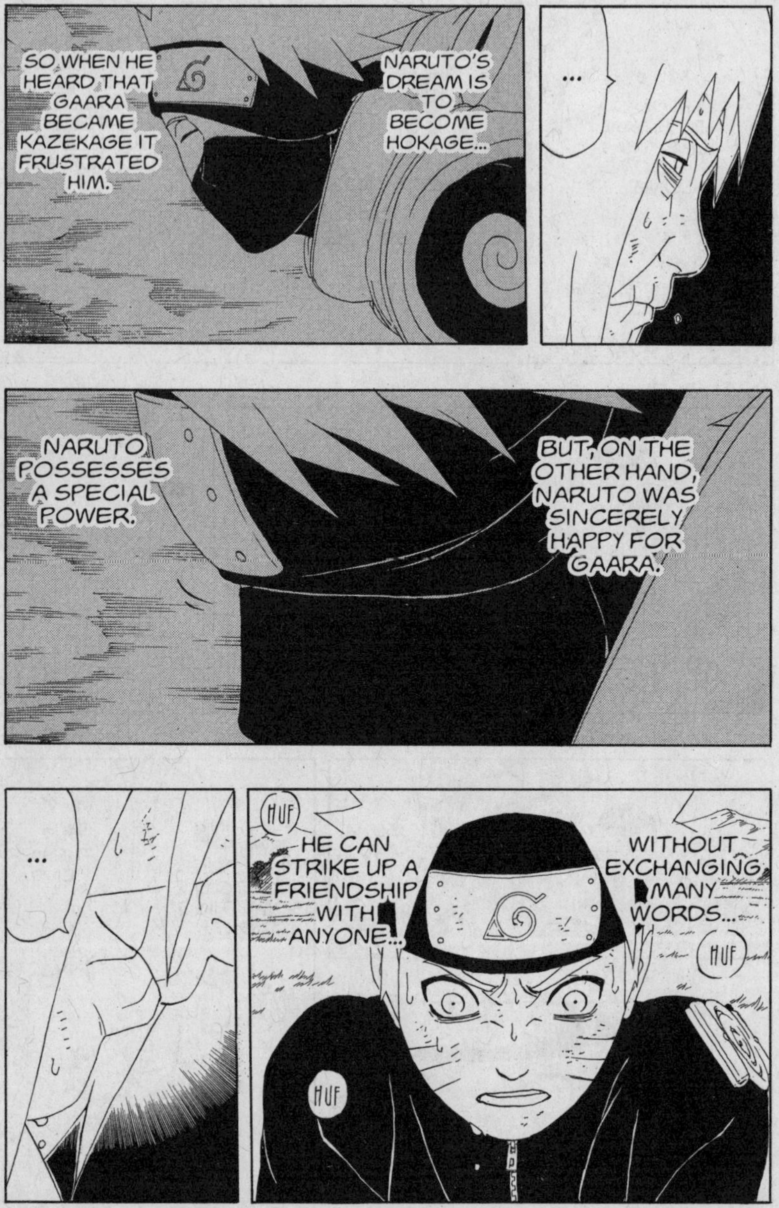
...
NARUTO'S DREAM IS TO BECOME HOKAGE...
SO WHEN HE HEARD THAT GAARA BECAME KAZEKAGE IT FRUSTRATED HIM.
BUT, ON THE OTHER HAND, NARUTO WAS SINCERELY HAPPY FOR GAARA.
NARUTO POSSESSES A SPECIAL POWER.
WITHOUT EXCHANGING MANY WORDS...
HUF
HE CAN STRIKE UP A FRIENDSHIP WITH ANYONE...
HUF
HUF
...

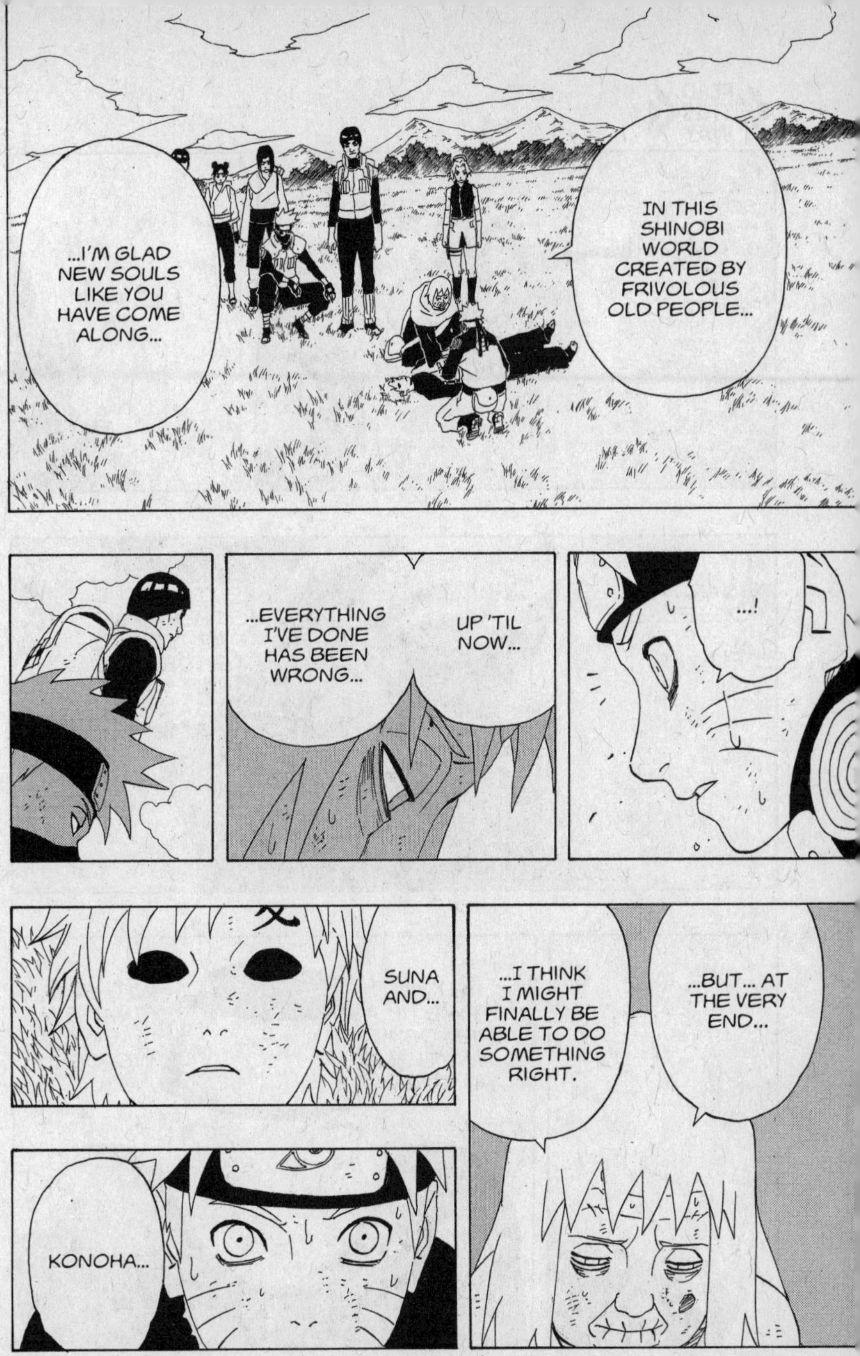
IN THIS SHINOBI WORLD CREATED BY FRIVOLOUS OLD PEOPLE...
...I'M GLAD NEW SOULS LIKE YOU HAVE COME ALONG...
...!
UP 'TIL NOW...
...EVERYTHING I'VE DONE HAS BEEN WRONG...
...BUT... AT THE VERY END...
...I THINK I MIGHT FINALLY BE ABLE TO DO SOMETHING RIGHT.
SUNA AND...
KONOHA...

READ THIS WAY

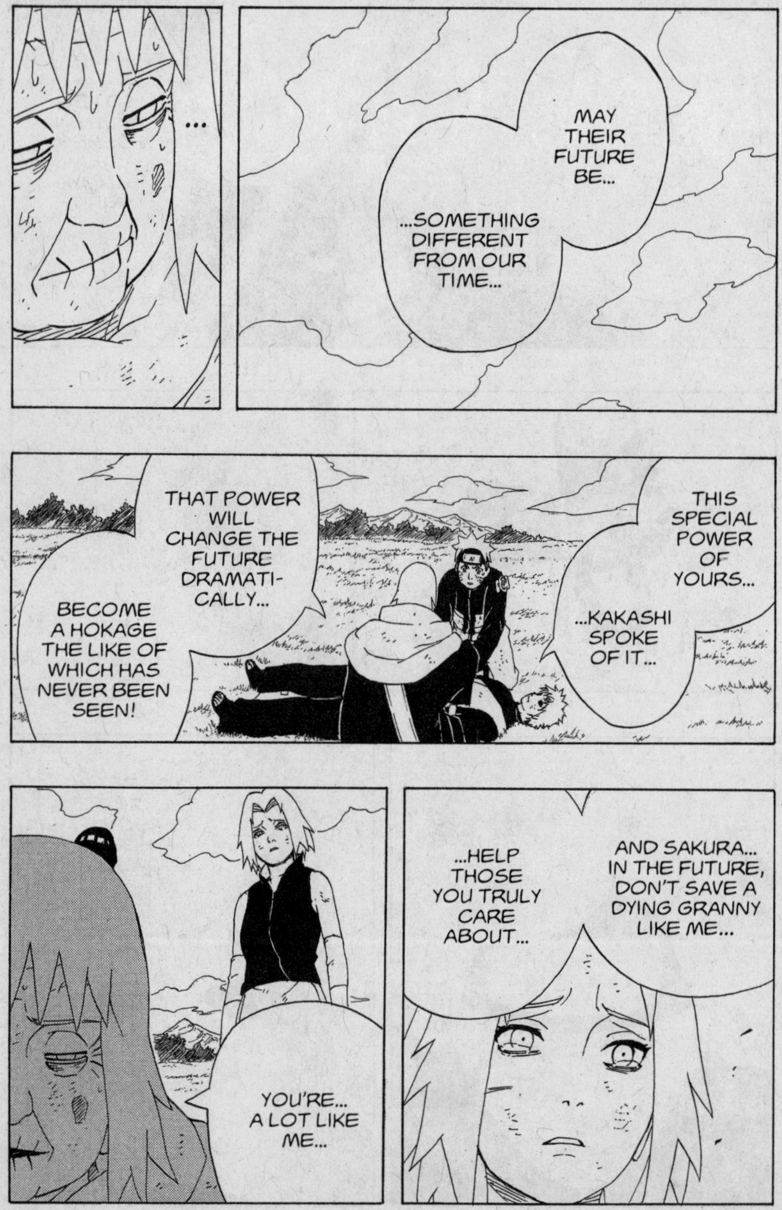

MAY THEIR FUTURE BE...
...SOMETHING DIFFERENT FROM OUR TIME...
...
THIS SPECIAL POWER OF YOURS...
...KAKASHI SPOKE OF IT...
THAT POWER WILL CHANGE THE FUTURE DRAMATICALLY...
BECOME A HOKAGE THE LIKE OF WHICH HAS NEVER BEEN SEEN!
AND SAKURA... IN THE FUTURE, DON'T SAVE A DYING GRANNY LIKE ME...
...HELP THOSE YOU TRULY CARE ABOUT...
YOU'RE... A LOT LIKE ME...

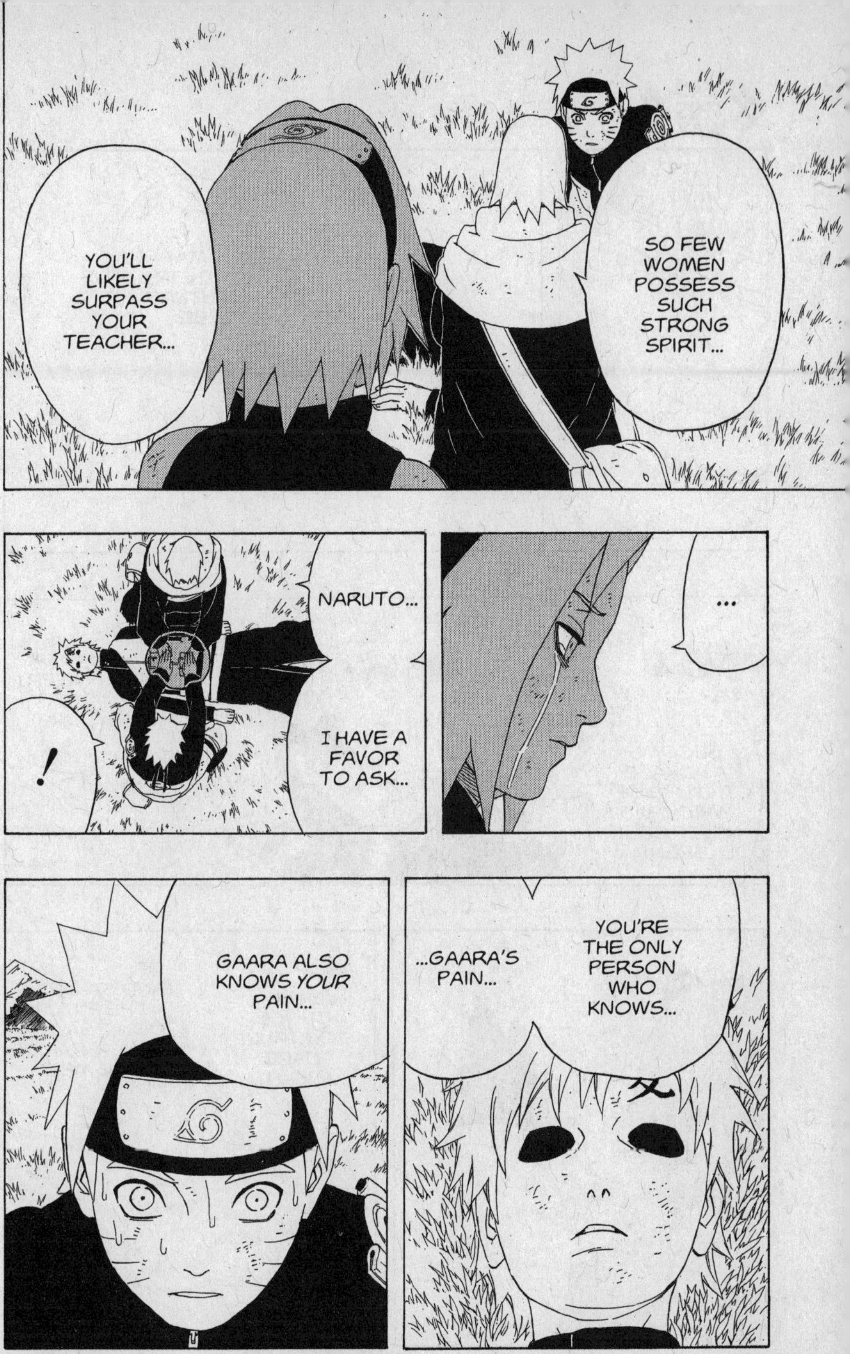
SO FEW WOMEN POSSESS SUCH STRONG SPIRIT...
YOU'LL LIKELY SURPASS YOUR TEACHER...
...
NARUTO...
I HAVE A FAVOR TO ASK...
!
YOU'RE THE ONLY PERSON WHO KNOWS...
...GAARA'S PAIN...
GAARA ALSO KNOWS *YOUR* PAIN...

READ THIS WAY

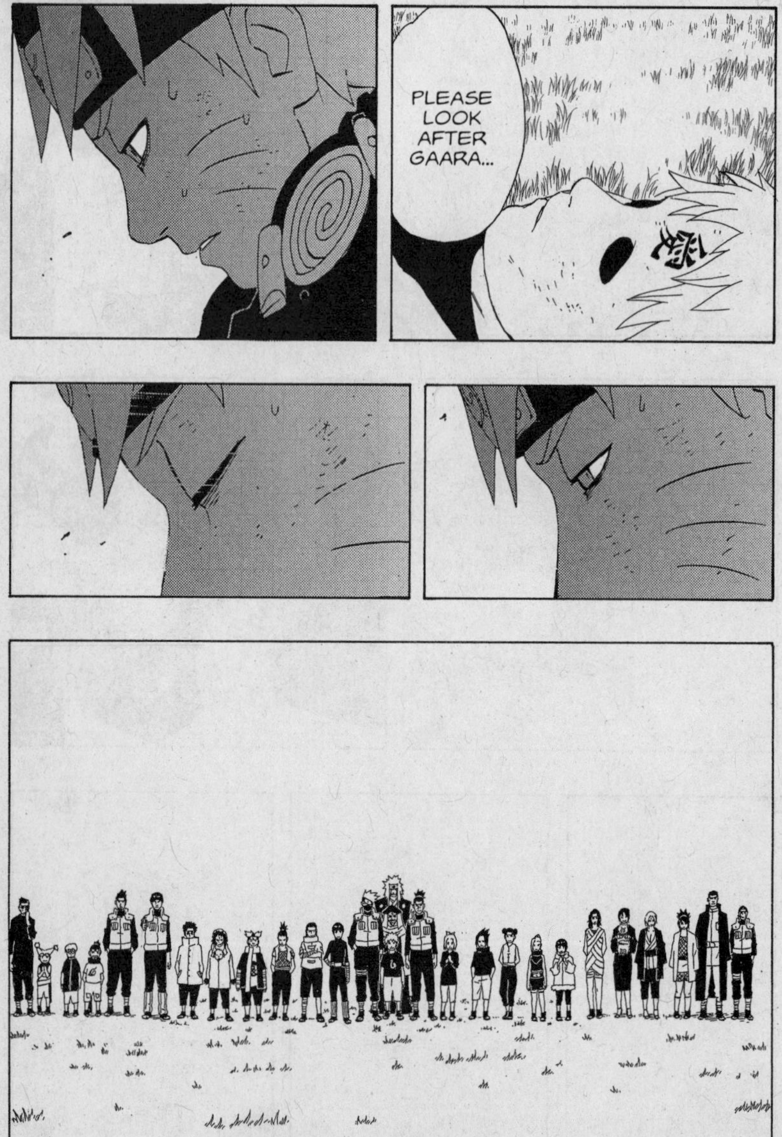
PLEASE LOOK AFTER GAARA...

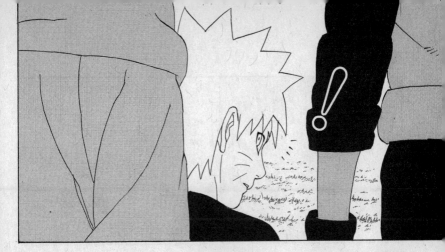

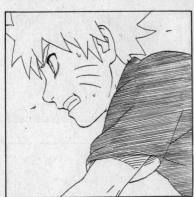

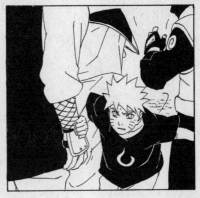

GAARA!

GAARA...

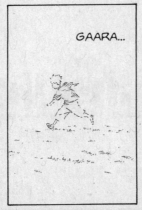

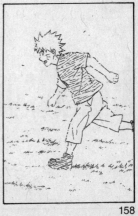

READ THIS WAY

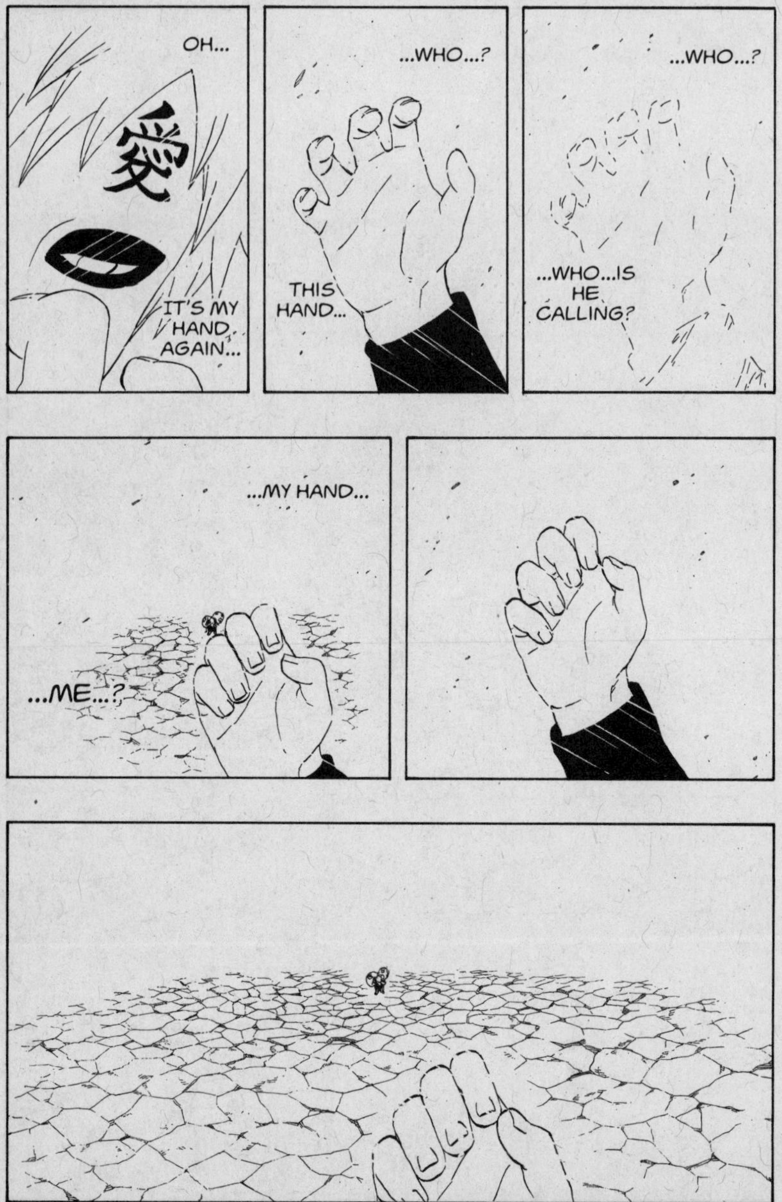
...WHO...?
...WHO...IS HE CALLING?
...WHO...?
THIS HAND...
OH...
愛
IT'S MY HAND AGAIN...
...MY HAND...
...ME...?

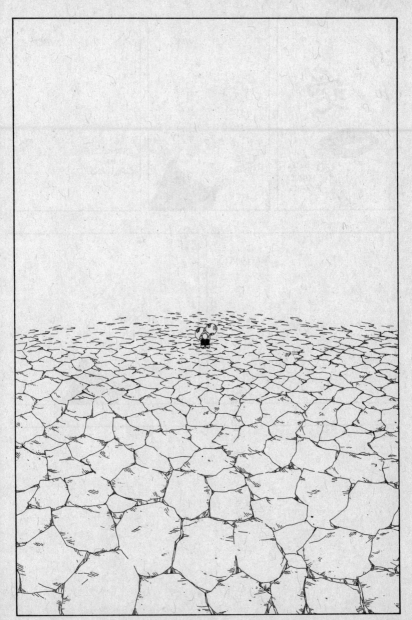

READ THIS WAY

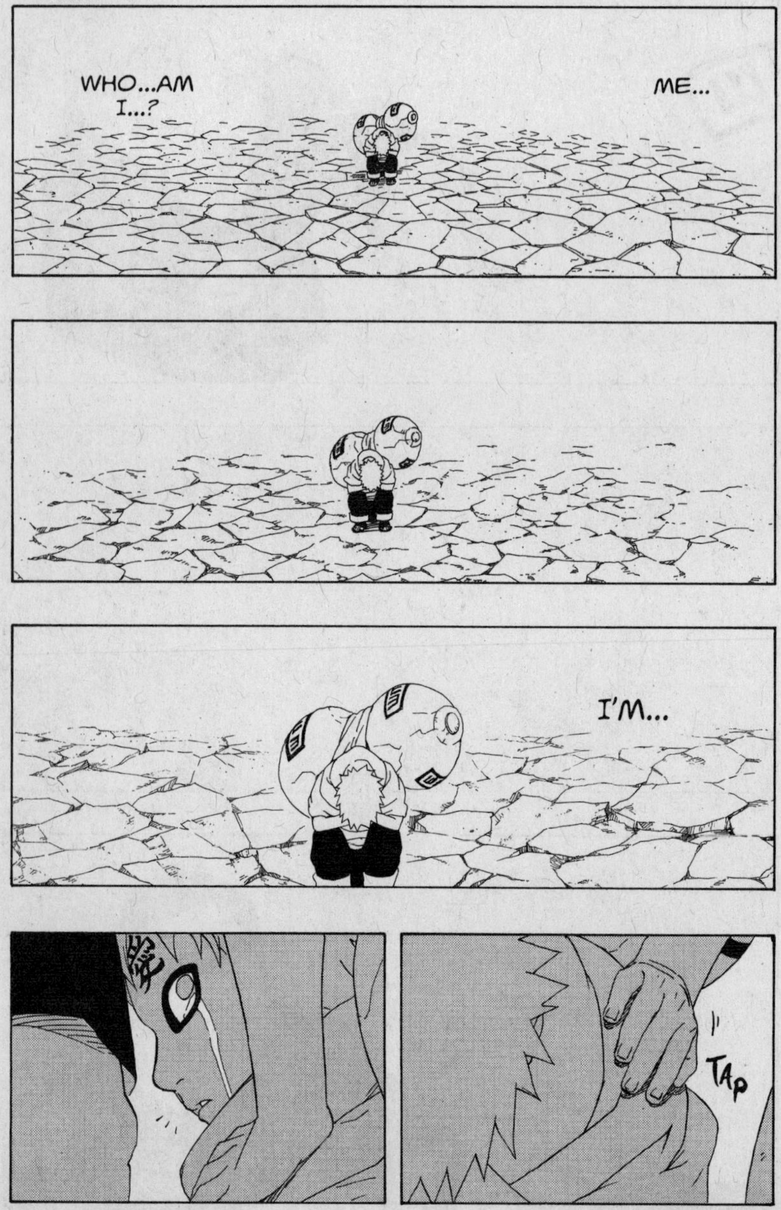
ME...
WHO...AM I...?
I'M...
TAP

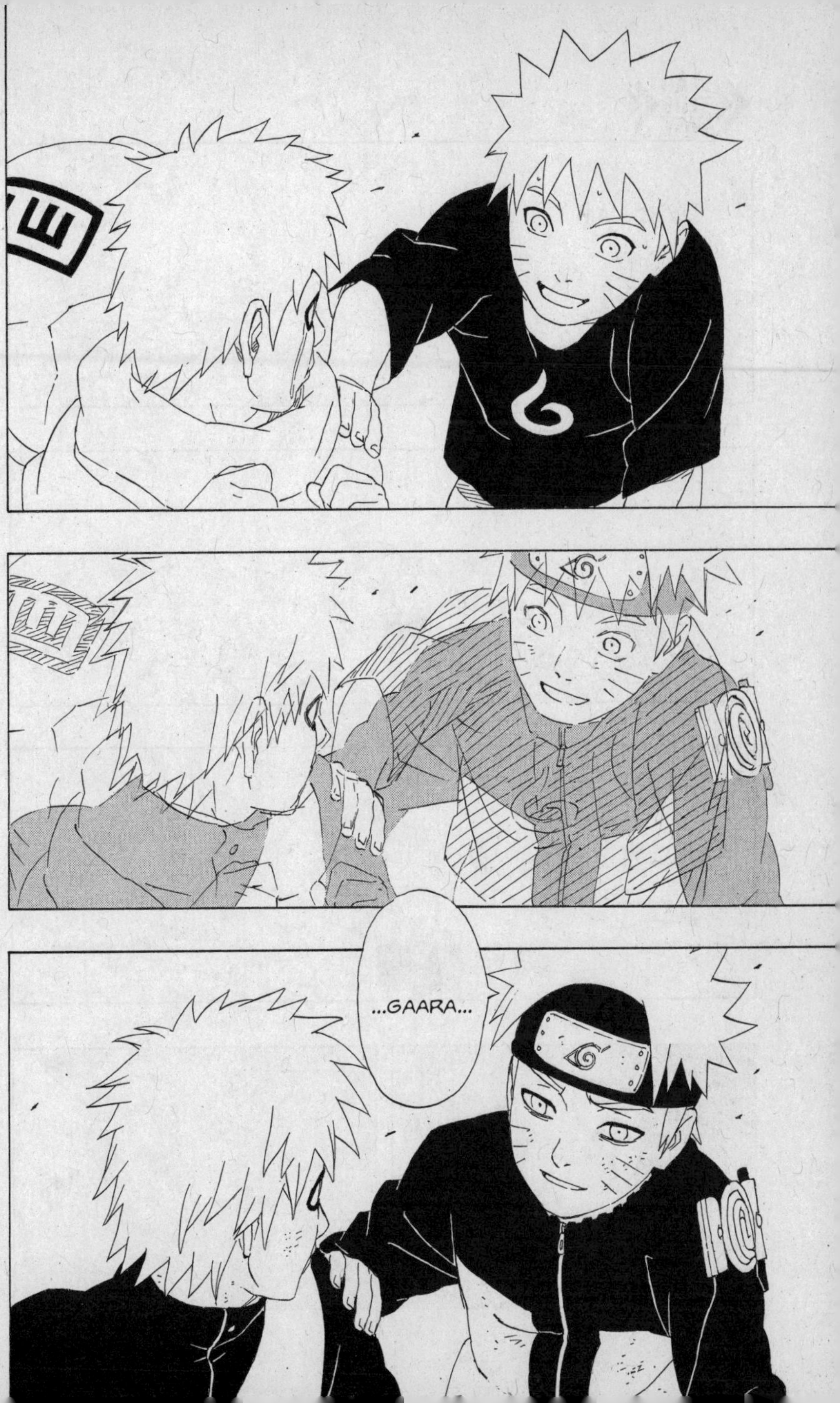
...GAARA...

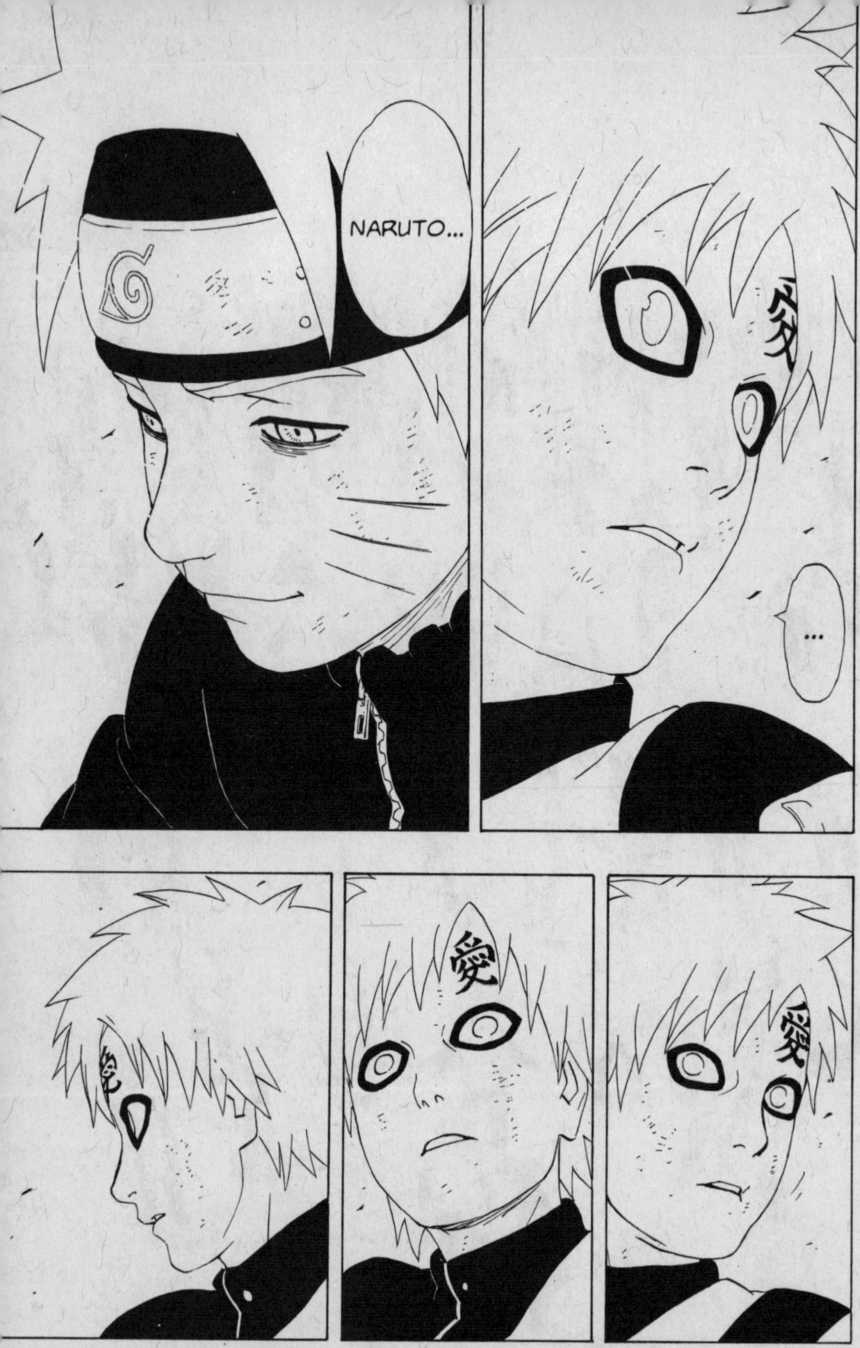
...
NARUTO...

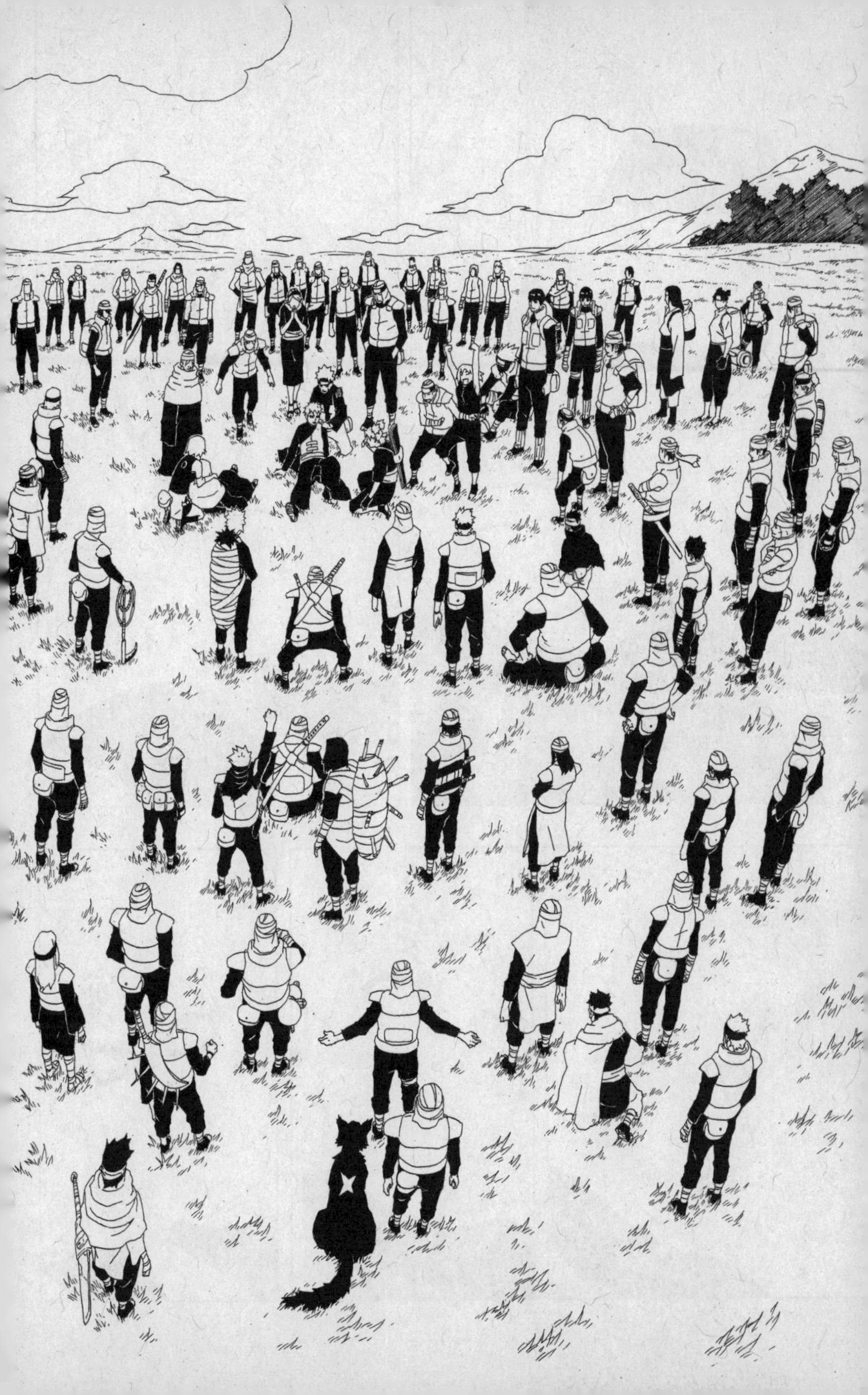

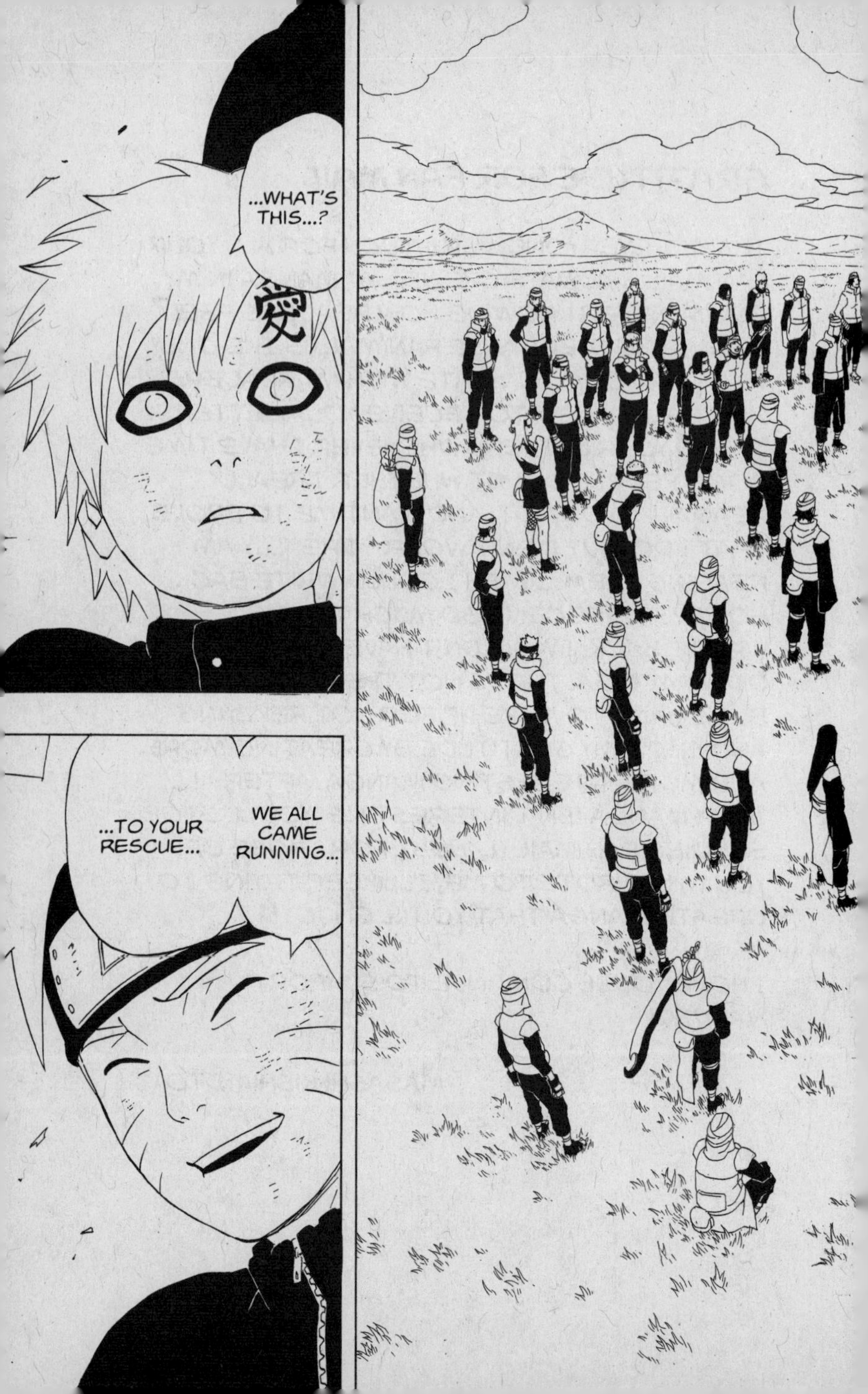
...WHAT'S THIS...?
WE ALL CAME RUNNING...
...TO YOUR RESCUE...

GRATITUDE FOR FAN MAIL

THANKS, EVERYONE, VERY MUCH FOR ALL YOUR FAN MAIL. I ALWAYS CREATE MY MANGA IN MY ROOM, NEVER KNOWING HOW READERS FEEL ABOUT IT. SO, BECAUSE FAN MAIL IS THE ONLY WAY I CAN COMMUNICATE WITH MY READERS, I'M REALLY HAPPY TO RECEIVE YOUR LETTERS. I READ YOUR LETTERS WHENEVER I HAVE TIME. SOME PEOPLE DOUBT WHETHER I REALLY READ THEM OR NOT, AND WANT ME TO PROVE THAT I DO. BUT DON'T WORRY. I REALLY AM READING THEM. I WISH I COULD WRITE BACK. HOWEVER, I RECEIVE SO MUCH THAT IF I WROTE BACK, I WOULDN'T HAVE TIME LEFT TO DO MY MANGA. THAT'S NOT THE WAY I'D LIKE IT, BUT I WANT TO MAKE UP FOR NOT REPLYING AND SHOW MY GRATITUDE BY CREATING MORE AND MORE INTERESTING MANGA. AFTER ALL, IF MY MANGA ISN'T INTERESTING, YOU'LL STOP SENDING FAN MAIL (*LAUGH*). FOR THOSE OF YOU WHO WROTE TO ME, I'LL KEEP TRYING TO CREATE MANGA THAT YOU'LL ENJOY!

I HOPE YOU'LL CONTINUE TO SUPPORT *NARUTO*!

MASASHI KISHIMOTO

Number 280: Trust!!

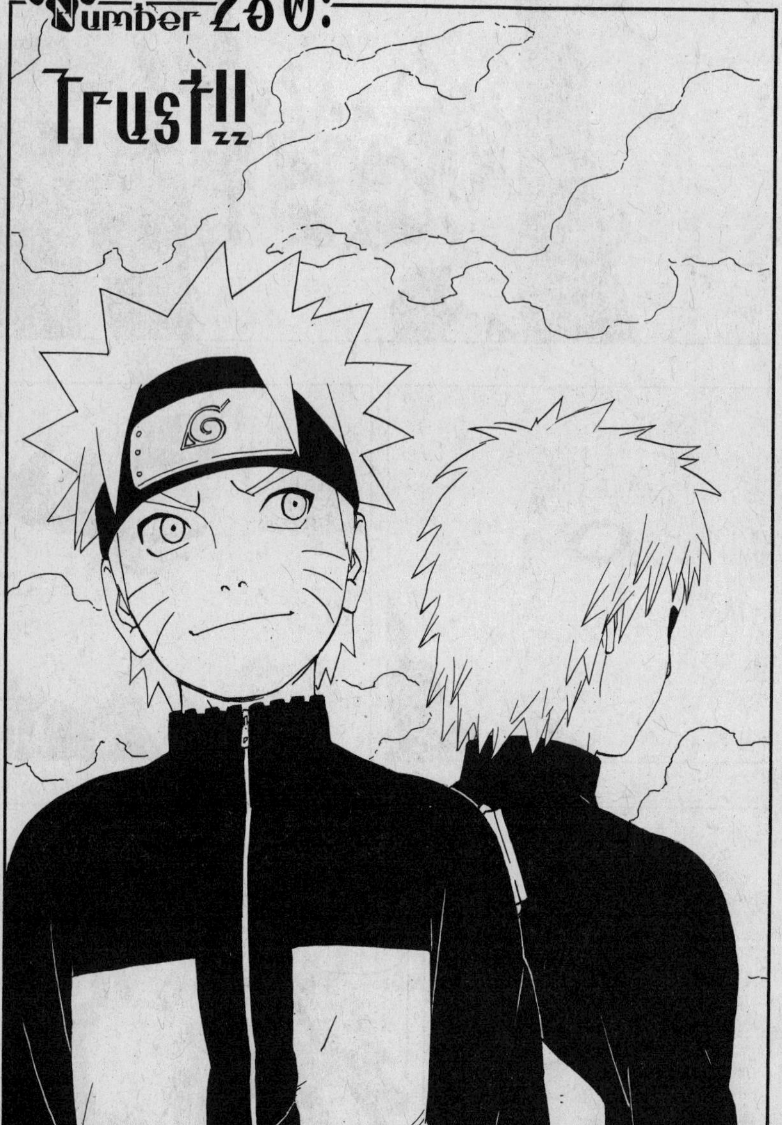

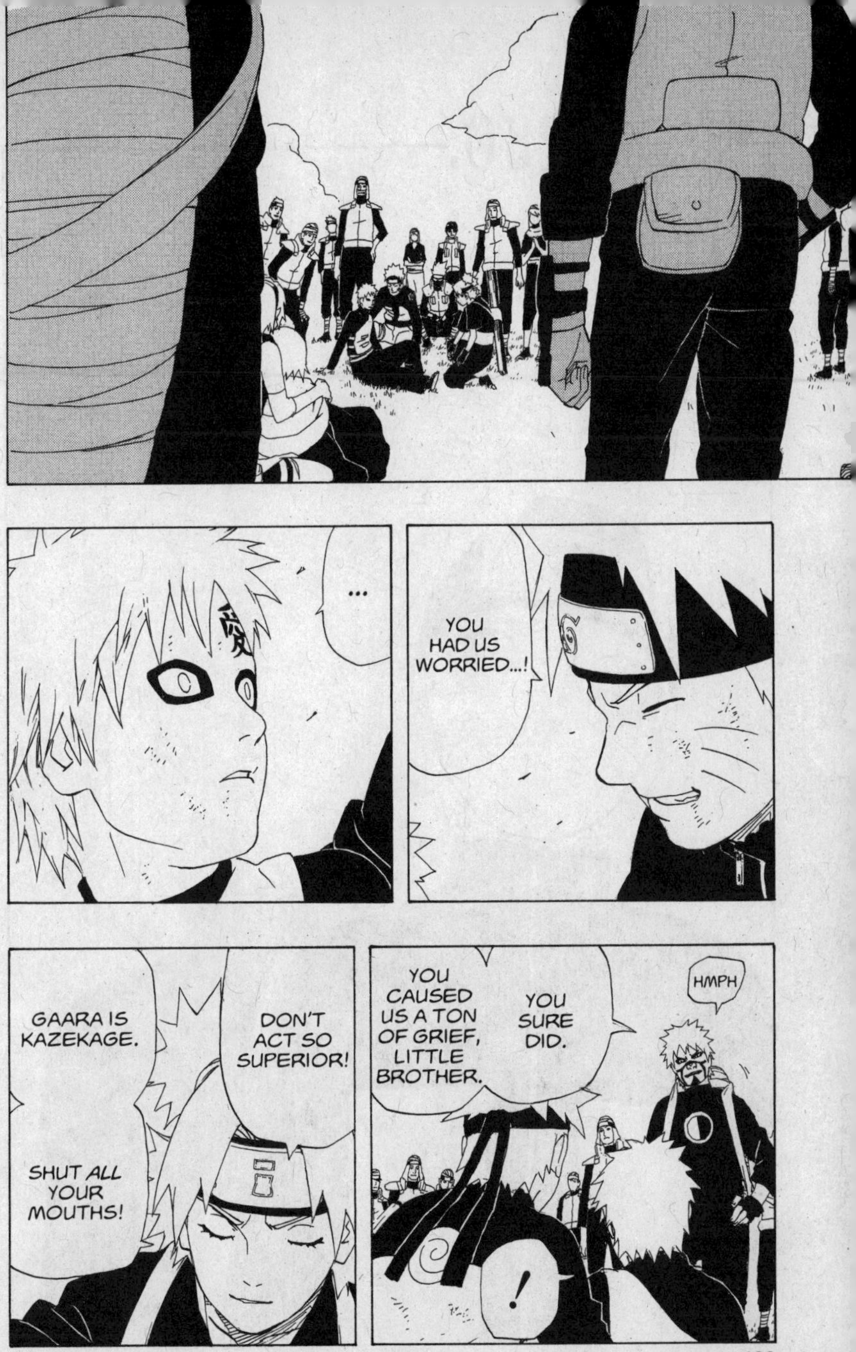
YOU HAD US WORRIED...!
...
HMPH
YOU CAUSED US A TON OF GRIEF, LITTLE BROTHER.
YOU SURE DID.
!
DON'T ACT SO SUPERIOR!
GAARA IS KAZEKAGE.
SHUT ALL YOUR MOUTHS!

READ THIS WAY

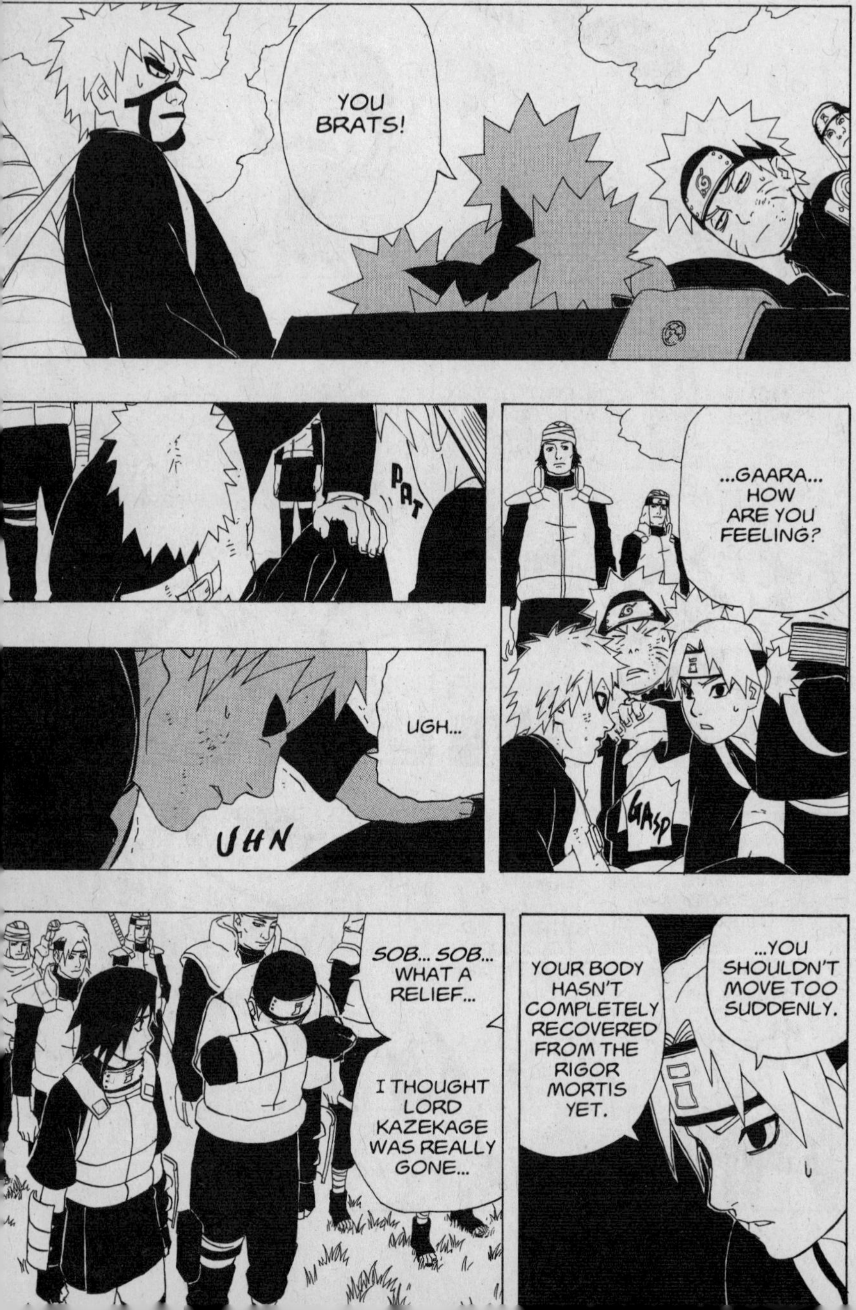
YOU BRATS!
...GAARA... HOW ARE YOU FEELING?
GASP
PAT
UGH...
UHN
...YOU SHOULDN'T MOVE TOO SUDDENLY.
YOUR BODY HASN'T COMPLETELY RECOVERED FROM THE RIGOR MORTIS YET.
SOB... SOB... WHAT A RELIEF...
I THOUGHT LORD KAZEKAGE WAS REALLY GONE...

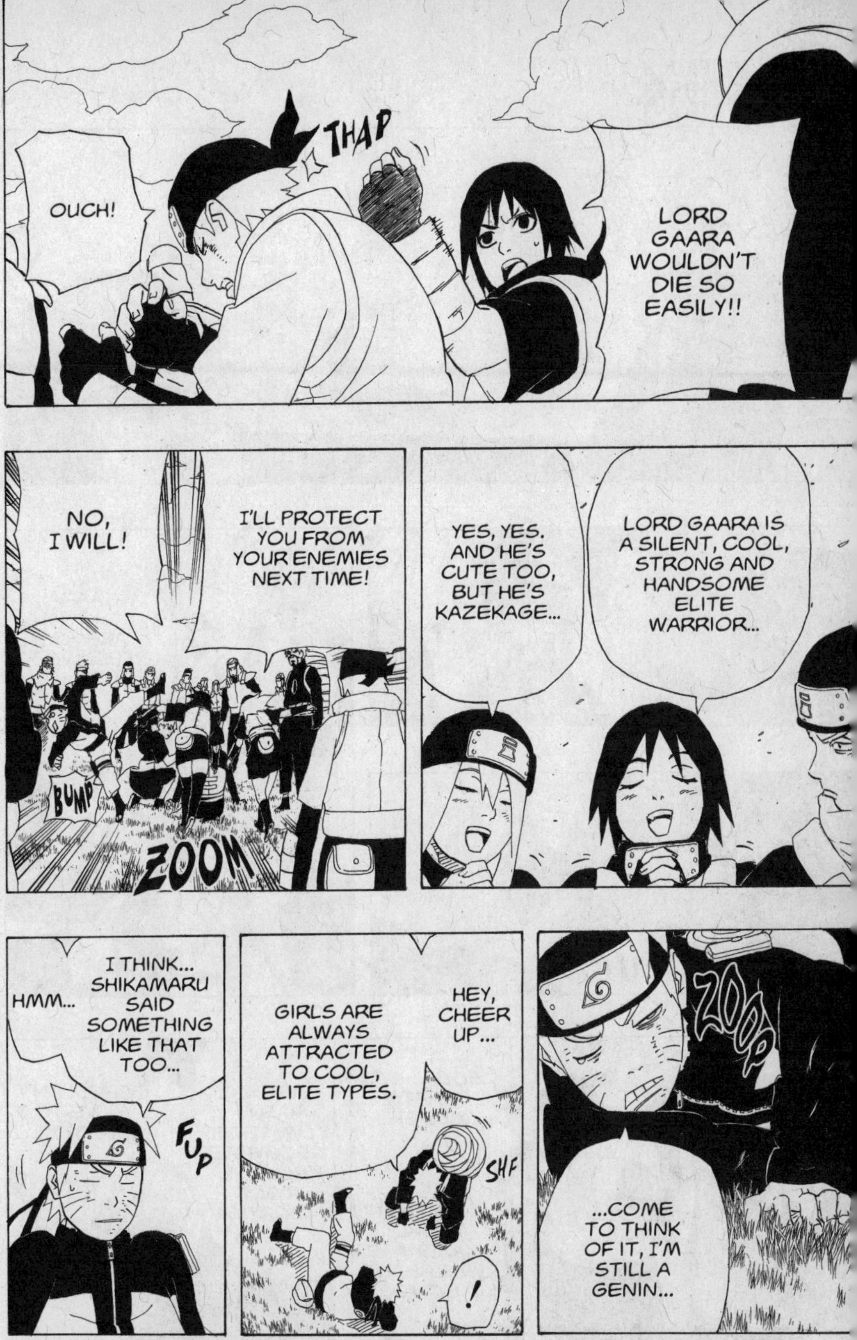
LORD GAARA WOULDN'T DIE SO EASILY!!
THAP
OUCH!
LORD GAARA IS A SILENT, COOL, STRONG AND HANDSOME ELITE WARRIOR...
YES, YES. AND HE'S CUTE TOO, BUT HE'S KAZEKAGE...
I'LL PROTECT YOU FROM YOUR ENEMIES NEXT TIME!
NO, I WILL!
BUMP
ZOOM
ZOOP
...COME TO THINK OF IT, I'M STILL A GENIN...
HEY, CHEER UP...
GIRLS ARE ALWAYS ATTRACTED TO COOL, ELITE TYPES.
SHF
!
I THINK... SHIKAMARU SAID SOMETHING LIKE THAT TOO...
HMM...
FUP

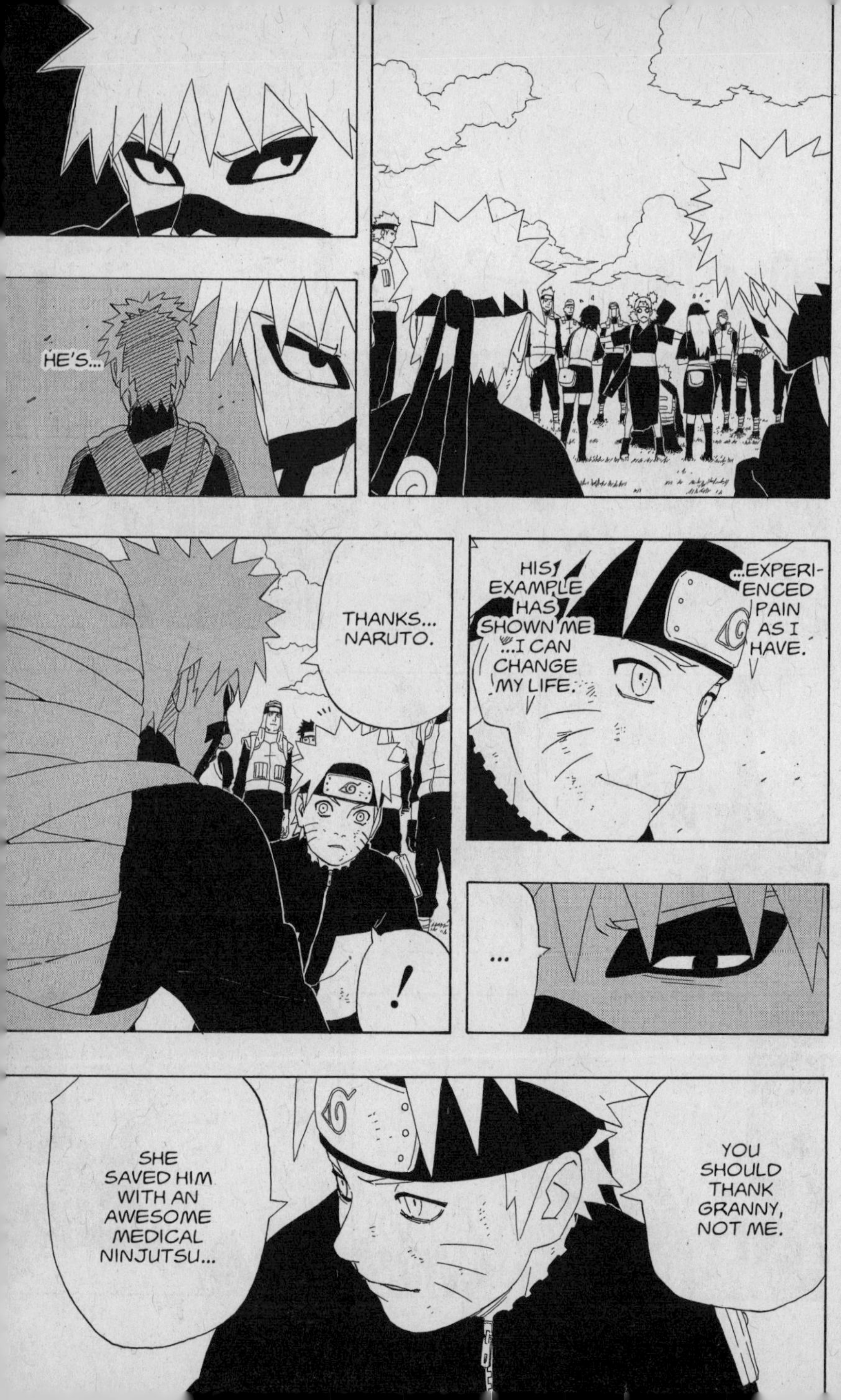
HE'S...
...EXPERIENCED PAIN AS I HAVE.
HIS EXAMPLE HAS SHOWN ME ...I CAN CHANGE MY LIFE.
...
THANKS... NARUTO.
!
YOU SHOULD THANK GRANNY, NOT ME.
SHE SAVED HIM WITH AN AWESOME MEDICAL NINJUTSU...

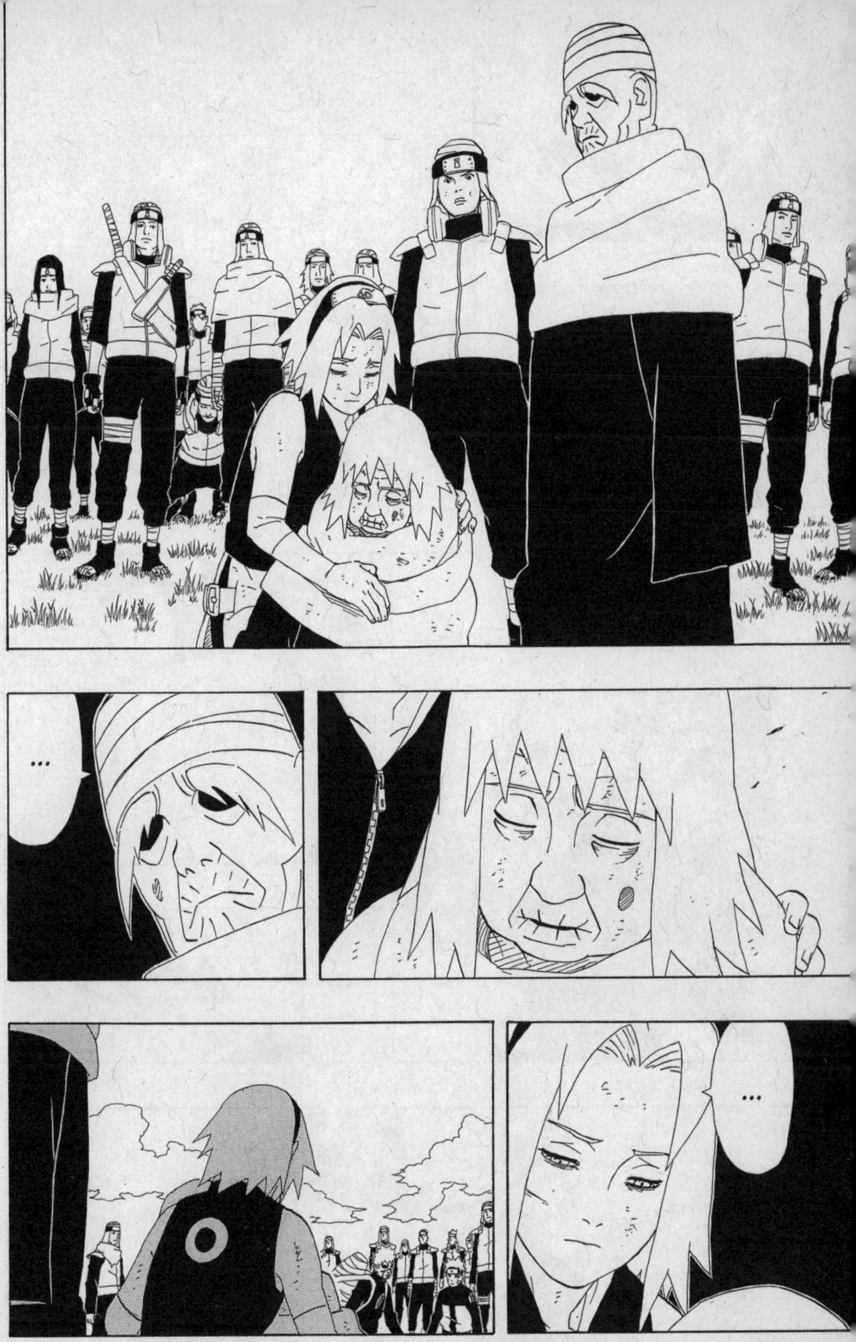
...
...

READ THIS WAY

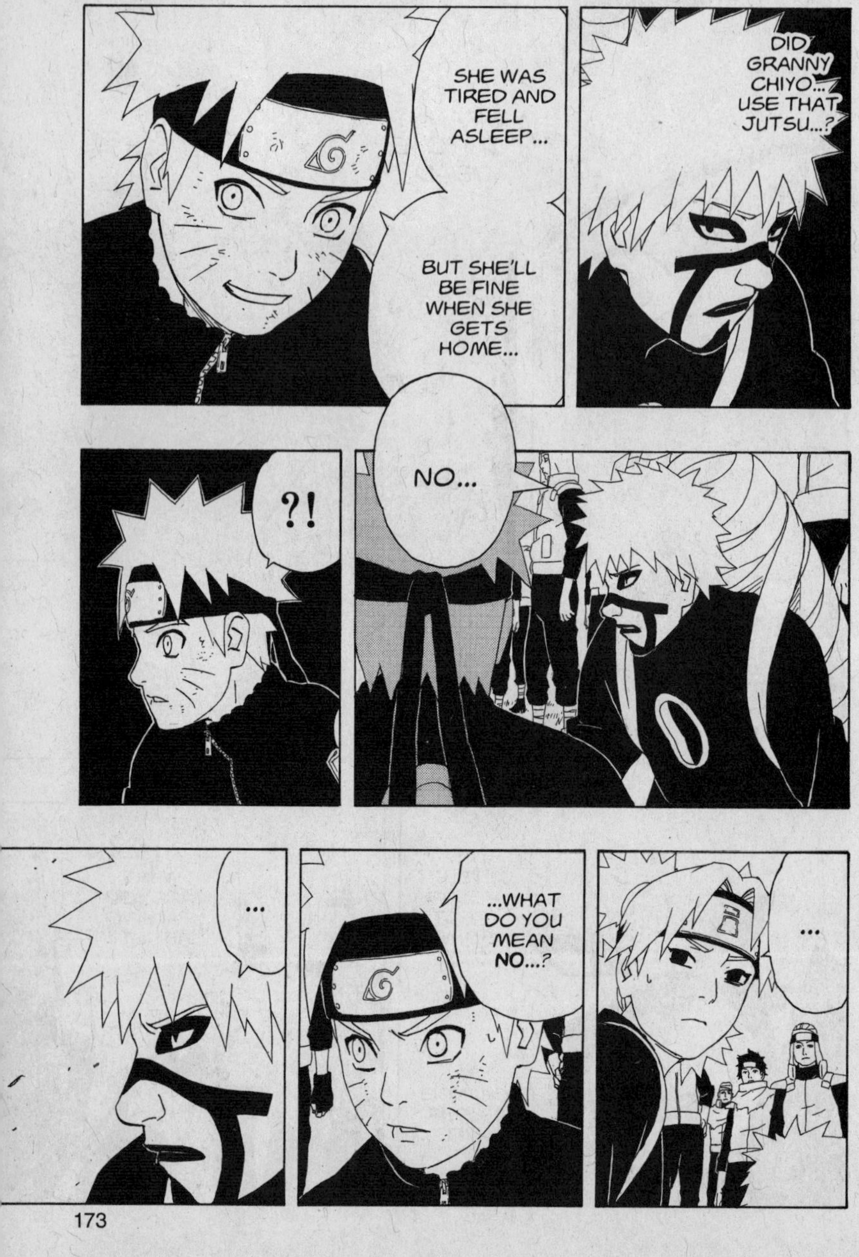

DID GRANNY CHIYO... USE THAT JUTSU...?
SHE WAS TIRED AND FELL ASLEEP...
BUT SHE'LL BE FINE WHEN SHE GETS HOME...
NO...
?!
...
...WHAT DO YOU MEAN NO...?
...

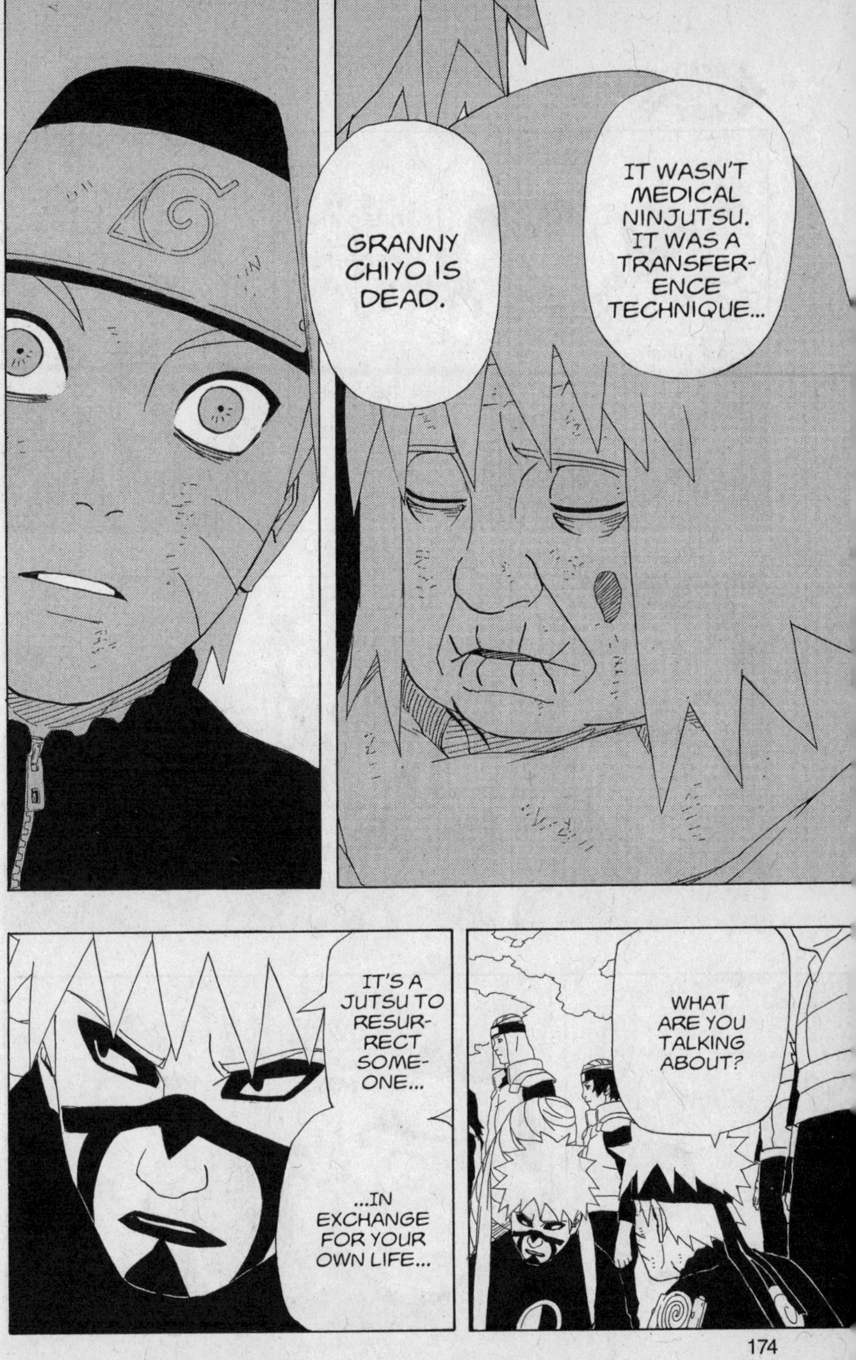
IT WASN'T MEDICAL NINJUTSU. IT WAS A TRANSFER-ENCE TECHNIQUE...
GRANNY CHIYO IS DEAD.
WHAT ARE YOU TALKING ABOUT?
IT'S A JUTSU TO RESUR-RECT SOME-ONE...
...IN EXCHANGE FOR YOUR OWN LIFE...

READ THIS WAY

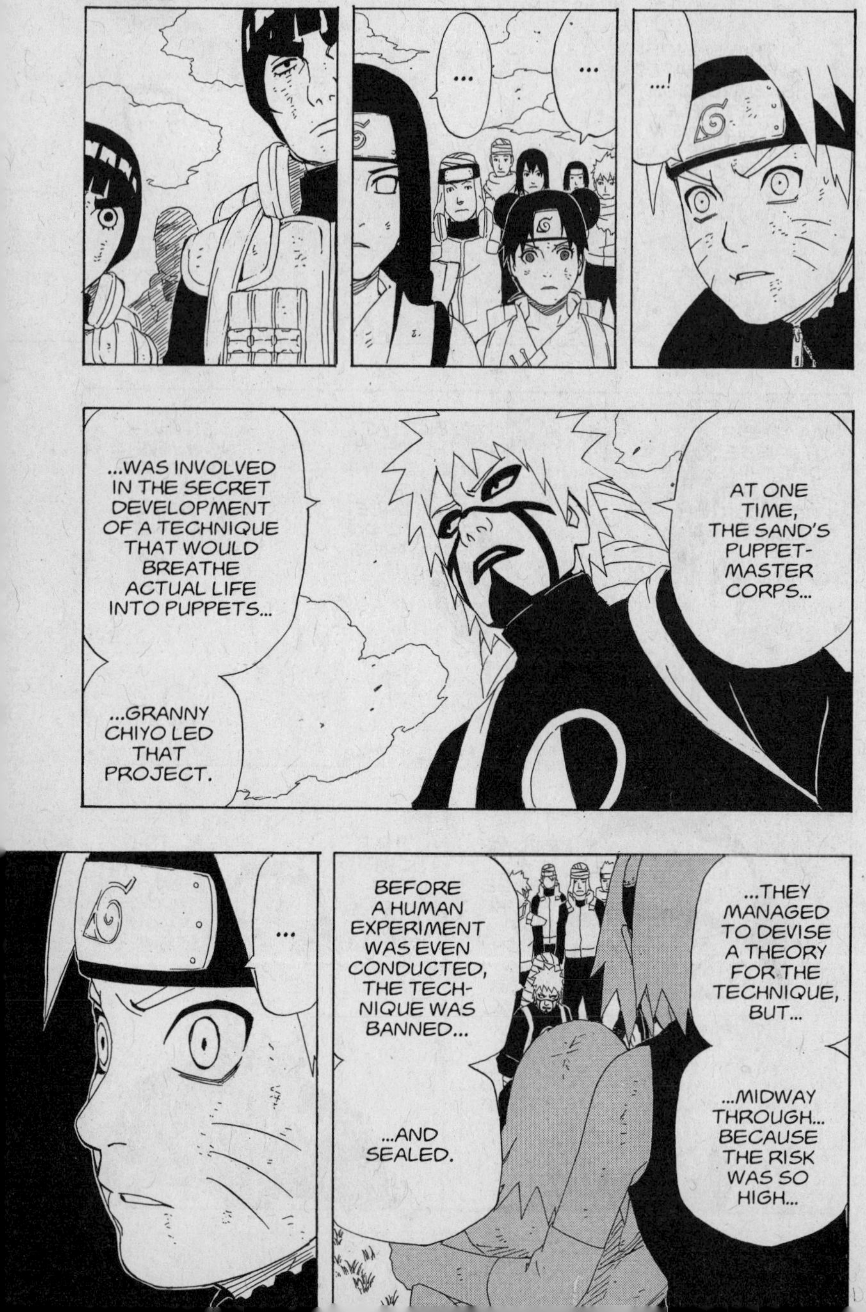

...!
...
...
AT ONE TIME, THE SAND'S PUPPET-MASTER CORPS...
...WAS INVOLVED IN THE SECRET DEVELOPMENT OF A TECHNIQUE THAT WOULD BREATHE ACTUAL LIFE INTO PUPPETS...
...GRANNY CHIYO LED THAT PROJECT.
...THEY MANAGED TO DEVISE A THEORY FOR THE TECHNIQUE, BUT...
...MIDWAY THROUGH... BECAUSE THE RISK WAS SO HIGH...
BEFORE A HUMAN EXPERIMENT WAS EVEN CONDUCTED, THE TECHNIQUE WAS BANNED...
...AND SEALED.
...

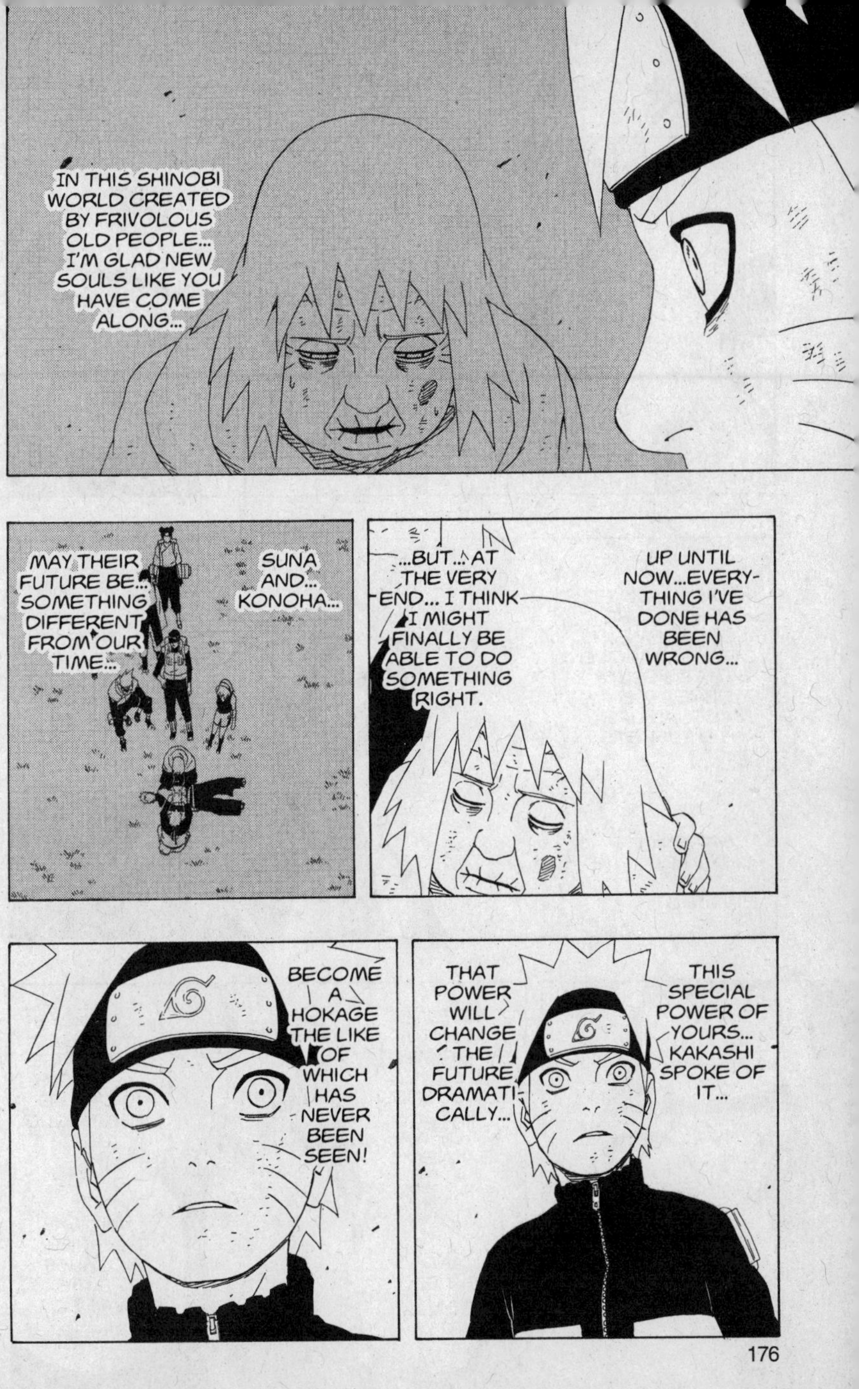
IN THIS SHINOBI WORLD CREATED BY FRIVOLOUS OLD PEOPLE... I'M GLAD NEW SOULS LIKE YOU HAVE COME ALONG...
UP UNTIL NOW...EVERYTHING I'VE DONE HAS BEEN WRONG...
...BUT... AT THE VERY END... I THINK I MIGHT FINALLY BE ABLE TO DO SOMETHING RIGHT.
SUNA AND... KONOHA...
MAY THEIR FUTURE BE... SOMETHING DIFFERENT FROM OUR TIME...
THIS SPECIAL POWER OF YOURS... KAKASHI SPOKE OF IT...
THAT POWER WILL CHANGE THE FUTURE DRAMATICALLY...
BECOME A HOKAGE THE LIKE OF WHICH HAS NEVER BEEN SEEN!

READ THIS WAY

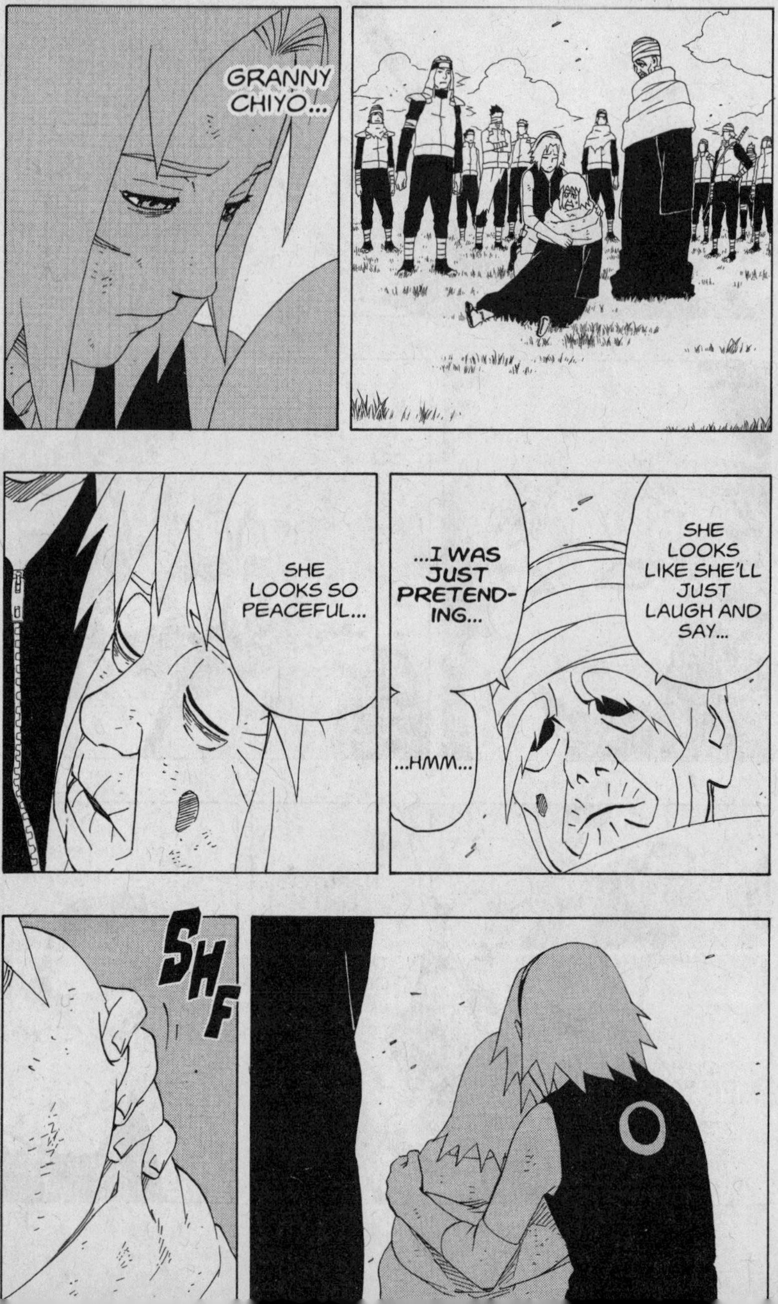
GRANNY CHIYO...
SHE LOOKS LIKE SHE'LL JUST LAUGH AND SAY...
...I WAS JUST PRETEND-ING...
...HMM...
SHE LOOKS SO PEACEFUL...
SHF

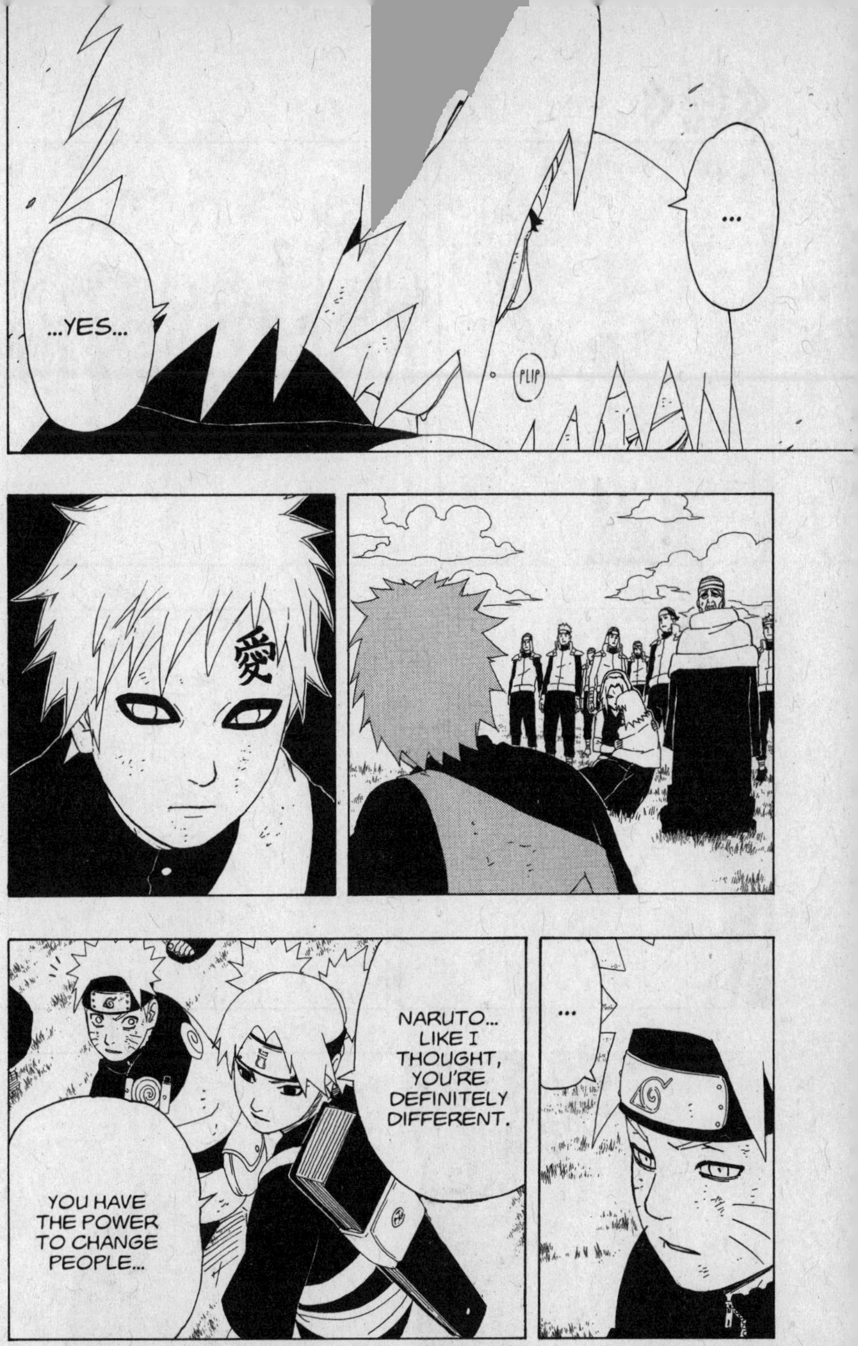
...
PLIP
...YES...
...
NARUTO... LIKE I THOUGHT, YOU'RE DEFINITELY DIFFERENT.
YOU HAVE THE POWER TO CHANGE PEOPLE...

READ THIS WAY

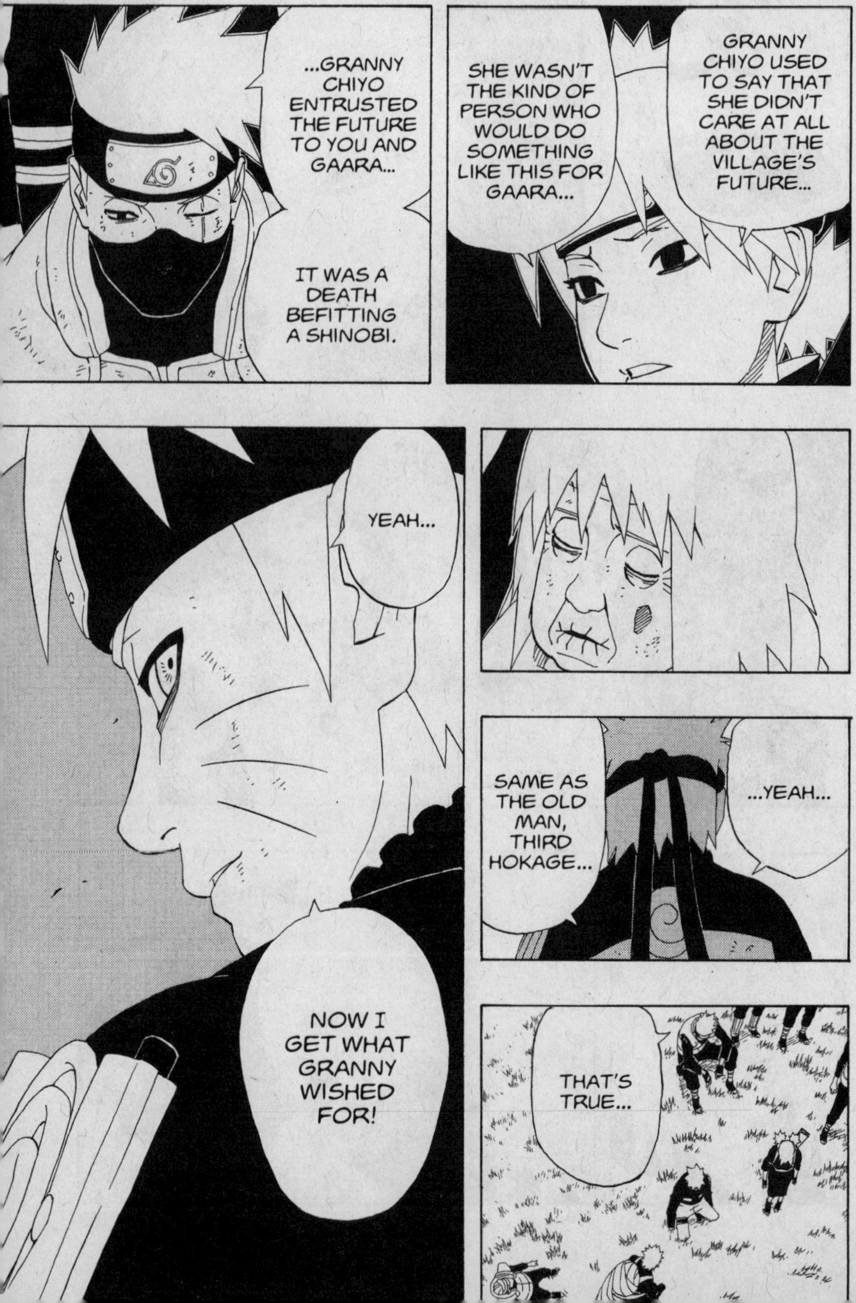
GRANNY CHIYO USED TO SAY THAT SHE DIDN'T CARE AT ALL ABOUT THE VILLAGE'S FUTURE...
SHE WASN'T THE KIND OF PERSON WHO WOULD DO SOMETHING LIKE THIS FOR GAARA...
...GRANNY CHIYO ENTRUSTED THE FUTURE TO YOU AND GAARA...
IT WAS A DEATH BEFITTING A SHINOBI.
YEAH...
...YEAH...
SAME AS THE OLD MAN, THIRD HOKAGE...
THAT'S TRUE...
NOW I GET WHAT GRANNY WISHED FOR!

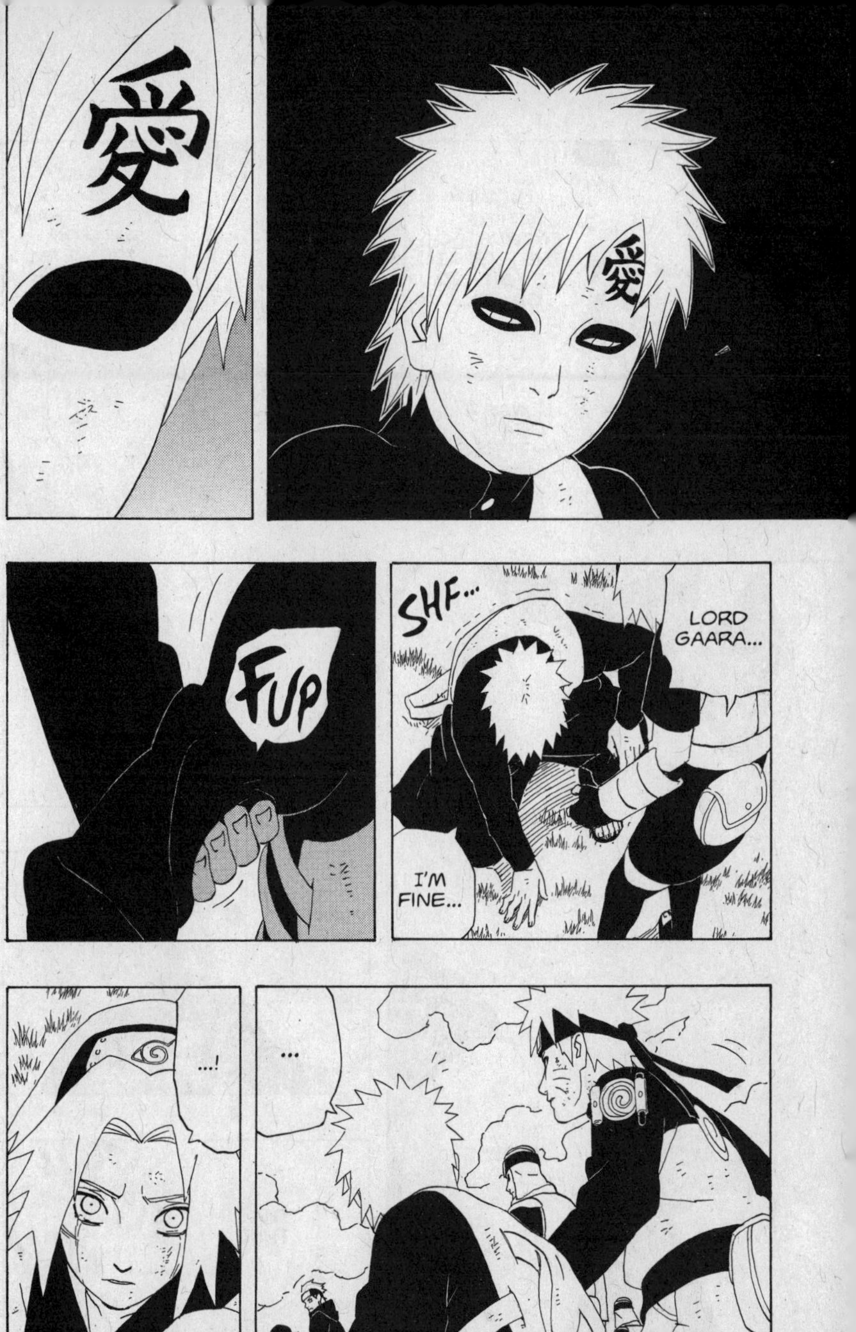
LORD GAARA...
SHF...
I'M FINE...
FUP
...
...!

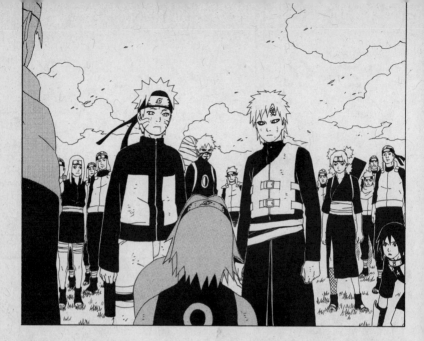

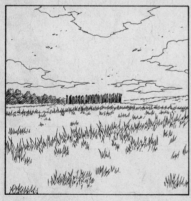

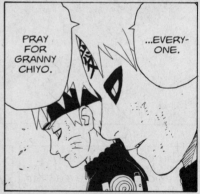

PRAY FOR GRANNY CHIYO.

...EVERY-ONE.

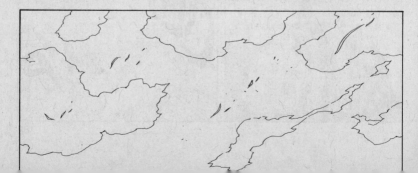

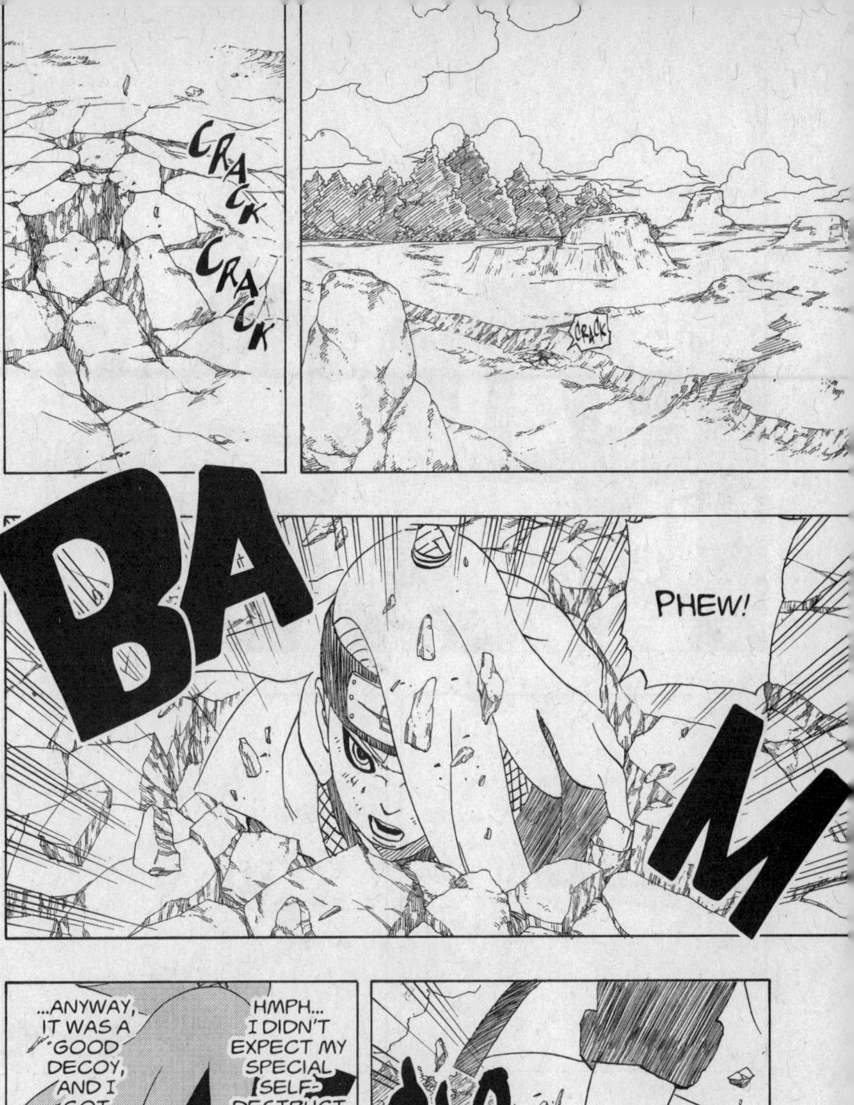
CRACK
CRACK CRACK
PHEW!
BAM
CLOMP
HMPH... I DIDN'T EXPECT MY SPECIAL SELF-DESTRUCT DOPPELGANGER TO BE FOILED...
...ANYWAY, IT WAS A GOOD DECOY, AND I GOT AWAY... HMMM?
KLAK
KLAK

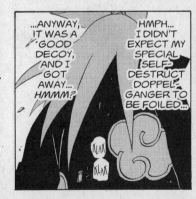

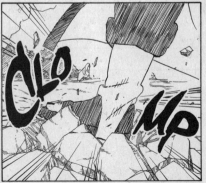

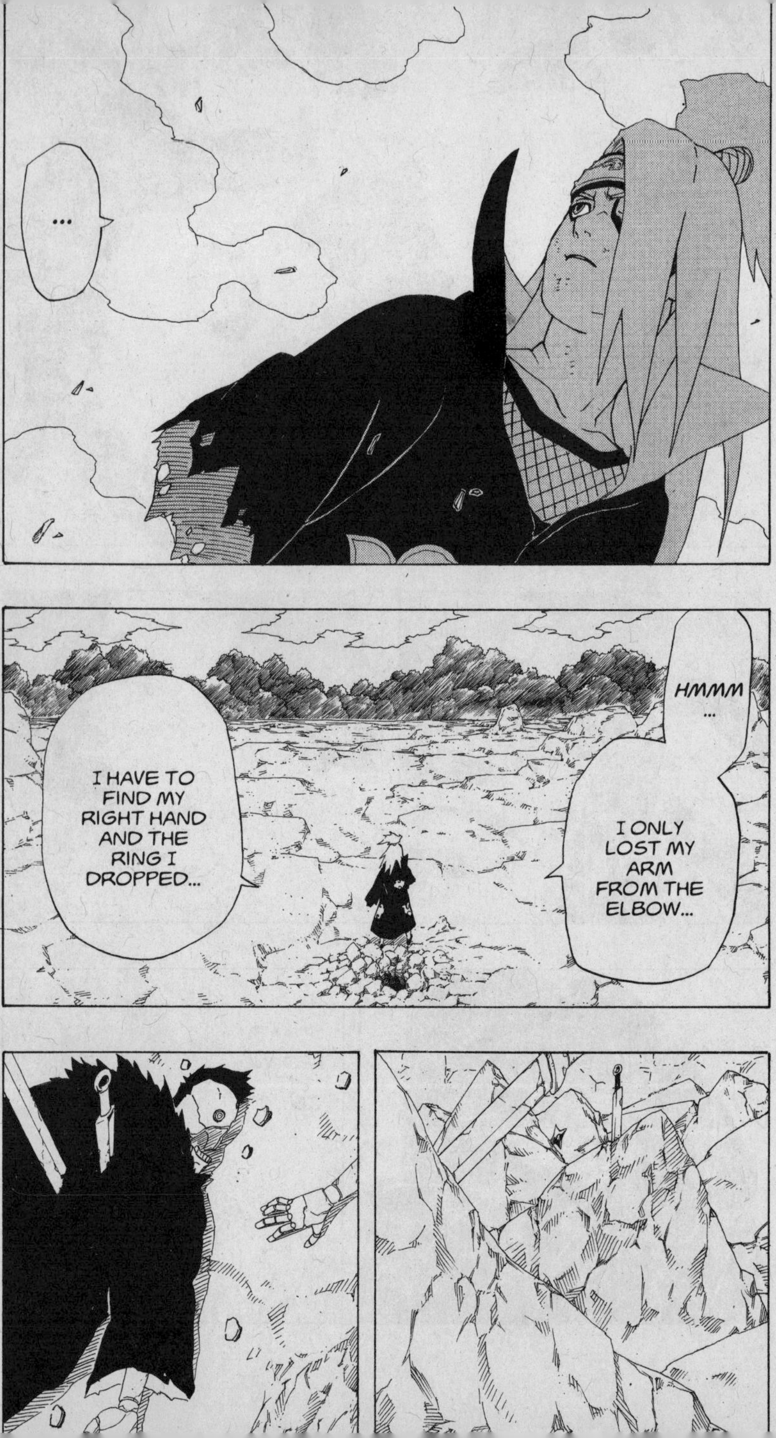
...
HMMM ...
I ONLY LOST MY ARM FROM THE ELBOW...
I HAVE TO FIND MY RIGHT HAND AND THE RING I DROPPED...

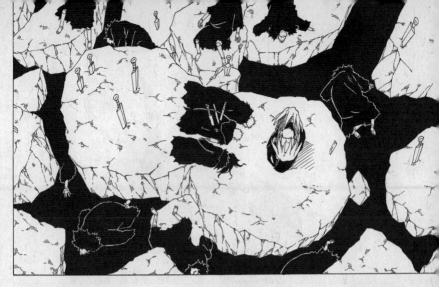

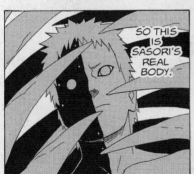

SO THIS IS SASORI'S REAL BODY.

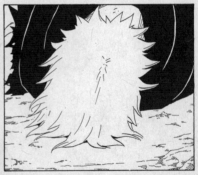

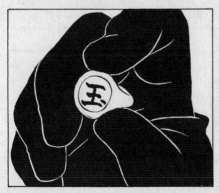

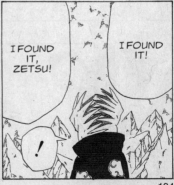

I FOUND IT, ZETSU!

I FOUND IT!

!

184

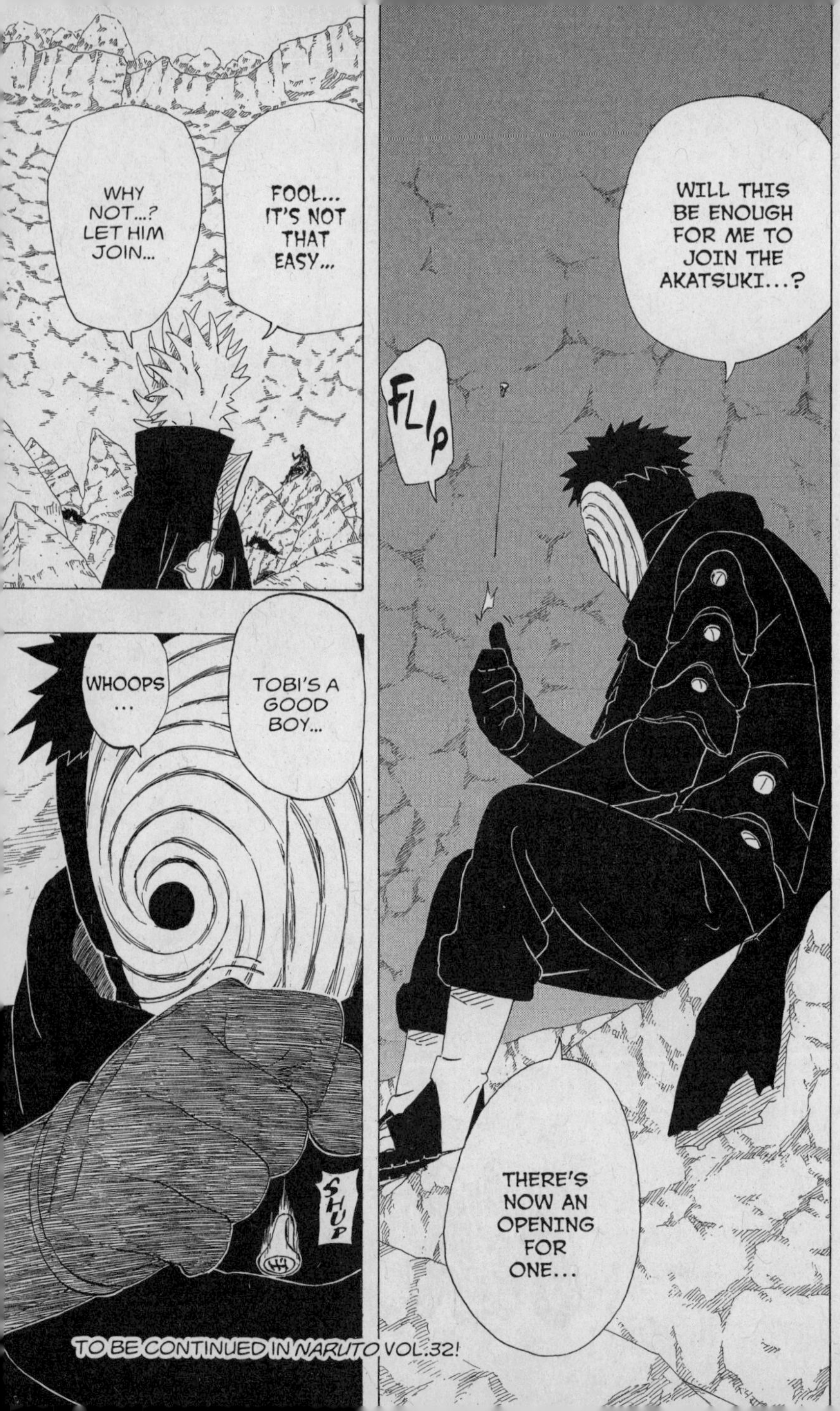
WILL THIS BE ENOUGH FOR ME TO JOIN THE AKATSUKI...?
FLIP
THERE'S NOW AN OPENING FOR ONE...
FOOL... IT'S NOT THAT EASY...
WHY NOT...? LET HIM JOIN...
TOBI'S A GOOD BOY...
WHOOPS ...
SHUP
TO BE CONTINUED IN NARUTO VOL.32!

NARUTO

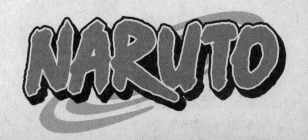

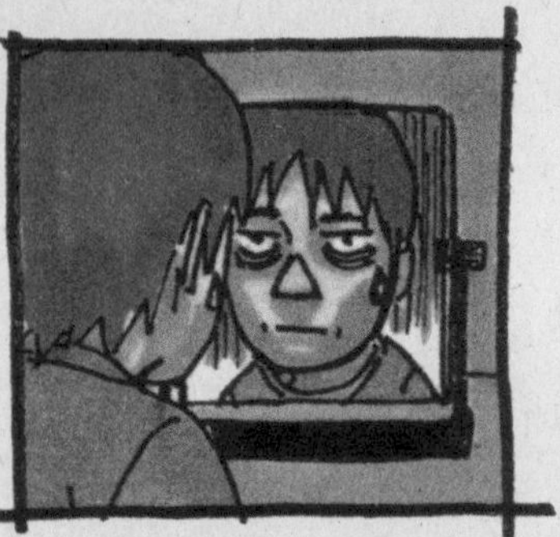

岸本斉史

It's 2006. I believe the serialization began in 1999, so that means we've entered our seventh year of publication! Long enough for kids that were just entering elementary school to now be in junior high... I recently started noticing how it seems like the years pass quicker and quicker. Where in the world did the time go?! When in the world did I become middle-aged?! Yikes...

—Masashi Kishimoto, 2006

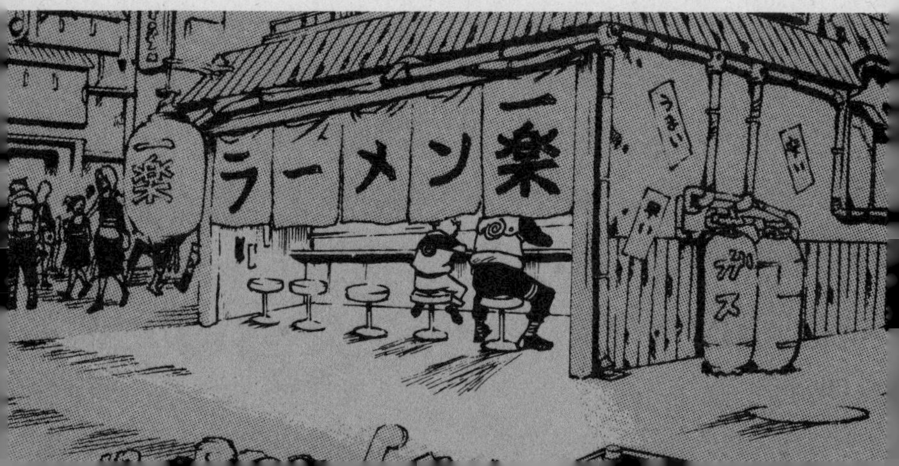

ラーメン
一楽
うまい

NARUTO

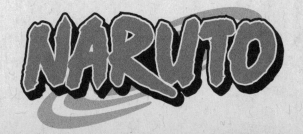

SHONEN JUMP MANGA EDITION

NARUTO

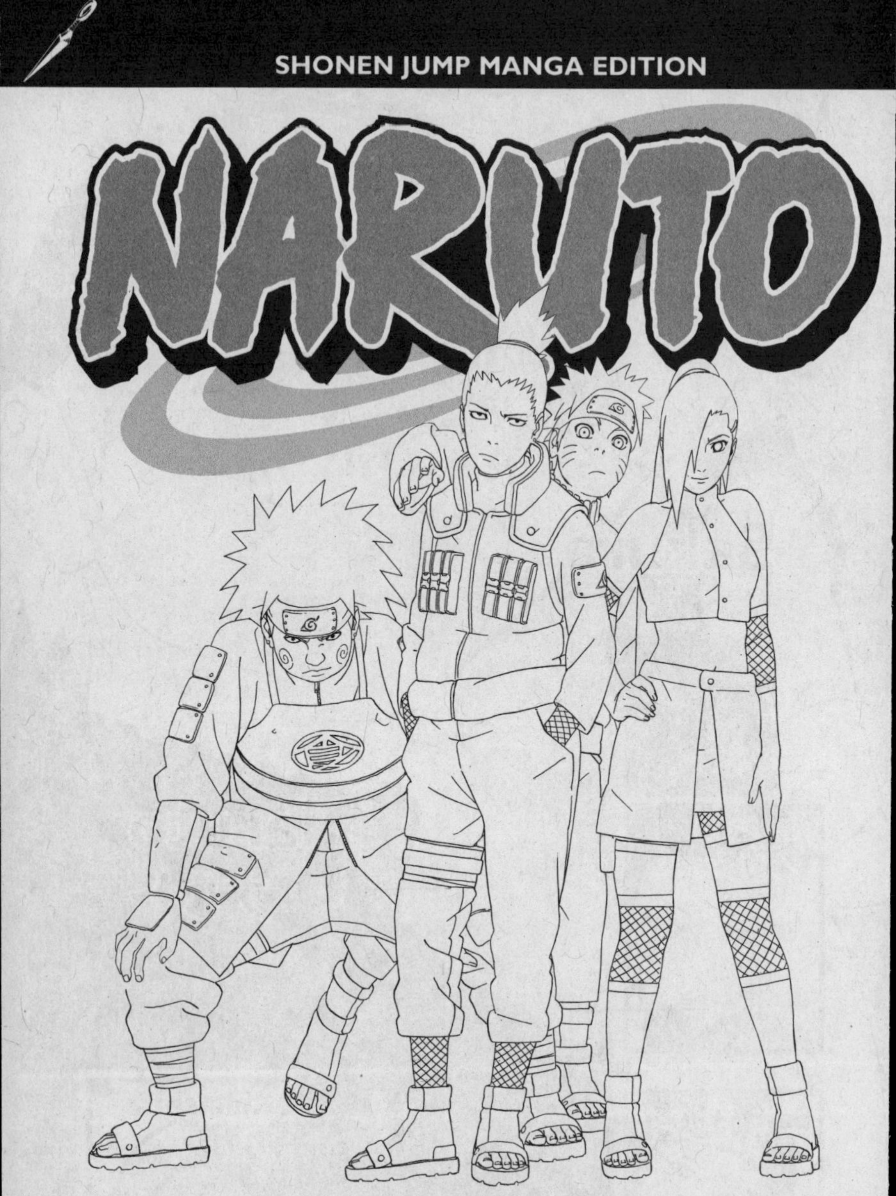

VOL. 32

THE SEARCH FOR SASUKE

STORY AND ART BY
MASASHI KISHIMOTO

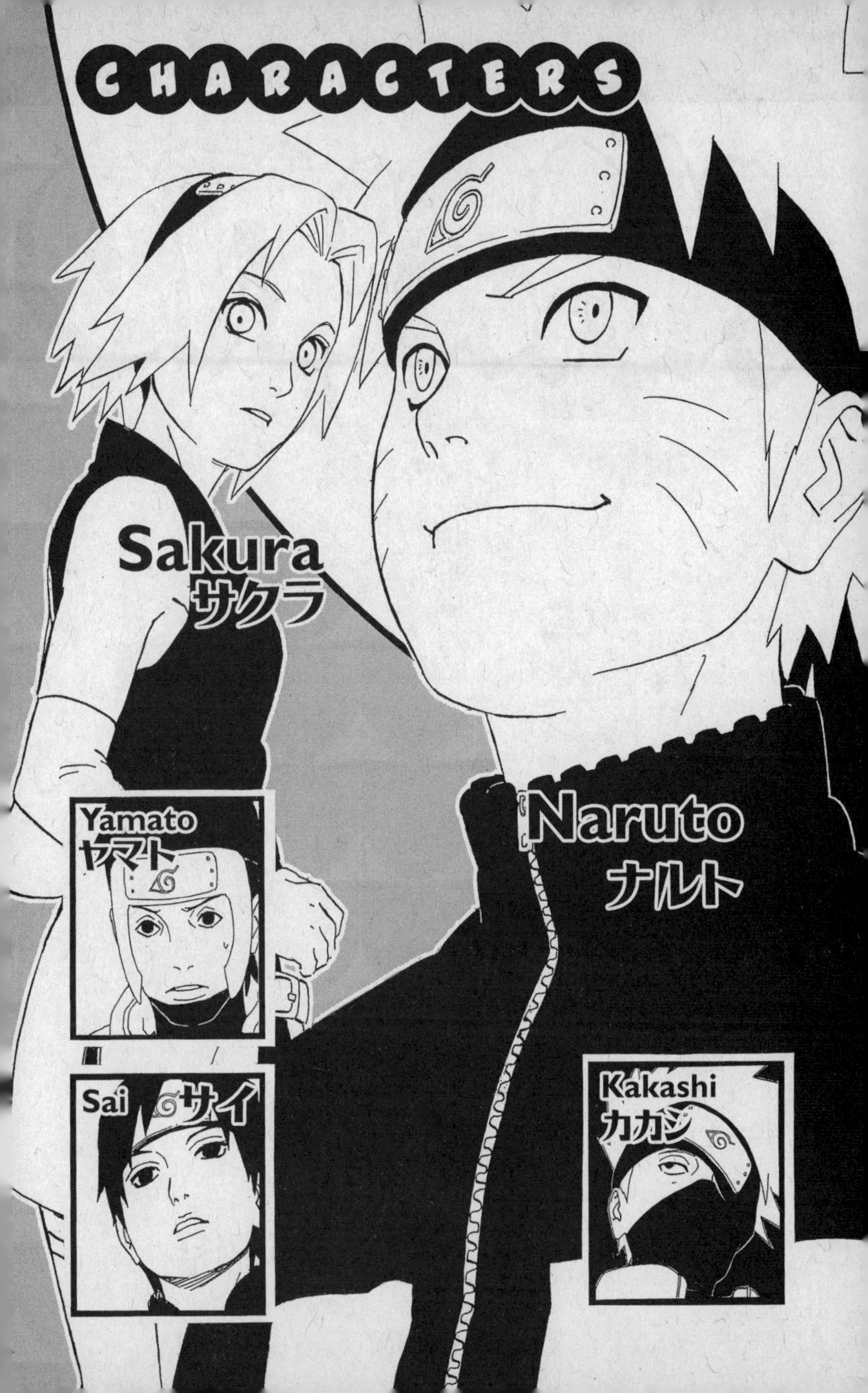
CHARACTERS
Sakura
サクラ
Naruto
ナルト
Yamato
ヤマト
Sai
サイ
Kakashi
カカシ

Tsunade
綱手
Shizune
シズネ
Danzo
ダンゾウ
Shikamaru
シカマル
Choji チョウジ
Ino
いの

The Story So Far...

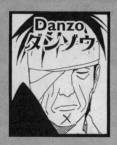

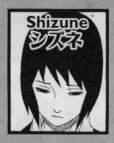

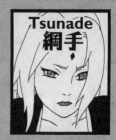

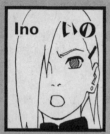

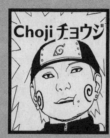

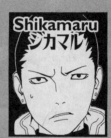

Naruto, the biggest troublemaker at the Ninja Academy in Konohagakure, finally becomes a ninja along with his classmates Sasuke and Sakura. During the Chûnin Selection Exams, Orochimaru and his henchmen launch *Operation Destroy Konoha*. To stop the attack and prevent the deaths of any more of Konoha's shinobi, Sarutobi, the Third Hokage, sacrifices his own life. In the wake of this tragedy, Lady Tsunade is sought out and declared Fifth Hokage.

Sasuke—lured by the Sound Ninja Four of Orochimaru—leaves Konohagakure. Naruto fights valiantly against Sasuke, but cannot stop his friend from following the possible path of darkness...

After two years, Naruto and his comrades reunite, each having grown and matured in attitude and aptitude. Gaara of the Sand has become Kazekage, and falls into the hands of the mysterious organization known as the Akatsuki.

After several fierce battles, Naruto and the others defeat rogue ninja Sasori and Deidara and recover Gaara. But their victory looks to be a bitter one as Gaara is dead. Or so it seems until Granny Chiyo, using a reincarnation jutsu, sacrifices her own life to resurrect the fallen Kazekage!

CONTENTS

Number 281: The Search for Sasuke!!

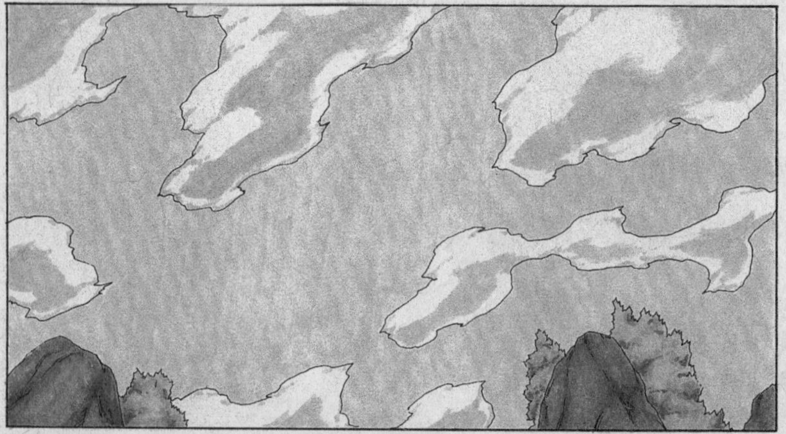

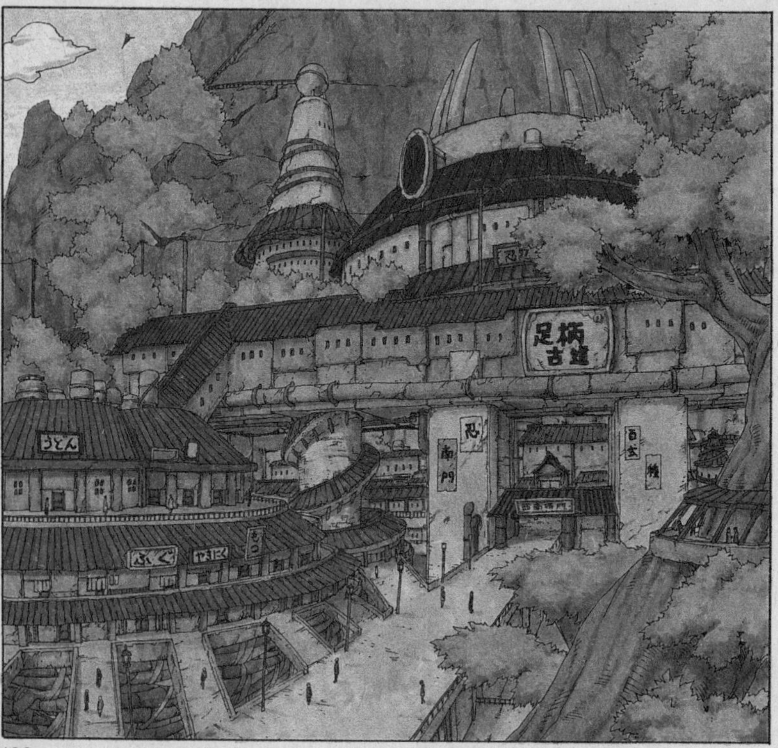
うどん
ふぐ
やきにく

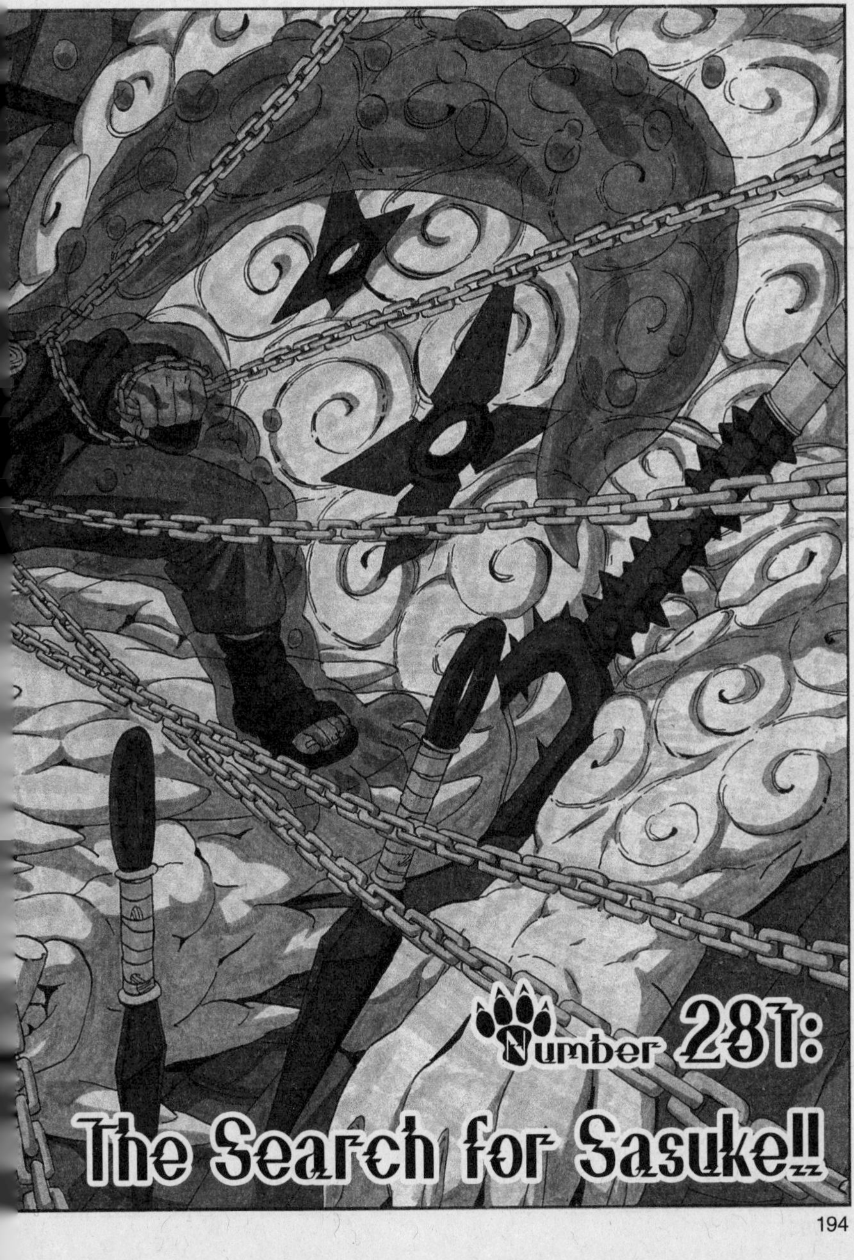
Number 281:
The Search for Sasuke!!

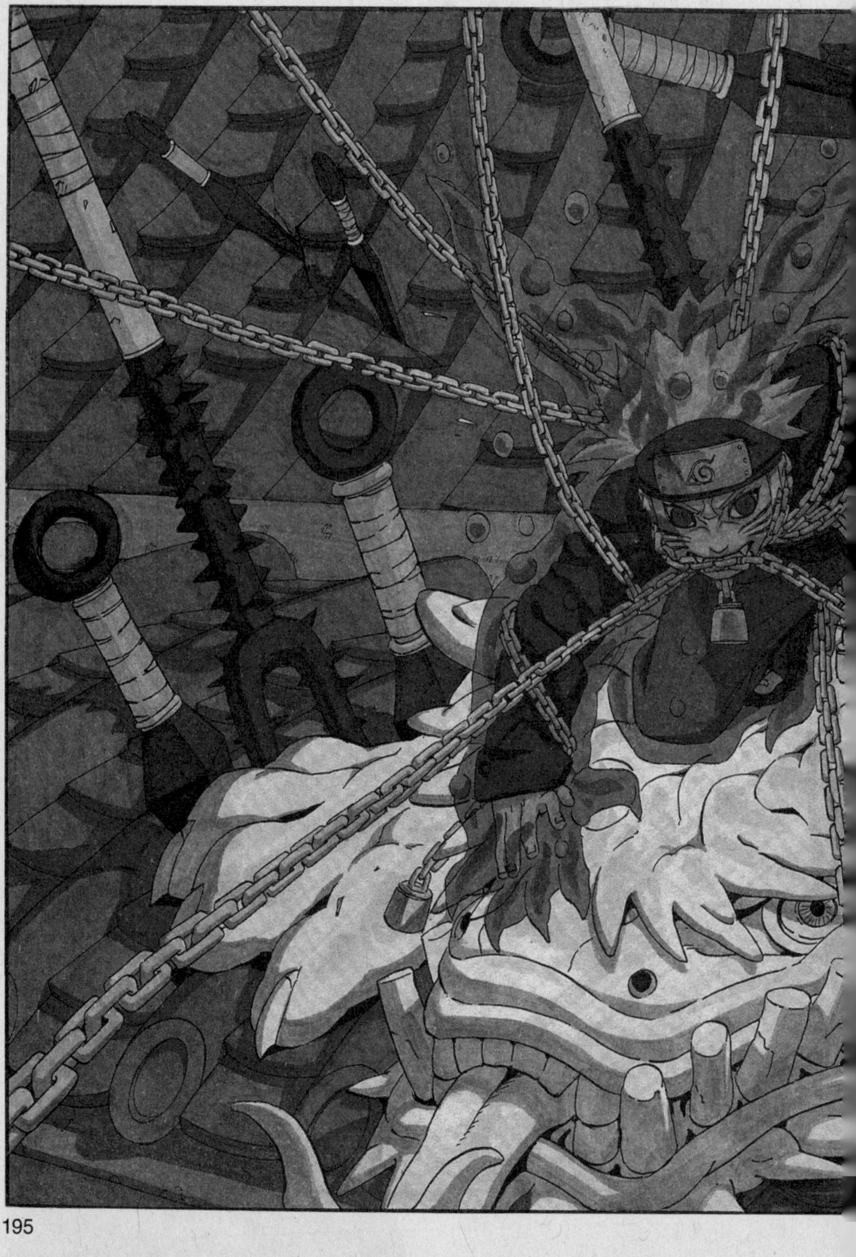

NARUTO

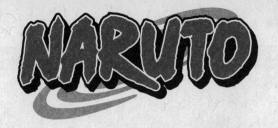

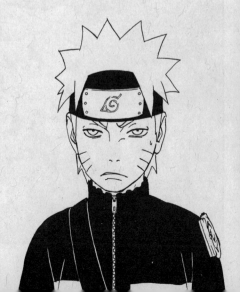

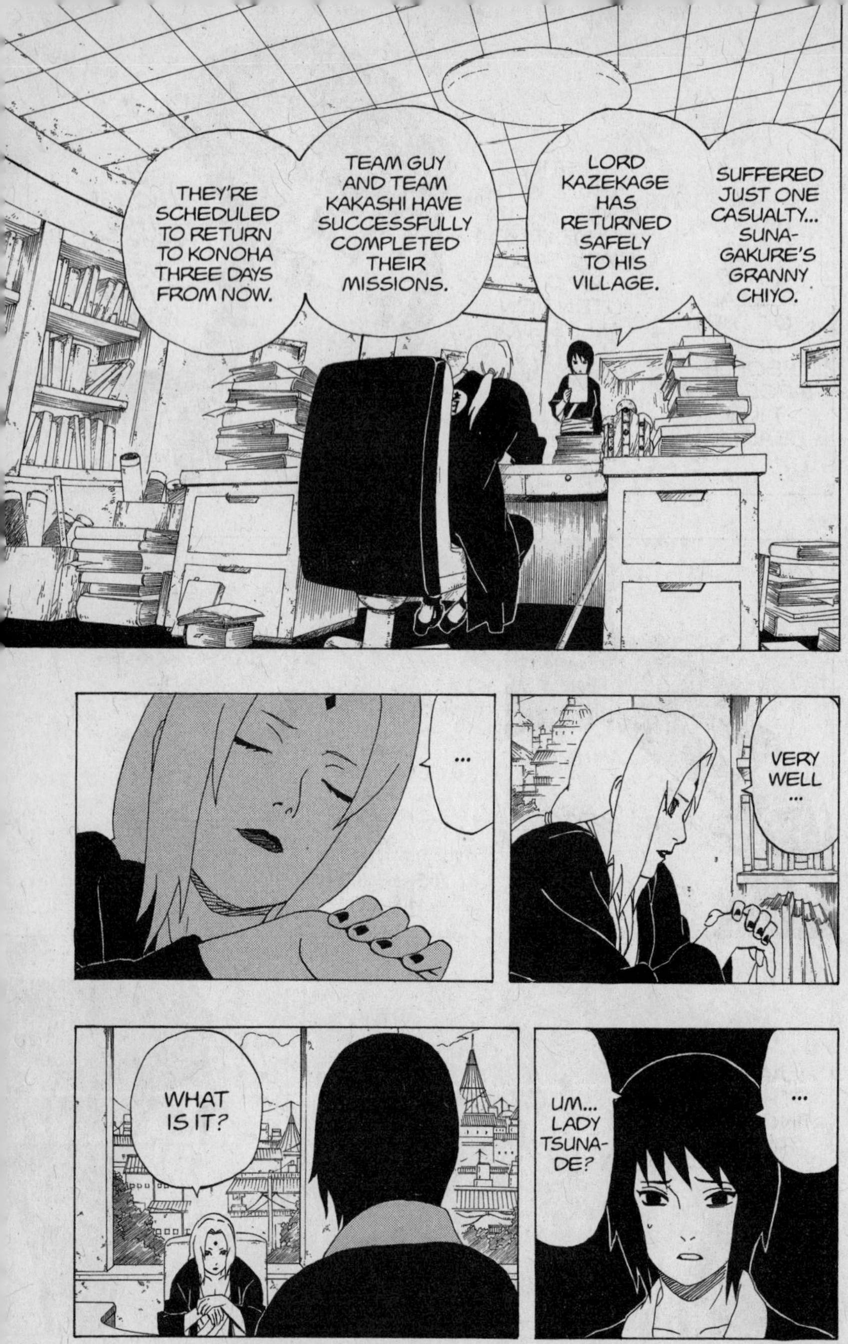
SUFFERED JUST ONE CASUALTY... SUNA-GAKURE'S GRANNY CHIYO.
LORD KAZEKAGE HAS RETURNED SAFELY TO HIS VILLAGE.
TEAM GUY AND TEAM KAKASHI HAVE SUCCESSFULLY COMPLETED THEIR MISSIONS.
THEY'RE SCHEDULED TO RETURN TO KONOHA THREE DAYS FROM NOW.
VERY WELL ...
...
...
UM... LADY TSUNA-DE?
WHAT IS IT?

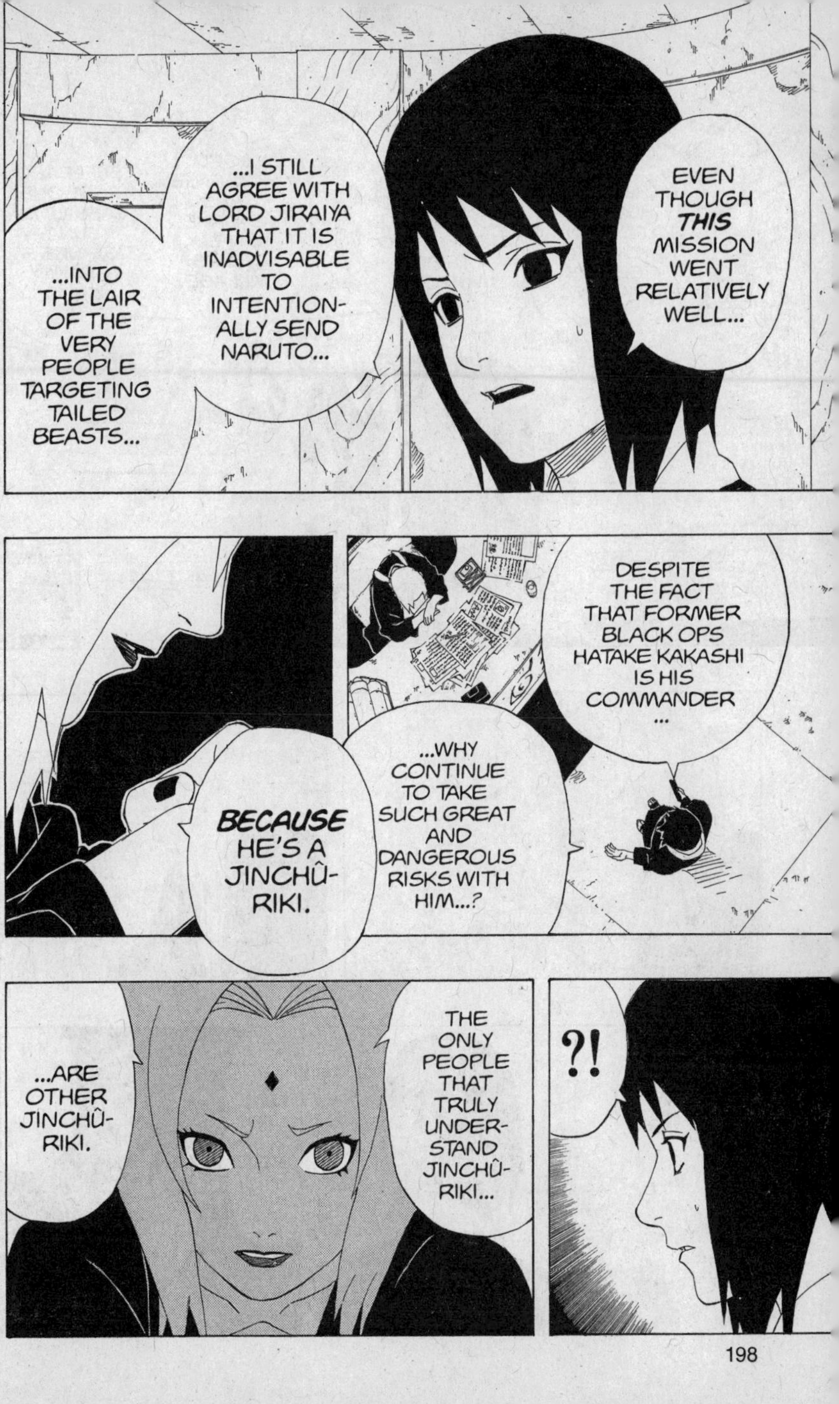
EVEN THOUGH ***THIS*** MISSION WENT RELATIVELY WELL...
...I STILL AGREE WITH LORD JIRAIYA THAT IT IS INADVISABLE TO INTENTION-ALLY SEND NARUTO...
...INTO THE LAIR OF THE VERY PEOPLE TARGETING TAILED BEASTS...
DESPITE THE FACT THAT FORMER BLACK OPS HATAKE KAKASHI IS HIS COMMANDER ...
...WHY CONTINUE TO TAKE SUCH GREAT AND DANGEROUS RISKS WITH HIM...?
BECAUSE HE'S A JINCHÛ-RIKI.
?!
THE ONLY PEOPLE THAT TRULY UNDER-STAND JINCHÛ-RIKI...
...ARE OTHER JINCHÛ-RIKI.

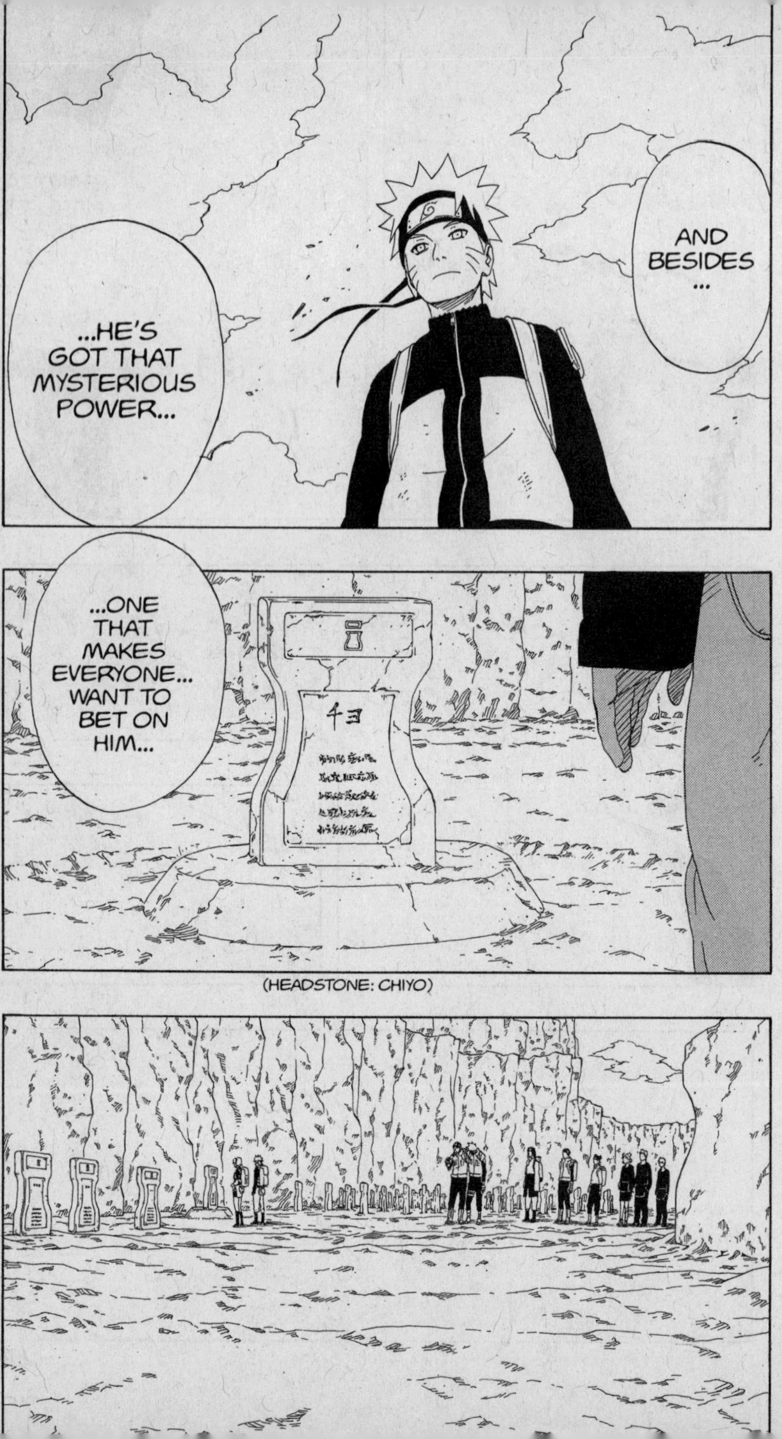
AND BESIDES ...
...HE'S GOT THAT MYSTERIOUS POWER...
...ONE THAT MAKES EVERYONE... WANT TO BET ON HIM...
(HEADSTONE: CHIYO)

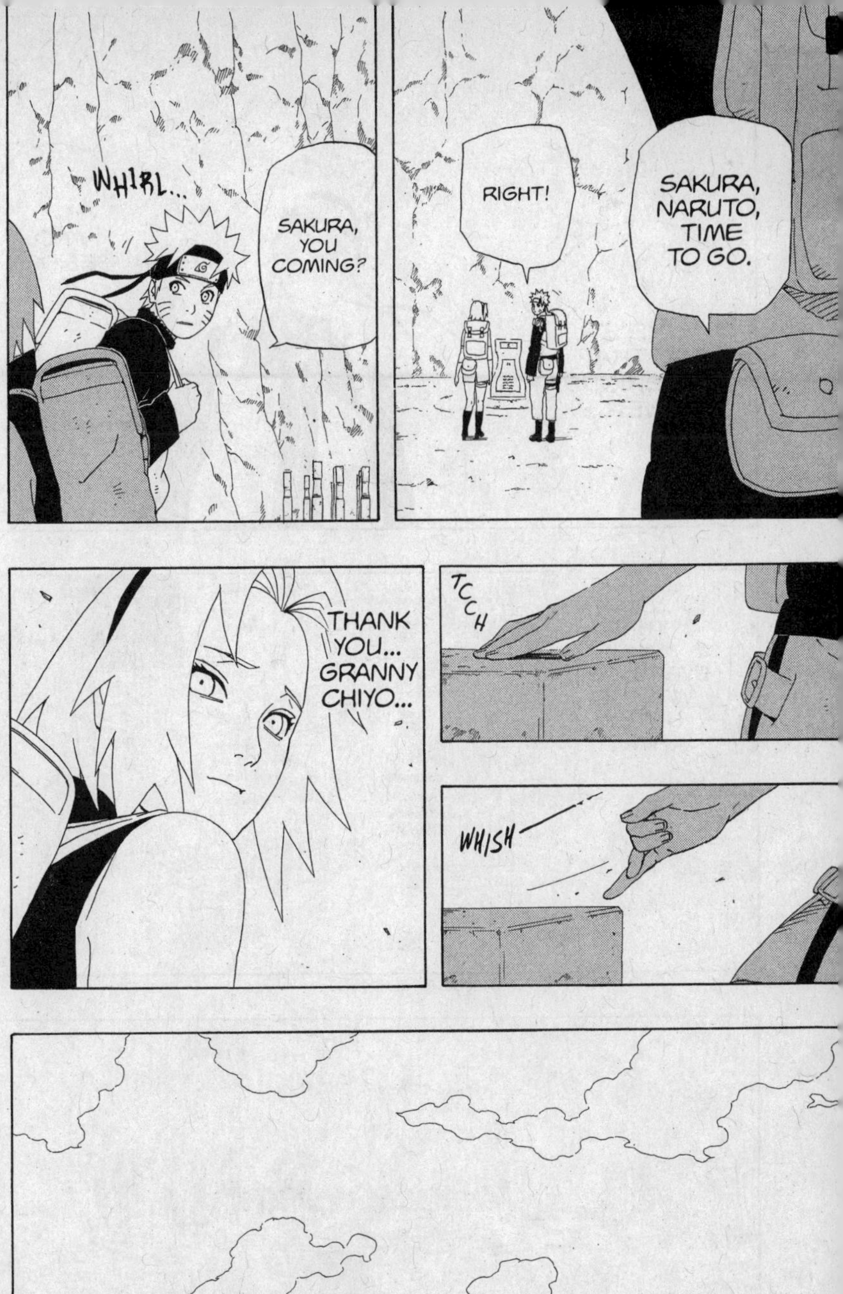
SAKURA, NARUTO, TIME TO GO.
RIGHT!
SAKURA, YOU COMING?
WHIRL...
TCCH
WHISH
THANK YOU... GRANNY CHIYO...

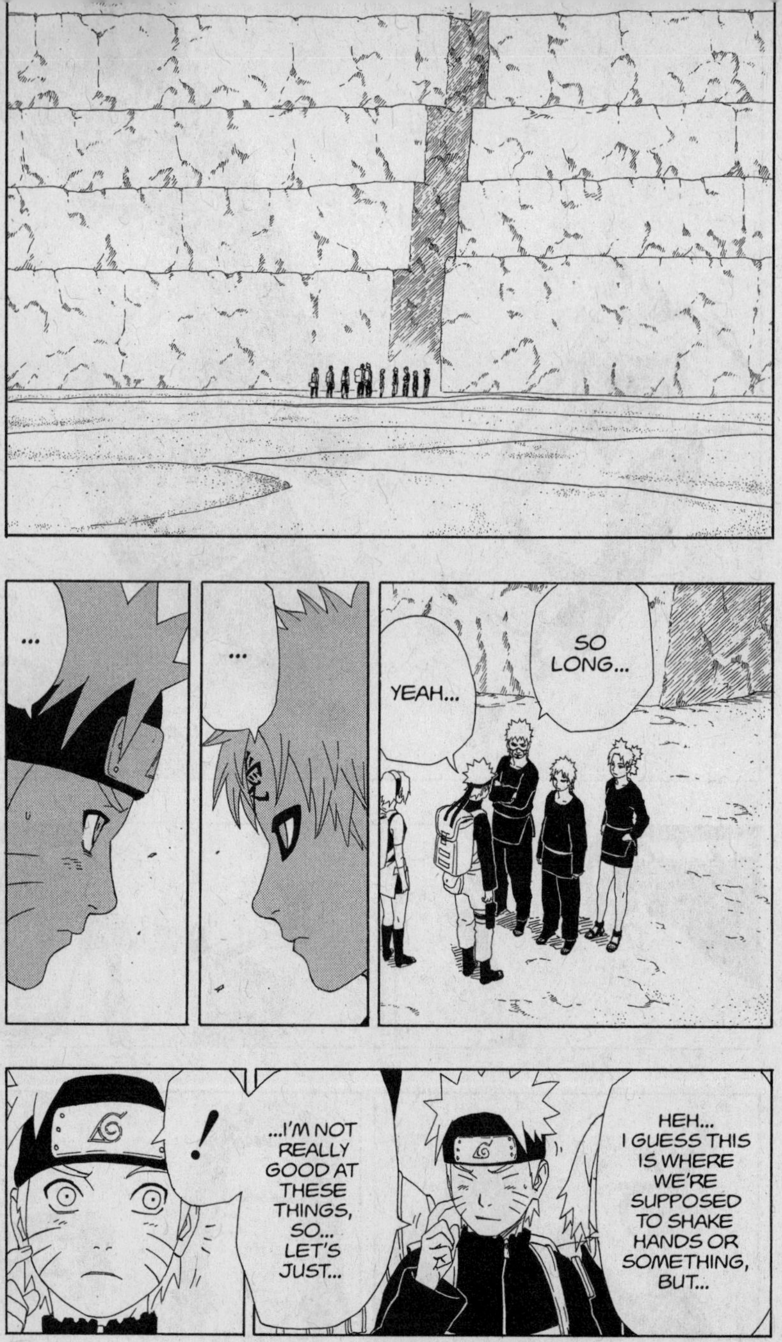
SO LONG...
YEAH...
...
...
HEH... I GUESS THIS IS WHERE WE'RE SUPPOSED TO SHAKE HANDS OR SOMETHING, BUT...
...I'M NOT REALLY GOOD AT THESE THINGS, SO... LET'S JUST...
!

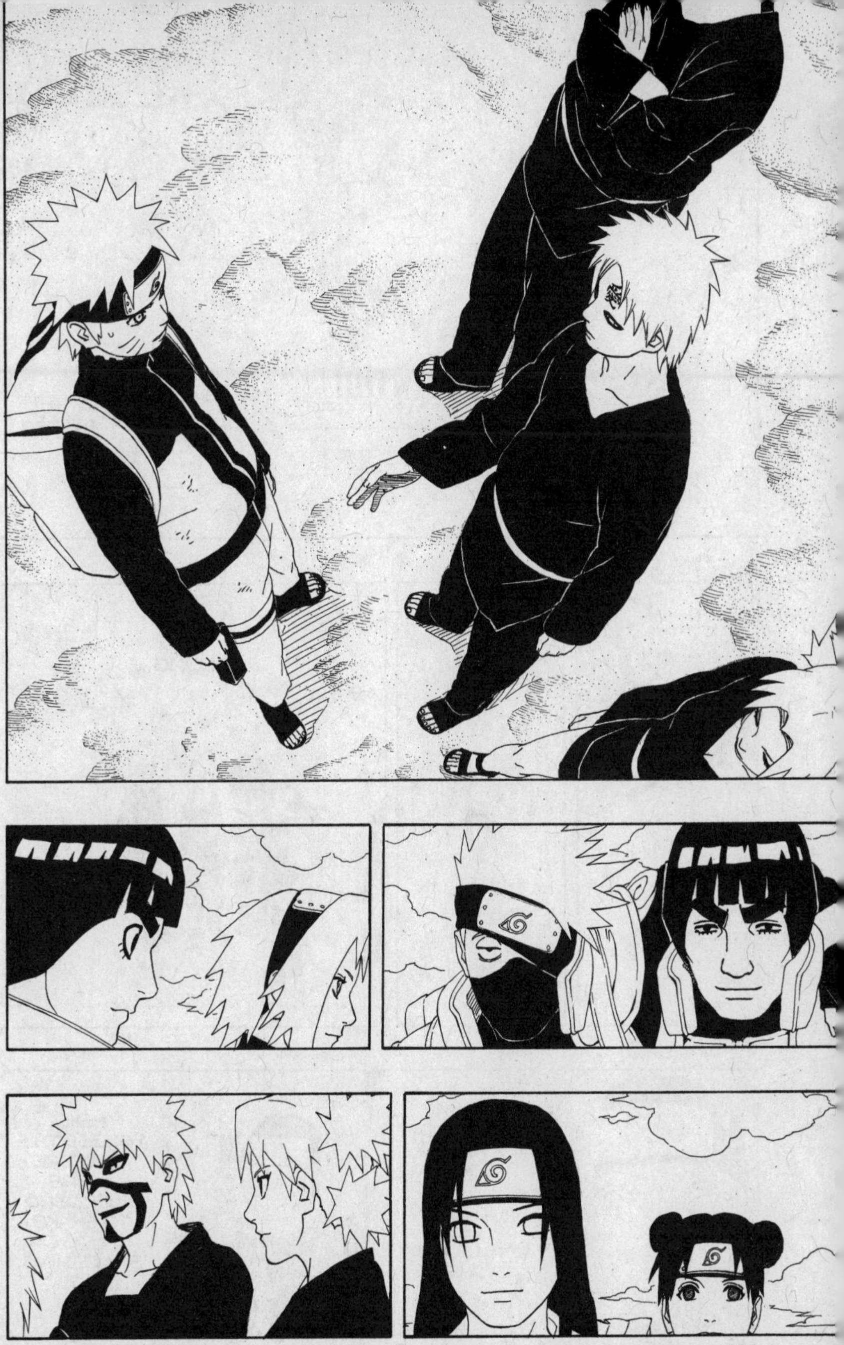

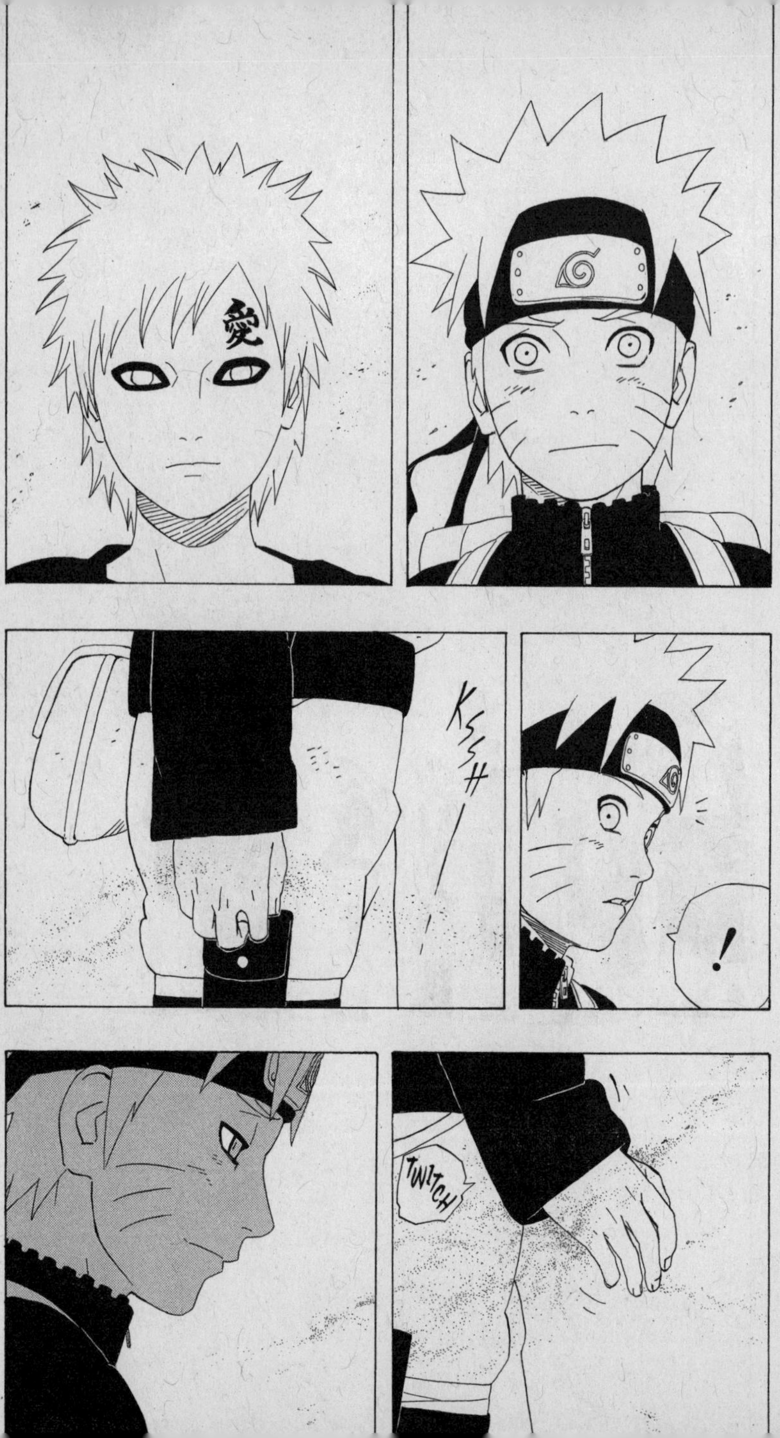
愛
!
KSSH
TWITCH

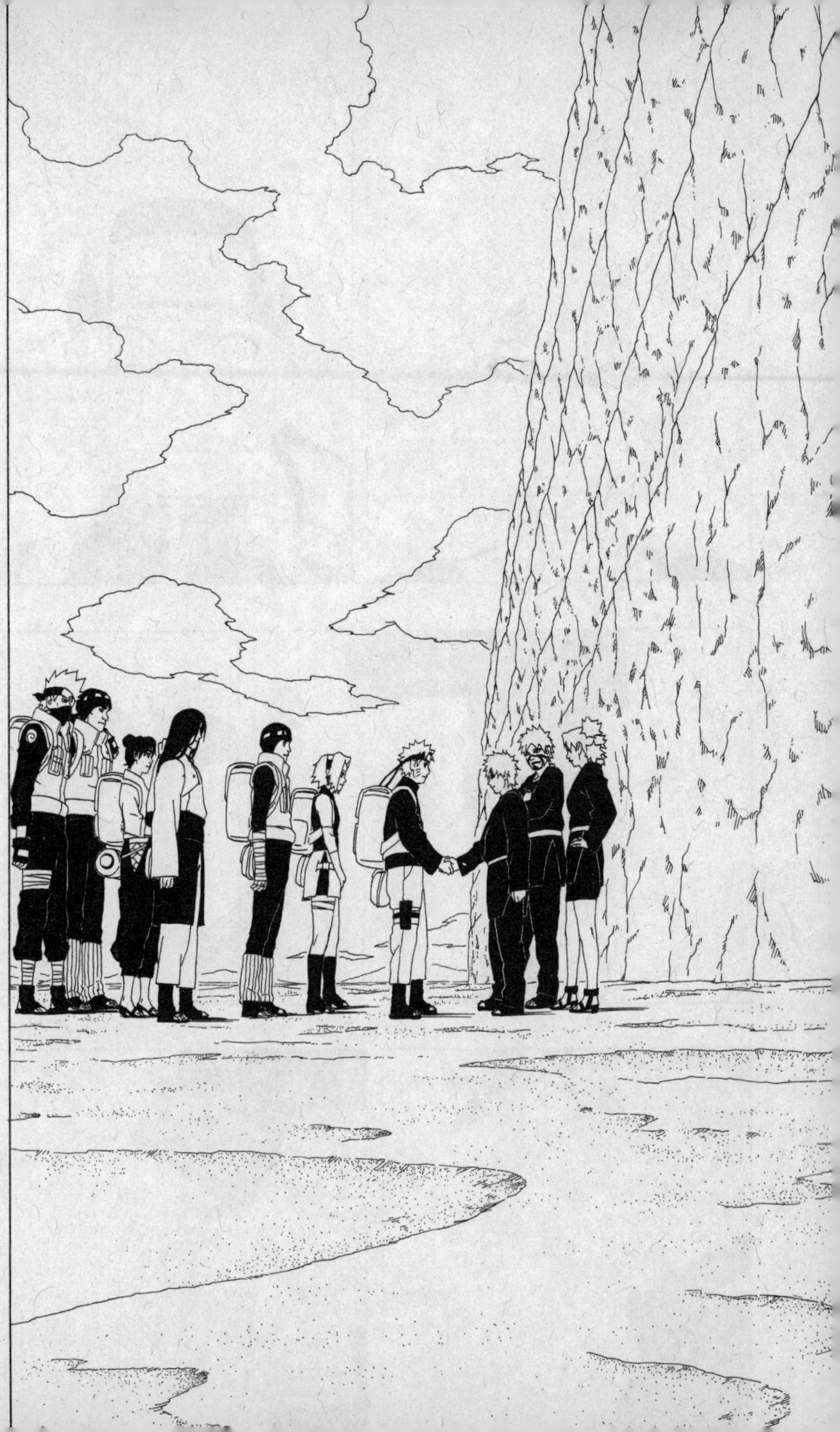

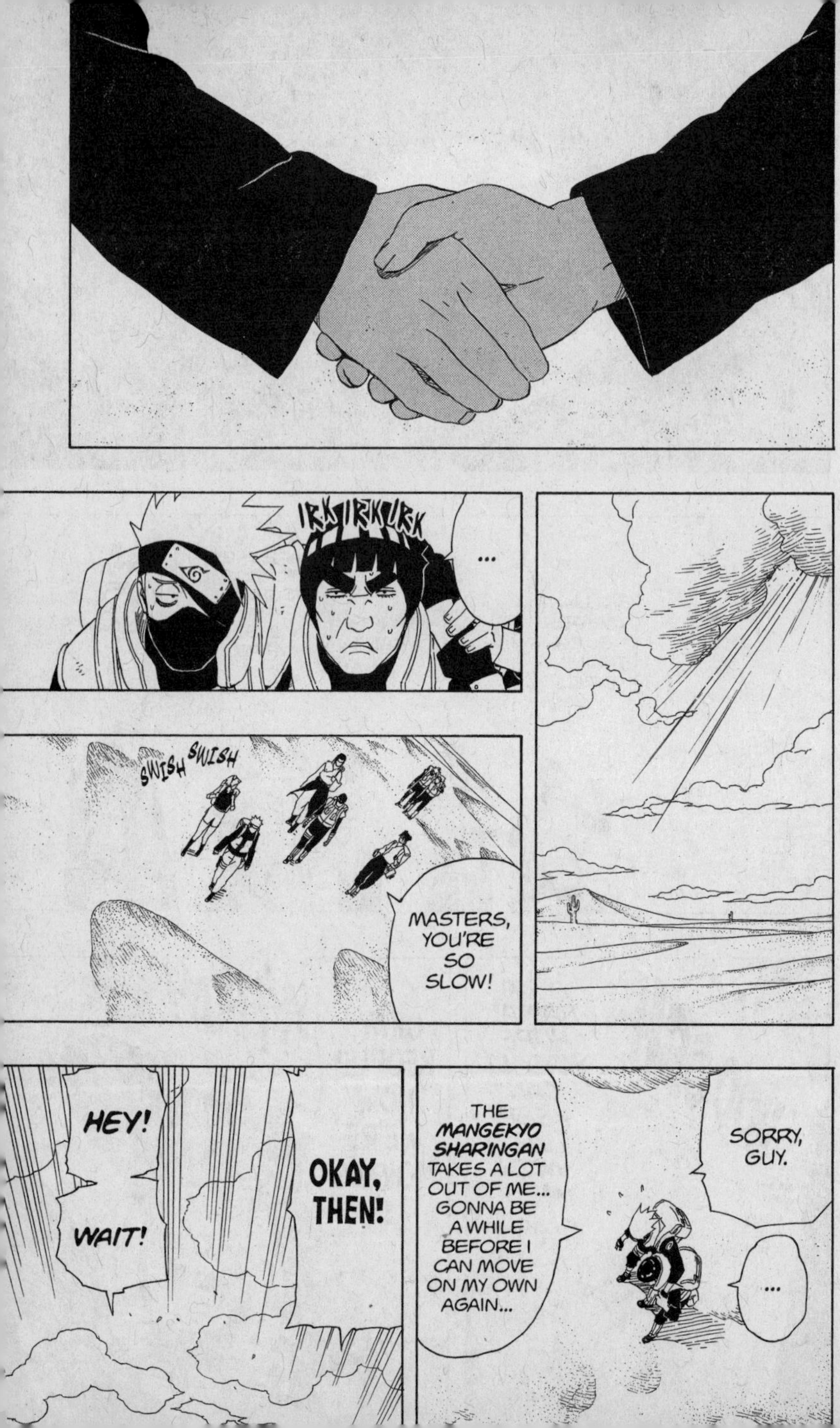
...
IRK IRK IRK
SWISH SWISH
MASTERS, YOU'RE SO SLOW!
SORRY, GUY.
THE *MANGEKYO SHARINGAN* TAKES A LOT OUT OF ME... GONNA BE A WHILE BEFORE I CAN MOVE ON MY OWN AGAIN...
...
OKAY, THEN!
HEY! WAIT!

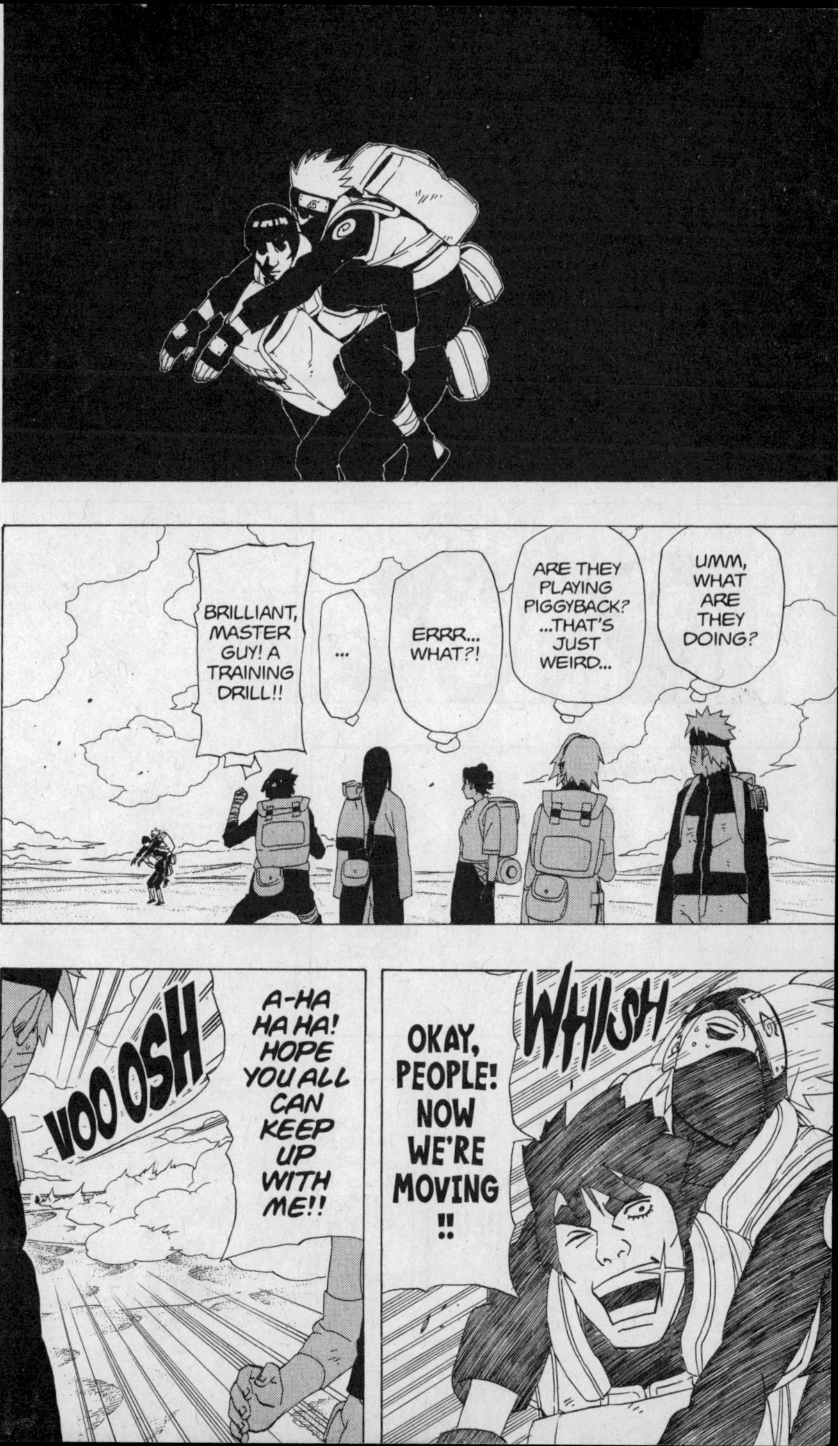
UMM, WHAT ARE THEY DOING?
ARE THEY PLAYING PIGGYBACK? ...THAT'S JUST WEIRD...
ERRR... WHAT?!
...
BRILLIANT, MASTER GUY! A TRAINING DRILL!!
WHISH
OKAY, PEOPLE! NOW WE'RE MOVING!!
A-HA HA HA! HOPE YOU ALL CAN KEEP UP WITH ME!!
VOOOSH

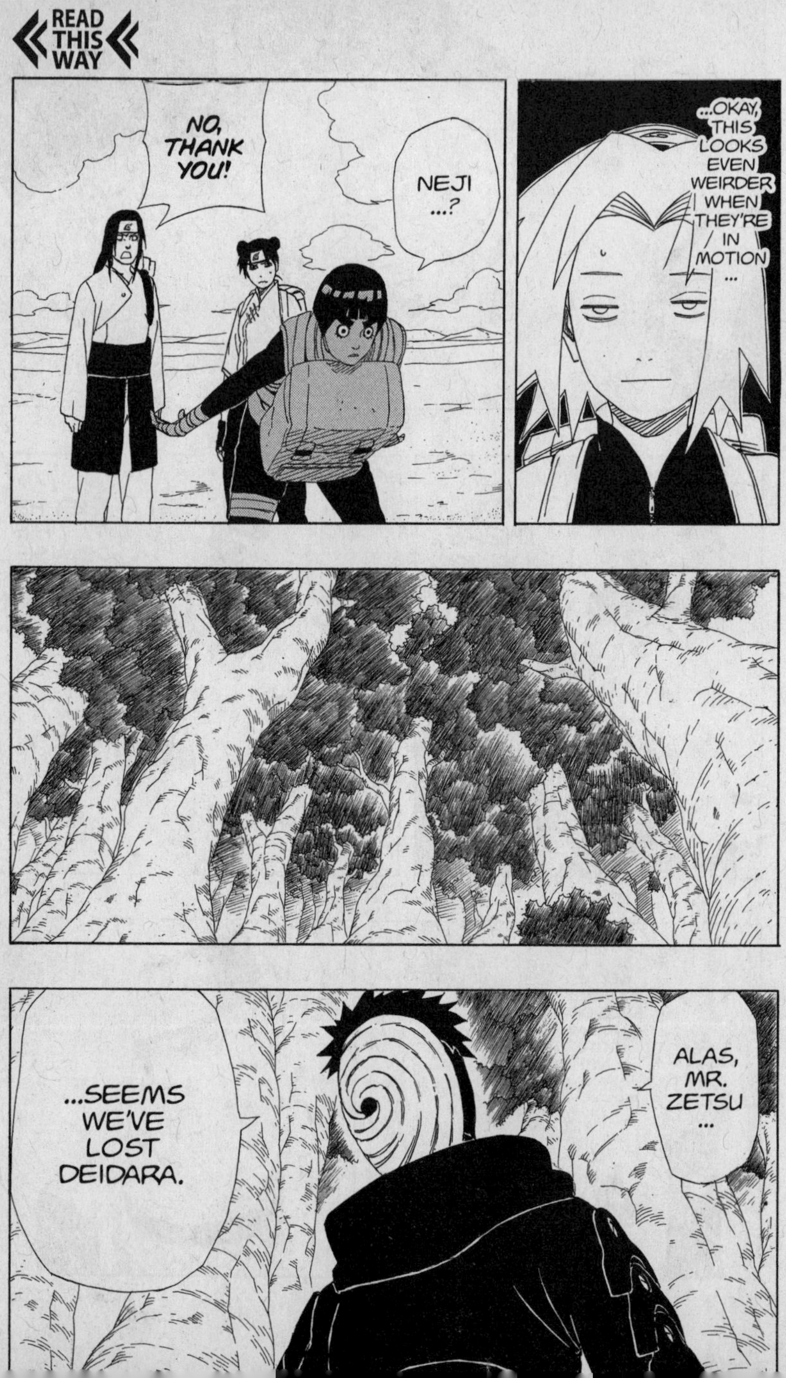
READ THIS WAY
...OKAY, THIS LOOKS EVEN WEIRDER WHEN THEY'RE IN MOTION...
NEJI...?
NO, THANK YOU!
ALAS, MR. ZETSU...
...SEEMS WE'VE LOST DEIDARA.

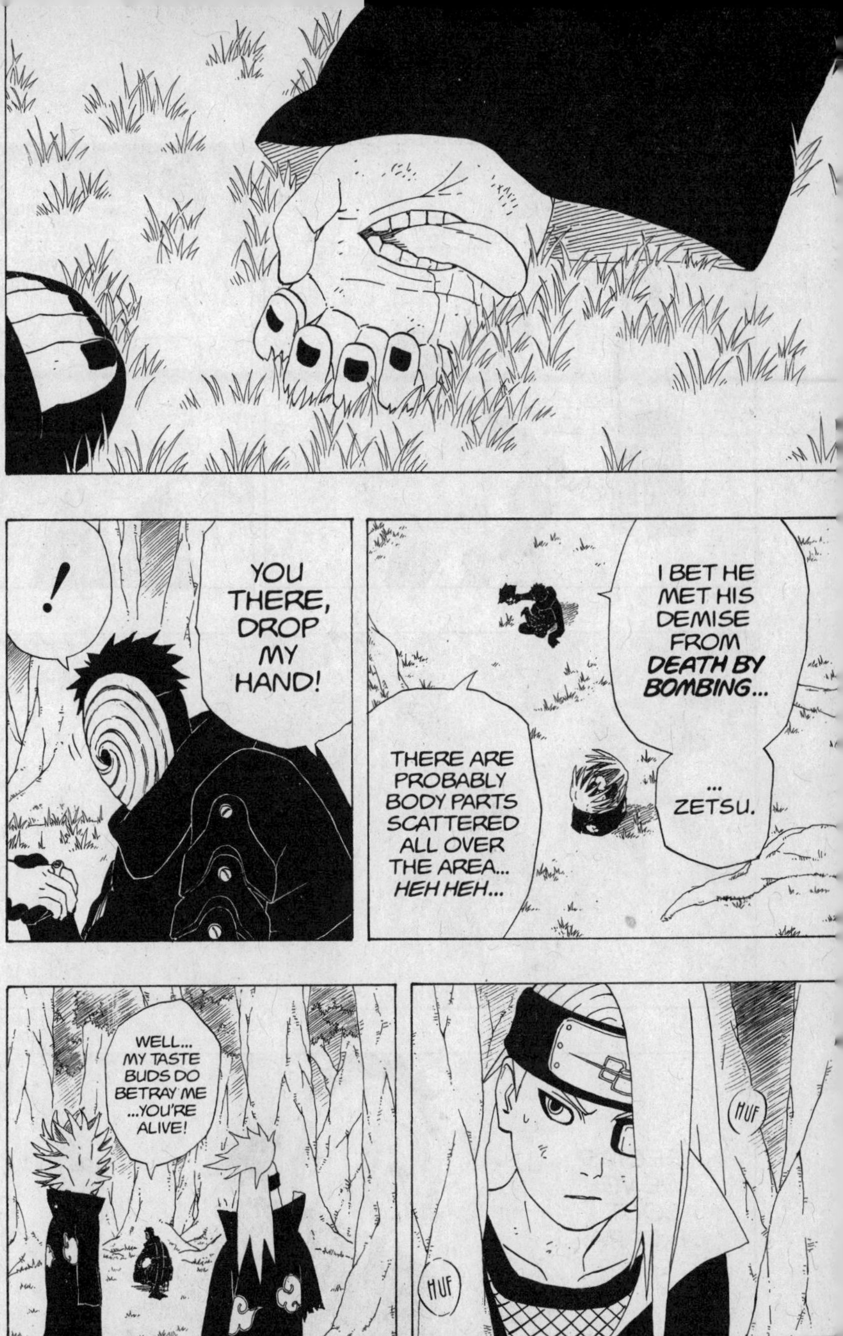

I BET HE MET HIS DEMISE FROM *DEATH BY BOMBING*...
... ZETSU.
THERE ARE PROBABLY BODY PARTS SCATTERED ALL OVER THE AREA... *HEH HEH*...
YOU THERE, DROP MY HAND!
!
HUF
HUF
WELL... MY TASTE BUDS DO BETRAY ME ...YOU'RE ALIVE!

READ THIS WAY

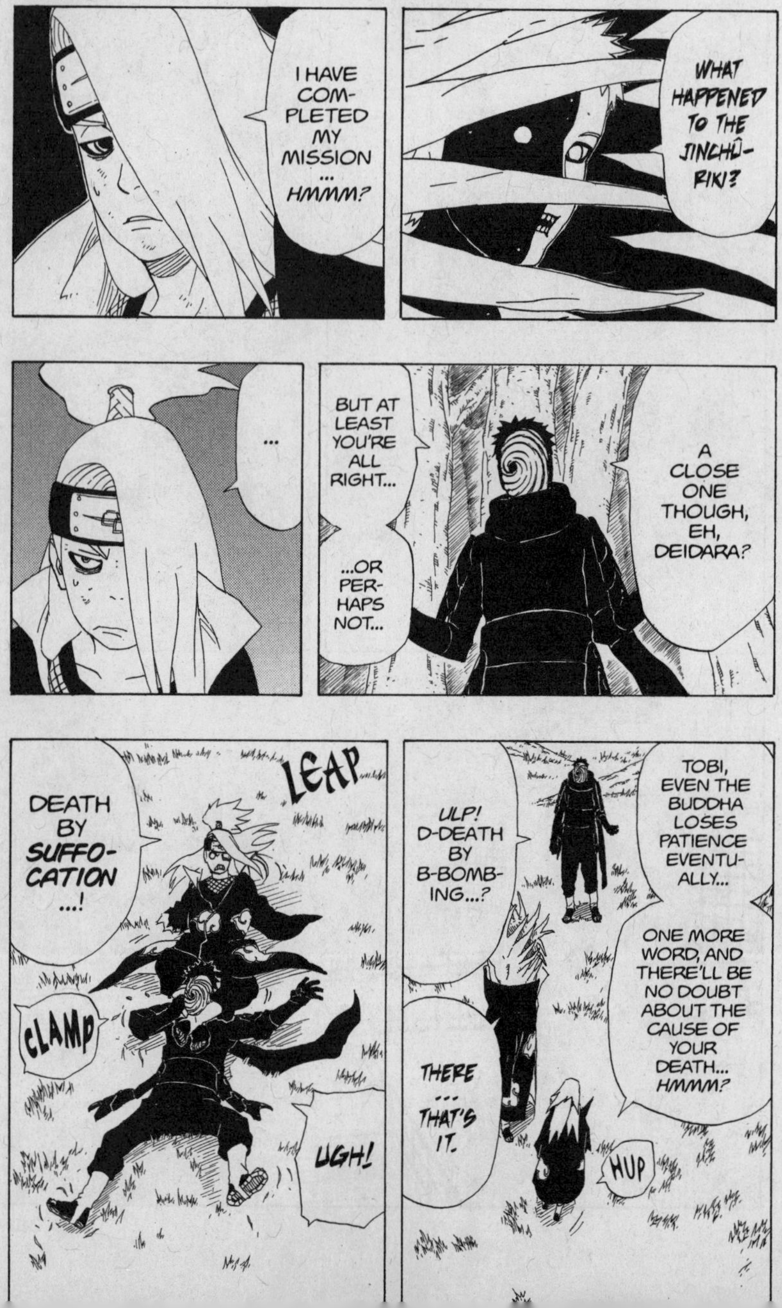
WHAT HAPPENED TO THE JINCHŪ-RIKI?
I HAVE COM-PLETED MY MISSION ... HMMM?
A CLOSE ONE THOUGH, EH, DEIDARA?
BUT AT LEAST YOU'RE ALL RIGHT...
...OR PER-HAPS NOT...
...
TOBI, EVEN THE BUDDHA LOSES PATIENCE EVENTU-ALLY...
ULP! D-DEATH BY B-BOMB-ING...?
ONE MORE WORD, AND THERE'LL BE NO DOUBT ABOUT THE CAUSE OF YOUR DEATH... HMMM?
THERE ... THAT'S IT.
HUP
LEAP
DEATH BY SUFFO-CATION ...!
CLAMP
UGH!

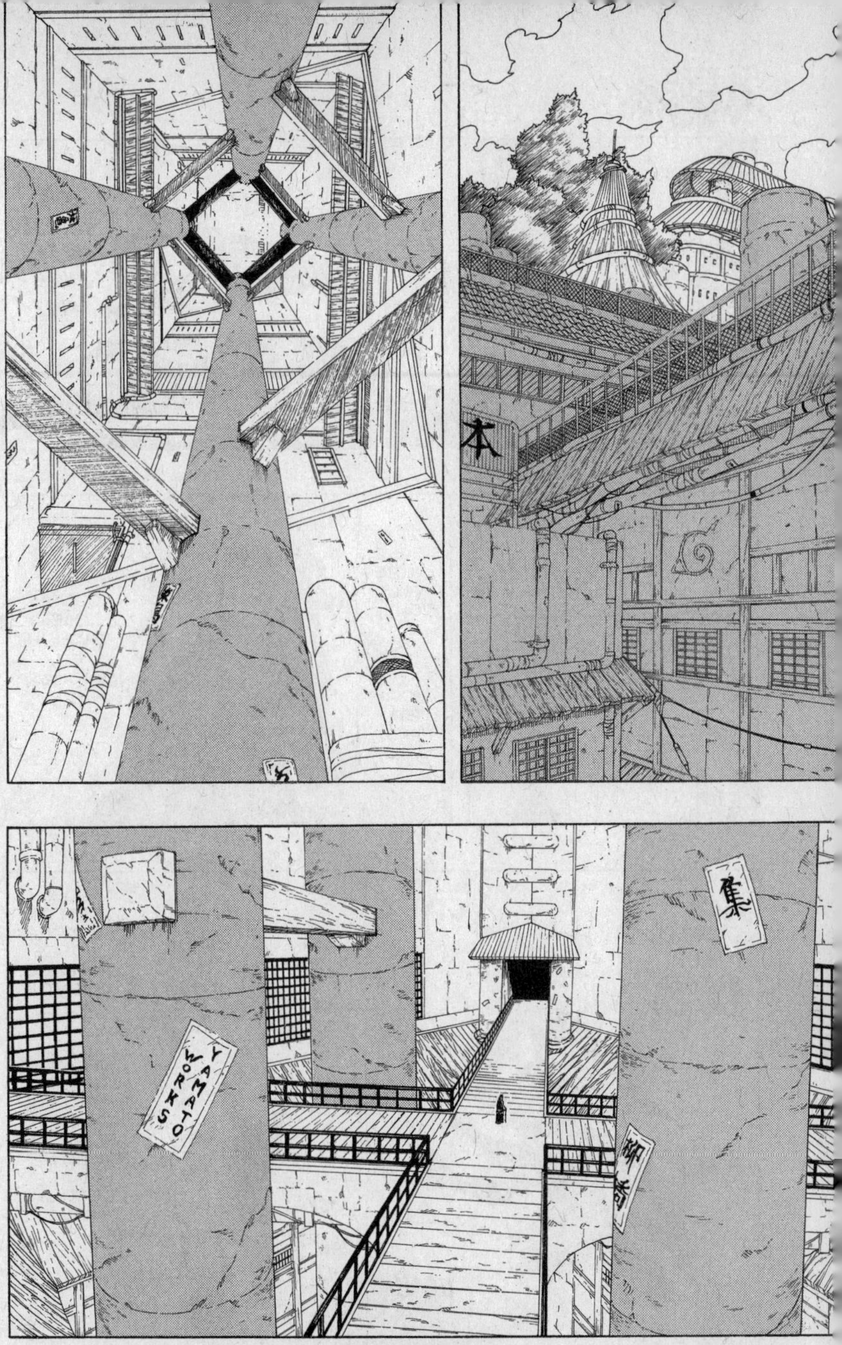
本
集
YAMATO WORKS

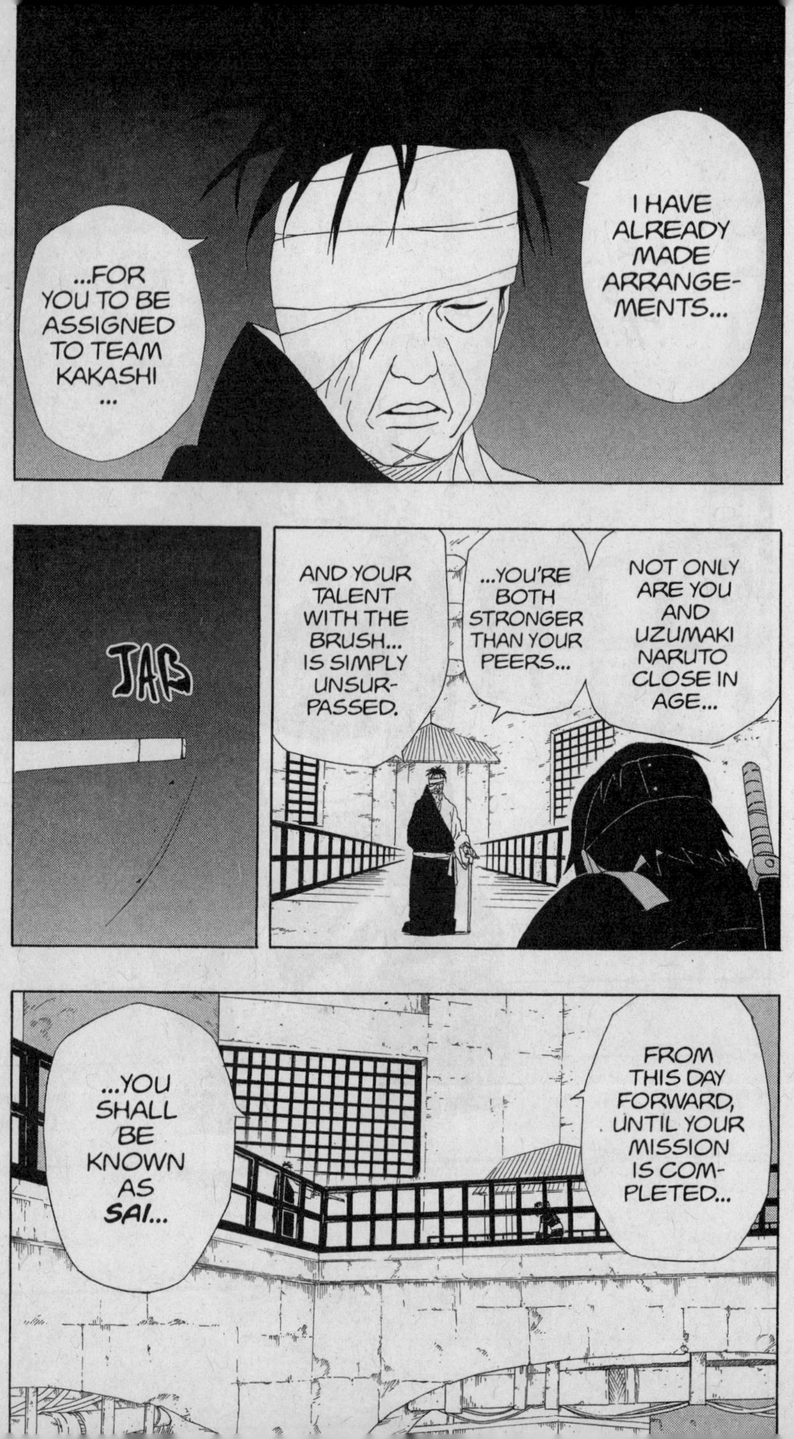
I HAVE ALREADY MADE ARRANGEMENTS...
...FOR YOU TO BE ASSIGNED TO TEAM KAKASHI ...
NOT ONLY ARE YOU AND UZUMAKI NARUTO CLOSE IN AGE...
...YOU'RE BOTH STRONGER THAN YOUR PEERS...
AND YOUR TALENT WITH THE BRUSH... IS SIMPLY UNSURPASSED.
JAB
FROM THIS DAY FORWARD, UNTIL YOUR MISSION IS COMPLETED...
...YOU SHALL BE KNOWN AS SAI...

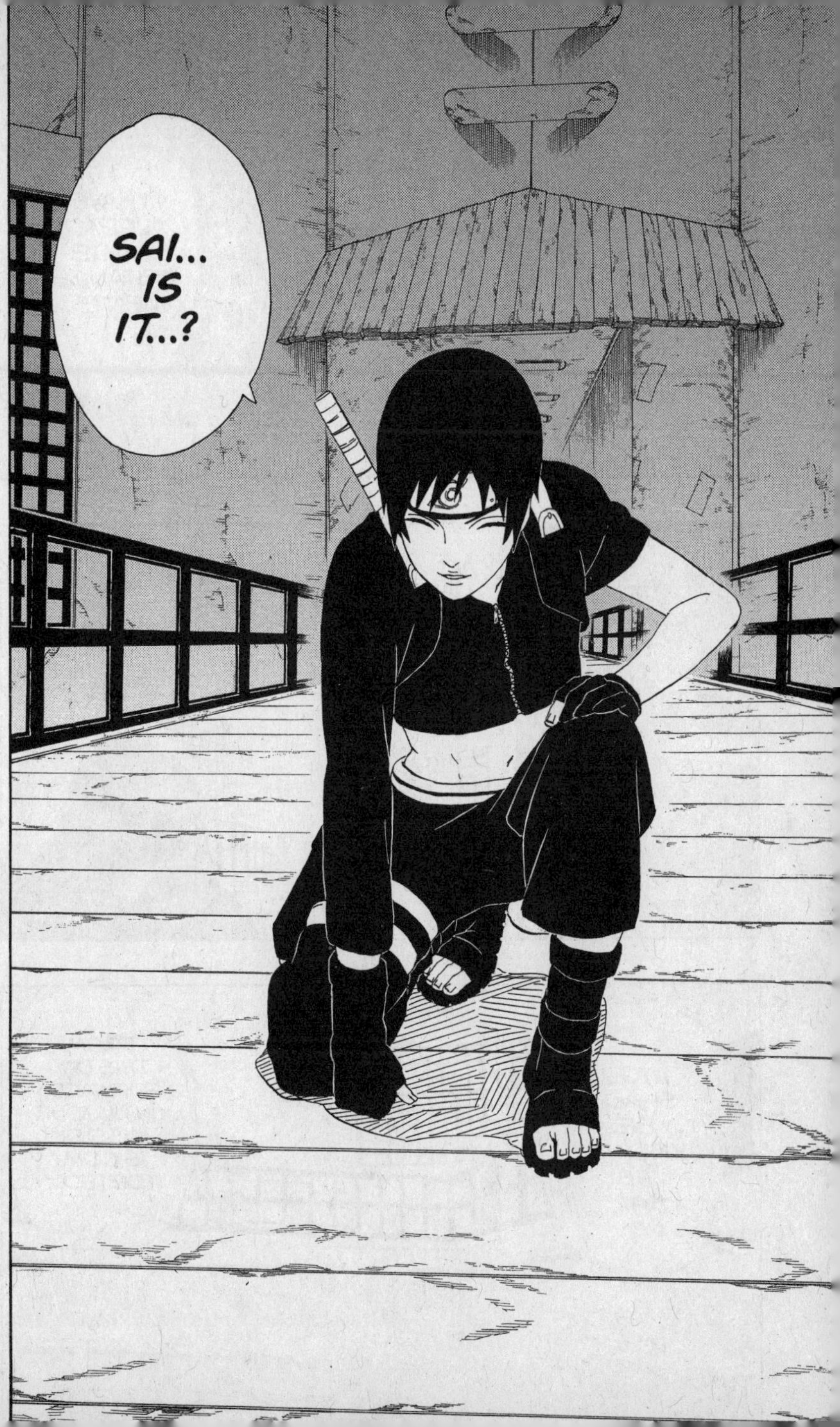
SAI... IS IT...?

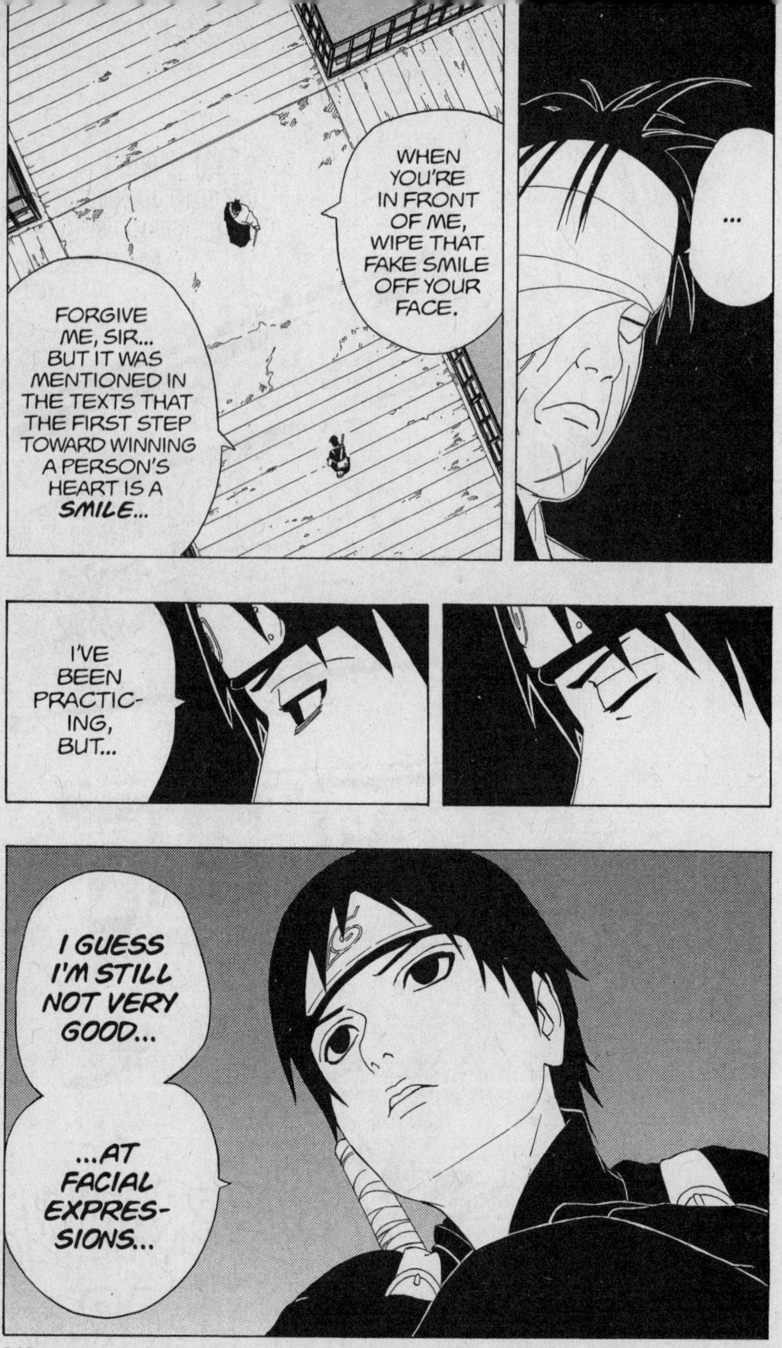
...
WHEN YOU'RE IN FRONT OF ME, WIPE THAT FAKE SMILE OFF YOUR FACE.
FORGIVE ME, SIR... BUT IT WAS MENTIONED IN THE TEXTS THAT THE FIRST STEP TOWARD WINNING A PERSON'S HEART IS A *SMILE*...
I'VE BEEN PRACTIC- ING, BUT...
I GUESS I'M STILL NOT VERY GOOD...
...AT FACIAL EXPRES- SIONS...

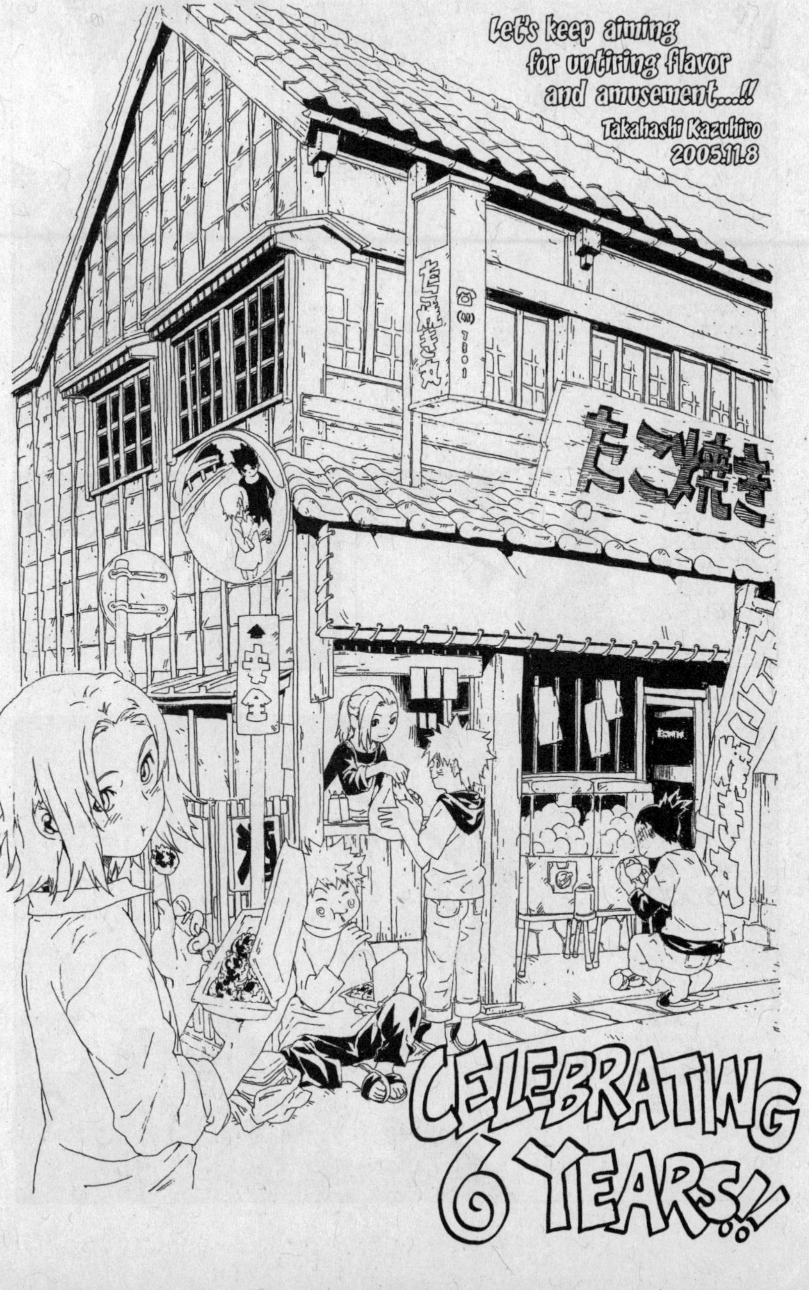
Let's keep aiming
for untiring flavor
and amusement...!!
Takahashi Kazuhiro
2005.11.8
たこ焼き
CELEBRATING
6 YEARS!!

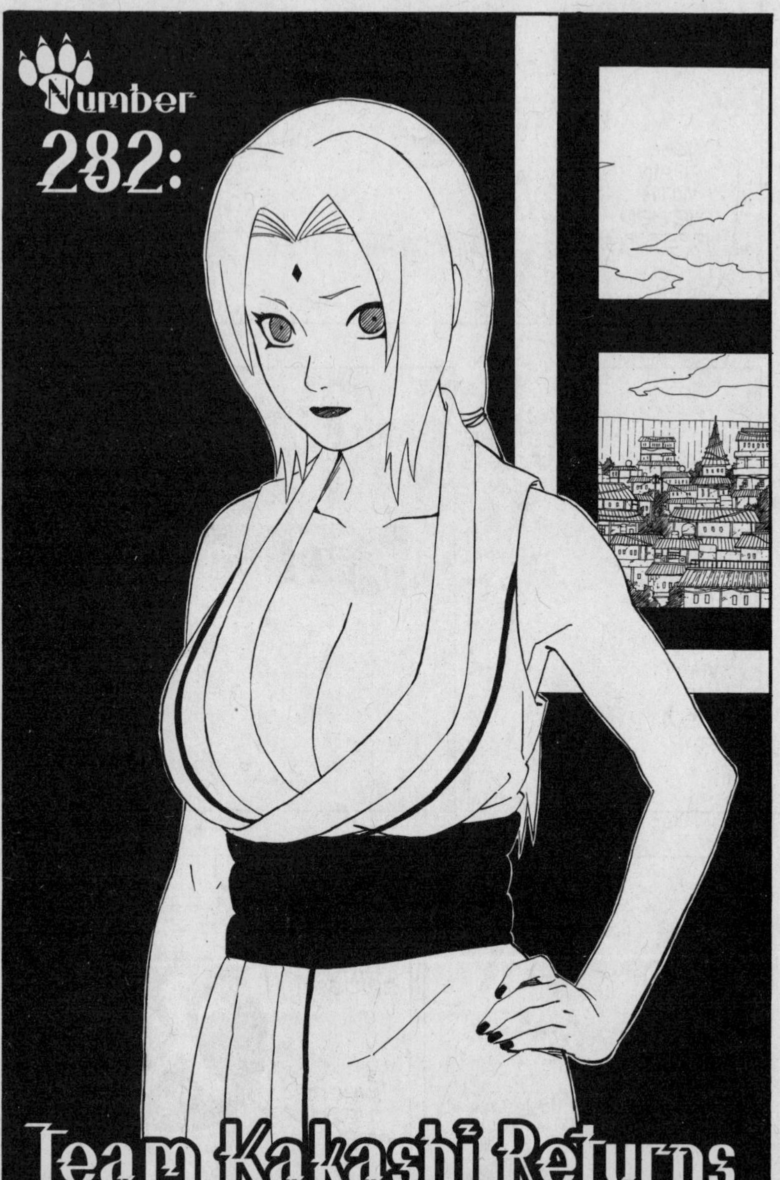
Number 282:
Team Kakashi Returns

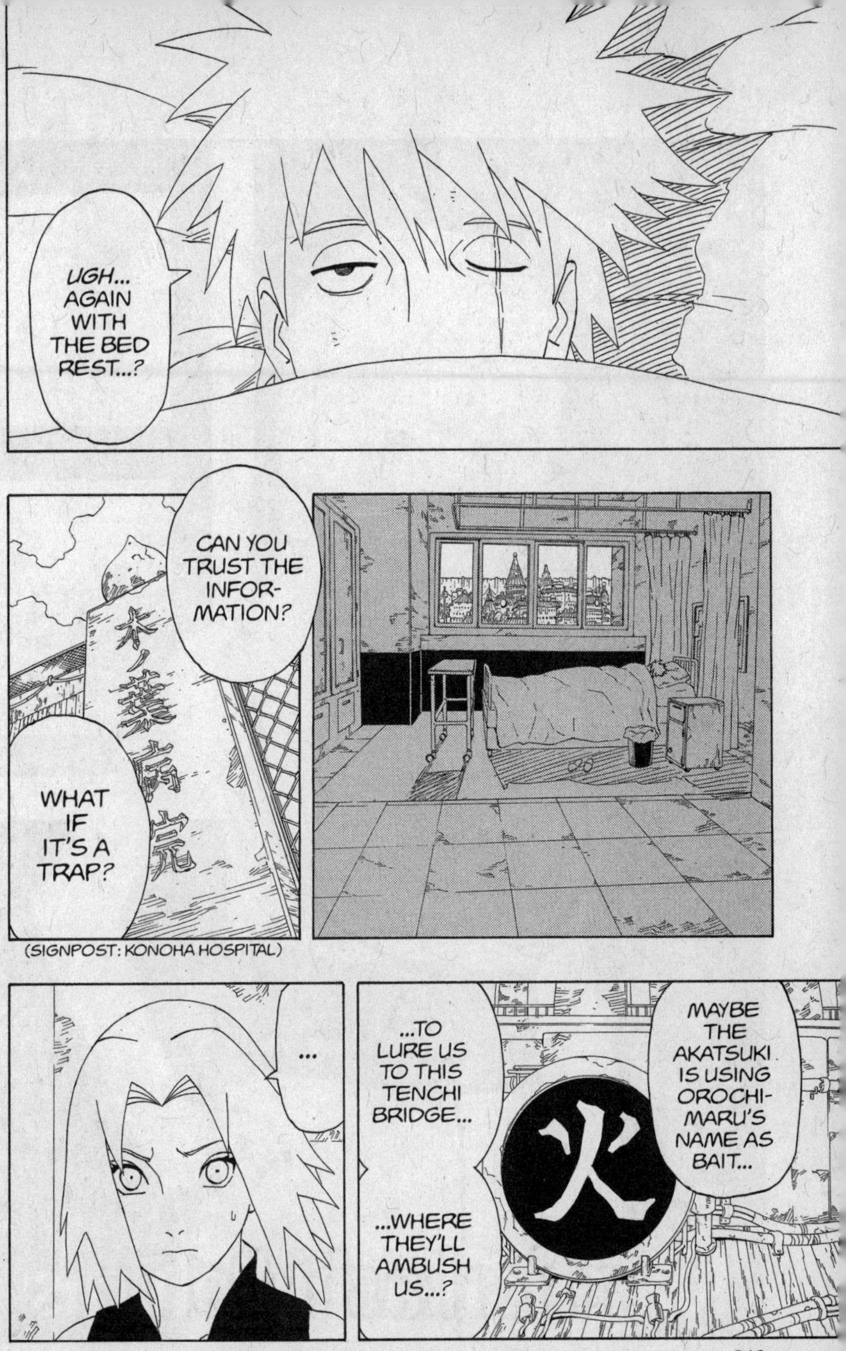
UGH... AGAIN WITH THE BED REST...?
CAN YOU TRUST THE INFORMATION?
WHAT IF IT'S A TRAP?
(SIGNPOST: KONOHA HOSPITAL)
MAYBE THE AKATSUKI IS USING OROCHIMARU'S NAME AS BAIT...
...TO LURE US TO THIS TENCHI BRIDGE...
...WHERE THEY'LL AMBUSH US...?
...

READ THIS WAY

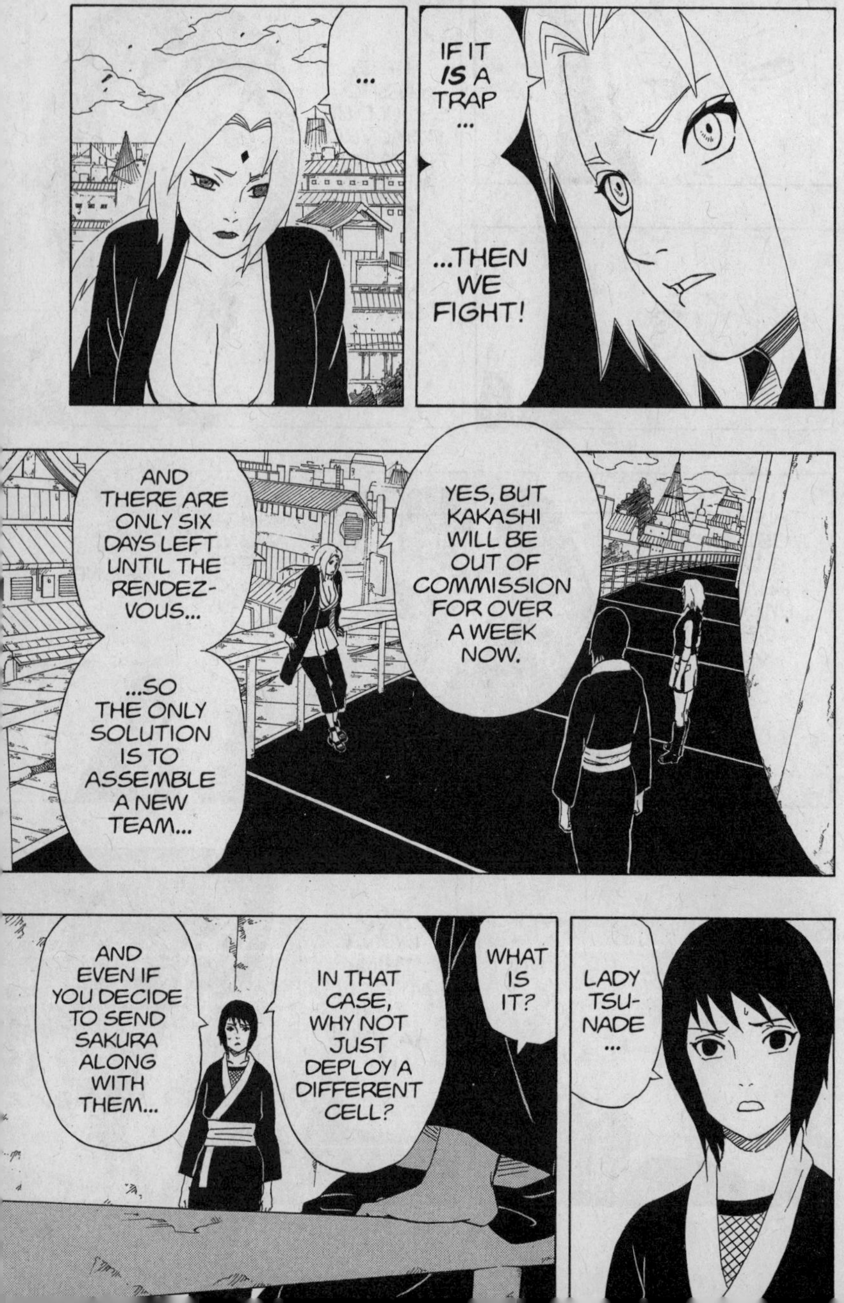
IF IT *IS* A TRAP ...
...THEN WE FIGHT!
...
YES, BUT KAKASHI WILL BE OUT OF COMMISSION FOR OVER A WEEK NOW.
AND THERE ARE ONLY SIX DAYS LEFT UNTIL THE RENDEZ-VOUS...
...SO THE ONLY SOLUTION IS TO ASSEMBLE A NEW TEAM...
LADY TSU-NADE ...
WHAT IS IT?
IN THAT CASE, WHY NOT JUST DEPLOY A DIFFERENT CELL?
AND EVEN IF YOU DECIDE TO SEND SAKURA ALONG WITH THEM...

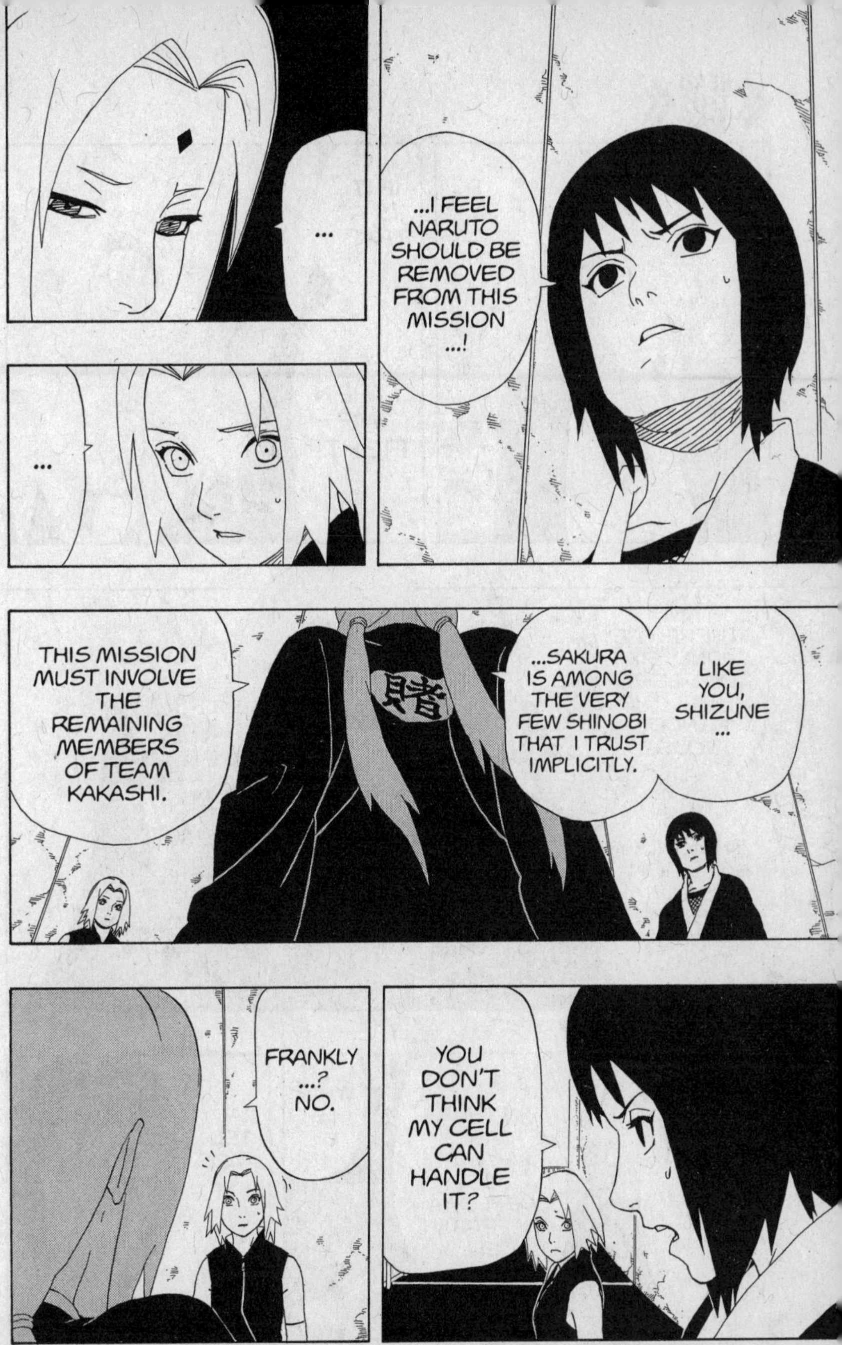
...I FEEL NARUTO SHOULD BE REMOVED FROM THIS MISSION ...!
...
...
...SAKURA IS AMONG THE VERY FEW SHINOBI THAT I TRUST IMPLICITLY.
LIKE YOU, SHIZUNE ...
THIS MISSION MUST INVOLVE THE REMAINING MEMBERS OF TEAM KAKASHI.
YOU DON'T THINK MY CELL CAN HANDLE IT?
FRANKLY ...? NO.

READ THIS WAY

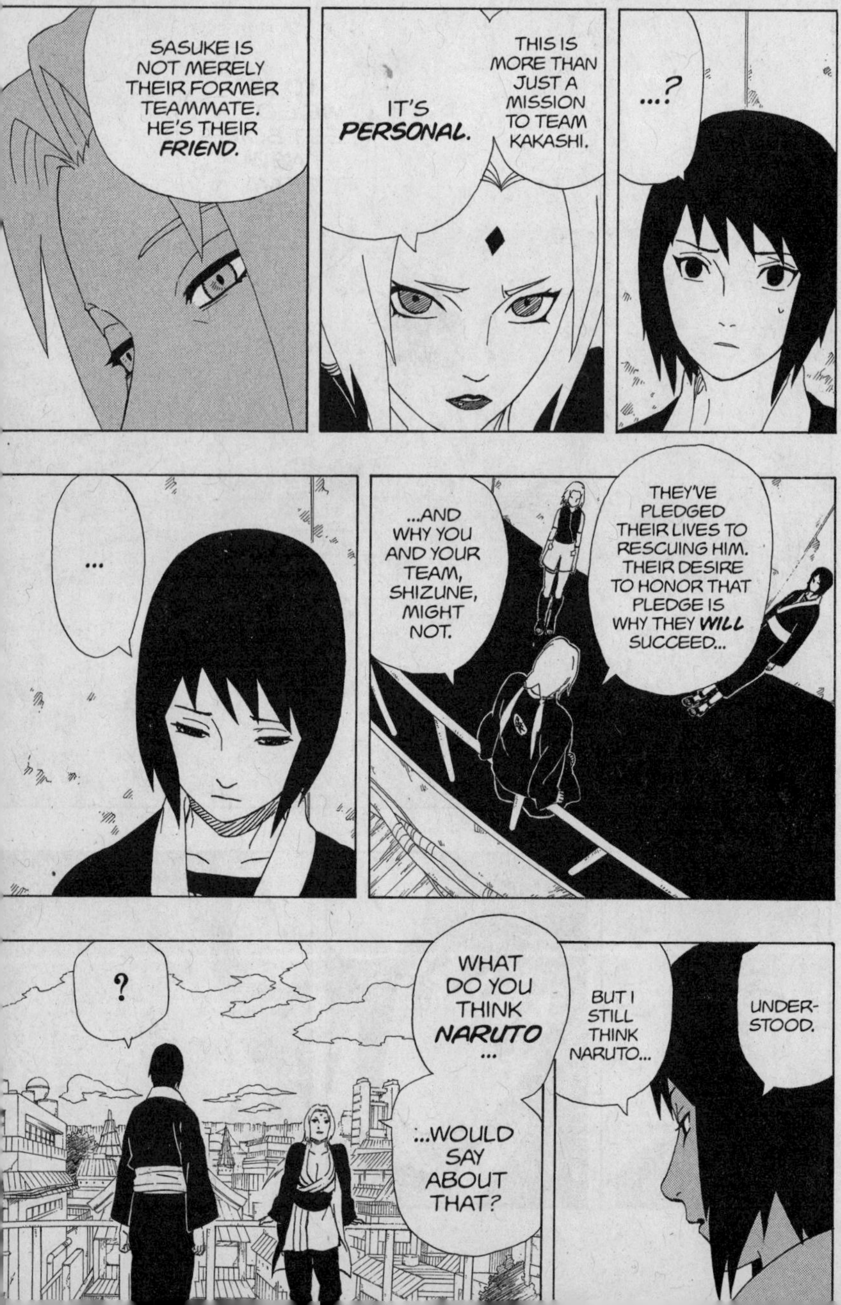
...?
THIS IS MORE THAN JUST A MISSION TO TEAM KAKASHI.
IT'S *PERSONAL.*
SASUKE IS NOT MERELY THEIR FORMER TEAMMATE. HE'S THEIR *FRIEND.*
THEY'VE PLEDGED THEIR LIVES TO RESCUING HIM. THEIR DESIRE TO HONOR THAT PLEDGE IS WHY THEY *WILL* SUCCEED...
...AND WHY YOU AND YOUR TEAM, SHIZUNE, MIGHT NOT.
...
UNDER-STOOD.
BUT I STILL THINK NARUTO...
WHAT DO YOU THINK *NARUTO* ...
...WOULD SAY ABOUT THAT?
?

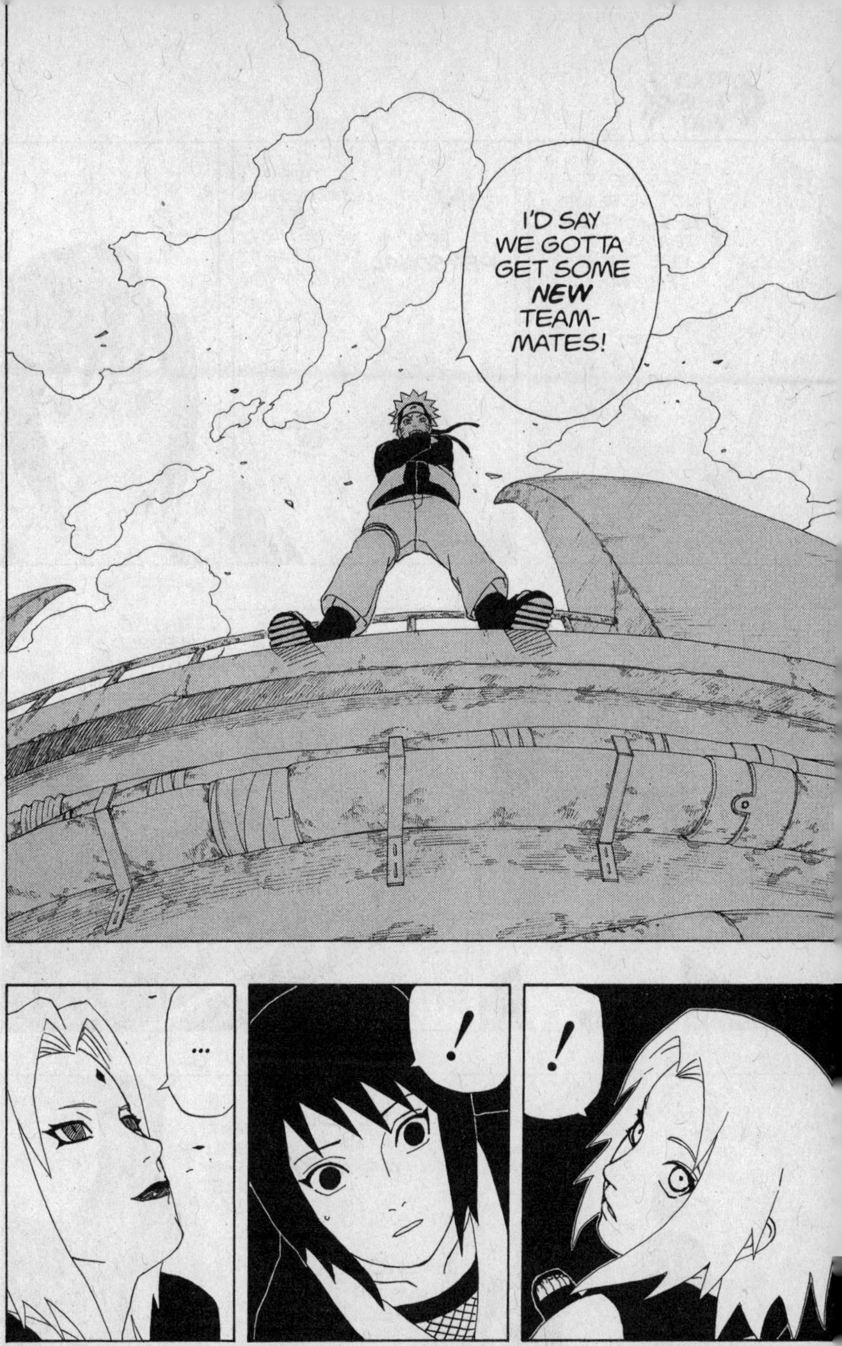
I'D SAY WE GOTTA GET SOME NEW TEAM-MATES!
!
!
...

READ THIS WAY

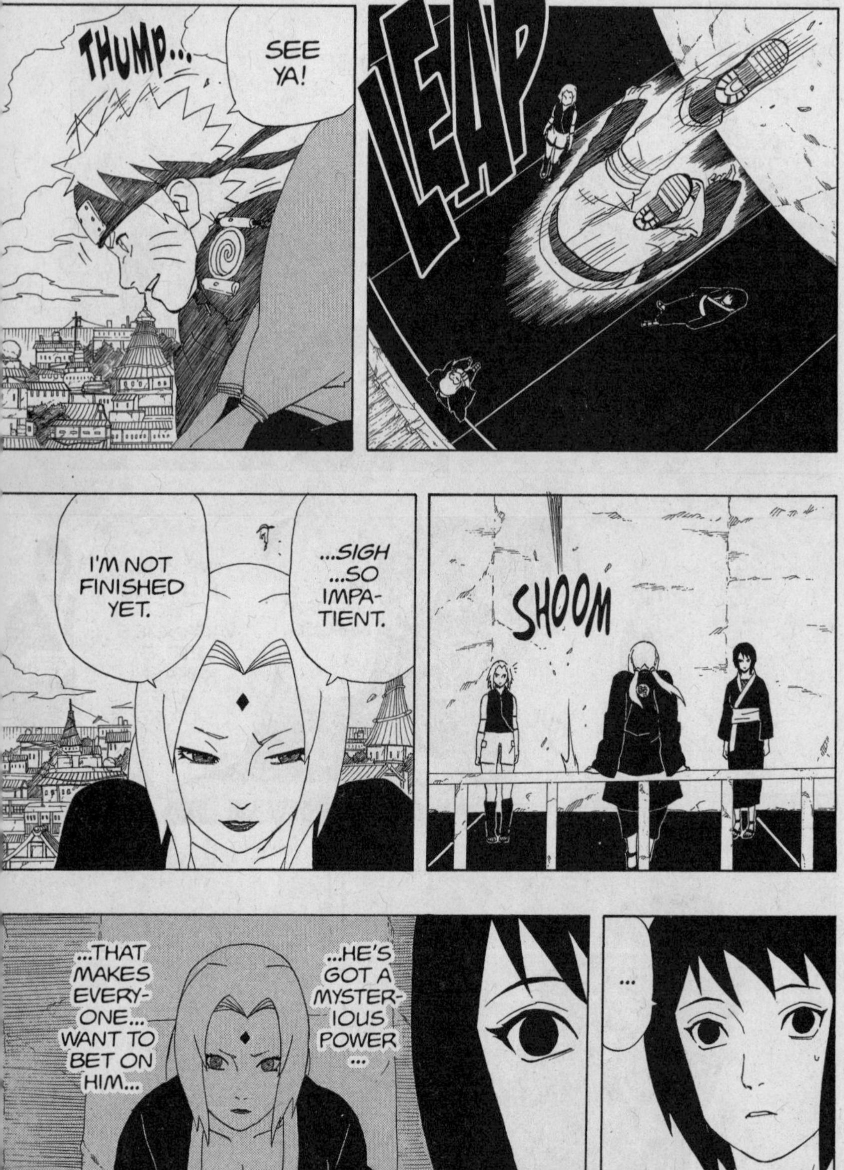

LEAP
THUMP...
SEE YA!
SHOOM
...SIGH ...SO IMPATIENT.
I'M NOT FINISHED YET.
...
...HE'S GOT A MYSTERIOUS POWER...
...THAT MAKES EVERYONE... WANT TO BET ON HIM...

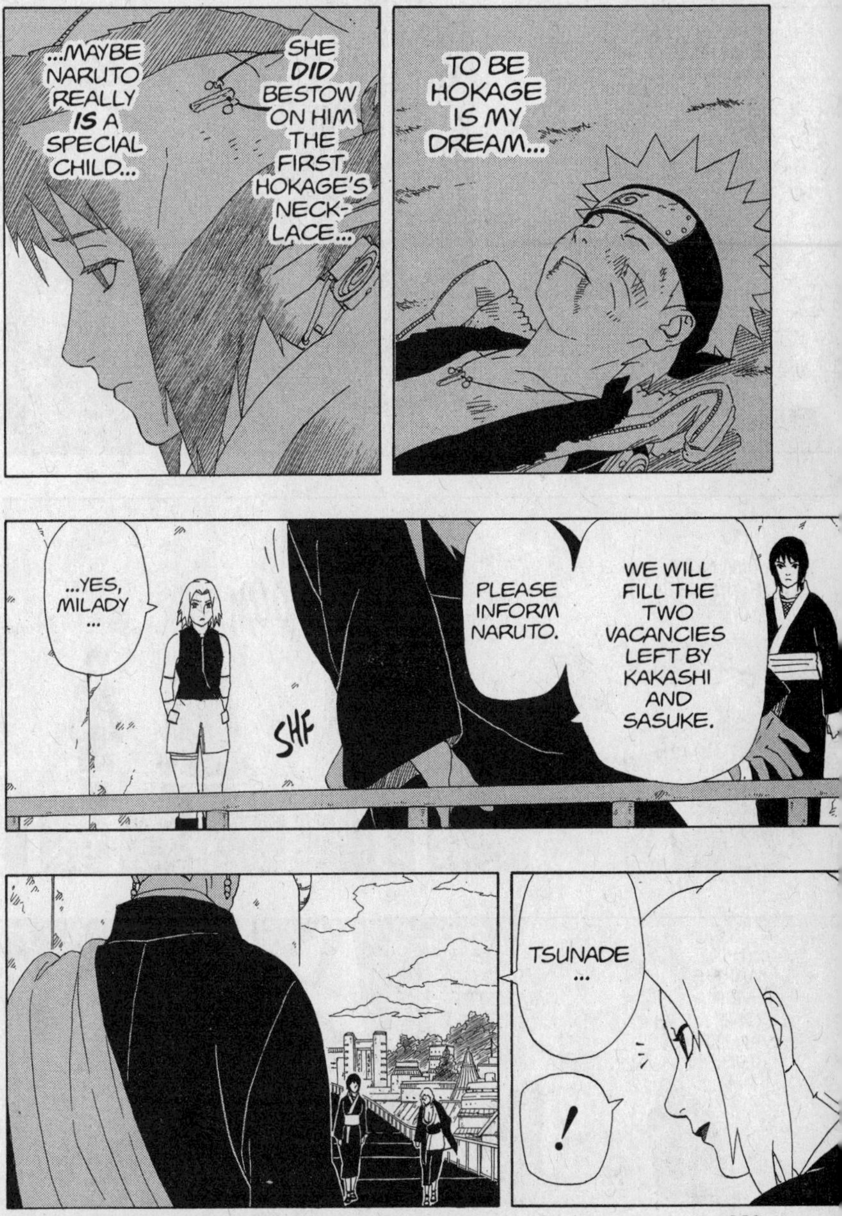
TO BE HOKAGE IS MY DREAM...
SHE DID BESTOW ON HIM THE FIRST HOKAGE'S NECK-LACE...
...MAYBE NARUTO REALLY IS A SPECIAL CHILD...
WE WILL FILL THE TWO VACANCIES LEFT BY KAKASHI AND SASUKE.
PLEASE INFORM NARUTO.
SHF
...YES, MILADY ...
TSUNADE ...
!

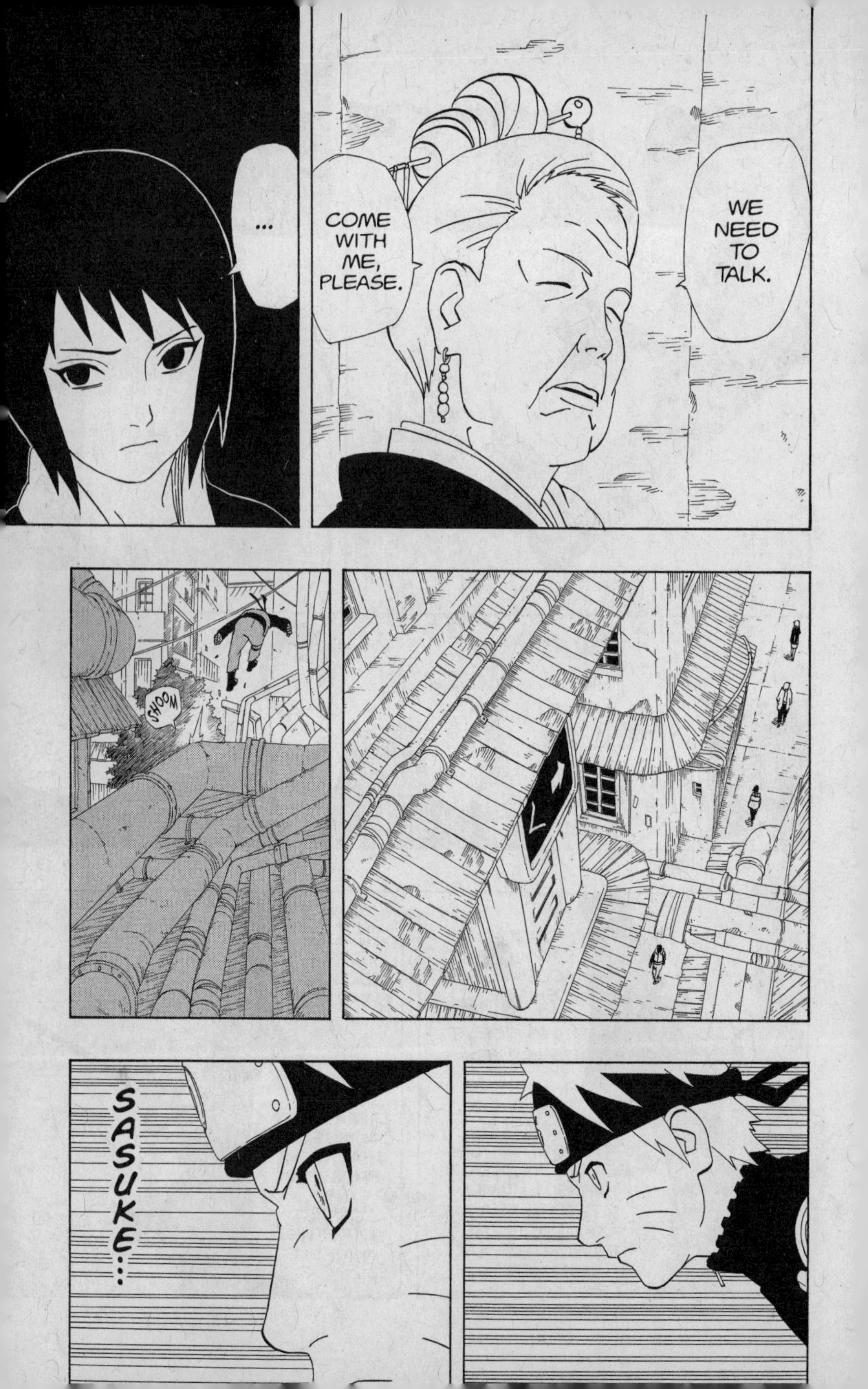
WE NEED TO TALK.
COME WITH ME, PLEASE.
...
SHOOM
SASUKE...

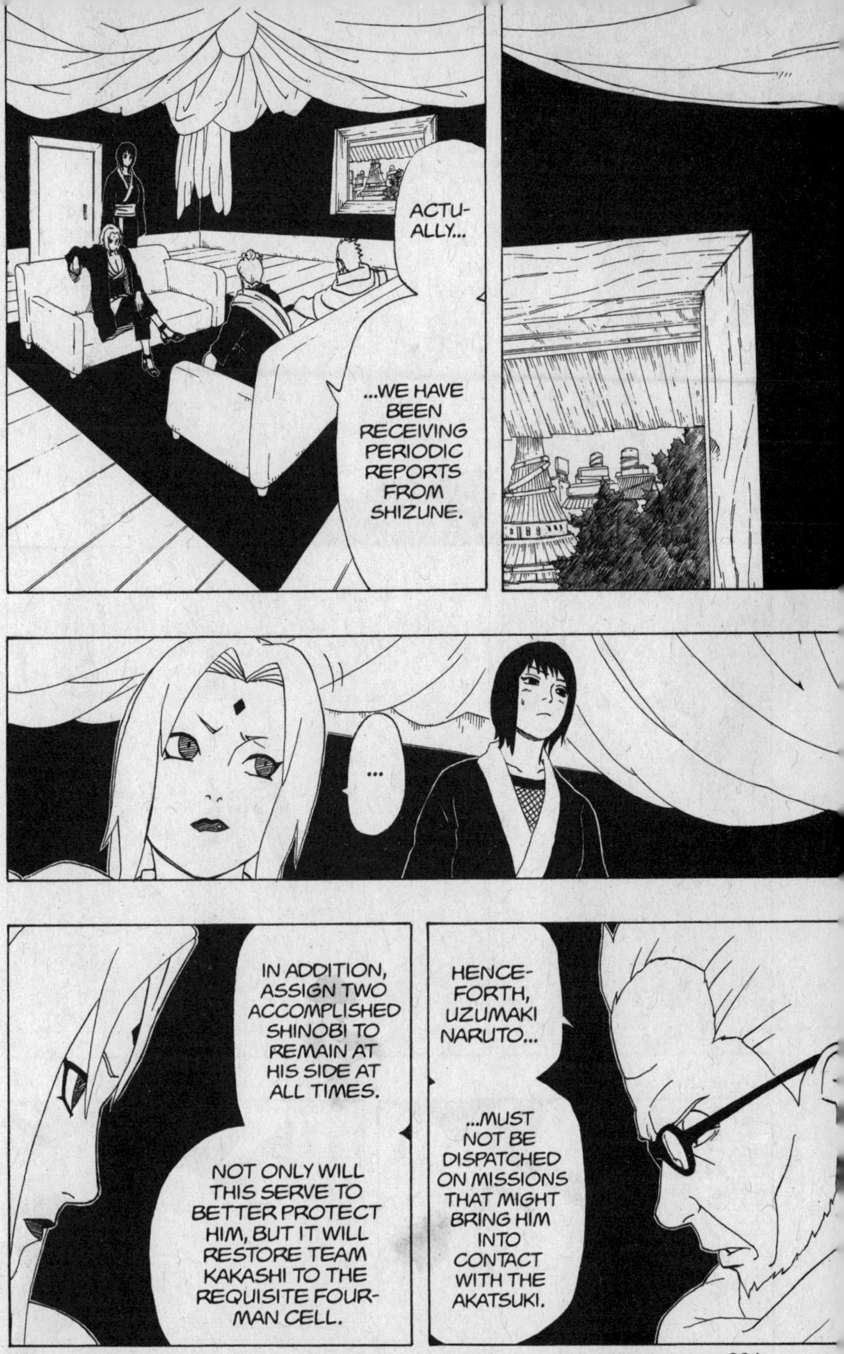
ACTU-ALLY...
...WE HAVE BEEN RECEIVING PERIODIC REPORTS FROM SHIZUNE.
...
HENCE-FORTH, UZUMAKI NARUTO...
...MUST NOT BE DISPATCHED ON MISSIONS THAT MIGHT BRING HIM INTO CONTACT WITH THE AKATSUKI.
IN ADDITION, ASSIGN TWO ACCOMPLISHED SHINOBI TO REMAIN AT HIS SIDE AT ALL TIMES.
NOT ONLY WILL THIS SERVE TO BETTER PROTECT HIM, BUT IT WILL RESTORE TEAM KAKASHI TO THE REQUISITE FOUR-MAN CELL.

READ THIS WAY

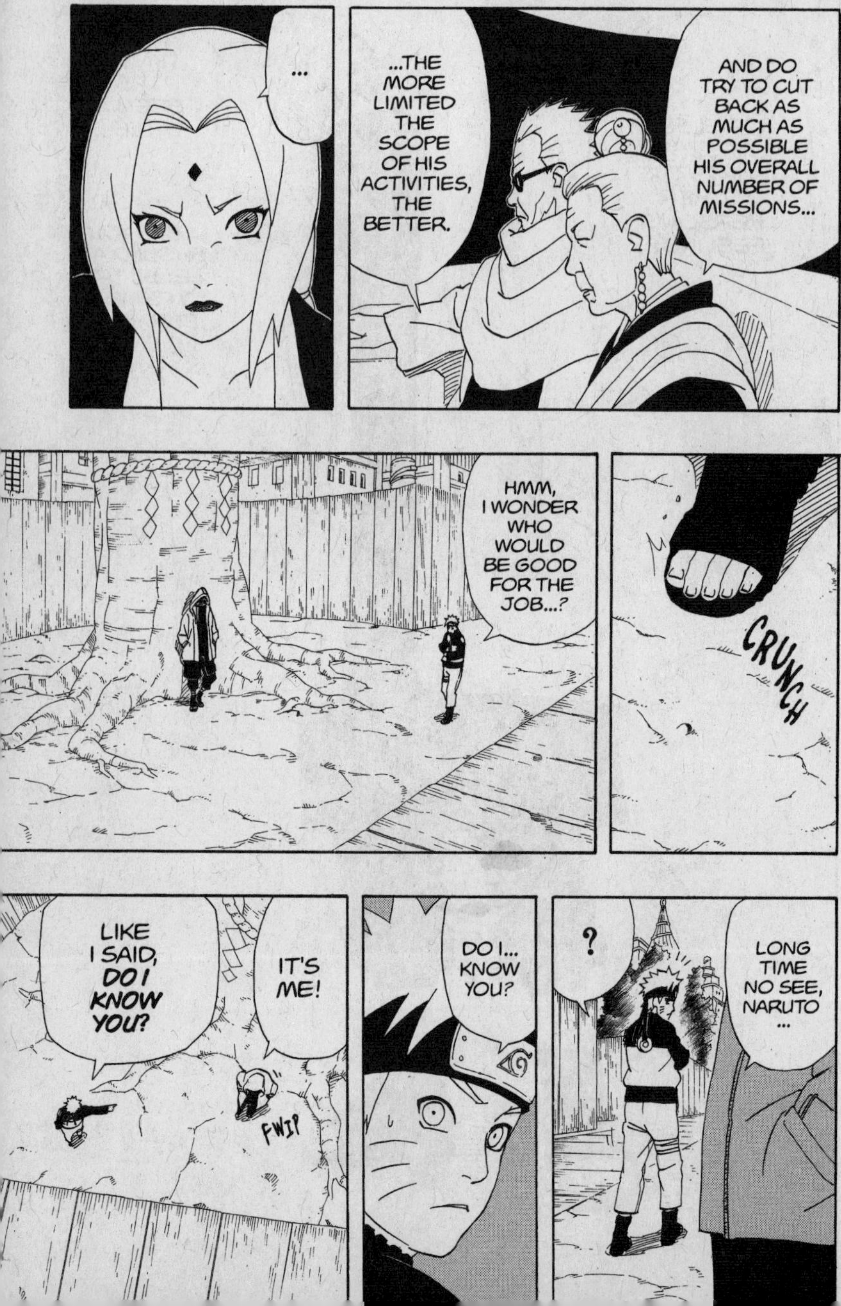

AND DO TRY TO CUT BACK AS MUCH AS POSSIBLE HIS OVERALL NUMBER OF MISSIONS...
...THE MORE LIMITED THE SCOPE OF HIS ACTIVITIES, THE BETTER.
...
CRUNCH
HMM, I WONDER WHO WOULD BE GOOD FOR THE JOB...?
LONG TIME NO SEE, NARUTO ...
?
DO I... KNOW YOU?
IT'S ME!
LIKE I SAID, **DO I KNOW YOU?**
FWIP

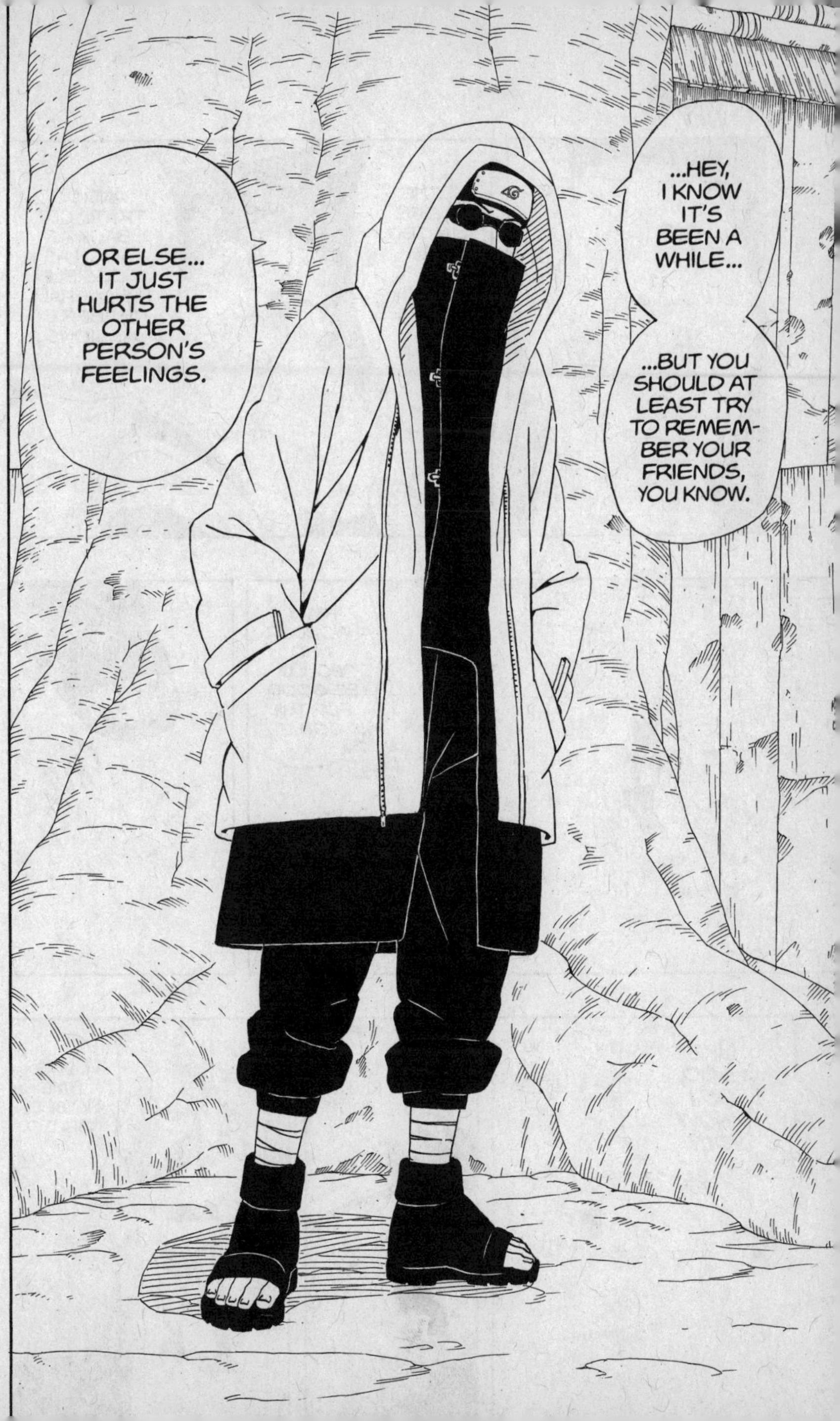
...HEY, I KNOW IT'S BEEN A WHILE...
...BUT YOU SHOULD AT LEAST TRY TO REMEM-BER YOUR FRIENDS, YOU KNOW.
OR ELSE... IT JUST HURTS THE OTHER PERSON'S FEELINGS.

READ THIS WAY

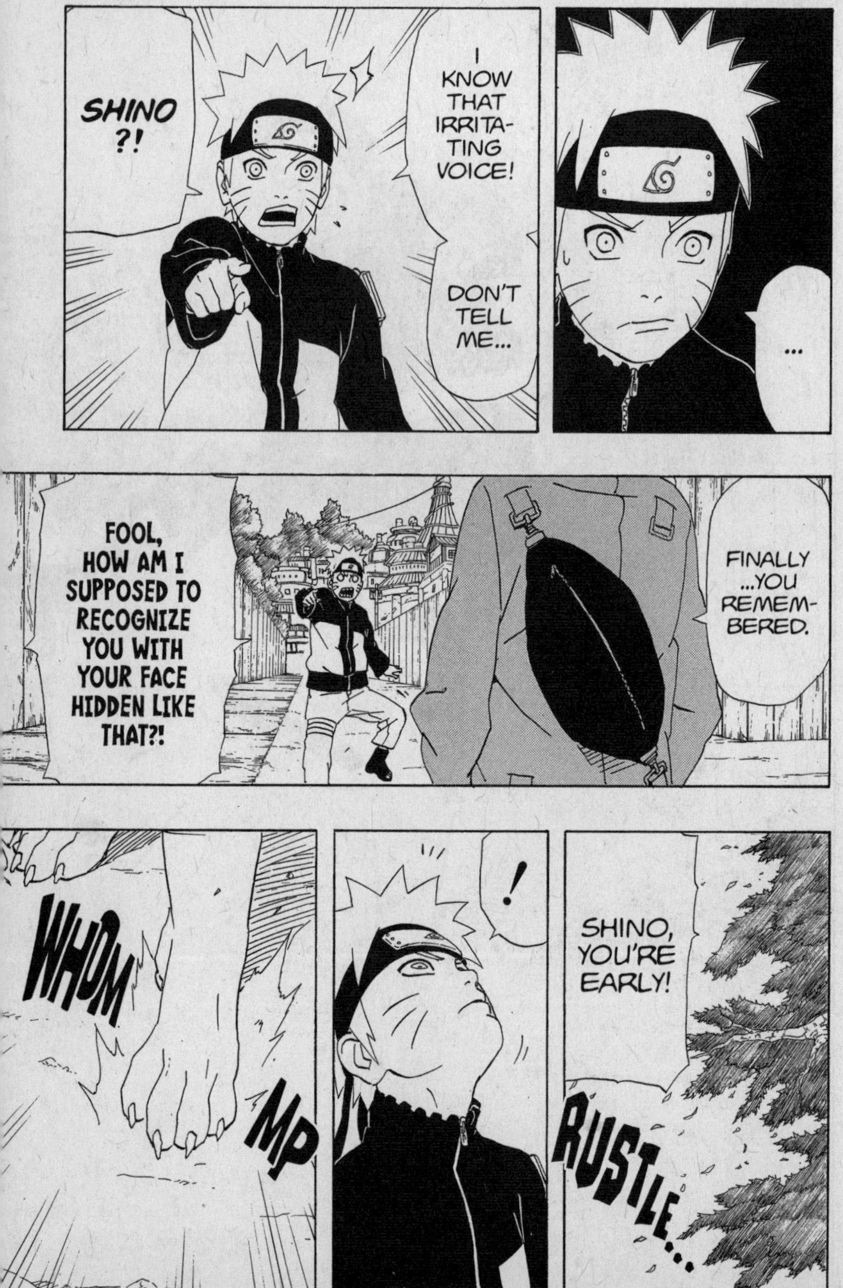
...
I KNOW THAT IRRITA-TING VOICE!
DON'T TELL ME...
SHINO ?!
FINALLY ...YOU REMEM-BERED.
FOOL, HOW AM I SUPPOSED TO RECOGNIZE YOU WITH YOUR FACE HIDDEN LIKE THAT?!
SHINO, YOU'RE EARLY!
RUSTLE...
!
WHUMMP

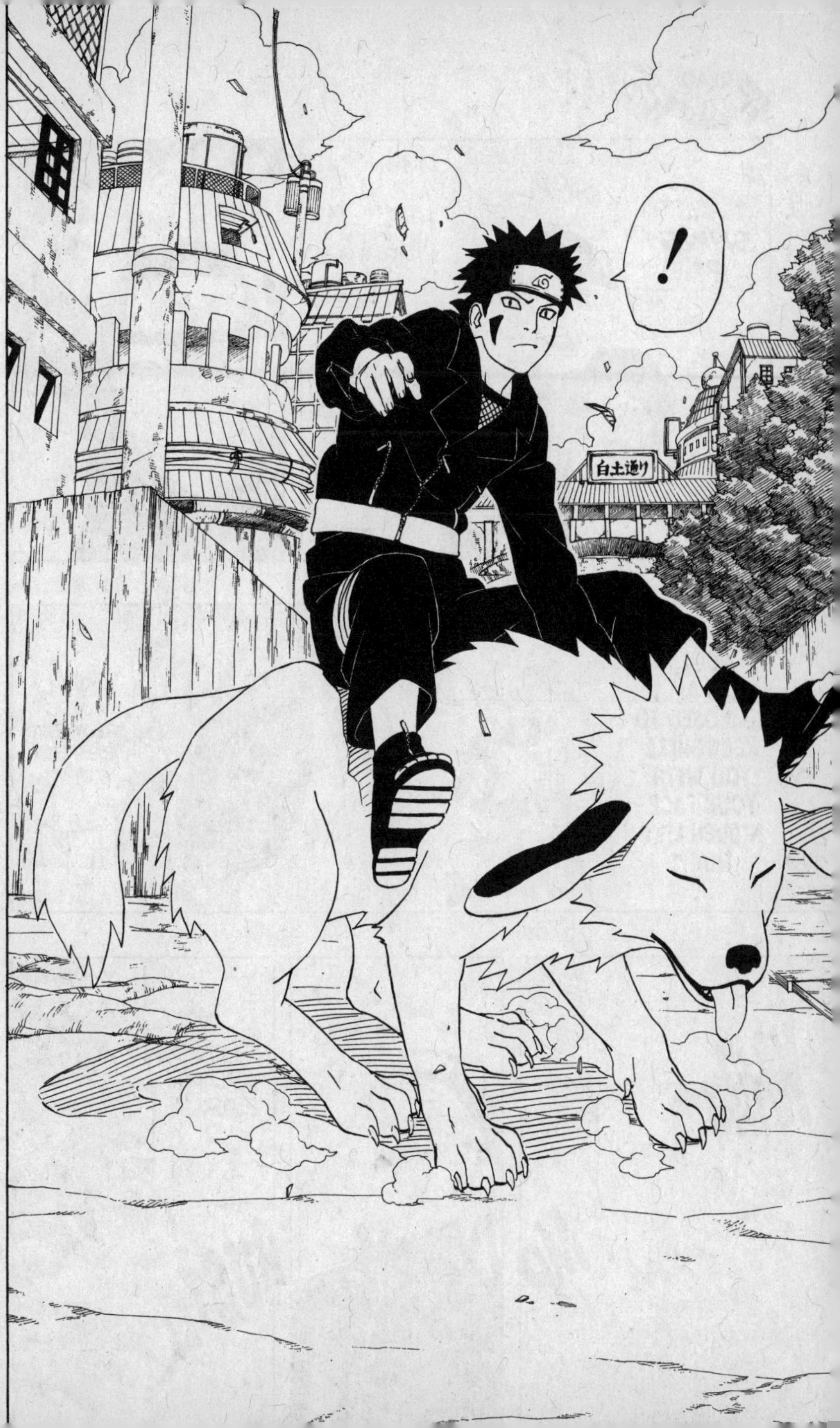
!
白土通り

READ THIS WAY

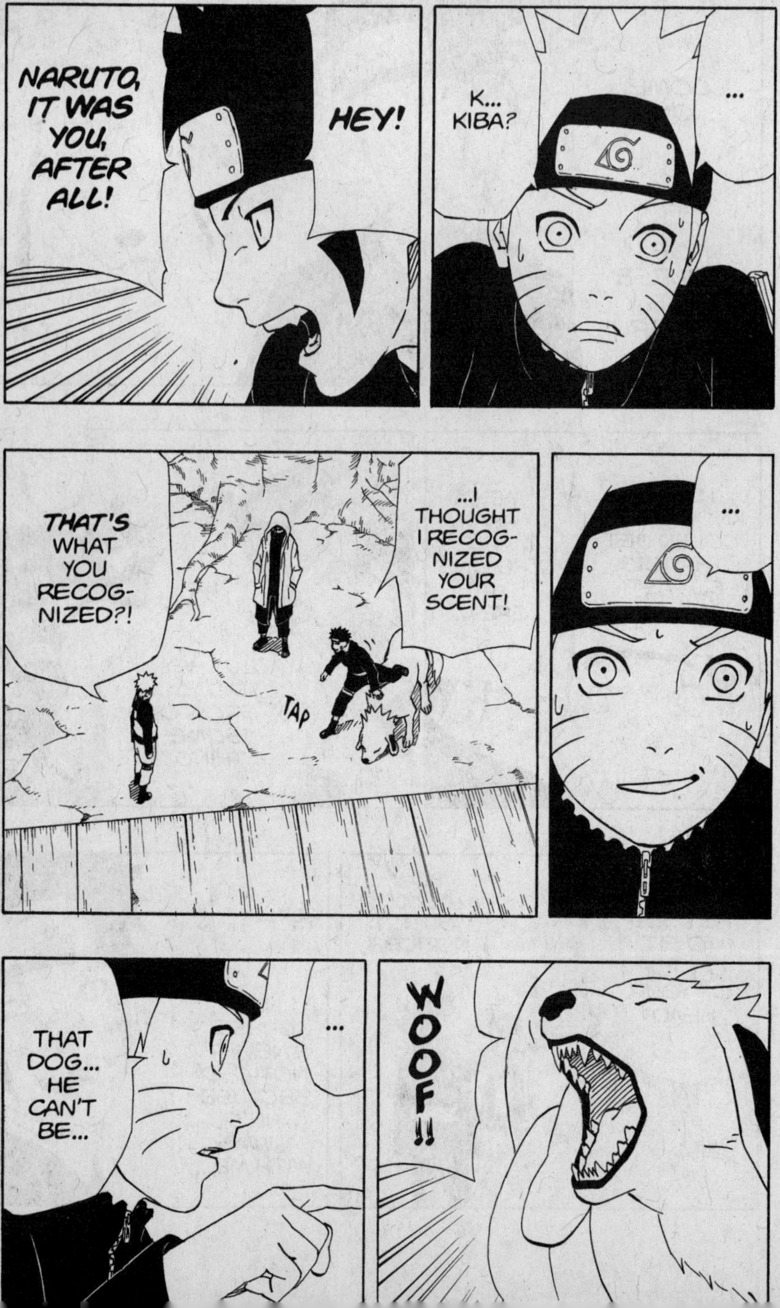
...
K... KIBA?
HEY!
NARUTO, IT WAS YOU, AFTER ALL!
...
...I THOUGHT I RECOGNIZED YOUR SCENT!
TAP
THAT'S WHAT YOU RECOGNIZED?!
WOOF!!
...
THAT DOG... HE CAN'T BE...

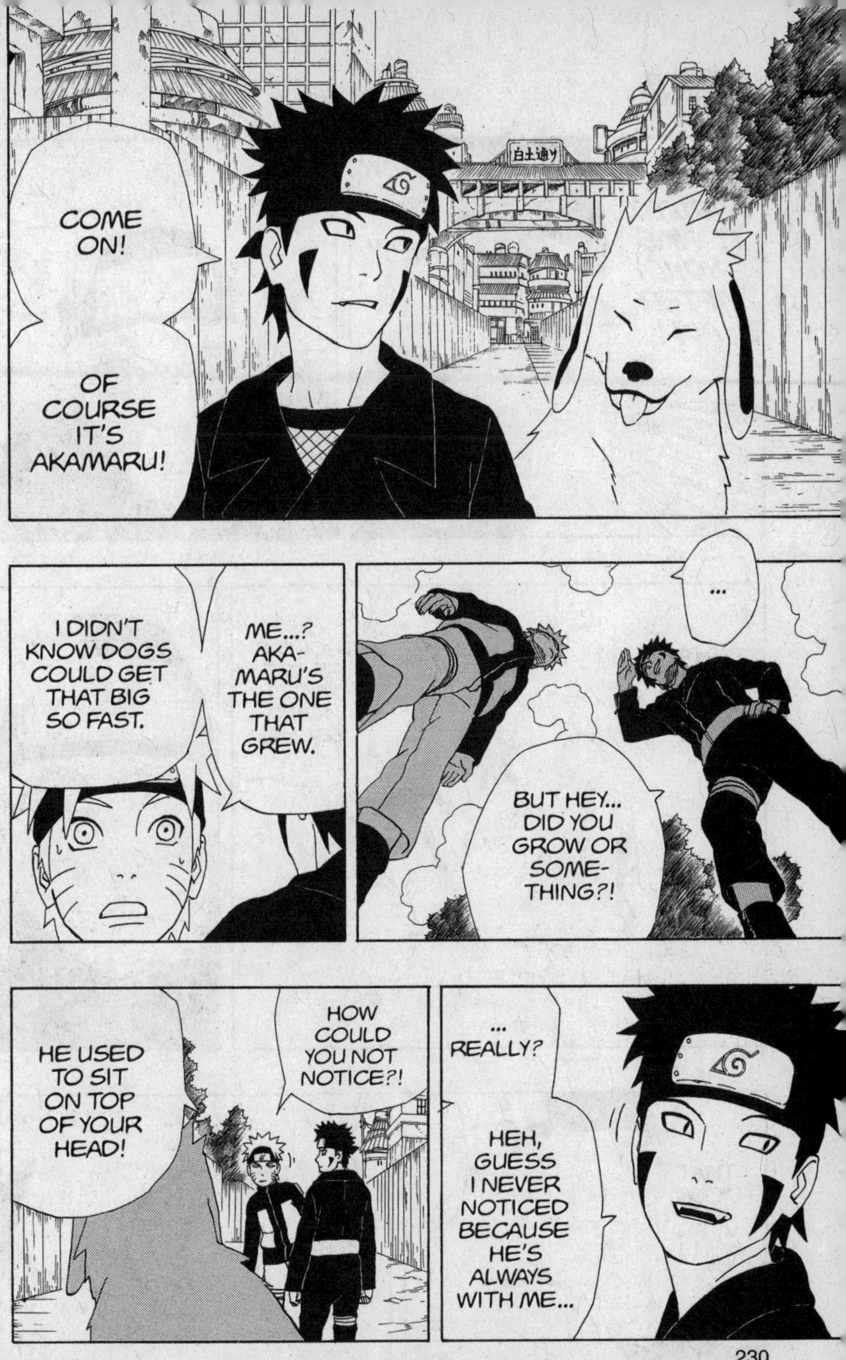
COME ON!
OF COURSE IT'S AKAMARU!
...
BUT HEY... DID YOU GROW OR SOME-THING?!
ME...? AKA-MARU'S THE ONE THAT GREW.
I DIDN'T KNOW DOGS COULD GET THAT BIG SO FAST.
...REALLY?
HEH, GUESS I NEVER NOTICED BECAUSE HE'S ALWAYS WITH ME...
HOW COULD YOU NOT NOTICE?!
HE USED TO SIT ON TOP OF YOUR HEAD!

READ THIS WAY

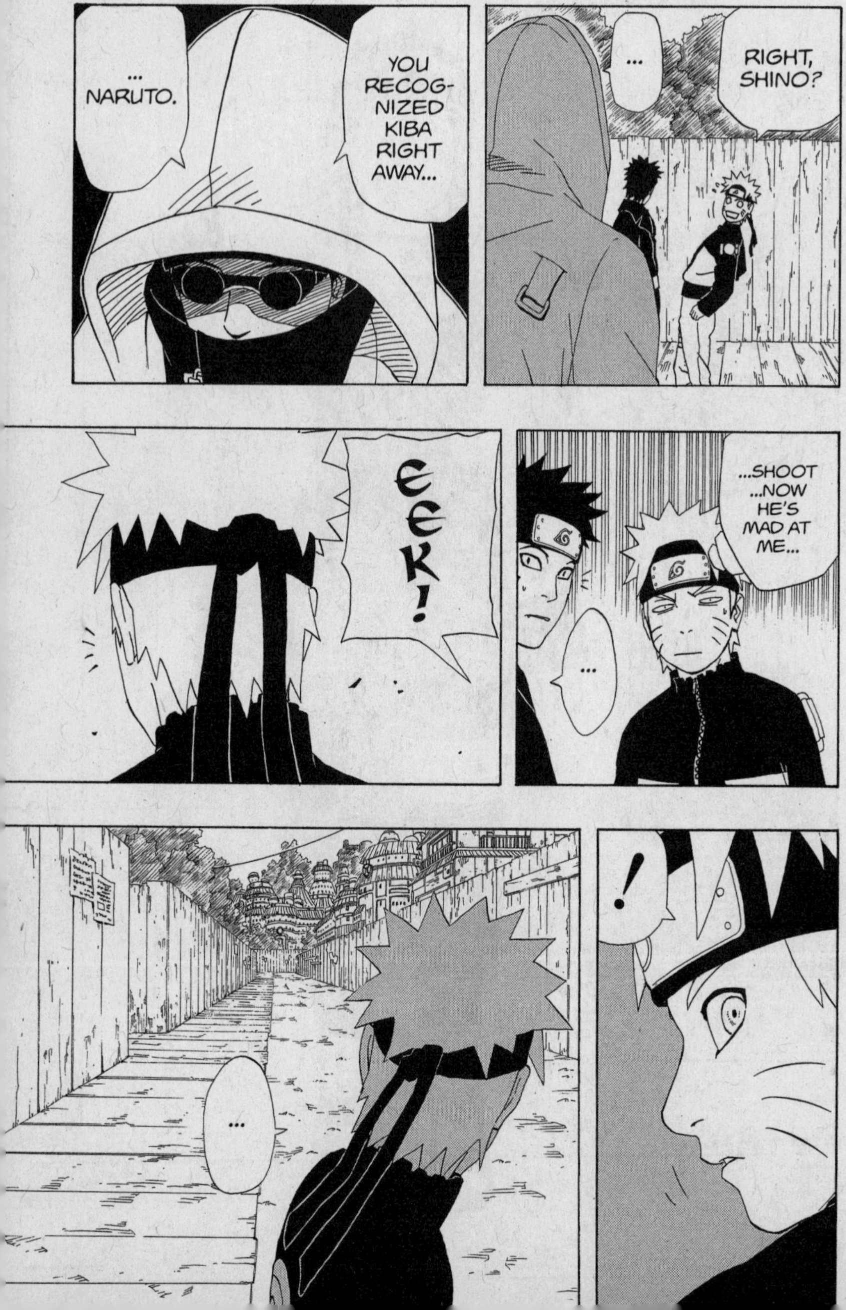
RIGHT, SHINO?
...
YOU RECOG-NIZED KIBA RIGHT AWAY...
... NARUTO.
...SHOOT ...NOW HE'S MAD AT ME...
...
EEK!
!
...

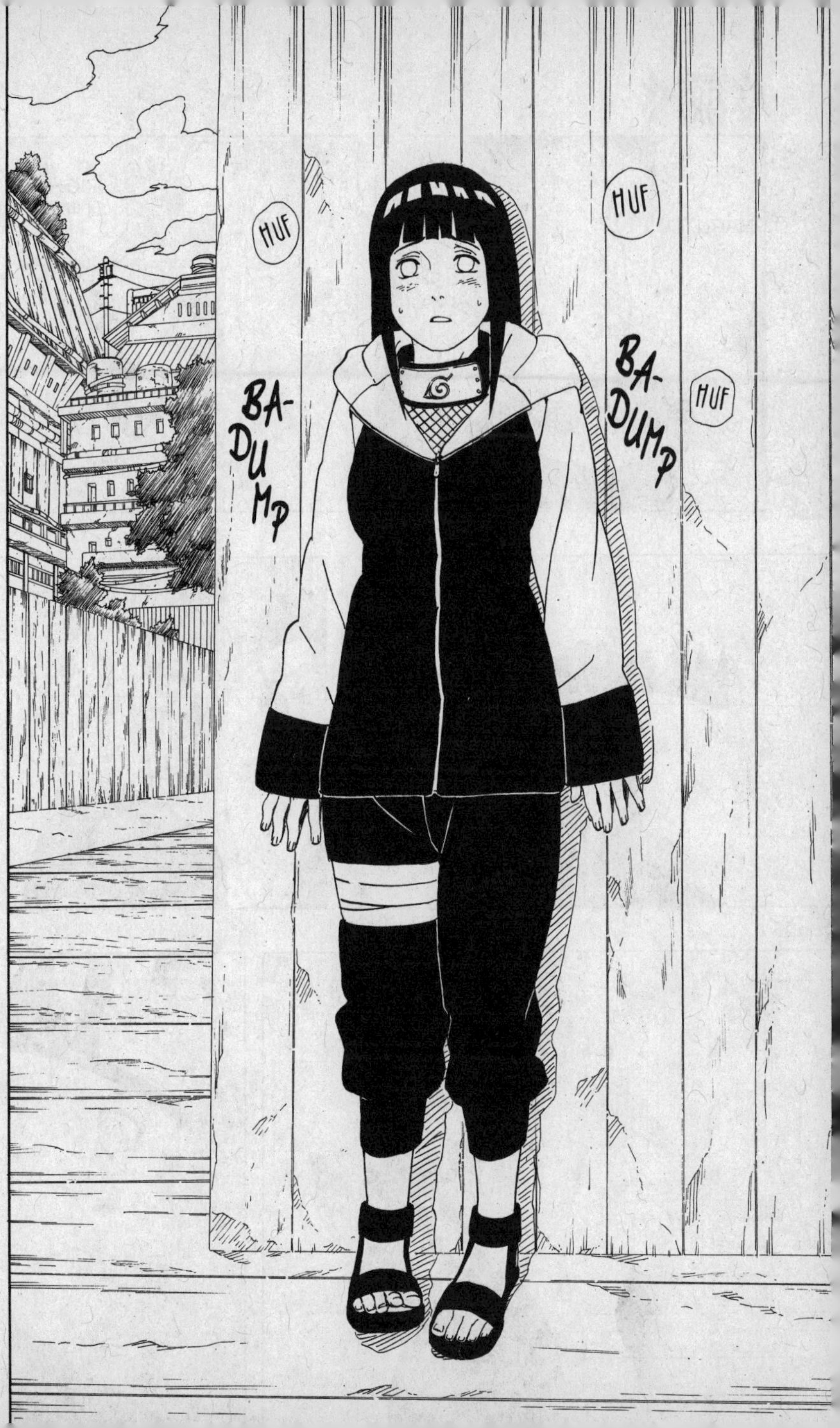
HUF
HUF
BA-DUMP
HUF
BA-DUMP

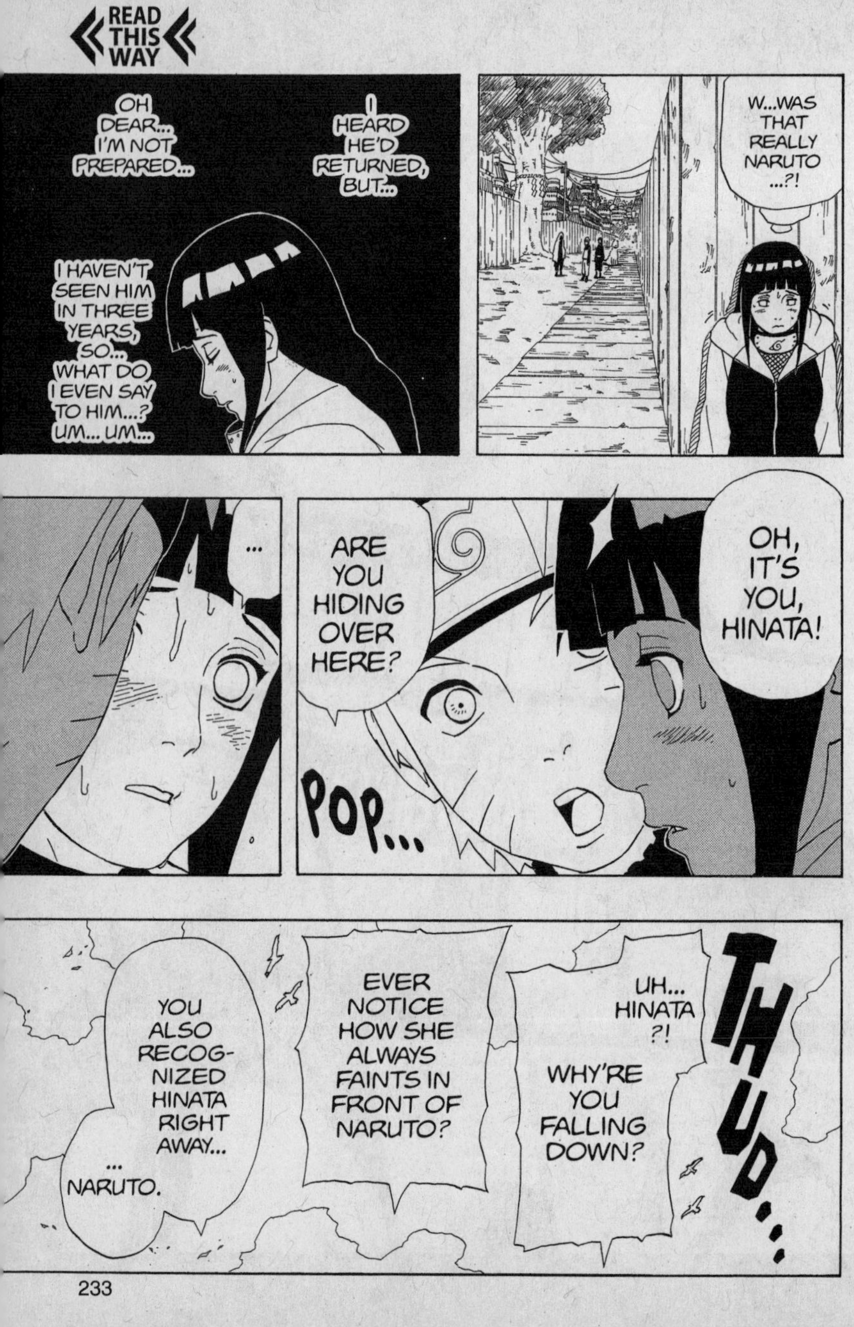
READ THIS WAY
W...WAS THAT REALLY NARUTO ...?!
I HEARD HE'D RETURNED, BUT...
OH DEAR... I'M NOT PREPARED...
I HAVEN'T SEEN HIM IN THREE YEARS, SO... WHAT DO I EVEN SAY TO HIM...? UM... UM...
OH, IT'S YOU, HINATA!
ARE YOU HIDING OVER HERE?
POP...
...
THUD...
UH... HINATA?!
WHY'RE YOU FALLING DOWN?
EVER NOTICE HOW SHE ALWAYS FAINTS IN FRONT OF NARUTO?
YOU ALSO RECOG-NIZED HINATA RIGHT AWAY...
... NARUTO.

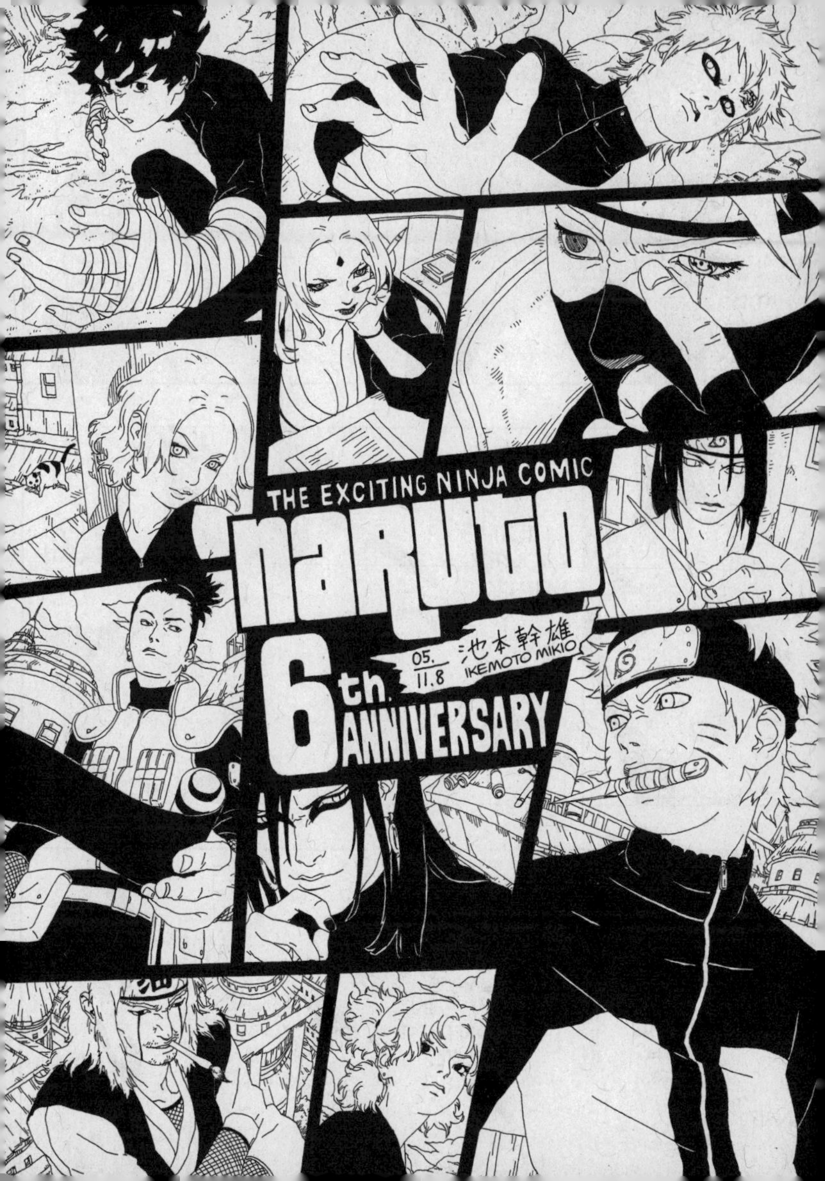
THE EXCITING NINJA COMIC
NARUTO
6th ANNIVERSARY
05.
11.8
池本幹雄
IKEMOTO MIKIO

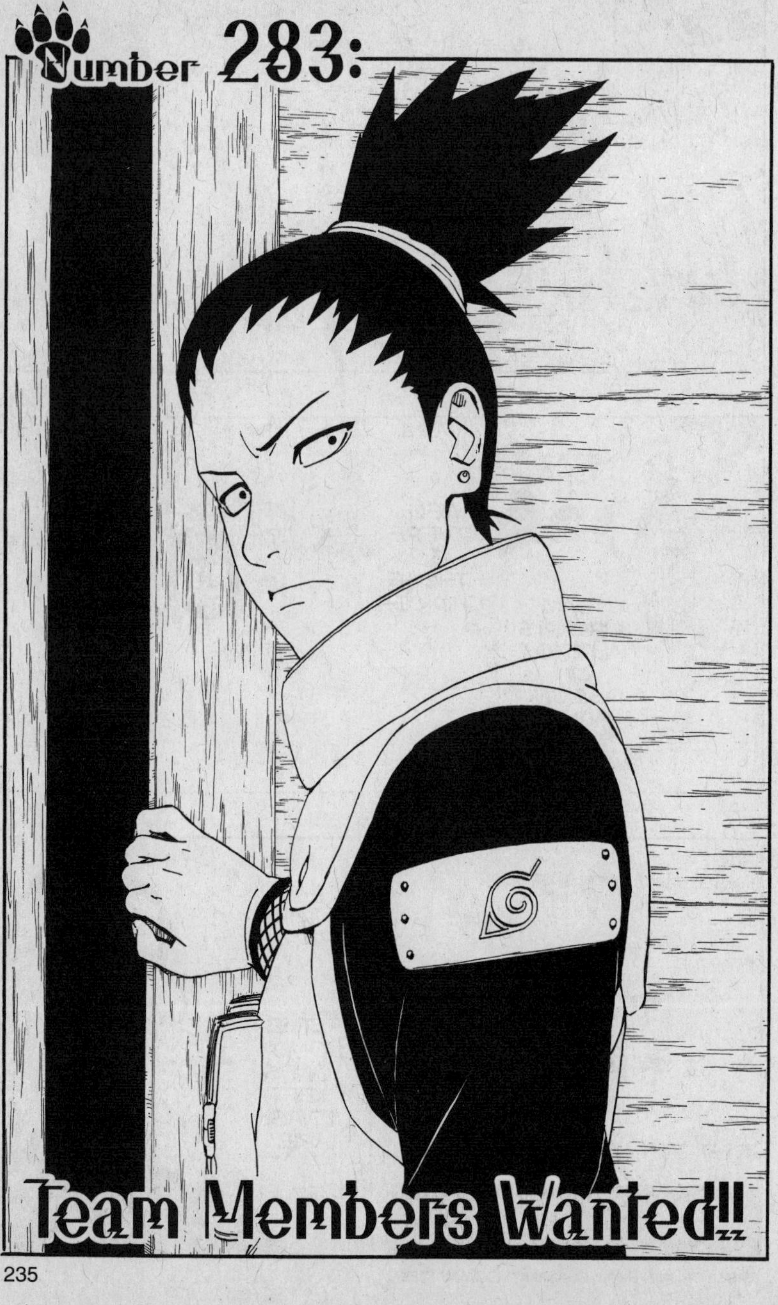
Number 283:
Team Members Wanted!!

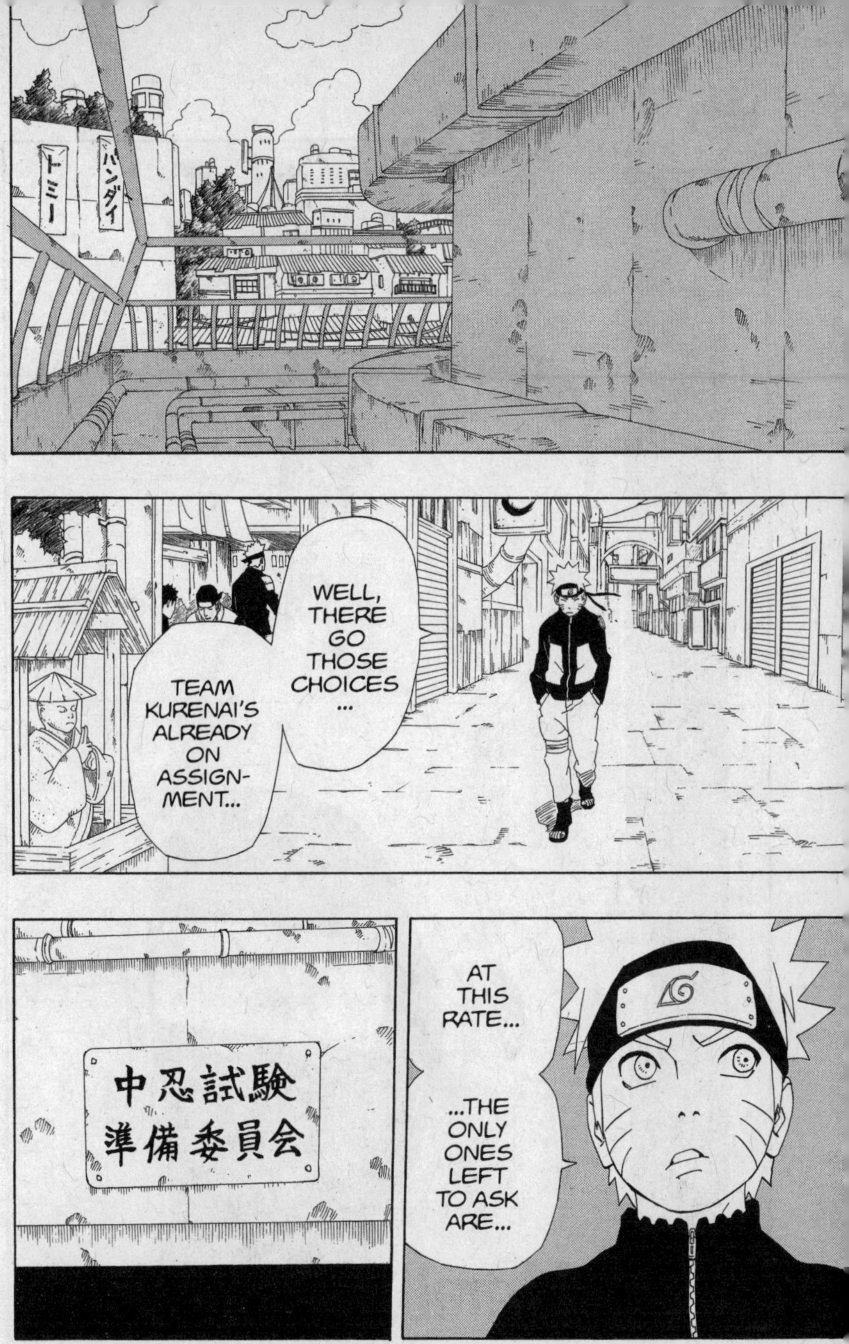
バンダイ
トミー
WELL, THERE GO THOSE CHOICES...
TEAM KURENAI'S ALREADY ON ASSIGNMENT...
AT THIS RATE...
...THE ONLY ONES LEFT TO ASK ARE...
中忍試験
準備委員会

(SIGN: CHÛNIN EXAM PLANNING COMMITTEE)

READ THIS WAY

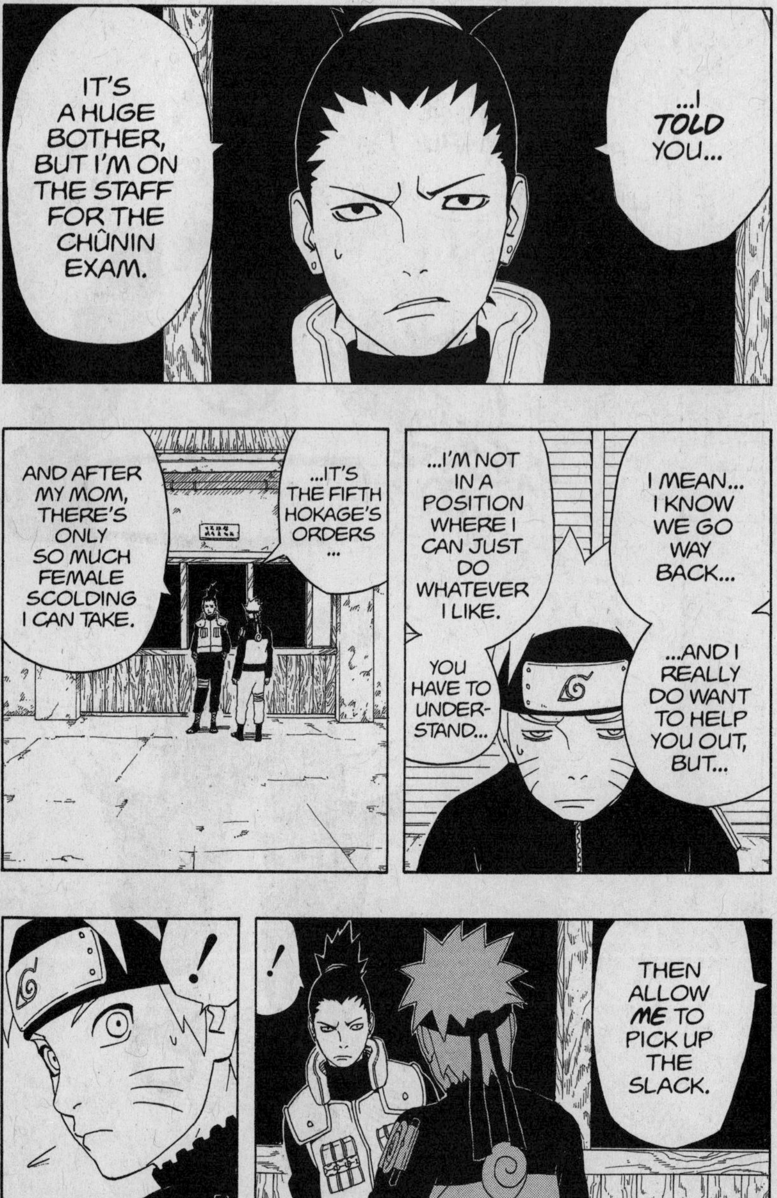

...I *TOLD* YOU...
IT'S A HUGE BOTHER, BUT I'M ON THE STAFF FOR THE CHÛNIN EXAM.
I MEAN... I KNOW WE GO WAY BACK...
...AND I REALLY DO WANT TO HELP YOU OUT, BUT...
...I'M NOT IN A POSITION WHERE I CAN JUST DO WHATEVER I LIKE.
YOU HAVE TO UNDER-STAND...
...IT'S THE FIFTH HOKAGE'S ORDERS...
AND AFTER MY MOM, THERE'S ONLY SO MUCH FEMALE SCOLDING I CAN TAKE.
THEN ALLOW *ME* TO PICK UP THE SLACK.
!
!

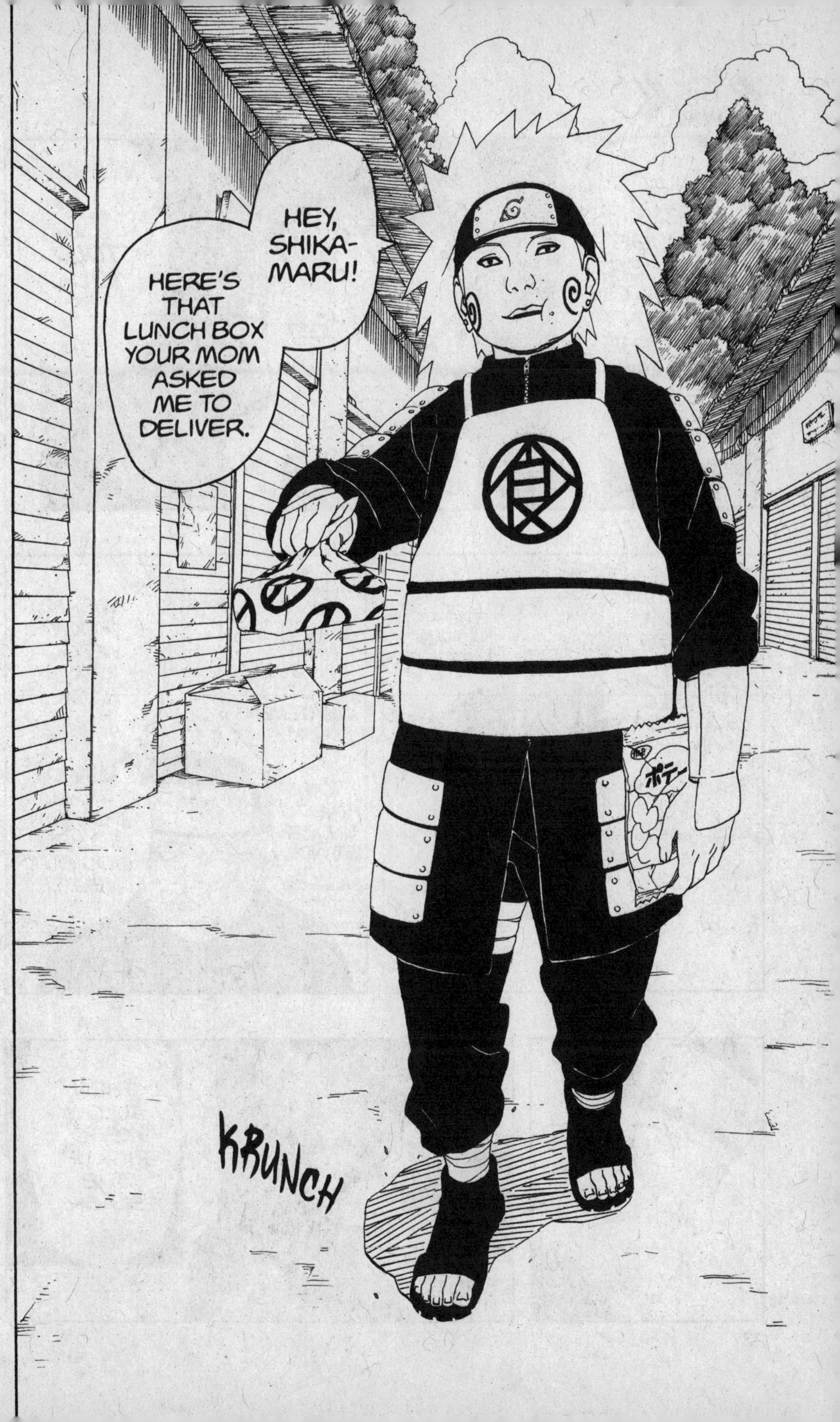
HEY, SHIKAMARU!
HERE'S THAT LUNCH BOX YOUR MOM ASKED ME TO DELIVER.
KRUNCH

READ THIS WAY

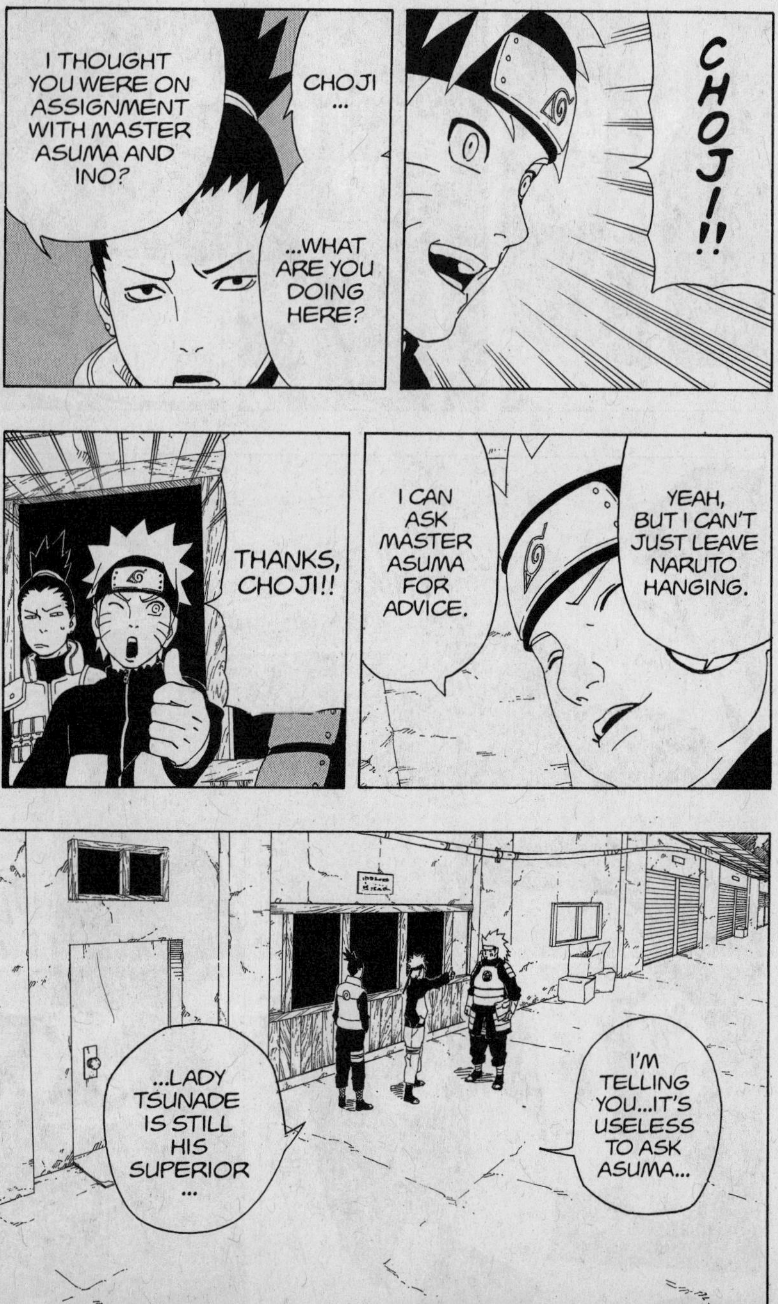
CHOJI!!
CHOJI ... ...WHAT ARE YOU DOING HERE?
I THOUGHT YOU WERE ON ASSIGNMENT WITH MASTER ASUMA AND INO?
YEAH, BUT I CAN'T JUST LEAVE NARUTO HANGING.
I CAN ASK MASTER ASUMA FOR ADVICE.
THANKS, CHOJI!!
I'M TELLING YOU...IT'S USELESS TO ASK ASUMA...
...LADY TSUNADE IS STILL HIS SUPERIOR ...

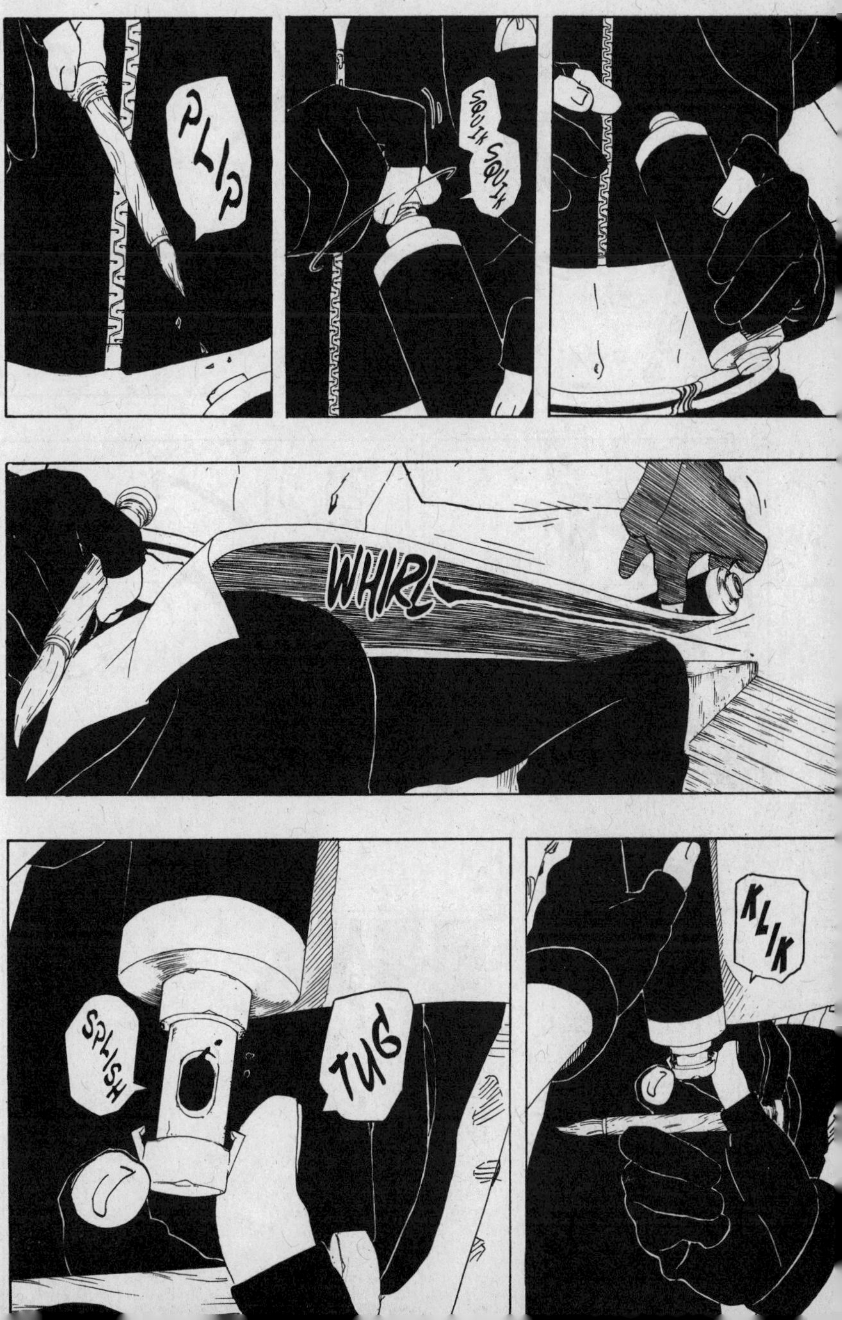
SQUIK SQUIK
PLIP
WHIRL
KLIK
TUG
SPLISH

READ THIS WAY

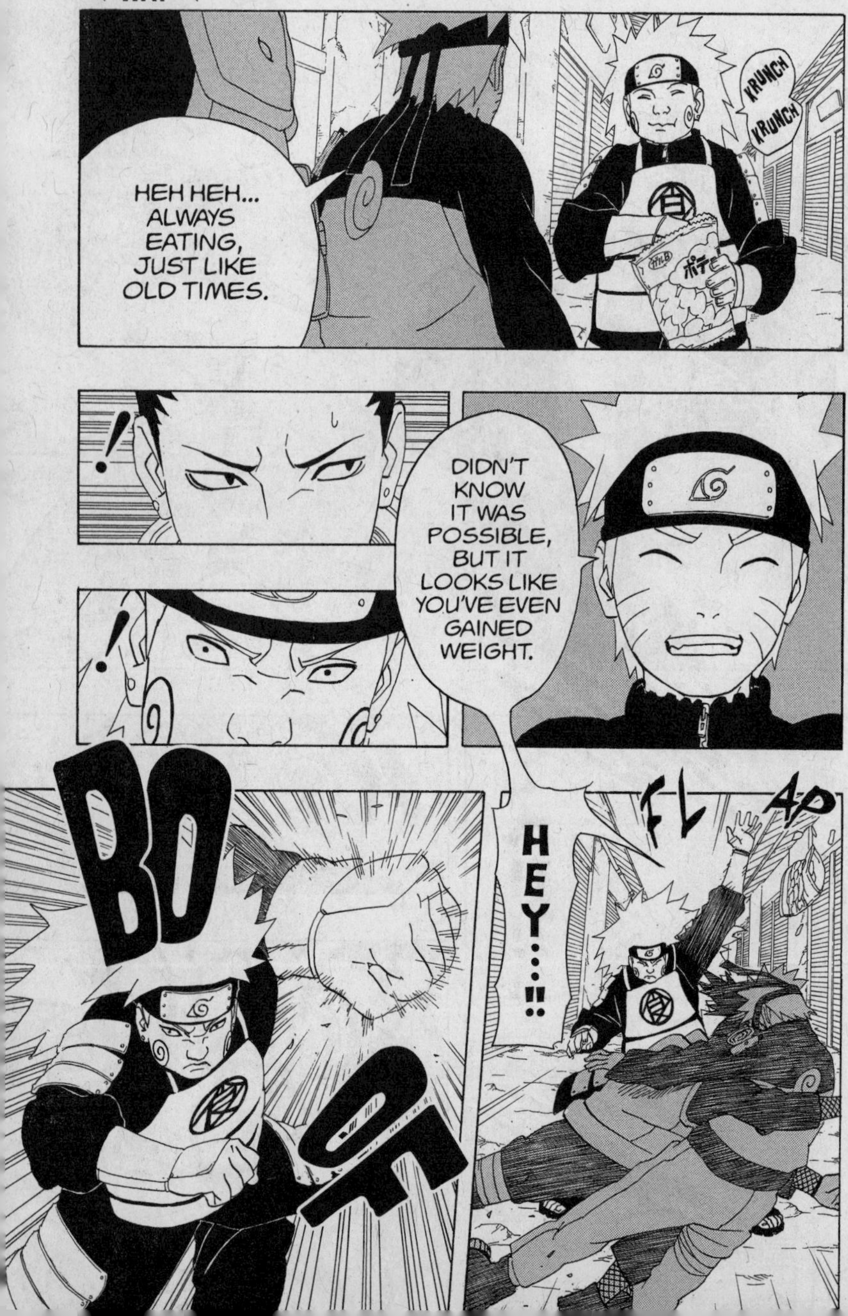
KRUNCH
KRUNCH
HEH HEH... ALWAYS EATING, JUST LIKE OLD TIMES.
DIDN'T KNOW IT WAS POSSIBLE, BUT IT LOOKS LIKE YOU'VE EVEN GAINED WEIGHT.
!
!
FLAP
HEY...!!
BOOF

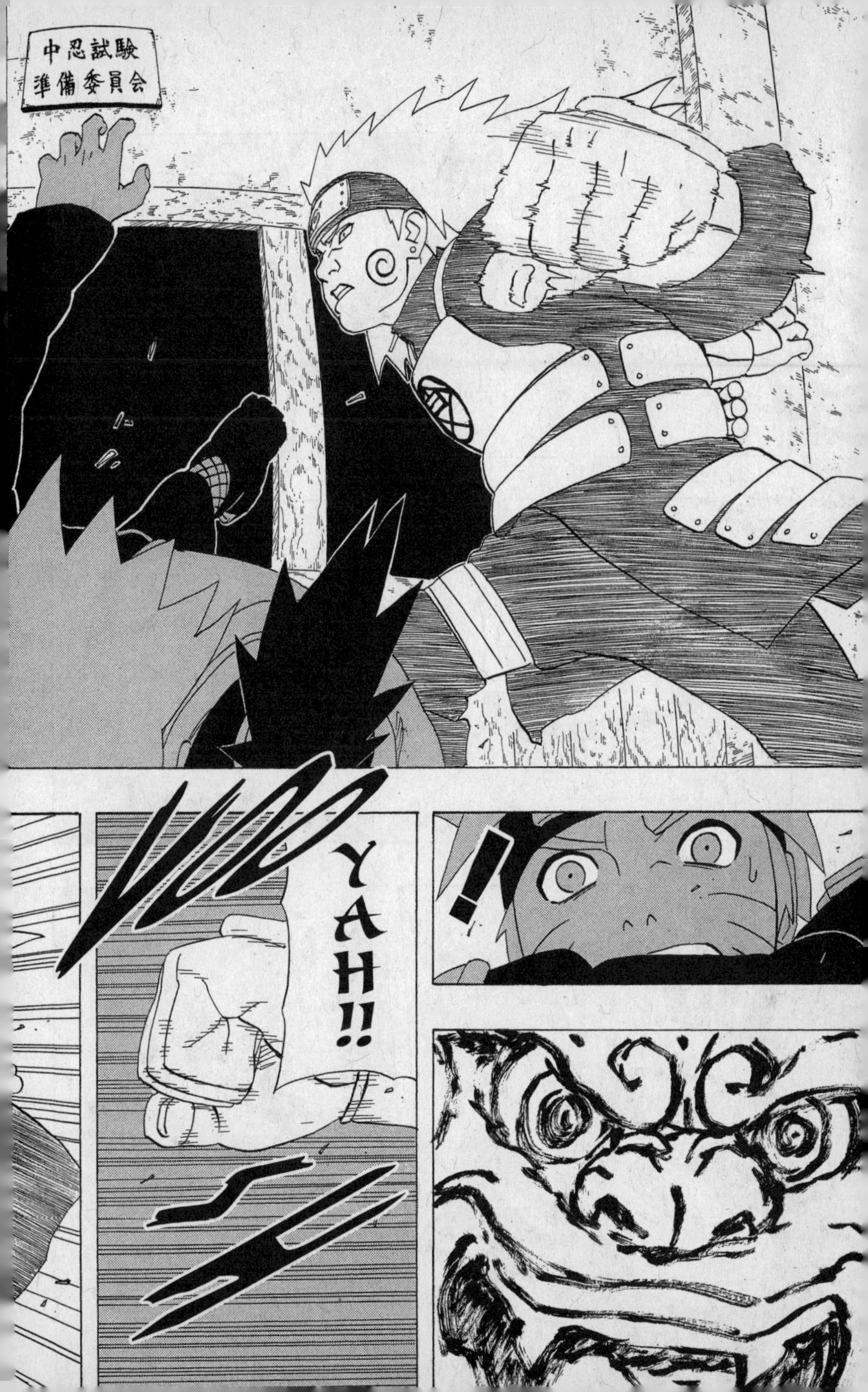
中忍試験
準備委員会
!
VOOYAH!!

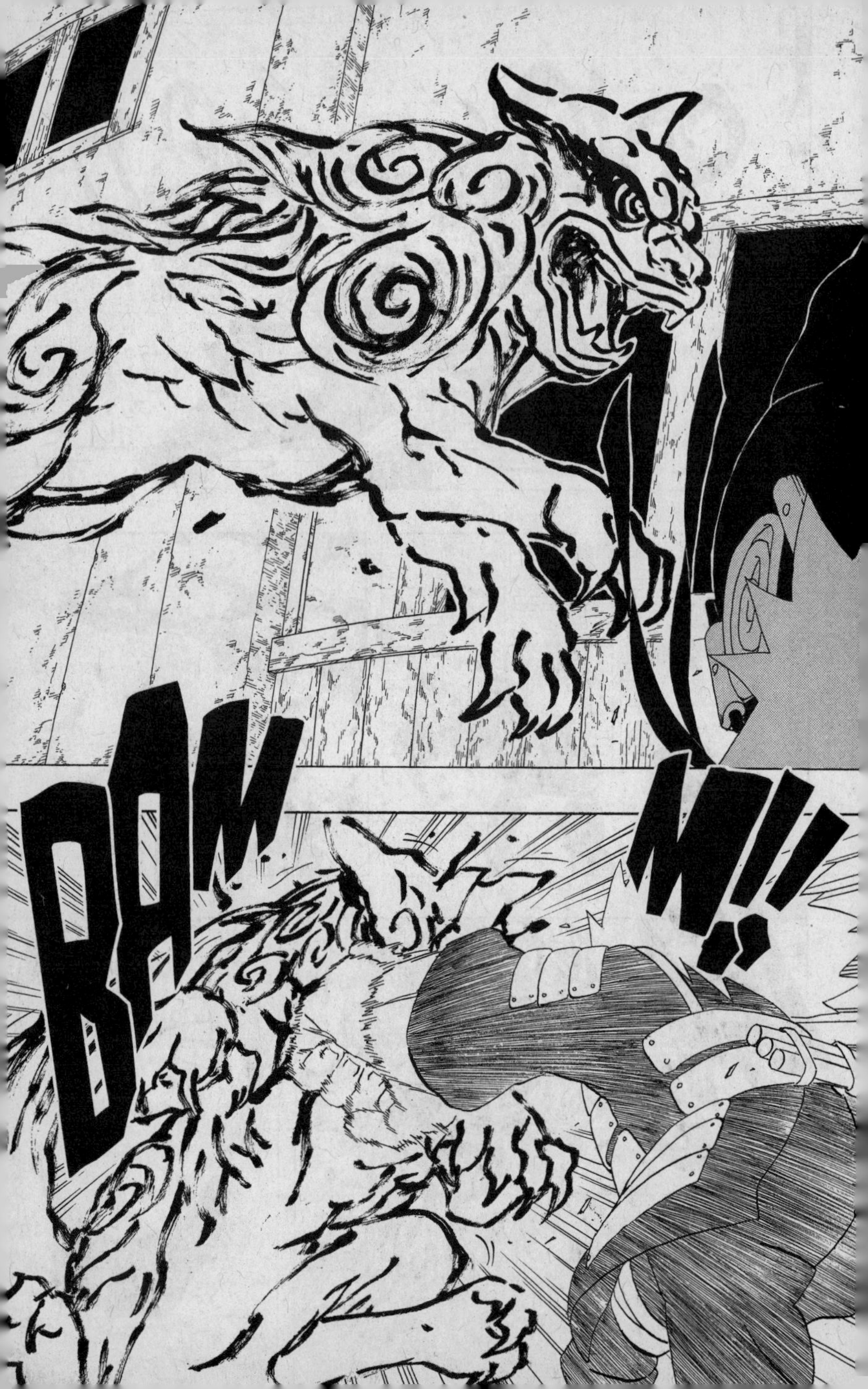
BAAM!!

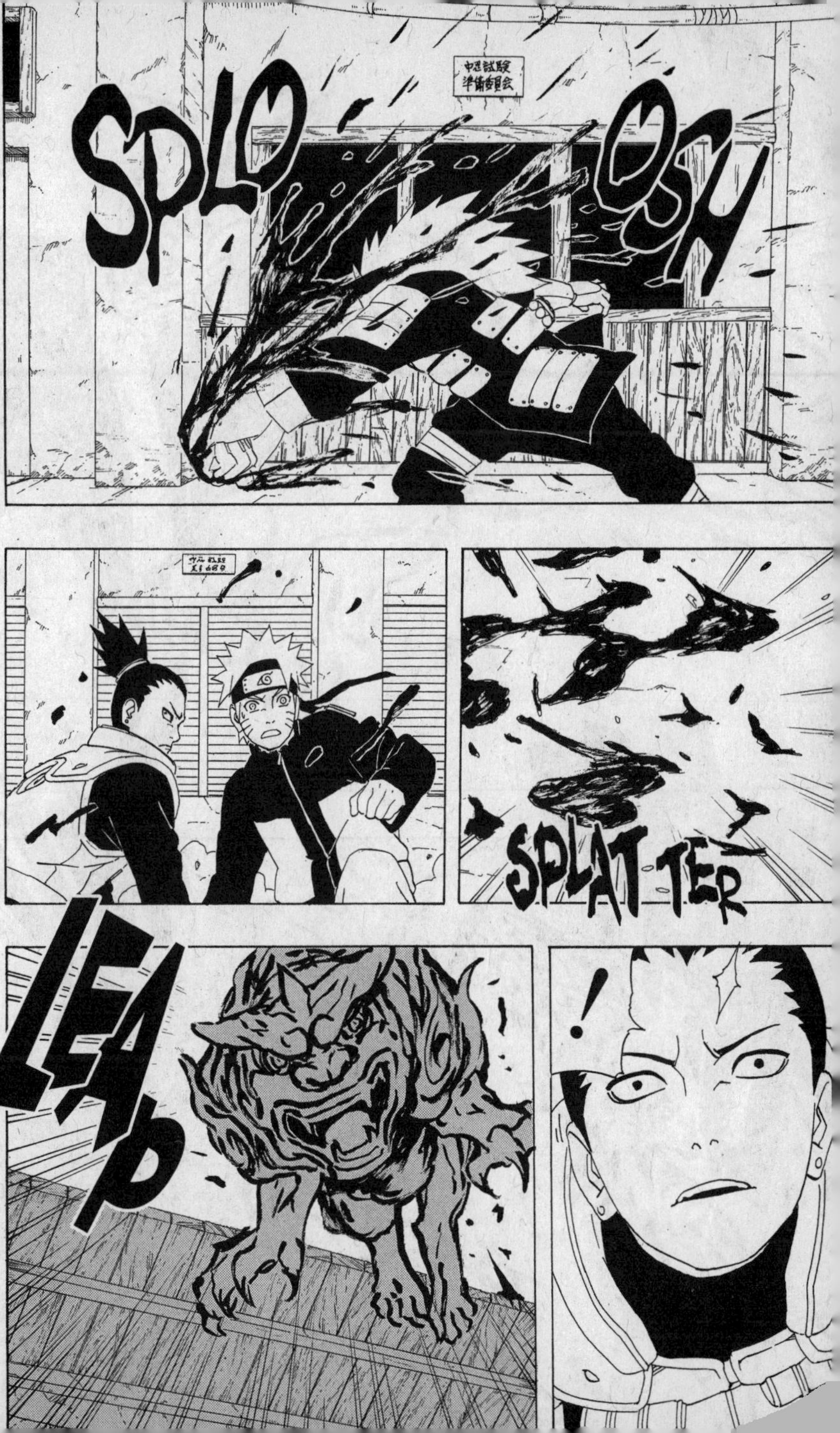
中忍試験
準備委員会
SPLOOSH
SPLATTER
!
LEAP

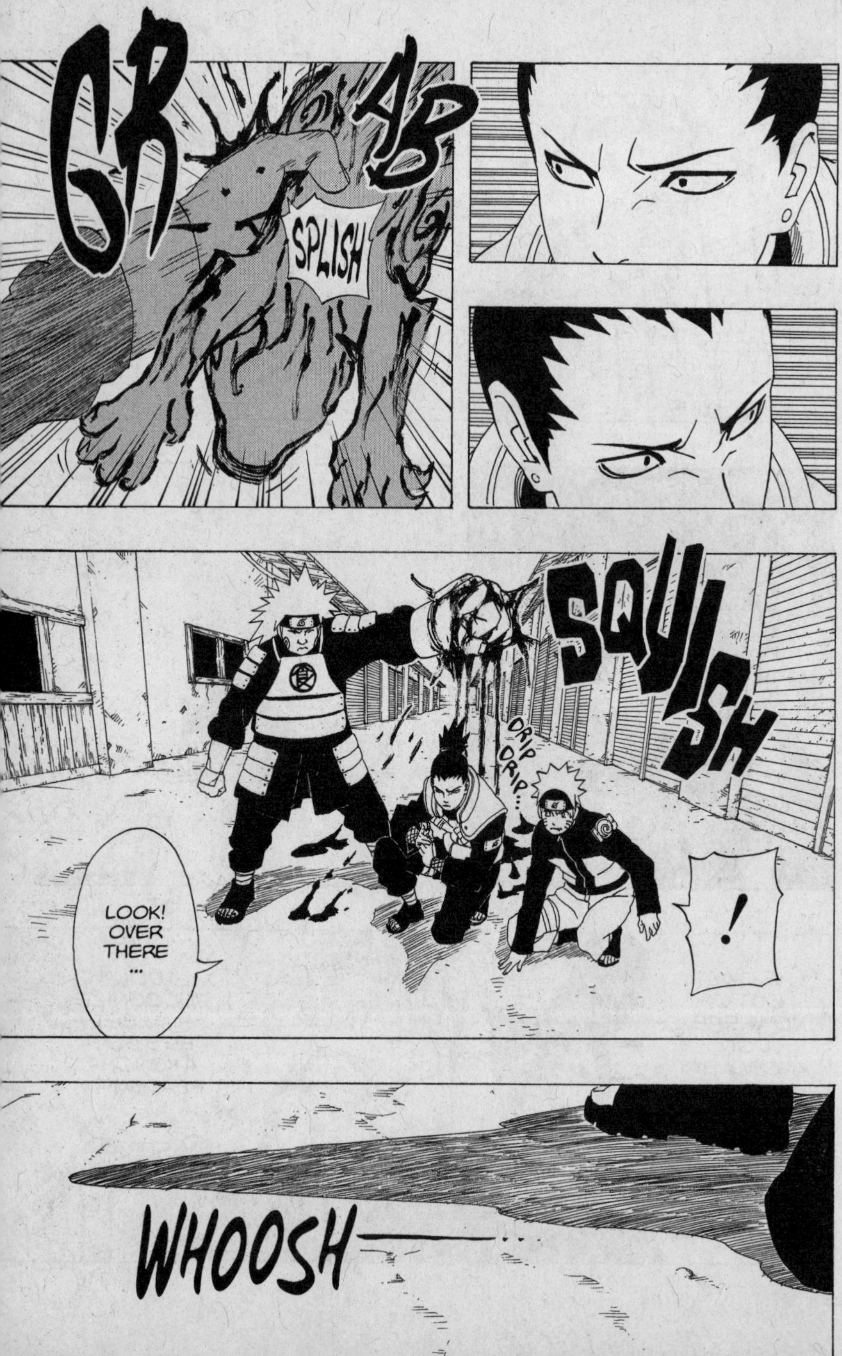
GRAB
SPLISH
SQUISH
DRIP DRIP...
!
LOOK! OVER THERE ...
WHOOSH

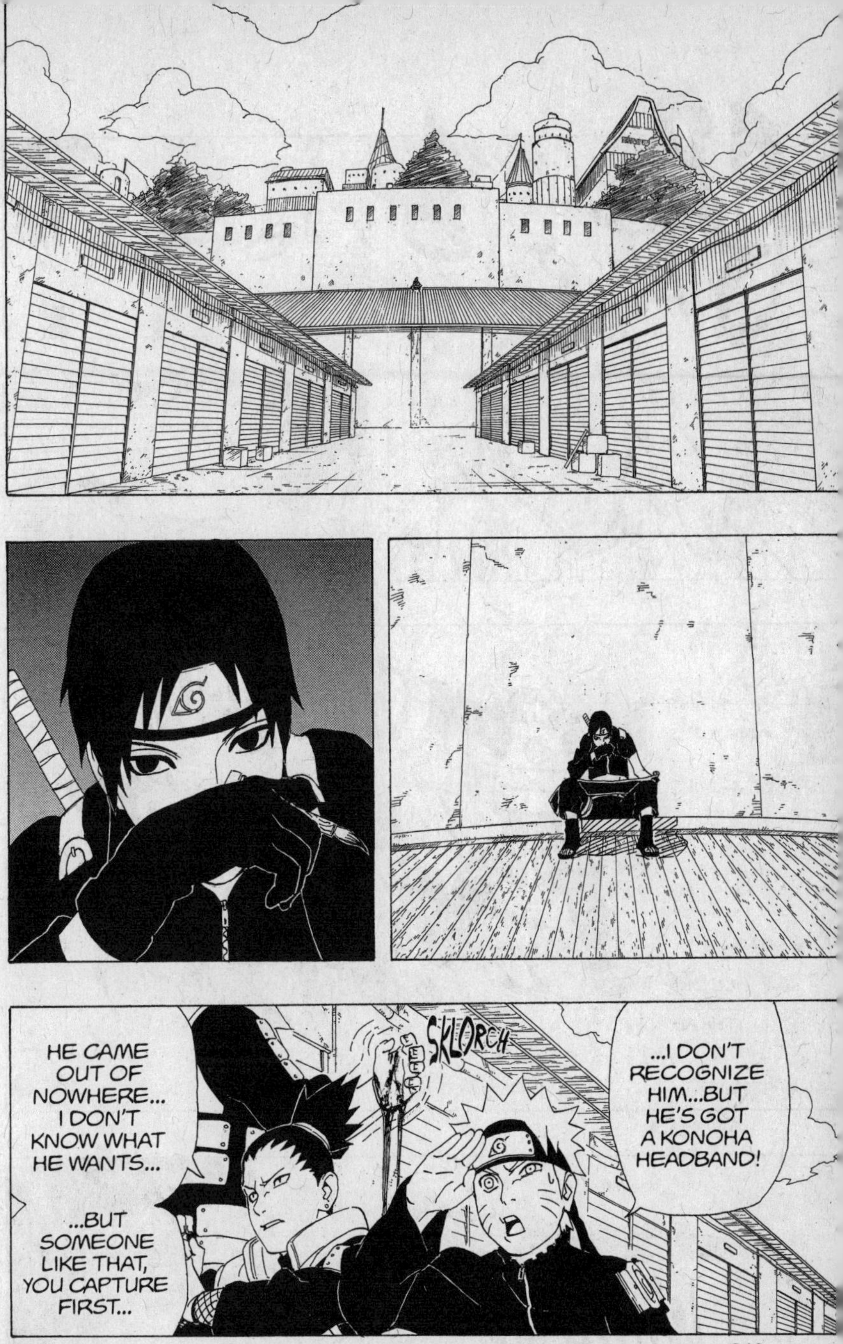
...I DON'T RECOGNIZE HIM...BUT HE'S GOT A KONOHA HEADBAND!
SKLORCH
HE CAME OUT OF NOWHERE... I DON'T KNOW WHAT HE WANTS...
...BUT SOMEONE LIKE THAT, YOU CAPTURE FIRST...

READ THIS WAY

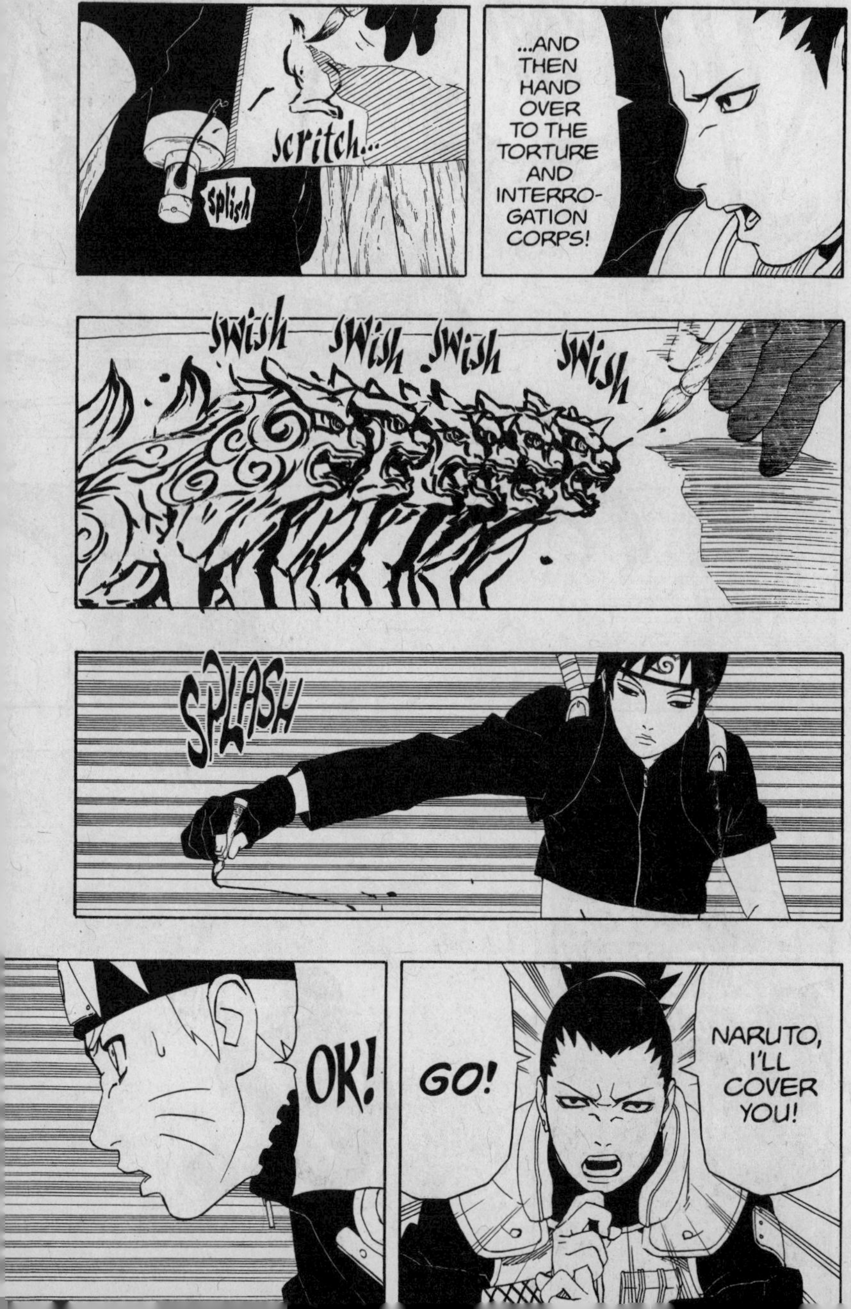
...AND THEN HAND OVER TO THE TORTURE AND INTERROGATION CORPS!
scritch...
splish
SWISH
SWISH
SWISH
SWISH
SPLASH
NARUTO, I'LL COVER YOU!
GO!
OK!

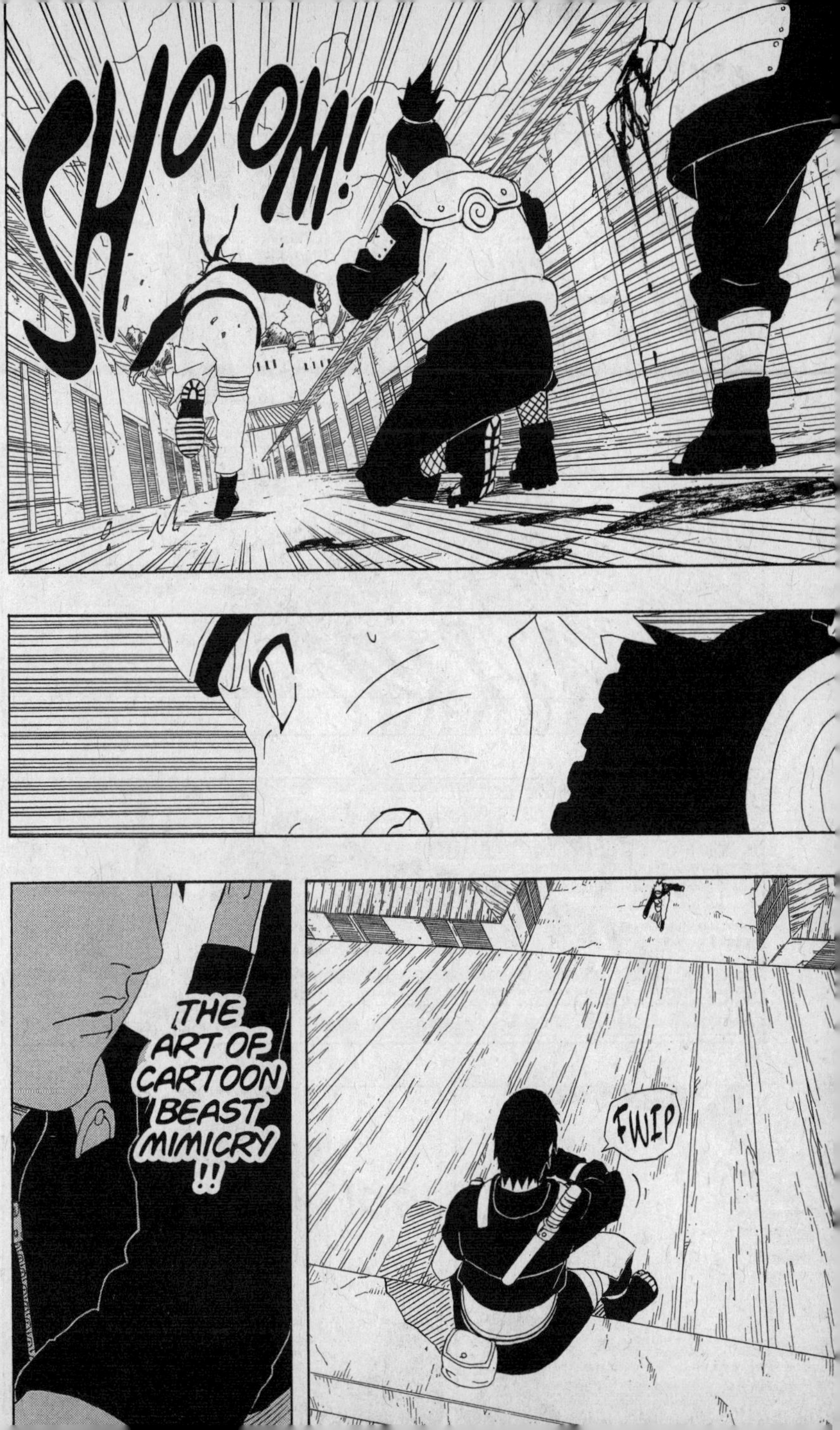
SHOOM!
FWIP
THE ART OF CARTOON BEAST MIMICRY!!

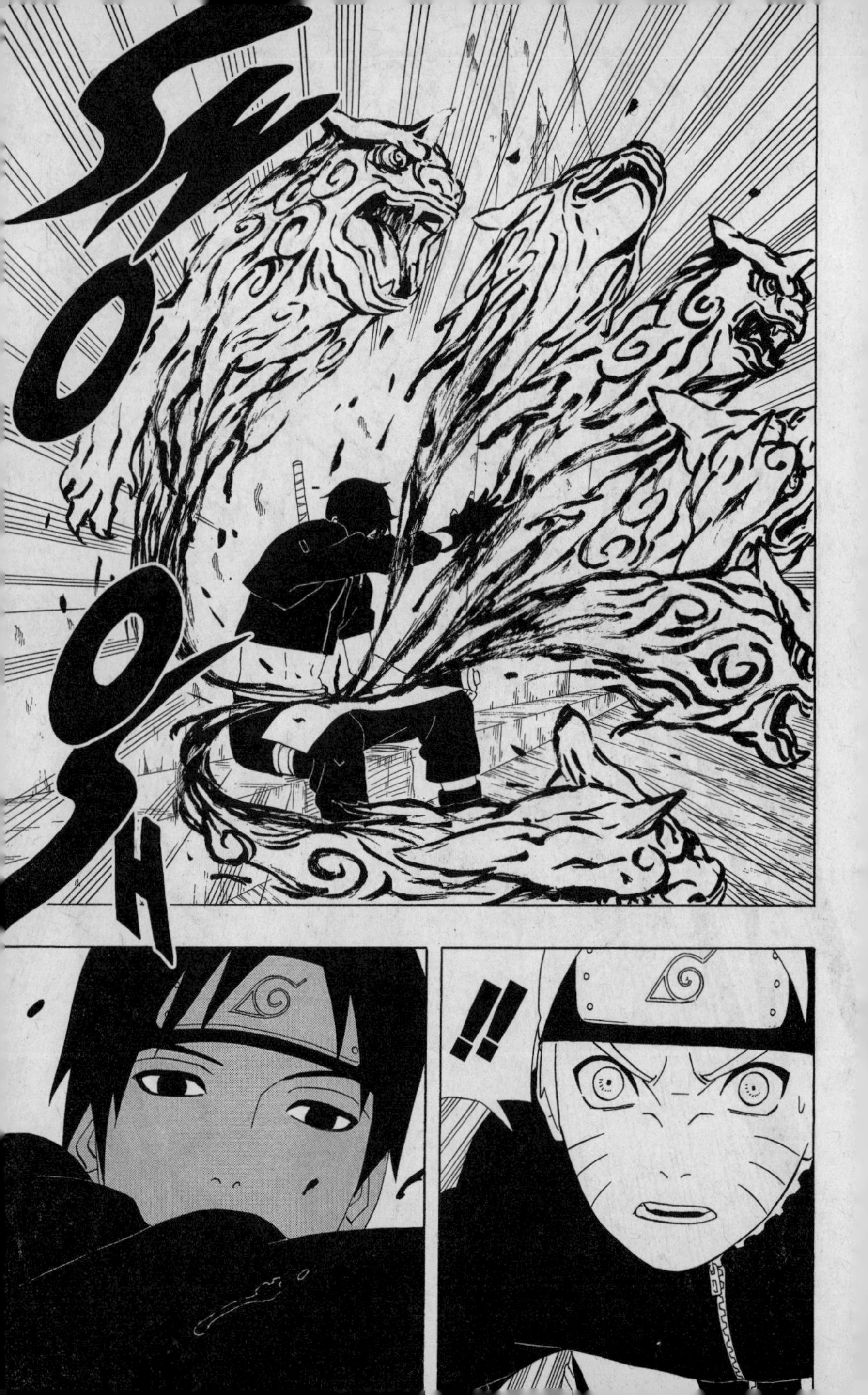
SHOOSH
!!

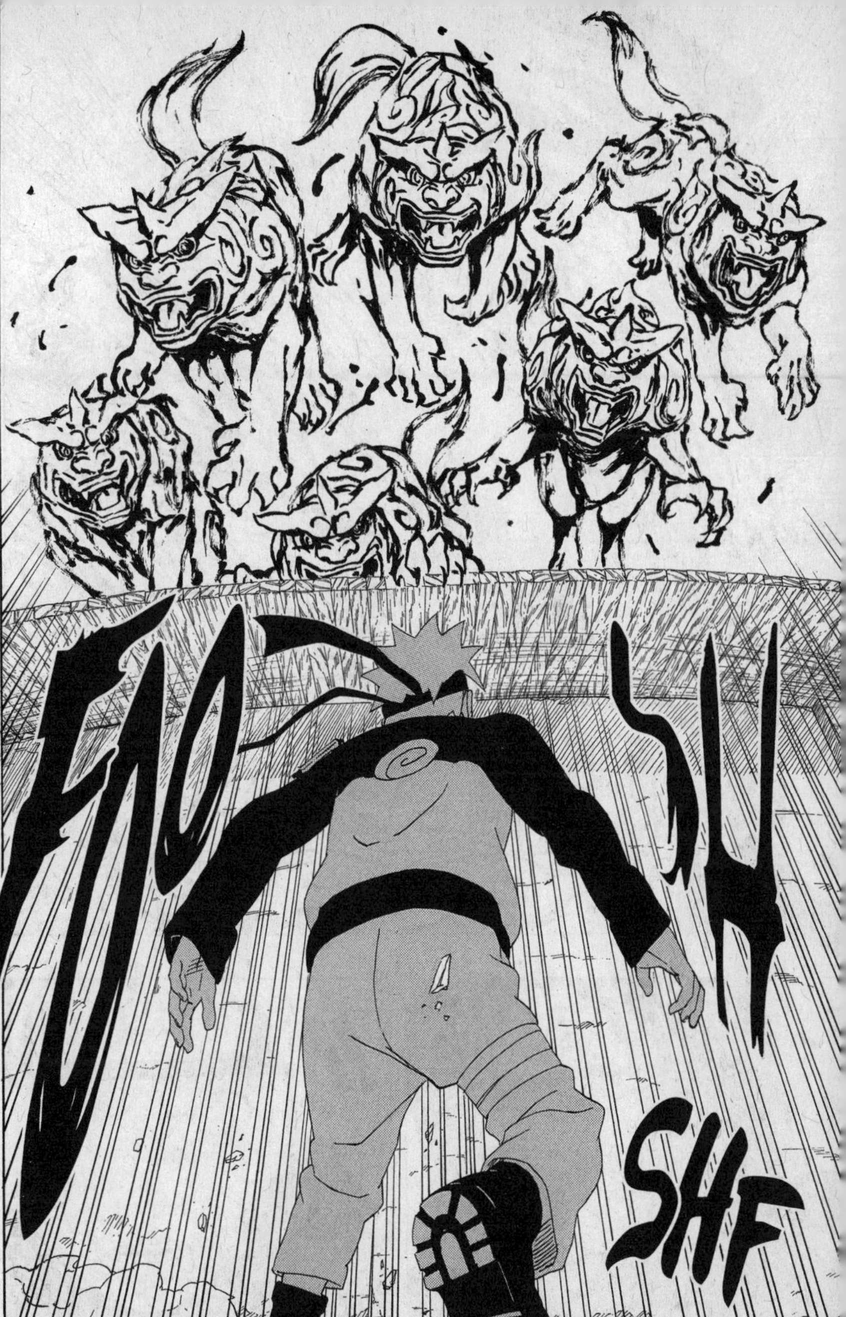
SHF

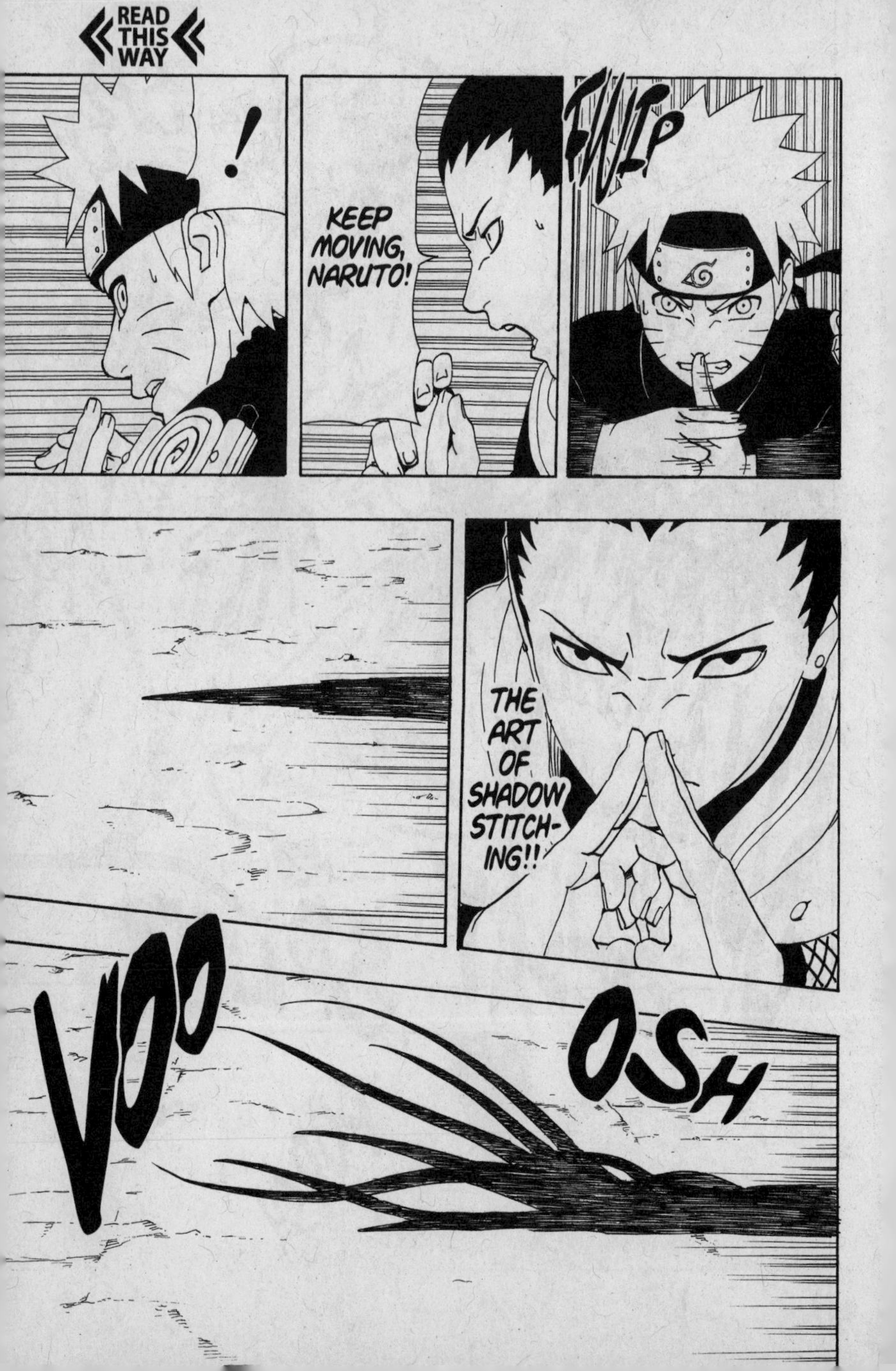
READ THIS WAY
FWIP
KEEP MOVING, NARUTO!
!
THE ART OF SHADOW STITCH-ING!!
VOOOSH

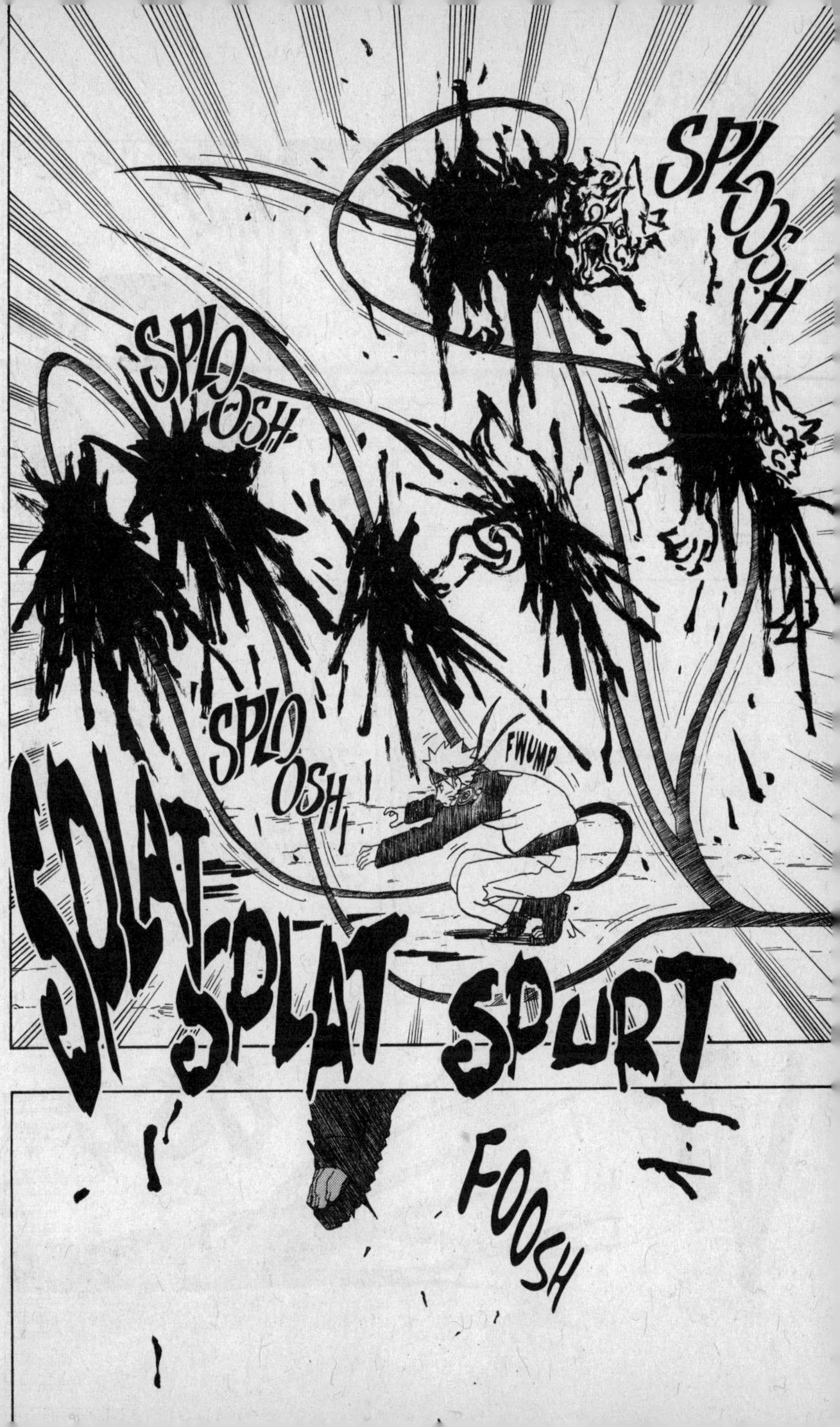
SPLOOSH
SPLOOSH
SPLOOSH
FWUMP
SPLAT
SPLAT
SPURT
FOOSH

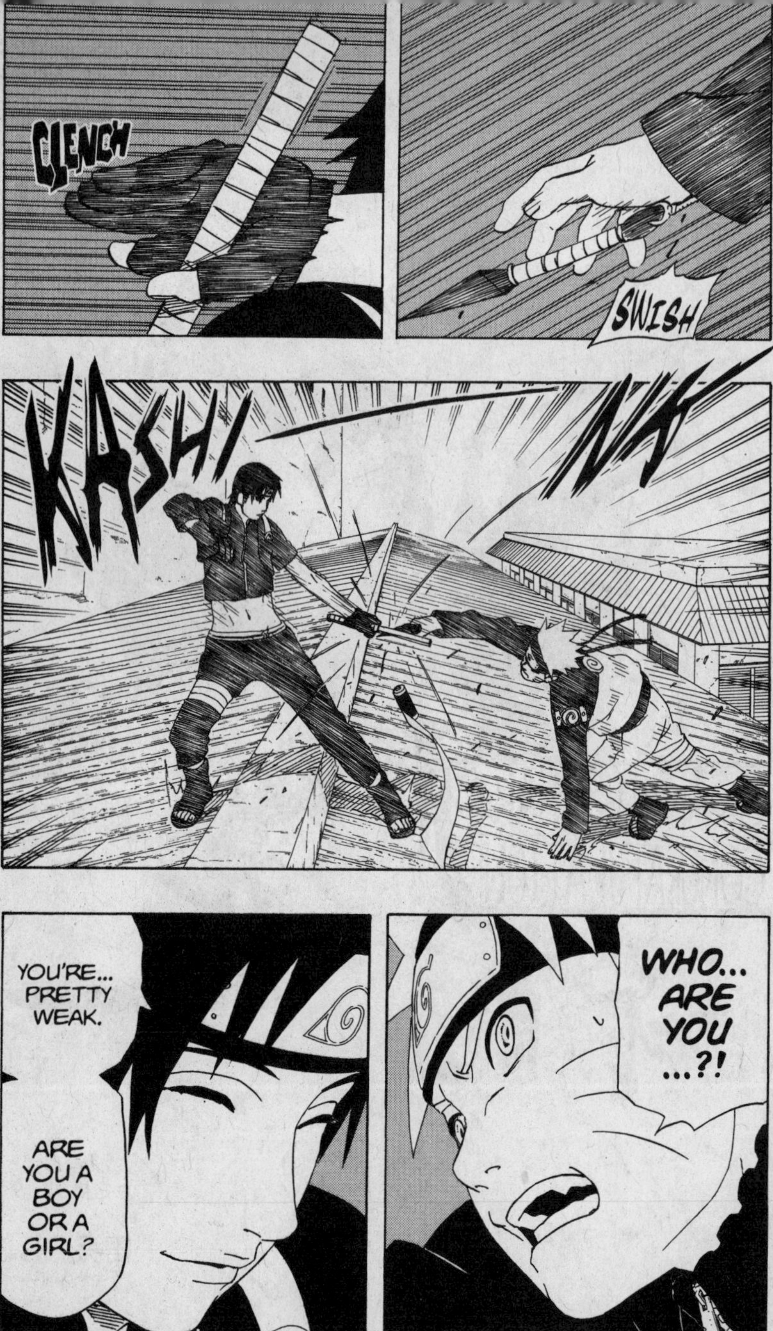
SWISH
CLENCH
KASHINK
WHO... ARE YOU ...?!
YOU'RE... PRETTY WEAK.
ARE YOU A BOY OR A GIRL?

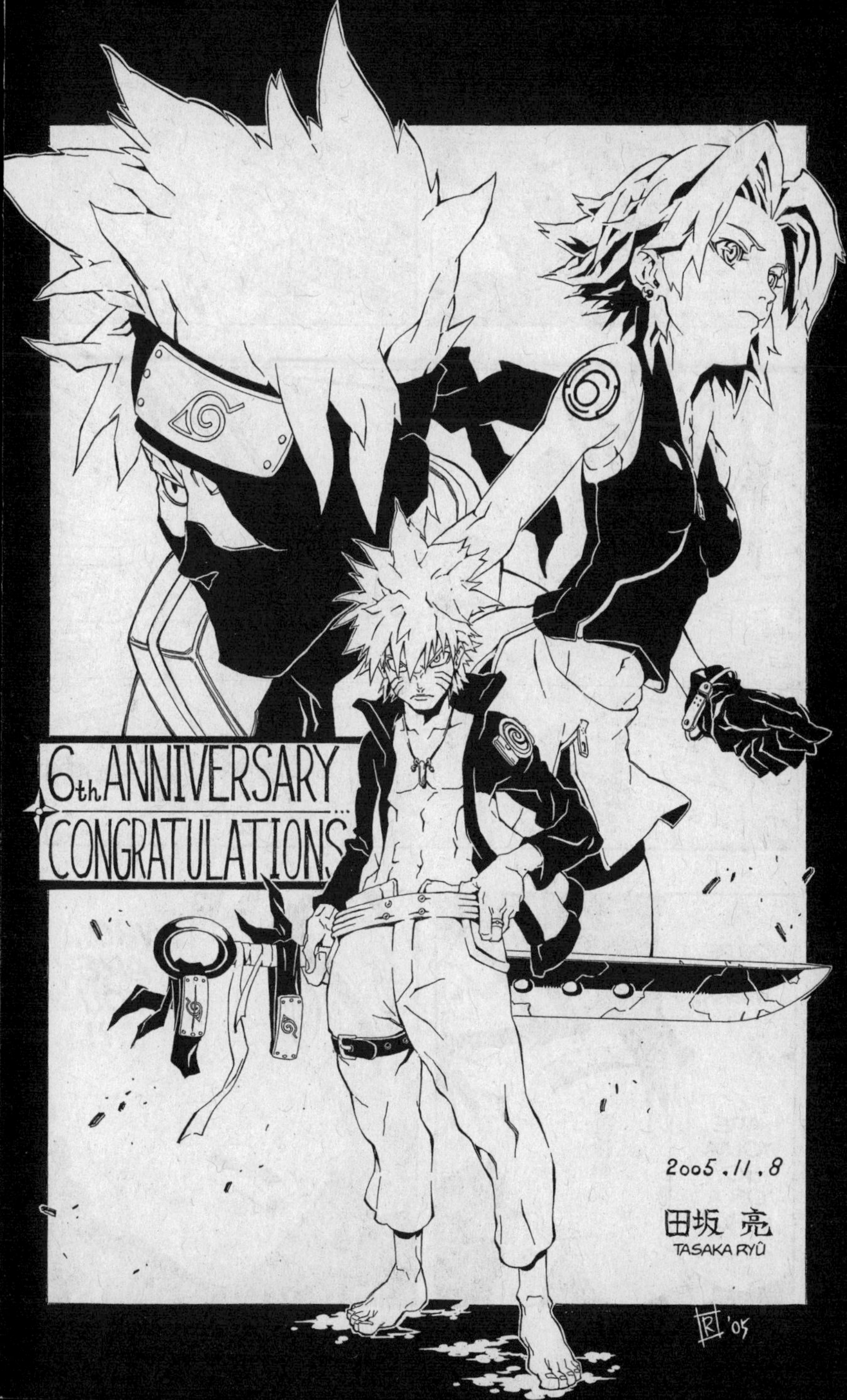
6th ANNIVERSARY
CONGRATULATIONS
2005.11.8
田坂 亮
TASAKA RYÛ
'05

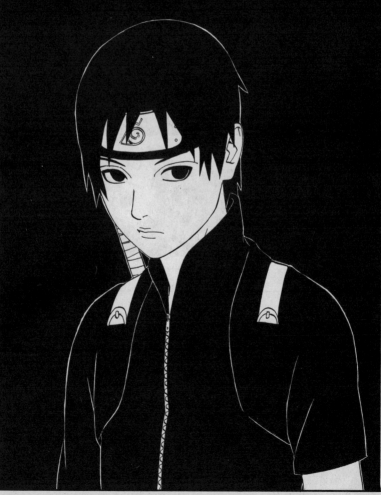

Number 284: The New
Cell...!!

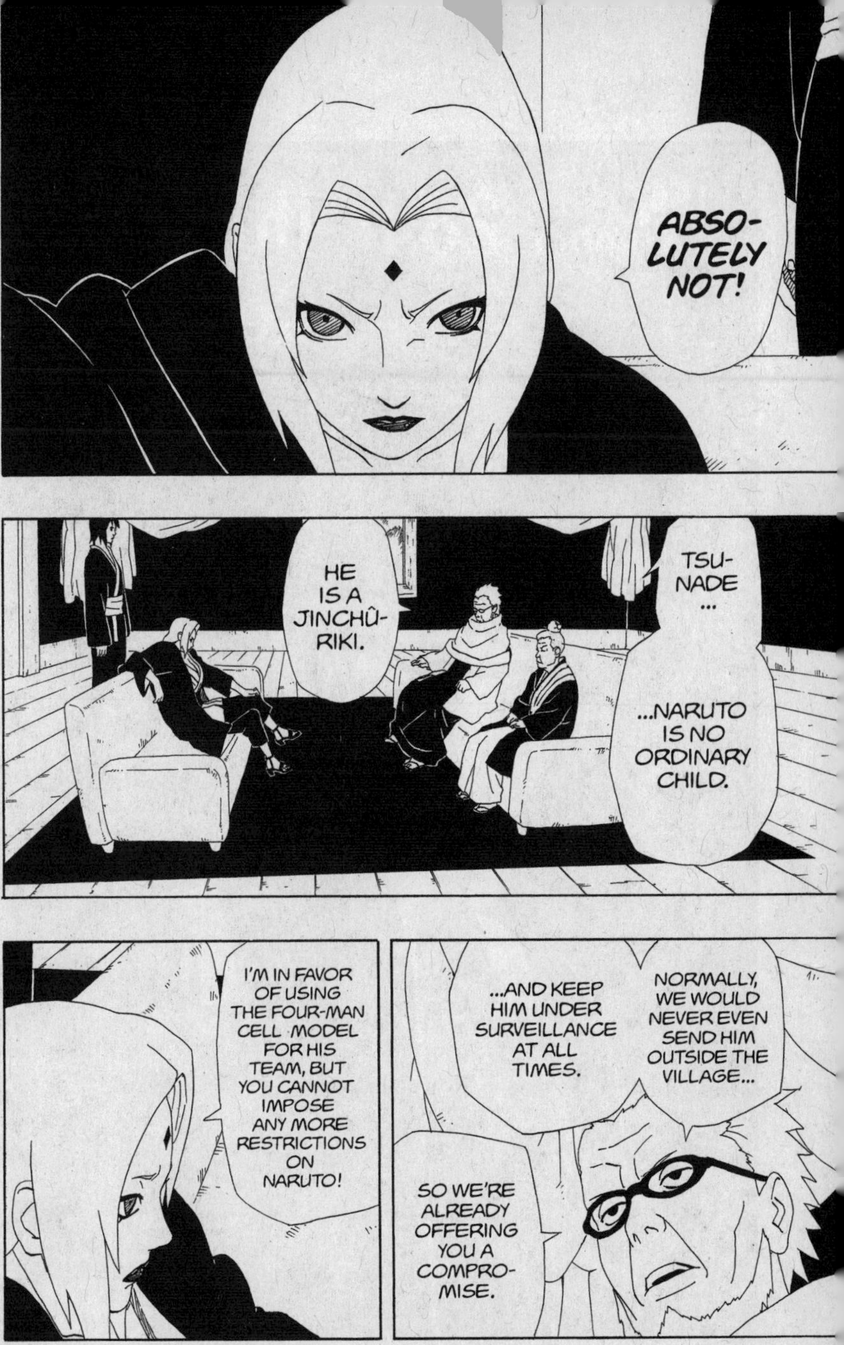
ABSO-LUTELY NOT!
TSU-NADE ...
...NARUTO IS NO ORDINARY CHILD.
HE IS A JINCHÛ-RIKI.
NORMALLY, WE WOULD NEVER EVEN SEND HIM OUTSIDE THE VILLAGE...
...AND KEEP HIM UNDER SURVEILLANCE AT ALL TIMES.
SO WE'RE ALREADY OFFERING YOU A COMPRO-MISE.
I'M IN FAVOR OF USING THE FOUR-MAN CELL MODEL FOR HIS TEAM, BUT YOU CANNOT IMPOSE ANY MORE RESTRICTIONS ON NARUTO!

READ THIS WAY

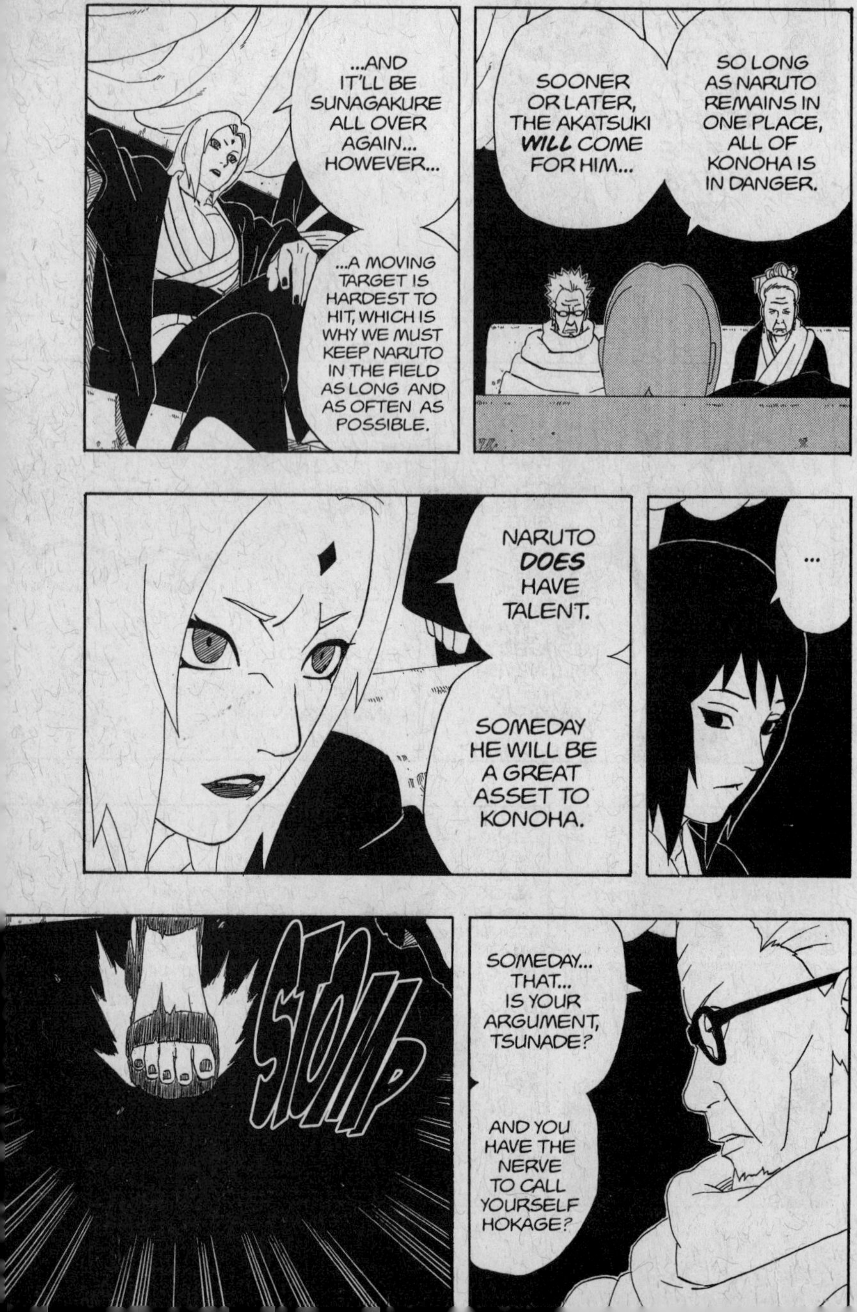
SO LONG AS NARUTO REMAINS IN ONE PLACE, ALL OF KONOHA IS IN DANGER.
SOONER OR LATER, THE AKATSUKI **WILL** COME FOR HIM...
...AND IT'LL BE SUNAGAKURE ALL OVER AGAIN... HOWEVER...
...A MOVING TARGET IS HARDEST TO HIT, WHICH IS WHY WE MUST KEEP NARUTO IN THE FIELD AS LONG AND AS OFTEN AS POSSIBLE.
...
NARUTO **DOES** HAVE TALENT.
SOMEDAY HE WILL BE A GREAT ASSET TO KONOHA.
SOMEDAY... THAT... IS YOUR ARGUMENT, TSUNADE?
AND YOU HAVE THE NERVE TO CALL YOURSELF HOKAGE?
STOMP

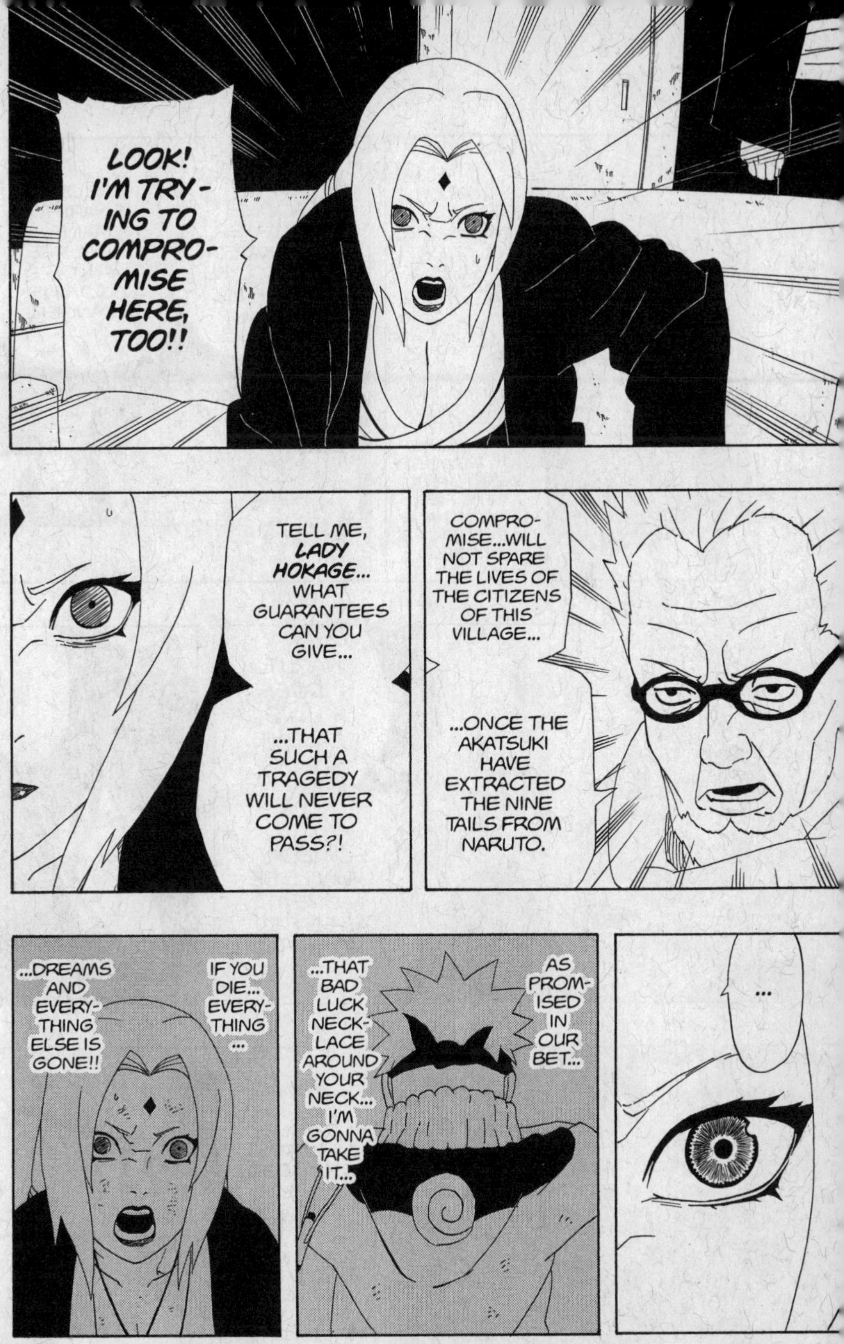
LOOK! I'M TRY-ING TO COMPRO-MISE HERE, TOO!!
COMPRO-MISE...WILL NOT SPARE THE LIVES OF THE CITIZENS OF THIS VILLAGE...
...ONCE THE AKATSUKI HAVE EXTRACTED THE NINE TAILS FROM NARUTO.
TELL ME, LADY HOKAGE... WHAT GUARANTEES CAN YOU GIVE...
...THAT SUCH A TRAGEDY WILL NEVER COME TO PASS?!
...
AS PROM-ISED IN OUR BET...
...THAT BAD LUCK NECK-LACE AROUND YOUR NECK... I'M GONNA TAKE IT...
IF YOU DIE... EVERY-THING...
...DREAMS AND EVERY-THING ELSE IS GONE!!

READ THIS WAY

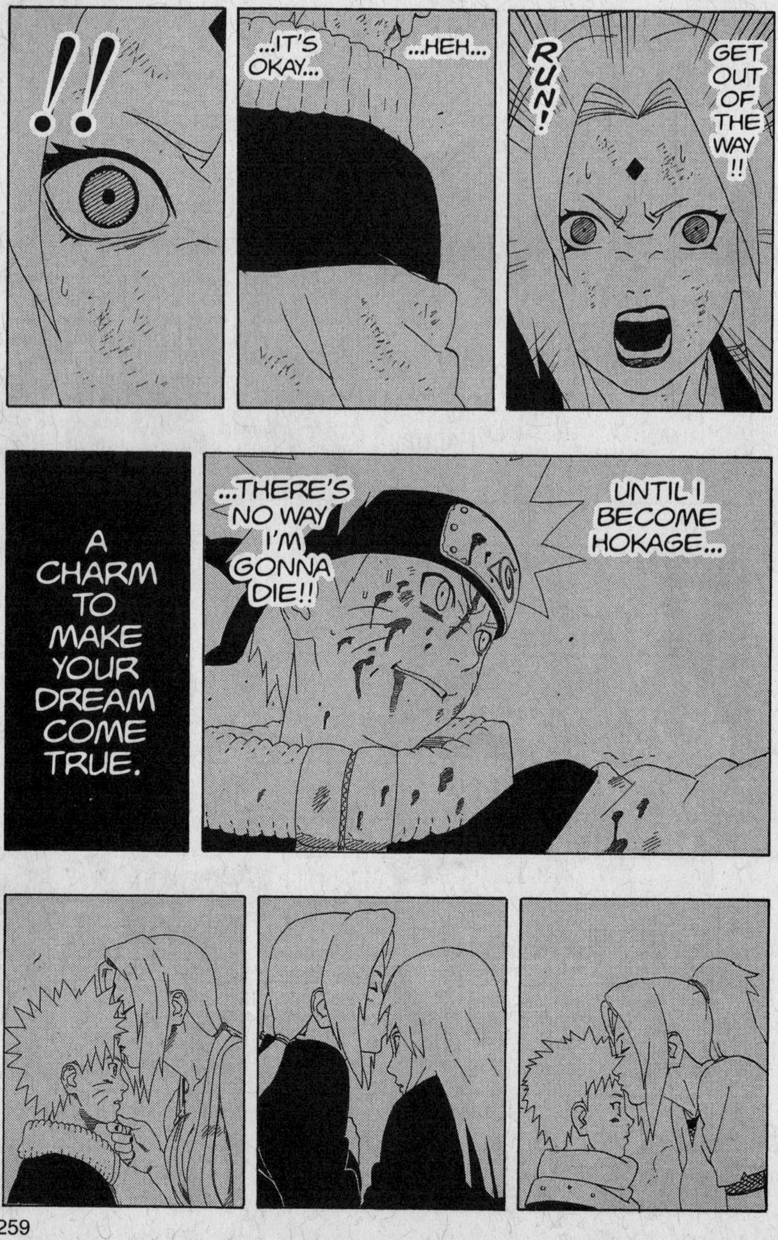
GET OUT OF THE WAY!!
RUN!
...HEH...
...IT'S OKAY...
!!
UNTIL I BECOME HOKAGE...
...THERE'S NO WAY I'M GONNA DIE!!
A CHARM TO MAKE YOUR DREAM COME TRUE.

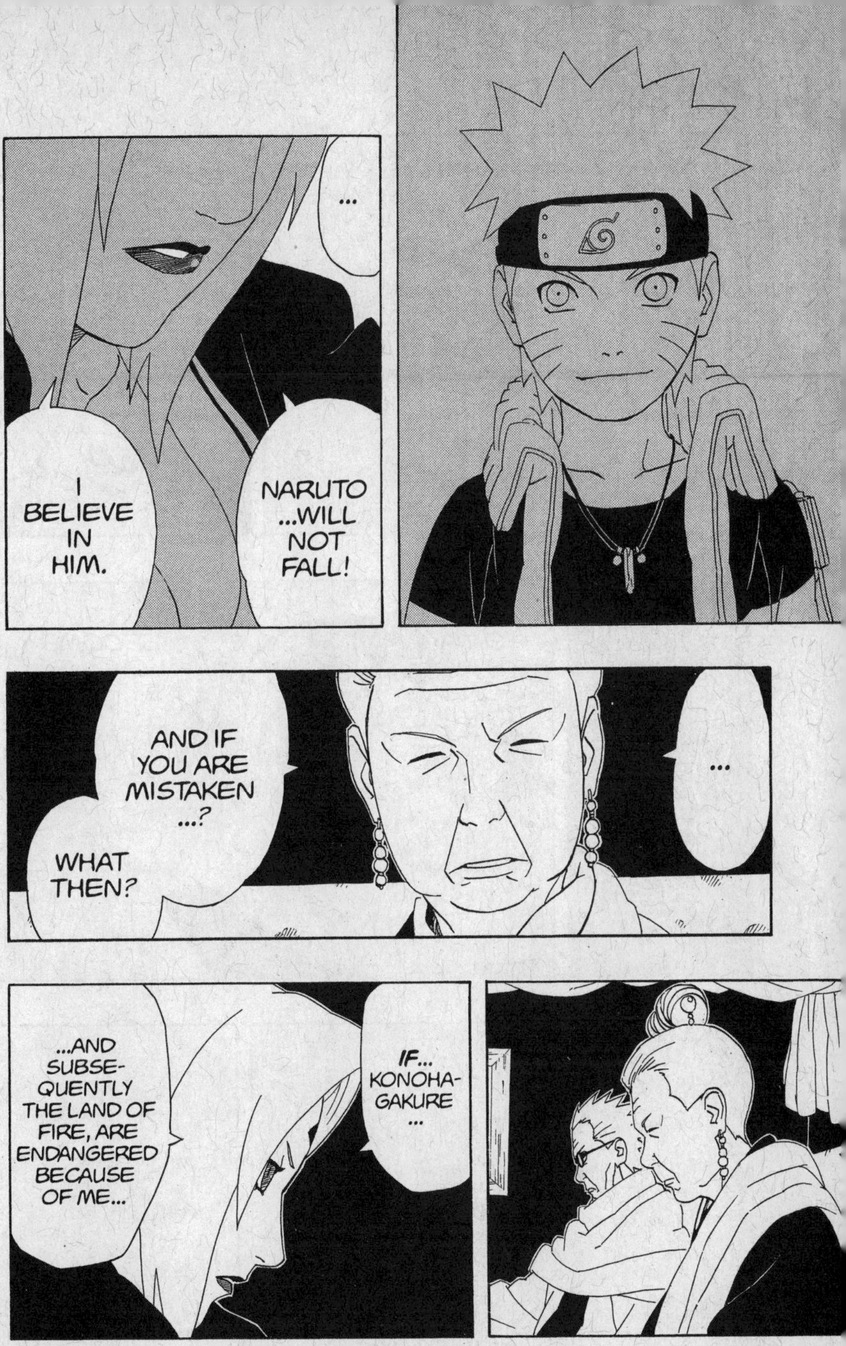
...
NARUTO ...WILL NOT FALL!
I BELIEVE IN HIM.
...
AND IF YOU ARE MISTAKEN ...?
WHAT THEN?
IF... KONOHAGAKURE ...
...AND SUBSEQUENTLY THE LAND OF FIRE, ARE ENDANGERED BECAUSE OF ME...

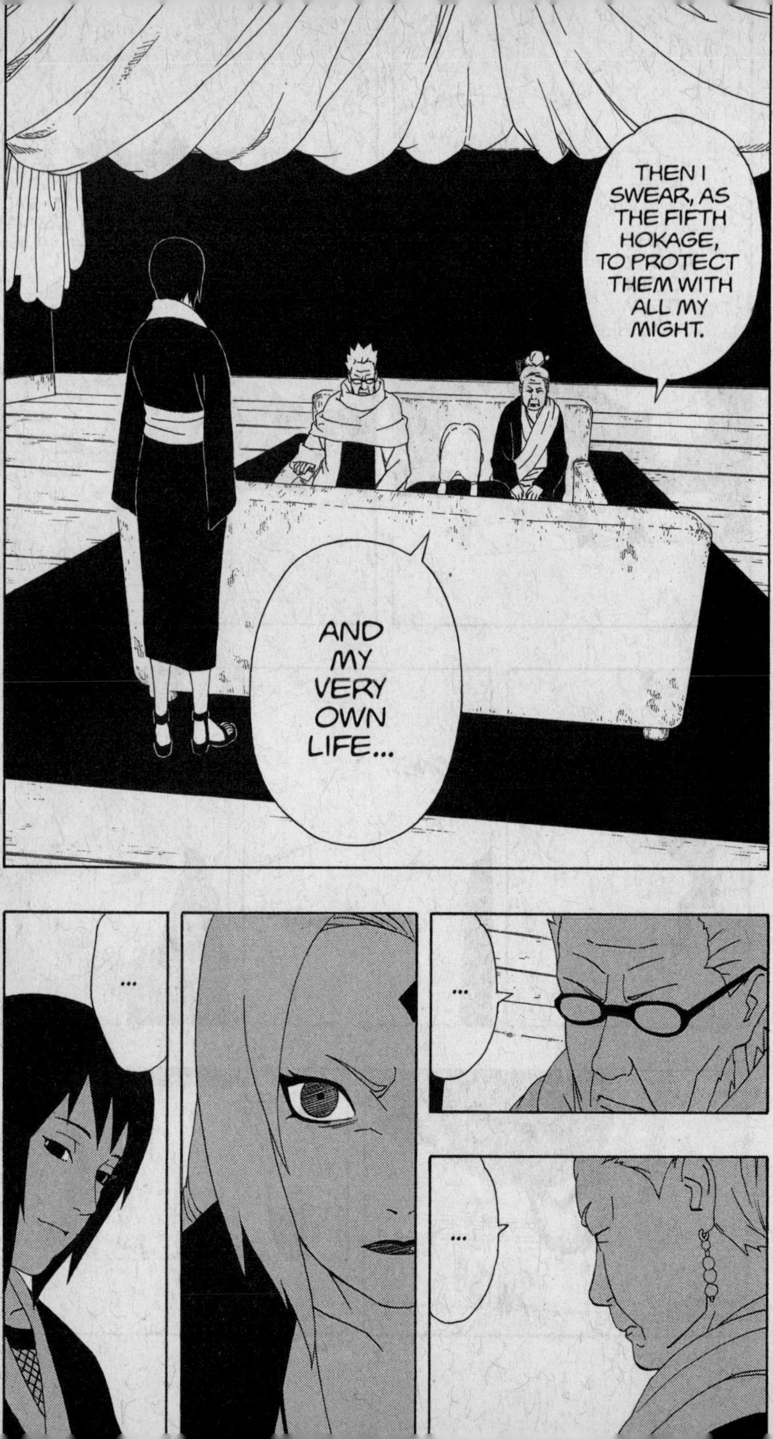
THEN I SWEAR, AS THE FIFTH HOKAGE, TO PROTECT THEM WITH ALL MY MIGHT.
AND MY VERY OWN LIFE...
...
...
...

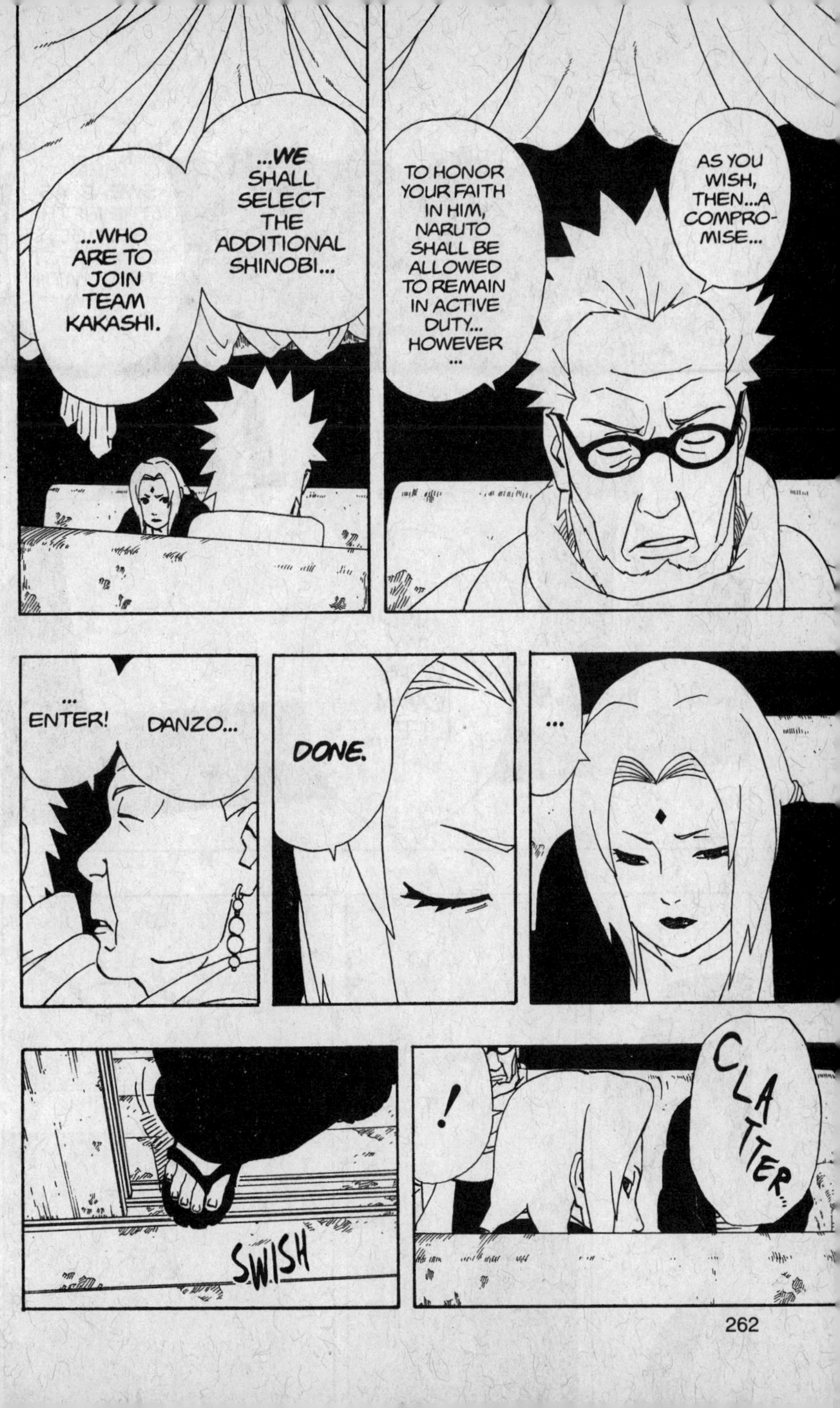
AS YOU WISH, THEN...A COMPROMISE...
TO HONOR YOUR FAITH IN HIM, NARUTO SHALL BE ALLOWED TO REMAIN IN ACTIVE DUTY... HOWEVER ...
...WE SHALL SELECT THE ADDITIONAL SHINOBI...
...WHO ARE TO JOIN TEAM KAKASHI.
...
DONE.
DANZO...
... ENTER!
CLATTER...
!
SWISH

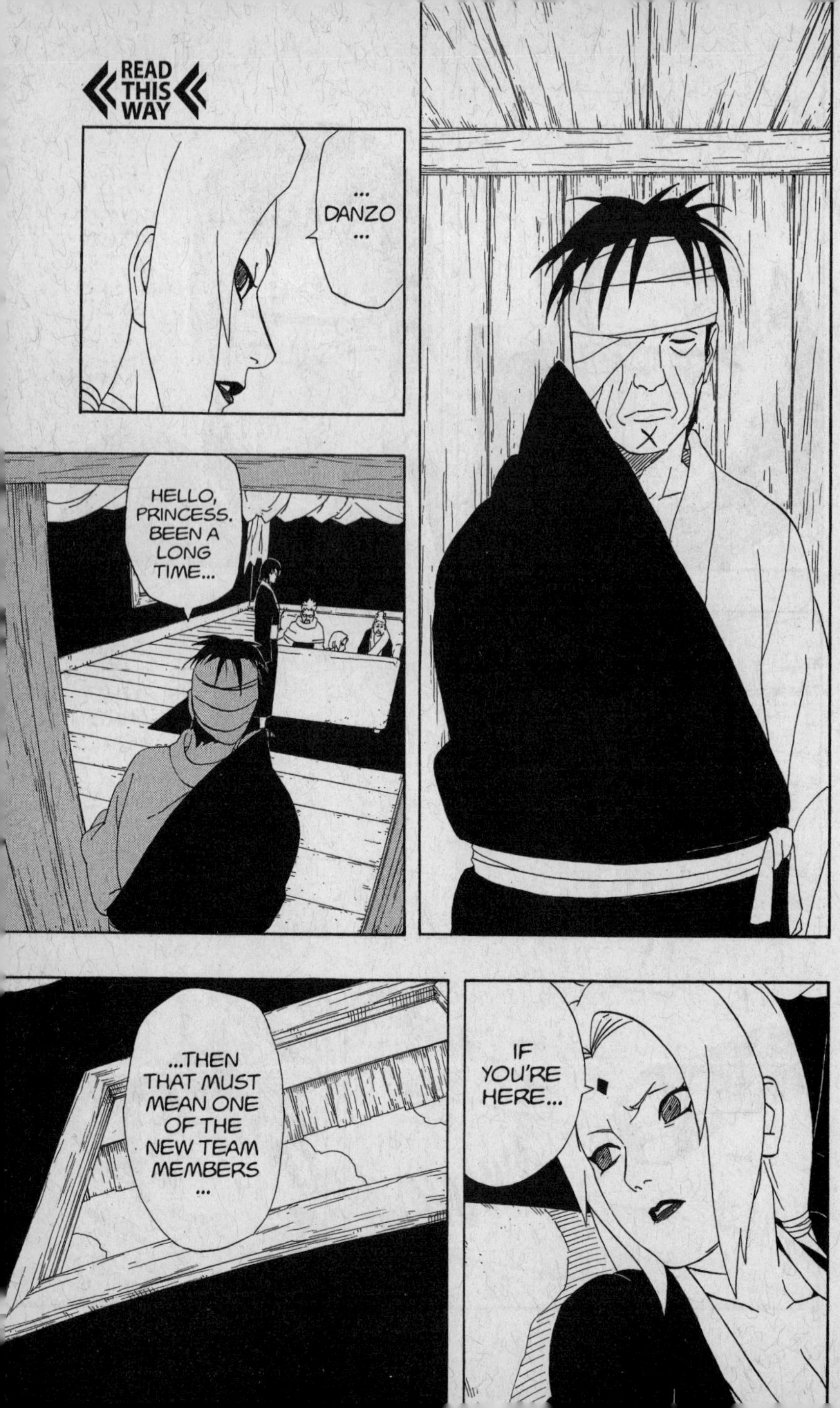
READ THIS WAY
... DANZO ...
HELLO, PRINCESS. BEEN A LONG TIME...
IF YOU'RE HERE...
...THEN THAT MUST MEAN ONE OF THE NEW TEAM MEMBERS ...

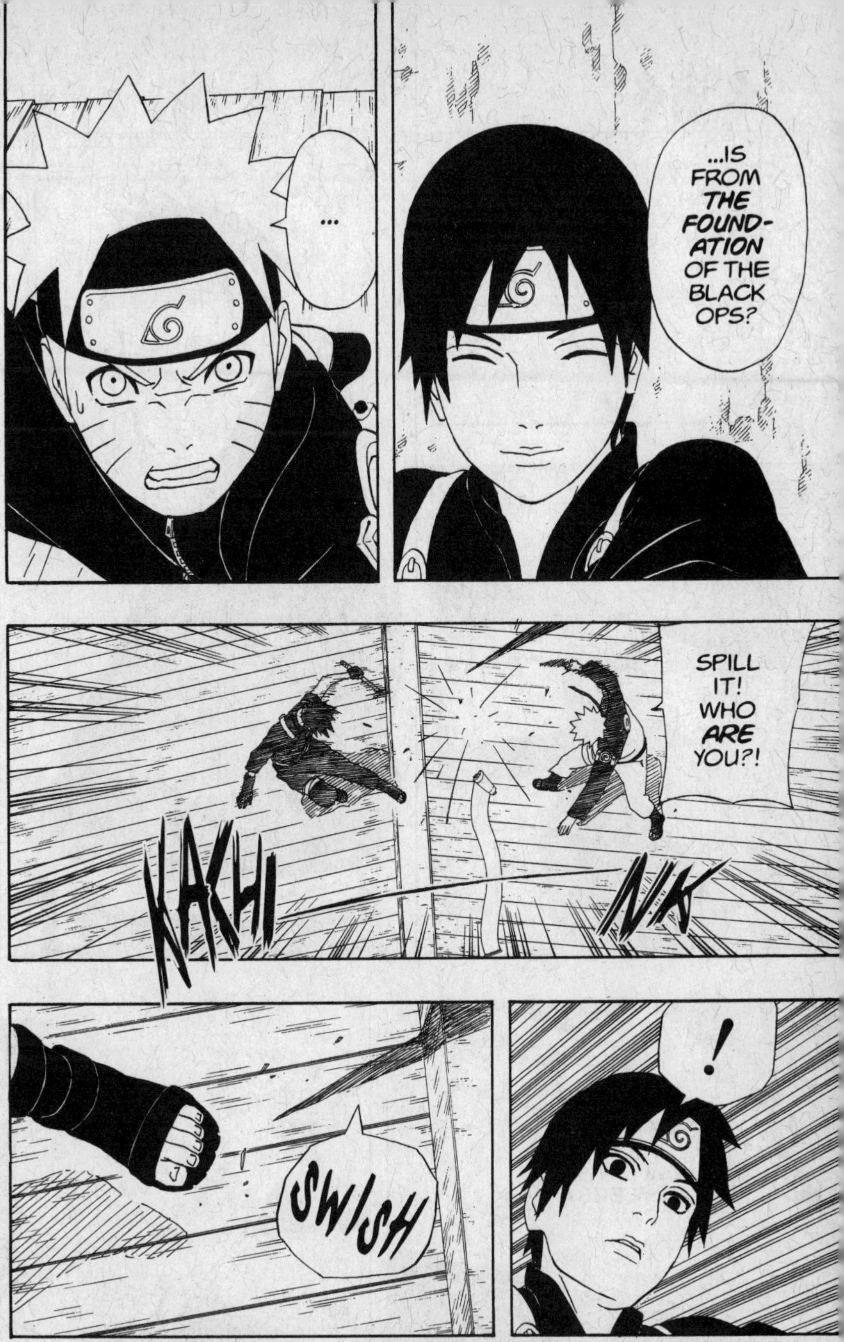

...IS FROM THE FOUNDATION OF THE BLACK OPS?
...
SPILL IT! WHO ARE YOU?!
KACHI
NK
!
SWISH

READ THIS WAY

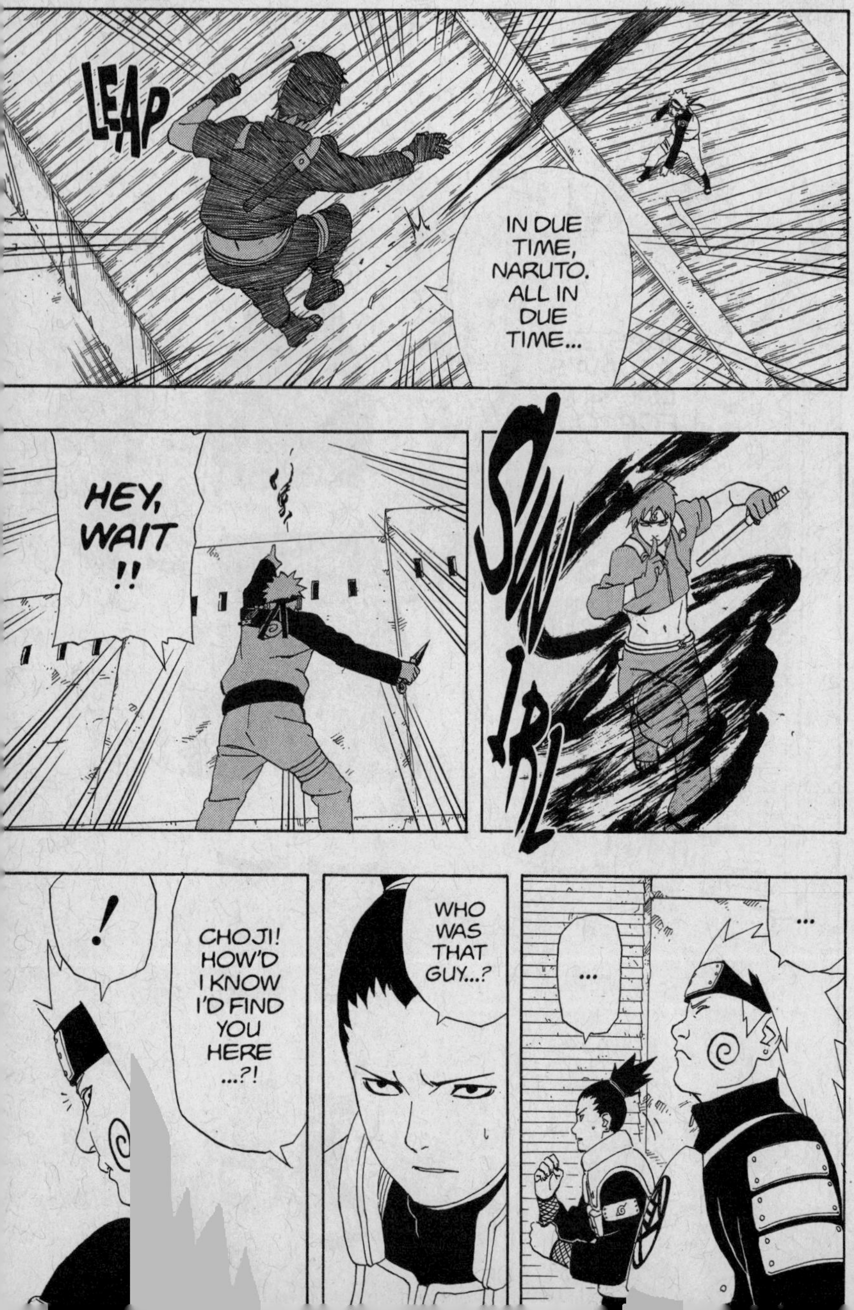
IN DUE TIME, NARUTO. ALL IN DUE TIME...
LEAP
SWIRL
HEY, WAIT!!
...
...
WHO WAS THAT GUY...?
CHOJI! HOW'D I KNOW I'D FIND YOU HERE...?!
!

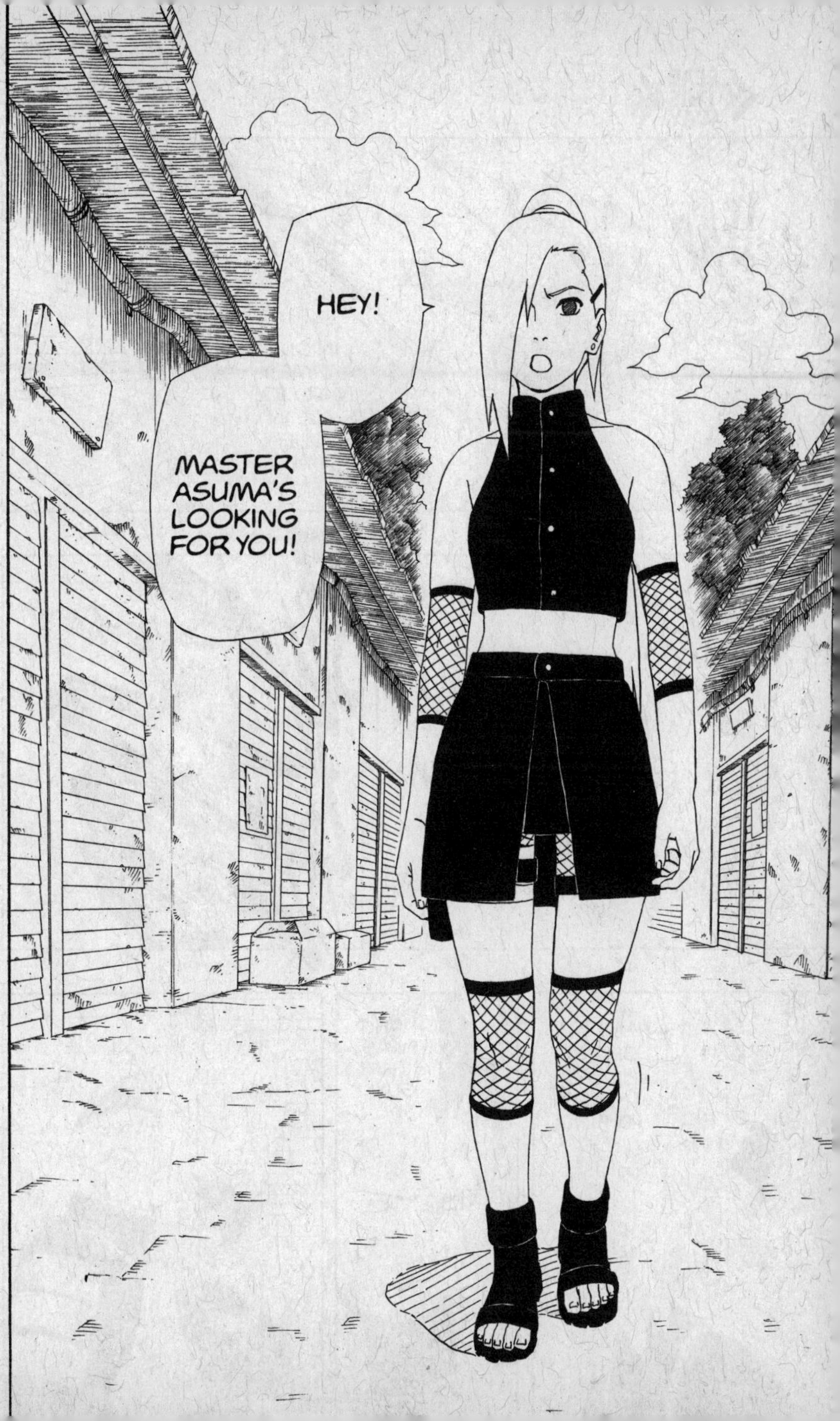
HEY!
MASTER ASUMA'S LOOKING FOR YOU!

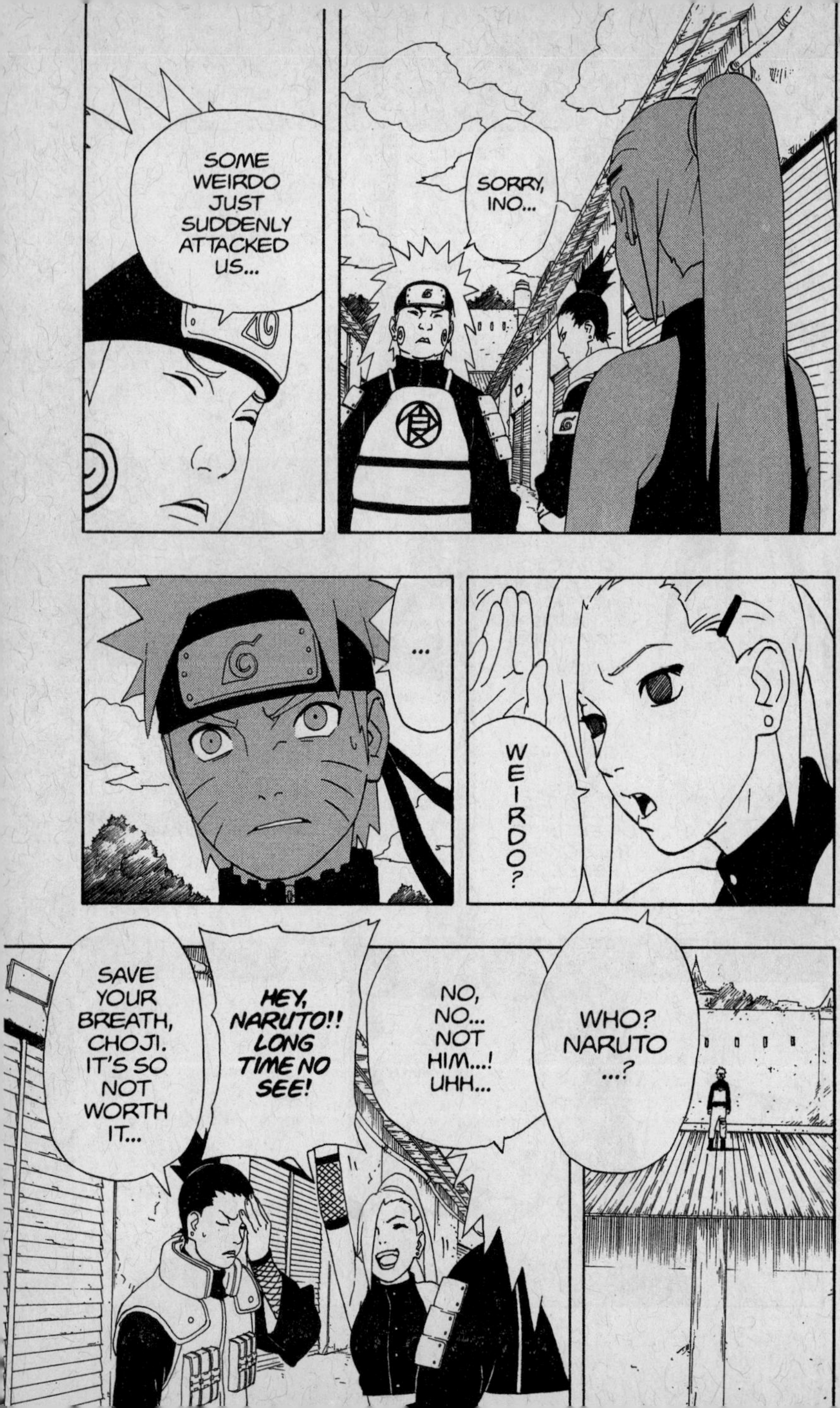
SORRY, INO...
SOME WEIRDO JUST SUDDENLY ATTACKED US...
WEIRDO?
...
WHO? NARUTO ...?
NO, NO... NOT HIM...! UHH...
HEY, NARUTO!! LONG TIME NO SEE!
SAVE YOUR BREATH, CHOJI. IT'S SO NOT WORTH IT...

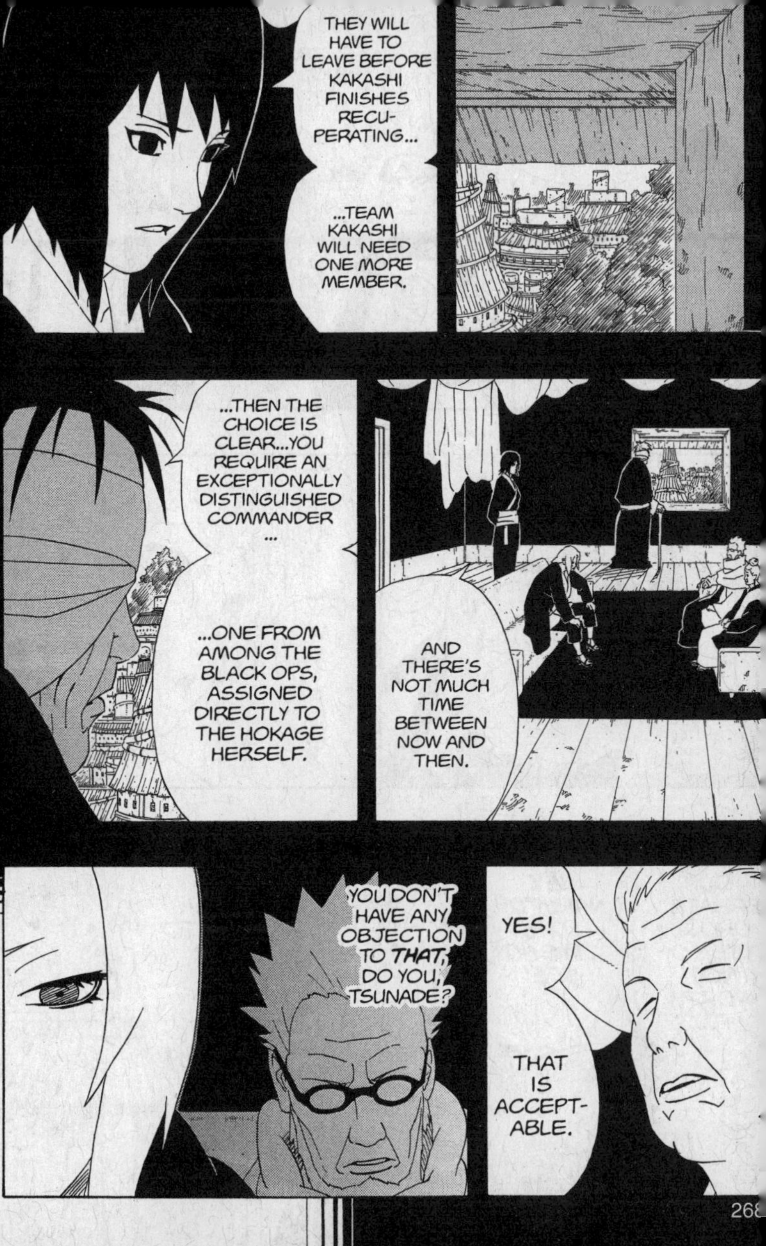
THEY WILL HAVE TO LEAVE BEFORE KAKASHI FINISHES RECU-PERATING...
...TEAM KAKASHI WILL NEED ONE MORE MEMBER.
AND THERE'S NOT MUCH TIME BETWEEN NOW AND THEN.
...THEN THE CHOICE IS CLEAR...YOU REQUIRE AN EXCEPTIONALLY DISTINGUISHED COMMANDER ...
...ONE FROM AMONG THE BLACK OPS, ASSIGNED DIRECTLY TO THE HOKAGE HERSELF.
YES!
THAT IS ACCEPT-ABLE.
YOU DON'T HAVE ANY OBJECTION TO *THAT*, DO YOU, TSUNADE?

READ THIS WAY

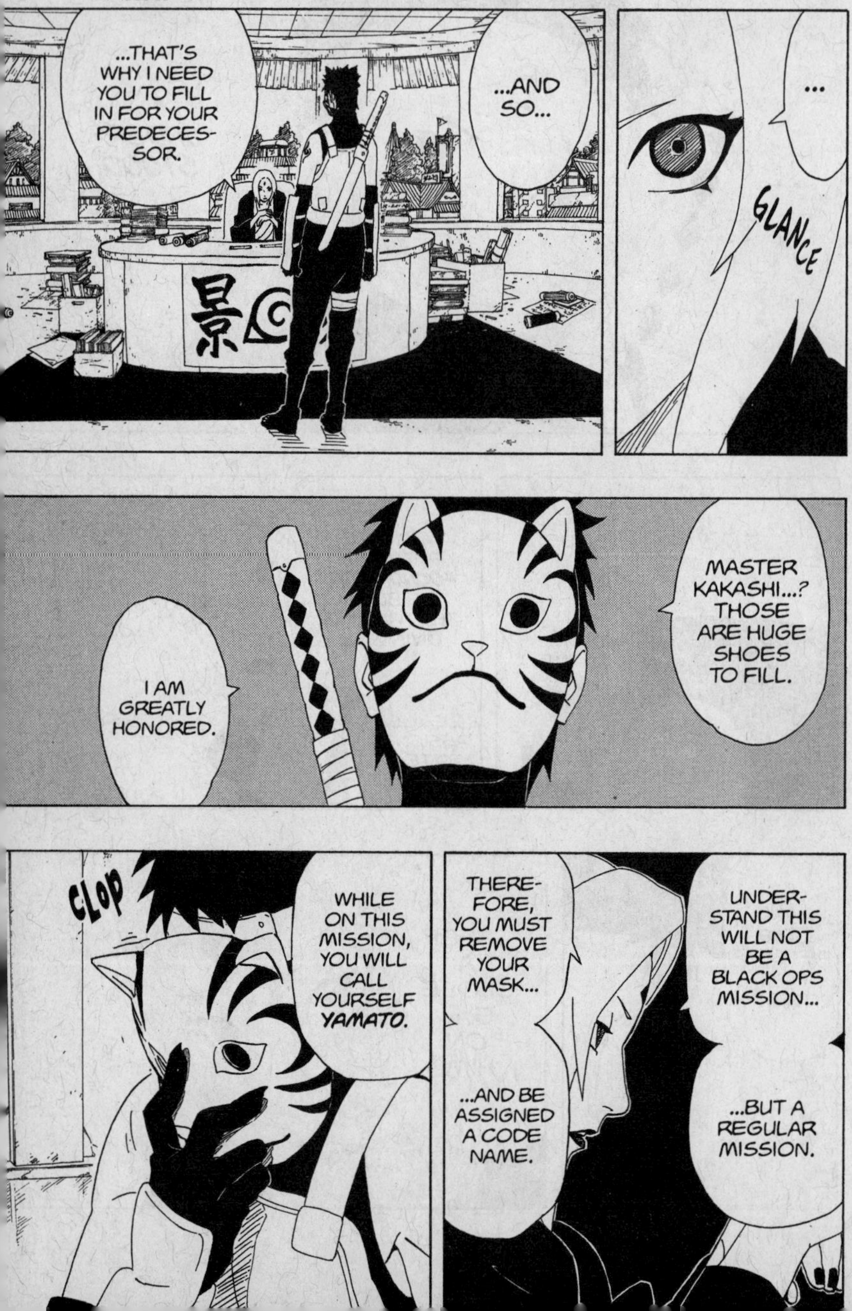
...
GLANCE
...AND SO...
...THAT'S WHY I NEED YOU TO FILL IN FOR YOUR PREDECES-SOR.
MASTER KAKASHI...? THOSE ARE HUGE SHOES TO FILL.
I AM GREATLY HONORED.
UNDER-STAND THIS WILL NOT BE A BLACK OPS MISSION...
...BUT A REGULAR MISSION.
THERE-FORE, YOU MUST REMOVE YOUR MASK...
...AND BE ASSIGNED A CODE NAME.
WHILE ON THIS MISSION, YOU WILL CALL YOURSELF *YAMATO.*
CLOP

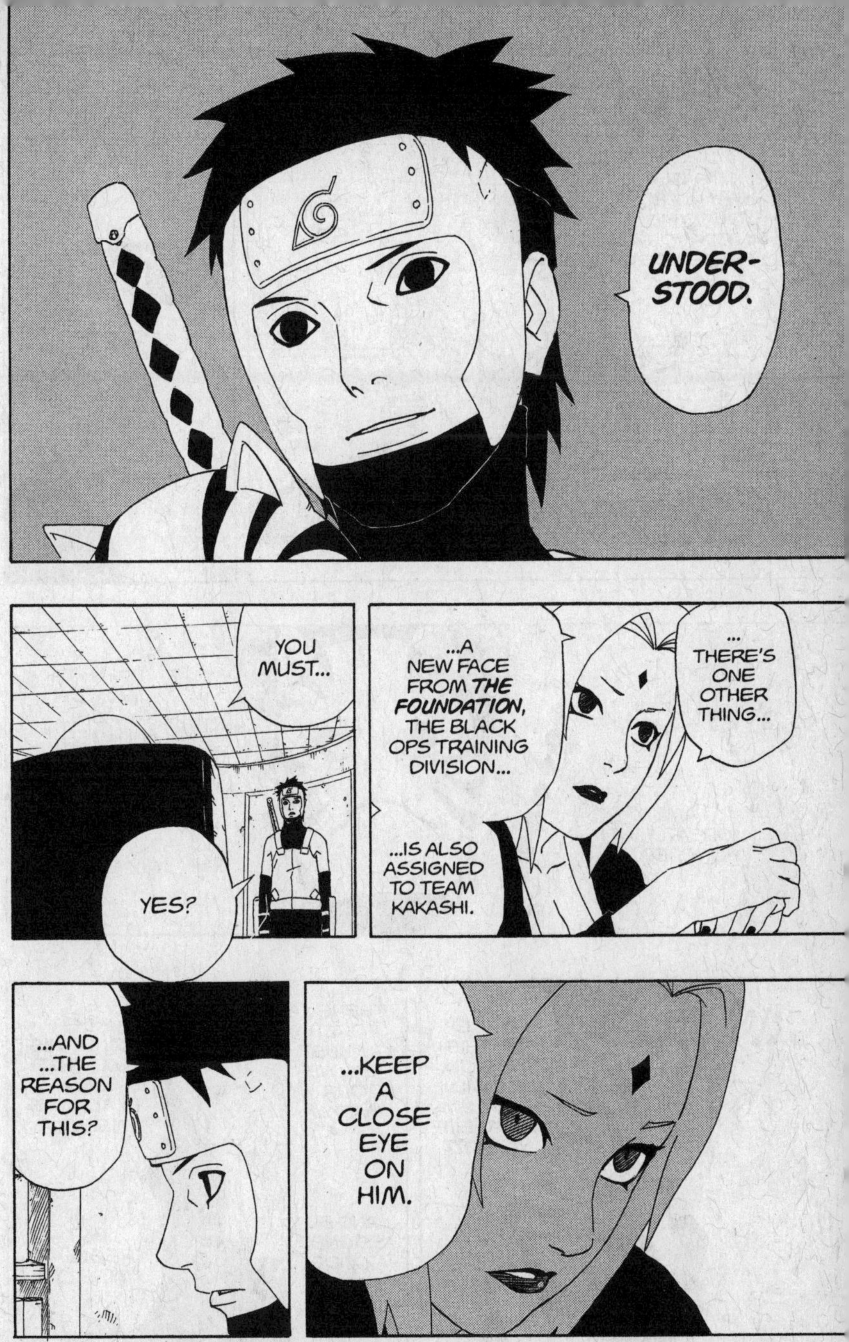
UNDER-STOOD.
...THERE'S ONE OTHER THING...
...A NEW FACE FROM THE FOUNDATION, THE BLACK OPS TRAINING DIVISION...
...IS ALSO ASSIGNED TO TEAM KAKASHI.
YOU MUST...
YES?
...KEEP A CLOSE EYE ON HIM.
...AND ...THE REASON FOR THIS?

READ THIS WAY

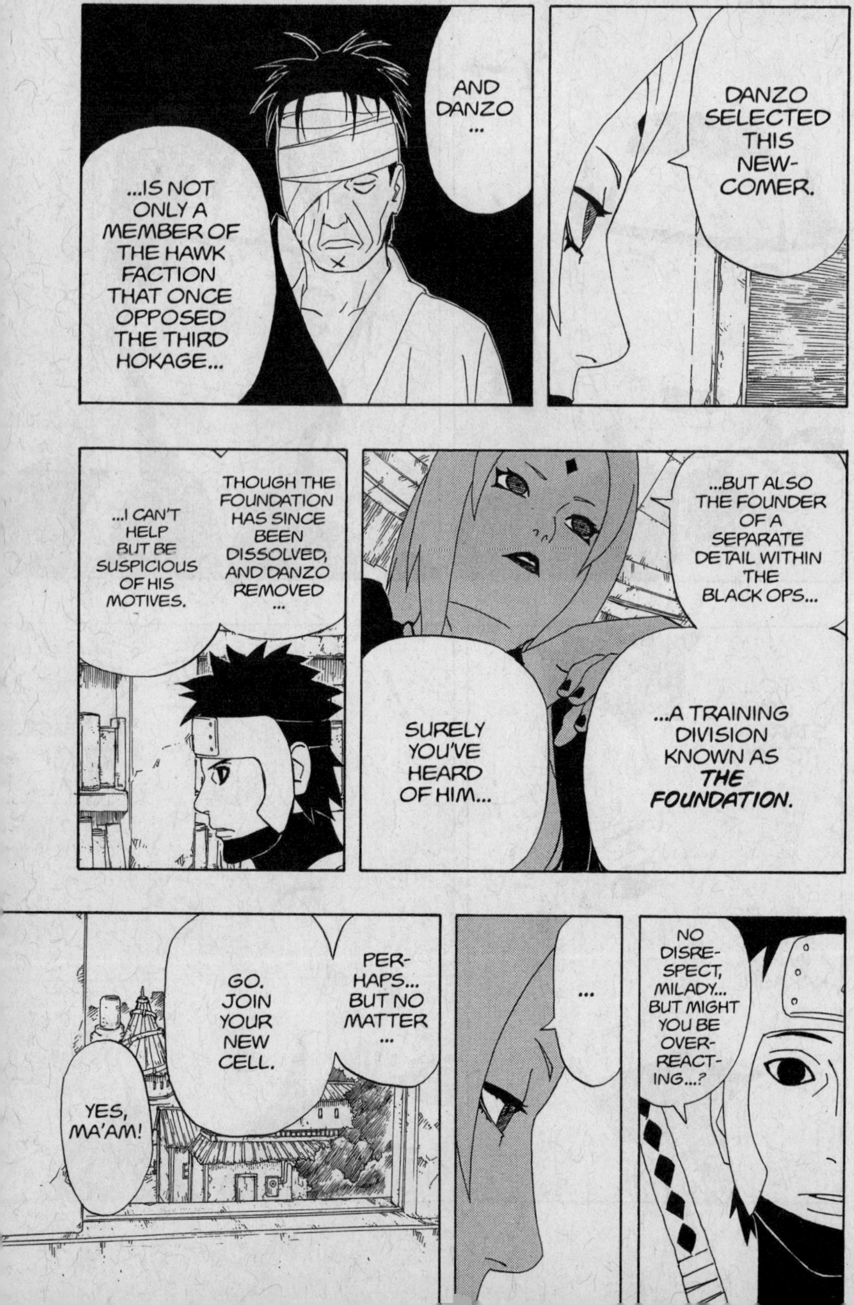
DANZO SELECTED THIS NEW-COMER.
AND DANZO ...
...IS NOT ONLY A MEMBER OF THE HAWK FACTION THAT ONCE OPPOSED THE THIRD HOKAGE...
...BUT ALSO THE FOUNDER OF A SEPARATE DETAIL WITHIN THE BLACK OPS...
...A TRAINING DIVISION KNOWN AS *THE FOUNDATION*.
SURELY YOU'VE HEARD OF HIM...
THOUGH THE FOUNDATION HAS SINCE BEEN DISSOLVED, AND DANZO REMOVED ...
...I CAN'T HELP BUT BE SUSPICIOUS OF HIS MOTIVES.
NO DISRE-SPECT, MILADY... BUT MIGHT YOU BE OVER-REACT-ING...?
...
PER-HAPS... BUT NO MATTER ...
GO. JOIN YOUR NEW CELL.
YES, MA'AM!

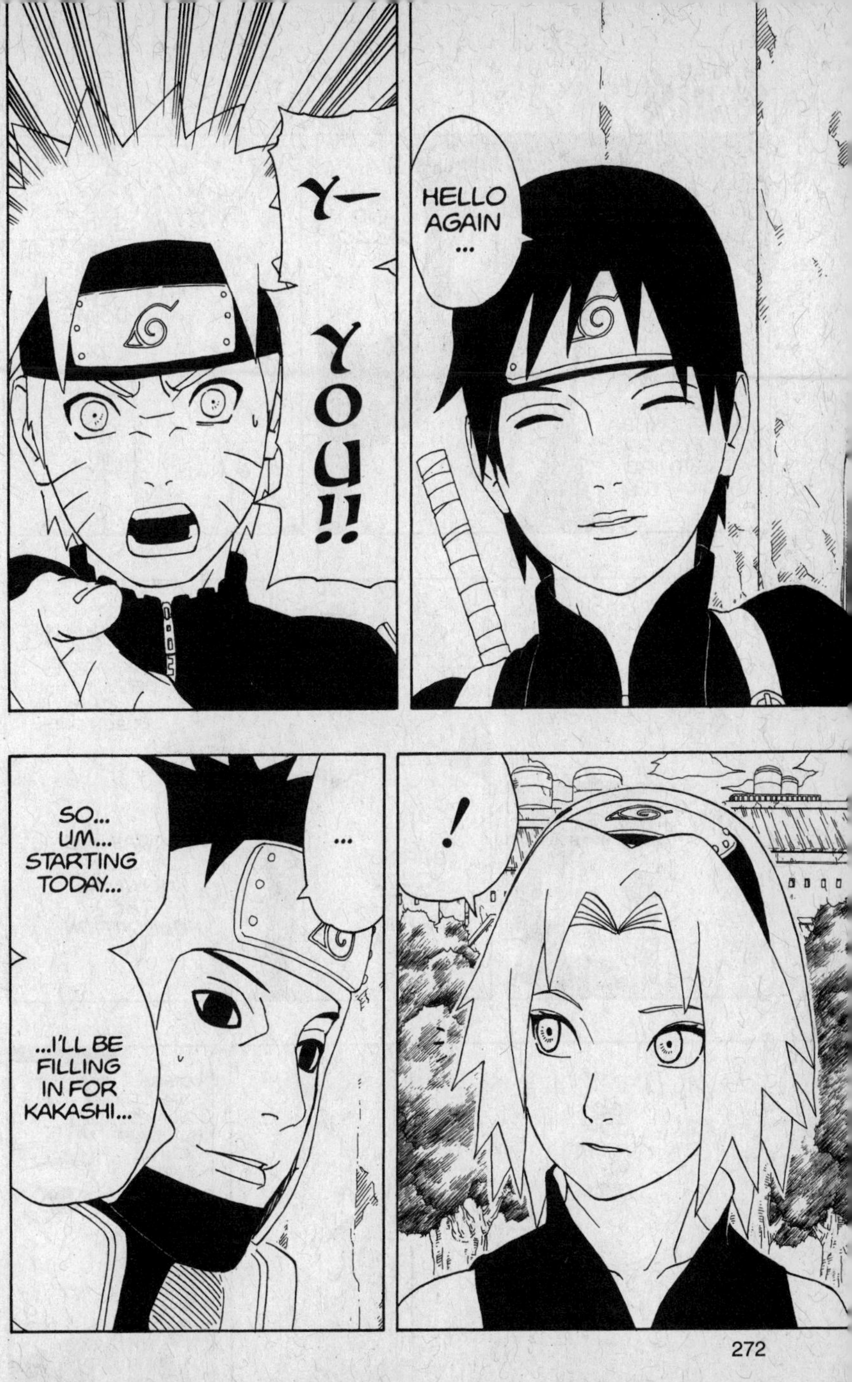
HELLO AGAIN ...
Y—
YOU!!
!
...
SO... UM... STARTING TODAY...
...I'LL BE FILLING IN FOR KAKASHI...

READ THIS WAY

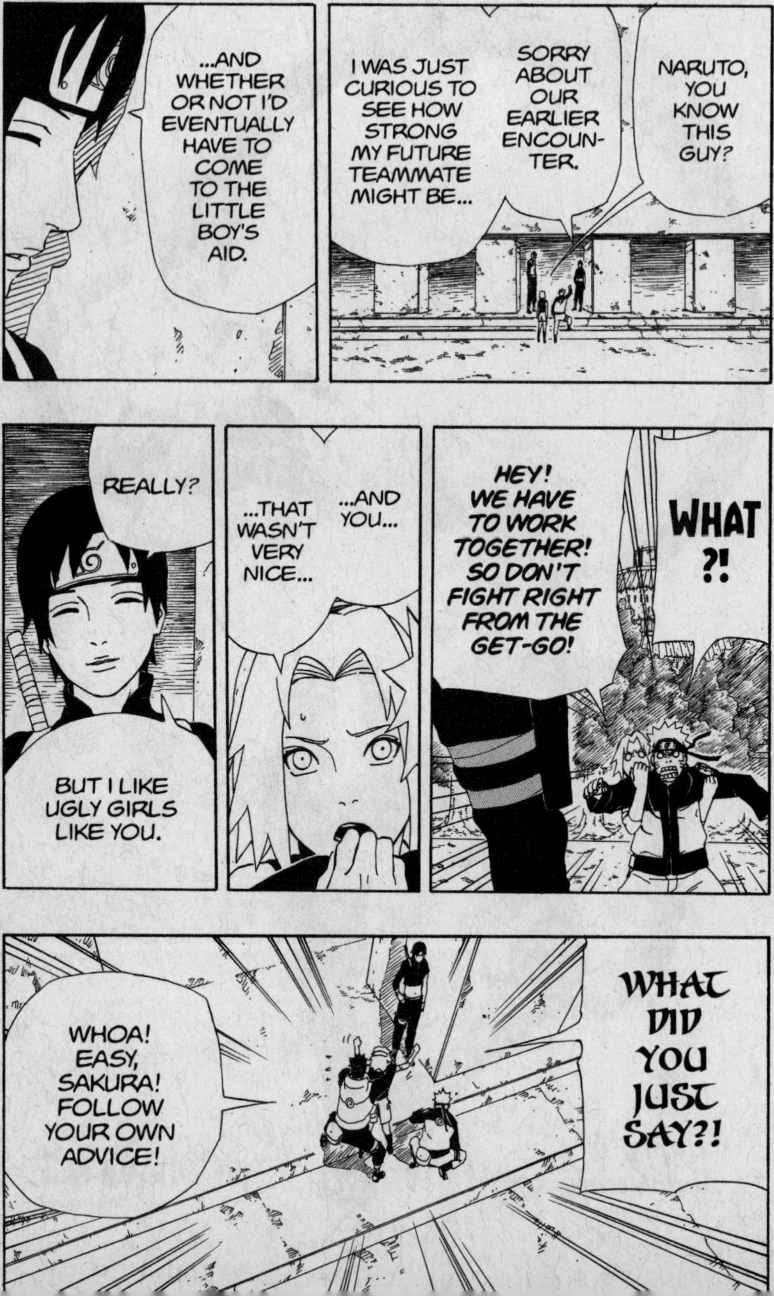

NARUTO, YOU KNOW THIS GUY?
SORRY ABOUT OUR EARLIER ENCOUNTER.
I WAS JUST CURIOUS TO SEE HOW STRONG MY FUTURE TEAMMATE MIGHT BE...
...AND WHETHER OR NOT I'D EVENTUALLY HAVE TO COME TO THE LITTLE BOY'S AID.
WHAT?!
HEY! WE HAVE TO WORK TOGETHER! SO DON'T FIGHT RIGHT FROM THE GET-GO!
...AND YOU...
...THAT WASN'T VERY NICE...
REALLY?
BUT I LIKE UGLY GIRLS LIKE YOU.
WHAT DID YOU JUST SAY?!
WHOA! EASY, SAKURA! FOLLOW YOUR OWN ADVICE!

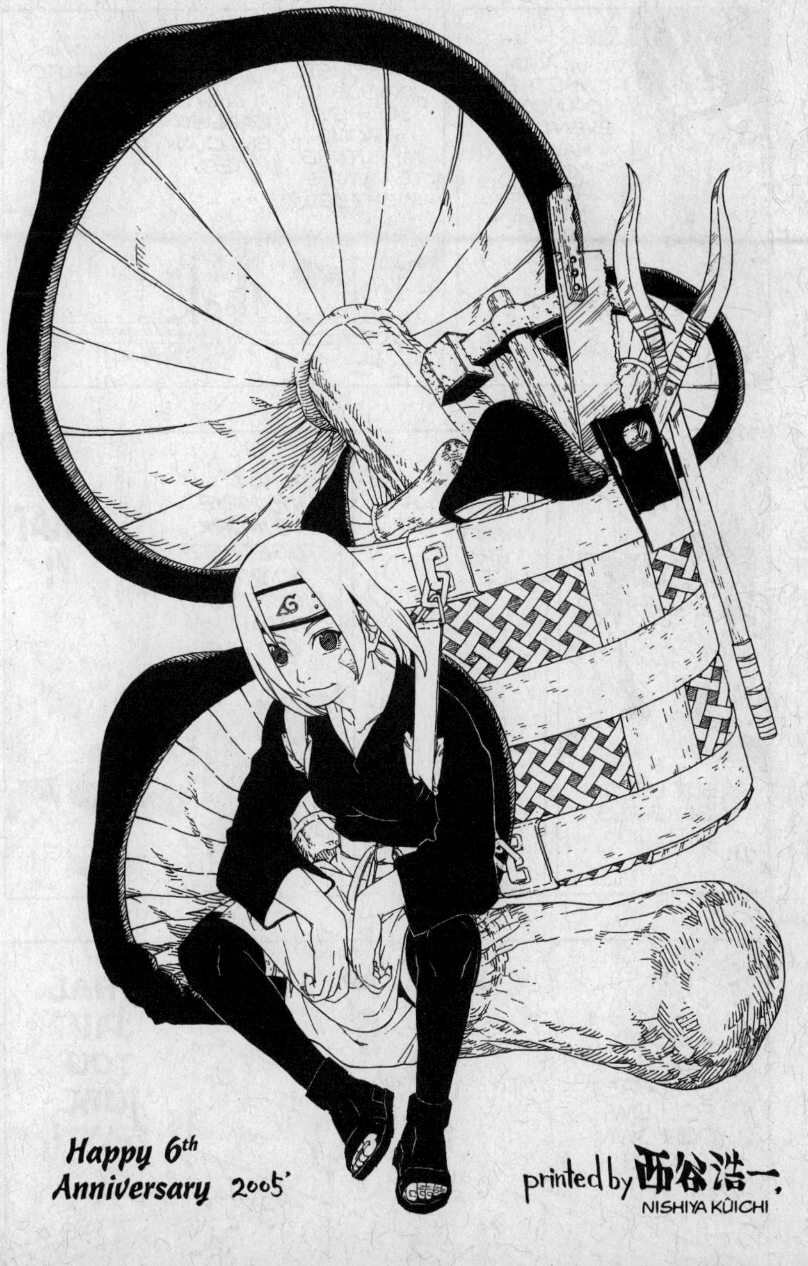
Happy 6th
Anniversary 2005'
printed by 西谷浩一,
NISHIYA KÛICHI

Number 285: The Foundation

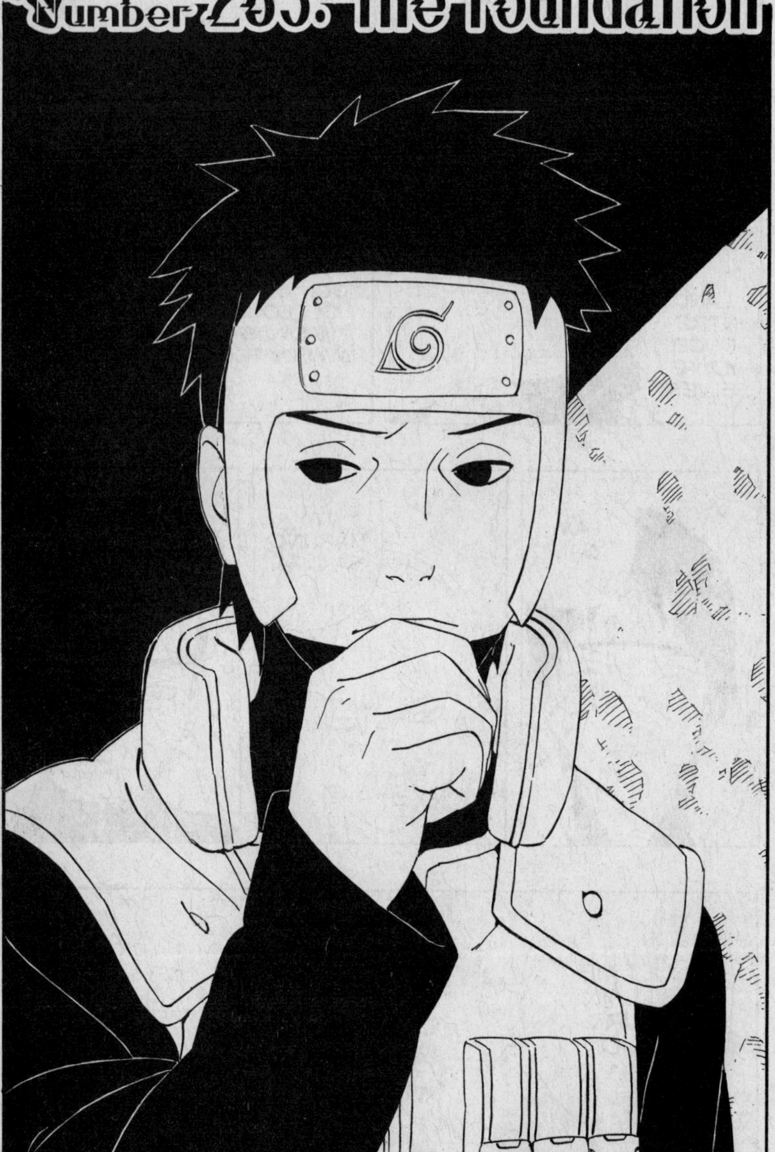

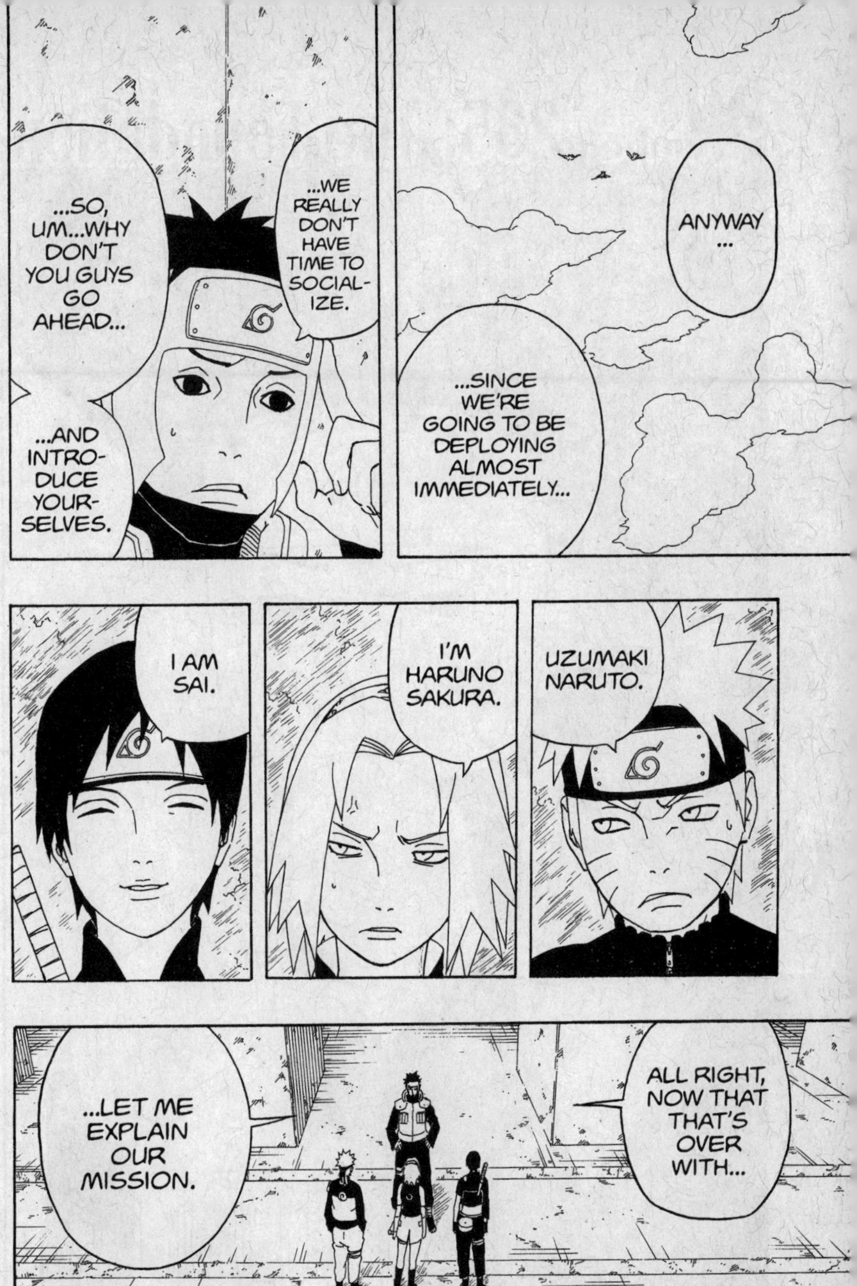
ANYWAY ...
...SINCE WE'RE GOING TO BE DEPLOYING ALMOST IMMEDIATELY...
...WE REALLY DON'T HAVE TIME TO SOCIAL-IZE.
...SO, UM...WHY DON'T YOU GUYS GO AHEAD...
...AND INTRO-DUCE YOUR-SELVES.
UZUMAKI NARUTO.
I'M HARUNO SAKURA.
I AM SAI.
ALL RIGHT, NOW THAT THAT'S OVER WITH...
...LET ME EXPLAIN OUR MISSION.

READ THIS WAY

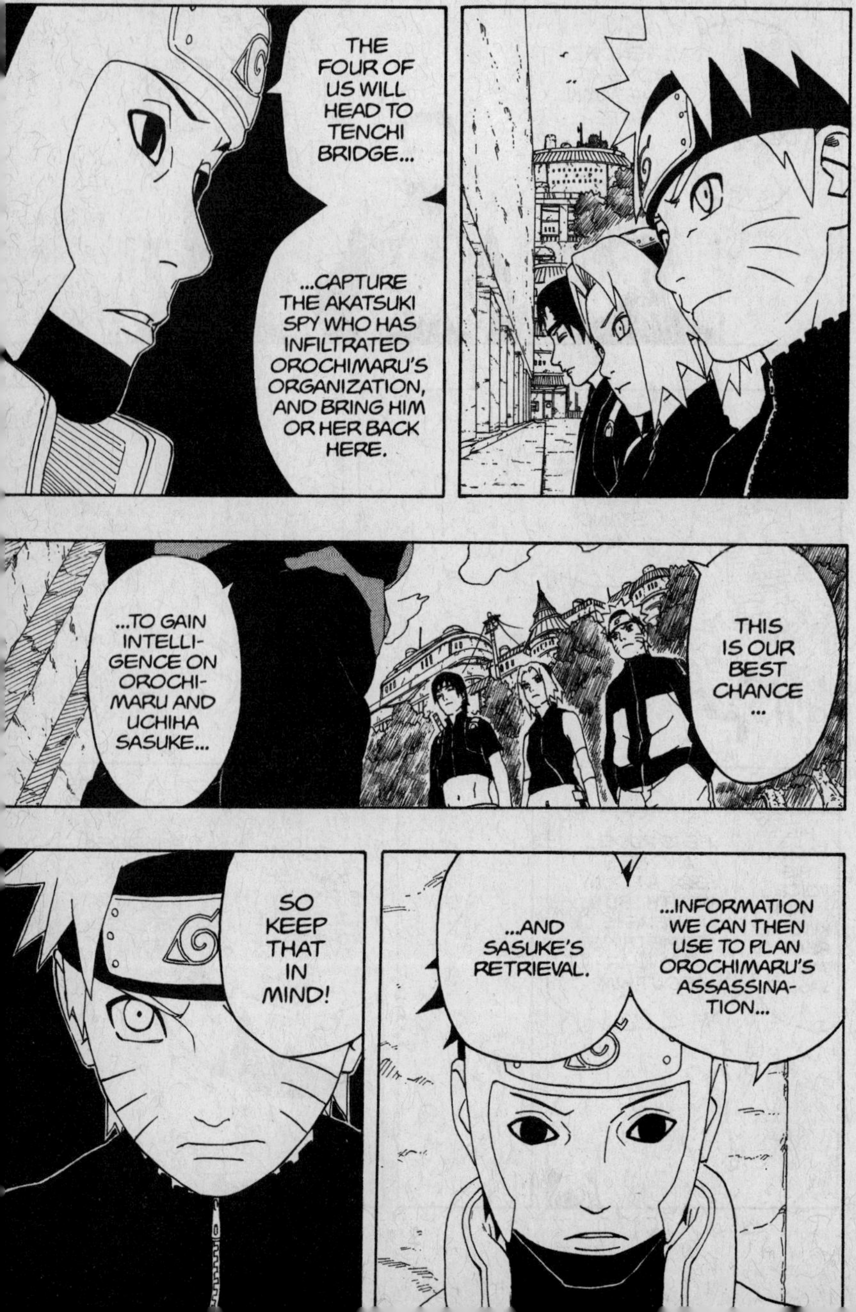
THE FOUR OF US WILL HEAD TO TENCHI BRIDGE...
...CAPTURE THE AKATSUKI SPY WHO HAS INFILTRATED OROCHIMARU'S ORGANIZATION, AND BRING HIM OR HER BACK HERE.
THIS IS OUR BEST CHANCE...
...TO GAIN INTELLIGENCE ON OROCHIMARU AND UCHIHA SASUKE...
...INFORMATION WE CAN THEN USE TO PLAN OROCHIMARU'S ASSASSINATION...
...AND SASUKE'S RETRIEVAL.
SO KEEP THAT IN MIND!

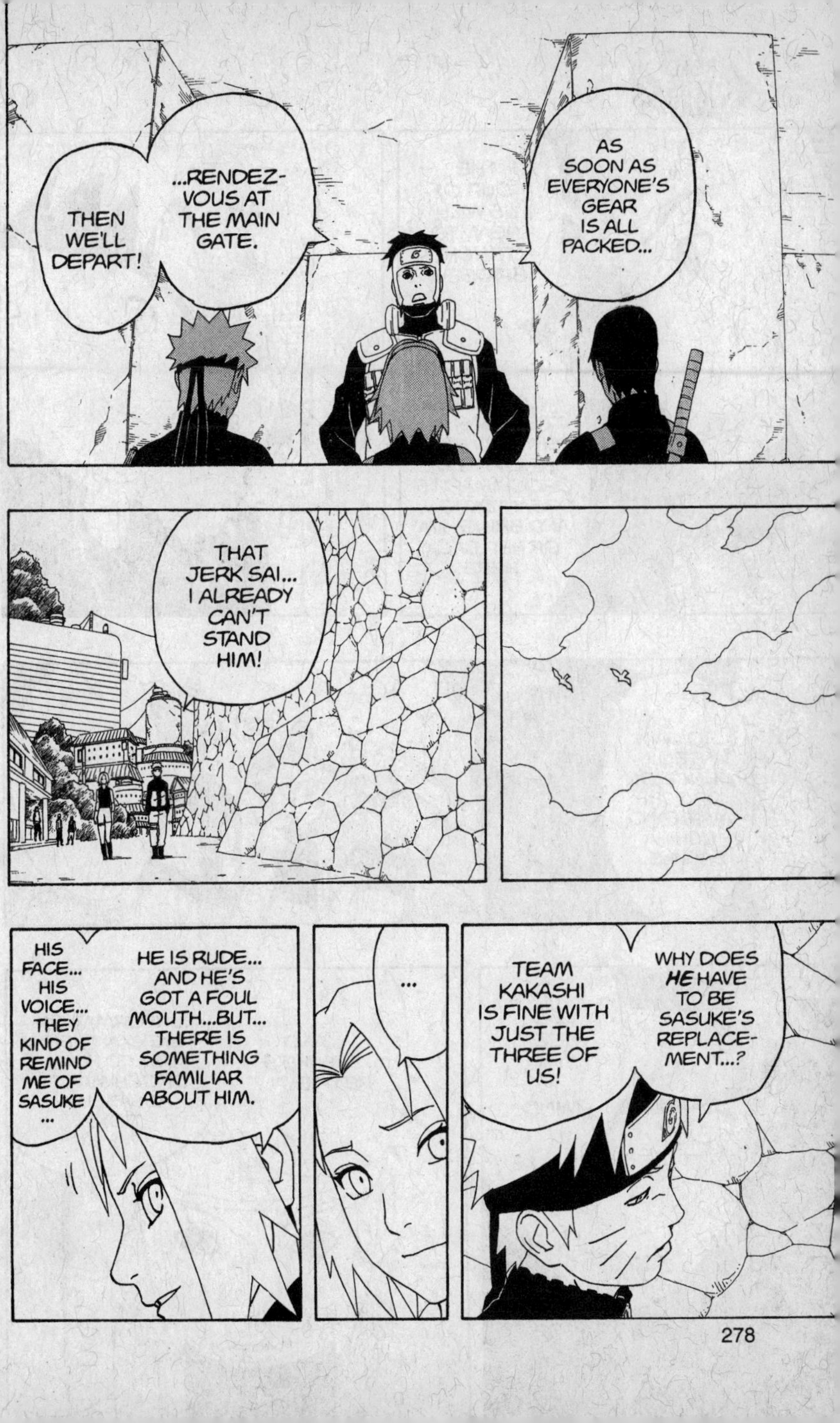
AS SOON AS EVERYONE'S GEAR IS ALL PACKED...
...RENDEZ-VOUS AT THE MAIN GATE.
THEN WE'LL DEPART!
THAT JERK SAI... I ALREADY CAN'T STAND HIM!
WHY DOES *HE* HAVE TO BE SASUKE'S REPLACEMENT...?
TEAM KAKASHI IS FINE WITH JUST THE THREE OF US!
...
HE IS RUDE... AND HE'S GOT A FOUL MOUTH...BUT... THERE IS SOMETHING FAMILIAR ABOUT HIM.
HIS FACE... HIS VOICE... THEY KIND OF REMIND ME OF SASUKE...

READ THIS WAY

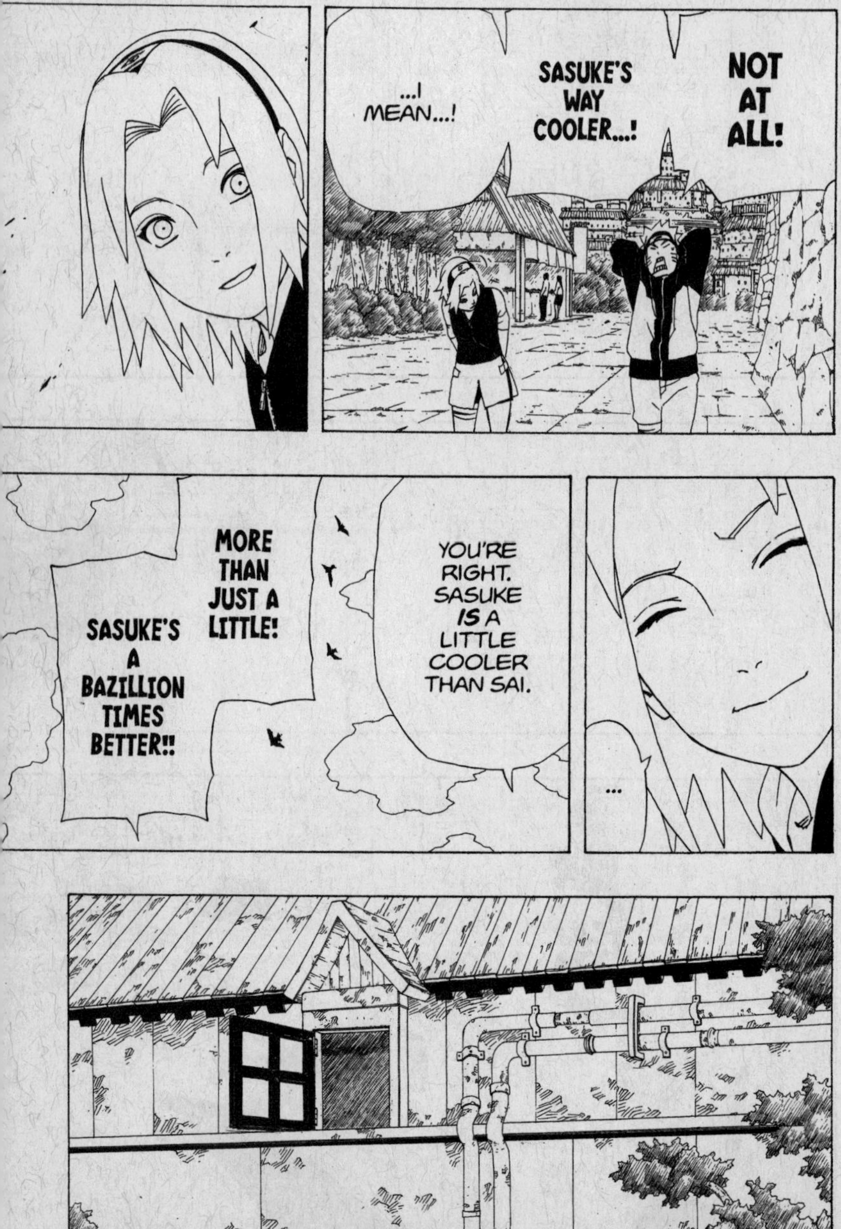
NOT AT ALL!
SASUKE'S WAY COOLER...!
...I MEAN...!
...
YOU'RE RIGHT. SASUKE IS A LITTLE COOLER THAN SAI.
MORE THAN JUST A LITTLE!
SASUKE'S A BAZILLION TIMES BETTER!!

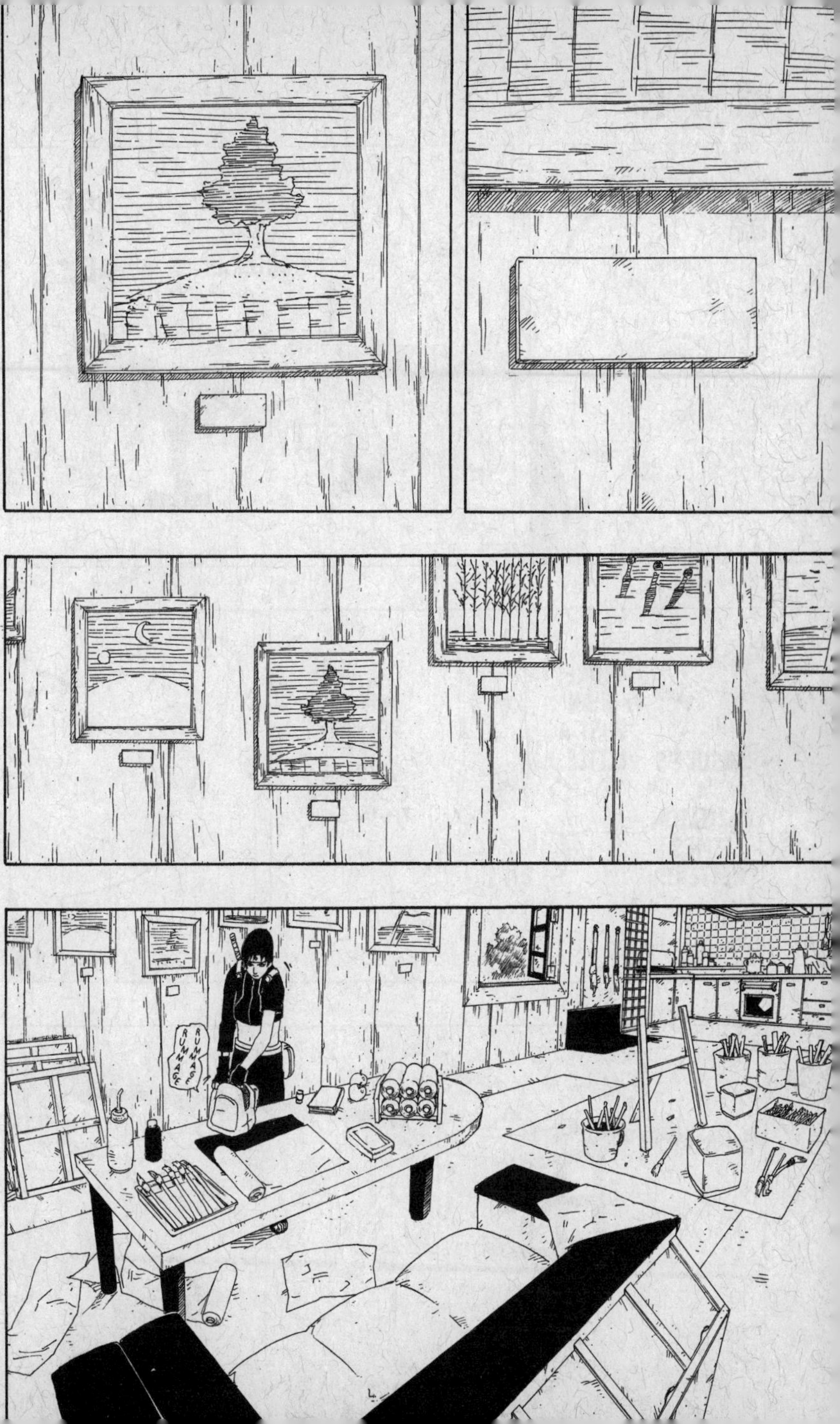
RUMMAGE RUMMAGE

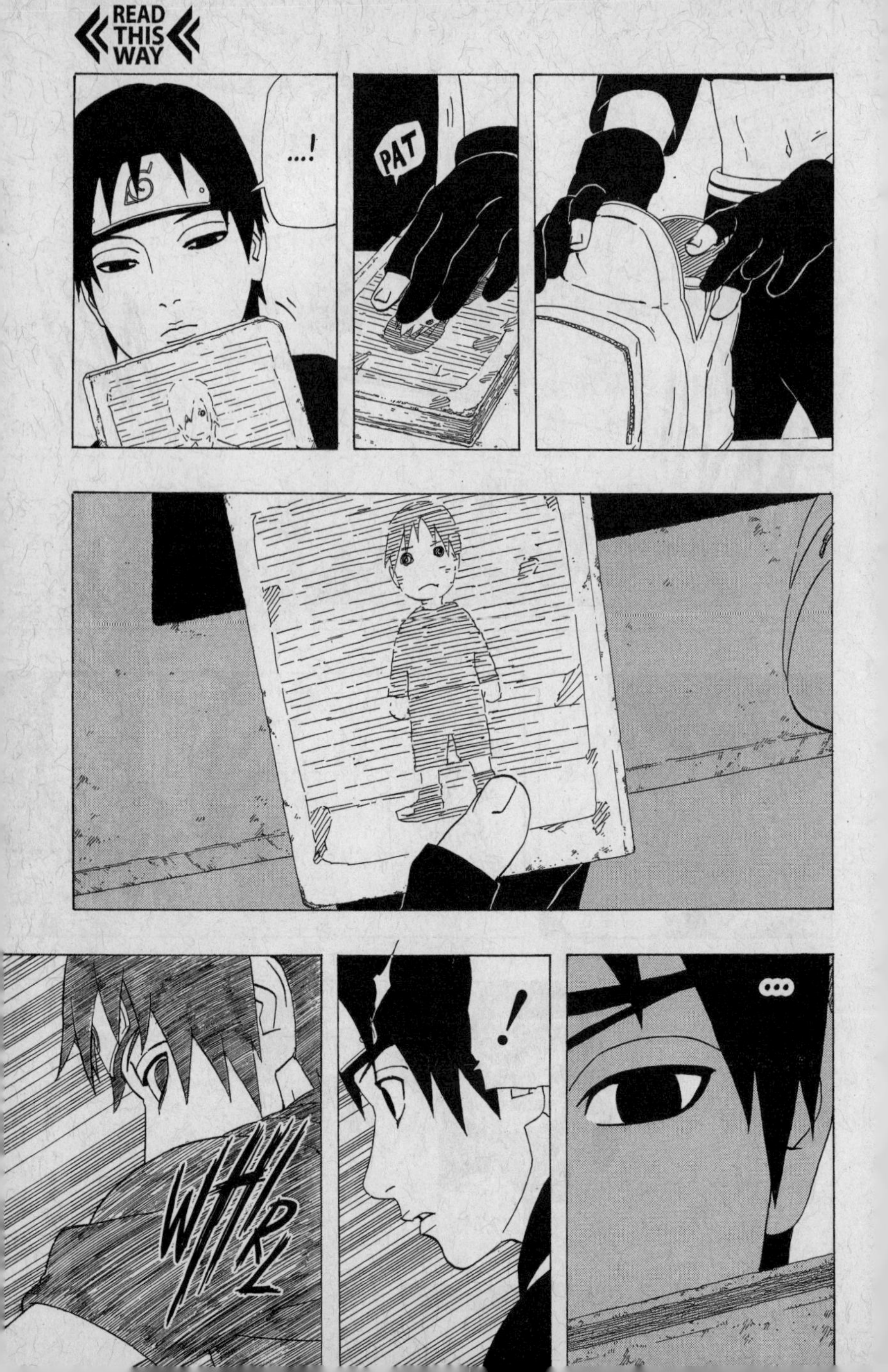
READ THIS WAY
PAT
...!
WHRL
...
!

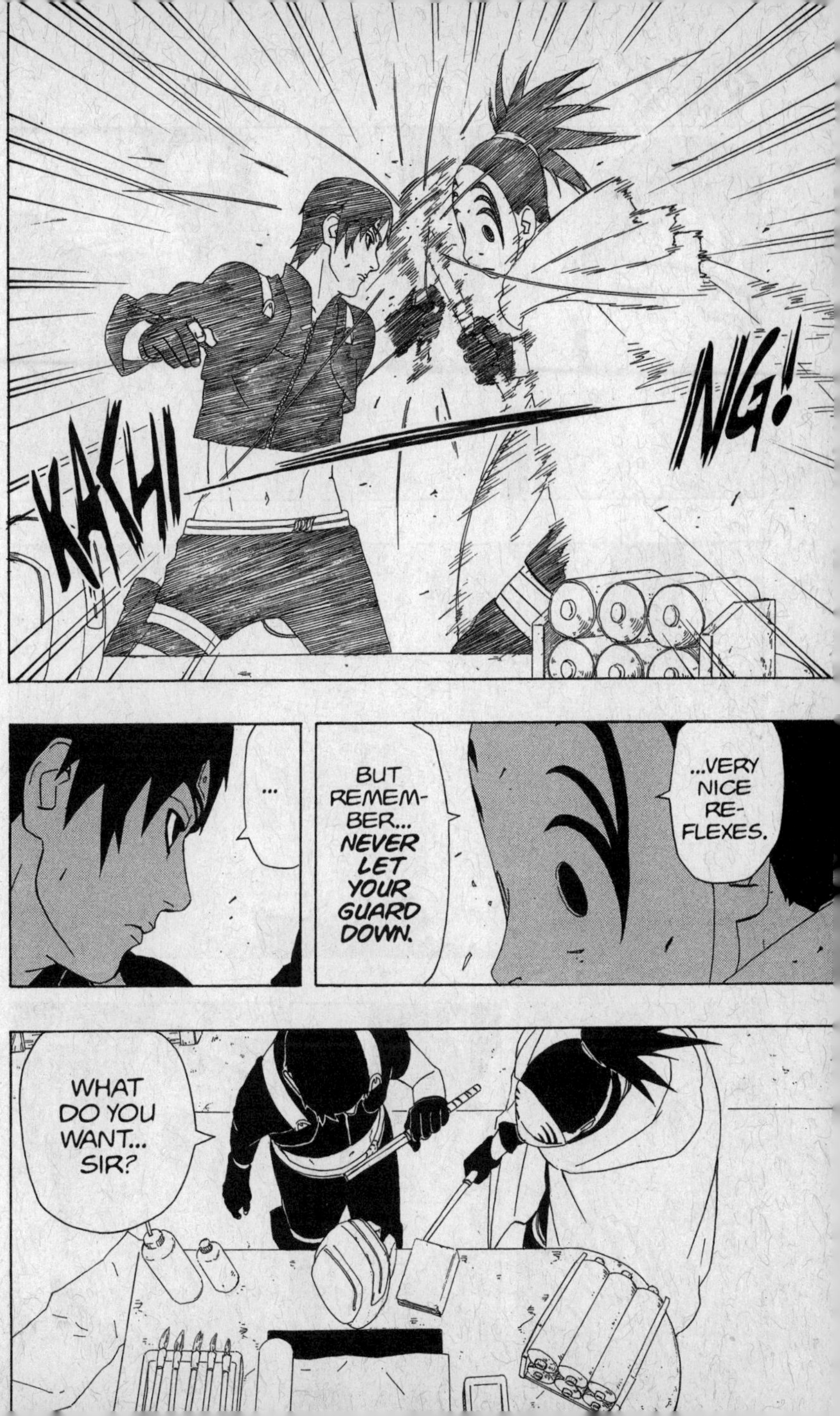
NG!
KACHI
...VERY NICE RE-FLEXES.
BUT REMEM-BER... NEVER LET YOUR GUARD DOWN.
...
WHAT DO YOU WANT... SIR?

READ THIS WAY

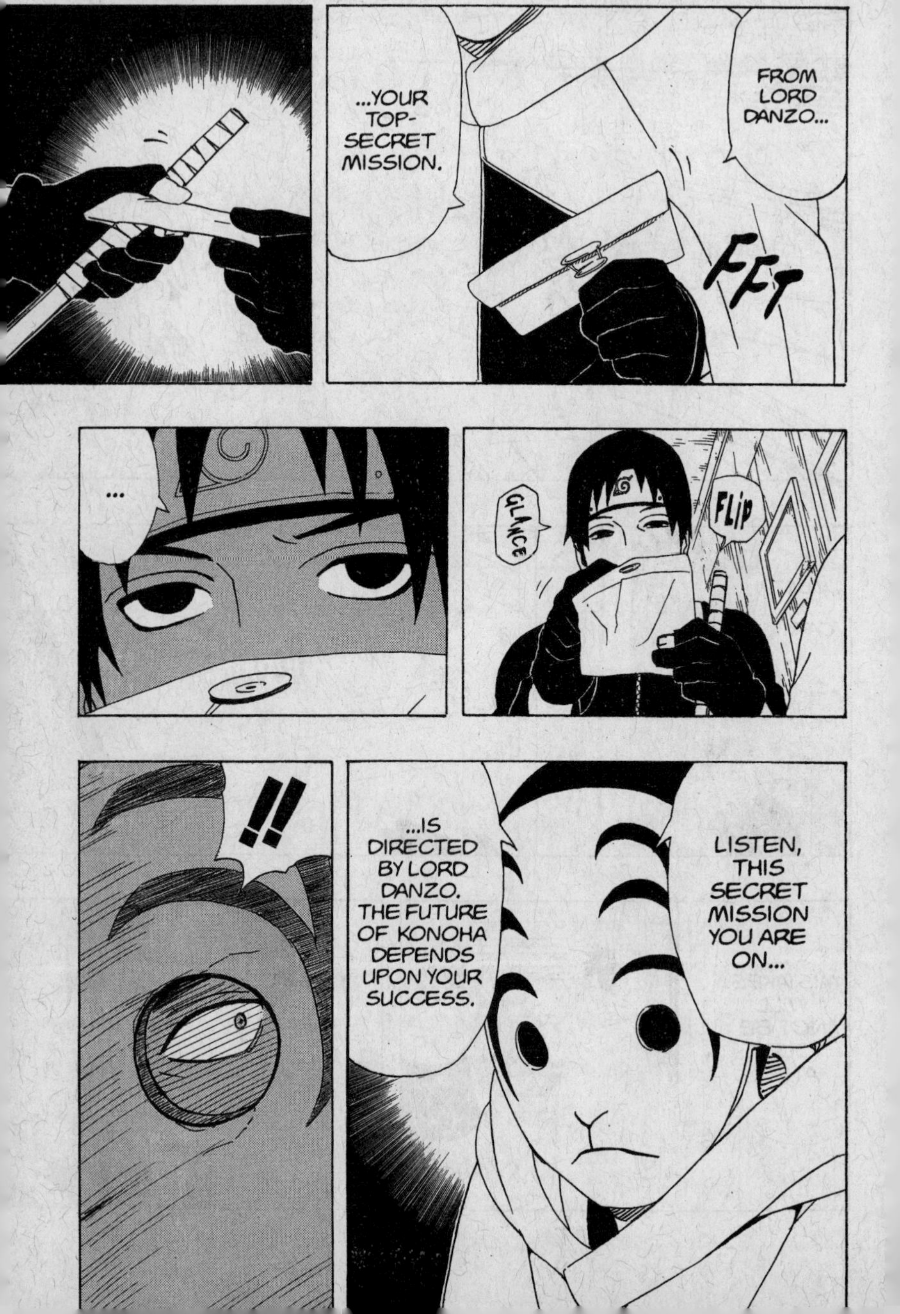
FROM LORD DANZO...
...YOUR TOP-SECRET MISSION.
FFT
FLIP
GLANCE
...
LISTEN, THIS SECRET MISSION YOU ARE ON...
...IS DIRECTED BY LORD DANZO. THE FUTURE OF KONOHA DEPENDS UPON YOUR SUCCESS.
!!

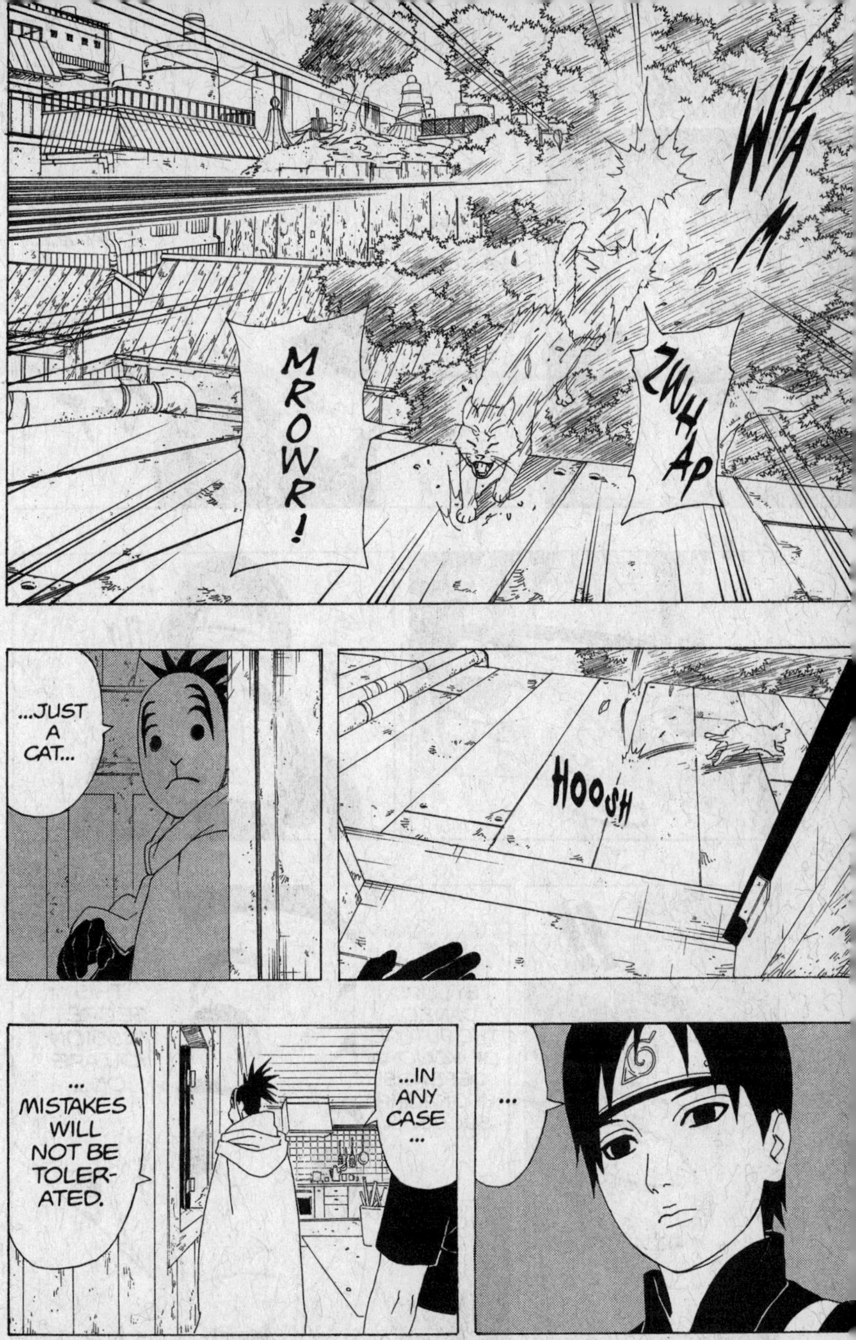
WHAM
ZWHAP
MROWR!
HOOSH
...JUST A CAT...
...
...IN ANY CASE ...
... MISTAKES WILL NOT BE TOLER-ATED.

READ THIS WAY

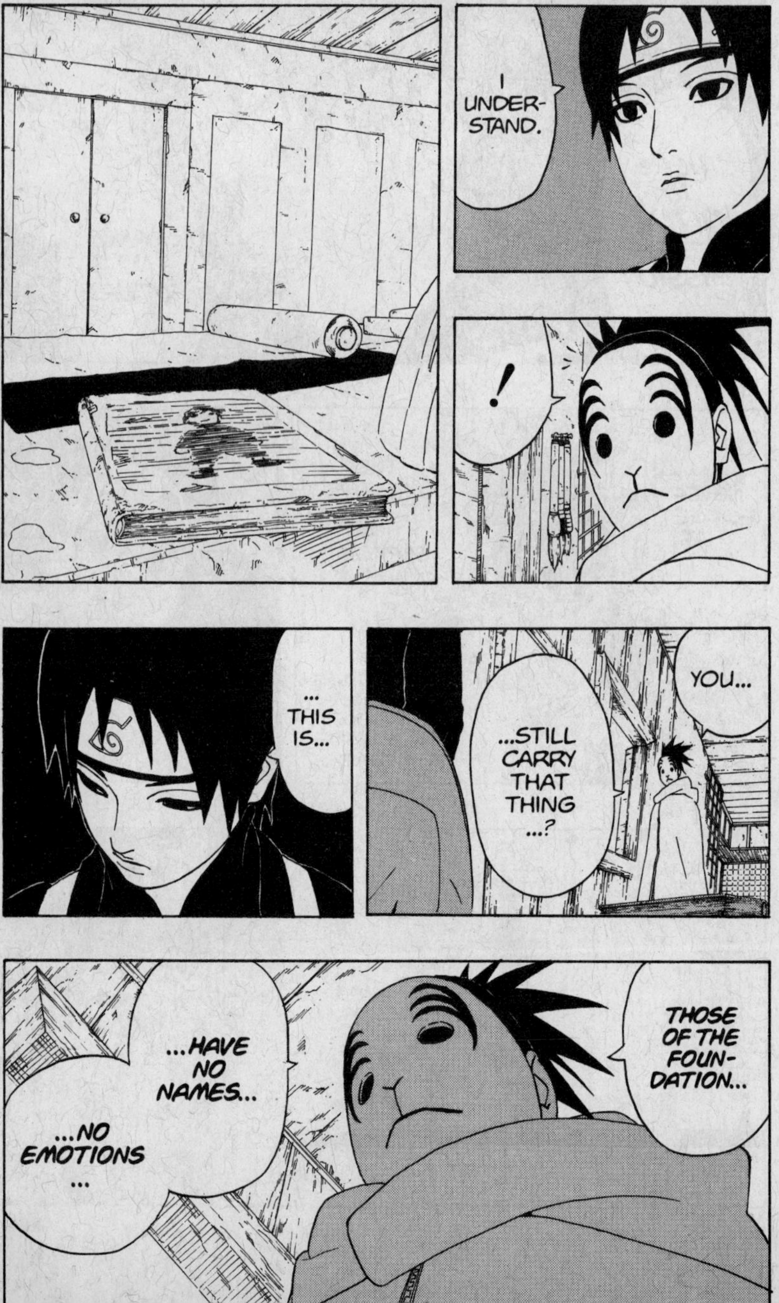
I UNDER-STAND.
!
YOU...
...STILL CARRY THAT THING ...?
... THIS IS...
THOSE OF THE FOUN-DATION...
...HAVE NO NAMES...
...NO EMOTIONS ...

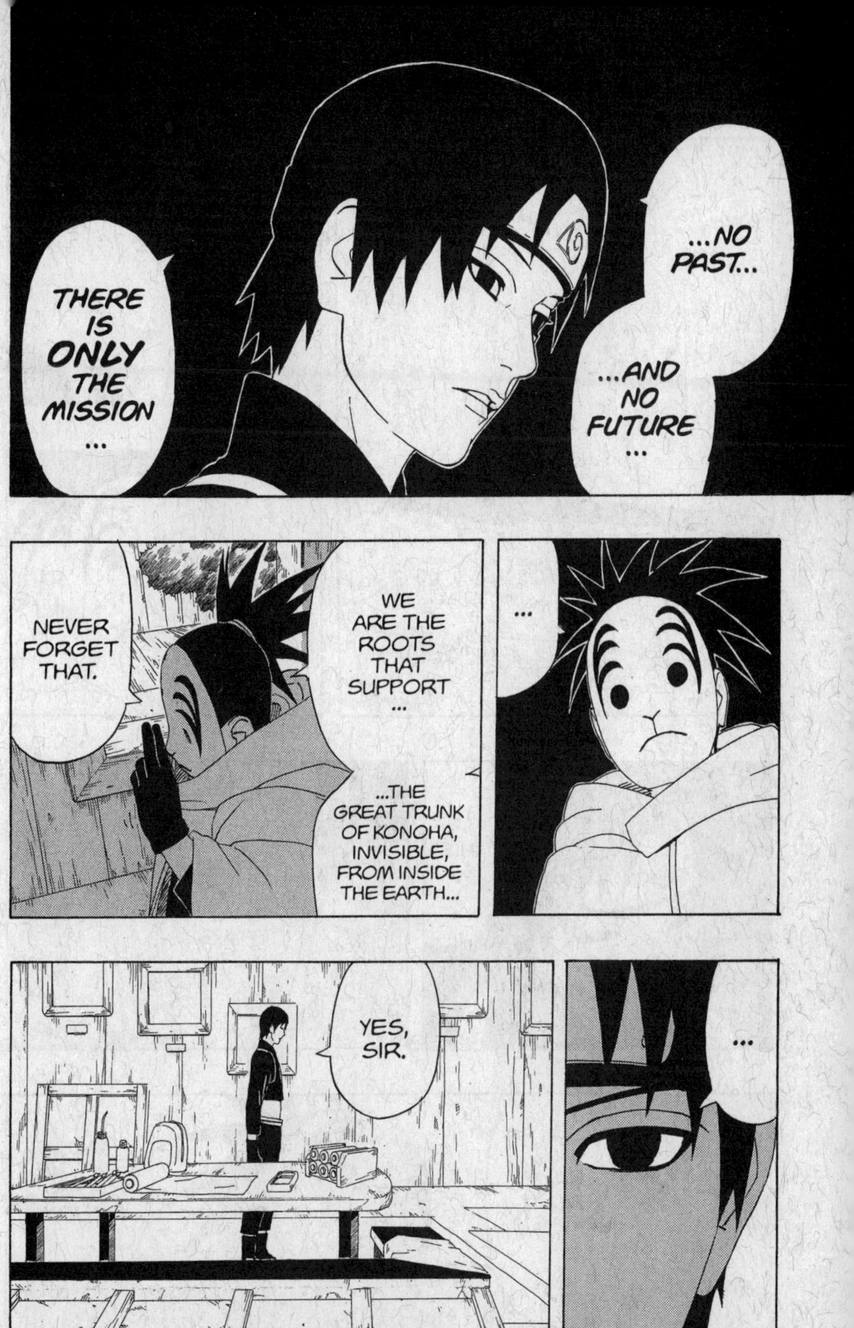
...NO PAST...
...AND NO FUTURE ...
THERE IS ONLY THE MISSION ...
...
WE ARE THE ROOTS THAT SUPPORT ...
...THE GREAT TRUNK OF KONOHA, INVISIBLE, FROM INSIDE THE EARTH...
NEVER FORGET THAT.
...
YES, SIR.

READ THIS WAY

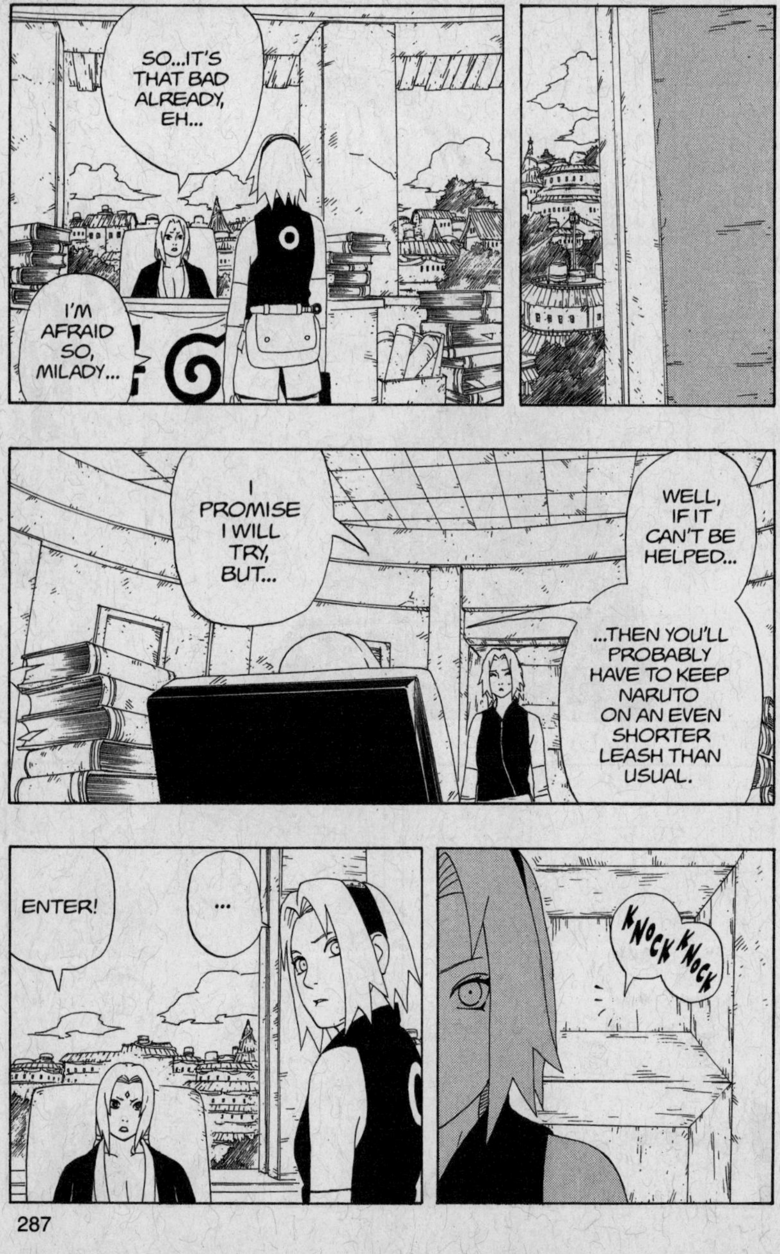

SO...IT'S THAT BAD ALREADY, EH...
I'M AFRAID SO, MILADY...
WELL, IF IT CAN'T BE HELPED...
...THEN YOU'LL PROBABLY HAVE TO KEEP NARUTO ON AN EVEN SHORTER LEASH THAN USUAL.
I PROMISE I WILL TRY, BUT...
KNOCK KNOCK
...
ENTER!

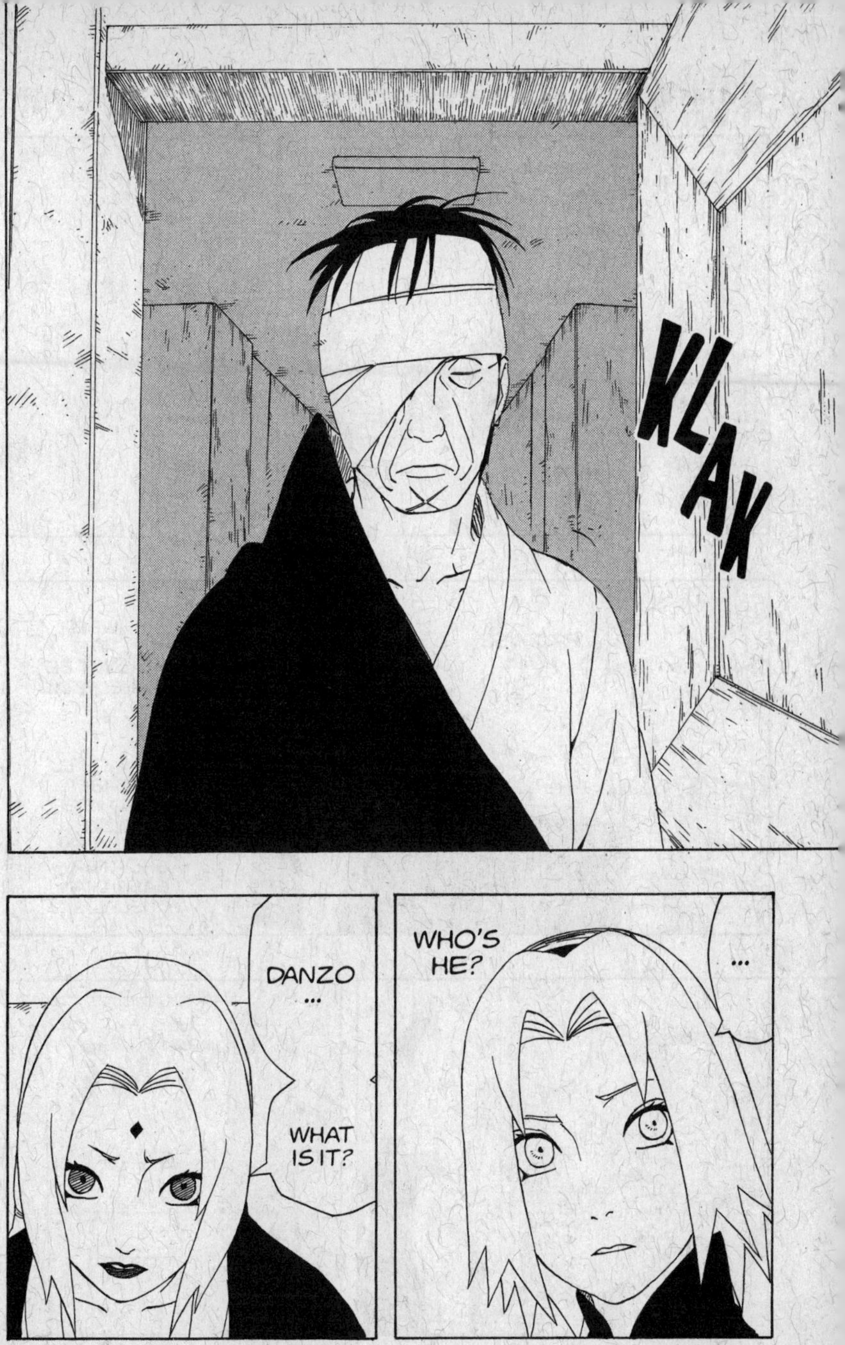
KLAK
...
WHO'S HE?
DANZO ...
WHAT IS IT?

READ THIS WAY

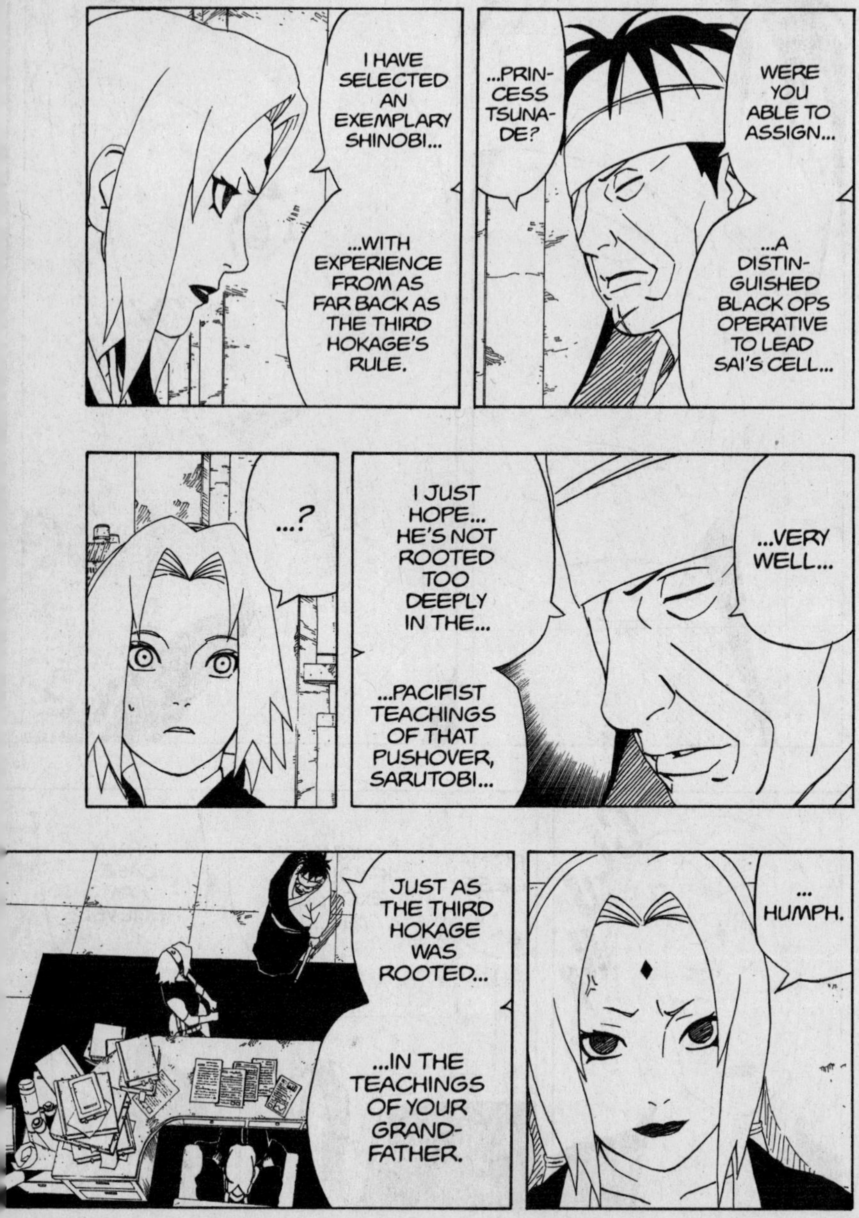

WERE YOU ABLE TO ASSIGN...
...A DISTINGUISHED BLACK OPS OPERATIVE TO LEAD SAI'S CELL...
...PRINCESS TSUNADE?
I HAVE SELECTED AN EXEMPLARY SHINOBI...
...WITH EXPERIENCE FROM AS FAR BACK AS THE THIRD HOKAGE'S RULE.
...VERY WELL...
I JUST HOPE... HE'S NOT ROOTED TOO DEEPLY IN THE...
...PACIFIST TEACHINGS OF THAT PUSHOVER, SARUTOBI...
...?
... HUMPH.
JUST AS THE THIRD HOKAGE WAS ROOTED...
...IN THE TEACHINGS OF YOUR GRANDFATHER.

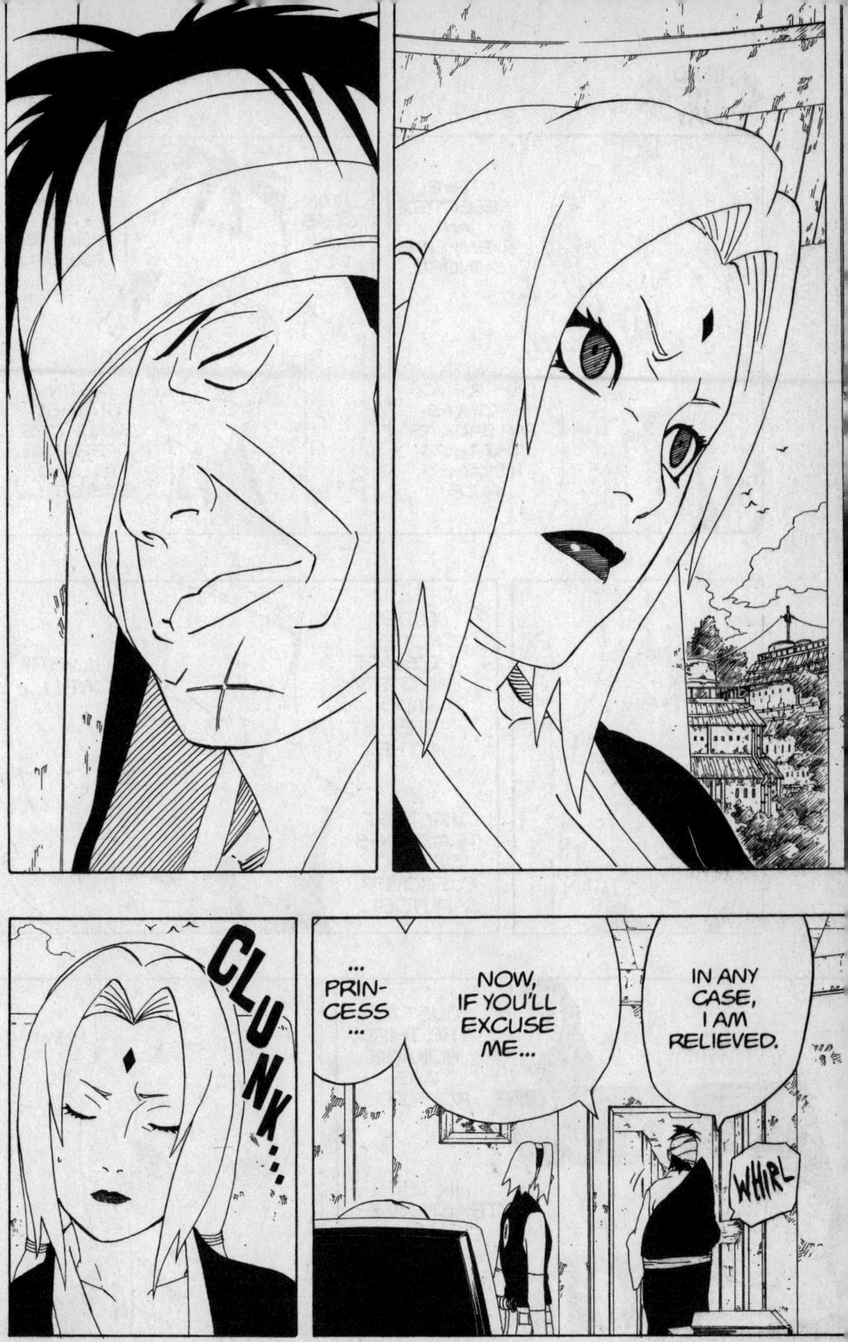
IN ANY CASE, I AM RELIEVED.
NOW, IF YOU'LL EXCUSE ME...
... PRINCESS ...
WHIRL
CLUNK...

READ THIS WAY

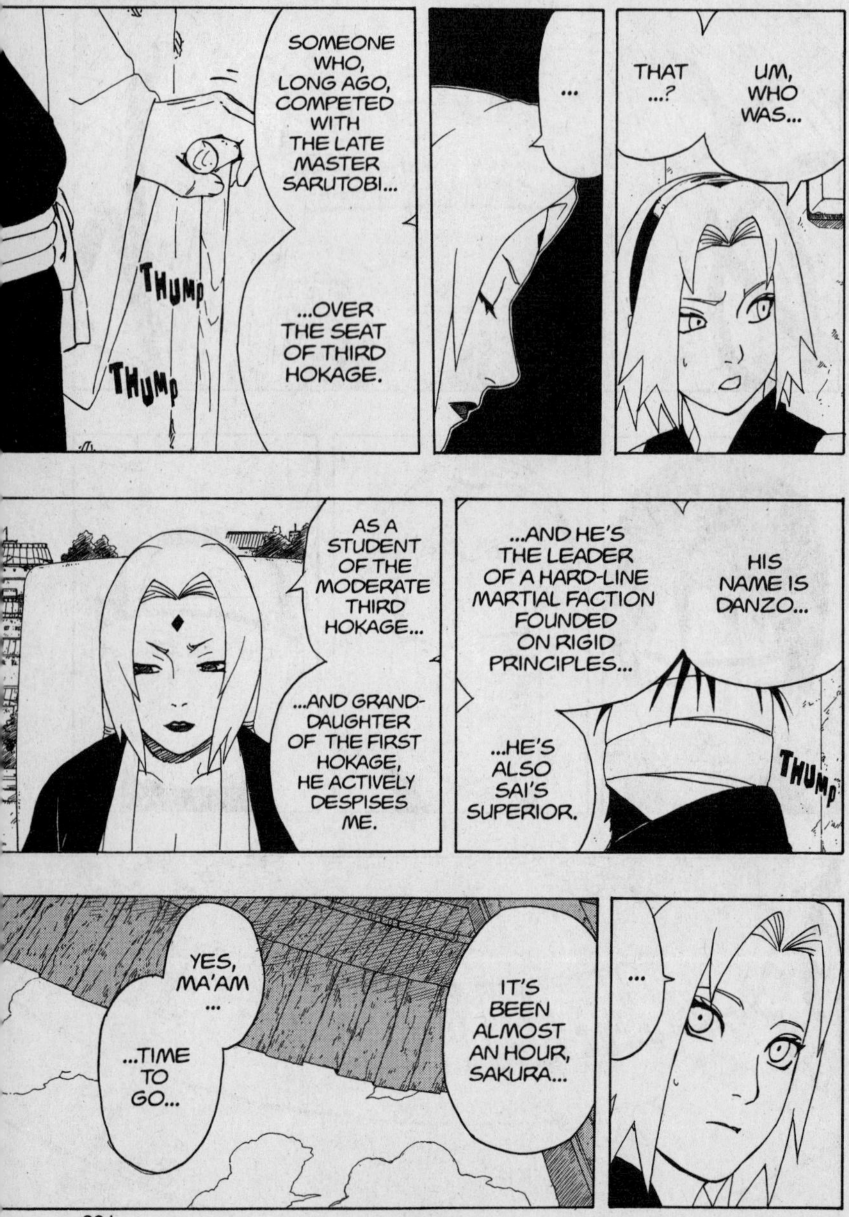
UM, WHO WAS...
THAT ...?
...
SOMEONE WHO, LONG AGO, COMPETED WITH THE LATE MASTER SARUTOBI...
...OVER THE SEAT OF THIRD HOKAGE.
THUMP
THUMP
HIS NAME IS DANZO...
...AND HE'S THE LEADER OF A HARD-LINE MARTIAL FACTION FOUNDED ON RIGID PRINCIPLES...
...HE'S ALSO SAI'S SUPERIOR.
THUMP
AS A STUDENT OF THE MODERATE THIRD HOKAGE...
...AND GRAND-DAUGHTER OF THE FIRST HOKAGE, HE ACTIVELY DESPISES ME.
...
IT'S BEEN ALMOST AN HOUR, SAKURA...
YES, MA'AM ...
...TIME TO GO...

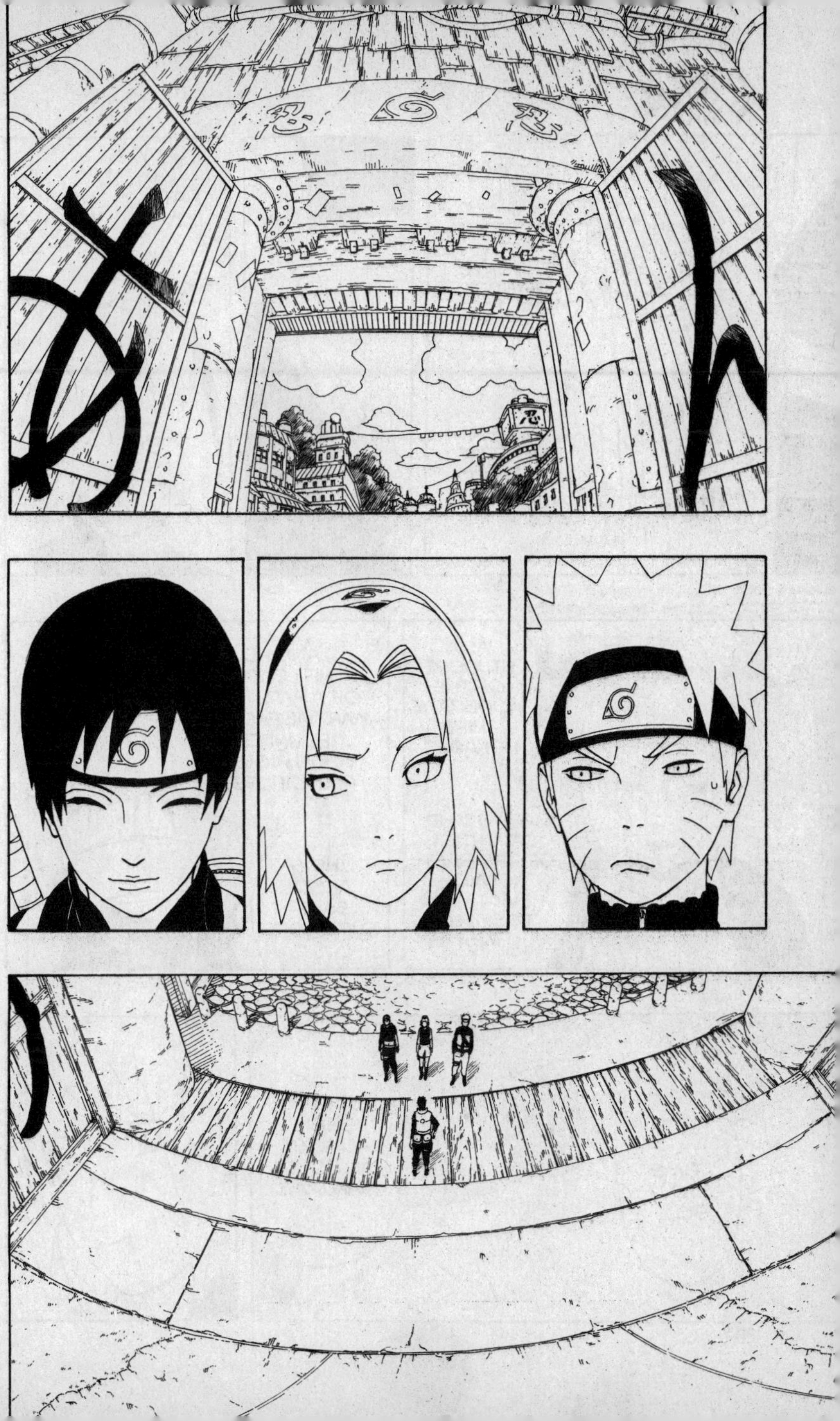

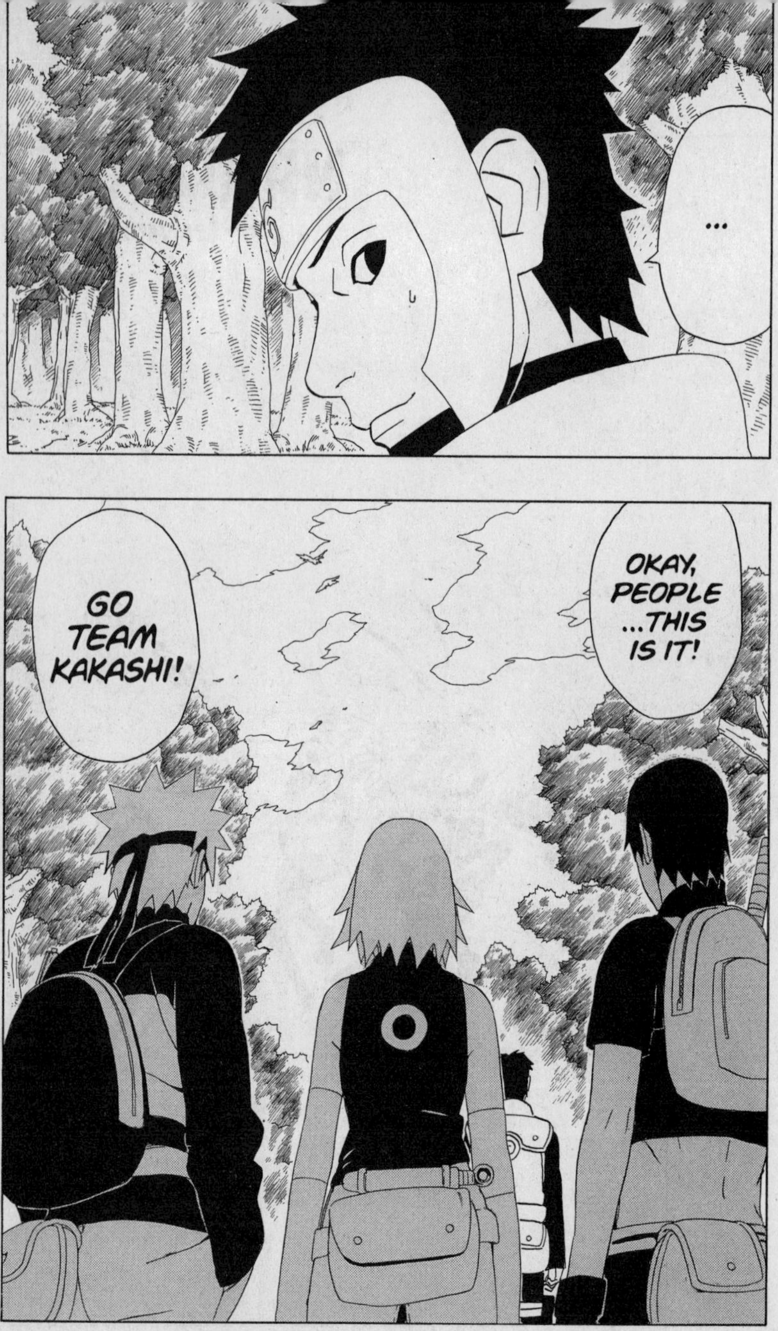
...
OKAY, PEOPLE ...THIS IS IT!
GO TEAM KAKASHI!

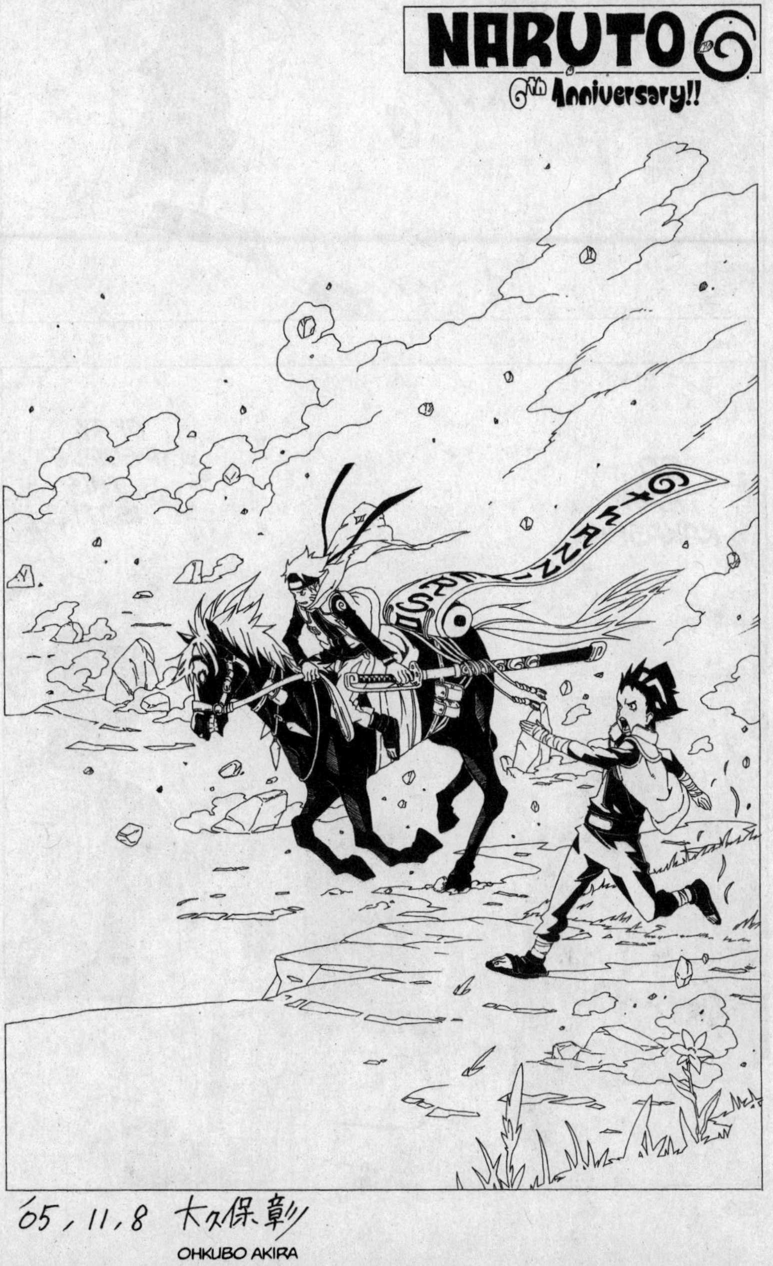
NARUTO
6th Anniversary!!

'05, 11, 8 大久保彰

OHKUBO AKIRA

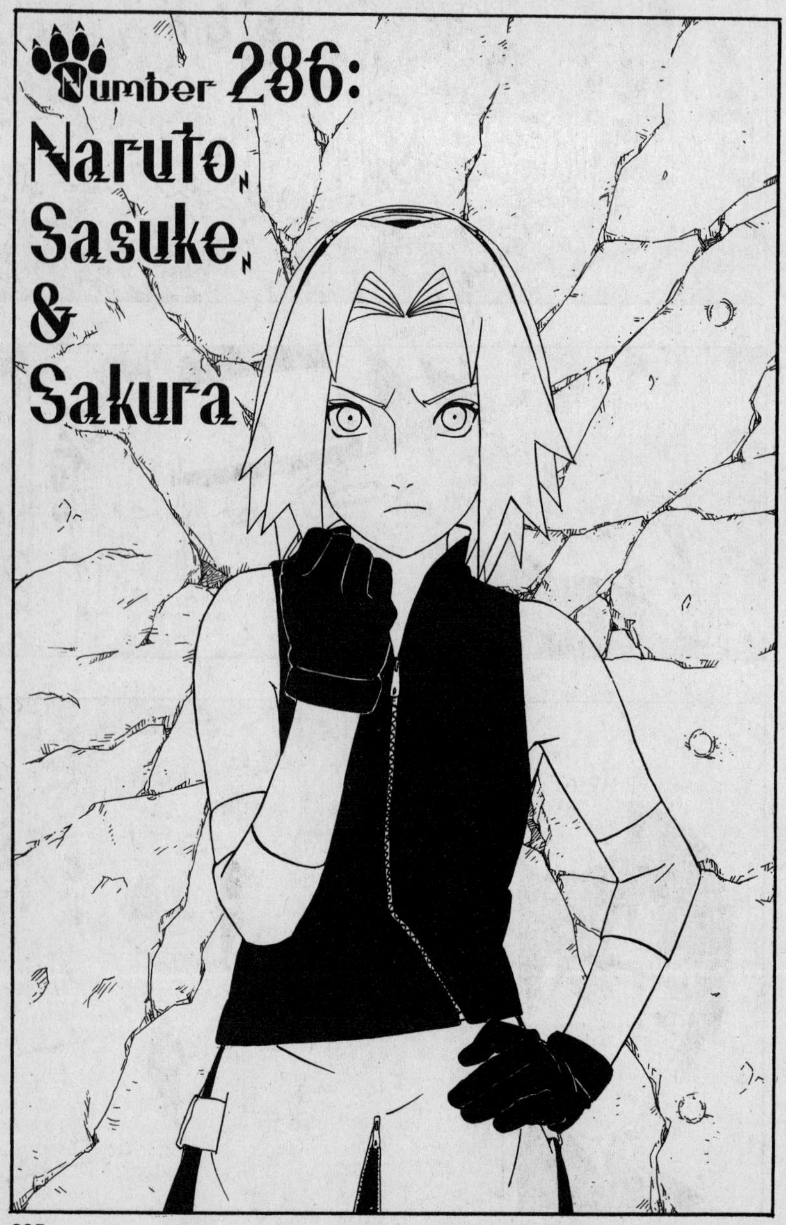
Number 286:
Naruto,
Sasuke,
&
Sakura

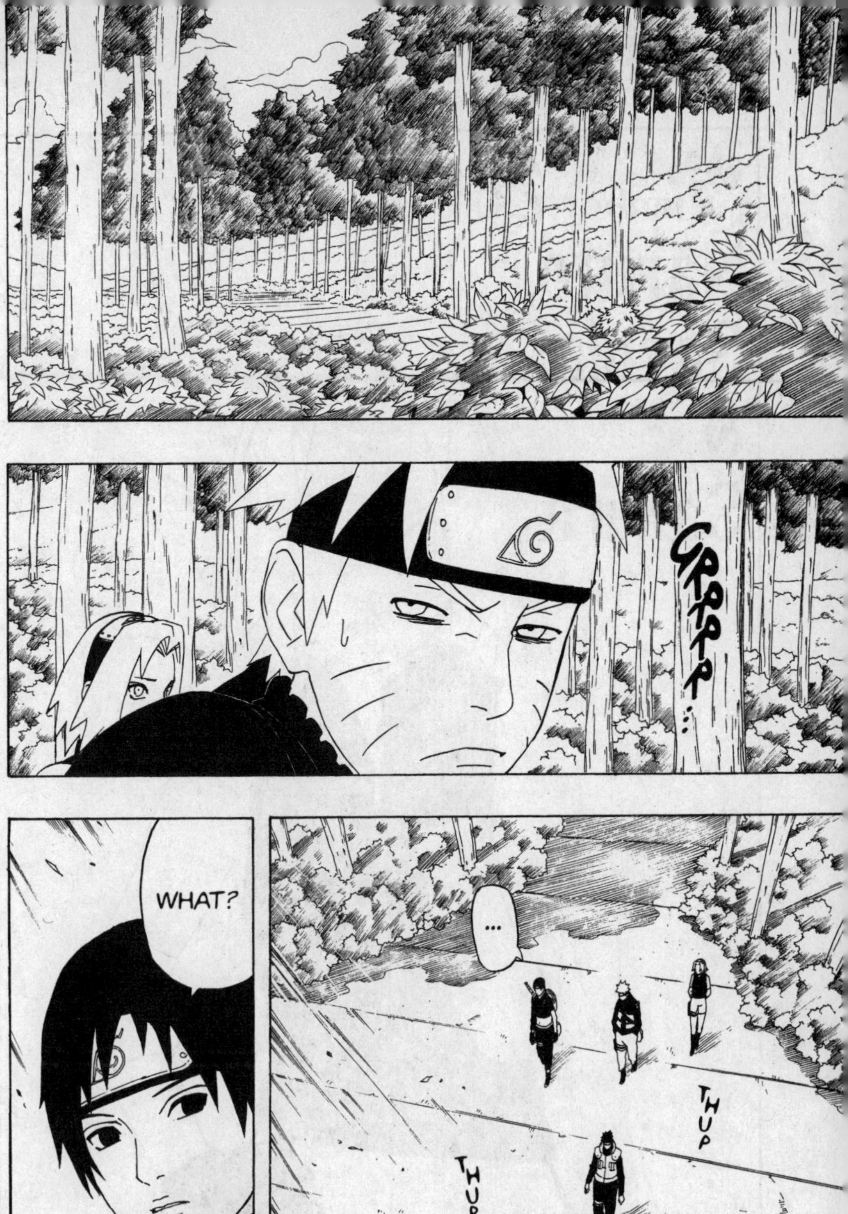
GRRRR...
...
THUP
THUP
WHAT?

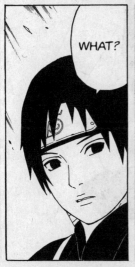

READ THIS WAY

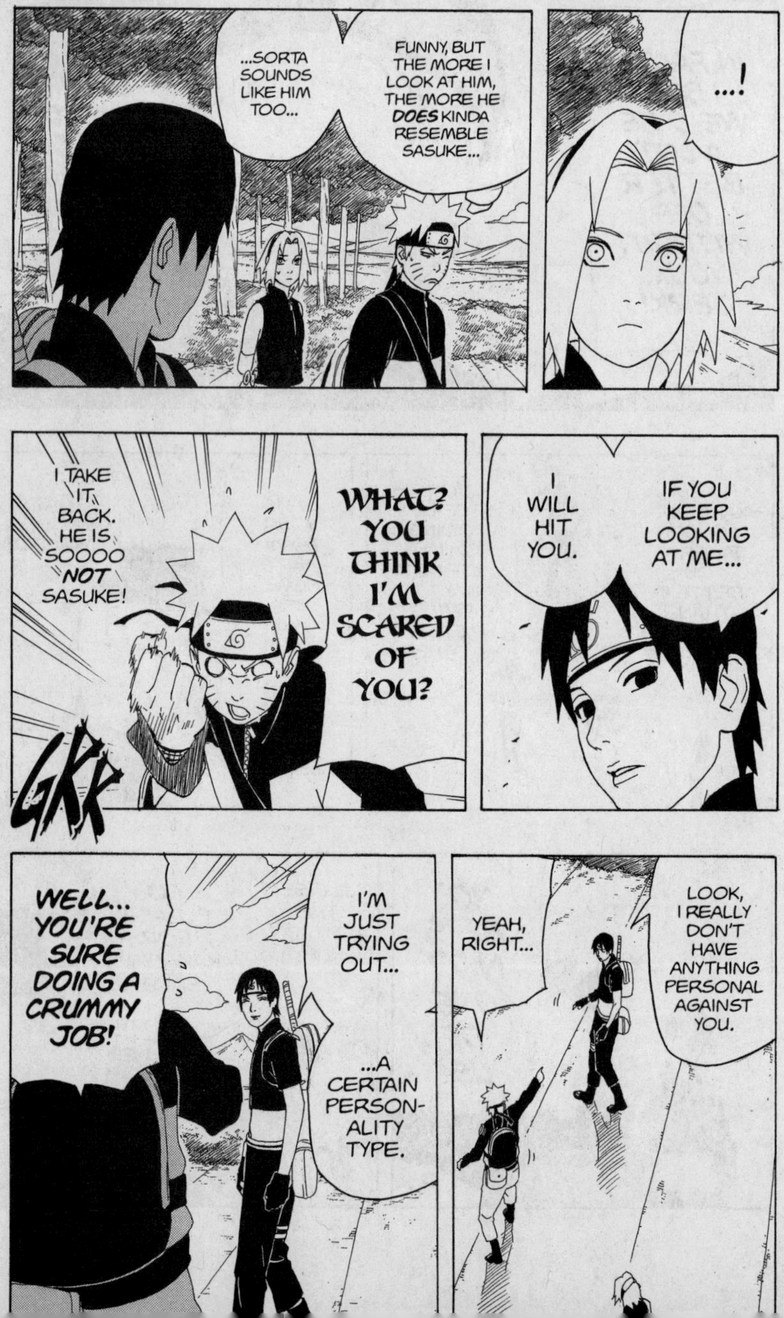
...!
FUNNY, BUT THE MORE I LOOK AT HIM, THE MORE HE DOES KINDA RESEMBLE SASUKE...
...SORTA SOUNDS LIKE HIM TOO...
IF YOU KEEP LOOKING AT ME...
I WILL HIT YOU.
WHAT? YOU THINK I'M SCARED OF YOU?
I TAKE IT BACK. HE IS SOOOO NOT SASUKE!
GRR
LOOK, I REALLY DON'T HAVE ANYTHING PERSONAL AGAINST YOU.
YEAH, RIGHT...
I'M JUST TRYING OUT...
...A CERTAIN PERSONALITY TYPE.
WELL... YOU'RE SURE DOING A CRUMMY JOB!

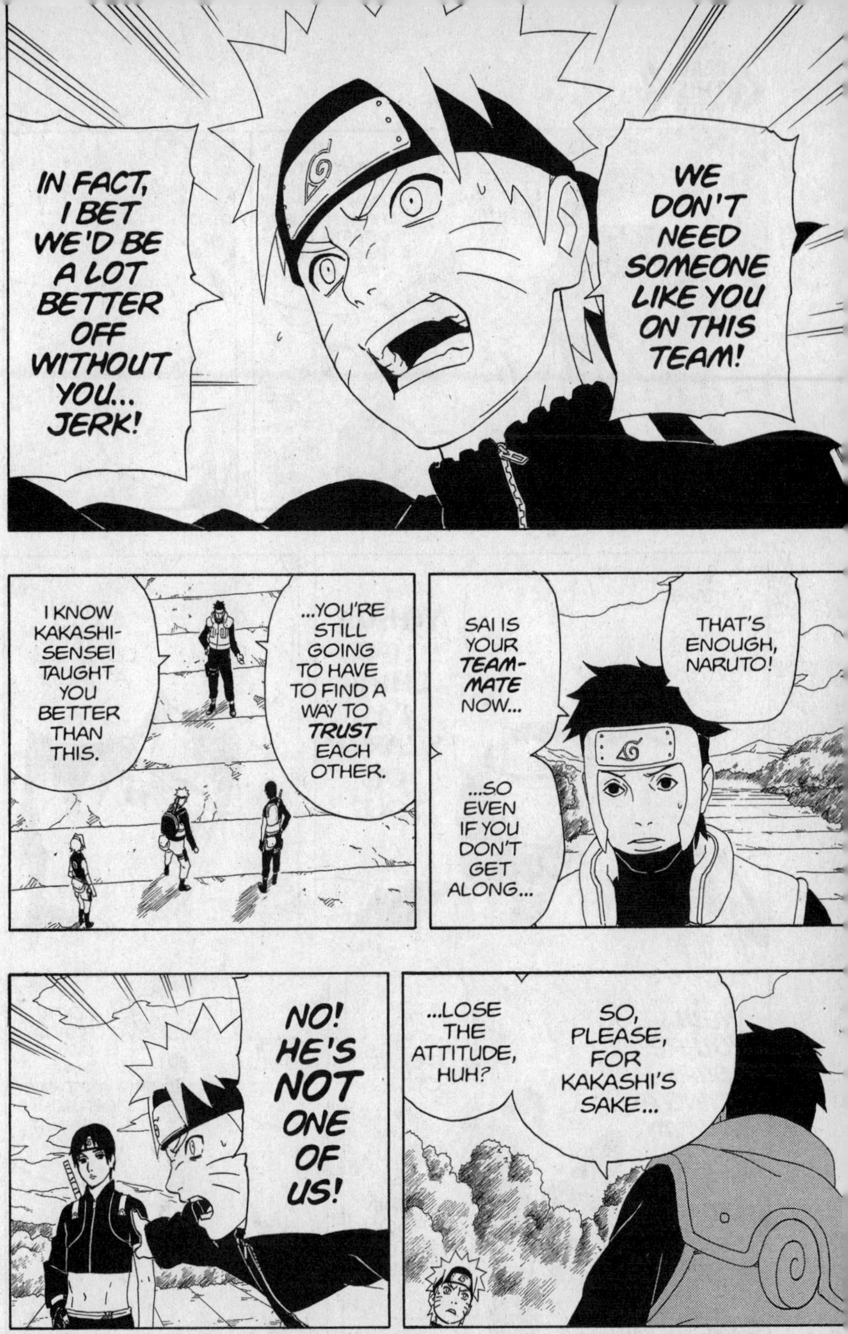
WE DON'T NEED SOMEONE LIKE YOU ON THIS TEAM!
IN FACT, I BET WE'D BE A LOT BETTER OFF WITHOUT YOU... JERK!
THAT'S ENOUGH, NARUTO!
SAI IS YOUR TEAMMATE NOW...
...SO EVEN IF YOU DON'T GET ALONG...
...YOU'RE STILL GOING TO HAVE TO FIND A WAY TO TRUST EACH OTHER.
I KNOW KAKASHI-SENSEI TAUGHT YOU BETTER THAN THIS.
SO, PLEASE, FOR KAKASHI'S SAKE...
...LOSE THE ATTITUDE, HUH?
NO! HE'S NOT ONE OF US!

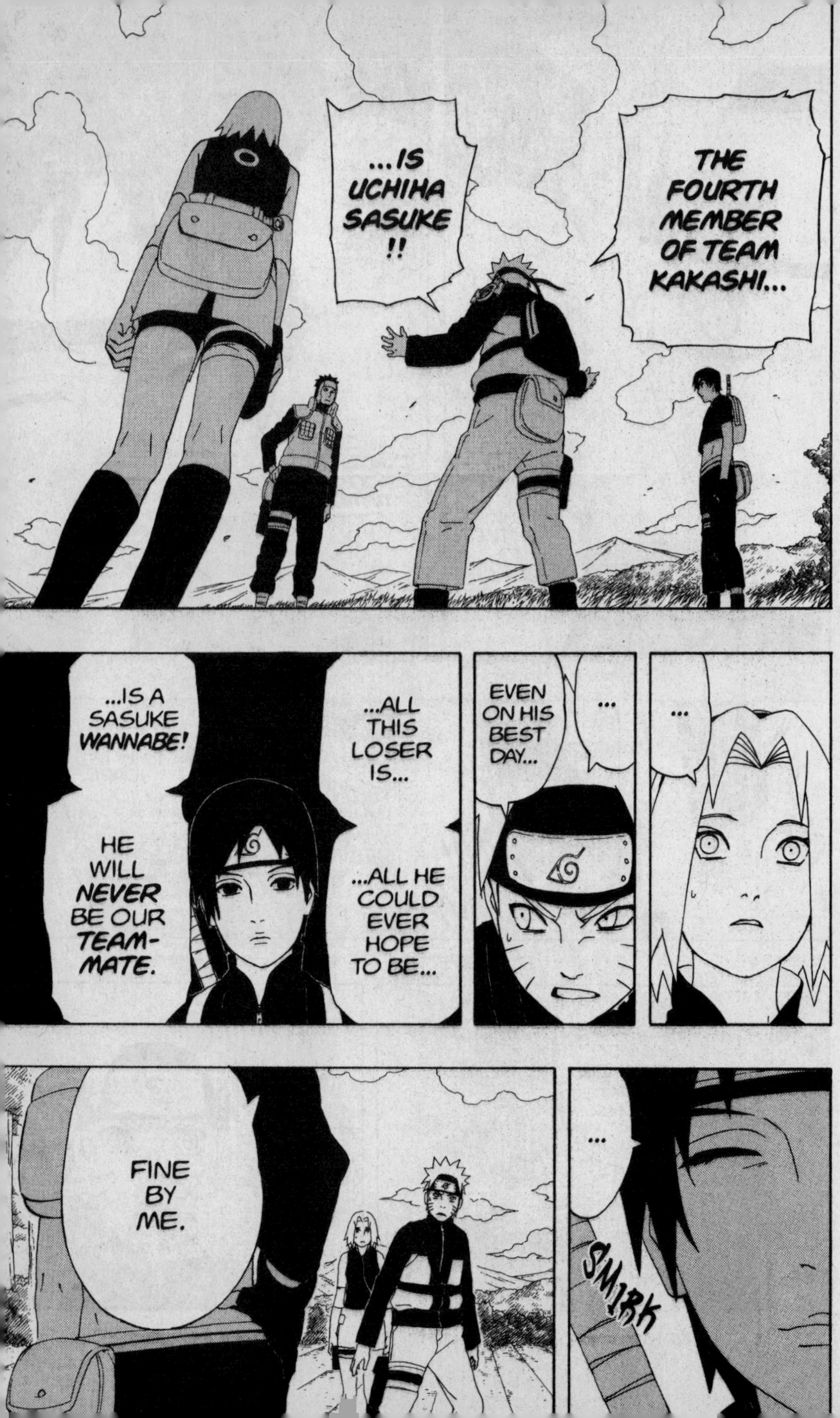
THE FOURTH MEMBER OF TEAM KAKASHI...
...IS UCHIHA SASUKE !!
...
...
EVEN ON HIS BEST DAY...
...ALL THIS LOSER IS...
...ALL HE COULD EVER HOPE TO BE...
...IS A SASUKE WANNABE!
HE WILL NEVER BE OUR TEAM-MATE.
...
SMIRK
FINE BY ME.

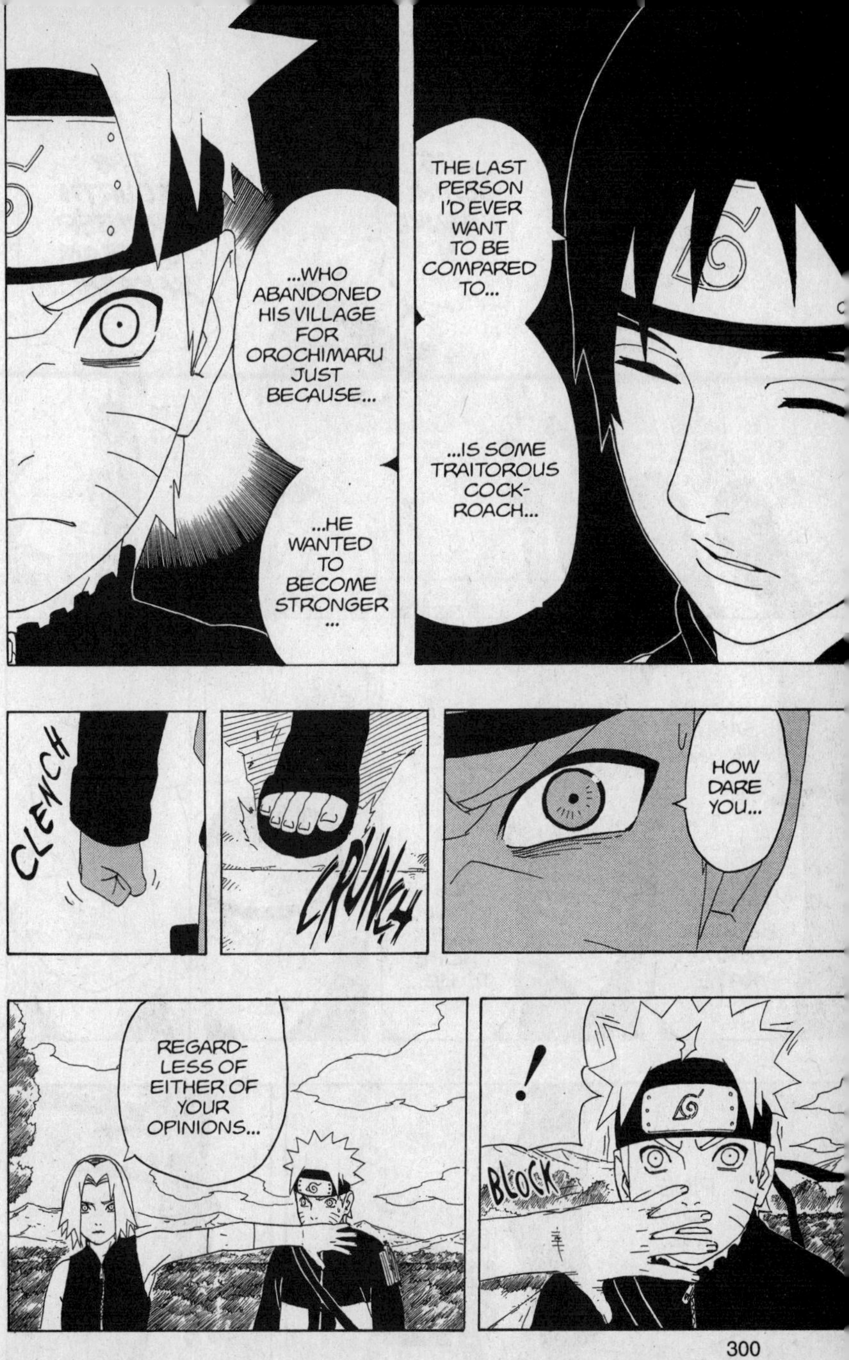
THE LAST PERSON I'D EVER WANT TO BE COMPARED TO...
...IS SOME TRAITOROUS COCK-ROACH...
...WHO ABANDONED HIS VILLAGE FOR OROCHIMARU JUST BECAUSE...
...HE WANTED TO BECOME STRONGER ...
HOW DARE YOU...
CRUNCH
CLENCH
!
BLOCK
REGARD-LESS OF EITHER OF YOUR OPINIONS...

READ THIS WAY

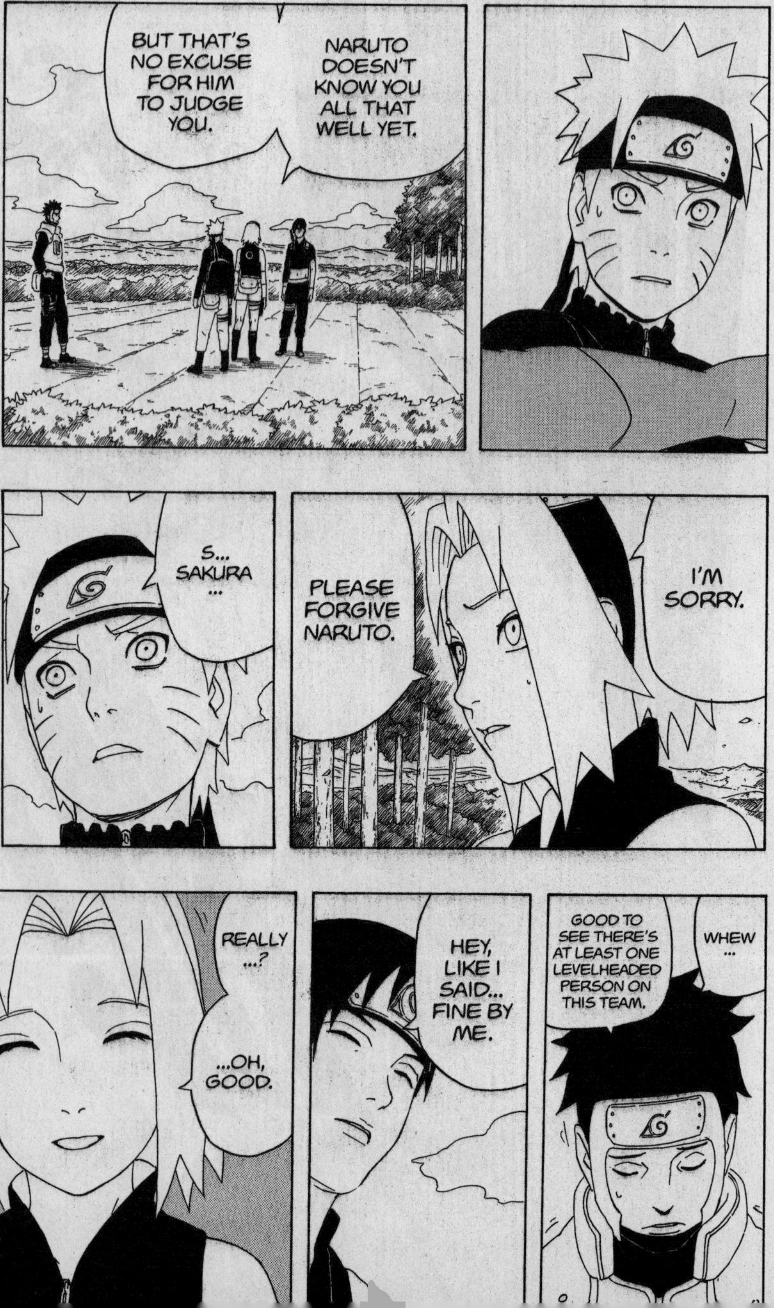
NARUTO DOESN'T KNOW YOU ALL THAT WELL YET.
BUT THAT'S NO EXCUSE FOR HIM TO JUDGE YOU.
I'M SORRY.
PLEASE FORGIVE NARUTO.
S... SAKURA ...
WHEW ...
GOOD TO SEE THERE'S AT LEAST ONE LEVELHEADED PERSON ON THIS TEAM.
HEY, LIKE I SAID... FINE BY ME.
REALLY ...?
...OH, GOOD.

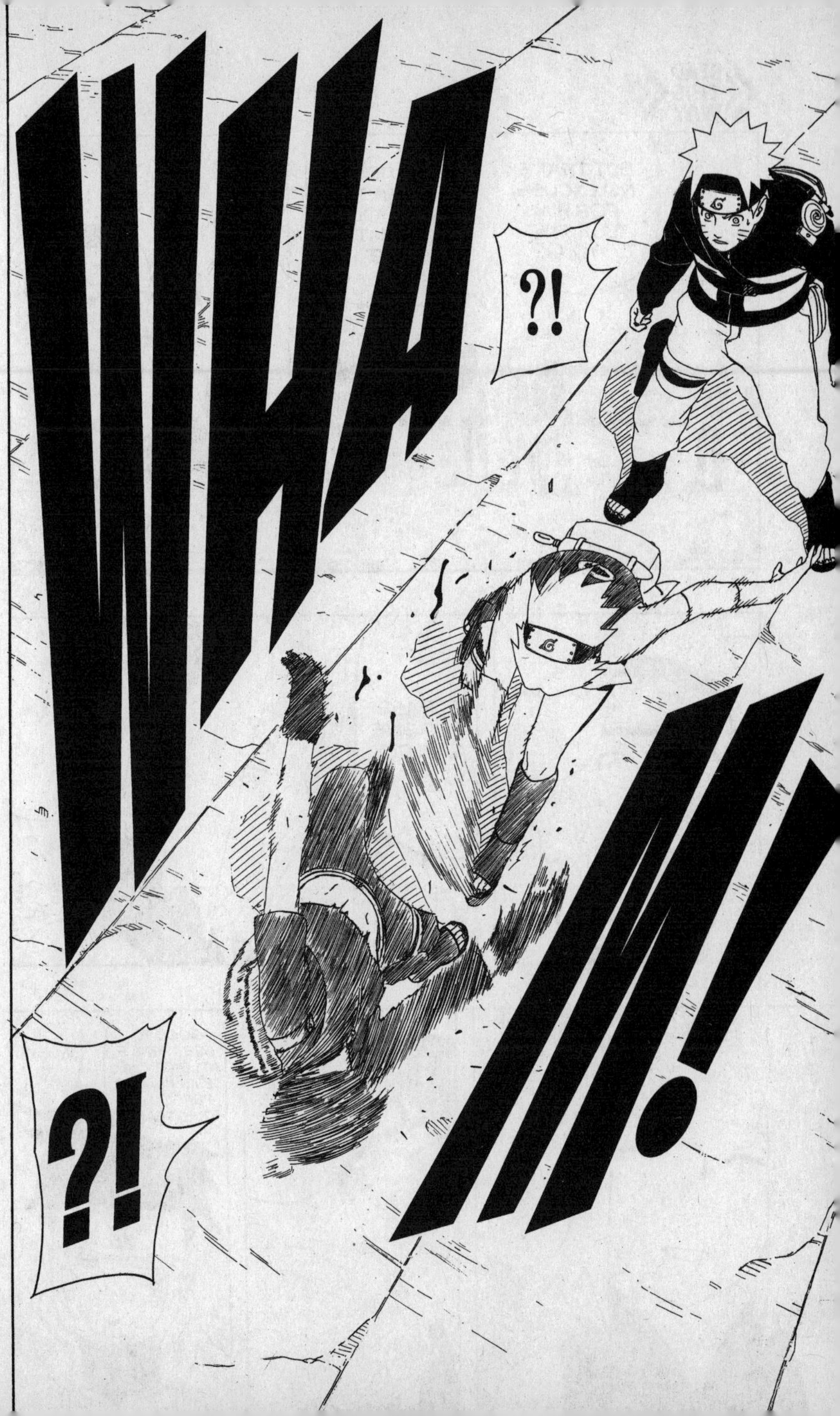
?!
WHAM!
?!

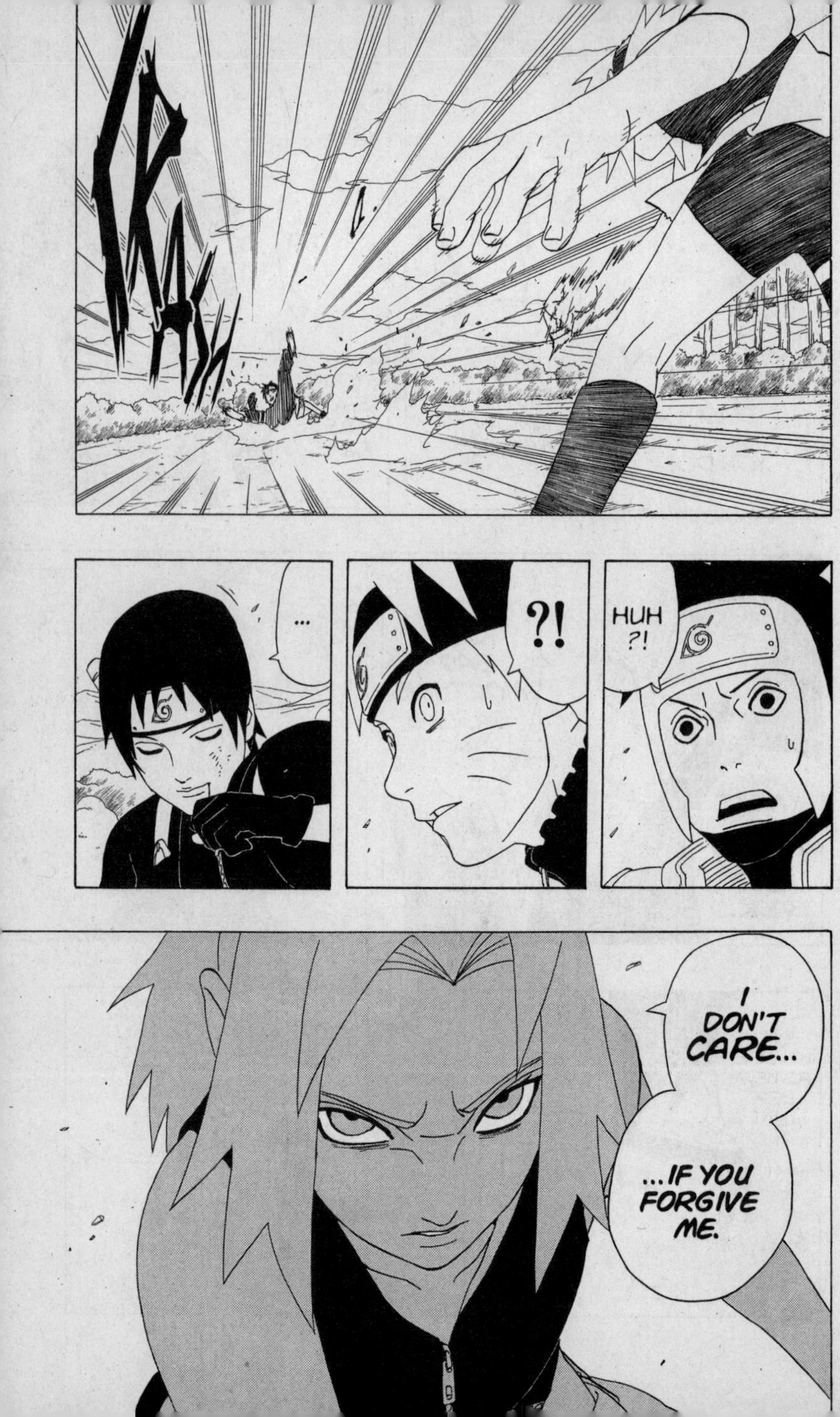
CRASH
HUH ?!
?!
...
I DON'T CARE...
...IF YOU FORGIVE ME.

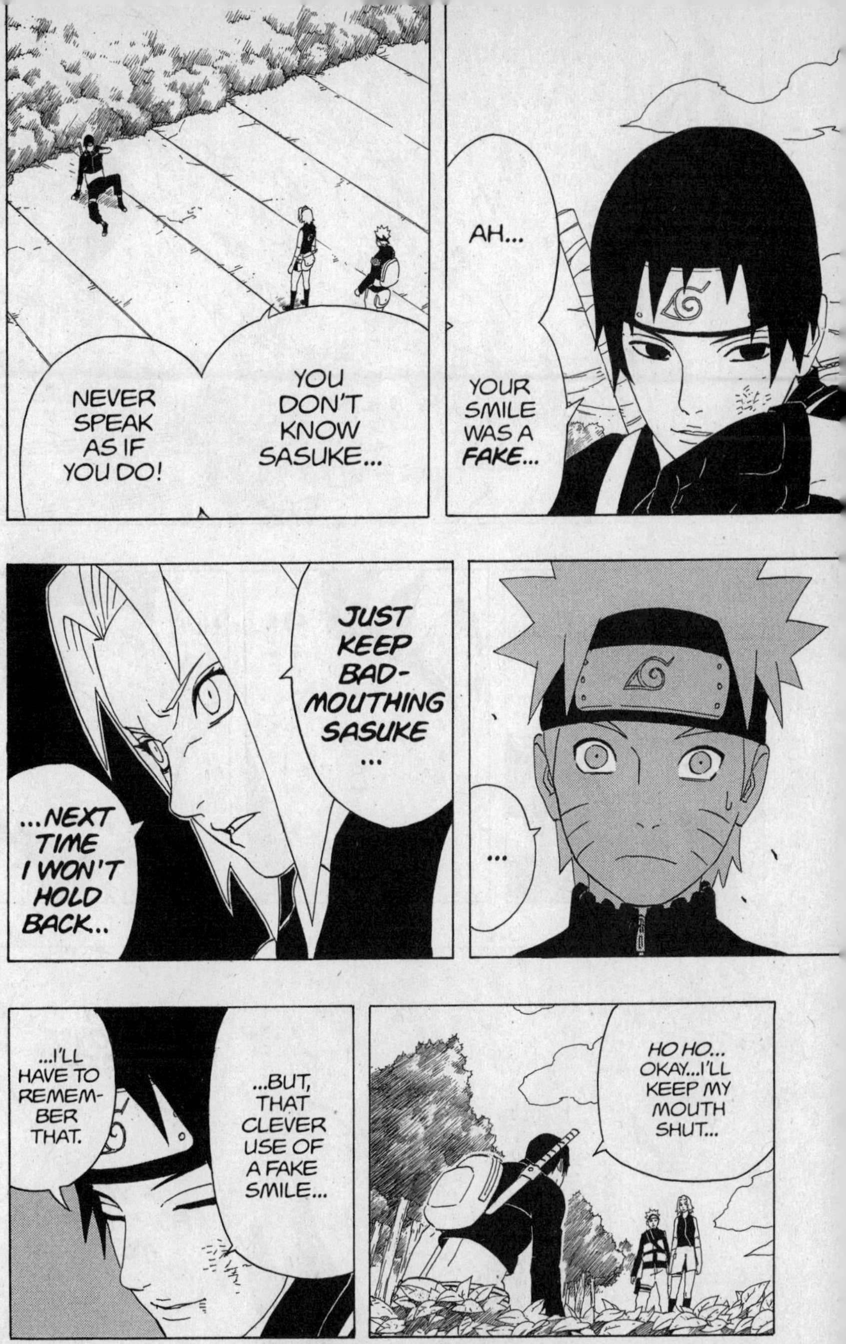
AH...
YOUR SMILE WAS A FAKE...
YOU DON'T KNOW SASUKE...
NEVER SPEAK AS IF YOU DO!
...
JUST KEEP BAD-MOUTHING SASUKE ...
...NEXT TIME I WON'T HOLD BACK...
HO HO... OKAY...I'LL KEEP MY MOUTH SHUT...
...BUT, THAT CLEVER USE OF A FAKE SMILE...
...I'LL HAVE TO REMEMBER THAT.

READ THIS WAY

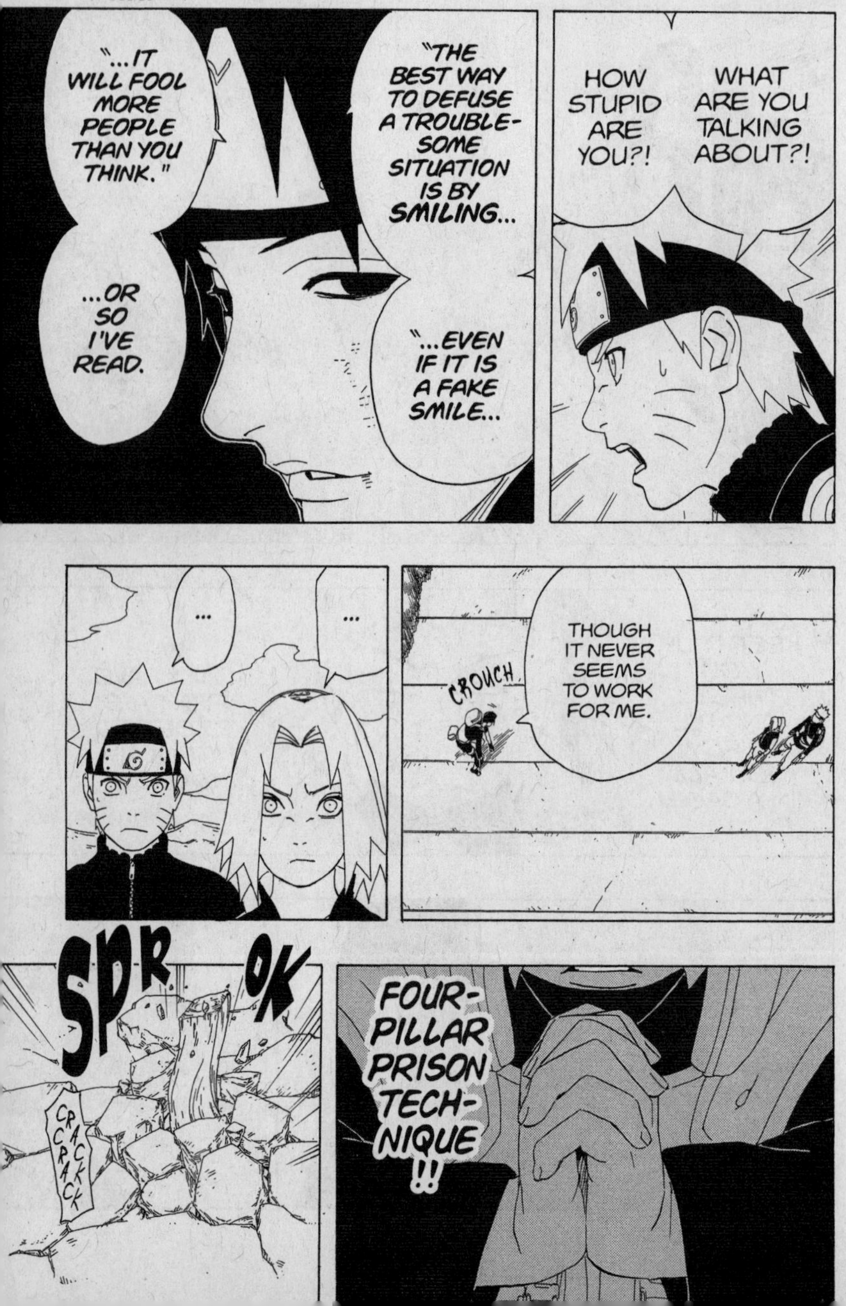
WHAT ARE YOU TALKING ABOUT?!
HOW STUPID ARE YOU?!
"THE BEST WAY TO DEFUSE A TROUBLE-SOME SITUATION IS BY SMILING...
"...EVEN IF IT IS A FAKE SMILE...
"...IT WILL FOOL MORE PEOPLE THAN YOU THINK."
...OR SO I'VE READ.
THOUGH IT NEVER SEEMS TO WORK FOR ME.
CROUCH
...
...
FOUR-PILLAR PRISON TECH-NIQUE!!
SPROK
CRACK CRACK

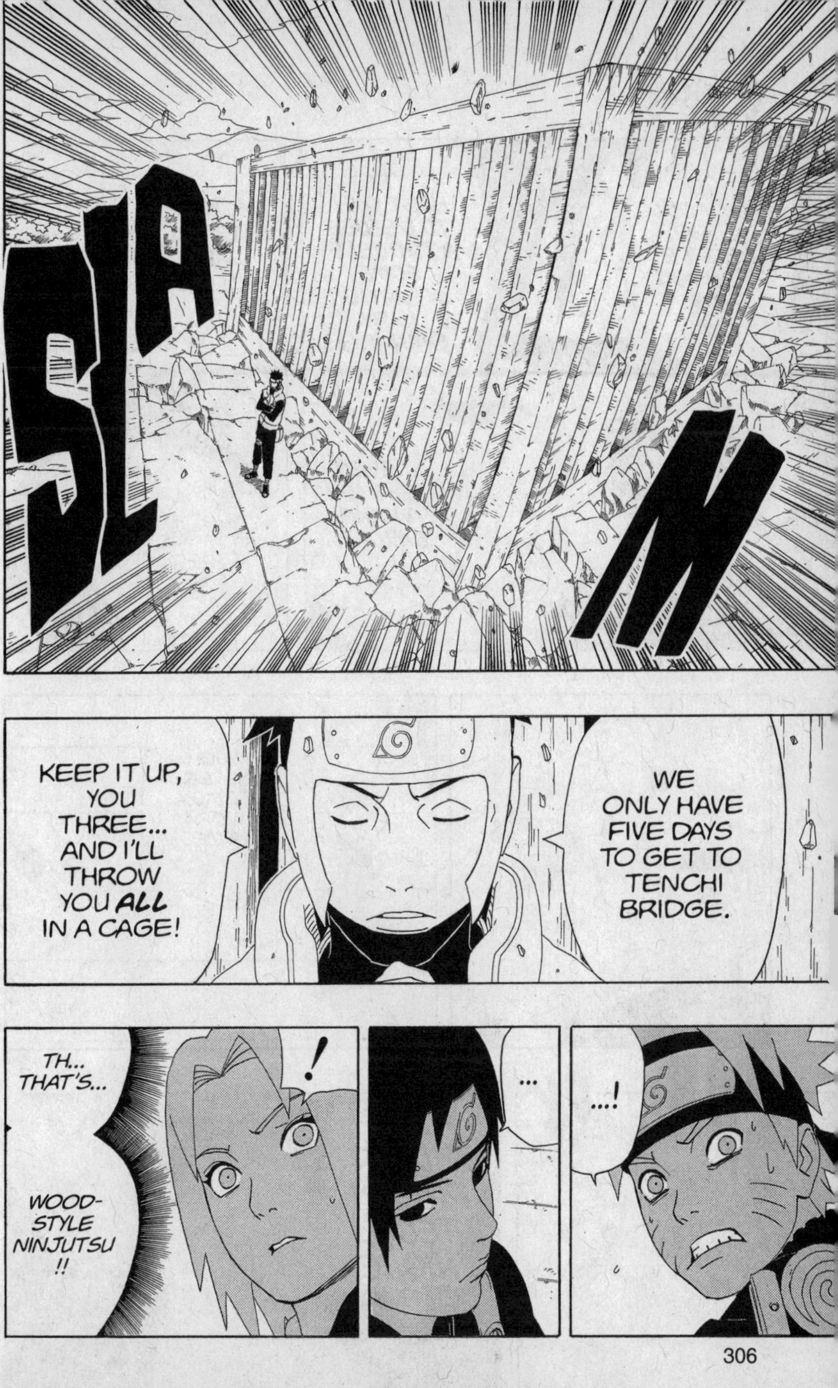
SLAM
WE ONLY HAVE FIVE DAYS TO GET TO TENCHI BRIDGE.
KEEP IT UP, YOU THREE... AND I'LL THROW YOU **ALL** IN A CAGE!
...!
...
!
TH... THAT'S...
WOOD-STYLE NINJUTSU !!

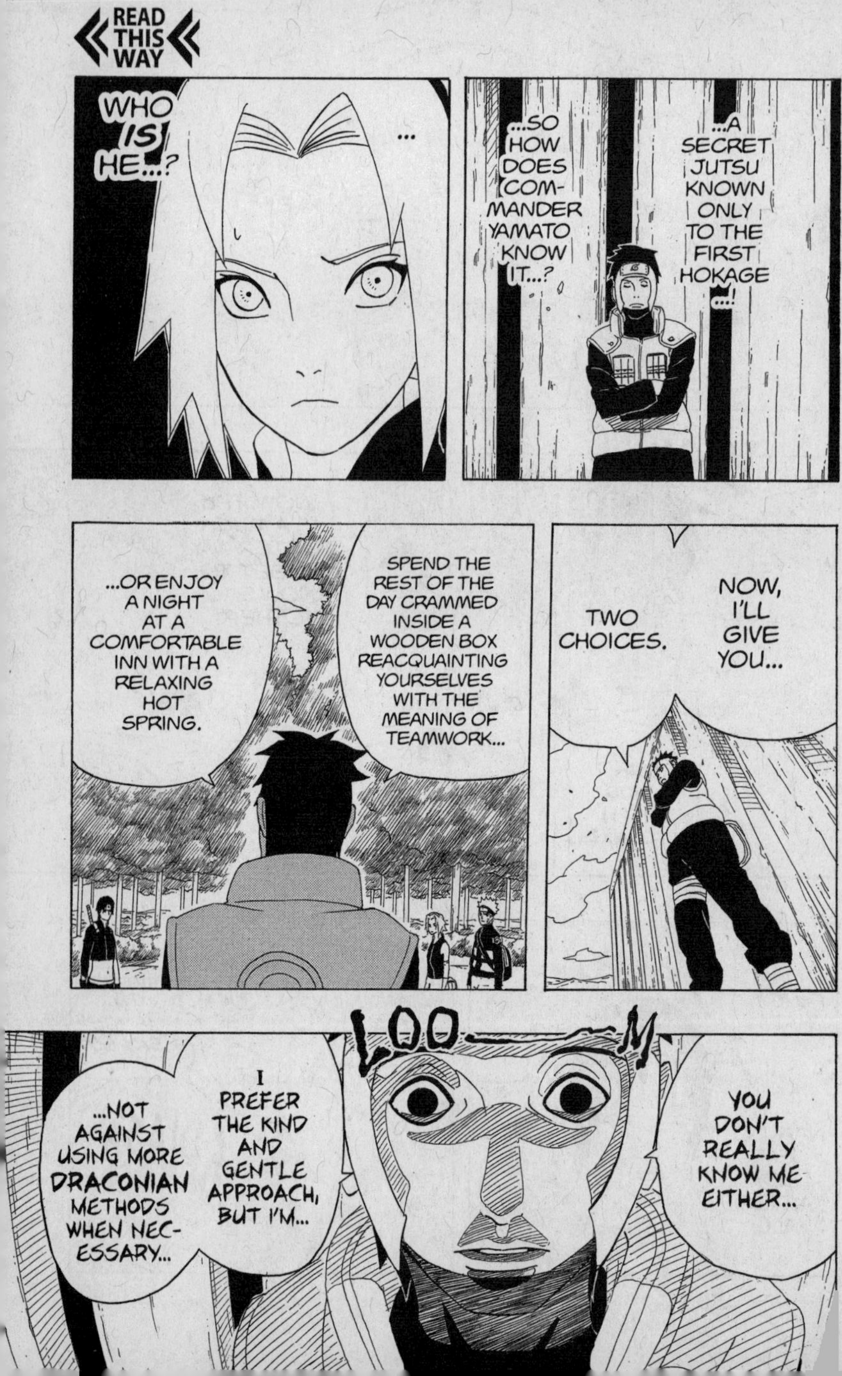
READ THIS WAY
...A SECRET JUTSU KNOWN ONLY TO THE FIRST HOKAGE ...!
...SO HOW DOES COMMANDER YAMATO KNOW IT...?
...
WHO IS HE...?
NOW, I'LL GIVE YOU...
TWO CHOICES.
SPEND THE REST OF THE DAY CRAMMED INSIDE A WOODEN BOX REACQUAINTING YOURSELVES WITH THE MEANING OF TEAMWORK...
...OR ENJOY A NIGHT AT A COMFORTABLE INN WITH A RELAXING HOT SPRING.
LOO—M
YOU DON'T REALLY KNOW ME EITHER...
I PREFER THE KIND AND GENTLE APPROACH, BUT I'M...
...NOT AGAINST USING MORE DRACONIAN METHODS WHEN NECESSARY...

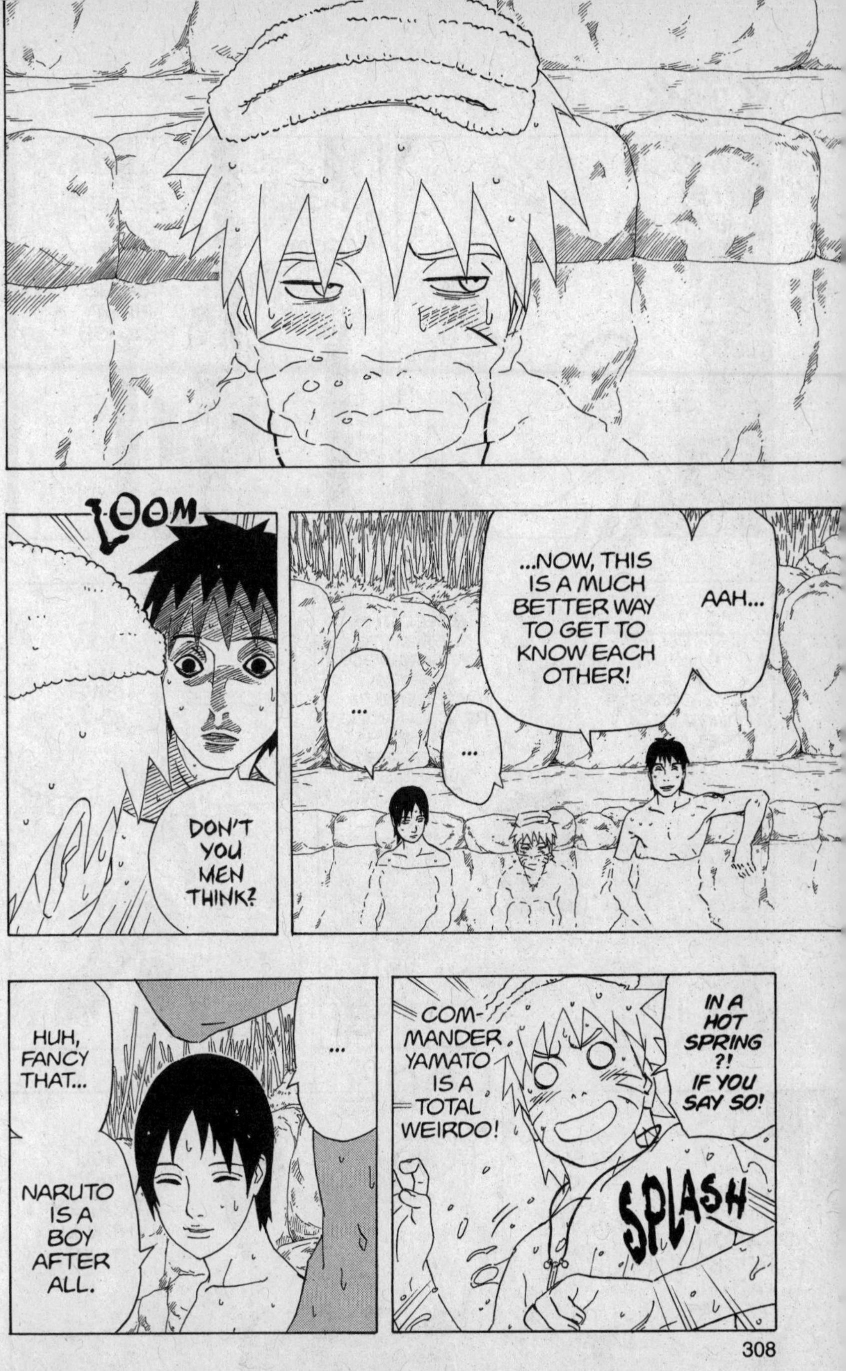
AAH...
...NOW, THIS IS A MUCH BETTER WAY TO GET TO KNOW EACH OTHER!
...
...
LOOM
...
...
DON'T YOU MEN THINK?
IN A HOT SPRING ?! IF YOU SAY SO!
COM-MANDER YAMATO IS A TOTAL WEIRDO!
SPLASH
...
HUH, FANCY THAT...
NARUTO IS A BOY AFTER ALL.

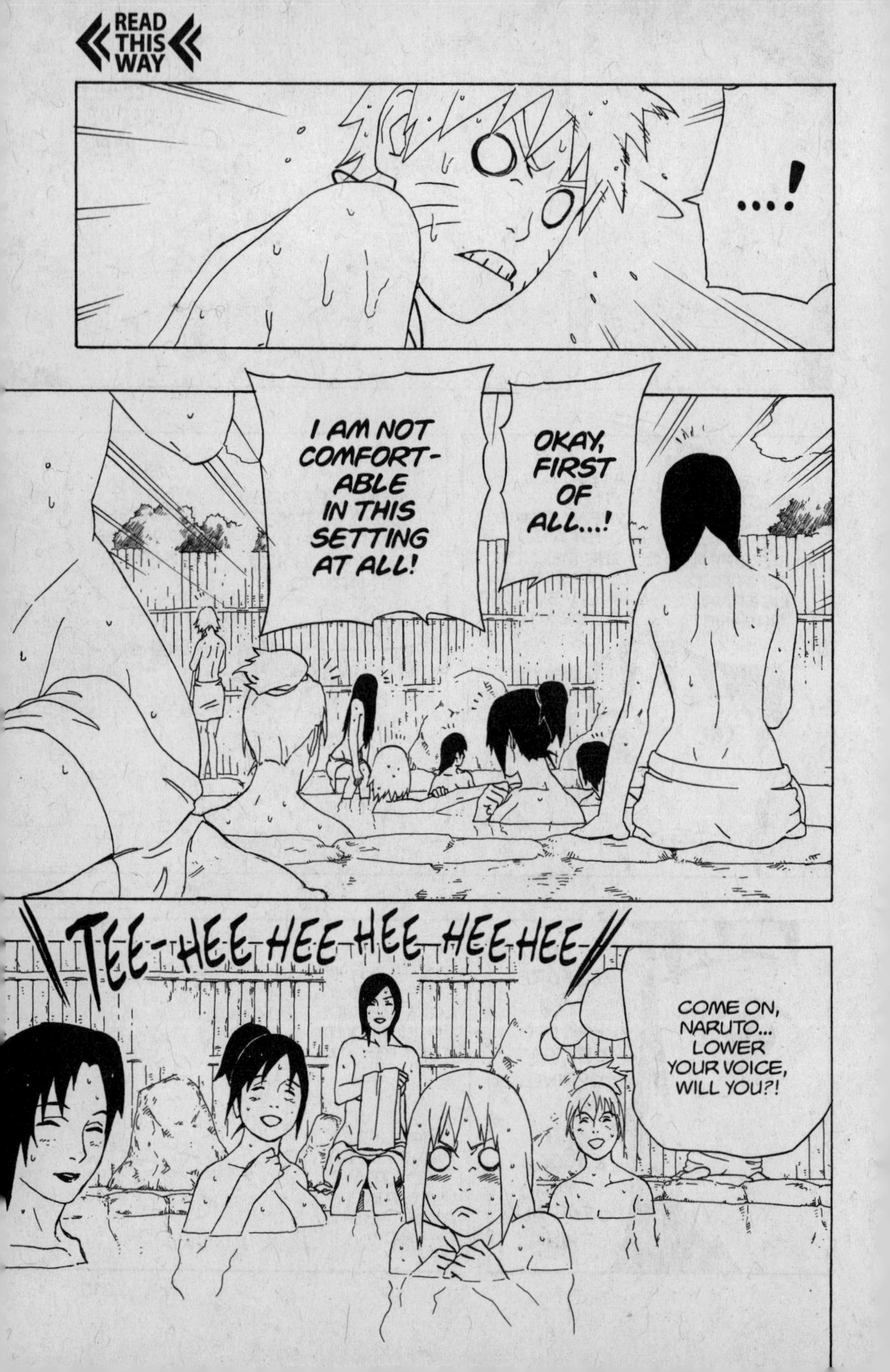
READ THIS WAY
...!
OKAY, FIRST OF ALL...!
I AM NOT COMFORTABLE IN THIS SETTING AT ALL!
TEE-HEE HEE HEE HEE HEE
COME ON, NARUTO... LOWER YOUR VOICE, WILL YOU?!

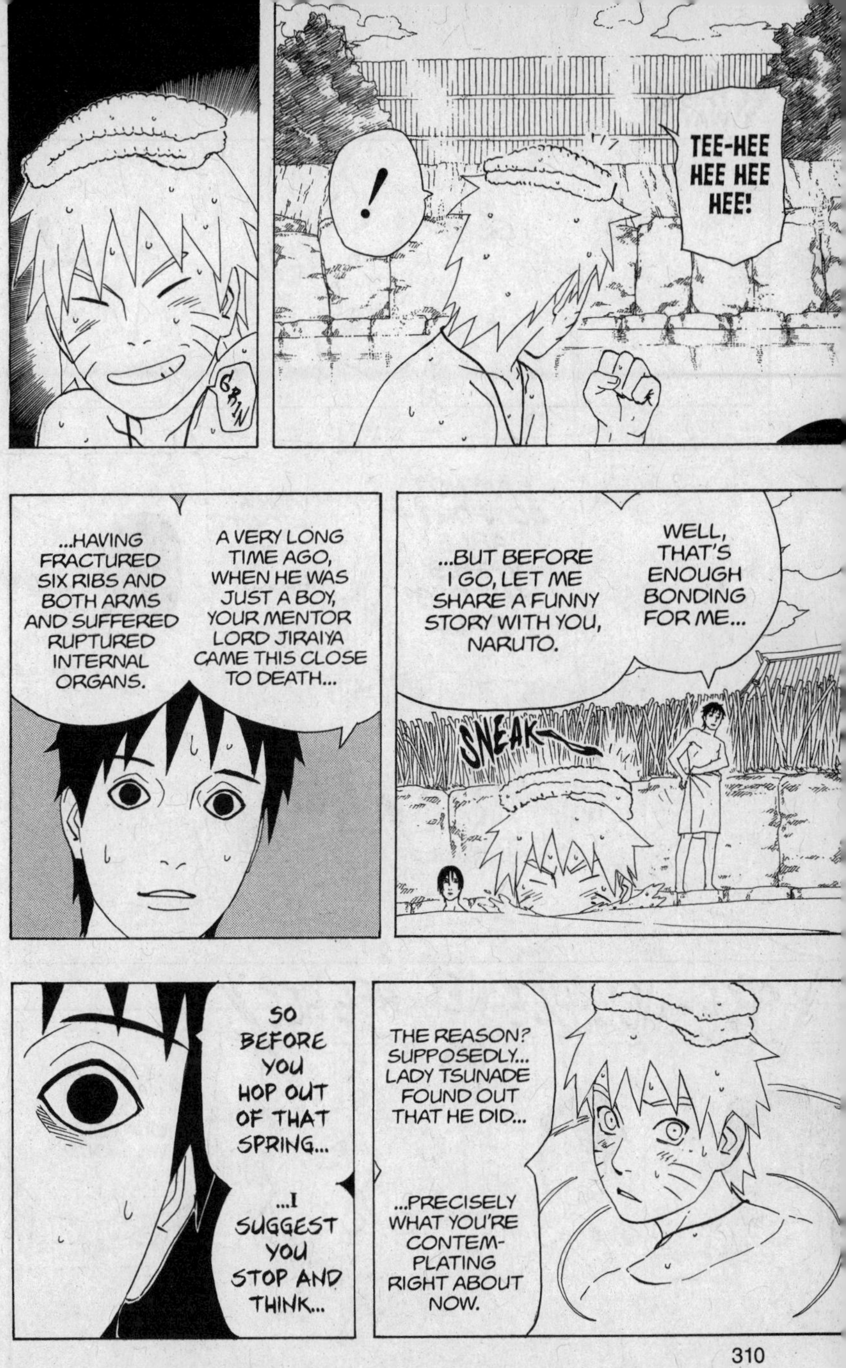
TEE-HEE HEE HEE HEE!
!
GRIN
WELL, THAT'S ENOUGH BONDING FOR ME...
...BUT BEFORE I GO, LET ME SHARE A FUNNY STORY WITH YOU, NARUTO.
SNEAK
A VERY LONG TIME AGO, WHEN HE WAS JUST A BOY, YOUR MENTOR LORD JIRAIYA CAME THIS CLOSE TO DEATH...
...HAVING FRACTURED SIX RIBS AND BOTH ARMS AND SUFFERED RUPTURED INTERNAL ORGANS.
THE REASON? SUPPOSEDLY... LADY TSUNADE FOUND OUT THAT HE DID...
...PRECISELY WHAT YOU'RE CONTEM-PLATING RIGHT ABOUT NOW.
SO BEFORE YOU HOP OUT OF THAT SPRING...
...I SUGGEST YOU STOP AND THINK...

READ THIS WAY

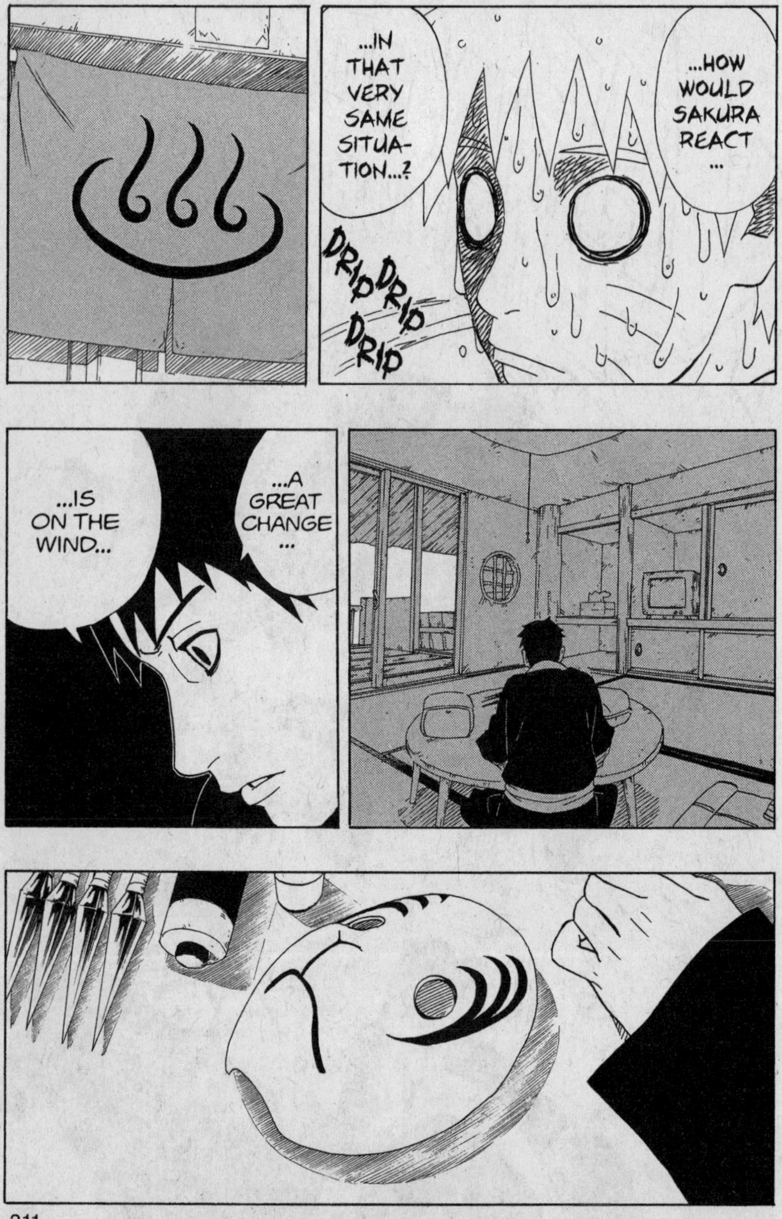

...HOW WOULD SAKURA REACT ...
...IN THAT VERY SAME SITUATION...?
DRIP DRIP DRIP
...A GREAT CHANGE ...
...IS ON THE WIND...

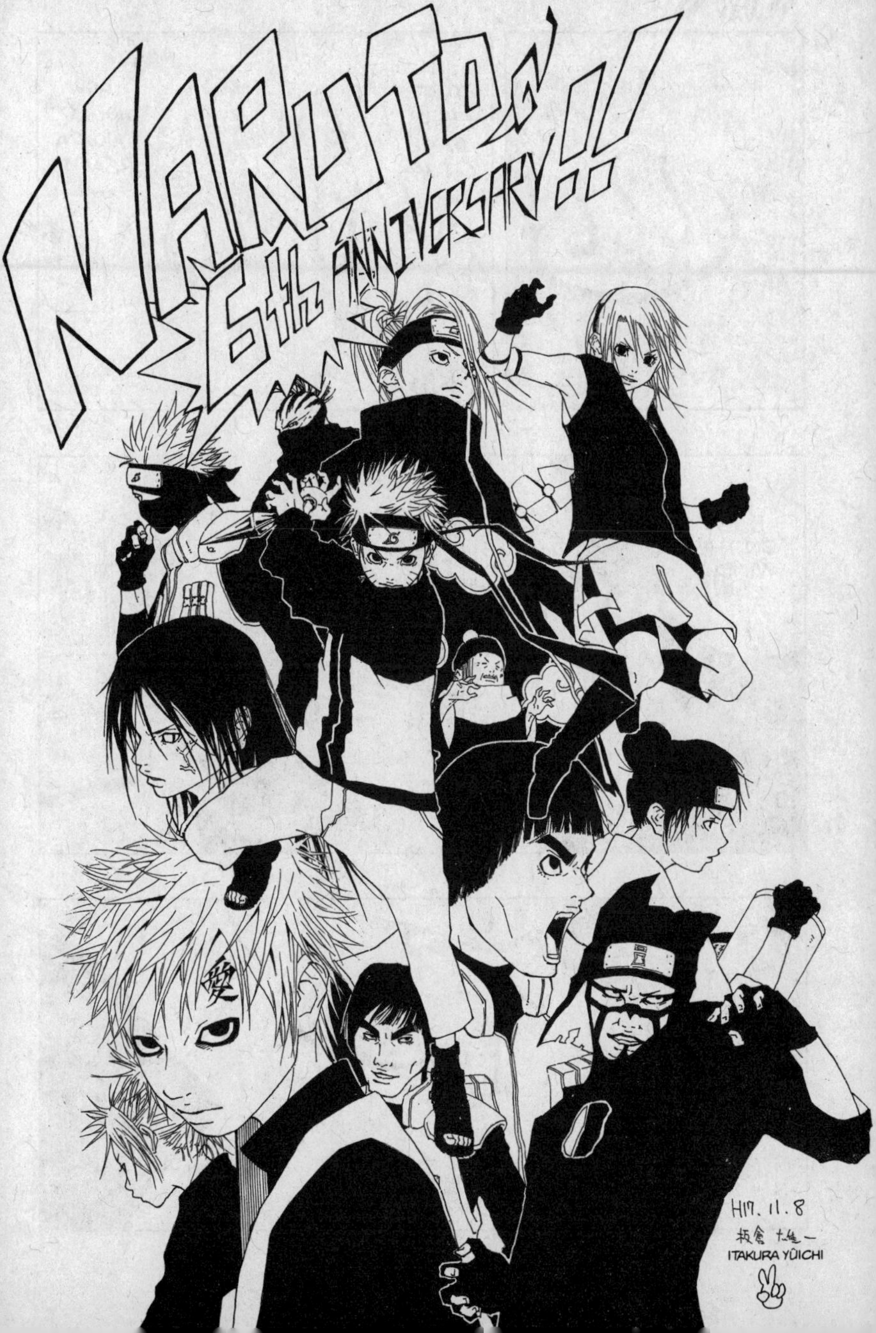
NARUTO 6th ANNIVERSARY!!
H17. 11. 8
ITAKURA YÛICHI

Number 287: Untitled

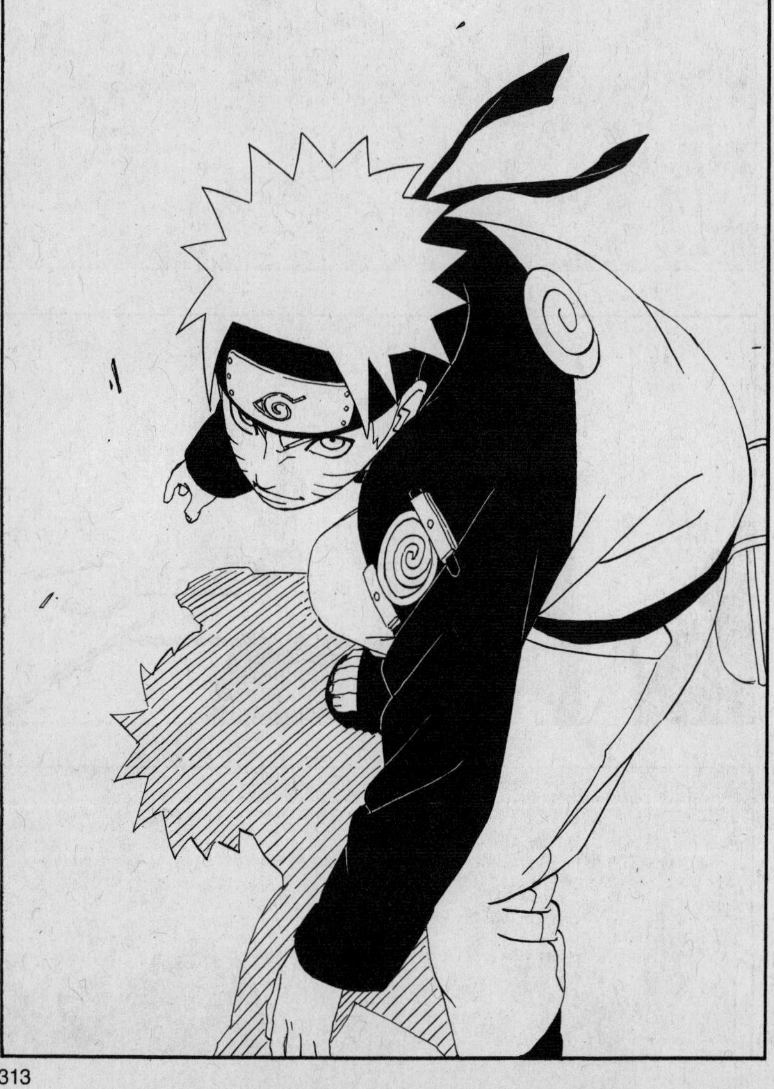

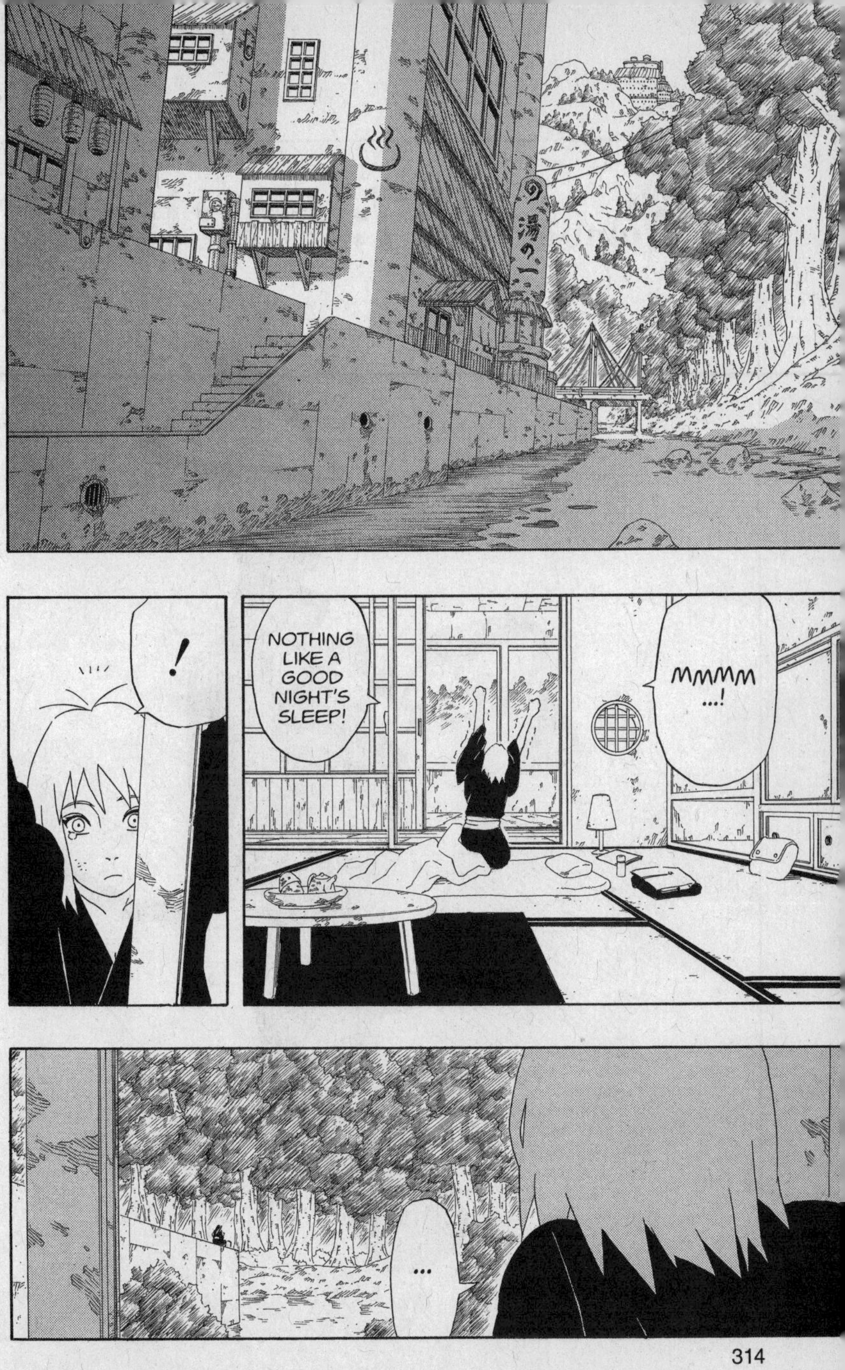
湯の一
MMMM ...!
NOTHING LIKE A GOOD NIGHT'S SLEEP!
!
...

READ THIS WAY

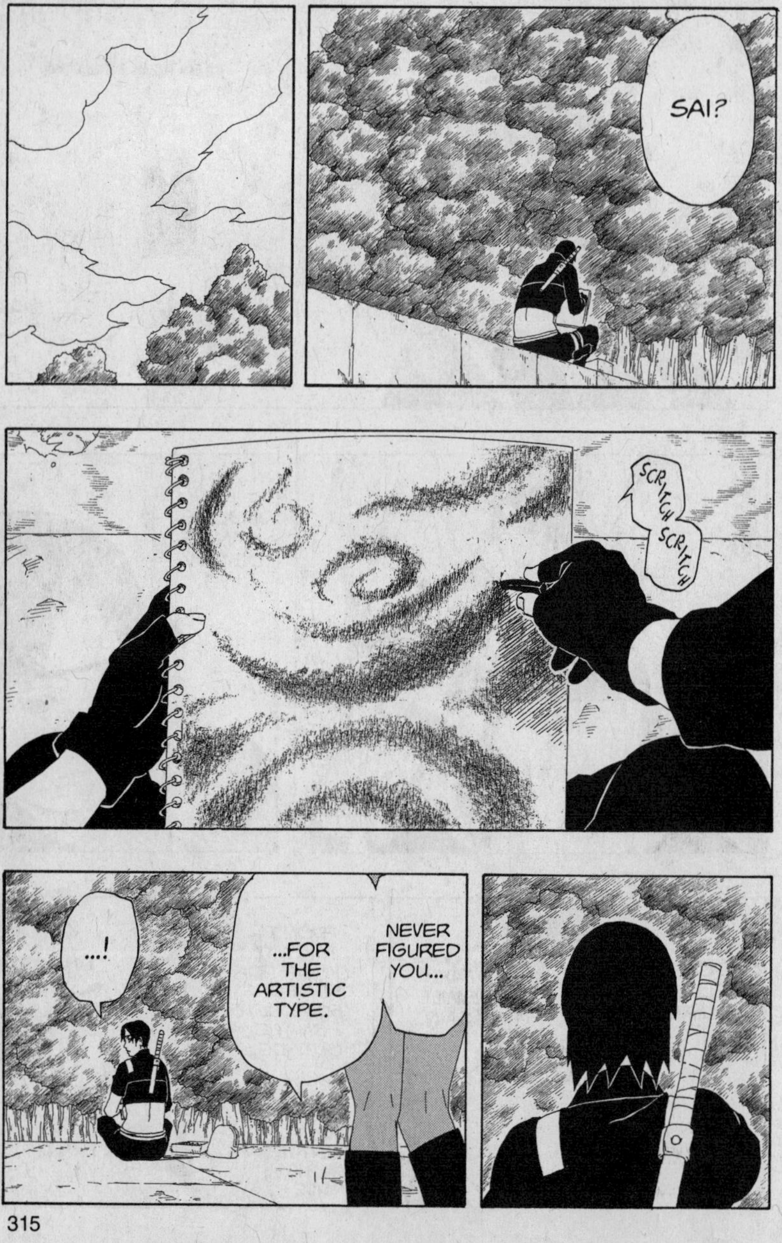
SAI?
SCRITCH SCRITCH
NEVER FIGURED YOU...
...FOR THE ARTISTIC TYPE.
...!

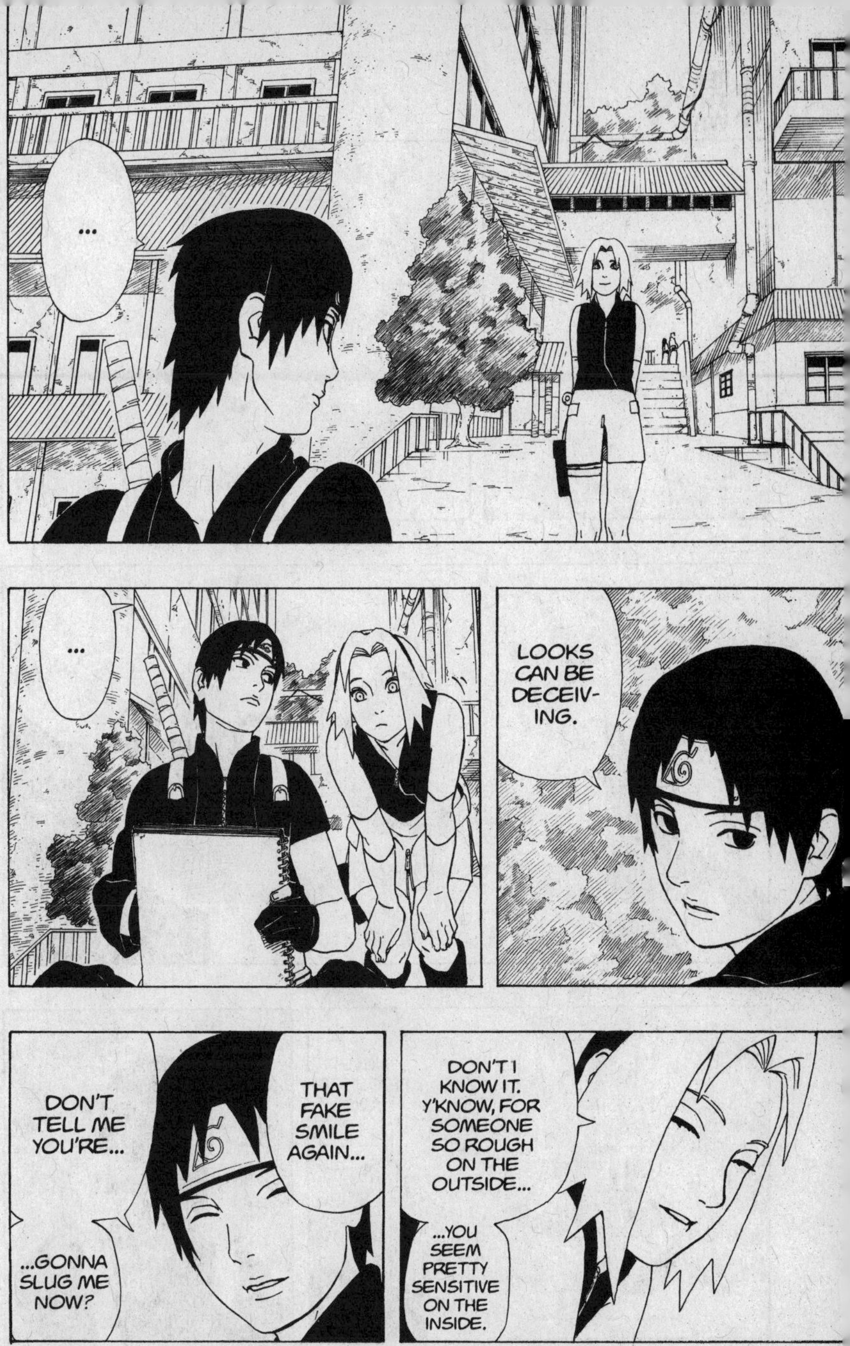
...
LOOKS CAN BE DECEIV-ING.
...
DON'T I KNOW IT. Y'KNOW, FOR SOMEONE SO ROUGH ON THE OUTSIDE...
...YOU SEEM PRETTY SENSITIVE ON THE INSIDE.
THAT FAKE SMILE AGAIN...
DON'T TELL ME YOU'RE...
...GONNA SLUG ME NOW?

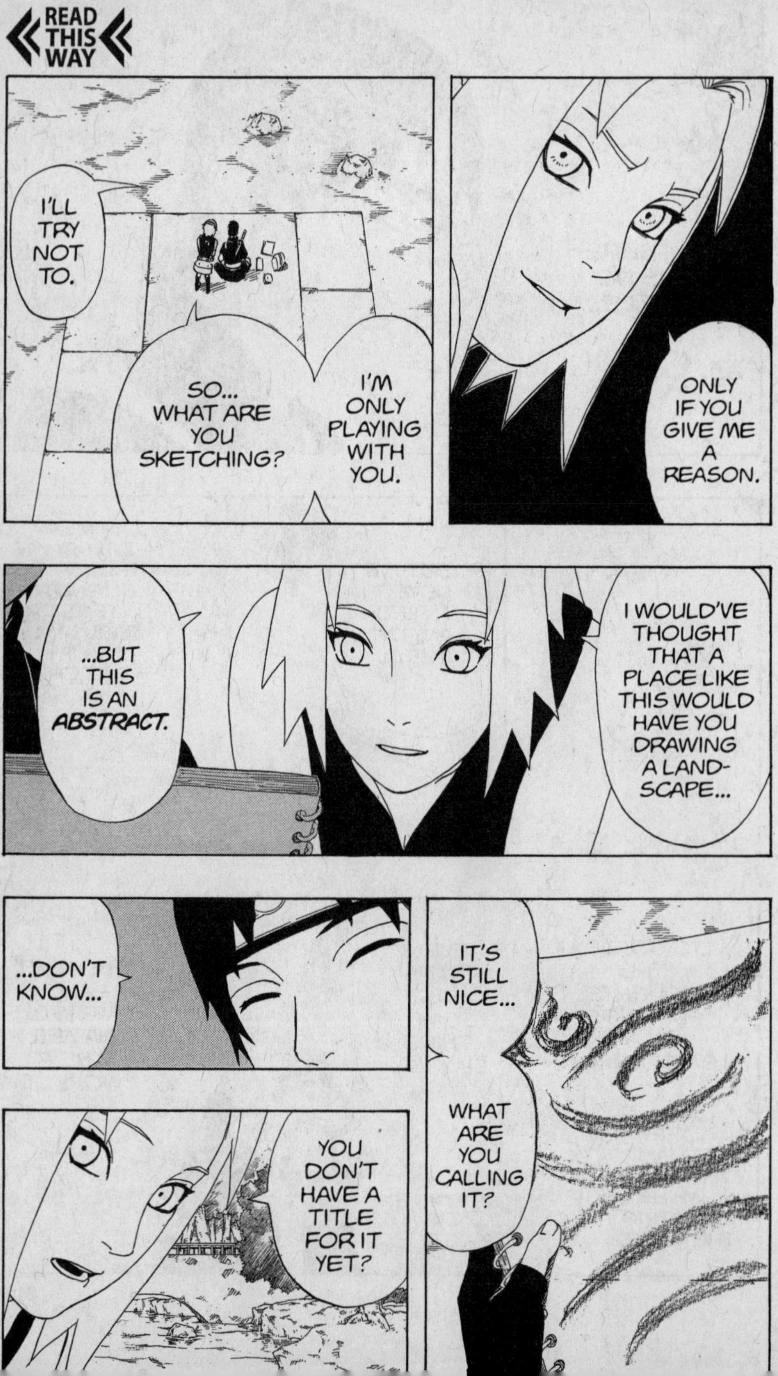
READ THIS WAY
ONLY IF YOU GIVE ME A REASON.
I'M ONLY PLAYING WITH YOU.
SO... WHAT ARE YOU SKETCHING?
I'LL TRY NOT TO.
I WOULD'VE THOUGHT THAT A PLACE LIKE THIS WOULD HAVE YOU DRAWING A LANDSCAPE...
...BUT THIS IS AN *ABSTRACT.*
IT'S STILL NICE...
WHAT ARE YOU CALLING IT?
...DON'T KNOW...
YOU DON'T HAVE A TITLE FOR IT YET?

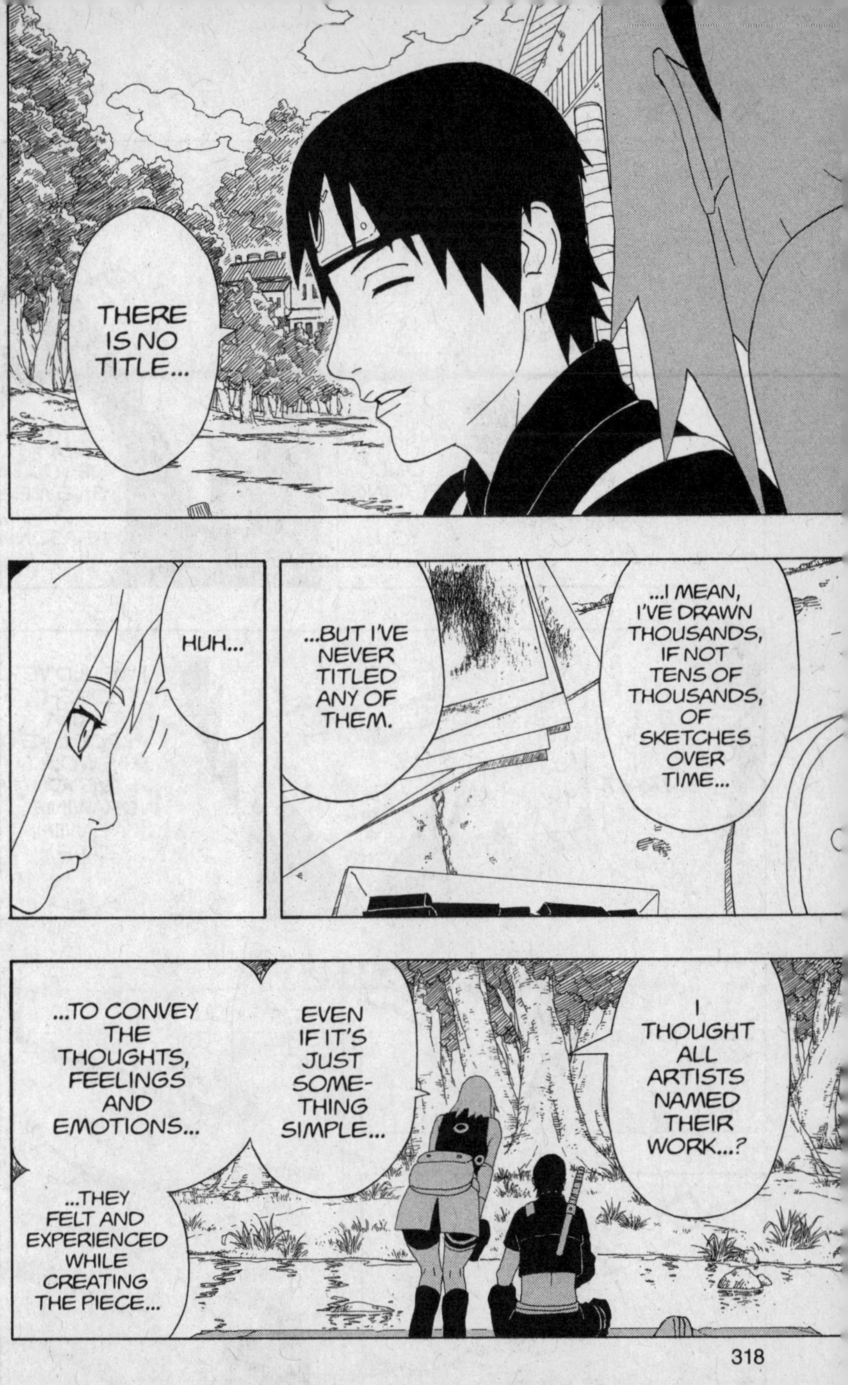
THERE IS NO TITLE...
...I MEAN, I'VE DRAWN THOUSANDS, IF NOT TENS OF THOUSANDS, OF SKETCHES OVER TIME...
...BUT I'VE NEVER TITLED ANY OF THEM.
HUH...
I THOUGHT ALL ARTISTS NAMED THEIR WORK...?
EVEN IF IT'S JUST SOME-THING SIMPLE...
...TO CONVEY THE THOUGHTS, FEELINGS AND EMOTIONS...
...THEY FELT AND EXPERIENCED WHILE CREATING THE PIECE...

READ THIS WAY

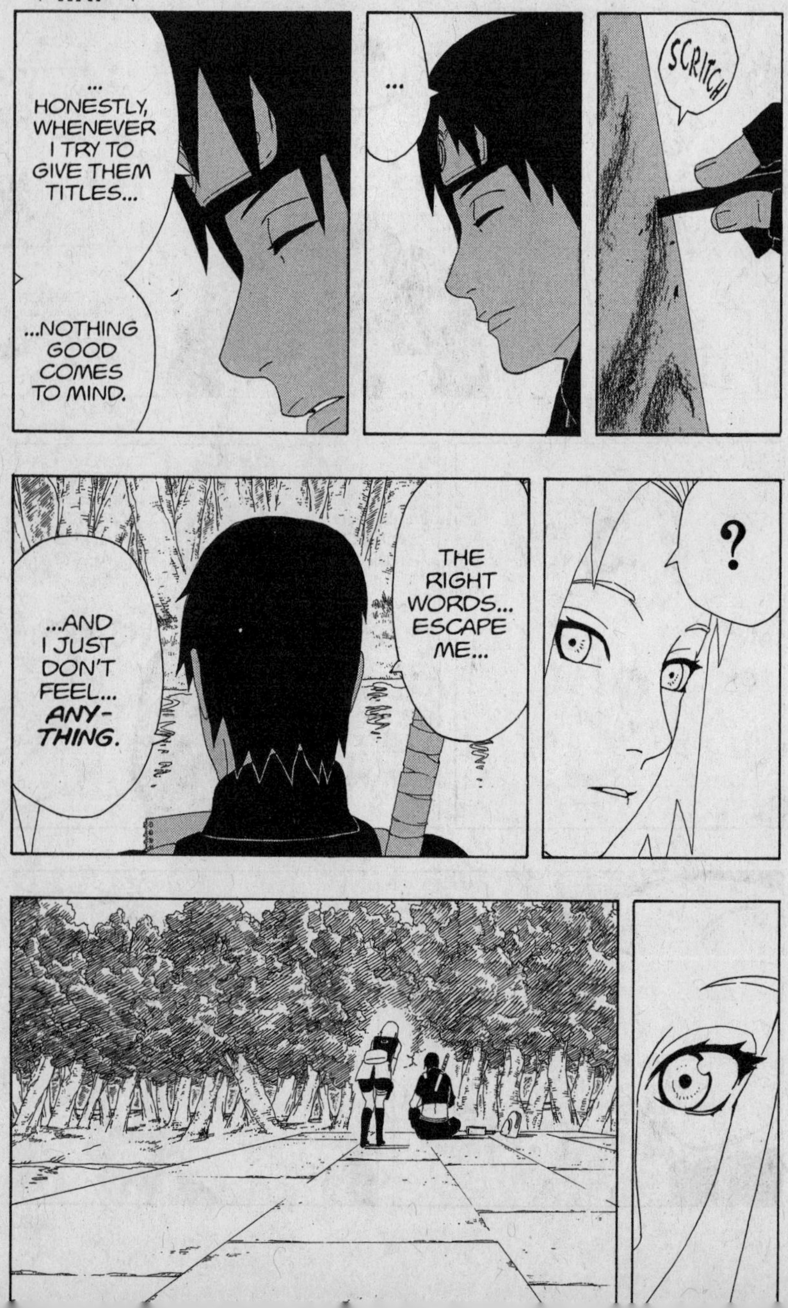
SCRITCH
...
... HONESTLY, WHENEVER I TRY TO GIVE THEM TITLES...
...NOTHING GOOD COMES TO MIND.
?
THE RIGHT WORDS... ESCAPE ME...
...AND I JUST DON'T FEEL... ANYTHING.

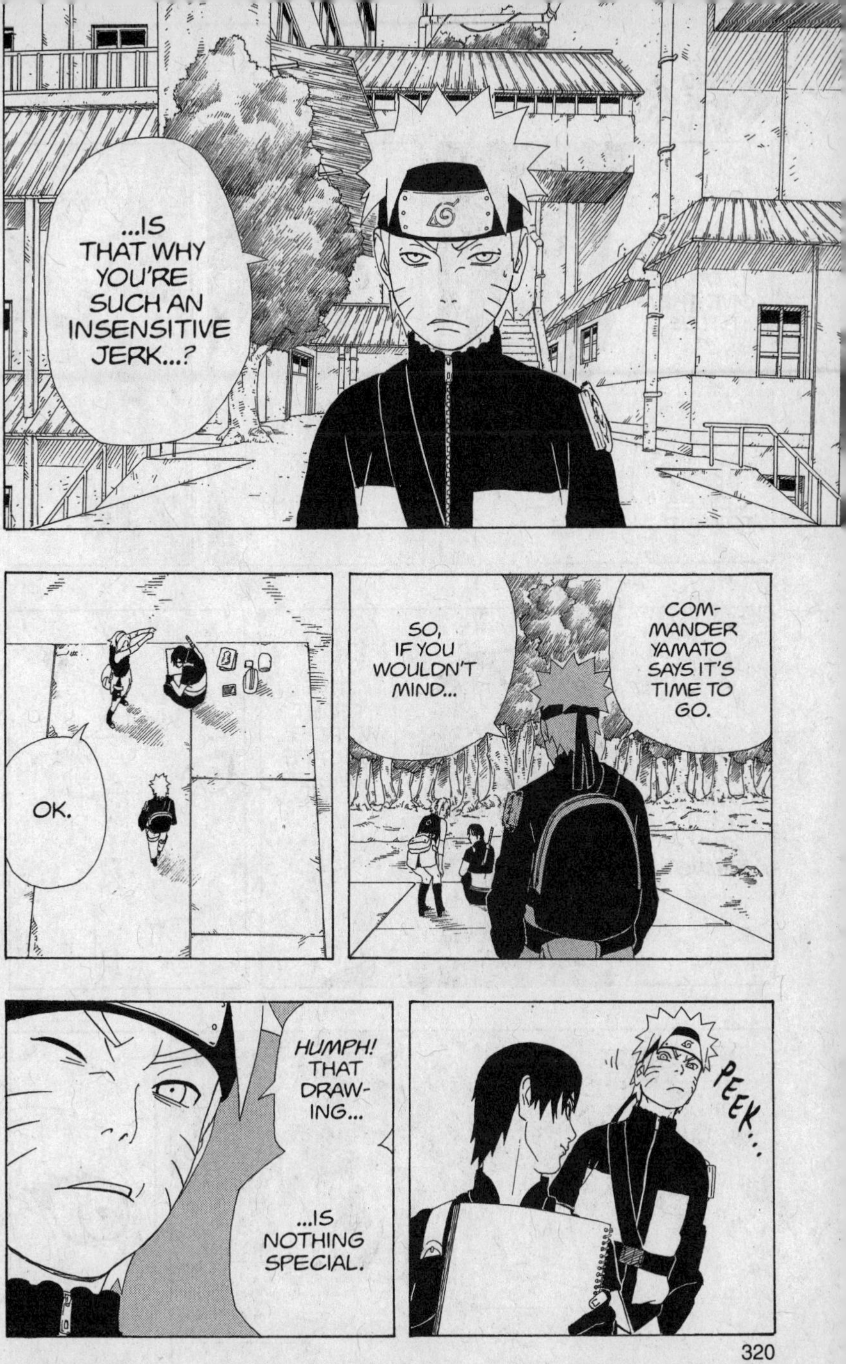
...IS THAT WHY YOU'RE SUCH AN INSENSITIVE JERK...?
COMMANDER YAMATO SAYS IT'S TIME TO GO.
SO, IF YOU WOULDN'T MIND...
OK.
PEEK...
HUMPH! THAT DRAWING...
...IS NOTHING SPECIAL.

READ THIS WAY

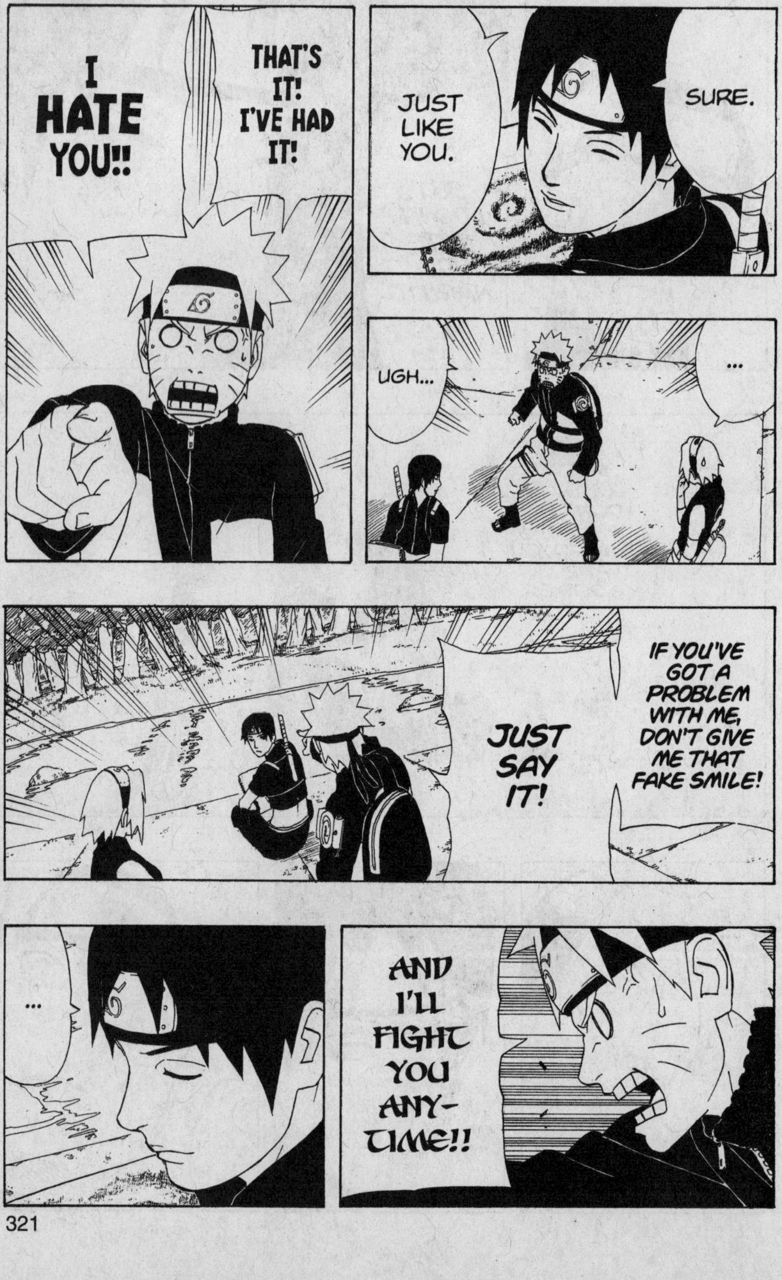
SURE.
JUST LIKE YOU.
...
UGH...
THAT'S IT! I'VE HAD IT!
I HATE YOU!!
IF YOU'VE GOT A PROBLEM WITH ME, DON'T GIVE ME THAT FAKE SMILE!
JUST SAY IT!
AND I'LL FIGHT YOU ANY-TIME!!
...

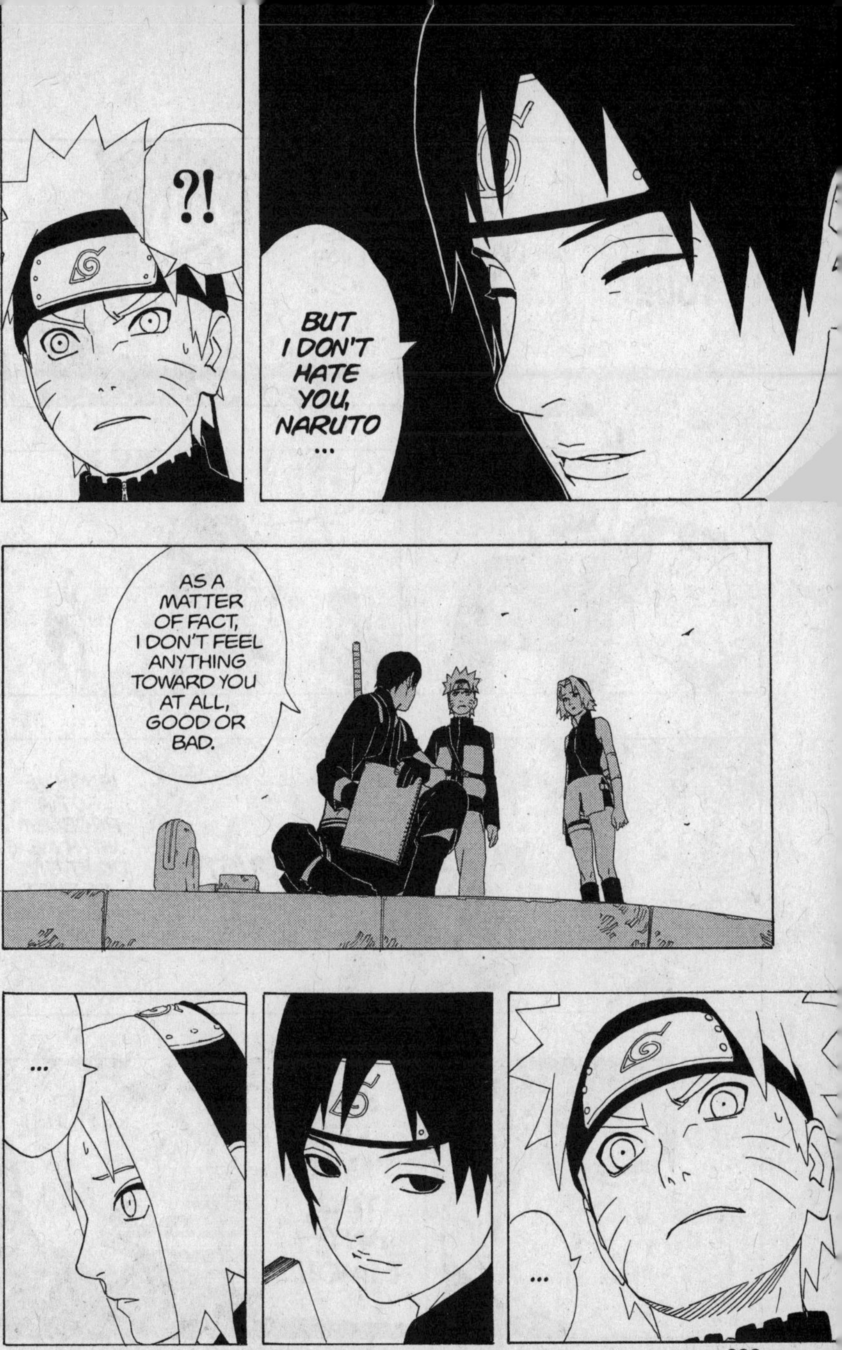
BUT I DON'T HATE YOU, NARUTO ...
?!
AS A MATTER OF FACT, I DON'T FEEL ANYTHING TOWARD YOU AT ALL, GOOD OR BAD.
...
...

READ THIS WAY

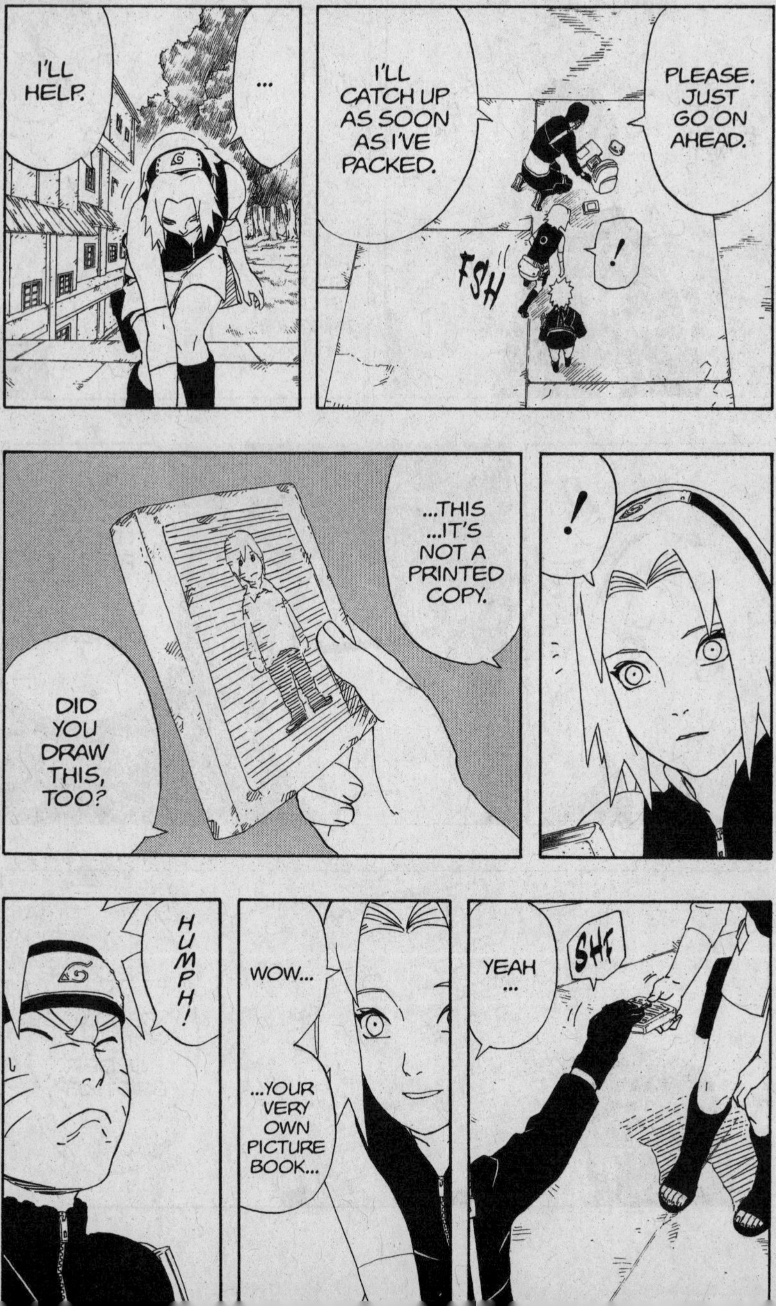
PLEASE. JUST GO ON AHEAD.
I'LL CATCH UP AS SOON AS I'VE PACKED.
!
FSH
...
I'LL HELP.
!
...THIS ...IT'S NOT A PRINTED COPY.
DID YOU DRAW THIS, TOO?
SHF
YEAH ...
WOW...
...YOUR VERY OWN PICTURE BOOK...
HUMPH!

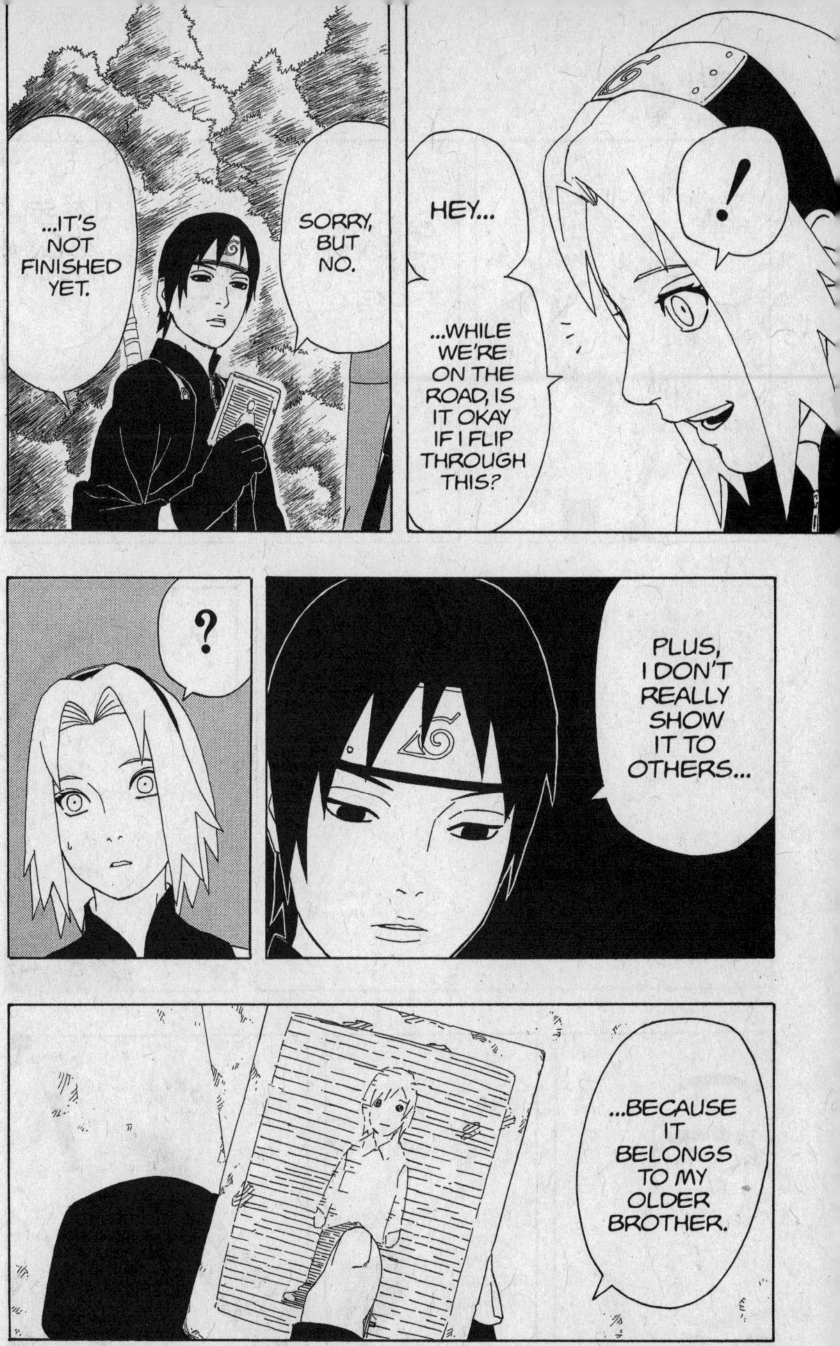
!
HEY...
...WHILE WE'RE ON THE ROAD, IS IT OKAY IF I FLIP THROUGH THIS?
SORRY, BUT NO.
...IT'S NOT FINISHED YET.
PLUS, I DON'T REALLY SHOW IT TO OTHERS...
?
...BECAUSE IT BELONGS TO MY OLDER BROTHER.

READ THIS WAY

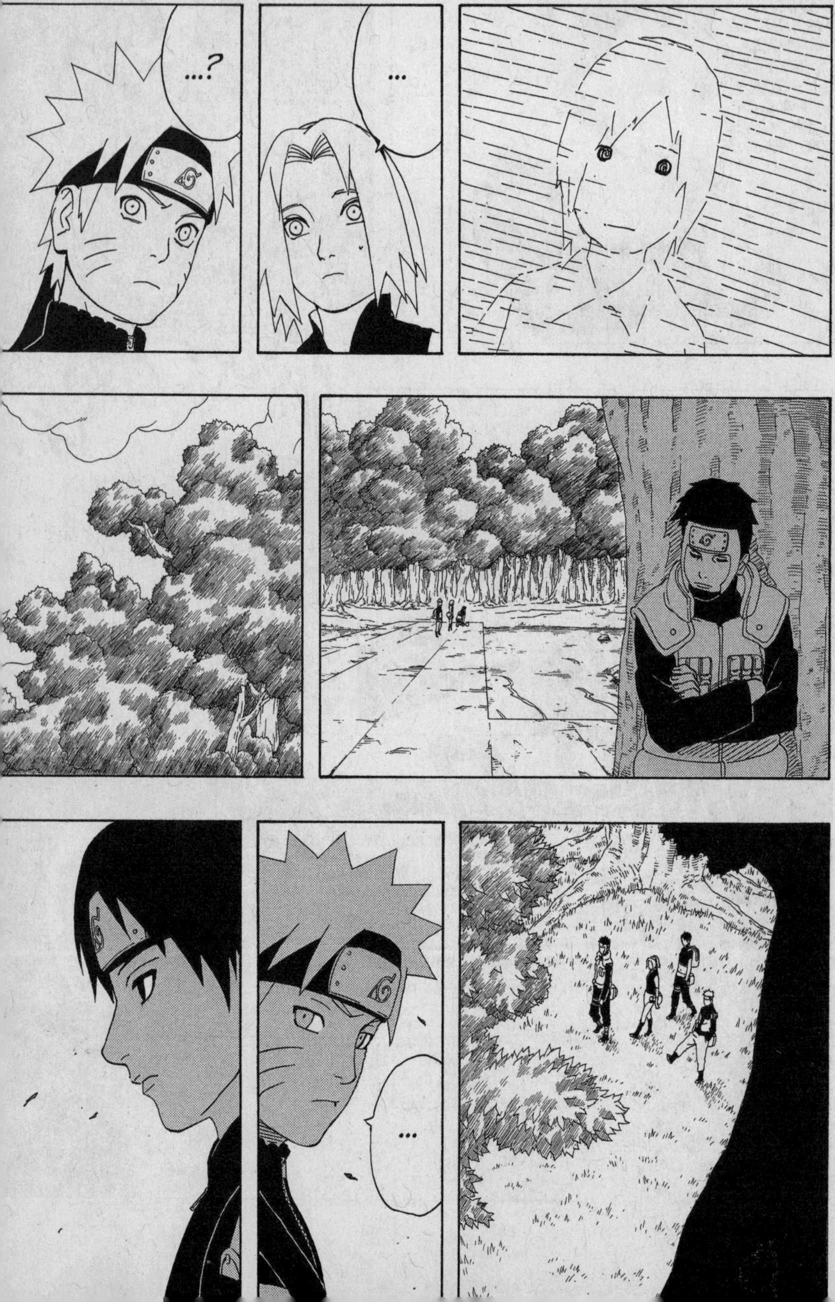
...
...?
...

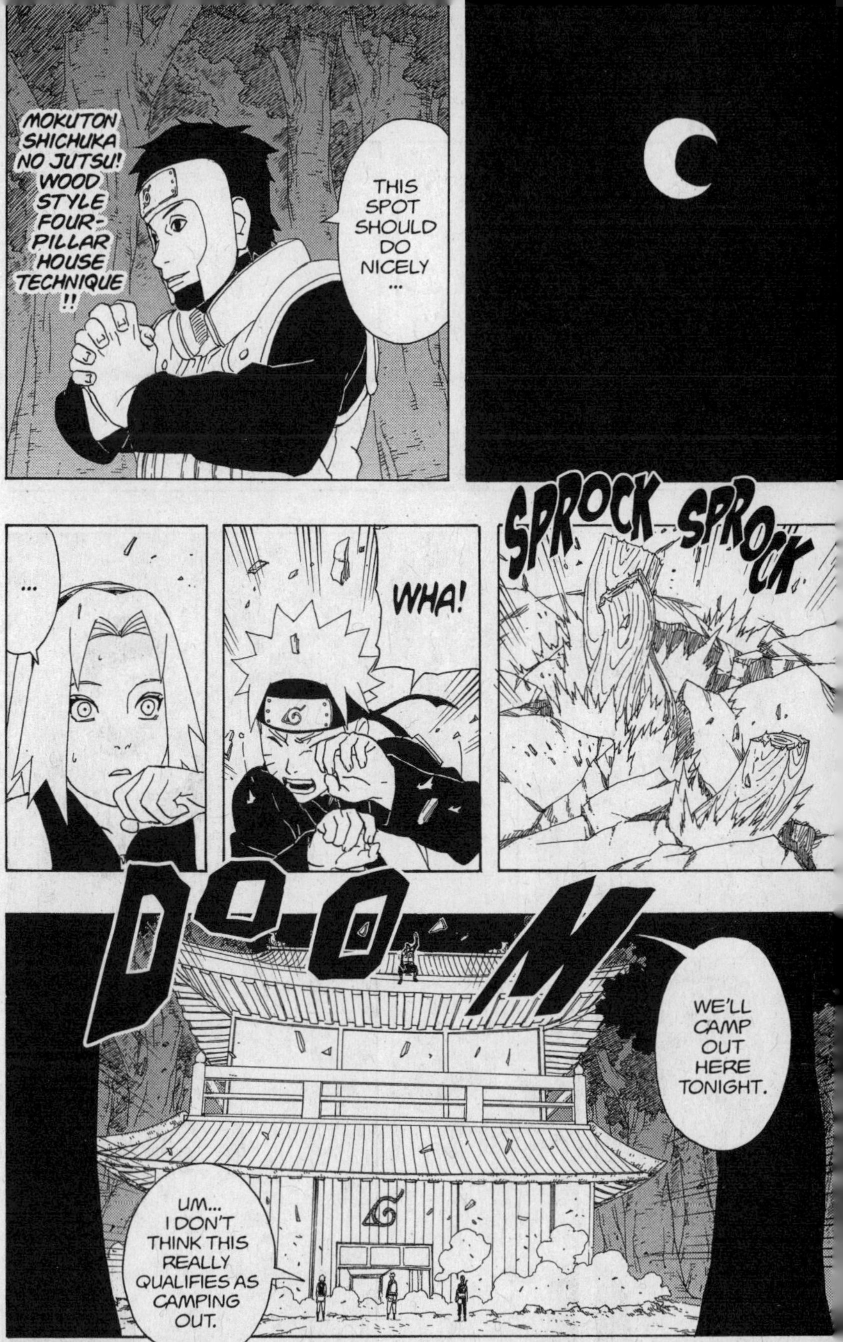
THIS SPOT SHOULD DO NICELY ...
MOKUTON SHICHUKA NO JUTSU! WOOD STYLE FOUR-PILLAR HOUSE TECHNIQUE !!
SPROCK SPROCK
WHA!
...
DOOM
WE'LL CAMP OUT HERE TONIGHT.
UM... I DON'T THINK THIS REALLY QUALIFIES AS CAMPING OUT.

READ THIS WAY

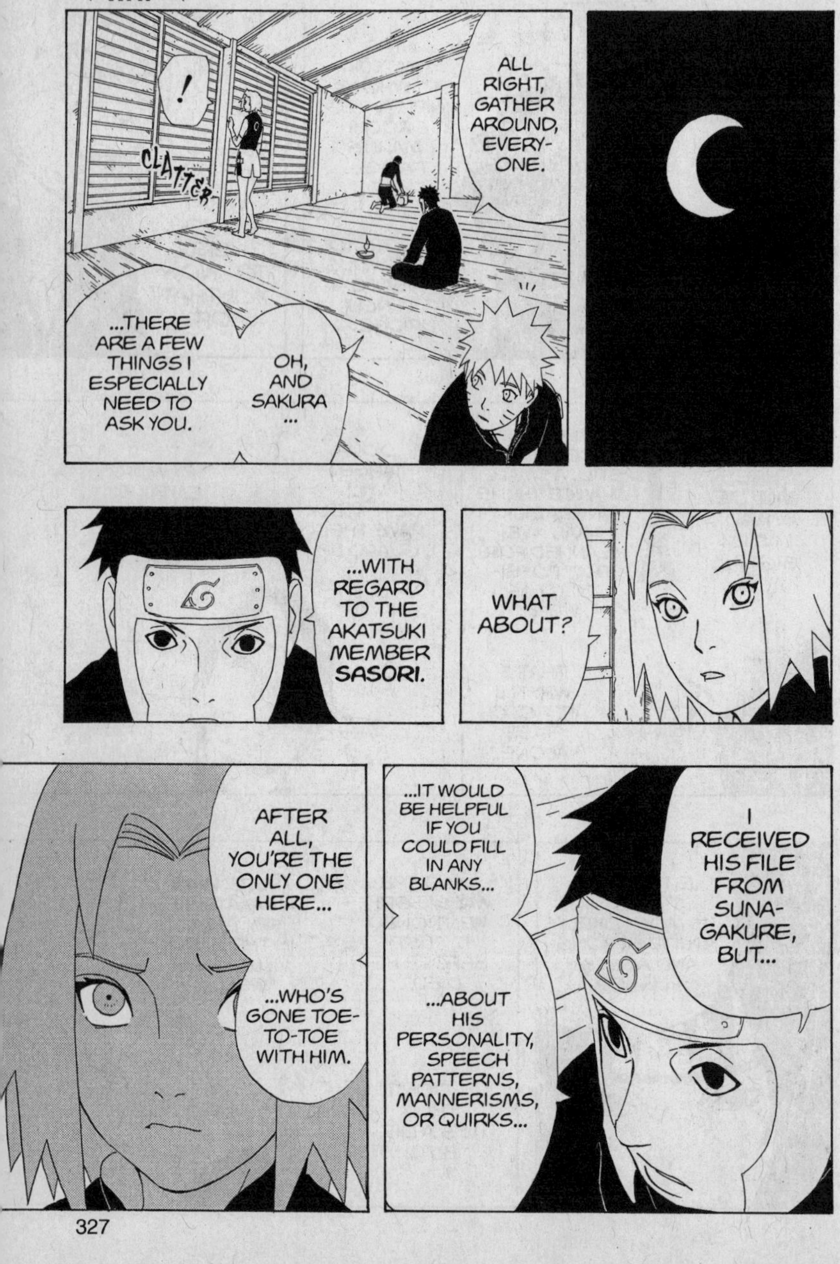
ALL RIGHT, GATHER AROUND, EVERYONE.
!
CLATTER
OH, AND SAKURA...
...THERE ARE A FEW THINGS I ESPECIALLY NEED TO ASK YOU.
WHAT ABOUT?
...WITH REGARD TO THE AKATSUKI MEMBER SASORI.
I RECEIVED HIS FILE FROM SUNAGAKURE, BUT...
...IT WOULD BE HELPFUL IF YOU COULD FILL IN ANY BLANKS...
...ABOUT HIS PERSONALITY, SPEECH PATTERNS, MANNERISMS, OR QUIRKS...
AFTER ALL, YOU'RE THE ONLY ONE HERE...
...WHO'S GONE TOE-TO-TOE WITH HIM.

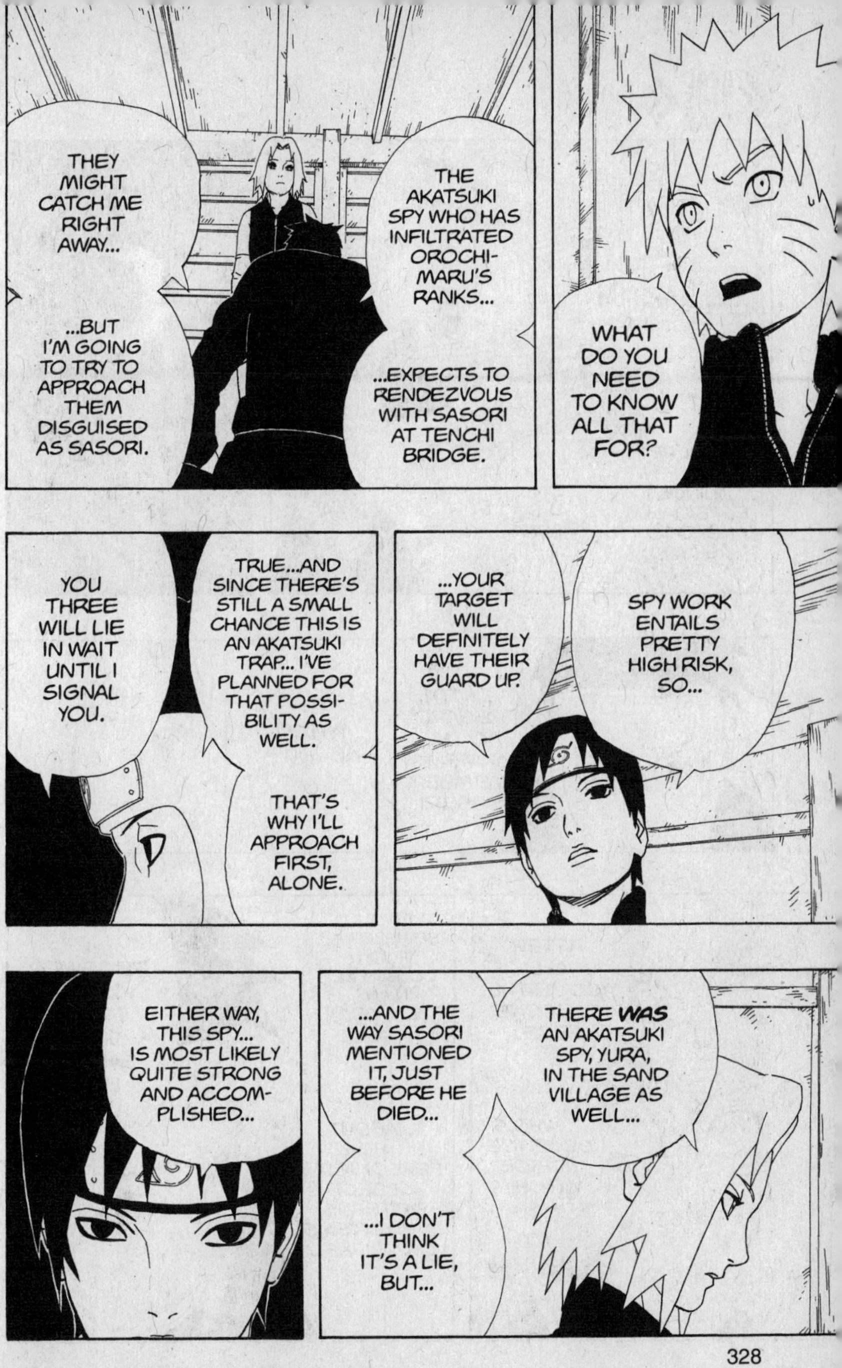
WHAT DO YOU NEED TO KNOW ALL THAT FOR?
THE AKATSUKI SPY WHO HAS INFILTRATED OROCHI-MARU'S RANKS...
...EXPECTS TO RENDEZVOUS WITH SASORI AT TENCHI BRIDGE.
THEY MIGHT CATCH ME RIGHT AWAY...
...BUT I'M GOING TO TRY TO APPROACH THEM DISGUISED AS SASORI.
SPY WORK ENTAILS PRETTY HIGH RISK, SO...
...YOUR TARGET WILL DEFINITELY HAVE THEIR GUARD UP.
TRUE...AND SINCE THERE'S STILL A SMALL CHANCE THIS IS AN AKATSUKI TRAP... I'VE PLANNED FOR THAT POSSI-BILITY AS WELL.
THAT'S WHY I'LL APPROACH FIRST, ALONE.
YOU THREE WILL LIE IN WAIT UNTIL I SIGNAL YOU.
THERE ***WAS*** AN AKATSUKI SPY, YURA, IN THE SAND VILLAGE AS WELL...
...AND THE WAY SASORI MENTIONED IT, JUST BEFORE HE DIED...
...I DON'T THINK IT'S A LIE, BUT...
EITHER WAY, THIS SPY... IS MOST LIKELY QUITE STRONG AND ACCOM-PLISHED...

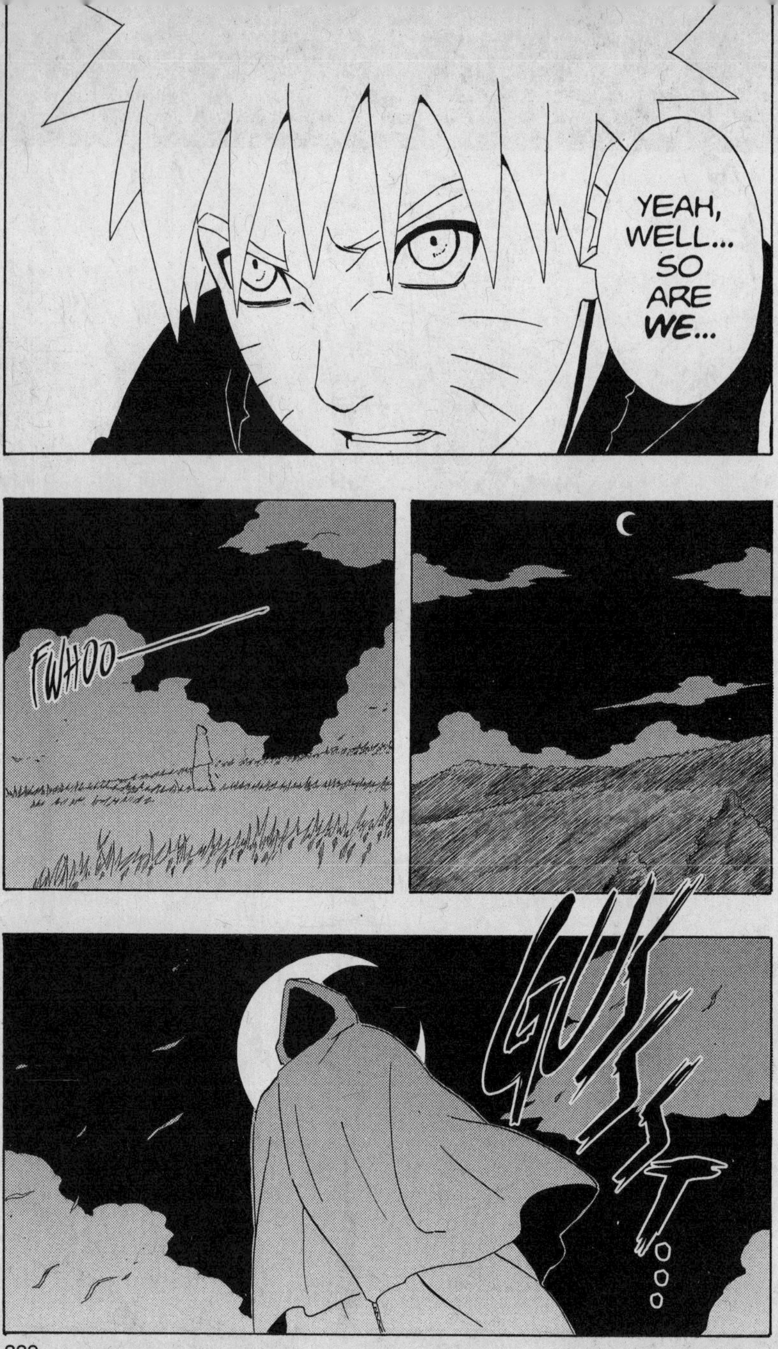
YEAH, WELL... SO ARE WE...
FWHOO
GUSH
T
O O O

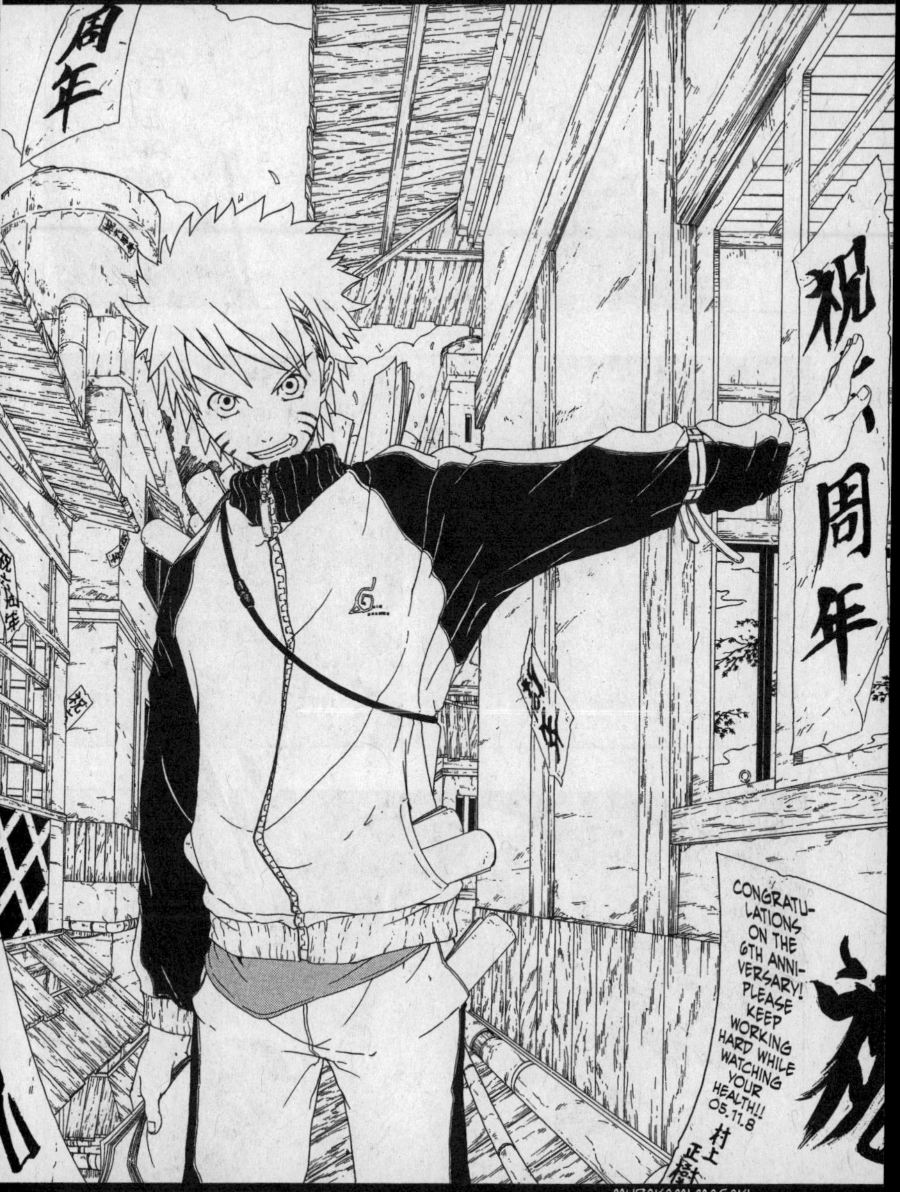
周年
祝六周年
CONGRATULATIONS ON THE 6TH ANNIVERSARY! PLEASE KEEP WORKING HARD WHILE WATCHING YOUR HEALTH!! 05.11.8
村上正樹
MURAKAMI MASAKI

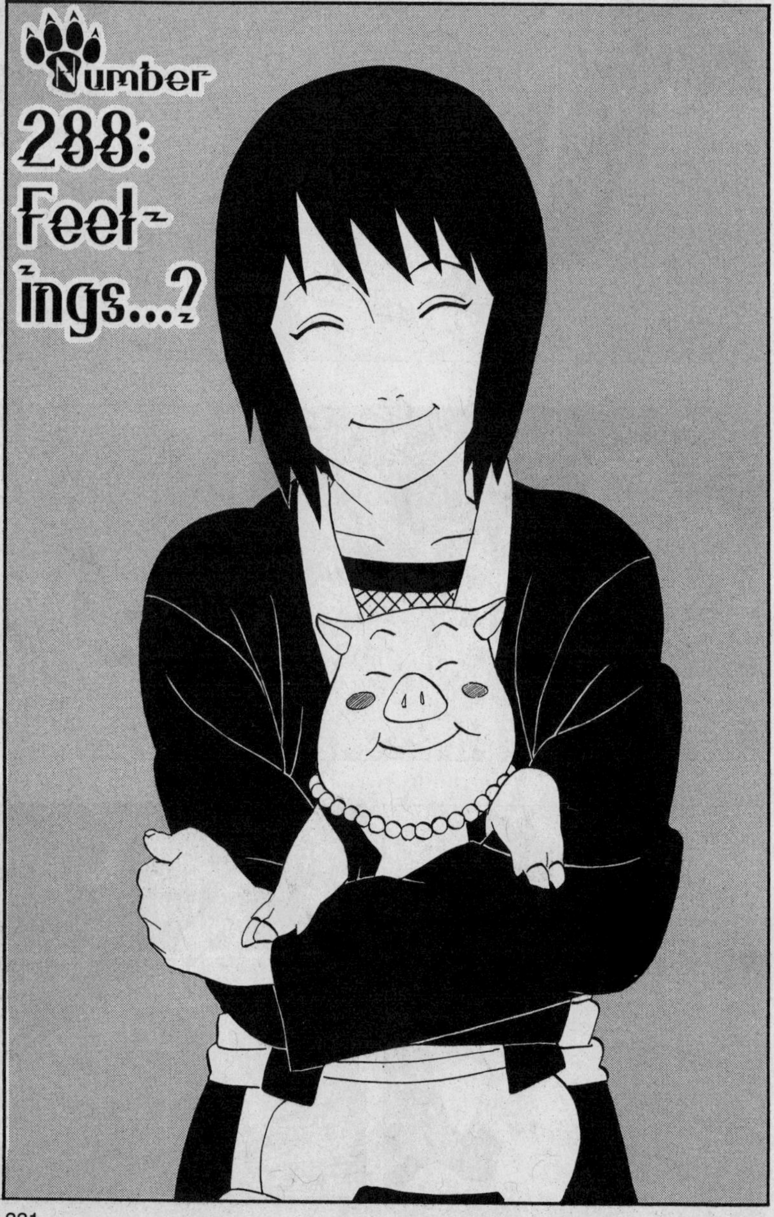
Number
288:
Feel-
ings...?

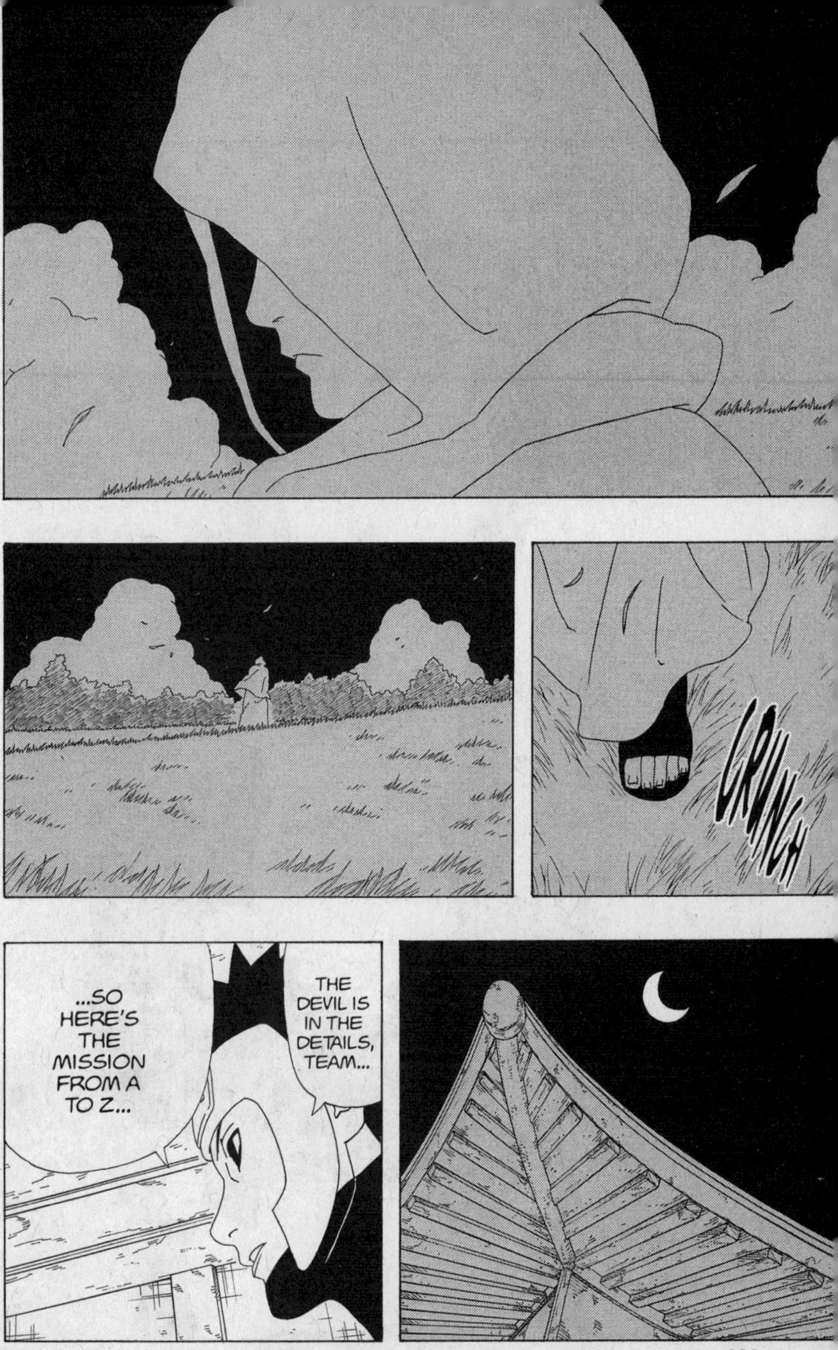
CRUNCH
THE DEVIL IS IN THE DETAILS, TEAM...
...SO HERE'S THE MISSION FROM A TO Z...

READ THIS WAY

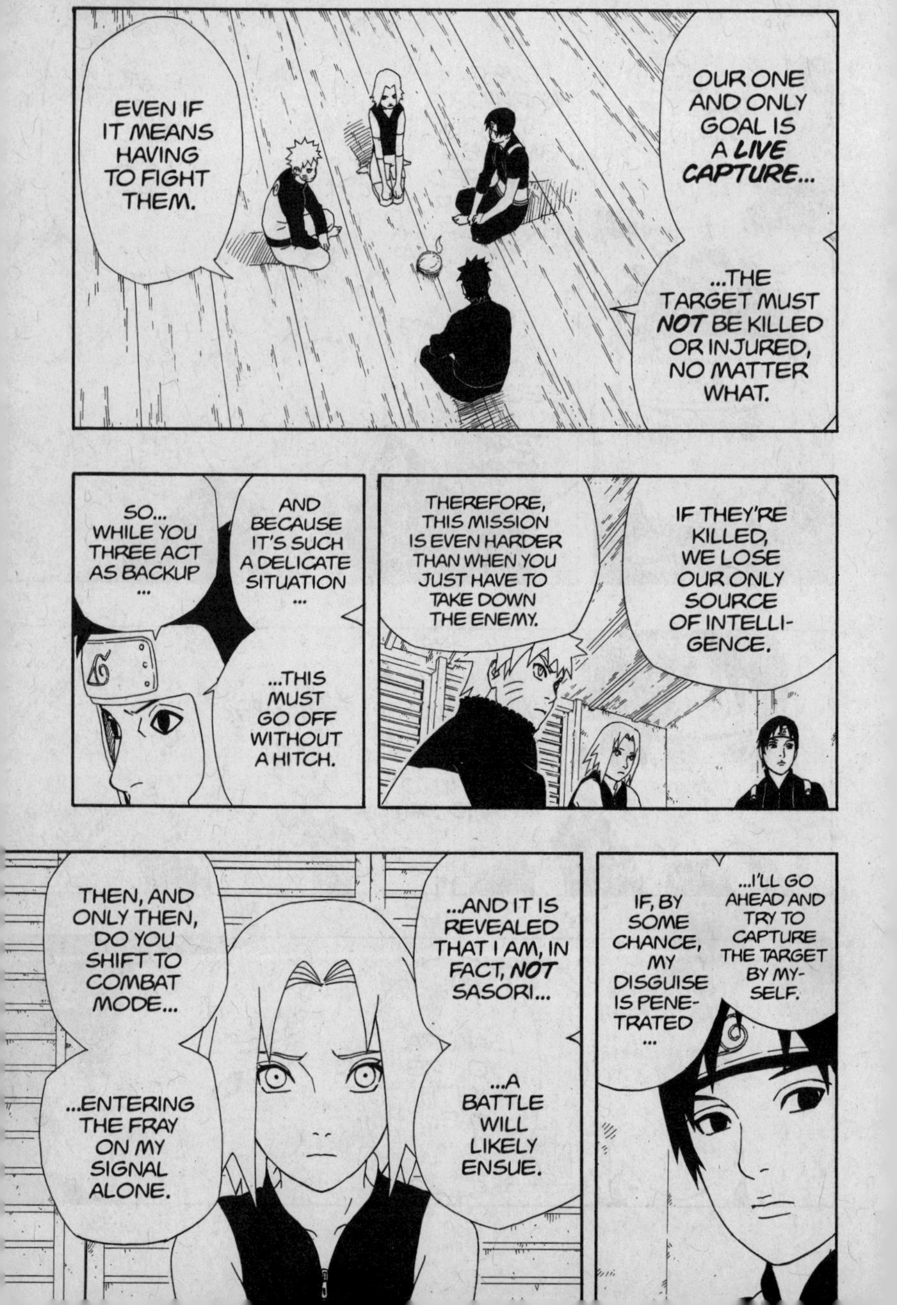
OUR ONE AND ONLY GOAL IS A *LIVE CAPTURE*...
...THE TARGET MUST *NOT* BE KILLED OR INJURED, NO MATTER WHAT.
EVEN IF IT MEANS HAVING TO FIGHT THEM.
IF THEY'RE KILLED, WE LOSE OUR ONLY SOURCE OF INTELLI-GENCE.
THEREFORE, THIS MISSION IS EVEN HARDER THAN WHEN YOU JUST HAVE TO TAKE DOWN THE ENEMY.
AND BECAUSE IT'S SUCH A DELICATE SITUATION...
...THIS MUST GO OFF WITHOUT A HITCH.
SO... WHILE YOU THREE ACT AS BACKUP...
...I'LL GO AHEAD AND TRY TO CAPTURE THE TARGET BY MY-SELF.
IF, BY SOME CHANCE, MY DISGUISE IS PENE-TRATED...
...AND IT IS REVEALED THAT I AM, IN FACT, *NOT* SASORI...
...A BATTLE WILL LIKELY ENSUE.
THEN, AND ONLY THEN, DO YOU SHIFT TO COMBAT MODE...
...ENTERING THE FRAY ON MY SIGNAL ALONE.

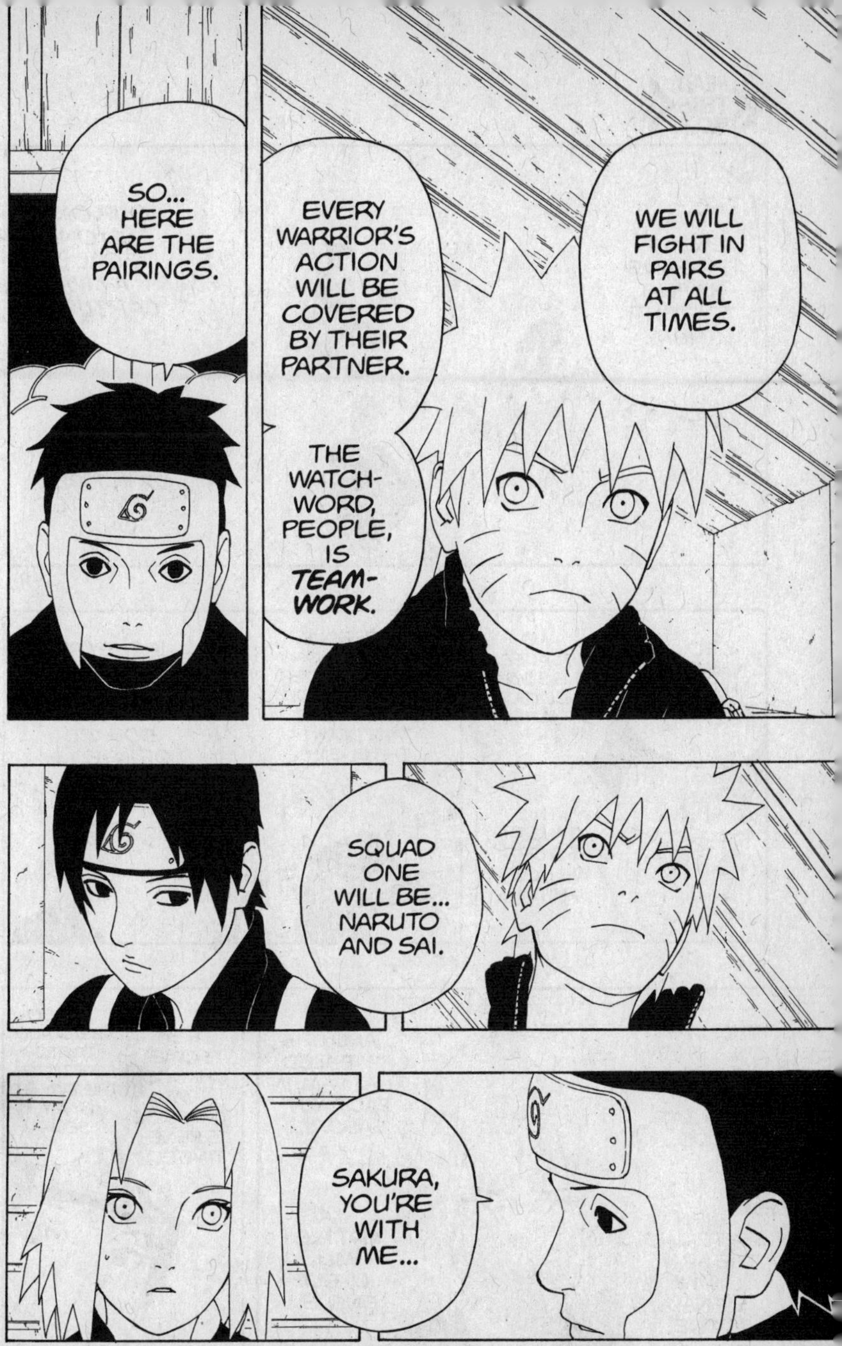
WE WILL FIGHT IN PAIRS AT ALL TIMES.
EVERY WARRIOR'S ACTION WILL BE COVERED BY THEIR PARTNER.
THE WATCHWORD, PEOPLE, IS *TEAMWORK.*
SO... HERE ARE THE PAIRINGS.
SQUAD ONE WILL BE... NARUTO AND SAI.
SAKURA, YOU'RE WITH ME...

READ THIS WAY

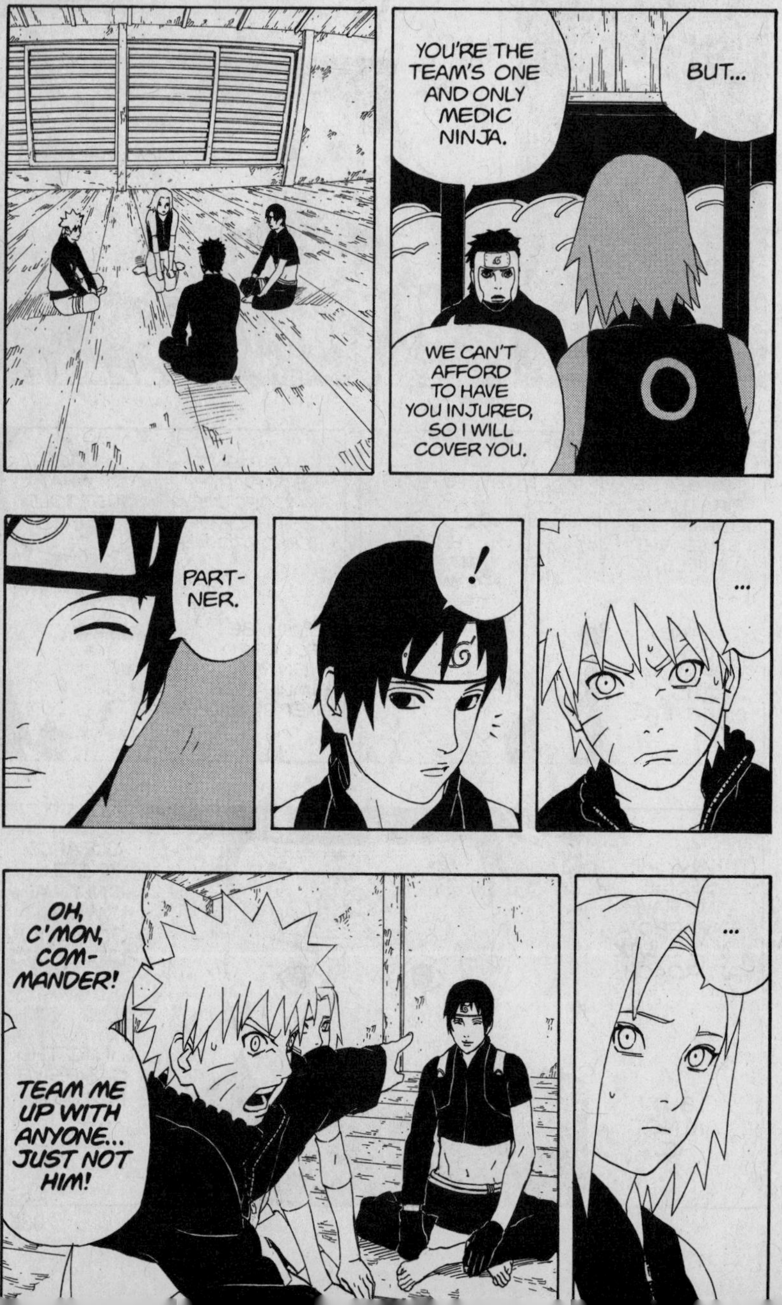
BUT...
YOU'RE THE TEAM'S ONE AND ONLY MEDIC NINJA.
WE CAN'T AFFORD TO HAVE YOU INJURED, SO I WILL COVER YOU.
...
!
PART-NER.
...
OH, C'MON, COM-MANDER!
TEAM ME UP WITH ANYONE... JUST NOT HIM!

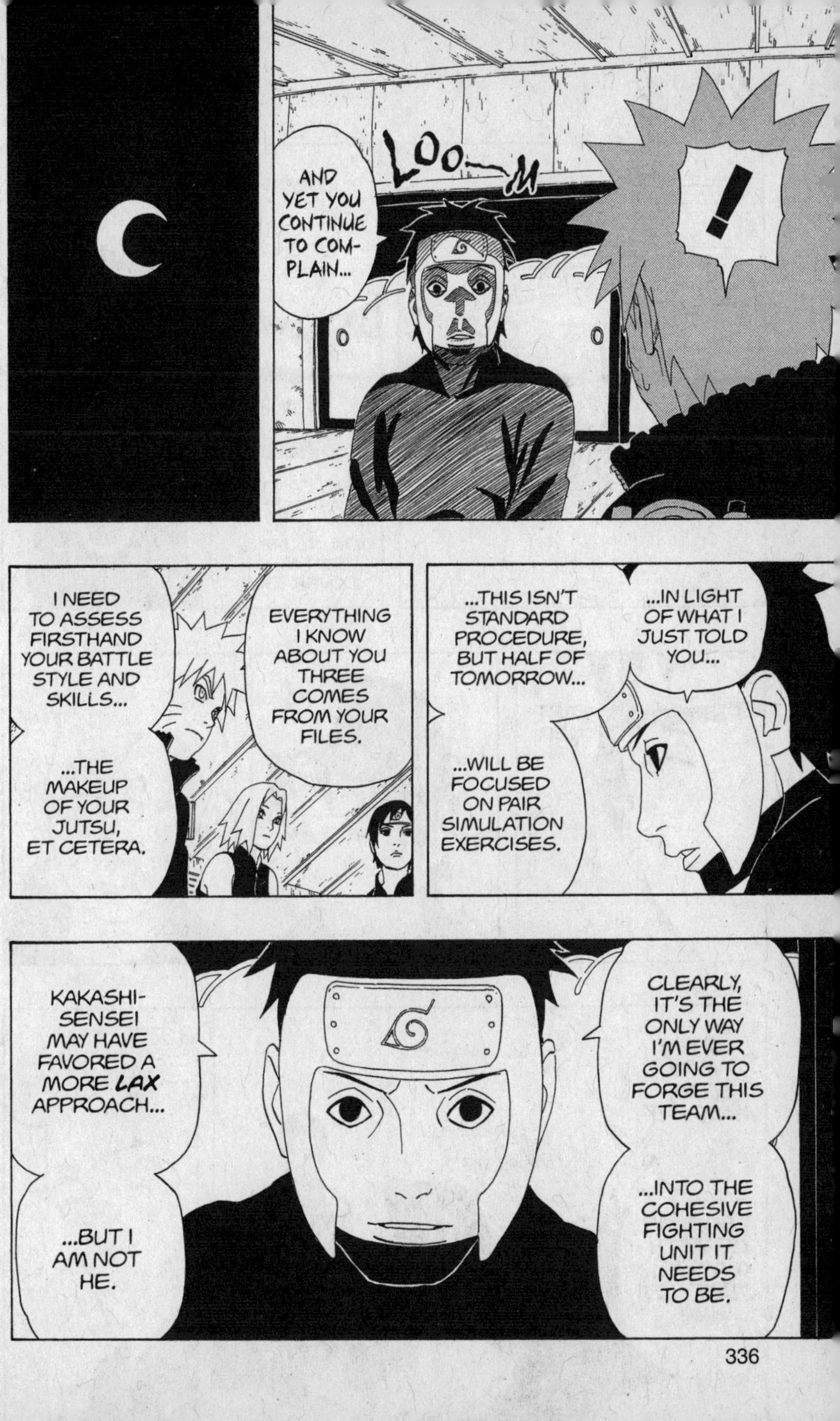
!
LOO—M
AND YET YOU CONTINUE TO COMPLAIN...
...IN LIGHT OF WHAT I JUST TOLD YOU...
...THIS ISN'T STANDARD PROCEDURE, BUT HALF OF TOMORROW...
...WILL BE FOCUSED ON PAIR SIMULATION EXERCISES.
EVERYTHING I KNOW ABOUT YOU THREE COMES FROM YOUR FILES.
I NEED TO ASSESS FIRSTHAND YOUR BATTLE STYLE AND SKILLS...
...THE MAKEUP OF YOUR JUTSU, ET CETERA.
CLEARLY, IT'S THE ONLY WAY I'M EVER GOING TO FORGE THIS TEAM...
...INTO THE COHESIVE FIGHTING UNIT IT NEEDS TO BE.
KAKASHI-SENSEI MAY HAVE FAVORED A MORE LAX APPROACH...
...BUT I AM NOT HE.

READ THIS WAY

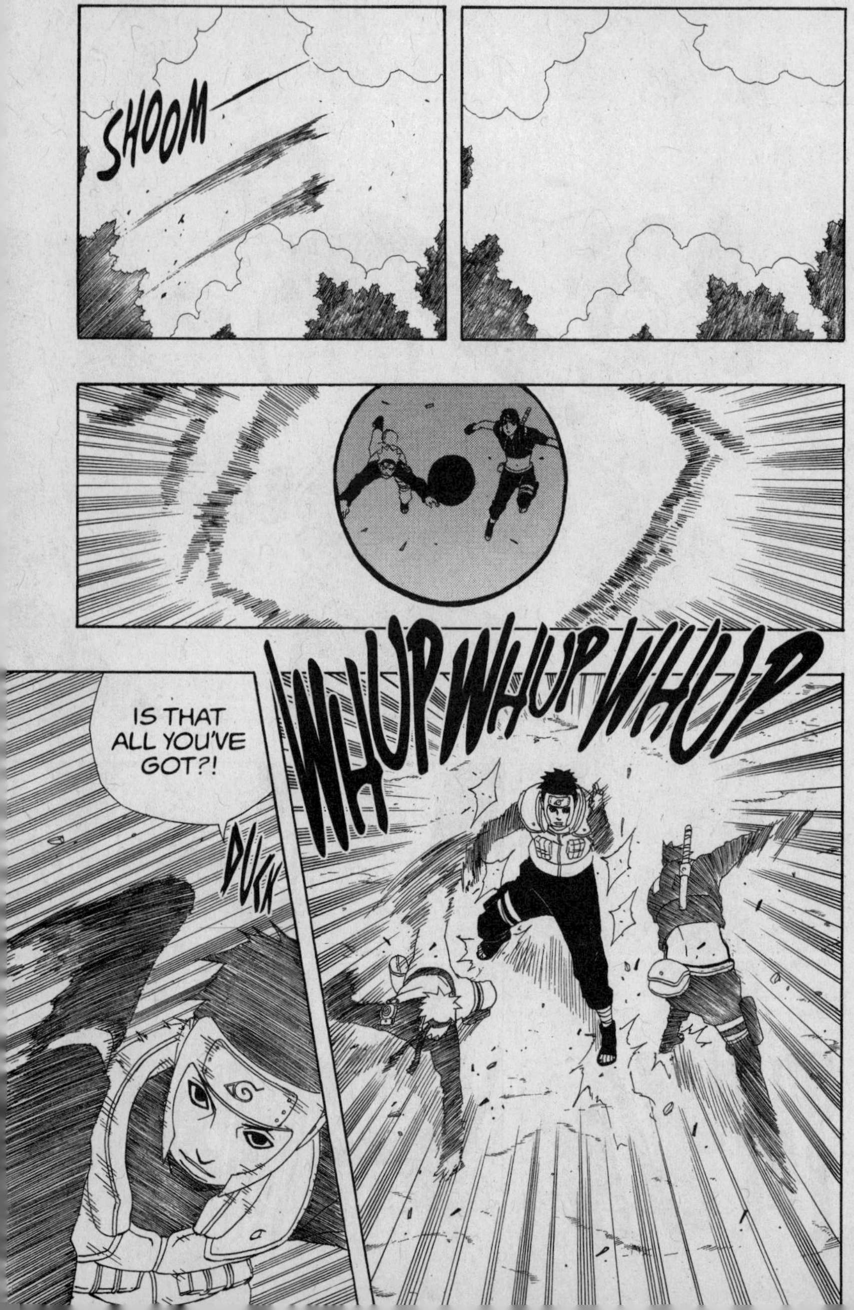
SHOOM
WHUP WHUP WHUP
IS THAT ALL YOU'VE GOT?!
DUCK

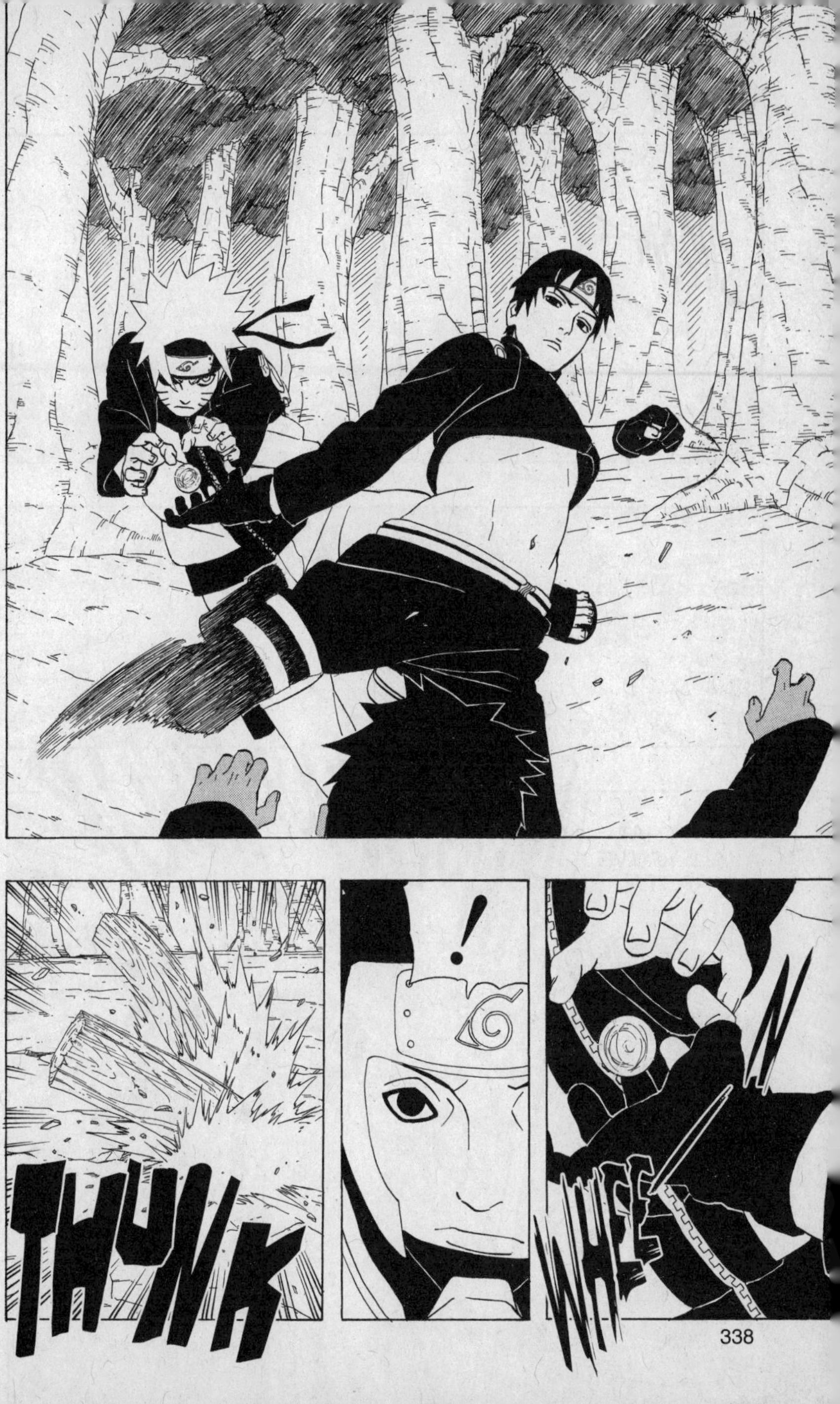

WHEE
!
THUNK

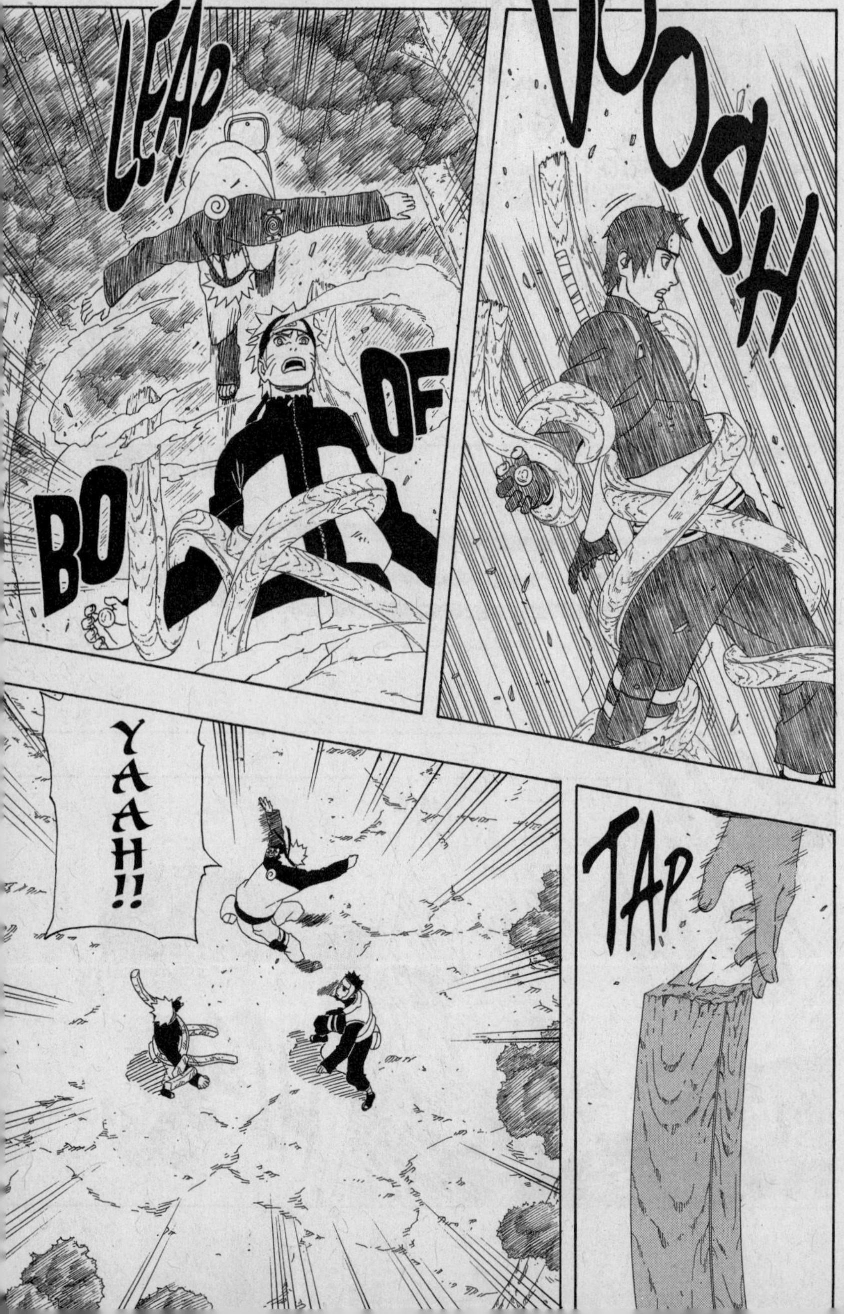
VOOSH
LEAP
BOOF
TAP
YAAH!!

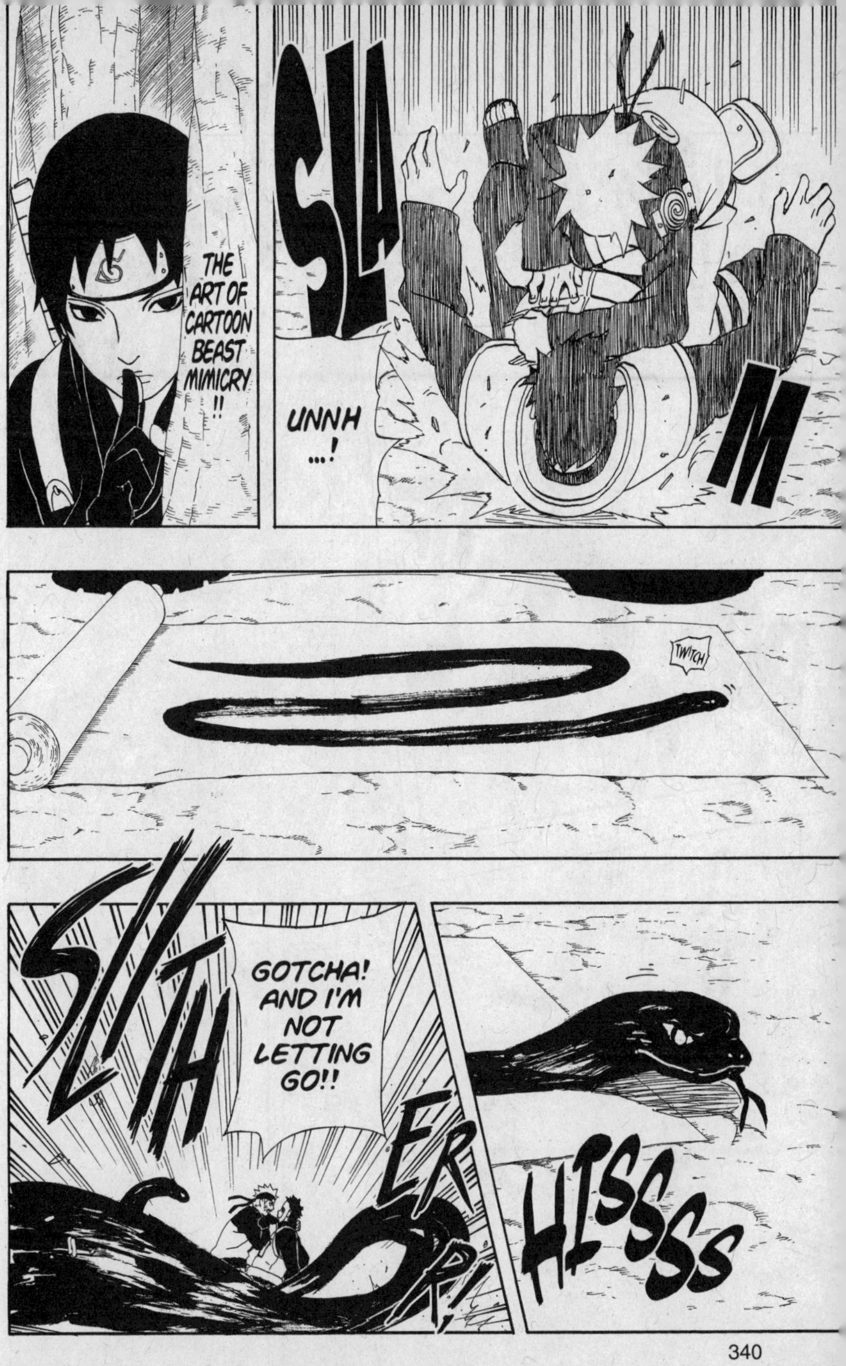
SLAM
UNNH ...!
THE ART OF CARTOON BEAST MIMICRY!!
TWITCH
HISSSS
SLITHER
R!
GOTCHA! AND I'M NOT LETTING GO!!

READ THIS WAY

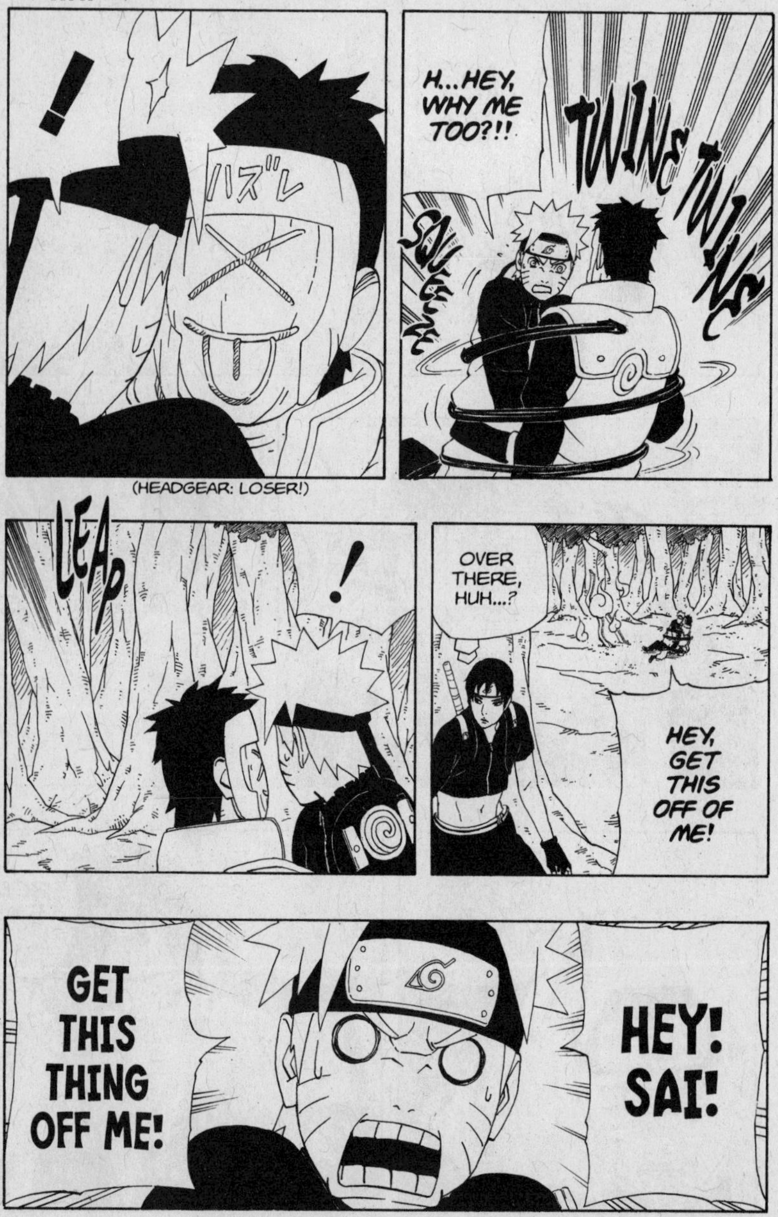
H...HEY, WHY ME TOO?!!
TWINE TWINE
SQUEEZE
!
ハズレ
(HEADGEAR: LOSER!)
OVER THERE, HUH...?
HEY, GET THIS OFF OF ME!
LEAP
!
HEY! SAI!
GET THIS THING OFF ME!

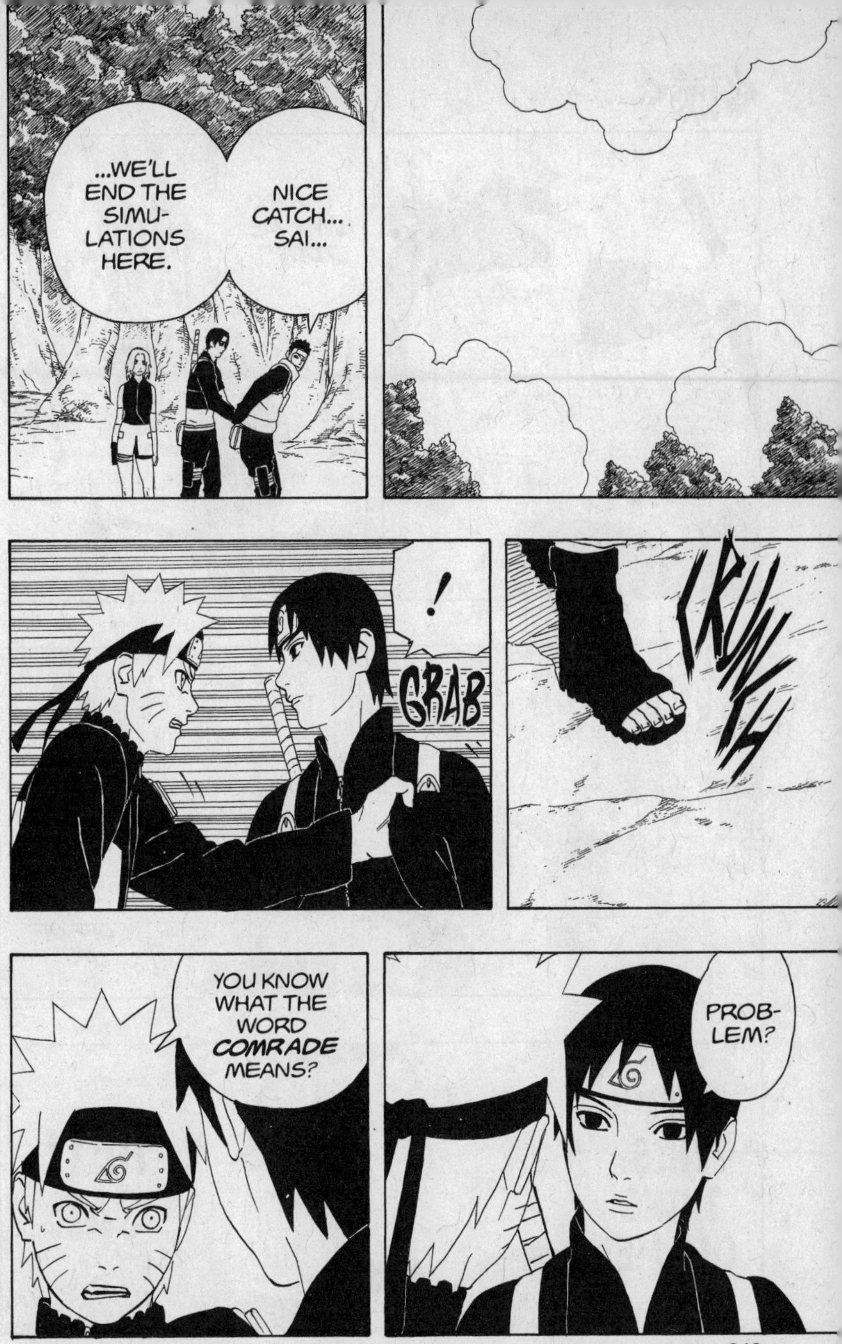
NICE CATCH... SAI...
...WE'LL END THE SIMULATIONS HERE.
CRUNCH
!
GRAB
PROBLEM?
YOU KNOW WHAT THE WORD COMRADE MEANS?

READ THIS WAY

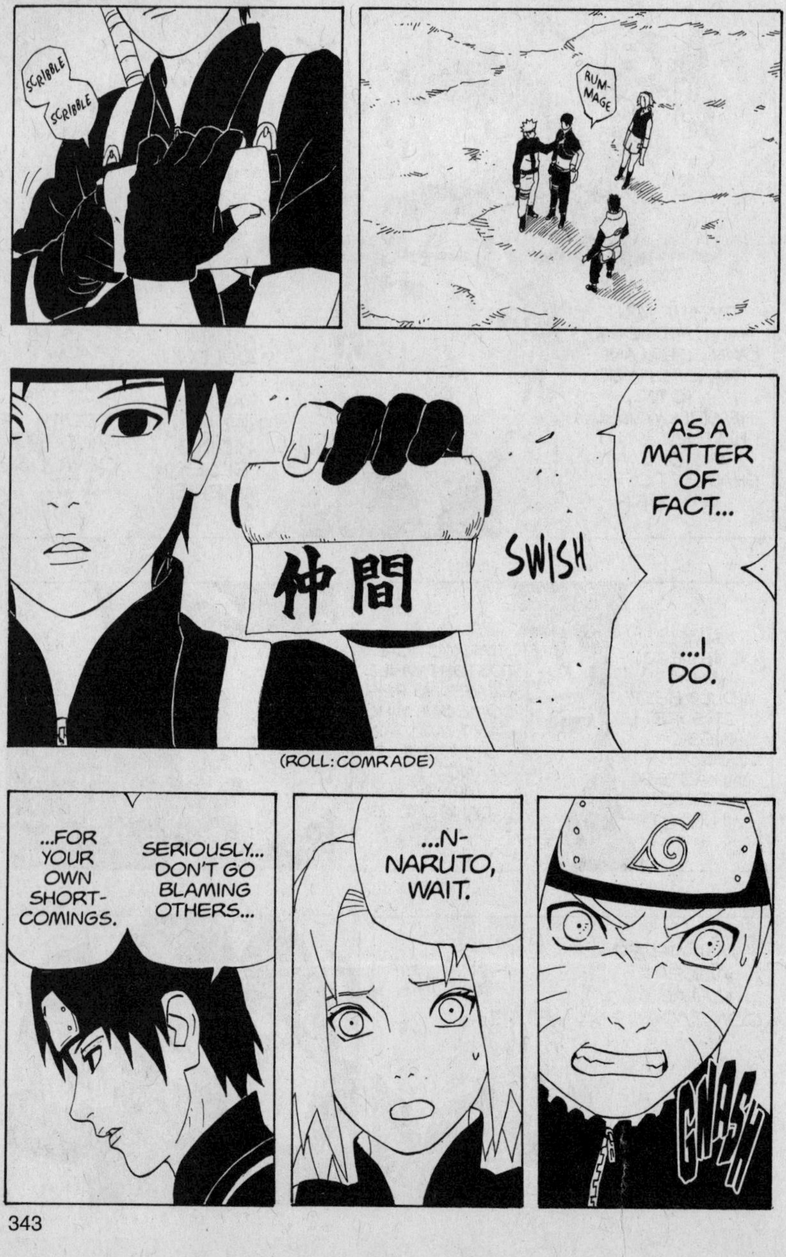
RUM-MAGE
SCRIBBLE SCRIBBLE
AS A MATTER OF FACT...
...I DO.
SWISH
仲間
(ROLL: COMRADE)
GNASH
...N-NARUTO, WAIT.
SERIOUSLY... DON'T GO BLAMING OTHERS...
...FOR YOUR OWN SHORT-COMINGS.

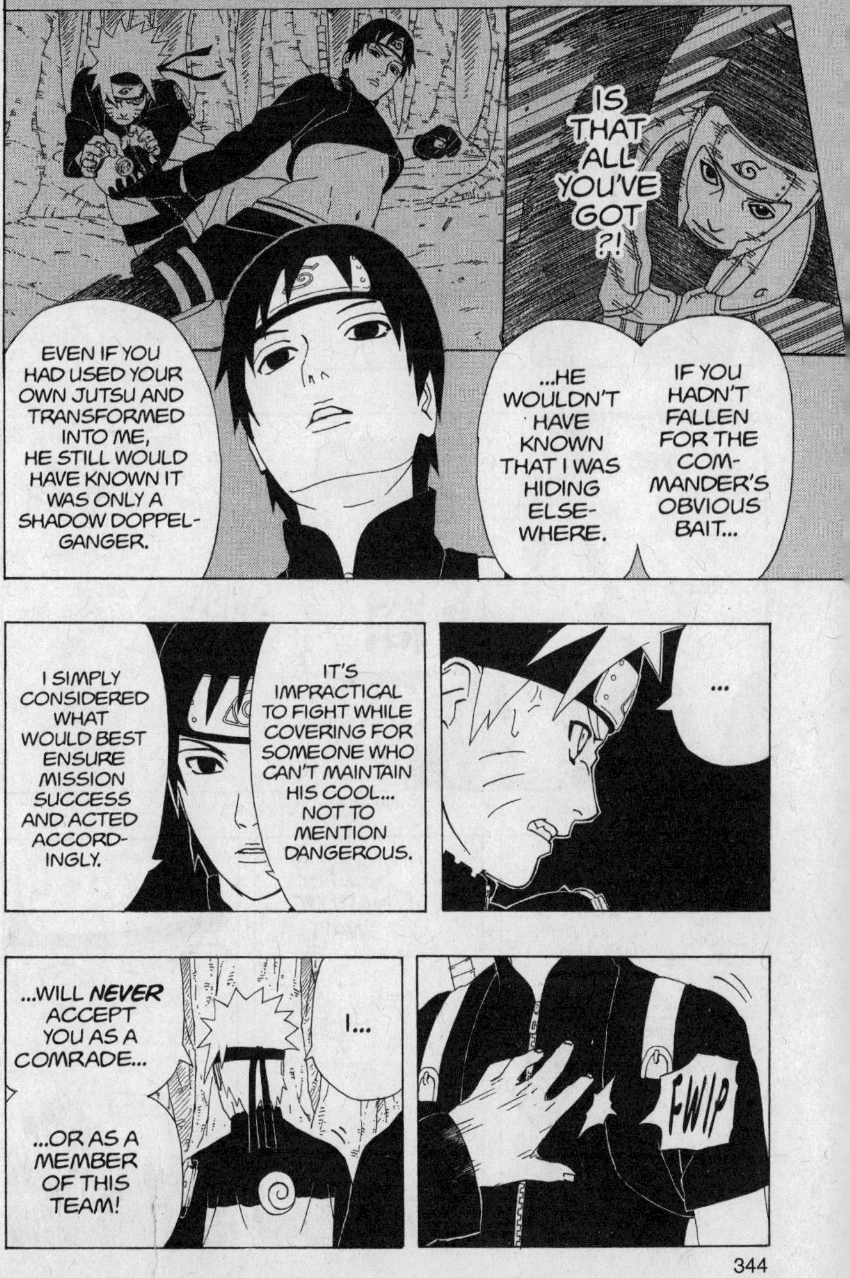
IS THAT ALL YOU'VE GOT ?!
IF YOU HADN'T FALLEN FOR THE COM-MANDER'S OBVIOUS BAIT...
...HE WOULDN'T HAVE KNOWN THAT I WAS HIDING ELSE-WHERE.
EVEN IF YOU HAD USED YOUR OWN JUTSU AND TRANSFORMED INTO ME, HE STILL WOULD HAVE KNOWN IT WAS ONLY A SHADOW DOPPEL-GANGER.
...
IT'S IMPRACTICAL TO FIGHT WHILE COVERING FOR SOMEONE WHO CAN'T MAINTAIN HIS COOL... NOT TO MENTION DANGEROUS.
I SIMPLY CONSIDERED WHAT WOULD BEST ENSURE MISSION SUCCESS AND ACTED ACCORD-INGLY.
FWIP
I...
...WILL **NEVER** ACCEPT YOU AS A COMRADE...
...OR AS A MEMBER OF THIS TEAM!

READ THIS WAY

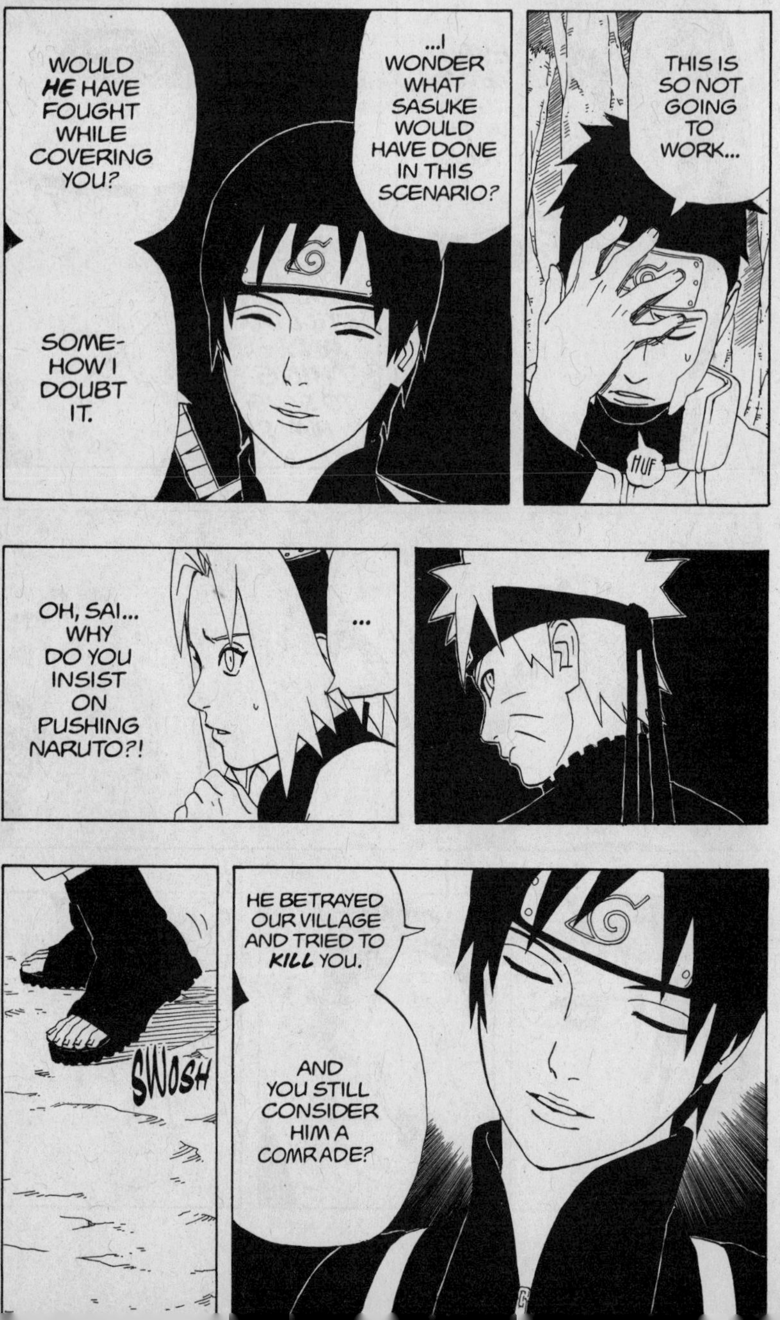
THIS IS SO NOT GOING TO WORK...
HUF
...I WONDER WHAT SASUKE WOULD HAVE DONE IN THIS SCENARIO?
WOULD *HE* HAVE FOUGHT WHILE COVERING YOU?
SOME-HOW I DOUBT IT.
...
OH, SAI... WHY DO YOU INSIST ON PUSHING NARUTO?!
HE BETRAYED OUR VILLAGE AND TRIED TO *KILL* YOU.
AND YOU STILL CONSIDER HIM A COMRADE?
SWOSH

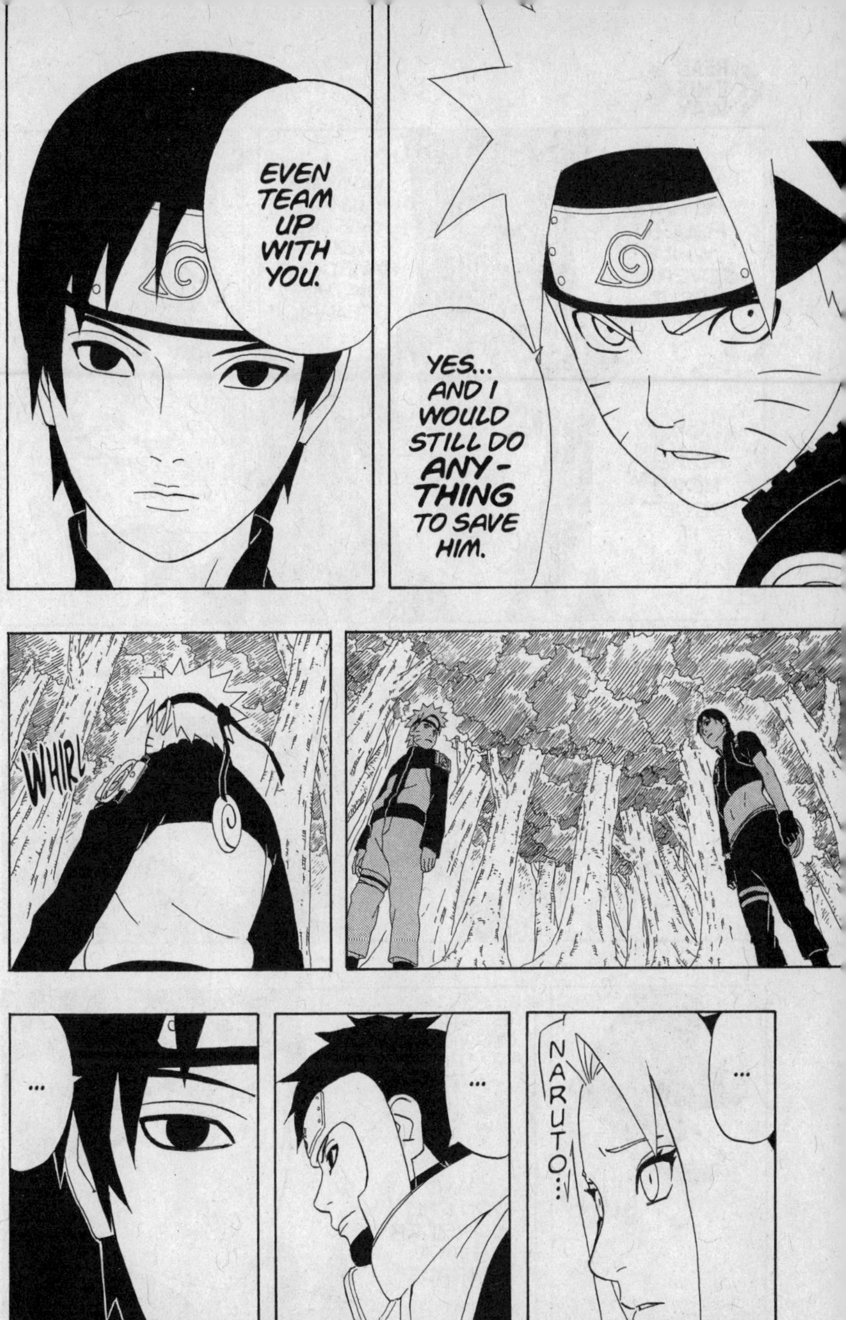
YES... AND I WOULD STILL DO ANY-THING TO SAVE HIM.
EVEN TEAM UP WITH YOU.
WHIRL
...
NARUTO...
...
...

READ THIS WAY

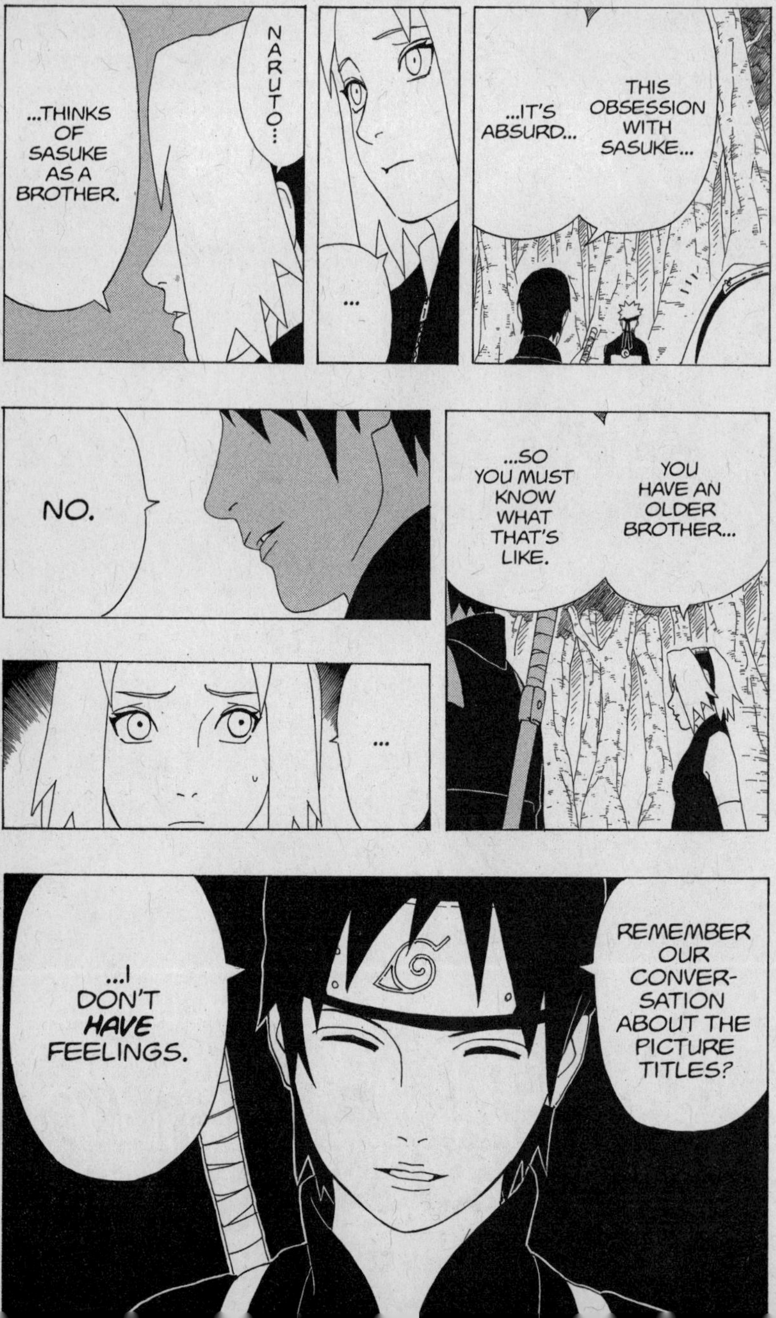
THIS OBSESSION WITH SASUKE...
...IT'S ABSURD...
NARUTO...
...
...THINKS OF SASUKE AS A BROTHER.
YOU HAVE AN OLDER BROTHER...
...SO YOU MUST KNOW WHAT THAT'S LIKE.
NO.
...
REMEMBER OUR CONVERSATION ABOUT THE PICTURE TITLES?
...I DON'T *HAVE* FEELINGS.

NARUTO

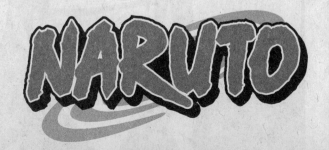

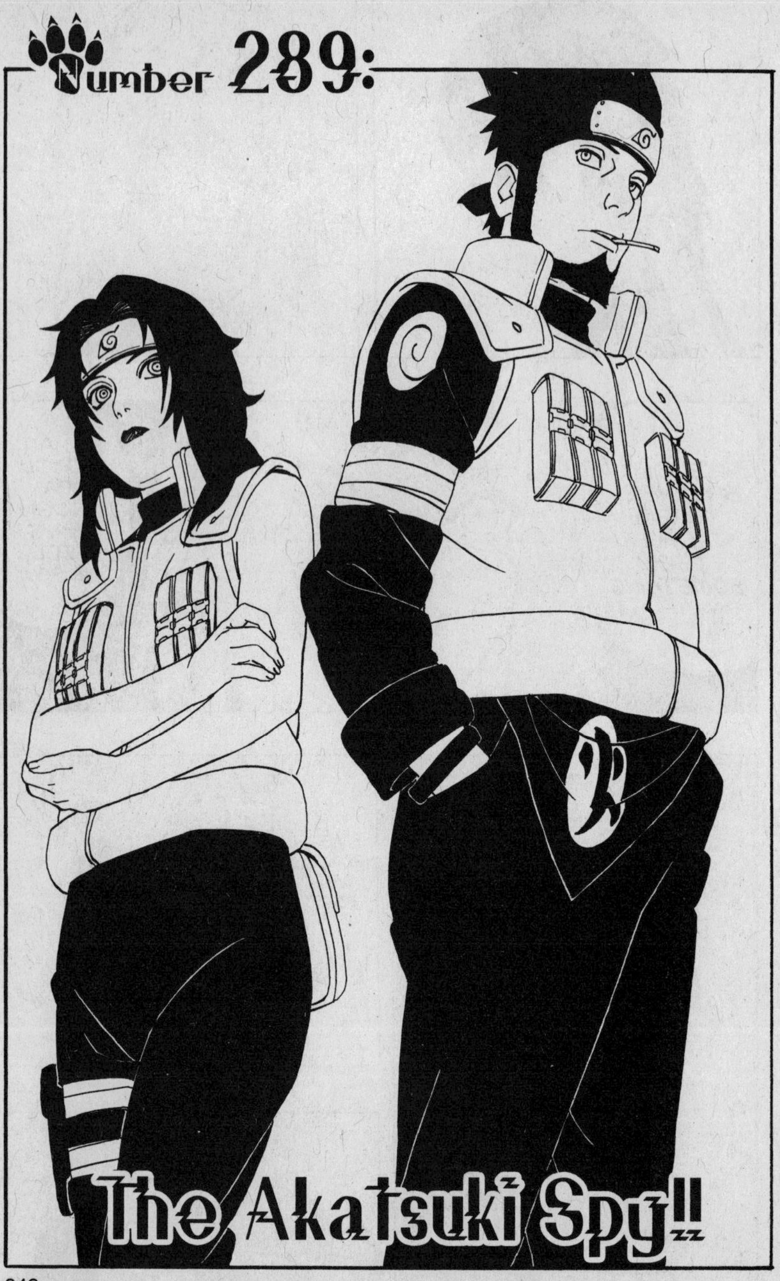
Number 289:
The Akatsuki Spy!!

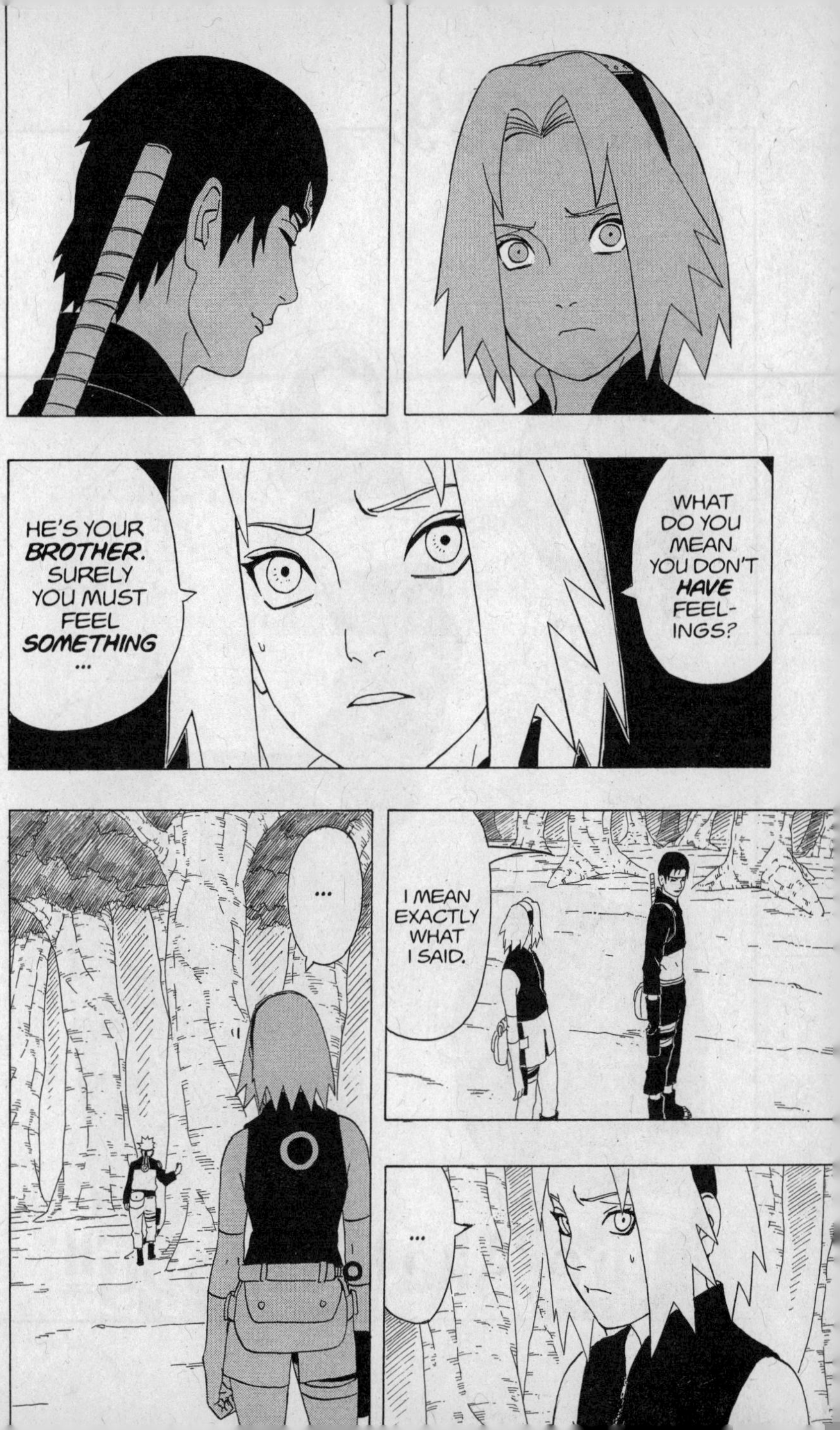
WHAT DO YOU MEAN YOU DON'T **HAVE** FEEL-INGS?
HE'S YOUR **BROTHER.** SURELY YOU MUST FEEL **SOMETHING** ...
I MEAN EXACTLY WHAT I SAID.
...
...

READ THIS WAY

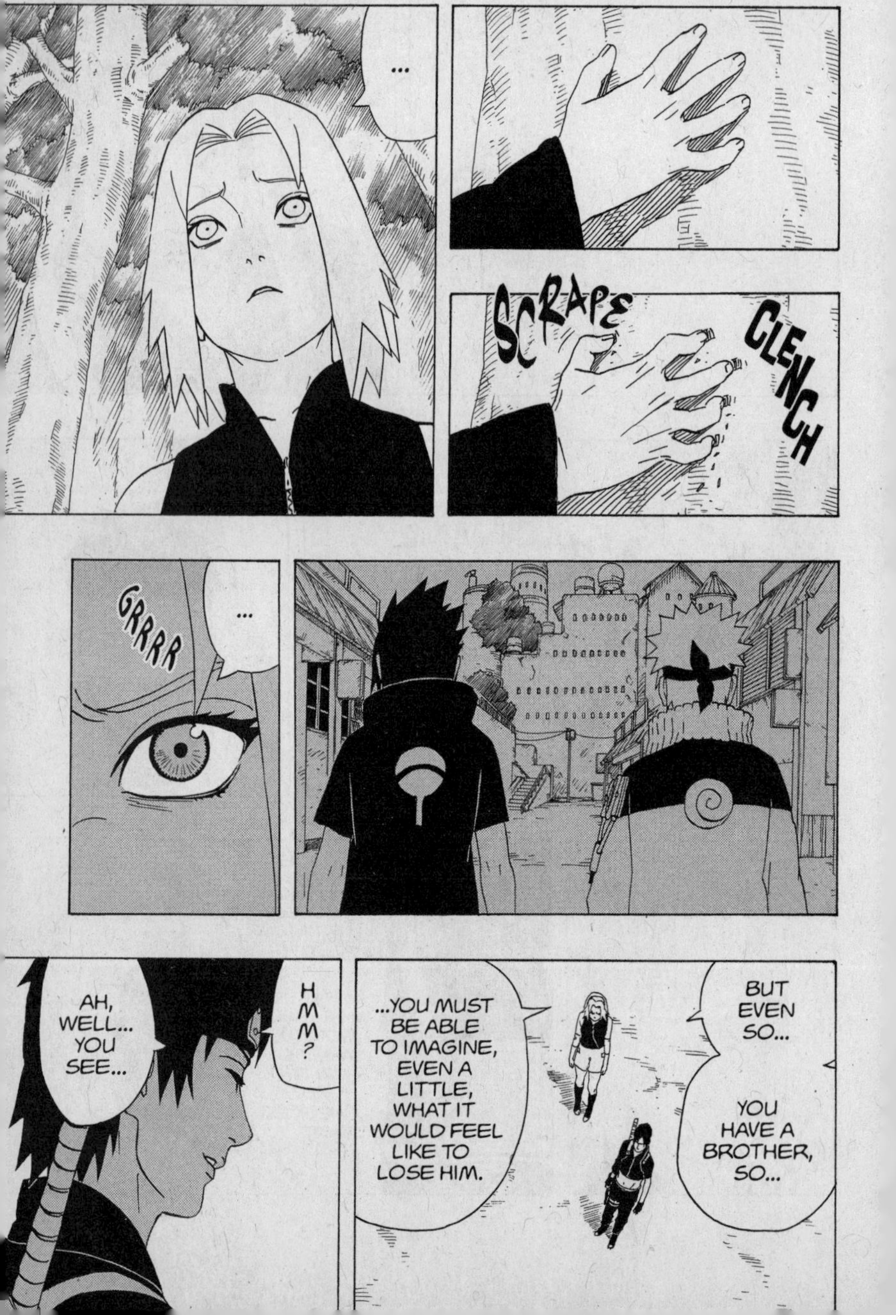
SCRAPE
CLENCH
...
GRRRR
...
BUT EVEN SO...
YOU HAVE A BROTHER, SO...
...YOU MUST BE ABLE TO IMAGINE, EVEN A LITTLE, WHAT IT WOULD FEEL LIKE TO LOSE HIM.
HMM?
AH, WELL... YOU SEE...

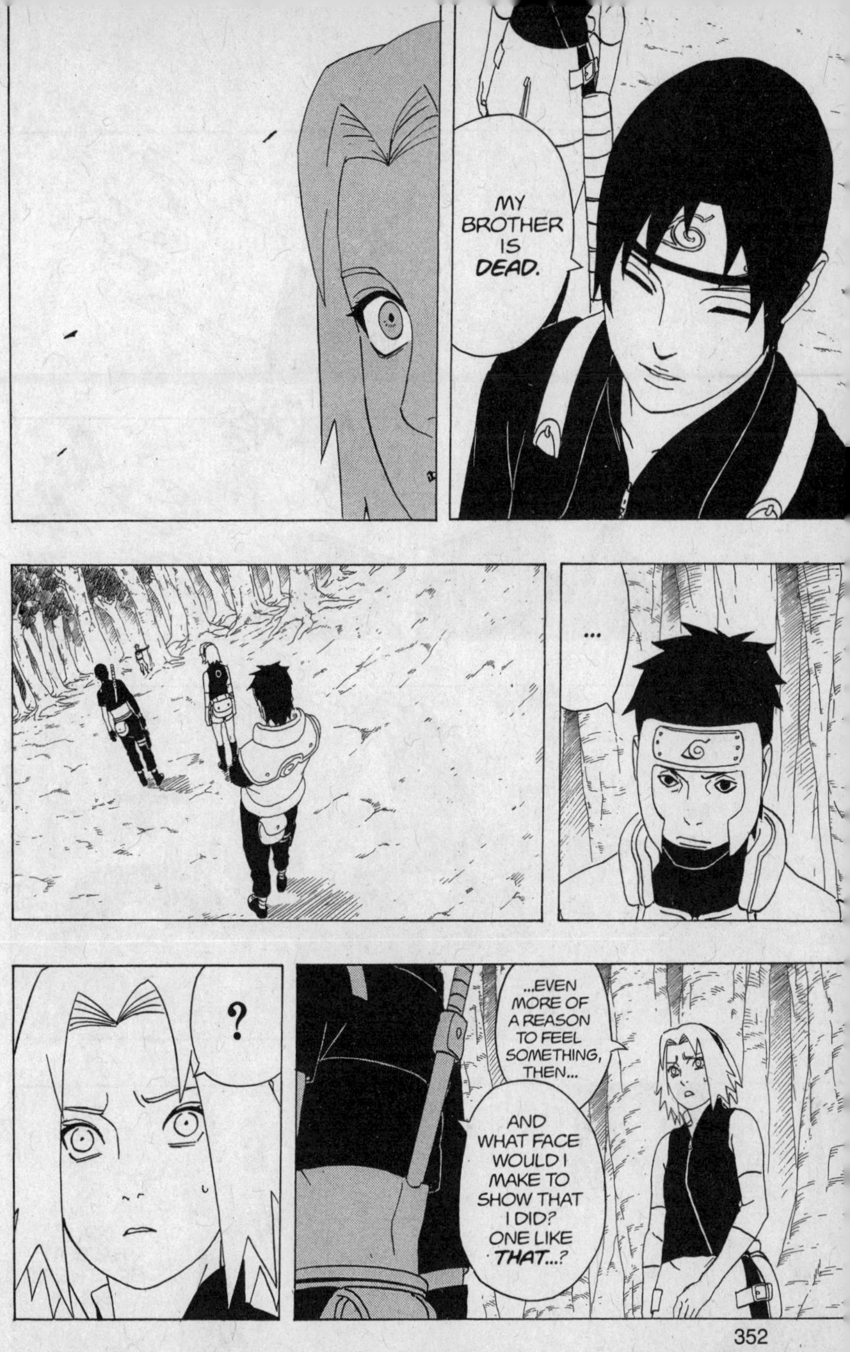
MY BROTHER IS DEAD.
...
...EVEN MORE OF A REASON TO FEEL SOMETHING, THEN...
AND WHAT FACE WOULD I MAKE TO SHOW THAT I DID? ONE LIKE THAT...?
?

READ THIS WAY

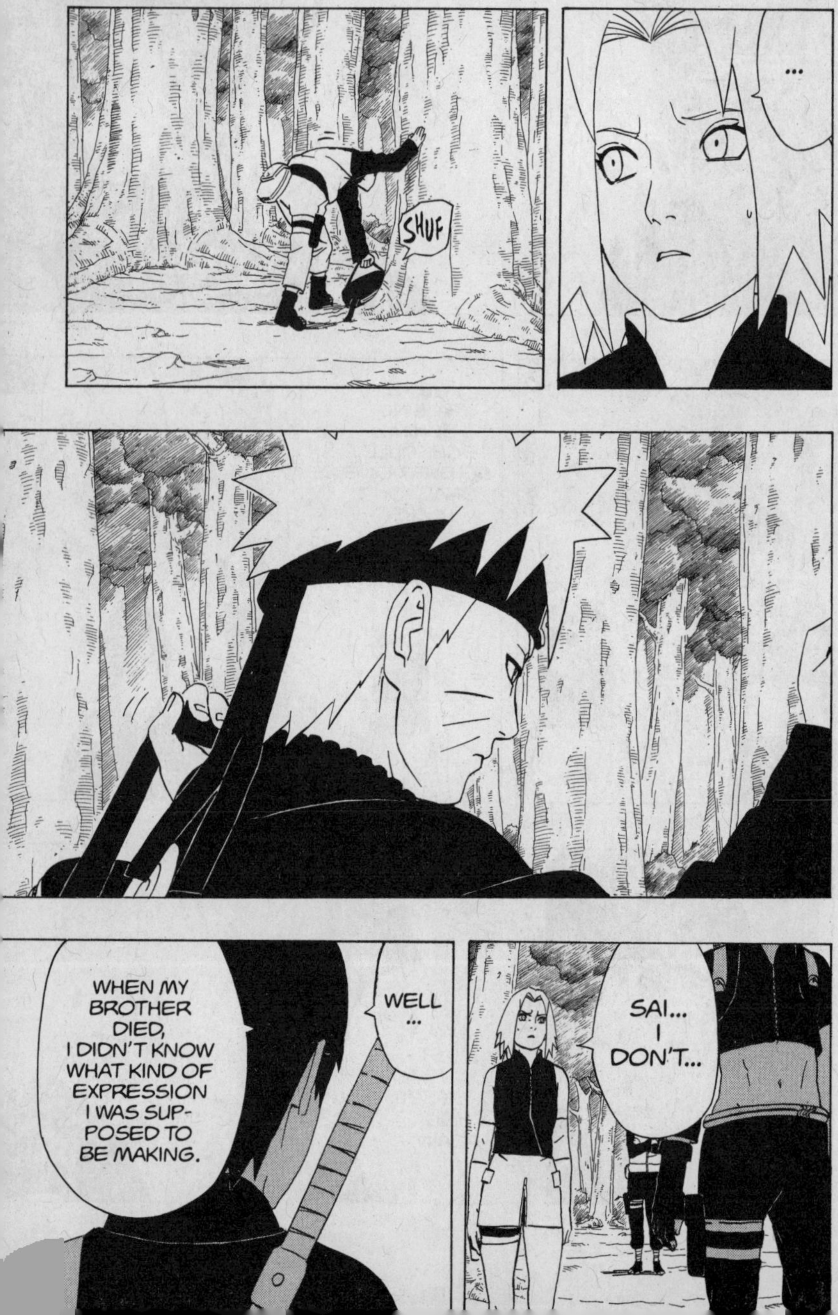
...
SHUF
SAI... I DON'T...
WELL ...
WHEN MY BROTHER DIED, I DIDN'T KNOW WHAT KIND OF EXPRESSION I WAS SUP-POSED TO BE MAKING.

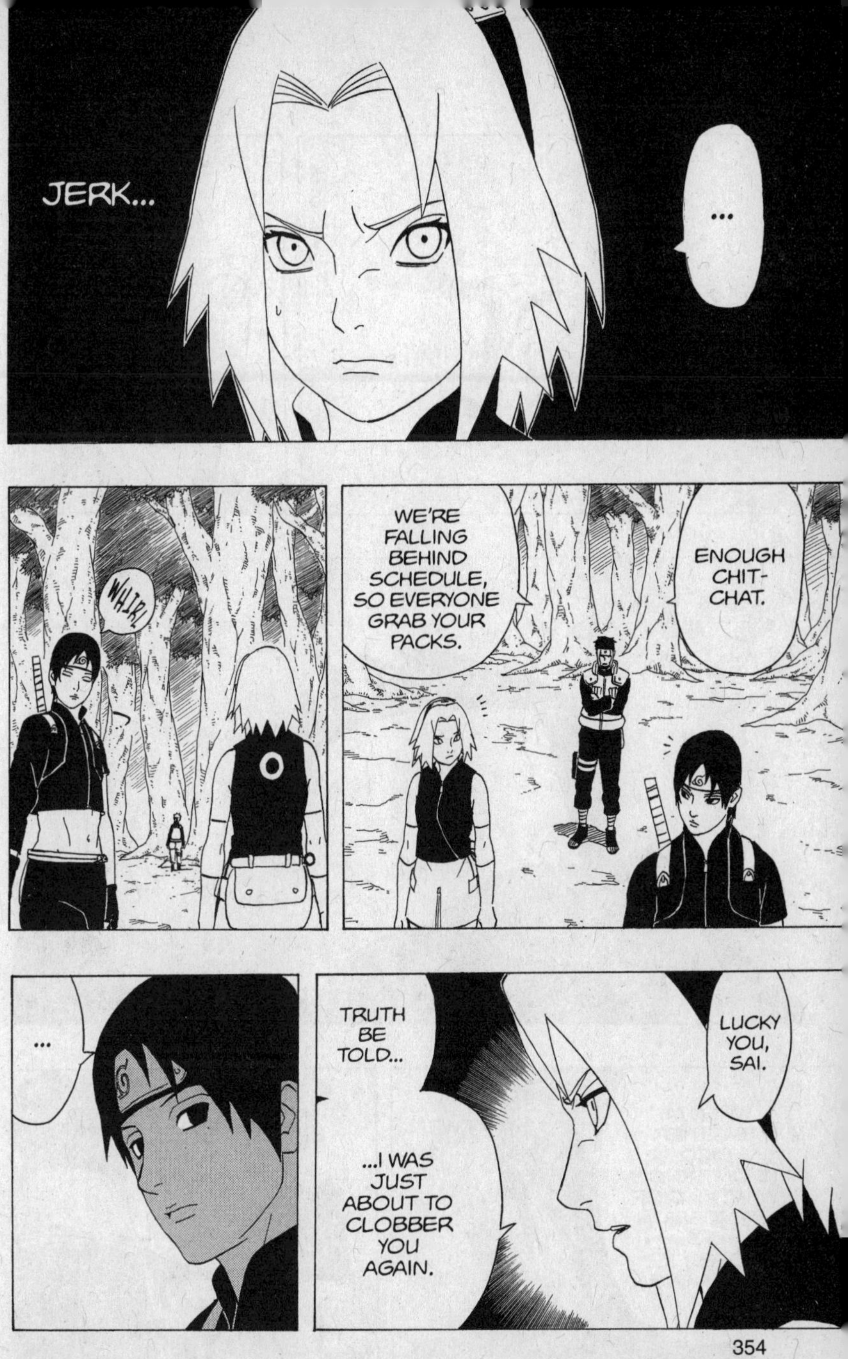
...
JERK...
ENOUGH CHIT-CHAT.
WE'RE FALLING BEHIND SCHEDULE, SO EVERYONE GRAB YOUR PACKS.
WHIR!
LUCKY YOU, SAI.
TRUTH BE TOLD...
...I WAS JUST ABOUT TO CLOBBER YOU AGAIN.
...

READ THIS WAY

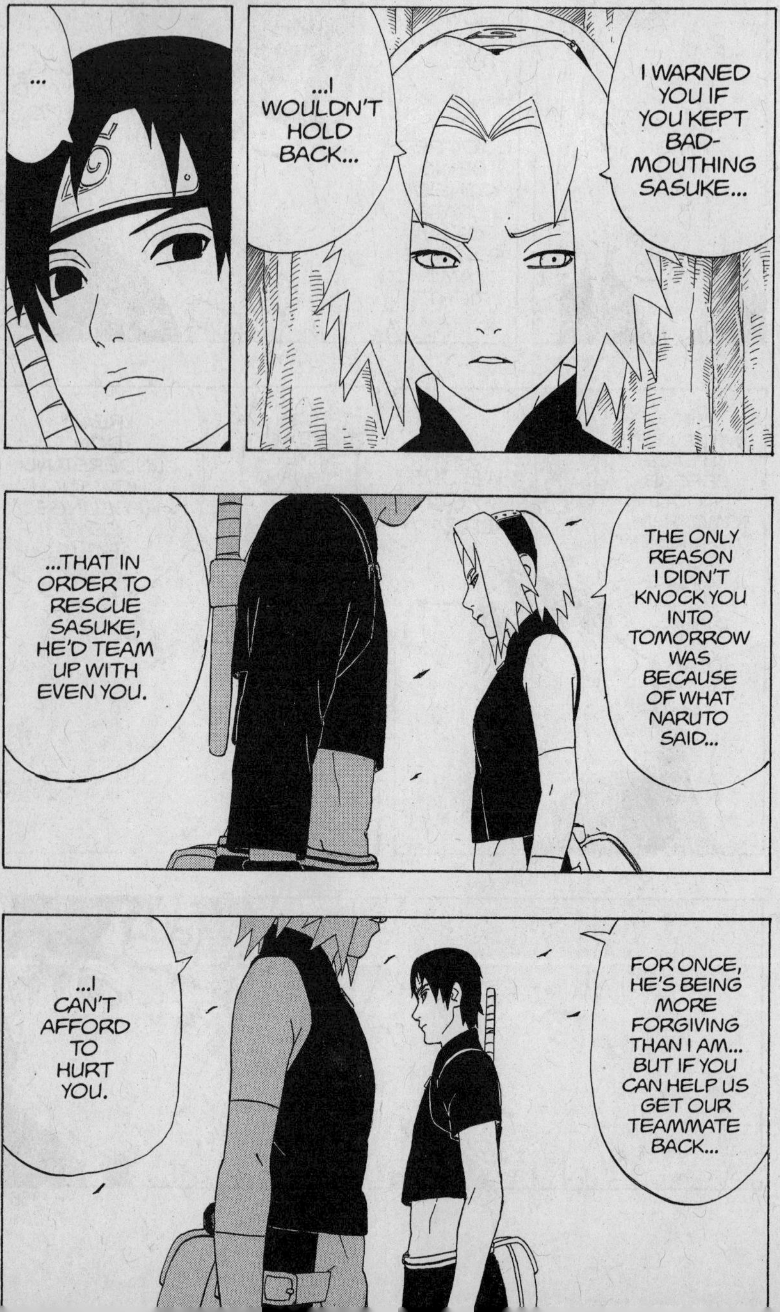
I WARNED YOU IF YOU KEPT BAD-MOUTHING SASUKE...
...I WOULDN'T HOLD BACK...
...
THE ONLY REASON I DIDN'T KNOCK YOU INTO TOMORROW WAS BECAUSE OF WHAT NARUTO SAID...
...THAT IN ORDER TO RESCUE SASUKE, HE'D TEAM UP WITH EVEN YOU.
FOR ONCE, HE'S BEING MORE FORGIVING THAN I AM... BUT IF YOU CAN HELP US GET OUR TEAMMATE BACK...
...I CAN'T AFFORD TO HURT YOU.

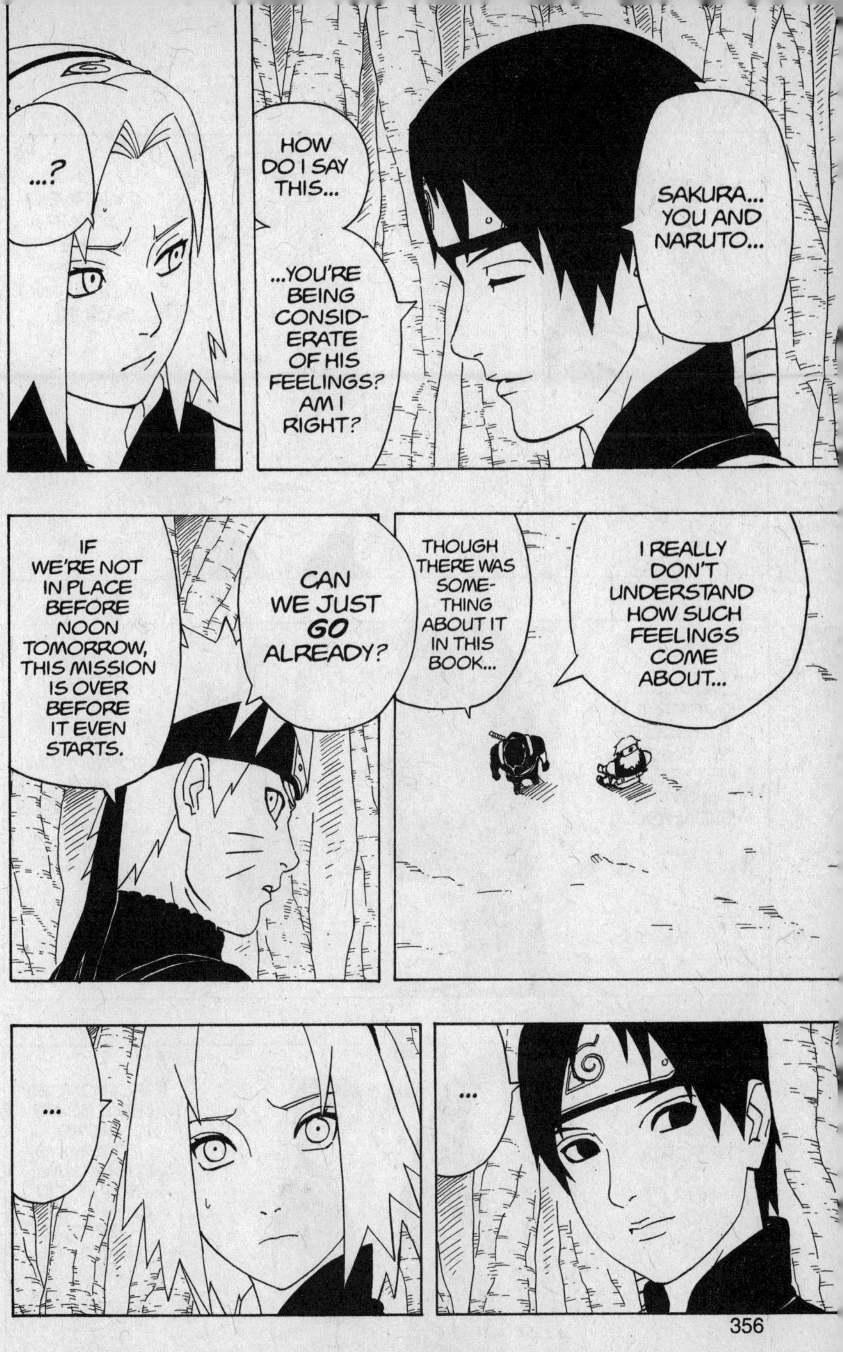
SAKURA... YOU AND NARUTO...
HOW DO I SAY THIS...
...YOU'RE BEING CONSIDERATE OF HIS FEELINGS? AM I RIGHT?
...?
I REALLY DON'T UNDERSTAND HOW SUCH FEELINGS COME ABOUT...
THOUGH THERE WAS SOMETHING ABOUT IT IN THIS BOOK...
CAN WE JUST **GO** ALREADY?
IF WE'RE NOT IN PLACE BEFORE NOON TOMORROW, THIS MISSION IS OVER BEFORE IT EVEN STARTS.
...
...

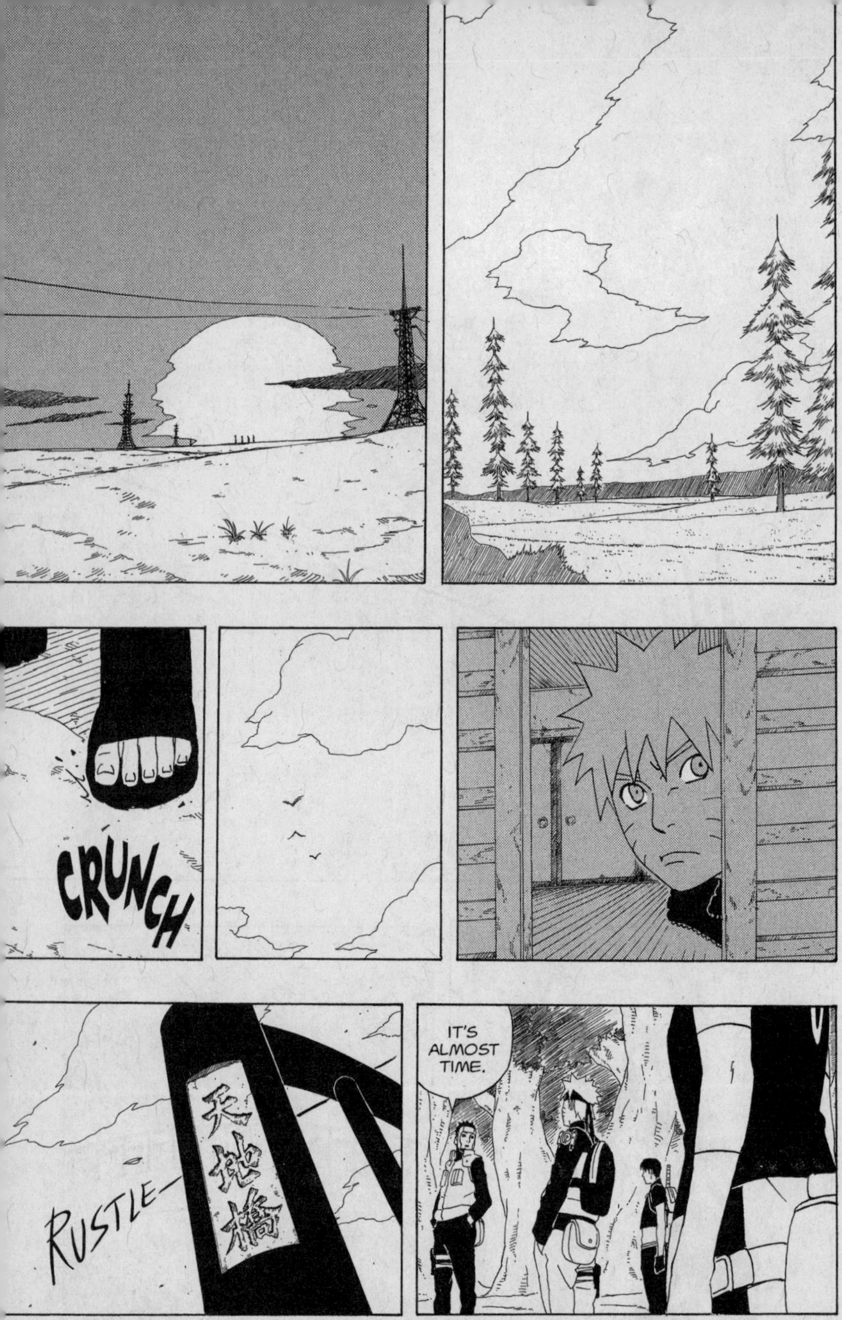
CRUNCH
IT'S ALMOST TIME.
天地橋
RUSTLE—

(POST: TENCHI BRIDGE)

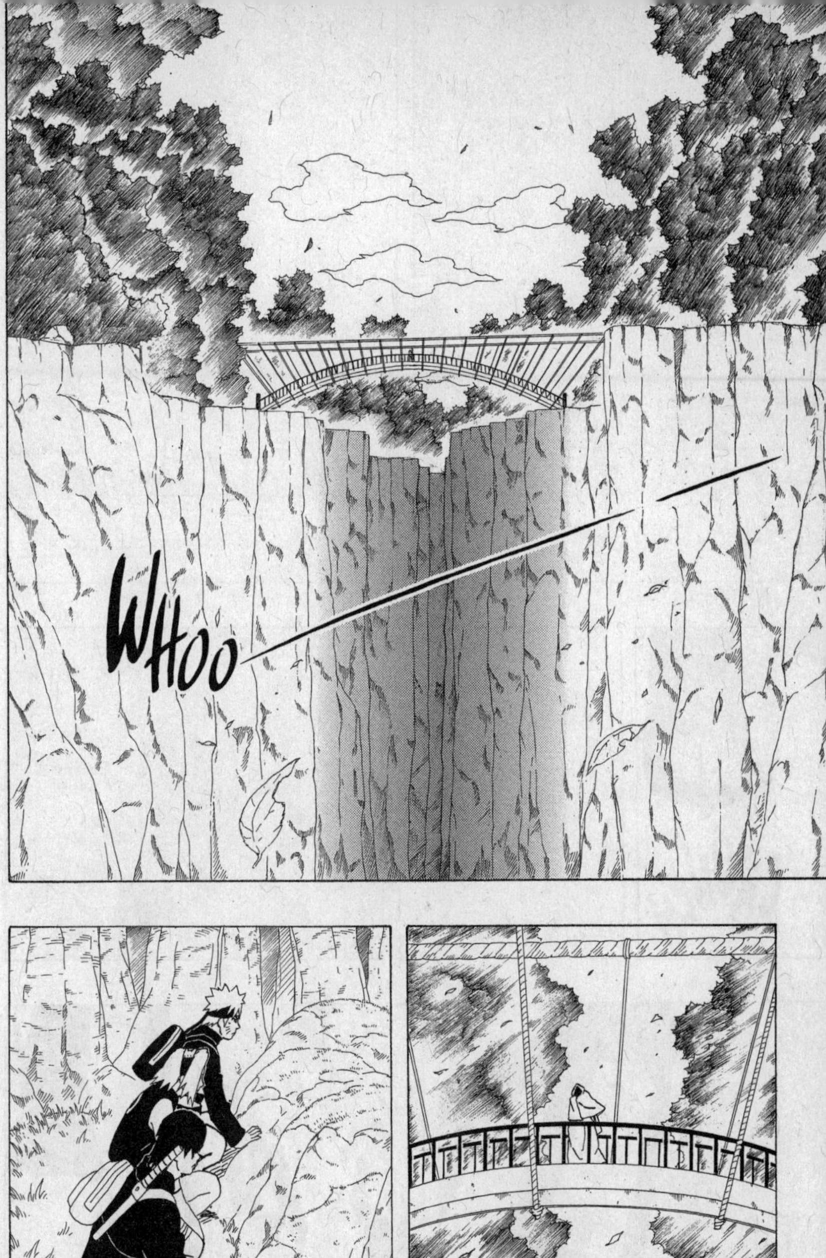
WHOO

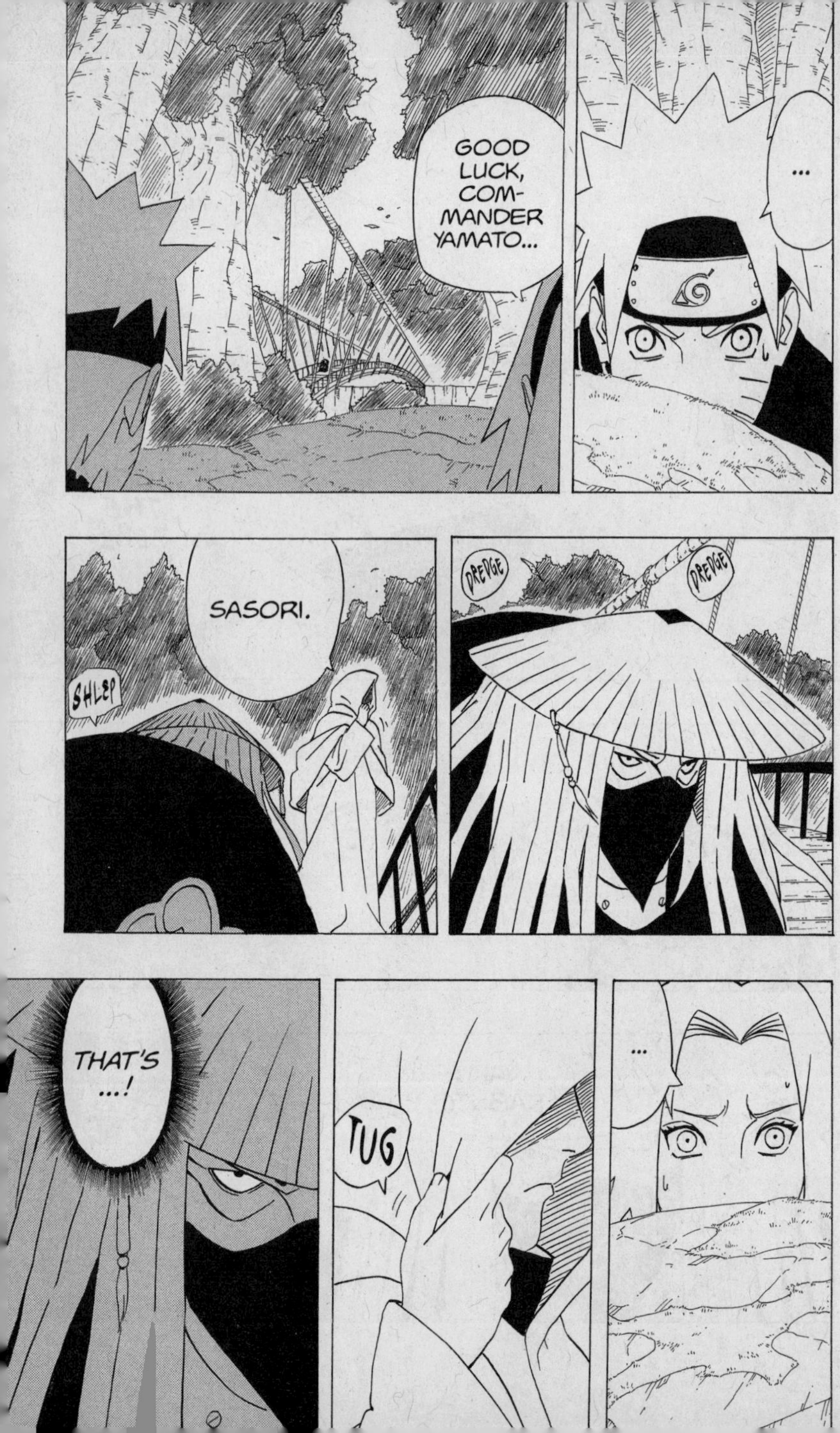
...
GOOD LUCK, COM- MANDER YAMATO...
DREDGE
DREDGE
SASORI.
SHLEP
...
TUG
THAT'S ...!

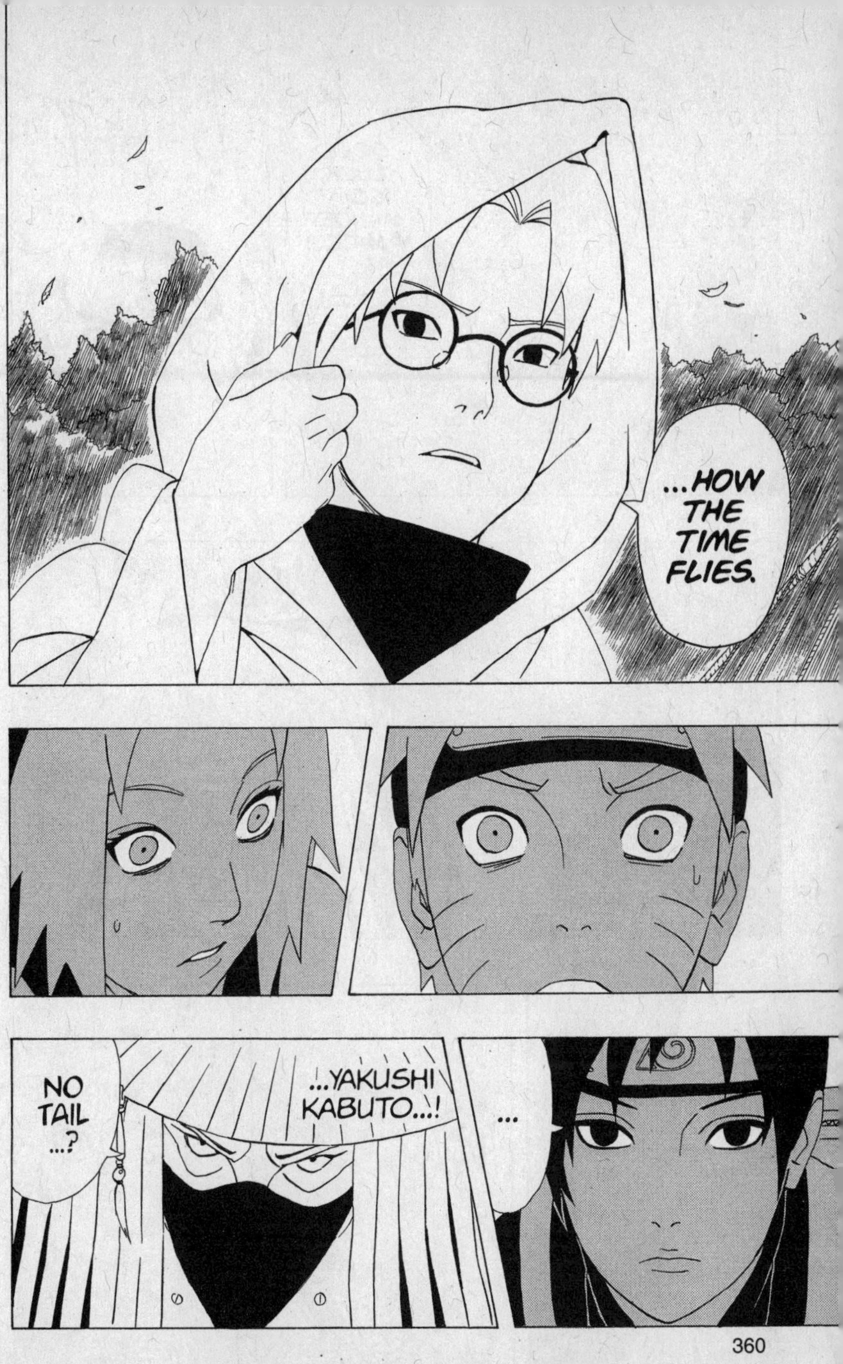
...HOW THE TIME FLIES.
...
...YAKUSHI KABUTO...!
NO TAIL ...?

READ THIS WAY

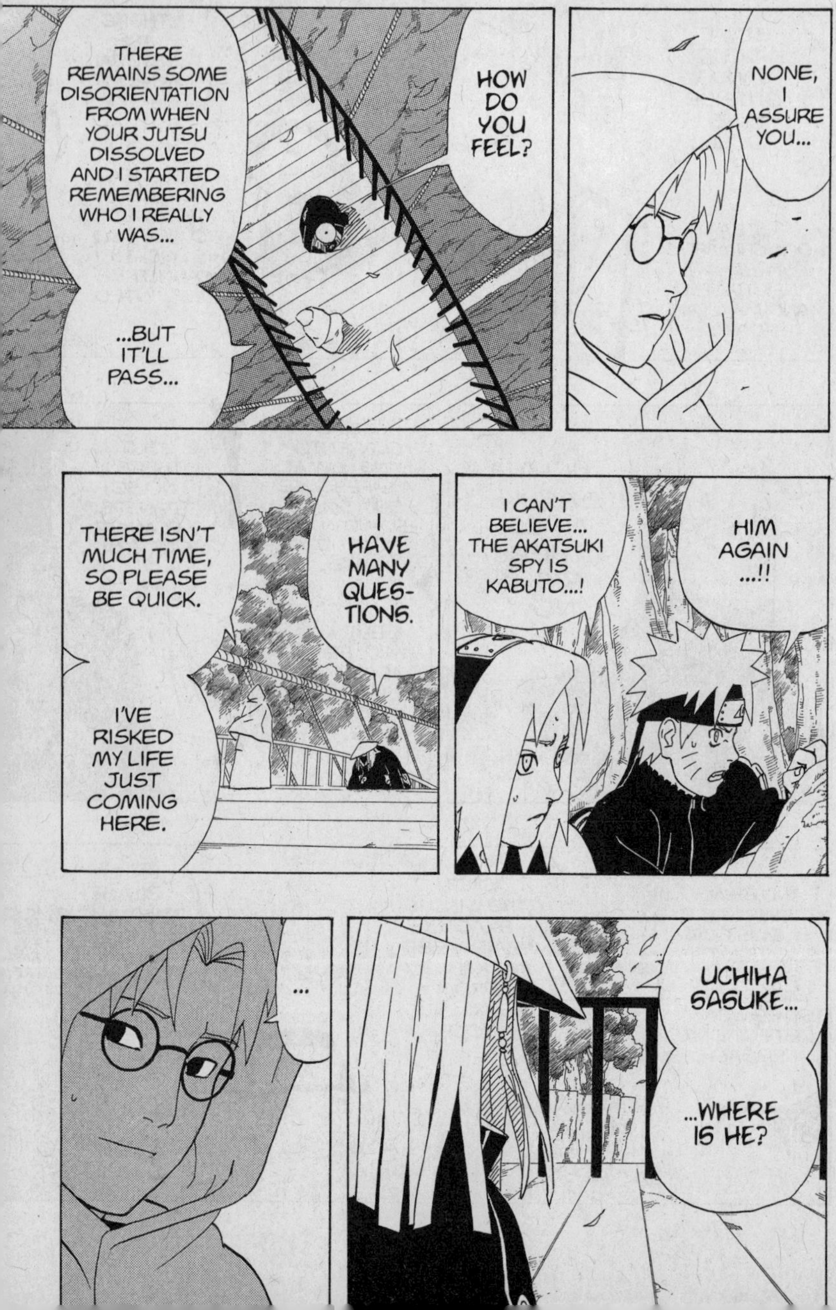
NONE, I ASSURE YOU...
HOW DO YOU FEEL?
THERE REMAINS SOME DISORIENTATION FROM WHEN YOUR JUTSU DISSOLVED AND I STARTED REMEMBERING WHO I REALLY WAS...
...BUT IT'LL PASS...
HIM AGAIN ...!!
I CAN'T BELIEVE... THE AKATSUKI SPY IS KABUTO...!
I HAVE MANY QUES-TIONS.
THERE ISN'T MUCH TIME, SO PLEASE BE QUICK.
I'VE RISKED MY LIFE JUST COMING HERE.
UCHIHA SASUKE...
...WHERE IS HE?
...

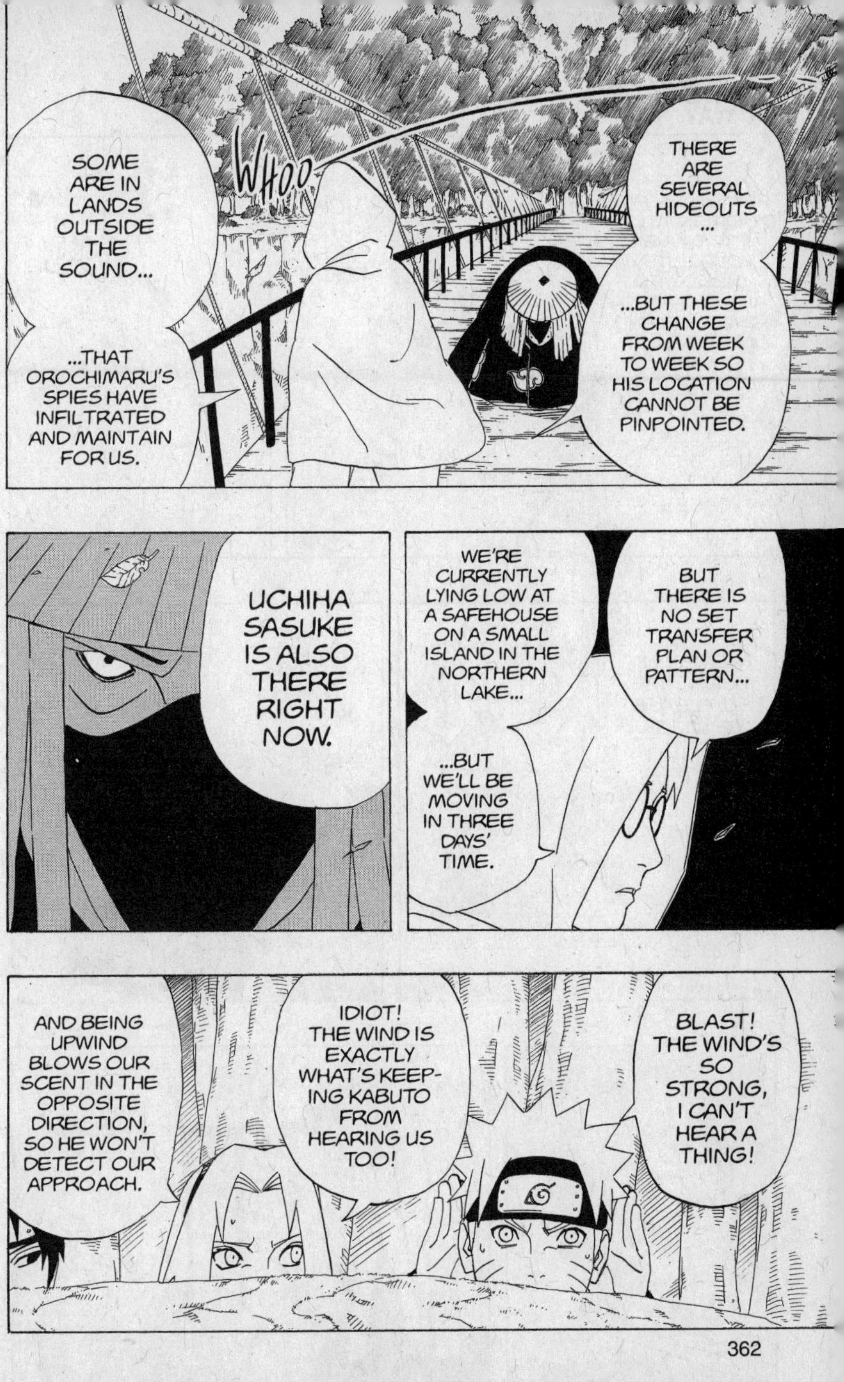
WHOO
THERE ARE SEVERAL HIDEOUTS ...
...BUT THESE CHANGE FROM WEEK TO WEEK SO HIS LOCATION CANNOT BE PINPOINTED.
SOME ARE IN LANDS OUTSIDE THE SOUND...
...THAT OROCHIMARU'S SPIES HAVE INFILTRATED AND MAINTAIN FOR US.
BUT THERE IS NO SET TRANSFER PLAN OR PATTERN...
WE'RE CURRENTLY LYING LOW AT A SAFEHOUSE ON A SMALL ISLAND IN THE NORTHERN LAKE...
...BUT WE'LL BE MOVING IN THREE DAYS' TIME.
UCHIHA SASUKE IS ALSO THERE RIGHT NOW.
BLAST! THE WIND'S SO STRONG, I CAN'T HEAR A THING!
IDIOT! THE WIND IS EXACTLY WHAT'S KEEP-ING KABUTO FROM HEARING US TOO!
AND BEING UPWIND BLOWS OUR SCENT IN THE OPPOSITE DIRECTION, SO HE WON'T DETECT OUR APPROACH.

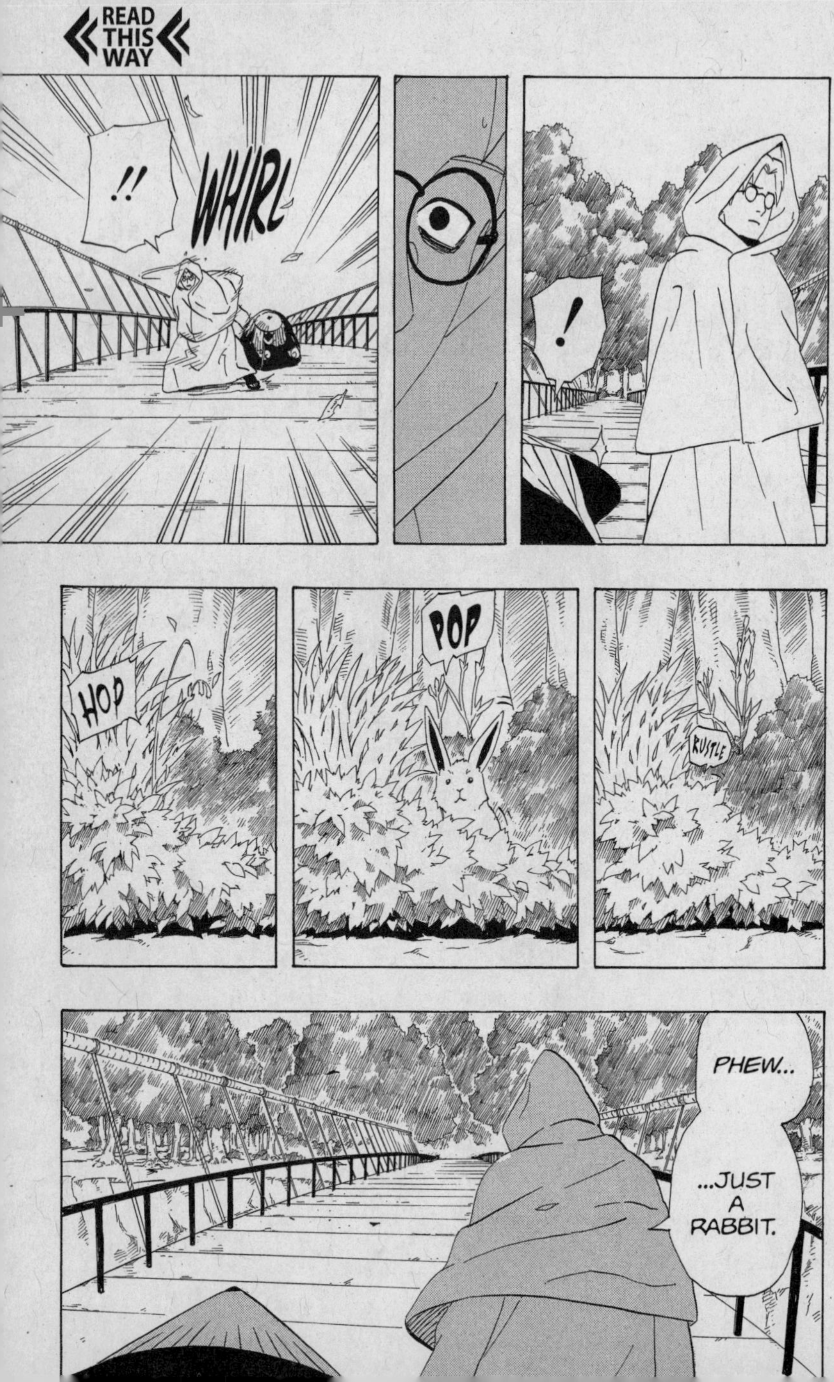
READ THIS WAY
!
!!
WHIRL
POP
HOP
RUSTLE
PHEW...
...JUST A RABBIT.

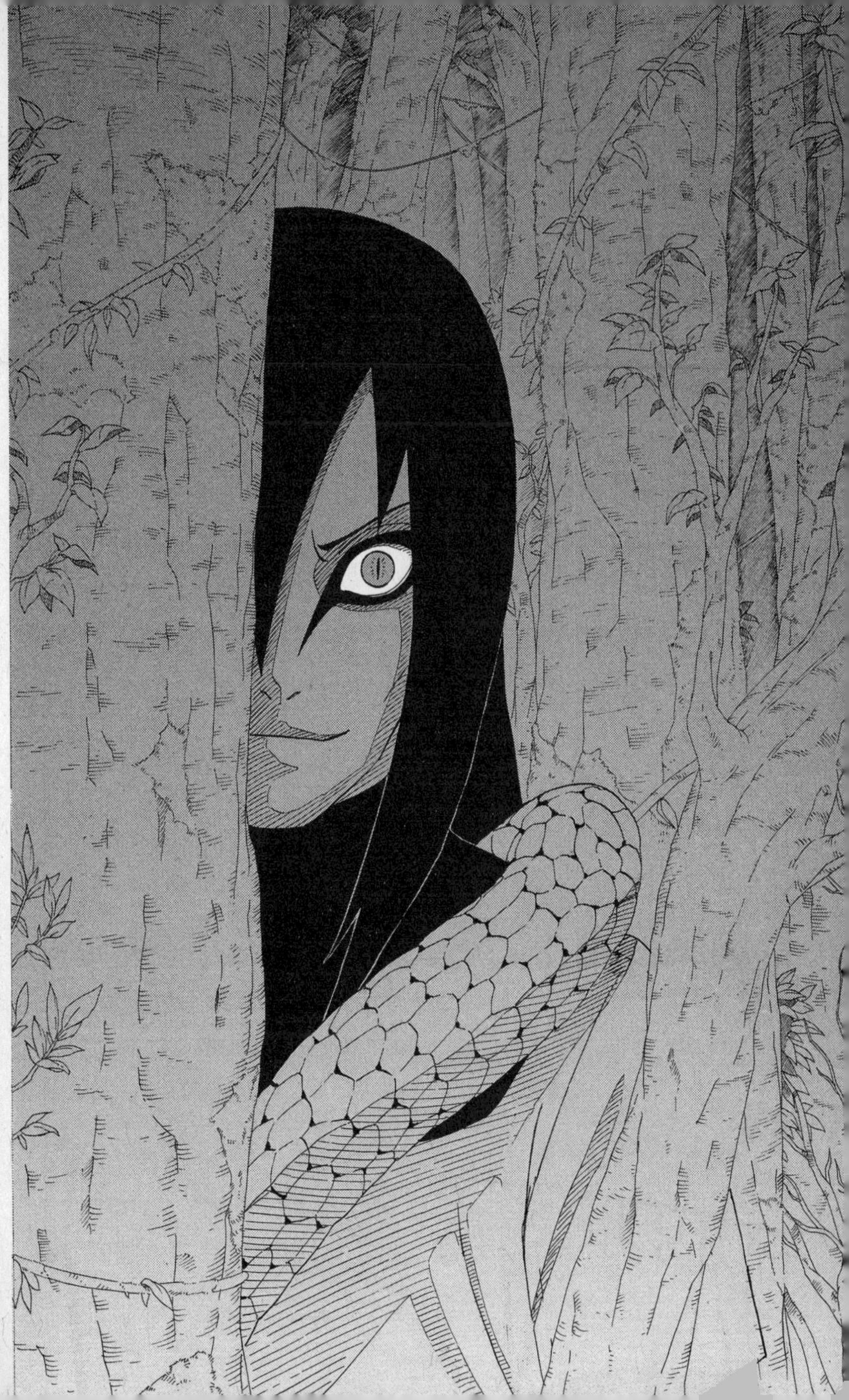

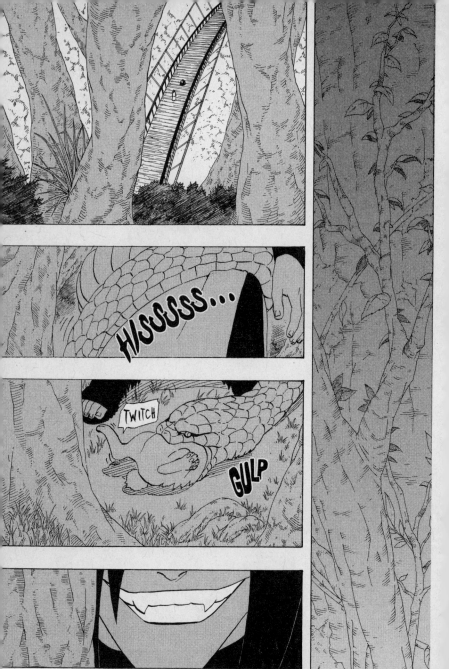

TO BE CONTINUED IN *NARUTO* VOLUME 33!

NARUTO

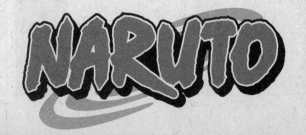

SHINE
SHINE
CHIRP
CHIRP

岸本斉史

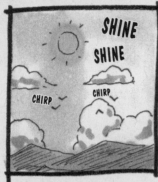

There is one period during each day that is my favorite time...The hour between 10 and 11 in the morning. The reason is that everything always seems so refreshing and delightful at that hour. But because of looming deadlines, I usually end up sleeping through it...That refreshing and delightful feeling...what was it like again?

—Masashi Kishimoto, 2006

一楽
ラーメン一楽

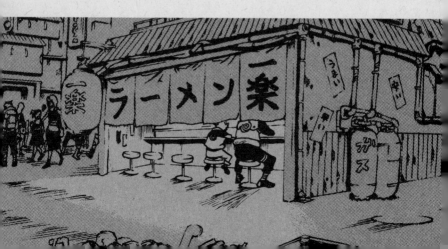

NARUTO

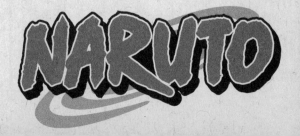

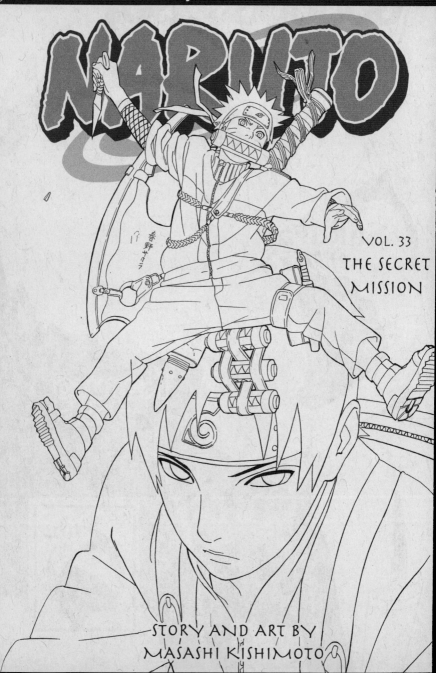

SHONEN JUMP MANGA EDITION

NARUTO

VOL. 33
THE SECRET
MISSION

STORY AND ART BY
MASASHI KISHIMOTO

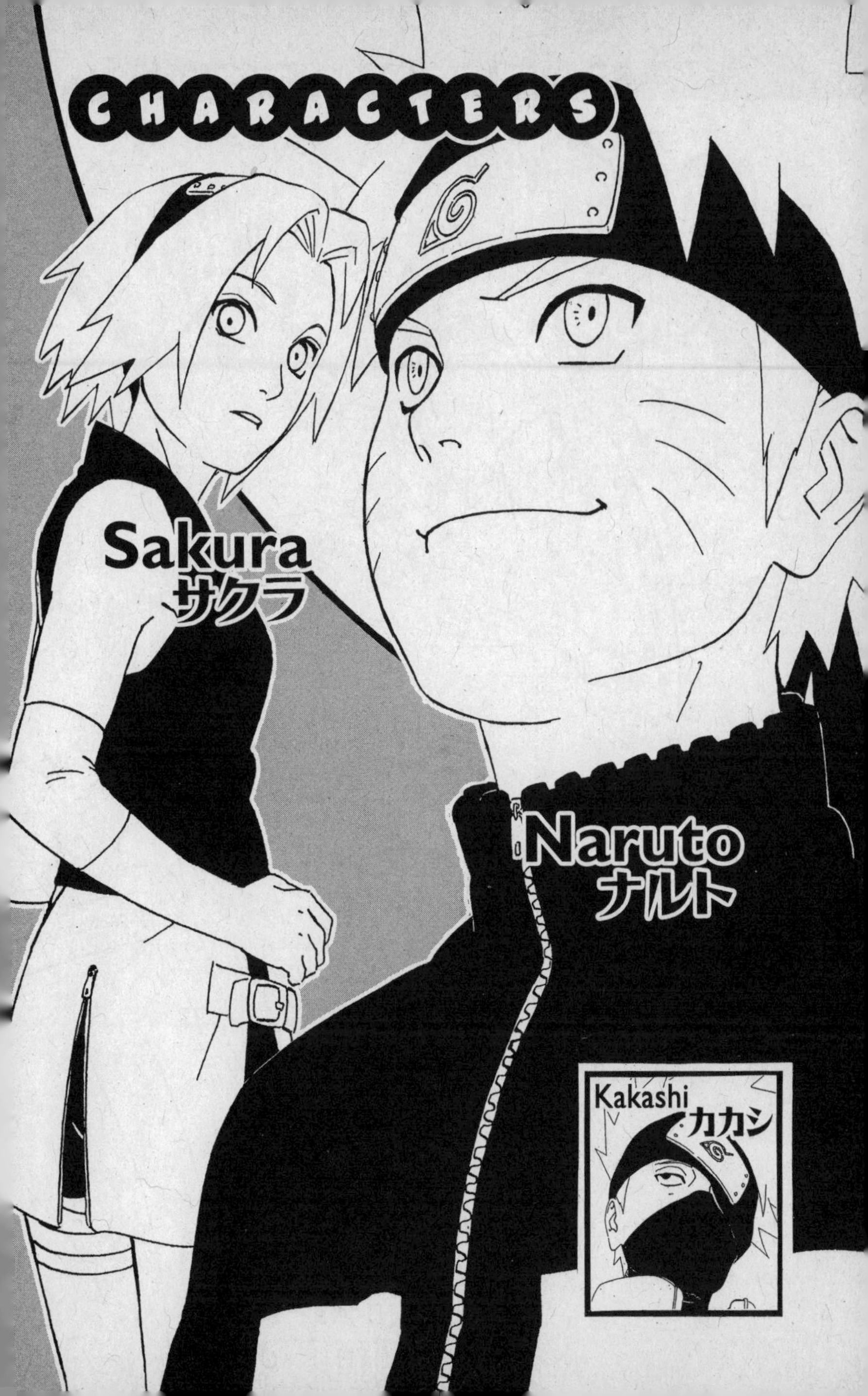
CHARACTERS
Sakura
サクラ
Naruto
ナルト
Kakashi
カカシ

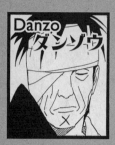

Danzo ダンゾウ

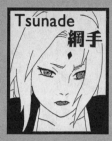

Tsunade 綱手

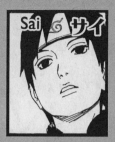

Sai サイ

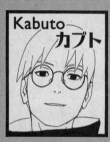

Kabuto カブト

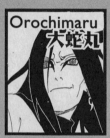

Orochimaru 大蛇丸

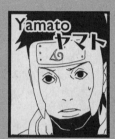

Yamato ヤマト

The Story So Far...

Against all odds, Uzumaki Naruto, the student least likely to graduate from the Ninja Academy in the village of Konohagakure, becomes a ninja along with his classmates and closest friends, Sasuke and Sakura. During the Chûnin Selection Exams, however, the turncoat ninja Orochimaru launches *Operation Destroy Konoha,* forcing Naruto's mentor, the Third Hokage, to sacrifice his own life to stop the attack and save the village.

Further tragedy follows when Sasuke succumbs to the lure of Orochimaru's power. Though Naruto fights valiantly to stop Sasuke from joining up with their worst enemy, he ultimately fails. After Sasuke flees with Orochimaru, Naruto vows to rescue his friend someday...

In the interim, two years pass and Naruto and his comrades once again confront the mysterious Akatsuki organization. But intelligence gained during that battle leads the new Team Kakashi to a secret rendezvous with an Akatsuki spy who turns out to be none other than the ever-duplicitous Kabuto! Unbeknownst to our heroes, the whole event takes place under the watchful snake eyes of Orochimaru...!

VOL. 33
THE SECRET MISSION

CONTENTS

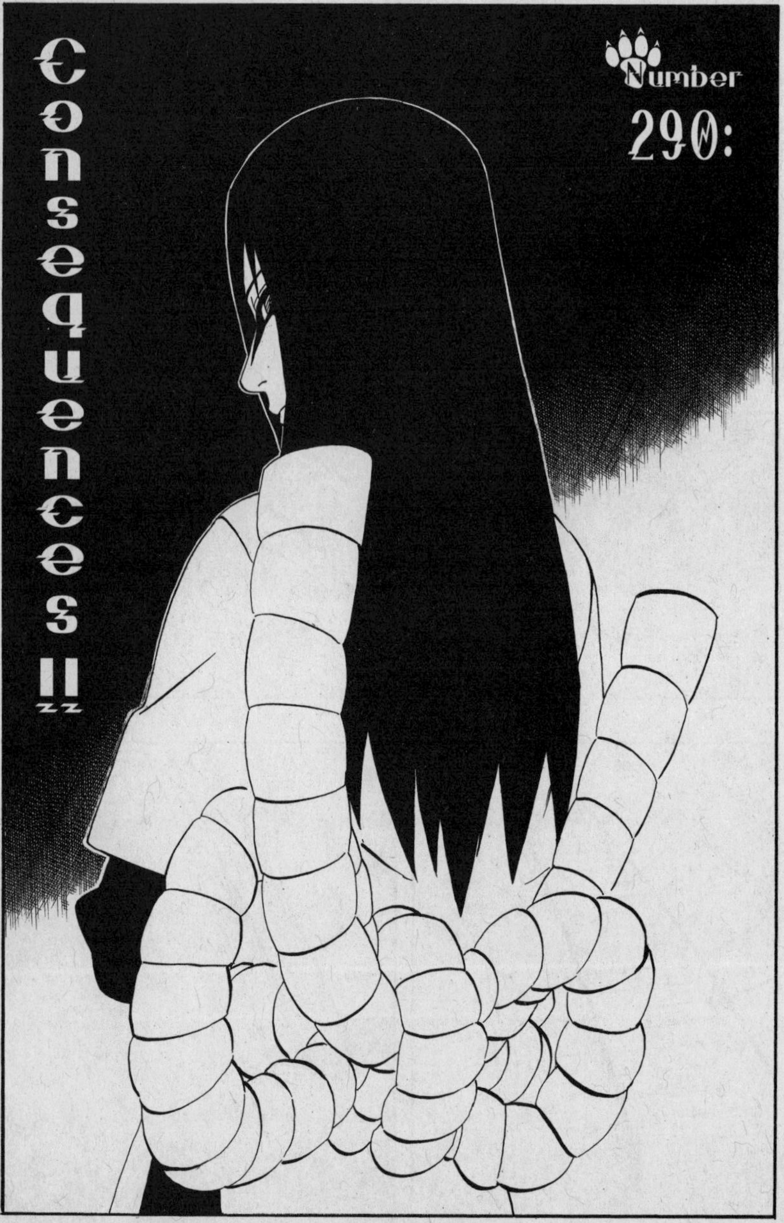
Number 290:
Consequences!!

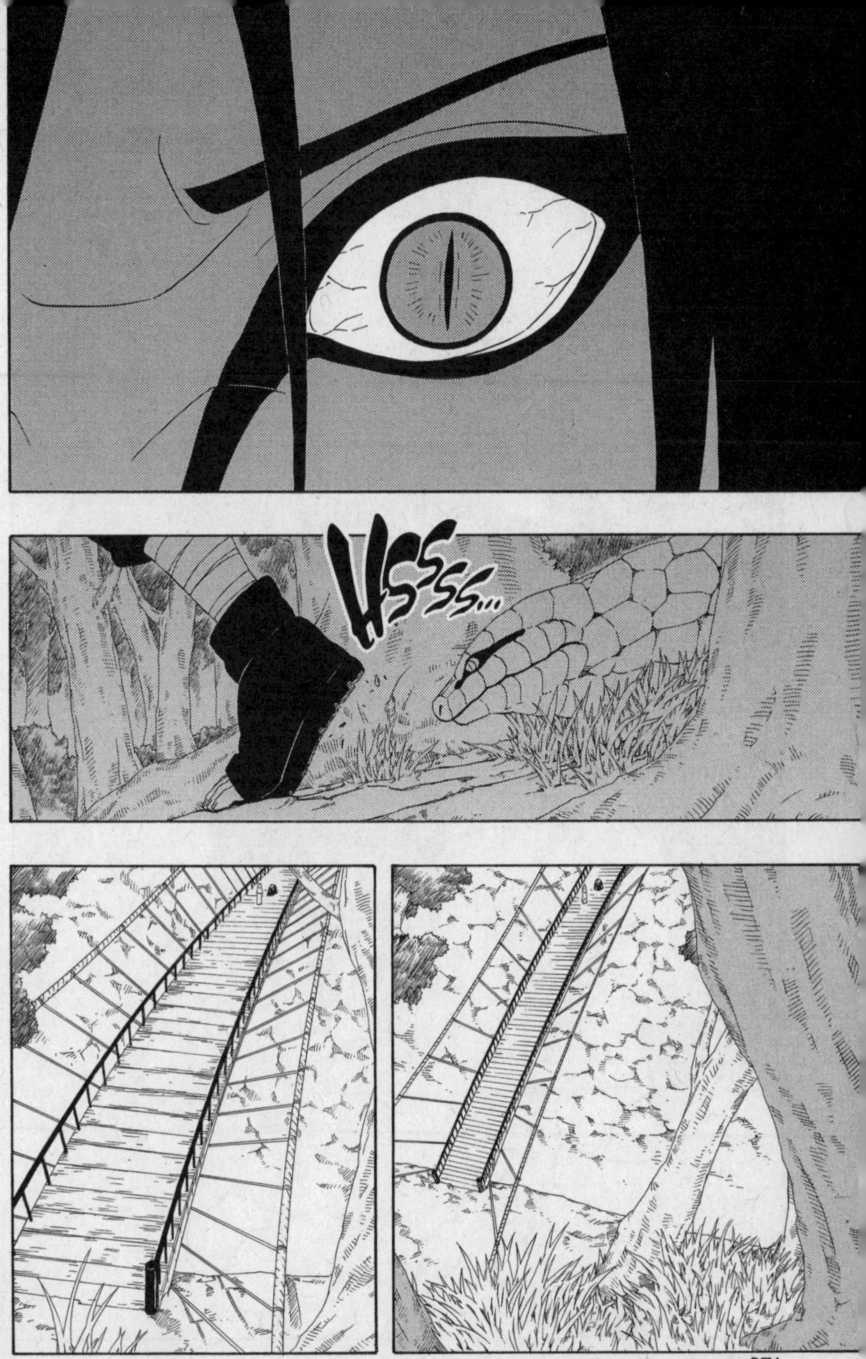
HSSSS...

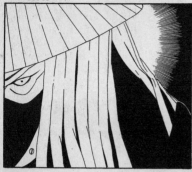

READ THIS WAY

SO...
... REGARDING THE MATTER YOU ASKED ME TO LOOK INTO...
...
THERE ARE STILL A FEW MORE THINGS I WANTED TO ASK HIM...
...BUT THE LONGER WE KEEP TALKING, THE GREATER THE CHANCE I MIGHT SLIP UP...
EVEN AFTER OROCHIMARU TRANSFERS BODIES, HE PUTS A PROTECTIVE JUTSU ON THE CELL SPECIMENS FROM THE OLD HOST BODY...
...SO I HAVE **NOT** BEEN ABLE TO ANALYZE THEM.
HOOSH
I SEE...
...

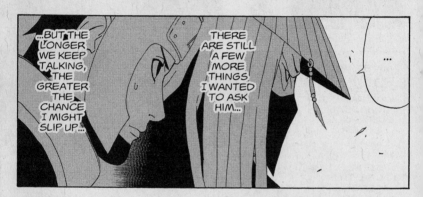

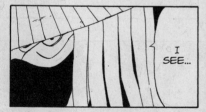

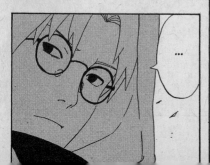

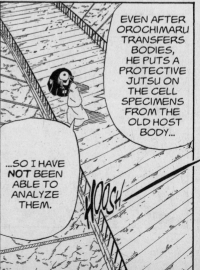

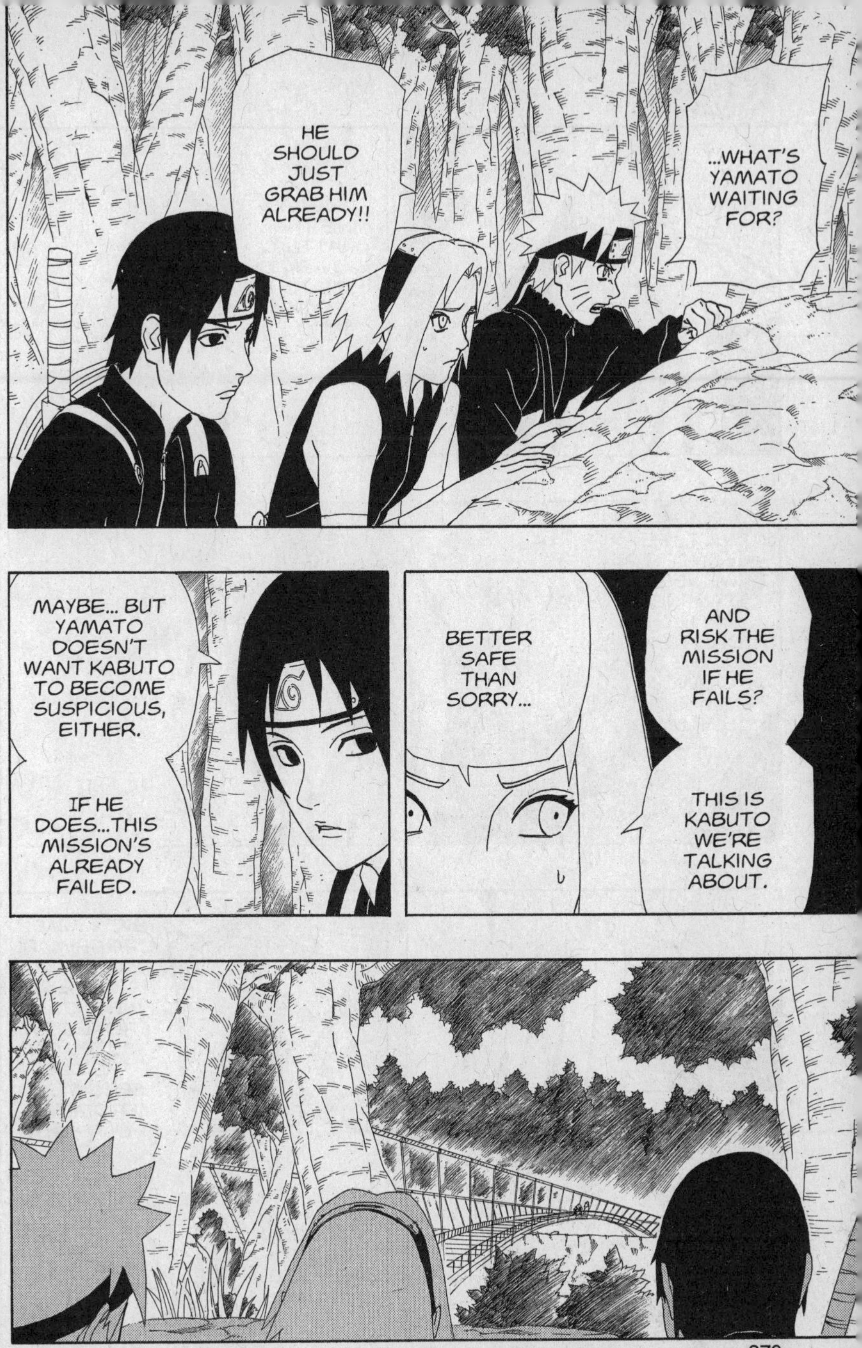
...WHAT'S YAMATO WAITING FOR?
HE SHOULD JUST GRAB HIM ALREADY!!
AND RISK THE MISSION IF HE FAILS?
THIS IS KABUTO WE'RE TALKING ABOUT.
BETTER SAFE THAN SORRY...
MAYBE... BUT YAMATO DOESN'T WANT KABUTO TO BECOME SUSPICIOUS, EITHER.
IF HE DOES...THIS MISSION'S ALREADY FAILED.

READ THIS WAY

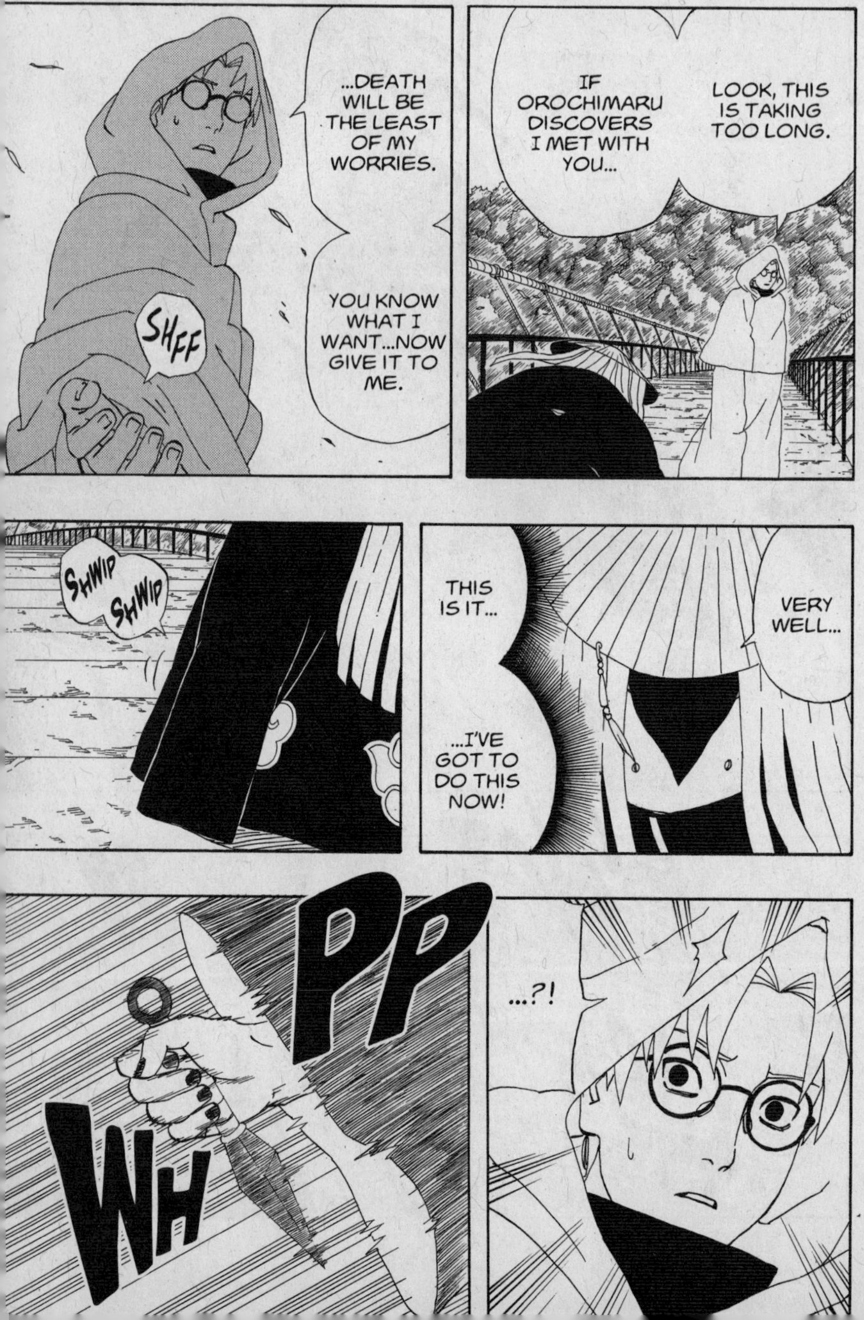
LOOK, THIS IS TAKING TOO LONG.
IF OROCHIMARU DISCOVERS I MET WITH YOU...
...DEATH WILL BE THE LEAST OF MY WORRIES.
YOU KNOW WHAT I WANT...NOW GIVE IT TO ME.
SHFF
VERY WELL...
THIS IS IT...
...I'VE GOT TO DO THIS NOW!
SHWIP SHWIP
...?!
WHPP

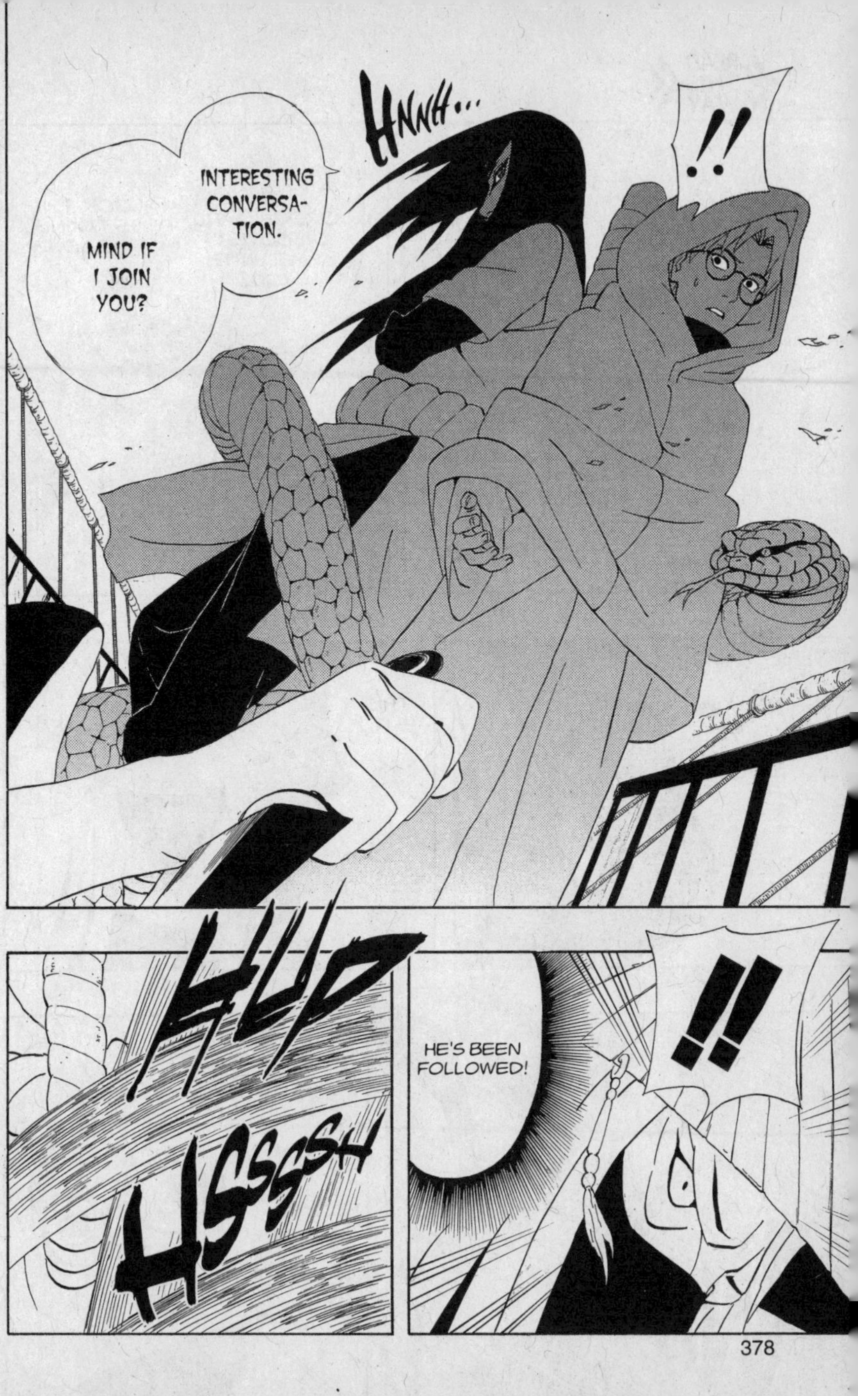
!!
HNNH...
INTERESTING CONVERSA-TION.
MIND IF I JOIN YOU?
!!
HE'S BEEN FOLLOWED!
KUD
HSSSH

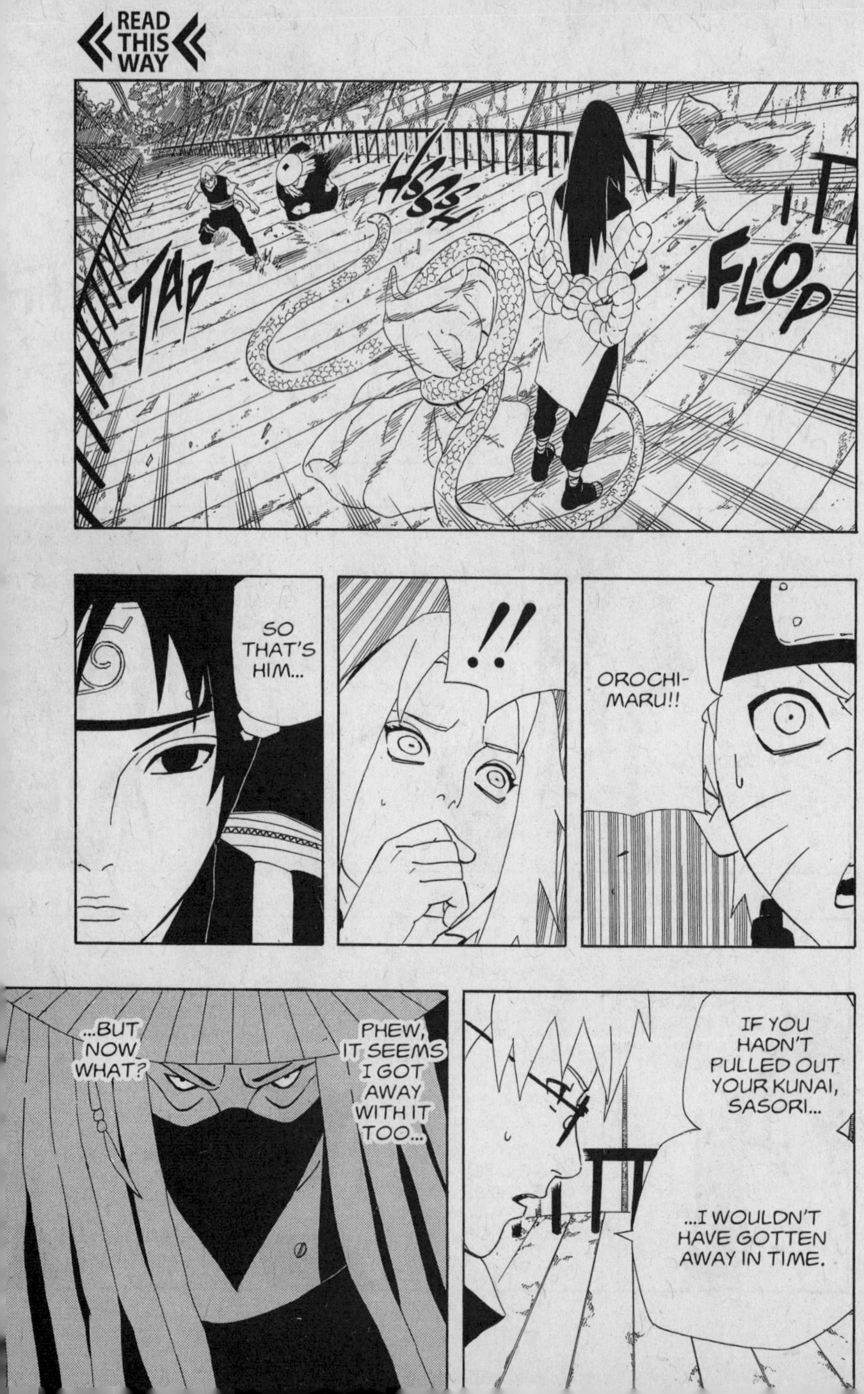
READ THIS WAY
FLOP
HSSH
TAP
OROCHI-MARU!!
!!
SO THAT'S HIM...
IF YOU HADN'T PULLED OUT YOUR KUNAI, SASORI...
...I WOULDN'T HAVE GOTTEN AWAY IN TIME.
PHEW, IT SEEMS I GOT AWAY WITH IT TOO...
...BUT NOW WHAT?

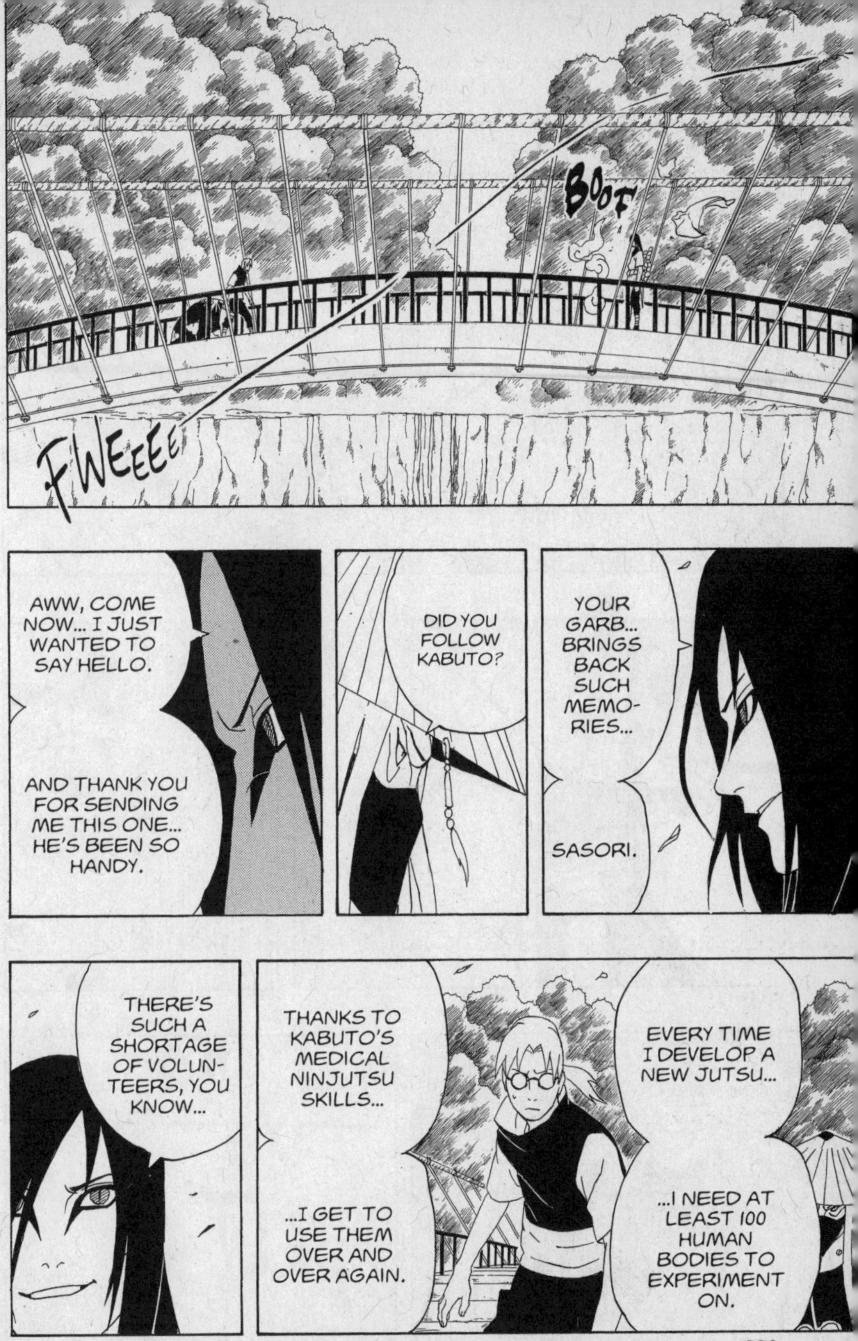
BOOF
FWEEEE
YOUR GARB... BRINGS BACK SUCH MEMO-RIES...
SASORI.
DID YOU FOLLOW KABUTO?
AWW, COME NOW... I JUST WANTED TO SAY HELLO.
AND THANK YOU FOR SENDING ME THIS ONE... HE'S BEEN SO HANDY.
EVERY TIME I DEVELOP A NEW JUTSU...
...I NEED AT LEAST 100 HUMAN BODIES TO EXPERIMENT ON.
THANKS TO KABUTO'S MEDICAL NINJUTSU SKILLS...
...I GET TO USE THEM OVER AND OVER AGAIN.
THERE'S SUCH A SHORTAGE OF VOLUN-TEERS, YOU KNOW...

READ THIS WAY

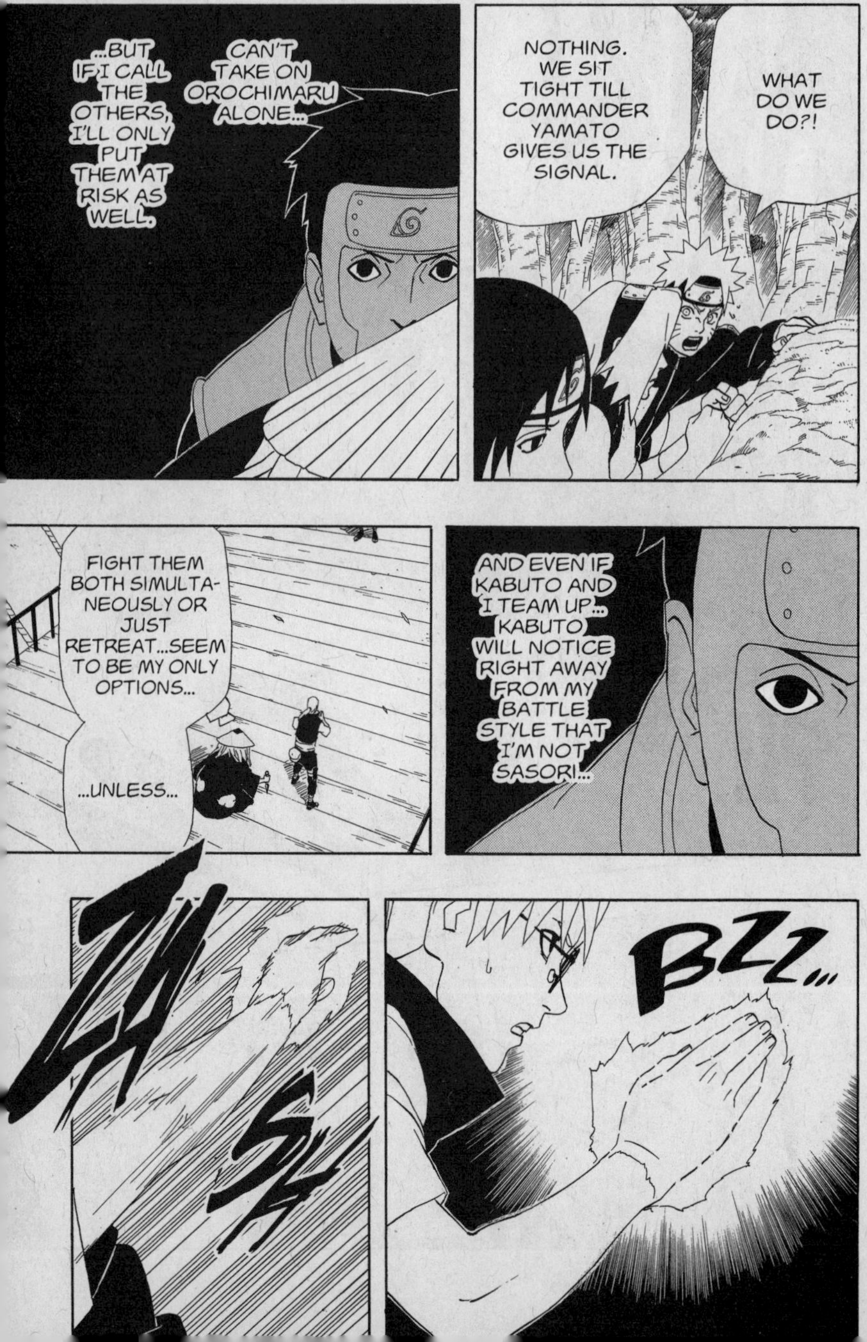
WHAT DO WE DO?!
NOTHING. WE SIT TIGHT TILL COMMANDER YAMATO GIVES US THE SIGNAL.
CAN'T TAKE ON OROCHIMARU ALONE...
...BUT IF I CALL THE OTHERS, I'LL ONLY PUT THEM AT RISK AS WELL.
AND EVEN IF KABUTO AND I TEAM UP... KABUTO WILL NOTICE RIGHT AWAY FROM MY BATTLE STYLE THAT I'M NOT SASORI...
FIGHT THEM BOTH SIMULTANEOUSLY OR JUST RETREAT...SEEM TO BE MY ONLY OPTIONS...
...UNLESS...
BZZ...

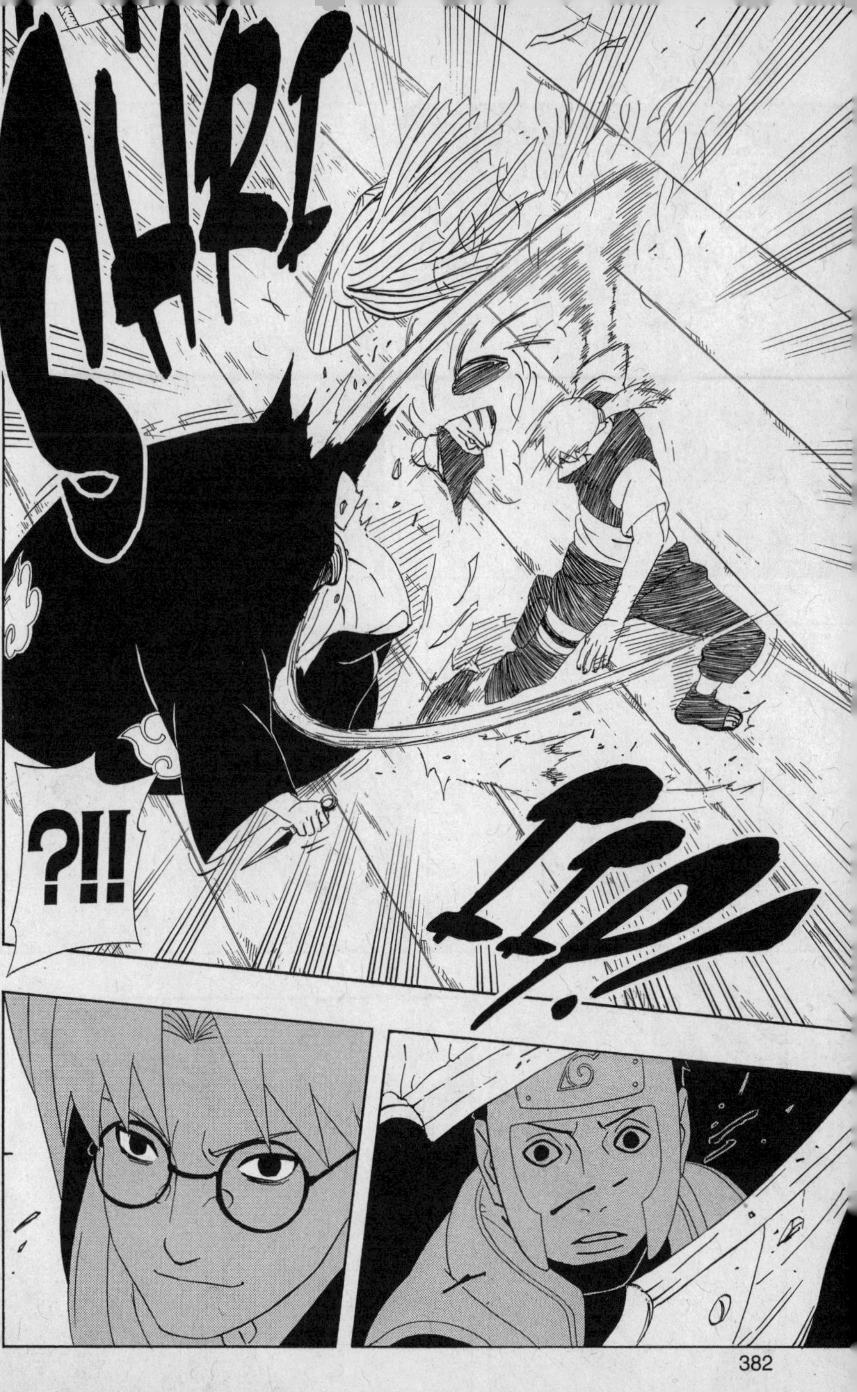
?!!

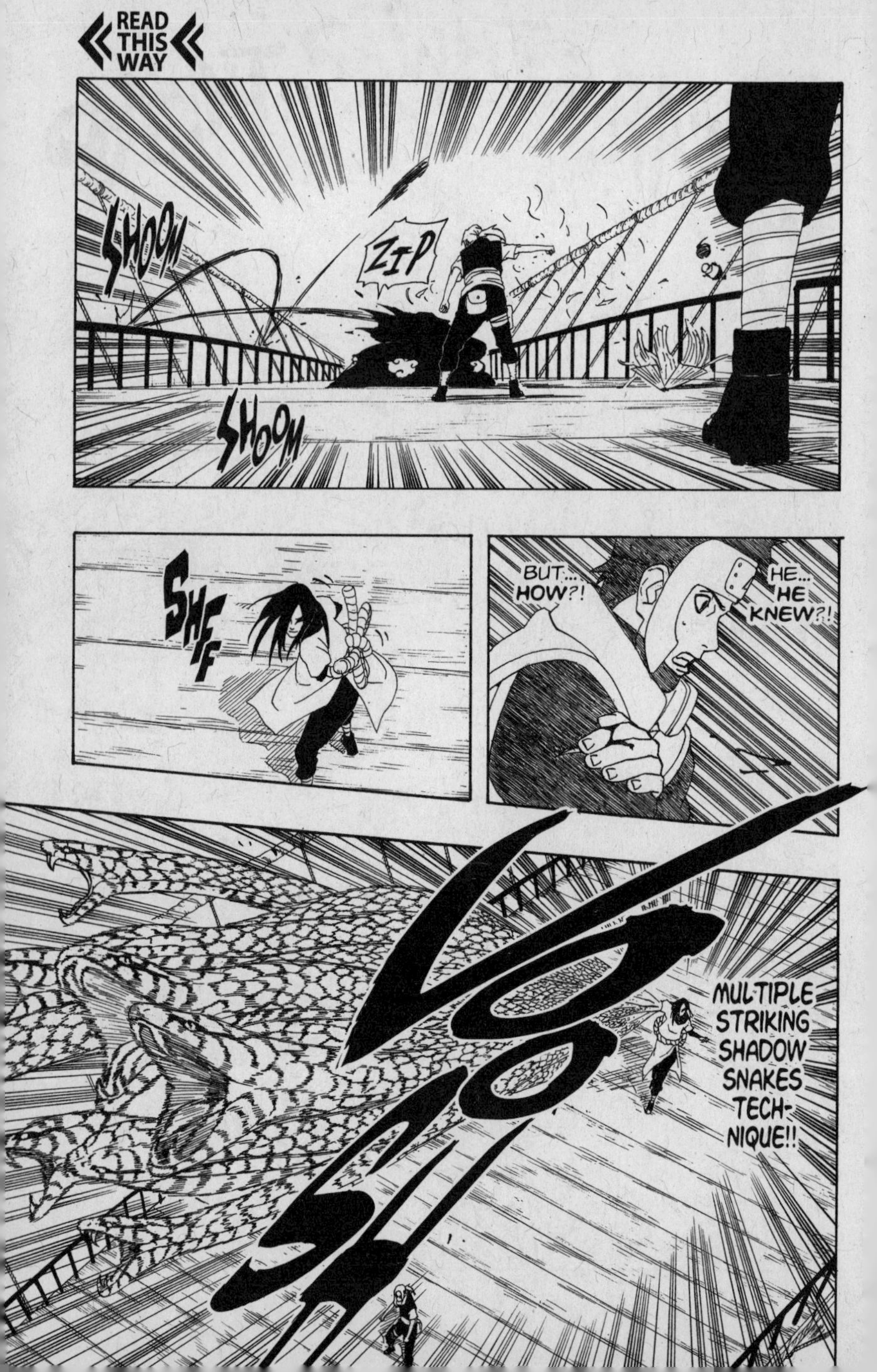
READ THIS WAY
ZIP
SHOOM
SHOOM
HE... HE KNEW?!
BUT... HOW?!
SHFF
MULTIPLE STRIKING SHADOW SNAKES TECH-NIQUE!!
VSSSH

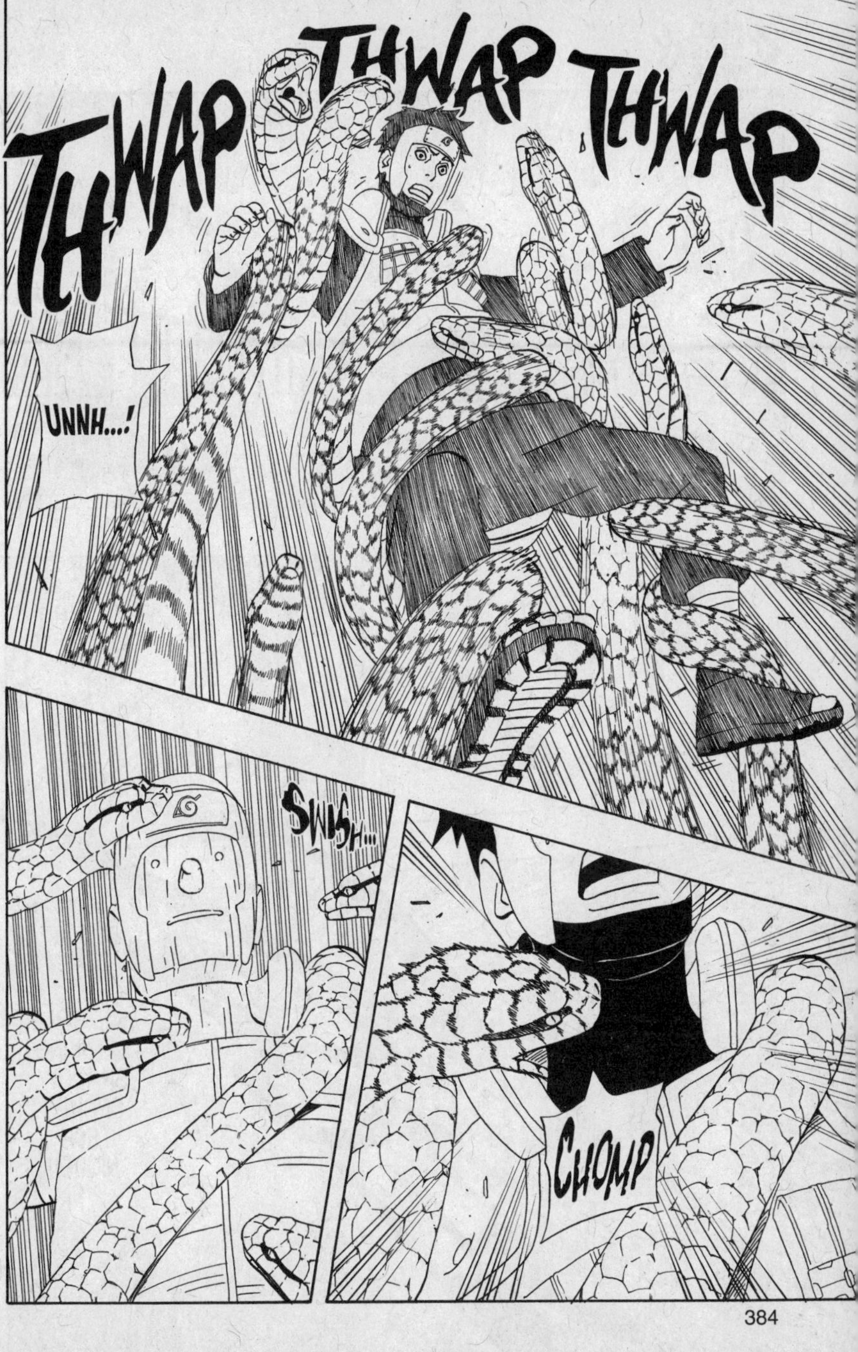
THWAP THWAP THWAP
UNNH...!
CHOMP
SWISH...

READ THIS WAY

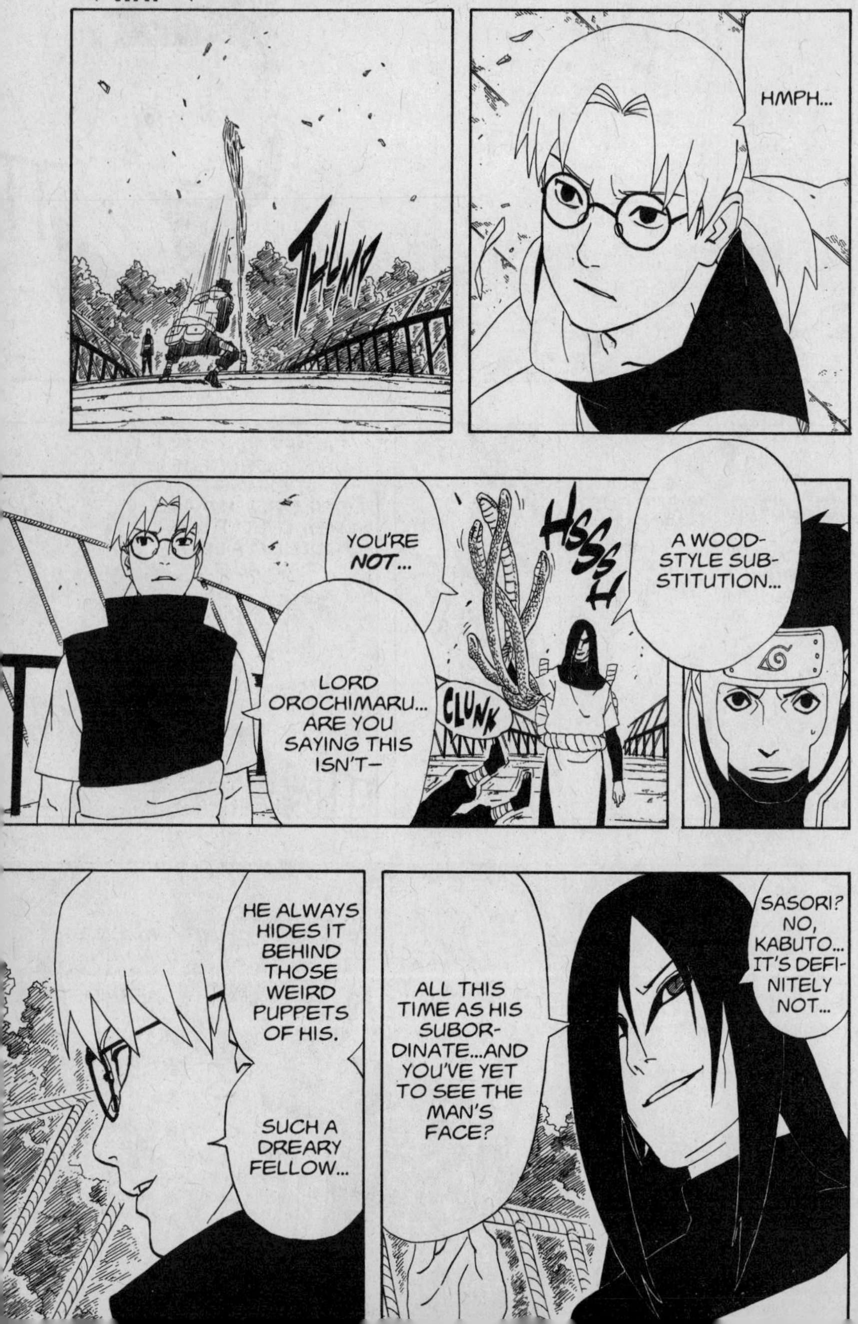
HMPH...
THUMP
A WOOD-STYLE SUBSTITUTION...
HSSSH
YOU'RE *NOT*...
CLUNK
LORD OROCHIMARU... ARE YOU SAYING THIS ISN'T—
SASORI? NO, KABUTO... IT'S DEFINITELY NOT...
ALL THIS TIME AS HIS SUBORDINATE...AND YOU'VE YET TO SEE THE MAN'S FACE?
HE ALWAYS HIDES IT BEHIND THOSE WEIRD PUPPETS OF HIS.
SUCH A DREARY FELLOW...

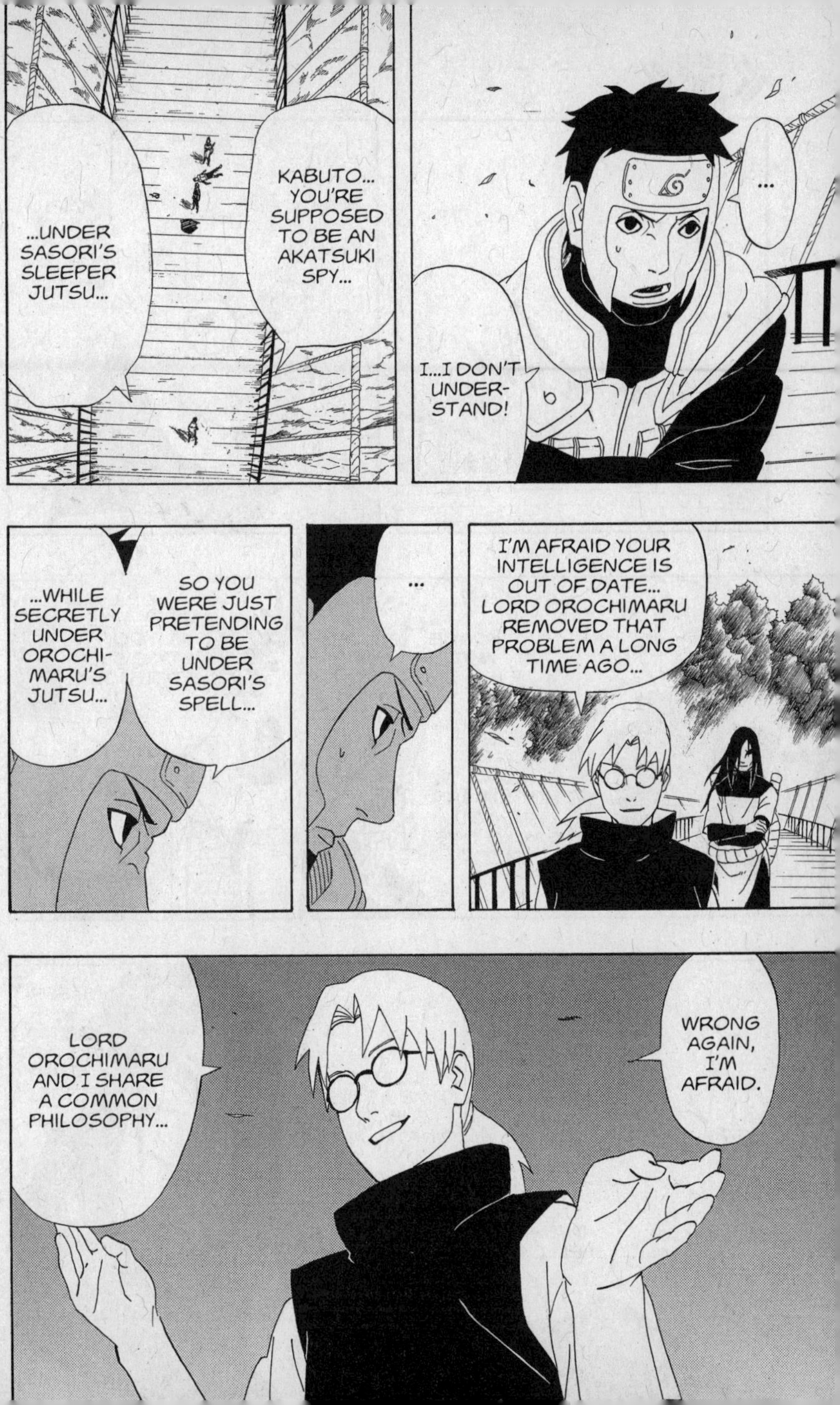
...
I...I DON'T UNDERSTAND!
KABUTO... YOU'RE SUPPOSED TO BE AN AKATSUKI SPY...
...UNDER SASORI'S SLEEPER JUTSU...
I'M AFRAID YOUR INTELLIGENCE IS OUT OF DATE... LORD OROCHIMARU REMOVED THAT PROBLEM A LONG TIME AGO...
...
SO YOU WERE JUST PRETENDING TO BE UNDER SASORI'S SPELL...
...WHILE SECRETLY UNDER OROCHIMARU'S JUTSU...
WRONG AGAIN, I'M AFRAID.
LORD OROCHIMARU AND I SHARE A COMMON PHILOSOPHY...

READ THIS WAY

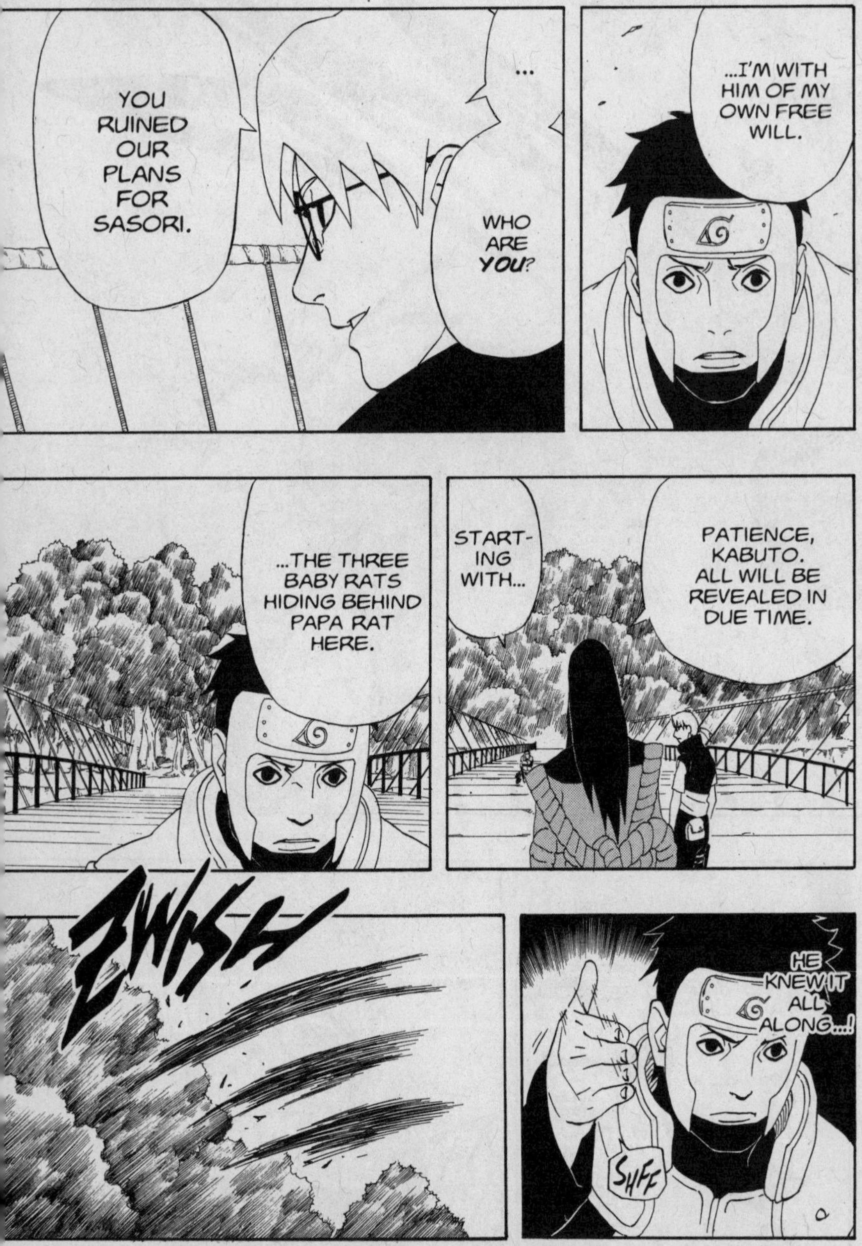
...I'M WITH HIM OF MY OWN FREE WILL.
...
WHO ARE *YOU*?
YOU RUINED OUR PLANS FOR SASORI.
PATIENCE, KABUTO. ALL WILL BE REVEALED IN DUE TIME.
STARTING WITH...
...THE THREE BABY RATS HIDING BEHIND PAPA RAT HERE.
HE KNEW IT ALL ALONG...!
SHFF
ZWISH

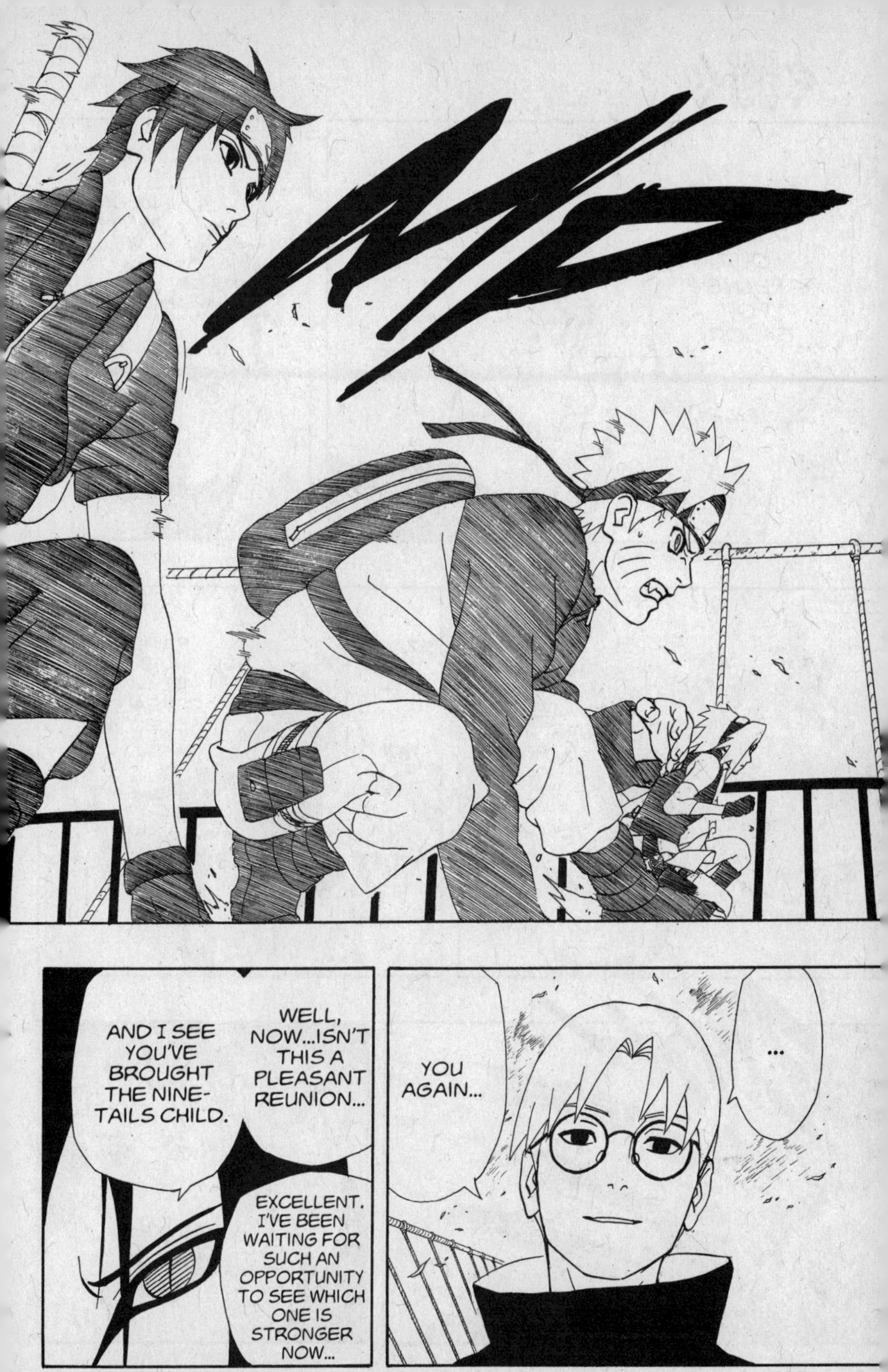
...
YOU AGAIN...
WELL, NOW...ISN'T THIS A PLEASANT REUNION...
AND I SEE YOU'VE BROUGHT THE NINE-TAILS CHILD.
EXCELLENT. I'VE BEEN WAITING FOR SUCH AN OPPORTUNITY TO SEE WHICH ONE IS STRONGER NOW...

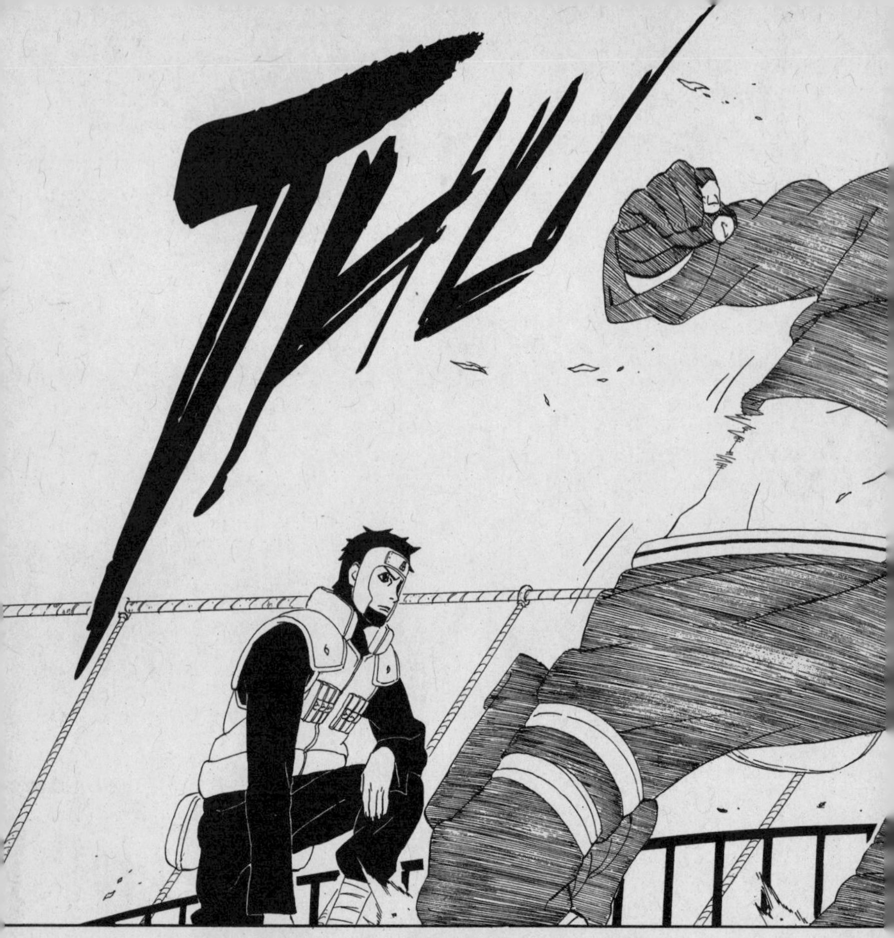
THUK

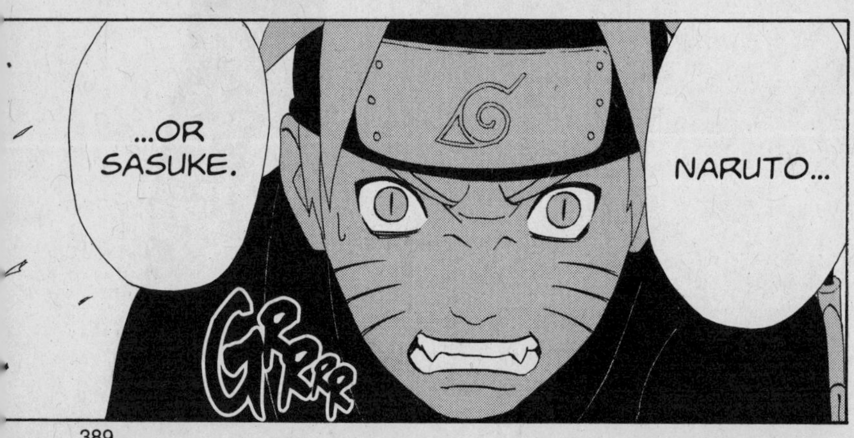
NARUTO...
...OR SASUKE.
GRRR

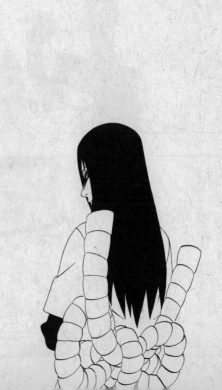

Number 291: Rage Trigger!!

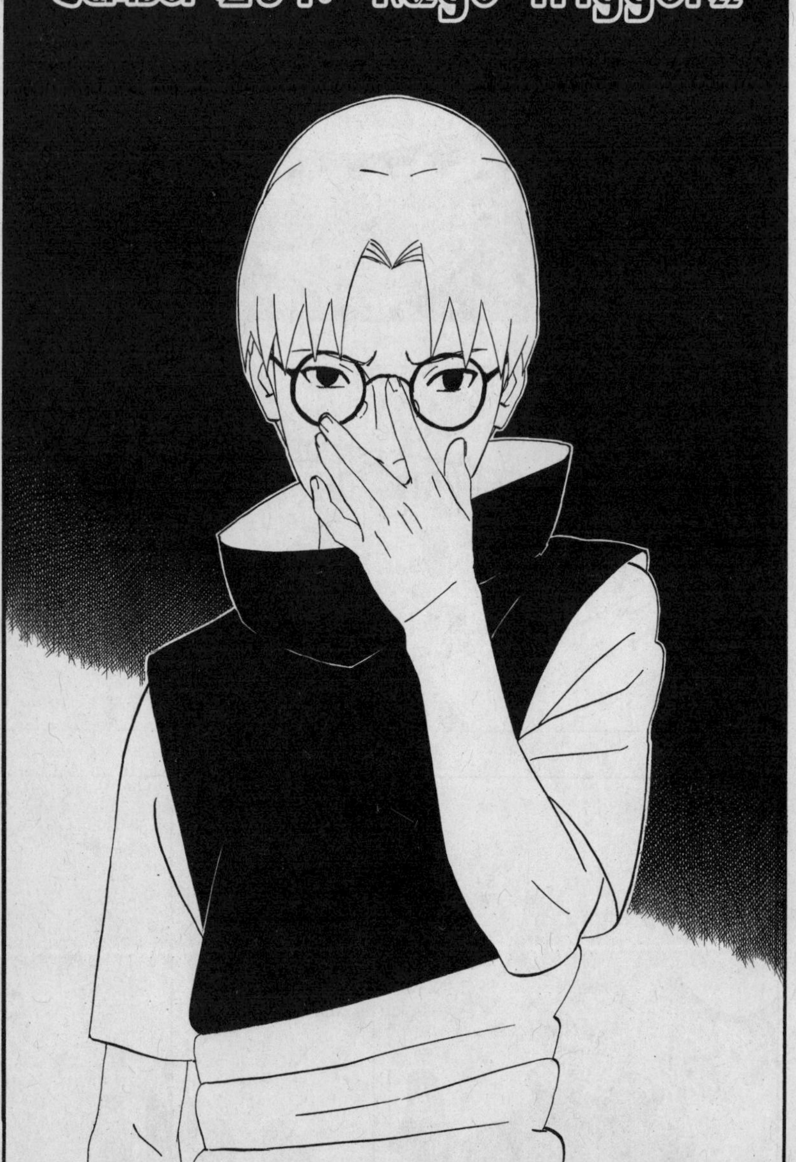

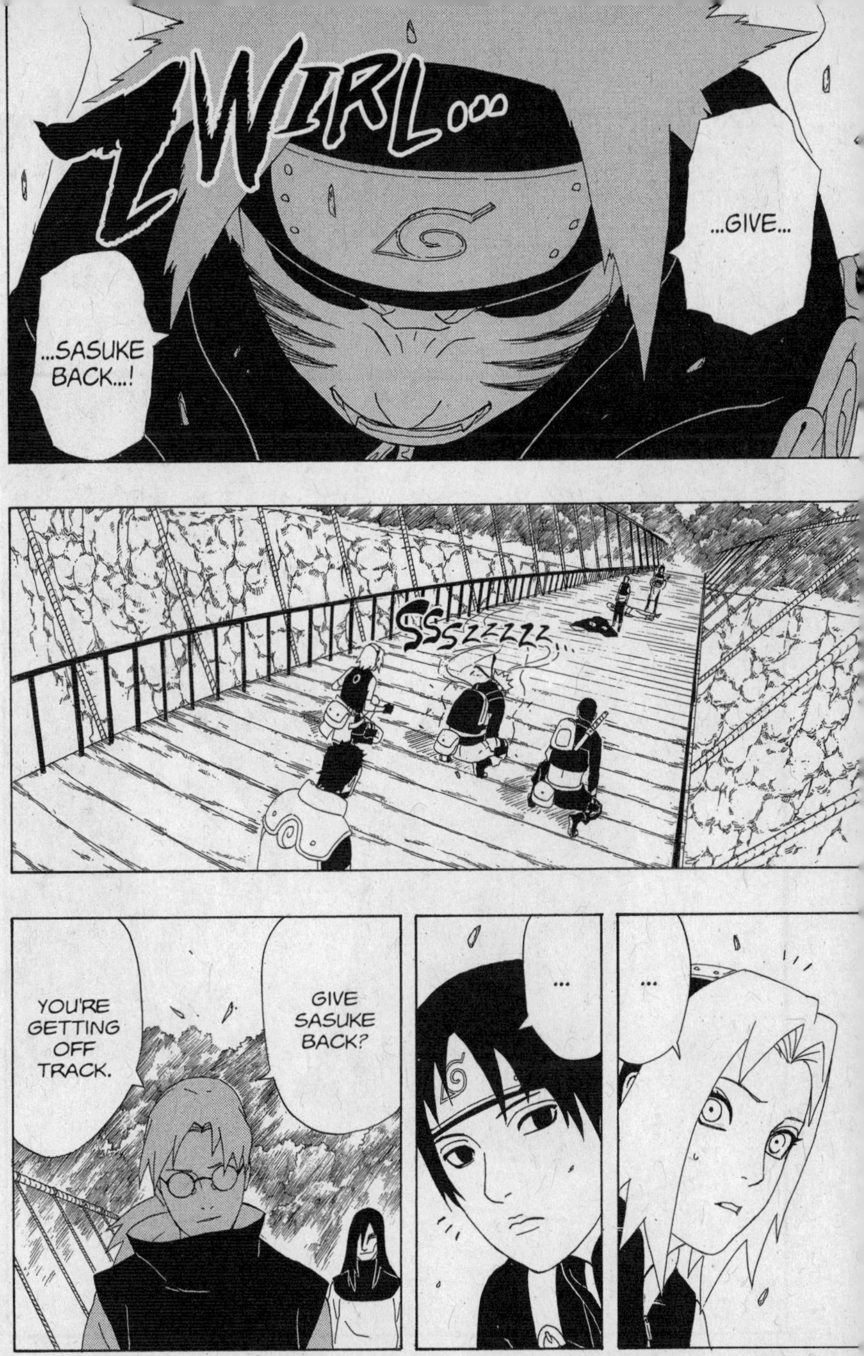
ZWIRL...
...GIVE...
...SASUKE BACK...!
SSSZZZZZZ...
...
...
GIVE SASUKE BACK?
YOU'RE GETTING OFF TRACK.

READ THIS WAY

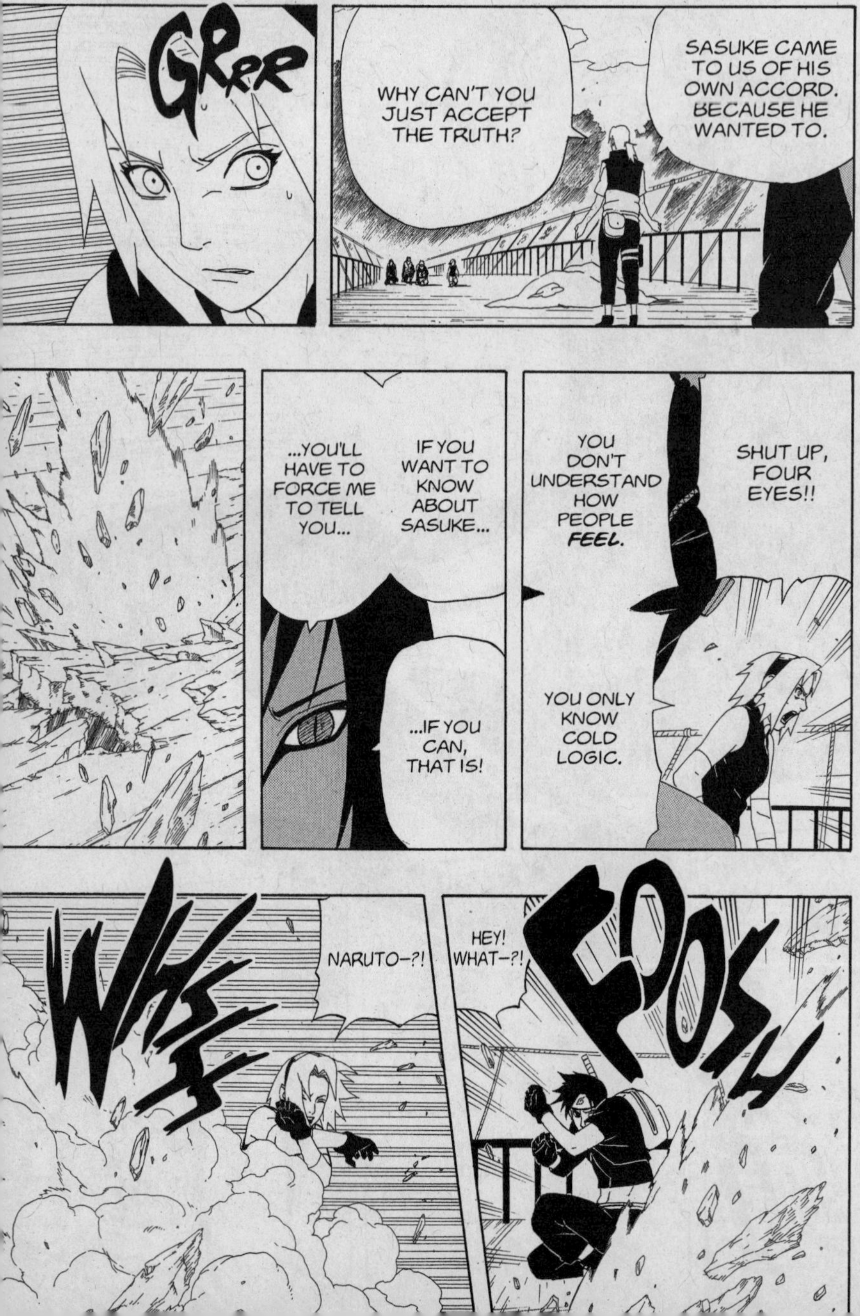
SASUKE CAME TO US OF HIS OWN ACCORD. BECAUSE HE WANTED TO.
WHY CAN'T YOU JUST ACCEPT THE TRUTH?
GRRR
SHUT UP, FOUR EYES!!
YOU DON'T UNDERSTAND HOW PEOPLE **FEEL.**
YOU ONLY KNOW COLD LOGIC.
IF YOU WANT TO KNOW ABOUT SASUKE...
...YOU'LL HAVE TO FORCE ME TO TELL YOU...
...IF YOU CAN, THAT IS!
HEY! WHAT–?!
FOOSH
NARUTO–?!
WHSH

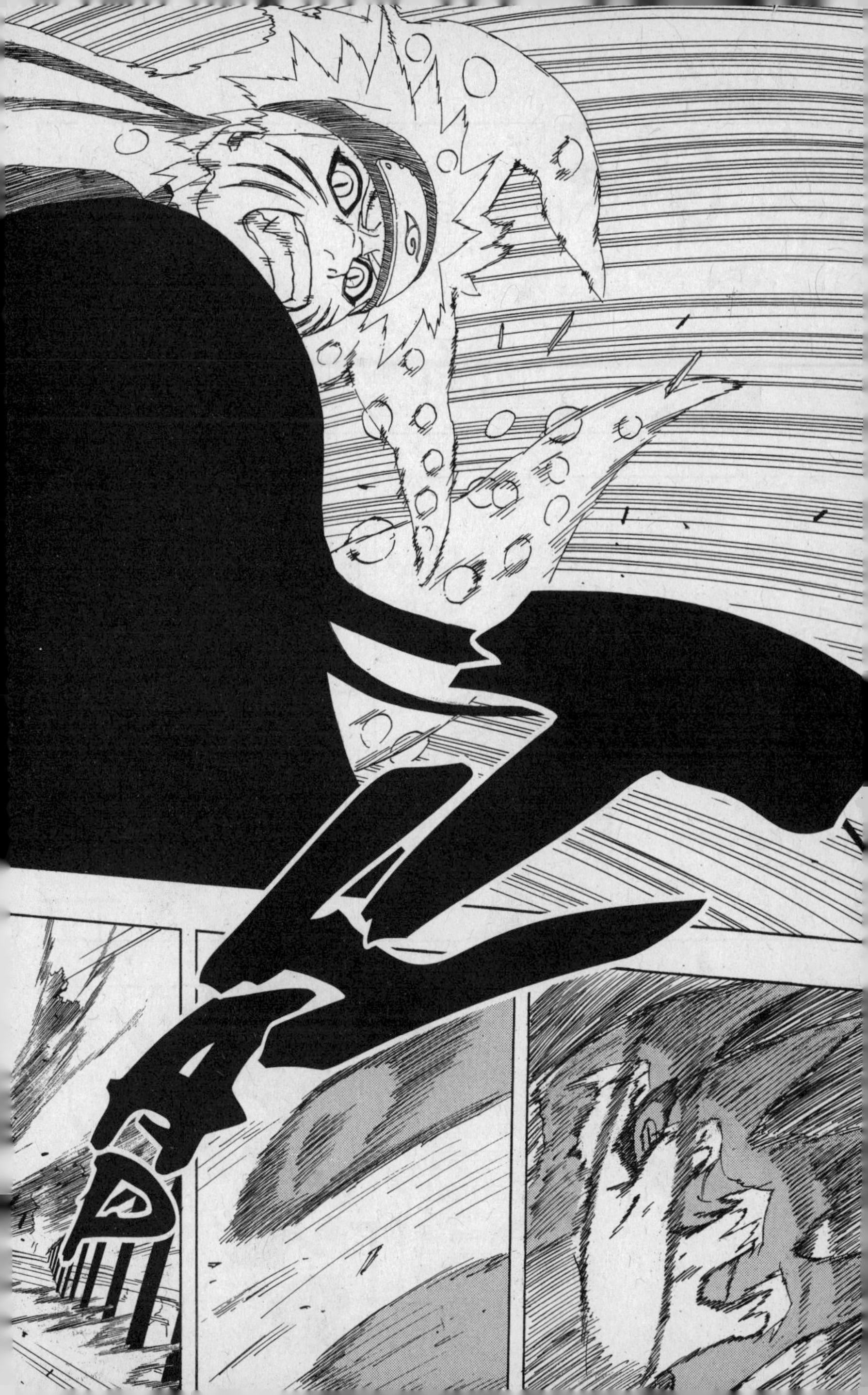

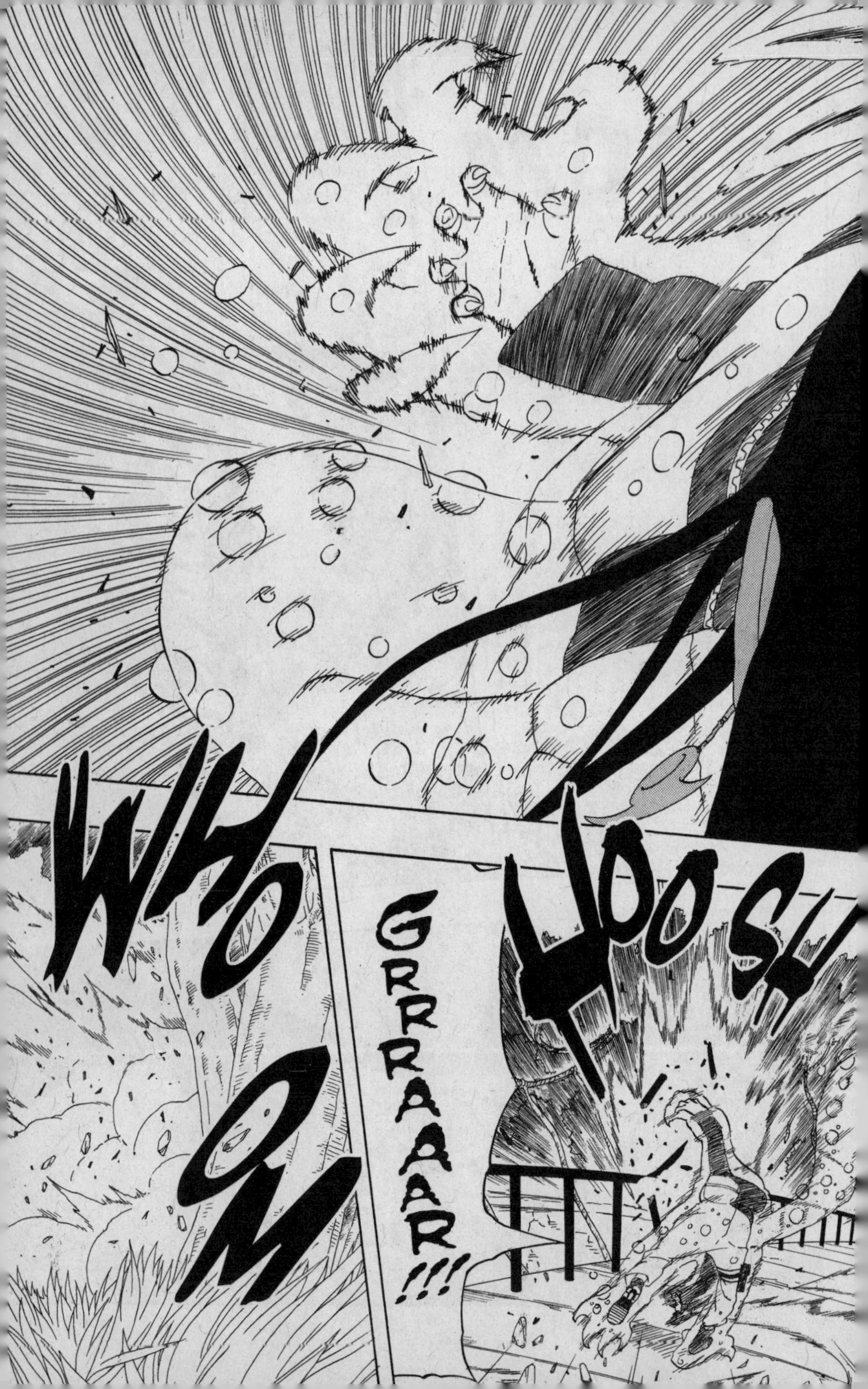
WHOOSH
GRRRAAAR!!!
WHOOM

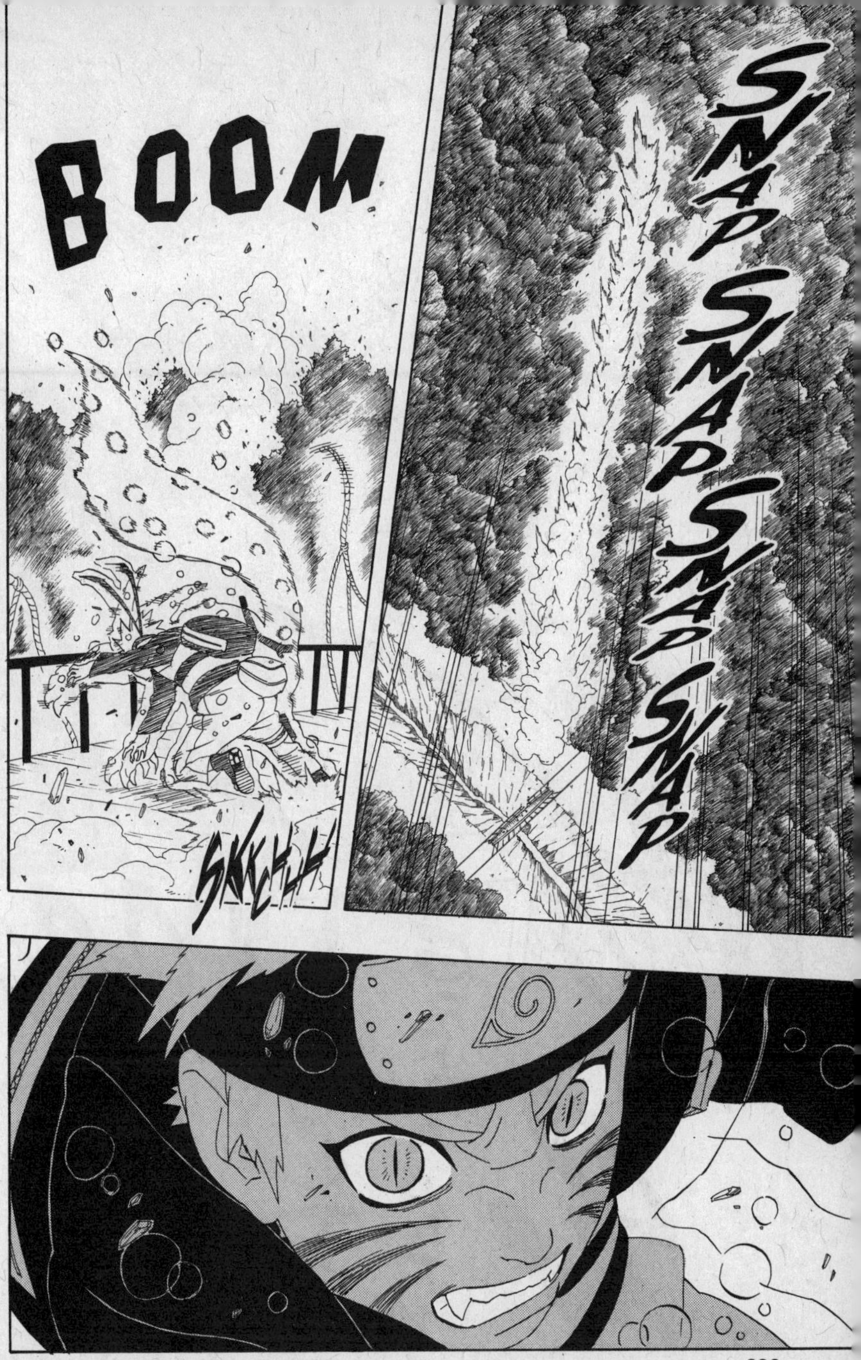
SNAP SNAP SNAP SNAP
BOOM

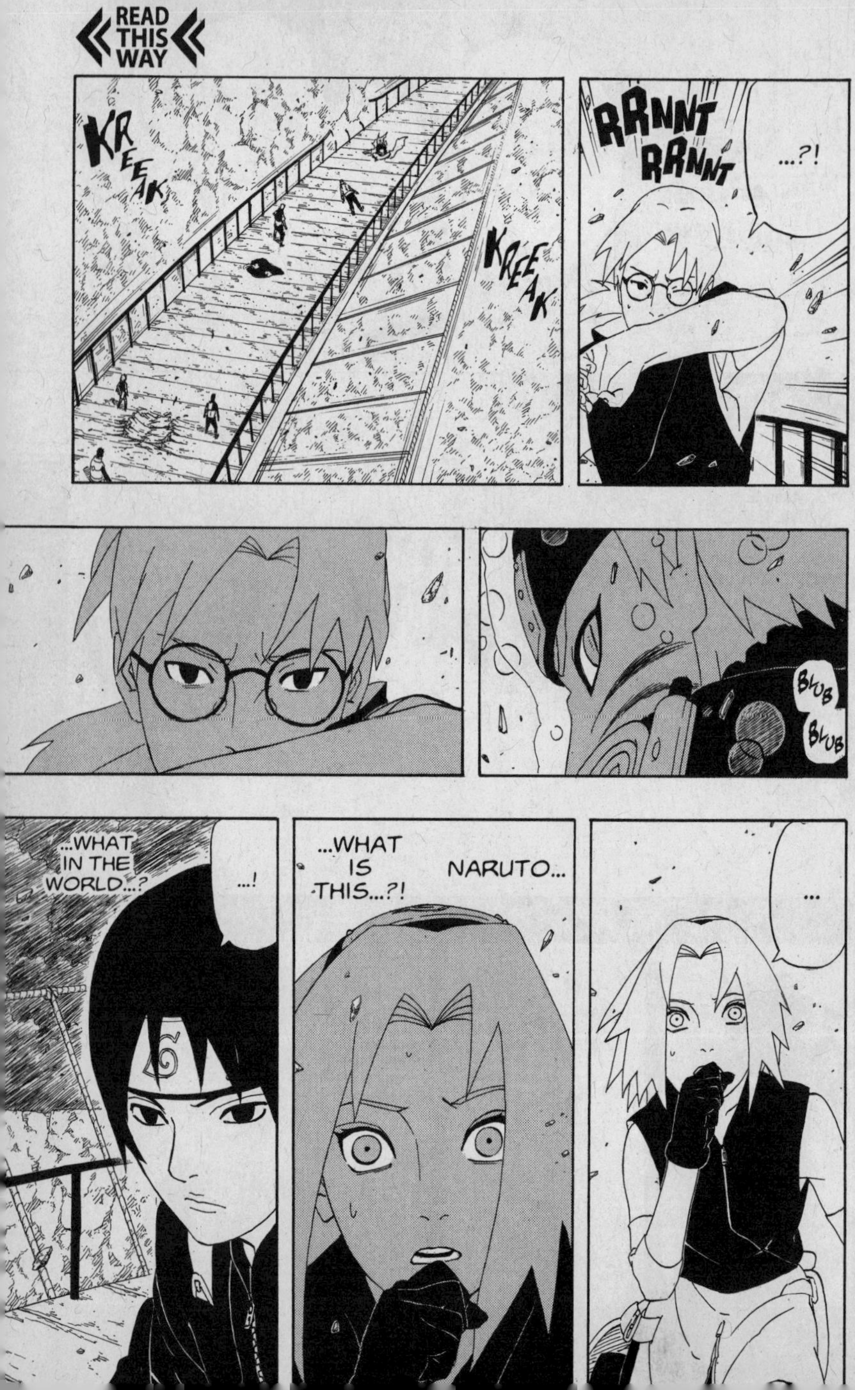
READ THIS WAY
RRNNT RRNNT
...?!
KREEAK
KREEAK
BLUB BLUB
...
NARUTO...
...WHAT IS THIS...?!
...!
...WHAT IN THE WORLD...?

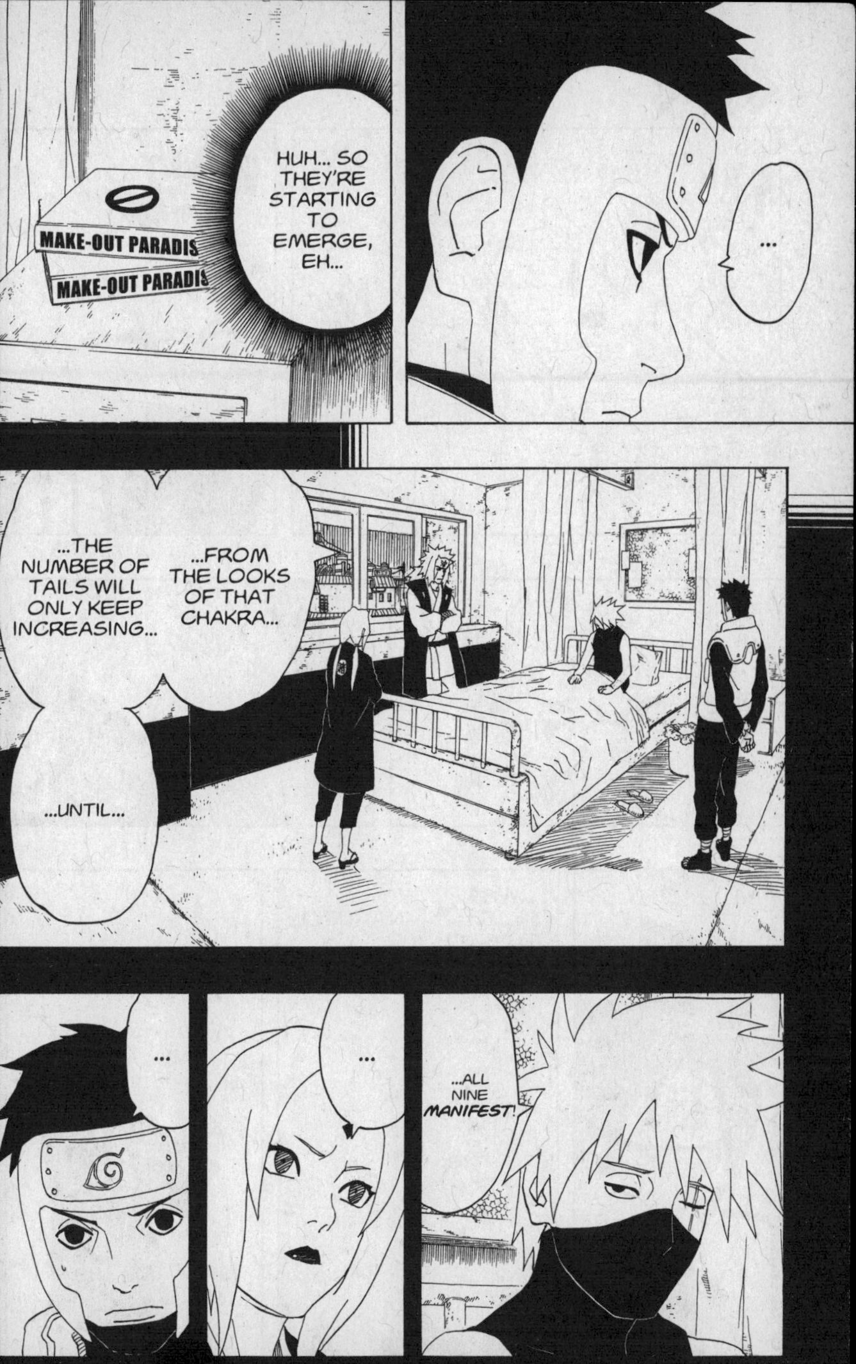
...
MAKE-OUT PARADIS
MAKE-OUT PARADIS
HUH... SO THEY'RE STARTING TO EMERGE, EH...
...FROM THE LOOKS OF THAT CHAKRA...
...THE NUMBER OF TAILS WILL ONLY KEEP INCREASING...
...UNTIL...
...ALL NINE *MANIFEST!*
...
...

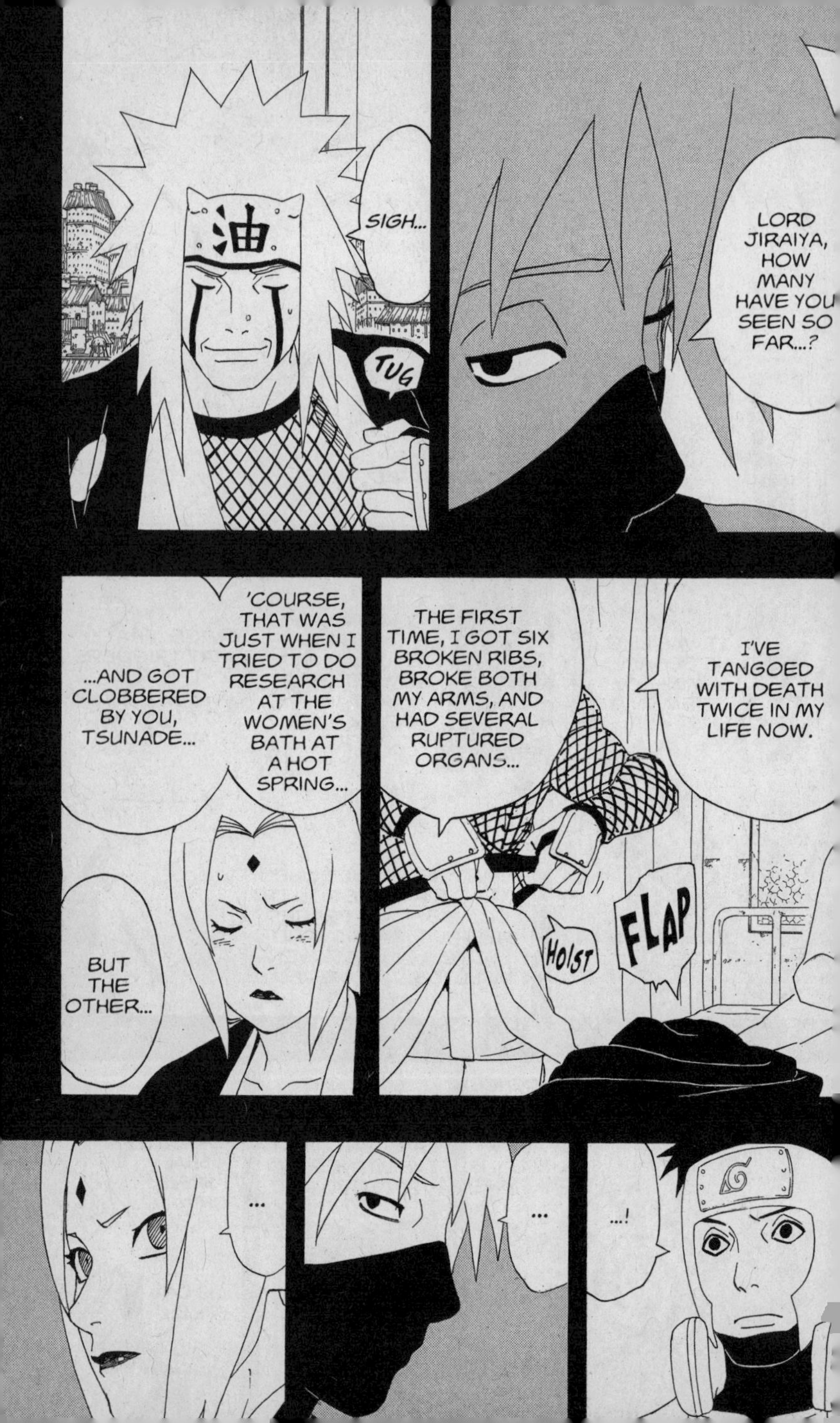
LORD JIRAIYA, HOW MANY HAVE YOU SEEN SO FAR...?
SIGH...
TUG
I'VE TANGOED WITH DEATH TWICE IN MY LIFE NOW.
THE FIRST TIME, I GOT SIX BROKEN RIBS, BROKE BOTH MY ARMS, AND HAD SEVERAL RUPTURED ORGANS...
FLAP
HOIST
'COURSE, THAT WAS JUST WHEN I TRIED TO DO RESEARCH AT THE WOMEN'S BATH AT A HOT SPRING...
...AND GOT CLOBBERED BY YOU, TSUNADE...
BUT THE OTHER...
...!
...
...

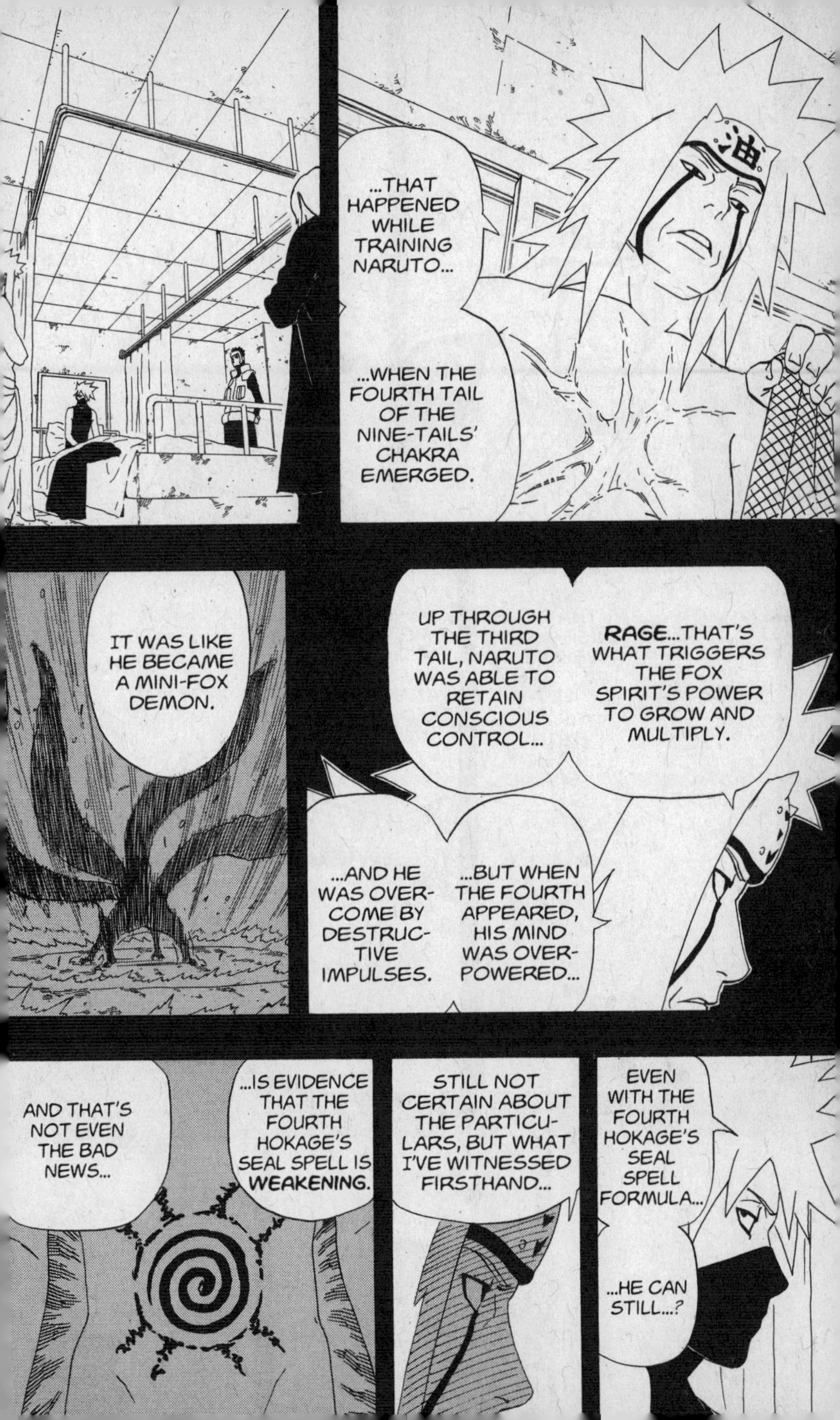
...THAT HAPPENED WHILE TRAINING NARUTO...
...WHEN THE FOURTH TAIL OF THE NINE-TAILS' CHAKRA EMERGED.
RAGE...THAT'S WHAT TRIGGERS THE FOX SPIRIT'S POWER TO GROW AND MULTIPLY.
UP THROUGH THE THIRD TAIL, NARUTO WAS ABLE TO RETAIN CONSCIOUS CONTROL...
...BUT WHEN THE FOURTH APPEARED, HIS MIND WAS OVER-POWERED...
...AND HE WAS OVER-COME BY DESTRUC-TIVE IMPULSES.
IT WAS LIKE HE BECAME A MINI-FOX DEMON.
EVEN WITH THE FOURTH HOKAGE'S SEAL SPELL FORMULA...
...HE CAN STILL...?
STILL NOT CERTAIN ABOUT THE PARTICU-LARS, BUT WHAT I'VE WITNESSED FIRSTHAND...
...IS EVIDENCE THAT THE FOURTH HOKAGE'S SEAL SPELL IS **WEAKENING**.
AND THAT'S NOT EVEN THE BAD NEWS...

READ THIS WAY

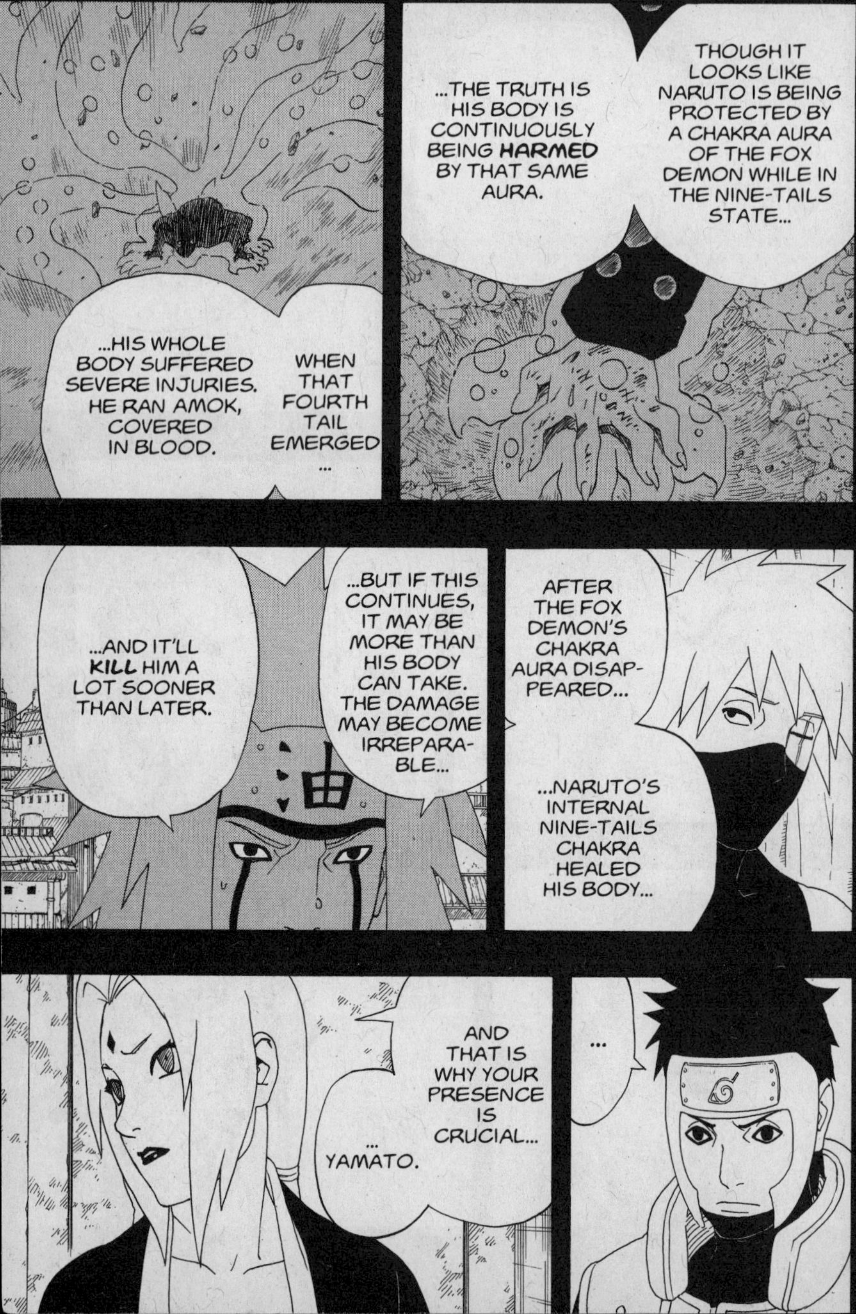
THOUGH IT LOOKS LIKE NARUTO IS BEING PROTECTED BY A CHAKRA AURA OF THE FOX DEMON WHILE IN THE NINE-TAILS STATE...
...THE TRUTH IS HIS BODY IS CONTINUOUSLY BEING **HARMED** BY THAT SAME AURA.
WHEN THAT FOURTH TAIL EMERGED...
...HIS WHOLE BODY SUFFERED SEVERE INJURIES. HE RAN AMOK, COVERED IN BLOOD.
AFTER THE FOX DEMON'S CHAKRA AURA DISAP-PEARED...
...NARUTO'S INTERNAL NINE-TAILS CHAKRA HEALED HIS BODY...
...BUT IF THIS CONTINUES, IT MAY BE MORE THAN HIS BODY CAN TAKE. THE DAMAGE MAY BECOME IRREPARA-BLE...
...AND IT'LL **KILL** HIM A LOT SOONER THAN LATER.
...
AND THAT IS WHY YOUR PRESENCE IS CRUCIAL...
...YAMATO.

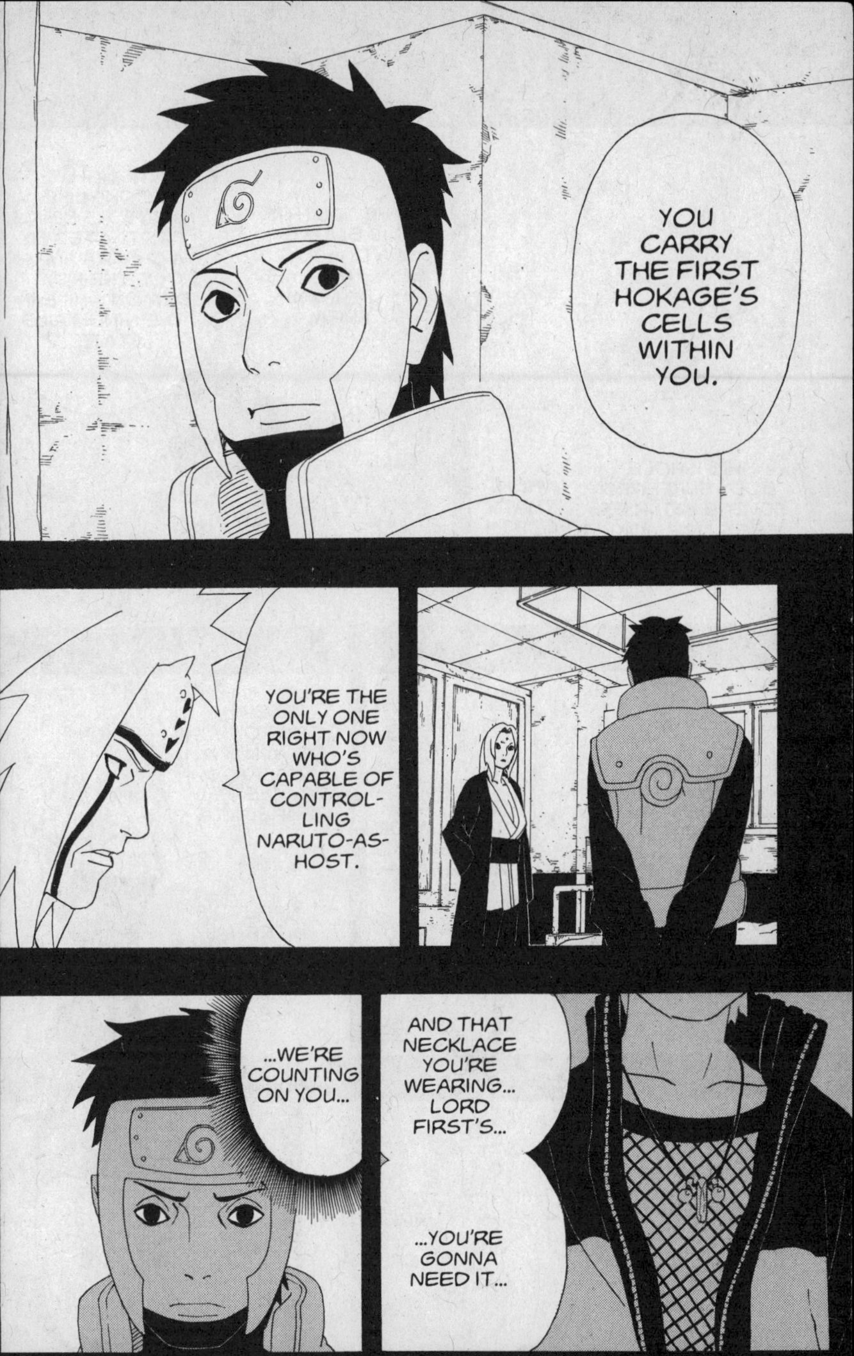
YOU CARRY THE FIRST HOKAGE'S CELLS WITHIN YOU.
YOU'RE THE ONLY ONE RIGHT NOW WHO'S CAPABLE OF CONTROL-LING NARUTO-AS-HOST.
AND THAT NECKLACE YOU'RE WEARING... LORD FIRST'S...
...YOU'RE GONNA NEED IT...
...WE'RE COUNTING ON YOU...

READ THIS WAY

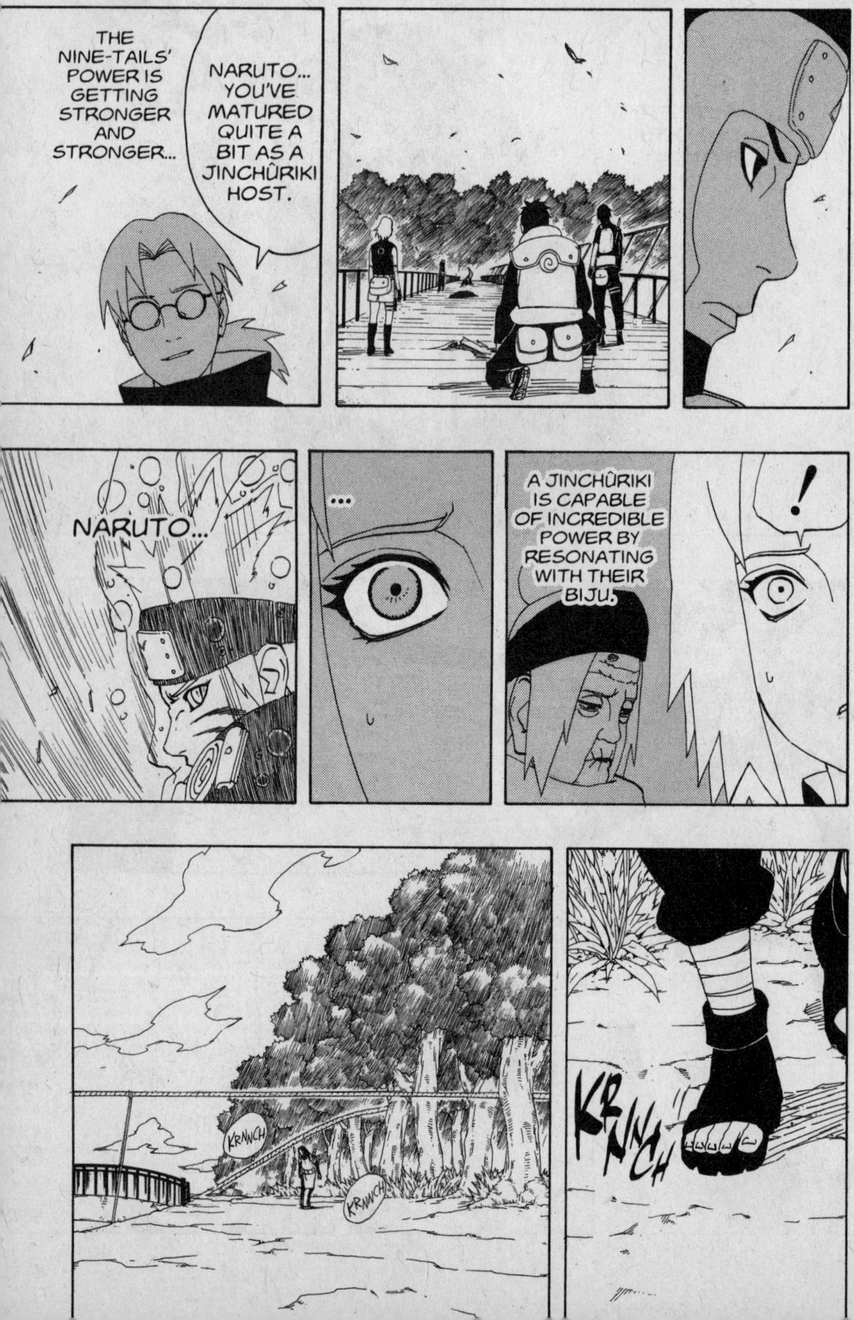

NARUTO... YOU'VE MATURED QUITE A BIT AS A JINCHÛRIKI HOST.
THE NINE-TAILS' POWER IS GETTING STRONGER AND STRONGER...
!
A JINCHÛRIKI IS CAPABLE OF INCREDIBLE POWER BY RESONATING WITH THEIR BIJU.
...
NARUTO...
KRNNCH
KRNNCH
KRNNCH

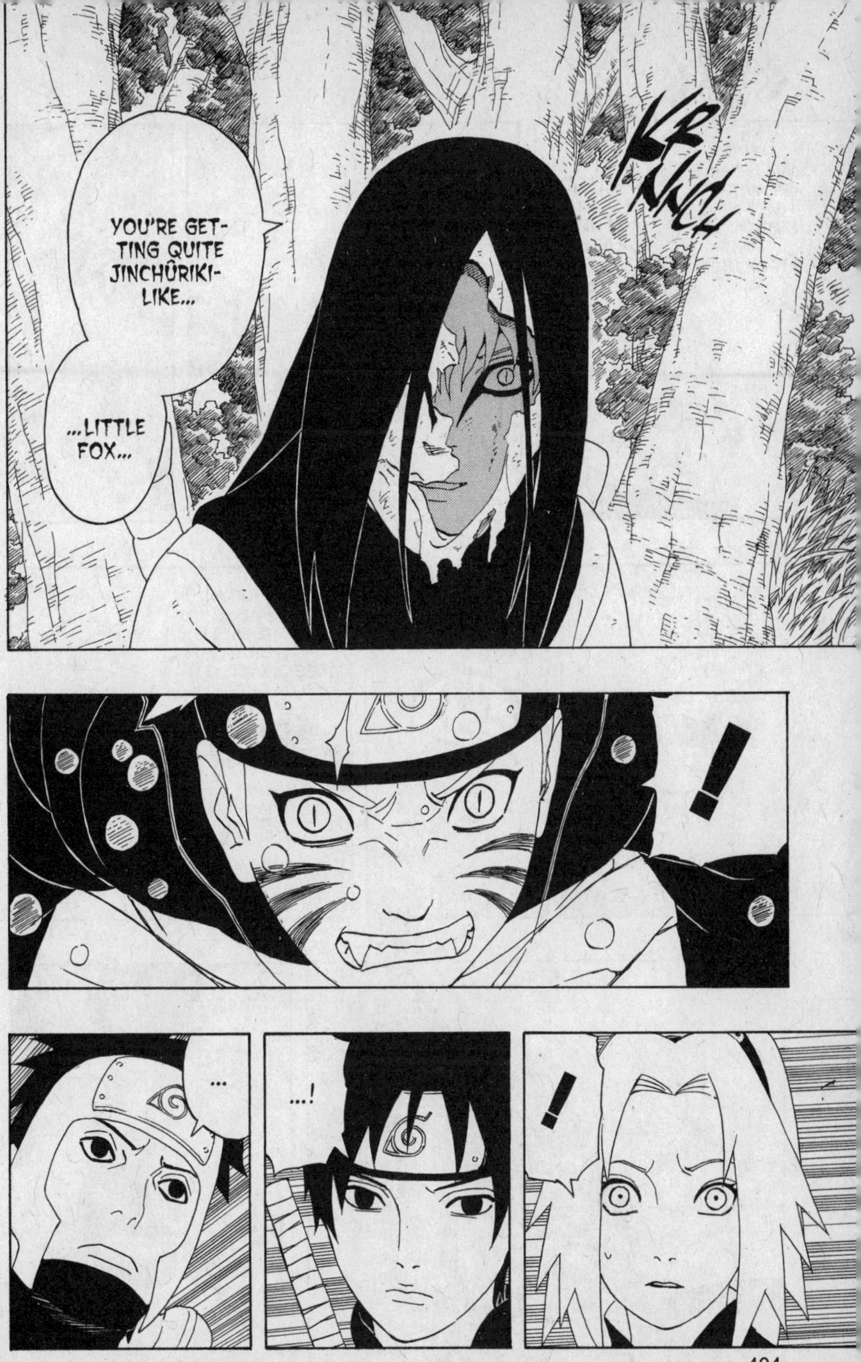
KRNNCH
YOU'RE GETTING QUITE JINCHÛRIKI-LIKE...
...LITTLE FOX...
!
!
...!
...

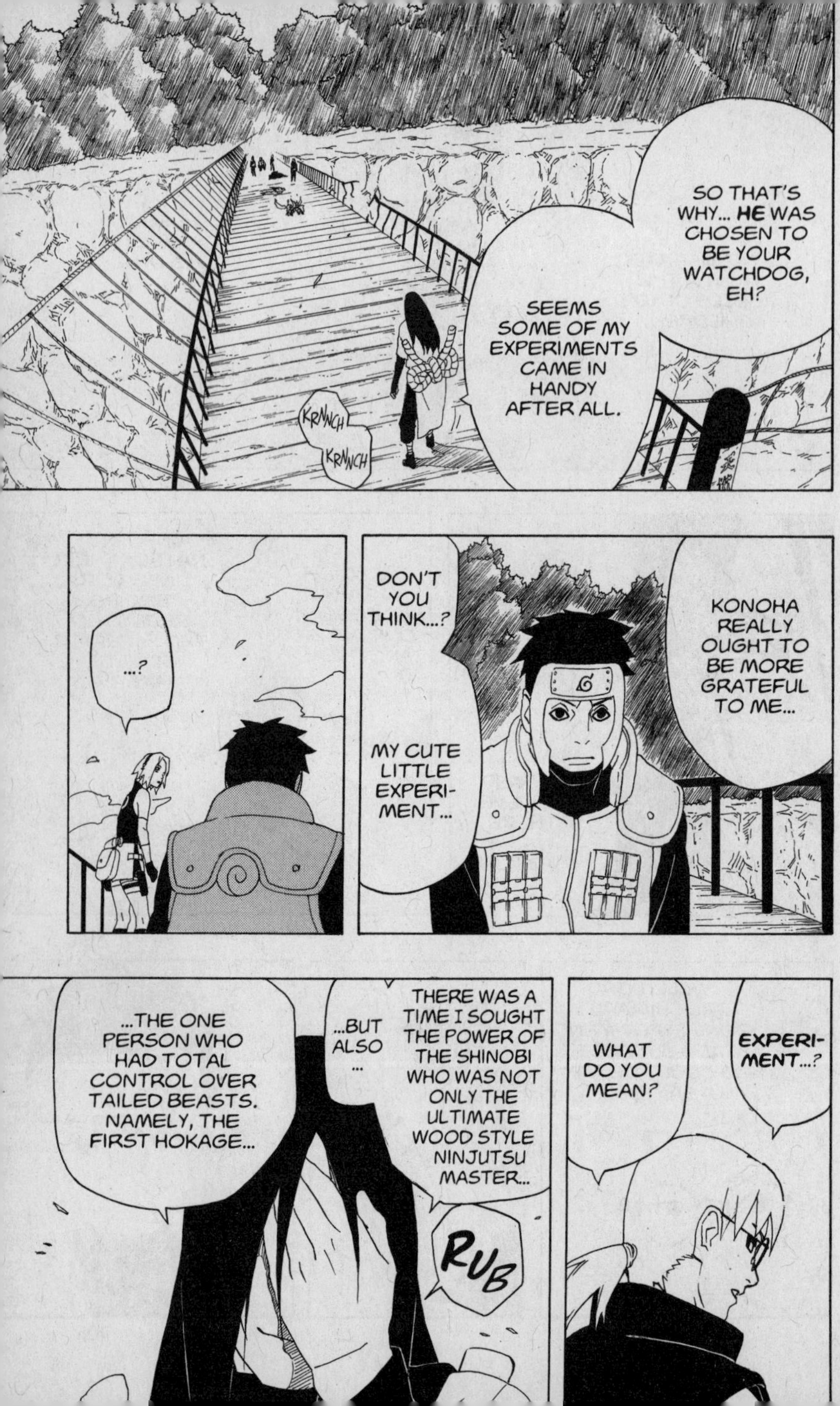
SO THAT'S WHY... **HE** WAS CHOSEN TO BE YOUR WATCHDOG, EH?
SEEMS SOME OF MY EXPERIMENTS CAME IN HANDY AFTER ALL.
KRNNCH
KRNNCH
KONOHA REALLY OUGHT TO BE MORE GRATEFUL TO ME...
DON'T YOU THINK...?
MY CUTE LITTLE EXPERIMENT...
...?
EXPERIMENT...?
WHAT DO YOU MEAN?
THERE WAS A TIME I SOUGHT THE POWER OF THE SHINOBI WHO WAS NOT ONLY THE ULTIMATE WOOD STYLE NINJUTSU MASTER...
...BUT ALSO ...
...THE ONE PERSON WHO HAD TOTAL CONTROL OVER TAILED BEASTS. NAMELY, THE FIRST HOKAGE...
RUB

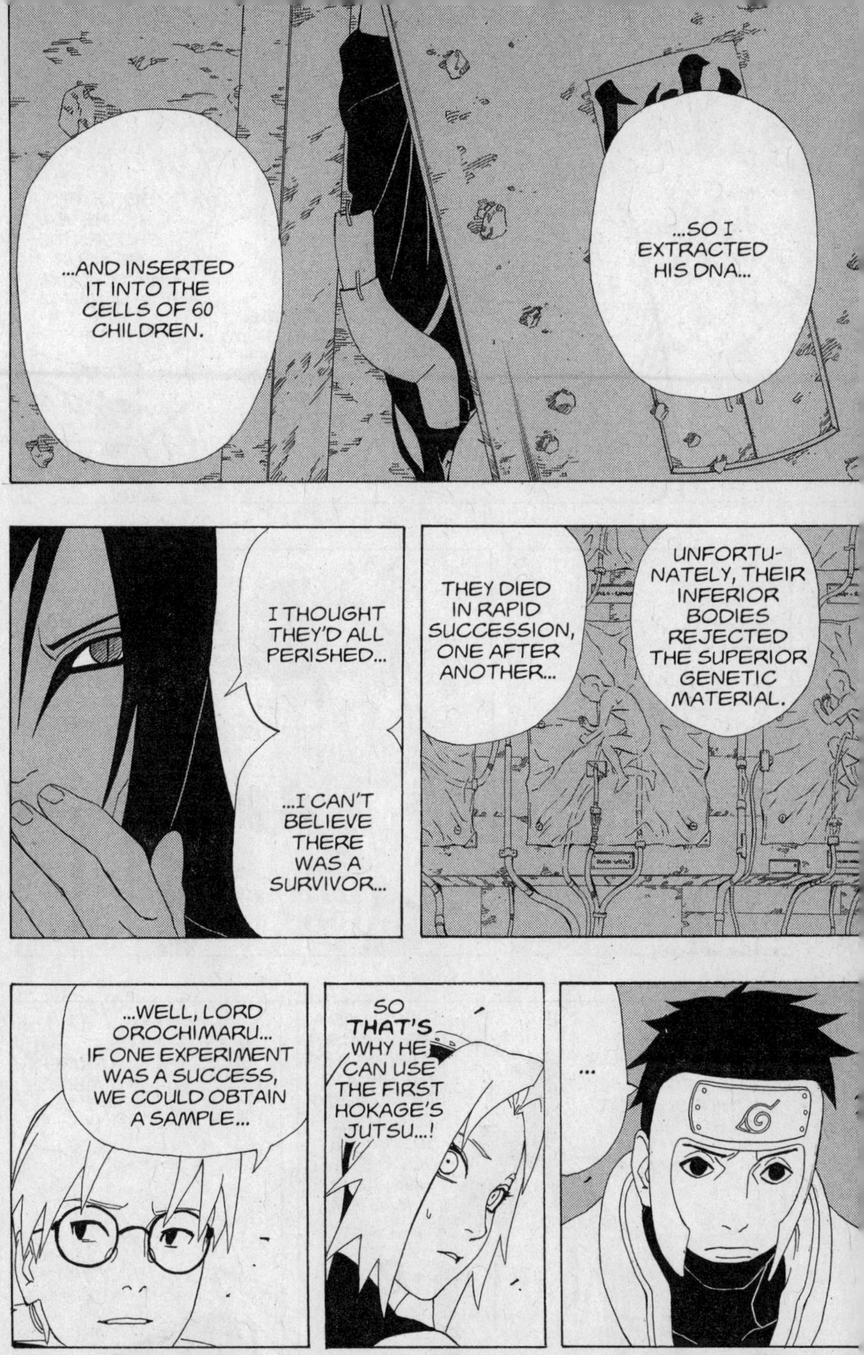
...SO I EXTRACTED HIS DNA...
...AND INSERTED IT INTO THE CELLS OF 60 CHILDREN.
UNFORTUNATELY, THEIR INFERIOR BODIES REJECTED THE SUPERIOR GENETIC MATERIAL.
THEY DIED IN RAPID SUCCESSION, ONE AFTER ANOTHER...
I THOUGHT THEY'D ALL PERISHED...
...I CAN'T BELIEVE THERE WAS A SURVIVOR...
...
SO **THAT'S** WHY HE CAN USE THE FIRST HOKAGE'S JUTSU...!
...WELL, LORD OROCHIMARU... IF ONE EXPERIMENT WAS A SUCCESS, WE COULD OBTAIN A SAMPLE...

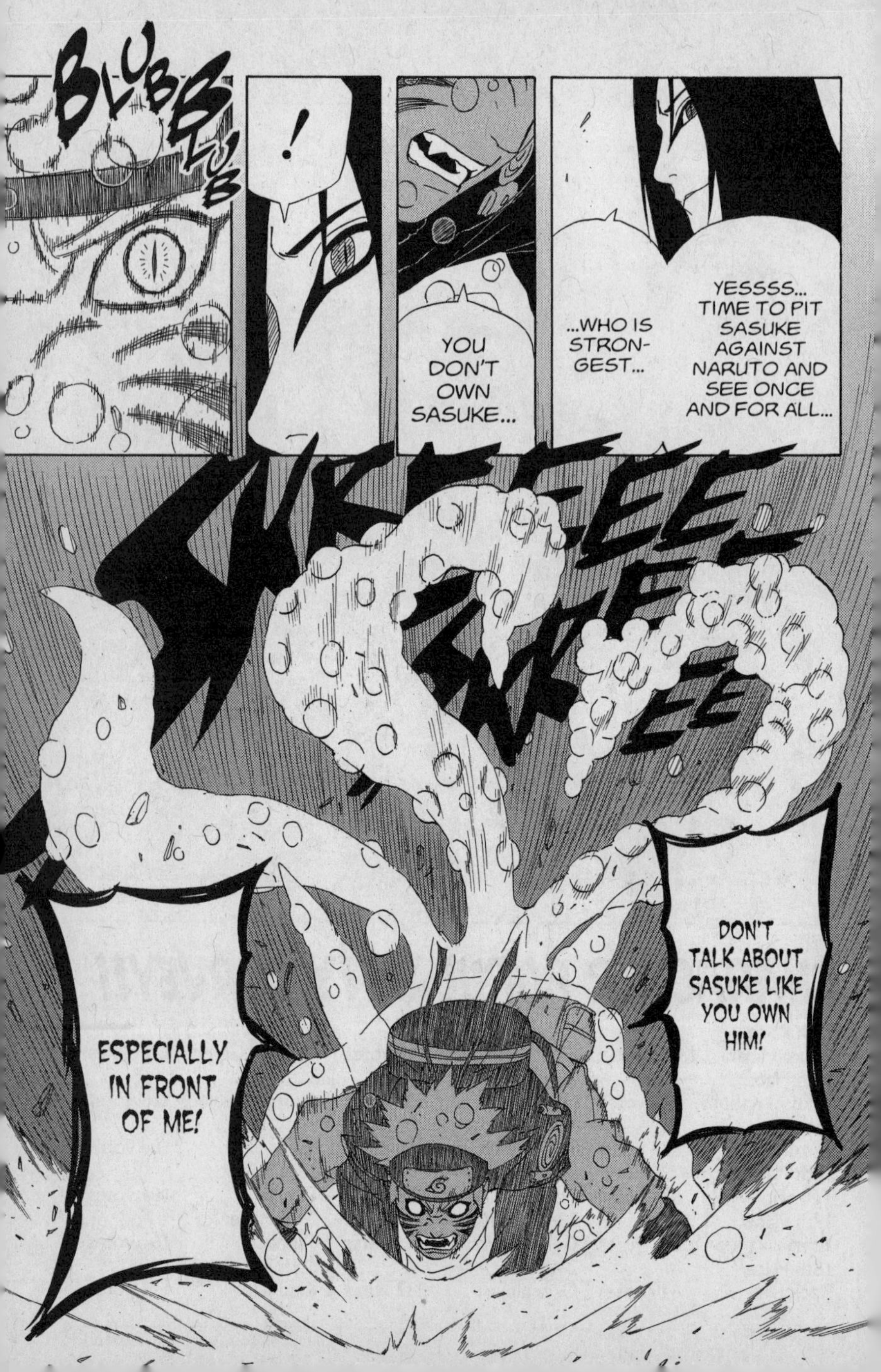
YESSSS... TIME TO PIT SASUKE AGAINST NARUTO AND SEE ONCE AND FOR ALL...
...WHO IS STRONG-GEST...
YOU DON'T OWN SASUKE...
!
BLUBB
BLUB
DON'T TALK ABOUT SASUKE LIKE YOU OWN HIM!
ESPECIALLY IN FRONT OF ME!

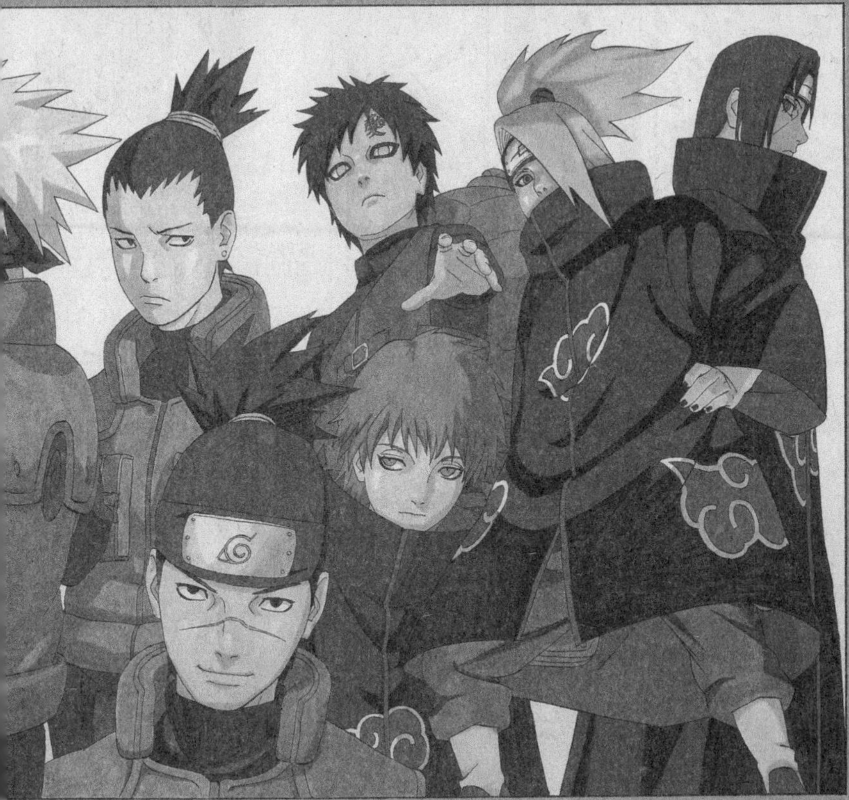

CHARACTER POPULARITY SURVEY!!

13th Place/ Hyuga Hinata	1,048 votes
14th Place/ Yakushi Kabuto	829 votes
15th Place/ Inuzuka Kiba	677 votes
16th Place/ Temari	671 votes
17th Place/ Yamanaka Ino	662 votes
18th Place/ Rock Lee	640 votes
19th Place/ Kankuro	519 votes
20th Place/ Might Guy	503 votes
21st Place/ Sarutobi Asuma	449 votes
22nd Place/ Tenten	395 votes
23rd Place/ Gekko Hayate	283 votes
24th Place/ Orochimaru	237 votes
25th Place/ Shiranui Genma	230 votes
26th Place/ Aburame Shino	226 votes
27th Place/ Haku	168 votes
28th Place/ Tayuya	164 votes
29th Place/ Tsunade	161 votes
30th Place/ Kimimaro	148 votes

(This poll conducted in Japan.)

Number 292: The Third Tail...!!

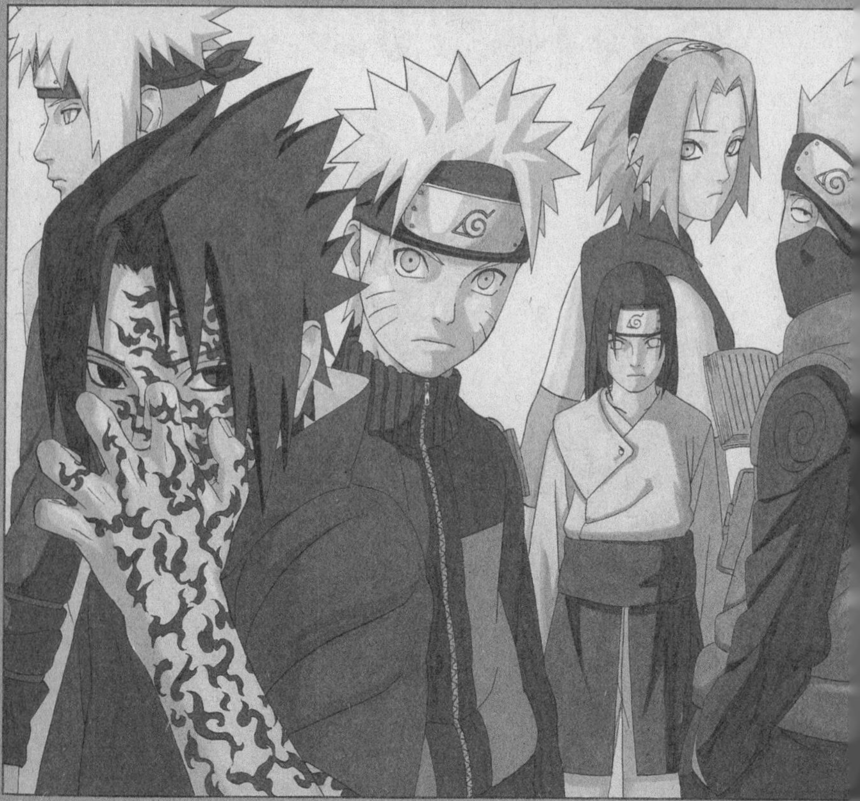

THE RESULTS OF THE SIXTH

1st Place/Uchiha Sasuke	3,242 votes	7th Place/Gaara	1,934 votes
2nd Place/Hatake Kakashi	2,916 votes	8th Place/Hyuga Neji	1,785 votes
3rd Place/Deidara	2,555 votes	9th Place/Fourth Hokage	1,458 votes
4th Place/Uzumaki Naruto	2,283 votes	10th Place/Nara Shikamaru	1,409 votes
5th Place/Umino Iruka	2,232 votes	11th Place/Uchiha Itachi	1,369 votes
6th Place/Sasori	1,949 votes	12th Place/Haruno Sakura	1,359 votes

NARUTO

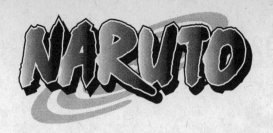

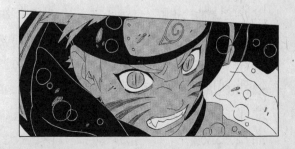

READ THIS WAY

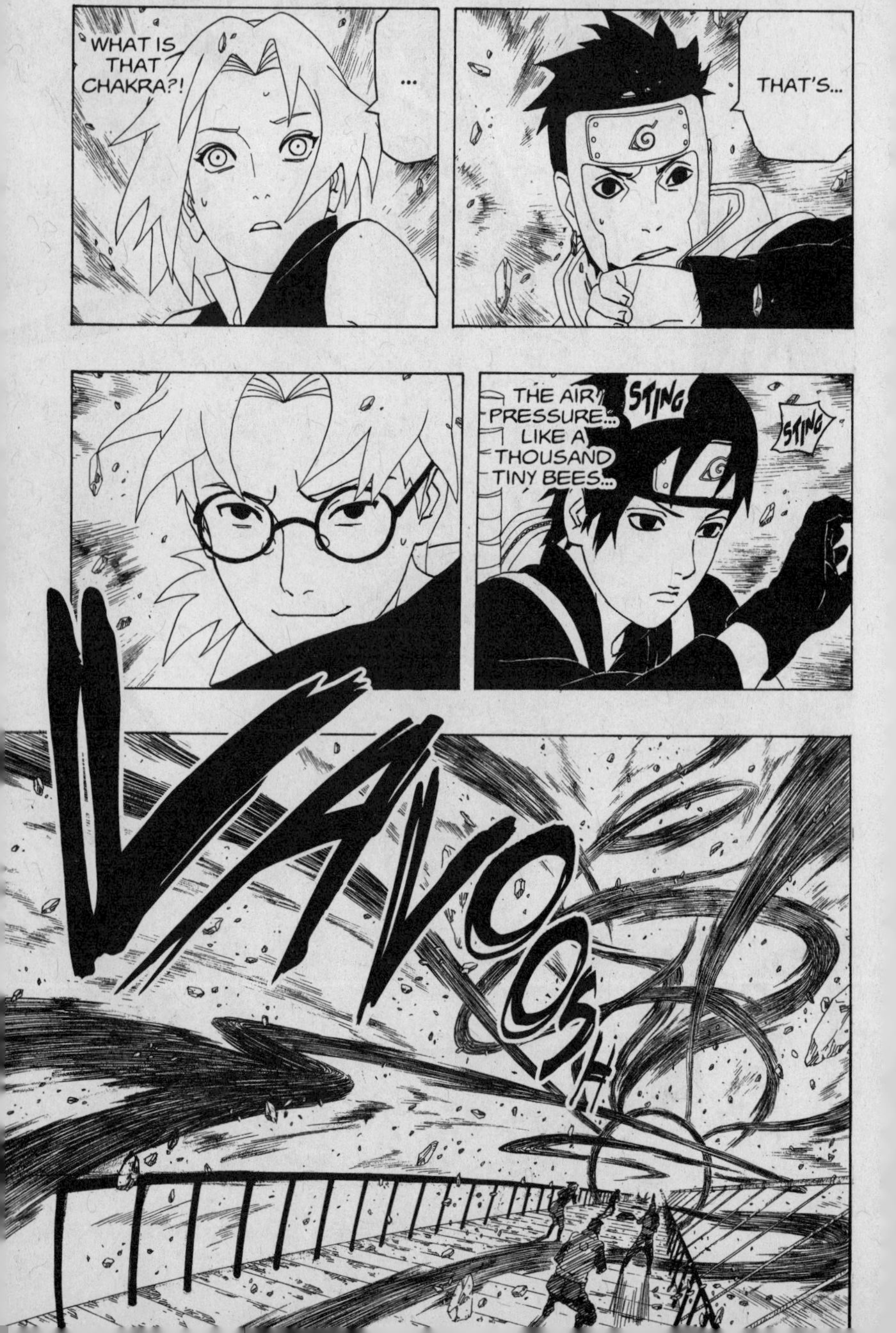
THAT'S...
...
WHAT IS THAT CHAKRA?!
STING
STING
THE AIR PRESSURE... LIKE A THOUSAND TINY BEES...
WOOSH!

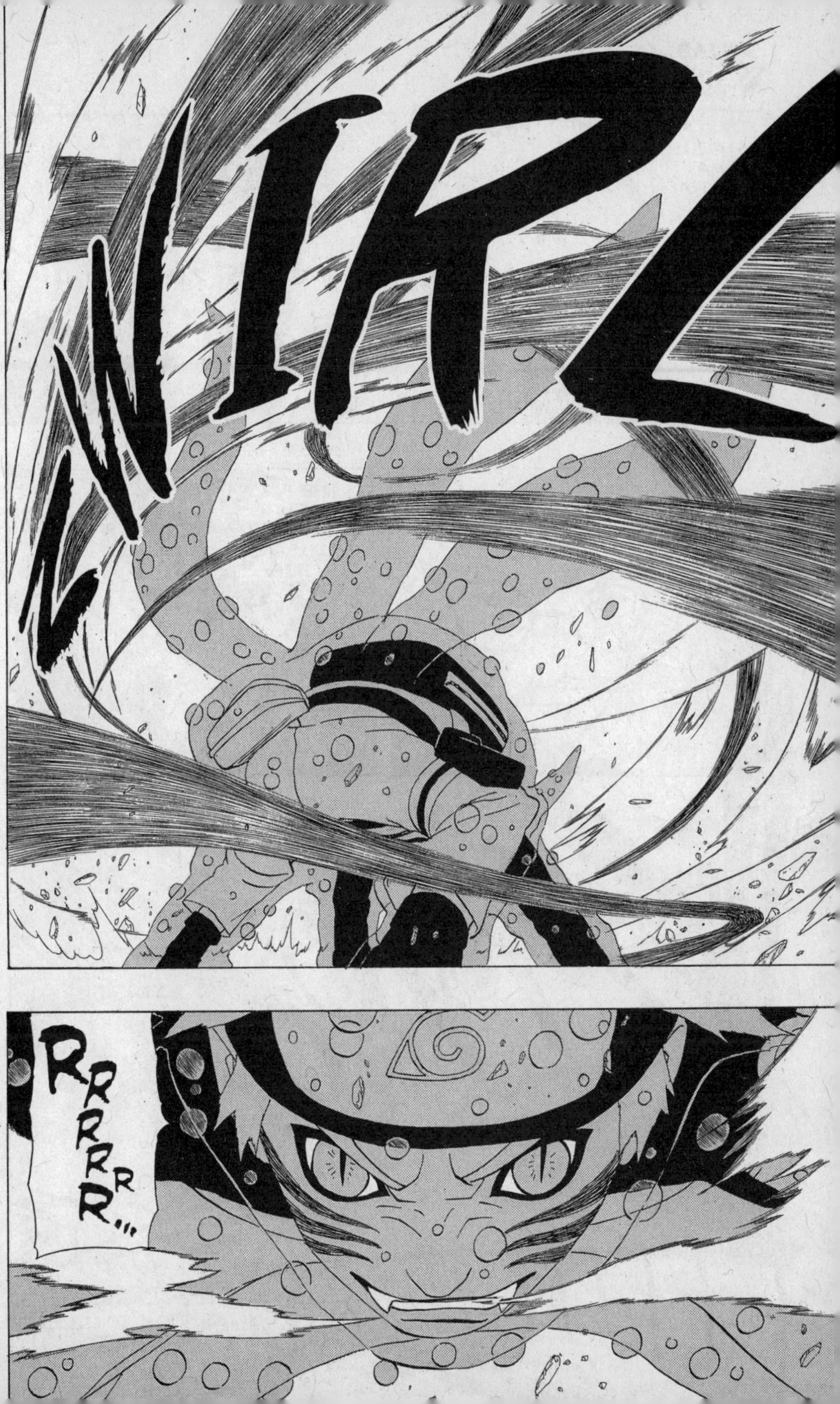
SWIRL
RRRRRR...

READ THIS WAY

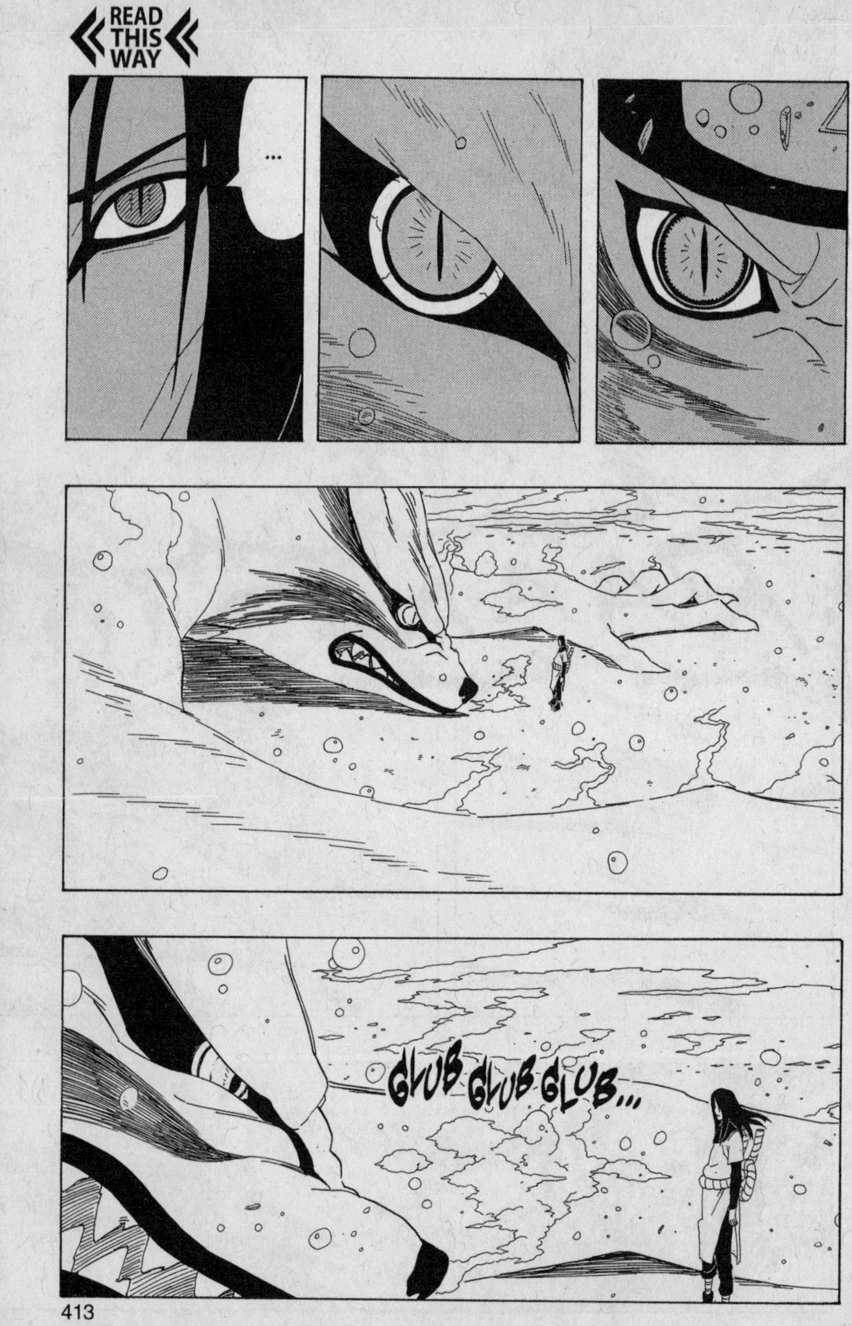
...
GLUB GLUB GLUB...

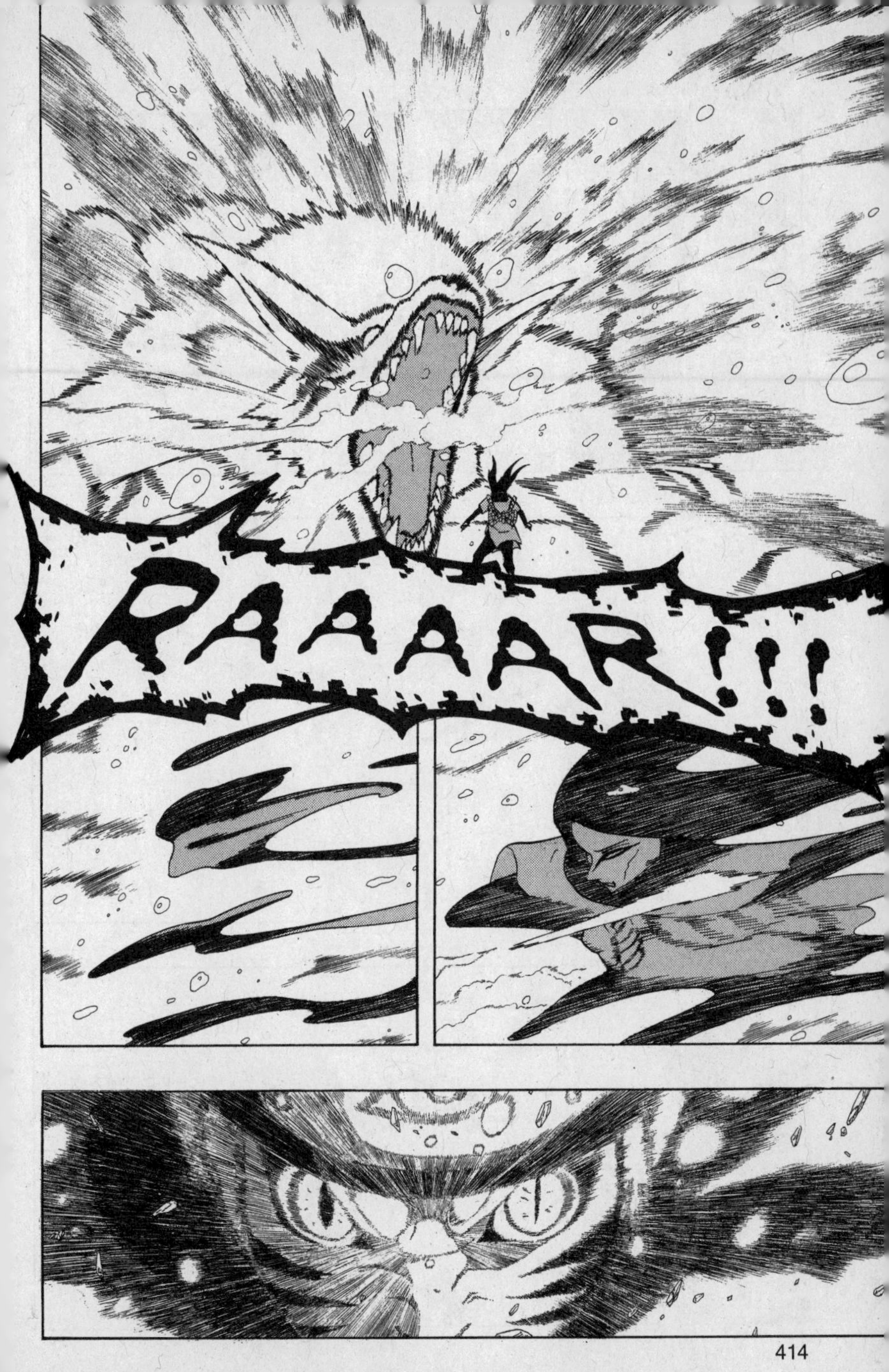
RAAAAR!!!

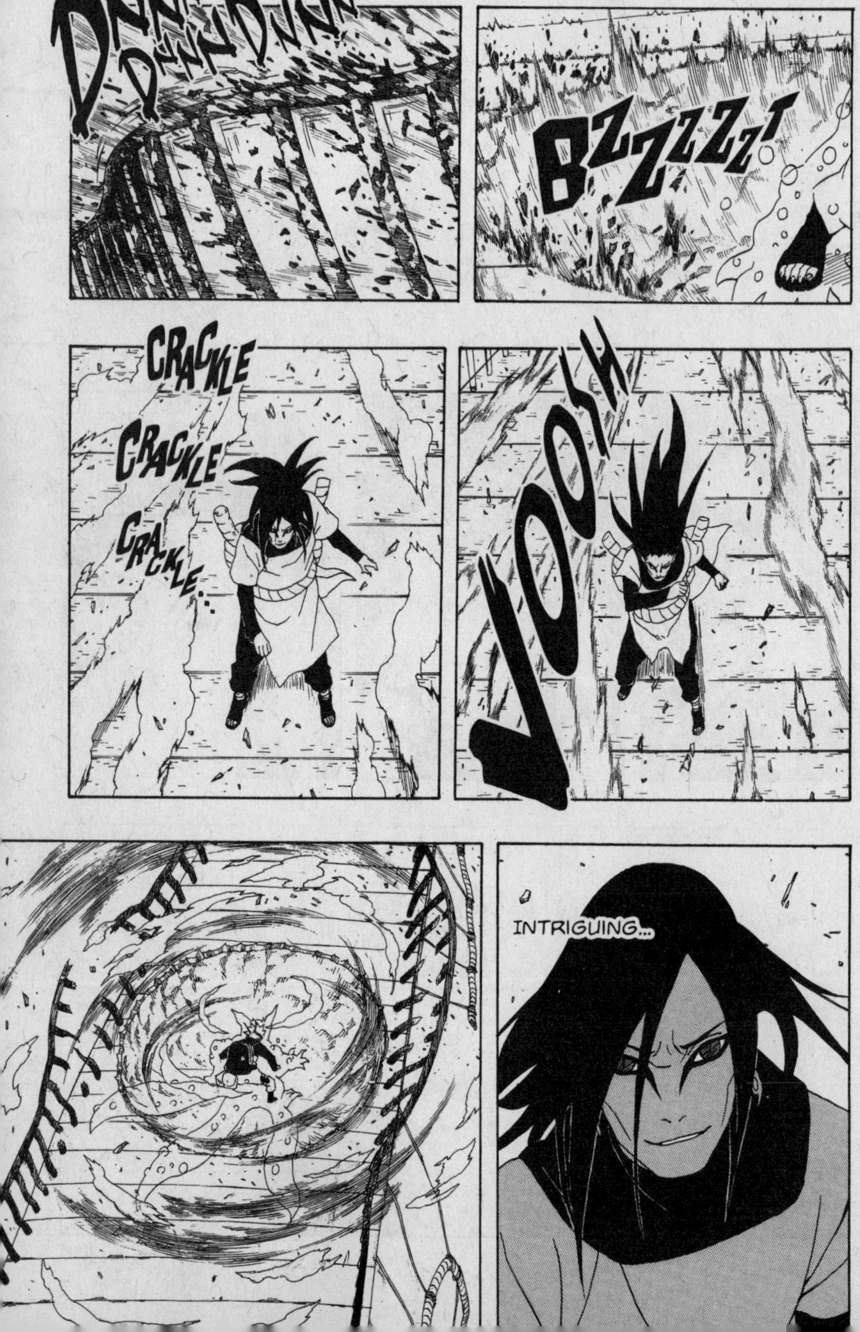
BZZZZZT
DNNN DNNN DNNN
VOOOSH
CRACKLE
CRACKLE
CRACKLE
INTRIGUING...

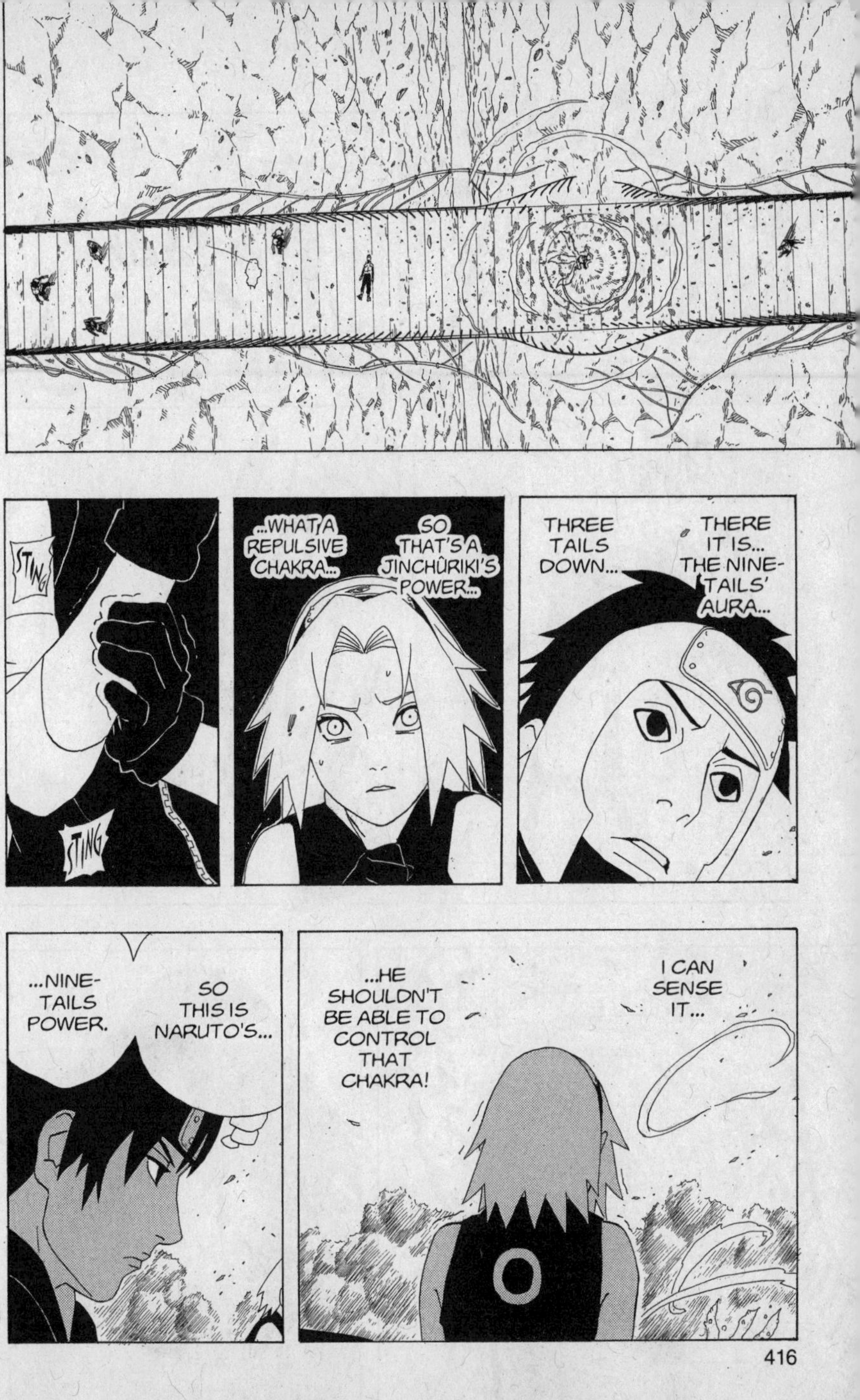
THERE IT IS... THE NINE-TAILS' AURA...
THREE TAILS DOWN...
SO THAT'S A JINCHÛRIKI'S POWER...
...WHAT A REPULSIVE CHAKRA...
STING
STING
I CAN SENSE IT...
...HE SHOULDN'T BE ABLE TO CONTROL THAT CHAKRA!
SO THIS IS NARUTO'S...
...NINE-TAILS POWER.

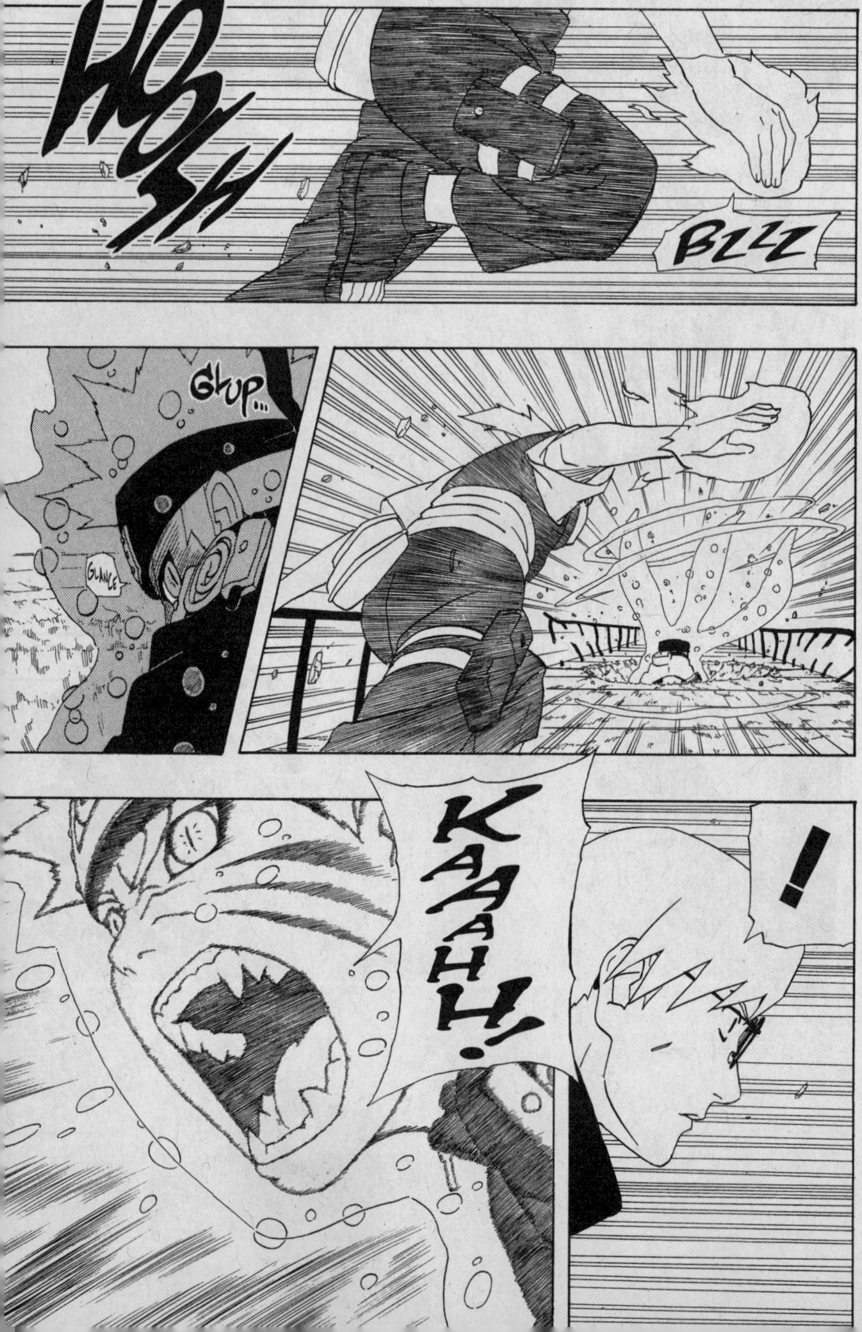
WHOSH
BZZZ
GULP...
GLANCE
!
KAAAHH!

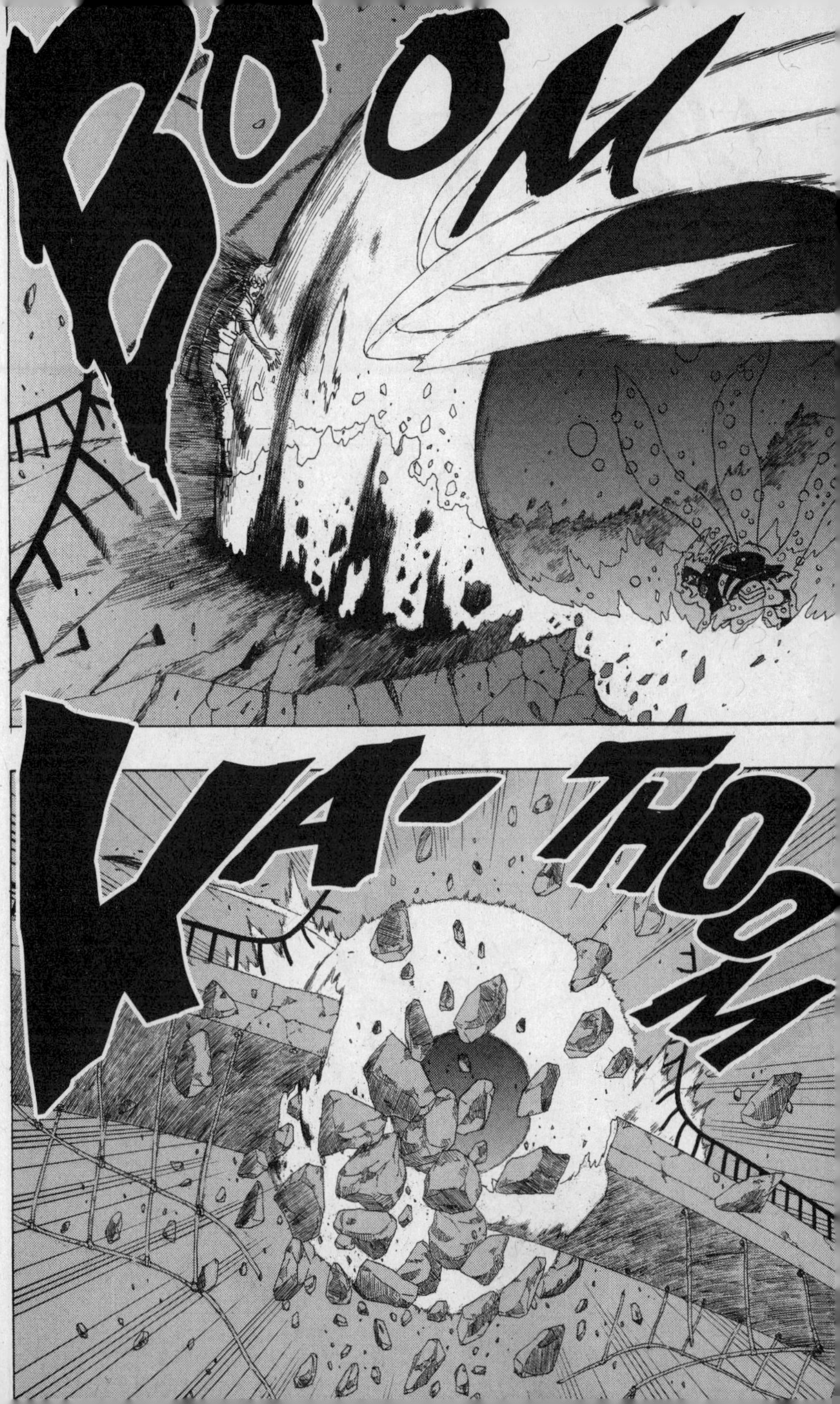
BOOM
KA-THOOM

READ THIS WAY

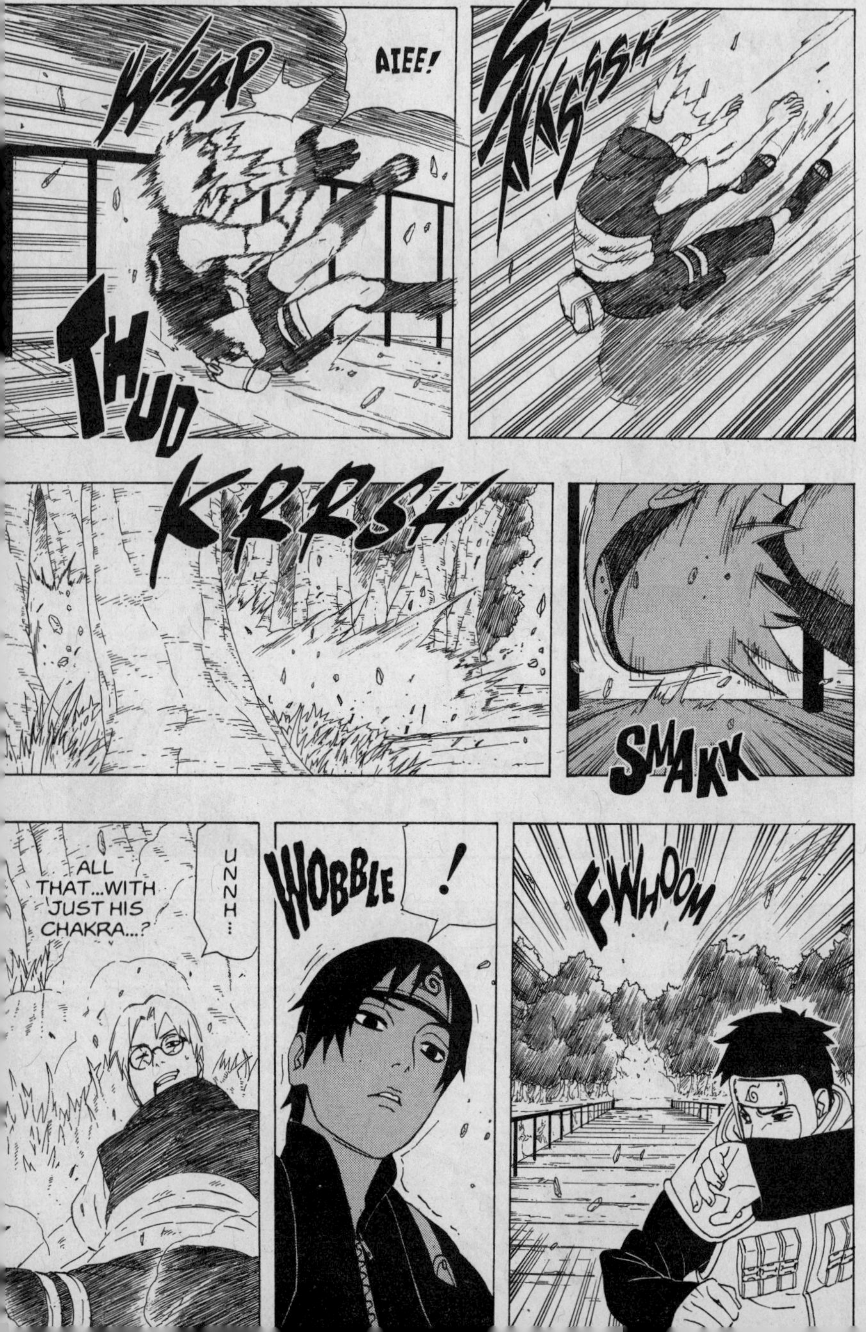
SHKSSSH
AIEE!
WHAP
THUD
SMAKK
KRRSH
FWHOOM
!
WOBBLE
UNNH...
ALL THAT...WITH JUST HIS CHAKRA...?

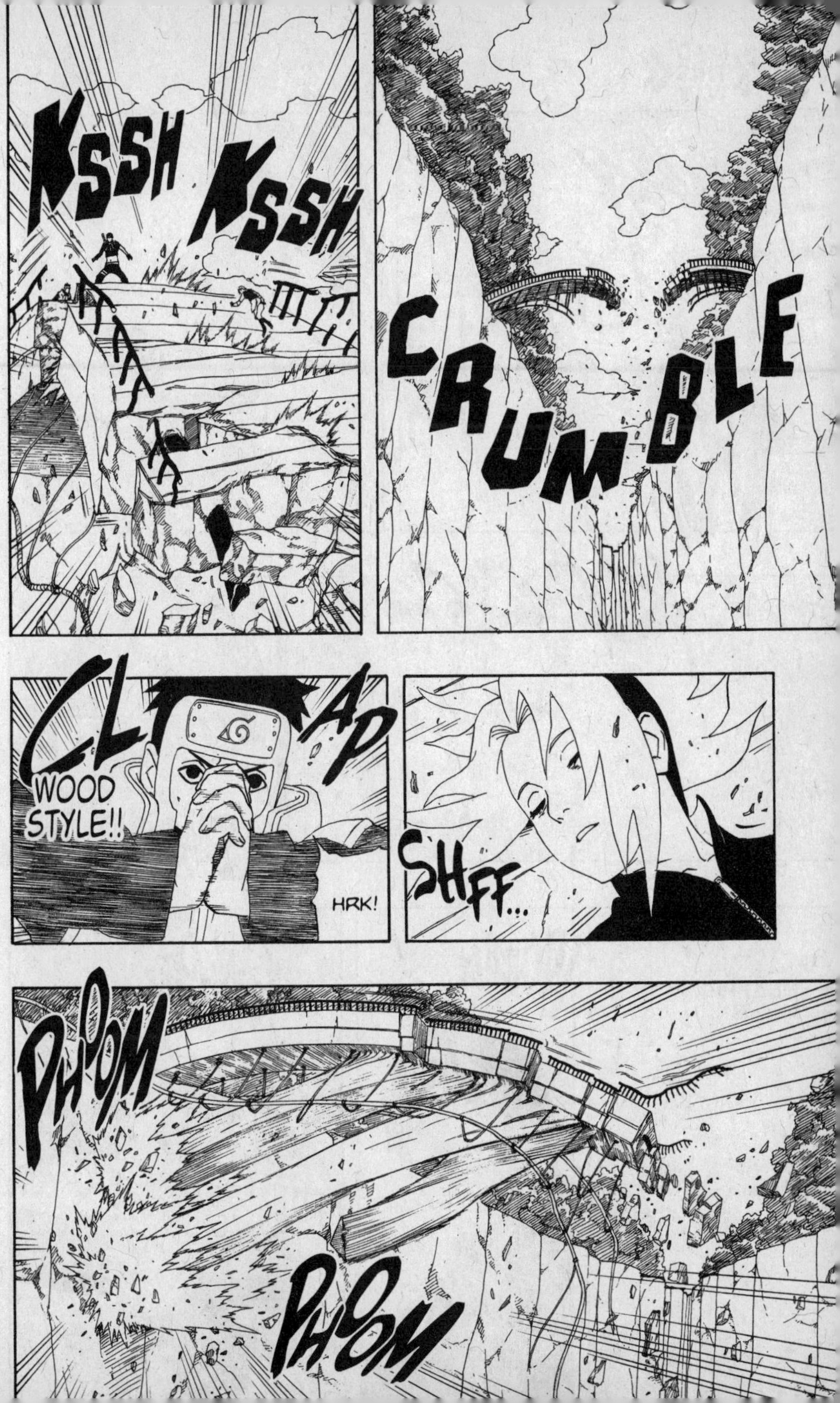
CRUMBLE
KSSH KSSH
SHFF...
CLAP
WOOD STYLE!!
HRK!
PHOOM
PHOOM

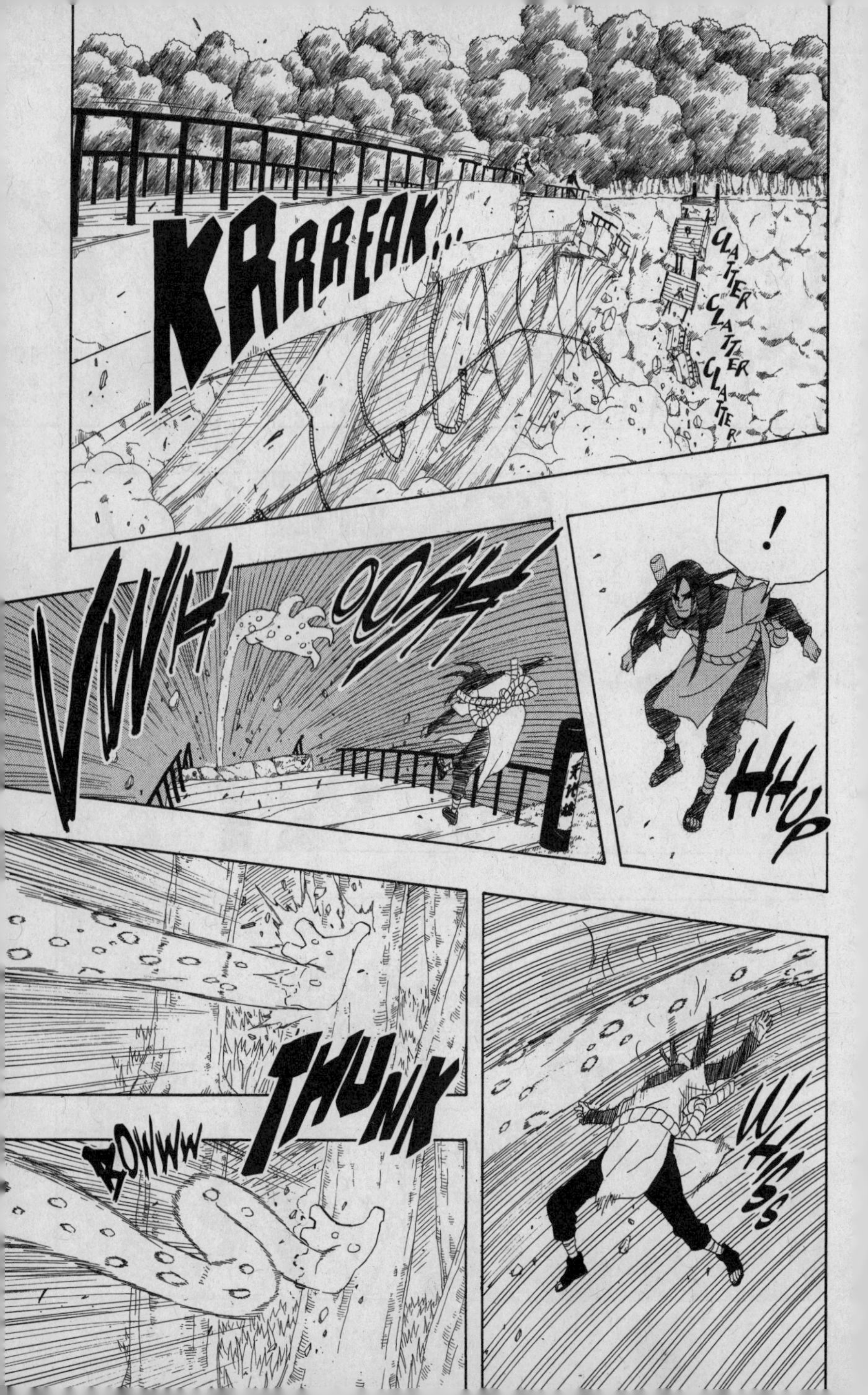
KRRREAK...
CLATTER CLATTER CLATTER
!
HHUP
VWWH OOSH
WHISS
THUNK
BOWWW

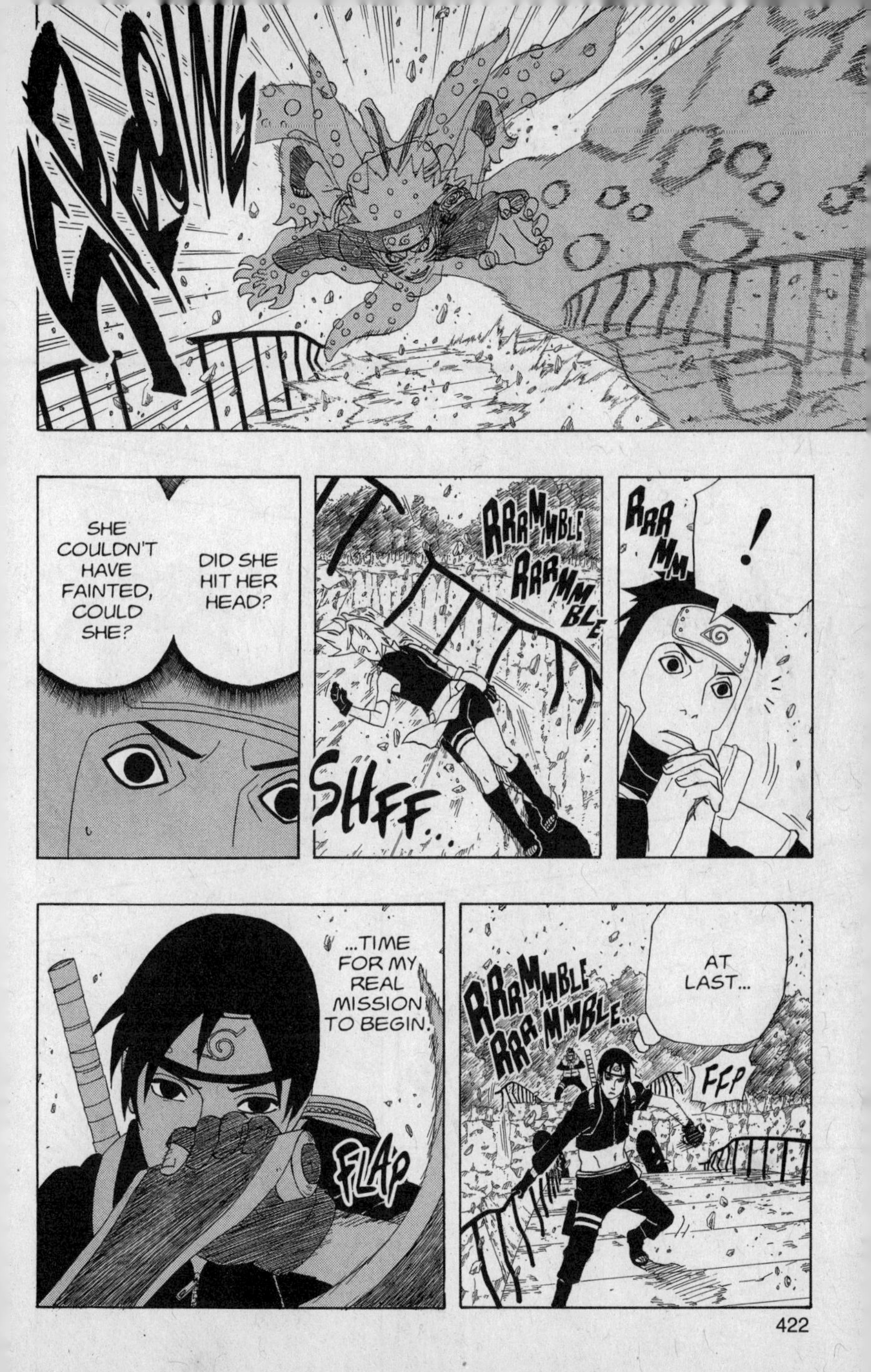
RRRMM
!
RRRMMBLE RRRMMBLE
SHFF...
DID SHE HIT HER HEAD?
SHE COULDN'T HAVE FAINTED, COULD SHE?
AT LAST...
RRRMMBLE RRRMMBLE...
FFP
...TIME FOR MY REAL MISSION TO BEGIN.
FLAP

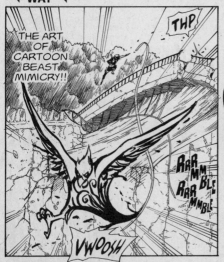

THE ART OF CARTOON BEAST MIMICRY!!

THP

RRR MM BLE

RRR MM BLE

VWOOSH

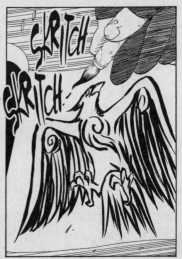

SKRITCH

SKRITCH

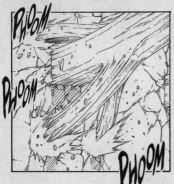

PHOOM

PHOOM

PHOOM

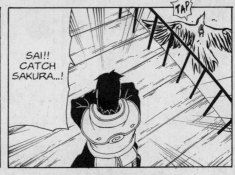

SAI!! CATCH SAKURA...!

TAP

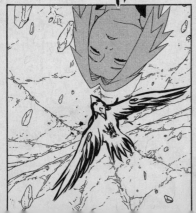

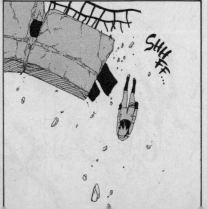

SHFFF...

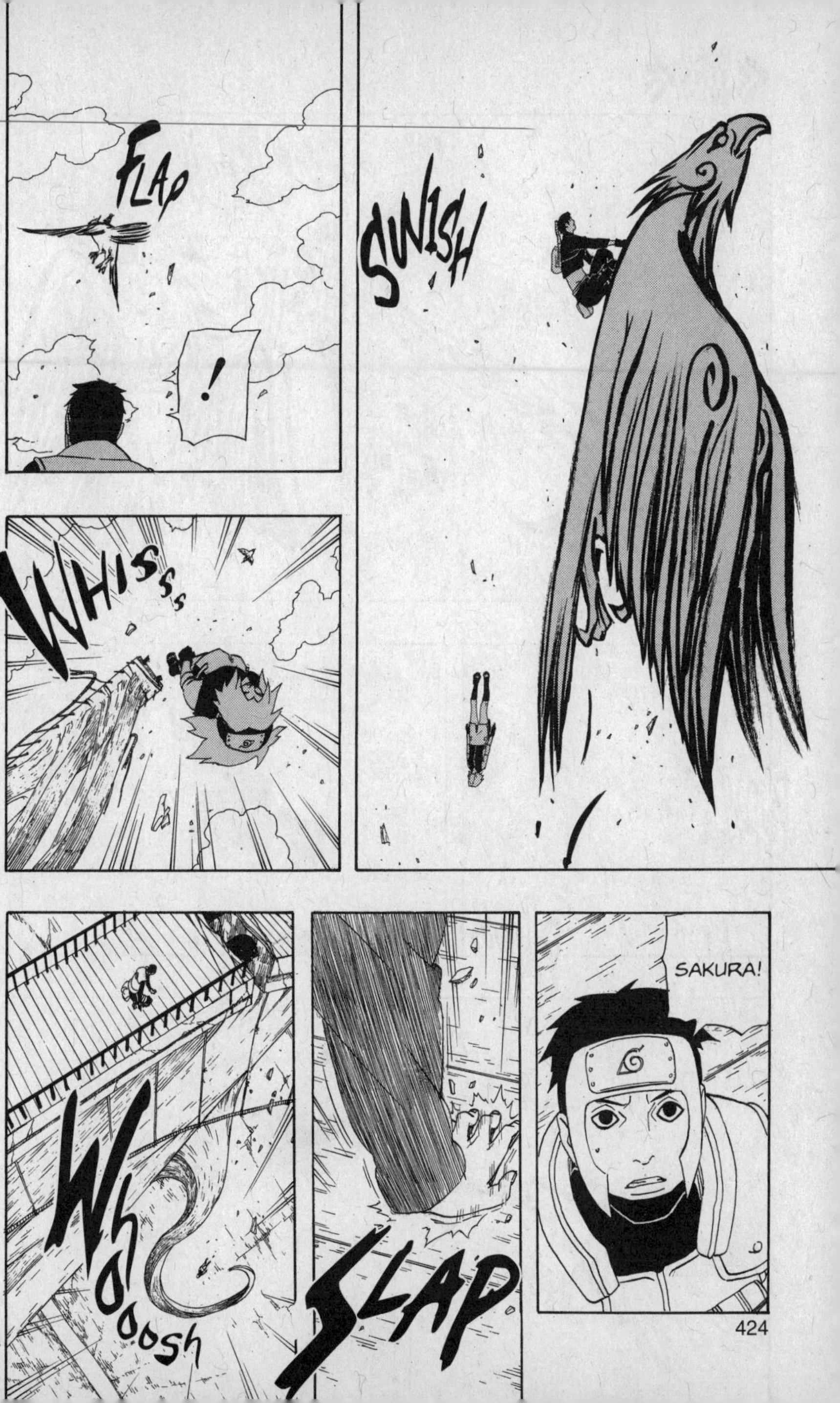
SWISH
FLAP
!
WHISSS
SAKURA!
SLAP
WHOOOSH

READ THIS WAY

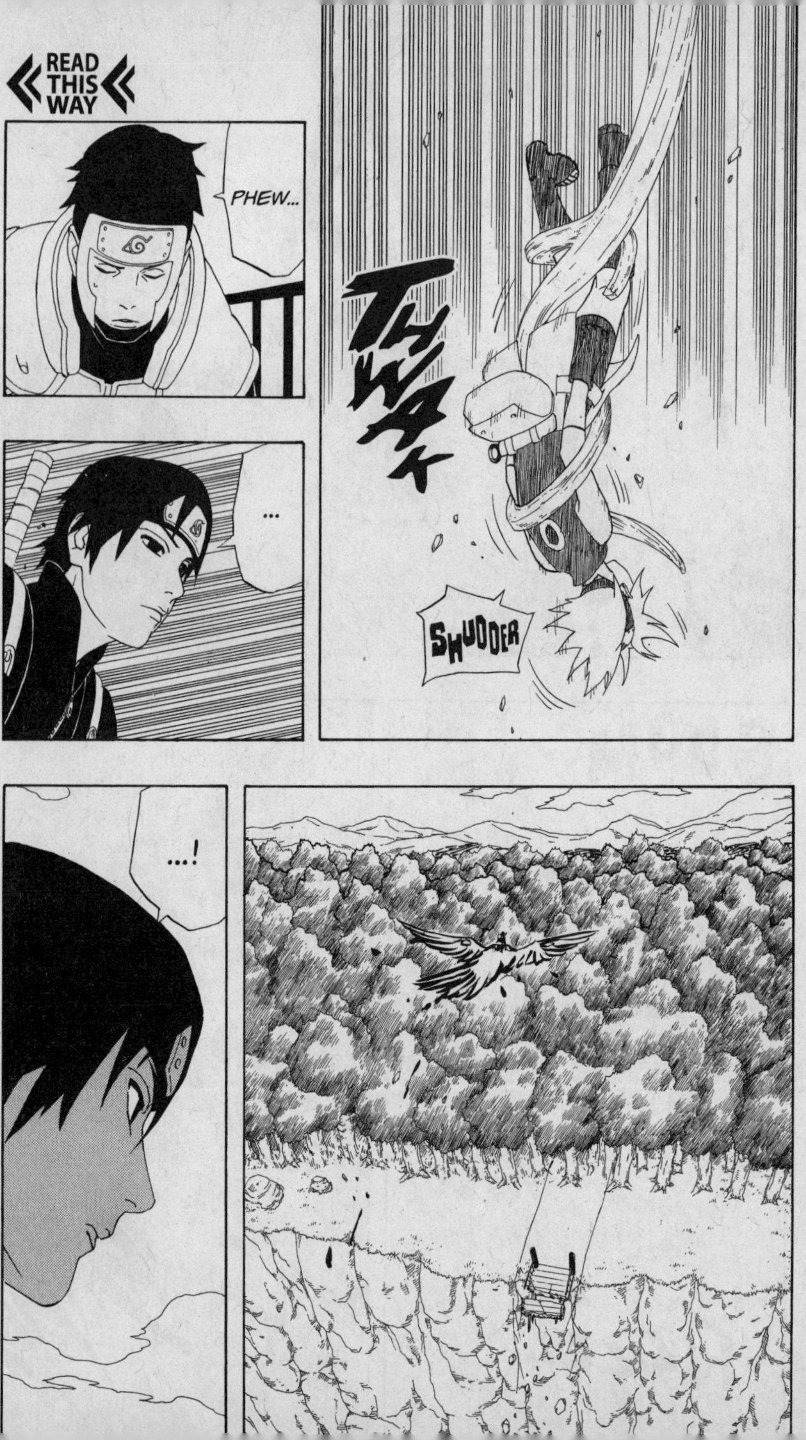
THWAK
SHUDDER
PHEW...
...
...!

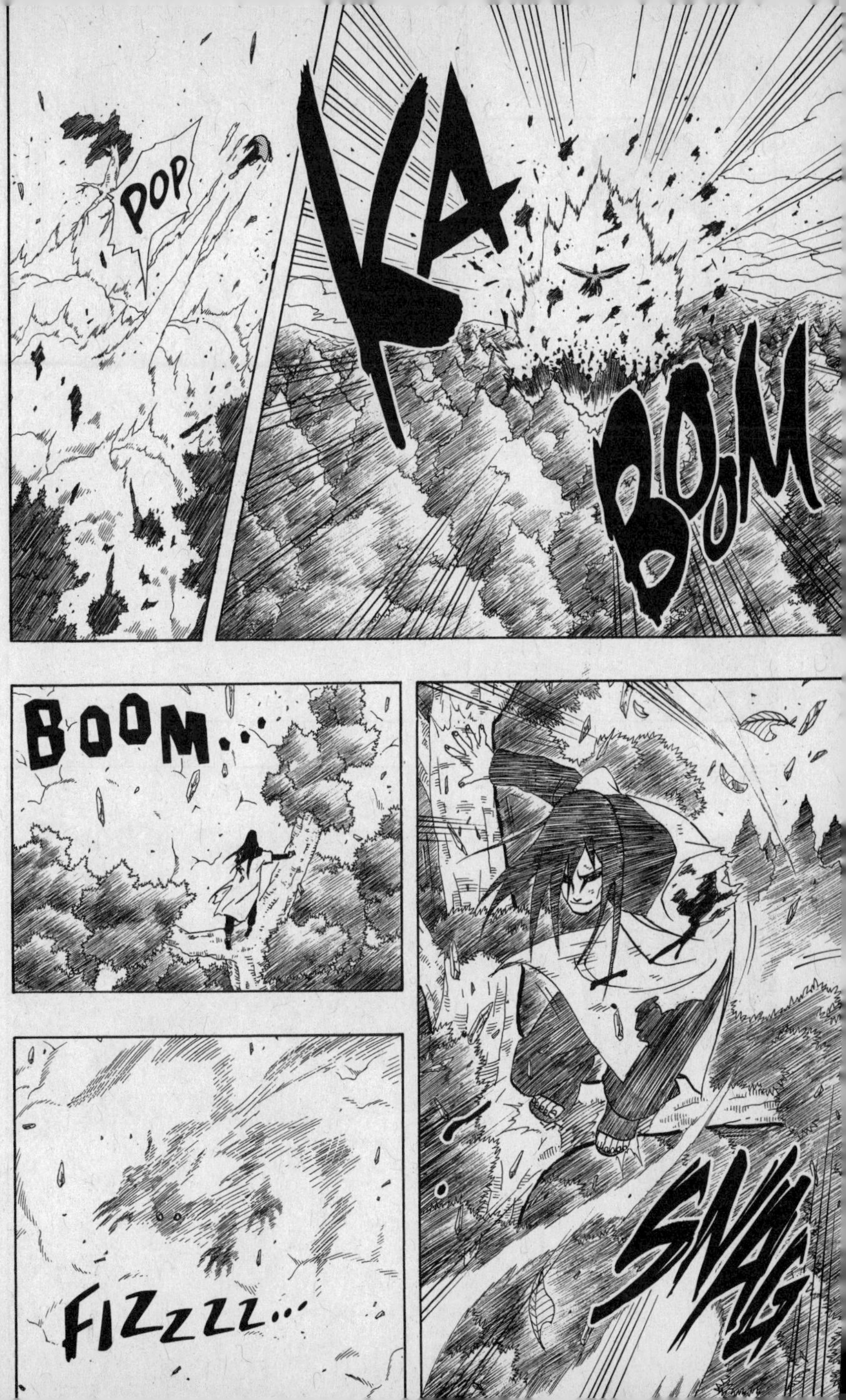
KA
BOOM
POP
SNAG
BOOM..
FIZZZZ...

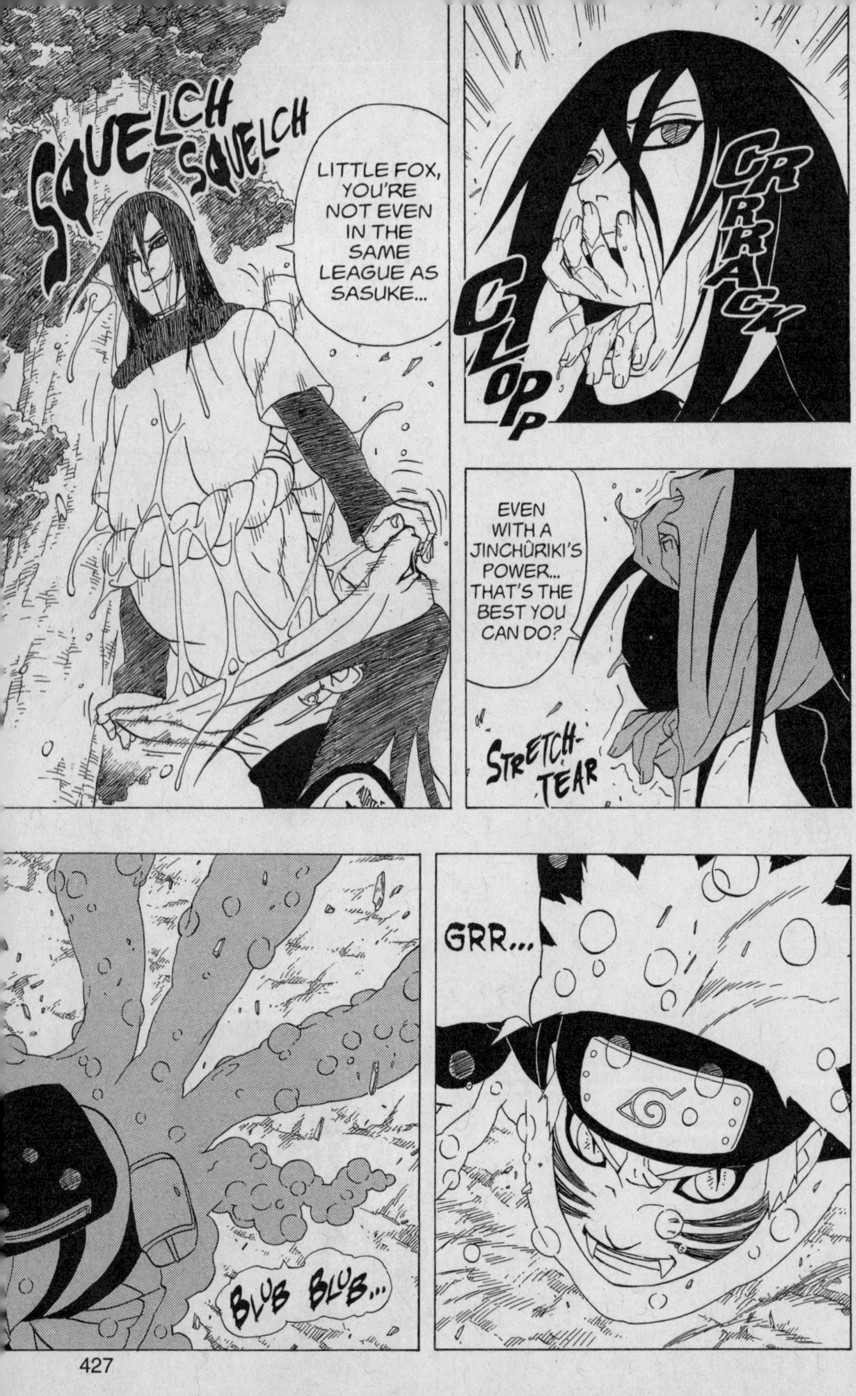
CRRRACK
CLOPP
EVEN WITH A JINCHÛRIKI'S POWER... THAT'S THE BEST YOU CAN DO?
STRETCH-TEAR
SQUELCH SQUELCH
LITTLE FOX, YOU'RE NOT EVEN IN THE SAME LEAGUE AS SASUKE...
GRR...
BLUB BLUB...

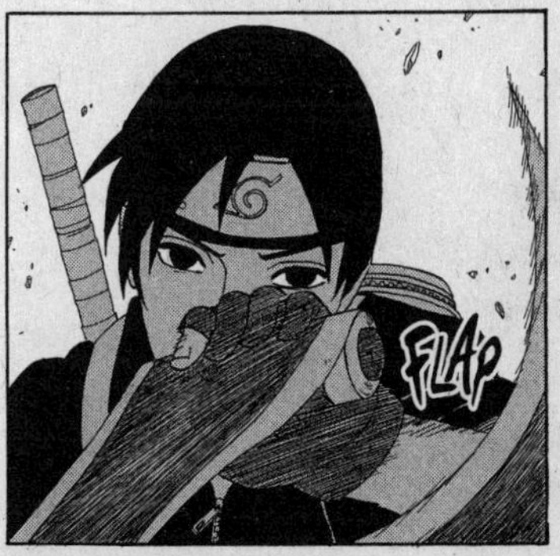
FLAP

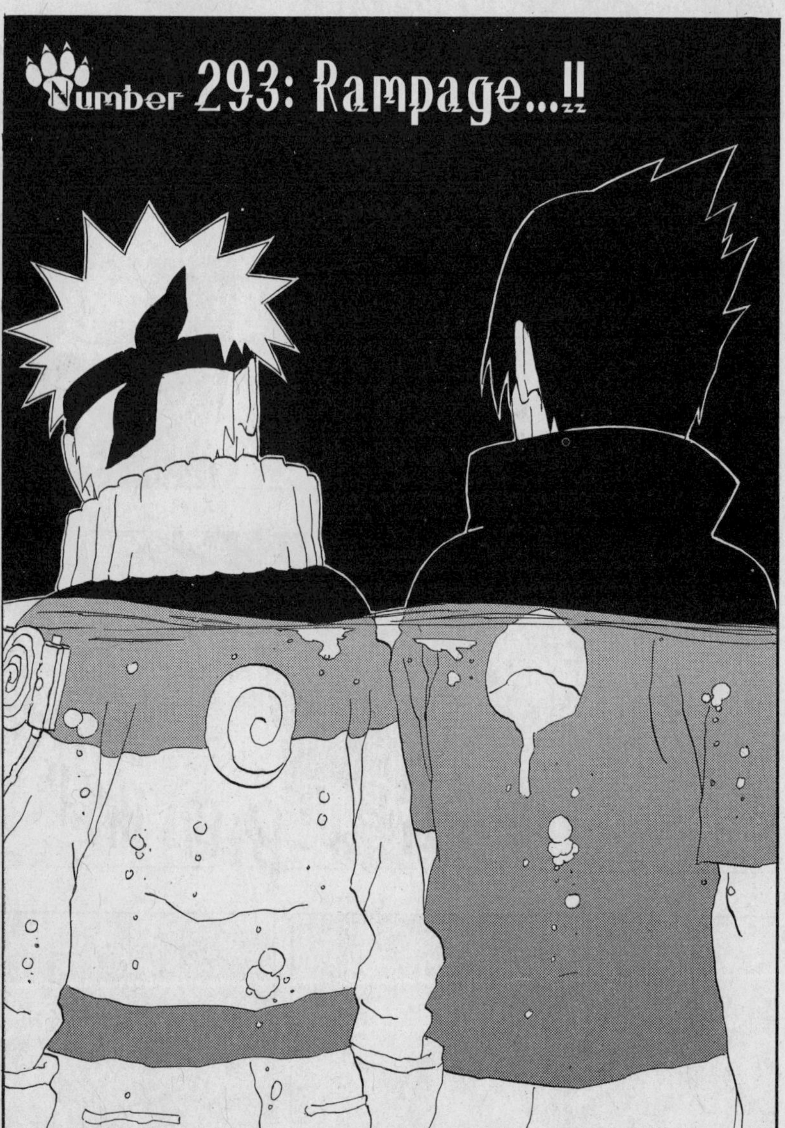
Number 293: Rampage...!!

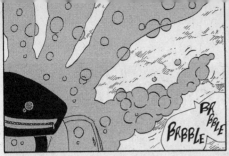

BR BBLE
BRBBLE

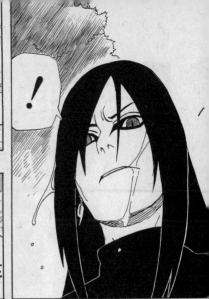

!

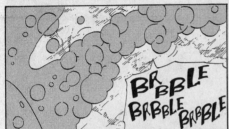

BR BBLE
BRBBLE
BRBBLE

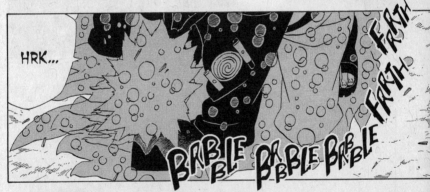

HRK...

FRRTH
FRRTH
FRRTH

BRBBLE BR BBLE BRBBLE

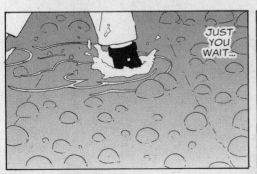

JUST
YOU
WAIT...

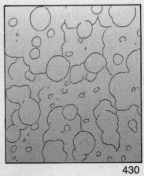

430

READ THIS WAY

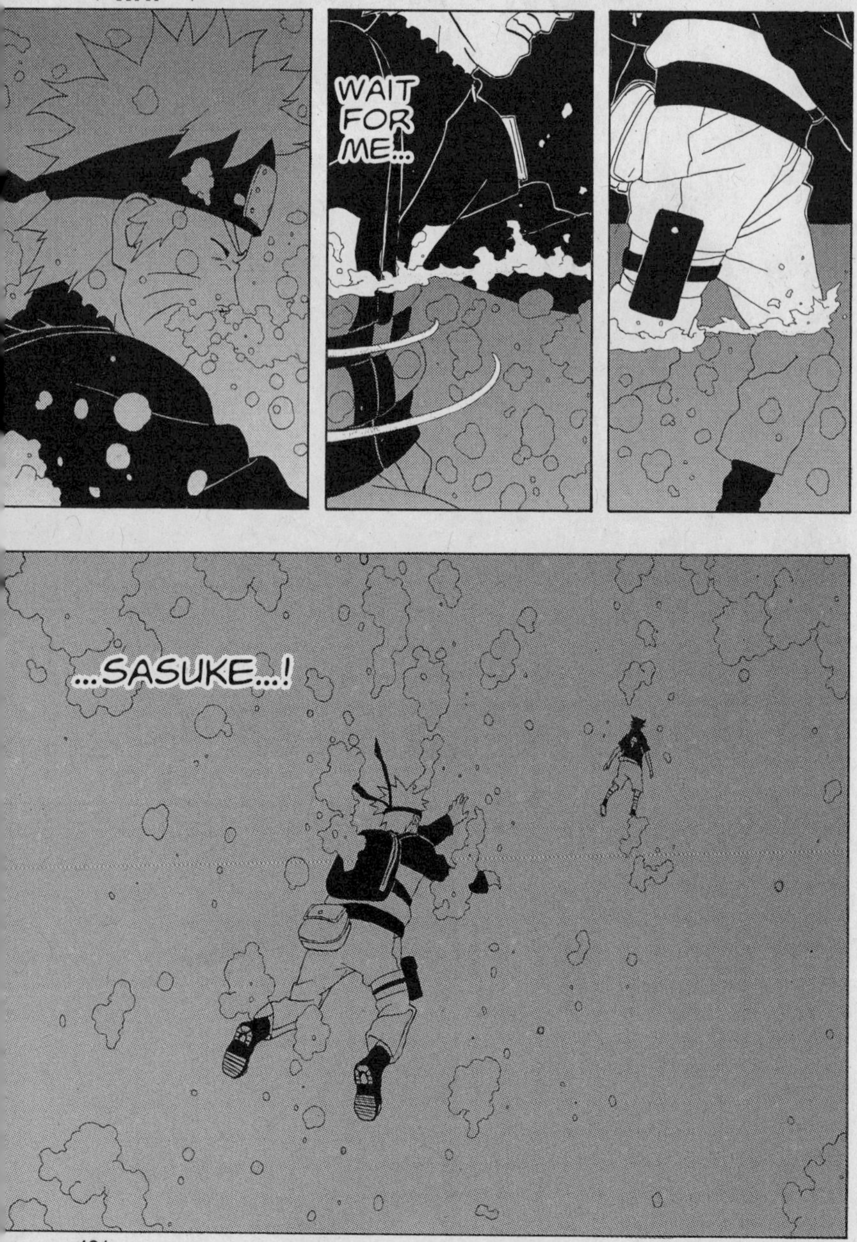

WAIT FOR ME...
...SASUKE...!

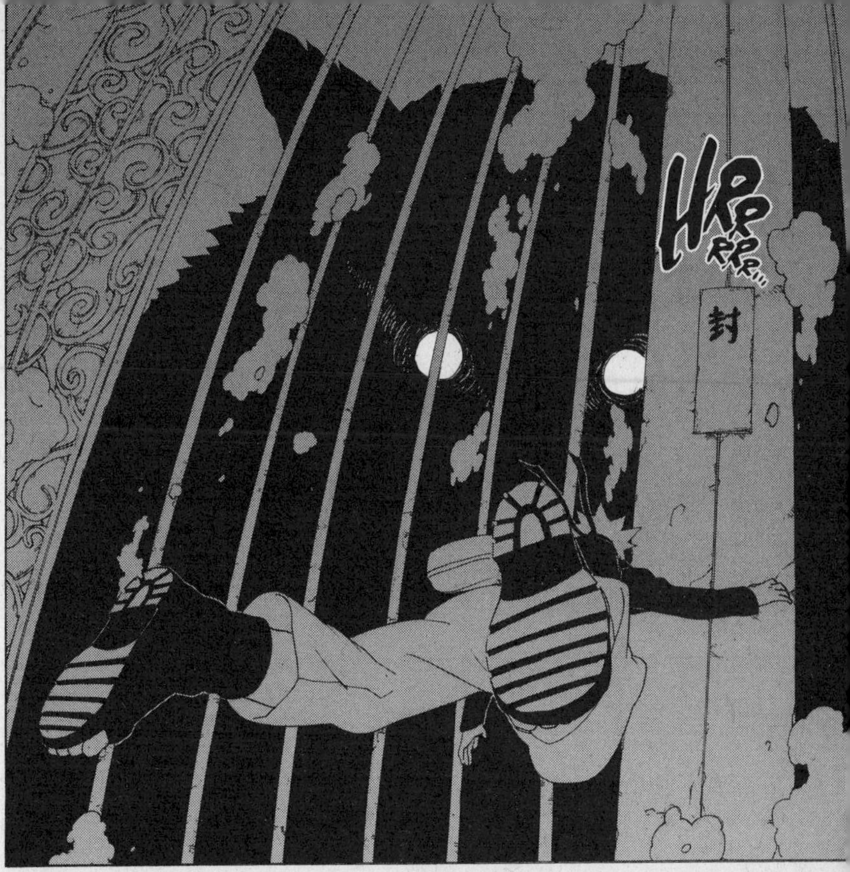
HRRRRR...
封
(SEAL)

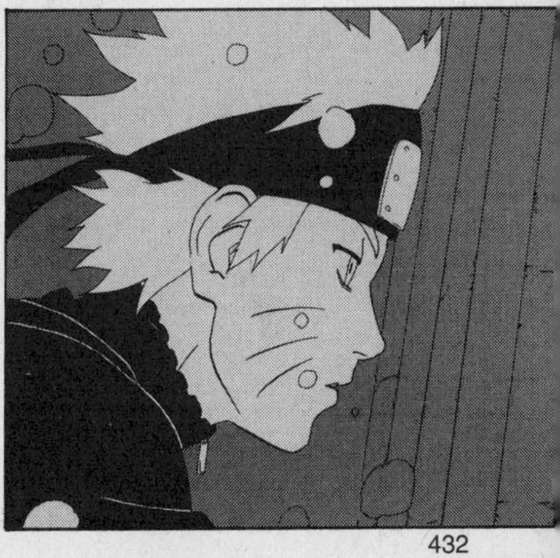

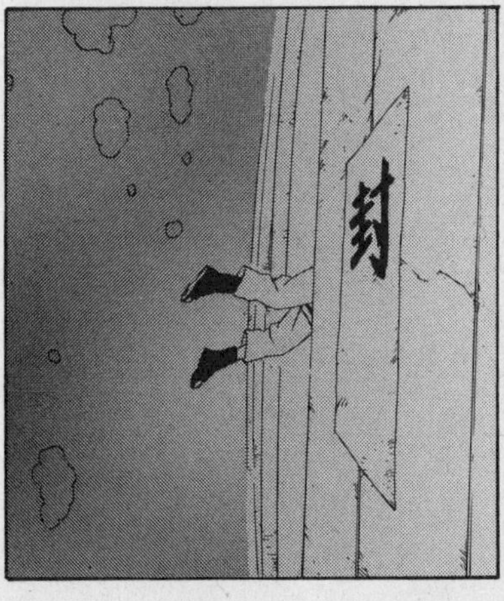
封

READ THIS WAY

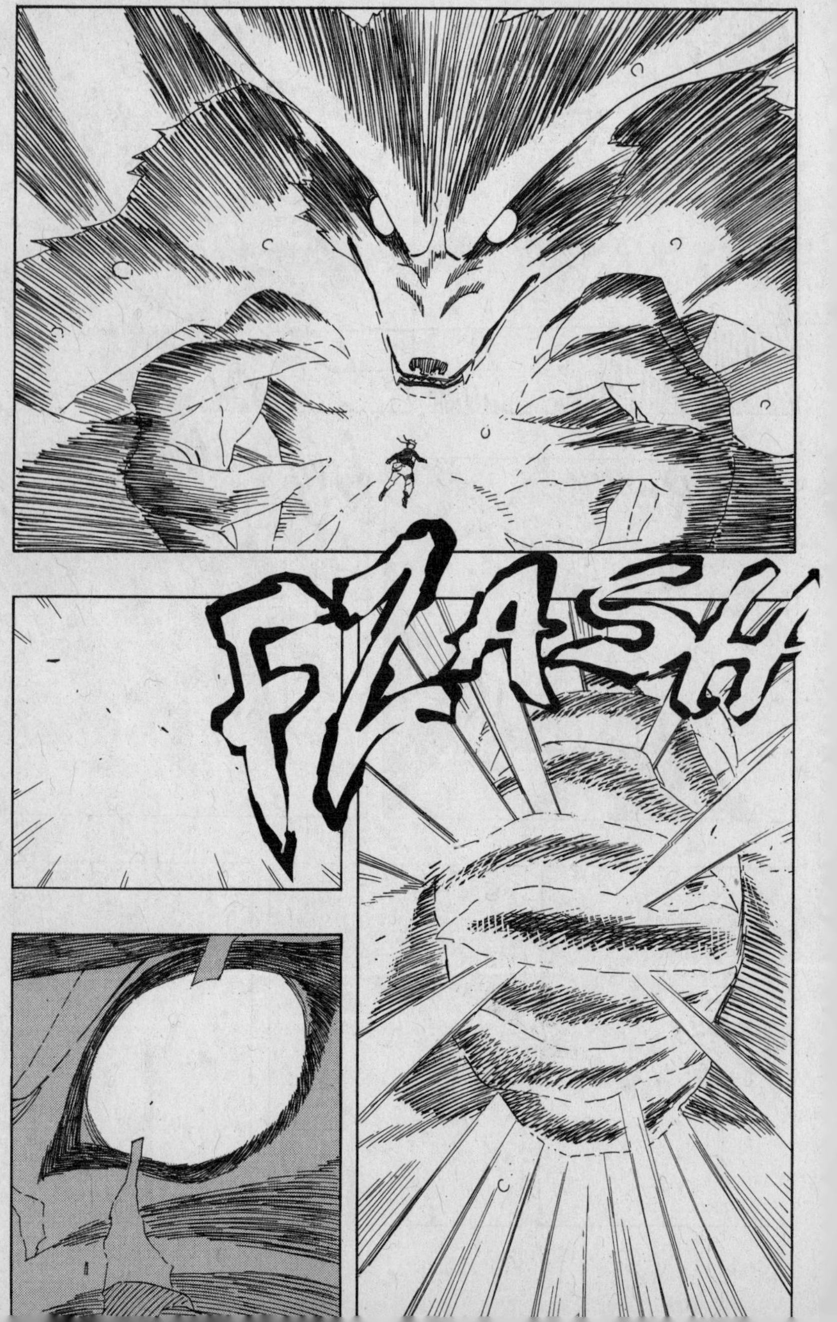
FLASH

SHRRP
SHRRP
SHRRP
SHRRP SHRRP
SHRRP
SHRRP
SHRRP
SHRRP
SKKrrkk
BLOP
TSSSSS

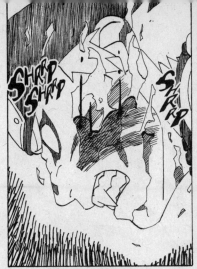

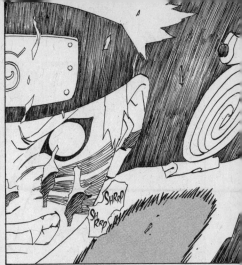

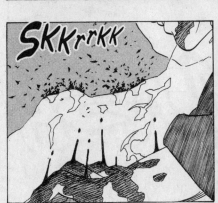

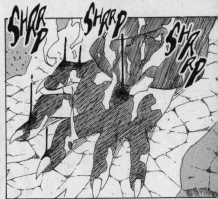

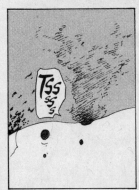

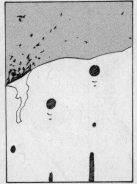

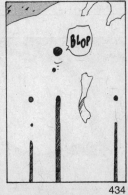

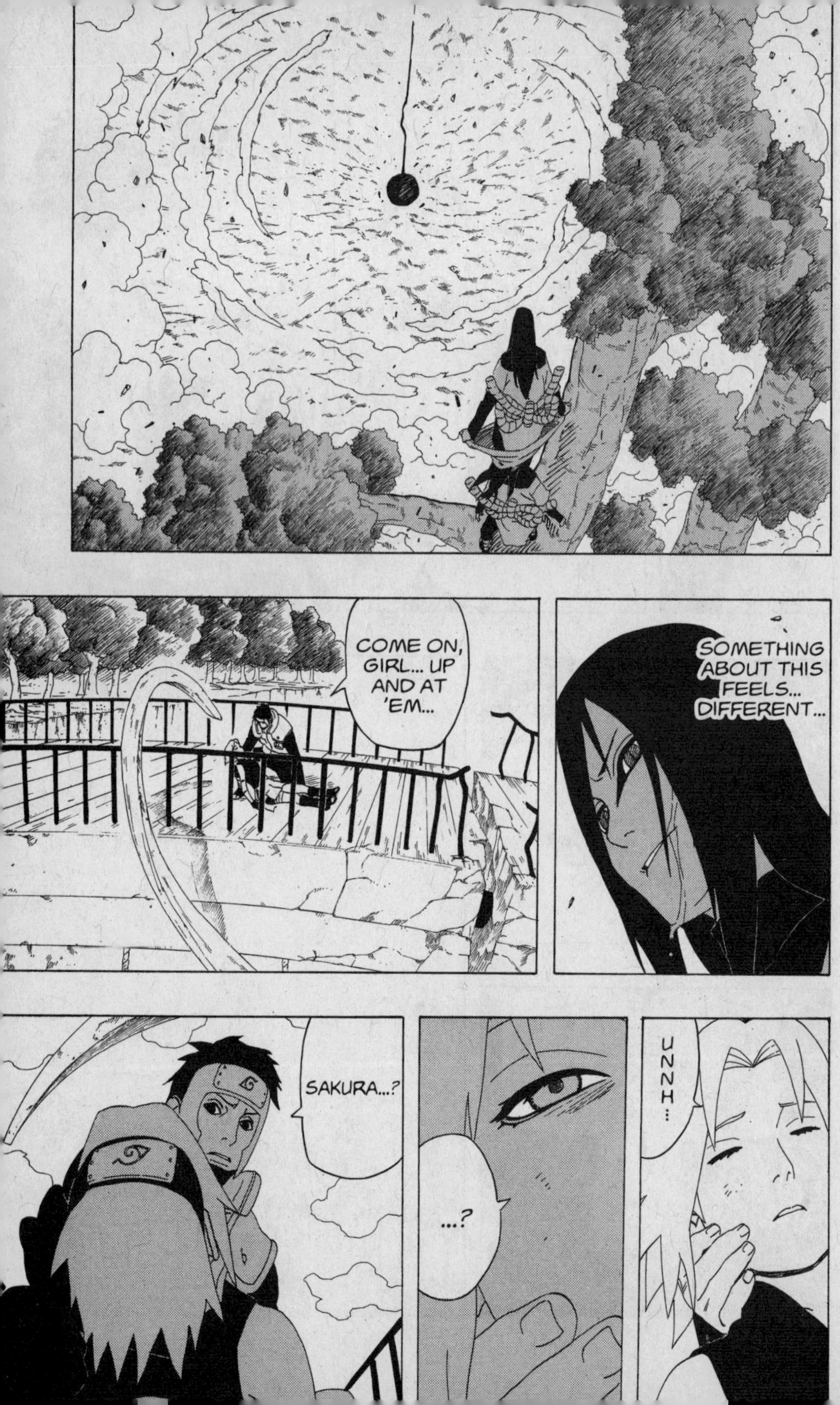
SOMETHING ABOUT THIS FEELS... DIFFERENT...
COME ON, GIRL... UP AND AT 'EM...
UNNH...
...?
SAKURA...?

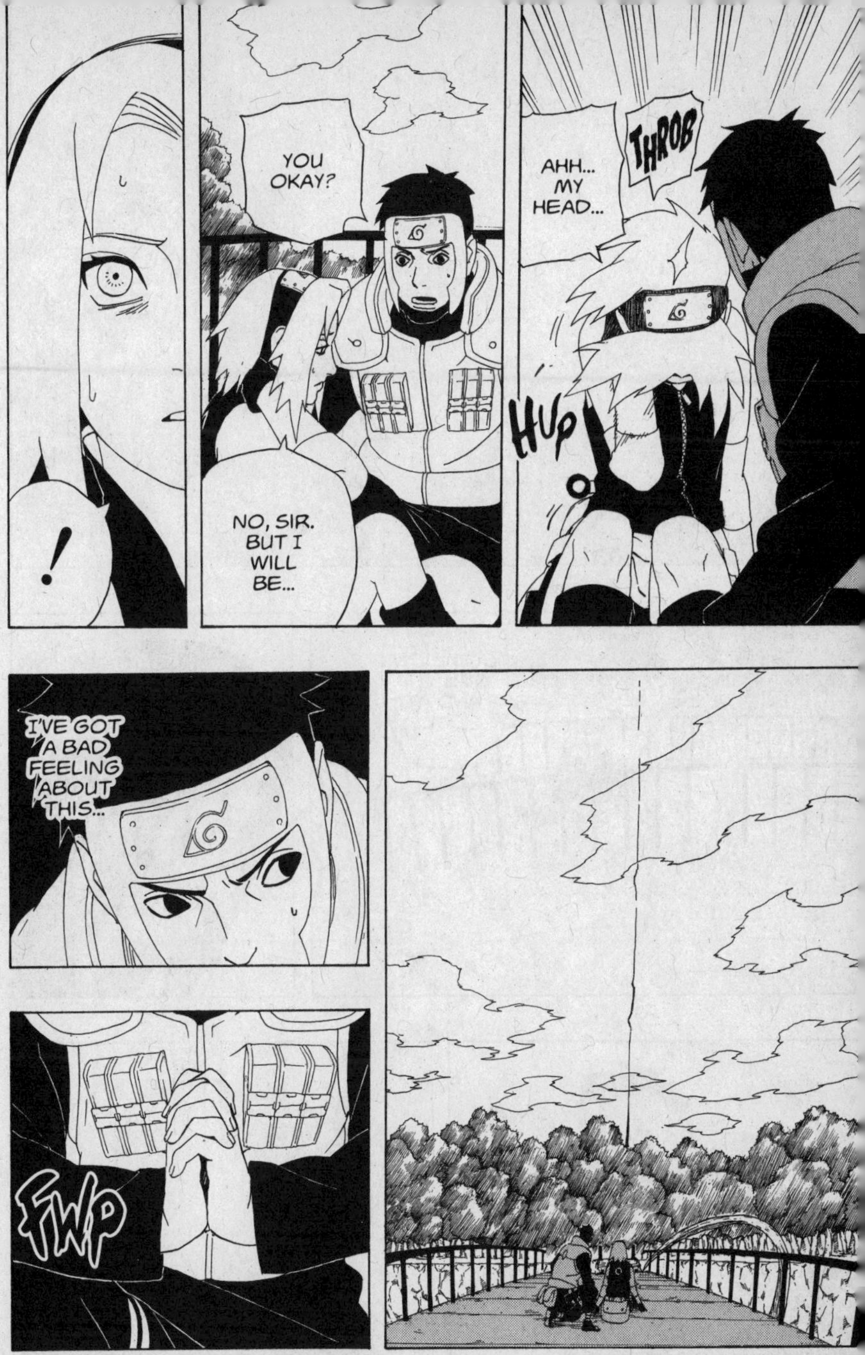
THROB
AHH... MY HEAD...
HUP
YOU OKAY?
NO, SIR. BUT I WILL BE...
!
I'VE GOT A BAD FEELING ABOUT THIS...
FWP

READ THIS WAY

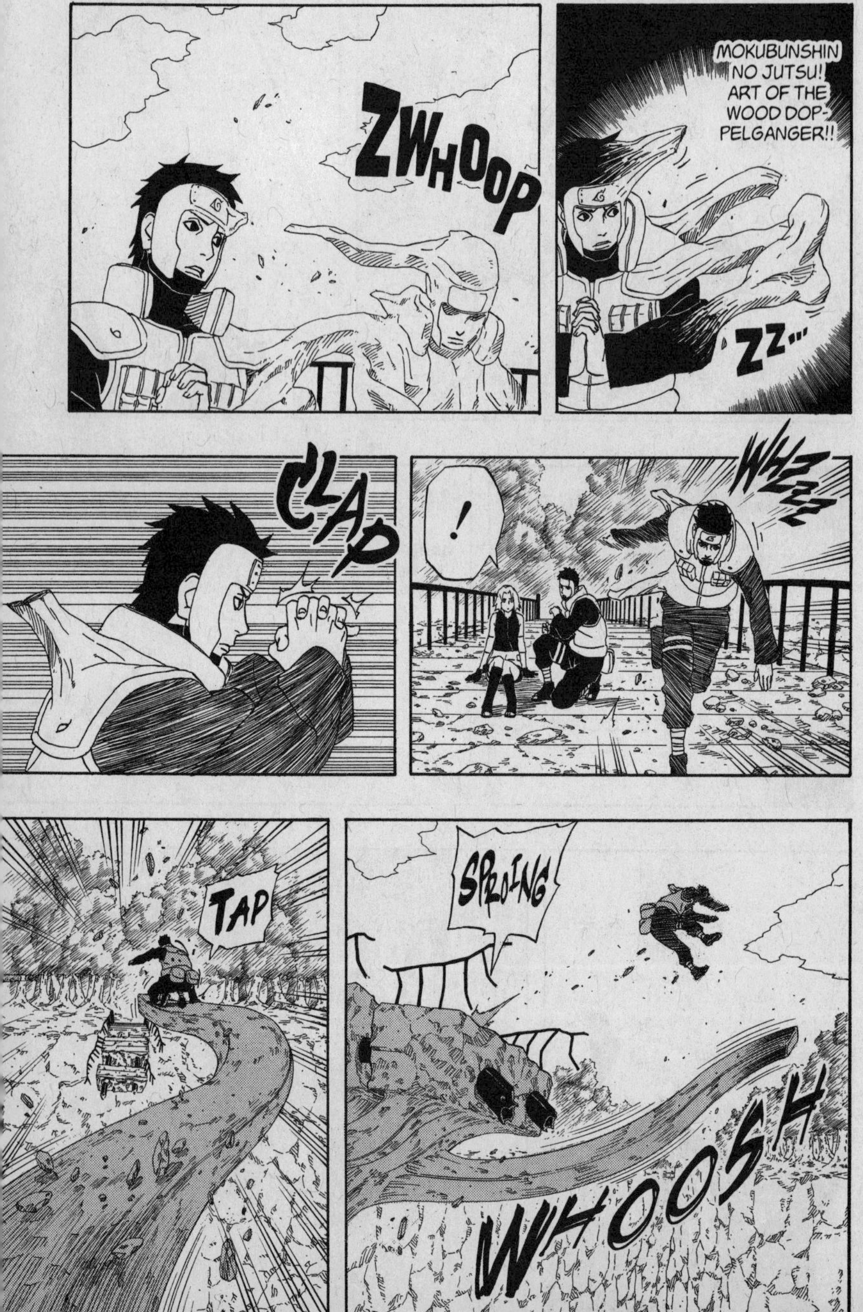
MOKUBUNSHIN NO JUTSU! ART OF THE WOOD DOP-PELGANGER!!
ZZ...
ZWHOOP
WHZZZ
!
CLAP
SPROING
WHOOSH
TAP

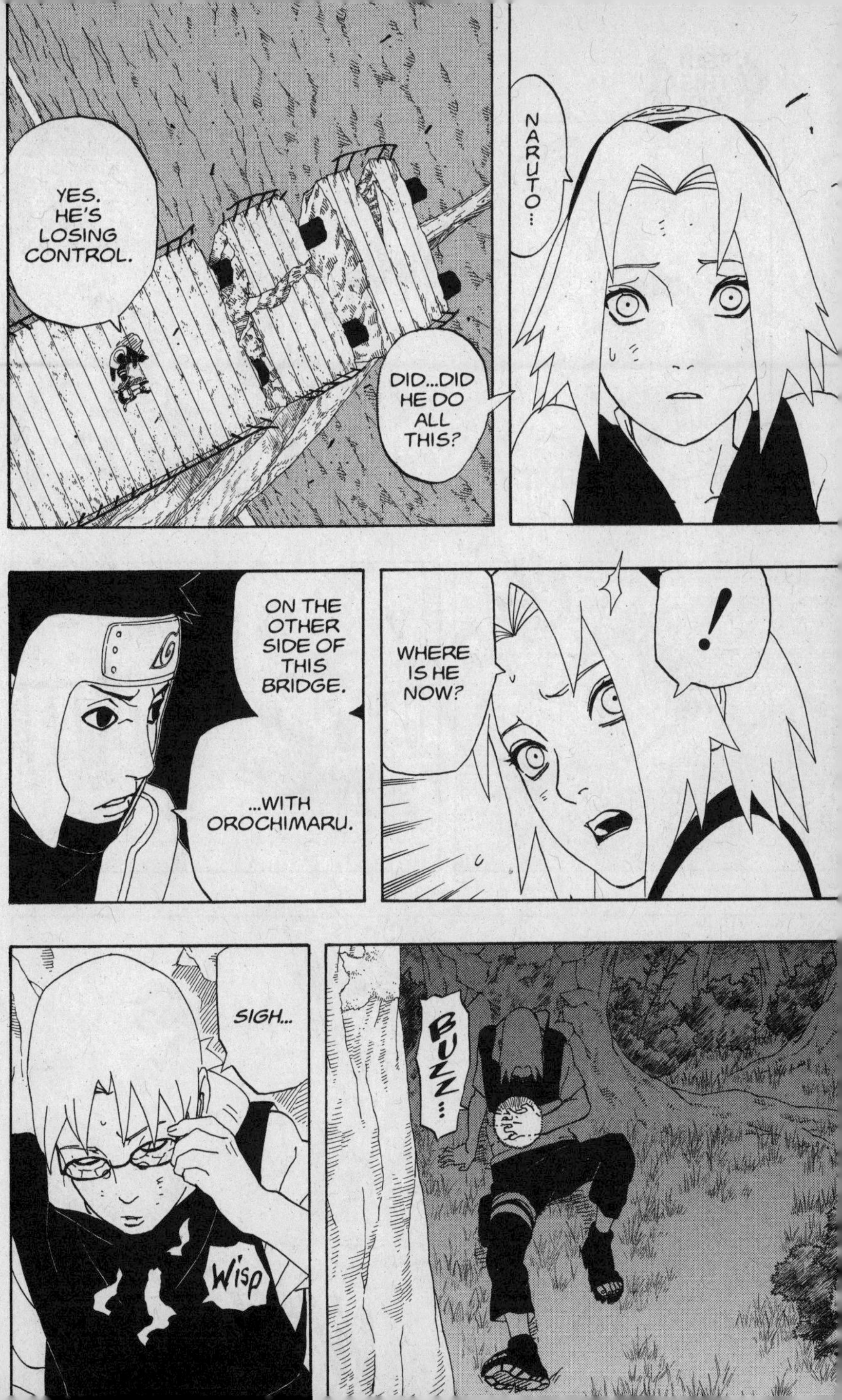
NARUTO...
DID...DID HE DO ALL THIS?
YES. HE'S LOSING CONTROL.
!
WHERE IS HE NOW?
ON THE OTHER SIDE OF THIS BRIDGE.
...WITH OROCHIMARU.
BUZZ...
SIGH...
Wisp

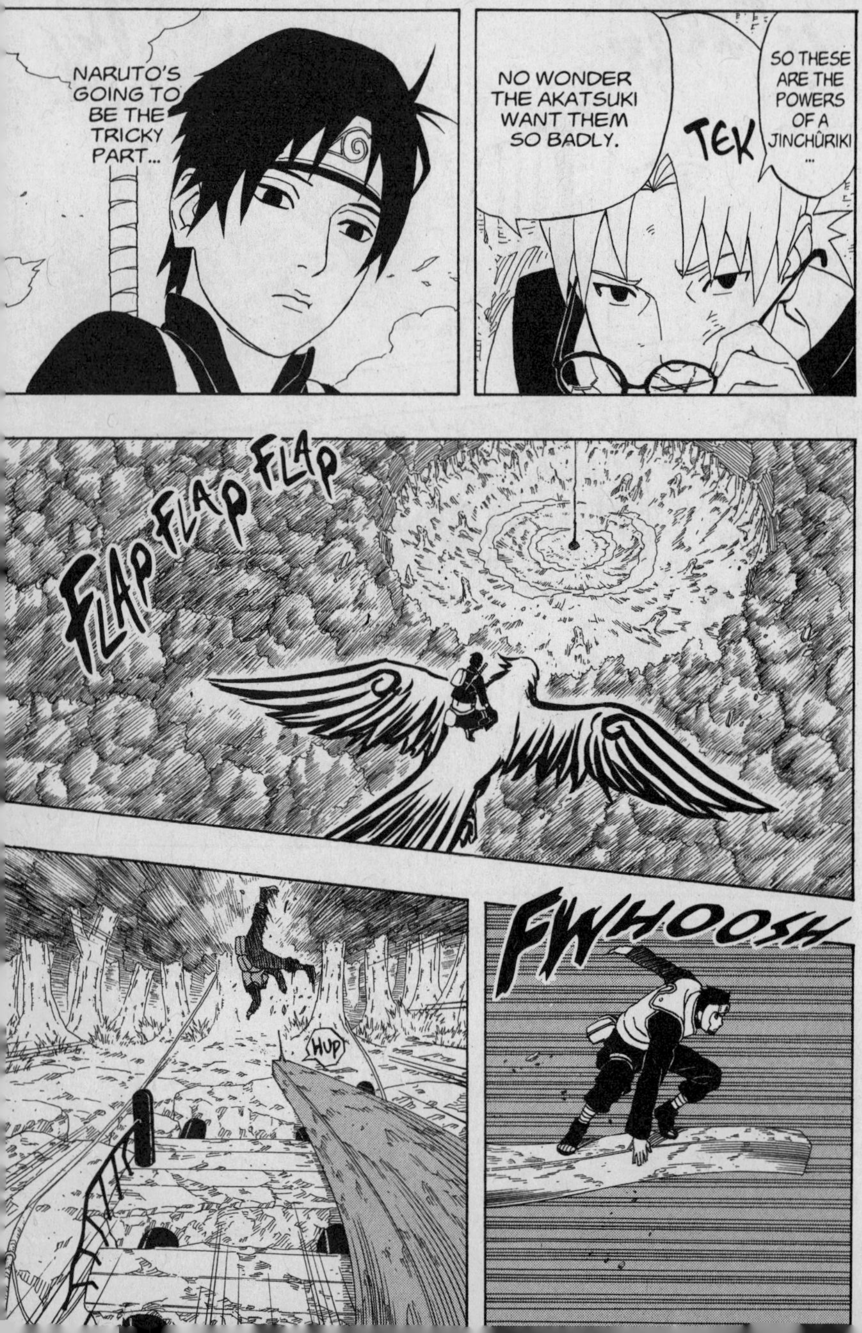
READ THIS WAY
SO THESE ARE THE POWERS OF A JINCHÛRIKI ...
TEK
NO WONDER THE AKATSUKI WANT THEM SO BADLY.
NARUTO'S GOING TO BE THE TRICKY PART...
FLAP FLAP FLAP
FWHOOSH
HUP

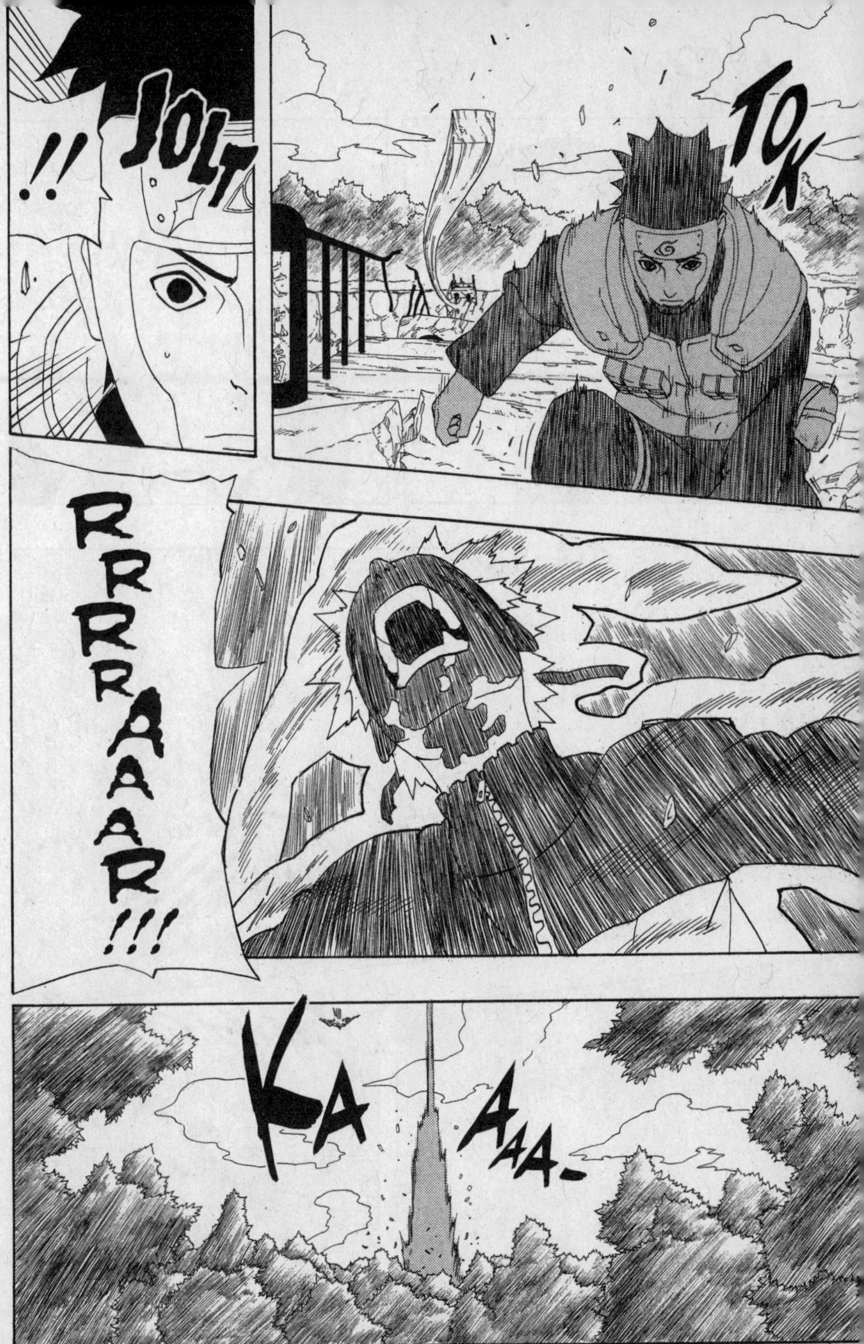
TOK
!!
JOLT
RRRRAAAR!!!
KA
AAA-

READ THIS WAY

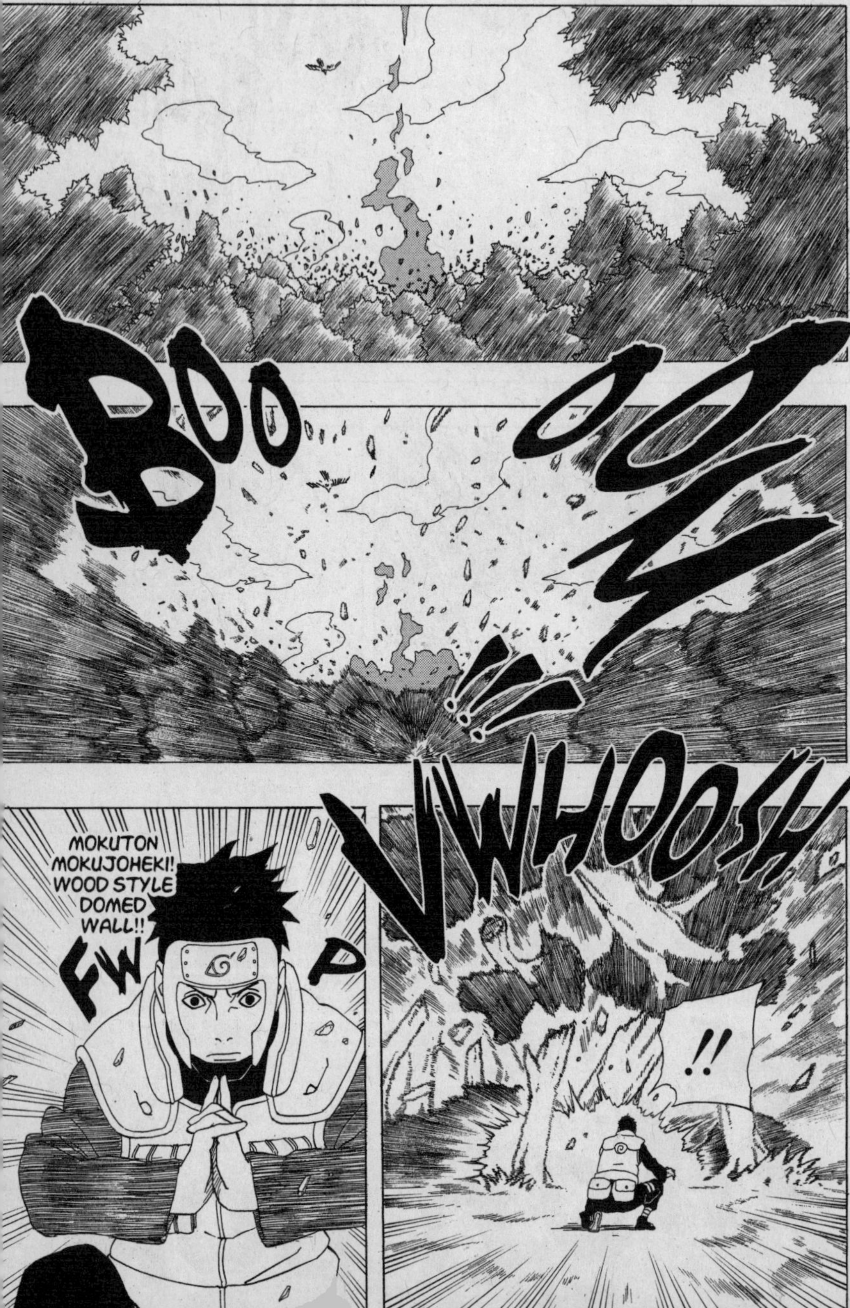
BOOOOM!!
VWHOOSH
!!
MOKUTON MOKUJOHEKI! WOOD STYLE DOMED WALL!!
FWP

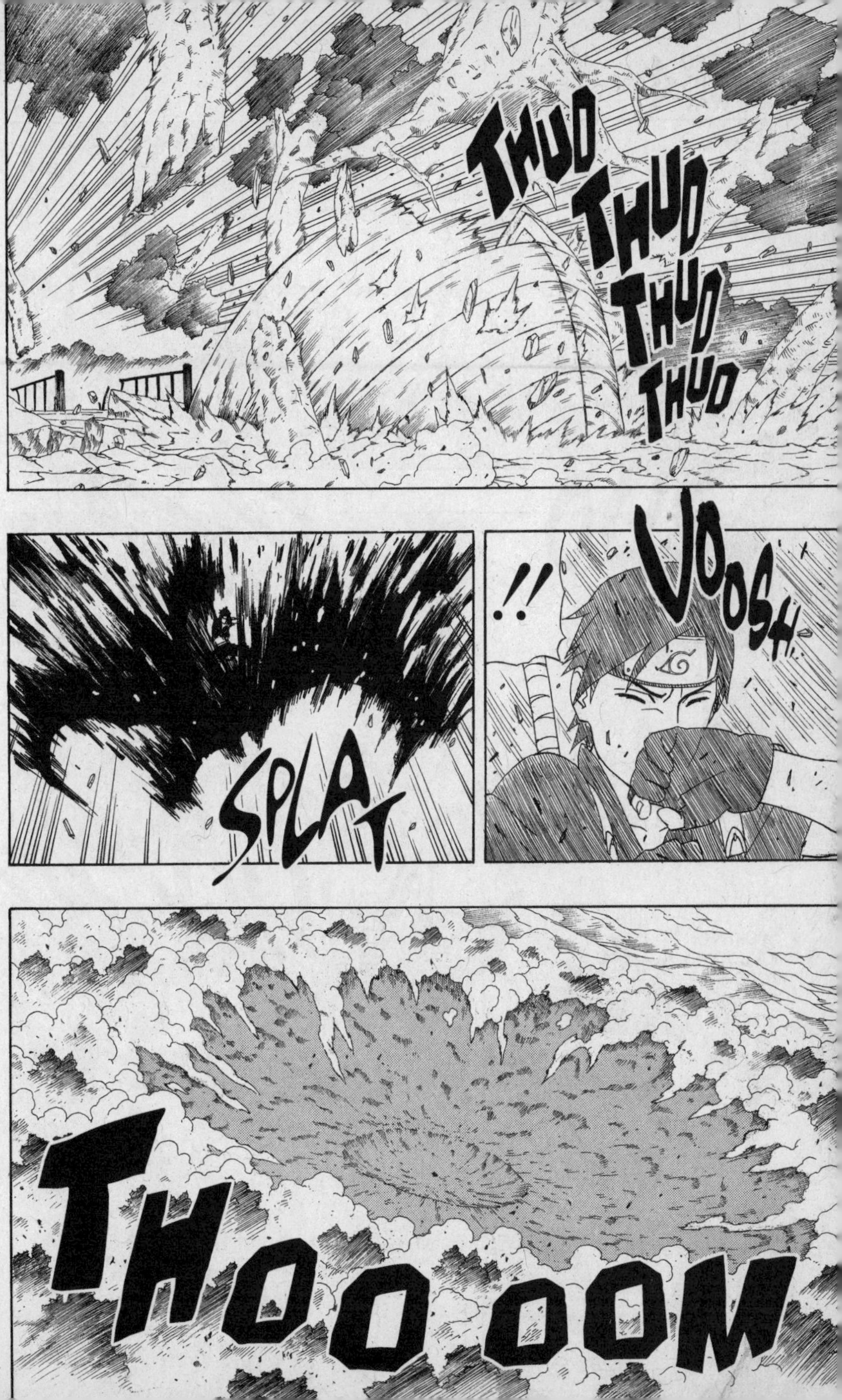
THUD
THUD
THUD
THUD
!!
VOOSH
SPLAT
THOOOOM

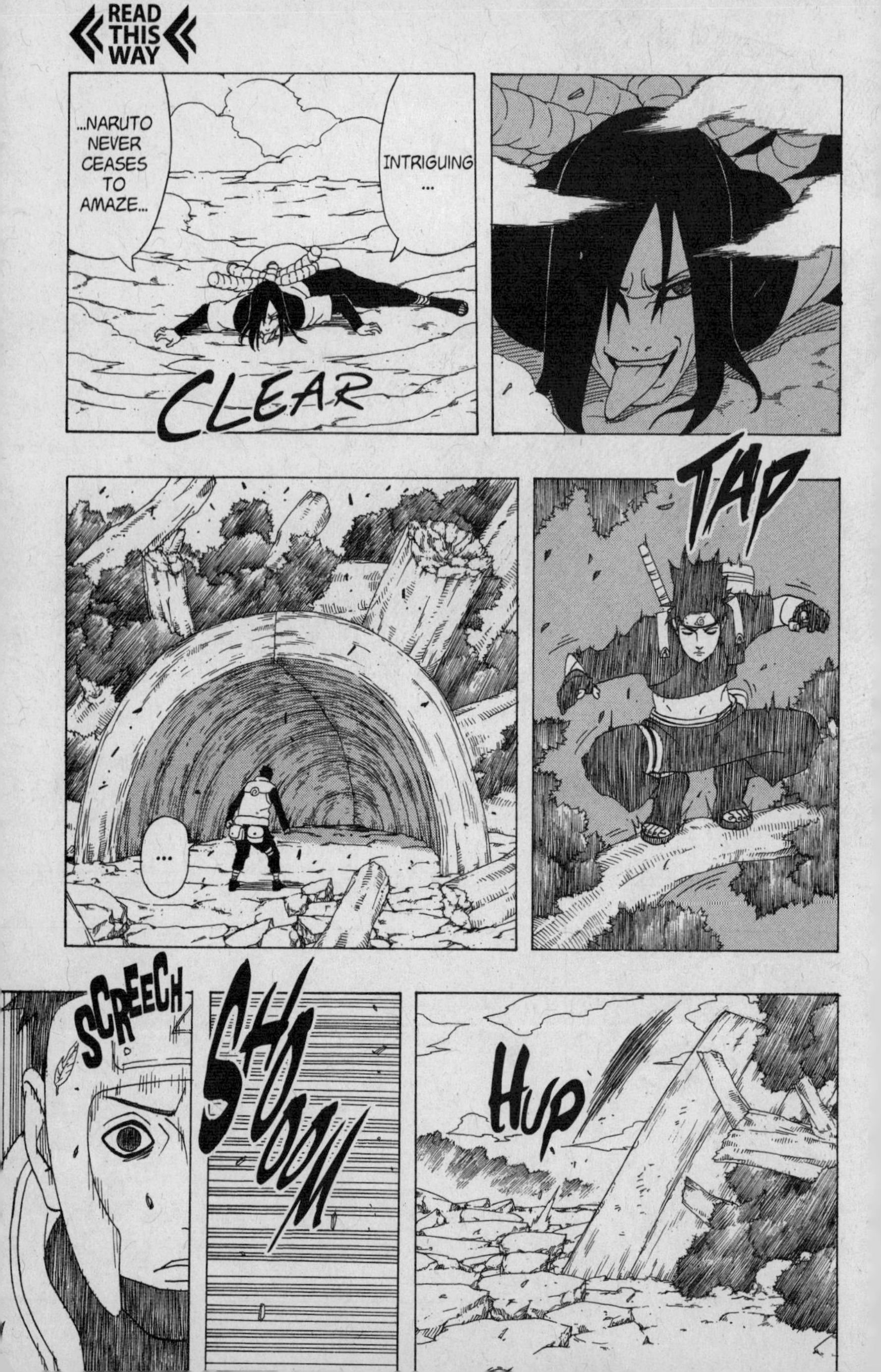
READ THIS WAY
INTRIGUING...
...NARUTO NEVER CEASES TO AMAZE...
CLEAR
TAP
...
HUP
SHOOM
SCREECH

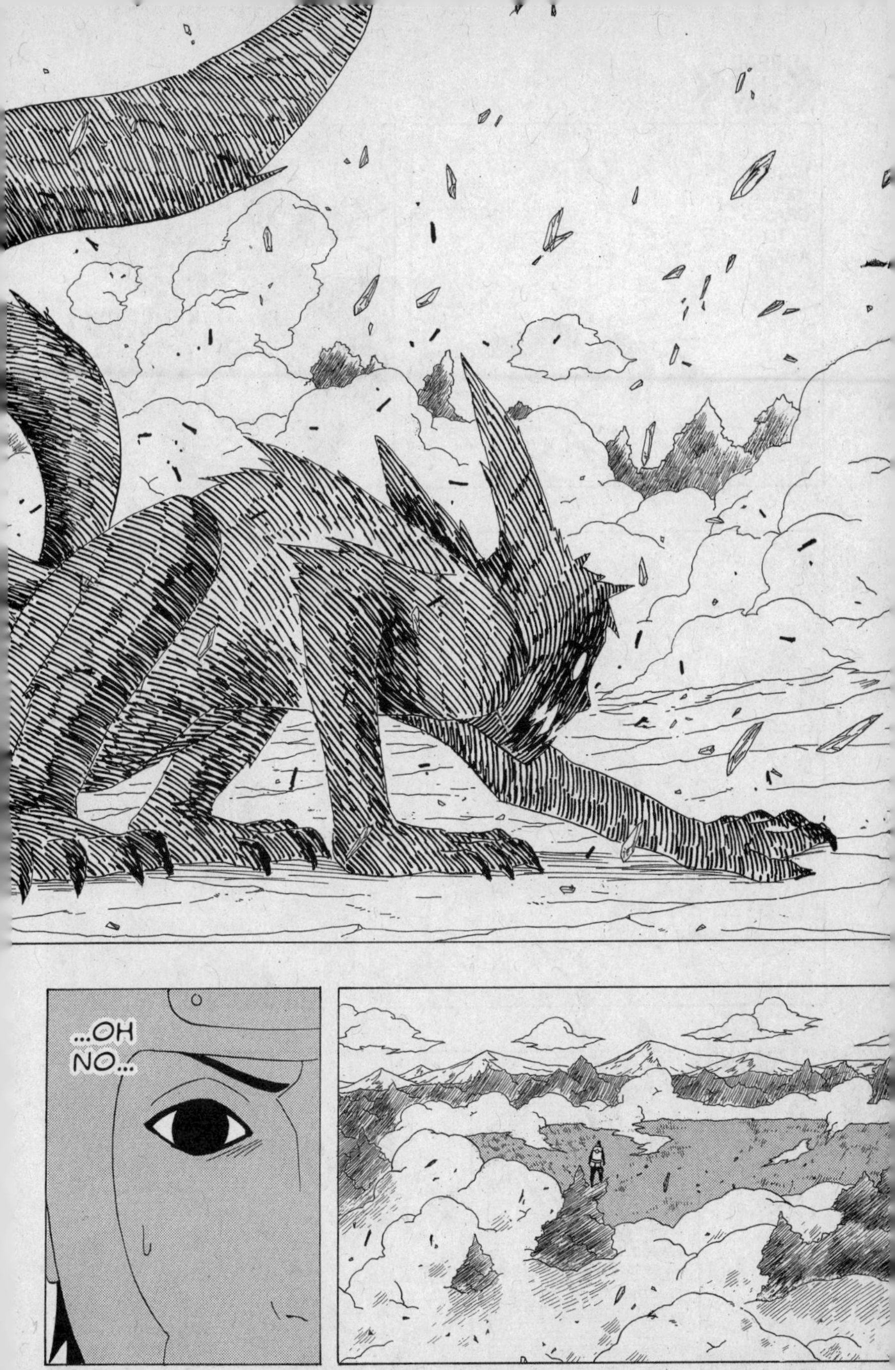
...OH NO...

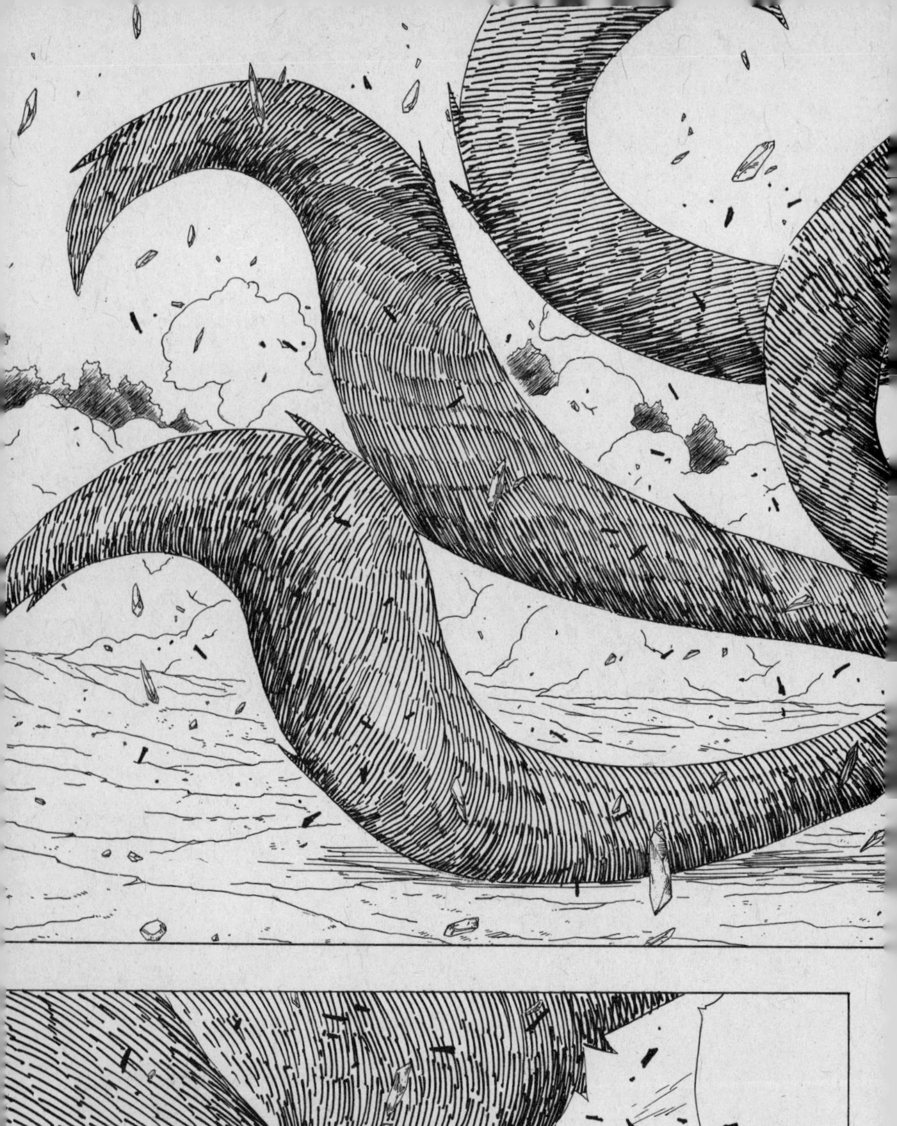

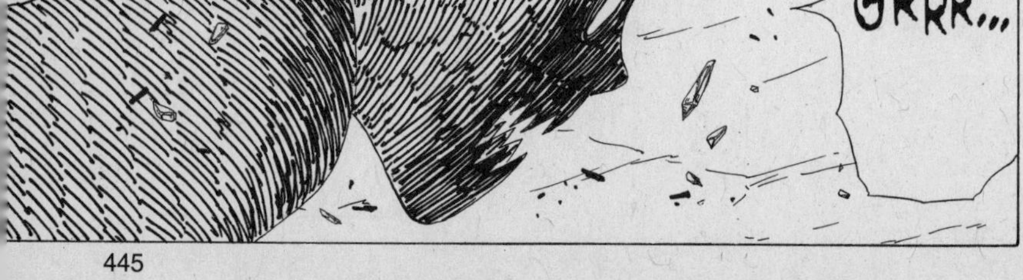
GRRR...

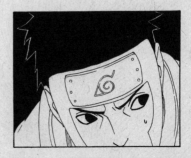

Number 294: The Fourth Tail...!!

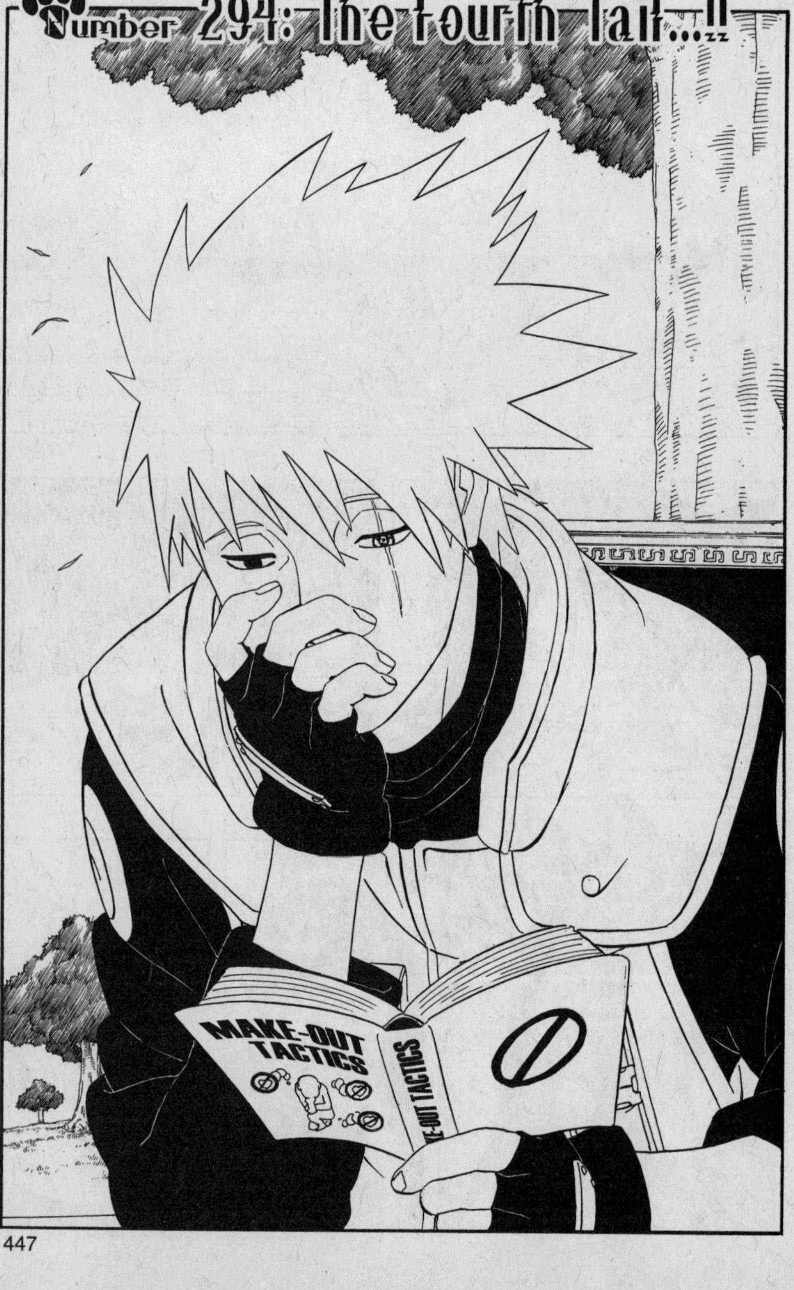
MAKE-OUT TACTICS
MAKE-OUT TACTICS

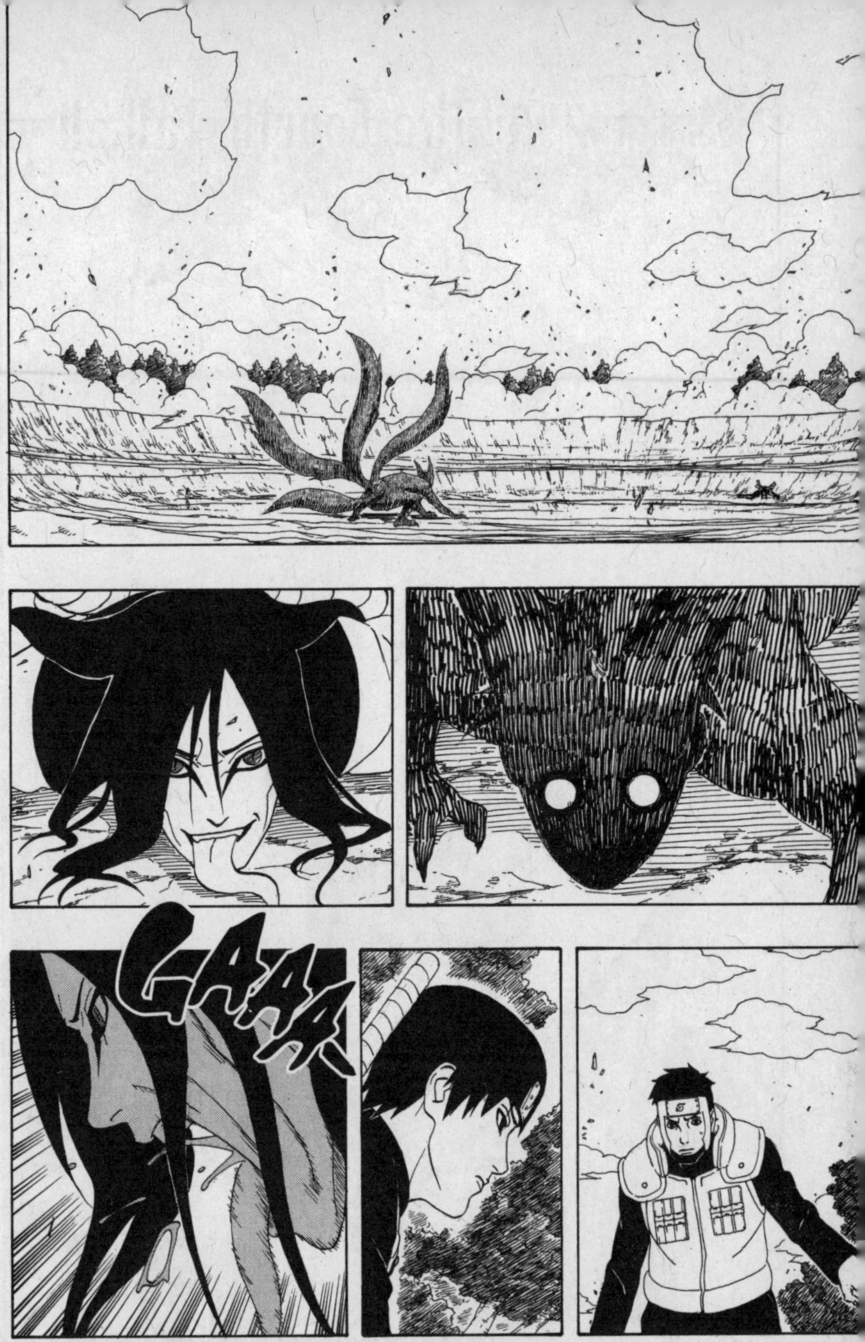
GAAA

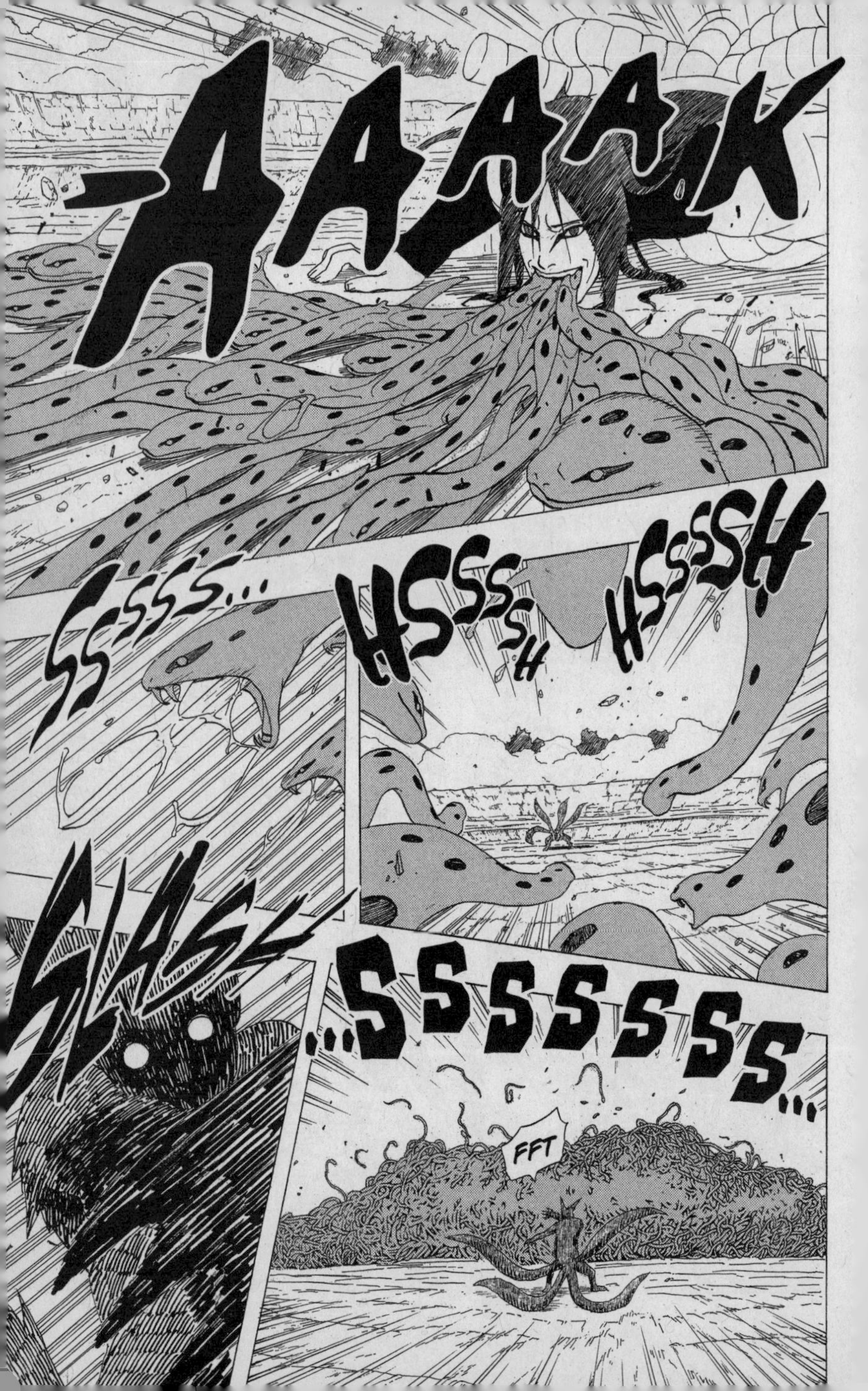
AAAAK
HSSSSH HSSSSH!
SSSSS...
...SSSSSSS...
FFT
SLASH

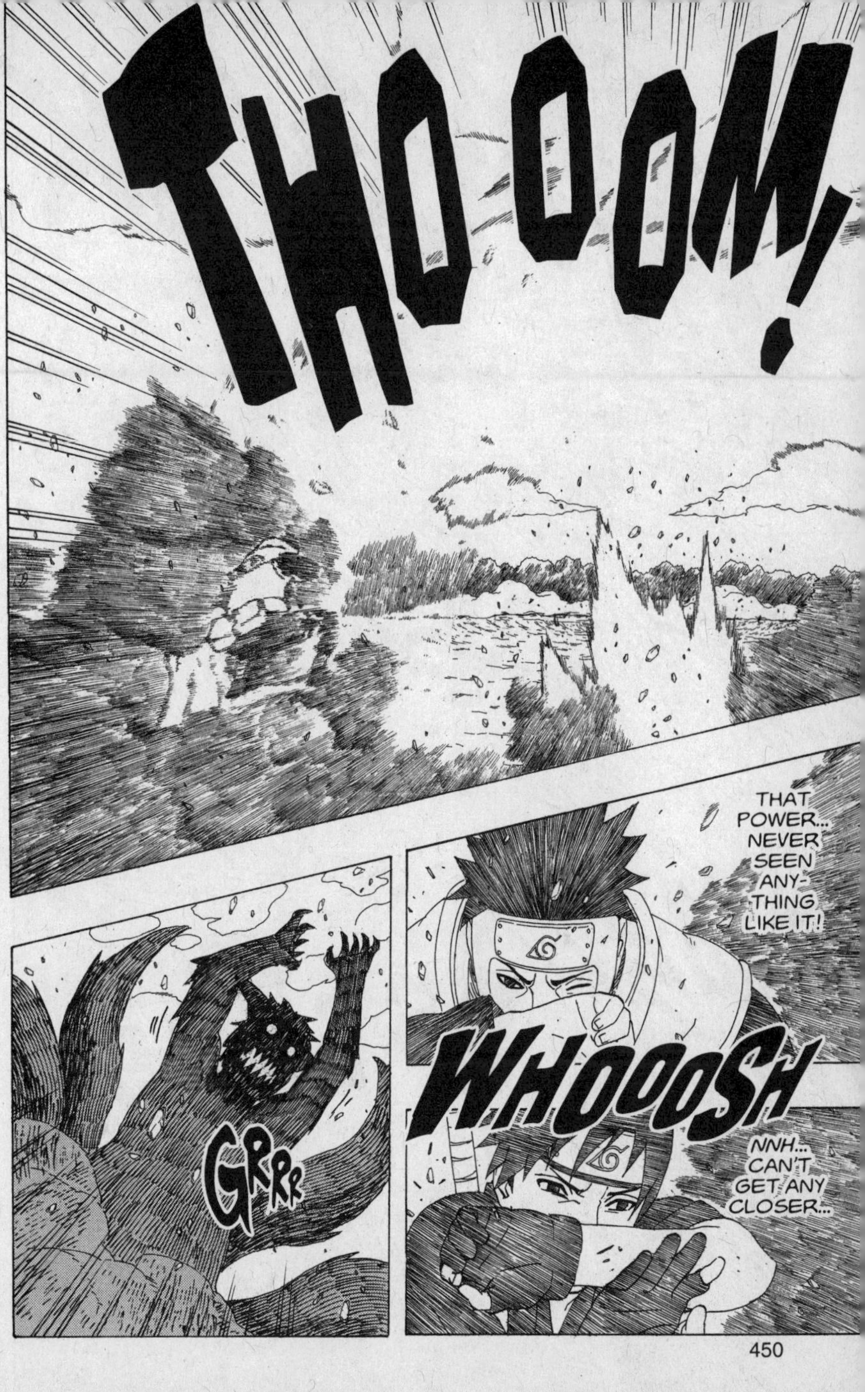
THOOOM!
THAT POWER... NEVER SEEN ANYTHING LIKE IT!
WHOOOSH
NNH... CAN'T GET ANY CLOSER...
GRRR

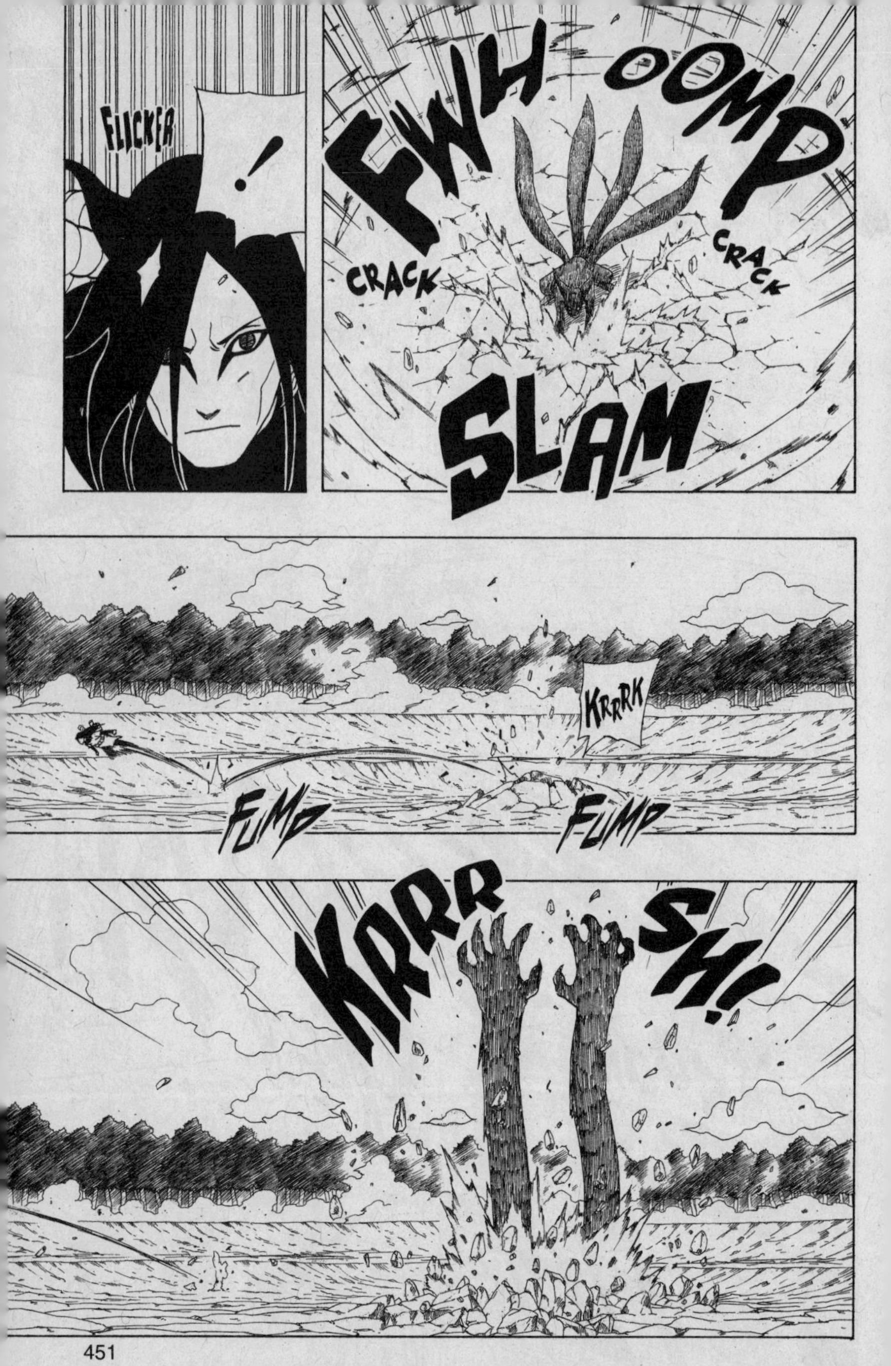
FWHOOMP
CRACK
CRACK
SLAM
FLICKER
!
KRRRK
FUMP
FUMP
KRRRSH!

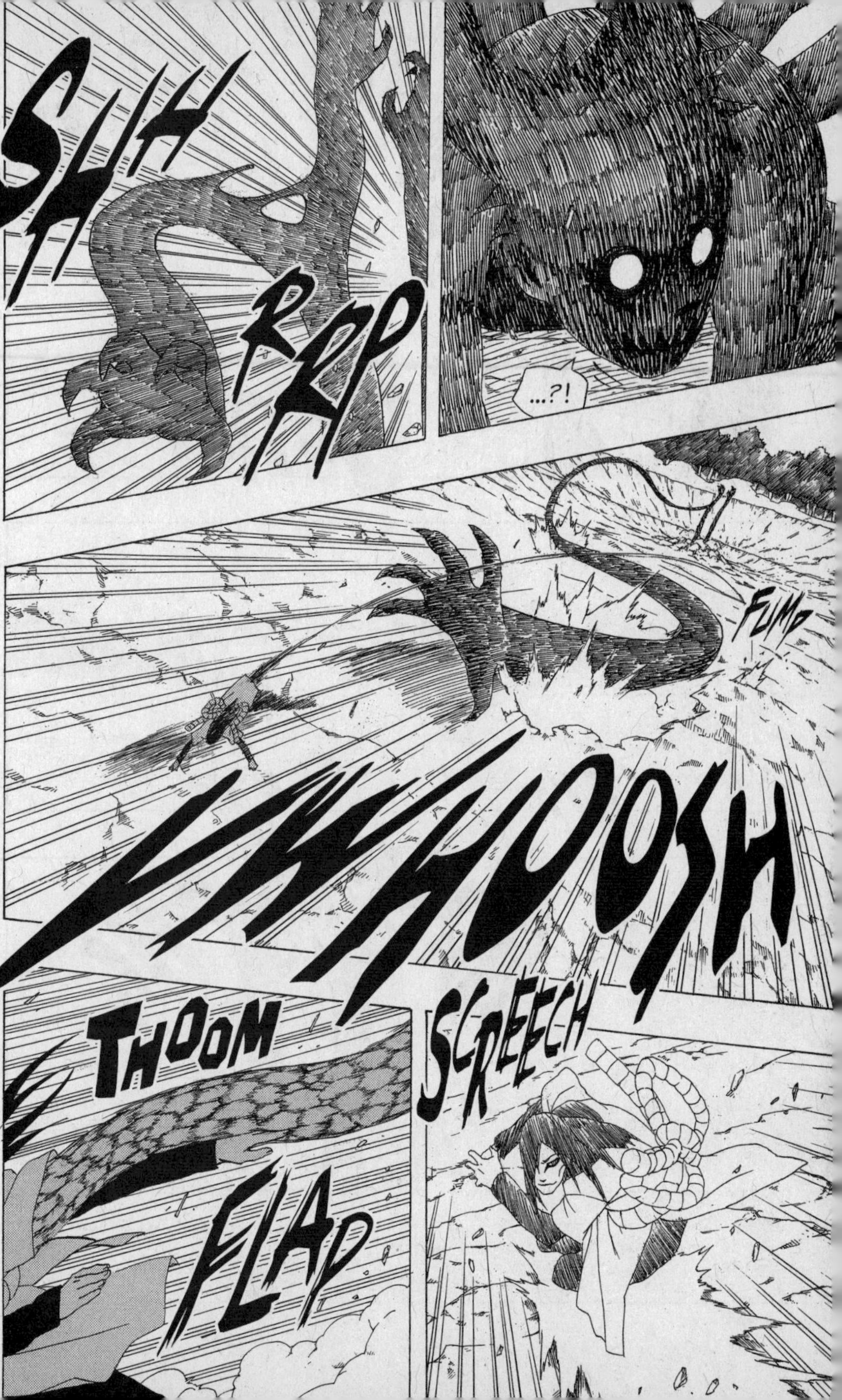
...?!
SHH
RAP
FUMP
WHOOSH
SCREECH
THOOM
FLAP

READ THIS WAY

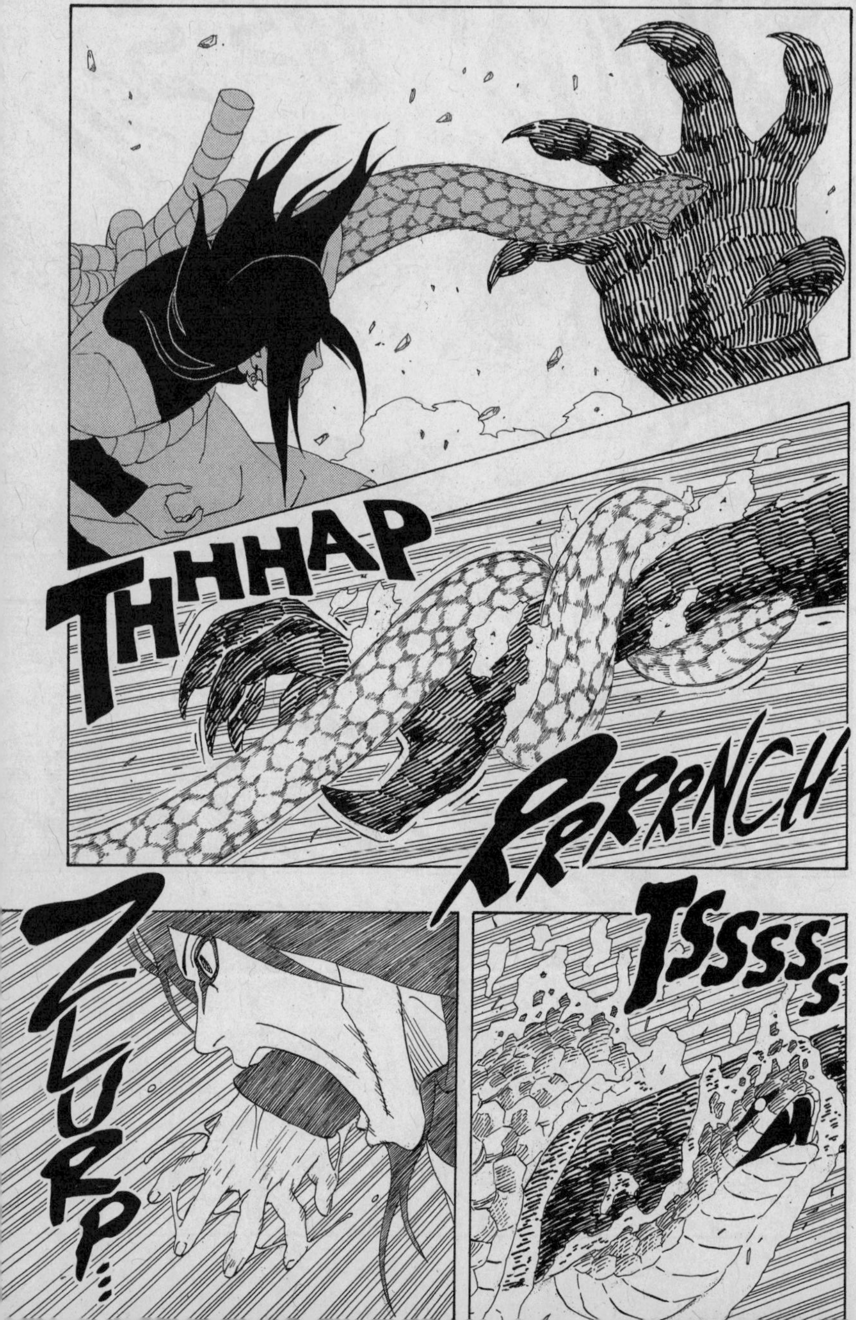
THHHAP
RRRRNCH
TSSSS
SLURP...

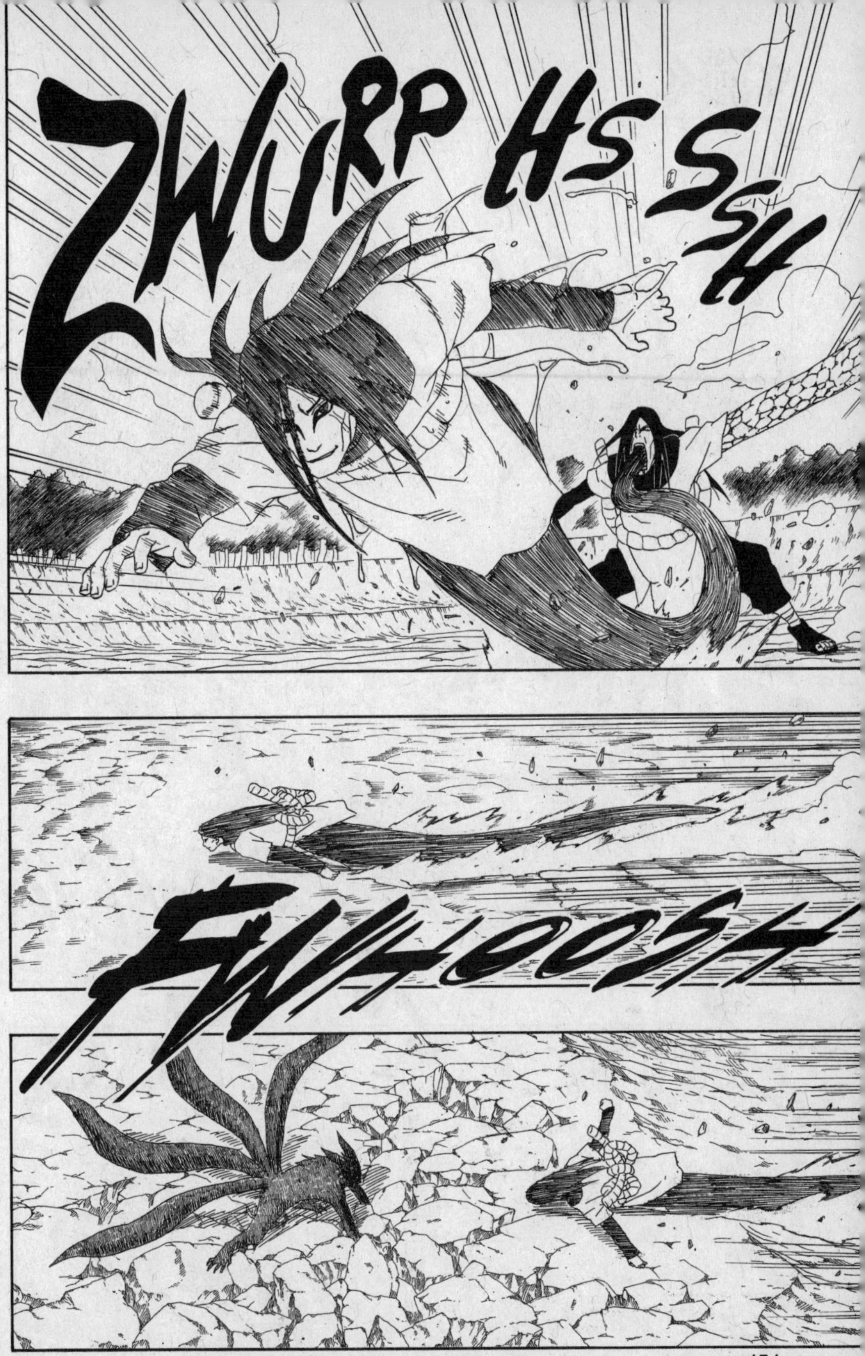
ZWURP
HSSSH
FWHOOSH

READ THIS WAY

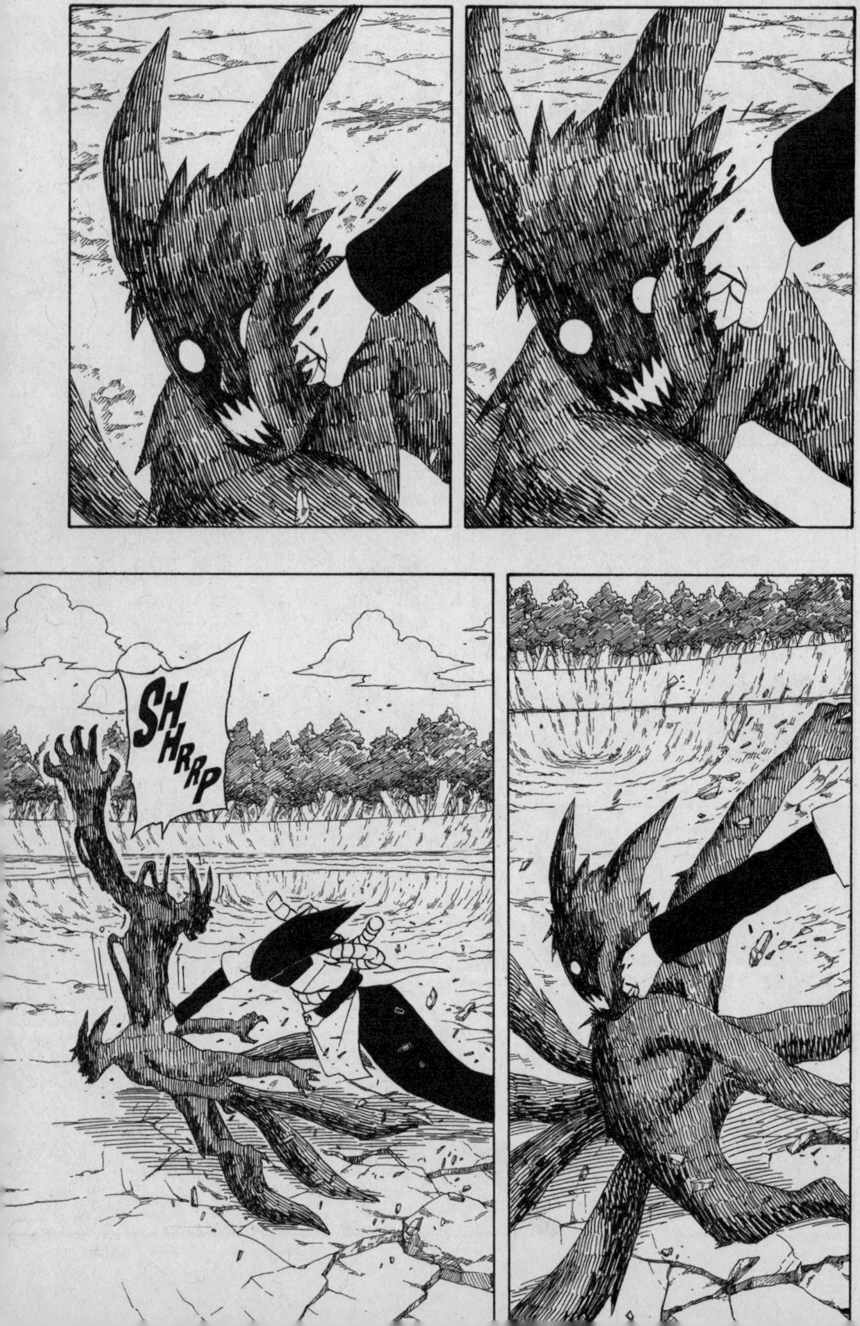
SHHRRP

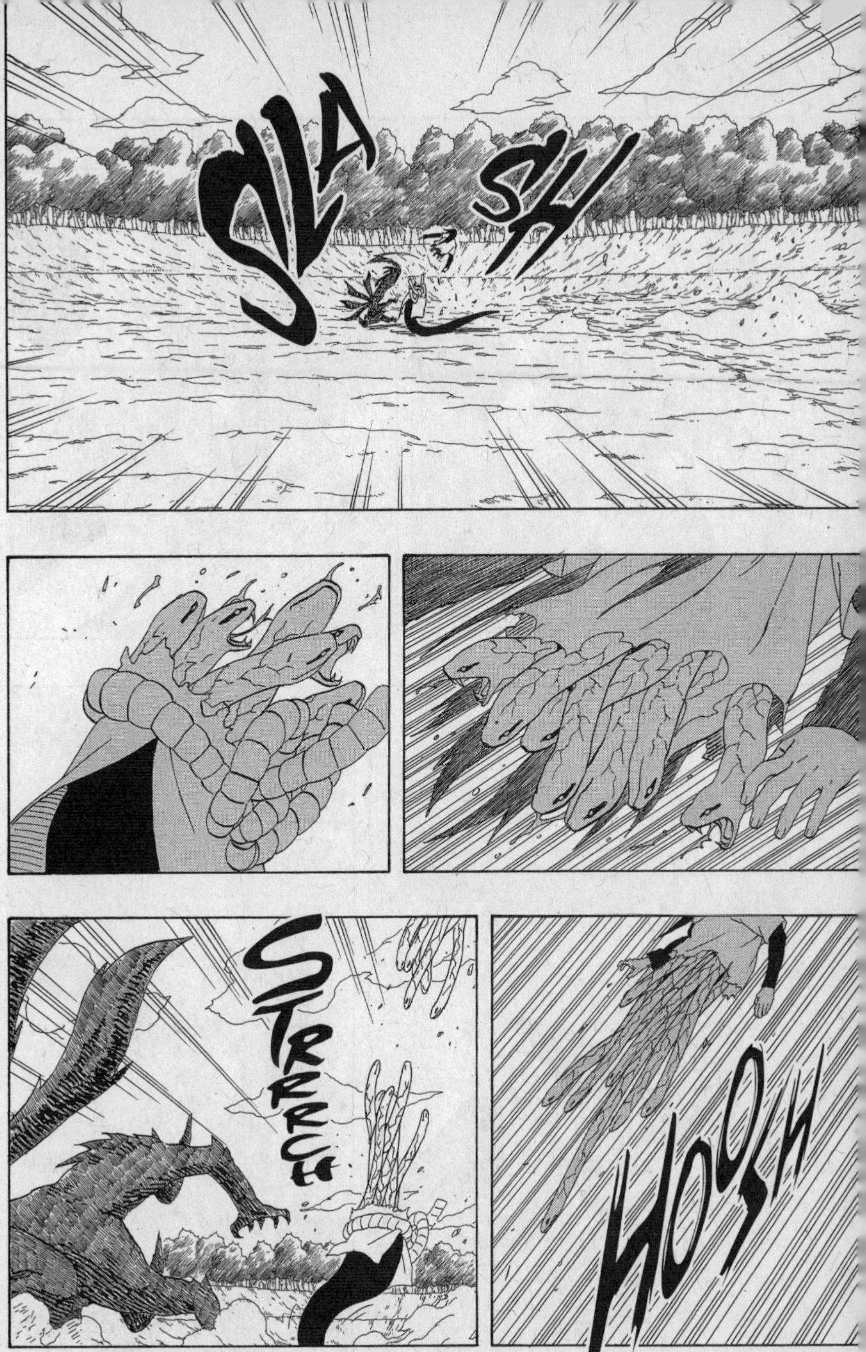
SLASH
WHOOSH
STRRRCH

READ THIS WAY

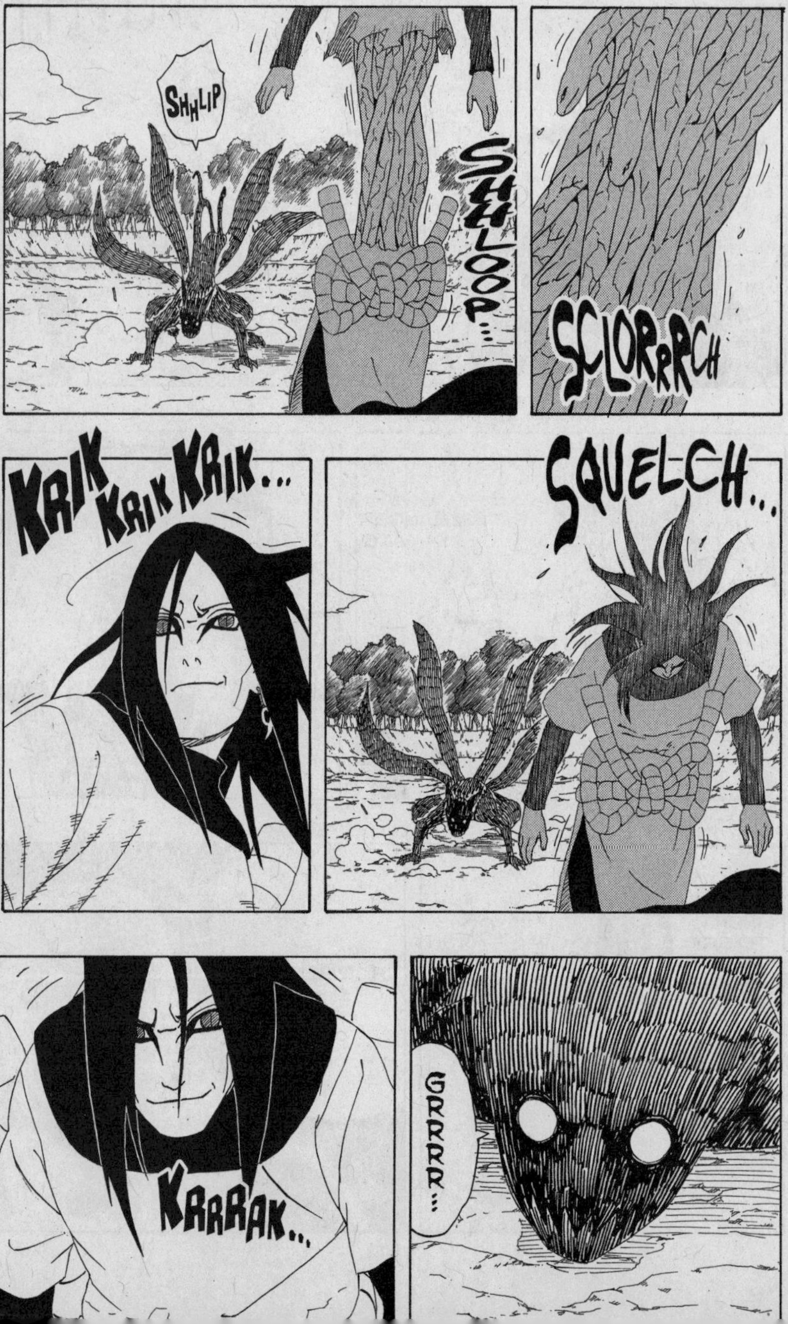
SCLORRRCH
SHHLIP
SHHHLOOP...
SQUELCH...
KRIK KRIK KRIK...
GRRRRR...
KRRRAK...

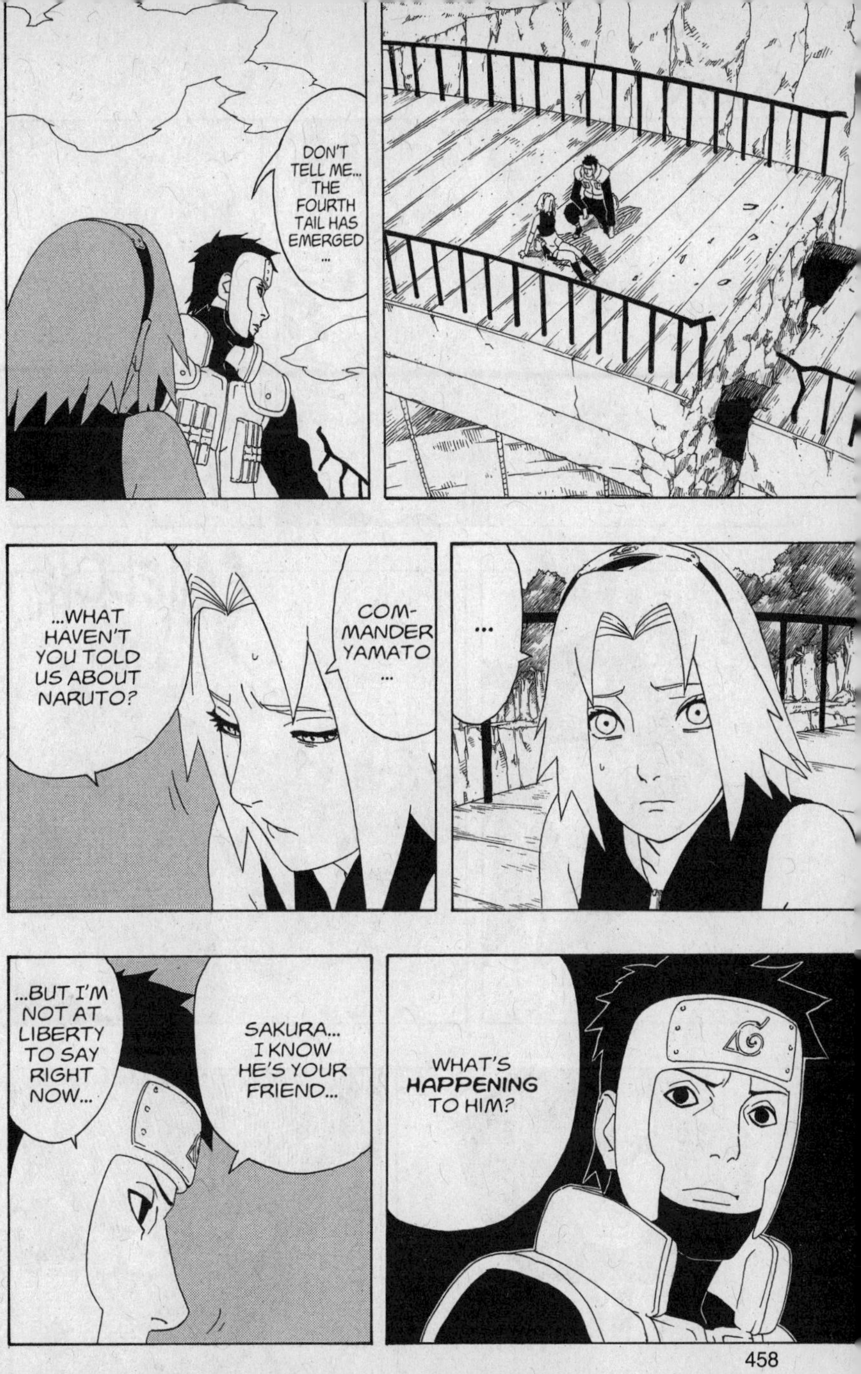
DON'T TELL ME... THE FOURTH TAIL HAS EMERGED...
...
COM-MANDER YAMATO...
...WHAT HAVEN'T YOU TOLD US ABOUT NARUTO?
WHAT'S **HAPPENING** TO HIM?
SAKURA... I KNOW HE'S YOUR FRIEND...
...BUT I'M NOT AT LIBERTY TO SAY RIGHT NOW...

READ THIS WAY

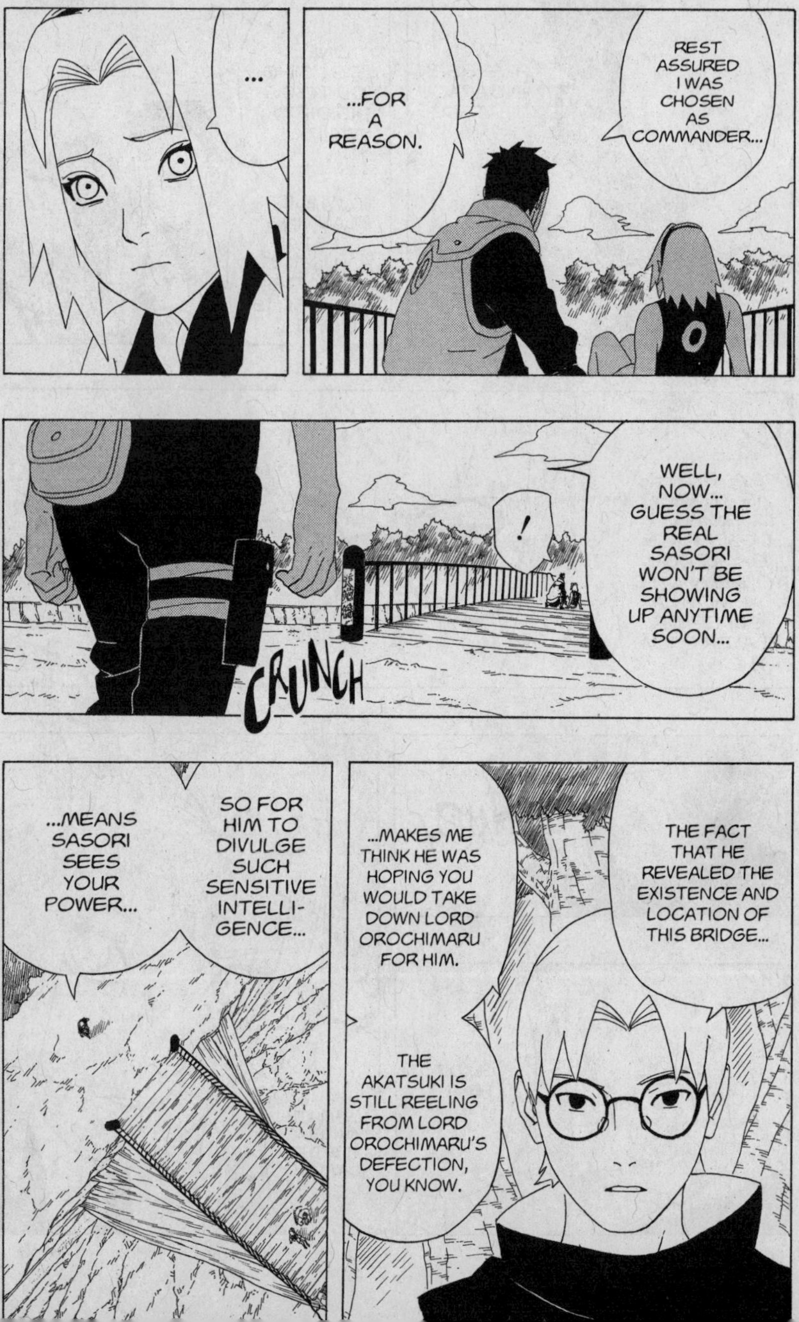
REST ASSURED I WAS CHOSEN AS COMMANDER...
...FOR A REASON.
...
WELL, NOW... GUESS THE REAL SASORI WON'T BE SHOWING UP ANYTIME SOON...
!
CRUNCH
THE FACT THAT HE REVEALED THE EXISTENCE AND LOCATION OF THIS BRIDGE...
...MAKES ME THINK HE WAS HOPING YOU WOULD TAKE DOWN LORD OROCHIMARU FOR HIM.
THE AKATSUKI IS STILL REELING FROM LORD OROCHIMARU'S DEFECTION, YOU KNOW.
SO FOR HIM TO DIVULGE SUCH SENSITIVE INTELLI-GENCE...
...MEANS SASORI SEES YOUR POWER...

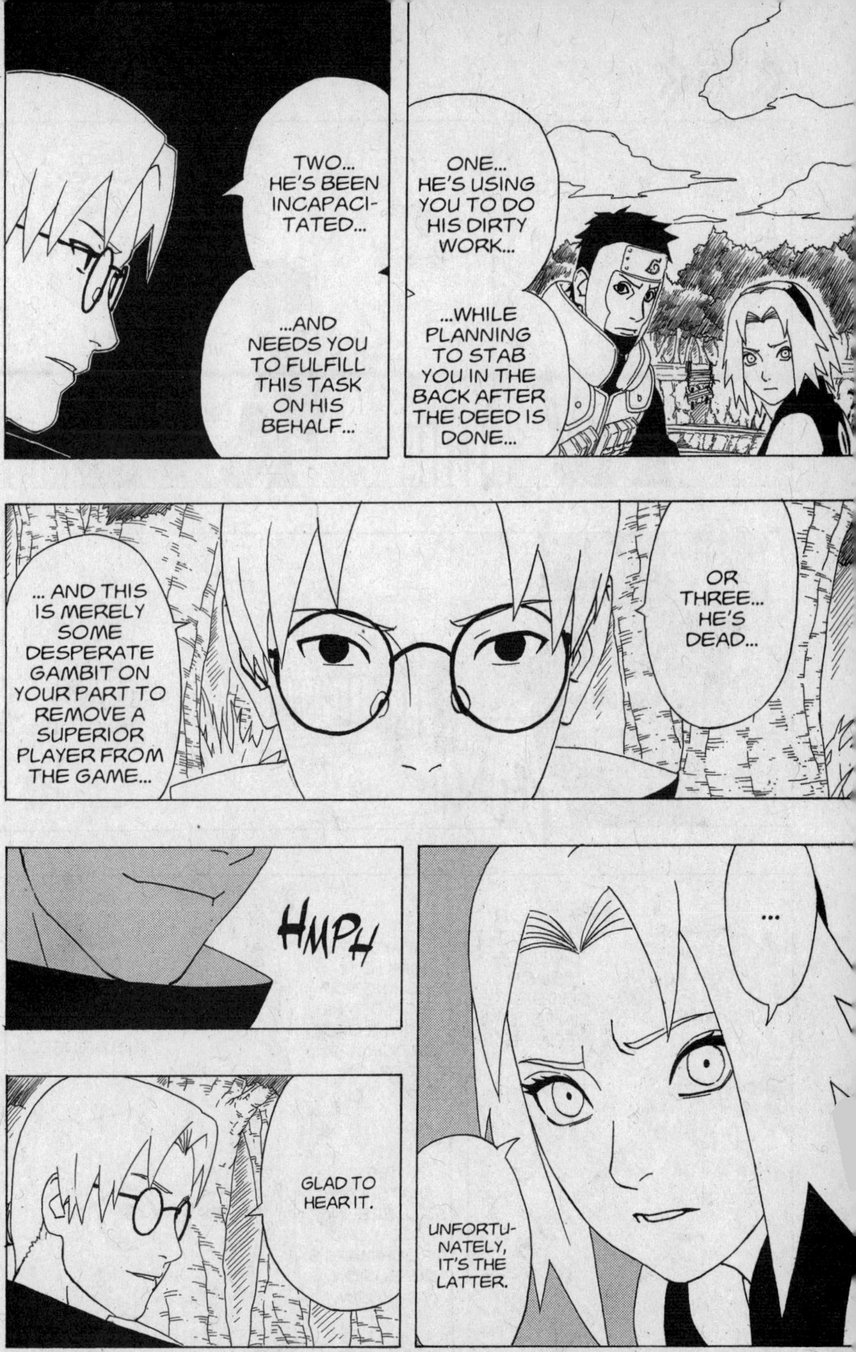
ONE... HE'S USING YOU TO DO HIS DIRTY WORK...
...WHILE PLANNING TO STAB YOU IN THE BACK AFTER THE DEED IS DONE...
TWO... HE'S BEEN INCAPACITATED...
...AND NEEDS YOU TO FULFILL THIS TASK ON HIS BEHALF...
OR THREE... HE'S DEAD...
... AND THIS IS MERELY SOME DESPERATE GAMBIT ON YOUR PART TO REMOVE A SUPERIOR PLAYER FROM THE GAME...
...
UNFORTUNATELY, IT'S THE LATTER.
HMPH
GLAD TO HEAR IT.

READ THIS WAY

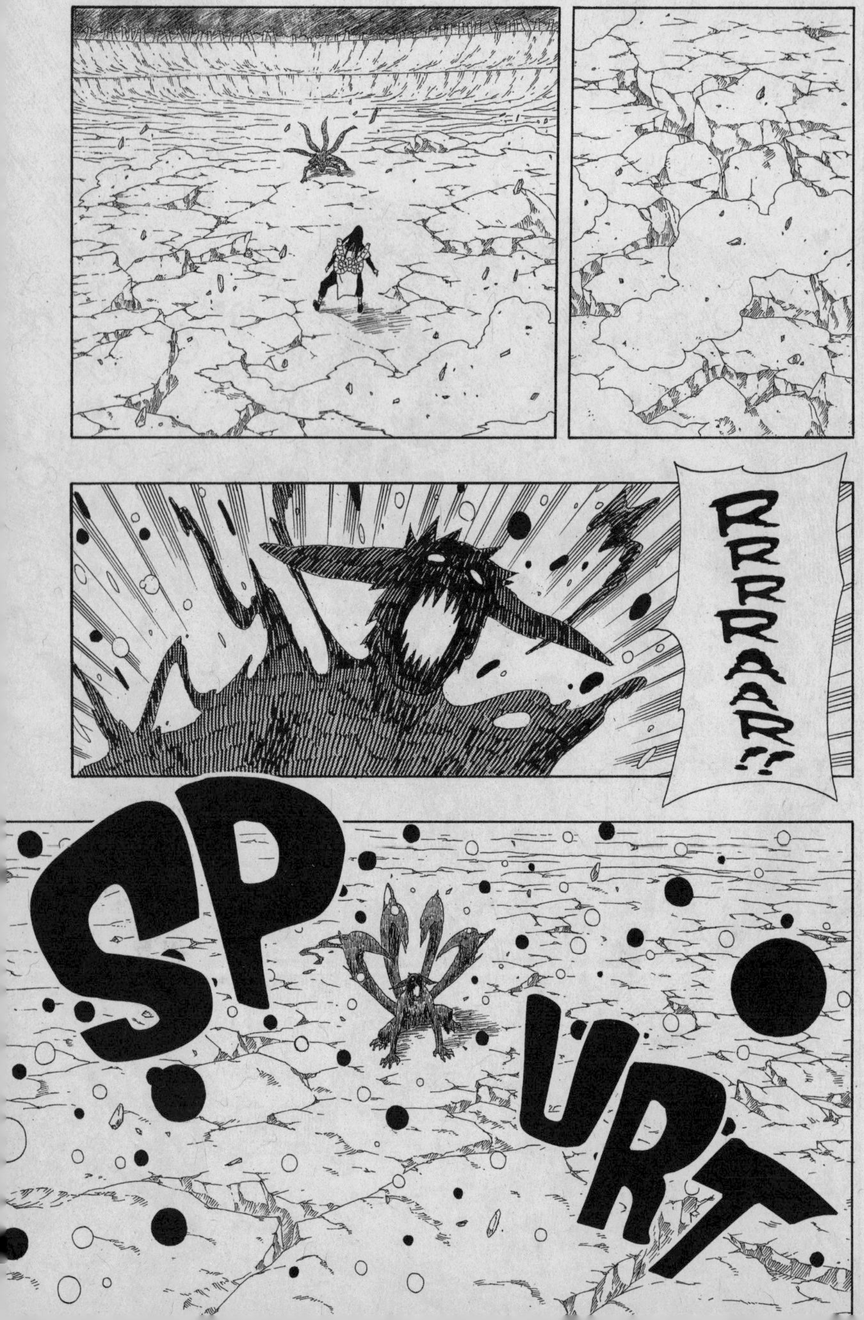
RRRRAAR!!
SPURT

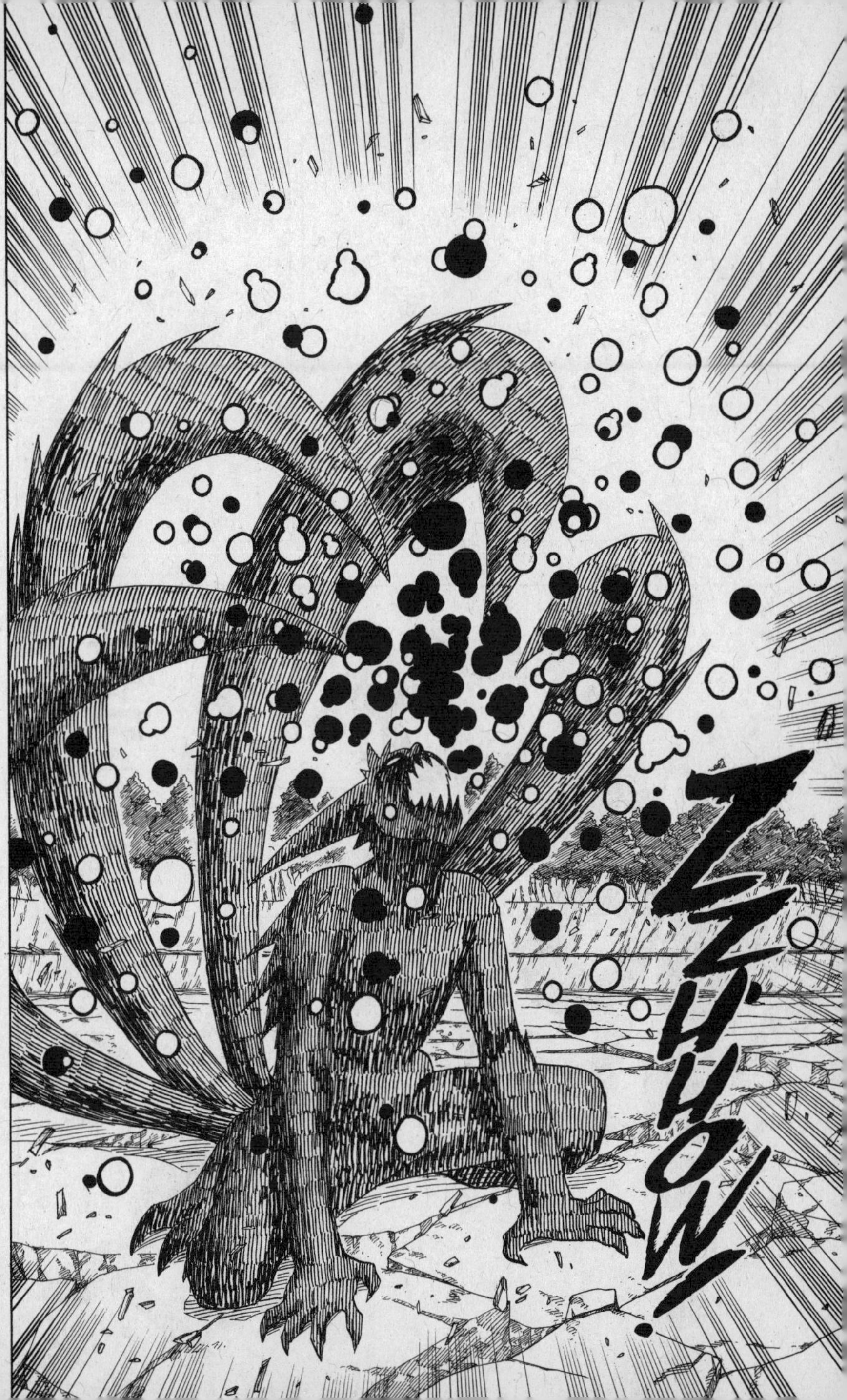
ZWUUOM!

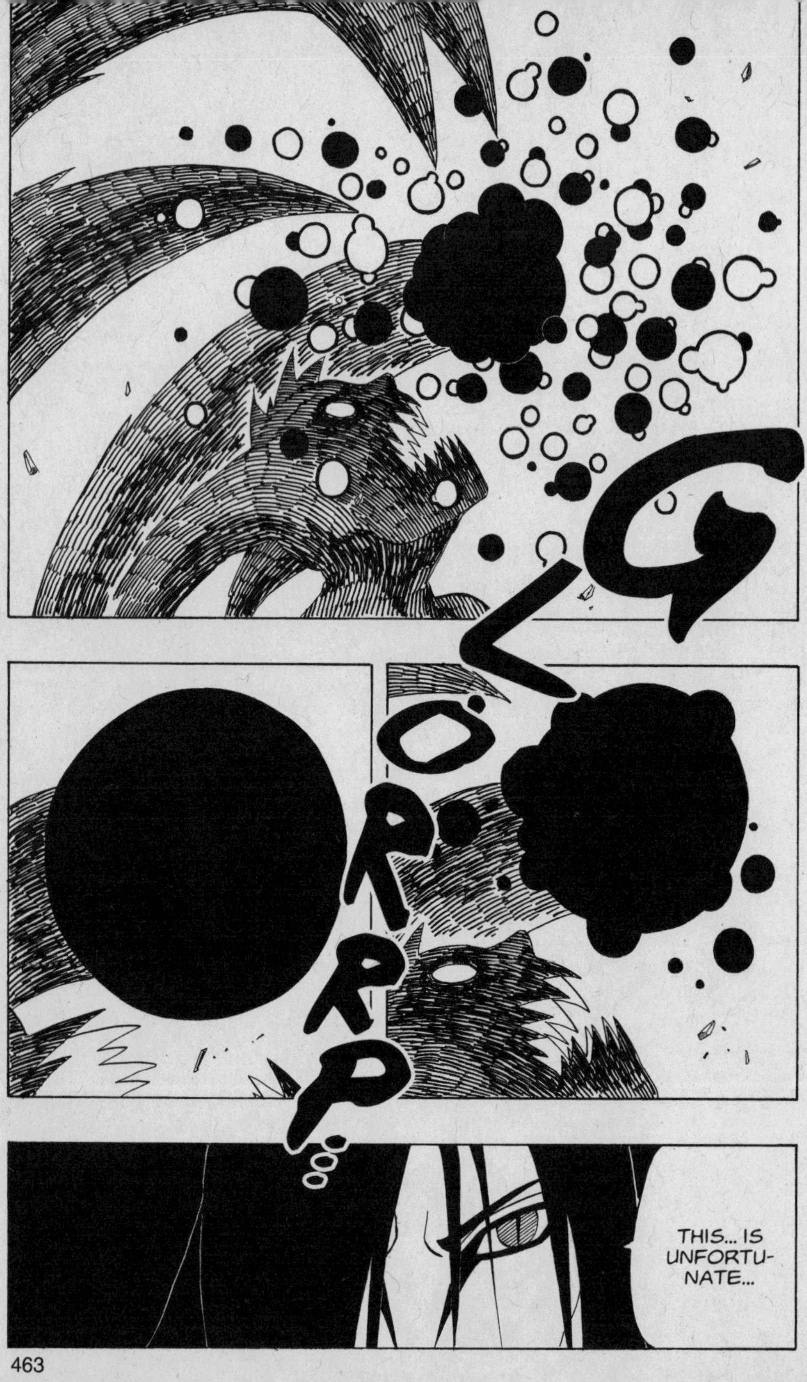
GLORRP...
THIS... IS UNFORTU-NATE...

NARUTO

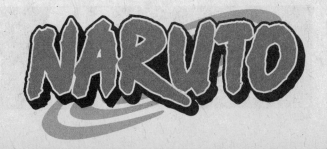

Number 295: Toward Nine Tails...!!

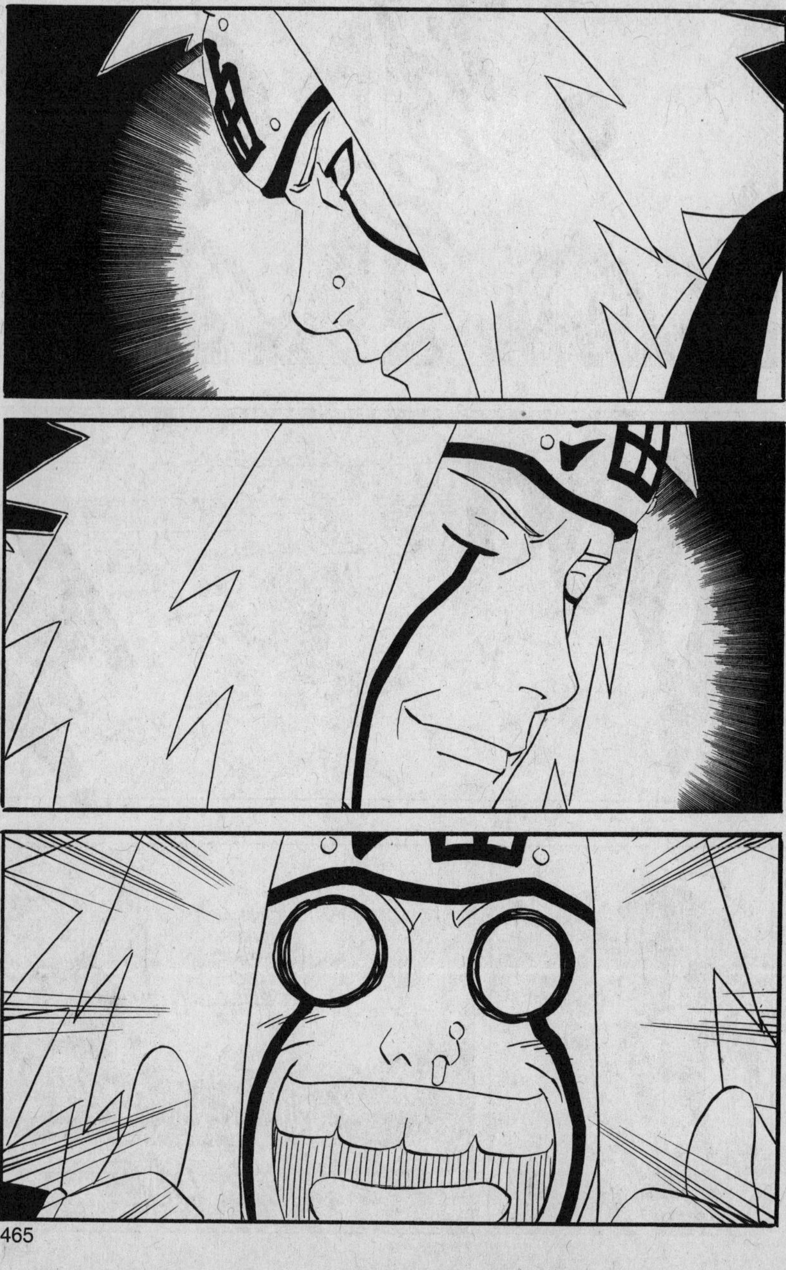

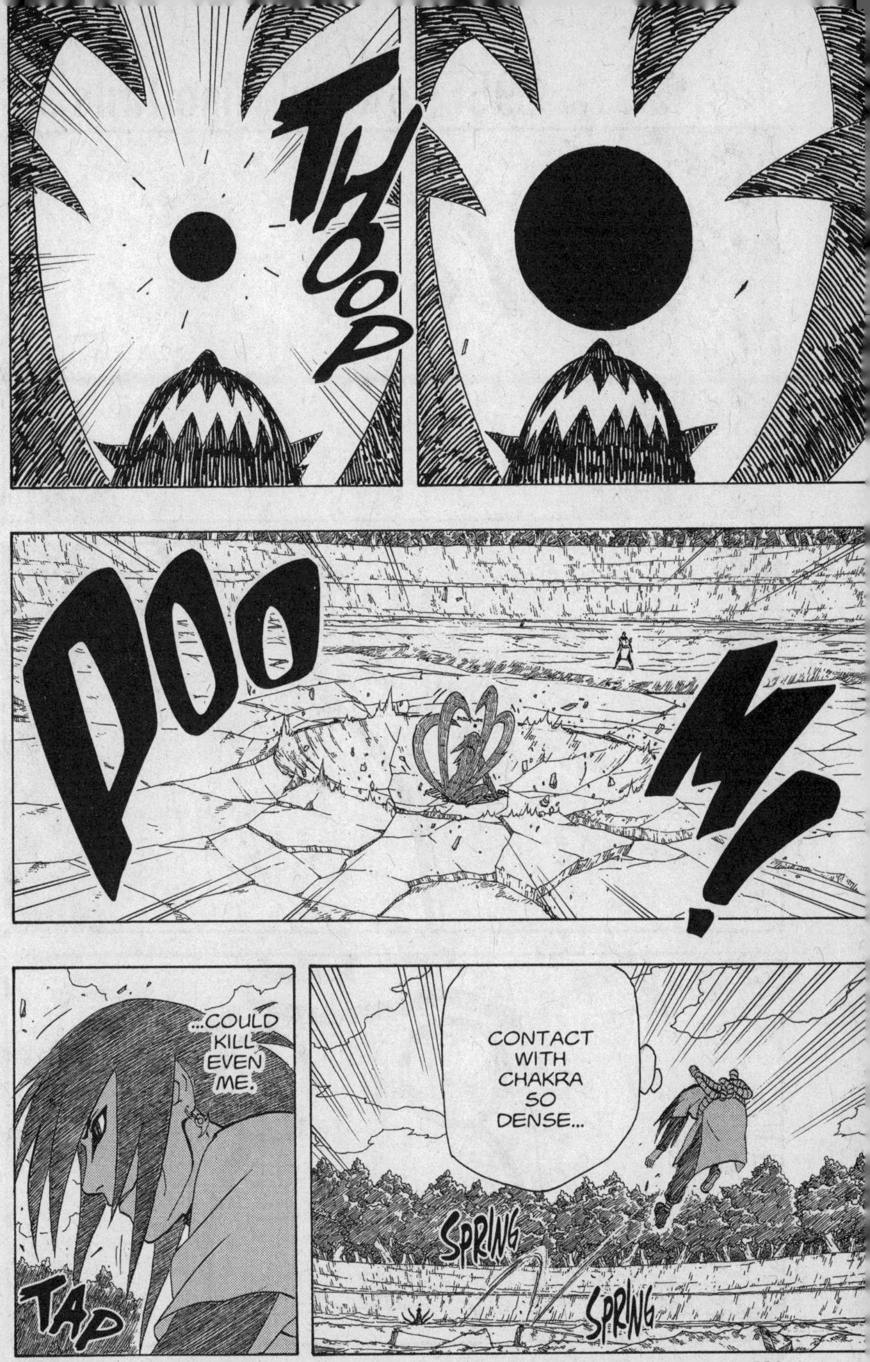
THOOP
DOOM!
CONTACT WITH CHAKRA SO DENSE...
SPRING
SPRING
...COULD KILL EVEN ME.
TAP

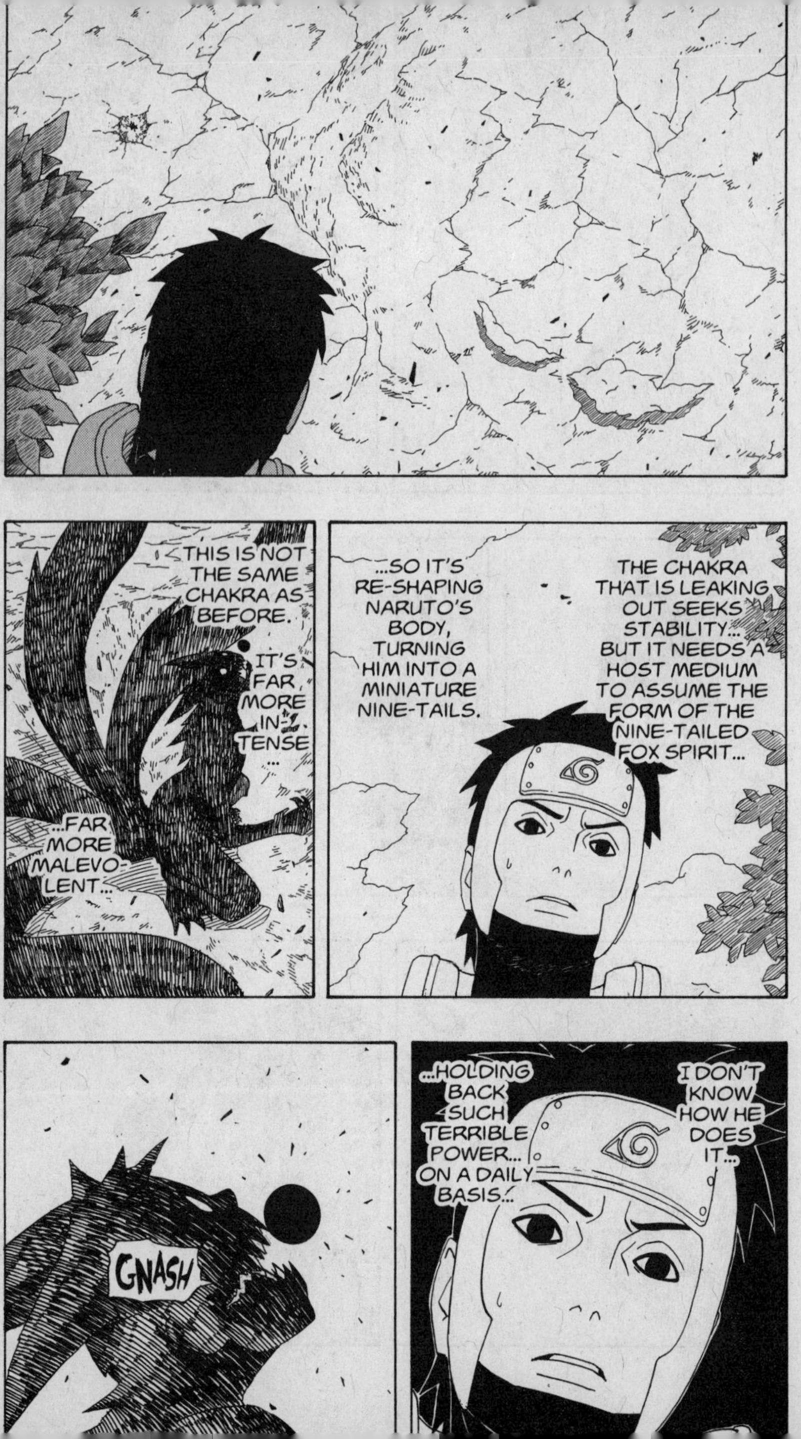
THE CHAKRA THAT IS LEAKING OUT SEEKS STABILITY... BUT IT NEEDS A HOST MEDIUM TO ASSUME THE FORM OF THE NINE-TAILED FOX SPIRIT...
...SO IT'S RE-SHAPING NARUTO'S BODY, TURNING HIM INTO A MINIATURE NINE-TAILS.
THIS IS NOT THE SAME CHAKRA AS BEFORE.
IT'S FAR, MORE IN-TENSE...
...FAR MORE MALEVO-LENT...
I DON'T KNOW HOW HE DOES IT...
...HOLDING BACK SUCH TERRIBLE POWER... ON A DAILY BASIS...
GNASH

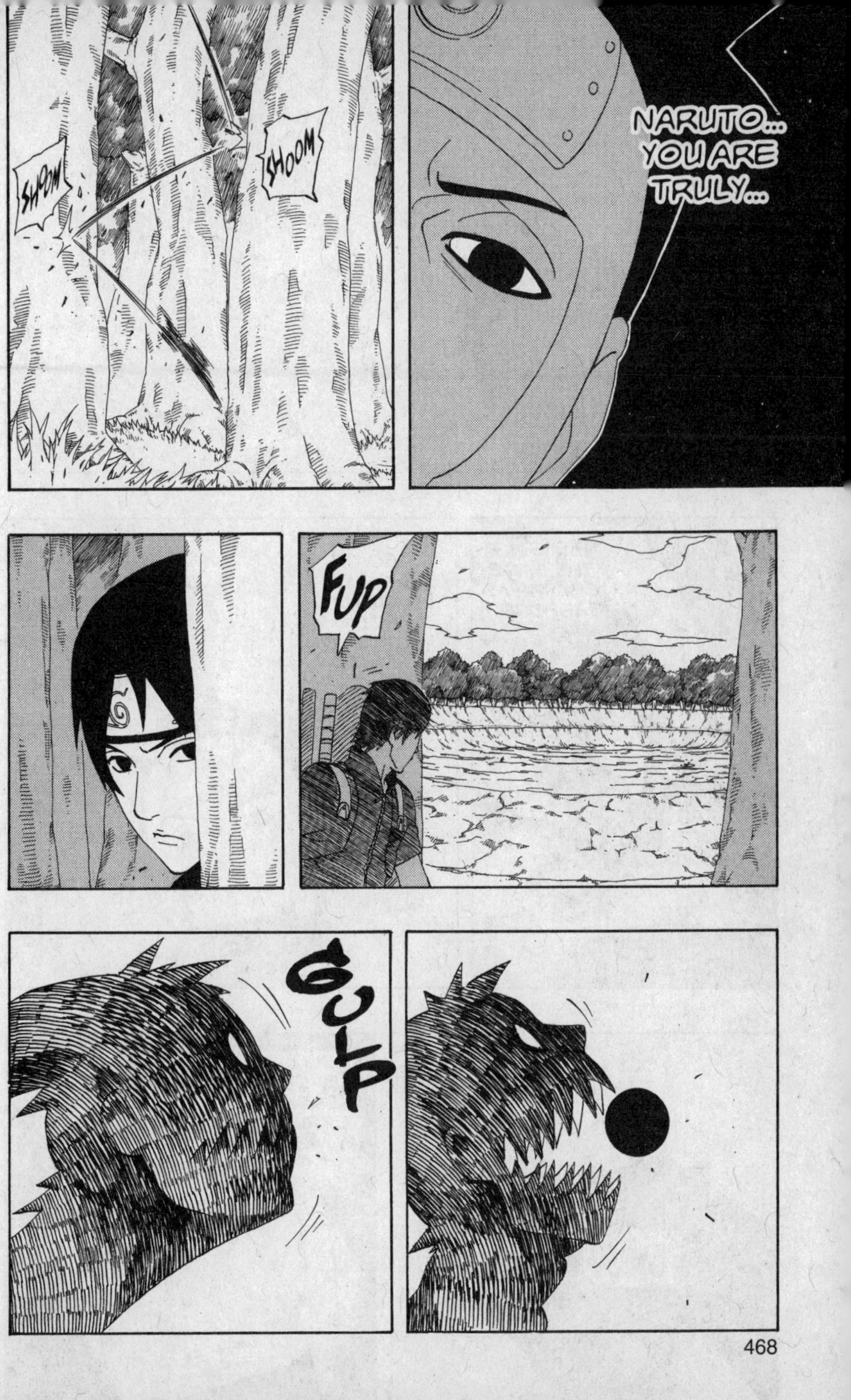
NARUTO... YOU ARE TRULY...
SHOOM
SHOOM
FUP
GULP

READ THIS WAY

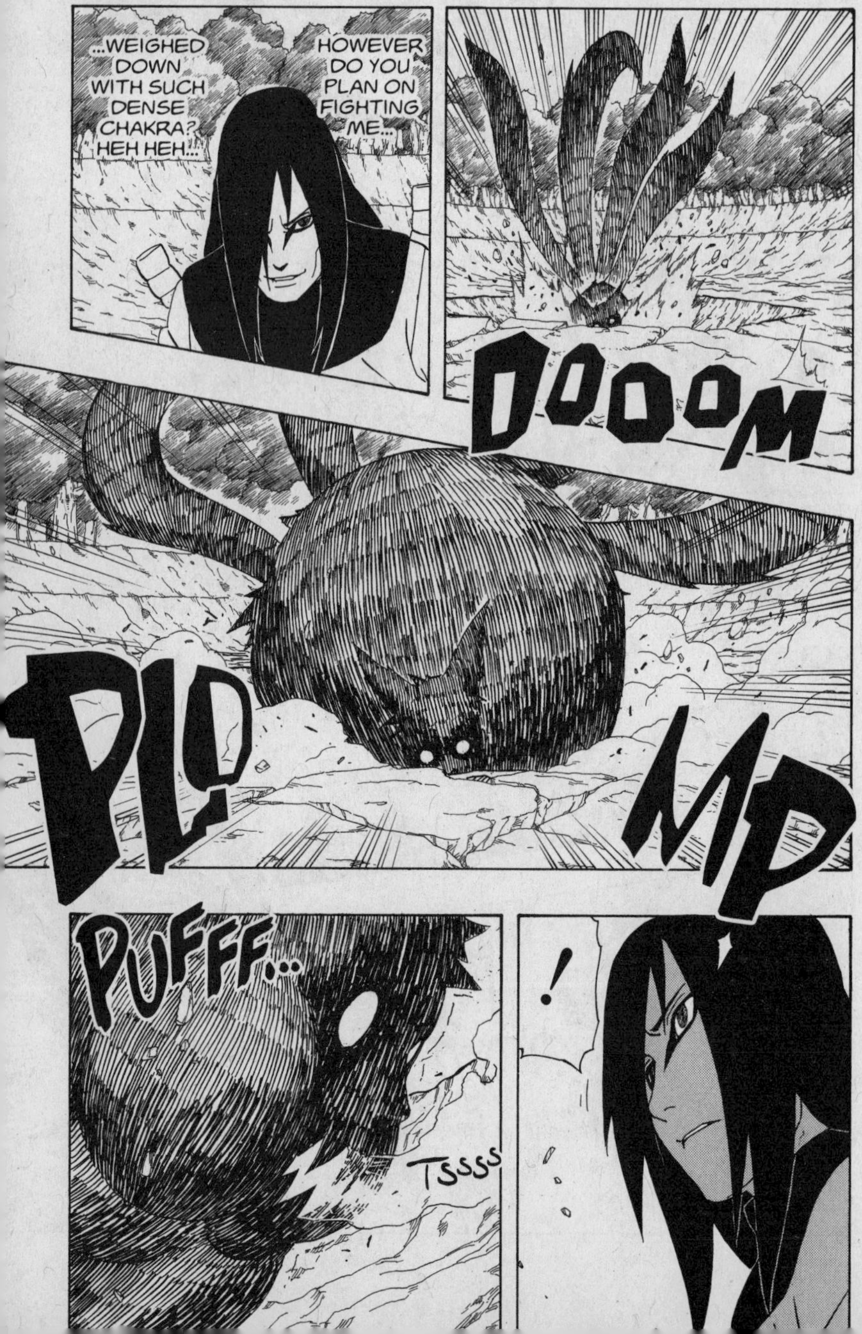
DOOOM
HOWEVER DO YOU PLAN ON FIGHTING ME...
...WEIGHED DOWN WITH SUCH DENSE CHAKRA? HEH HEH...
PLOMP
!
PUFFF...
TSSSS

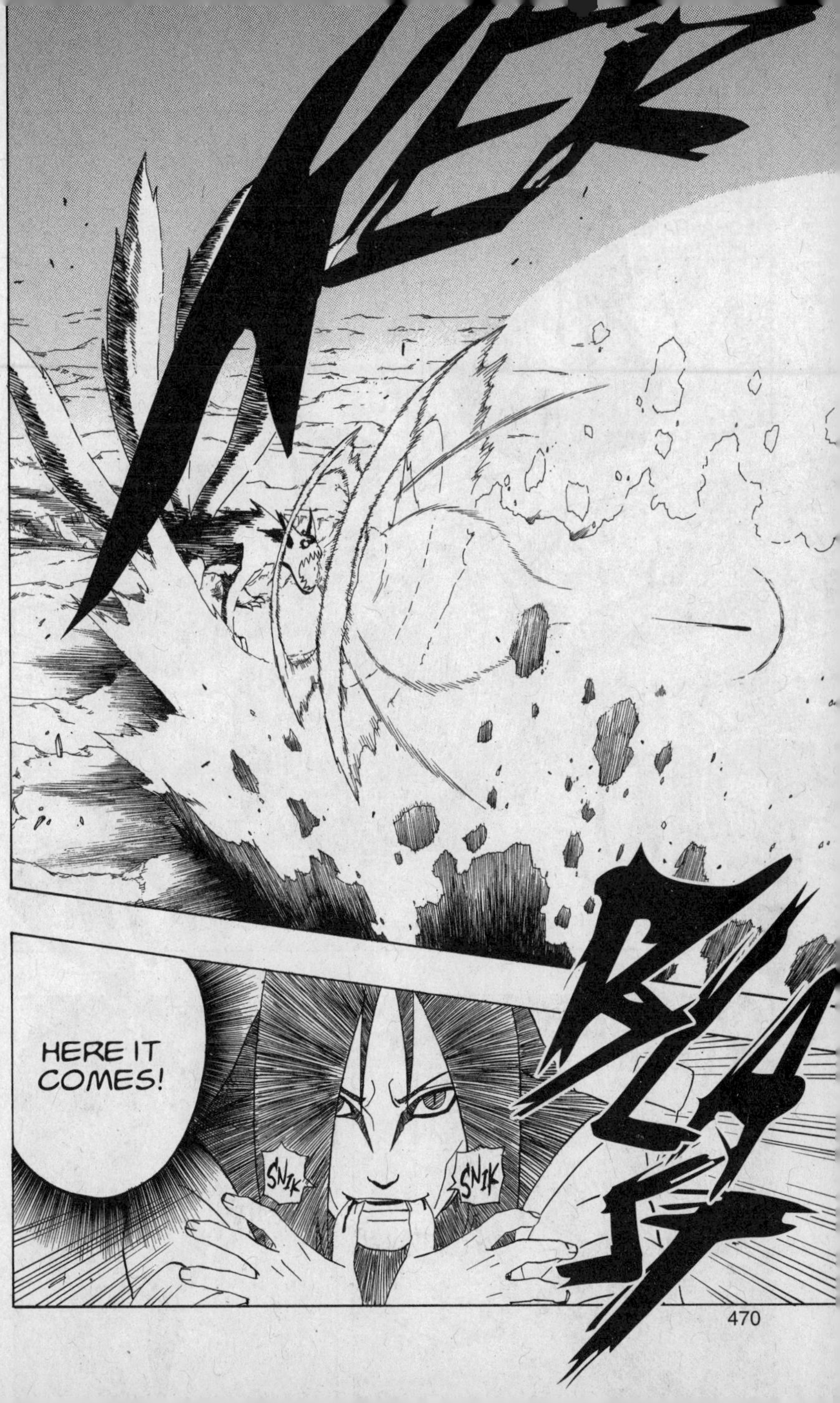
HERE IT COMES!
SNIK
SNIK

READ THIS WAY

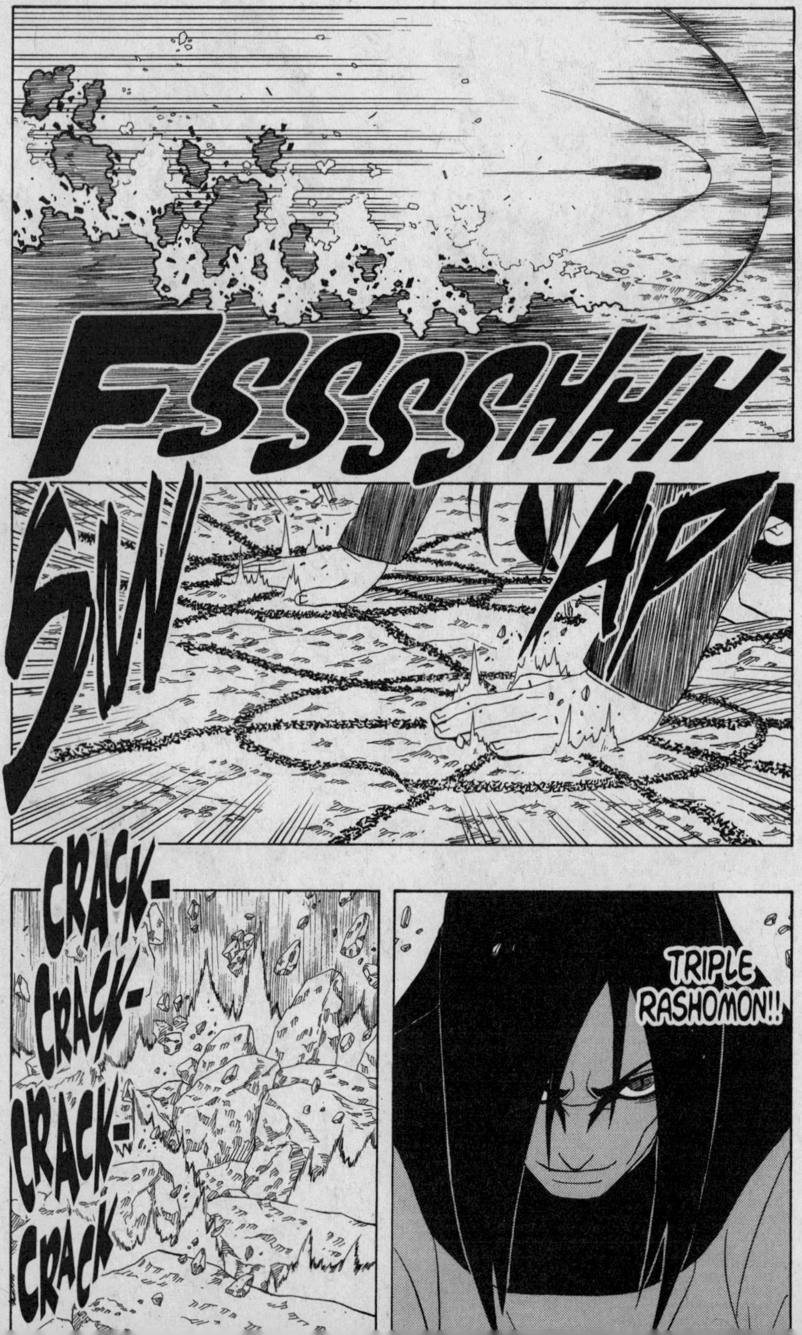
FSSSHH
SWAP
TRIPLE RASHOMON!!
CRACK-CRACK-CRACK-CRACK

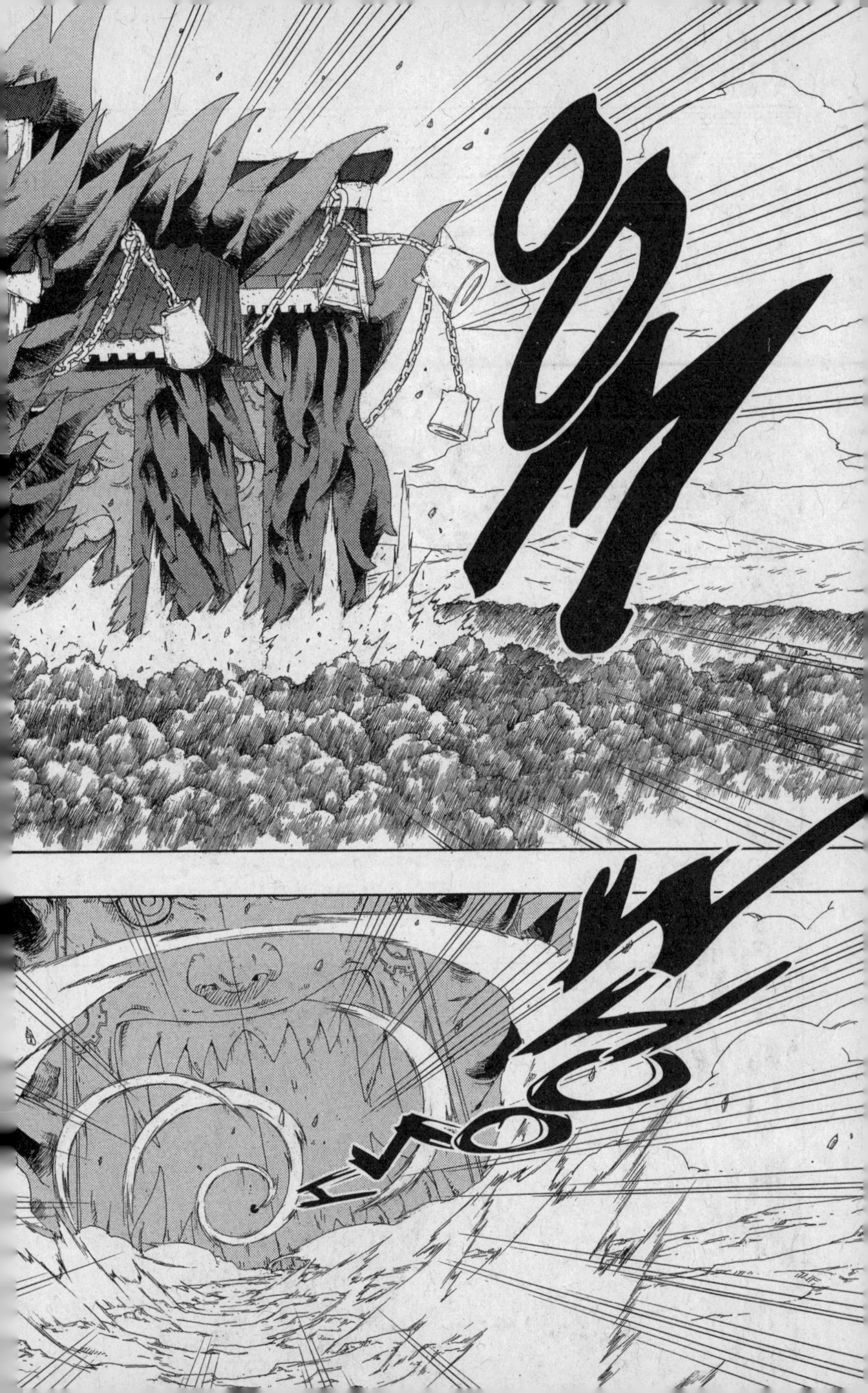

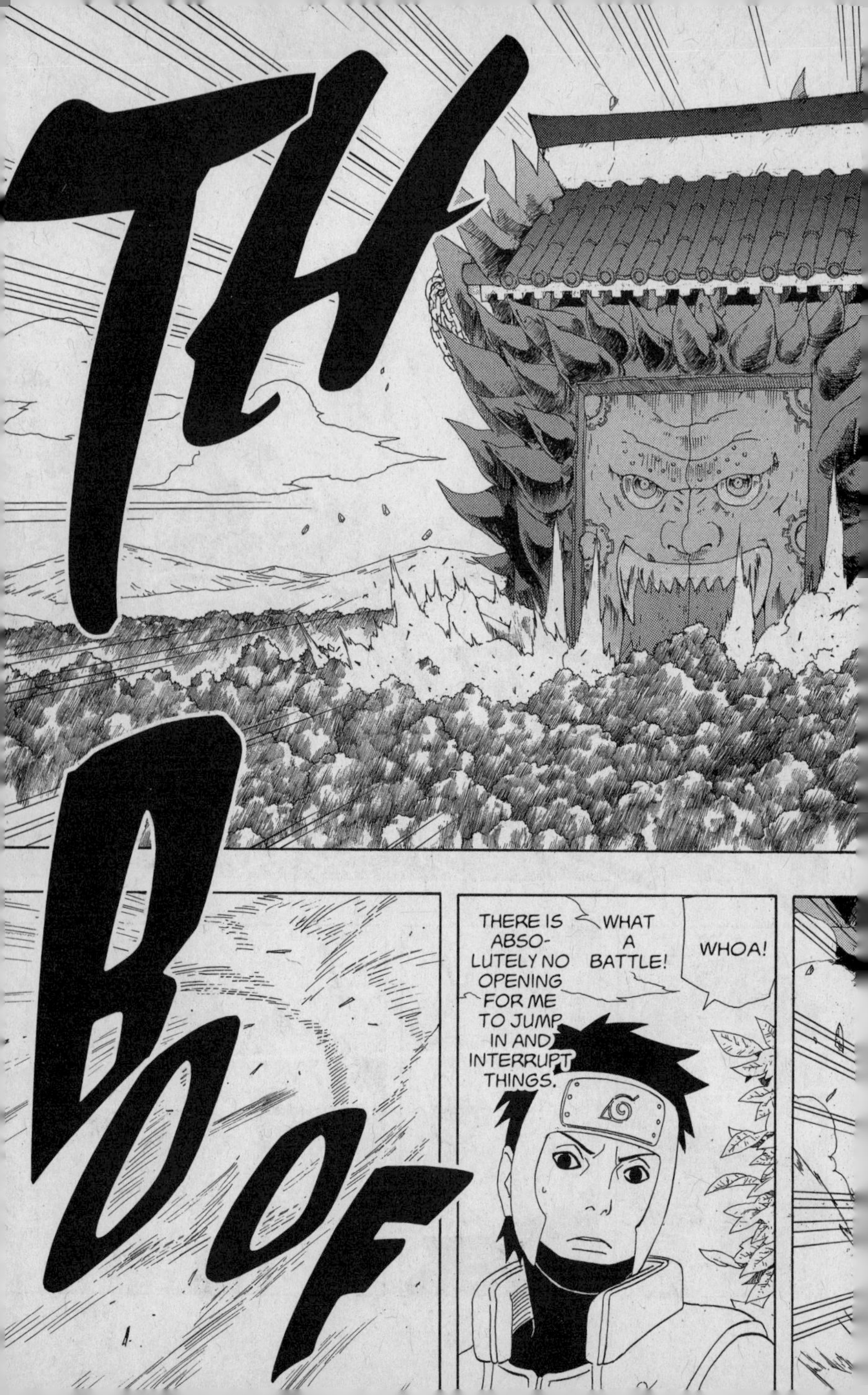
THBOOF
WHOA!
WHAT A BATTLE!
THERE IS ABSOLUTELY NO OPENING FOR ME TO JUMP IN AND INTERRUPT THINGS.

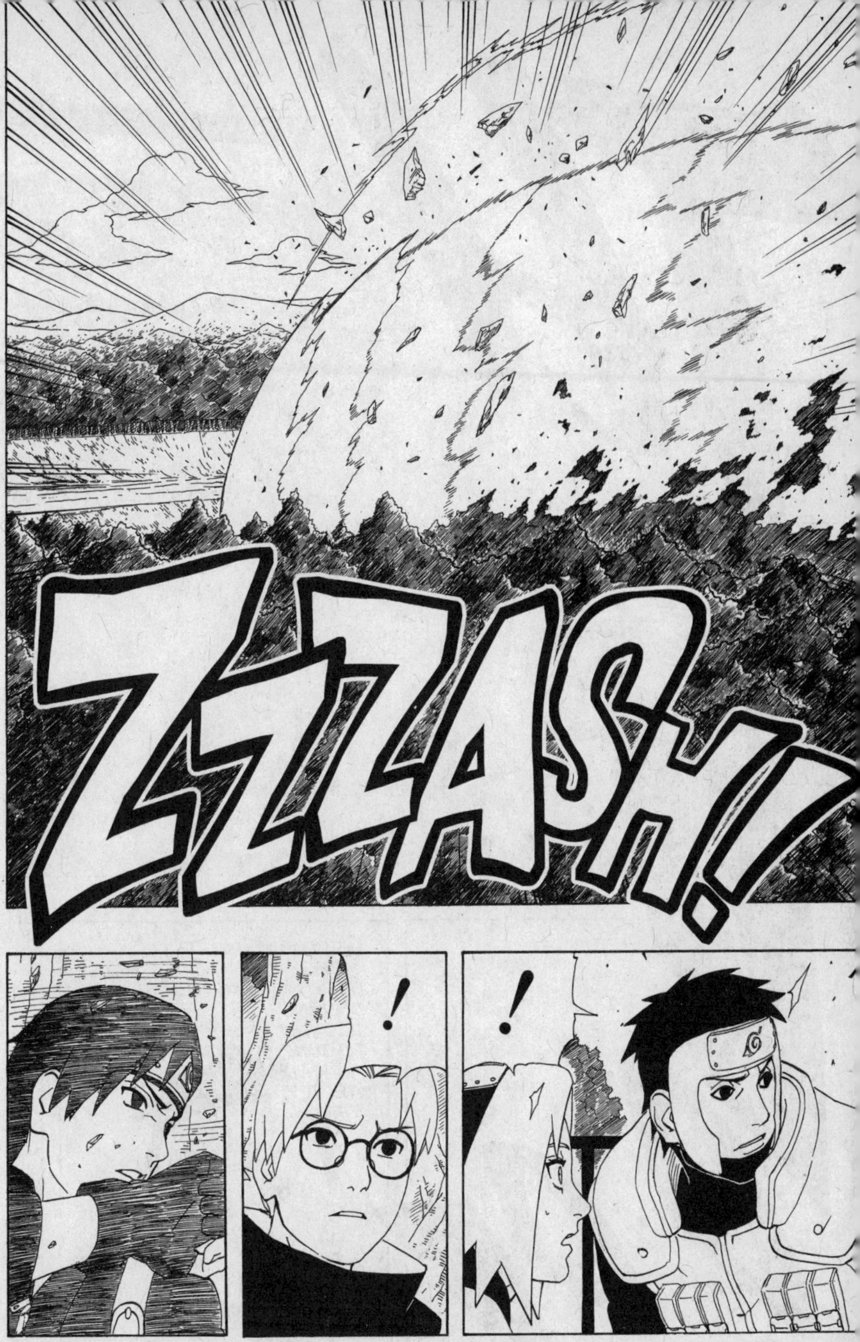
ZZZASH!!
!
!

READ THIS WAY

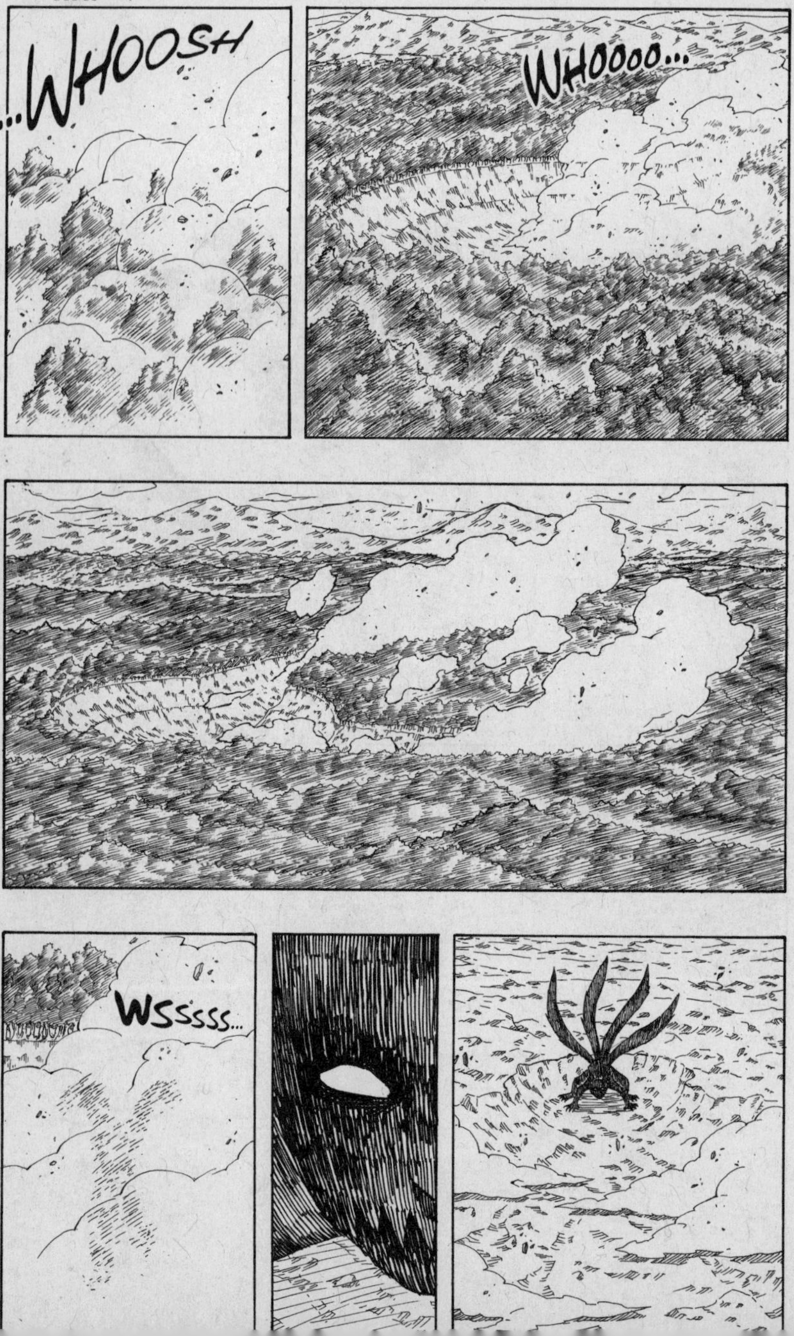
WHOOOO...
...WHOOSH
WSSSSS...

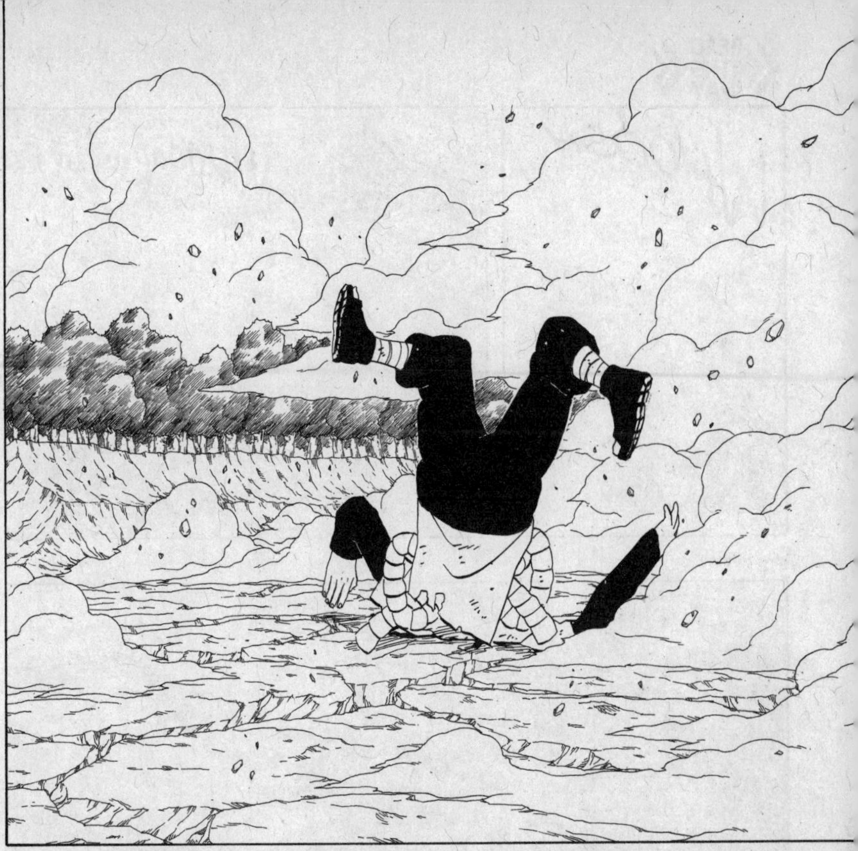
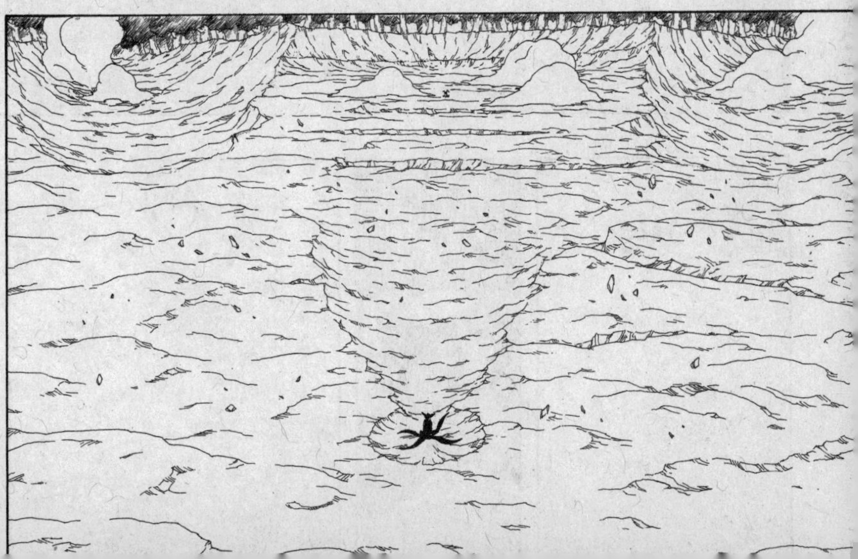

READ THIS WAY

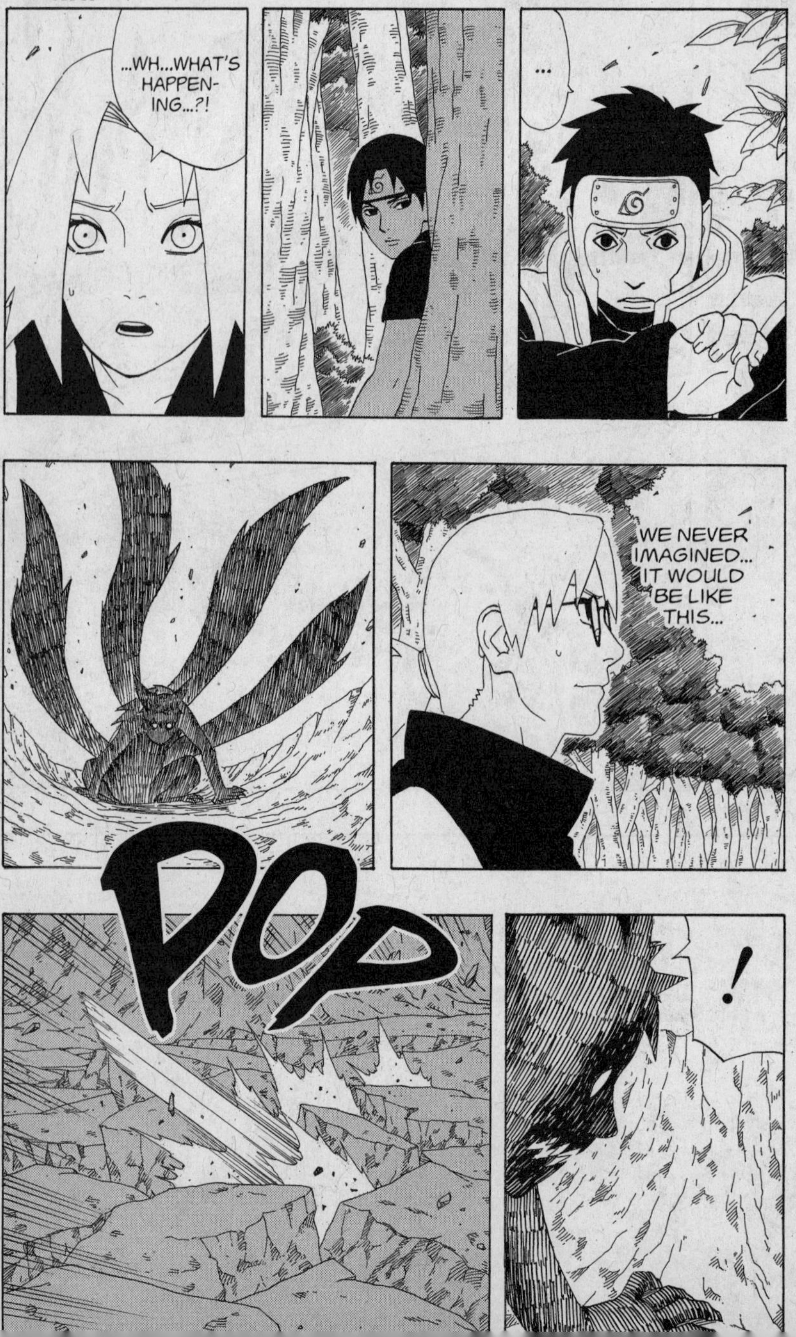
...
...WH...WHAT'S HAPPEN-ING...?!
WE NEVER IMAGINED... IT WOULD BE LIKE THIS...
!
POP

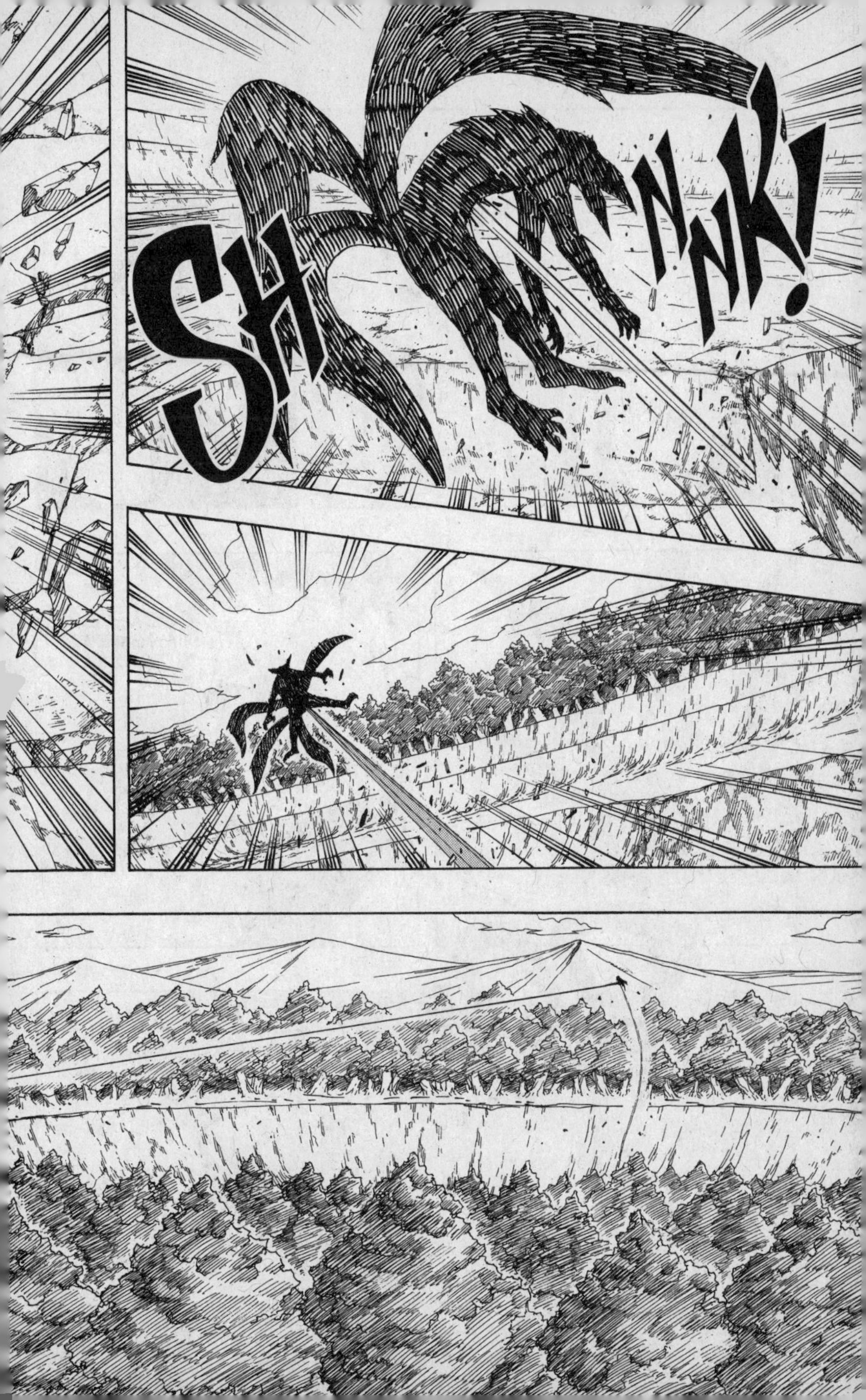
SHTNNK!

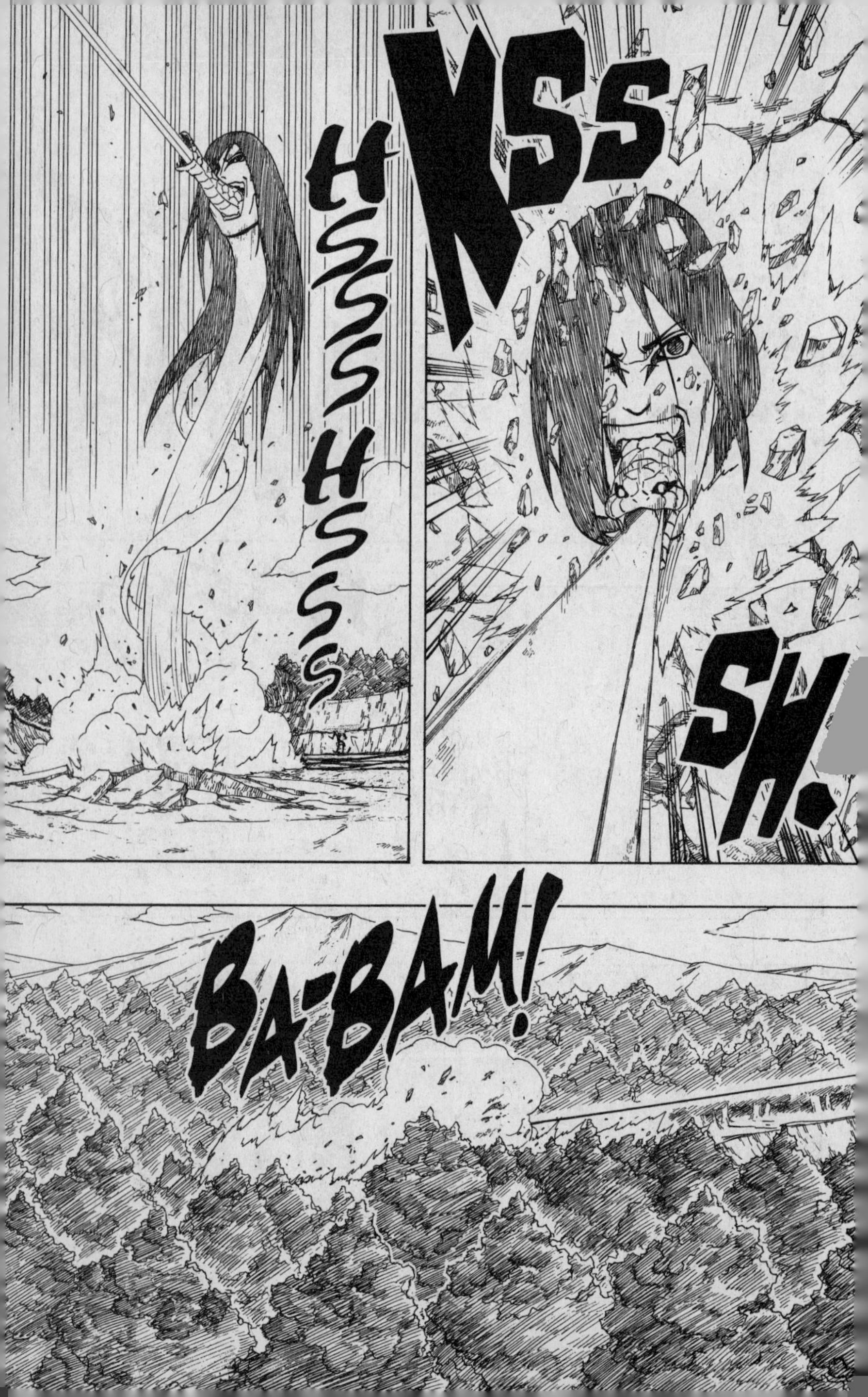

KSS
SH.
HSSSHSSSS
BA-BAM!

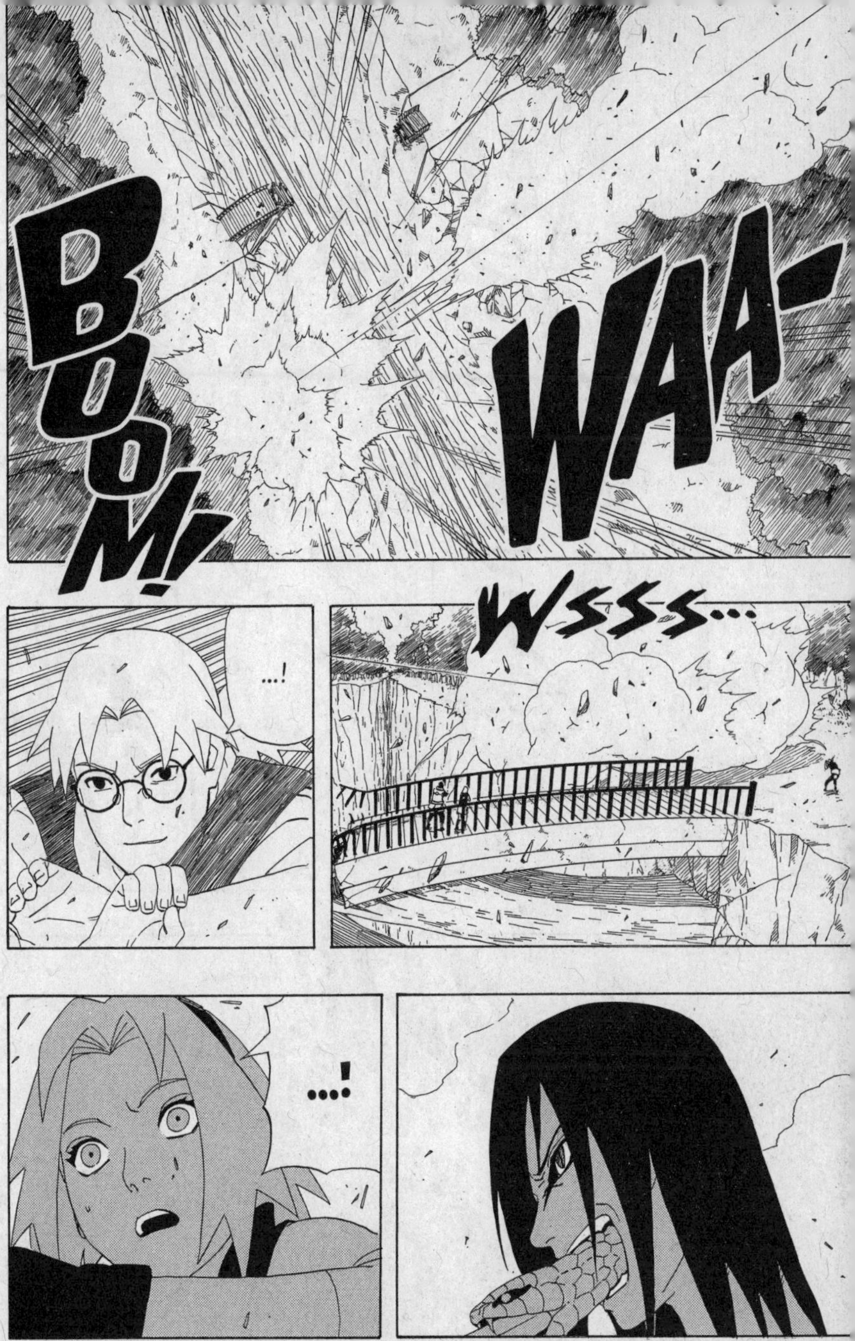
WAA-
BOOM!
WSSS...
...!
...!

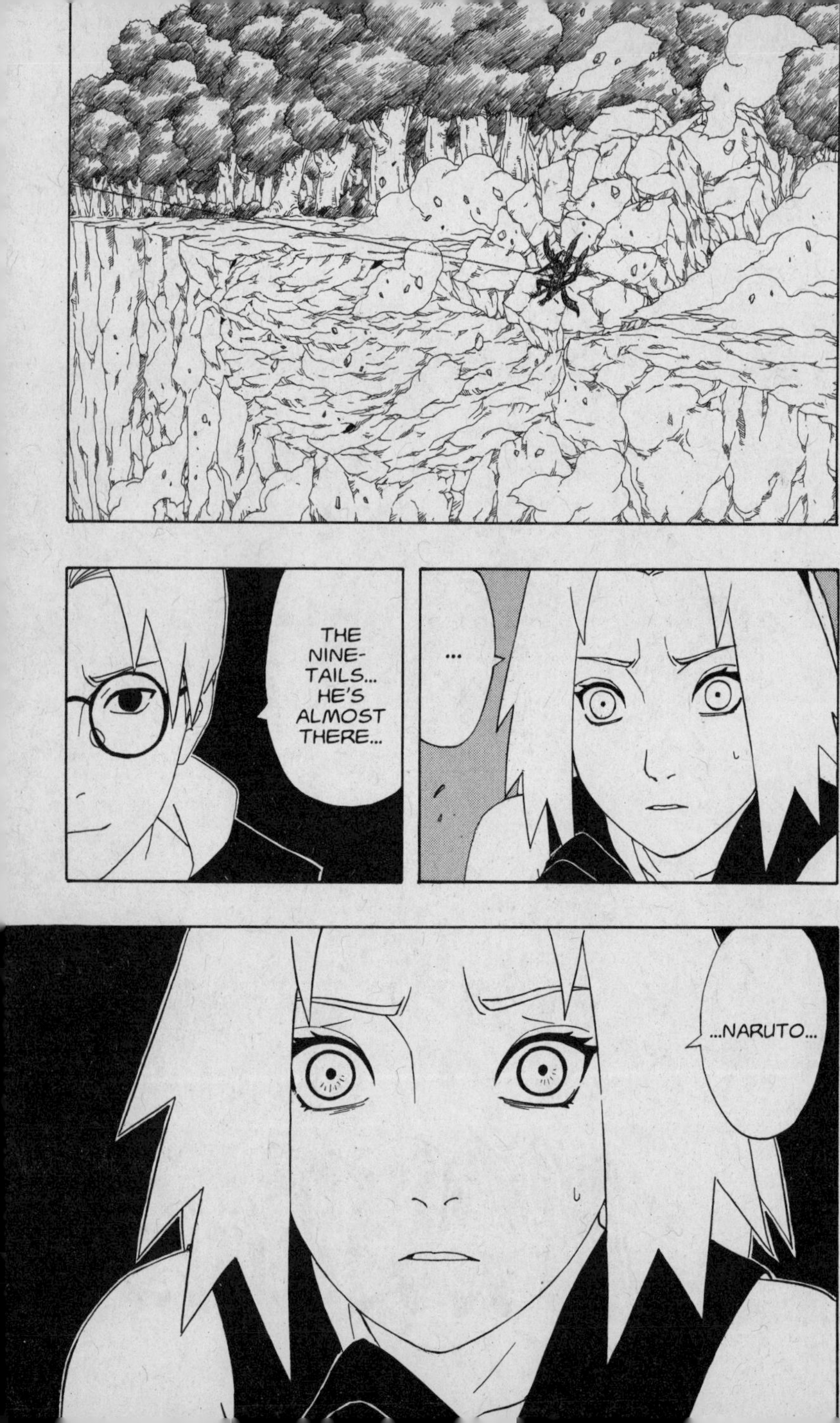
...
THE NINE-TAILS... HE'S ALMOST THERE...
...NARUTO...

NARUTO

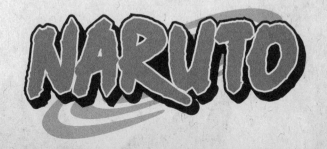

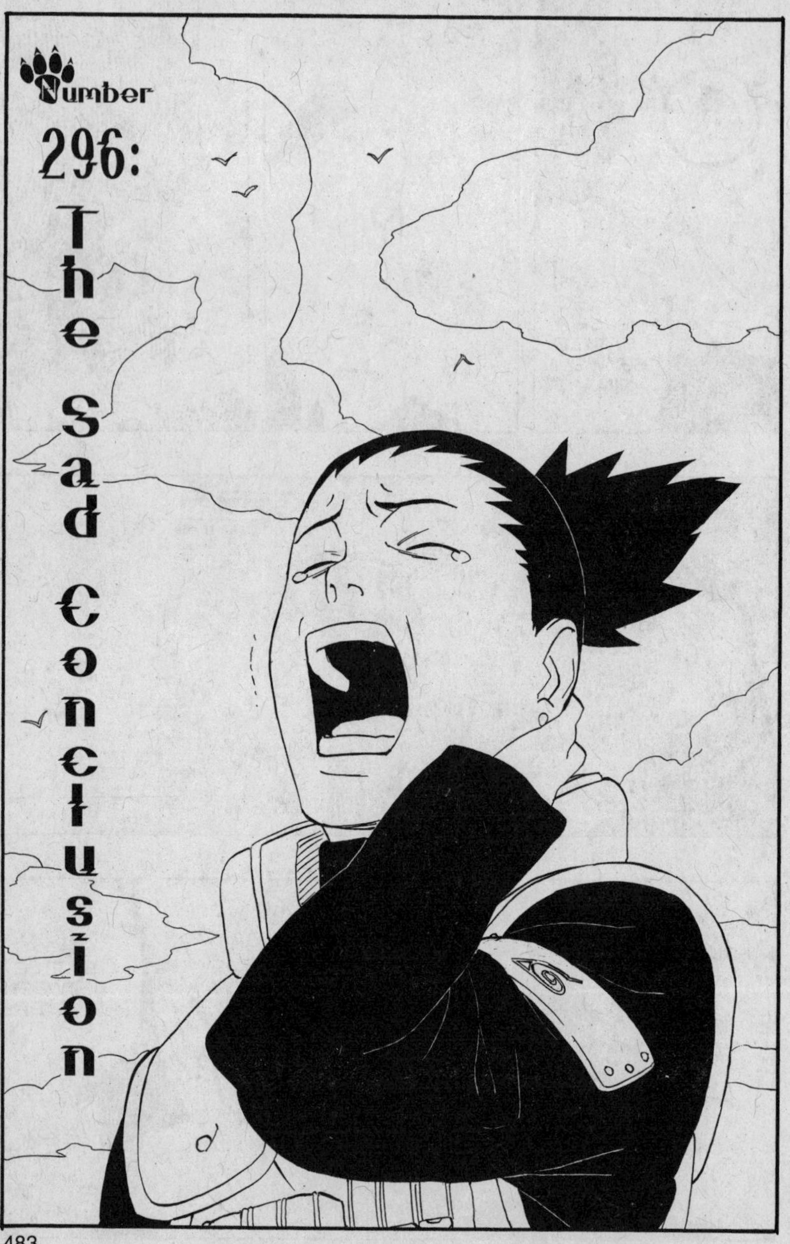
Number
296:
The Sad Conclusion

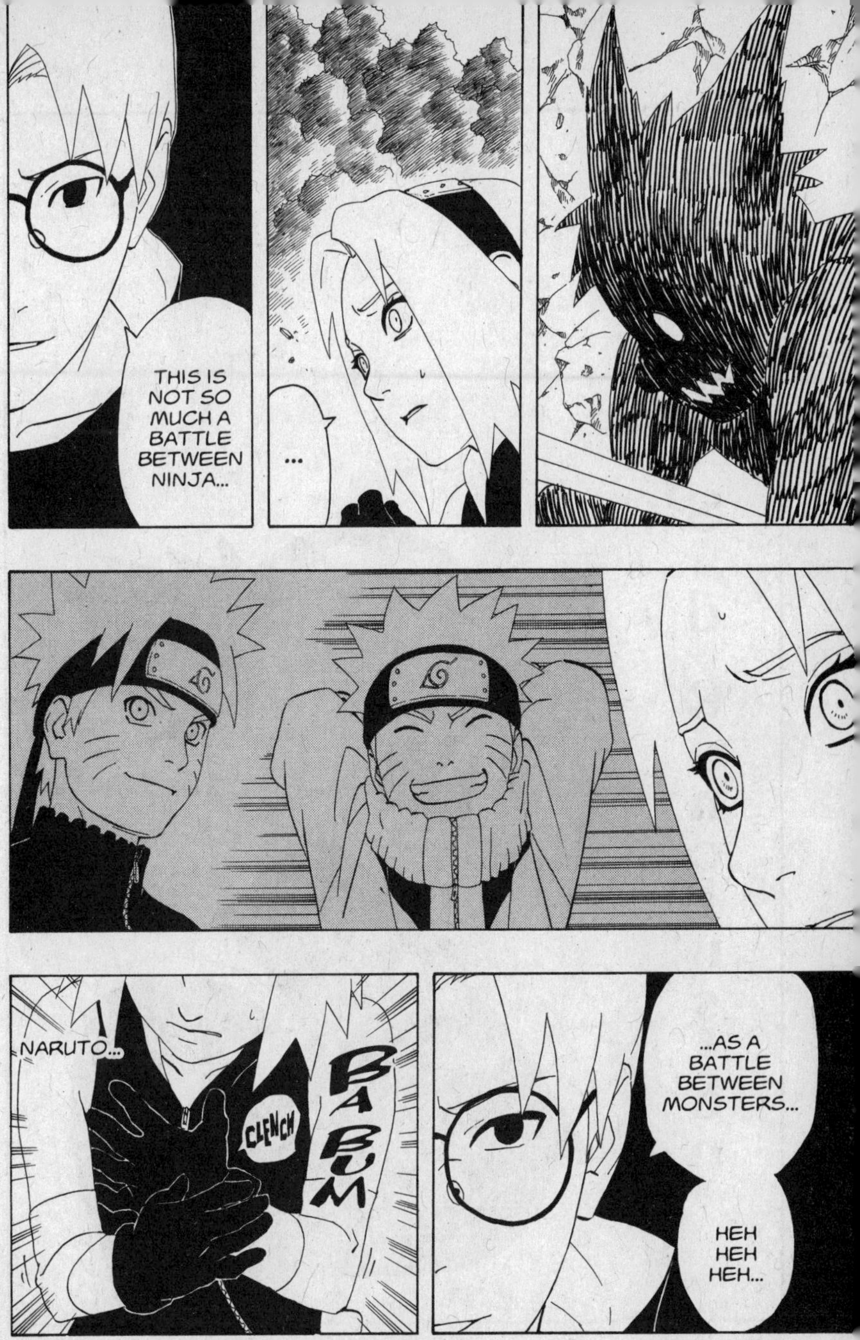
...
THIS IS NOT SO MUCH A BATTLE BETWEEN NINJA...
...AS A BATTLE BETWEEN MONSTERS...
HEH HEH HEH...
BABUM
NARUTO...
CLENCH

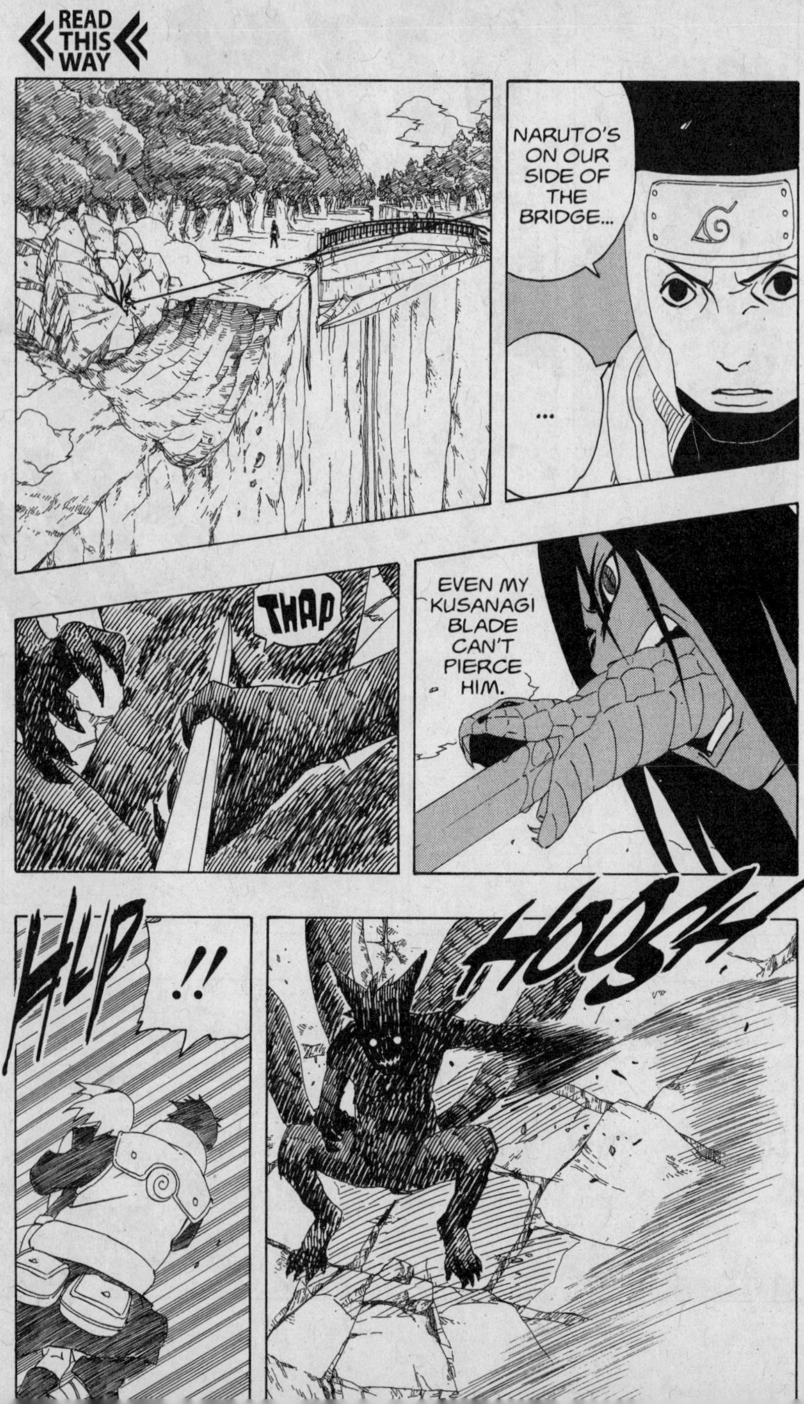
READ THIS WAY
NARUTO'S ON OUR SIDE OF THE BRIDGE...
...
EVEN MY KUSANAGI BLADE CAN'T PIERCE HIM.
THAP
HOOSH!
HUP!!

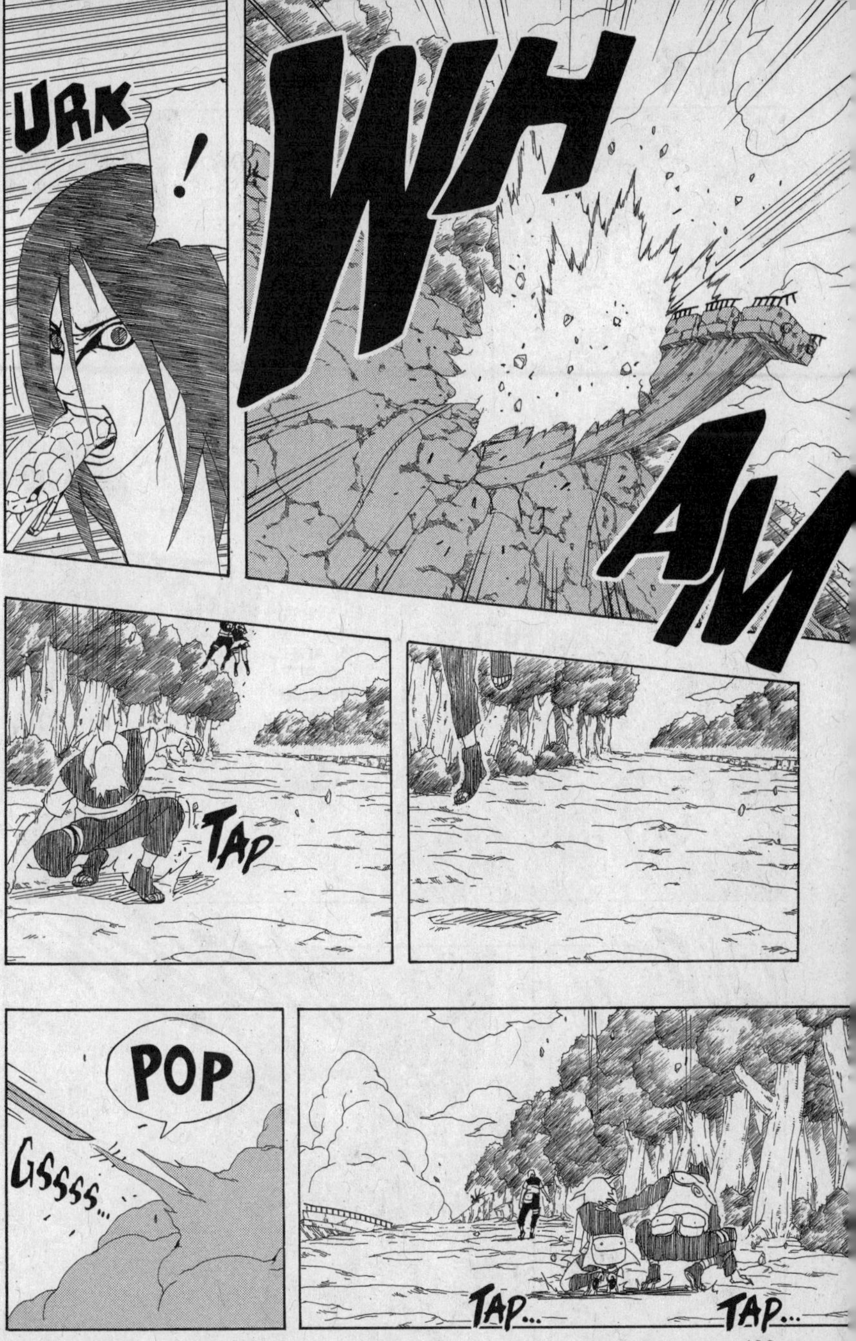
WHAM
URK
!
TAP
TAP...
TAP...
POP
GSSSS...

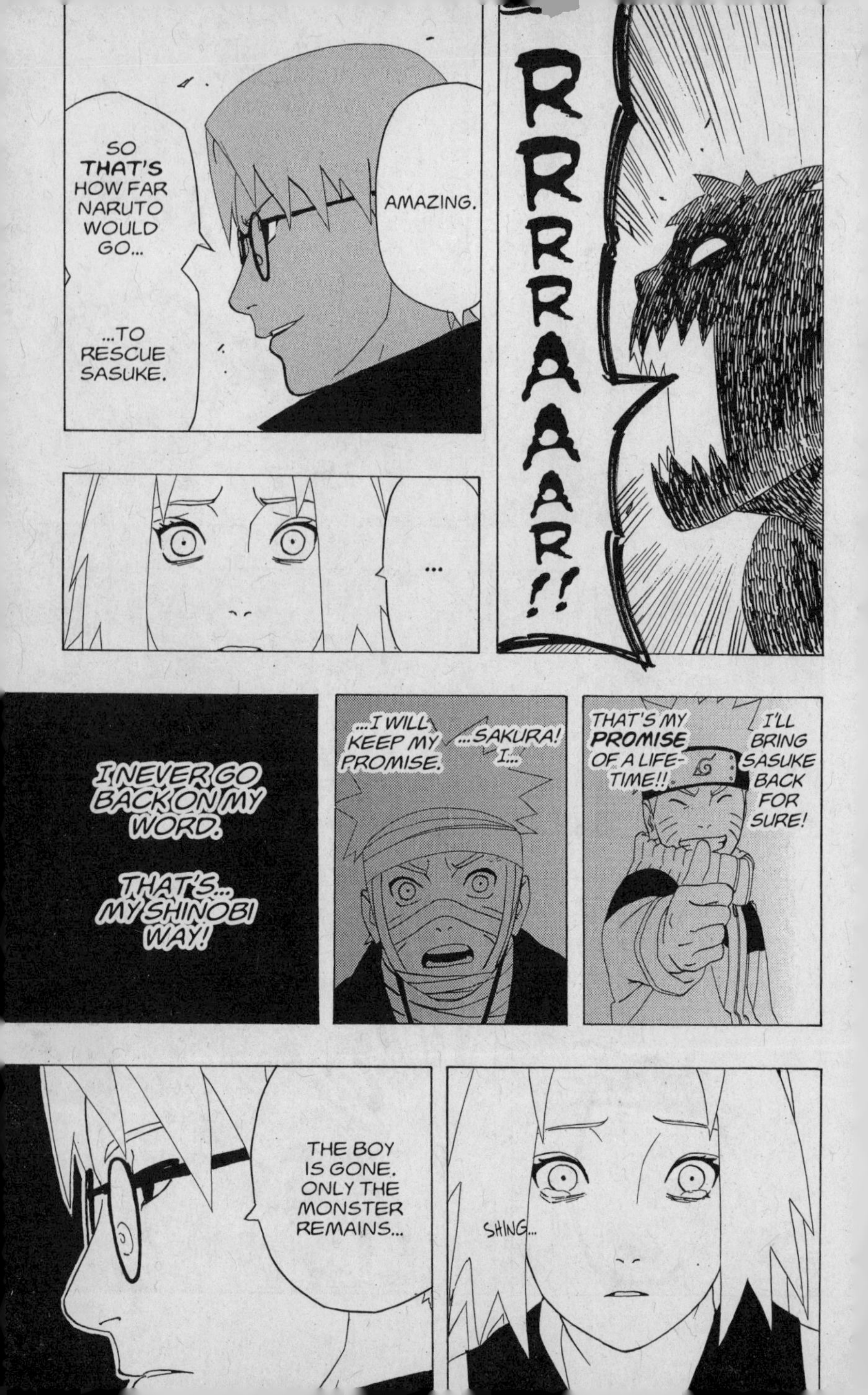
RRRRAAAAR!!
AMAZING.
SO THAT'S HOW FAR NARUTO WOULD GO...
...TO RESCUE SASUKE.
...
I'LL BRING SASUKE BACK FOR SURE!
THAT'S MY PROMISE OF A LIFE-TIME!!
...SAKURA! I...
...I WILL KEEP MY PROMISE.
I NEVER GO BACK ON MY WORD.
THAT'S... MY SHINOBI WAY!
SHING...
THE BOY IS GONE. ONLY THE MONSTER REMAINS...

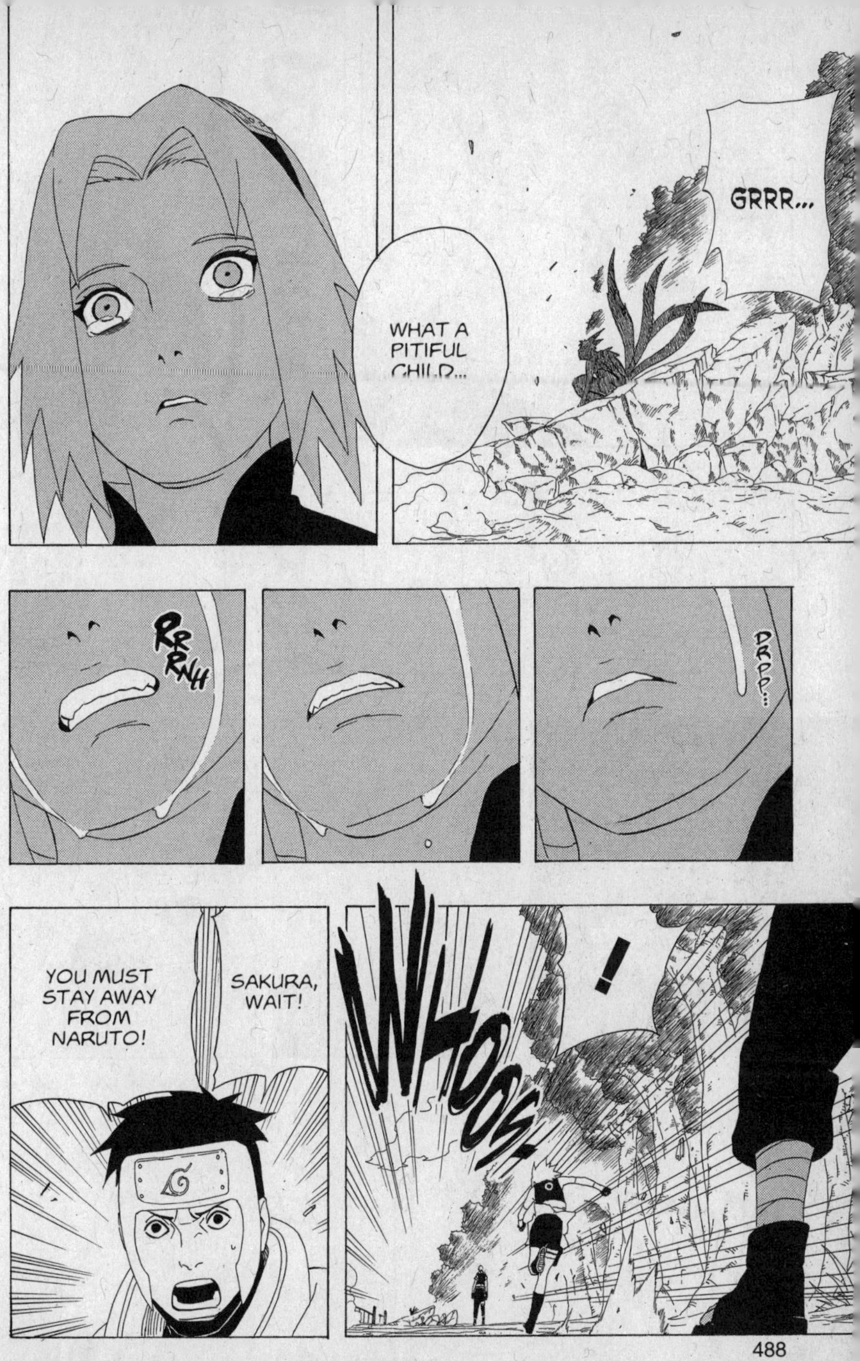
GRRR...
WHAT A PITIFUL CHILD...
DRPP...
RRRNH
WHOOSH
!
SAKURA, WAIT!
YOU MUST STAY AWAY FROM NARUTO!

READ THIS WAY

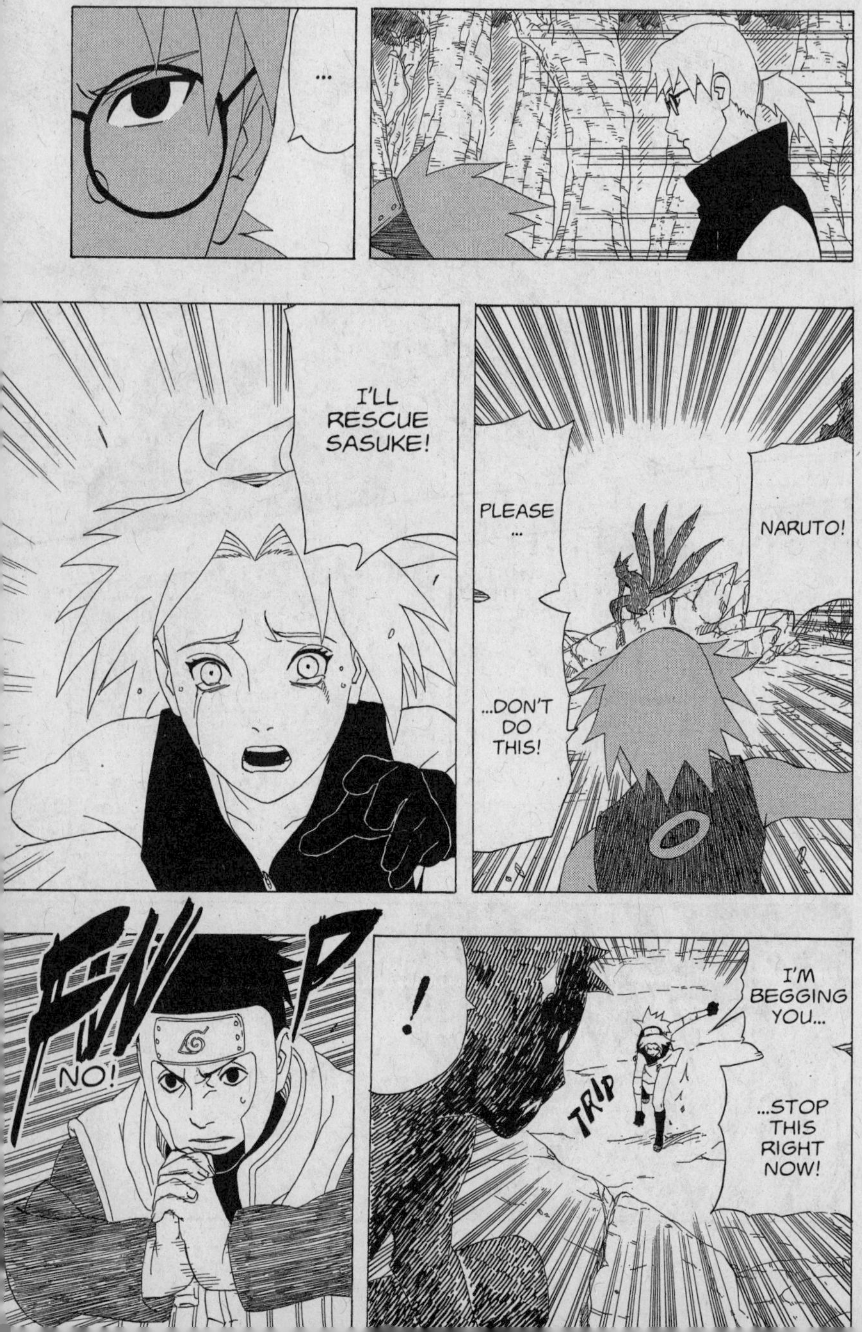
...
NARUTO!
PLEASE ...
...DON'T DO THIS!
I'LL RESCUE SASUKE!
I'M BEGGING YOU...
!
...STOP THIS RIGHT NOW!
TRIP
NO!

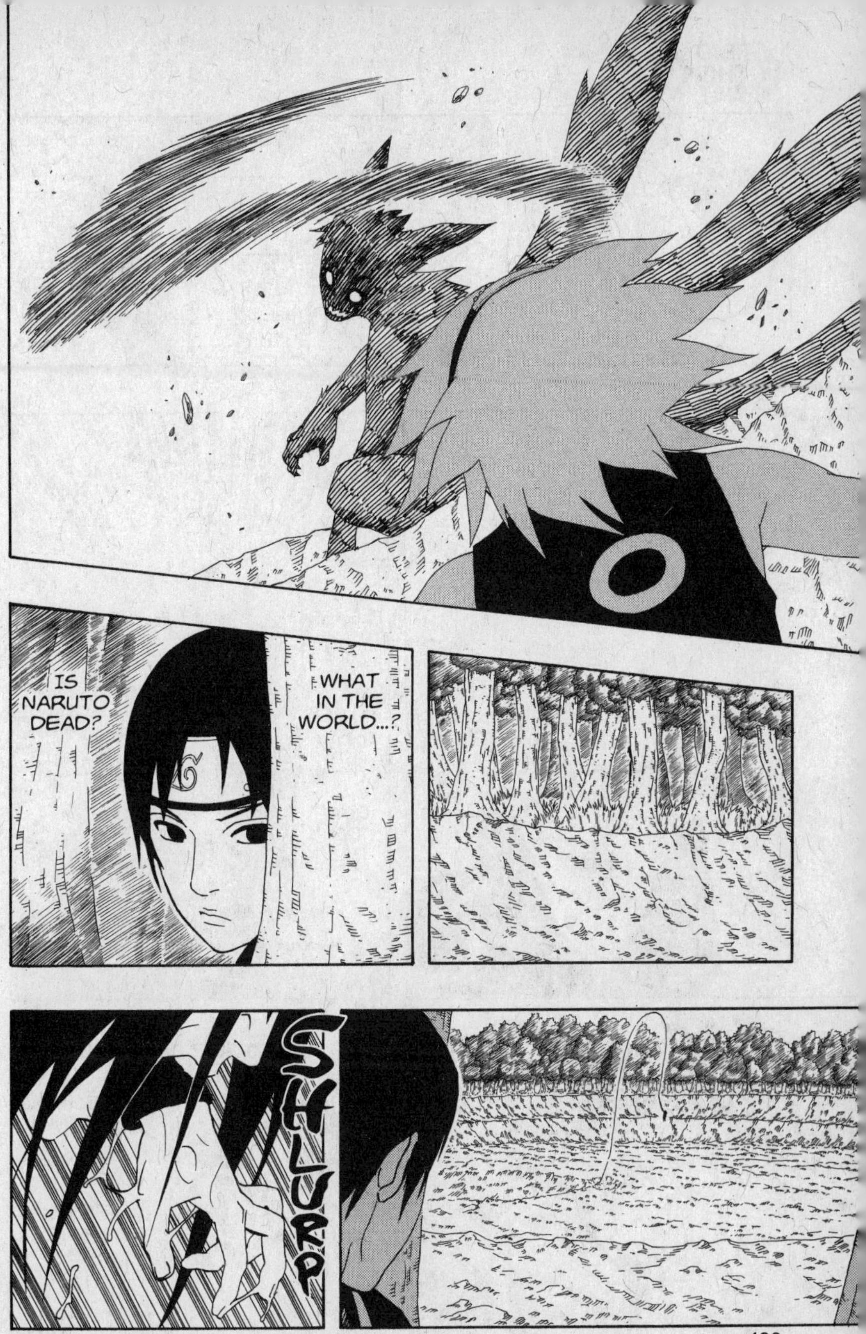
WHAT IN THE WORLD...?
IS NARUTO DEAD?
SHLURP

READ THIS WAY

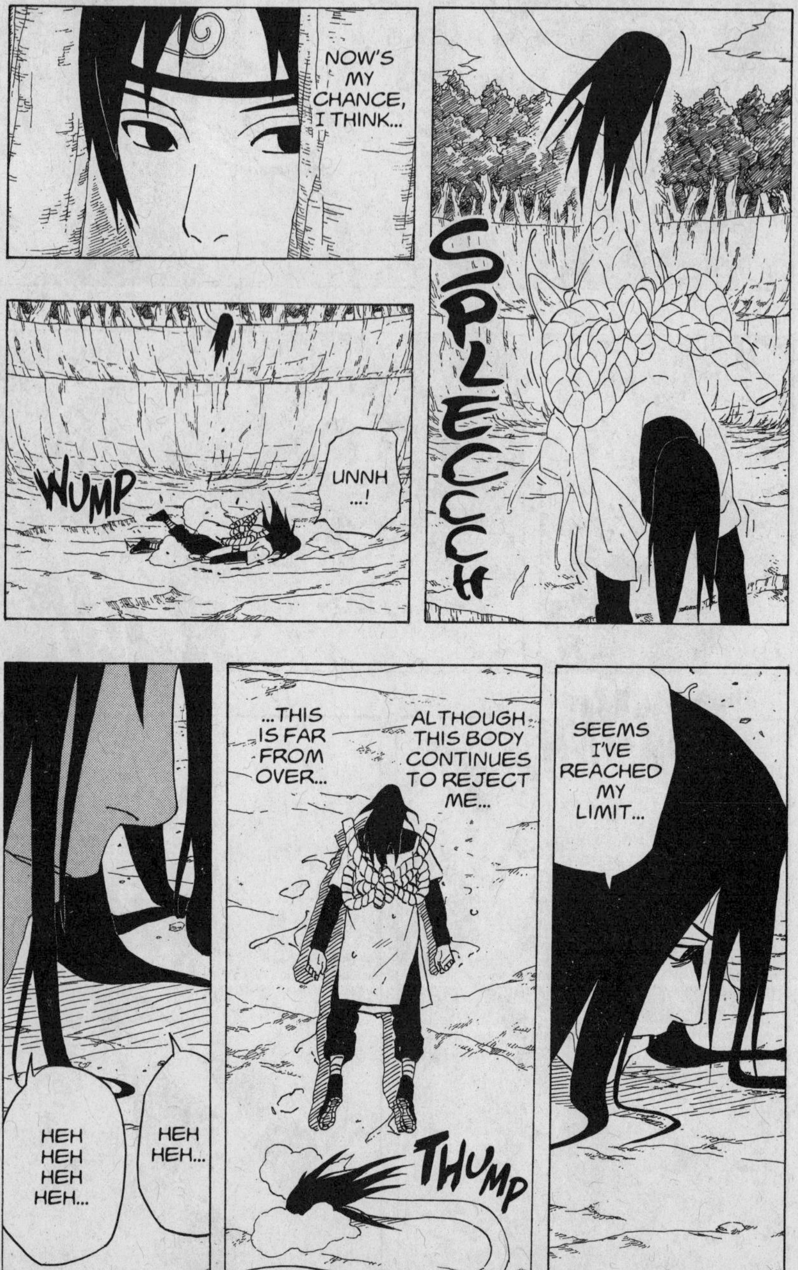
SPLECCCH
NOW'S MY CHANCE, I THINK...
WUMP
UNNH ...!
SEEMS I'VE REACHED MY LIMIT...
ALTHOUGH THIS BODY CONTINUES TO REJECT ME...
...THIS IS FAR FROM OVER...
THUMP
HEH HEH...
HEH HEH HEH HEH...

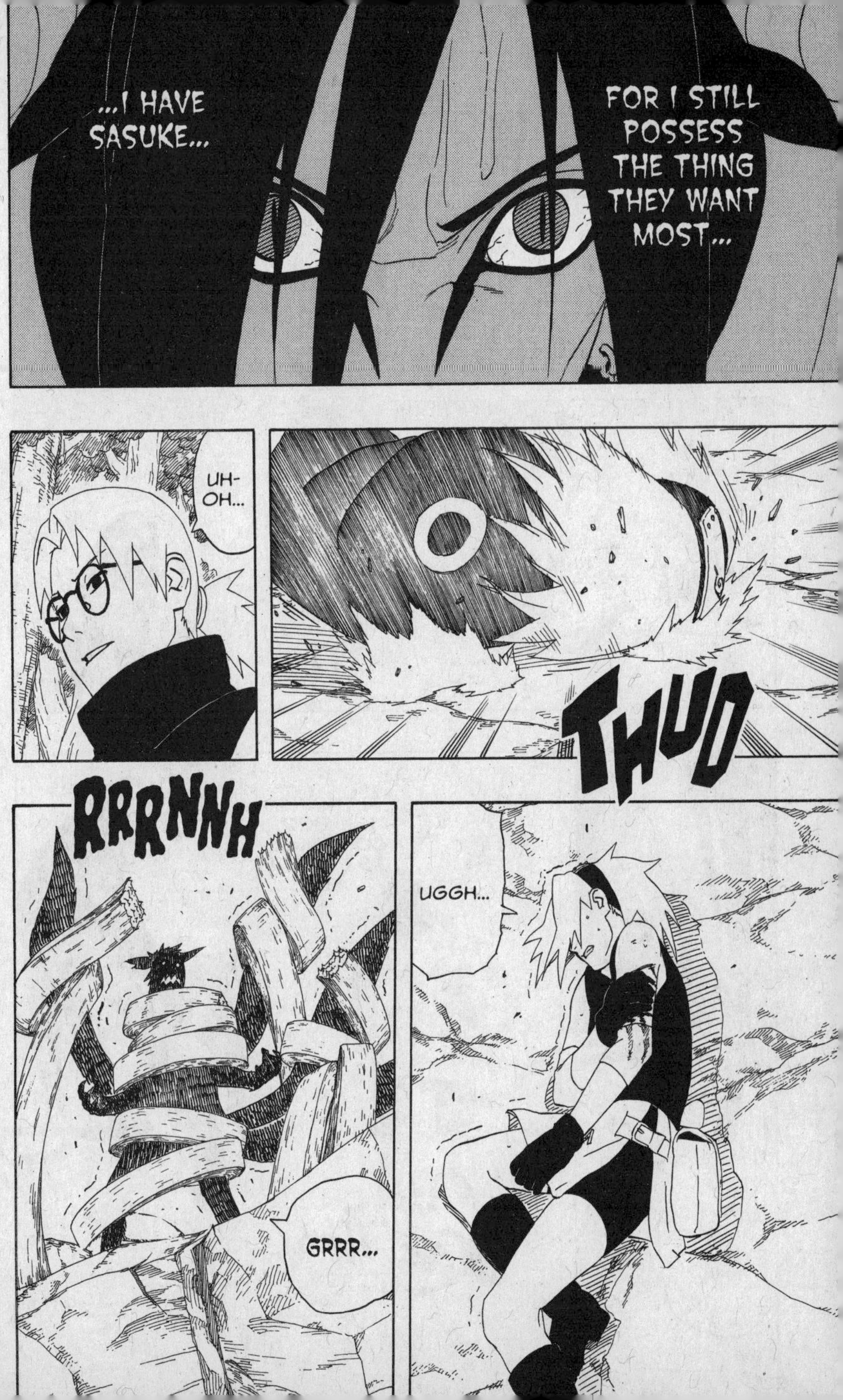
FOR I STILL POSSESS THE THING THEY WANT MOST...
...I HAVE SASUKE...
THUD
UH-OH...
UGGH...
RRRNNH
GRRR...

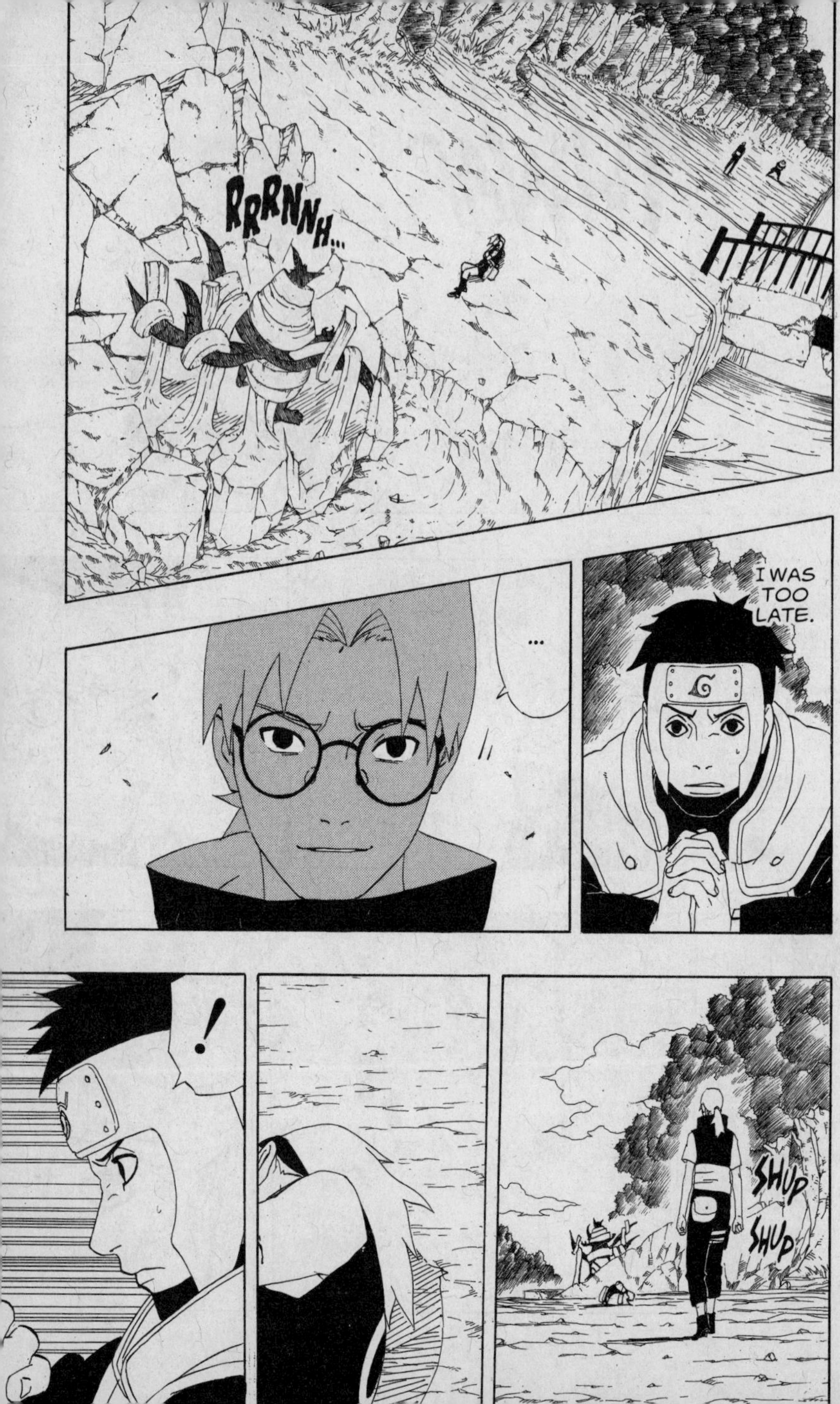
RRRNNH...
I WAS TOO LATE.
...
SHUP
SHUP
!

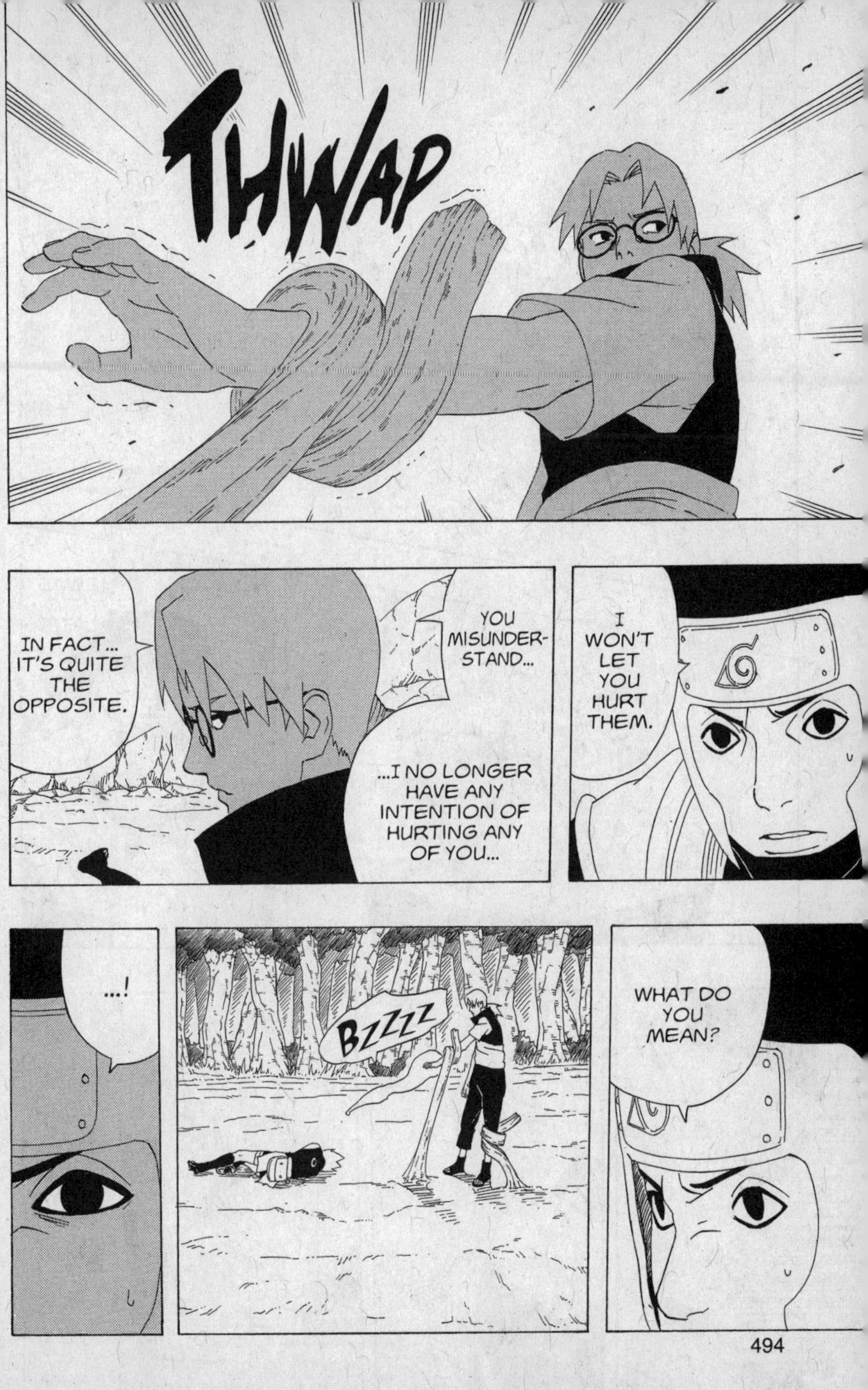
THWAP
I WON'T LET YOU HURT THEM.
YOU MISUNDER-STAND...
...I NO LONGER HAVE ANY INTENTION OF HURTING ANY OF YOU...
IN FACT... IT'S QUITE THE OPPOSITE.
WHAT DO YOU MEAN?
BZZZZ
...!

READ THIS WAY

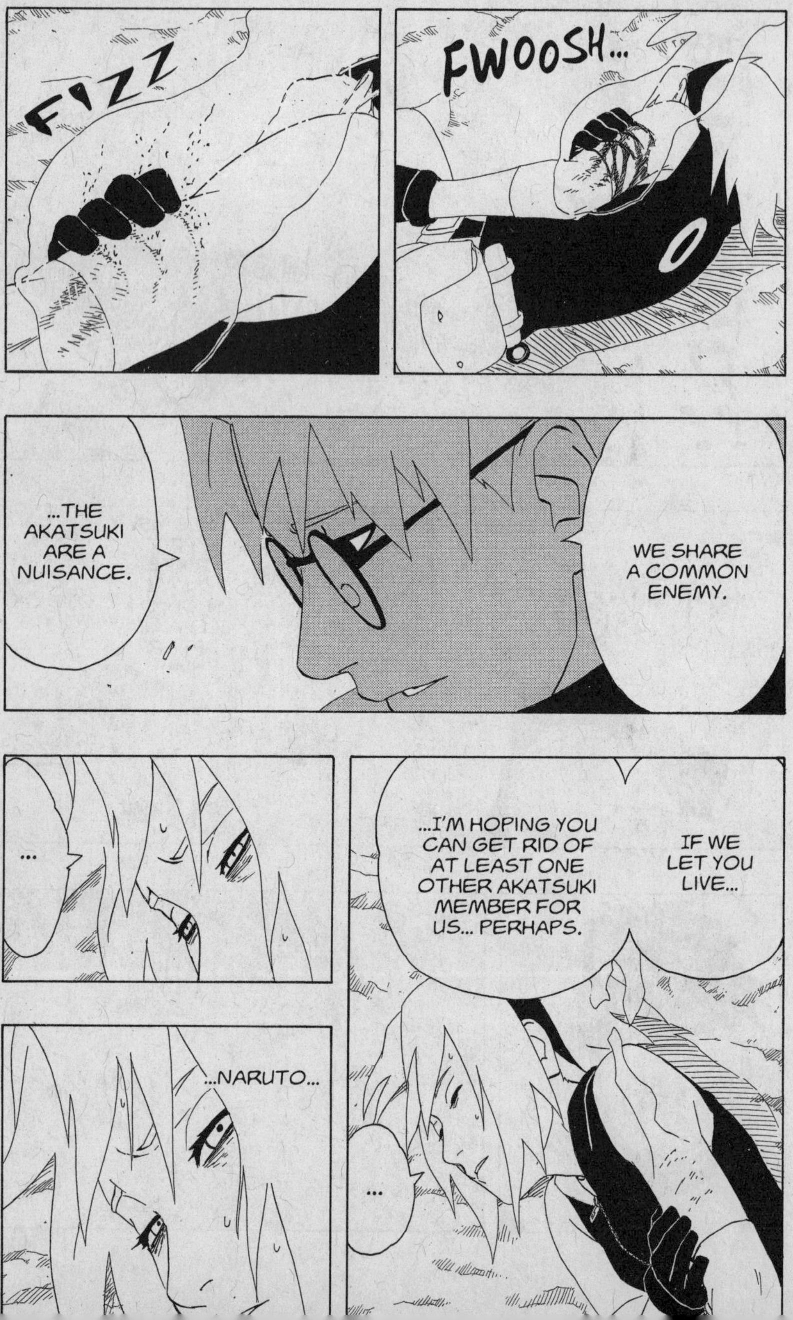
FWOOSH...
FIZZ
WE SHARE A COMMON ENEMY.
...THE AKATSUKI ARE A NUISANCE.
IF WE LET YOU LIVE...
...I'M HOPING YOU CAN GET RID OF AT LEAST ONE OTHER AKATSUKI MEMBER FOR US... PERHAPS.
...
...
...NARUTO...

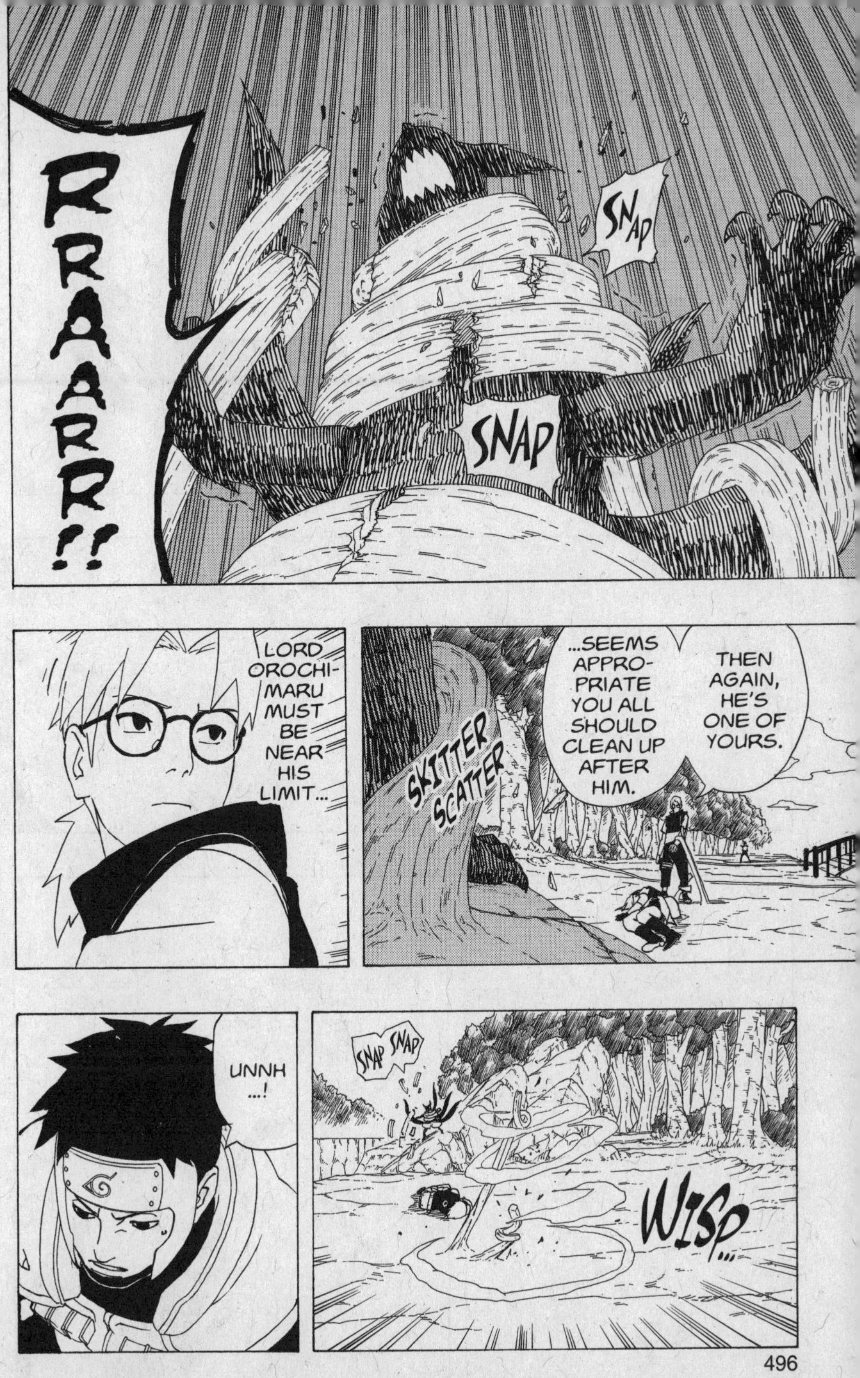
SNAP
SNAP
RRAARRR!!
THEN AGAIN, HE'S ONE OF YOURS.
...SEEMS APPROPRIATE YOU ALL SHOULD CLEAN UP AFTER HIM.
SKITTER SCATTER
LORD OROCHIMARU MUST BE NEAR HIS LIMIT...
SNAP SNAP
WISP...
UNNH ...!

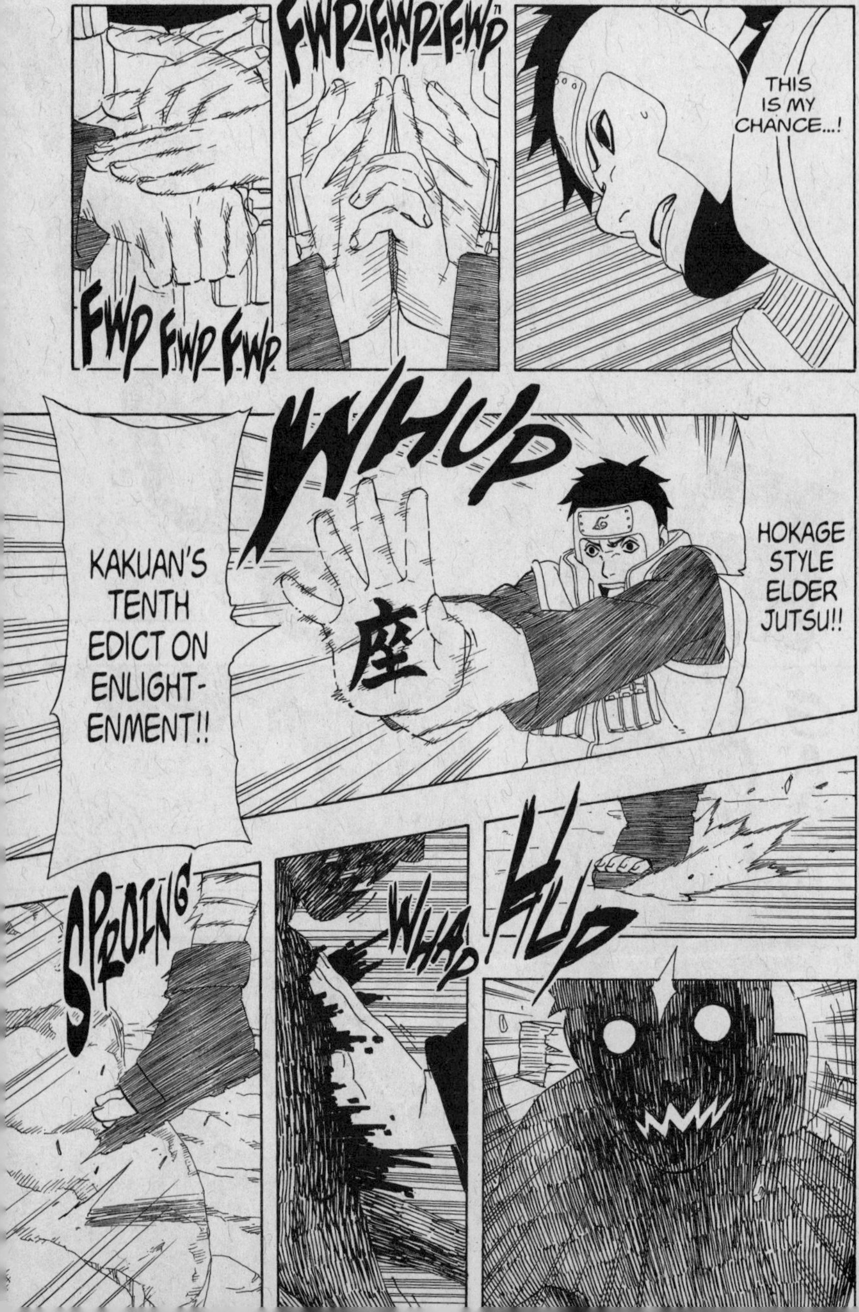
THIS IS MY CHANCE...!
FWP FWP FWP
FWP FWP FWP
HOKAGE STYLE ELDER JUTSU!!
WHUP
座
KAKUAN'S TENTH EDICT ON ENLIGHT-ENMENT!!
KUP
WHAP
SPROING

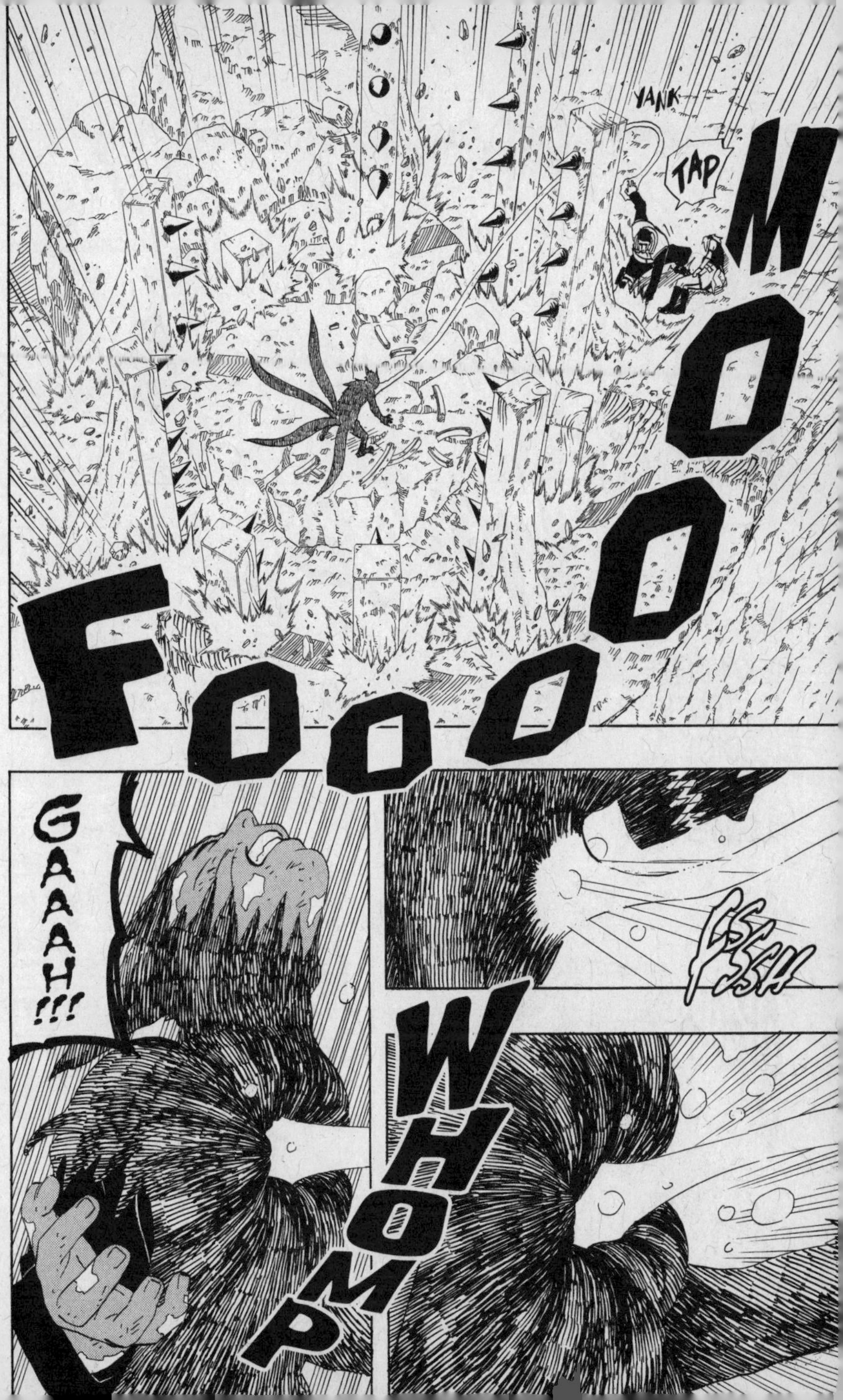
YANK
TAP
FOOOOOOM
PSSH
WHOMP
GAAAH!!!

READ THIS WAY

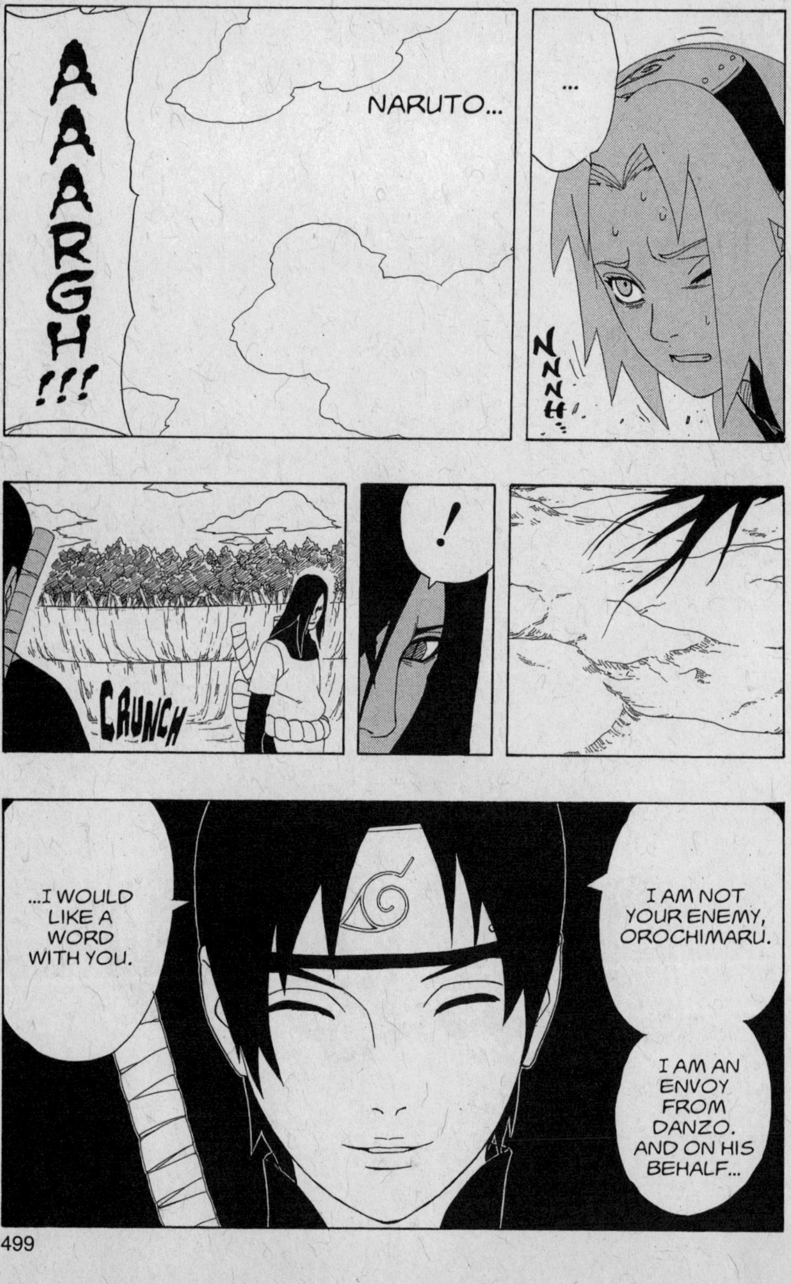
...
NNNH...
NARUTO...
AAAARGH!!!
!
CRUNCH
I AM NOT YOUR ENEMY, OROCHIMARU.
I AM AN ENVOY FROM DANZO. AND ON HIS BEHALF...
...I WOULD LIKE A WORD WITH YOU.

NARUTO

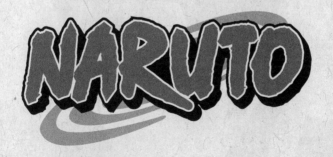

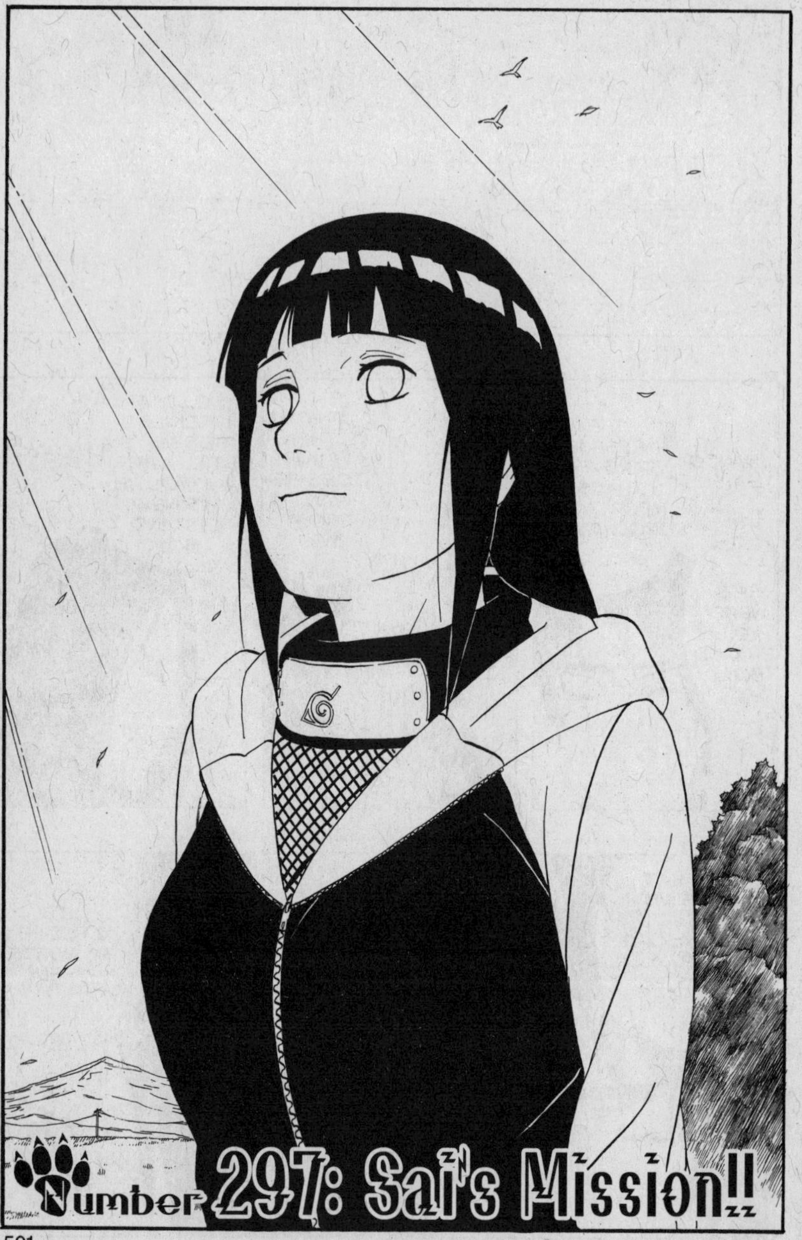
Number 297: Sai's Mission!!

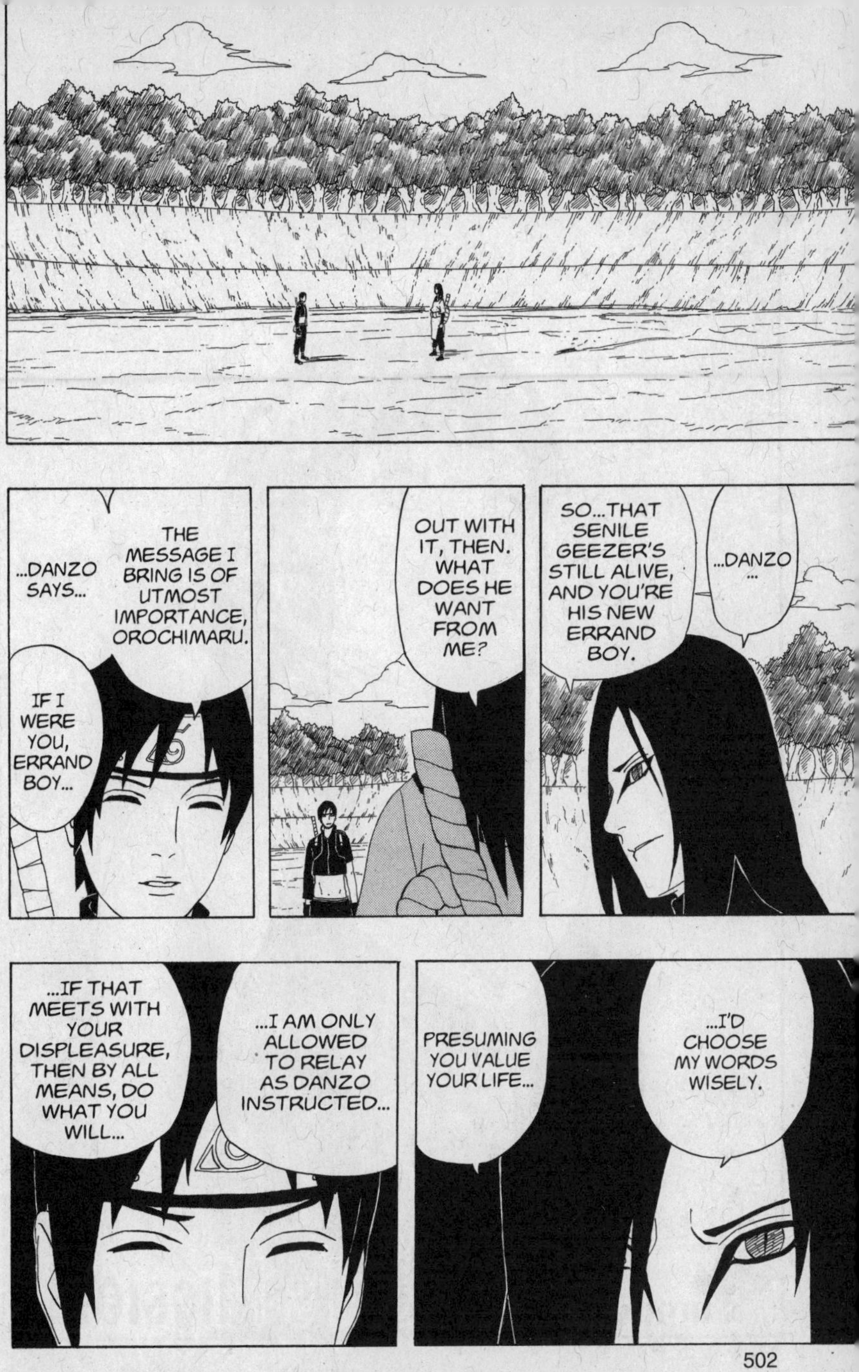
...DANZO ...
SO...THAT SENILE GEEZER'S STILL ALIVE, AND YOU'RE HIS NEW ERRAND BOY.
OUT WITH IT, THEN. WHAT DOES HE WANT FROM ME?
THE MESSAGE I BRING IS OF UTMOST IMPORTANCE, OROCHIMARU.
...DANZO SAYS...
IF I WERE YOU, ERRAND BOY...
...I'D CHOOSE MY WORDS WISELY.
PRESUMING YOU VALUE YOUR LIFE...
...I AM ONLY ALLOWED TO RELAY AS DANZO INSTRUCTED...
...IF THAT MEETS WITH YOUR DISPLEASURE, THEN BY ALL MEANS, DO WHAT YOU WILL...

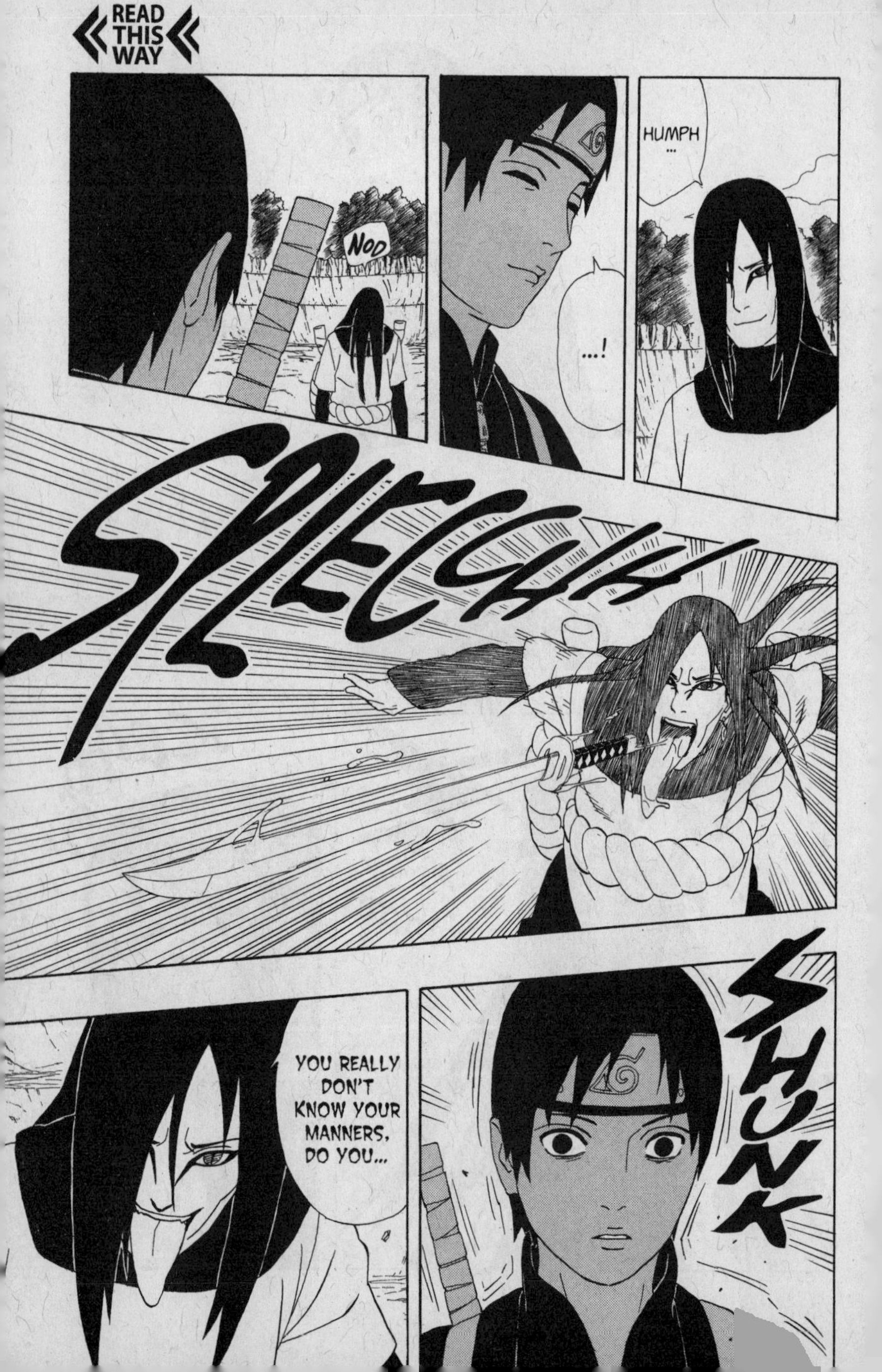
READ THIS WAY
HUMPH ...
...!
NOD
SPLECHA!
SHUNK
YOU REALLY DON'T KNOW YOUR MANNERS, DO YOU...

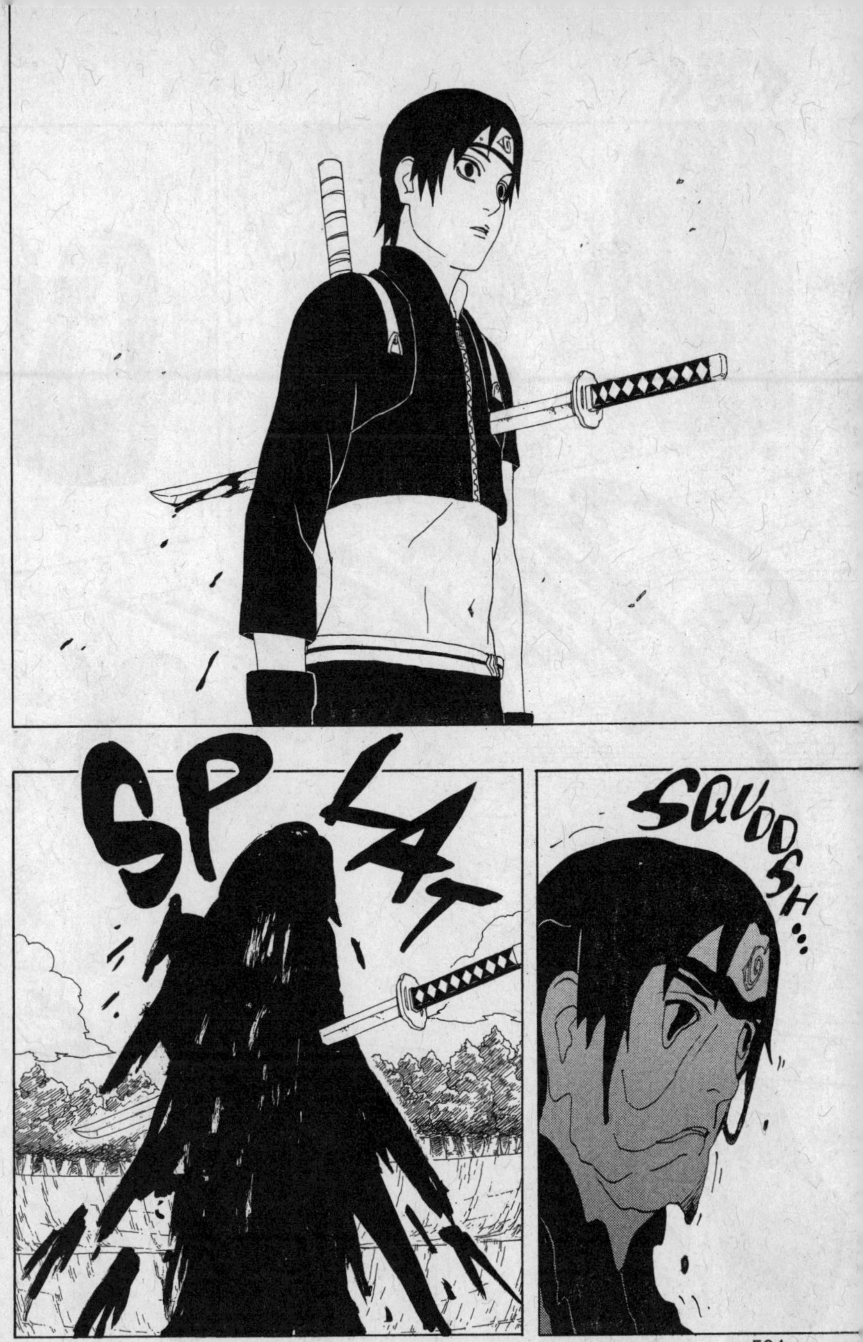
SQUOOSH...
SPLAT

READ THIS WAY

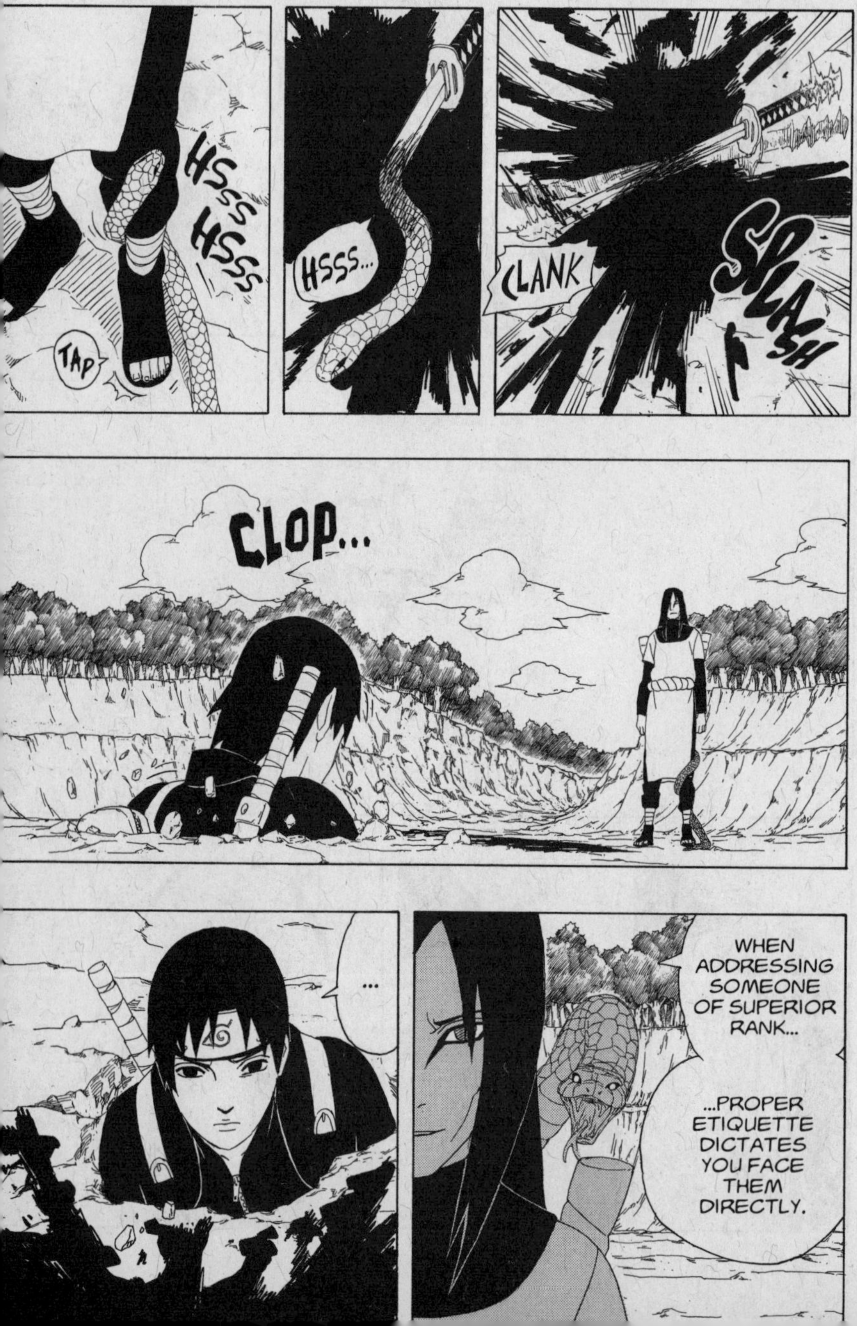
CLANK
SPLASH
HSSS...
HSSS HSSS
TAP
CLOP...
WHEN ADDRESSING SOMEONE OF SUPERIOR RANK...
...PROPER ETIQUETTE DICTATES YOU FACE THEM DIRECTLY.
...

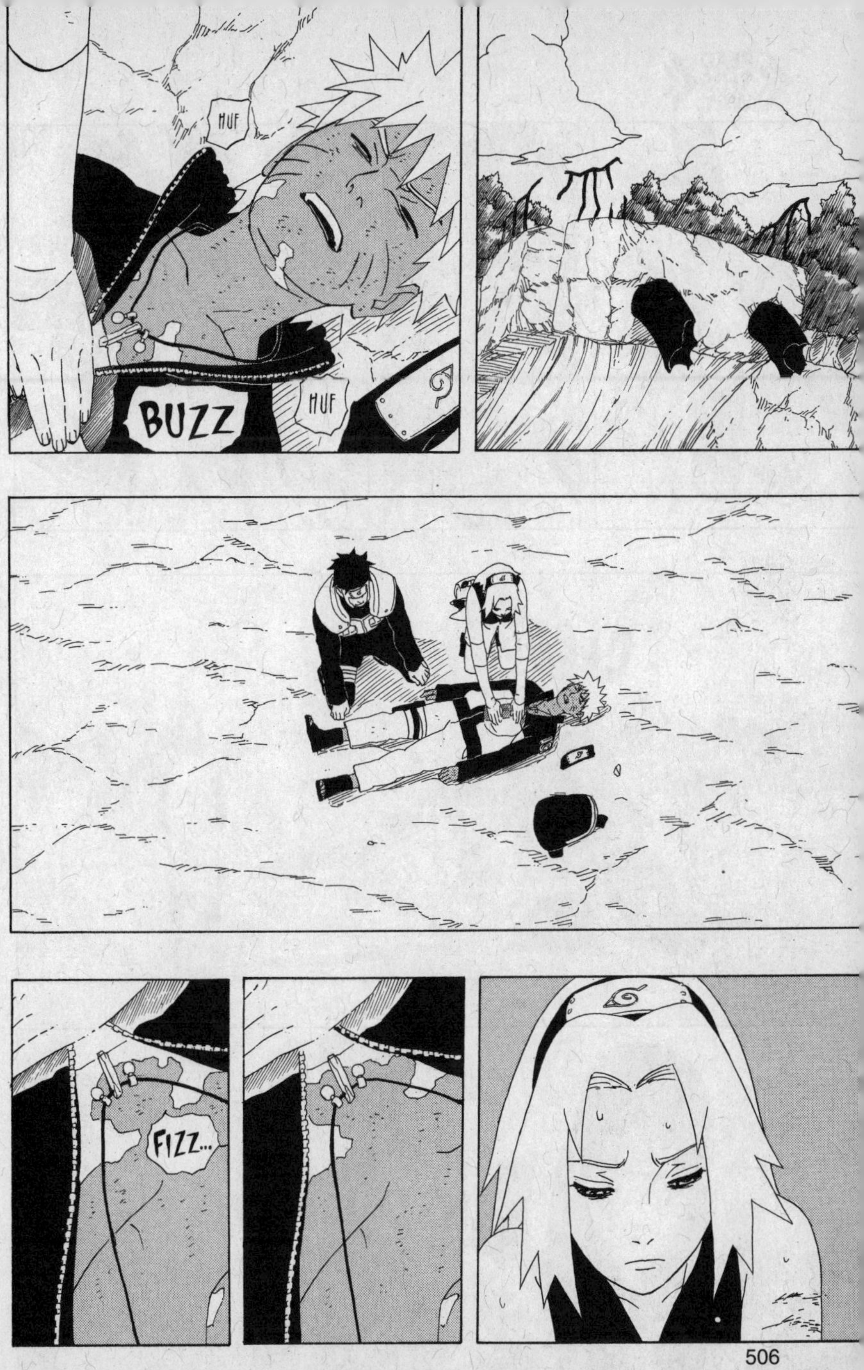
HUF
HUF
BUZZ
FIZZ...

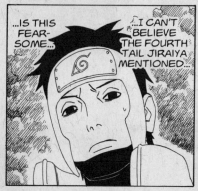

READ THIS WAY

IN THE PAST, THE NINE-TAILS' CHAKRA GAVE NARUTO ACCELERATED HEALING...
...SO, WHY IS THIS TAKING SO LONG?
...I CAN'T BELIEVE THE FOURTH TAIL JIRAIYA MENTIONED...
...IS THIS FEARSOME...
HAH!
BUZZ...
BA BUM
UNH...!

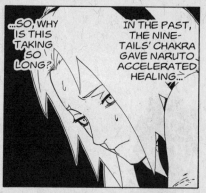

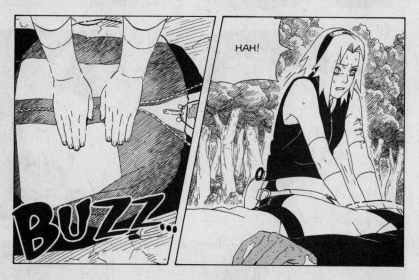

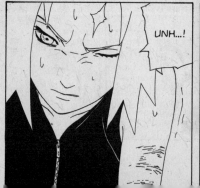

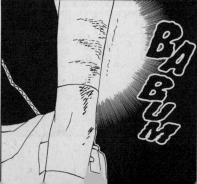

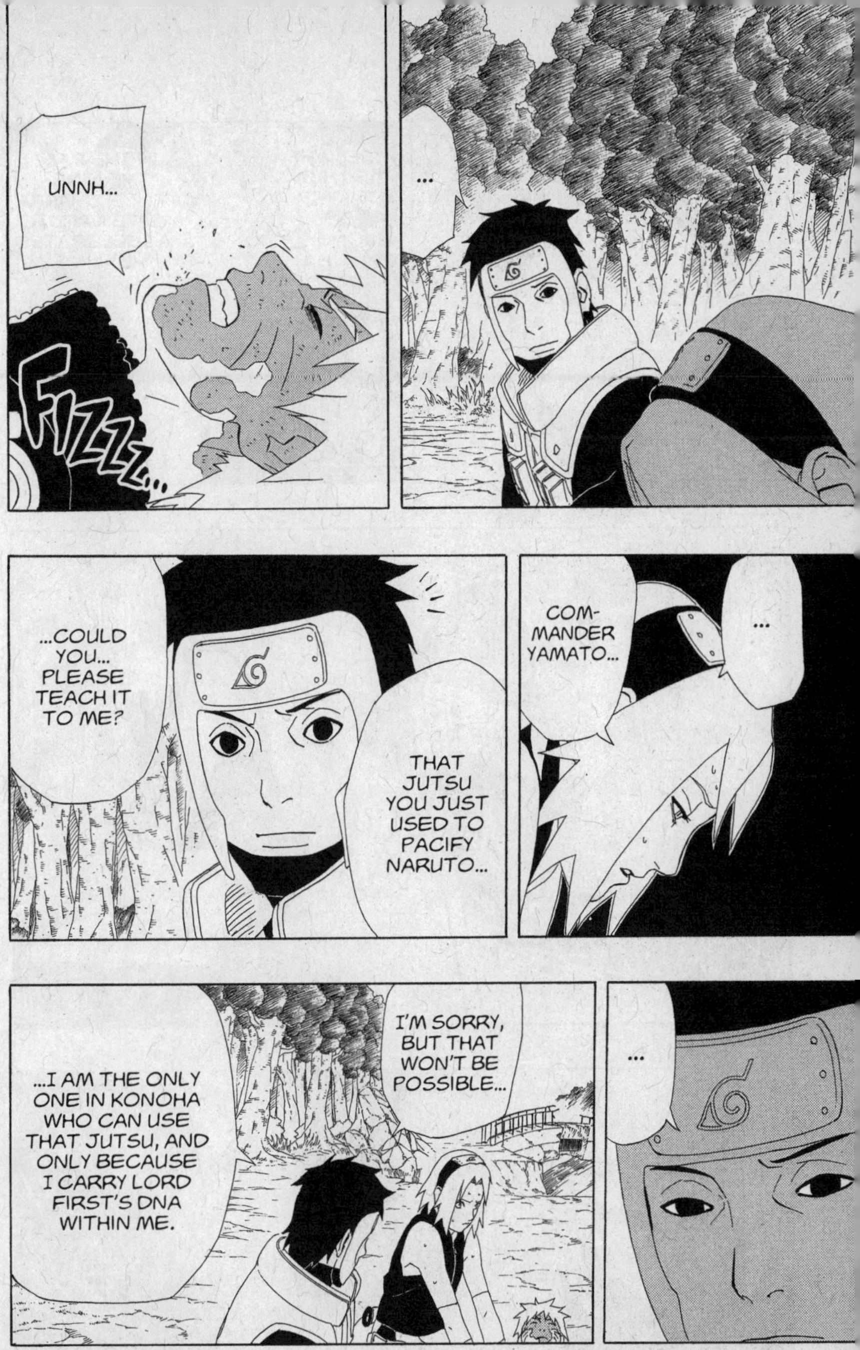
...
UNNH...
FIZZZZ...
...
COM-MANDER YAMATO...
THAT JUTSU YOU JUST USED TO PACIFY NARUTO...
...COULD YOU... PLEASE TEACH IT TO ME?
...
I'M SORRY, BUT THAT WON'T BE POSSIBLE...
...I AM THE ONLY ONE IN KONOHA WHO CAN USE THAT JUTSU, AND ONLY BECAUSE I CARRY LORD FIRST'S DNA WITHIN ME.

READ THIS WAY

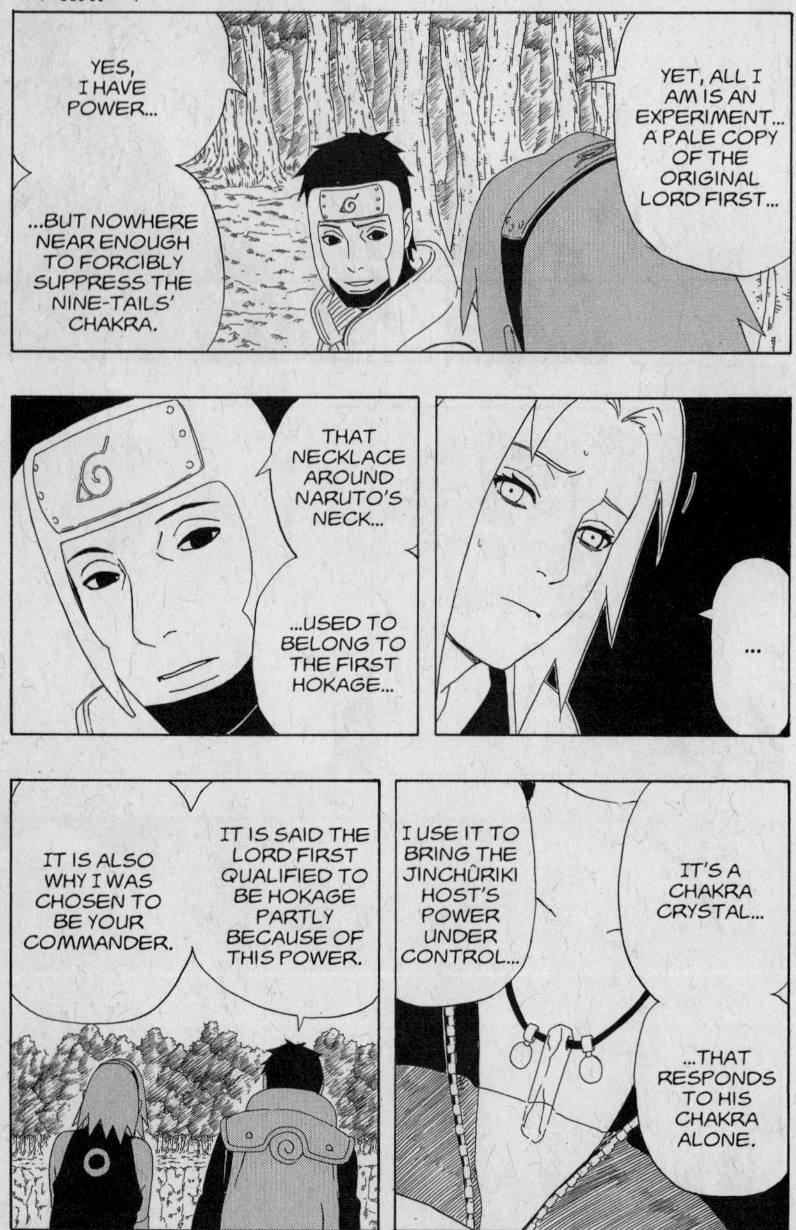
YET, ALL I AM IS AN EXPERIMENT... A PALE COPY OF THE ORIGINAL LORD FIRST...
YES, I HAVE POWER...
...BUT NOWHERE NEAR ENOUGH TO FORCIBLY SUPPRESS THE NINE-TAILS' CHAKRA.
...
THAT NECKLACE AROUND NARUTO'S NECK...
...USED TO BELONG TO THE FIRST HOKAGE...
IT'S A CHAKRA CRYSTAL...
...THAT RESPONDS TO HIS CHAKRA ALONE.
I USE IT TO BRING THE JINCHÛRIKI HOST'S POWER UNDER CONTROL...
IT IS SAID THE LORD FIRST QUALIFIED TO BE HOKAGE PARTLY BECAUSE OF THIS POWER.
IT IS ALSO WHY I WAS CHOSEN TO BE YOUR COMMANDER.

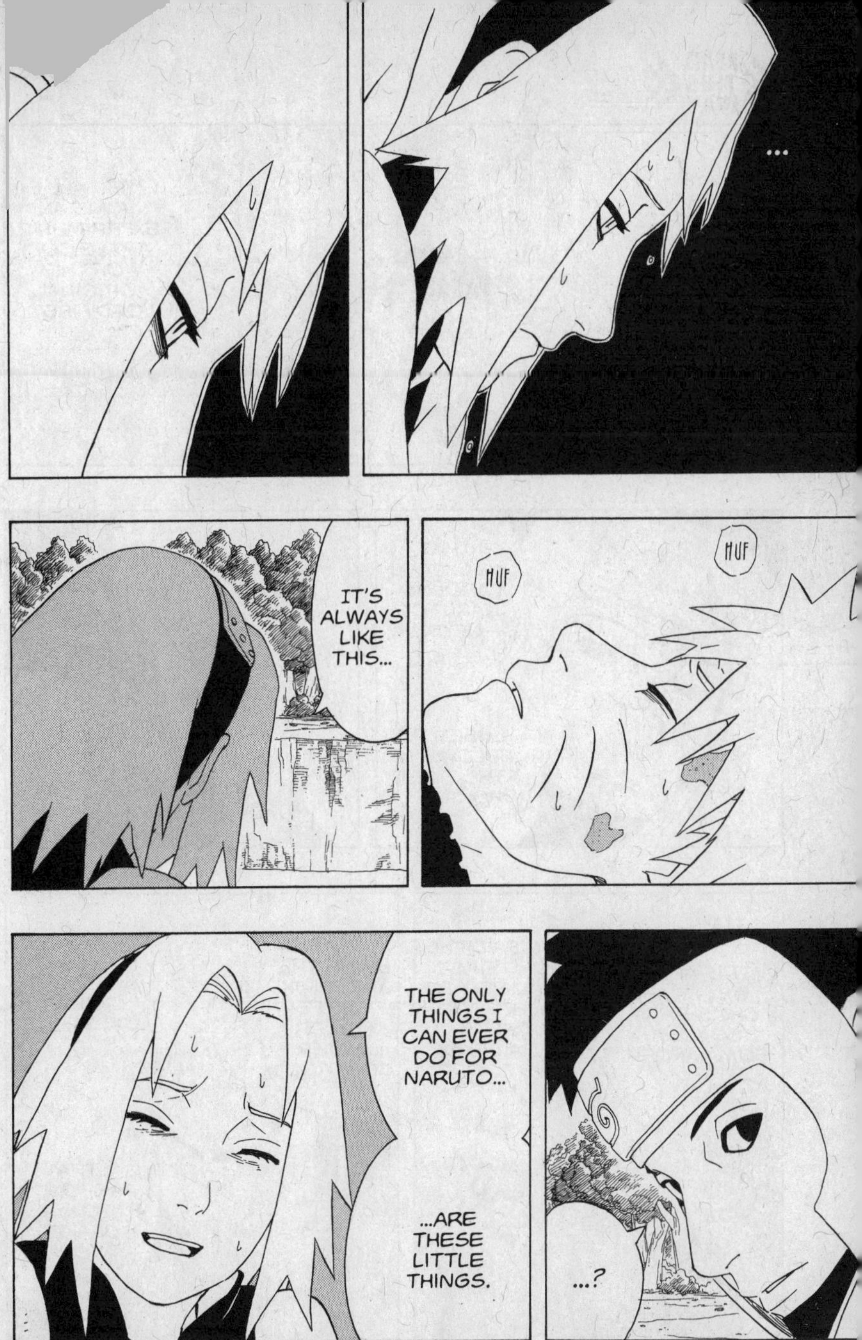
...
HUF
HUF
IT'S ALWAYS LIKE THIS...
...?
THE ONLY THINGS I CAN EVER DO FOR NARUTO...
...ARE THESE LITTLE THINGS.

READ THIS WAY

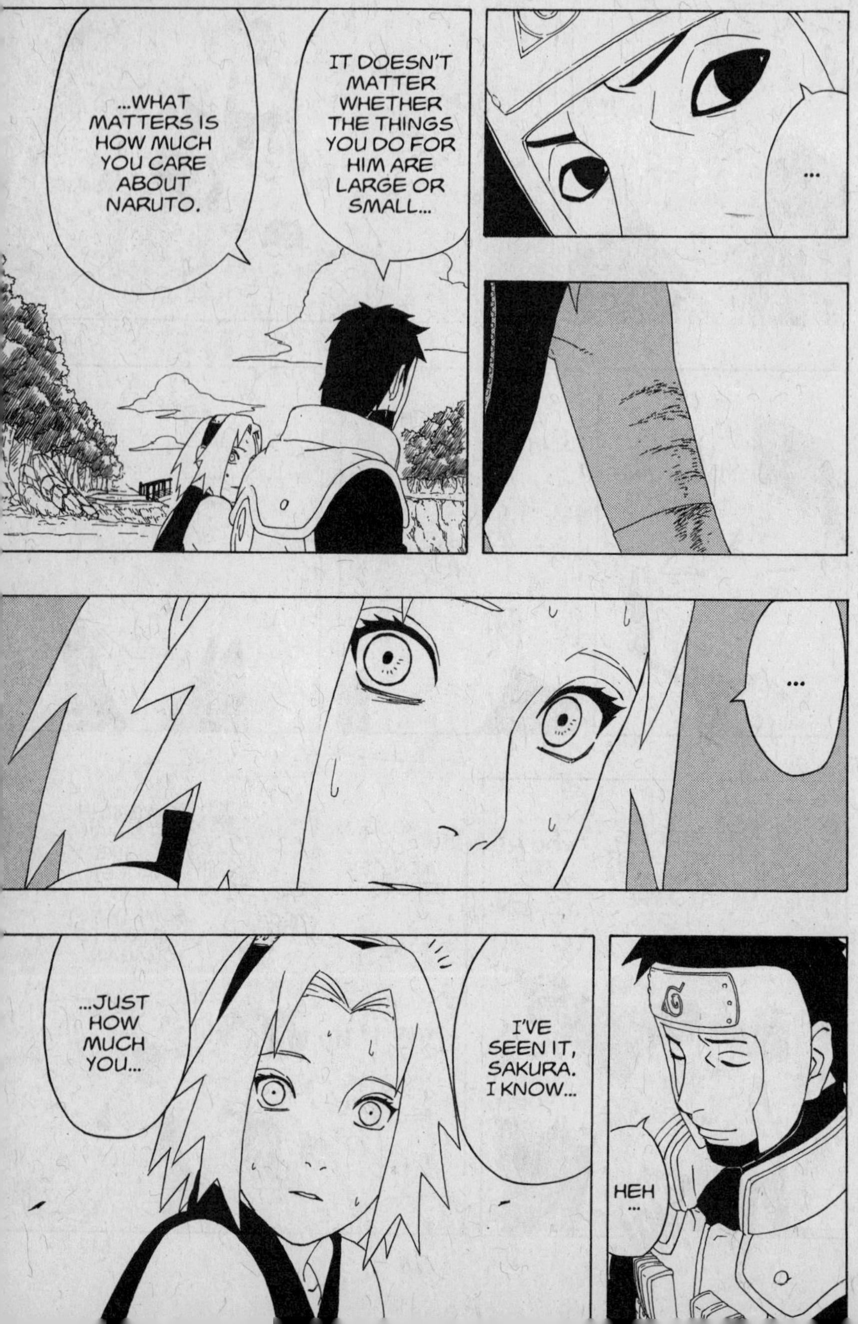
...
IT DOESN'T MATTER WHETHER THE THINGS YOU DO FOR HIM ARE LARGE OR SMALL...
...WHAT MATTERS IS HOW MUCH YOU CARE ABOUT NARUTO.
...
HEH ...
I'VE SEEN IT, SAKURA. I KNOW...
...JUST HOW MUCH YOU...

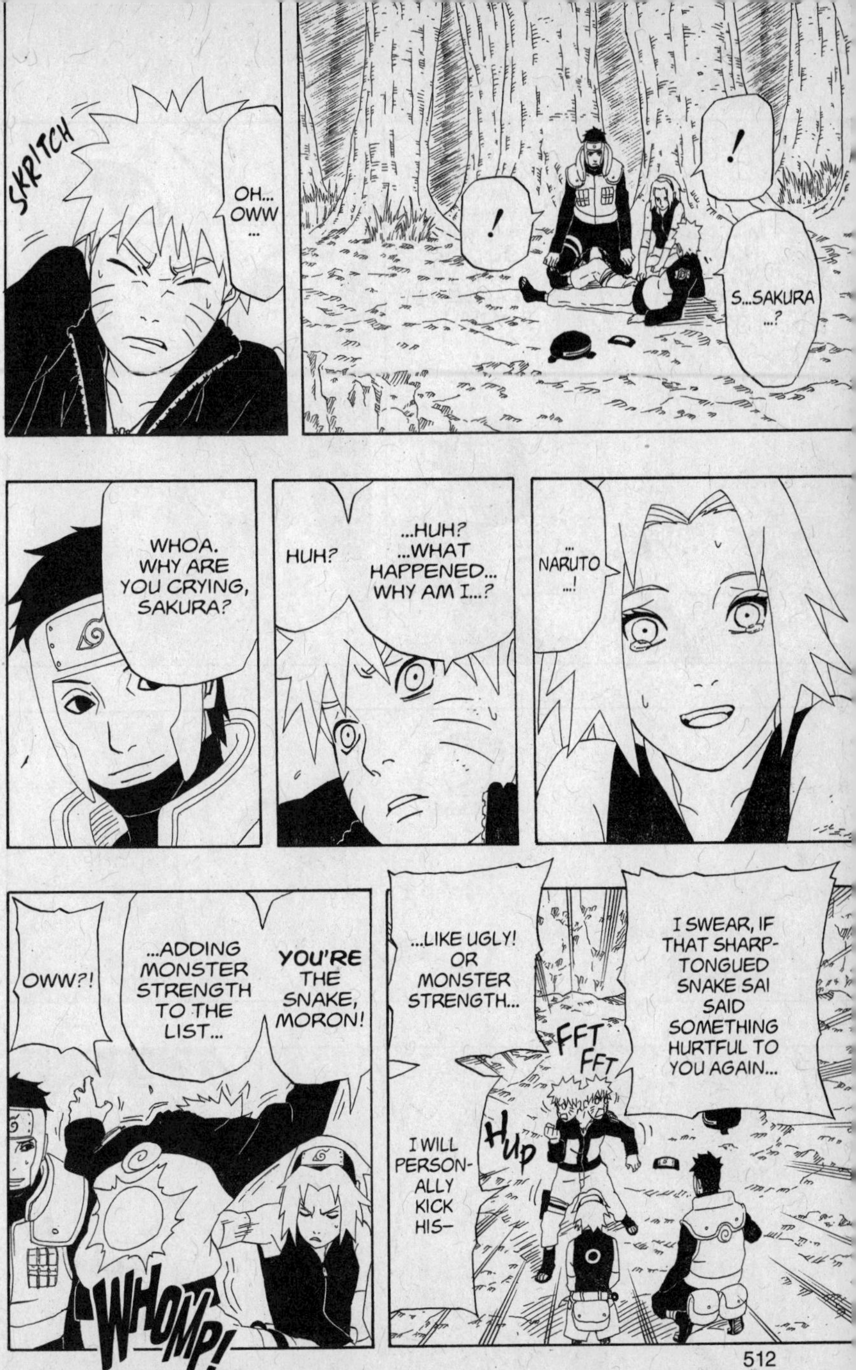
!
S...SAKURA ...?
!
SKRITCH
OH... OWW ...
... NARUTO ...!
...HUH? ...WHAT HAPPENED... WHY AM I...?
HUH?
WHOA. WHY ARE YOU CRYING, SAKURA?
I SWEAR, IF THAT SHARP-TONGUED SNAKE SAI SAID SOMETHING HURTFUL TO YOU AGAIN...
...LIKE UGLY! OR MONSTER STRENGTH...
FFT FFT
HUP
I WILL PERSON-ALLY KICK HIS–
YOU'RE THE SNAKE, MORON!
...ADDING MONSTER STRENGTH TO THE LIST...
OWW?!
WHOMP!

READ THIS WAY

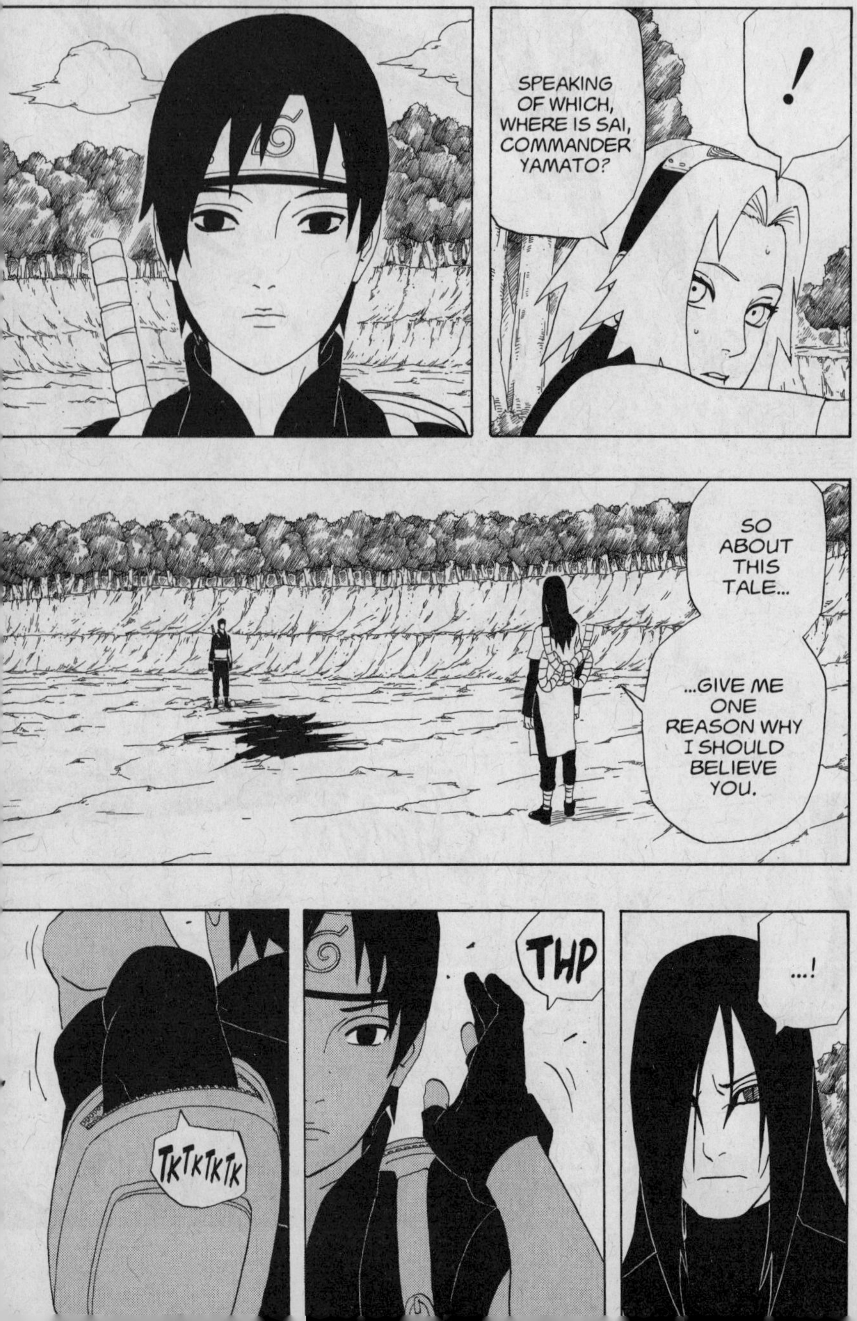
!
SPEAKING OF WHICH, WHERE IS SAI, COMMANDER YAMATO?
SO ABOUT THIS TALE...
...GIVE ME ONE REASON WHY I SHOULD BELIEVE YOU.
...!
THP
TKTKTKTK

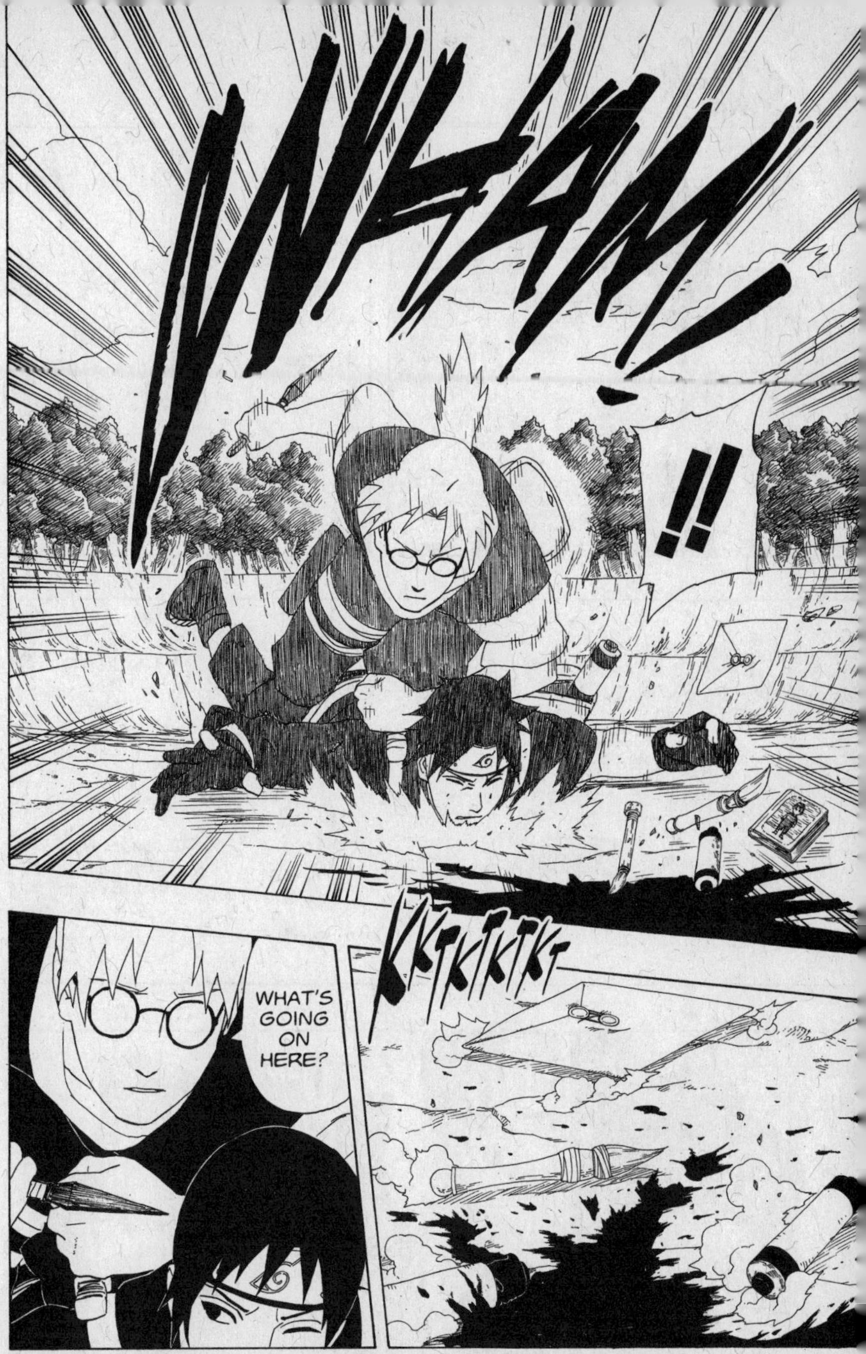
WHAM!
!!
KKTKTKTKT
WHAT'S GOING ON HERE?

READ THIS WAY

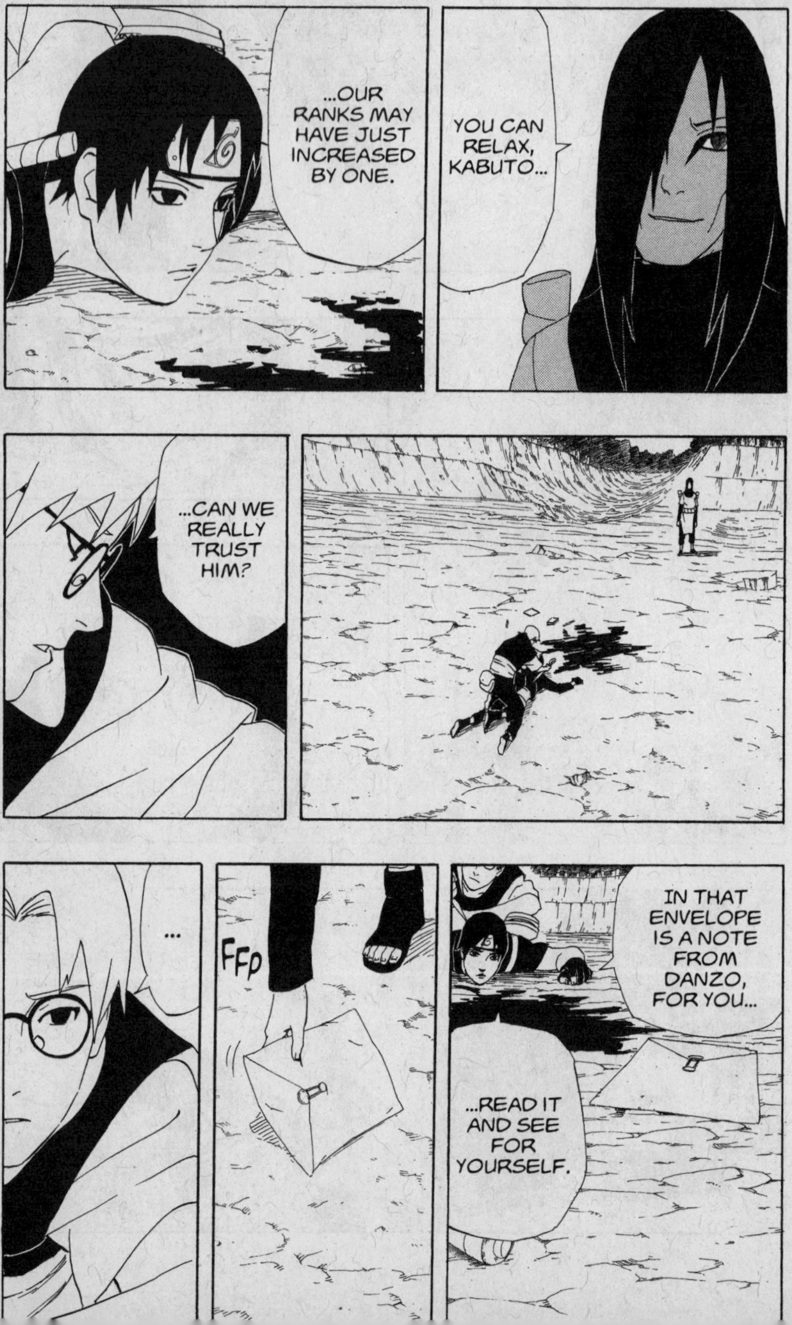
YOU CAN RELAX, KABUTO...
...OUR RANKS MAY HAVE JUST INCREASED BY ONE.
...CAN WE REALLY TRUST HIM?
IN THAT ENVELOPE IS A NOTE FROM DANZO, FOR YOU...
...READ IT AND SEE FOR YOURSELF.
FFP
...

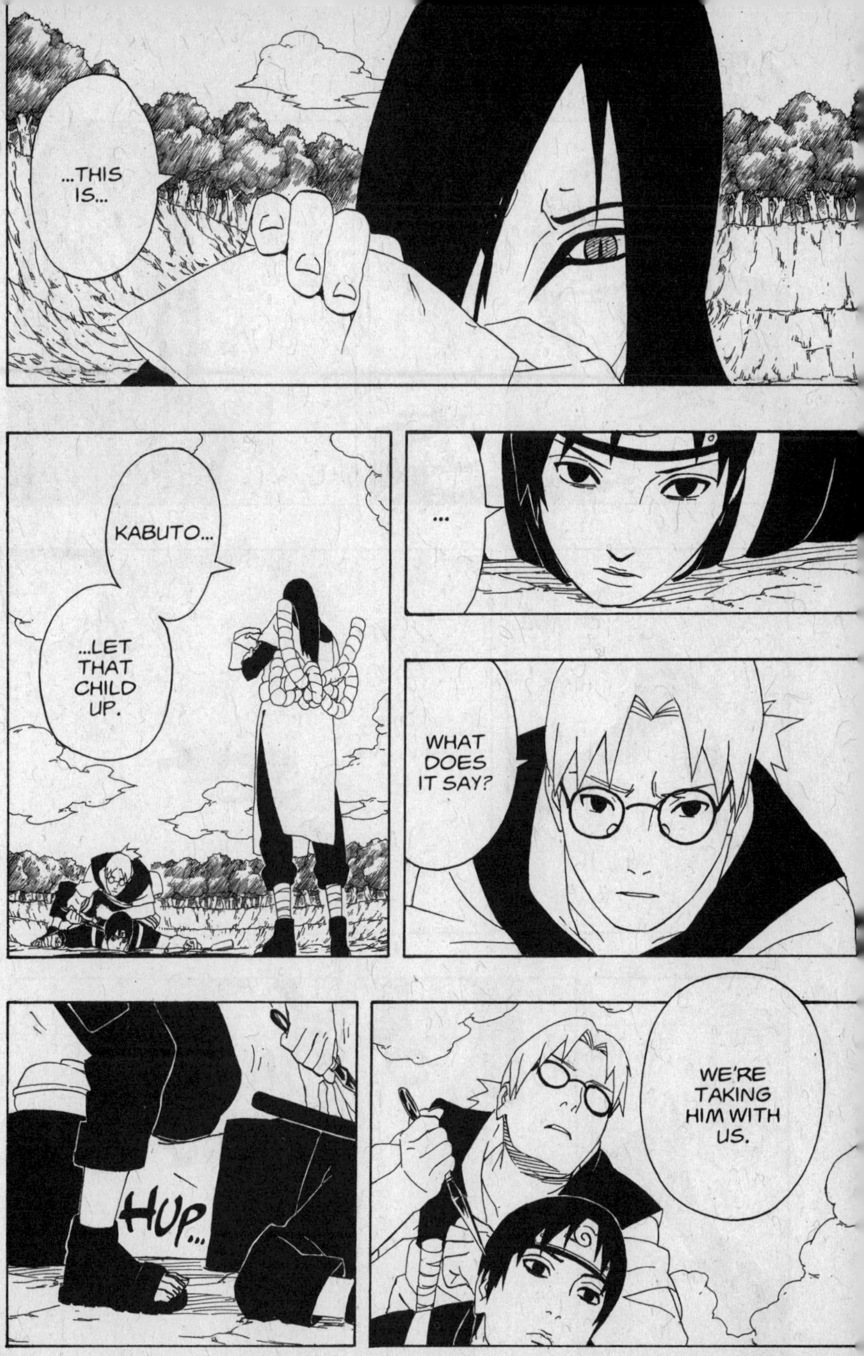
...THIS IS...
...
WHAT DOES IT SAY?
KABUTO...
...LET THAT CHILD UP.
WE'RE TAKING HIM WITH US.
HUP...

READ THIS WAY

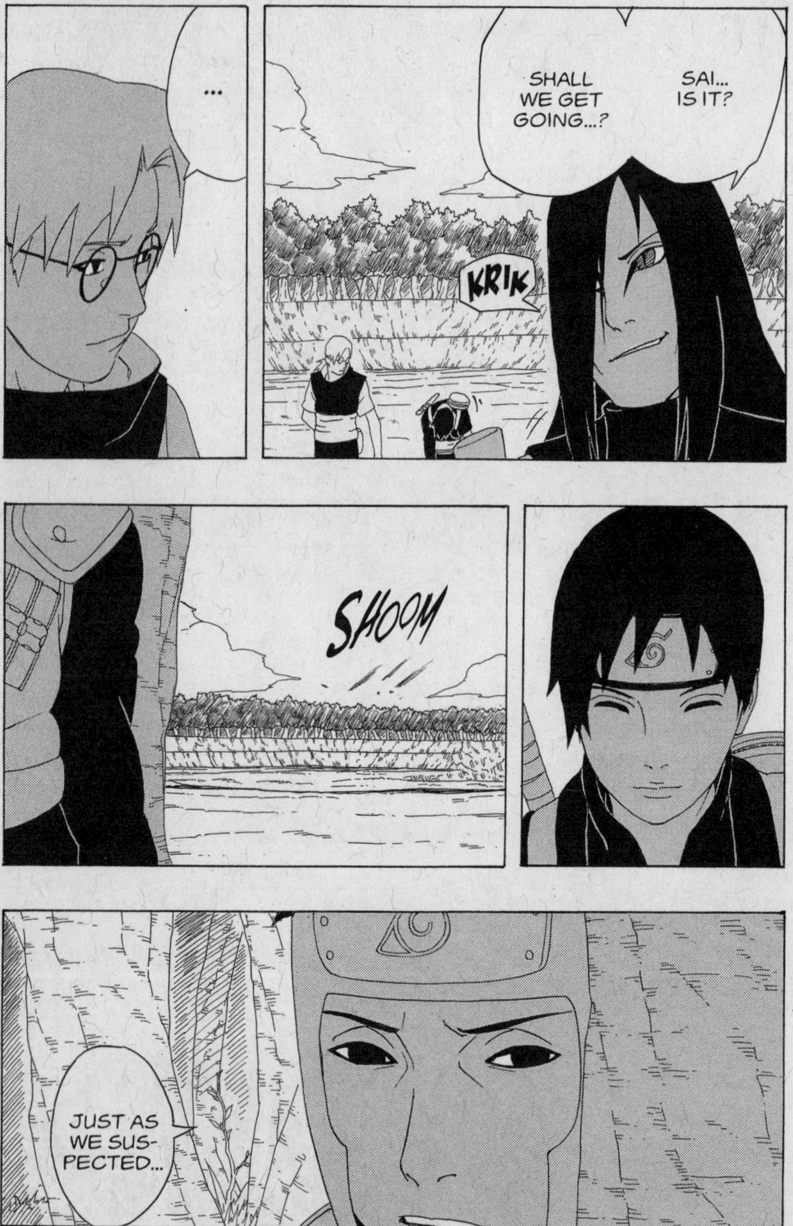
SAI... IS IT?
SHALL WE GET GOING...?
KRIK
...
SHOOM
JUST AS WE SUS-PECTED...

NARUTO

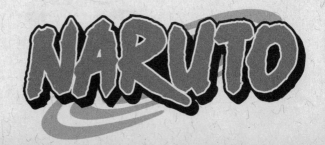

Number 298: The Secret Mission...!!

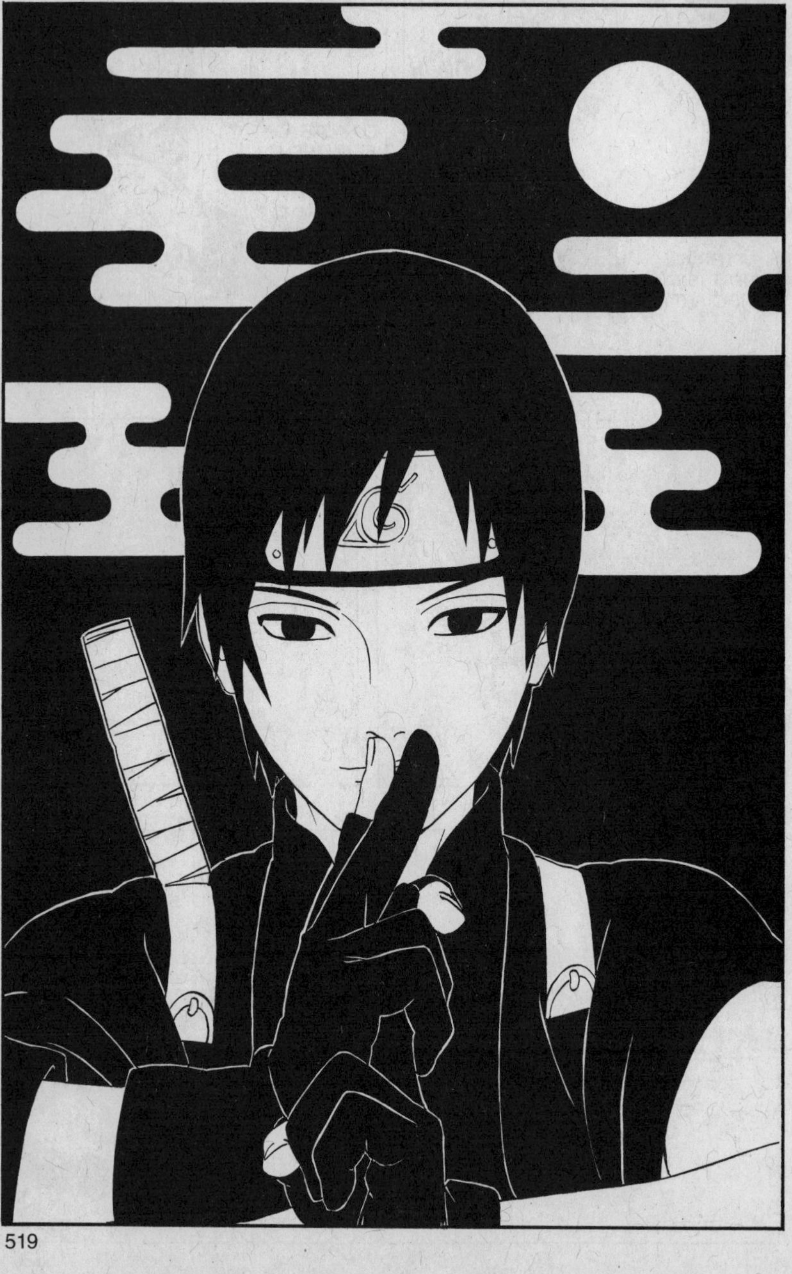

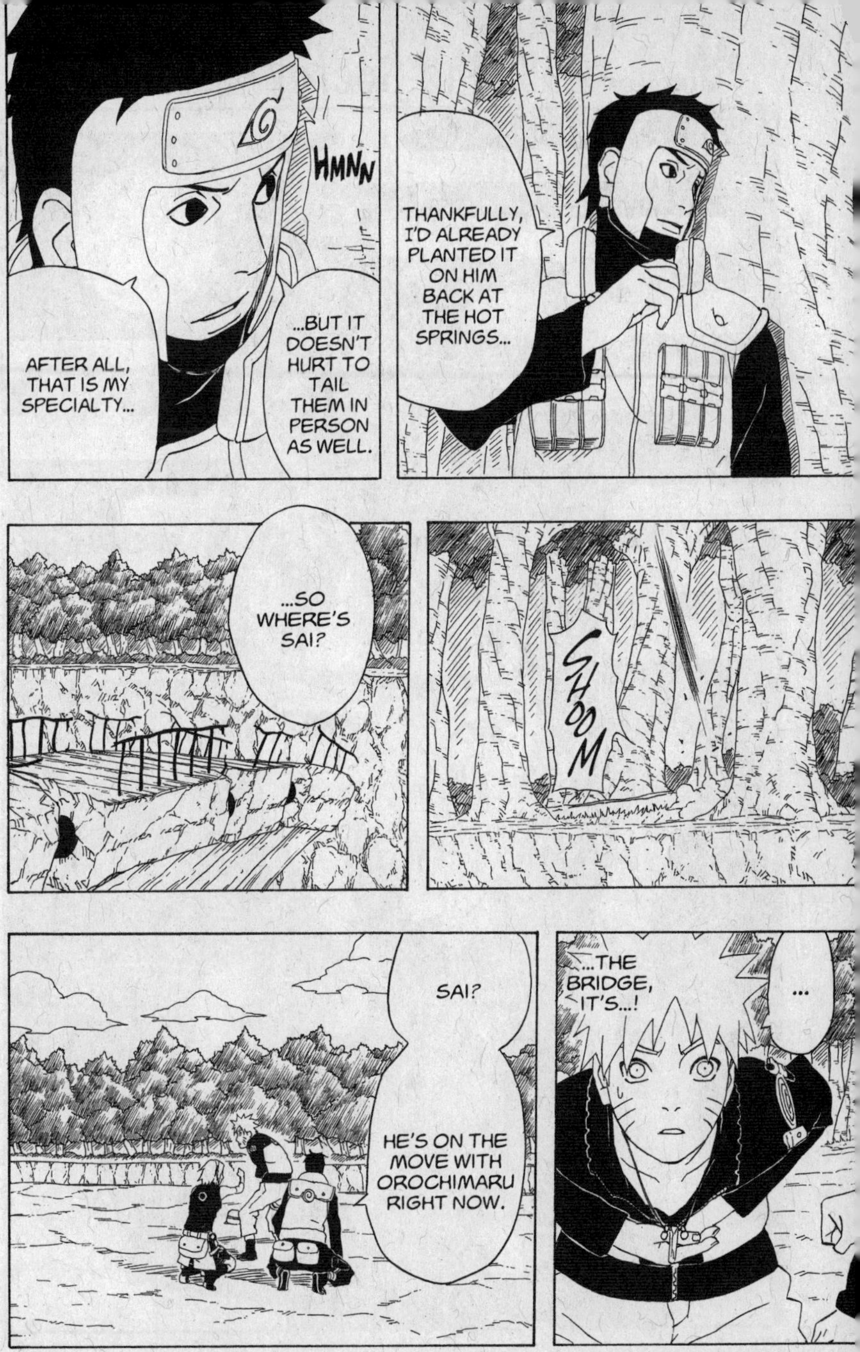
THANKFULLY, I'D ALREADY PLANTED IT ON HIM BACK AT THE HOT SPRINGS...
HMNN
AFTER ALL, THAT IS MY SPECIALTY...
...BUT IT DOESN'T HURT TO TAIL THEM IN PERSON AS WELL.
SHOOM
...SO WHERE'S SAI?
...
...THE BRIDGE, IT'S...!
SAI?
HE'S ON THE MOVE WITH OROCHIMARU RIGHT NOW.

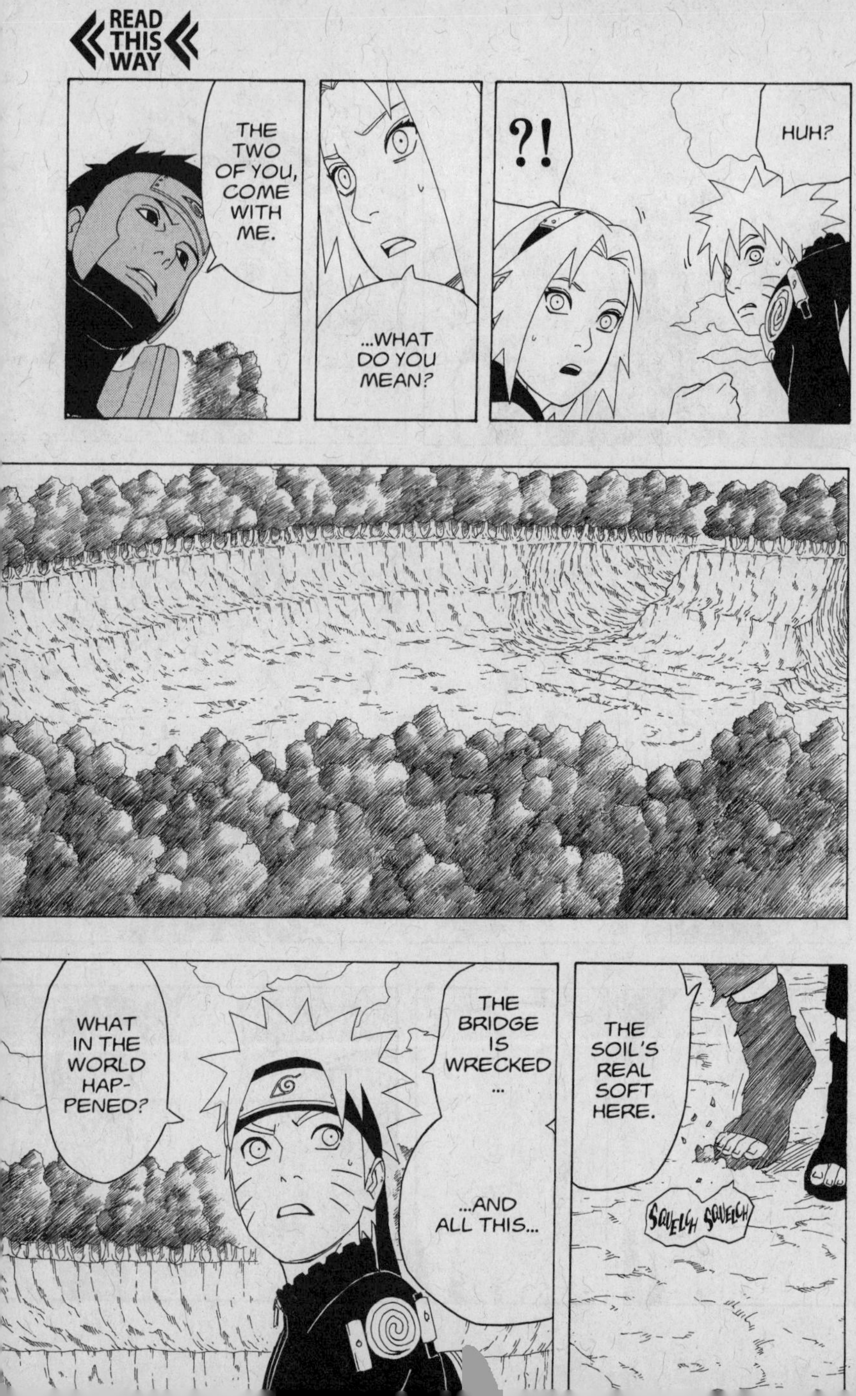
READ THIS WAY
HUH?
?!
...WHAT DO YOU MEAN?
THE TWO OF YOU, COME WITH ME.
THE SOIL'S REAL SOFT HERE.
SQUELCH SQUELCH
THE BRIDGE IS WRECKED...
...AND ALL THIS...
WHAT IN THE WORLD HAP-PENED?

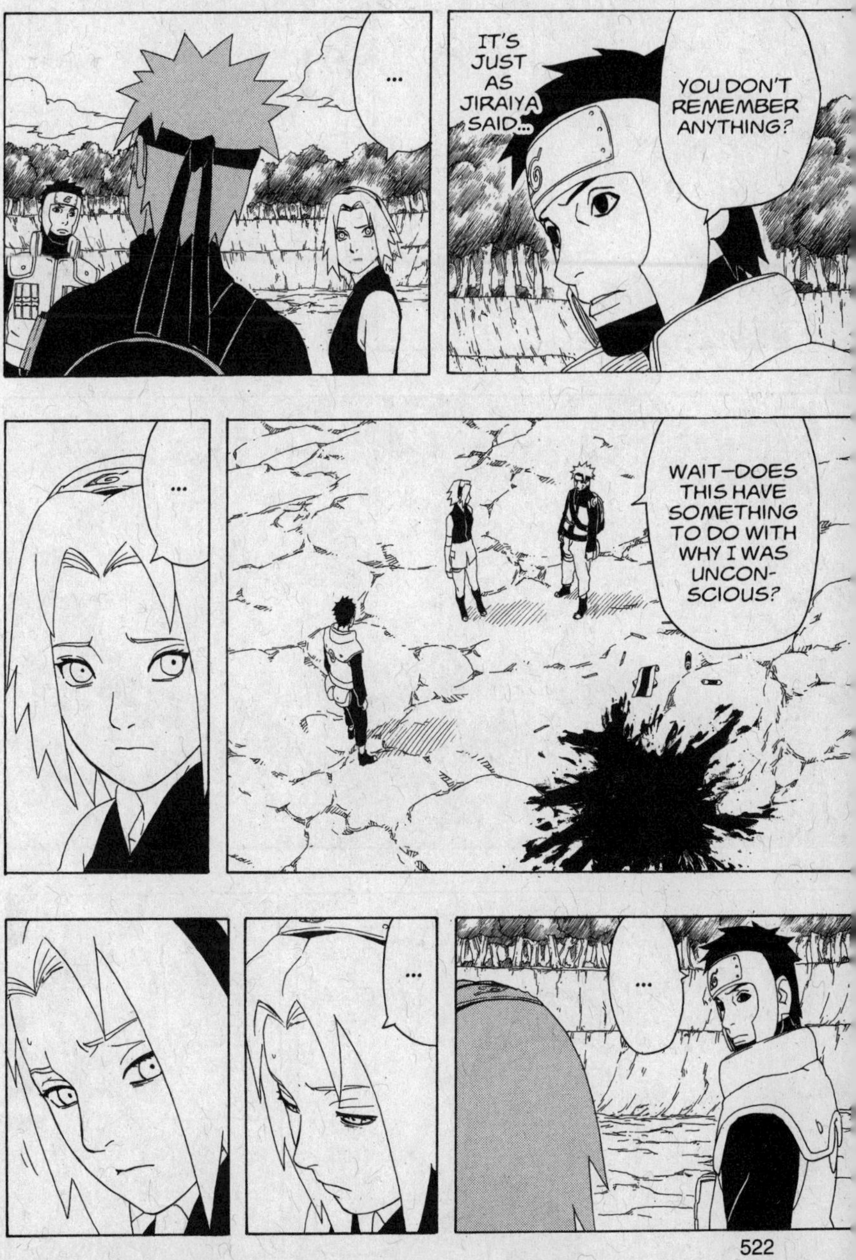
IT'S JUST AS JIRAIYA SAID...
YOU DON'T REMEMBER ANYTHING?
...
WAIT—DOES THIS HAVE SOMETHING TO DO WITH WHY I WAS UNCON-SCIOUS?
...
...
...

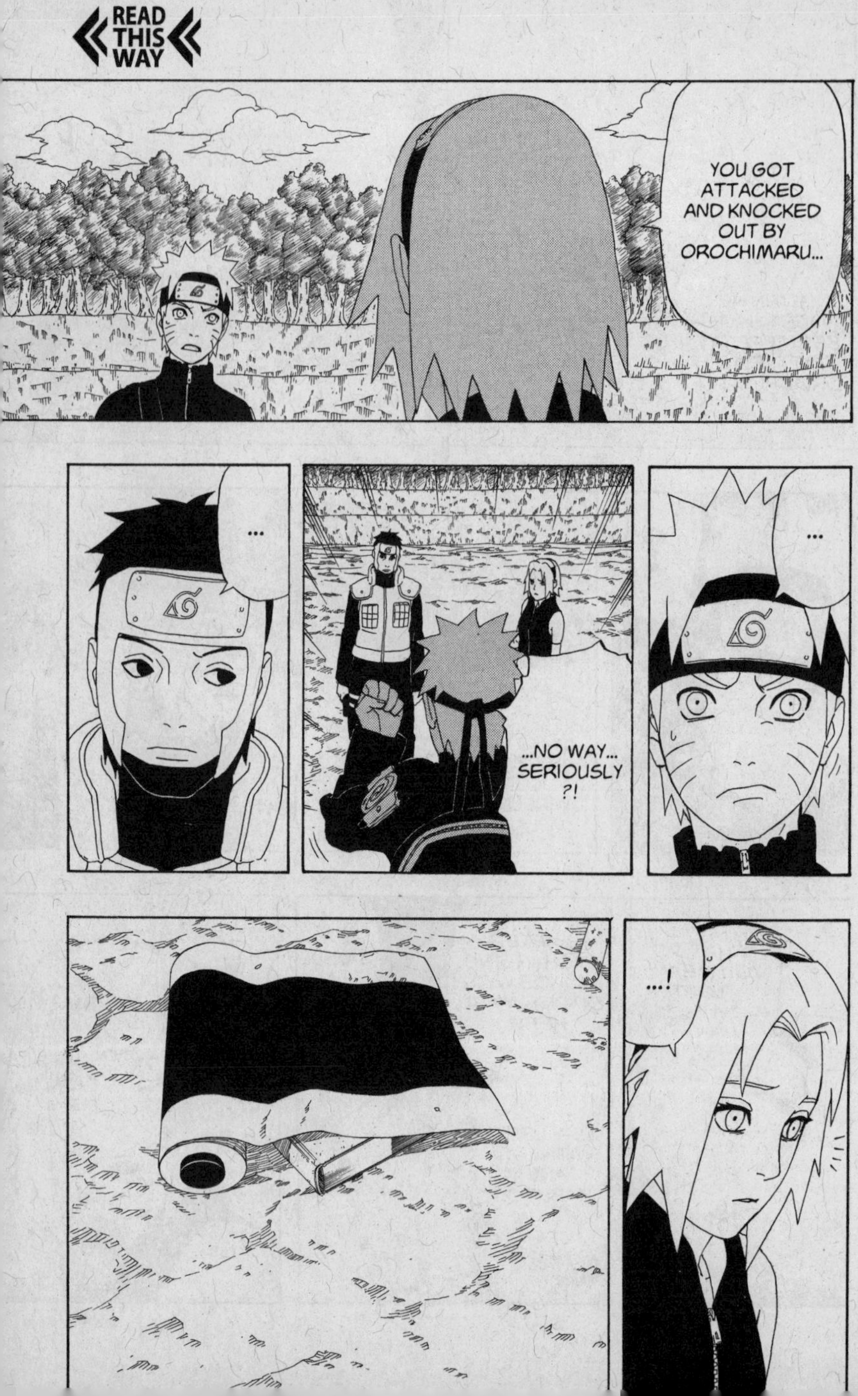
READ THIS WAY
YOU GOT ATTACKED AND KNOCKED OUT BY OROCHIMARU...
...
...NO WAY... SERIOUSLY?!
...
...!

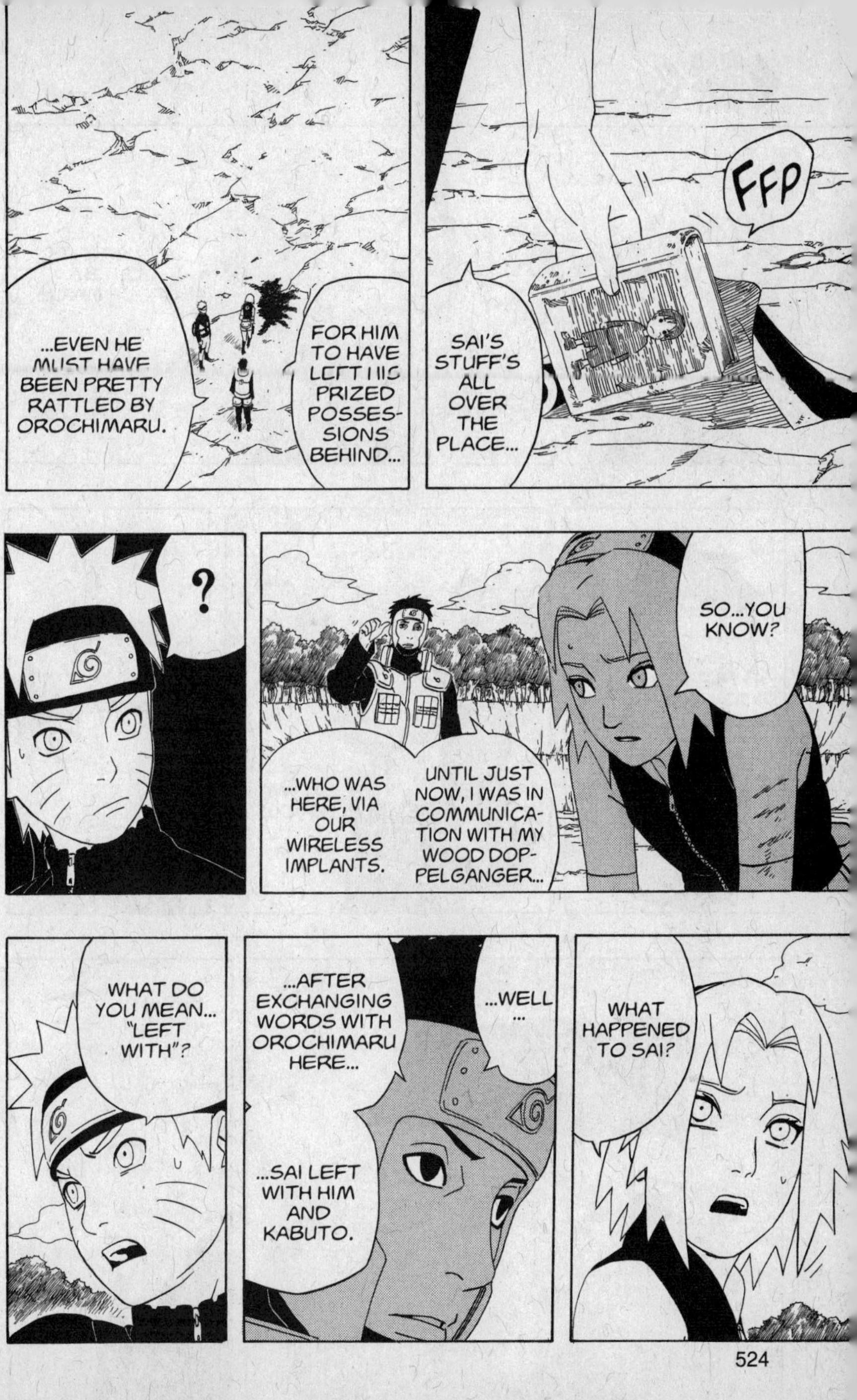
FFP
SAI'S STUFF'S ALL OVER THE PLACE...
FOR HIM TO HAVE LEFT HIS PRIZED POSSESSIONS BEHIND...
...EVEN HE MUST HAVE BEEN PRETTY RATTLED BY OROCHIMARU.
SO...YOU KNOW?
UNTIL JUST NOW, I WAS IN COMMUNICATION WITH MY WOOD DOPPELGANGER...
...WHO WAS HERE, VIA OUR WIRELESS IMPLANTS.
?
WHAT HAPPENED TO SAI?
...WELL ...
...AFTER EXCHANGING WORDS WITH OROCHIMARU HERE...
...SAI LEFT WITH HIM AND KABUTO.
WHAT DO YOU MEAN... "LEFT WITH"?

READ THIS WAY

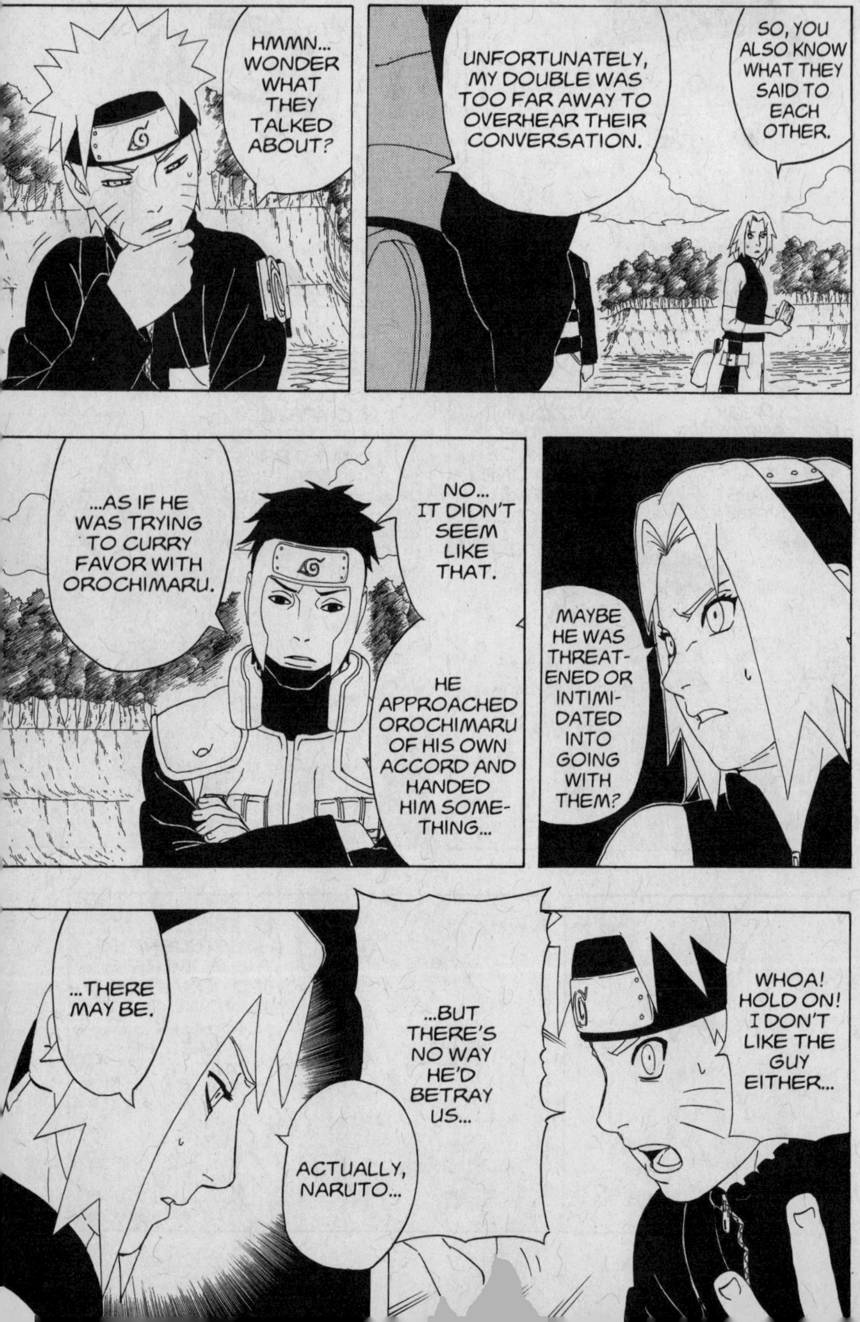
SO, YOU ALSO KNOW WHAT THEY SAID TO EACH OTHER.
UNFORTUNATELY, MY DOUBLE WAS TOO FAR AWAY TO OVERHEAR THEIR CONVERSATION.
HMMN... WONDER WHAT THEY TALKED ABOUT?
MAYBE HE WAS THREAT-ENED OR INTIMI-DATED INTO GOING WITH THEM?
NO... IT DIDN'T SEEM LIKE THAT.
HE APPROACHED OROCHIMARU OF HIS OWN ACCORD AND HANDED HIM SOME-THING...
...AS IF HE WAS TRYING TO CURRY FAVOR WITH OROCHIMARU.
WHOA! HOLD ON! I DON'T LIKE THE GUY EITHER...
...BUT THERE'S NO WAY HE'D BETRAY US...
ACTUALLY, NARUTO...
...THERE MAY BE.

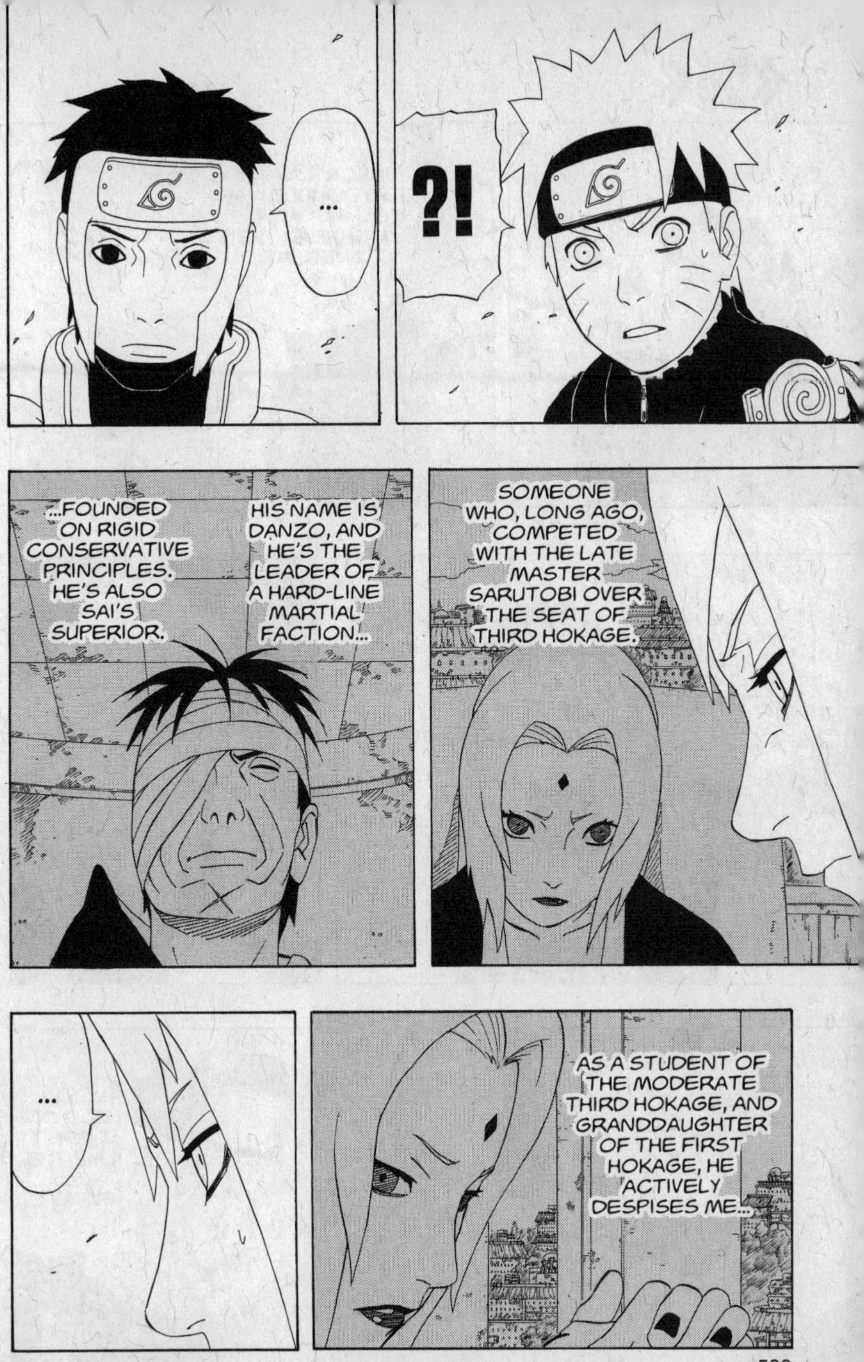
?!
...
SOMEONE WHO, LONG AGO, COMPETED WITH THE LATE MASTER SARUTOBI OVER THE SEAT OF THIRD HOKAGE.
HIS NAME IS DANZO, AND HE'S THE LEADER OF A HARD-LINE MARTIAL FACTION...
...FOUNDED ON RIGID CONSERVATIVE PRINCIPLES. HE'S ALSO SAI'S SUPERIOR.
AS A STUDENT OF THE MODERATE THIRD HOKAGE, AND GRANDDAUGHTER OF THE FIRST HOKAGE, HE ACTIVELY DESPISES ME...
...

READ THIS WAY

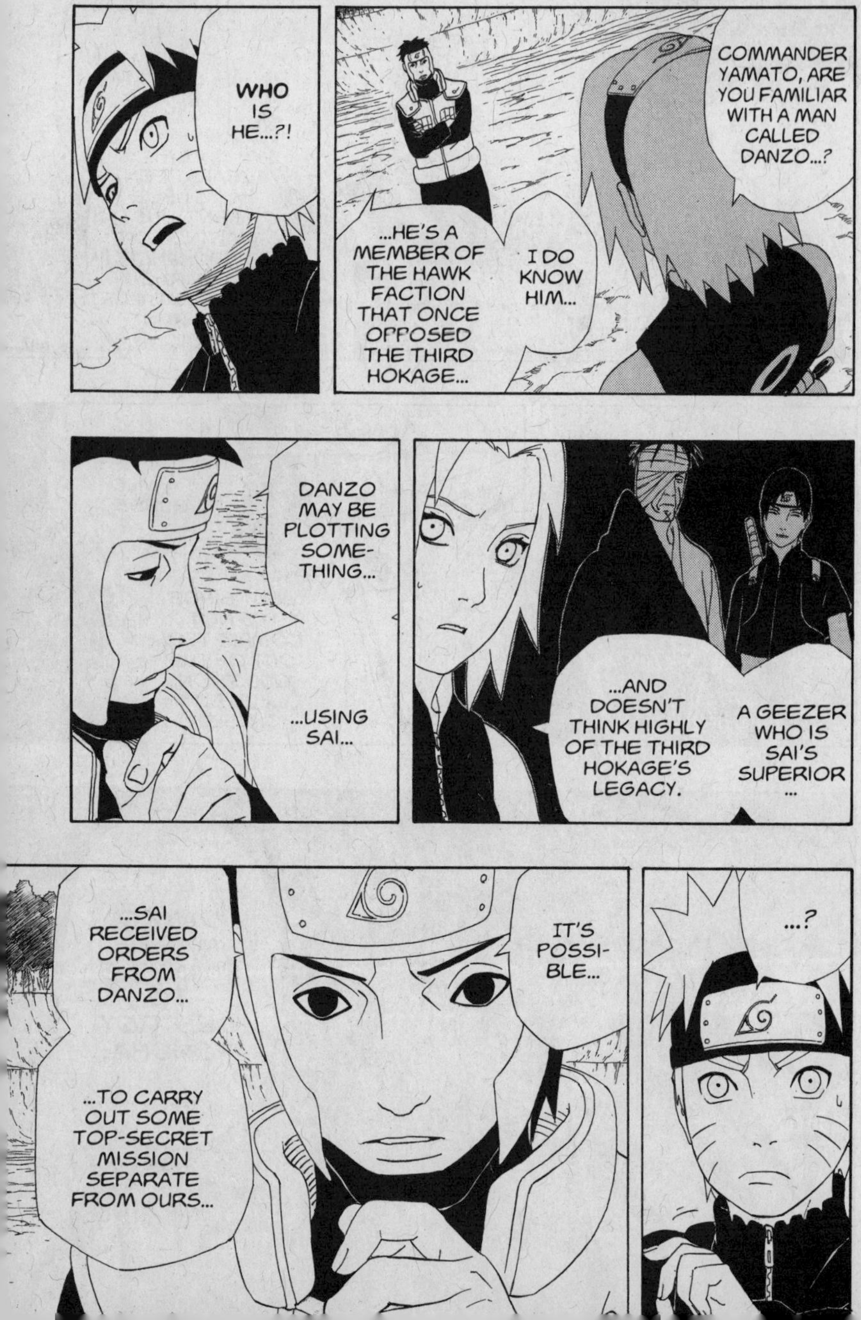
COMMANDER YAMATO, ARE YOU FAMILIAR WITH A MAN CALLED DANZO...?
I DO KNOW HIM...
...HE'S A MEMBER OF THE HAWK FACTION THAT ONCE OPPOSED THE THIRD HOKAGE...
WHO IS HE...?!
A GEEZER WHO IS SAI'S SUPERIOR...
...AND DOESN'T THINK HIGHLY OF THE THIRD HOKAGE'S LEGACY.
DANZO MAY BE PLOTTING SOME-THING...
...USING SAI...
...?
IT'S POSSI-BLE...
...SAI RECEIVED ORDERS FROM DANZO...
...TO CARRY OUT SOME TOP-SECRET MISSION SEPARATE FROM OURS...

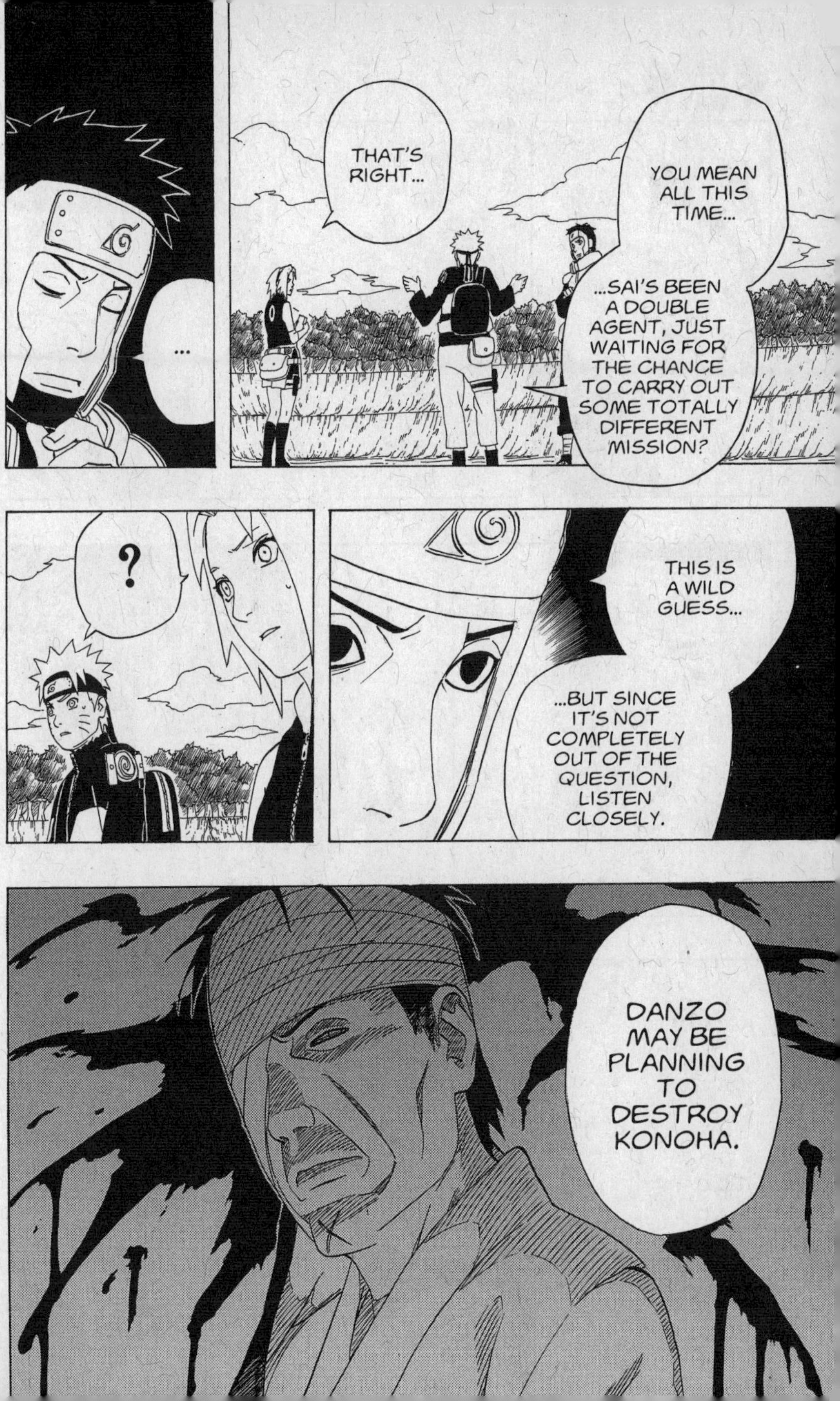
YOU MEAN ALL THIS TIME...
...SAI'S BEEN A DOUBLE AGENT, JUST WAITING FOR THE CHANCE TO CARRY OUT SOME TOTALLY DIFFERENT MISSION?
THAT'S RIGHT...
...
THIS IS A WILD GUESS...
...BUT SINCE IT'S NOT COMPLETELY OUT OF THE QUESTION, LISTEN CLOSELY.
?
DANZO MAY BE PLANNING TO DESTROY KONOHA.

READ THIS WAY

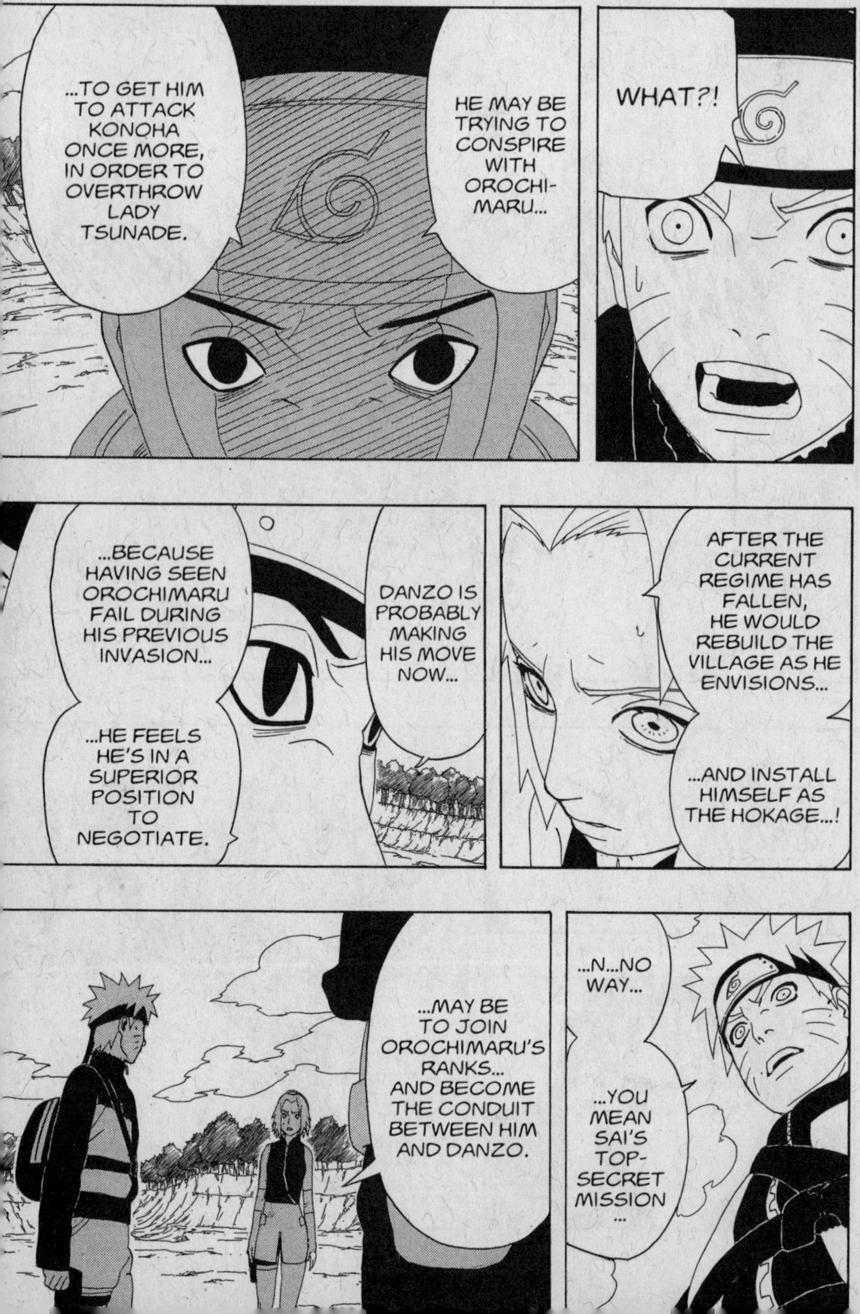
WHAT?!
HE MAY BE TRYING TO CONSPIRE WITH OROCHI-MARU...
...TO GET HIM TO ATTACK KONOHA ONCE MORE, IN ORDER TO OVERTHROW LADY TSUNADE.
AFTER THE CURRENT REGIME HAS FALLEN, HE WOULD REBUILD THE VILLAGE AS HE ENVISIONS...
...AND INSTALL HIMSELF AS THE HOKAGE...!
DANZO IS PROBABLY MAKING HIS MOVE NOW...
...BECAUSE HAVING SEEN OROCHIMARU FAIL DURING HIS PREVIOUS INVASION...
...HE FEELS HE'S IN A SUPERIOR POSITION TO NEGOTIATE.
...N...NO WAY...
...YOU MEAN SAI'S TOP-SECRET MISSION ...
...MAY BE TO JOIN OROCHIMARU'S RANKS... AND BECOME THE CONDUIT BETWEEN HIM AND DANZO.

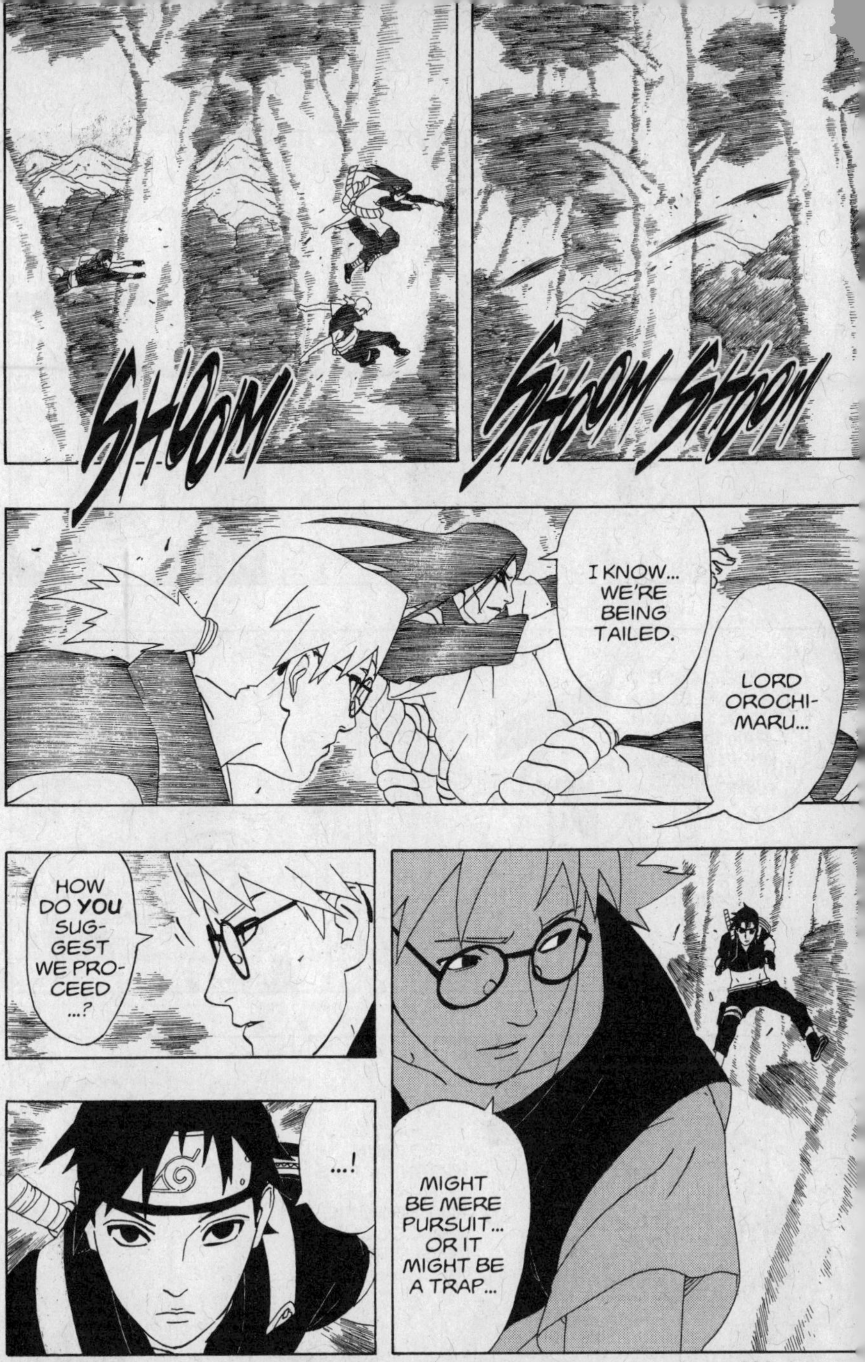
SHOOM SHOOM
SHOOM
LORD OROCHIMARU...
I KNOW... WE'RE BEING TAILED.
MIGHT BE MERE PURSUIT... OR IT MIGHT BE A TRAP...
HOW DO **YOU** SUGGEST WE PROCEED ...?
...!

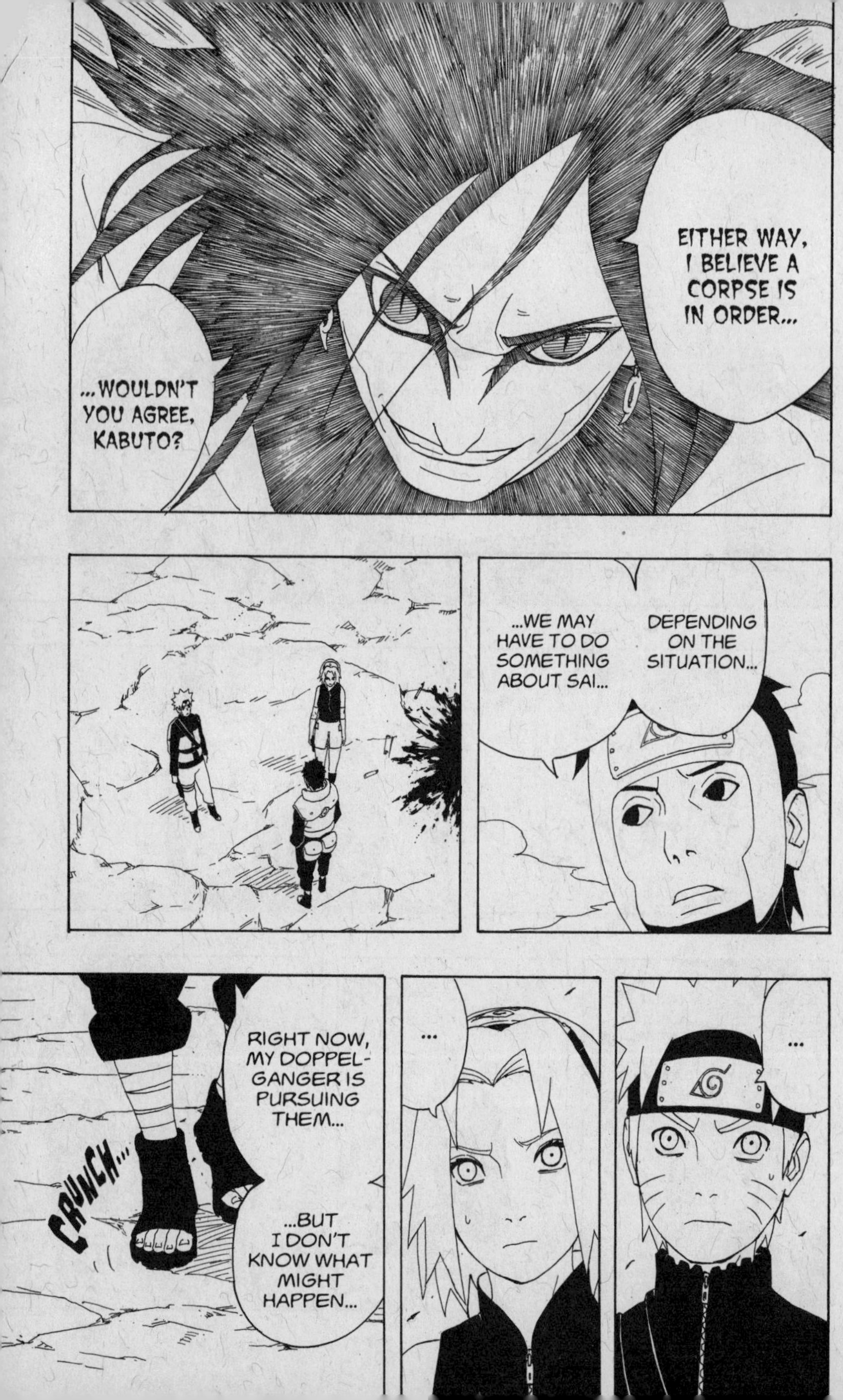
EITHER WAY, I BELIEVE A CORPSE IS IN ORDER...
...WOULDN'T YOU AGREE, KABUTO?
DEPENDING ON THE SITUATION...
...WE MAY HAVE TO DO SOMETHING ABOUT SAI...
...
...
RIGHT NOW, MY DOPPEL-GANGER IS PURSUING THEM...
...BUT I DON'T KNOW WHAT MIGHT HAPPEN...
CRUNCH...

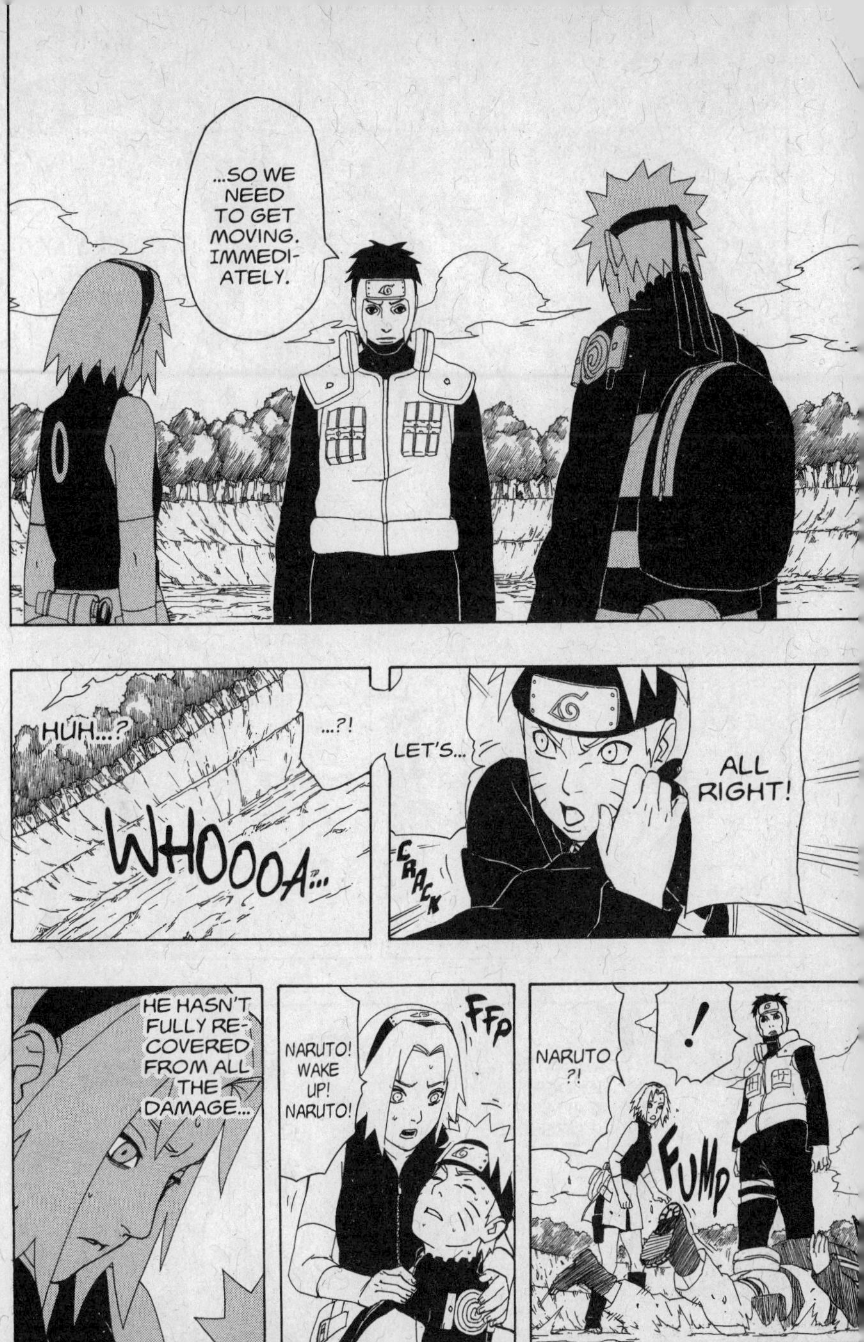
...SO WE NEED TO GET MOVING. IMMEDIATELY.
ALL RIGHT!
LET'S...
CRACK
...?!
HUH...?
WHOOOA...
!
NARUTO ?!
FUMP
FFP
NARUTO! WAKE UP! NARUTO!
HE HASN'T FULLY RE-COVERED FROM ALL THE DAMAGE...

READ THIS WAY

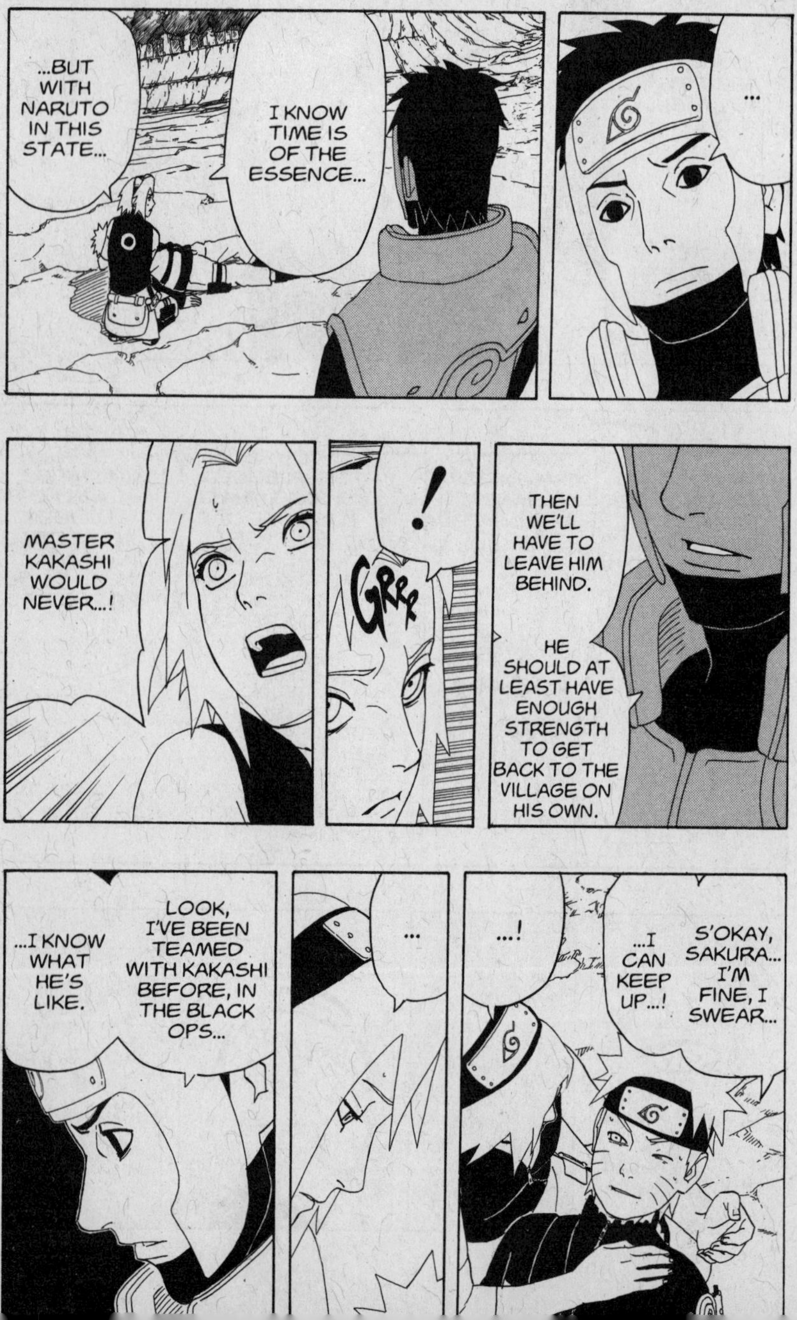
...
I KNOW TIME IS OF THE ESSENCE...
...BUT WITH NARUTO IN THIS STATE...
THEN WE'LL HAVE TO LEAVE HIM BEHIND.
HE SHOULD AT LEAST HAVE ENOUGH STRENGTH TO GET BACK TO THE VILLAGE ON HIS OWN.
!
GRrr
MASTER KAKASHI WOULD NEVER...!
S'OKAY, SAKURA... I'M FINE, I SWEAR...
...I CAN KEEP UP...!
...!
...
LOOK, I'VE BEEN TEAMED WITH KAKASHI BEFORE, IN THE BLACK OPS...
...I KNOW WHAT HE'S LIKE.

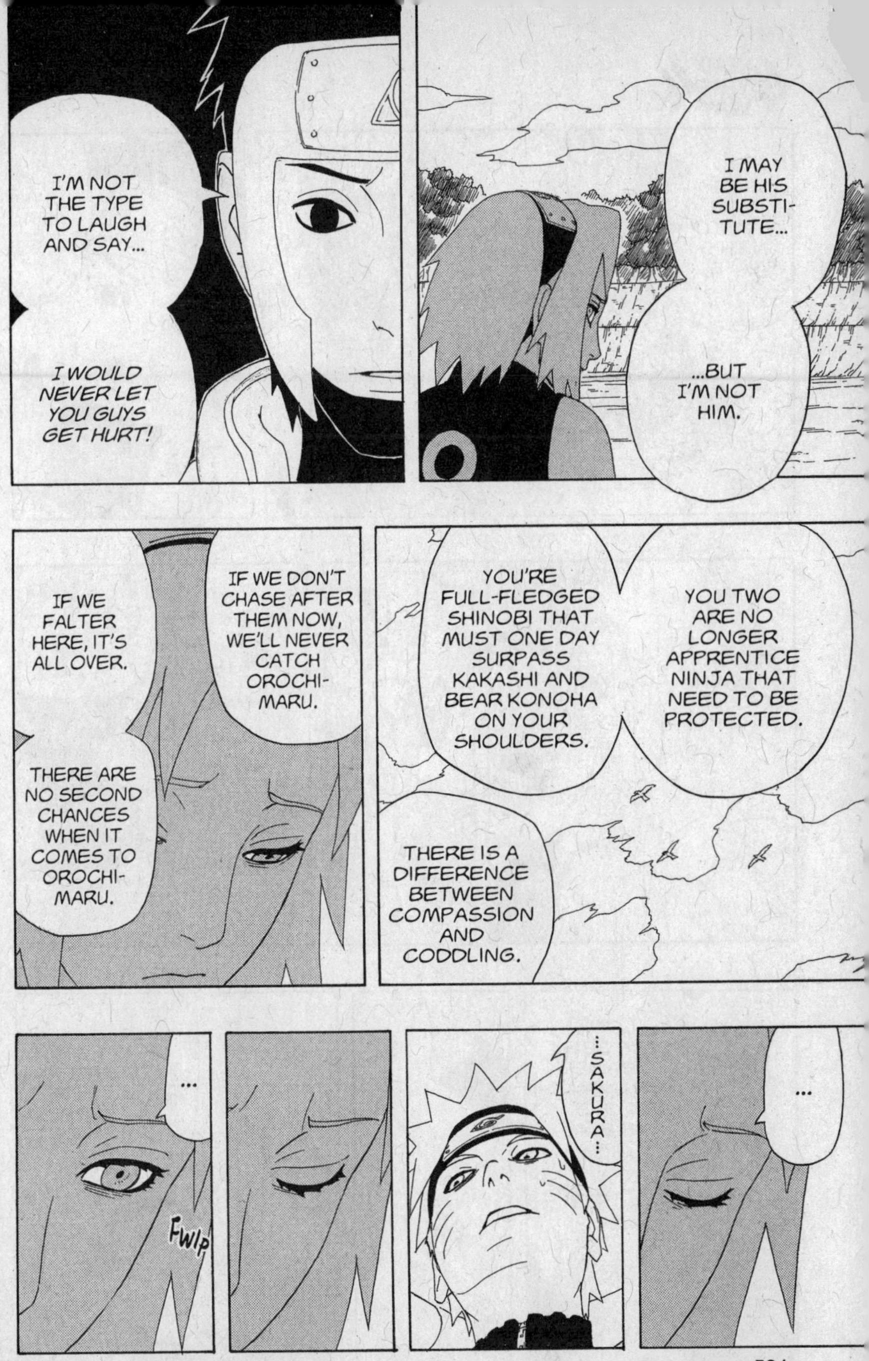
I MAY BE HIS SUBSTITUTE...
...BUT I'M NOT HIM.
I'M NOT THE TYPE TO LAUGH AND SAY...
I WOULD NEVER LET YOU GUYS GET HURT!
YOU TWO ARE NO LONGER APPRENTICE NINJA THAT NEED TO BE PROTECTED.
YOU'RE FULL-FLEDGED SHINOBI THAT MUST ONE DAY SURPASS KAKASHI AND BEAR KONOHA ON YOUR SHOULDERS.
THERE IS A DIFFERENCE BETWEEN COMPASSION AND CODDLING.
IF WE DON'T CHASE AFTER THEM NOW, WE'LL NEVER CATCH OROCHIMARU.
IF WE FALTER HERE, IT'S ALL OVER.
THERE ARE NO SECOND CHANCES WHEN IT COMES TO OROCHIMARU.
...
...SAKURA...
...
FWIP

READ THIS WAY

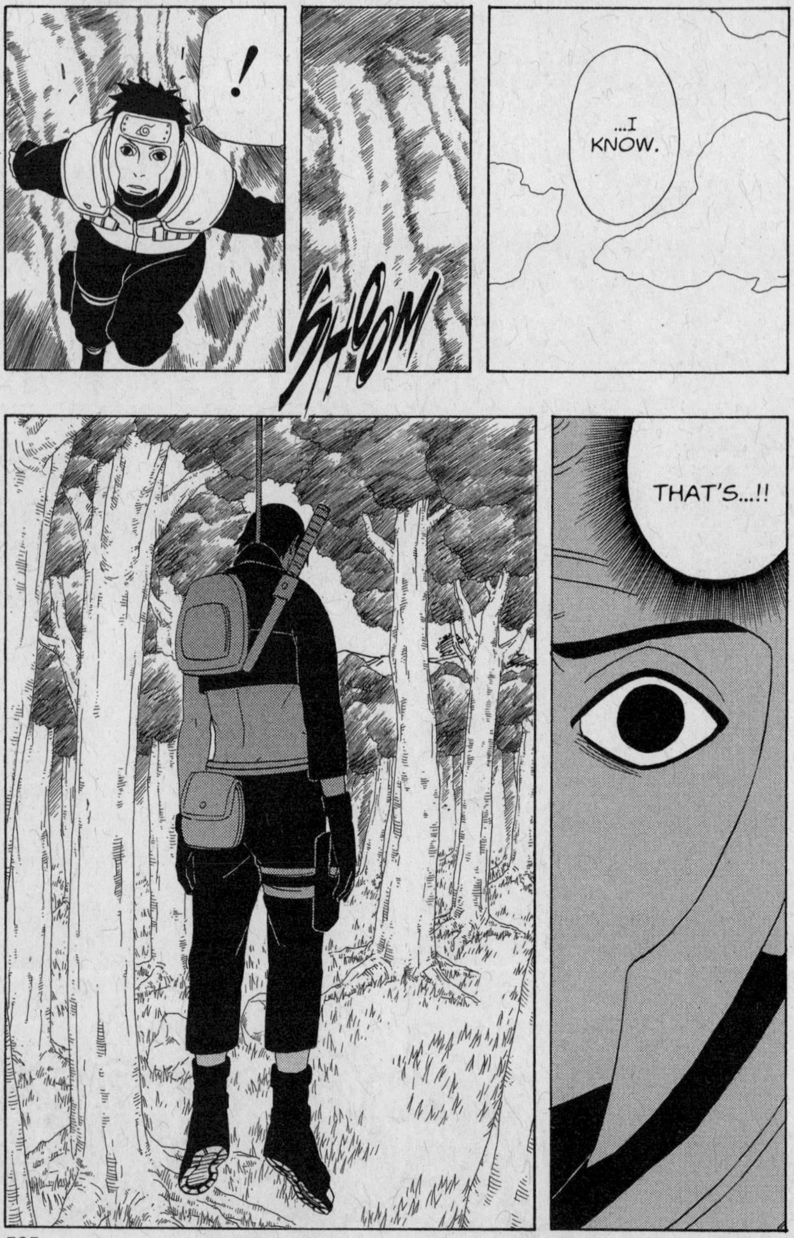
...I KNOW.
SHOOM
!
THAT'S...!!

NARUTO

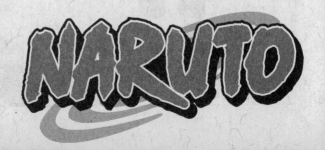

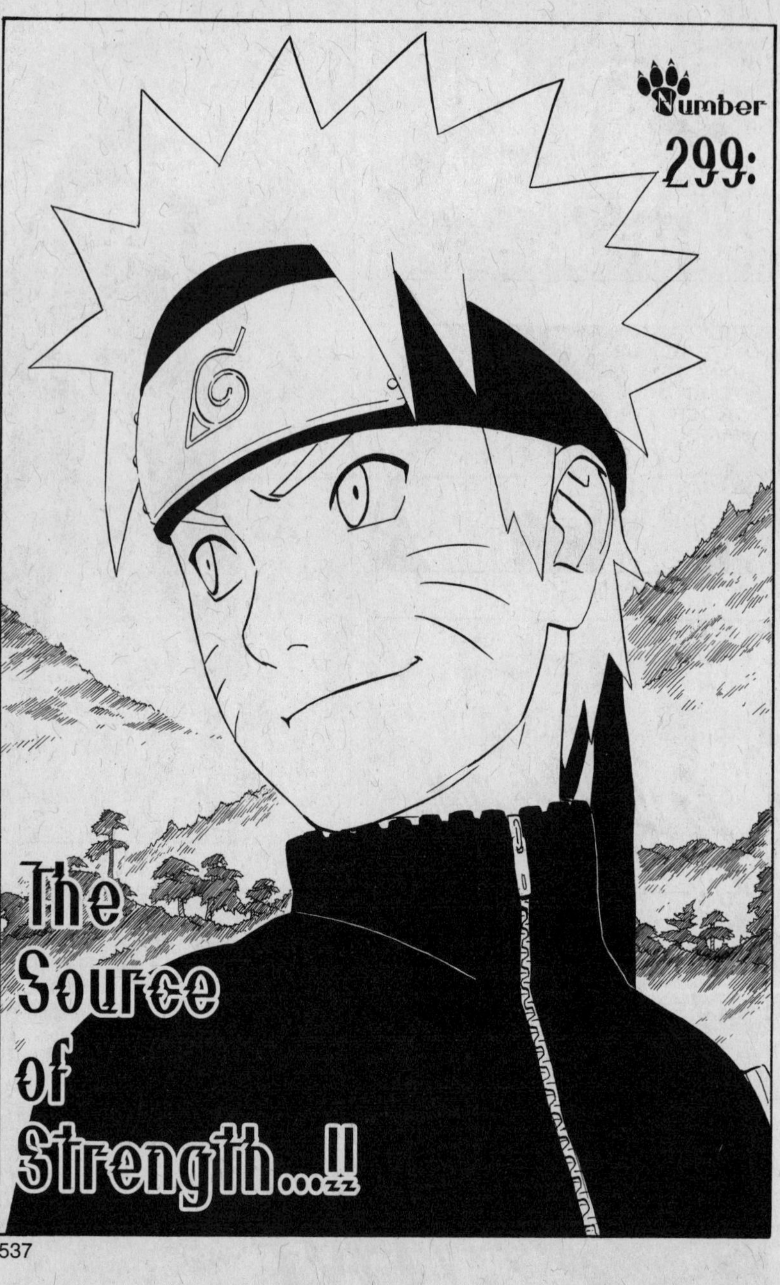
Number 299:
The Source of Strength...!!

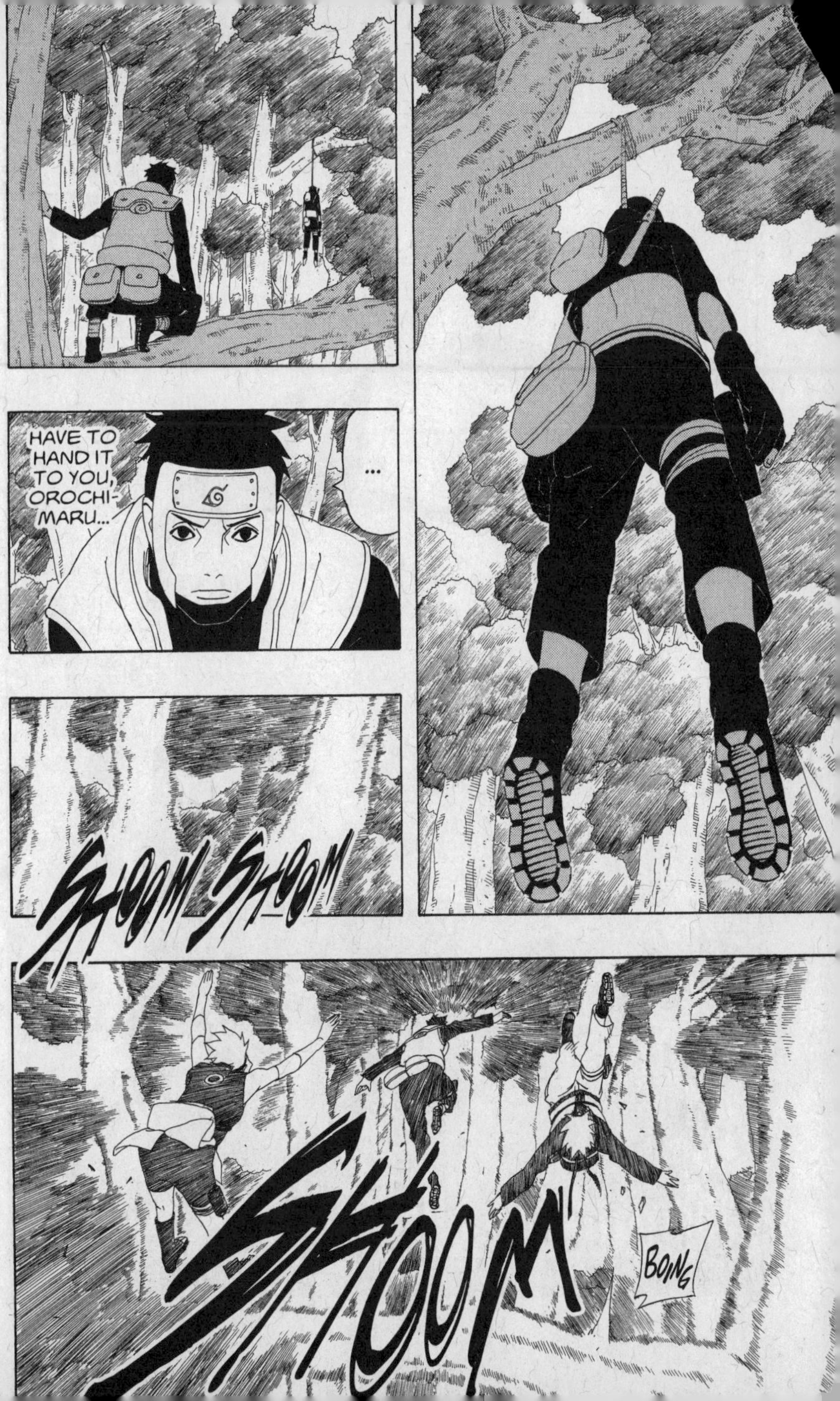
...
HAVE TO HAND IT TO YOU, OROCHIMARU...
SHOOM SHOOM
SHOOM
BOING

READ THIS WAY

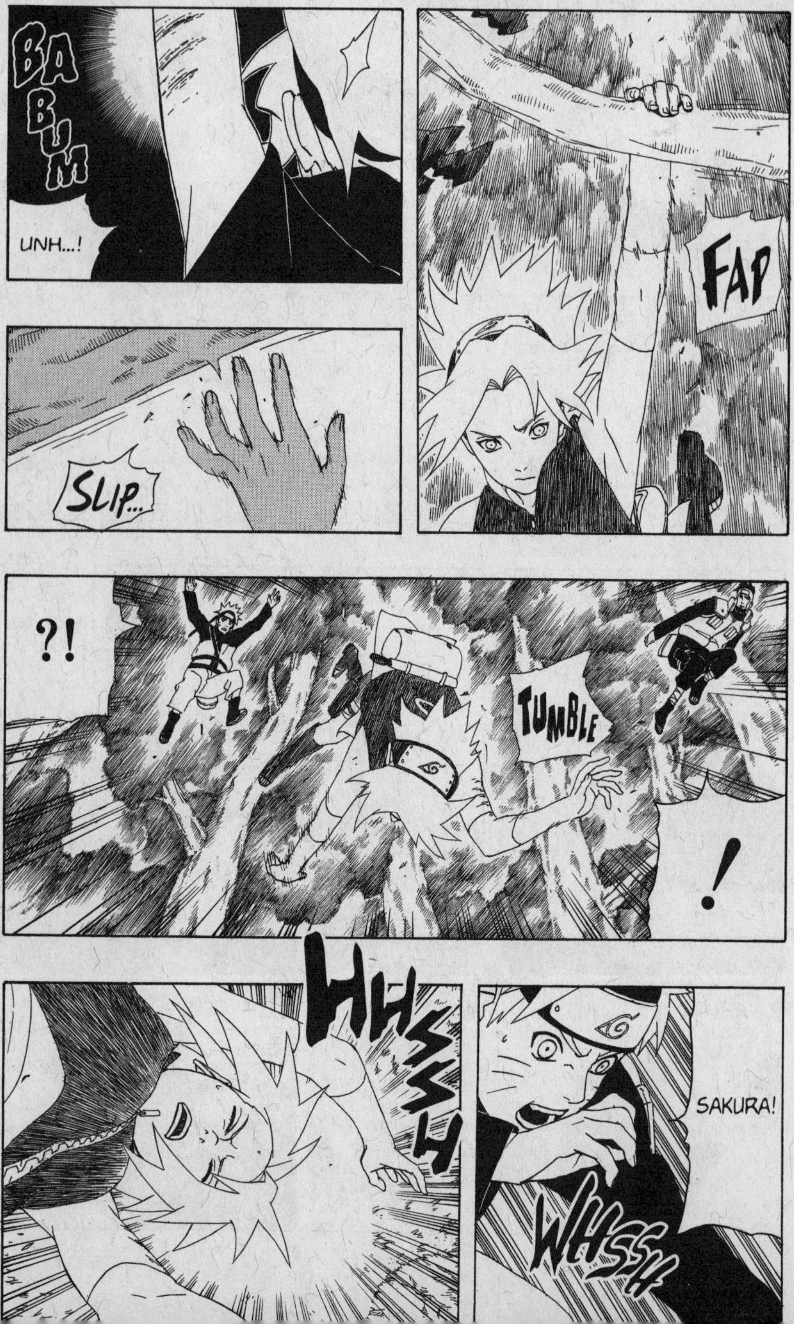
FAP
BABUM
UNH...!
SLIP...
TUMBLE
?!
!
SAKURA!
WHSSH
WHSSSH

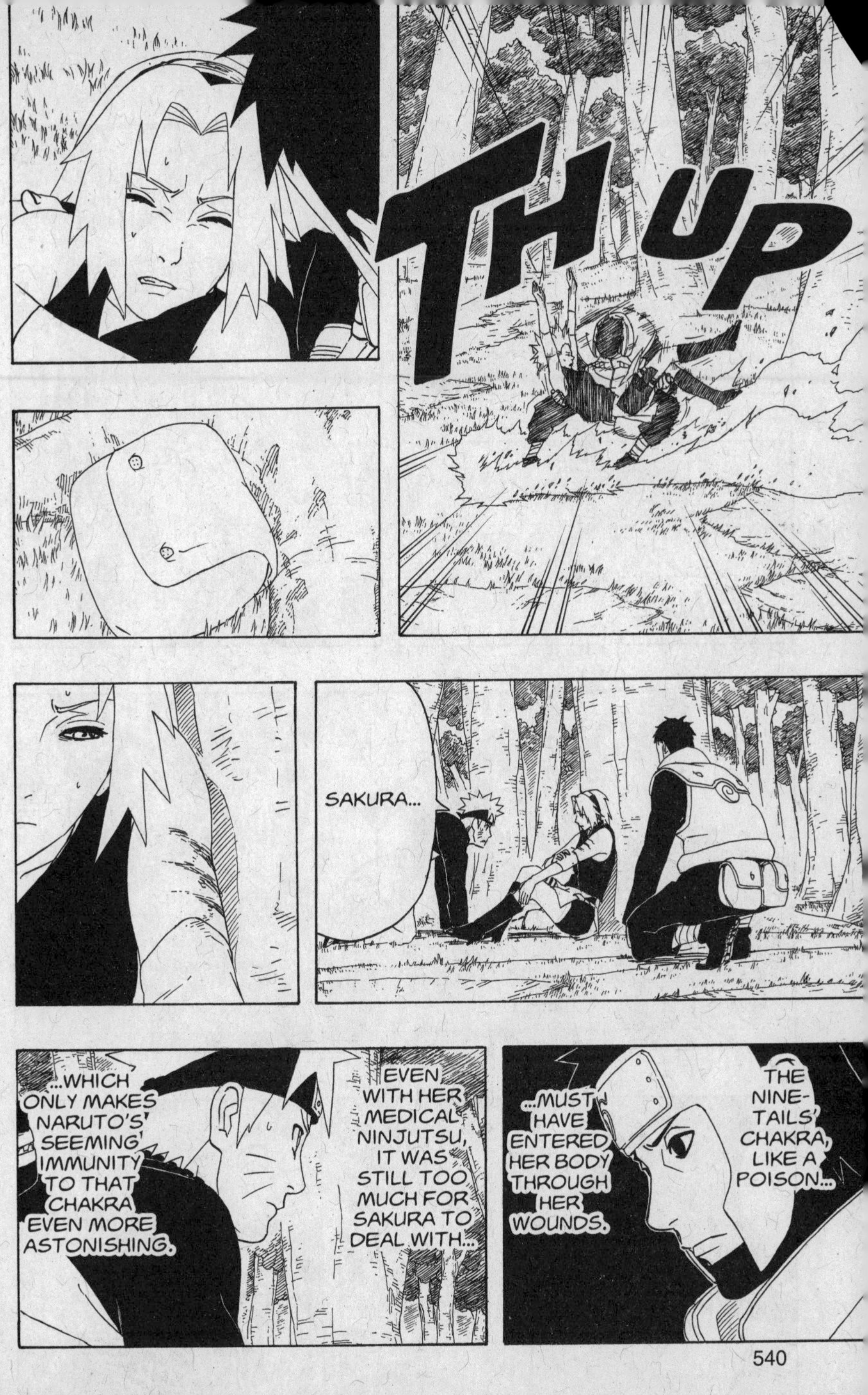
THUP
SAKURA...
THE NINE-TAILS' CHAKRA, LIKE A POISON...
...MUST HAVE ENTERED HER BODY THROUGH HER WOUNDS.
EVEN WITH HER MEDICAL NINJUTSU, IT WAS STILL TOO MUCH FOR SAKURA TO DEAL WITH...
...WHICH ONLY MAKES NARUTO'S SEEMING IMMUNITY TO THAT CHAKRA EVEN MORE ASTONISHING.

READ THIS WAY

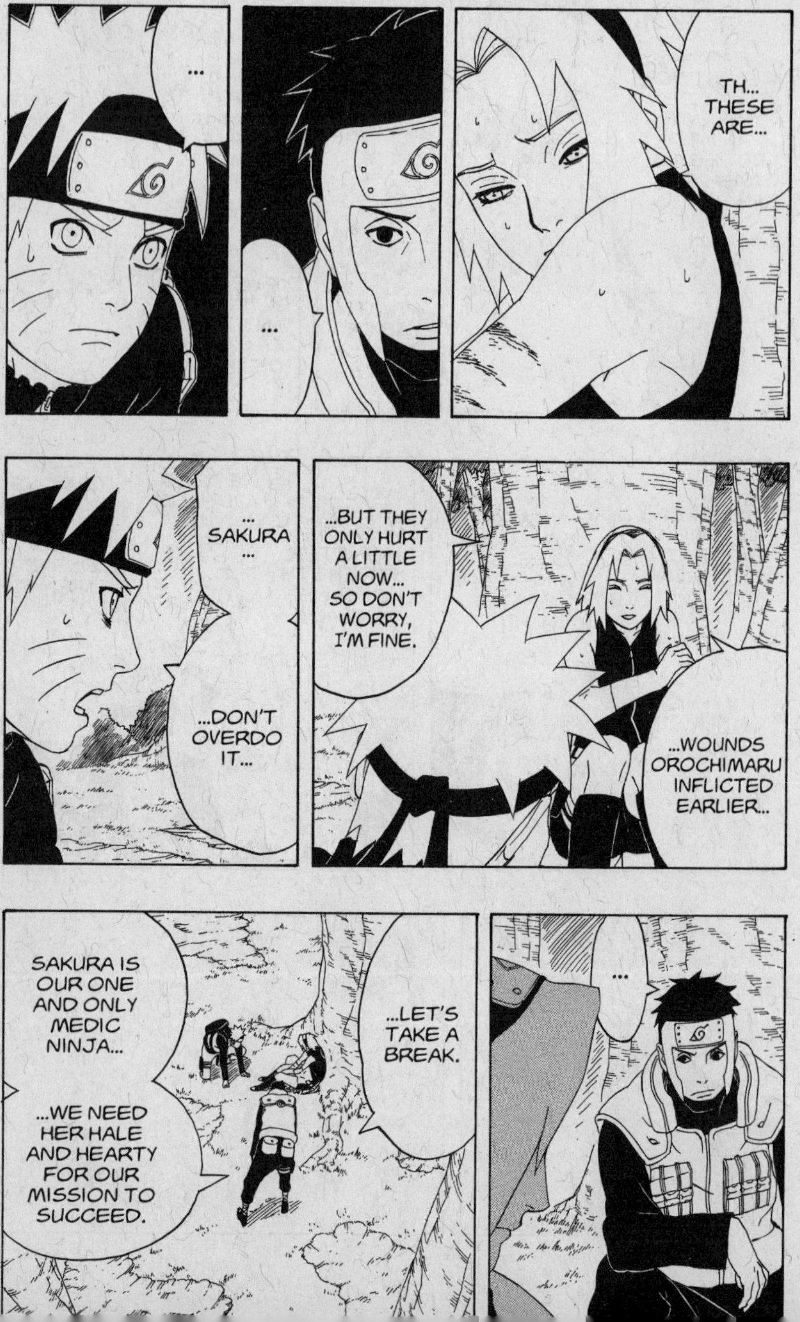
TH... THESE ARE...
...
...
...WOUNDS OROCHIMARU INFLICTED EARLIER...
...BUT THEY ONLY HURT A LITTLE NOW... SO DON'T WORRY, I'M FINE.
... SAKURA ...
...DON'T OVERDO IT...
...
...LET'S TAKE A BREAK.
SAKURA IS OUR ONE AND ONLY MEDIC NINJA...
...WE NEED HER HALE AND HEARTY FOR OUR MISSION TO SUCCEED.

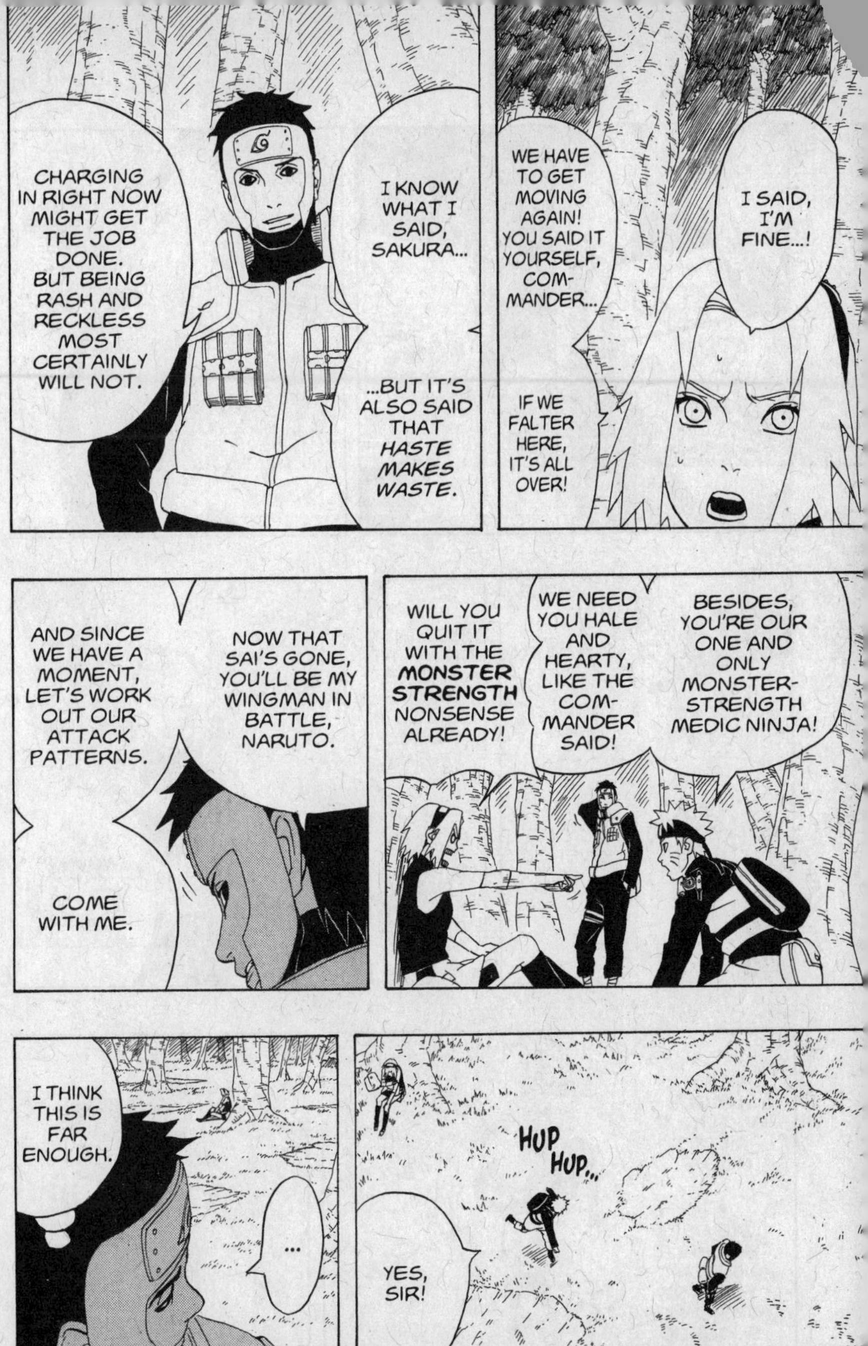
I SAID, I'M FINE...!
WE HAVE TO GET MOVING AGAIN! YOU SAID IT YOURSELF, COMMANDER...
IF WE FALTER HERE, IT'S ALL OVER!
I KNOW WHAT I SAID, SAKURA...
...BUT IT'S ALSO SAID THAT *HASTE MAKES WASTE.*
CHARGING IN RIGHT NOW MIGHT GET THE JOB DONE. BUT BEING RASH AND RECKLESS MOST CERTAINLY WILL NOT.
BESIDES, YOU'RE OUR ONE AND ONLY MONSTER-STRENGTH MEDIC NINJA!
WE NEED YOU HALE AND HEARTY, LIKE THE COMMANDER SAID!
WILL YOU QUIT IT WITH THE **MONSTER STRENGTH** NONSENSE ALREADY!
NOW THAT SAI'S GONE, YOU'LL BE MY WINGMAN IN BATTLE, NARUTO.
AND SINCE WE HAVE A MOMENT, LET'S WORK OUT OUR ATTACK PATTERNS.
COME WITH ME.
HUP HUP...
YES, SIR!
I THINK THIS IS FAR ENOUGH.
...

READ THIS WAY

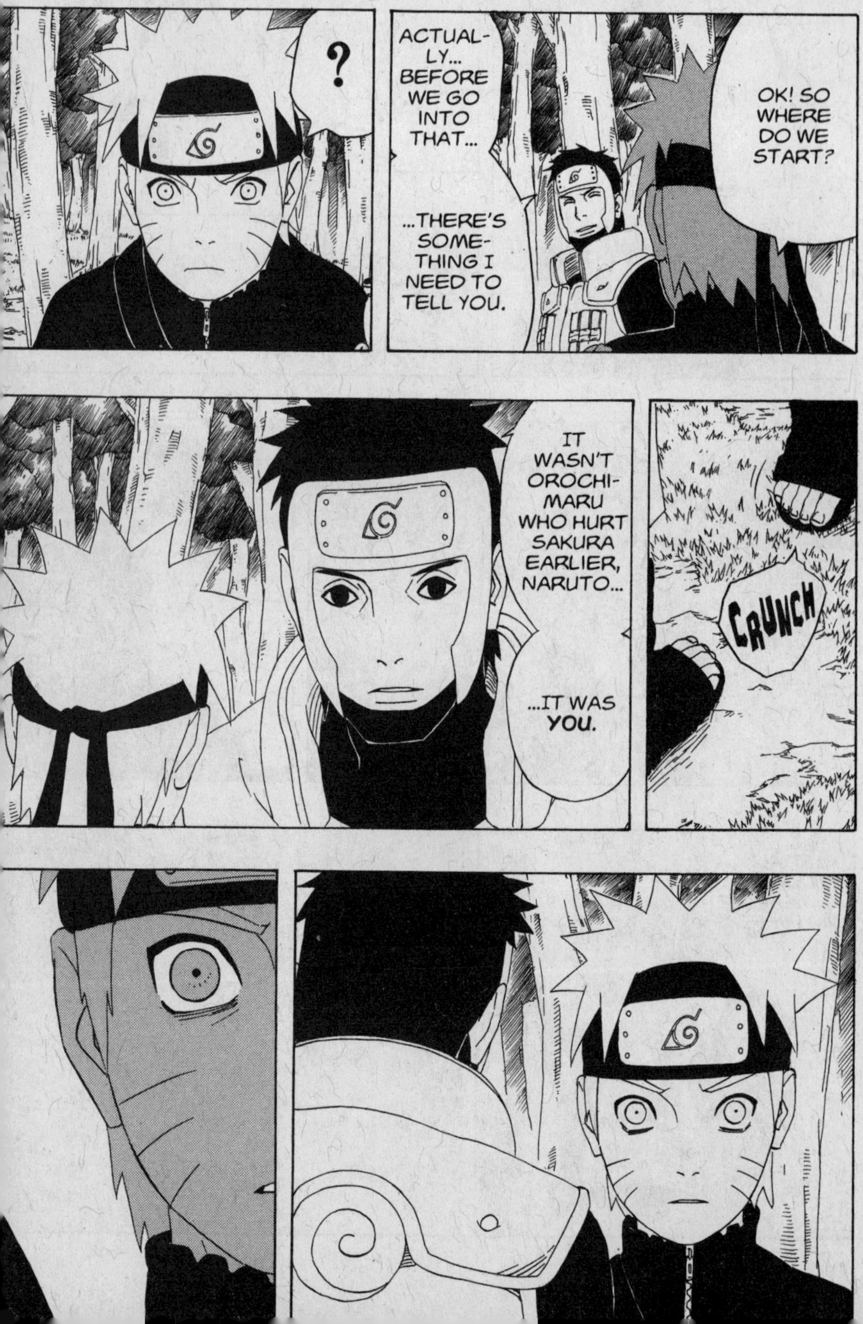
OK! SO WHERE DO WE START?
ACTUAL-LY... BEFORE WE GO INTO THAT...
...THERE'S SOME-THING I NEED TO TELL YOU.
?
CRUNCH
IT WASN'T OROCHI-MARU WHO HURT SAKURA EARLIER, NARUTO...
...IT WAS YOU.

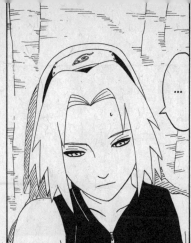

...

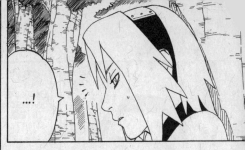

...!

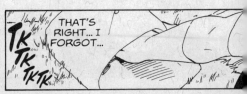

THAT'S RIGHT... I FORGOT...

TK TK TKTK

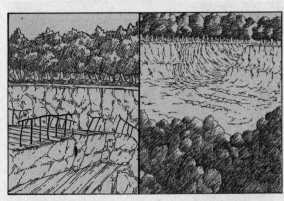

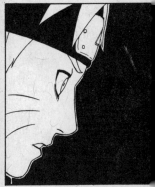

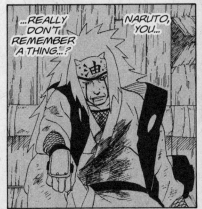

NARUTO, YOU...

...REALLY DON'T REMEMBER A THING...?

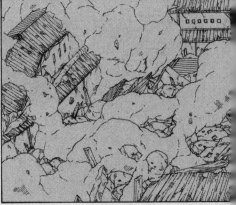

READ THIS WAY

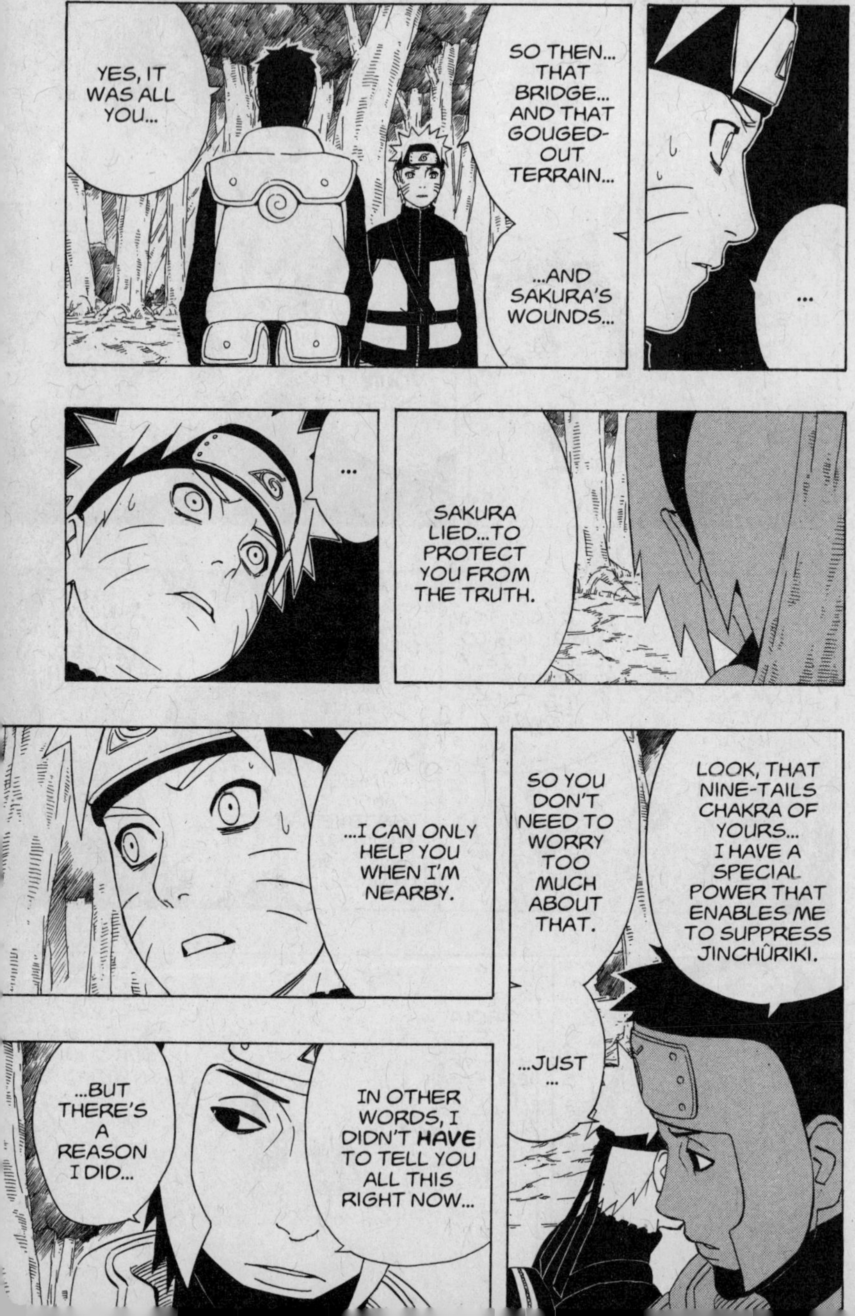
...
SO THEN... THAT BRIDGE... AND THAT GOUGED-OUT TERRAIN...
...AND SAKURA'S WOUNDS...
YES, IT WAS ALL YOU...
SAKURA LIED...TO PROTECT YOU FROM THE TRUTH.
...
LOOK, THAT NINE-TAILS CHAKRA OF YOURS... I HAVE A SPECIAL POWER THAT ENABLES ME TO SUPPRESS JINCHÛRIKI.
SO YOU DON'T NEED TO WORRY TOO MUCH ABOUT THAT.
...JUST ...
...I CAN ONLY HELP YOU WHEN I'M NEARBY.
IN OTHER WORDS, I DIDN'T **HAVE** TO TELL YOU ALL THIS RIGHT NOW...
...BUT THERE'S A REASON I DID...

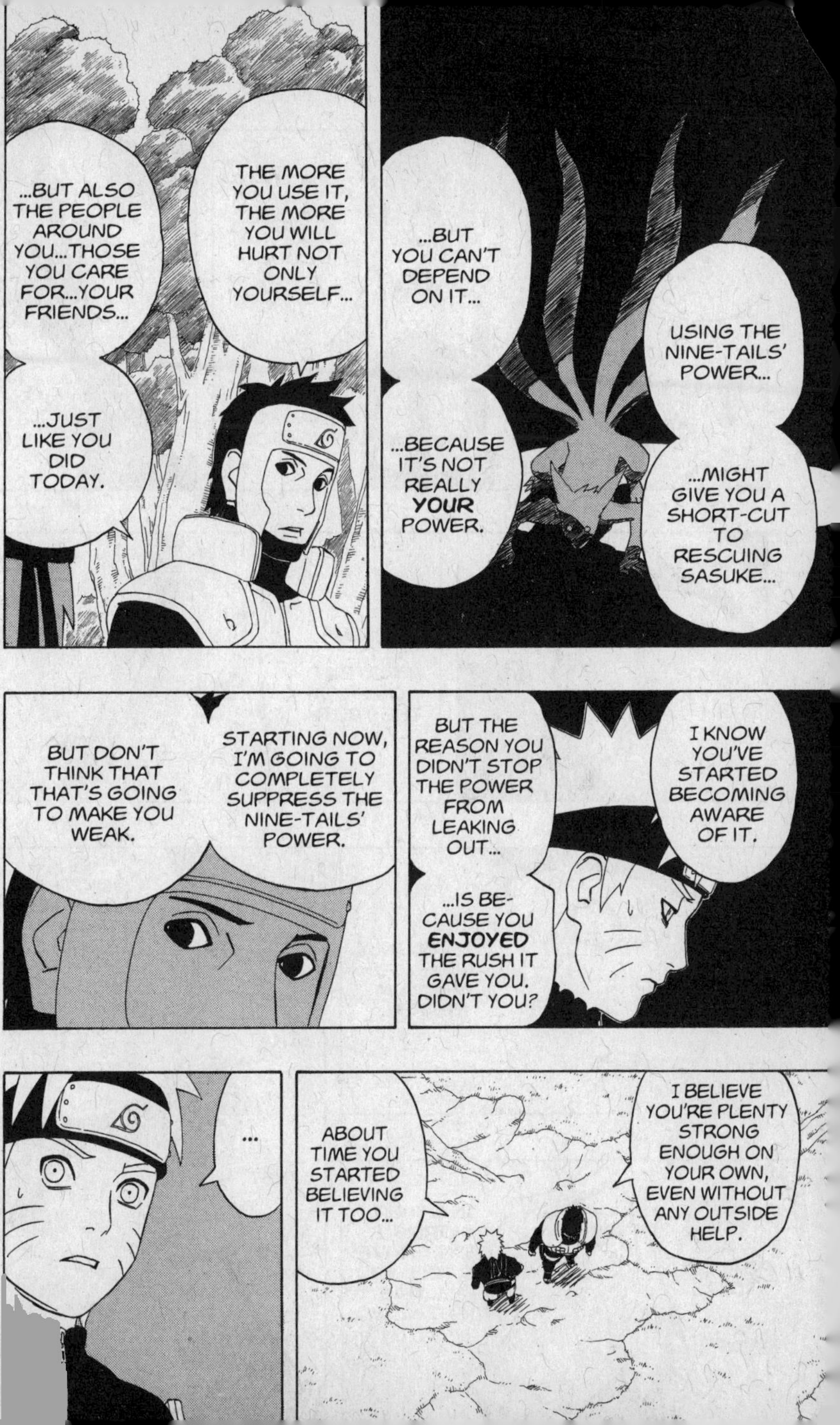
USING THE NINE-TAILS' POWER...
...MIGHT GIVE YOU A SHORT-CUT TO RESCUING SASUKE...
...BUT YOU CAN'T DEPEND ON IT...
...BECAUSE IT'S NOT REALLY **YOUR** POWER.
THE MORE YOU USE IT, THE MORE YOU WILL HURT NOT ONLY YOURSELF...
...BUT ALSO THE PEOPLE AROUND YOU...THOSE YOU CARE FOR...YOUR FRIENDS...
...JUST LIKE YOU DID TODAY.
I KNOW YOU'VE STARTED BECOMING AWARE OF IT.
BUT THE REASON YOU DIDN'T STOP THE POWER FROM LEAKING OUT...
...IS BECAUSE YOU **ENJOYED** THE RUSH IT GAVE YOU. DIDN'T YOU?
STARTING NOW, I'M GOING TO COMPLETELY SUPPRESS THE NINE-TAILS' POWER.
BUT DON'T THINK THAT THAT'S GOING TO MAKE YOU WEAK.
I BELIEVE YOU'RE PLENTY STRONG ENOUGH ON YOUR OWN, EVEN WITHOUT ANY OUTSIDE HELP.
ABOUT TIME YOU STARTED BELIEVING IT TOO...
...

READ THIS WAY

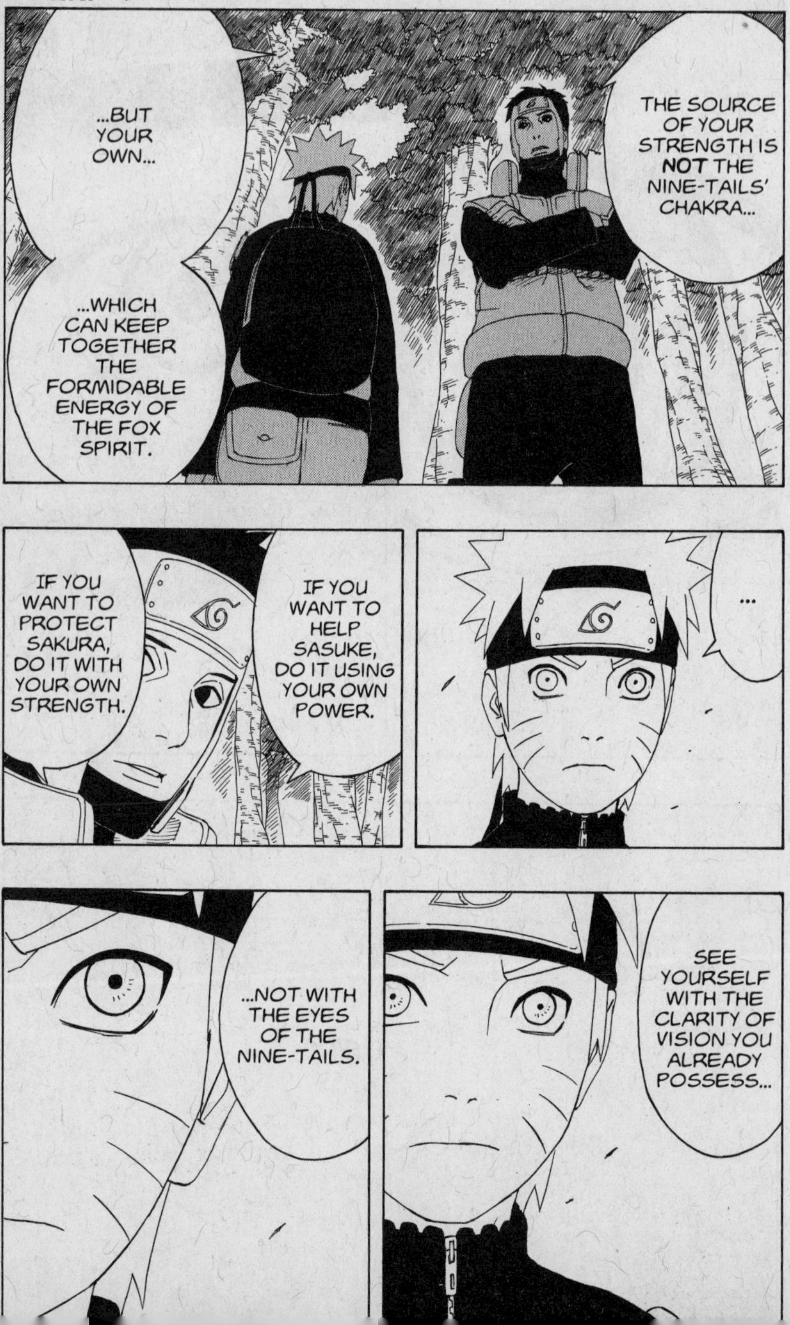
THE SOURCE OF YOUR STRENGTH IS **NOT** THE NINE-TAILS' CHAKRA...
...BUT YOUR OWN...
...WHICH CAN KEEP TOGETHER THE FORMIDABLE ENERGY OF THE FOX SPIRIT.
...
IF YOU WANT TO HELP SASUKE, DO IT USING YOUR OWN POWER.
IF YOU WANT TO PROTECT SAKURA, DO IT WITH YOUR OWN STRENGTH.
SEE YOURSELF WITH THE CLARITY OF VISION YOU ALREADY POSSESS...
...NOT WITH THE EYES OF THE NINE-TAILS.

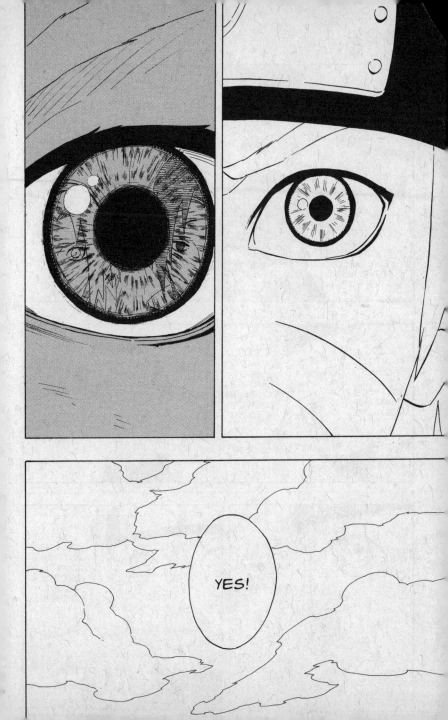

YES!

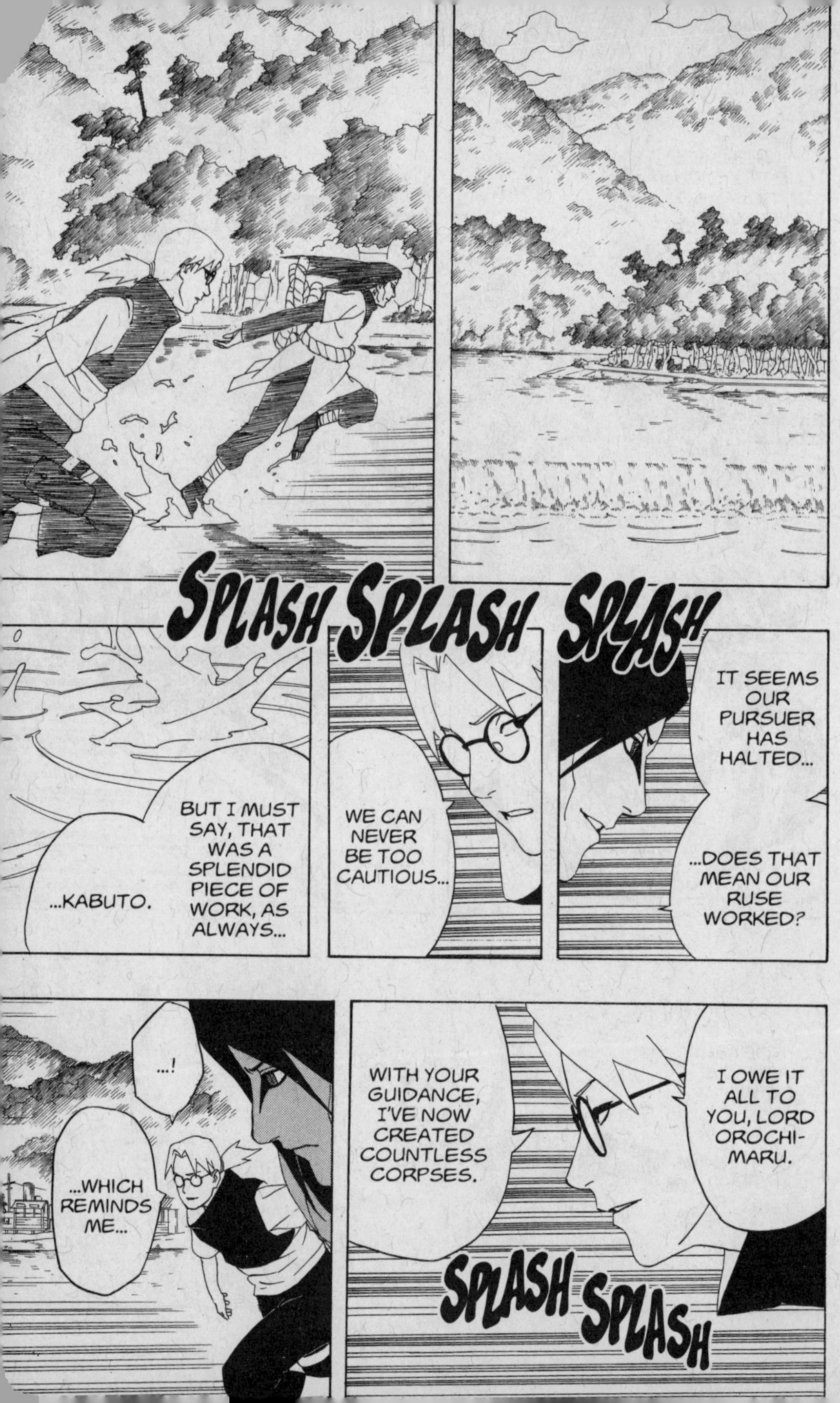
SPLASH SPLASH SPLASH
IT SEEMS OUR PURSUER HAS HALTED...
...DOES THAT MEAN OUR RUSE WORKED?
WE CAN NEVER BE TOO CAUTIOUS...
BUT I MUST SAY, THAT WAS A SPLENDID PIECE OF WORK, AS ALWAYS...
...KABUTO.
I OWE IT ALL TO YOU, LORD OROCHI-MARU.
WITH YOUR GUIDANCE, I'VE NOW CREATED COUNTLESS CORPSES.
SPLASH SPLASH
...!
...WHICH REMINDS ME...

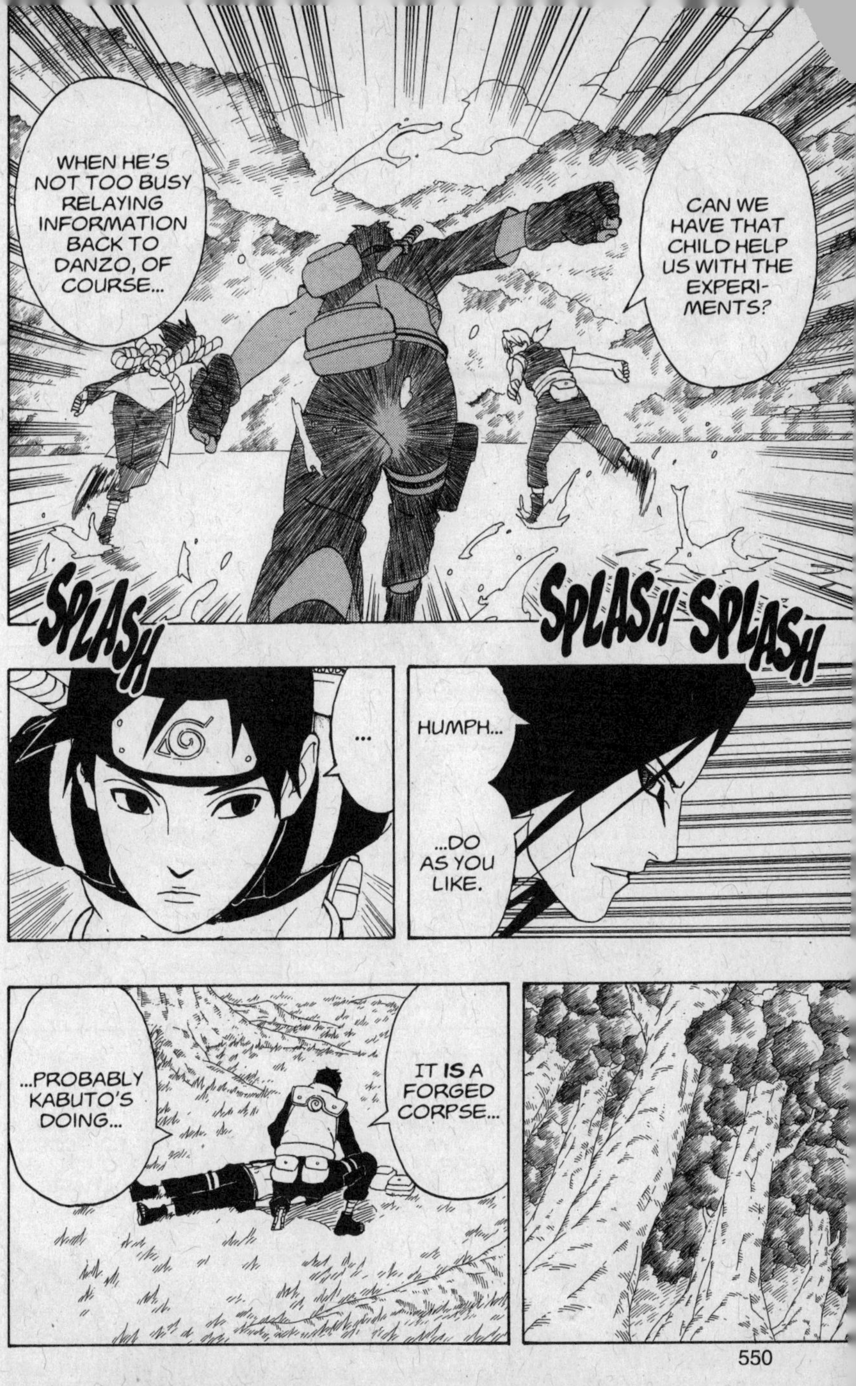
CAN WE HAVE THAT CHILD HELP US WITH THE EXPERI- MENTS?
WHEN HE'S NOT TOO BUSY RELAYING INFORMATION BACK TO DANZO, OF COURSE...
SPLASH SPLASH
SPLASH
HUMPH...
...DO AS YOU LIKE.
...
IT **IS** A FORGED CORPSE...
...PROBABLY KABUTO'S DOING...

READ THIS WAY

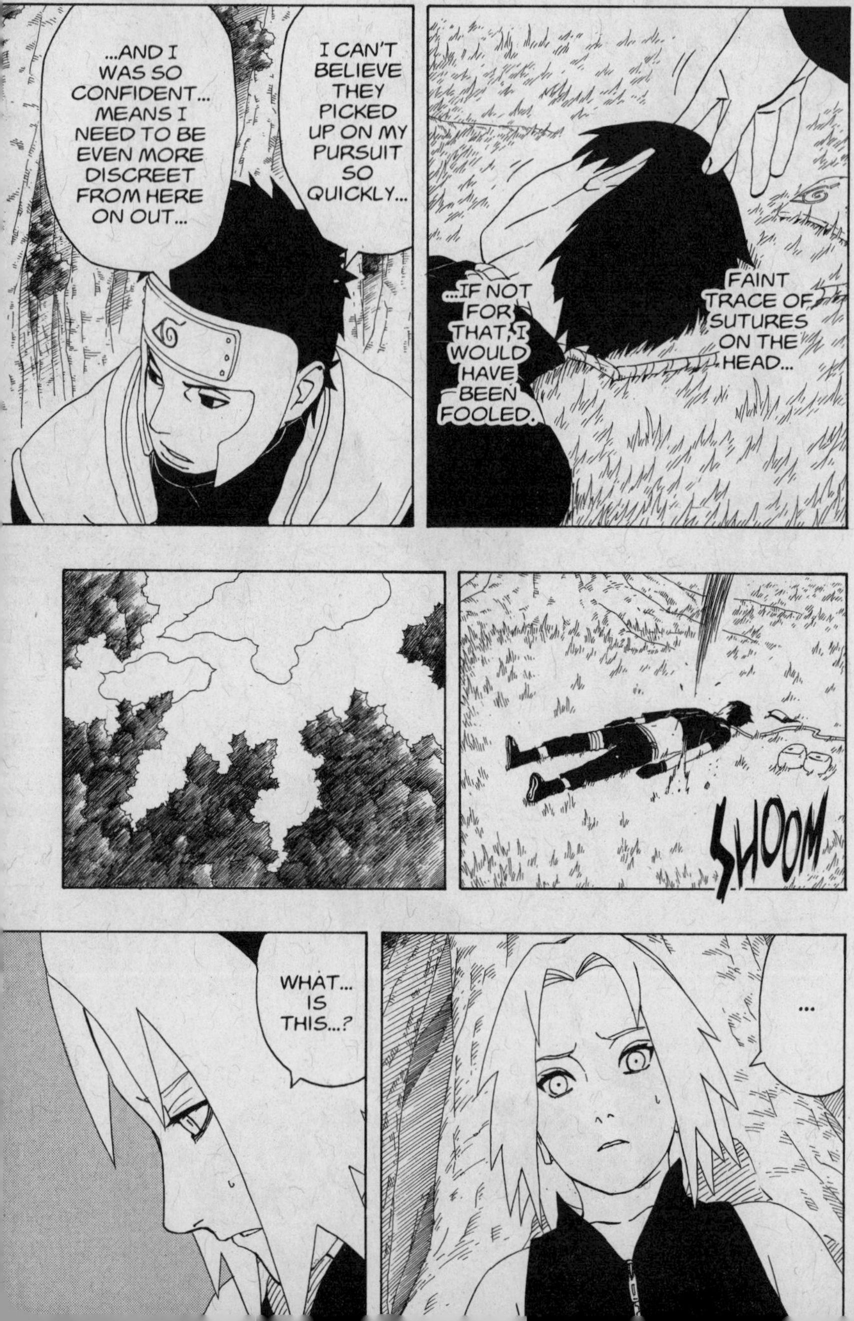
FAINT TRACE OF SUTURES ON THE HEAD...
...IF NOT FOR THAT, I WOULD HAVE BEEN FOOLED.
I CAN'T BELIEVE THEY PICKED UP ON MY PURSUIT SO QUICKLY...
...AND I WAS SO CONFIDENT... MEANS I NEED TO BE EVEN MORE DISCREET FROM HERE ON OUT...
SHOOM
...
WHAT... IS THIS...?

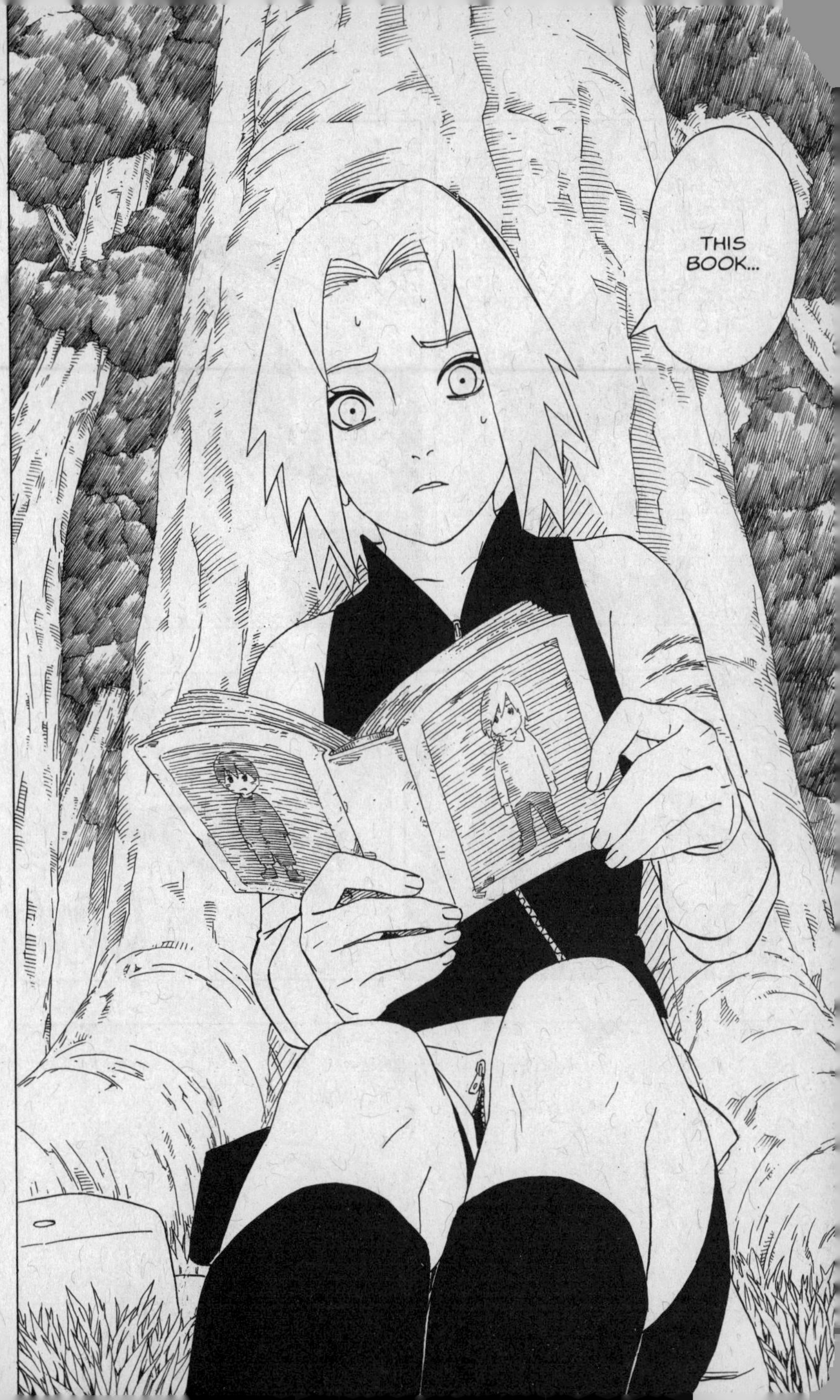
THIS BOOK...

READ THIS WAY

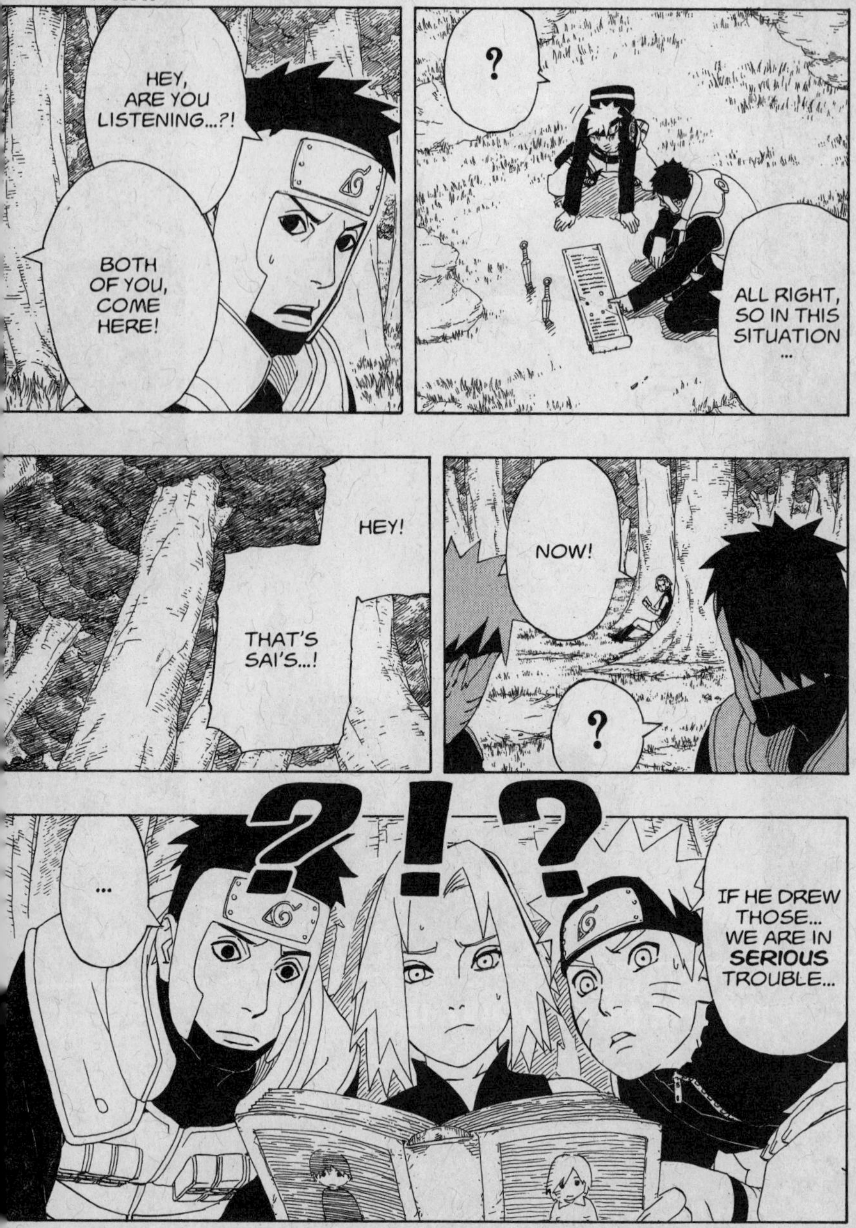
?
ALL RIGHT, SO IN THIS SITUATION ...
HEY, ARE YOU LISTENING...?!
BOTH OF YOU, COME HERE!
NOW!
?
HEY!
THAT'S SAI'S...!
?!?
IF HE DREW THOSE... WE ARE IN **SERIOUS** TROUBLE...
...

TO BE CONTINUED IN *NARUTO* VOLUME 34!

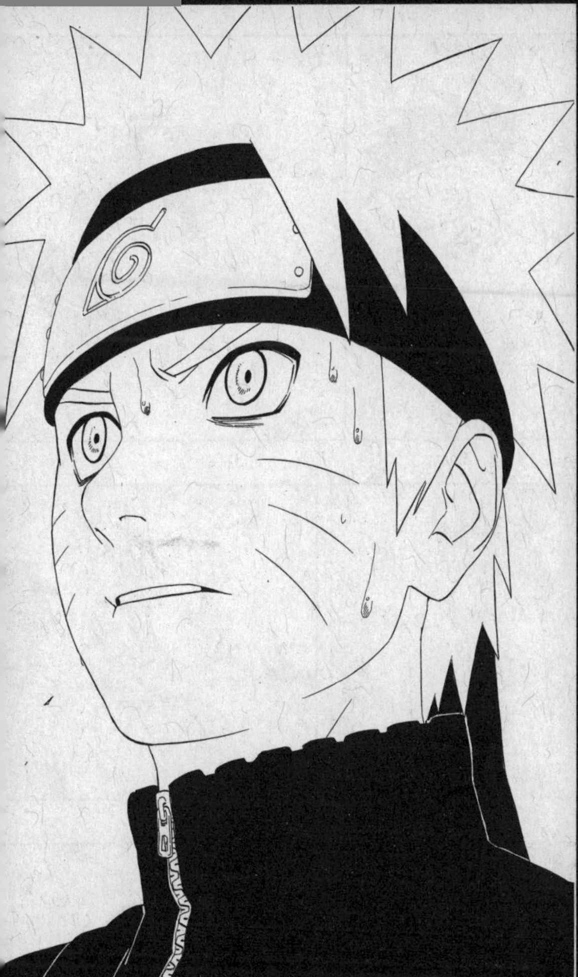

IN THE NEXT VOLUME...

THE REUNION

Naruto finally finds Sasuke! But Sasuke won't return to Konoha without a fight. This time it might take all of the new Team Kakashi to bring him down—and bring him back.

NARUTO 3-IN-1 EDITION VOLUME 12 AVAILABLE SEPTEMBER 2015!

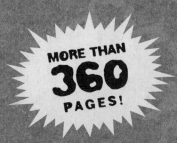
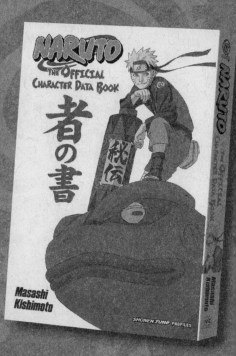

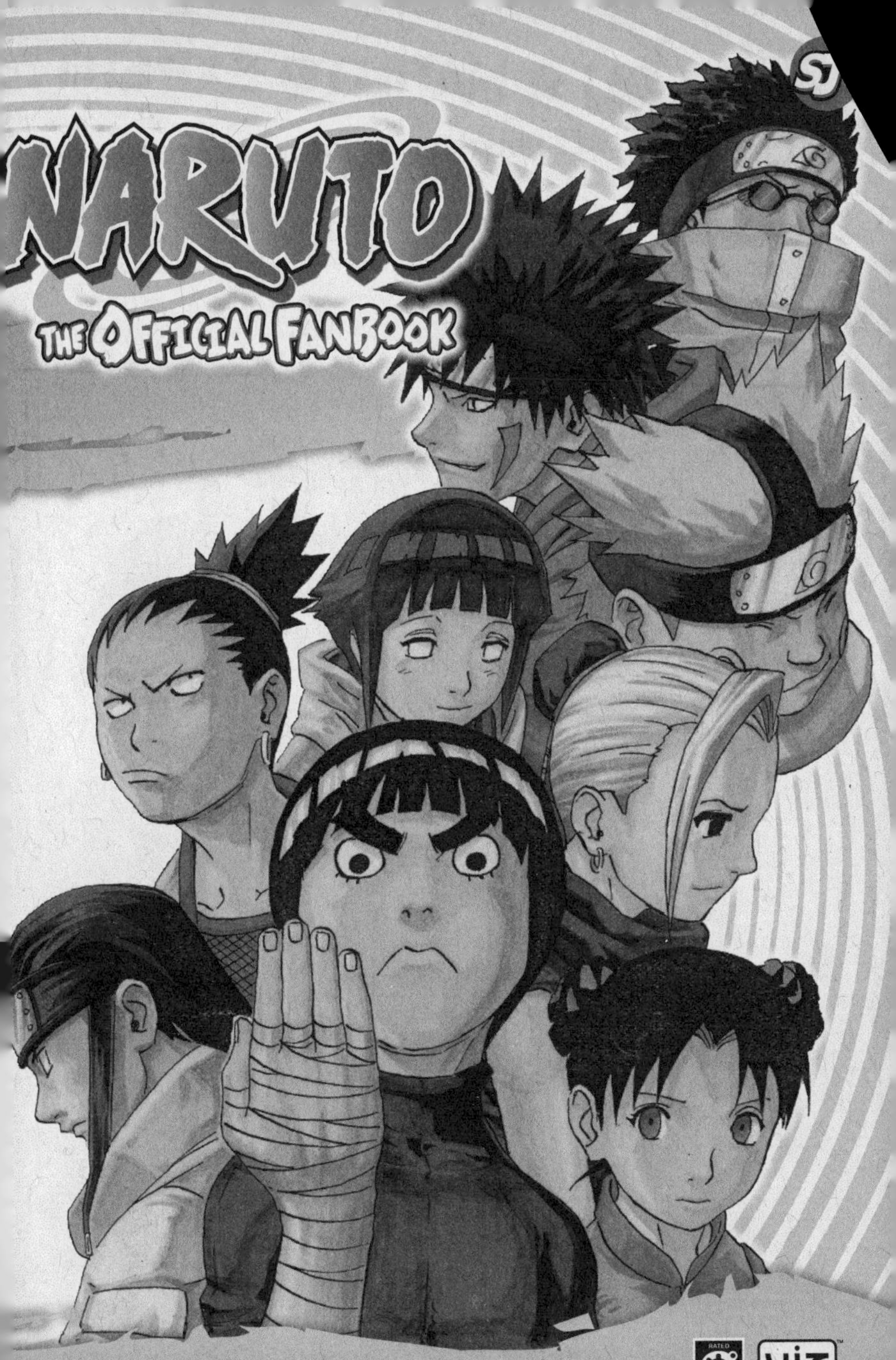
NARUTO
THE OFFICIAL FANBOOK

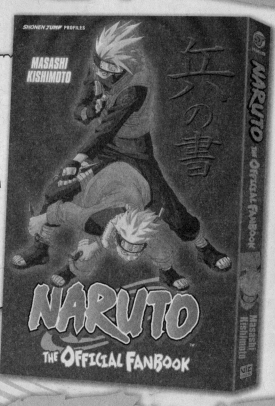
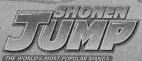

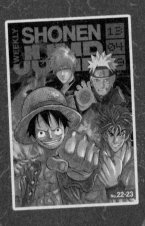
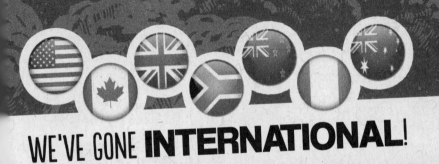

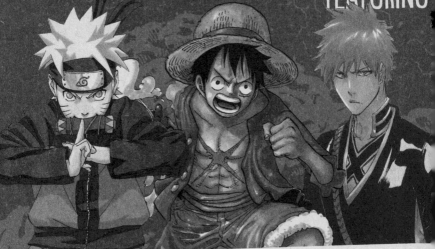

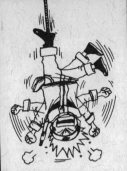

You're Reading in the Wrong Direction!!

Whoops! Guess what? You're starting at the wrong end of the comic!

...It's true! In keeping with the original Japanese format, **Naruto** is meant to be read from right to left, starting in the upper-right corner.

Unlike English, which is read from left to right, Japanese is read from right to left, meaning that action, sound effects and word-balloon order are completely reversed...something which can make readers unfamiliar with Japanese feel pretty backwards themselves. For this reason, manga or Japanese comics published in the U.S. in English have sometimes been published "flopped"—that is, printed in exact reverse order, as though seen from the other side of a mirror.

By flopping pages, U.S. publishers can avoid confusing readers, but the compromise is not without its downside. For one thing, a character in a flopped manga series who once wore in the original Japanese version a T-shirt emblazoned with "M A Y" (as in "the merry month of") now wears one which reads "Y A M"! Additionally, many manga creators in Japan are themselves unhappy with the process, as some feel the mirror-imaging of their art alters their original intentions.

We are proud to bring you Masashi Kishimoto's **Naruto** in the original unflopped format. For now, though, turn to the other side of the book and let the ninjutsu begin...!

—Editor

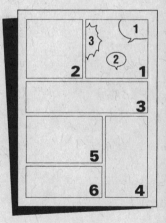